Test Booklet No. 3947351

Test Booklet Code CH1

MEDACE
NEET (UG)
SELF ASSESSMENT KIT

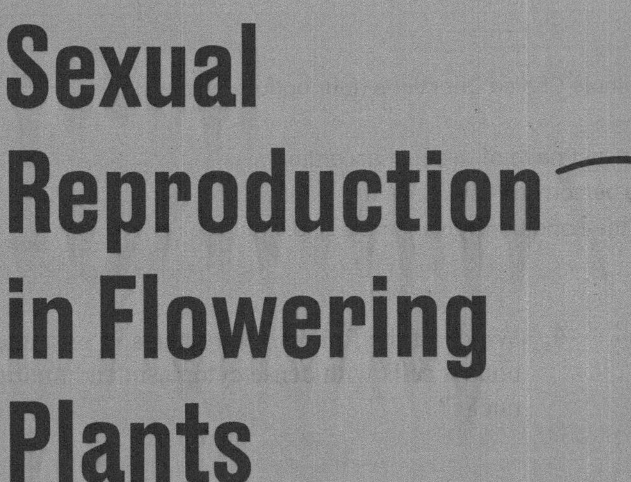

Sexual Reproduction in Flowering Plants

Topics Covered

Flower, Pre-fertilisation Structure and Event

Pollination and Double Fertilisation

Post-fertilisation : Events and Structure, Polyembryony and Apomixis

Important Instructions

- This Booklet Contains – Three Topic Tests and One Test on Complete Chapter.
- Each question carries 4 marks.
- For each correct response, the candidate will get 4 marks. And for every incorrect response, 1 mark will be additionally deducted from total score.
- Use **Blue/Black** point pen only for filling the OMR.
- Rough work is to be done in the space provided for this purpose in the test booklet only.

Name of the Candidate (In Capitals)

____

____

Candidate's Signature __________

Invigilator's Signature __________

Facsimile signature stamp of center superintendent__________

Do not open this booklet until you start attempting the test

Topical Follow Thru

Test 1

Syllabus	Flower structure	Development of male and female gametophytes

For deeper insight, **Scan the QR Code**

Important Instructions

- The test is of 30 minutes duration and contains 15 Multiple Choice Questions (four options with a single correct answer).
- Choose the correct option and fill the OMR given on the last page of this test accordingly.
- At some instances, you may find more than 1 option to be correct. In such circumstances, you have to judge the most appropriate answer as per the conditions given in the question.

1. Which of the following statements about the endothecium layer of the microsporangial wall is incorrect?

(a) It is located below the epidermis.
(b) It plays a role in nourishing the developing pollen grains.
(c) It serves as a protective layer.
(d) It assists in the dehiscence of the anther.

2. The type of ovule in which the nucellus becomes horse-shoe shaped is

(a) anatropous ovule
(b) orthotropous ovule
(c) amphitropous ovule
(d) circinotropous ovule

3. Consider the following sequence of microsporogenesis. The ploidy levels are enclosed in the brackets.

Sporogenous tissue (A) → PMC (B) → Microspore tetrad (C) → Pollen grains (n)

Choose the correct answer from the following options.

(a) A-2n, B-n, C-2n
(b) A-2n, B-2n, C-2n
(c) A-2n, B-2n, C-n
(d) A-2n, B-n, C-n

4. Which of the following structures in an anther houses cells with dense cytoplasm and multiple nuclei?

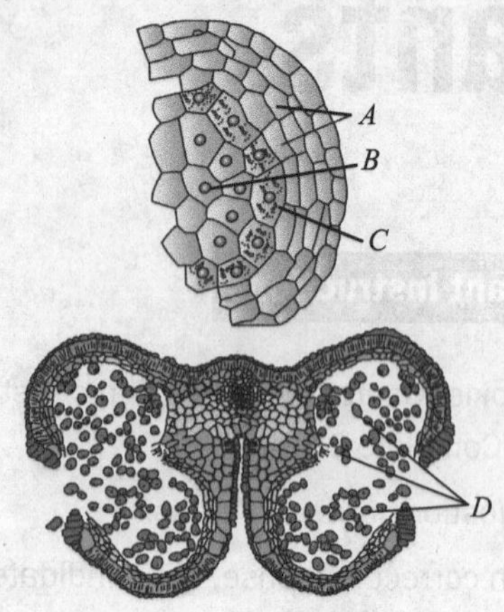

(a) A
(b) B
(c) C
(d) D

5. The correct sequence of four layers of microsporangia from outer to inner side is

(a) epidermis - tapetum - middle layers - endothecium
(b) endothecium - epidermis - tapetum - middle layers
(c) epidermis - endothecium - middle layers - tapetum
(d) tapetum - endothecium - middle layers - epidermis

6. Match List I with List II.

	List I		List II
A.	Vegetative cell	1.	Composed of sporopollenin
B.	Generative cell	2.	Involved in the formation of the pollen tube
C.	Exine	3.	Composed of cellulose and pectin
D.	Intine	4.	Divides to form two sperm cells

Choose the correct answer from the options given below.

	A	B	C	D		A	B	C	D
(a)	4	3	2	1	(b)	2	4	1	3
(c)	2	1	4	3	(d)	3	1	4	2

7. Given below are two statements.

Statement I Pollen grains are generally spherical shaped and measured about 25-50 μm in diameter.

Statement II In order to develop into pollen grains from microspores, the anthers get dehydrated.

In the light of the above statements, choose the correct answer from the options given below.

(a) Statement I is incorrect, but statement II is correct

(b) Both statement I and statement II are correct

(c) Both statement I and statement II are incorrect

(d) Statement I is correct, but statement II is incorrect

8. Given below are the two statements; one is labelled as Assertion (A) and the other is labelled as Reason (R).

Assertion (A) The functional megaspore undergoes three successive meiotic divisions, resulting in an eight-nucleate embryo sac.

Reason (R) The equational division ensures the formation of genetically identical daughter nuclei in the embryo sac.

In the light of the above statements, choose the correct answer from the options given below.

(a) A is false, but R is true.

(b) Both A and R are true and R is the correct explanation of A.

(c) Both A and R are true, but R is not the correct explanation of A.

(d) A is true, but R is false.

9. Read the following statements.

I. A funicle is a stalk through which the placenta is attached to ovule.

II. The micropyle is the protective envelope around the ovule.

III. The ovule body fuses with the nucellus in the region called the hilum.

IV. Chalaza represents the basal part of an ovule.

V. Micropyle encircles the ovule at the tip where the nucellus is present.

How many of the above statements are correct?

(a) Four (b) Three (c) One (d) Two

10. Select the incorrectly matched pair.

(a) Filiform apparatus - guides the pollen grain into synergids

(b) Egg apparatus - constituted by the grouping of three cells at the micropylar end

(c) Antipodals - three in number, located at the chalazal end

(d) Central cell - bears two polar nuclei

11. Given below are two statements.

Statement I Severe allergies and bronchial afflictions can lead to chronic respiratory disorders due to pollen grains.

Statement II *Parthenium* is considered as a contaminant and has become ubiquitous in occurrence and causes pollen allergy.

In the light of the above statements, choose the correct answer from the options given below.

(a) Statement I is incorrect, but statement II is correct.

(b) Both statement I and statement II are correct.

(c) Both statement I and statement II are incorrect.

(d) Statement I is correct, but statement II is incorrect.

12. In about 40% of angiosperms, the ...A... divides mitotically to give rise to ...B... before ...C... are shed (3-celled stage).

	A	B	C
(a)	vegetative cell	pollen grains	two male gametes
(b)	generative cell	pollen grains	two male gametes
(c)	generative cell	two male gametes	pollen grains
(d)	vegetative cell	two male gametes	pollen grains

13. In the ovule, the hilum represents the point of attachment between
(a) integuments and nucellus
(b) chalaza and nucellus
(c) funicle and nucellus
(d) micropyle and integuments

14. Which one of the following is surrounded by callose wall?
(a) Male gamete (b) Pollen grain
(c) Anther (d) Microspore mother cell

15. Which of the following statement is incorrect regarding pollen development?
(a) Microsporogenesis results in the formation of haploid microspores.
(b) Dehydration of the anther is essential for microspore dissociation.
(c) Each microspore tetrad contains genetically identical cells.
(d) A single microsporangium produces millions of pollen grains.

■ **Response Index**

01	(a)	(b)	(c)	(d)	10	(a)	(b)	(c)	(d)	19	(a)	(b)	(c)	(d)
02	(a)	(b)	(c)	(d)	11	(a)	(b)	(c)	(d)	20	(a)	(b)	(c)	(d)
03	(a)	(b)	(c)	(d)	12	(a)	(b)	(c)	(d)	21	(a)	(b)	(c)	(d)
04	(a)	(b)	(c)	(d)	13	(a)	(b)	(c)	(d)	22	(a)	(b)	(c)	(d)
05	(a)	(b)	(c)	(d)	14	(a)	(b)	(c)	(d)	23	(a)	(b)	(c)	(d)
06	(a)	(b)	(c)	(d)	15	(a)	(b)	(c)	(d)	24	(a)	(b)	(c)	(d)
07	(a)	(b)	(c)	(d)	16	(a)	(b)	(c)	(d)	25	(a)	(b)	(c)	(d)
08	(a)	(b)	(c)	(d)	17	(a)	(b)	(c)	(d)					
09	(a)	(b)	(c)	(d)	18	(a)	(b)	(c)	(d)					

■ **Performance Scanner**

> 90% Excellent !	You have mastered these topics. The concepts of these topics are at your fingertips. Move on to the next test and maintain this momentum.
76-90% Very Good !	You have a good command over these topics. Revise these topics again after a few days and enhance your performance.
60-75% Good !	You have a wide scope to learn for these topics. Revise these topics again.
<60% Not Satisfactory!	You have a long way ahead of you to master these topics. Revise it thoroughly.

Test 2

Syllabus
- Pollination-types, agencies and examples
- Outbreeding devices
- Pollen-pistil interaction
- Double fertilisation

For deeper insight, **Scan the QR Code**

Important Instructions
- The test is of 30 minutes duration and contains 15 Multiple Choice Questions (four options with a single correct answer).
- Choose the correct option and fill the OMR given on the last page of this test accordingly.
- At some instances, you may find more than 1 option to be correct. In such circumstances, you have to judge the most appropriate answer as per the conditions given in the question.

1. Flowering plants exhibit a remarkable variety of adaptations to achieve efficient pollination. Which of the following adaptations is least likely to promote cross-pollination?
(a) Brightly coloured petals with a sweet fragrance.
(b) Stamens positioned above the pistil within a flower.
(c) Production of sticky pollen grains.
(d) Flowers that open only at night.

2. Consider the following statements.
I. Autogamy guarantees seed set, but limits genetic variation in offspring.
II. Geitonogamy promotes genetic diversity, but is less efficient than xenogamy.
III. Plants with brightly coloured, fragrant flowers and sticky pollen primarily rely on wind pollination.
IV. Self-compatible plants can exhibit both autogamy and xenogamy, depending on pollinator availability.

V. In *Viola*, only chasmogamous flowers are found.

Which of the following is most likely true?

(a) Only statements I and IV are correct.
(b) Only statements I, III and V are correct.
(c) Only statements I, IV and V are correct.
(d) Only statements I and III are correct.

3. Choose the incorrect statement about cleistogamy.

(a) Cleistogamous flowers are invariably autogamous.
(b) In such flowers, the anther and stigma lie close to each other.
(c) Anthers undergo dehiscence before pollination.
(d) It brings genetically different types of pollen grains to the stigma.

4. Among the following, which one is not an advantage of xenogamy?

(a) Similar types of offsprings are formed
(b) Increased heterosis is observed
(c) Fertility increases
(d) An increase in vigor of offspring is observed

5. Match List I with List II.

List I	List II
A. Chasmogamy	1. Transfer of pollen grains from the anther to the stigma of another flower of the same plant.
B. Cleistogamy	2. Transfer of pollen grains from anther to the stigma of a different plant.
C. Xenogamy	3. Flowers in which the anthers and stigma lie close to each other.
D. Geitonogamy	4. Flowers with exposed anthers and stigma.

Choose the correct option from the following.

	A	B	C	D		A	B	C	D
(a)	4	3	2	1	(b)	3	1	2	4
(c)	2	4	1	3	(d)	3	4	1	2

6. Given below are two statements.

Statement I Pollen grains coming in contact with the stigma is a chance factor in both wind and water pollination.
Statement II Pollination by water is more common amongst abiotic pollinations.

In the light of the above statements, choose the correct answer from the options given below.

(a) Statement I is incorrect, but statement II is correct.
(b) Both statement I and statement II are correct.
(c) Both statement I and statement II are incorrect.
(d) Statement I is correct, but statement II is incorrect.

7. Consider the following statements and identify the incorrect one regarding hydrophily.

(a) It is quite rare in flowering plants and is limited to about 50 genera, mostly dicotyledons.
(b) Water is regular mode of transport for male gametes among the lower plant groups.
(c) Water pollinated plants are *Vallisneria* and *Hydrilla* which grow in fresh water.
(d) In water-pollinated species, pollen grains are protected from wetting by a mucilaginous covering.

8. Select which of the following is not adaptable by plants to prevent self-pollination?

(a) Pollen and stigma receptivity are not synchronised
(b) Anther and stigma placed at different positions
(c) Production of unisexual flower
(d) Encourage inbreeding by self-incompatibility

9. Which of the following statements are incorrect?

I. Most of the insect pollinated flowers are large, colourful, fragrant and rich in nectar.
II. For harvesting the nectar, the biotic agent comes only in contact with the stigma.
III. The body of animal gets a coating of pollen grains, which are generally sticky in nature.
IV. The flowers pollinated by flies and butterflies secrete foul odours to attract these animals.
V. When the flowers are small, a number of flowers are clustered into an inflorescence to make them conspicuous.

Choose the correct answer from the options given below.

(a) I and IV
(b) II and IV
(c) I and III
(d) IV and V

10. The production of a particular type of flowers (w.r.t. sexuality) in papaya prevents

(a) Both autogamy and geitonogamy
(b) xenogamy only
(c) geitonogamy only
(d) Both xenogamy and geitonogamy

11. Analyse the following statements.

I. Self-incompatibility prevents pollen of the same plant from fertilising ovules.
II. Monoecious plants cannot undergo autogamy, but still have a chance of geitonogamy.
III. Self-incompatibility is a more effective barrier to inbreeding compared to having separate male and female flowers on the same plant (monoecy).
IV. All flowering plants exhibit some form of mechanism to prevent self-pollination.

Which of the following is most likely true?
(a) Statements I, II and IV are correct.
(b) Statements I, II and III are correct.
(c) Statements II, III and IV are correct.
(d) Statements II and III are correct.

12. The ability of pistil to recognise the pollen followed by its acceptance or rejection is the result of
(a) compatibility of pollen grain and pistil
(b) incompatibility of pollen grain and pistil
(c) a continuous dialogue between pollen grain and pistil
(d) a discontinuous dialogue between pollen grain and pistil

13. An experiment investigates pollen germination. Pollen grains from a flower are placed on a specific solution to observe pollen tube growth under a microscope. What is the most suitable solution for this experiment?
(a) Distilled water (b) Sugar solution
(c) Alcohol solution (d) Oil

14. Match List I with List II.

	List I		List II
A.	Syngamy	1.	Zygote
B.	Triple fusion	2.	Removal of anthers
C.	Emasculation	3.	PEN
D.	Bagging	4.	Amphimixis
		5.	Covering of flower

Choose the correct answer from the options given below.

	A	B	C	D
(a)	4,1	3	2	5
(b)	2	4, 5	1	3
(c)	1, 3	2	5	4
(d)	3	4, 2	4	1

15. Given below are the two statements; one is labelled as Assertion (A) and the other is labelled as Reason (R).

Assertion (A) Chasmogamous flowers require pollinating agents.

Reason (R) Cleistogamous flowers do not expose at all.

In the light of the above statements, choose the correct answer from the options given below.
(a) A is false, but R is true
(b) Both A and R are true and R is the correct explanation of A
(c) Both A and R are true, but R is not the correct explanation of A
(d) A is true, but R is false

Response Index

01	a	b	c	d	10	a	b	c	d	19	a	b	c	d
02	a	b	c	d	11	a	b	c	d	20	a	b	c	d
03	a	b	c	d	12	a	b	c	d	21	a	b	c	d
04	a	b	c	d	13	a	b	c	d	22	a	b	c	d
05	a	b	c	d	14	a	b	c	d	23	a	b	c	d
06	a	b	c	d	15	a	b	c	d	24	a	b	c	d
07	a	b	c	d	16	a	b	c	d	25	a	b	c	d
08	a	b	c	d	17	a	b	c	d					
09	a	b	c	d	18	a	b	c	d					

Performance Scanner

> 90% Excellent !	You have mastered these topics. The concepts of these topics are at your fingertips. Move on to the next test and maintain this momentum.
76-90% Very Good !	You have a good command over these topics. Revise these topics again after a few days and enhance your performance.
60-75% Good !	You have a wide scope to learn for these topics. Revise these topics again.
<60% Not Satisfactory!	You have a long way ahead of you to master these topics. Revise it thoroughly.

Test 3

Syllabus

- Post-fertilisation events-Development of endosperm and embryo
- Development of seed and formation of fruit
- Special modes-apomixis, parthenocarpy, polyembryony
- Significance of seed and fruit formation

For deeper insight, Scan the QR Code 

Important Instructions

- The test is of 30 minutes duration and contains 15 Multiple Choice Questions (four options with a single correct answer).
- Choose the correct option and fill the OMR given on the last page of this test accordingly.
- At some instances, you may find more than 1 option to be correct. In such circumstances, you have to judge the most appropriate answer as per the conditions given in the question.

1. The liquid found inside a young coconut represents which stage of endosperm development?

(a) Cellular tissue
(b) Free-nuclear endosperm
(c) Embryo
(d) Seed coat

2. Analyse the following statements.

I. The Primary Endosperm Nucleus (PEN) undergoes repeated mitotic divisions, forming a triploid endosperm tissue.
II. Free nuclear endosperm refers to a stage with numerous free nuclei within a large central vacuole, lacking cell walls.
III. The triploid endosperm serves as a source of nutrition for the developing embryo.
IV. Free nuclear type of endosperm development is always present in all angiosperms.
V. Seed coats are derived from the tissues surrounding the developing endosperm.

Which of the following is most likely true?

(a) Statements I, II and III are correct.
(b) Statements II, III, IV and V are correct.
(c) Statements I, III and V are correct.
(d) Statements I, IV and V are correct.

3. Which of the following matches are correct regarding the stages of embryonic development in plants with their descriptions?

	List I	List II
1.	Zygote	Provides assured nutrition
2.	Proembryo	First stage of cell division
3.	Globular stage	Heart-shaped structure
4.	Mature embryo	Fully developed with organs

Choose the correct match.

(a) 1 and 2 (b) 3 and 4
(c) 1 and 3 (d) 2 and 4

4. Identify the correct statement(s) with respect to the embryo sac of flowering plants.

I. Scutellum represents a single cotyledon that is found present in monocot seeds.
II. In the process of dicot embryo development, a globular embryo forms after a heart-shaped embryo.
III. Epicotyl and hypocotyl are the parts of the embryonal axis found above and below the level of cotyledons, respectively.
IV. Lower end of embryonal axis has the radicle and root cap enclosed in coleorhiza.

V. Albuminous seed retains endosperm as it is not completely consumed during embryo development.

(a) I, III, IV and V
(b) I and II
(c) II and III
(d) I, II and III

5. Consider the following paragraph.

The stalk-like part below the seed leaves is called the _______. It ends in the root tip (radicle).

Grass embryos have a single cotyledon, called a _______, located on the side of the embryonic axis.

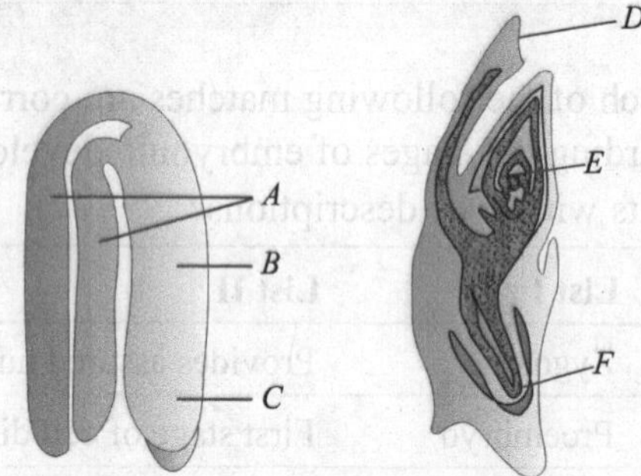

Choose the correct option w.r.t. the given blanks, respectively.

(a) A and D (b) A and F
(c) C and E (d) B and D

6. In a seed of maize, scutellum is considered as cotyledon because it

(a) protects the embryo
(b) contains food for the embryo
(c) absorbs food materials and supplies them to the embryo
(d) converts itself into a monocot leaf

7. The edible part of apple is

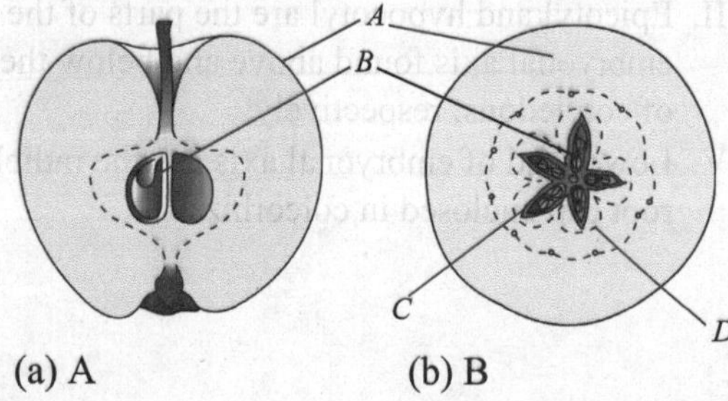

(a) A (b) B
(c) C (d) D

8. Match the items given in List I with their examples given in List II and choose the correct option given below.

	List I (Items)		List II (Examples)
A.	Ovary	1.	Groundnut, mustard
B.	Wall of ovary	2.	Guava, orange, mango
C.	Fleshy fruits	3.	Pericarp
D.	Dry fruits	4.	Fruit

A B C D
(a) 1 4 3 2
(b) 4 3 2 1
(c) 1 3 2 4
(d) 3 4 1 2

9. Given below are two statements.

Statement I Seeds have better adaptive strategies for dispersal to new habitats.

Statement II The hard seed coat provides protection to the young embryo.

In the light of the above statements, choose the correct answer from the options given below.

(a) Statement I is incorrect, but statement II is correct
(b) Both statement I and statement II are correct
(c) Both statement I and statement II are incorrect
(d) Statement I is correct, but statement II is incorrect

10. Match List I with List II.

	List I		List II
A.	False fruit	1.	Cashew
B.	Corolla	2.	Falls off
C.	Perisperm	3.	Castor
D.	Persistent endosperm	4.	Beet

Choose the correct answer from the options given below.

A B C D
(a) 4 3 2 1
(b) 2 4 1 3
(c) 1 2 4 3
(d) 3 1 4 2

11. Some seeds can lose viability within few months, whereas some can be alive for hundred of years. A recent record of 2000 years old viable seed is of

(a) date palm
(b) lupine
(c) castor
(d) *Amorphophallus*

12. Choose an incorrect statement about the significance of polyembryony.

(a) Provides uniform seedling like parents.
(b) Seedlings are free from disease.
(c) Seedlings develop better root system.
(d) Suitable for large-scale production of variable plants.

13. If endosperm has 36 number of chromosomes, then the number of chromosomes of nucellus, male gametes, synergids, antipodals, female gamete and integument, respectively is

(a) 12, 12, 12, 12, 12, 12
(b) 12, 12, 24, 24, 12, 24
(c) 24, 12, 12, 12, 12, 24
(d) 24, 12, 24, 24, 12, 24

14. Given below are two statements; one is labelled as the Assertion (A) and the other is labelled as the Reason (R).

Assertion (A) Endosperm development preceeds embryo development.

Reason (R) Development of endosperm before embryo is an adaptation to provide assured nutrition to the developing embryo.

In the light of the above statements, choose the correct answer from the options given below.

(a) A is false, but R is true
(b) Both A and R are true and R is the correct explanation of A
(c) Both A and R are true, but R is not the correct explanation of A
(d) A is true, but R is false

15. Thalamus contributes in the fruit formation in case of false fruits. How many of the following satisfy this criteria?

Apple, Cashewnut, Strawberry, Banana, Mango, Grapes

(a) Two (b) Three
(c) Four (d) Five

Response Index

01	ⓐ	ⓑ	ⓒ	ⓓ	10	ⓐ	ⓑ	ⓒ	ⓓ	19	ⓐ	ⓑ	ⓒ	ⓓ
02	ⓐ	ⓑ	ⓒ	ⓓ	11	ⓐ	ⓑ	ⓒ	ⓓ	20	ⓐ	ⓑ	ⓒ	ⓓ
03	ⓐ	ⓑ	ⓒ	ⓓ	12	ⓐ	ⓑ	ⓒ	ⓓ	21	ⓐ	ⓑ	ⓒ	ⓓ
04	ⓐ	ⓑ	ⓒ	ⓓ	13	ⓐ	ⓑ	ⓒ	ⓓ	22	ⓐ	ⓑ	ⓒ	ⓓ
05	ⓐ	ⓑ	ⓒ	ⓓ	14	ⓐ	ⓑ	ⓒ	ⓓ	23	ⓐ	ⓑ	ⓒ	ⓓ
06	ⓐ	ⓑ	ⓒ	ⓓ	15	ⓐ	ⓑ	ⓒ	ⓓ	24	ⓐ	ⓑ	ⓒ	ⓓ
07	ⓐ	ⓑ	ⓒ	ⓓ	16	ⓐ	ⓑ	ⓒ	ⓓ	25	ⓐ	ⓑ	ⓒ	ⓓ
08	ⓐ	ⓑ	ⓒ	ⓓ	17	ⓐ	ⓑ	ⓒ	ⓓ					
09	ⓐ	ⓑ	ⓒ	ⓓ	18	ⓐ	ⓑ	ⓒ	ⓓ					

Performance Scanner

> 90% Excellent !	You have mastered these topics. The concepts of these topics are at your fingertips. Move on to the next test and maintain this momentum.
76-90% Very Good !	You have a good command over these topics. Revise these topics again after a few days and enhance your performance.
60-75% Good !	You have a wide scope to learn for these topics. Revise these topics again.
<60% Not Satisfactory!	You have a long way ahead of you to master these topics. Revise it thoroughly.

Chapter Break Thru

Syllabus	• Flower structure • Development of male and female gametophytes • Pollination-types, agencies and examples • Outbreeding devices	• Pollen-pistil Interaction • Double fertilisation • Post-fertilisation events-Development of endosperm and embryo	• Development of seed and formation of fruit • Special modes-Apomixis, parthenocarpy, polyembryony • Significance of seed and fruit formation

Important Instructions

- The test is of 1 hour duration and contains 50 Multiple-Choice Questions (Four options with a single correct answer).
- Choose the correct option and fill the OMR given on the last page of this test accordingly.
- At some instances, you may find more than 1 option to be correct. In such circumstances, you have to judge the most appropriate answer as per the conditions given in the question.

1. Among the following, which one is not the function of the tapetum layer of the microsporangial layer?

(a) To provide nutrition to pollen grains
(b) To produce sporopollenin
(c) To help in the dehiscence of anther
(d) To secrete callase enzyme

2. Analyse the following statements.

I. Microsporangia within the anther undergo meiosis to produce haploid microspores.
II. Microspores mature directly into pollen grains without further development.
III. Pollen sacs develop longitudinally within the anther, typically two per lobe.
IV. The wall of the mature pollen sac remains single-layered throughout development.

Which of the following is most likely true?

(a) Only statements I and III are correct.
(b) Only statements II and IV are correct.
(c) Only statements I, II, and III are correct.
(d) Only statements III and IV are correct.

3. Given below are the two statements; one is labelled as Assertion (A) and the other is labelled as Reason (R).

Assertion (A) The exine of a pollen grain is a hard, sporopollenin-rich layer.

Reason (R) Pollen grains need protection during dispersal and germination.

In the light of the above statements, choose the correct answer from the options given below.

(a) A is false, but R is true.
(b) Both A and R are true and R is the correct explanation of A.
(c) Both A and R are true, but R is not the correct explanation of A.
(d) A is true, but R is false.

4. The development of microsporangia leads to the formation of

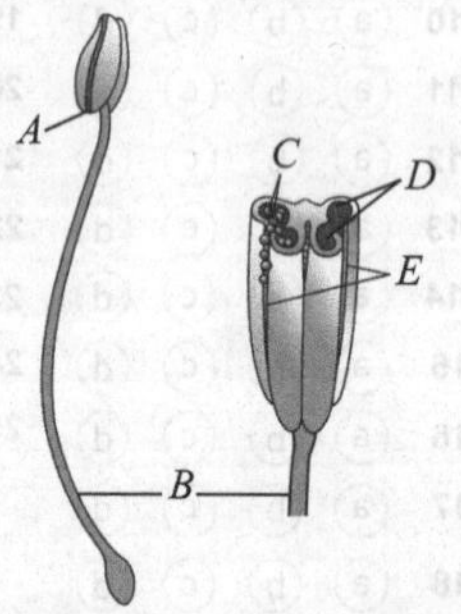

(a) A (b) B
(c) C (d) D

5. Given below are two statements.

Statement I The vegetative cell has an abundant food reserve.

Statement II The generative cell is small and possesses an irregularly shaped nucleus.

In the light of the above statements, choose the correct answer from the options given below.

(a) Statement I is incorrect, but statement II is correct.
(b) Both statement I and statement II are correct.
(c) Both statement I and statement II are incorrect.
(d) Statement I is correct, but statement II is incorrect.

6. Pollen grains from certain plants can trigger allergic reactions in some individuals. What is the most likely reason why pollen grains from some plants can cause these reactions?
(a) Presence of essential vitamins in the pollen.
(b) Specific substances within the pollen that the immune system misidentifies as harmful.
(c) High sugar content in the pollen causing irritation.
(d) Colour pigments in the pollen causing skin reactions.

7. Which of the following statements are incorrect regarding the pollen grains?
I. Pollen tablets formed from pollen grains are used as food supplements.
II. A large number of pollen products are consumed as tablets and syrups.
III. They are generally used to increase the performance of football players and cattles.
IV. The viability of pollen grains depends upon the temperature and humidity.
V. Carrot grass came to India with imported rice as a contaminant and causes pollen allergy.
Choose the correct option from the following.
(a) III and V (b) I and IV
(c) II and IV (d) I and V

8. Out of the following, how many have more than one ovule?
Wheat, Papaya, Paddy, Watermelon, Orchids
(a) Two (b) Three
(c) Four (d) One

9. Match List I with List II.

	List I		List II
A.	Funicle	1.	Basal part of ovules
B.	Integument	2.	Nutritive mass of cells
C.	Chalaza	3.	Stalk that attach ovule to placenta
D.	Nucellus	4.	Protective envelopes

Choose the correct option from the following.
(a) A-4, B-1, C-3, D-2
(b) A-3, B-4, C-1, D-2
(c) A-4, B-2, C-1, D-3
(d) A-3, B-2, C-4, D-1

10. The given figure shows a diagrammatic view of a typical anatropous ovule, in which some parts are marked as A, B, C and D. Identify the correct part where three antipodal cells lie and which acts as basal point of ovule.

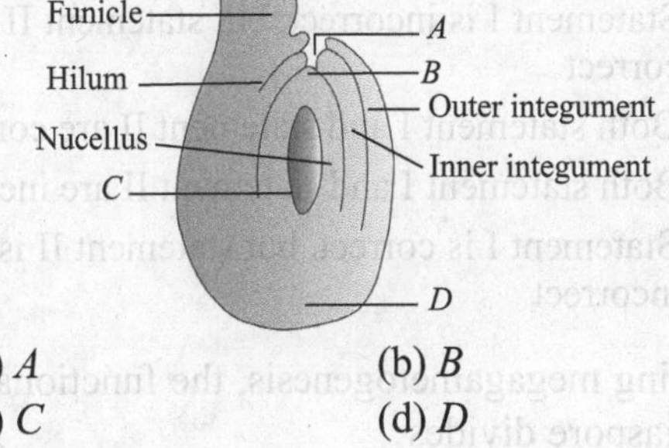

(a) *A* (b) *B*
(c) *C* (d) *D*

11. Given below are two statements.
Statement I The single functional megaspore develops into a female gametophyte.
Statement II The nucleus of the functional megaspore divides meiotically to form 4 nuclei which move to opposite poles.
In the light of the above statements, choose the correct answer from the options given below.
(a) Statement I is incorrect, but statement II is correct
(b) Both statement I and statement II are correct
(c) Both statement I and statement II are incorrect
(d) Statement I is correct, but statement II is incorrect

12. Select the incorrect statements w.r.t. embryo sac.
I. Two sequential mitotic divisions result in 8 celled stages of the embryo sac.
II. The nuclear divisions are strictly free nuclear in embryo sac development.
III. Four of the eight nuclei are surrounded by cell walls and organised into cells.
IV. Polar nuclei are situated above the egg apparatus in the large central cell when chalazal end is considered at top.
V. A characteristic distribution of the cells is seen within the embryo sac.

Choose the correct option from the following.
(a) I, II and V (b) II, III and V
(c) I, III and IV (d) II, IV and V

13. Given below are two statements.

Statement I Four cells are grouped together at the micropylar end to form the egg apparatus.

Statement II Egg apparatus consists of three synergids and one egg cell.

In the light of the above statements, choose the correct answer from the options given below.
(a) Statement I is incorrect, but statement II is correct
(b) Both statement I and statement II are correct
(c) Both statement I and statement II are incorrect
(d) Statement I is correct, but statement II is incorrect

14. During megagametogenesis, the functional megaspore divides
(a) two times (b) three times
(c) one time (d) four times

15. Which of the following flowers ensures seed production even when pollinators are absent?
(a) Cleistogamous (b) Chasmogamous
(c) Geitonogamous (d) Xenogamous

16. Given below are the two statements; one is labelled as the Assertion (A) and the other is labelled as the Reason (R).

Assertion (A) Insects visit flower to gather honey.

Reason (R) Insects gets floral rewards, e.g. nectar for helping in pollination.

In the light of the above statements, choose the correct answer from the options given below.
(a) A is false, but R is true
(b) Both A and R are true and R is the correct explanation of A
(c) Both A and R are true, but R is not the correct explanation of A
(d) A is true, but R is false

17. Given below are two statements.

Statement I Wind-pollinated flowers are typically brightly coloured and fragrant to attract insects for pollination.

Statement II Wind-pollinated flowers often have numerous, lightweight pollen grains for efficient airborne dispersal.

In light of the above statements, choose the correct answer from the options given below.
(a) Statement I is incorrect, but statement II is correct
(b) Both statement I and statement II are correct
(c) Both statement I and statement II are incorrect
(d) Statement I is correct, but statement II is incorrect

18. Match the type of cross pollination given in List I with their feature given in List II.

List I		List II	
A.	Zoophily	1.	Pollinatin by birds
B.	Ornithophily	2.	Pollination by insects
C.	Entomophily	3.	Pollination by bats
D.	Chiropterophily	4.	Pollination by animals

Select the correct answer using the codes given below.
(a) A-3; B-2; C-1; D-4
(b) A-1; B-2; C-3; D-4
(c) A-4; B-1; C-2; D-3
(d) A-4; B-2; C-1; D-3

19. While most flowering plants rely on other methods for pollen dispersal, a select group of about 30 genera, predominantly monocots, utilise water as the medium for pollen transport.

Among the following, which is an example of a freshwater flowering plant that uses water pollination?
(a) Marine algae (b) *Vallisneria*
(c) *Zostera* (d) Water hyacinth

20. Which of the following statements about self-incompatibility are correct?

I. It is a mechanism to prevent outbreeding.
II. It provides a biochemical barrier to self-fertilisation.
III. It ensures cross-fertilisation.
IV. It is controlled by pollen-pistil interaction.
V. It is regulated by a series of multiple alleles.

Choose the correct statements.
(a) I, II and V (b) III and IV
(c) I, III and IV (d) II, III, IV and V

21. Given below are two statements.

Statement I In some flowering plants, pollen release and stigma receptivity are not synchronised, preventing self-pollination.

Statement II Self-pollination is always detrimental to flowering plants and all species have evolved mechanisms to prevent it.
In the light of the above statements, choose the correct answer from the options given below.
(a) Statement I is incorrect, but statement II is correct
(b) Both statement I and statement II are correct
(c) Both statement I and statement II are incorrect
(d) Statement I is correct, but statement II is incorrect

22. Which of the following statement is incorrect about emasculation?
(a) Emasculation is the removal of stamens from the bisexual flowers.
(b) Emasculated flowers are bagged in order to prevent self-pollination.
(c) It is one of the steps for artificial hybridisation.
(d) It is done after the desiccation of anthers, using a pair of forceps.

23. Refer to the given diagram and select the correct option regarding processes A, B and C.

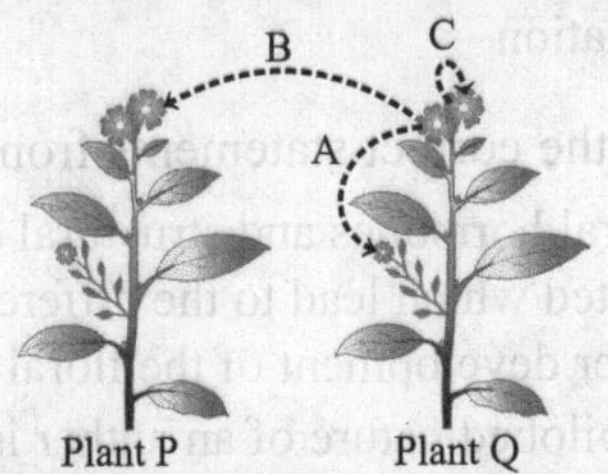

(a) In process B, synchrony is required in pollen release and stigma receptivity
(b) Process C can result into inbreeding depression
(c) Wind serves as agent for process B if plant P and Q belong to genus–*Salvia*
(d) Processes A, B and C introduce genetic variability in the offspring of sexually reproducing plants A and B

24. Which of the following statement is most likely true concerning non-albuminous seeds?
(a) They have a thick fleshy cotyledon filled with stored food reserves.
(b) They possess a well-developed endosperm that nourishes the developing embryo.
(c) They rely solely on the external environment for nutrients after germination.
(d) Their embryos are small and undifferentiated, lacking stored food.

25. Given below are two statements.
Statement I Endosperm is formed as a result of triple fusion.
Statement II Endosperm provides nutrition to the developing embryo.
In the light of the above statements, choose the correct answer from the options given below.
(a) Statement I is incorrect, but statement II is correct
(b) Both statement I and statement II are correct
(c) Both statement I and statement II are incorrect
(d) Statement I is correct, but statement II is incorrect

26. Given below are the two statements; one is labelled as Assertion (A) and the other is labelled as Reason (R)
Assertion (A) Pea is an ex-albuminous seed.
Reason (R) Endosperm is absent in pea seed.
In the light of the above statements, choose the correct answer from the options given below.
(a) A is false, but R is true
(b) Both A and R are true and R is the correct explanation of A
(c) Both A and R are true, but R is not the correct explanation of A
(d) A is true, but R is false

27. Select the incorrect option with respect to fruit.
(a) It works as a source of energy for animals
(b) It protects seeds
(c) It helps in the dispersal of seeds
(d) Its water content gets reduced and it gets dried on maturation

28. Identify the structure most likely rich in stored food reserves to nourish the developing embryo.

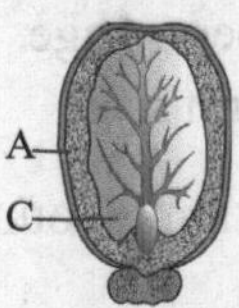

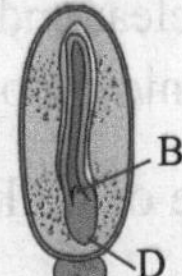

(a) A and B
(b) B and C
(c) C and A
(d) D and A

29. Given below are two statements.
Statement I Apomixis is the only method of seed production in all species of Asteraceae and grasses.

Statement II In apomixis, a diploid egg cell develops into an embryo without requiring fertilisation, mimicing asexual reproduction.

In the light of the above statements, choose the correct answer from the options given below.

(a) Statement I is incorrect, but statement II is correct
(b) Both statement I and statement II are correct
(c) Both statement I and statement II are incorrect
(d) Statement I is correct, but statement II is incorrect

30. Considering the limitations of hybrid seeds, which of the following applications of apomixis would be most advantageous for farmers?

(a) Apomixis can eliminate the need for pollination in crop production.
(b) Apomixis can create new hybrid varieties with improved characteristics.
(c) Apomixis can allow farmers to reuse seeds from hybrid crops for planting in subsequent generations.
(d) Apomixis can reduce the overall cost of producing hybrid seeds.

31. Which of the following is true about the endosperm in cereals like wheat, rice and maize?

(a) It is always persistant in the mature seed.
(b) It is completely consumed before seed maturation.
(c) It varies greatly in persistence across different species.
(d) It is only present during seed germination.

32. Which stage of endosperm development involves successive nuclear divisions without cell wall formation?

(a) Cellular endosperm stage
(b) Triploid endosperm stage
(c) Free-nuclear endosperm stage
(d) Embryonic endosperm stage

33. Which type of pollination is found in the given figure?

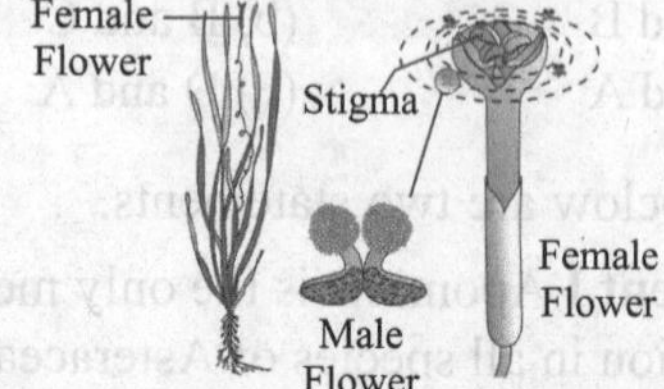

(a) Wind pollination (b) Water pollination
(c) Insect pollination (d) Ant pollination

34. Given below are two statements.

Statement I Endosperm development is crucial as it provides structural support to the developing embryo.

Statement II The primary endosperm cell divides repeatedly to form a triploid endosperm tissue which provides nutrition to the developing embryo.

In the light of the above statements, choose the correct answer from the options given below.

(a) Statement I is incorrect, but statement II is correct.
(b) Both statement I and statement II are correct
(c) Both statement I and statement II are incorrect
(d) Statement I is correct, but statement II is incorrect

35. The main disadvantage of cleistogamous flowers in terms of genetic diversity is that

(a) they do not produce seeds
(b) they ensure only self-pollination, leading to less genetic variation
(c) they require external pollinators
(d) they depend on environmental factors for pollination

36. Identify the correct statements from the following.

I. Several hormones and structural changes are initiated which lead to the differentiation and further development of the floral primordium.
II. The bilobed nature of an anther is very distinct in the longitudinal section of the anther.
III. The anther is tetragonal structure consisting of four microsporangia located at the corners, two in each lobe.
IV. The pollen sacs are extended longitudinally all throughout the length of an anther and are packed with pollen grains.

Choose the correct answer from the options given below.

(a) I and II (b) II and IV
(c) I, III and IV (d) II and III

37. Which plants are mentioned as examples that produce both chasmogamous and cleistogamous flowers?

(a) *Vallisneria* and coconut
(b) *Viola, Oxalis* and *Commelina*
(c) Wheat, rice and maize
(d) Pea, groundnut and beans

38. How does the presence of a vegetative cell in the pollen grain contribute to the overall process of fertilisation in flowering plants?

(a) By providing energy for the pollen grain
(b) By protecting the generative cell from external damage
(c) By forming the pollen tube that delivers sperm cells to the ovule
(d) By ensuring the genetic diversity of the offspring

39. What does the given figure represent?

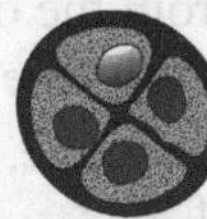

(a) An enlarged view of a pollen tetrad
(b) The formation of endosperm tissue
(c) The stages of seed germination
(d) The process of fertilisation in flowering plants

40. Given below are two statements; one is labelled as Assertion (A) and other one is labelled as Reason (R).

Assertion (A) Autogamy is the transfer of pollen grains from the anther to the stigma of the same flower.

Reason (R) Autogamy in flowers with exposed anther and stigma is common.

In the light of above statements, choose the correct answer from the options given below.

(a) A is false, but R is true
(b) Both A and R are true, and R is the correct explanation of A
(c) Both A and R are true, but R is not the correct explanation of A
(d) A is true, but R is false

41. Some of the stages of a microspore maturing into a pollen grain are given below. Identify the correct order of these stages in which they occur and select the correct options.

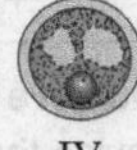

I II III IV

(a) I → II → III → IV
(b) II → IV → I → III
(c) II → I → IV → III
(d) IV → III → II → I

42. If the endothecium layer of the microsporangium was genetically modified to lose its ability to function, what impact would this have on the anther.

(a) The pollen grains would become inviable due to lack of nutrients
(b) The anther would fail to dehisce, preventing pollen release.
(c) The sporogenous tissue would not form, halting pollen production.
(d) The tapetum would compensate by increasing its protective role.

43. Consider the following figures and identify the correct option.

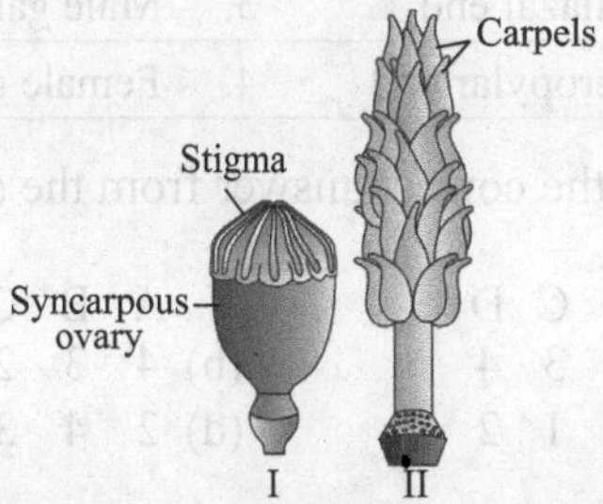

(a) Syncarpous pistil of *Papaver*, Apocarpous gynoecium of *Michelia*
(b) Apocarpous gynoecium of *Hibiscus*, Syncarpous pistil of rose
(c) Apocarpous gynoecium of *Michelia*, Syncarpous pistil of *Papaver*
(d) Syncarpous pistil of rose, Apocarpous gynoecium of *Hibiscus*

44. Why is it significant for tapetal cells to have dense cytoplasm and often more than one nucleus?

(a) It enhances their protective function for the microsporangium
(b) It aids in the synthesis and transport of nutrients to the developing pollen grains.
(c) It allows them to undergo meiosis and produce pollen grains
(d) It ensures the structural integrity of the microsporangium

45. Given below are two statements.

Statement I A group of compactly arranged homogenous cells called the sporogenous tissue occupies the centre of each microsporangium.

Statement II Sporogenous tissues have dense cytoplasm and generally have more than one nucleus, and is present in mature anther.
In the light of the above statements, choose the correct answer from the options given below.
(a) Statement I is incorrect, but statement II is correct
(b) Both statement I and statement II are correct
(c) Both statement I and statement Ii are incorrect
(d) Statement I is correct, but statement II is incorrect

46. Match List I with List II.

List I		List II	
A.	Pollen grains	1.	Antipodal cells
B.	Embryo sac	2.	Synergid cells
C.	Chalazal end	3.	Male gametophyte
D.	Micropylar end	4.	Female gametophyte

Choose the correct answer from the options given below.

	A	B	C	D		A	B	C	D
(a)	1	2	3	4	(b)	4	3	2	1
(c)	3	4	1	2	(d)	2	4	3	1

47. Which of the following best describes the nature of the nuclear divisions during the formation of the embryo sac?
(a) These are synchronous, followed by simultaneous cell wall formation.
(b) They are strictly free nuclear, with mitotic divisions not immediately followed by cell wall formation.
(c) They are accompanied by cytoplasmic divisions to form distinct cells.
(d) They involve a mix of free nuclear and cell wall formations at each stage.

48. Given below are two statements, one is labelled as Assertion (A) and other is labelled as Reason (R).
Assertion (A) In monosporic development, the degeneration of three megaspores is a common feature in flowering plants.
Reason (R) The degeneration of three megaspores allows the functional megaspore to develop into a highly specialised embryo sac.
In the light of above statements, choose the correct answer from the options given below.
(a) A is false, but R is true
(b) Both A and R are true, and R is the correct explanation of A
(c) Both A and R are true, but R is not the correct explanation of A
(d) A is true, but R is false

49. If the haploid number in a flowering plant is 8, what shall be the number of chromosomes in integuments, antipodal cells, synergid cells and endosperm, respectively?
(a) 16, 8, 8, 24
(b) 8, 8, 16, 24
(c) 16, 16, 16, 24
(d) 8, 8, 8, 16

50. Male gametes or sperms are developed from generative cell by
(a) meiotic division
(b) mitotic division
(c) amitotic division
(d) vegetative division

Scan for online chapter test

Response Index

01 ⓐ ⓑ ⓒ ⓓ	14 ⓐ ⓑ ⓒ ⓓ	27 ⓐ ⓑ ⓒ ⓓ	40 ⓐ ⓑ ⓒ ⓓ
02 ⓐ ⓑ ⓒ ⓓ	15 ⓐ ⓑ ⓒ ⓓ	28 ⓐ ⓑ ⓒ ⓓ	41 ⓐ ⓑ ⓒ ⓓ
03 ⓐ ⓑ ⓒ ⓓ	16 ⓐ ⓑ ⓒ ⓓ	29 ⓐ ⓑ ⓒ ⓓ	42 ⓐ ⓑ ⓒ ⓓ
04 ⓐ ⓑ ⓒ ⓓ	17 ⓐ ⓑ ⓒ ⓓ	30 ⓐ ⓑ ⓒ ⓓ	43 ⓐ ⓑ ⓒ ⓓ
05 ⓐ ⓑ ⓒ ⓓ	18 ⓐ ⓑ ⓒ ⓓ	31 ⓐ ⓑ ⓒ ⓓ	44 ⓐ ⓑ ⓒ ⓓ
06 ⓐ ⓑ ⓒ ⓓ	19 ⓐ ⓑ ⓒ ⓓ	32 ⓐ ⓑ ⓒ ⓓ	45 ⓐ ⓑ ⓒ ⓓ
07 ⓐ ⓑ ⓒ ⓓ	20 ⓐ ⓑ ⓒ ⓓ	33 ⓐ ⓑ ⓒ ⓓ	46 ⓐ ⓑ ⓒ ⓓ
08 ⓐ ⓑ ⓒ ⓓ	21 ⓐ ⓑ ⓒ ⓓ	34 ⓐ ⓑ ⓒ ⓓ	47 ⓐ ⓑ ⓒ ⓓ
09 ⓐ ⓑ ⓒ ⓓ	22 ⓐ ⓑ ⓒ ⓓ	35 ⓐ ⓑ ⓒ ⓓ	48 ⓐ ⓑ ⓒ ⓓ
10 ⓐ ⓑ ⓒ ⓓ	23 ⓐ ⓑ ⓒ ⓓ	36 ⓐ ⓑ ⓒ ⓓ	49 ⓐ ⓑ ⓒ ⓓ
11 ⓐ ⓑ ⓒ ⓓ	24 ⓐ ⓑ ⓒ ⓓ	37 ⓐ ⓑ ⓒ ⓓ	50 ⓐ ⓑ ⓒ ⓓ
12 ⓐ ⓑ ⓒ ⓓ	25 ⓐ ⓑ ⓒ ⓓ	38 ⓐ ⓑ ⓒ ⓓ	
13 ⓐ ⓑ ⓒ ⓓ	26 ⓐ ⓑ ⓒ ⓓ	39 ⓐ ⓑ ⓒ ⓓ	

Performance Scanner

> 90% Excellent !	You have mastered this chapter. The concepts of this chapter are at your fingertips. Move on to the next chapter and maintain this momentum.
76-90% Very Good !	You have a good command over this chapter. Revise the chapter again after a few days and enhance your performance.
60-75% Good !	You have a wide scope to learn for this chapter. Revise this chapter again.
<60% Not Satisfactory!	You have a long way ahead of you to master this chapter. Revise it thoroughly.

Test Booklet No. **3947352**

Test Booklet Code **CH2**

MEDACE
NEET (UG)
SELF ASSESSMENT KIT

Human Reproduction

Topics Covered

Male and Female Reproductive System

Gametogenesis and Menstrual Cycle

Fertilisation and Post-Fertilisation Changes

Important Instructions

- This Booklet Contains – Three Topic Tests and One Test on Complete Chapter.
- Each question carries 4 marks.
- For each correct response, the candidate will get 4 marks. And for every incorrect response, 1 mark will be additionally deducted from total score.
- Use **Blue/Black** point pen only for filling the OMR.
- Rough work is to be done in the space provided for this purpose in the test booklet only.

Name of the Candidate (In Capitals) ______

______

Candidate's Signature ______

Invigilator's Signature ______

Facsimile signature stamp of center superintendent ______

Do not open this booklet until you start attempting the test

Topical Follow Thru

Test 1

Syllabus Male and female reproductive systems; Microscopic anatomy of testis

For deeper insight, **Scan the QR Code**

Important Instructions

- The test is of 30 minutes duration and contains 15 Multiple Choice Questions (four options with a single correct answer).
- Choose the correct option and fill the OMR given on the last page of this test accordingly.
- At some instances, you may find more than 1 option to be correct. In such circumstances, you have to judge the most appropriate answer as per the conditions given in the question.

1. Each seminiferous tubule is lined on the interior side by two types of cells, which are

(a) interstitial cells and Leydig cells
(b) male germ cells and interstitial cells
(c) spermatogonia and Sertoli cells
(d) spermatogonia and Leydig cells

2. Which of the following structures contribute to the seminal plasma, the fluid part of semen?

(a) Seminal vesicle and Prostate gland
(b) Seminal vesicle, Prostate gland and Bulbourethral gland
(c) Prostate gland, Urethra and Bulbourethral gland
(d) Seminal vesicle and Bulbourethral gland

3. Select the incorrect match.

(a) Mons pubis - A cushion of fatty tissue covered by skin and pubic hair.
(b) Labia majora - Fleshy folds of tissue, which extend down from the mons pubis and surround the vaginal opening.
(c) Labia minora - Paired folds of tissue under the labia majora.
(d) Clitoris - A tiny finger-like structure which lies at the upper junction of the two labia minora below the urethral opening.

4. Identify the correct path of milk production and its expulsion out of the mammary glands.

I. Mammary ducts
II. Mammary ampulla
III. Nipples
IV. Mammary alveoli
V. Lactiferous ducts
VI. Mammary tubules

Choose the correct answer from the options given below.

(a) IV, VI, I, II, V, III
(b) IV, I, II, V, VI, III
(c) IV, II, I, V, VI, III
(d) III, VI, V, II, I, IV

5. Given below are two statements.

Statement I Male sex accessory ducts includes rete testis, vasa efferentia, epididymis and vesicles.

Statement II The secretion of male accessory glands constitutes the seminal plasma which is rich in fructose, calcium and certain enzymes.

In the light of the above statements, choose the correct answer from the options given below.

(a) Statement I is incorrect, but statement II is correct
(b) Both statement I and statement II are correct
(c) Both statement I and statement II are incorrect
(d) Statement I is correct, but statement II is incorrect

6. Identify the correct set of internal structure of testis from innermost coat to outermost coat.

(a) Tunica vaginalis, tunica vasculosa, tunica albuginea
(b) Tunica vasculosa, tunica albuginea, tunica vaginalis

(c) Tunica vasculosa, tunica vaginalis, tunica albuginea
(d) Tunica albuginea, tunica vasculosa, tunica vaginalis

7. Read the following statements.

I. The shape of the uterus is like an inverted pear and is also called the womb.
II. The uterus is supported by ligaments attached to the abdominal wall.
III. The uterus opens into the vagina through a narrow cervix.
IV. Perimetrium, myometrium and endometrium are the three wall of uterus
V. The endometrium exhibits strong contractions during the delivery of the baby.

Choose the set of correct statements from the options given below.
(a) I, II, III, IV and V
(b) I, III and IV
(c) I, IV and V
(d) I, III, and V

8. Match List I with List II.

List I		List II	
A.	Interstitial cells	1.	Functional unit of paired male organ
B.	Prostate gland	2.	Androgens
C.	Sertoli cells	3.	Club shaped, paired
D.	Seminal vesicles	4.	Unpaired, enhances motility of spermatozoa
E.	Testicular lobule	5.	Provides nutrition for spermatogonia

Choose the correct option.
(a) A–2, B–3, C–5, D–4, E–1
(b) A–5, B–4, C–2, D–3, E–1
(c) A–2, B–4, C–5, D–3, E–1
(d) A–2, B–4, C–1, D–3, E–5

9. Given below are two statements; one is labelled as Assertion (A) and the other is labelled as Reason (R).

Assertion (A) The isthmus is the longest part of the Fallopian tube, which connects ampulla to the uterus.

Reason (R) The isthmus contains ciliated epithelial cells that help the movement of the ovum from the ampulla to the uterus.

In the light of the above statements, choose the correct answer from the options given below:
(a) A is false, but R is true
(b) Both A and R are true and R is the correct explanation of A
(c) Both A and R are correct, but R is not the correct explanation of A
(d) A is true, but R is false

10. Identify A, B & C from the following diagram.

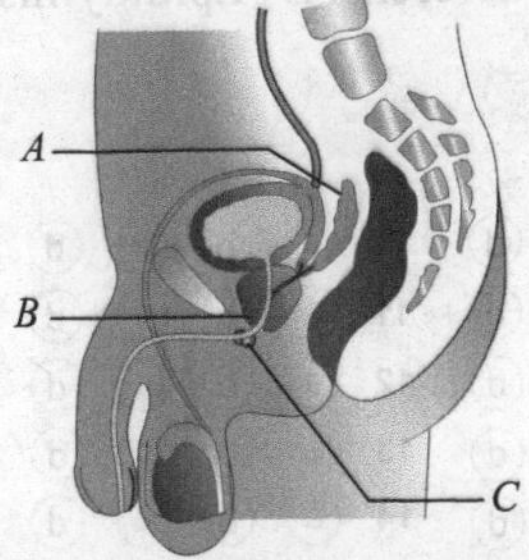

(a) A–Seminal vesicle, B–Bulbourethral gland, C–Prostate gland
(b) A–Seminal vesicle, B–Prostate gland, C–Bulbourethral gland
(c) A–Prostate gland, B–Bulbourethral gland, C–Seminal vesicle
(d) A–Prostate gland, B–Seminal vesicle, C–Bulbourethral gland

11. Structure which is essential for the maturation and storage of sperms is
(a) epididymis (b) vasa efferentia
(c) testes (s) seminal vesicle

12. In females, birth canal is formed by
(a) cervix and vagina
(b) vagina only
(c) cervical canal and vagina
(d) vagina, cervix and womb

13. If the Cowper's gland is surgically removed, which of the following functions in the male reproductive system would be directly affected?
(a) Spermatogenesis
(b) Spermiation
(c) Motility of sperm
(d) Lubrication of penis

14. Given below is a flowchart depicting process of sperm transportation in human males.

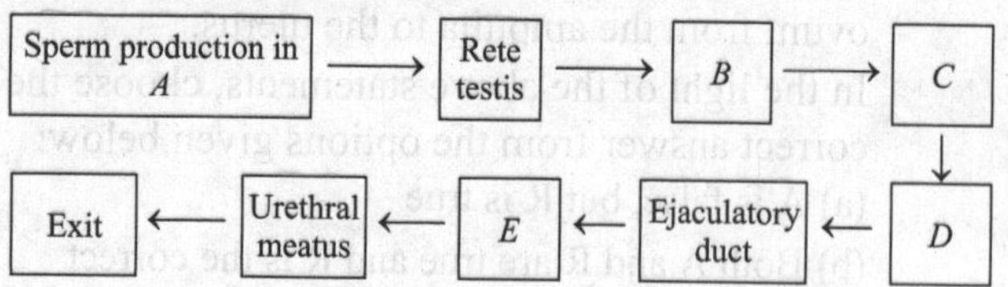

Choose the correct labelling for *A-E* from the given options.

(a) *A*–Vasa efferentia, *B*–Seminiferous tubules, *C*–Epididymis, *D*–Vas deferens, *E*–Urethra

(b) *A*–Seminiferous tubule, *B*–Vasa efferentia, *C*–Vas deferens, *D*–Epididymis, *E*–Urethra

(c) *A*–Vas deferens, *B*–Seminiferous tubules, *C*–Epididymis, *D*–Vasa efferentia, *E*–urethra

(d) *A*–Seminiferous tubules, *B*–Vasa efferentia, *C*–Epididymis, *D*–Vas deferens, *E*–Urethra

15. Select the incorrect statement.

(a) Seminal gland is derived from the mesonephric duct

(b) Prostaglandins in seminal gland secretions suppress female immune response to foreign semen

(c) Secretion of seminal gland is acidic in nature

(d) Inner layer of seminal gland is comprised of pseudostratified columnar epithelium

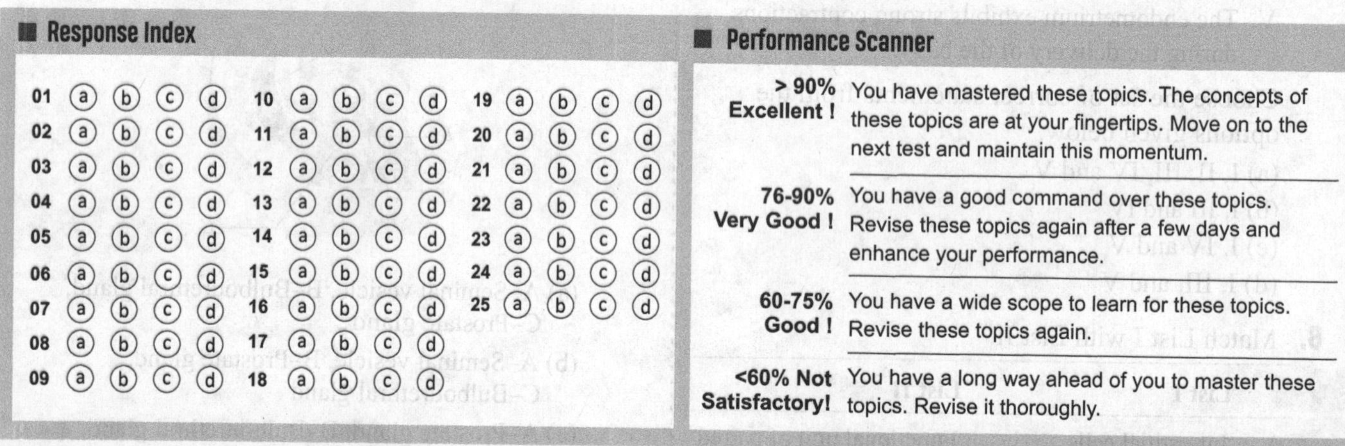

Test 2

Syllabus • Gametogenesis-Spermatogenesis and oogenesis • Microscopic anatomy of ovary; Menstrual cycle

For deeper insight, **Scan the QR Code**

Important Instructions

- The test is of 30 minutes duration and contains 15 Multiple Choice Questions (four options with a single correct answer).
- Choose the correct option and fill the OMR given on the last page of this test accordingly.
- At some instances, you may find more than 1 option to be correct. In such circumstances, you have to judge the most appropriate answer as per the conditions given in the question.

1. When does a human female have the maximum number of primary oocytes in her ovaries?

(a) At puberty

(b) Early in her fertile years

(c) At menopause

(d) At birth

2. Sertoli cells are responsible for spermatogenesis procedure and it's regulation by releasing two hormones at different times. These hormones released in turn, are

(a) FSH and LH

(b) testosterone and inhibin

(c) inhibin and testosterone

(d) relaxin and GnRH

3. Match List I with List II.

	List I		List II
A.	Follicular phase	1.	Event occur due to increased secretion of LH.
B.	Menstrual phase	2.	Regresses to form corpus albicans
C.	Luteal phase	3.	Breakdown of endometrium lining of uterus and blood vessels
D.	Ovulatory phase	4.	One primodial follicle develops into a mature Graafian follicle

Choose the correct answer from the options given below.

	A	B	C	D
(a)	4	3	1	2
(b)	2	4	3	1
(c)	4	3	2	1
(d)	2	3	1	4

4. How many spermatids will form 100 sperms?

(a) 100 (b) 25
(c) 50 (d) 400

5. In the given diagram, what are the functions of *A* and *B*?

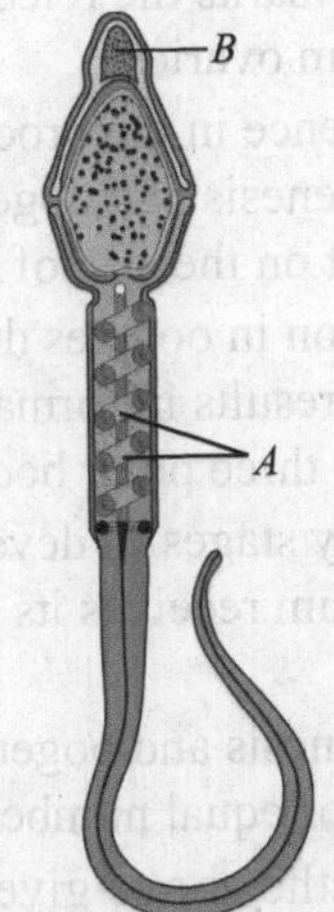

(a) *A* forms tail, whereas *B* provides energy for motility
(b) *A* contains hydrolytic enzymes, whereas *B* facilitates sperm motility
(c) *A* maintains structure of sperm, whereas *B* is filled with enzyme
(d) *A* provides energy for motility, whereas *B* contains hydrolytic enzymes

6. Consider the following paragraph and fill in the blanks with correct options.

Luteinizing hormones acts on …I…, while Follicle stimulating acts on …II… . The former hormone helps in stimulating spermatogenesis by synthesis and secretion of androgen while, the latter is important to stimulate …III… .

(a) I–Leydig cells, II–Sertoli cells, III–Spermiation
(b) I–Interstitial cells, II–Sertoli cells, III–Spermiogenesis
(c) I–Sertoli cells, II–Interstitial cells, III–Spermiogenesis
(d) I–Leydig cells, II–Sertoli cells, III–fertilisation

7. Given below is a flowchart representing the phases of spermatogenesis. Choose the correct labels for *A* to *D* act of the given options.

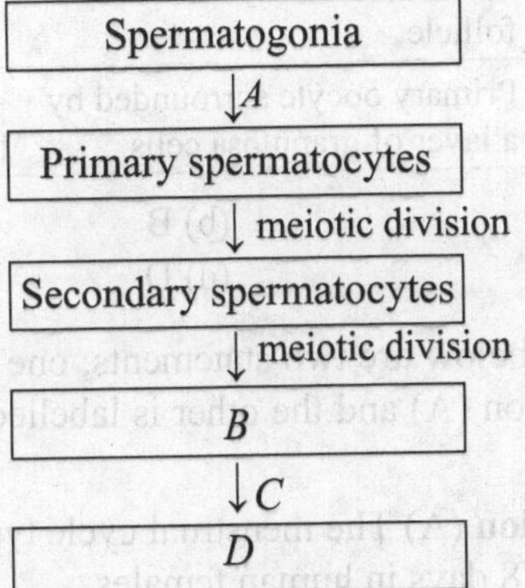

(a) *A*–Meiosis, *B*–Spermatids, *C*–Differentiation, *D*–Spermatozoa
(b) *A*–Mitosis, *B*–Spermatids, *C*–Mitosis, *D*–Spermatozoa
(c) *A*–Mitosis, *B*–Spermatids, *C*–Differentiation, *D*–Spermatozoa
(d) *A*–Meiosis, *B*–Spermatozoa, *C*–Mitosis, *D*–Spermatids

8. Which among the following has haploid set of chromosomes in human?

(a) Oogonia (b) Primary oocyte
(c) Secondary oocyte (d) Zygote

9. Given below are two statements; one is labelled as Assertion (A) and other is labelled as Reason (R).

Assertion (A) The release of an ovum from ovary is known as ovulation.

Reason (R) Rapid secretion of FSH induces rupturing of Graafian follicle and thereby the release of ovum.

In the light of the above statements, choose the correct answer from the options given below.

(a) A is false, but R is true
(b) Both A and R are true and R is the correct explanation of A
(c) Both A and R are true, but R is not the correct explanation of A
(d) A is true, but R is false

10. Select the incorrect match.

A.	Degenerative process of follicles or eggs in ovary	– Regression
B.	Result of unequal division in primary oocyte	– Polar body
C.	Fluid filled cavity in tertiary follicle	– Antrum
D.	Primary oocyte surrounded by a layer of granulosa cells	– Primary follicle

(a) A (b) B
(c) C (d) D

11. Given below are two statements; one is labelled as Assertion (A) and the other is labelled as Reason (R).

Assertion (A) The menstrual cycle typically lasts about 28 days in human females.

Reason (R) The luteal phase, which occurs after ovulation, is consistently around 14 days long in most women.

In the light of the above statements, choose the correct answer from the options given below.

(a) A is false, but R is true
(b) Both A and R are true, and R is the correct explanation of A
(c) Both A and R are true, but R is not the correct explanation of A
(d) A is true, but R is false

12. The role of gonadotropin releasing hormone is to stimulate the production of
(a) progesterone and oestrogen
(b) inhibin and LH
(c) FSH and LH
(d) oestrogen and androgen

13. LH level declines during luteal phase, why?
(a) Level of oestrogen and progesterone inclines
(b) Level of oestrogen and progesterone declines
(c) Level of oestrogen inclines and level of progesterone declines
(d) Level of oestrogen declines and level of progesterone inclines

14. Given below are two statements.

Statement I Estrous cycle in non-primates is exactly similar to menstrual cycle in human and differs only in terms of absence of blood flow that is menstrual flow.

Statement II The period of heat in estrous females marks the high oestrogen level in blood which increases the urge for copulation.

In the light of the above statements, choose the correct answer from the options given below.

(a) Statement I is incorrect, but statement II is correct
(b) Both statement I and statement II are correct
(c) Both statement I and statement II are incorrect
(d) Statement I is correct, but statement II is incorrect

15. Find the correct statements.

I. Ovulation marks the release of secondary oocyte from ovaries.
II. The difference in the process of spermatogenesis and oogenesis does not have any impact on the size of sperm and ova.
III. Cell division in oocytes during meiosis I and meiosis II results in formation of one large egg and two or three polar bodies.
IV. At the early stages of development, the newly formed ovum receives its nutrition from cytoplasm.
V. Spermiogenesis and oogenesis results into formation of equal number of daughter cells.

In the light of the above given statement, choose correct answer from the options given below.
(a) Only I
(b) I, III and V
(c) I, III and IV
(d) I and V

■ **Response Index**

01	(a)	(b)	(c)	(d)	10	(a)	(b)	(c)	(d)	19	(a)	(b)	(c)	(d)
02	(a)	(b)	(c)	(d)	11	(a)	(b)	(c)	(d)	20	(a)	(b)	(c)	(d)
03	(a)	(b)	(c)	(d)	12	(a)	(b)	(c)	(d)	21	(a)	(b)	(c)	(d)
04	(a)	(b)	(c)	(d)	13	(a)	(b)	(c)	(d)	22	(a)	(b)	(c)	(d)
05	(a)	(b)	(c)	(d)	14	(a)	(b)	(c)	(d)	23	(a)	(b)	(c)	(d)
06	(a)	(b)	(c)	(d)	15	(a)	(b)	(c)	(d)	24	(a)	(b)	(c)	(d)
07	(a)	(b)	(c)	(d)	16	(a)	(b)	(c)	(d)	25	(a)	(b)	(c)	(d)
08	(a)	(b)	(c)	(d)	17	(a)	(b)	(c)	(d)					
09	(a)	(b)	(c)	(d)	18	(a)	(b)	(c)	(d)					

■ **Performance Scanner**

> 90% Excellent !	You have mastered these topics. The concepts of these topics are at your fingertips. Move on to the next test and maintain this momentum.
76-90% Very Good !	You have a good command over these topics. Revise these topics again after a few days and enhance your performance.
60-75% Good !	You have a wide scope to learn for these topics. Revise these topics again.
<60% Not Satisfactory!	You have a long way ahead of you to master these topics. Revise it thoroughly.

Test 3

Syllabus

- Fertilisation, embryo development upto blastocyst formation
- Implantation : Pregnancy and placenta formation
- Parturition
- Lactation

For deeper insight, **Scan the QR Code**

Important Instructions

- The test is of 30 minutes duration and contains 15 Multiple Choice Questions (four options with a single correct answer).
- Choose the correct option and fill the OMR given on the last page of this test accordingly.
- At some instances, you may find more than 1 option to be correct. In such circumstances, you have to judge the most appropriate answer as per the conditions given in the question.

1. During fertilisation, spermatozoa does not pass through

(a) Birth canal (b) Uterine tube
(c) Infundibulum (d) Isthmus

2. Given below are two statements; one is labelled as Assertion (A) and the other is labelled as Reason (R).

Assertion (A) Not all copulations lead to fertilisation and pregnancy.

Reason (R) The ovum released by the ovary is transported to the ampullary region where fertilisation takes place.

In the light of the above statements, choose the correct answers from the options given below.

(a) A is false, but R is true
(b) Both A and R are true and R is the correct explanation of A
(c) Both A and R are true, but R is not the correct explanation of A
(d) A is true, but R is false

3. Arrange the events of fertilisation in the correct sequence.

I. Entry of sperm into egg cytoplasm
II. Karyogamy
III. Acrosomal reaction
IV. Zygote formation
V. Completion of meiosis-II in ovum

Choose the correct option.

(a) III → I → V → II → IV
(b) II → III → I → IV → V
(c) I → III → II → IV → V
(d) III → II → IV → I → V

4. Morulation is followed by blastulation, stage of blastula formation, which leads to implantation of embryo with uterine walls. Which structure of blastocyst adheres with the wall to support pregnancy?

(a) Blastocoel
(b) Trophoblast
(c) Inner cell mass
(d) Blastocoel and trophoblast

5. Match the List I with List II.

List I	List II
A. Endometrium	1. Widest part of Fallopian tube, site of gametes fusion
B. Oviduct or Fallopian tube opening	2. Uterine lining which supports the implantation during pregnancy
C. Ampulla	3. Ensures collection of ova after ovulation
D. Fimbriae	4. Provides pathway for ova and guides sperm to reach upto ova

Choose the correct answer from the options given below.

	A	B	C	D
(a)	3	1	4	2
(b)	2	4	1	3
(c)	1	3	2	4
(d)	1	2	4	3

6. Given below are two statements.

Statement I After implantation, finger-like projections appear on the trophoblast called chorionic villi which are surrounded by the uterine tissue and maternal blood.

Statement II The chorionic villi and uterine tissue become interdigitated with each other and jointly form a structural and functional unit between the developing embryo (foetus) and maternal body called the placenta.

In the light of the above statements, choose the correct answers from the options given below.

(a) Statement I is incorrect, but statement II is correct.
(b) Both statement I and statement II are correct.
(c) Both statement I and statement II are incorrect.
(d) Statement I is correct, but statement II is incorrect.

7. Select the correct order of phases of embryo development.

(a) Zygote, morula, blastula, and gastrula
(b) Zygote, blastula, morula, and gastrula
(c) Zygote, gastrula, morula, and blastula
(d) Morula, gastrula, blastula, and zygote

8. Which quality makes oxytocin a very important hormone?

(a) It induces parturition as well as milk ejection
(b) It induces parturition as well as triggers relaxin hormone
(c) It induces placenta dissolution and milk ejection
(d) It induces parturition and placenta dissolution

9. To keep a check of embryo development, multiple sonographies are done. In which month of pregnancy, heartbeat of embryo can be observed?

(a) After one month
(b) After 3 months
(c) After 6 months
(d) In the ninth month

10. Which structure in the given diagram is responsible for the development of 3 germ layers, i.e. ectoderm, mesoderm, and endoderm?

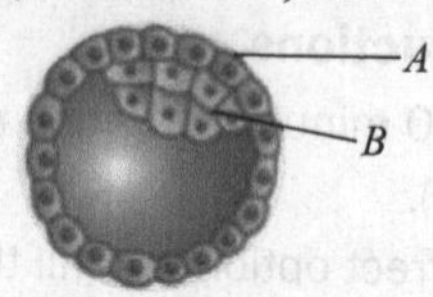

(a) A – ectoderm and mesoderm, B – endoderm
(b) A – all 3 germ layer
(c) B – all 3 germ layer
(d) A – ectoderm B – mesoderm and endoderm

11. Select the incorrect match.

	Embryonic development		Duration of pregnancy
A.	Development of limbs and digits of foetus	–	Second month
B.	Development of external genital organ	–	Third month
C.	First movement of foetus	–	Four month
D.	Body is covered with fine hair	–	24 weeks

(a) A (b) B
(c) C (d) D

12. Foetal ejection reflex is a result of

(a) Signals from the cervix only
(b) Signals from the mother's nervous system
(c) Signals from the ovaries
(d) Signals from the fully developed foetus and the placenta

13. Select the correct match.

(a) Prolactin - Placenta
(b) Progesterone - Corpus luteum
(c) Oxytocin - Ovary
(d) Relaxin -Pituitary

14. Given below are two statements.

Statement I The average duration of human pregnancy, known as the gastrulation period, is about 9 months.

Statement II The expulsion of the baby out of the uterus through the birth canal is called parturition.

In the light of the above statements, choose the correct answer from the options given below.

(a) Statement I is incorrect, but statement II is correct.
(b) Both statement I and statement II are correct.
(c) Both statement I and statement II are incorrect.
(d) Statement I is correct, but statement II is incorrect.

15. Which of the following statement is incorrect?

(a) Meiotic division of the secondary oocyte is completed prior to ovulation.
(b) Receptors for sperm binding in mammals are present on zona pellucida.
(c) Release of oxytocin is an important component of initiation of parturition in humans.
(d) Colostrum contains several antibodies absolutely essential to develop resistance for the new-born babies.

Response Index

01	a	b	c	d	10	a	b	c	d	19	a	b	c	d
02	a	b	c	d	11	a	b	c	d	20	a	b	c	d
03	a	b	c	d	12	a	b	c	d	21	a	b	c	d
04	a	b	c	d	13	a	b	c	d	22	a	b	c	d
05	a	b	c	d	14	a	b	c	d	23	a	b	c	d
06	a	b	c	d	15	a	b	c	d	24	a	b	c	d
07	a	b	c	d	16	a	b	c	d	25	a	b	c	d
08	a	b	c	d	17	a	b	c	d					
09	a	b	c	d	18	a	b	c	d					

Performance Scanner

> 90% Excellent !	You have mastered these topics. The concepts of these topics are at your fingertips. Move on to the next test and maintain this momentum.
76-90% Very Good !	You have a good command over these topics. Revise these topics again after a few days and enhance your performance.
60-75% Good !	You have a wide scope to learn for these topics. Revise these topics again.
<60% Not Satisfactory!	You have a long way ahead of you to master these topics. Revise it thoroughly.

Chapter Break Thru

Syllabus	• Male and female reproductive systems • Microscopic anatomy of testis and ovary • Gametogenesis-spermatogenesis and oogenesis	• Menstrual cycle • Fertilisation, embryo development upto blastocyst formation, implantation	• Pregnancy and placenta formation • Parturition • Lactation

Important Instructions

- The test is of 1 hour duration and contains 50 Multiple-Choice Questions (Four options with a single correct answer).
- Choose the correct option and fill the OMR given on the last page of this test accordingly.
- At some instances, you may find more than 1 option to be correct. In such circumstances, you have to judge the most appropriate answer as per the conditions given in the question.

1. Which part of a sperm produce the energy to facilitate the motility of sperm in the female body after coitus?

(a) Head (b) Middle piece
(c) Tail (d) Neck

2. Identify the correct sequence in the light of sperm transportation through male accessory reproductive ducts.

I. Vas deferens II. Epididymis
III. Rete testis IV. Vasa efferentia
V. Ejaculatory duct

(a) V, IV, I, II, III (b) IV, V, III, I, II
(c) III, IV, II, I, V (d) III, I, II, IV, V

3. Identify the structures that are responsible for constituting the seminal plasma.

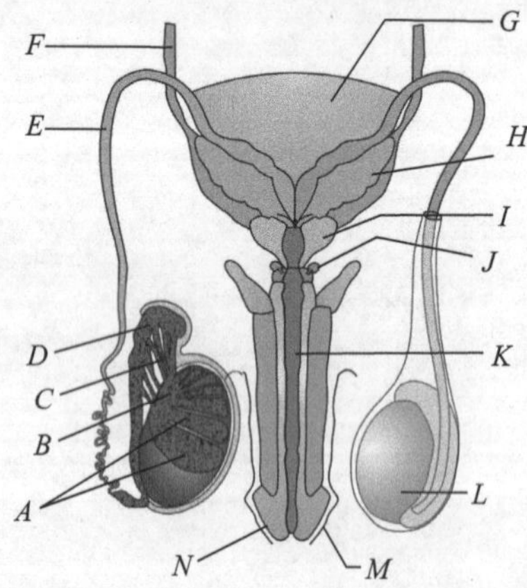

(a) A, B, C and D
(b) H, I and J
(c) B, C and D
(d) G, H, I and J

4. Identify the incorrect statement w.r.t. human male reproduction system.

(a) The scrotum helps in maintaining the low temperature of the testes (2–2.5°C lower than the normal internal body temperature) necessary only for longevity of sperm.
(b) Each testis has about 250 compartments called testicular lobules.
(c) Testicular lobule contains one to three highly coiled seminiferous tubules in which sperms are produced.
(d) In adults, each testis is oval in shape, with a length of about 4 to 5 cm and a width of about 2 to 3 cm.

5. How does the respirational needs of a foetus get fulfilled despite being enclosed in the amniotic cavity?

(a) Active transport of oxygen and carbon dioxide molecules occurs through placenta.
(b) Pinocytosis of oxygen and carbon dioxide molecules occurs through placenta.
(c) Diffusion of oxygen and carbon dioxide molecule occurs through placenta.
(d) Foetus does not require respiration until birth.

6. Gestation period of human is 9 months long. During entire period the foetus keeps growing, organogenesis confirms the embryo development. Multiple sonographies are performed to monitor the proper growth of organs, etc. In which duration of pregnancy, the doctor can determine the gender of the embryo?

(a) 12-14 weeks (b) 14-16 weeks
(c) 16-18 weeks (d) At the end of pregnancy

7. Identify the inverted pear shaped structure where embryo or foetus is developed.

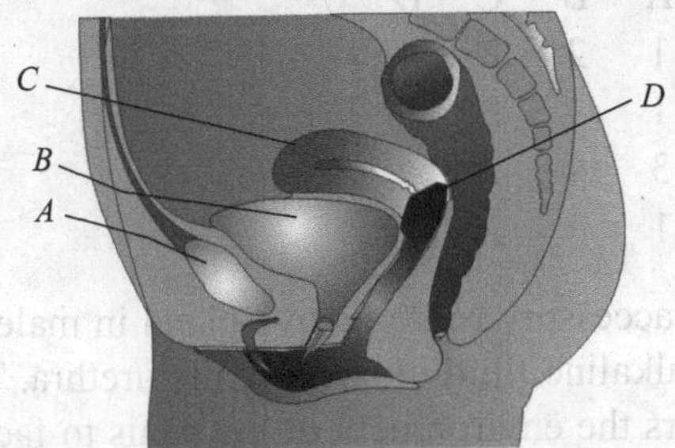

(a) A (b) B
(c) C (d) D

8. Identify the haploid cells among the following.
(a) Spermatogonia and oogonia
(b) Primary spermatocytes and primary oocytes
(c) Primary spermatocytes and secondary oocytes
(d) Secondary spermatocytes and secondary oocytes

9. Which of the following represents the correct order of spermatogenesis?
(a) Spermatogonia, Spermatocytes, Spermatozoa, Spermatid
(b) Spermatid, Spermatogonia, Spermatocytes, Sperm
(c) Spermatogonia, Primary Spermatocytes, Secondary Spermatocytes, Spermatid
(d) Spermatogonia, Spermatid, Spermatocytes, Sperm

10. Which stage of ovarian follicle development is also called as Graafian follicle?
(a) Primary follicle
(b) Secondary follicle
(c) Tertiary follicle
(d) Mature tertiary follicle

11. Which phases are included in the menstrual cycle?
A. Follicular/proliferative phase
B. Luteal/secretory phase
C. Menses phase
D. Maturation phase
Select the correct combination.
(a) A and B (b) C and D
(c) A, B and C (d) A, B, C and D

12. Identify the incorrect statement describing menstrual flow.
(a) Menarche refers to the onset of menstrual flow in a female.
(b) Unsignificant and abrupt inclination can be observed in GnRH level at the time of menopause.
(c) A female normally loses about 100mL blood during one menstrual cycle.
(d) Menstrual blood clots inside the uterus.

13. Which one of the following correctly matches the events occurring during the menstrual cycle?
(a) Proliferative phase -Rapid regeneration of myometrium and maturation of Graafian follicle.
(b) Corpus luteum -Secretory phase and increased secretion of progesterone.
(c) Menstruation -Breakdown of myometrium and ovum not fertilized.
(d) Ovulation -LH and FSH attain peak level and sharp fall in the secretion of progesterone

14. What causes the onset of puberty in males?
(a) Increase in secretion of testosterone by testis
(b) Decrease in secretion of testosterone by testis
(c) Increase in secretion of GnRH by hypothalamus
(d) Decrease in secretion of GnRH by hypothalamus

15. After release into the vagina, sperms start moving towards the ovum. At what location does the sperm infuses with the ova resulting in fertilisation?
(a) Ampulla (b) Uterus
(c) Cervix (d) Isthmus

16. Given below are two statements; one is labelled as Assertion (A) and the other is labelled as Reason (R).
Assertion (A) Polyspermy in humans is screened by the zona pellucida layer of the egg.
Reason (R) Zona pellucida is a barrier around the mammalian eggs which becomes impermeable to other sperms immediately after the penetration by one sperm cell.

In the light of the above statements, choose the correct answer from the options given below.

(a) A is false, but R true
(b) Both A and R are true and R is the correct explanation of A
(c) Both A and R are true, but R is not the correct explanation of A
(d) A is true, but R false

17. Consider the following options and identify incorrect one about how cleavage differs from mitosis.

(a) There is no growth phase in cleavage
(b) Consumption of oxygen increases in cleavage
(c) Nucleocytoplasmic ratio decreases in cleavage
(d) Cytoplasmic volume increase in cleavage

18. Identify the incorrect statement with respect to female reproductive system.

(a) Ovaries are the primary sex organs which remain embedded inside the abdominal cavity.
(b) At the junction of labia minora, homologous structure to penis is found.
(c) Anterior urethral opening and posterior vaginal orifice are the parts of vulva.
(d) The presence or absence of hymen is a reliable indicator of virginity or sexual experience.

19. Lowering of which hormonal level promotes milk ejection after parturition?

(a) Oxytocin and prolactin
(b) Progesterone and oestrogen
(c) Prolactin and hCG
(d) Relaxin and hPL

20. Which hormone is significantly detectable in the urine of pregnant women?

(a) LH
(b) Progesterone
(c) FSH
(d) HCG

21. Match the List I with List II.

	List I		List II
A	Leydig's cell	1.	Testosterone
B	Proliferative phase	2.	Progesterone
C	Secretory phase	3.	Estrogen
D	Spermatogenesis	4.	GnRH

Choose the correct answer from the options given below.

	A	B	C	D
(a)	1	2	3	4
(b)	1	4	3	2
(c)	3	4	2	1
(d)	1	3	2	4

22. An accessory reproductive gland in male secretes an alkaline fluid into the penile urethra. This fluid alters the environment of the penis to facilitate the unrestricted movement of matured sperms after ejaculation. Identify the gland.

(a) Seminal vesicle
(b) Prostate gland
(c) Cowper's gland
(d) Sertoli cells

23. Given below are two statements.

Statement I A secondary oocyte is formed after fertilisation.

Statement II One oogonium is responsible for production of one secondary oocyte.

In the light of the above statements, choose the correct answers from the options given below.

(a) Statement I is incorrect, but statement II is correct
(b) Both statement I and statement II are correct
(c) Both statement I and statement II are incorrect
(d) Statement I is correct, but statement II is incorrect

24. Given below are two statements; one is labelled as Assertion (A) and the other is labelled as Reason (R).

Assertion (A) The development of the Graafian follicle is essential for ovulation.

Reason (R) The Graafian follicle produces estrogen, which triggers the surge of Luteinizing Hormone (LH) necessary for ovulation.

In the light of the above statements, choose the correct answer from the options given below.

(a) A is false, but R is true
(b) Both A and R are true and R is the correct explanation of A.
(c) Both A and R are correct, but R is not the correct explanation of A.
(d) A is true, but R is false

25. Given below are two statements.

Statement I Breast are the sexual characters of female which start growing at the time of puberty.

Statement II Prolactin hormones remain inactive till the female gets menarche. Menarche indicates the activation time of prolactin.

In the light of the above statements, choose the most appropriate answer from the options given below.

(a) Statement I is incorrect, but statement II is correct.
(b) Both statement I and statement II are correct.
(c) Both statement I and statement II are incorrect.
(d) Statement I is correct, but statement II is incorrect.

26. Identify the correct statements about menstrual cycle in human female.

I. Breakdown of endometrial lining and blood vessels shows the possibility of pregnancy in the woman.
II. LH surge is the major event of the menstrual cycle which happens mid- cycle and results into the ovulation.
III. Corpus luteum is a temporary endocrine gland of the uterus which secrete oestrogen and progesterone.
IV. Menstruation happens due to higher levels of progesterone and oestrogen released by corpus luteum.
V. Maintenance of endometrium by progesterone is necessary for implantation of embryo and pregnancy.

Choose the correct answer out of the given options.

(a) I, IV and II (b) I, III and IV
(c) II, IV and I (d) II, III and V

27. Select the incorrect match.

(a) Ootid - Haploid ovum
(b) Block the entry of additional sperms - Corona radiata
(c) Embryo with 8 to 16 blastomeres - Morula
(d) Outer layer of blastocyst - Trophoblast

28. Read the following statements.

I. The embryo's heart forms after one month of pregnancy.
II. Limbs and digits develop by the end of the first trimester.
III. By the end of 16 weeks, most of the major organ systems are formed.
IV. The first movements of the foetus are observed during the fifth month.
V. Eyelids separate and eyelashes are formed by the end of the sixth month.

Choose the correct set of statements from the options given below.

(a) III, IV and V
(b) I, II and III
(c) II, III and V
(d) I, IV and V

29. Given below are two statements.

Statement I Parturition is the process of childbirth, where the foetus is expelled from the mother's uterus.

Statement II During parturition, the hormone oxytocin stimulates uterine contractions while, relaxin causes the pelvic ligaments to relax to prepare the uterus for child birth.

In the light of the above statements, choose the correct answers from the options given below.

(a) Statement I is incorrect, but statement II is correct.
(b) Both statement I and statement II are correct.
(c) Both statement I and statement II are incorrect.
(d) Statement I is correct, but statement II is incorrect.

30. Match the List I with List II.

	List I		List II
A.	Hymen	1.	Cervical canal along with vagina
B.	Birth canal	2.	Female accessory ducts
C.	Fallopian tubes	3.	Fleshy folds of tissue, which surrounds the vaginal opening
D.	Labia majora	4.	Membrane covering the vaginal opening partially

Choose the correct answer from the options given below.

	A	B	C	D
(a)	4	1	3	2
(b)	1	4	3	2
(c)	4	1	2	3
(d)	3	4	1	2

31. Given below are two statements; one is labelled as Assertion (A) and the other as Reason (R).

Assertion (A) In females, vaginal tract has a low pH.

Reason (R) Alkaline secretions of semen neutralize the acid in vagina.

In the light of the above statements, choose the correct answer from the options given below.

(a) A is false, but R is true.

(b) Both A and R are true and R is the correct explanation of A

(c) Both A and R are true, but R is not the correct explanation of A

(d) A is true, but R is false

32. Following are the events involved in a successful fertilisation.

A. Binding to the zona pellucida

B. Completion of meiosis II

C. Formation of diploid nucleus

D. Penetration by acrosomes

E. Fusion with vitelline membrane

Choose the correct order from the options given below.

(a) A-D-E-B-C

(b) D-A-E-B-C

(c) D-A-B-E-C

(d) A-D-B-E-C

33. Following is the diagram of the cyclical changes in a human female in a month. Which of the following is the reason for lower secretion of Y following their peak phase?

(a) Hyper secretion of oestrogen

(b) Menopause

(c) Ovulation

(d) Increased secretion of progesterone

34. Following is the pictorial representation of a stage in embryogenesis in humans. Which of the following statements about the same is correct?

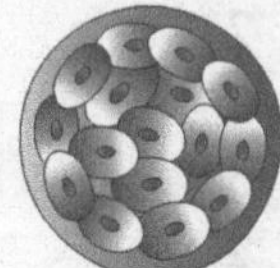

I. The structure is derived from a single diploid cell.

II. Individual cells of the structure are called blastomeres.

III. Implantation into the endometrium occurs in this stage.

IV. Blastocoel appears in the stage preceding this.

V. Germinal layers separate in this stage.

Choose the correct answer from the options given below

(a) III and IV (b) II, III and IV

(c) I and II (d) I only

35. Select the incorrect statement.

(a) Zona pellucida is secreted by the ovum itself

(b) Corona radiata is a primary egg membrane

(c) Hyaluronic acid which binds corona radiata cells is a mucopolysaccharide

(d) Zona pellucida is extracellular material that is composed of various glycoproteins

36. Given below are two statements; one is labelled as Assertion (A) and the other as Reason (R).

Assertion (A) Fertilisation by multiple sperms can lead to polyploidy.

Reason (R) During fusion, the nuclei of the gametes fuse together.

In the light of the above statements, choose the correct answer from the options given below.

(a) A is false, but R is true.

(b) Both A and R are true and R is the correct explanation of A

(c) Both A and R are true, but R is not the correct explanation of A

(d) A is true, but R is false

37. Following is the diagram of the male reproductive system. The secretion from which of the following structure would add the substrate on which the midpiece of spermatozoa would work?

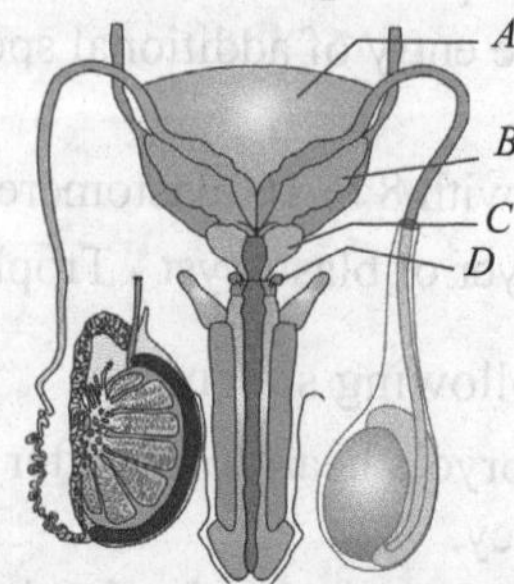

(a) B (b) A

(c) D (d) C

38. In a population of 10 primary spermatocytes, half gets killed. Remaining spermatocytes undergo meiosis I and II to form spermatids. Again 25% of the spermatids die, and the remaining undergoes spermiogenesis. 20% of the products of spermiogenesis die. If the remaining undergo spermiation, calculate how many would form a zygote?
(a) 12 (b) 15
(c) 1 (d) 4

39. Match List I with List II.

	List I		List II
A.	Rete testis	1.	Innervated
B.	Alveoli	2.	Sperm transport
C.	Urethral meatus	3.	Milk secretion
D.	Clitoris	4.	Release of semen

Choose the correct answer from the options given below.
(a) A-2,B-3,C-4,D-1
(b) A-4,B-3,C-2,D-1
(c) A-4,B-1,C-2,D-3
(d) A-2,B-1,C-4,D-3

40. Given below are two statements; one is labelled as Assertion (A) and the other is labelled as Reason (R).
Assertion (A) Pregnant mother can sometimes transmit viral pathogens to the foetus.
Reason (R) Placenta is the medium of exchange between the foetal and maternal blood.
In the light of the above statements, choose the correct answer from the options given below.
(a) A is false, but R is true.
(b) Both A and R are true and R is the correct explanation of A
(c) Both A and R are true, but R is not the correct explanation of A
(d) A is true, but R is false

41. Under secretion of gonadotropins can cause which of the following in males?
A. Low pitched voice.
B. Masculine body
C. Low sperm count
D. Under developed testes
E. Low testosterone

Choose the correct answer from the options given below.
(a) A,C and E (b) B and C
(c) A and B (d) C, D and E

42. Following is the diagram of the male gamete. Which of the following part enters the secondary oocyte prior to fusion of the nucleus?

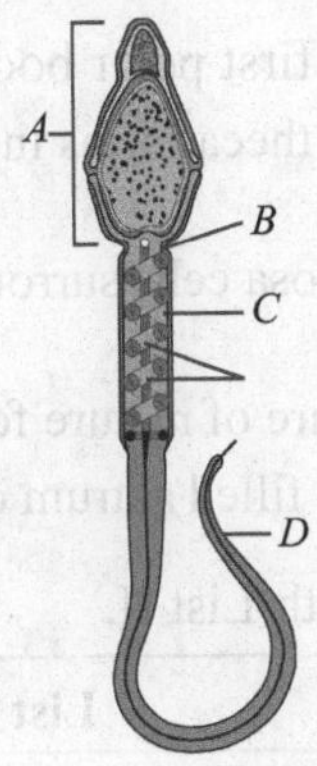

(a) A and B (b) A, B and C
(c) Only A (d) A and C

43. Hormone profiling in a woman reveals high levels of FSH, LH and estrogen and low levels of progesterone. Which of the following can be inferred from this data?
(a) The woman has attained menopause.
(b) The woman has not attained puberty.
(c) It is the proliferative phase of the woman.
(d) Recent fertilization event has taken place.

44. Polyspermy is the condition where one ootid is fertilised by more than one sperm. This condition is prevented by the
(a) Corona radiata cells
(b) Zona pellucida
(c) Vitelline membrane
(d) Theca interna

45. Choose the correct pathway of milk ejection from the mammary glands.
(a) Mammary lobes → alveoli → ampulla → mammary duct
(b) Alveoli → mammary duct → mammary tubules → ampulla
(c) Alveoli → mammary tubules → mammary duct → lactiferous duct
(d) Mammary lobes → mammary tubules → ampulla → mammary duct

46. If normal contractions do not initiate in a female at the end of gestation then the doctors will inject synthetic version of which hormone?

(a) Relaxin
(b) Oxytocin
(c) Oestrogen
(d) Prolactin

47. When does the first polar body form?

(a) When a new theca forms in the primary follicle.
(b) When granulosa cells surround the primary oocyte.
(c) Prior to rupture of mature follicle.
(d) When a fluid filled antrum develops.

48. Match List I with List II.

	List I		List II
A.	Progesterone	1.	Stimulates corpus luteum
B.	Relaxin	2.	Inhibits menstruation
C.	hCG	3.	Breast development
D.	Oestrogen	4.	Loosens the pelvic muscles

Choose the correct answer from the options given below.

(a) A-3, B-4, C-1, D-2
(b) A-2, B-1, C-4, D-3
(c) A-3, B-1, C-4, D-2
(d) A-2, B-4, C-1, D-3

49. Given below are two statements.

Statement I Uterine contraction and oxytocin levels have stimulatory effect on one another.

Statement II Foetal ejection reflex stimulates the anterior pituitary of the pregnant female.

In the light of the above statements, choose the correct answer from the options given below.

(a) Statement I is incorrect, but statement II is correct.
(b) Both statement I and statement II are correct.
(c) Both statement I and statement II are incorrect
(d) Statement I is correct, but statement II is incorrect

50. Which of the following function would be impaired if inner cell mass loses their totipotent nature?

(a) Lack of differentiation into other cell types.
(b) Absence of chorionic villi
(c) Implantation would fail
(d) No placenta formation

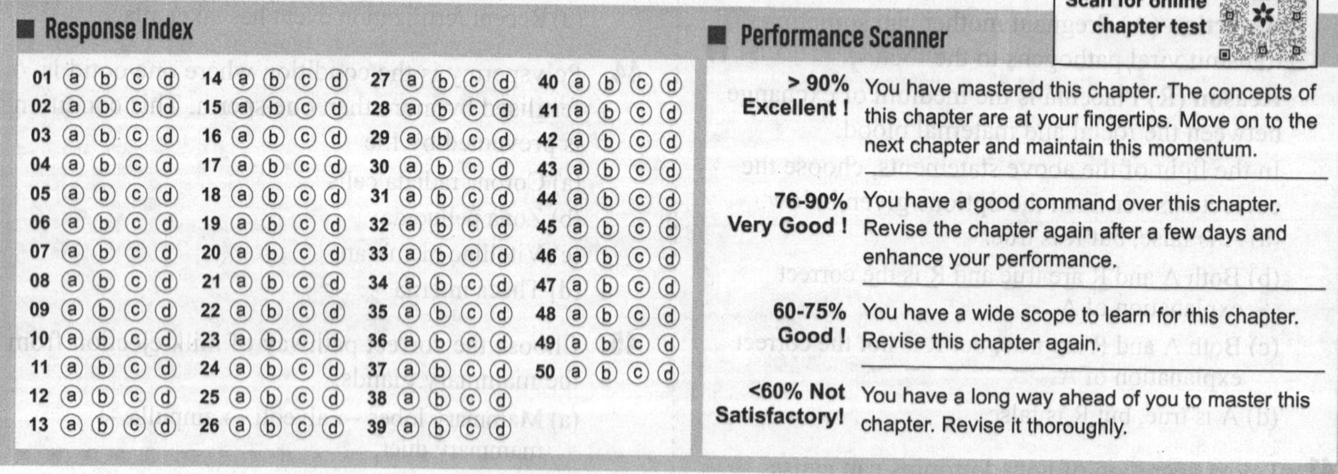

Test Booklet No. 3947353

Test Booklet Code CH3

MEDACE

NEET (UG)

SELF ASSESSMENT KIT

Reproductive Health

Topics Covered

Reproductive Health, Population Explosion and Birth Control

MTP, STIs and Infertility

Important Instructions

- This Booklet Contains – Two Topic Tests and One Test on Complete Chapter.
- Each question carries 4 marks.
- For each correct response, the candidate will get 4 marks. And for every incorrect response, 1 mark will be additionally deducted from total score.
- Use **Blue/Black** point pen only for filling the OMR.
- Rough work is to be done in the space provided for this purpose in the test booklet only.

Name of the Candidate (In Capitals)

____

____

Candidate's Signature ________

Invigilator's Signature ________

Facsimile signature stamp of center superintendent ________

Do not open this booklet until you start attempting the test

Topical Follow Thru

Test 1

Syllabus
- Need for reproductive health
- Birth control-Need and Methods
- Contraception
- Amniocentesis

For deeper insight, **Scan the QR Code** 

Important Instructions
- The test is of 30 minutes duration and contains 25 Multiple Choice Questions (four options with a single correct answer).
- Choose the correct option and fill the OMR given on the last page of this test accordingly.
- At some instances, you may find more than 1 option to be correct. In such circumstances, you have to judge the most appropriate answer as per the conditions given in the question.

1. Intensely lactating mothers generally do not conceive due to complex physiological changes. Which of the following best explains this phenomenon?

(a) Prolonged suppression of GnRH leading to reduced levels of LH and FSH.

(b) Hypersecretion of gonadotropins resulting in an ovulation.

(c) Disruption of gamete transport mechanisms within the Fallopian tubes.

(d) Direct inhibition of the fertilisation process by lactation-induced hormones.

2. Identify the incorrect set which is not the part of reproductive health program and its strategies in India.

(a) Gender equality, women empowerment, foeticide prevention.

(b) Sex education, birth control, sexually transmitted disease.

(c) Awareness about reproduction, birth control methods, post-natal care of mother and child.

(d) Medical facilities, drug research, awareness about problems associated to reproduction.

3. The contraceptive methods that involve a role of hormone are

(a) barrier method, pills

(b) emergency contraceptive pills, implants

(c) Cu-T, emergency contraceptives

(d) barrier methods, Cu-T

4. An increase in the population growth of an area is possible due to

(a) Low MMR and high IMR

(b) Both low MMR and IMR

(c) Both high MMR and IMR

(d) High MMR and low IMR

5. Amniocentesis is performed to check the disorder, involves the :

(a) Removal of a small sample of chorionic villi

(b) Insertion of needle into the amniotic sac to collect fluid

(c) Analysis of fetal blood cells

(d) Ultrasound examination of the foetus

6. Read the following statements about lactational amenorrhea and select the correct statements.

I. Phase of absence of menstrual flow.

II. Absence of ovulation.

III. Natural method of contraception as chances of pregnancy are almost nil.

IV. This method includes phagocytosis of sperms.

V. Natural fertility rate decreases even after the lactational amenorrhea.

Choose the correct answer from the options given below.

(a) I, II and III

(b) II and III

(c) IV and V

(d) I, II, IV and V

7. Given below are two statements; one is labelled as Assertion (A) and the other is labelled as Reason (R).

Assertion (A) Periodic abstinence a natural method of contraception, means abstaining from coitus from day 1 to 5 of the menstrual cycle.

Reason (R) Periodic abstinence is one such method in which the couples avoid or abstain from coitus when ovulation could be expected.

In the light of the above statements, choose the correct answer from the options given below.

(a) A is false, but R is true.
(b) Both A and R are true and R is the correct explanation of A.
(c) Both A and R are true, but R is not the correct explanation of A.
(d) A is true, but R is false.

8. Select incorrect statement w.r.t condoms.

(a) These are effective barriers for insemination.
(b) They do not interfere with the coital act.
(c) These help in reducing the risk of STDs.
(d) They are 100% reliable.

9. Identify which of the following contraceptive methods involve hormones:

(a) Lactational amenorrhea, oral contraceptive pills, emergency contraceptive pills
(b) Barrier methods, lactational amenorrhea, oral contraceptive pills
(c) Cu-T, oral contraceptive pills, Natural methods
(d) Oral contraceptive pills, emergency contraceptive pills, barrier methods.

10. Given below are two statements.

Statement I To maintain a good reproductive health, it is required that adolescent boys and girls are properly being educated about the sexual relationships, sexual infections, their consequences and other relatable matters.

Statement II Early sex education or reproductive education in schools or at home will pollute the young brains and they will not be able to focus on positive attributes of reproductive health.

In the light of the above statements, choose the correct answer from the options given below.

(a) Statement I is incorrect, but statement II is correct.
(b) Both statement I and statement II are correct.
(c) Both statement I and statement II are incorrect.
(d) Statement I is correct, but statement II is incorrect.

11. Norplant is the new form of birth control and it

(a) allows ovulation but does not allow fertilisation
(b) makes the cervical mucus thin to prevent sperm entry into the uterus
(c) has progestin as the active ingredient
(d) is effective for a maximum of 1 year

12. The given diagram is of a contraceptive.

Following are the mode of action w.r.t. this contraceptive except one. Select the odd one

(a) It prevents ovulation.
(b) It prevents implantation.
(c) It contains a non-steroidal preparation.
(d) It alter the quality of cervical mucus.

13. Which of the following features are correct with respect to Copper-T device ?

I. It prevents fertilisation.
II. It releases Cu^{2+} that is toxic to function of sperm.
III. Enhances luteal activities.
IV. Can be inserted with or without the help of expert nurses.
V. Suppresses sperm motility.

Choose the correct answer from the options given below.

(a) I and II
(b) I and IV
(c) I, II and V
(d) IV Only

14. Match the List I with List II.

List I	List II
A. Coitus interruptus	1. avoid insemination
B. Lactational amenorrhea	2. inhibit ovulation
C. Pills	3. ovulation and the menstrual cycle do not occur
D. Sterilisation	4. blocks gamete transport

Choose the correct answer from the options given below.

	A	B	C	D
(a)	1	2	3	4
(b)	1	4	3	2
(c)	1	4	2	3
(d)	1	3	2	4

15. Select the incorrect match w.r.t. contraceptives.
(a) Saheli - Non-steroidal pills
(b) Multiload 375 - Steroid containing IUD
(c) LNG-20 - Hormone containing IUD
(d) Vaults - Barriers

16. To which of the following population categories does India belongs to?
(a) High birth rate and high mortality rate
(b) Low birth rate and low mortality rate
(c) Low birth rate and high mortality rate
(d) High birth rate and low mortality rate

17. 'RU486' also known as Mifepristone is
(a) a steroid having affinity for progesterone hormone receptor
(b) a contraceptive pill taken daily
(c) a non-hormonal pill that taken daily
(d) a non-steroid acts by inhibiting oestrogen activity

18. Given below are two statements, one is labelled as Assertion (A) and the other is labelled as Reason (R).

Assertion (A) Zero population growth should be achieved as early as possible to control human population.

Reason (R) This demands a couple to have more than two children.

In the light of the above statements, choose the correct answer from the options given below.
(a) A is false, but R is true.
(b) Both A and R are true and R is the correct explanation of A.
(c) Both A and R are true, but R is not the correct explanation of A.
(d) A is true, but R is false.

19. Spermicidal creams used as the coating of diaphragms, vaults and cervical caps are meant
(a) for lubrication
(b) to provide medication
(c) for increasing effectiveness
(d) to prevent infection

20. Which of the following statements are correct?
I. India is the second largest populated country in the world.
II. 11 July is observed as world population day.
III. 'Hum do, Humare Do' slogan encourages family planning.
IV. RCH programmes resulted in bringing down the population growth rate to a significant level.
Choose the correct answer from the options given below.
(a) II and IV
(b) I, II and IV
(c) II and III
(d) I and III

21. Consider the following statements. Choose the incorrect one.
(a) Female condoms are internal condoms
(b) Vaults are reusable, but needs expert's administration
(c) IUDs are one of the most widely accepted methods of contraception in India
(d) Breast cancer is a potential ill-effect of using contraceptive methods

22. A women 'X' is consuming Mala -D as a method of contraceptive. Given below graphs shows the levels of progesterone in her body. Which of the following graph is correct for women 'X'?

(a)
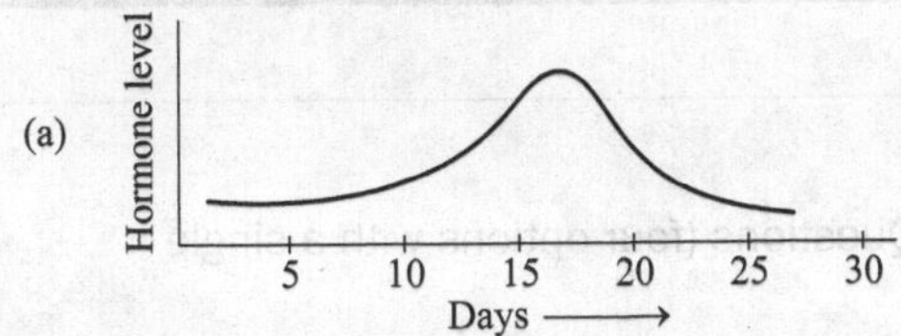

(b)
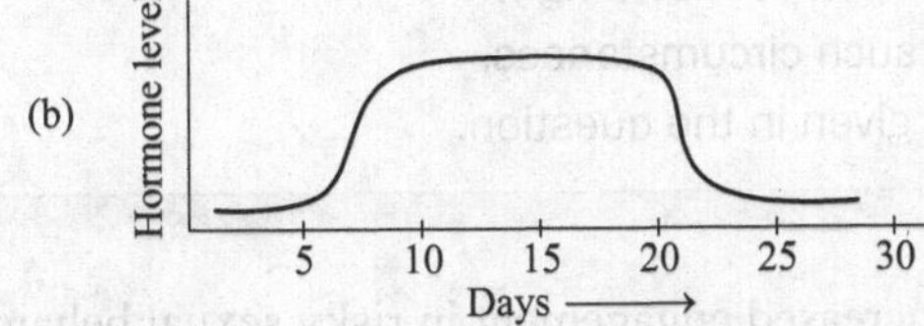

(c)
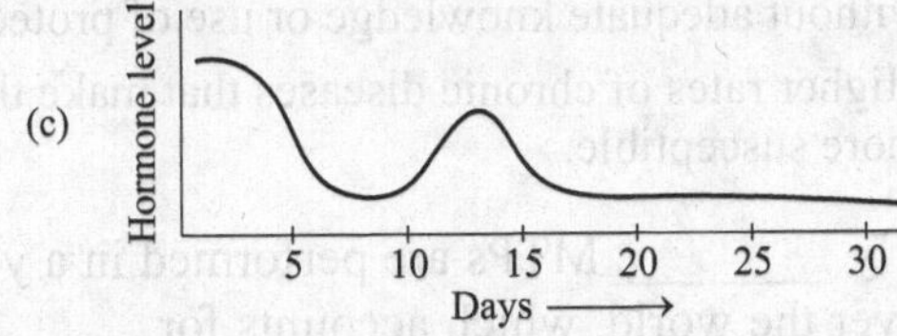

(d)
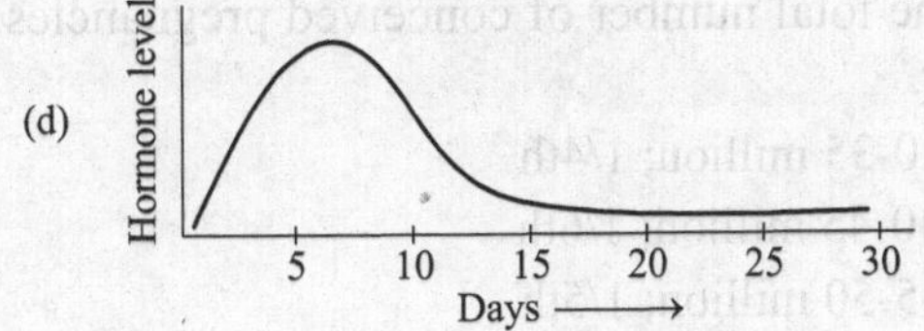

23. Which of the following contraceptive technique is safest?
(a) Rhythm method
(b) Use of physical barriers
(c) Termination of unwanted pregnancies
(d) Sterilisation techniques

24. The mode of action of vaginal diaphragm involves
(a) prevention of ova to come in the uterus
(b) prevention of sperm to come in contact with ova
(c) acting as a spermicidal agent
(d) prevention of implantation of zygote in the uterus.

25. Ovulation does not occur in lactating womens because of the release of.......
(a) prolactin
(b) inhibit
(c) prostaglandin
(d) oxytocin

Response Index

01	ⓐ ⓑ ⓒ ⓓ		10	ⓐ ⓑ ⓒ ⓓ		19	ⓐ ⓑ ⓒ ⓓ							
02	ⓐ ⓑ ⓒ ⓓ		11	ⓐ ⓑ ⓒ ⓓ		20	ⓐ ⓑ ⓒ ⓓ							
03	ⓐ ⓑ ⓒ ⓓ		12	ⓐ ⓑ ⓒ ⓓ		21	ⓐ ⓑ ⓒ ⓓ							
04	ⓐ ⓑ ⓒ ⓓ		13	ⓐ ⓑ ⓒ ⓓ		22	ⓐ ⓑ ⓒ ⓓ							
05	ⓐ ⓑ ⓒ ⓓ		14	ⓐ ⓑ ⓒ ⓓ		23	ⓐ ⓑ ⓒ ⓓ							
06	ⓐ ⓑ ⓒ ⓓ		15	ⓐ ⓑ ⓒ ⓓ		24	ⓐ ⓑ ⓒ ⓓ							
07	ⓐ ⓑ ⓒ ⓓ		16	ⓐ ⓑ ⓒ ⓓ		25	ⓐ ⓑ ⓒ ⓓ							
08	ⓐ ⓑ ⓒ ⓓ		17	ⓐ ⓑ ⓒ ⓓ										
09	ⓐ ⓑ ⓒ ⓓ		18	ⓐ ⓑ ⓒ ⓓ										

Performance Scanner

> 90% Excellent !	You have mastered these topics. The concepts of these topics are at your fingertips. Move on to the next test and maintain this momentum.
76-90% Very Good !	You have a good command over these topics. Revise these topics again after a few days and enhance your performance.
60-75% Good !	You have a wide scope to learn for these topics. Revise these topics again.
<60% Not Satisfactory!	You have a long way ahead of you to master these topics. Revise it thoroughly.

Test 2

Syllabus	• Medical Termination of Pregnancy (MTP) • Sexually Transmitted Diseases (STDs)	• Infertility and assisted reproductive technologies IVF, ZIFT, GIFT (Elementary idea for general awareness)	For deeper insight, **Scan the QR Code** 

Important Instructions

- The test is of 30 minutes duration and contains 25 Multiple Choice Questions (four options with a single correct answer).
- Choose the correct option and fill the OMR given on the last page of this test accordingly.
- At some instances, you may find more than 1 option to be correct. In such circumstances, you have to judge the most appropriate answer as per the conditions given in the question.

1. Among the listed sexually transmitted diseases, which is correct regarding HIV, hepatitis-B, gonorrhoea, trichomoniasis?

(a) Trichomoniasis is a STI, whereas other are not
(b) Gonorrhoea is a viral disease, whereas other are bacterial
(c) HIV is a pathogen, whereas others are diseases
(d) Hepatitis-B is eradicated completely, whereas other are not

2. Identify the incorrect statement with respect to MTP.

(a) MTPs have a significant role in decreasing the size of population.
(b) Government of India legalised MTP in 1981 with some restrictions.
(c) MTPs is considered relatively safe during the first trimester of pregnancy.
(d) The MTP amendment Act 2017 was enacted by Indian government with the intention of reducing illegal abortions and consequent maternal mortality.

3. Though all persons are vulnerable to sexually transmitted infections, their incidences are reported to be very high among adolescents. Why?

(a) More frequent use of communal facilities like gyms and public pools.
(b) Weaker immune system compared to other age groups.
(c) Increased engagement in risky sexual behaviors without adequate knowledge or use of protection.
(d) Higher rates of chronic diseases that make them more susceptible.

4. Nearly ________ MTPs are performed in a year all over the world, which accounts for ________ of the total number of conceived pregnancies in a year.

(a) 30-35 million; 1/4th
(b) 40-45 million; 1/6th
(c) 45-50 million; 1/5th
(d) 50-55 million; 1/3rd

5. Following are the reasons why, in India, despite the activation of multiple laws against abortions, unsafe abortions are still frequently reported. Find the incorrect reason.

(a) People, especially women, are not aware of the information delivered by the government.
(b) Government hospitals are not well equipped and abortion services are not readily available.
(c) People do not want to risk their prestige in cases of pregnancies that occur due to unwanted reasons, such as rape or extramarital relations.
(d) People take unfair advantage of laws that favor abortion.

6. Given below are two statements.

Statement I All reproductive tract infections are curable if diagnosed at the early stage.

Statement II Cancer in the reproductive system can be a potential reason of sexually transmitted diseases.
In the light of the above statements, choose the correct answer from the options given below.
(a) Statement I is incorrect, but statement II is correct.
(b) Both statement I and statement II are correct.
(c) Both statement I and statement II are incorrect.
(d) Statement I is correct, but statement II is incorrect.

7. Given below are two statements; one is labelled as Assertion (A) and the other is labelled as Reason (R).
Assertion (A) The Medical Termination Amendment Act, 2017 allows the termination of pregnancy under certain circumstances, although it never supports the female foeticide.
Reason (R) MTP act allows the termination of pregnancy in the case, if continuation of pregnancy has potential risk of mental or physical injury to the pregnant woman.
In the light of the above statements, choose the correct answers from the options given below.
(a) A is false, but R is true.
(b) Both A and R are true and R is the correct explanation of A.
(c) Both A and R are true, but R is not the correct explanation of A.
(d) A is true, but R is false.

8. Sexually transmitted infections (STIs) can lead to severe complications if not detected and treated early. Despite the importance of early detection, various factors deter people from seeking timely diagnosis and treatment. Which of the following statements best explains why early detection and treatment of STIs are often neglected?
(a) Infected individuals usually have strong immune responses that mask symptoms.
(b) Most STIs have highly visible and painful early symptoms, prompting immediate treatment.
(c) Early symptoms of STIs are usually mild, and the social stigma associated with these infections prevents individuals from seeking prompt diagnosis and treatment.
(d) The majority of STIs do not cause serious long-term health complications, making early treatment unnecessary.

9. Match List I with List II.

List I	List II
A. Trichomoniasis	1. *Human Papilloma Virus*
B. Gonorrhoea	2. Human Immunodeficiency Virus
C. Genital warts	3. *Trichomonas vaginalis*
D. AIDS	4. *Neisseria gonorrhoeae*

Choose the correct answer from the options given below.

	A	B	C	D
(a)	4	3	2	1
(b)	3	4	2	1
(c)	3	4	1	2
(d)	2	1	4	3

10. Given below are two statements.
Statement I Embryo with more than 8 blastomeres introduced into the uterus to complete their further development is called IUI.
Statement II The semen collected either from the husband or a healthy donor is artificially transferred into the uterus is called IUT.
In the light of above statements, choose the correct answers from the options given below.
(a) Statement I is incorrect, but statement II is correct
(b) Both statement I and statement II are correct
(c) Both statement I and statement II are incorrect
(d) Statement I is correct, but statement II is incorrect

11. Pick odd one out from each series given below.
I. Hepatitis-B, gonnorrhoea, trichomoniasis and chlamydiasis
II. Ectopic pregnancies, still births, pelvic inflammatory diseases, syphilis
III. ZIFT, IUI, AI, GIFT
Choose the correct answer from the options given below.
(a) Hepatitis-B, syphilis and ZIFT
(b) Gonorrhoea, pelvic inflammatory diseases and IUI
(c) Trichomoniasis, still births and GIFT
(d) Chlamydiasis, Ectopic pregnancy and AI

12. Which statement is correct with respect to test tube baby?
(a) A baby developing from an unfertilized egg.
(b) A foetus developed in a test tube.
(c) Fertilisation happening outside the female body in a lab.
(d) The embryo formed by *in-vivo* fertilisation is transferred to assist women who cannot conceive.

13. In the process of IVF, what is the site of implantation of embryo at 16 celled stage?
(a) Fallopian tube (b) Cervix
(c) Uterus (d) Ampulla

14. Match List I with List II.

	List I		List II
A.	GIFT	1.	Sperms are collected and purified to directly inject into the ovum
B.	IVF	2.	Sperms are allowed to fuse with ovum in a petridish in the lab environment
C.	ICSI	3.	Semen is released in the vagina of female through syringe
D.	AI	4.	Ovum is extracted from one female and transferred into the reproductive environment of another female

Choose the correct answer from the options given below.

	A	B	C	D		A	B	C	D
(a)	4	3	1	2	(b)	3	2	1	4
(c)	1	3	2	4	(d)	4	2	1	3

15. Given below are two statements.
Statement I MTP is essential to keep the sex ratio in proper manner.
Statement II Medical termination of pregnancy is useful for those females who became pregnant due to sexual assault or due to extra marital relationships.
In the light of the above statements, choose the correct answer from the options given below.
(a) Statement I is incorrect, but statement II is correct.
(b) Both statement I and statement II are correct.
(c) Both statement I and statement II are incorrect.
(d) Statement I is correct, but statement II is incorrect.

16. Which of the following statement is incorrect about STDs?
I. These are called silent infection.
II. STD's lead to changing pattern of sexual behaviour
III. Abstinence results into STD infection.
III. Pathogens of STDs develop resistance to antibiotics.
Choose the correct option.
(a) I and II (b) IV only
(c) III only (d) III and IV

17. Given below are two statements.
Statement I Both ZIFT and IUT are embryo transfer technique.
Statement II In both ZIFT and IUT the number of cells in zygote is same.
In the light of the above statements, choose the correct answer from the options given below.
(a) Statement I is incorrect, but statement II is correct.
(b) Both statement I and statement II are correct.
(c) Both statement I and statement II are incorrect.
(d) Statement I is correct, but statement II is incorrect.

18. GIFT technique is useful for woman's
I. Whose fimbriae fail to capture ovum.
II. Whose cervics produce antibodies against sperm
III. Who have atleast one potent Fallopian tube.
IV. Who have weak uterus
Choose correct option.
(a) I and II (b) I, II and III
(c) II, III and IV (d) I, II and IV

19. If the sperm count of a male is very low than which technique can help in fertilisation?
(a) Interauterine transfer
(b) Gamete intracytoplasmic Fallopian transfer
(c) Artificial insemination
(d) Intracytoplasmic spem injection

20. Which of the following is the correct sequence of events in development of test tube baby?
(a) Removal of unfertilised ovum → *In vitro* fusion of sperm and ovum → Development of zygote up to 32 cell stage → Embryo transfer into the uterus of mother
(b) Fusion of sperm and ovum *in vitro* → Removal of unfertilised ovum and transfer in to the uterus

of mother → Formation and development of zygote up to 32 cell stage

(c) Embryo transfer into the uterus of mother → Formation and development of zygote up to 32 cell stage → Fusion of sperm and ovum *in vitro* → Removal of unfertilised ovum

(d) Formation and development of zygote up to 32 cell stage → Fusion of sperm and ovum *in vitro* → Removal of unfertilised ovum → Embryo transfer into the uterus

21. Given below are two statements; one is labelled as Assertion (A) and the other is labelled as Reason (R).

Assertion (A) Test tube baby has raised sexual legal problems.

Reason (R) It involves *in vitro* fetilisation followed by embryo transfer.

In the light of the above statements, choose the correct answer from the options given below.

(a) A is false, but R is true.

(b) Both A and R are true and R is the correct explanation of A.

(c) Both A and R are true, but R is not the correct explanation of A.

(d) A is true, but R is false.

22. Ethical principles in support of abortion do not include

(a) a woman's right to autonomous choice

(b) a woman has no moral obligation or duty to carry a foetus

(c) fertilisation does not automatically bestow moral status on a foetus

(d) abortion is of utilitarian value to a woman

23. What is the latest stage of pregnancy when an abortion can be under taken pursuant to the Medical Termination of Pregnancy Act, 1971?

(a) 26 weeks (b) 24 weeks

(c) 28 weeks (d) 20 weeks

24. Which of the following is wrongly matched?

(a)	IUT	–	Semen collected from husband or donor is artificially introduced either into the vagina or into the uterus
(b)	GIFT	–	Transfer of embryos with more than 8 blastomeres into the Fallopian tube
(c)	ICSI	–	Sperm directly injected into the ovum
(d)	ZIFT	–	Transfer of embryos with up to 8 blastomeres into the Fallopian tube

25. Given below are two statements.

Statement I Inability to conceive or produce children even after 2 years of unprotected cohabitation is called infertility.

Statement II The season of infertility can be immunological, physical, psychological.

In the light of the above statements, choose the correct answer from the options given below.

(a) Statement I is incorrect, but statement II is correct.

(b) Both statement I and statement II are correct.

(c) Both statement I and statement II are incorrect.

(d) Statement I is correct, but statement II is incorrect.

Response Index

01 (a) (b) (c) (d)	10 (a) (b) (c) (d)	19 (a) (b) (c) (d)
02 (a) (b) (c) (d)	11 (a) (b) (c) (d)	20 (a) (b) (c) (d)
03 (a) (b) (c) (d)	12 (a) (b) (c) (d)	21 (a) (b) (c) (d)
04 (a) (b) (c) (d)	13 (a) (b) (c) (d)	22 (a) (b) (c) (d)
05 (a) (b) (c) (d)	14 (a) (b) (c) (d)	23 (a) (b) (c) (d)
06 (a) (b) (c) (d)	15 (a) (b) (c) (d)	24 (a) (b) (c) (d)
07 (a) (b) (c) (d)	16 (a) (b) (c) (d)	25 (a) (b) (c) (d)
08 (a) (b) (c) (d)	17 (a) (b) (c) (d)	
09 (a) (b) (c) (d)	18 (a) (b) (c) (d)	

Performance Scanner

> 90% Excellent !	You have mastered these topics. The concepts of these topics are at your fingertips. Move on to the next test and maintain this momentum.
76-90% Very Good !	You have a good command over these topics. Revise these topics again after a few days and enhance your performance.
60-75% Good !	You have a wide scope to learn for these topics. Revise these topics again.
<60% Not Satisfactory!	You have a long way ahead of you to master these topics. Revise it thoroughly.

Chapter Break Thru

Syllabus	• Need for reproductive health and prevention of sexually transmitted diseases (STD); Amniocentesis;	• Birth control-Need and Methods, • Contraception and Medical Termination of Pregnancy (MTP);	• Infertility and assisted reproductive technologies - IVF, ZIFT, GIFT (Elementary idea for general awareness).

Important Instructions

- The test is of 1 hour duration and contains 30 Multiple-Choice Questions (Four options with a single correct answer).
- Choose the correct option and fill the OMR given on the last page of this test accordingly.
- At some instances, you may find more than 1 option to be correct. In such circumstances, you have to judge the most appropriate answer as per the conditions given in the question.

1. Saheli is an oral contraceptive that acts by
(a) stimulating oestrogen secretion.
(b) inhibiting oestrogen activity.
(c) stimulating progesterone activity.
(d) increasing level of oestrogen and progesterone.

2. Given below are two statements.
Statement I India is the first country in the world to initiate action plans and programmes at national level to attain total reproductive health as a social goal.
Statement II The primary concern of RCH programmes is to control population rate of India.
In the light of the above statements, choose the correct answer from the options given below.
(a) Statement I is incorrect, but statement II is correct.
(b) Both statement I and statement II are correct.
(c) Both statements I and statement II are incorrect.
(d) Statement I is correct, but statement II is incorrect.

3. Identify the incorrect statement.
(a) Amniocentesis is a prenatal test in which a sample of amniotic fluid is taken from the uterus using a thin needle.
(b) Amniocentesis is used to detect certain genetic disorders, such as Down syndrome, haemophilia, and sickle-cell anaemia, to assess foetal viability.
(c) Implementing a legal ban on amniocentesis for sex determination is essential to combat the rising issue of female foeticide.
(d) Amniocentesis is a non-invasive prenatal test.

4. Read the following statements.
I. The world population increased from about 2 billion in 1900 to about 6 billion by 2000.
II. The population of India was approximately 350 million at the time of independence.
III. By 2000, the world population had reached 7.2 billion.
IV. A rapid decline in death rate, MMR, and IMR contributed to the population growth.
V. India's population crossed 1.2 billion in May 2011.
Choose the correct answer from the options given below:
(a) I, II, IV, V
(b) I, III, IV, V
(c) II, III, IV, V
(d) I, II, III, IV

5. Find the odd pair of contraceptives based on their working method.
(a) Cervical cap, fem shield
(b) Coitus interruptus, lactational amenorrhea
(c) Saheli, Lippe's loop
(d) Condom, diaphragm

6. From the following procedures, how many of these can be employed in IVF?

IUI, ZIFT, IUT, GIFT, ICSI

(a) Two (b) Three
(c) Four (d) Five

7. Which statement is incorrect regarding the following diagram?

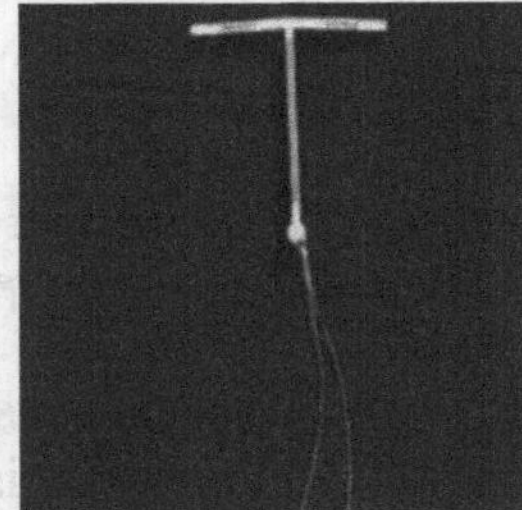

(a) It inhibits sperm motility.
(b) It is a contraceptive device, which is inserted by doctors or expert nurses in the uterus through vagina.
(c) It is a non-medicated IUD, which make the uterus unsuitable for implantation and the cervix hostile to the sperms.
(d) It is one of most widely accepted contraceptive in India.

8. Which of the following is incorrectly matched?

(a) Multiload 375 –Copper releasing IUD
(b) Mala-D –Steroidal pills
(c) Saheli –Barrier
(d) LNG-20 –Hormone releasing IUD

9. Given below are two statements; one is labelled as Assertion (A) and the other is labelled as Reason (R).

Assertion (A) Amniocentesis is the best method to accurately determine the gender of developing embryo as well as it can be done to check the paternity.

Reason (R) Amniocentesis is necessary to predetermine the possibility of multiple disorders developing in the baby such as chromosomal disorders, etc.

In the light of the above statements, choose the correct answers from the options given below.

(a) A is false, but R is true
(b) Both A and R are true and R is the correct explanation of A
(c) Both A and R are true, but R is not the correct explanation of A
(d) A is true, but R is false

10. Identify the incorrect statement with respect to procedure, legal use and requirements of MTP.

(a) MTP is legal in the case of child may develop physical and mental abnormalities
(b) MTP between 12 to 24 week need atleast one registered medical practitioner validity.
(c) MTP is advised in the case of potential risk of maternal mortality.
(d) MTP requires specific medical or legal justifications, especially for pregnancies beyond 12 weeks.

11. The following sexually transmitted diseases are caused by bacteria, except

(a) gonorrhoea (b) syphilis
(c) trichomoniasis (d) chlamydiasis

12. The sexually transmitted disease that mainly affects cervix, uterus and Fallopian tubes in women is

(a) gonorrhoea (b) syphilis
(c) genital herpes (d) chlamydiasis

13. What is the term for medical condition in which the fertilised egg implants and develops outside the uterus, usually in Fallopian tube?

(a) Ectopic pregnancy
(b) Extra uterine pregnancy
(c) Amenorrhea
(d) Cervical pregnancy

14. Following are the symptoms of STDs except,

(a) itching and fluid discharge
(b) pain and swelling
(c) ectopic pregnancies, stillbirth
(d) high blood pressure and frequent urination

15. Match List I with List II.

	List I		List II
A.	MTP amendment	1.	2011
B.	Family planning program activation in India	2.	1971
C.	World population reached 7.2 billion	3.	2017
D.	MTP legalisation in India	4.	1951

Choose the correct answer from the options given below.

	A	B	C	D
(a)	3	4	1	2
(b)	2	3	4	1
(c)	4	3	2	1
(d)	2	1	4	3

16. The method suggested by the doctor to a female who cannot produce ovum, but can provide suitable environment for fertilisation is

(a) IVF (b) GIFT
(c) ICSI (d) ZIFT

17. Arrange the steps involved in ZIFT (Zygote Intra Fallopian Transfer) in the correct sequence.

A. Transfer to the Fallopian tubes
B. Ovarian stimulation and egg retrieval
C. Fertilisation in the laboratory
D. Zygote culture

Choose the correct sequence from the options below:

(a) B, C, D, A (b) A, B, C, D
(c) B, D, C, A (d) C, B, A, D

18. *In vitro* fertilisation involves transferring which of the following into the Fallopian tube?

(a) Only a zygote
(b) Only an embryo up to the 8-cell stage
(c) Either a zygote or an early embryo up to the 8-cell stage
(d) An embryo at the 32-cell stage

19. The test-tube baby program utilizes which of the following techniques?

(a) Artificial insemination (AI)
(b) Zygote Intra Fallopian Transfer (ZIFT)
(c) Intrauterine Insemination (IUI)
(d) Gamete Intra Fallopian Transfer (GIFT)

20. AI is the method of ART suggested to the couples because of

(a) very low sperm count
(b) inability to produce ovum
(c) genetic disease in one partner
(d) no proper environment for fertilisation

21. Given below are two statements; one is labelled as Assertion (A) and the other is labelled as Reason (R).

Assertion (A) Introduction of sex education in schools should be encouraged to provide the right information to the young people, discouraging myths and misconceptions about sex-related aspects.

Reason (R) Proper information about reproductive organs, adolescence and related changes, safe and hygienic sexual practices, sexually transmitted diseases (STD), AIDS, etc., would help people, especially those in the adolescent age group, to lead a reproductively healthy life.

In the light of the above statements, choose the correct answer from the options given below:

(a) A is false, but R is true
(b) Both A and R are true and R is the correct explanation of A
(c) Both A and R are true, but R is not the correct explanation of A
(d) A is true, but R is false

22. Select the incorrect match.

(a) Semen without sperm -Condom
(b) No ovulation - Pills
(c) Reduce fertilization - Cu-T
(d) Prevent insemination - Coitus interruptus

23. Which of the following birth control measures can be considered the safest and most effective as well?

(a) Terminalisation of unwanted pregnancy
(b) Sterilisation technique
(c) Barrier method
(d) The use of withdrawal method

24. Find out the incorrect statement(s) in the light of methods of contraception or pregnancy terminations.

I. Induced abortions are performed in the case of failure of contraceptive pills or other methods of contraception.
II. Miscarriages are the part of contraception in case of unwanted pregnancy.
III. Vasectomy is performed in males to restrict the passage of sperms.
IV. Tubectomy is performed in females to block the passage of ovum through Fallopian tubes.
V. Surgical methods are terminal methods to prevent pregnancies.

Choose the correct answer from the options given below.

(a) I and II (b) II only
(c) I, III and IV (d) II and V

25. Select the most appropriate definition of infertility.

(a) Couple is unable to produce children inspite of unprotected sexual cohabitation.
(b) Infertility is defined as the inability to produce a viable offspring and is always due to defects/abnormalities in the female partner.
(c) Infertility is due to immature sex organs.
(d) Infertility means that a couple can conceive but cannot maintain a pregnancy beyond the first trimester.

26. Match List I with List II.

List I		List II	
A.	Artificial insemination	1.	Test of the chromosomal pattern
B.	Amniocentesis	2.	Embryo transfer in the uterus of mother
C.	ICSI	3.	Injection of sperms in uterus or vagina
D.	Test-tube baby	4.	Procedure to inject sperm into ovum directly

Choose the correct answer from the options given below.

	A	B	C	D
(a)	3	1	4	2
(b)	2	3	1	4
(c)	2	4	1	3
(d)	4	3	2	1

27. Given below are two statements.

Statement I Assistive reproductive technologies are the requirement of the modern world as it is the most suitable method to achieve pregnancy or to produce baby through surrogacy.

Statement II For surrogacy, only male sperm is required and the ovum of the surrogate mother is used.

In the light of the above statements, choose the correct answer from the options given below.

(a) Statement I is incorrect, but statement II is correct
(b) Both statement I and statement II are correct
(c) Both statement I and statement II are incorrect
(d) Statement I is correct, but statement II is incorrect

28. Match List I with List II.

List I		List II	
A.	Cervical caps	1.	Rubber or plastic cap which is hemispherical in shape and gets fit over the cervix
B.	Vaults	2.	Shows local antifertility effect by releasing toxic cytokines
C.	Sponge (Foam)	3.	Rubber-made barriers used by females to cover cervix during coitus
D.	Cu- T	4.	Contains spermicide, acts upon the membrane of sperms.

Choose the correct answer from the options given below.

	A	B	C	D
(a)	3	1	4	2
(b)	4	3	2	1
(c)	4	2	1	3
(d)	1	3	2	4

29. Given below are two statements; one is labelled as Assertion (A) and the other is labelled as Reason (R).

Assertion (A) Intra Cytoplasmic Sperm Injection (ICSI) is an effective assisted reproductive technology used to address male infertility, which involves injecting a single sperm directly into an egg to fertilize it during the IVF process.

Reason (R) Zygote Intra Fallopian Transfer (ZIFT) involves transferring a fertilized egg (zygote) into the fallopian tube to ensure natural implantation, particularly beneficial in cases where other methods of fertilisation have failed.

In the light of the above statements, choose the correct answer from the options given below:

(a) A is false, but R is true.
(b) Both A and R are true and R is the correct explanation of A.
(c) Both A and R are true, but R is not the correct explanation of A.
(d) A is true, but R is false.

30. Venereal diseases can spread through

I. Sterile needles.
II. Blood transfusion from infected individual.
III. Kissing.
IV. Infected mother to foetus.
V. Inheritance from parents.

Choose the correct answer from the options given below

(a) I, II, III and IV
(b) II, IV and V
(c) II, III, IV and V
(d) II, III and IV

Response Index

01 ⓐ ⓑ ⓒ ⓓ	14 ⓐ ⓑ ⓒ ⓓ	27 ⓐ ⓑ ⓒ ⓓ	40 ⓐ ⓑ ⓒ ⓓ
02 ⓐ ⓑ ⓒ ⓓ	15 ⓐ ⓑ ⓒ ⓓ	28 ⓐ ⓑ ⓒ ⓓ	41 ⓐ ⓑ ⓒ ⓓ
03 ⓐ ⓑ ⓒ ⓓ	16 ⓐ ⓑ ⓒ ⓓ	29 ⓐ ⓑ ⓒ ⓓ	42 ⓐ ⓑ ⓒ ⓓ
04 ⓐ ⓑ ⓒ ⓓ	17 ⓐ ⓑ ⓒ ⓓ	30 ⓐ ⓑ ⓒ ⓓ	43 ⓐ ⓑ ⓒ ⓓ
05 ⓐ ⓑ ⓒ ⓓ	18 ⓐ ⓑ ⓒ ⓓ	31 ⓐ ⓑ ⓒ ⓓ	44 ⓐ ⓑ ⓒ ⓓ
06 ⓐ ⓑ ⓒ ⓓ	19 ⓐ ⓑ ⓒ ⓓ	32 ⓐ ⓑ ⓒ ⓓ	45 ⓐ ⓑ ⓒ ⓓ
07 ⓐ ⓑ ⓒ ⓓ	20 ⓐ ⓑ ⓒ ⓓ	33 ⓐ ⓑ ⓒ ⓓ	46 ⓐ ⓑ ⓒ ⓓ
08 ⓐ ⓑ ⓒ ⓓ	21 ⓐ ⓑ ⓒ ⓓ	34 ⓐ ⓑ ⓒ ⓓ	47 ⓐ ⓑ ⓒ ⓓ
09 ⓐ ⓑ ⓒ ⓓ	22 ⓐ ⓑ ⓒ ⓓ	35 ⓐ ⓑ ⓒ ⓓ	48 ⓐ ⓑ ⓒ ⓓ
10 ⓐ ⓑ ⓒ ⓓ	23 ⓐ ⓑ ⓒ ⓓ	36 ⓐ ⓑ ⓒ ⓓ	49 ⓐ ⓑ ⓒ ⓓ
11 ⓐ ⓑ ⓒ ⓓ	24 ⓐ ⓑ ⓒ ⓓ	37 ⓐ ⓑ ⓒ ⓓ	50 ⓐ ⓑ ⓒ ⓓ
12 ⓐ ⓑ ⓒ ⓓ	25 ⓐ ⓑ ⓒ ⓓ	38 ⓐ ⓑ ⓒ ⓓ	
13 ⓐ ⓑ ⓒ ⓓ	26 ⓐ ⓑ ⓒ ⓓ	39 ⓐ ⓑ ⓒ ⓓ	

Performance Scanner

> 90% Excellent !	You have mastered this chapter. The concepts of this chapter are at your fingertips. Move on to the next chapter and maintain this momentum.
76-90% Very Good !	You have a good command over this chapter. Revise the chapter again after a few days and enhance your performance.
60-75% Good !	You have a wide scope to learn for this chapter. Revise this chapter again.
<60% Not Satisfactory!	You have a long way ahead of you to master this chapter. Revise it thoroughly.

Scan for online chapter test

Scan for online unit test

Space for Rough Work

Space for Rough Work

Test Booklet No. **3947354**

Test Booklet Code **CH4**

MED ACE

NEET (UG)

SELF ASSESSMENT KIT

Principles of Inheritance and Variation

Topics Covered

Genetic Terms and Inheritance of One Gene

Inheritance of Two Genes

Sex-determination, Mutation and Genetic Disorders

Important Instructions

- This Booklet Contains – Three Topic Tests and One Test on Complete Chapter.
- Each question carries 4 marks.
- For each correct response, the candidate will get 4 marks. And for every incorrect response, 1 mark will be additionally deducted from total score.
- Use **Blue/Black** point pen only for filling the OMR.
- Rough work is to be done in the space provided for this purpose in the test booklet only.

Name of the Candidate (In Capitals)

____

____

Candidate's Signature ______________

Invigilator's Signature ______________

Facsimile signature stamp of center superintendent______________

Do not open this booklet until you start attempting the test

Topical Follow Thru

Test 1

Syllabus	• Mendelian Inheritance- I : Deviations from Mendelism- • Incomplete dominance • Co-dominance	• Multiple alleles and Inheritance of blood groups • Pleiotropy	For deeper insight, **Scan the QR Code** 

Important Instructions

- The test is of 30 minutes duration and contains 15 Multiple Choice Questions (four options with a single correct answer).
- Choose the correct option and fill the OMR given on the last page of this test accordingly.
- At some instances, you may find more than 1 option to be correct. In such circumstances, you have to judge the most appropriate answer as per the conditions given in the question.

1. In Snapdragon, if a pink flower plant from the F_1 progeny is back-crossed with its dominant parent, what would be the expected phenotypic ratio of the offspring?

(a) 100% red flowers

(b) 50% red flowers and 50% white flowers

(c) 50% red flowers and 50% pink flowers

(d) 100% pink flowers

2. Identify the incorrect statement from the following.

(a) Externally observable characters of an individual are called phenotype.

(b) Law of segregation of gametes was proposed by Mendel.

(c) The law of dominance is used to explain the expression of both of the parental traits in monohybrid cross in the F_1 generation.

(d) The homozygous parent produce similar gametes.

3. Match List I with List II.

	List I (Types of crosses)		List II (Phenotypic ratio)
A.	Monohybrid cross	1.	1 : 2 : 1
B.	Test cross	2.	1 : 1
C.	Incomplete dominance	3.	9 : 3 : 3 : 1
D.	Dihybrid cross	4.	3 : 1

Choose the correct answer from the codes given below.

	A	B	C	D
(a)	4	2	1	3
(b)	4	3	1	2
(c)	2	4	1	3
(d)	1	3	4	2

4. Select incorrect statement w.r.t. reciprocal cross.

(a) It helps to know whether the alleles are present on sex chromosomes or autosomes

(b) It is made to eliminate the effect of nuclear traits

(c) Two individuals with contrast genotypes are involved

(d) Results are not changed for autosomal traits

5. On which type of plants does the Mendel's laws of inheritance is applicable?

(a) Plants that reproduce asexually

(b) Plants that reproduce sexually

(c) Plants that reproduce vegetatively

(d) Mendel's laws of inheritance are independent of mode of reproduction

6. In classic experiments on pea plants, Mendel did not study which of the following traits?

(a) The arrangement of flowers

(b) The pigmentation of seeds

(c) The round or wrinkled morphology of seeds

(d) The anatomy of pods

7. What led Mendel to propose that the factor controlling any character is discrete and independent?
(a) Results of F_3 generation of a cross
(b) Cross pollination of F_1 generation with recessive parent
(c) Observations that the offspring of a cross made between the plants having two contrasting characters shows only one character without any blending
(d) Self-pollination of F_1 offsprings

8. Identify the incorrect statement regarding experiments on *Pisum sativum* by Gregor Mendel.
(a) He conducted hybridisation experiment on garden peas for seven years (1856-1863)
(b) It was for the first time that statistical analysis and mathematical logic were applied to problems in biology
(c) His experiments had a small sampling size, which gave less credibility to the data that he collected
(d) He investigated characters in the garden pea plant that were manifested as two opposite traits

9. Read the following statements with respect to law of dominance.
I. Characters are controlled by discrete units called factors.
II. Homozygous genotype produces similar kind of gametes.
III. Factors always occur in pairs.
IV. In a dissimilar pair of factors, one member of pair dominates the other.
V. During gamete formation, traits segregate from each other and passes to different gametes.
Choose the correct set of statement from the options given below.
(a) I, III and IV (b) II, IV and V
(c) III and V (d) Only V

10. Given below are two statements.
Statement I The law of dominance is used to explain the expression of only one of the parental characters in a monohybrid cross in F_1 generation.
Statement II The law of dominance is the universal law.
In the light of the above statements, choose the correct answers from the options given below.
(a) Statement I is incorrect, but statement II is correct
(b) Both statement I and statement II are correct
(c) Both statement I and statement II are incorrect
(d) Statement I is correct, but statement II is incorrect

11. The most popularly known blood grouping is the ABO grouping. It is named ABO and not ABC, because "O" in it refers to having
(a) no antigens on RBCs
(b) other antigens besides A and B on RBCs
(c) overdominance of this type on the genes for A and B types
(d) one antibody only - either anti–A or anti–B on RBCs

12. Which of the following characteristics represent 'Inheritance of blood groups in humans?
1. Dominance 2. Co-dominance
3. Multiple allele 4. Incomplete dominance
5. Pleiotropy
(a) 2, 3 and 5 (b) 1, 2 and 3
(c) 2, 4 and 5 (d) 1, 3 and 5

13. Choose the correct match.
(a) Multiple alleles – Presence of more than one allele for a gene at different gene locus
(b) Codominance – Alleles for I^A and i for blood group A in humans
(c) Incomplete dominance – F_1 hybrid resembles both dominance parents
(d) Pleiotropy – A gene produces multiple phenotypic effect

14. Match the List I with List II.

List I	List II
A. Dominance	1. Present at the same locus of homologous chromosome
B. Co-dominance	2. In a heterozygous organism, only one allele expresses itself
C. Incomplete dominance	3. In a heterozygous organism, both alleles express themselves fully
D. Multiple alleles	4. Intermediate characteristic appears in heterozygous organism

Choose the correct answer from given below.

	A	B	C	D		A	B	C	D
(a)	1	3	4	2	(b)	2	3	1	4
(c)	2	3	4	1	(d)	3	2	4	1

15. Given below are two statements; one is labelled as Assertion (A) and the other is labelled as Reason (R).

Assertion (A) The law of segregation states that the two alleles of a gene pair segregate from each other during gamete formation.

Reason (R) Alleles are different forms of a gene and are present on homologous chromosomes.

In the light of the above statements, choose the correct answer from the options given below.

(a) A is false, but R is true

(b) Both A and R are true and R is the correct explanation of A

(c) Both A and R are correct, but R is not the correct explanation of A

(d) A is true, but R is false

Response Index

01	a	b	c	d	10	a	b	c	d	19	a	b	c	d
02	a	b	c	d	11	a	b	c	d	20	a	b	c	d
03	a	b	c	d	12	a	b	c	d	21	a	b	c	d
04	a	b	c	d	13	a	b	c	d	22	a	b	c	d
05	a	b	c	d	14	a	b	c	d	23	a	b	c	d
06	a	b	c	d	15	a	b	c	d	24	a	b	c	d
07	a	b	c	d	16	a	b	c	d	25	a	b	c	d
08	a	b	c	d	17	a	b	c	d					
09	a	b	c	d	18	a	b	c	d					

Performance Scanner

> 90% Excellent !	You have mastered these topics. The concepts of these topics are at your fingertips. Move on to the next test and maintain this momentum.
76-90% Very Good !	You have a good command over these topics. Revise these topics again after a few days and enhance your performance.
60-75% Good !	You have a wide scope to learn for these topics. Revise these topics again.
<60% Not Satisfactory!	You have a long way ahead of you to master these topics. Revise it thoroughly.

Test 2

Syllabus

- Mendelian Inheritance- II : Elementary idea of polygenic inheritance
- Chromosome theory of inheritance
- Chromosomes and genes
- Linkage and crossing over

For deeper insight, **Scan the QR Code**

Important Instructions

- The test is of 30 minutes duration and contains 25 Multiple Choice Questions (four options with a single correct answer).
- Choose the correct option and fill the OMR given on the last page of this test accordingly.
- At some instances, you may find more than 1 option to be correct. In such circumstances, you have to judge the most appropriate answer as per the conditions given in the question.

1. From the cross of AABb × aaBb, the genotypes AaBB : AaBb : Aabb : aabb will be obtained in the ratio- Polymeric

(a) 0 : 3 :1 : 0 (b) 1 : 2 : 1 : 0

(c) 1 : 1 : 1 : 1 (d) 1 : 1 : 1 :0

2. In Mendel's experiments with garden pea, round seed shape (RR) was dominant over wrinkled seeds (rr), yellow colour of seed (YY) was dominant over green colour of seed (yy). What are the expected phenotypes in the F_2 generation of the cross RRYY × rryy?

(a) Only round seeds with green colour

(b) Only wrinkled seeds with yellow colour

(c) Only wrinkled seeds with green colour

(d) Round seeds with yellow colour, and wrinkled seeds with yellow colour

3. How many different genotypes are produced in the F_2 generation from the self-pollination of a dihybrid F_1 plant?

(a) 4 (b) 3
(c) 9 (d) 1

4. In a cross between a pure tall plant with violet flower and a pure short plant with white flower. How many short plants are produced in F_2 generation out of 16?

(a) 1 (b) 3
(c) 4 (d) 9

5. How many different types of gametes can be formed by F_1 progeny, resulting from the following cross : AABBCC x aabbcc?

(a) 3 (b) 8
(c) 27 (d) 64

6. In a dihybrid cross, if you get 9:3:3:1 ratio, it denotes that

(a) the alleles of two genes are interacting with each other
(b) it is a multigenic inheritance
(c) it is a case of multiple allelism
(d) the alleles of two genes are segregating independently

7. Who observed that the behaviour of chromosomes parallels the behaviour of genes and used chromosome movement to explain Mendel's laws?

(a) Hugo de Vries (b) Sutton and Boveri
(c) Beadle and Tatum (d) TH Morgan

8. Given diagram refers to

Meiosis I - anaphase Meiosis I - anaphase
Meiosis II - anaphase Meiosis II - anaphase
Germ cells Germ cells

(a) Linkage
(b) Crossing over
(c) Dominance
(d) Independent assortment

9. Independent assortment is absent in case of

(a) Genes located on homologous chromosomes
(b) Genes located on the same chromosome
(c) Genes located on non-homologous chromosomes
(d) It does not get affected by the location of genes

10. Given below are two statements; one is labelled as Assertion (A) and the other is labelled as Reason (R).

Assertion (A) The chromosomal theory of inheritance suggested that genes are located on chromosomes.

Reason (R) The discovery of non-Mendelian inheritance patterns, such as linked genes, supported the chromosomal theory.

In the light of the above statements, choose the correct answer from the options given below.

(a) A is false, but R is true
(b) Both A and R are true and R is the correct explanation of A
(c) Both A and R are correct, but R is not the correct explanation of A
(d) A is true, but R is false

11. Which of the following will not result in variations among siblings?

(a) Crossing over
(b) Linkage
(c) Mutation
(d) Independent assortment of genes

12. *Drosophila melanogaster* is found to be very suitable for genetic studies because

I. they could be grown in simple synthetic medium in the laboratory
II. they complete their life-cycle in about 2 days
III. a single mating could produce a large number of progenies
IV. male and females are clearly distinguishable
V. it has many hereditary variations that can be seen with low power microscopes

Select correct set of statements.

(a) I, II, III, IV and V (b) I, III, IV and V
(c) III, IV and V (d) Only IV

13. How many linkage group are there in bacteria *E.coli*?

(a) One (b) Two
(c) Four (d) None

14. About genes of a linkage group, which of the following statement is correct?
(a) They stimulate the mitotic spindle formation during cell division
(b) They cannot be accurately positioned on a genetic linkage map
(c) They experience genetic recombination at reduced frequencies during meiosis
(d) They demonstrate co-inheritance due to their physical proximity on the same chromosome

15. In a test cross involving F_1 dihybrid flies, more parental type offsprings were produced than the recombinant type offsprings. This indicates
(a) chromosomes failed to separate during meiosis
(b) the two genes are linked and present on the same chromosome
(c) Both of the characters are controlled by more than one gene
(d) the genes are located on two different chromosomes

16. Mendel stated that, when two pairs of traits are combined in a hybrid, segregation of one pair of characters is independent of the other pair of characters. The phenomenon which is exception to this statement is
(a) purity of gametes (b) linkage
(c) multiple allele (d) co-dominance

17. Which type of cross is performed for the determination of map distance ?
(a) Reciprocal cross (b) Dihybrid cross
(c) Test cross (d) Monohybrid cross

18. The longer the chromosome of an organism, the more genetic variability it gets from
(a) linkage
(b) independent assortment
(c) mutation
(d) crossing over

19. Chromosome map is important to know
(a) occurrence of genes in a random sequence on the chromosome
(b) the strength of linkage between two genes and the chance of recombination
(c) recombination frequency that is inversely proportional to the distance between the genes
(d) exact physical distance amongst genes

20. ___A___ employed the frequency of recombination between gene pairs on ___B___ to measure the distance between genes and chart their positions on that chromosome?

	A	B
(a)	Sturtevant	different chromosomes
(b)	Morgan	same chromosome
(c)	Sturtevant	same chromosome
(d)	Morgan	different chromosomes

21. What map unit (CentiMorgan) is adopted in the construction of genetic maps?
(a) A unit of distance between two expressed genes, representing a 10% frequency of crossing over between them during meiosis
(b) A unit of distance between two expressed genes, representing a 100% frequency of crossing over between them during meiosis
(c) A unit of distance between genes on chromosomes, representing a 1% frequency of crossing over between them during meiosis
(d) A unit of distance between genes on chromosomes, representing a 50% frequency of crossing over between them during meiosis

22. Distance between the genes and percentage of recombination shows
(a) a direct relationship
(b) an inverse relationship
(c) a parallel relationship
(d) no relationship

23. A polygenic trait is controlled by 3 genes, i.e., A, B and C. In a cross AaBbCc × AaBbCc, the phenotypic ratio of the offsprings was observed as : 1 : 6 : X : 20 : X : 6 : 1 What is the possible value of X ?
(a) 3 (b) 9
(c) 15 (d) 25

24. Given below are two statements.
Statement I Inheritance of polygenic traits is controlled by multiple genes, each with two alleles.
Statement II Polygenic traits exhibit continuous variation, often represented by a bell-shaped curve.
In the light of above statements, choose the correct answers from the options given below.

(a) Statement I is incorrect, but statement II is correct

(b) Both statement I and statement II are correct

(c) Both statement I and statement II are incorrect

(d) Statement I is correct, but statement II is incorrect

25. Match the List I with List II.

	List I		List II
A.	Linkage	1.	Many genes govern a single character
B.	Polygenic inheritance	2.	Genes inherited together due to proximity on chromosome.
C.	Recombinant	3.	Random distribution of alleles during gamete formation.
D.	Independent assortment	4.	New combination of gene occurs in pachytene stage

Choose the correct answer from the options given below.

	A	B	C	D
(a)	2	4	3	1
(b)	1	2	3	4
(c)	2	1	4	3
(d)	4	3	2	1

■ **Response Index**

01	ⓐ	ⓑ	ⓒ	ⓓ	10	ⓐ	ⓑ	ⓒ	ⓓ	19	ⓐ	ⓑ	ⓒ	ⓓ
02	ⓐ	ⓑ	ⓒ	ⓓ	11	ⓐ	ⓑ	ⓒ	ⓓ	20	ⓐ	ⓑ	ⓒ	ⓓ
03	ⓐ	ⓑ	ⓒ	ⓓ	12	ⓐ	ⓑ	ⓒ	ⓓ	21	ⓐ	ⓑ	ⓒ	ⓓ
04	ⓐ	ⓑ	ⓒ	ⓓ	13	ⓐ	ⓑ	ⓒ	ⓓ	22	ⓐ	ⓑ	ⓒ	ⓓ
05	ⓐ	ⓑ	ⓒ	ⓓ	14	ⓐ	ⓑ	ⓒ	ⓓ	23	ⓐ	ⓑ	ⓒ	ⓓ
06	ⓐ	ⓑ	ⓒ	ⓓ	15	ⓐ	ⓑ	ⓒ	ⓓ	24	ⓐ	ⓑ	ⓒ	ⓓ
07	ⓐ	ⓑ	ⓒ	ⓓ	16	ⓐ	ⓑ	ⓒ	ⓓ	25	ⓐ	ⓑ	ⓒ	ⓓ
08	ⓐ	ⓑ	ⓒ	ⓓ	17	ⓐ	ⓑ	ⓒ	ⓓ					
09	ⓐ	ⓑ	ⓒ	ⓓ	18	ⓐ	ⓑ	ⓒ	ⓓ					

■ **Performance Scanner**

> 90% Excellent !	You have mastered these topics. The concepts of these topics are at your fingertips. Move on to the next test and maintain this momentum.
76-90% Very Good !	You have a good command over these topics. Revise these topics again after a few days and enhance your performance.
60-75% Good !	You have a wide scope to learn for these topics. Revise these topics again.
<60% Not Satisfactory!	You have a long way ahead of you to master these topics. Revise it thoroughly.

Test 3

Syllabus

- Sex determination-In humans, birds, honey bee
- Sex linked inheritance-Haemophilia, colour blindness
- Mendelian disorders in humans-Thalassemia
- Chromosomal disorders in humans-Down's syndrome, Turner's and Klinefelter's syndromes

For deeper insight, **Scan the QR Code**

Important Instructions

- The test is of 30 minutes duration and contains 25 Multiple Choice Questions (four options with a single correct answer).
- Choose the correct option and fill the OMR given on the last page of this test accordingly.
- At some instances, you may find more than 1 option to be correct. In such circumstances, you have to judge the most appropriate answer as per the conditions given in the question.

1. Among the following option, which one does not show male heterogamety?

(a) Grasshopper (b) *Drosophila*

(c) Human beings (d) Birds

2. Find the incorrect match regarding mutation.

(a) Point mutation - Involves a change in a single nucleotide base

(b) Insertion mutation - Adds one or more nucleotides to the DNA sequence

(c) Deletion mutation - Removes one or more nucleotides from the DNA sequence

(d) Substitution mutation - Involves the insertion of a segment of DNA from one chromosome to another

3. Read the following statements with respect to sex determination.

I. In haplo-diploid sex determination system, the males do not have father and thus cannot have sons, but have a grandfather and can have grandsons.

II. Worker bees are developed by the unfertilised eggs by means of parthenogenesis.

III. The females are diploid having 32 chromosomes and males are haploid, i.e., having 16 chromosomes.

IV. In XO type of sex-determination, male have half number of chromosomes than the female.

V. The sex determination in honey bee is based on the number of sets of chromosomes an individual receives.

Choose the incorrect set of answers from the options given below.

(a) I, III and IV (b) II and IV
(c) III and V (d) Only V

4. Identify the disease unrelated to abnormalities in human blood among the following.

(a) Diabetes mellitus type 1
(b) Haemophilia A
(c) Sickle cell anaemia
(d) Beta-thalassemia major

5. Which statement about sex determination is incorrect?

(a) In fruit flies, males are heterogametic.
(b) Half of male grasshopper sperm lack a sex chromosome.
(c) In domesticated fowls, offspring sex is determined by the type of sperm.
(d) Human males have one sex chromosome notably shorter than the other.

6. Among the following which one is not a physical mutagen?

(a) X- rays (b) β-rays
(c) Acridine (d) UV rays

7. Consider the following statements.

I. Point mutation arises due to change in single base pair.

II. Chromosomal aberration is commonly observed in cancer cells.

III. Nitrous acid is mutagenic to only replicating DNA.

IV. Aneuploidy occurs due to the variation in one or more haploid sets of chromosomes.

V. UV radiation can cause mutation.

Choose the correct set of statements from the options given below.

(a) I, II and V (b) I and IV
(c) Only IV (d) I, II, III, IV and V

8. Find the incorrect match.

(a)	Birds	–	Heterogametic females
(b)	Mammals	–	Heterogametic males
(c)	Grasshopper	–	ZW – ZZ type sex determination
(d)	Honey bee	–	Haplo-diploid sex determination

9. Among the following, which one is not true for the pedigree analysis?

(a) It is important to know the possibility of a recessive gene
(b) It is used to study the inheritance of human as well as plant, traits
(c) It may indicate harmfulness of marriage between close relatives
(d) It is used for genetic counselling

10. In human genetics, pedigree analysis is used to study the inheritance pattern of a specific gene across generations. Which type of trait corresponds to the characteristic being examined in this analysis?

(1) Quantitative trait (2) Mendelian trait
(3) Polygenic trait (4) Non-Mendelian trait

Choose the correct option.

(a) only 1 (b) only 2
(c) only 3 (d) 2 and 4

11. What is represented in the pedigree analysis by the given symbol?

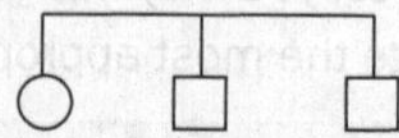

(a) Dizygotic twins
(b) Siblings
(c) Monozygotic twins
(d) Parents with single child

12. Analyze the genetic composition of the first generation in the given pedigree, which option represents an autosomal recessive disease?

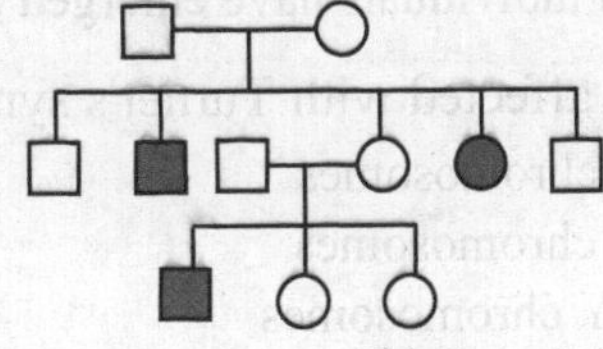

(a) Aa, Aa (b) Aa, AA
(c) AA, AA (d) aa, aa

13. Sterile condition in man associated with sex chromosomal abnormality is usually due to
(a) moderate increase in Y complement
(b) reduction in X complement
(c) large increase in Y complement
(d) increase is X complement

14. Holandric genes are located on
(a) autosomes
(b) sex-chromosomes as well as autosomes
(c) X-chromosomes
(d) Y-chromosomes

15. In a couple, where both the husband's father and the wife's mother were colour blind, while the wife's father was not colourblind and the husband's mother was neither colour blind nor a carrier, what percentage of their male children are expected to be colourblind?
(a) 1/4 (b) 1/2
(c) 3/4 (d) 0

16. Given below are two statements.
Statement I Haemophilic male baby can be born to a normal couple, if the mother is carrier for haemophilia (XX^h).
Statement II The progeny of a colourblind woman and a normal man will consist of 50% colourblind boys and 50% carrier girls.
In the light of above statements, choose the correct answers from the options given below.
(a) Statement I is incorrect, but statement II is correct
(b) Both statement I and statement II are correct
(c) Both statement I and statement II are incorrect
(d) Statement I is correct, but statement II is incorrect

17. Which triplet of nucleotides in the DNA sequence corresponds to the amino acid valine in sickle cell anaemia?
(a) G G G (b) A G G
(c) G A G (d) G U G

18. Which of the following points are true about phenylketonuria disease?
I. It occurs due to mutation in phenylalanine hydroxylase enzyme.
II. It occurs due to mutation in tyrosine hydroxylase enzyme.
III. It is autosomal recessive trait.
IV. It is an example of polygenic inheritance.
V. It follows Mendelian inheritance.
Choose the correct options.
(a) I, III and V (b) I and III
(c) II, III and V (d) III, IV and V

19. Which one of following statement is not true about thalassemia?
(a) There is different types of thalassemia, depending on the in globin chain mutations in genes.
(b) It is caused by mutations in the DNA of cells which make up the haemoglobin.
(c) There is two type of thalassemia, α and β.
(d) Four genes are necessary to make beta-globin chains.

20. Match the List I with List II.

	List I (Types of Heterogamety)		List II (Examples)
A.	XX - XO type	1.	Birds
B.	XX - XY type	2.	Grasshopper
C.	ZW - ZZ type	3.	Butterflies
D.	ZO - ZZ type	4.	*Drosophila*

Choose the correct answer from the options given below.

	A	B	C	D		A	B	C	D
(a)	4	3	2	1	(b)	2	4	1	3
(c)	1	2	4	3	(d)	3	1	4	2

21. Which of the following statement is incorrect regarding chromosomal aberrations?
(a) Chromosomal aberrations can be caused by exposure to mutagens.
(b) Chromosomal aberrations involve a change in a single gene only.

(c) Chromosomal aberrations can lead to genetic disorders such as Down syndrome.
(d) Chromosomal aberrations can be detected through techniques like karyotyping.

22. Usually the recessive character is expressed only when present in double recessive condition. However, single recessive gene can express itself in human beings when the gene present on
(a) any autosomes
(b) the X-chromosome of the female
(c) the X-chromosome of the male
(d) either can autosome or X-chromosome

23. Choose the incorrect statement about Klinefelter's syndrome.
(a) The affected individual possesses 45 chromosomes
(b) Phenotypically, these individuals are males
(c) Individuals have small testes
(d) Affected individuals have enlarged breasts

24. Individuals affected with Turner's syndrome possess
(a) 44 + Y0 chromosomes
(b) 44 + X0 chromosomes
(c) 44+ XXY chromosomes
(d) 45 + X0 chromosomes

25. Which of the following symptoms is not typically associated with Down's syndrome?
(a) Flat face profile
(b) Simian crease
(c) Poor reflexes
(d) Polydactyly

Response Index

01	a	b	c	d	10	a	b	c	d	19	a	b	c	d
02	a	b	c	d	11	a	b	c	d	20	a	b	c	d
03	a	b	c	d	12	a	b	c	d	21	a	b	c	d
04	a	b	c	d	13	a	b	c	d	22	a	b	c	d
05	a	b	c	d	14	a	b	c	d	23	a	b	c	d
06	a	b	c	d	15	a	b	c	d	24	a	b	c	d
07	a	b	c	d	16	a	b	c	d	25	a	b	c	d
08	a	b	c	d	17	a	b	c	d					
09	a	b	c	d	18	a	b	c	d					

Performance Scanner

> 90% Excellent !	You have mastered these topics. The concepts of these topics are at your fingertips. Move on to the next test and maintain this momentum.
76-90% Very Good !	You have a good command over these topics. Revise these topics again after a few days and enhance your performance.
60-75% Good !	You have a wide scope to learn for these topics. Revise these topics again.
<60% Not Satisfactory!	You have a long way ahead of you to master these topics. Revise it thoroughly.

Chapter Break Thru

Syllabus			
Syllabus	• Mendelian Inheritance : • Deviations from Mendelism-Incomplete dominance, Co-dominance, Multiple alleles and Inheritance of blood groups, Pleiotropy	• Elementary idea of polygenic inheritance; Chromosome theory of inheritance; Chromosomes and genes; Sex determination-In humans, birds, honey bee; Linkage and crossing over	• Sex linked inheritance-Haemophilia colour blindness; Mendelian disorders in humans-Thalassemia; Chromosomal disorders in humans; Down's syndrome, Turner's and Klinefelter's syndromes

Important Instructions

- The test is of 1 hour duration and contains 50 Multiple-Choice Questions (Four options with a single correct answer).
- Choose the correct option and fill the OMR given on the last page of this test accordingly.
- At some instances, you may find more than 1 option to be correct. In such circumstances, you have to judge the most appropriate answer as per the conditions given in the question.

1. If a women is homozygous normal and her husband is heterozygous for a genetically inherited recessive disease than what is the possibility that they will have a healthy child?

(a) 1 out of 4 (b) 2 out of 4
(c) 3 out of 4 (d) 4 out of 4

2. Select the incorrect match.

(a) Factor - Mendel
(b) Genes - Wilhelm Johannsen
(c) Alleles - William Bateson
(d) Genetics - Reginald Punnett

3. Choose the incorrect statement w.r.t. wild type allele.

(a) It is the phenotype found most commonly in nature
(b) It is the dominant allele
(c) It is designated by a small letter if it is recessive or a capital letter if it is dominant
(d) The occurrence of mutations in wild type alleles is a fundamental aspect of genetic variation and evolution

4. Given below are two statements.

Statement I Variation refers to the differences in traits among individuals of the same species, which can arise from genetic, environmental, or a combination of both factors.

Statement II Alleles are alternative form of a gene that governs contrasting characters of different traits.

In the light of the above statements, choose the correct answer from the options given below.

(a) Statement I is incorrect, but statement II is correct
(b) Both statement I and statement II are correct
(c) Both statement I and statement II are incorrect
(d) Statement I is correct, but statement II is incorrect

5. Given alongside is a simplified representation of the human sex-chromosomes from a karyotype. Observe them carefully.

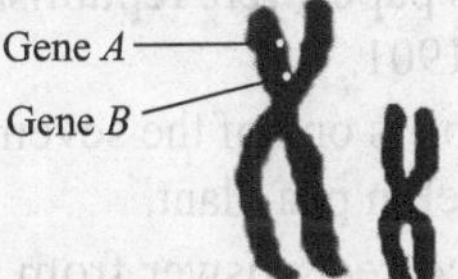

Based on your understanding, identify the genetic disease that gene '*A*' and '*B*' represent.

(a) Colour blindness and phenylketonuria
(b) Skin colour and myotonic dystrophy
(c) Haemophilia and colour blindness
(d) Thalassemia and sickle cell anaemia

6. Given below are two statements; one is labelled as Assertion (A) and the other is labelled as Reason (R).

Assertion (A) In a monohybrid cross, the F_2 generation shows a phenotypic ratio of 3:1.

Reason (R) Mendel's law of segregation states that allele pairs separate or segregate during gamete formation, and randomly unite at fertilisation.

In the light of the above statements, choose the correct answer from the options given below.

(a) A is false, but R is true

(b) Both A and R are true and R is the correct explanation of A

(c) Both A and R are true, but R is not the correct explanation of A

(d) A is true, but R is false

7. A woman married a man having ABO blood type 'A' and their child had blood type 'O'. She remarried again, so the blood group of her second husband is 'B' and the blood group of their child is AB.

Based on the given information what can be the possible genotype and the name of her of the women blood type?

(a) ii, blood type O (b) I^AI^B, blood type AB

(c) I^Ai, blood type A (d) I^B blood type B

8. Identify the incorrect statements from the following.

I. Mendel was the first biologist to discover that chromosomes are responsible for inheritance.

II. An organism with two couples of the same allele is homozygous for that trait.

III. Mendel took only those traits for his studies, which did not show linkage, interaction and incomplete dominance.

IV. Mendel's paper were republished in the journal Flora in 1901.

V. Leaf shape is one of the seven characters studied by Mendel in pea plant.

Choose the correct answer from the option given below.

(a) I, II and III (b) I and V

(c) II and III (d) IV and V

9. In wheat, when a green plant was self-fertilised, the progeny had 20 green seedling and 14 white seedling; this result indicates that the parents were

(a) true breeding

(b) homozygous for one allele

(c) heterozygous for one allele

(d) heterozygous for two duplicate alleles

10. Given below are two statements.

Statement I Test cross is used to determine as unknown genotype within one breeding generation.

Statement II The outcome ratio of test cross is 3:1, if unknown genotype is heterozygous.

In the light of above statements, choose the correct answers from the options given below.

(a) Statement I is incorrect, but statement II is correct

(b) Both statement I and statement II are correct

(c) Both statement I and statement II are incorrect

(d) Statement I is correct, but statement II is incorrect

11. In a monohybrid cross, when F_1 is crossed with homozygous dominant parent, then which type of offsprings will be obtained?

(a) Dominant recessive, 3 : 1

(b) Only recessive

(c) Dominant recessive, 1 : 1

(d) No recessive

12. During the gamete formation, the gametes may carry either the dominant or the recessive allele. This is the basis of

(a) law of independent assortment

(b) incomplete dominance

(c) principle of segregation

(d) complementary genes

13. Which of the following structure does not possess genes occurring in pairs?

(a) Zygote (b) Somatic cell

(c) Embryo (d) Gametes

14. What would be the expected type of plants in the F_1 generation if a dwarf plant, treated with the plant hormone gibberellin, is crossed with another dwarf plant?

(a) All tall (b) Intermediate plants

(c) Both tall and dwarf (d) All dwarf

15. Select the incorrect match.

(a) Incomplete dominance - Flower colour of Snapdragon

(b) Dominance - Yellow seed colour of pea

(c) Codominance - Human blood group

(d) Multiple allelism - Intermediate size of starch grain in pea seed

16. A man with blood group 'AB' marries a woman with blood group 'O'. Which blood groups will not be found in offsprings?

(a) A,B and AB only (b) A,B, AB and O

(c) O only (d) AB and O only

17. Mendel crossed round and wrinkled seed varieties of garden peas. All offspring in F_1 were round. When round hybrid plants were selfed, 1064 number of seeds were obtained in F_2 generation in which round and wrinkled seeds were around

(a) 787 and 277, respectively
(b) 277 and 787, respectively
(c) 354 and 710, respectively
(d) 710 and 354, respectively

18. Given below are two statements; one is labelled as Assertion (A) and the other is labelled as Reason (R).

Assertion (A) Theoretically, in a linkage experiment, 50 per cent of offspring can exhibit non-parental combinations for linked genes.

Reason (R) Distantly located linked genes sometimes show 100 per cent crossing over.

In the light of the above statements, choose the correct answer from the options given below.

(a) A is false, but R is true
(b) Both A and R are true and R is the correct explanation of A
(c) Both A and R are correct, but R is not the correct explanation of A
(d) A is true, but R is false

19. Two genes R and Y are located very close on the chromosome. When plants with RRYY and rryy genotypes are crossed, the F_2 generation will show

(a) Higher number of the non-parental types
(b) Higher number of the parental types
(c) 3:1 ratio
(d) The expected 9:3:3:1 ratio

20. A pea plant produces gametes with the genotypes RY, rY , Ry and ry having two characters. What is the corresponding genotype of the pea plant?

(a) rrYY (b) RrYY
(c) RrYy (d) rryy

21. In a dihybrid cross, the ratio 9:3:3:1 represents

(a) 9 individual out of 16 would have one dominant and one recessive character
(b) 3 individual out of 16 would be dominant for both character
(c) only one individual would be recessive for both the character
(d) 2 individual out of 16 would be dominant for both character

22. In a dihybrid cross, between two heterozygous plants (AaBb x AaBb), assuming independent assortment, what is the probability of obtaining an offspring that is homozygous recessive for both traits?

(a) 1/16 (b) 1/8
(c) 3/16 (d) 1/4

23. Match the List I with List II.

	List I		List II
A.	Independent assortment	1.	Alleles sorting into gametes independently
B.	Chromosomal theory of inheritance	2.	Genes are located on chromosomes
C.	Mendel's Law of segregation	3.	In a heterozygote, one allele may conceal the presence of another allele
D.	Mendel's Law of Dominance	4.	The random distribution of alleles for a single gene into gametes during meiosis.

Choose the correct answer from the options given below.

(a) A-1, B-2, C-3, D-4 (b) A-3, B-4, C-1, D-2
(c) A-1, B-2, C-4, D-3 (d) A-3, B-1, C-2, D-4

24. Given below are two statements.

Statement I Thomas Hunt Morgan and his colleagues used *Drosophila melanogaster* to experimentally verify the chromosomal theory of inheritance because these flies complete their life cycle in about two weeks and produce a large number of progenies.

Statement II *Drosophila melanogaster* were found suitable for genetic studies because they could be grown on a complex medium and had indistinguishable sexes.

In the light of the above statements, choose the correct answer from the options given below

(a) Statement I is incorrect, but statement II is correct
(b) Both statement I and statement II are correct
(c) Both statement I and statement II are incorrect
(d) Statement I is correct, but statement II is incorrect

25. Mendel conducted a number of crosses and studies but could never discover linkage. What could be the reason for this?

I. Some genes are linked but they are too far apart for crossing over to be distinguished from independent assortment.

II. Linked genes were never tested for the same time in same cross.

III. The seven genes were present on the 7 chromosomes.

IV. The genes underwent mutations during subsequent crossings.

Choose the correct options.

(a) I and II (b) II and III
(c) III and IV (d) Only IV

26. If map distance between genes A and B is 5 units, between B and C is 13 units and between C and A is 8 units, the order of genes on the linkage map will be so that

(a) C lies in the middle
(b) B lies opposite to A
(c) B cannot lie on the same side of C
(d) A lies opposite to C

27. Given below are two statements; one is labelled as Assertion (A) and the other is labelled as Reason (R).

Assertion (A) Thalassemia is caused by mutations in the genes responsible for haemoglobin production.

Reason (R) Thalassemia can be effectively treated by increasing dietary iron intake.

In the light of the above statements, choose the correct answer from the options given below.

(a) A is false, but R is true
(b) Both A and R are true and R is the correct explanation of A
(c) Both A and R are correct, but R is not the correct explanation of A
(d) A is true, but R is false

28. Which of the following is true about polygenes?

(a) Genes involved in qualitative inheritance
(b) Genes involved in quantitative inheritance
(c) Genes involved in multiple allelism
(d) Genes responsible for secondary sexual characters

29. In polygenic inheritance, a trait is controlled by two pairs of genes. Two individuals which are heterozygous for both genes, crossed each other, such type of cross produces the phenotypic ratio of:

(a) 1 : 2 : 1
(b) 9 : 3 : 3 : 1
(c) 1 : 4 : 6 : 4 : 1
(d) 1 : 6 : 15 : 20 : 15 : 6 : 1

30. In which organism the male is heterogametic and female has one chromosome more than the male?

(a) Grasshopper (b) Birds
(c) Human (d) Honey bee

31. In the haplo diploid sex-determination system of honey bees, females are ___A___ and workers are ___B___.

	A	B
(a)	Haploid	diploid
(b)	Diploid	diploid
(c)	Haploid	haploid
(d)	Diploid	haploid

32. Choose the incorrect statement about deletion.

(a) The loss in intermediary segment of DNA is designated as deletion.
(b) Deletions can be detected during pairing of non-homologous chromosomes.
(c) In plants, deletion is not easily transmitted to the offspring.
(d) The break in chromosomes may be caused by several agents like chemicals, drugs and radiations.

33. Given below is the partial sequence of the β-chain of haemoglobin from a person with sickle cell anaemia, identify the amino acid substitution at the blank circle ◯

Val-His-Leu-Thr-Pro-◯-Glu-Lys

What is the amino acid at the blank circle in sickle cell anaemia?

(a) Val (b) Glu
(c) Lys (d) Ala

34. Which symbol is used in pedigree analysis to represent an unspecified sex?

(a) Circle (b) Square
(c) Diamond (d) Triangle

35. A tobacco plant heterozygous for albinism (a recessive character) is self-pollinated and 1200 seeds are subsequently germinated. How many seedlings would have the parental genotype?

(a) 1250 (b) 600
(c) 300 (d) 2250

36. Given below is a pedigree chart showing the inheritance of a certain trait in humans.

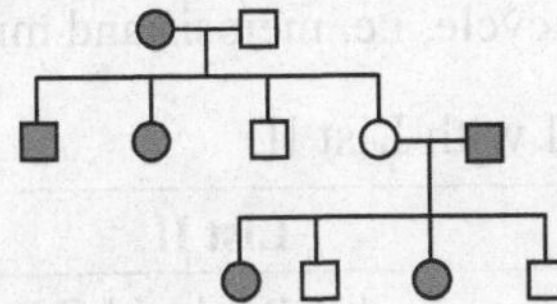

What is the inheritance pattern for this trait?
(a) Dominant X-linked
(b) Dominant Y-linked
(c) Recessive X-linked
(d) Recessive Y-linked

37. If a genetic disease is transferred from a phenoty- pically normal but carrier female to only some of the male offspring, the disease is likely to be
(a) Phenylketonuria (b) Sickle cell anaemia
(c) Colour blindness (d) Myotonic dystrophy

38. Below is a family tree illustrating the inheritance pattern of myotonic dystrophy, a genetic disorder inherited in an autosomal dominant manner.

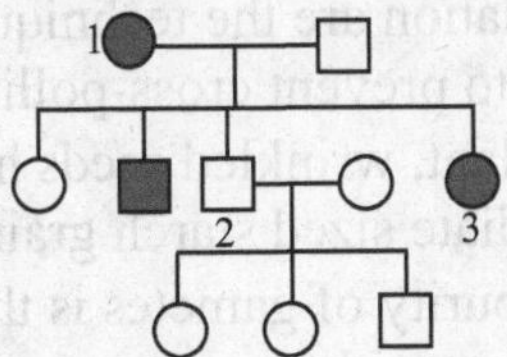

The genotypes of person 1, 2 and 3 in this family tree are

	1 2 3		1 2 3
(a)	Mm mm Mm	(b)	MM MM mm
(c)	Mm MM Mm	(d)	Mm Mm mm

39. Sickle cell anaemia is a mendelian disorder. If both parents are carriers for the trait, what is the probability that their child will also be a carrier?
(a) 25% (b) 50%
(c) 75% (d) 100%

40. Given below are two statements.
Statement I Colour blindness is a sex-linked recessive disorder.
Statement II Males have only one Y chromosome, so if they inherit the defective gene, they will be colourblind.
In the light of above statements, choose the correct answers from the options given below.
(a) Statement I is incorrect, but statement II is correct
(b) Both statement I and statements II are correct
(c) Both statements I and statements II are incorrect
(d) Statement I is correct, but statement II is incorrect

41. The incorrect statement regarding haemophilia is that
(a) the possibility of a female becoming a haemophilic is extremely rare
(b) a single protein that is a part of the cascade of proteins involved in the clotting of blood is affected
(c) Queen victoria was a carrier of the disease
(d) it is a autosome-linked recessive blood disease

42. In humans, PKU (Phenylketonuria) occurs due to the absence of which enzyme?
(a) Pyruvate dehydrogenase
(b) Adenosine deaminase
(c) Phenylalanine hydroxylase
(d) Phenylalanine dehydrogenase

43. Thalassemia is transmitted when
(a) both parents are affected
(b) both parents are unaffected carriers
(c) one parent is affected and the other is a carrier
(d) both parents are unaffected and non-carriers

44. Read the following statements.
I. Down's syndrome was first described by Langdon Down.
II. Klinefelter's syndrome is characterised by the absence of one X chromosome in females, leading to short stature and infertility.
III. Turner's syndrome results from the presence of an extra X chromosome in males, causing underdeveloped testes and infertility.
IV. Down's syndrome is the most common chromosomal disorder.
V. Turner's syndrome affects only females, while Klinefelter's syndrome affects only males.
Choose the correct set of statements from the options given below.
(a) I, II and III are correct.
(b) II, III and IV are correct.
(c) III, IV and V are correct.
(d) I, IV and V are correct.

45. If a haploid chromosome number in an organism is 23, the trisomic number will be

(a) 24 (b) 27
(c) 47 (d) 45

46. Select the incorrect match.

(a) Down's syndrome – 21- trisomy
(b) Turner's syndrome – $(2n-2)$ monosomy
(c) Klinefelter syndrome – (44 + XXY)
(d) Supermale – (44 + XYY)

47. Match the List I with List II.

List I	List II
A. Allele	1. Expressed only when it is present in the homozygous state
B. Recessive allele	2. Express more than one characters
C. Pleiotropy	3. Human skin colour
D. Polygenic inheritance	4. Different forms of the same gene

Choose the correct answer from the options given below

	A	B	C	D
(a)	1	2	3	4
(b)	4	2	3	1
(c)	3	2	1	4
(d)	4	1	2	3

48. Identify the incorrect statement from the following options.

(a) The probability of the progeny being heterozygous for both the alleles is 4/16th in dihybrid cross
(b) The genes for the seven characters chosen by Mendel are located on four chromosomes
(c) Gamete formation for polyhybrid cross can be easily done with the help of fork line method
(d) The independent assortment of genes occur in both cell cycle, i.e. meiosis and mitosis

49. Match List I with List II.

List I	List II
A. Wild type	1. Reginald C Punnett
B. Phenotype	2. Phenotype found in nature
C. Punnett square	3. 1:1:1:1
D. Dihybrid test cross	4. Appearance of an individual

Choose the correct correct answers from the options given below.

	A	B	C	D
(a)	1	2	4	3
(b)	2	4	1	3
(c)	1	2	3	4
(d)	2	4	3	1

50. Consider the following statements

I. Human male individual is hemizygous for sexual characters.
II. Mutant traits are mostly dominant in a population.
III. Emasculation are the techniques used by Mendel to prevent cross-pollination.
IV. In pea plant, wrinkled seeds have intermediate sized starch grains.
V. Law of purity of gametes is the only law of inheritance with exception.

Choose the incorrect set of statements from the options given below.

(a) II, III and V (b) I, II and III
(c) I, II, III, IV and V (d) II, III, IV and V

Scan for online chapter test

Response Index

01	ⓐ ⓑ ⓒ ⓓ	14	ⓐ ⓑ ⓒ ⓓ	27	ⓐ ⓑ ⓒ ⓓ	40	ⓐ ⓑ ⓒ ⓓ
02	ⓐ ⓑ ⓒ ⓓ	15	ⓐ ⓑ ⓒ ⓓ	28	ⓐ ⓑ ⓒ ⓓ	41	ⓐ ⓑ ⓒ ⓓ
03	ⓐ ⓑ ⓒ ⓓ	16	ⓐ ⓑ ⓒ ⓓ	29	ⓐ ⓑ ⓒ ⓓ	42	ⓐ ⓑ ⓒ ⓓ
04	ⓐ ⓑ ⓒ ⓓ	17	ⓐ ⓑ ⓒ ⓓ	30	ⓐ ⓑ ⓒ ⓓ	43	ⓐ ⓑ ⓒ ⓓ
05	ⓐ ⓑ ⓒ ⓓ	18	ⓐ ⓑ ⓒ ⓓ	31	ⓐ ⓑ ⓒ ⓓ	44	ⓐ ⓑ ⓒ ⓓ
06	ⓐ ⓑ ⓒ ⓓ	19	ⓐ ⓑ ⓒ ⓓ	32	ⓐ ⓑ ⓒ ⓓ	45	ⓐ ⓑ ⓒ ⓓ
07	ⓐ ⓑ ⓒ ⓓ	20	ⓐ ⓑ ⓒ ⓓ	33	ⓐ ⓑ ⓒ ⓓ	46	ⓐ ⓑ ⓒ ⓓ
08	ⓐ ⓑ ⓒ ⓓ	21	ⓐ ⓑ ⓒ ⓓ	34	ⓐ ⓑ ⓒ ⓓ	47	ⓐ ⓑ ⓒ ⓓ
09	ⓐ ⓑ ⓒ ⓓ	22	ⓐ ⓑ ⓒ ⓓ	35	ⓐ ⓑ ⓒ ⓓ	48	ⓐ ⓑ ⓒ ⓓ
10	ⓐ ⓑ ⓒ ⓓ	23	ⓐ ⓑ ⓒ ⓓ	36	ⓐ ⓑ ⓒ ⓓ	49	ⓐ ⓑ ⓒ ⓓ
11	ⓐ ⓑ ⓒ ⓓ	24	ⓐ ⓑ ⓒ ⓓ	37	ⓐ ⓑ ⓒ ⓓ	50	ⓐ ⓑ ⓒ ⓓ
12	ⓐ ⓑ ⓒ ⓓ	25	ⓐ ⓑ ⓒ ⓓ	38	ⓐ ⓑ ⓒ ⓓ		
13	ⓐ ⓑ ⓒ ⓓ	26	ⓐ ⓑ ⓒ ⓓ	39	ⓐ ⓑ ⓒ ⓓ		

Performance Scanner

> 90% Excellent !	You have mastered this chapter. The concepts of this chapter are at your fingertips. Move on to the next chapter and maintain this momentum.
76-90% Very Good !	You have a good command over this chapter. Revise the chapter again after a few days and enhance your performance.
60-75% Good !	You have a wide scope to learn for this chapter. Revise this chapter again.
<60% Not Satisfactory!	You have a long way ahead of you to master this chapter. Revise it thoroughly.

Test Booklet No. **3947355**

Test Booklet Code **CH5**

MEDACE

NEET (UG)

SELF ASSESSMENT KIT

Molecular Basis of Inheritance

Topics Covered

Genetic Material, DNA Packaging and Replication

Transcription and Translation

Regulation of Gene Expression, HGP and DNA Fingerprinting

Important Instructions

- This Booklet Contains – Three Topic Tests and One Test on Complete Chapter.
- Each question carries 4 marks.
- For each correct response, the candidate will get 4 marks. And for every incorrect response, 1 mark will be additionally deducted from total score.
- Use **Blue/Black** point pen only for filling the OMR.
- Rough work is to be done in the space provided for this purpose in the test booklet only.

Name of the Candidate (In Capitals)

____

____

Candidate's Signature ______________

Invigilator's Signature ______________

Facsimile signature stamp of center superintendent______________

Do not open this booklet until you start attempting the test

Topical Follow Thru

Test 1

Syllabus
- Search for genetic material and DNA as Genetic material
- Structure of DNA and RNA
- DNA Packaging
- DNA replication
- Central dogma

For deeper insight, **Scan the QR Code** 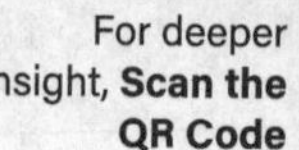 

Important Instructions
- The test is of 30 minutes duration and contains 15 Multiple Choice Questions (four options with a single correct answer).
- Choose the correct option and fill the OMR given on the last page of this test accordingly.
- At some instances, you may find more than 1 option to be correct. In such circumstances, you have to judge the most appropriate answer as per the conditions given in the question.

1. Identify the correct match of the organism with its DNA length.

1. $\phi \times 174$ - 5386 nucleotides
2. Bacteriophage lambda - 4.6×10^6 bp
3. *Escherichia coli* - 3.3×10^9 bp
4. Human (haploid content) - 48502 bp

How many pair shows the correct match?
(a) One
(b) Two
(c) Three
(d) Four

2. Given below are two statements; one is labelled as Assertion (A) and the other is labelled as Reason (R).

Assertion (A) There is a uniform distance between the two strands of the DNA helix.

Reason The bases in two strands are paired through hydrogen bonds forming base pairs.

In the light of the above statements, choose the correct answer from the options given below.
(a) A is false, but R is true
(b) Both A and R are true and R is the correct explanation of A
(c) Both A and R are true, but R is not the correct explanation of A
(d) A is true, but R is false

3. Given figure represents the DNA double helix model, proposed by Watson and Crick (1953). Select the option that shows correct measurement of *A*, *B* and *C* marked in the figure.

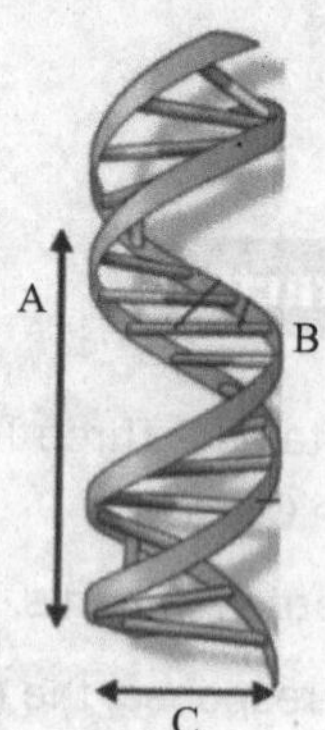

(a) *A*–3.4 nm, *B*–0.34 nm, *C*–2 nm
(b) *A*–34 nm, *B*–3.4 nm, *C*–20 nm
(c) *A*–3.4 Å, *B*–0.34 Å, *C*–20Å
(d) *A*–34 Å, *B*–3.4 Å, *C*–2 Å

4. Given below are two statements.

Statement I Nucleosomes consist of DNA wrapped around histone proteins, forming the fundamental repeating unit of chromatin.

Statement II Centromeres compact DNA into a tightly organised structure that ensures its orderly distribution during cell division.

In the light of the above statements, choose the correct answer from the options given below.

(a) Statement I is incorrect, but statement II is correct
(b) Both statement I and statement II are correct
(c) Both statement I and statement II are incorrect
(d) Statement I is correct, but statement II is incorrect

5. Which of the following structures from the following diagram are positively and negatively charged, respectively?

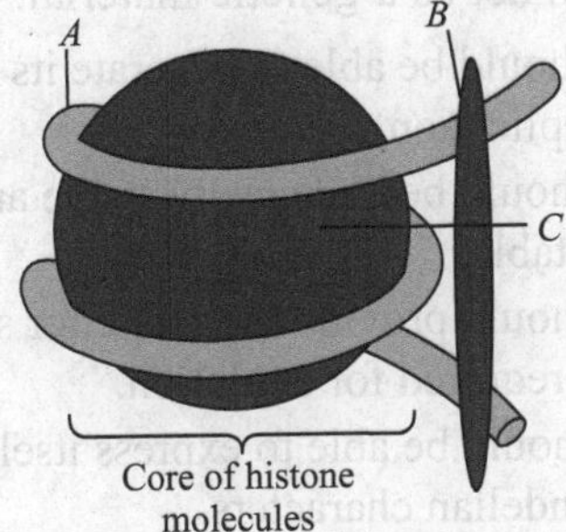

(a) *A* and *B* (b) *B* and *C*
(c) *B* and *A* (d) *C* and *A*

6. Match the following components or observations with their significance or role in Griffith's experiment on bacterial transformation.

	Components/ Observations		Significance/Roles
A.	Heat-killed S-type bacteria	1.	Showed that hereditary material could transform bacteria.
B.	Live R-type bacteria	2.	Confirmed that genetic information could be transferred between bacteria.
C.	Mixture of heat-killed S-type bacteria and live R-type bacteria	3.	Provided evidence, that transformation required direct interaction between cells.
D.	Smooth (S) colonies observed in mice	4.	Demonstrated the necessity of a specific bacterial structure for virulence.

Choose the correct option from the following.

	A	B	C	D
(a)	3	1	4	2
(b)	2	4	1	3
(c)	4	1	3	2
(d)	3	1	2	4

7. Identify the correct order of organisation of genetic material from largest to smallest.

(a) Genome, Chromosome, Nucleotide, Gene
(b) Genome, Chromosome, Gene, Nucleotide
(c) Chromosome, Genome, Nucleotide, Gene
(d) Chromosome, Gene, Genome, Nucleotide

8. Which of the following statement about the RNA world hypothesis is incorrect?

(a) RNA molecules are capable of both storing genetic information and catalysing biochemical reactions.
(b) The RNA world hypothesis proposes that RNA preceded DNA as the primary genetic material in early life forms.
(c) DNA had evolve from RNA through chemical modifications that increased its stability.
(d) The RNA world hypothesis suggests that proteins played a key role in early cellular processes before RNA molecules evolved.

9. Which of the following researchers proved that DNA in chromosomes also replicates semi-conservatively?

(a) Avery, MacLeod, and McCarty
(b) Taylor and colleagues
(c) Alfred Hershey and Martha Chase
(d) Griffith

10. In Hershey-Chase's experiment, when the radioactive viruses were allowed to infect *E. coli*, what was observed?

I. *E. coli* which was infected by viruses with radioactive DNA became radioactive.
II. *E. coli* which was infected by viruses with radioactive protein did not become radioactive.
III. *E. coli* which was infected by viruses with radioactive DNA did not become radioactive.
IV. *E. coli* which was infected by viruses with radioactive protein became radioactive.

(a) I and II were observed
(b) II and III were observed
(c) III and IV were observed
(d) I and IV were observed

11. Consider the following statements.

Statement I New DNA strand is synthesised by the addition of nucleotides at 5′–OH group.

Statement II DNA synthesis occurs in 5′-3′ direction.

In the light of the above statements, choose the correct answer from the options given below.

(a) Statement I is incorrect, but statement II is correct

(b) Both statement I and statement II are correct

(c) Both statement I and statement II are incorrect

(d) Statement I is correct, but statement II is incorrect

12. DNA replication at the replication fork requires the coordinated action of several enzymes. Identify the enzyme that specifically catalyses the unwinding of the parental DNA strands to create a replication bubble, facilitating the progression of the replication machinery.

(a) Topoisomerase

(b) Helicase

(c) Endonuclease

(d) Polymerase

13. Given below are two statements.

Statement I The DNA-dependent DNA polymerase is the key enzyme of DNA replication and it utilises a DNA template to facilitate the polymerisation of deoxynucleotides.

Statement II DNA replication in eukaryotes is semiconservative, semi-discontinuous and bidirectional.

In the light of the above statements, choose the correct answer from the options given below.

(a) Statement I is incorrect, but statement II is correct

(b) Both statement I and statement II are correct

(c) Both statement I and statement II are incorrect

(d) Statement I is correct, but statement II is incorrect

14. Read the following statements about a molecule that can act as a genetic material.

I. It should be able to generate its replica (Replication).

II. It should be chemically stable and structurally unstable.

III. It should provide the scope for slow changes that are required for evolution.

IV. It should be able to express itself in the form of Mendelian characters.

V. It should undergo mutation.

Choose the correct answer from the options given below.

(a) III and IV (b) I, III, IV and V

(c) I, II and V (d) III and V

15. A segment of DNA has 120 adenine and 120 cytosine bases. What will be the total number of nucleotide present in the segment?

(a) 120 (b) 60

(c) 480 (d) 240

Response Index

01	ⓐ ⓑ ⓒ ⓓ	10	ⓐ ⓑ ⓒ ⓓ	19	ⓐ ⓑ ⓒ ⓓ
02	ⓐ ⓑ ⓒ ⓓ	11	ⓐ ⓑ ⓒ ⓓ	20	ⓐ ⓑ ⓒ ⓓ
03	ⓐ ⓑ ⓒ ⓓ	12	ⓐ ⓑ ⓒ ⓓ	21	ⓐ ⓑ ⓒ ⓓ
04	ⓐ ⓑ ⓒ ⓓ	13	ⓐ ⓑ ⓒ ⓓ	22	ⓐ ⓑ ⓒ ⓓ
05	ⓐ ⓑ ⓒ ⓓ	14	ⓐ ⓑ ⓒ ⓓ	23	ⓐ ⓑ ⓒ ⓓ
06	ⓐ ⓑ ⓒ ⓓ	15	ⓐ ⓑ ⓒ ⓓ	24	ⓐ ⓑ ⓒ ⓓ
07	ⓐ ⓑ ⓒ ⓓ	16	ⓐ ⓑ ⓒ ⓓ	25	ⓐ ⓑ ⓒ ⓓ
08	ⓐ ⓑ ⓒ ⓓ	17	ⓐ ⓑ ⓒ ⓓ		
09	ⓐ ⓑ ⓒ ⓓ	18	ⓐ ⓑ ⓒ ⓓ		

Performance Scanner

> 90% Excellent !	You have mastered these topics. The concepts of these topics are at your fingertips. Move on to the next test and maintain this momentum.
76-90% Very Good !	You have a good command over these topics. Revise these topics again after a few days and enhance your performance.
60-75% Good !	You have a wide scope to learn for these topics. Revise these topics again.
<60% Not Satisfactory!	You have a long way ahead of you to master these topics. Revise it thoroughly.

Test 2

Syllabus
- Transcription
- Genetic code
- Translation
- Protein biosynthesis

For deeper insight, Scan the QR Code 

Important Instructions
- The test is of 30 minutes duration and contains 15 Multiple Choice Questions (four options with a single correct answer).
- Choose the correct option and fill the OMR given on the last page of this test accordingly.
- At some instances, you may find more than 1 option to be correct. In such circumstances, you have to judge the most appropriate answer as per the conditions given in the question.

1. The heterogenous nuclear RNA is
(a) the *m*RNA in which molecules are free to associate with ribosomes, facilitating the process of translation, where the *m*RNA is decoded to synthesise proteins
(b) synthesised and processed within the nucleus of a eukaryotic cell and undergoes several modifications
(c) the primary transcript that is initially synthesised during the process of *m*RNA formation
(d) a type of RNA that is a key structural and functional component of ribosomes, the cellular machinery responsible for protein synthesis

2. A mutation involving the insertion or deletion of a single or two nucleotides in a gene is most likely to cause
(a) a silent mutation with no change in amino acid sequence
(b) a change in a single amino acid due to a different codon (missense mutation)
(c) no change in the reading frame beyond the point of insertion/deletion
(d) a shift in the reading frame from the point of insertion/deletion potentially affects the entire protein sequence

3. The presence of which of the following specifies the starting point for RNA polymerase to bind and initiate RNA synthesis?

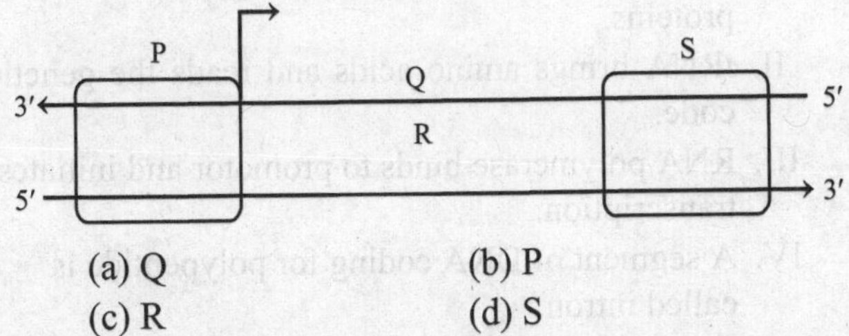

(a) Q (b) P
(c) R (d) S

4. ______ and ______ transiently associate with ______, altering its specificity for initiation and termination, respectively.

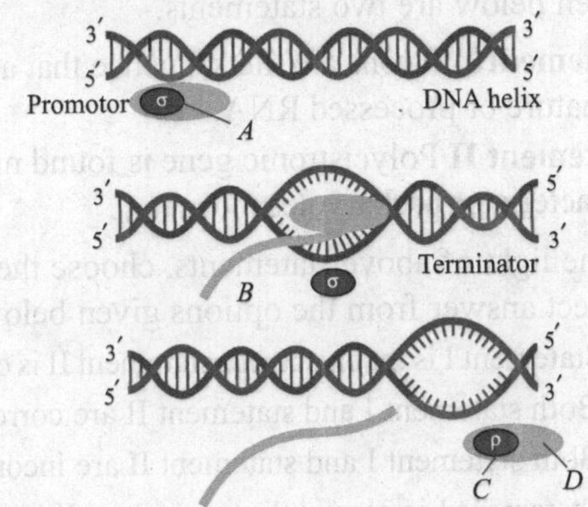

Identify *A*, *B*, *C* and *D* and fill the given blank by choosing the appropriate option.
(a) *A*, *B* and *C* (b) *A*, *C* and *D*
(c) *A*, *D* and *C* (d) *A*, *B* and *D*

5. Match List I with List II.

	List I		List II
A.	Activation of amino acid	1.	Aminoacyl *t*RNA synthetase
B.	Transfer of activated amino acid to *t*RNA	2.	Additional sequences required for an efficient translation process
C.	Initiation of polypeptide chain synthesis	3.	Aminoacylation of *t*RNA
D.	Untranslated regions	4.	Methionine

Choose the correct answer from the options given below.

	A	B	C	D		A	B	C	D
(a)	3	1	4	2	(b)	2	4	1	3
(c)	2	4	3	1	(d)	1	3	2	4

6. Which of the following statement about transcription is incorrect?

(a) Transcription involves copying a specific segment of DNA, utilising only one strand, into a complementary RNA molecule.

(b) The entire DNA molecule participates in transcription, with the active region designated as the transcription unit.

(c) During RNA copying (transcription), a terminator at the 3' end (downstream) halts the process on the DNA strand serving as the template.

(d) The coding strand possesses a sequence complementary to the newly formed RNA transcript, with thymine (T) replacing uracil (U).

7. Given below are two statements.

Statement I Introns are the sequence that appear in mature or processed RNA.

Statement II Polycistronic gene is found mostly in bacteria or prokaryotes.

In the light of above statements, choose the correct answer from the options given below.

(a) Statement I is incorrect, but statement II is correct

(b) Both statement I and statement II are correct

(c) Both statement I and statement II are incorrect

(d) Statement I is correct, but statement II is incorrect

8. Match the List I with List II.

	List I	List II
A.	Initiation factor	1. *m*RNA
B.	Soluble RNA	2. *r*RNA
C.	RNA polymerase-II transcribe	3. *t*RNA
D.	RNA polymerase-I transcribe	4. σ (sigma)

Choose the correct answer from the options given below.

	A	B	C	D		A	B	C	D
(a)	1	2	4	3	(b)	4	3	1	2
(c)	4	3	2	1	(d)	3	2	1	4

9. The enzyme polynucleotide phosphorylase facilitates the synthesis of RNA molecules with defined sequences in a template-independent manner, providing valuable tools for studying the code. This was given by

(a) Severo Ochoa (b) Har Gobind Khorana

(c) Marshall Nirenberg (d) George Gamow

10. Given below are two statements.

Statement I The anticodon loop of tRNA binds to a specific amino acid based on its complementary sequence.

Statement II The amino acid attachment site of *t*RNA is located at the 5' end of the acceptor arm.

In the light of above statements, choose the correct answer from the options given below.

(a) Statement I is incorrect, but statement II is correct

(b) Both statement I and statement II are correct

(c) Both statement I and statement II are incorrect

(d) Statement I is correct, but statement II is incorrect

11. Large deletions or rearrangements in DNA are easier to detect as compared to point mutations because

(a) point mutations affect only a single base pair, while deletions and rearrangements involve larger DNA segments.

(b) point mutations alter protein structure to a lesser extent compared to deletions and rearrangements.

(c) point mutations always have a visible effect on the organism, while deletions and rearrangements might not.

(d) point mutations occur more frequently than deletions and rearrangements.

12. Select the correct statement with respect to the post-transcriptional modifications.

(a) This process involve conversion of *sn*RNA into *m*RNA.

(b) In capping, methyl guanosine triphosphate is added to the 3′-end

(c) It leads to removal of exons and joining of introns in a definite order.

(d) It includes tailing where adenylate residues are added at 3′-end in a template independent manner.

13. Consider the following statements.

I. *r*RNA provides the template for synthesis of proteins.

II. *t*RNA brings amino acids and reads the genetic code.

III. RNA polymerase binds to promotor and initiates transcription.

IV. A segment of DNA coding for polypeptide is called intron.

V. *m*RNA is transcribed by RNA polymerase-II.

Choose the correct answer from the options given below.

(a) I and II

(b) I and III

(c) II, III and V

(d) I, II and IV

14. Consider the following statements about the genetic code.

I. Every codon specifies a single amino acid, with a few exceptions (Universal code).

II. Three consecutive nucleotides (triplet) form a codon and there are 64 possible codons that code for amino acids.

III. Degeneracy of the code implies that multiple codons can code for the same amino acid.

IV. The genetic code is unambiguous, meaning a single codon cannot code for more than one amino acid.

V. Stop codons (UAA, UAG, UGA) also specify an amino acid and terminate translation.

Choose the correct combination of statements that are true.

(a) I, II and V (b) I, III and IV

(c) II, III and V (d) I, IV and V

15. If there are 999 bases in an RNA that codes for a protein with 333 amino acids and the base at position 901 is deleted such that the length of the RNA becomes 998 bases, how many codons will be altered?

(a) 1 (b) 333

(c) 33 (d) 11

Response Index

01	a	b	c	d	10	a	b	c	d	19	a	b	c	d
02	a	b	c	d	11	a	b	c	d	20	a	b	c	d
03	a	b	c	d	12	a	b	c	d	21	a	b	c	d
04	a	b	c	d	13	a	b	c	d	22	a	b	c	d
05	a	b	c	d	14	a	b	c	d	23	a	b	c	d
06	a	b	c	d	15	a	b	c	d	24	a	b	c	d
07	a	b	c	d	16	a	b	c	d	25	a	b	c	d
08	a	b	c	d	17	a	b	c	d					
09	a	b	c	d	18	a	b	c	d					

Performance Scanner

> 90% Excellent !	You have mastered these topics. The concepts of these topics are at your fingertips. Move on to the next test and maintain this momentum.
76-90% Very Good !	You have a good command over these topics. Revise these topics again after a few days and enhance your performance.
60-75% Good !	You have a wide scope to learn for these topics. Revise these topics again.
<60% Not Satisfactory!	You have a long way ahead of you to master these topics. Revise it thoroughly.

Test 3

Syllabus	Gene expression and regulation-*Lac* Operon	Genome and human genome project	DNA finger printing	For deeper insight, **Scan the QR Code**

Important Instructions

- The test is of 30 minutes duration and contains 15 Multiple Choice Questions (four options with a single correct answer).
- Choose the correct option and fill the OMR given on the last page of this test accordingly.
- At some instances, you may find more than 1 option to be correct. In such circumstances, you have to judge the most appropriate answer as per the conditions given in the question.

1. Considering the *lac* operon and identify where does the RNA polymerase binds to initiate transcription?

(a) Operator gene

(b) Promoter gene

(c) Repressor binding site

(d) Promotor region

2. Choose the correct option.

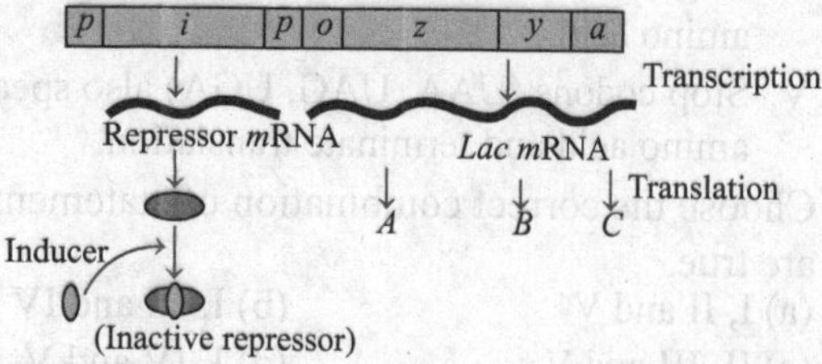

(a) A-β-galactosides, *B*-Permease, *C*-Transacetylase
(b) *A*- Transacetylase, *B*-Repressor, *C*-Permease
(c) *A*-Permease, *B*-Transacetylase, *C*-β-galactosides
(d) *A*-Permease, *B*-β-galactosides, *C*-Transacetylase

3. Choose the correct match from the following.
(a) Sequence annotation- Assigning functions to different regions of a sequenced genome
(b) Expressed Sequence Tags (ESTs) - Analyses DNA sequence to predict gene functions
(c) Bacterial Artificial Chromosomes (BACs) - Cloning vector for large DNA fragments.
(d) Yeast Artificial Chromosomes (YACs) - Cloning vector for large DNA fragments.

4. Analyse the following statements and choose the correct option.
(a) An operon can have more than one operator and repressor.
(b) Common promotor and regulatory genes can regulate a monocistronic structural gene.
(c) Allolactose interacts with repressor and activates it.
(d) For the metabolism of lactose, the 3 gene products in *lac* operon are required.

5. Control of gene expression can take place at multiple levels. Here are given some events showing the levels where control of gene expression takes place.
1. DNA replication
2. Transcription
3. Splicing regulation
4. Translation

Choose the correct option.
(a) 1 and 2
(b) 1, 3 and 4
(c) 2, 3 and 4
(d) 2 and 4

6. Considering DNA fingerprinting, which of the following statements is least likely to be true?
(a) Repetitive DNA sequences are used for identification due to their high variability between individuals.
(b) Polymorphism in non-coding DNA regions forms the basis of the technique.
(c) Northern blotting separates DNA fragments based on size after restriction enzyme digestion.
(d) Restriction endonucleases cleave DNA at specific recognition sequences.

7. *E. coli* cells with a mutated *z*-gene of the *lac* operon cannot grow in medium containing only lactose as the source of energy. Which of the following correctly justify the above statement?
(a) In the presence of glucose *E. coli* cells do not utilise lactose
(b) They cannot transport lactose from the medium into the cell
(c) The *lac* operon is constitutively active in these cells
(d) They cannot synthesise functional beta-galactosidase

8. Which organisation played a leading role in coordinating the human genome project?
1. US Department of Energy
2. National Institute of Health
3. Human Genome Organisation
4. Wellcome Trust (UK)

Choose the correct option.
(a) 1 and 2
(b) 1, 2 and 4
(c) 2 and 3
(d) 3 and 4

9. Find the incorrect statement with respect to HGP.
(a) The HGP's initial cost estimates likely underestimated the true financial investment required for sequencing the entire human genome.
(b) The vast amount of data generated by the HGP highlighted the need for advancements in data storage technologies.
(c) The HGP primarily focused on sequencing the human genome without considering the ethical implications of such research.
(d) The estimated amount of data from a single human cell, if stored in printed form, would require a significant number of books, highlighting the data management challenge.

10. Which of the following approach is used to identify all the genes expressed as RNA?
(a) Sequence annotation
(b) Expressed Sequence Tags (ESTs)
(c) Bacterial Artificial Chromosomes (BAC)
(d) Yeast Artificial Chromosomes (YAC)

11. Which of the following statement does not reflect a surprising discovery about the human genome?

(a) The human genome contains a vast amount of DNA, with an estimated 3×10^9 base pairs.

(b) The size of human genes can vary greatly, with some genes being much larger than others.

(c) The human genome contains a significant portion of repetitive DNA sequences, suggesting they might play a role in protein-coding.

(d) The functions of over half of the discovered human genes remain unknown, highlighting the complexity of gene regulation.

12. Given below are two statements.

Statement I Scientists have identified about 1.4 million locations where single-base DNA differences (SNPs) occur in humans.

Statement II This SNP information is primarily useful for identifying protein-coding genes in the human genome.

In the light of above statements, choose the correct answer from the options given below.

(a) Statement I is incorrect, but statement II is correct

(b) Both statement I and statement II are correct

(c) Both statement I and statement II are incorrect

(d) Statement I is correct, but statement II is incorrect

13. Given below are the two statements; one is labelled as Assertion (A) and the other is labelled as Reason (R).

Assertion (A) VNTR analysis is a highly polymorphic technique for DNA fingerprinting.

Reason (R) VNTR loci exhibit a high degree of variation in the number of tandem repeats between individuals.

In the light of the above statements, choose the correct answer from the options given below.

(a) A is false, but R is true

(b) Both A and R are true and R is the correct explanation of A

(c) Both A and R are true, but R is not the correct explanation of A

(d) A is true, but R is false

14. Given below are two statements.

Statement I Beta-galactose is synthesised by *E. coli.*

Statement II Beta-galactosidase catalyses the hydrolysis of lactose into falactose and fructose.

In the light of above statements, choose the correct answer from the options given below.

(a) Statement I is incorrect, but statement II is correct

(b) Both statement I and statement II are correct

(c) Both statement I and statement II are incorrect

(d) Statement I is correct, but statement II is incorrect

15. Given below are the two statements; one is labelled as Assertion (A) and the other is labelled as Reason (R)

Assertion (A) Studying DNA variations in non-human organisms like *C. elegans* provides limited insights into human health due to significant differences in their genetic makeup.

Reason (R) *C. elegans* and humans share a considerable portion of genes, allowing us to study genes potentially relevant to human health.

In the light of the above statements, choose the correct answer from the options given below.

(a) A is false, but R is true

(b) Both A and R are true and R is the correct explanation of A

(c) Both A and R are true, but R is not the correct explanation of A

(d) A is true, but R is false

Response Index

01	a	b	c	d	10	a	b	c	d	19	a	b	c	d
02	a	b	c	d	11	a	b	c	d	20	a	b	c	d
03	a	b	c	d	12	a	b	c	d	21	a	b	c	d
04	a	b	c	d	13	a	b	c	d	22	a	b	c	d
05	a	b	c	d	14	a	b	c	d	23	a	b	c	d
06	a	b	c	d	15	a	b	c	d	24	a	b	c	d
07	a	b	c	d	16	a	b	c	d	25	a	b	c	d
08	a	b	c	d	17	a	b	c	d					
09	a	b	c	d	18	a	b	c	d					

Performance Scanner

> 90% Excellent !	You have mastered these topics. The concepts of these topics are at your fingertips. Move on to the next test and maintain this momentum.
76-90% Very Good !	You have a good command over these topics. Revise these topics again after a few days and enhance your performance.
60-75% Good !	You have a wide scope to learn for these topics. Revise these topics again.
<60% Not Satisfactory!	You have a long way ahead of you to master these topics. Revise it thoroughly.

Chapter Break Thru

Syllabus

- Search for genetic material and DNA as genetic material
- Structure of DNA and RNA
- DNA packaging
- DNA replication
- Central dogma
- Transcription
- Genetic code
- Translation (protein biosynthesis)
- Gene expression and regulation-lac operon
- Genome and human genome project
- DNA fingerprinting

Important Instructions

- The test is of 1 hour duration and contains 50 Multiple-Choice Questions (Four options with a single correct answer).
- Choose the correct option and fill the OMR given on the last page of this test accordingly.
- At some instances, you may find more than 1 option to be correct. In such circumstances, you have to judge the most appropriate answer as per the conditions given in the question.

1. If RNA consists of 666 bases that codes for a protein with 222 amino acid and the base at position 600 is inserted such that the length of the RNA becomes 667 bases, then the number of codons being altered will be

(a) 11 (b) 24 (c) 22 (d) 2

2. A researcher observes a cell undergoing rapid protein synthesis. He then analyse the chromatin structure of this cell and find a significant increase in the proportion of lightly stained regions. What can be concluded from this observation?

(a) The cell is rich in inactive genes located in heterochromatin.

(b) The cell is replicating its DNA and the euchromatin is undergoing unwinding.

(c) The cell is actively transcribing genes located in the euchromatin regions.

(d) The cell is undergoing cell division and the heterochromatin is condensing.

3. Which of the following statements are correct regarding the historical and structural aspects of DNA?

I. DNA was first identified as an acidic substance in the nucleus by James Watson in 1869.

II. The double helix model of DNA was proposed in 1953 based on X-ray diffraction data produced by Maurice Wilkins and Rosalind Franklin.

III. Erwin Chargaff observed that in double-stranded DNA, the ratios between adenine and thymine and guanine and cytosine are constant and equal to one.

IV. The base pairing property of DNA means that if the sequence of bases in one strand is known, the sequence in the other strand can be predicted.

V. The two double-stranded DNA molecules produced during replication are not identical to the parental DNA molecule.

(a) I, II and V (b) II, III and IV
(c) I, III and IV (d) II, IV and V

4. Given below are some statements.

I. In a species, if amount of thymine is 20%, then the amount of cytosine will be more than 20%.
II. DNA replicates semiconservationly.
III. Presence of thymine in DNA confers it stability.
IV. Anticodon loop of tRNA possess condons complementary to the condons on DNA.
V. RNA is more stable than DNA.

Choose the correct options from the options given below.

(a) I, II and IV (b) II, III and V
(c) II, III and IV (d) I, II and III

5. Given below are the two statements; one is labelled as Assertion (A) and the other is labelled as Reason (R).

Assertion (A) Repetitive sequences make up very large portion of human genome.
Reason (R) Repetitive sequence do not have direct coding functions in the genome.
In the light of the above statements, choose the correct answer from the options given below.

(a) A is false, but R is true
(b) Both A and R are true and R is the correct explanation of A
(c) Both A and R are true, but R is not the correct explanation of A
(d) A is true, but R is false

6. The flow of information in some viruses occurs in a particular direction.

$$\overset{A}{\circlearrowright}\text{DNA} \underset{D}{\overset{B}{\rightleftharpoons}} m\text{RNA} \xrightarrow{C} \text{Protein}$$

With the help of this flowchart, name the alphabet which explains the process of flow of information in viruses.

(a) B (b) A
(c) D (d) C

7. Given below are the two statements; one is labelled as Assertion (A) and the other is labelled as Reason (R).

Assertion (A) RNA acts as a genetic material in a variety of life forms.
Reason (R) RNA plays a fundamental role in the evolution of essential life processes like metabolism, translation and splicing.

In the light of the above statements, choose the correct answer from the options given below.

(a) A is false, but R is true
(b) Both A and R are true and R is the correct explanation of A
(c) Both A and R are true, but R is not the correct explanation of A
(d) A is true, but R is false

8. After growing the cells in 15N medium, they were transferred to a medium with normal 14N. The DNA extracted from these cells at various time intervals was separated on a CsCl gradient. Which density profile would most likely be observed in the first generation after the transfer?

(a) A single band with intermediate density.
(b) Two bands, one heavy and one light with equal intensity.
(c) A single heavy band with reduced intensity.
(d) A single light band with reduced intensity.

9. Given below are two statements.

Statement I Histones are the positively charged basic amino acids that are rich in lysine and arginine.
Statement II The positive charge of lysine and arginine is present in their main chain.
In the light of the above statements, choose the correct answer from the options given below.

(a) Statement I is incorrect, but statement II is correct
(b) Both statement I and statement II are correct
(c) Both statement I and statement II are incorrect
(d) Statement I is correct, but statement II is incorrect

10. Match List I with List II.

List I	List II
A. RNA polymerase	1. Catalyse polymerisation
B. RNA polymerase- III	2. Catalyse process of elongation
C. DNA polymerase	3. Joins DNA segment
D. DNA ligase	4. transcription of *sn*RNA

Choose the correct answer from the options given below.

	A	B	C	D		A	B	C	D
(a)	1	3	2	4	(b)	2	4	1	3
(c)	1	2	3	4	(d)	3	2	4	1

11. Given below are two statements.

Statement I A specific DNA sequence located upstream of a gene acts as the binding site for RNA polymerase-II, initiating transcription in eukaryotes.

Statement II A distinct DNA region positioned downstream of a gene signals the termination of the RNA synthesis process during transcription.

In the light of above statements, choose the correct answer from the options given below.

(a) Statement I is incorrect, but statement II is correct
(b) Both statement I and statement II are correct
(c) Both statement I and statement II are incorrect
(d) Statement I is correct, but statement II is incorrect

12. Consider the following statements about Frederick Griffith's experiment with *Streptococcus pneumoniae*.

I. Smooth (S) strain bacteria have a polysaccharide coat and form shiny colonies.
II. Rough (R) strain bacteria lack a polysaccharide coat and form rough colonies.
III. Mice injected with the S-strain (virulent) die from pneumonia infection.
IV. Heat-killed S-strain bacteria, when injected alone, do not kill mice.

Which of the following option is correct?

(a) I, II and III
(b) I, II, III and IV
(c) II, III and IV
(d) I, III and IV

13. Given below are the two statements; one is labelled as Assertion (A) and the other is labelled as Reason (R).

Assertion (A) The first phase of translation involves activation of amino acids in the presence of ATP.

Reason (R) Amino acids are joined by hydrogen bonds.

In the light of the above statements, choose the correct answer from the options given below.

(a) A is false, but R is true
(b) Both A and R are true and R is the correct explanation of A
(c) Both A and R are true, but R is not the correct explanation of A
(d) A is true, but R is false

14. Which enzyme in prokaryotes is responsible for synthesising messenger RNA (*m*RNA) from DNA?

(a) RNA-dependent RNA polymerase-I
(b) DNA-dependent DNA polymerase-I
(c) DNA-dependent RNA polymerase
(d) DNA-dependent DNA polymerase-III

15. Given below are two statements; one is labelled as Assertion (A) and the other is labelled as Reason (R).

Assertion (A) Griffith's experiment with *Streptococcus pneumoniae* demonstrated that genetic material could be transferred between bacteria, resulting in a change in phenotype.

Reason (R) Griffith's experiment conclusively identified DNA as the genetic material responsible for transformation in bacteria.

In the light of the above statements, choose the correct answer from the options given below.

(a) A is false, but R is true
(b) Both A and R are true and R is the correct explanation of A
(c) Both A and R are true, but R is not the correct explanation of A
(d) A is true, but R is false

16. During *hn*RNA processing, which of the following modifications occurs at both the 5' and 3' ends?

(a) Addition of methyl groups
(b) Removal of introns
(c) Shortening of the transcript
(d) Addition of nucleotides in a template-independent manner

17. Given below are two statements.

Statement I The Hershey-Chase experiment involved attaching radioactive bacteriophages to *E. coli* bacteria, followed by removal of the viral coats using a blender.

Statement II Radioactivity detected in the bacteria after coat removal confirmed that DNA, not protein, from the virus was transferred to the host bacteria.

In the light of the above statements, choose the correct answer from the options given below.

(a) Statement I is incorrect, but statement II is correct
(b) Both statement I and statement II are correct
(c) Both statement I and statement II are incorrect
(d) Statement I is correct, but statement II is incorrect

18. Match List I with List II.

	List I		List II
A.	*m*RNA	1.	Soluble
B.	*r*RNA	2.	Genetic RNA
C.	*t*RNA	3.	Precursor *m*RNA
D.	*hn*RNA	4.	Stable

Choose the correct answer from the options given below.

	A	B	C	D		A	B	C	D
(a)	4	3	2	1	(b)	2	4	1	3
(c)	1	2	3	4	(d)	3	2	4	1

19. Choose the correct statement.

(a) The coding strand has the same polarity (3' to 5') as the *m*RNA transcript.

(b) RNA polymerase can transcribe from either DNA strand in a transcription unit.

(c) The promotor region is always located upstream (towards the 5' end) of the coding strand.

(d) The terminator sequence marks the end of the coding strand and RNA polymerase detaches here.

20. Match the following features with the type of frameshift mutation they most likely cause.

	List I (Features)		List II (Types of Mutation)
A.	Elongation continues with incorrect amino acids incorporated.	1.	Deletion of a single nucleotide
B.	Chain termination immediately after the mutation site.	2.	Insertion of a single nucleotide
C.	Altered amino acid sequence from the mutation point onwards.		

(a) A-1, B-2, C-1 (b) A-2, B-1, C-1 and 2

(c) A-1, B-2, C-2 (d) A-1, B-2, C-1 and 2

21. Which technique is used to determine the unique nucleotide sequences of specific DNA regions in individuals?

(a) Sequence annotation

(b) DNA fingerprinting

(c) Expressed sequence tags

(d) Sequence nucleotide polymorphism

22. Which of the following statement is incorrect about goals of HGP?

(a) To identify all the approximately 20,000 -25,000 genes in human DNA.

(b) To determine the sequence of the 3 billion bp.

(c) To store information in databases.

(d) Mapping all the functional proteins encoded by the human genome.

23. Given below are two statements.

Statement I In prokaryotes, the primary mechanism for regulating gene expression is controlling the rate of transcription initiation.

Statement II The binding of repressors to operator regions directly prevents RNA polymerase from binding to the promoter.

In the light of the above statements, choose the correct answer from the options given below.

(a) Statement I is incorrect, but statement II is correct

(b) Both statement I and statement II are correct

(c) Both statement I and statement II are incorrect

(d) Statement I is correct, but statement II is incorrect

24. The Human Genome Project (HGP) provided valuable insights into human biology and the DNA sequences of non-human model organisms. Which of the following pairs of model organisms have been sequenced as part of efforts to understand their natural capabilities and contribute to various fields such as health care and agriculture?

I. *Caenorhabditis elegans* and *Drosophila*

II. *Arabidopsis* and *E. coli*

III. Yeast and rice

Choose the correct option.

(a) I and II

(b) II and III

(c) I and III

(d) I, II and III

25. During DNA replication, which strand is synthesised in short fragments?

(a) Leading strand

(b) Lagging strand

(c) Continuous strand

(d) RNA template strand

26. Choose the incorrect statement about the control of gene expression in eukaryotes.

(a) The control of gene expression is complex in eukaryotes.
(b) Histones play a major role in the regulation of gene expression.
(c) Histones are gene repressor.
(d) They mask the gene activity.

27. Cytidine is

(a) Cytosine + Ribose sugar + Phosphate
(b) Cytosine + Ribose sugar
(c) Cytosine + Deoxyribose sugar + Phosphate
(d) Cytosine + Deoxyribose sugar

28. Given below are two statements; one is labelled as Assertion (A) and the other is labelled as Reason (R).

Assertion (A) Base ratio A + T / C + G is used for the identification of species.

Reason (R) The base ratio A+ T / C + G is specific for a species.

In the light of the above statements, choose the correct answer from the options given below.

(a) A is false, but R is true
(b) Both A and R are true and R is the correct explanation of A
(c) Both A and R are true, but R is not the correct explanation of A
(d) A is true, but R is false

29. Read the following statements about DNA and RNA and choose the incorrect statement.

(a) The presence of a 2'-OH group in DNA makes it more stable and less reactive compared to DNA.
(b) RNA can directly code for protein synthesis, while DNA requires RNA as an intermediary.
(c) Due to its stability, DNA is a better suited genetic material for most organisms.
(d) Mutations occur more frequently in RNA due to its higher reactivity.

30. Which sequence of codons specifies for leucine–threonine-proline?

(a) CUC–GCU–CCC
(b) AAA–ACC–CCC
(c) UUG–AGC–UAG
(d) CUA–ACA–CCU

31. During RNA processing, an additional chain of 200-300 adenine units is attached at a point

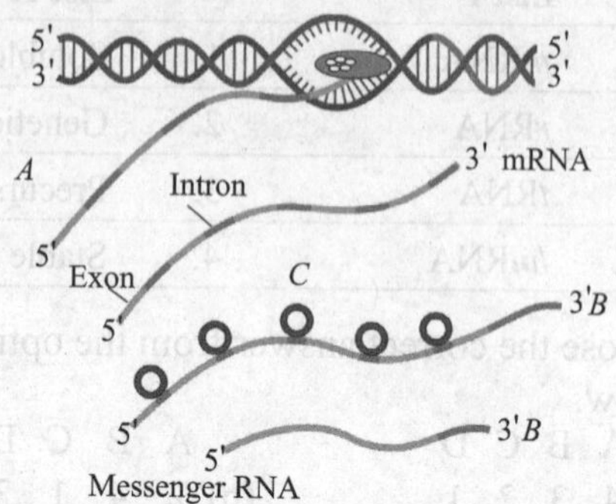

Choose the correct option which represents this process.

(a) A
(b) B
(c) C
(d) Both B and C

32. Given below are two statements; one is labelled as Assertion (A) and the other is labelled as Reason (R).

Assertion (A) Aminoacyl *t*RNA synthetase are enzymes that load the individual amino acids onto the *t*RNAs.

Reason (R) The tRNA molecules are transcribed by RNA polymerase-III.

In the light of the above statements, choose the correct answer from the options given below.

(a) A is false, but R is true
(b) Both A and R are true and R is the correct explanation of A
(c) Both A and R are true, but R is not the correct explanation of A
(d) A is true, but R is false

33. How similar is the genetic makeup (base sequence) between two random humans?

(a) Only 20% identical
(b) Around 90% identical
(c) Nearly identical, with about 99.9% similarity
(d) Highly variable, with a difference of more than 5%

34. Why cannot glucose and galactose act as an inducer for *lac* operon?

(a) Because they cannot bind with the repressor
(b) Because they can bind with the promotor
(c) Because they can bind with the operator
(d) Because they can bind with the regulator

35. The Human Genome Project (HGP) completed in the year

(a) 2003 (b) 2015
(c) 2013 (d) 2005

36. Given below are two statements.

Statement I The human genome project has enabled a shift in research from studying individual genes to investigating entire genomes.

Statement II This shift necessitates collaboration only between public sector scientists across the globe.

In the light of the above statements, choose the correct answer from the options given below.

(a) Statement I is incorrect, but statement II is correct
(b) Both statement I and statement II are correct
(c) Both statement I and statement II are incorrect
(d) Statement I is correct, but statement II is incorrect

37. Choose the incorrect statement about translation.

(a) Activation of amino acid is known as aminoacylation of *t*RNA
(b) The amino acids are attached to the tRNA by high energy bond
(c) The starting amino acid is methionine in eukaryotes
(d) The UTR is present only at 5' end

38. Which term refers to the existence of different versions of a gene or genetic sequence within a population?

(a) Polymorphism
(b) VNTR (Variable Number Tandem Repeat)
(c) Satellite DNA
(d) Mutation

39. Read the following statements about salient features of genetic code.

I. The codon is triplet.
II. One codon codes for only one amino acid hence it is ambiguous and specific.
III. The code is degenerate.
IV. The code is nearly universal with some exceptions.
V. The codon has punctuation.

Which of the following option is correct?

(a) I, II and IV (b) II, III, IV and V
(c) I, III and IV (d) III and IV

40. Match List I with List II.

	List I		List II
A.	*z* gene	1.	Transacetylase
B.	*y* gene	2.	Repressor
C.	*a* gene	3.	β-galactose
D.	*i* gene	4.	Permease

Choose the correct answer from the options given below.

	A	B	C	D		A	B	C	D
(a)	2	1	4	3	(b)	2	4	3	1
(c)	3	1	2	4	(d)	3	4	1	2

41. Given below are two statements.

Statement I DNA fingerprinting employes the principle of polymorphism in DNA sequences.

Statement II DNA sample hybridised with DNA probe when kept in contact with X-ray film results into photographic image of DNA bands

In the light of the above statements, choose the correct answer from the options given below.

(a) Statement I is incorrect, but statement II is correct
(b) Both statement I and statement II are correct
(c) Both statement I and statement II are incorrect
(d) Statement I is correct, but statement II is incorrect

42. Given below are two statements; one is labelled as Assertion (A) and the other is labelled as Reason (R).

Assertion (A) The replication of DNA does not initiate randomly at any place in DNA, but begins at a specific region known as the origin of replication.

Reason (R) In recombinant DNA procedures, vectors are required because they provide the origin of replication necessary for the propagation of DNA.

In the light of the above statements, choose the correct answer from the options given below.

(a) A is false, but R is true
(b) Both A and R are true and R is the correct explanation of A
(c) Both A and R are true, but R is not the correct explanation of A
(d) A is true, but R is false

43. Consider the following statements and choose the incorrect answer from the options given below

(a) *r*RNA provides the template for synthesis of proteins.

(b) *t*RNA brings amino acids and reads the genetic code.

(c) RNA polymerase binds to promoter and initiates transcription.

(d) *m*RNA is transcribs by RNA polymeras-II.

44. The ribosomal unit that attaches to *m*RNA to form *m*RNA-subunit complex is

(a) larger subunit

(b) smaller subunit

(c) Both units

(d) depends upon the function of the protein

45. If the length of *E. coli* DNA is 1.36 mm. How many base pairs are there in *E. coli*?

(a) 2.5 million base pairs

(b) 4 million base pairs

(c) 6.5 million base pairs

(d) 8 million base pairs

46. Viruses having RNA genome have a shorter lifespan mutate and evolve faster because

(a) RNA is unstable, hence mutate at faster rate

(b) RNA is stable, hence mutate at faster rate

(c) RNA is stable and mutate at slower rate

(d) RNA is unstable and mutate at slower rate

47. Function of helix-destabilising proteins is to

(a) keep uncoiled strands of DNA apart

(b) resist uncoiling of DNA under normal conditions

(c) repair DNA molecule during replication

(d) keep DNA helix tightly coiled

48. Consider the following statements.

Statement I Structural genes produce *m*RNA when operator gene is turned on by an inducer.

Statement II Promotor gene base sequence determines which strand of DNA acts as template.

In the light of the above statements, choose the correct answer from the options given below.

(a) Statement I is incorrect, but statement II is correct

(b) Both statement I and statement II are correct

(c) Both statement I and statement II are incorrect

(d) Statement I is correct, but statement II is incorrect

49. In *lac* operon model, feedback repression is

(a) when the end product starts the process

(b) when the end product does not form

(c) when the end product halt the process

(d) when the start product stop the process

50. Which of the following characters are required for protein synthesis?

I. DNA to provide the base sequence.

II. 20 types of amino acids.

III. Genetic type of RNA.

IV. Non-genetic type of RNA such as *m*RNA, *r*RNA, *t*RNA.

V. ATP/GTP as source of energy.

Choose the correct answer from the options given below

(a) I, II and III are required

(b) I, II, IV and V are required

(c) III and V are required

(d) I and V are required

Scan for online chapter test

■ **Response Index**

01	ⓐ ⓑ ⓒ ⓓ	14	ⓐ ⓑ ⓒ ⓓ	27	ⓐ ⓑ ⓒ ⓓ	40	ⓐ ⓑ ⓒ ⓓ
02	ⓐ ⓑ ⓒ ⓓ	15	ⓐ ⓑ ⓒ ⓓ	28	ⓐ ⓑ ⓒ ⓓ	41	ⓐ ⓑ ⓒ ⓓ
03	ⓐ ⓑ ⓒ ⓓ	16	ⓐ ⓑ ⓒ ⓓ	29	ⓐ ⓑ ⓒ ⓓ	42	ⓐ ⓑ ⓒ ⓓ
04	ⓐ ⓑ ⓒ ⓓ	17	ⓐ ⓑ ⓒ ⓓ	30	ⓐ ⓑ ⓒ ⓓ	43	ⓐ ⓑ ⓒ ⓓ
05	ⓐ ⓑ ⓒ ⓓ	18	ⓐ ⓑ ⓒ ⓓ	31	ⓐ ⓑ ⓒ ⓓ	44	ⓐ ⓑ ⓒ ⓓ
06	ⓐ ⓑ ⓒ ⓓ	19	ⓐ ⓑ ⓒ ⓓ	32	ⓐ ⓑ ⓒ ⓓ	45	ⓐ ⓑ ⓒ ⓓ
07	ⓐ ⓑ ⓒ ⓓ	20	ⓐ ⓑ ⓒ ⓓ	33	ⓐ ⓑ ⓒ ⓓ	46	ⓐ ⓑ ⓒ ⓓ
08	ⓐ ⓑ ⓒ ⓓ	21	ⓐ ⓑ ⓒ ⓓ	34	ⓐ ⓑ ⓒ ⓓ	47	ⓐ ⓑ ⓒ ⓓ
09	ⓐ ⓑ ⓒ ⓓ	22	ⓐ ⓑ ⓒ ⓓ	35	ⓐ ⓑ ⓒ ⓓ	48	ⓐ ⓑ ⓒ ⓓ
10	ⓐ ⓑ ⓒ ⓓ	23	ⓐ ⓑ ⓒ ⓓ	36	ⓐ ⓑ ⓒ ⓓ	49	ⓐ ⓑ ⓒ ⓓ
11	ⓐ ⓑ ⓒ ⓓ	24	ⓐ ⓑ ⓒ ⓓ	37	ⓐ ⓑ ⓒ ⓓ	50	ⓐ ⓑ ⓒ ⓓ
12	ⓐ ⓑ ⓒ ⓓ	25	ⓐ ⓑ ⓒ ⓓ	38	ⓐ ⓑ ⓒ ⓓ		
13	ⓐ ⓑ ⓒ ⓓ	26	ⓐ ⓑ ⓒ ⓓ	39	ⓐ ⓑ ⓒ ⓓ		

■ **Performance Scanner**

> 90% Excellent !	You have mastered this chapter. The concepts of this chapter are at your fingertips. Move on to the next chapter and maintain this momentum.
76-90% Very Good !	You have a good command over this chapter. Revise the chapter again after a few days and enhance your performance.
60-75% Good !	You have a wide scope to learn for this chapter. Revise this chapter again.
<60% Not Satisfactory!	You have a long way ahead of you to master this chapter. Revise it thoroughly.

Test Booklet No. **3947356**

Test Booklet Code **CH6**

MEDACE
NEET (UG)
SELF ASSESSMENT KIT

Evolution

Topics Covered

Origin of Life and Evidence of Evolution

Theories of Evolution, Speciation (Hardy-Weinberg Law and Geographical Isolation)

Brief Account of Evolution, Origin and Evolution of Man

Important Instructions

- This Booklet Contains – Three Topic Tests and One Test on Complete Chapter.
- Each question carries 4 marks.
- For each correct response, the candidate will get 4 marks. And for every incorrect response, 1 mark will be additionally deducted from total score.
- Use **Blue/Black** point pen only for filling the OMR.
- Rough work is to be done in the space provided for this purpose in the test booklet only.

Name of the Candidate (In Capitals) ________________

____

Candidate's Signature ________________

Invigilator's Signature ________________

Facsimile signature stamp of center superintendent________________

Do not open this booklet until you start attempting the test

Topical Follow Thru

Test 1

Syllabus
- Origin of life
- Biological evolution and evidences for biological evolution (from Paleontology, comparative anatomy, embryology and molecular evidence)

For deeper insight, **Scan the QR Code**

Important Instructions
- The test is of 30 minutes duration and contains 15 Multiple Choice Questions (four options with a single correct answer).
- Choose the correct option and fill the OMR given on the last page of this test accordingly.
- At some instances, you may find more than 1 option to be correct. In such circumstances, you have to judge the most appropriate answer as per the conditions given in the question.

1. The theory of spontaneous generation, which was a prevalent belief before, was conclusively disapproved by
(a) Darwin
(b) Louis Pasteur
(c) Oparin and Haldane
(d) SL Miller

2. Given below are two statements; one is labelled as Assertion (A) and the other is labelled as Reason (R).

Assertion (A) Early earth had no atmosphere.
Reason (R) The surface of early earth was in molten state.
In the light of the above statements, choose the correct answer from the options given below.
(a) A is false, but R is true.
(b) Both A and R are true and R is the correct explanation of A.
(c) Both A and R are true, but R is not the correct explanation of A.
(d) A is true, but R is false.

3. Read the following statements.
I. Fossils are the preserved remains of hard parts of organisms found in rocks, which accumulate as sediments.
II. A cross-section of earth's crust displays the sequential layering of sediments over time.
III. Sediments of different ages contain fossils of various life-forms that most likely perished during the formation of those sediments.
IV. Fossils of all organisms, whether modern or extinct, can be found in every geological layer.
V. Analysing fossils in sedimentary layers helps determine the geological period in which the organisms lived, showing that new life forms have emerged at different times in earth's history.

Choose the correct set of statements from the options given below.
(a) I, II, III and IV
(b) I, II, IV and V
(c) II, III, IV and V
(d) I, II, III and V

4. Select the incorrect match w.r.t. theories of evolution and their discoverers.
(a) Biological evolution - Charles Darwin
(b) Biogenesis - Louis Pasteur
(c) Chemical evolution - SL Miller
(d) Panspermia - Early Greek thinkers

5. In 1953, SL Miller simulated the conditions of early Earth in a laboratory setting and provided experimental proof for the emergence of the first life forms from pre-existing non-living organic molecules. Which of the following best describes the conditions of early earth that were simulated?
(a) High temperature, volcanic storms, reducing atmosphere containing CH_4, NH_3, etc.
(b) Low temperature, volcanic storms, reducing atmosphere
(c) Low temperature, volcanic storms, atmosphere rich in oxygen
(d) High temperature, volcanic storms, non-reducing atmosphere

6. Consider the evolutionary history of life on earth and the adaptive strategies employed by various life forms. Which of the following sequences best represent the general trend observed in the movement of life forms during this evolutionary process?
(a) Terrestrial environments to aquatic environments
(b) Arid terrestrial environments to humid terrestrial environments
(c) Freshwater aquatic environments to saline marine environments
(d) Aquatic environments to terrestrial environments

7. Evidences that were produced by Darwin in support of evolution include the following, except
(a) species diversity
(b) geographical distribution
(c) oceanic islands
(d) anthropogenic selection

8. The atmosphere of early earth probably contained no O_2 until the emergence of organisms that
(a) were chemoautotrophic
(b) were oxygen-respiring
(c) used hydrogen sulfide as a hydrogen source for photosynthesis
(d) used water as a hydrogen source for photosynthesis

9. Given below are two statements.
Statement I Darwin's theory of evolution was solely based on his observations during the voyage of the HMS Beagle and did not consider any external influences or contemporary work.
Statement II Wallace independently formulated the theory of natural selection after extensive studies in the Amazon and Malay Archipelago and observed that the geological history of earth is independent of biological history of earth.
In the light of above statements, choose the correct answers from the options given below.
(a) Statement I is incorrect, but statement II is correct.
(b) Both statement I and statement II are correct.
(c) Both statement I and statement II are incorrect.
(d) Statement I is correct, but statement II is incorrect.

10. Match List I with List II.

	List I (Primitive earth)		List II (Conditions)
A.	Reducing atmosphere	1.	Combined with ammonia
B.	Surface of earth	2.	Received UV rays
C.	Hydrogen	3.	Less amount of energy
D.	Oxygen	4.	Escaped

Choose the correct answer from the options given below.

	A	B	C	D		A	B	C	D
(a)	4	3	2	1	(b)	2	4	1	3
(c)	3	2	1	4	(d)	3	2	4	1

11. Consider the following diagram and identify the correct option.

(a) same origin, but different functions
(b) different functions and different origin
(c) different origin, but same function
(d) neither same origin nor same function

12. Whales, bats, cheetah and human share similarities in the pattern of bones of forelimbs. This is .... evolution and these structures are ....
(a) convergent, analogous
(b) divergent, homologous
(c) disruptive, analogous
(d) directional, homologous

13. Choose the incorrect statement about theories of origin of life.
(a) Theory of special creation states that life was created as such by some supernatural power.
(b) Theory of panspermia states that life came on earth from other planets by the transfer of spores.
(c) Experiments by SL Miller gave evidence for the chemical evolution given by Oparin and Haldane.
(d) Theory of biogenesis states that life has originated automatically from the non-living materials.

14. Embryological support for evolution given by Ernst Haeckel includes the
(a) presence of hair all over the body in adult human
(b) absence of tail bone and presence of wisdom tooth
(c) absence of vestigial gill slits in human's embryo
(d) presence of row of vestigial gill slits in embryo of all vertebrates

15. Which of the following is considered as direct evidence of evolution?
(a) Paleontological evidence
(b) Embryological evidence
(c) Evidences from comparative anatomy and morphology
(d) Adaptive radiation

Response Index

01	a	b	c	d	10	a	b	c	d	19	a	b	c	d
02	a	b	c	d	11	a	b	c	d	20	a	b	c	d
03	a	b	c	d	12	a	b	c	d	21	a	b	c	d
04	a	b	c	d	13	a	b	c	d	22	a	b	c	d
05	a	b	c	d	14	a	b	c	d	23	a	b	c	d
06	a	b	c	d	15	a	b	c	d	24	a	b	c	d
07	a	b	c	d	16	a	b	c	d	25	a	b	c	d
08	a	b	c	d	17	a	b	c	d					
09	a	b	c	d	18	a	b	c	d					

Performance Scanner

> 90% Excellent !	You have mastered these topics. The concepts of these topics are at your fingertips. Move on to the next test and maintain this momentum.
76-90% Very Good !	You have a good command over these topics. Revise these topics again after a few days and enhance your performance.
60-75% Good !	You have a wide scope to learn for these topics. Revise these topics again.
<60% Not Satisfactory!	You have a long way ahead of you to master these topics. Revise it thoroughly.

Test 2

Syllabus

- Darwin's contribution, modern synthetic theory of evolution;
- Mechanism of evolution- Variation (mutation and recombination) and natural Selection with examples, types of natural selection;
- Gene flow and genetic drift
- Hardy-Weinberg's principle
- Adaptive radiation

For deeper insight, **Scan the QR Code**

Important Instructions

- The test is of 30 minutes duration and contains 15 Multiple Choice Questions (four options with a single correct answer).
- Choose the correct option and fill the OMR given on the last page of this test accordingly.
- At some instances, you may find more than 1 option to be correct. In such circumstances, you have to judge the most appropriate answer as per the conditions given in the question.

1. In a famous experiment, A Weismann cut off the tails of newborn mice generation after generation. At the end of experiment, tails of mice neither disappeared nor shortened. This experiment

(a) supported Darwin's theory of natural selection

(b) proved that the tail is an essential organ of vertebrates

(c) disproved de Vries mutation theory

(d) showed that Lamarck was wrong in his theory of inheritance of acquired characters

2. Which of the following best describes the emergence of antibiotic-resistant bacteria?

(a) Adaptive radiation

(b) Transduction

(c) Presence of pre-existing variation in the population

(d) Divergent evolution

3. Today, again the faith in Lamarck's theory has been revived by some people due to the fact that

(a) if the environment influences the genes of the organisms, the acquired change will be transmitted to the next generation

(b) genetic studies refuted the Darwinism

(c) mutation theory supports the Lamarckism

(d) germplasm theory supports the Lamarckism

4. Due to ...., pouched mammals of Australia survived because of lack of competition from any other mammals.

(a) continental drift (b) convergent evolution

(c) speciation (d) fragmentation

5. Read the following statements related to Darwin's theory of evolution.

I. More offsprings are produced than that can survive.

II. Individuals in a population vary in their traits.

III. Individuals with advantageous traits are more likely to survive and reproduce.

IV. Traits are passed from parents to offspring.

V. New traits arise spontaneously in each generation.

Choose the correct set of statements from the options given below.

(a) I, II, III and IV (b) I, II, III and V

(c) I, II, IV and V (d) I, III, IV and V

6. What are the two key concepts of Darwinian theory of evolution?

(a) Natural selection and convergent evolution

(b) Natural selection and divergent evolution

(c) Natural selection and branching descent

(d) Natural selection and relative fitness

Test 2

Syllabus

- Darwin's contribution, modern synthetic theory of evolution;
- Mechanism of evolution- Variation (mutation and recombination) and natural Selection with examples, types of natural selection;
- Gene flow and genetic drift
- Hardy-Weinberg's principle
- Adaptive radiation

For deeper insight, **Scan the QR Code**

Important Instructions

- The test is of 30 minutes duration and contains 15 Multiple Choice Questions (four options with a single correct answer).
- Choose the correct option and fill the OMR given on the last page of this test accordingly.
- At some instances, you may find more than 1 option to be correct. In such circumstances, you have to judge the most appropriate answer as per the conditions given in the question.

1. In a famous experiment, AWeismann cut off the tails of newborn mice generation after generation. At the end of experiment, tails of mice neither disappeared nor shortened. This experiment

(a) supported Darwin's theory of natural selection

(b) proved that the tail is an essential organ of vertebrates

(c) disproved de Vries mutation theory

(d) showed that Lamarck was wrong in his theory of inheritance of acquired characters

2. Which of the following best describes the emergence of antibiotic-resistant bacteria?

(a) Adaptive radiation

(b) Transduction

(c) Presence of pre-existing variation in the population

(d) Divergent evolution

3. Today, again the faith in Lamarck's theory has been revived by some people due to the fact that

(a) if the environment influences the genes of the organisms, the acquired change will be transmitted to the next generation

(b) genetic studies refuted the Darwinism

(c) mutation theory supports the Lamarckism

(d) germplasm theory supports the Lamarckism

4. Due to ...., pouched mammals of Australia survived because of lack of competition from any other mammals.

(a) continental drift (b) convergent evolution

(c) speciation (d) fragmentation

5. Read the following statements related to Darwin's theory of evolution.

I. More offsprings are produced than that can survive.

II. Individuals in a population vary in their traits.

III. Individuals with advantageous traits are more likely to survive and reproduce.

IV. Traits are passed from parents to offspring.

V. New traits arise spontaneously in each generation.

Choose the correct set of statements from the options given below.

(a) I, II, III and IV (b) I, II, III and V

(c) I, II, IV and V (d) I, III, IV and V

6. What are the two key concepts of Darwinian theory of evolution?

(a) Natural selection and convergent evolution

(b) Natural selection and divergent evolution

(c) Natural selection and branching descent

(d) Natural selection and relative fitness

(c) Both statement I and statement II are incorrect.

(d) Statement I is correct, but statement II is incorrect.

15. Match the List I with List II.

	List I		List II
A	Genetic drift	1.	Migration of a section of population to another place
B	Gene flow	2.	Change in the allele frequencies of a population due to random events.
C	Founder effect	3.	Mutation caused speciation
D	Saltation	4.	Small group forms new population and reduces size of population.

Choose the correct answer from the options given below.

	A	B	C	D		A	B	C	D
(a)	3	2	4	1	(b)	2	1	4	3
(c)	1	2	4	3	(d)	3	4	1	2

Response Index

01	a b c d	10	a b c d	19	a b c d
02	a b c d	11	a b c d	20	a b c d
03	a b c d	12	a b c d	21	a b c d
04	a b c d	13	a b c d	22	a b c d
05	a b c d	14	a b c d	23	a b c d
06	a b c d	15	a b c d	24	a b c d
07	a b c d	16	a b c d	25	a b c d
08	a b c d	17	a b c d		
09	a b c d	18	a b c d		

Performance Scanner

> 90% Excellent !	You have mastered these topics. The concepts of these topics are at your fingertips. Move on to the next test and maintain this momentum.
76-90% Very Good !	You have a good command over these topics. Revise these topics again after a few days and enhance your performance.
60-75% Good !	You have a wide scope to learn for these topics. Revise these topics again.
<60% Not Satisfactory!	You have a long way ahead of you to master these topics. Revise it thoroughly.

Test 3

Syllabus
- Evolution of animals and plants
- Human evolution

For deeper insight, **Scan the QR Code** 

Important Instructions
- The test is of 30 minutes duration and contains 15 Multiple Choice Questions (four options with a single correct answer).
- Choose the correct option and fill the OMR given on the last page of this test accordingly.
- At some instances, you may find more than 1 option to be correct. In such circumstances, you have to judge the most appropriate answer as per the conditions given in the question.

1. Sphenopsids and ginkgos evolved during
(a) Quaternary
(b) Jurassic
(c) Cretaceous
(d) Devonian

2. Devonian epoch is known as golden age of
(a) reptiles (b) fishes
(c) dinosaur (d) birds

3. There are two opposing views about origin of modern man. According to one view, *Homo erectus* in Asia was the ancestor of modern man. A study of variation of DNA however suggested African origin of modern man. What kind of observation on DNA variation could suggest this?
(a) Greater variation in Asia than in Africa
(b) Greater variation in Africa than in Asia
(c) Similar variation in Africa and Asia
(d) Variation only in Asia and no variation in Africa

4. Given below are two statements.
Statement I *Australopithecus* was the connecting link between apes and man.
Statement II *Australopithecus* had an erect posture and showed bipedal movement.
In the light of the above statements, choose the correct answer from the options given below.
(a) Statement I is incorrect, but statement II is correct
(b) Both statement I and statement II are correct
(c) Both statement I and statement II are incorrect
(d) Statement I is correct, but statement II is incorrect

5. It is believed that lobe-finned fishes are the ancestors of amphibians, although there are no specimens of these left with us. Find the most appropriate reason for this belief.
(a) The ability of both lobe-finned fishes and amphibians to live in water and on land.
(b) Lobe-finned fishes are the only fishes that can breathe air.
(c) Lobe-finned fishes are found exclusively in freshwater environments.
(d) Lobe-finned fishes have more complex brains than other types of fishes.

6. Which of the following statement is incorrect w.r.t. rise of mammals?
(a) Mammals were viviparous and protected their unborn young one inside the mother's body.
(b) Mammals were more intelligent in sensing and avoiding danger at least.
(c) When reptiles came down, mammals took over this earth.
(d) Due to continental drift, mammals thrived because of lack of competition from marsupials.

7. Given below are two statements.

Statement I By the time of 500 mya, invertebrates had already formed and were active, marking a significant milestone in the evolution of complex life forms from single-celled organisms.

Statement II Jawless fish, one of the earliest forms of vertebrates, probably evolved around 350 mya, representing an important step in the evolution of more complex fish and eventually terrestrial vertebrates.

In the light of the above statements, choose the correct answer from the options given below.

(a) Statement I is incorrect, but statement II is correct.

(b) Both statement I and statement II are correct.

(c) Both statement I and statement II are incorrect.

(d) Statement I is correct, but statement II is incorrect.

8. Identify the correct statement.

(a) *Ichthyosaurus* is fish like reptile found probably around 200 mya.

(b) *Tyrannosaurus rex* was about 200 feet in height and had huge fearsome dagger like teeth.

(c) About 65 mya, in quaternary period, the dinosaurs suddenly disappeared from the earth.

(d) When reptiles came down, birds took over this earth.

9. What is the most accepted sequence of human evolution?

(a) *Australopithecus* → *Ramapithecus* → *Homo habilis* → *Homo sapiens*

(b) *Ramapithecus* → *Homo habilis* → *Homo erectus* → *Homo sapiens*

(c) *Australopithecus* → *Ramapithecus* → *Homo erectus* → *Homo habilis* → *Homo sapiens*

(d) *Homo erectus* → *Homo habilis* → *Homo sapiens* → *Australopithecus*

10. Which of the following is a characteristic feature of *Ramapithecus*?

(a) *Ramapithecus* exhibited more man-like features compared to its predecessors.

(b) *Ramapithecus* exhibited more ape-like features than its predecessors.

(c) They existed about 3-4 mya.

(d) They were hairy and walked like modern human.

11. Which of the following characteristic features was not shown by *Dryopithecus*?

(a) More ape-like features

(b) Semi-erect posture

(c) Bipedal locomotion

(d) Hairy

12. Consider the following statements.

I. *Homo habilis* was the first hominid with brain capacity ranging between 650-800 cc.

II. Studies suggest that first organisms that invaded land were plants.

III. Saltations are large mutations and directionless, while Darwinian variations are small and directional.

IV. Jawless fish evolved around 250 mya.

V. About 15 mya, primates called *Dryopithecus* and *Ramapithecus* were existing.

Choose the option containing correct statements.

(a) I and II

(b) I, II, III and V

(c) III and IV

(d) II, III and IV

13. Given below are two statements; one is labelled as Assertion (A) and the other is labelled as Reason (R).

Assertion (A) *Homo habilis* is considered the first human-like being and had brain capacities between 650-800cc.

Reason (R) *Homo habilis* hunted with stone weapons and consumed a varied diet that included both fruit and meat.

In the light of the above statements, choose the correct answer from the options given below.

(a) A is false, but R is true.

(b) Both A and R are true and R is the correct explanation of A.

(c) Both A and R are correct, but R is not the correct explanation of A.

(d) A is true, but R is false.

14. Consider the following statements regarding *Homo erectus*?

I. Fossils of *Homo erectus* were obtained from diverse site of Africa, Java and China.

II. *Homo erectus* survived about 14-15 million years ago during Late Miocene to Pilocene.

III. *Homo erectus* species include Java man, Pecking man, etc.

IV. The forelimbs, skull and brain of *Homo erectus* resembled with monkeys.

Choose the correct statements from the options given below.

(a) I and II

(b) III and IV

(c) I and IV

(d) I and III

15. Among the following, which one is known for using hides to protect their body?

(a) *Homo habilis*

(b) *Homo erectus*

(c) *Ramapithecus*

(d) Neanderthal man

Response Index

01	a	b	c	d	10	a	b	c	d	19	a	b	c	d
02	a	b	c	d	11	a	b	c	d	20	a	b	c	d
03	a	b	c	d	12	a	b	c	d	21	a	b	c	d
04	a	b	c	d	13	a	b	c	d	22	a	b	c	d
05	a	b	c	d	14	a	b	c	d	23	a	b	c	d
06	a	b	c	d	15	a	b	c	d	24	a	b	c	d
07	a	b	c	d	16	a	b	c	d	25	a	b	c	d
08	a	b	c	d	17	a	b	c	d					
09	a	b	c	d	18	a	b	c	d					

Performance Scanner

> 90% Excellent !	You have mastered these topics. The concepts of these topics are at your fingertips. Move on to the next test and maintain this momentum.
76-90% Very Good !	You have a good command over these topics. Revise these topics again after a few days and enhance your performance.
60-75% Good !	You have a wide scope to learn for these topics. Revise these topics again.
<60% Not Satisfactory!	You have a long way ahead of you to master these topics. Revise it thoroughly.

Chapter Break Thru

Syllabus	• Origin of life; • Biological evolution and evidences for biological evolution (from Paleontology, comparative anatomy, embryology and molecular evidence);	• Darwin's contribution, modern synthetic theory of evolution; • Mechanism of evolution- Variation (mutation and recombination) and natural selection with examples, types of natural selection;	• Gene flow and genetic drift; • Hardy-Weinberg's principle; • Adaptive radiation; • Evolution of animals and plants • Human evolution

Important Instructions

- The test is of 1 hour duration and contains 30 Multiple-Choice Questions (four options with a single correct answer).
- Choose the correct option and fill the OMR given on the last page of this test accordingly.
- At some instances, you may find more than 1 option to be correct. In such circumstances, you have to judge the most appropriate answer as per the conditions given in the question.

1. According to the chemical theory of the origin of life, which of the following events is believed to have occurred first?

(a) The formation of protobionts
(b) The synthesis of organic monomers
(c) The synthesis of organic polymers
(d) The formation of DNA-based genetic systems

2. In 1953, Stanley L Miller simulated early earth conditions in a lab to provide experimental proof for the origin of first life's form from pre-existing non-living organic molecules. Which of the following conditions did he create?

(a) An oxygen-rich atmosphere with low temperature and volcanic storms
(b) A reducing atmosphere with high temperature and volcanic storms
(c) A non-reducing atmosphere with high temperature and volcanic storms
(d) A reducing atmosphere with low temperature and volcanic storms

3. Which of the following best defines the concept of evolution?

(a) The process by which species adapt to their environment over time.
(b) The process by which new species are created through genetic mutations.
(c) The process of change in all forms of life over generations.
(d) The process by which organisms grow and develop from a single cell.

4. Read the following statements.

I. The universe is almost 20 billion years old.
II. The Big Bang theory suggests that a singular huge explosion led to the formation of the universe.
III. The earth was formed about 4.5 billion years back in the solar system of the Andromeda galaxy.
IV. The early earth had no atmosphere, and gases like water vapour, methane, carbon dioxide, and ammonia were released from the molten mass.
V. Life appeared on earth almost four billion years ago, about 500 million years after its formation.

Choose the correct answers from the options given below.

(a) I, II and IV are correct.
(b) I, II, IV and V are correct.
(c) II, III and V are correct.
(d) II and IV are correct.

5. The correct order of geological period from older to recent time is

(a) Permian → Jurassic → Triassic → Tertiary
(b) Triassic → Jurassic → Cretaceous → Tertiary
(c) Jurassic → Cretaceous → Permian → Triassic
(d) Cretaceous → Jurassic → Triassic → Permian

6. Which theory is based on the concept that species change over generations through descent with modification?

(a) The theory of recapitulation, also known as 'ontogeny recapitulates phylogeny'.
(b) Oparin's theory, also known as the 'primordial soup' theory.
(c) The theory of organic evolution.
(d) The theory of chemical evolution.

7. Which of the following statements are incorrect regarding the evolution of humans?

I. The skull of adult chimpanzee is more like adult human skull than baby chimpanzee skull.
II. The skull of baby chimpanzee is more like adult human skull than adult chimpanzee skull.
III. *Dryopithecus* existed about 15 mya.
IV. *Dryopithecus* was more human-like.
V. *Australopithecines* probably lived in East African grasslands.

Choose the correct answer from the options given below

(a) I and II (b) I and III
(c) I and IV (d) II, III and IV

8. Given below are two statements; one is labelled as Assertion (A) and the other is labelled as Reason (R).

Assertion (A) Convergent evolution leads to formation of analogous organs.
Reason (R) Convergent evolution leads to adaptation by different species to similar environments independently, despite different evolutionary origins.

In the light of the above statements, choose the correct answer from the options given below

(a) A is false, but R is true.
(b) Both A and R are true and R is the correct explanation of A.
(c) Both A and R are correct, but R is not the correct explanation of A.
(d) A is true, but R is false.

9. Match the List I with List II.

	List I		List II
A.	Darwin	1.	Chemical evolution before life
B.	Oparin	2.	Use and disuse of organs
C.	Lamarck	3.	Continental drift
D.	Australian Marsupials	4.	Evolution by natural selection

Choose the correct answer out of the options given below.

	A	B	C	D		A	B	C	D
(a)	4	1	2	3	(b)	2	4	1	3
(c)	3	4	2	1	(d)	4	1	3	2

10. Referring to the provided diagram, which type of natural selection best describes the change observed in the moth, *Biston betularia*?

(a) Stabilising (b) Disruptive
(c) Directional (d) Artificial

11. According to Hugo de Vries, mutation is

(a) non-inheritable minor variations
(b) small and directional and they can bring the change when they accumulate
(c) large and cause speciation, named saltation
(d) slow and gradual change which takes a lot of time to proceed

12. Match the List I with List II.

	List I		List II
A.	Homologous organ	1.	Perform similar function
B.	Analogous organ	2.	Similar environmental pressure
C.	Divergent evolution	3.	Similar embryonic origin
D.	Convergent evolution	4.	Common ancestry

Choose the correct answer from the options given below.

	A	B	C	D
(a)	4	3	1	2
(b)	3	1	4	2
(c)	3	4	2	1
(d)	1	4	3	2

13. Select the incorrect pair.
(a) Carboniferous period – Early reptiles
(b) Triassic period – Therapsids
(c) Devonian period – Progymnosperms
(d) Permian period – Synapsids

14. Choose the correct sequence of geological time scale.
(a) Eon, Era, Period, Epoch
(b) Eon, Epoch, Era, Period
(c) Eon, Era, Epoch, Period
(d) Eon, Epoch, Period, Era

15. What are the criteria of Darwinian fitness?
I. High mutation rate.
II. Superior physical strength and high reproduction rate.
III. The ability to survive and reproduce.
IV. Successful passing of genes to the next generation.
V. Adaptability to environmental changes.
Choose the correct answer.
(a) I, II and V (b) III and IV
(c) Only III (d) III, IV and V

16. The diagram compares placental mammals and Australian marsupials that exhibit similar adaptations. Which of the following best explains the evolutionary mechanisms leading to these similarities?

Placental mammals	Australian marsupials
Mole	Marsupial mole
Anteater	Numbat (anteater)
Mouse	Marsupial mouse
Lemur	Spotted cuscus

(a) Adaptive radiation resulting from geographical isolation
(b) Convergent evolution due to similar environmental pressures
(c) Homologous organs within closely related species
(d) Divergent evolution from a common ancestor

17. Following diagram is related to the family tree of dinosaurs.

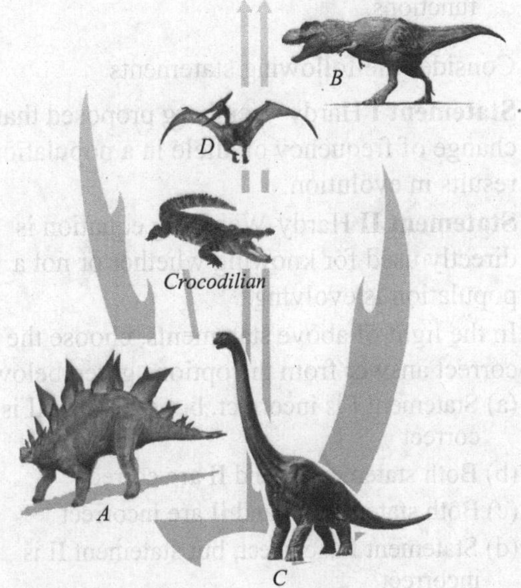

Which dinosaur was a dominant carnivore of the Late Cretaceous period known for its massive size and powerful bite.
(a) D (b) B
(c) A (d) C

18. Based on the given diagram, which of the following statement is incorrect in relation to the depicted limb structures of different species?

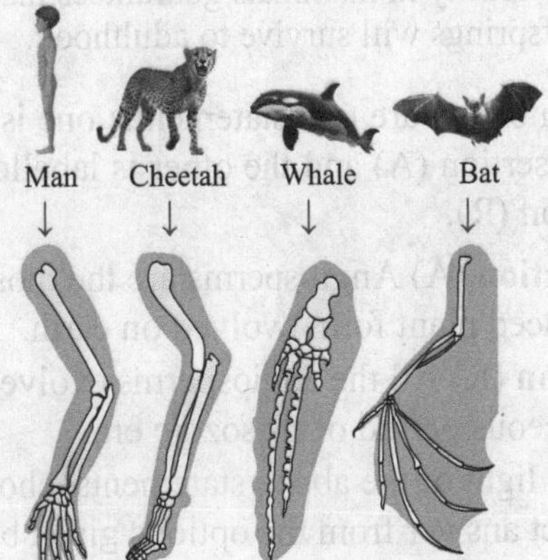

(a) Despite the different functions of these limbs, they all share a similar bone structure.
(b) The whale's flipper, although used for swimming, shows a similar skeletal structure to the limbs of terrestrial animals
(c) The similar bone structure across different species is due to divergent evolution, from common ancestry.
(d) All depicted limbs are examples of analogous structures that have evolved for different functions.

19. Consider the following statements.

Statement I Hardy-Weinberg proposed that change of frequency of allele in a population results in evolution.

Statement II Hardy-Weinberg equation is directly used for knowing whether or not a population is evolving.

In the light of above statements, choose the correct answer from the options given below.
(a) Statement I is incorrect, but statement II is correct
(b) Both statements I and II are correct
(c) Both statements I and II are incorrect
(d) Statement I is correct, but statement II is incorrect

20. Why is viviparity considered to be a more evolved reproductive strategy?
(a) Viviparity ensures that offsprings are born with a fully developed immune system.
(b) The young ones are protected by a thick shell.
(c) The young ones are protected inside the mother's body and are looked after once they are born, leading to higher chances of survival.
(d) Viviparity in mammals guarantees that all offsprings will survive to adulthood.

21. Given below are two statements; one is labelled as Assertion (A) and the other is labelled as Reason (R).

Assertion (A) Angiosperms are the most advanced plant form evolved on earth.

Reason (R) All the angiosperms evolved in cretaceous period of mesozoic era.

In the light of the above statements, choose the correct answer from the options given below.
(a) A is false, but R is true.
(b) Both A and R are true and R is the correct explanation of A.
(c) Both A and R are correct, but R is not the correct explanation of A.
(d) A is true, but R is false.

22. Which of the following hominids is known to have had the largest cranial capacity?
(a) *Australopithecus* (b) *Dryopithecus*
(c) *Ramapithecus* (d) Neanderthal man

23. According to Hardy-Weinberg equilibrium, the original population is said to be in genetic equilibrium, except when
(a) population size is very large
(b) random mating is not occurring
(c) no selection occur
(d) no immigration takes place

24. Which of the following were ancestors of modern day frogs and salamanders?
(a) Coelacanth (b) Reptiles
(c) Toad (d) *Amphioxus*

25. Darwinism explains all the following, except
(a) within each species, there are variations
(b) organisms tend to produce more number of offspring that can survive
(c) offspring with better traits that overcome competition are best suited for the environment
(d) variations are inherited from parents to offspring through genes

26. What is the primary driving force behind adaptive radiation?
(a) Genetic drift (b) Mutation
(c) Natural selection (d) Gene flow

27. Choose the incorrect statement about the *Homo sapiens sapiens.*
(a) Involves evolution of culture rather than that of anatomy.
(b) Appeared during ice age between 100000 - 75,000 years ago.
(c) Agriculture was started by humans around 10,000 years back.
(d) It started making its settlements.

28. Choose the incorrect statement about Big-Bang theory of 'origin of universe'.

(a) Universe was formed as a result of thermonuclear explosion.
(b) The explosion resulted in cataclysmic eruption of hot, energy-rich subatomic particle.
(c) The simplest gases helium and hydrogen were formed as a result of explosion.
(d) As a result of explosion, universe expanded and its temperature increased in the following years.

29. Match the following lists.

	List I		List II
A.	Mutation	1.	A drastic reduction in population size brought about by severe pressure or a calamity.
B.	Genetic drift	2.	Individuals and their alleles, move into or out of populations.
C.	Gene flow	3.	A heritable change in DNA.
D.	Bottleneck effect	4.	Random fluctuation in allele over time due to chance occurrences alone.

Codes

	A	B	C	D
(a)	3	4	2	1
(b)	4	3	2	1
(c)	1	2	3	4
(d)	2	1	4	3

30. The equation $(p + q)^2 = p^2 + 2pq + q^2 = 1$ is commonly applied in which field of biological study?

(a) The study of the structure and function of genetic material
(b) The inheritance patterns of specific traits
(c) The statistical analysis of biological data
(d) The analysis of allele frequency distributions within populations

Response Index

01	ⓐ	ⓑ	ⓒ	ⓓ	14	ⓐ	ⓑ	ⓒ	ⓓ	27	ⓐ	ⓑ	ⓒ	ⓓ	40	ⓐ	ⓑ	ⓒ	ⓓ
02	ⓐ	ⓑ	ⓒ	ⓓ	15	ⓐ	ⓑ	ⓒ	ⓓ	28	ⓐ	ⓑ	ⓒ	ⓓ	41	ⓐ	ⓑ	ⓒ	ⓓ
03	ⓐ	ⓑ	ⓒ	ⓓ	16	ⓐ	ⓑ	ⓒ	ⓓ	29	ⓐ	ⓑ	ⓒ	ⓓ	42	ⓐ	ⓑ	ⓒ	ⓓ
04	ⓐ	ⓑ	ⓒ	ⓓ	17	ⓐ	ⓑ	ⓒ	ⓓ	30	ⓐ	ⓑ	ⓒ	ⓓ	43	ⓐ	ⓑ	ⓒ	ⓓ
05	ⓐ	ⓑ	ⓒ	ⓓ	18	ⓐ	ⓑ	ⓒ	ⓓ	31	ⓐ	ⓑ	ⓒ	ⓓ	44	ⓐ	ⓑ	ⓒ	ⓓ
06	ⓐ	ⓑ	ⓒ	ⓓ	19	ⓐ	ⓑ	ⓒ	ⓓ	32	ⓐ	ⓑ	ⓒ	ⓓ	45	ⓐ	ⓑ	ⓒ	ⓓ
07	ⓐ	ⓑ	ⓒ	ⓓ	20	ⓐ	ⓑ	ⓒ	ⓓ	33	ⓐ	ⓑ	ⓒ	ⓓ	46	ⓐ	ⓑ	ⓒ	ⓓ
08	ⓐ	ⓑ	ⓒ	ⓓ	21	ⓐ	ⓑ	ⓒ	ⓓ	34	ⓐ	ⓑ	ⓒ	ⓓ	47	ⓐ	ⓑ	ⓒ	ⓓ
09	ⓐ	ⓑ	ⓒ	ⓓ	22	ⓐ	ⓑ	ⓒ	ⓓ	35	ⓐ	ⓑ	ⓒ	ⓓ	48	ⓐ	ⓑ	ⓒ	ⓓ
10	ⓐ	ⓑ	ⓒ	ⓓ	23	ⓐ	ⓑ	ⓒ	ⓓ	36	ⓐ	ⓑ	ⓒ	ⓓ	49	ⓐ	ⓑ	ⓒ	ⓓ
11	ⓐ	ⓑ	ⓒ	ⓓ	24	ⓐ	ⓑ	ⓒ	ⓓ	37	ⓐ	ⓑ	ⓒ	ⓓ	50	ⓐ	ⓑ	ⓒ	ⓓ
12	ⓐ	ⓑ	ⓒ	ⓓ	25	ⓐ	ⓑ	ⓒ	ⓓ	38	ⓐ	ⓑ	ⓒ	ⓓ					
13	ⓐ	ⓑ	ⓒ	ⓓ	26	ⓐ	ⓑ	ⓒ	ⓓ	39	ⓐ	ⓑ	ⓒ	ⓓ					

Performance Scanner

> 90% Excellent !	You have mastered this chapter. The concepts of this chapter are at your fingertips. Move on to the next chapter and maintain this momentum.
76-90% Very Good !	You have a good command over this chapter. Revise the chapter again after a few days and enhance your performance.
60-75% Good !	You have a wide scope to learn for this chapter. Revise this chapter again.
<60% Not Satisfactory!	You have a long way ahead of you to master this chapter. Revise it thoroughly.

Scan for online chapter test

Scan for online unit test

Space for Rough Work

Test Booklet No. 3947357

Test Booklet Code CH7

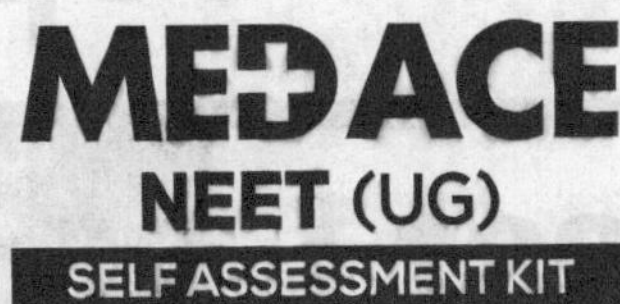

Human Health and Diseases

Topics Covered

Common Human Diseases

Immunity

Cancer, AIDS, Alcohol and Drug Abuse

Important Instructions

- This Booklet Contains – Three Topic Tests and One Test on Complete Chapter.
- Each question carries 4 marks.
- For each correct response, the candidate will get 4 marks. And for every incorrect response, 1 mark will be additionally deducted from total score.
- Use **Blue/Black** point pen only for filling the OMR.
- Rough work is to be done in the space provided for this purpose in the test booklet only.

Name of the Candidate (In Capitals) ____________

____

Candidate's Signature ____________

Invigilator's Signature ____________

Facsimile signature stamp of center superintendent____________

Do not open this booklet until you start attempting the test

Topical Follow Thru

Test 1

Syllabus Concept of health and diseases; Pathogens; parasites causing human diseases (malaria, filariasis, ascariasis, typhoid, pneumonia, common cold, amoebiasis, ringworm, dengue, chikungunya)

For deeper insight, **Scan the QR Code** 

Important Instructions

- The test is of 30 minutes duration and contains 25 Multiple Choice Questions (four options with a single correct answer).
- Choose the correct option and fill the OMR given on the last page of this test accordingly.
- At some instances, you may find more than 1 option to be correct. In such circumstances, you have to judge the most appropriate answer as per the conditions given in the question.

1. Gray to bluish coloured lips and nails are observed in a person suffering from

(a) Pneumonia
(b) Tuberculosis
(c) Pulmonary edema
(d) Common cold

2. What is the target location of the human body for *Streptococcus pneumoniae*?

(a) Bronchioles of respiratory tract
(b) Nostrils
(c) Central nervous system
(d) Alveoli of lungs

3. Which of the following is not true about pathogens?

(a) Most of the pathogens are parasites.
(b) Pathogenic attack causes defect in functionality of body cells.
(c) Pathogens get immersed into the environment of human body.
(d) Pathogens do not affect the internal vital organs of the human body.

4. Find the set of diseases which are spread by bacterial agents.

(a) Tetanus, diphtheria, cholera
(b) Tetanus, AIDS, smallpox
(c) Diphtheria, smallpox, cholera
(d) Ascariasis, malaria, dengue

5. Given below are two statements; one is labelled as Assertion (A) and the other is labelled as Reason (R).

Assertion (A) Filarial worms transmitted by mosquito bites reach the spine and block nerves.

Reason (R) Elephantiasis is caused by blocked lymph vessels, not nerves.

In the light of the above statements, choose the correct answer from the options given below.

(a) A is false, but R is true.
(b) Both A and R are true and R is the correct explanation of A.
(c) Both A and R are true, but R is not the correct explanation of A.
(d) A is true, but R is false.

6. Match List I with List II.

	List I (Pathogens)		List II (Diseases)
A.	Helminths	1.	Malaria
B.	Protozoan	2.	Ringworm
C.	Fungus	3.	Polio
D.	Virus	4.	Ascariasis

Choose the correct answer from the options given below.

	A	B	C	D		A	B	C	D
(a)	3	1	4	2	(b)	4	1	2	3
(c)	3	1	2	4	(d)	2	3	1	4

7. Given below are two statements.

Statement I A person with a healthy immune system might not experience any sign or symptom upon exposure to a common infectious agent.

Statement II The absence of signs and symptoms always indicates a complete state of health, encompassing physical, mental and social well-being.

In the light of the above statements, choose the correct answer from the options given below.

(a) Statement I is incorrect, but statement II is correct.
(b) Both statement I and statement II are correct.
(c) Both statement I and statement II are incorrect.
(d) Statement I is correct, but statement II is incorrect.

8. Which of the following is not a characteristic symptom of common cold?

(a) Nasal congestion and discharge
(b) Sore throat
(c) Hoarseness
(d) Consistent fever and chills

9. Which of the following statement is true about haemozoin?

(a) It is a precursor molecule for haemoglobin synthesis.
(b) It is a waste product released by healthy red blood cells.
(c) It is a toxin formed by the breakdown of haemoglobin during the malarial cycle, causing chills and fever.
(d) It is an antibody produced by the human immune system to fight *Plasmodium* parasites.

10. A 25-year-old patient suffers from persistent constipation with stools containing mucus and blood clots.

Based on the provided information, which of the following modes of transmission is most likely for this patient's condition?

(a) Direct airborne transmission through coughing or sneezing
(b) Contact with infected mosquito bites
(c) Sharing contaminated glasses, utensils or consuming faecally contaminated food/water
(d) Sexual contact with an infected individual

11. Which of the following statement about malarial infection is incorrect?

(a) Gametocytes develop from sporozoites in the salivary gland of *Anopheles* mosquitoes.
(b) The infection causes high fever that recurs every three to four days.
(c) Sporozoites initially replicate inside liver cells before attacking and rupturing Red Blood Cells (RBCs).
(d) When a female *Anopheles* mosquito bites an infected individual, the parasites enter the mosquito's body and continue their development.

12. The causative agents of ringworm belong to the genus

(a) *Wuchereria* and *Trichophyton*
(b) *Trichophyton* and *Microsporum*
(c) *Haemophilus* and *Epidermophyton*
(d) *Epidermophyton* and *Entamoeba*

13. Houseflies are implicated in the transmission of amoebiasis because they act as

(a) reservoir hosts for the parasite
(b) definitive hosts for the parasite
(c) intermediate hosts for the parasite
(d) mechanical vectors for the parasite

14. A public health campaign is launched to reduce the incidence of typhoid in a community. Which of the following interventions would be least effective in achieving this goal?

(a) Promotion of handwashing with soap after using the toilet
(b) Chlorination of municipal water supplies
(c) Encouraging consumption of properly cooked and packaged food
(d) Educational workshops on proper cough etiquette and respiratory hygiene

15. Select the correct pair representing the causative agent of typhoid fever and its confirmatory test.

(a) *Plasmodium vivax*/UTI test
(b) *Streptococcus typhi*/Anthrone test
(c) *Salmonella typhi*/Anthrone test
(d) *Salmonella typhi*/Widal test

16. What did the discovery of normal body temperature in persons with blackbile demonstrate?

(a) It represented the good humor hypothesis of health.

(b) It disproved the good humor hypothesis of health.

(c) It represented the necessity of reflective thought.

(d) It demonstrates the relationship between temperature and personality.

17. Which of the following best describes the role of mind and mental state in maintaining health as per modern biology?

(a) The mind and mental state have no significant impact on health.

(b) The mind and mental state influence the immune system, which maintains health.

(c) The immune system independently maintains health without any influence from the mind.

(d) Health is solely determined by genetic and lifestyle factors.

18. Given below are steps of life cycle of malaria.

I. Sexual cycle
II. Transmission to human (injects sporozoites)
III. Intraerythrocytic cycle
IV. Transmission to mosquito
V. Liver cells rupture and merozoites released.
VI. Sporozoites enter liver and infect hepatocytes.

Choose the correct option showing the appropriate sequence of the life cycle of malaria.

(a) II → III → VI → I → IV → V

(b) II → VI → V → III → I → IV

(c) II → III → I → VI → V → IV

(d) III → II → I → VI → IV → V

19. Given below are two statements.

Statement I Rhino viruses primarily infect the nose and respiratory passage, but not the lungs.

Statement II The common cold is primarily prevented through first generation vaccines.

In the light of the above statements, choose the correct answer from the options given below.

(a) Statement I is incorrect, but statement II is correct.

(b) Both statement I and statement II are correct.

(c) Both statement I and statement II are incorrect.

(d) Statement I is correct, but statement II is incorrect.

20. Which of the following public health strategy is most effective in preventing the spread of chikungunya?

(a) Vaccination programms

(b) Quarantine of infected individual

(c) Antiviral medications programme

(d) Mosquito control and reduction of breeding sites

21. Identify the correct statements from the following.

I. Maintenance of personal and public hygiene is very important for prevention and control of many infectious diseases.

II. Measures for personal hygiene include, keeping the body clean, consumption of clean drinking water, food, vegetables etc.

III. Personal and public hygiene measures are crucial for the prevention and control of infectious diseases.

IV. For diseases transmitted through food and water, such as typhoid and amoebiasis, it is crucial to control insect vectors.

V. Introducing Gambusia fish in ponds helps to control mosquito larvae.

Choose the correct statements from the options given below.

(a) I, II and IV
(b) I, II and V
(c) I, II, III and V
(d) II, III and IV

22. If a community implements both mosquito control measures and sanitation improvements, which disease control outcome is most likely to be observed?

(a) Decrease in the incidence of both filariasis and ascariasis

(b) Decrease in the incidence of ascariasis only

(c) Decrease in the incidence of filariasis only

(d) No change in the incidence of either disease

23. Houseflies serve as mechanical carriers for *Entamoeba histolytica*. What does this imply about their role in the transmission of the parasite?

(a) Houseflies are biological hosts that amplify the parasite population.

(b) Houseflies ingest the parasite and replicate it within their bodies

(c) Houseflies physically transport the parasite from contaminated sources to food.

(d) Houseflies bite humans to transmit the parasite directly into the blood stream.

24. Given below are two statements; one is labelled as Assertion (A) and other one is labelled as Reason (R).

Assertion (A) Pathogen must adapt to the host environment to survive and cause disease.

Reason (R) Pathogens entering the gut need to resist the low pH and digestive enzymes of the stomach.

In the light of the above statements, choose the correct answer from the options given below.

(a) A is false, but R is true.

(b) Both A and R are true and R is the correct explanation of A.

(c) Both A and R are true but R is not the correct explanation of A.

(d) A is true, but R is false.

25. Match the following diseases with their vectors/ agents.

List I (Diseases)		List II (Vectors/agents)	
A.	Malaria	1.	*Salmonella typhi*
B.	Typhoid	2.	*Plasmodium*
C.	Pneumonia	3.	*Haemophilus influenzae*
D.	Amoebiasis	4.	*Entamoeba histolytica*

Choose the correct answer from the options given below.

	A	B	C	D		A	B	C	D
(a)	2	1	3	4	(b)	3	4	2	1
(c)	1	2	4	3	(d)	3	2	1	4

Response Index

01	a	b	c	d	10	a	b	c	d	19	a	b	c	d
02	a	b	c	d	11	a	b	c	d	20	a	b	c	d
03	a	b	c	d	12	a	b	c	d	21	a	b	c	d
04	a	b	c	d	13	a	b	c	d	22	a	b	c	d
05	a	b	c	d	14	a	b	c	d	23	a	b	c	d
06	a	b	c	d	15	a	b	c	d	24	a	b	c	d
07	a	b	c	d	16	a	b	c	d	25	a	b	c	d
08	a	b	c	d	17	a	b	c	d					
09	a	b	c	d	18	a	b	c	d					

Performance Scanner

> 90% Excellent !	You have mastered these topics. The concepts of these topics are at your fingertips. Move on to the next test and maintain this momentum.
76-90% Very Good !	You have a good command over these topics. Revise these topics again after a few days and enhance your performance.
60-75% Good !	You have a wide scope to learn for these topics. Revise these topics again.
<60% Not Satisfactory!	You have a long way ahead of you to master these topics. Revise it thoroughly.

Test 2

Syllabus Basic concepts of immunology
Vaccines

For deeper insight, **Scan the QR Code**

Important Instructions

- The test is of 30 minutes duration and contains 25 Multiple Choice Questions (four options with a single correct answer).
- Choose the correct option and fill the OMR given on the last page of this test accordingly.
- At some instances, you may find more than 1 option to be correct. In such circumstances, you have to judge the most appropriate answer as per the conditions given in the question.

1. What is the main characteristic of acquired immunity which makes it a specific immunity?

(a) Acquired immunity can recognise various pathogens and foreign molecules and acts upon them.

(b) Acquired immunity is specific to several kind of pathogens and acts upon them.

(c) Acquired immunity results in the production of antibodies for specific protein containing pathogens.

(d) Acquired immunity can specifically recognise the virus carrying pathogens.

2. Match List I with List II.

	List I		List II
A.	Cellular barriers	1.	PMNL-neutrophils
B.	Physical barriers	2.	Saliva in mouth
C.	Cytokine barrier	3.	Mucus lining in respiratory, digestive and urogenital tracts
D.	Physiological barrier	4.	Secreted protein by virus-infected cells.

Choose the correct match.

(a) A-2, B-3, C-4, D-1
(b) A-2, B-4, C-1, D-3
(c) A-3, B-2, C-1, D-4
(d) A-1, B-3, C-4, D-2

3. Given below are two statements.

Statement I The attack of pathogen leads to the production of some proteins called antibodies.

Statement II The cell-mediated immunity is mediated by B-lymphocytes.

In the light of the above statements, choose the correct answer from the options given below.

(a) Statement I is incorrect, but statement II is correct.
(b) Both statement I and statement II are correct.
(c) Both statement I and statement II are incorrect.
(d) Statement I is correct, but statement II is incorrect.

4. Consider the following statements.

I. IgE antibodies are produced in an allergic reaction.
II. Spleen is a primary lymphoid organ.
III. Immunoglobins are proteins showing binding capacity for antigens.
IV. Peyer's patches are found in small intestine and constitute secondary lymphoid organs.

Choose the correct statements from the options given below.

(a) I, II and III
(b) I, III and IV
(c) II, III and IV
(d) I, II and IV

5. Which of the following components are involved in allergic reaction?

(a) IgE and mast cells
(b) IgG and mast cells
(c) IgA and mast cells
(d) IgG and basophils

6. Given below are two statements; one is labelled as Assertion (A) and the other is labelled as Reason (R).

Assertion (A) Colostrum, the yellowish fluid secreted by mothers in the initial days of lactation, is rich in antibodies.

Reason (R) Colostrum provides active immunity to the newborn, protecting them from various infections.

In the light of the above statements, choose the correct answer from the options given below.

(a) A is false, but R is true.
(b) Both A and R are true and R is the correct explanation of A.
(c) Both A and R are true, but R is not the correct explanation of A.
(d) A is true, but R is false.

7. Consider the given statements regarding vaccination.

I. Vaccines work by creating an immune system memory for a specific disease, allowing for a faster response later.
II. The vaccines are capable to generate memory B-cells only that recognise the pathogen quickly on subsequent exposure.
III. In tetanus and snakebite cases, patients receive injections containing preformed antibodies or antitoxins.
IV. A type of immunisation, providing long-term protection, is called passive immunisation.
V. Recombinant DNA technology eliminates the risk of reactivation in vaccines, making them inherently safer than traditional vaccines made from weakened pathogens.

Choose the correct set of statements from the following options.

(a) I, III and V
(b) II, IV and V
(c) I, III and IV
(d) II, III and IV

8. The given diagram shows the diagrammatic representation of lymph nodes. Identify the correct organ represented by the alphabets for the following statements.

The immature lymphocytes differentiate into antigen-sensitive lymphocytes in the ………… . The ………… are specialised sites where lymphocytes encounter antigens and mature into immune cells.

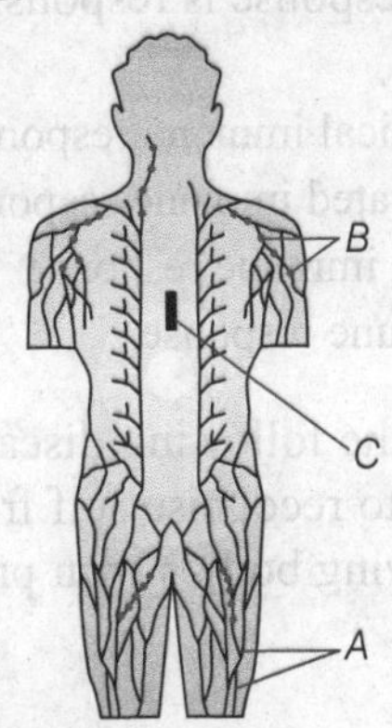

(a) *B* and *C*, respectively
(b) *A* and *B*, respectively
(c) *C* and *A*, respectively
(d) *C* and *B*, respectively

9. Match List I with List II.

	List I		List II
A.	Allergens	1.	IgE type antibody
B.	Spleen	2.	Trap microorganisms
C.	Bone marrow	3.	Reservoir of erythrocytes
D.	Lymph nodes	4.	Primary lymphoid organ

Choose the correct match.

(a) A-2, B-3, C-4, D-1
(b) A-2, B-4, C-1, D-3
(c) A-3, B-2, C-1, D-4
(d) A-1, B-3, C-4, D-2

10. A patient experiences excessive sneezing, watery eyes and a runny nose after exposure to certain flowers. What class of medication would likely provide the fastest relief for these symptoms?

(a) Antibiotics (b) Antiseptics
(c) Antihistamines (d) Antipyretics

11. A type of protein that inhibits viral replication by synthesising enzymes that inhibit protein synthesis and replication of the viral genome is

(a) perforin
(b) immunoglobulin
(c) thrombin
(d) interferon

12. Transplantation of tissues/organs fails often due to non-acceptance by patient's body. Which type of immune response is responsible for such reactions?
(a) Physiological immune response
(b) Cell-mediated immune response
(c) Hormonal immune response
(d) Autoimmune response

13. In which of the following diseases, immune system fails to recognise self from non-self and starts destroying body's own proteins?
(a) Asthma
(b) Taeniasis
(c) Rheumatoid arthritis
(d) Polio

14. Which of the following best demonstrates the ability of the vertebrate immune system to distinguish between "self" and "non-self" molecules?
(a) Phagocytosis of dead body cells by white blood cells
(b) Increased mucus production in the respiratory tract
(c) Fever as a response to infection
(d) Production of antibodies specific to a particular virus

15. Approximately what percentage of lymphoid tissue in the human body is comprised by MALT?
(a) 10% (b) 25%
(c) 50% (d) 75%

16. Which of the following statements best describes immunity?
(a) It is the body's ability to grow and develop.
(b) It is the body's ability to defend itself from disease-causing organisms.
(c) It is the process of acquiring diseases to build resistance.
(d) It is the state of being completely free from any foreign agents.

17. Which of the following mechanism is a part of innate immune response?
(a) Production of antibodies by B-cells
(b) Secretion of interferons by virus-infected cells
(c) Activation of memory T-cells
(d) Clonal expansion of B-cells.

18. Which of the following are the component of innate immunity?
I. Skin and mucous membranes
II. Antibodies
III. Saliva
IV. Humoral response
V. Leucocytes
Choose the correct answer from the options given below.
(a) I and II (b) II and V
(c) I, III and V (d) III and V

19. Consider the following statements.
I. Vaccination can create a quick immune response to deadly microbes.
II. The hepatitis-B vaccine is an example of passive immunisation.
III. Antitoxins are used to neutralize toxins produced by pathogens.
IV. Vaccines generate memory cells that can last for years.
V. Recombinant DNA technology has increased the production of antigenic polypeptides of pathogen in bacteria or yeast.
Which of the following combination of statements is correct?
(a) I, II and III (b) II and IV
(c) I, III, IV and V (d) Only V

20. In the structure of an immunoglobulin, which terminal has antigen-binding site?
(a) N-terminal
(b) C-terminal
(c) N-terminal of heavy chain and C-terminal of light chain
(d) C-terminal of heavy chain and N-terminal of light chain

21. Given below are two statements.

Statement I Higher vertebrates have developed memory-based acquired immunity which provides the ability to differentiate foreign organisms from self cells.

Statement II Auto-immune diseases occur when the immune system mistakenly attacks the body's own cells.

In the light of the above statements, choose the correct answer from the options given below.

(a) Statement I is incorrect, but statement II is correct.

(b) Both statement I and statement II are correct.

(c) Both statement I and statement II are incorrect.

(d) Statement I is correct, but statement II is incorrect.

22. Which of the following correctly explains an epitope?

(a) It is the region of antibody that binds with antigen

(b) It is the region of antigen that elicit secretion of specific antibody

(c) It is the heavy chain of an antibody

(d) It is the light chain of an antibody

23. What is a common environmental factor that may increase sensitivity to allergens in modern urban life?

(a) Increased exposure to outdoor pollutants

(b) Lowered immunity due to a protected environment in early life

(c) Higher levels of physical exercise

(d) Increased exposure to sunlight

24. The main function of the spleen in the immune system is the

(a) Production of antibodies

(b) Maturation of B-lymphocytes

(c) Filtering blood and trapping blood-borne microorganisms

(d) Production of lymph

25. The ...... is quite large at the time of birth, but keeps reducing in size with age and by the time puberty is attained, it reduces to a very small size.

(a) thymus

(b) spleen

(c) lymph nodes

(d) bone marrow

Response Index

01	a	b	c	d	10	a	b	c	d	19	a	b	c	d
02	a	b	c	d	11	a	b	c	d	20	a	b	c	d
03	a	b	c	d	12	a	b	c	d	21	a	b	c	d
04	a	b	c	d	13	a	b	c	d	22	a	b	c	d
05	a	b	c	d	14	a	b	c	d	23	a	b	c	d
06	a	b	c	d	15	a	b	c	d	24	a	b	c	d
07	a	b	c	d	16	a	b	c	d	25	a	b	c	d
08	a	b	c	d	17	a	b	c	d					
09	a	b	c	d	18	a	b	c	d					

Performance Scanner

> 90% Excellent !	You have mastered these topics. The concepts of these topics are at your fingertips. Move on to the next test and maintain this momentum.
76-90% Very Good !	You have a good command over these topics. Revise these topics again after a few days and enhance your performance.
60-75% Good !	You have a wide scope to learn for these topics. Revise these topics again.
<60% Not Satisfactory!	You have a long way ahead of you to master these topics. Revise it thoroughly.

Test 3

Syllabus
- Cancer, HIV and AIDS
- Adolescence
- Drug and alcohol abuse
- Tobacco abuse

For deeper insight, **Scan the QR Code**

Important Instructions

- The test is of 30 minutes duration and contains 15 Multiple Choice Questions (four options with a single correct answer).
- Choose the correct option and fill the OMR given on the last page of this test accordingly.
- At some instances, you may find more than 1 option to be correct. In such circumstances, you have to judge the most appropriate answer as per the conditions given in the question.

1. Transmission of HIV from infected mother to her child occurs through
(a) liver (b) blood
(c) skin (d) placenta

2. Mark the incorrect statement about AIDS/HIV.
(a) The initial clinical observations of AIDS occurred in 1981.
(b) HIV is not spread by mosquitoes.
(c) HIV destroys the T-helper cells.
(d) HIV infection never co-exists with other infections.

3. HIV responsible for AIDS in human is a
(a) *ss*DNA virus (b) *ds*DNA virus
(c) *ss*RNA virus (d) *ds*RNA virus

4. Read the following statements about cancer.
I. Metastasis is the most feared property of benign tumours.
II. The majority of cancers are managed through a multimodal approach combining surgery, radiotherapy and chemotherapy.
III. CT and MRI are useful to detect cancers of the internal organs.
IV. Cancer cells are characterised by invasion of local tissue and uncontrolled growth.
V. Analgesics help in destroying the tumour.

Choose the correct set of statements from the options given below.
(a) II, III and IV (b) I, III and V
(c) I, IV and V (d) II, IV and V

5. Which of the following statement is correct?
(a) All viruses are oncogenic.
(b) All tumours are cancerous.
(c) Normal cells show the property of contact inhibition.
(d) Antigens against cancer -specific chemicals are used for detection of certain cancers.

6. Some plant parts of *Cannabis sativa* when combined, produce different psychoactive effects. Which of the following best shows this?
(a) Thorns and colourful petals
(b) Roots and sweet fruit
(c) Flower tops and leaves
(d) Seeds and bark

7. A feel-good brain chemical (neurotransmitter) has its movement blocked by a certain illegal drug. Which drug most likely disrupts this movement?
(a) Morphine
(b) Cocaine
(c) Atropine
(d) Heroin

8. Identify the incorrect statement about opioids.
(a) Opioids serve as CNS depressants.
(b) PNS possess receptors for opioids.
(c) Opioids are powerful painkillers and sedatives.
(d) Opioids are consumed by snorting or through injections.

9. Match List I with List II.

	List I		List II
A.	Smack	1.	Hallucinogenic
B.	*Datura*	2.	Coke
C.	*Erythroxylum*	3.	Used in surgeries as sedative
D.	Morphine	4.	Diacetylmorphine

Choose the correct combination.

(a) A - 4, B - 1, C - 2, D - 3
(b) A - 2, B - 1, C - 4, D - 3
(c) A - 1, B - 2, C - 4, D - 3
(d) A - 2, B - 3, C - 1, D - 4

10. Choose the correct option with respect to given sentence.

Nicotine stimulates ...I... gland to release ...II... into blood circulation, both of which raise blood pressure and ...III... heart rate.

(a) I–adrenal, II–adrenaline, III–decrease
(b) I–adrenal, II–adrenaline and nor-adrenaline, III–increase
(c) I–thymus, II–nor-adrenaline, III–increase
(d) I–thymus, II–nor-adrenaline, III–decrease

11. Which of the following drug normally helps in preventing depression and insomnia?

(a) Opioids (b) Cannabinoids
(c) Amphetamines (d) Coca alkaloids

12. Given below are two statements.

Statement I Cancerous cells spread to distant site by a property called contact inhibition.

Statement II Majority of drugs are obtained from flowering plants, while some are isolated from fungal strains.

In the light of the above statements, choose the correct answer from the options given below.

(a) Statement I is incorrect, but statement II is correct.
(b) Both statement I and statement II are correct.
(c) Both statement I and statement II are incorrect.
(d) Statement I is correct, but statement II is incorrect.

13. The chemical structure of a drug is given below.

Identify the role of this drug from the following options.

(a) Hallucinogenic properties
(b) Used by sportsperson
(c) Produces a sense of increased energy
(d) Used as a depressant that slows down body functions

14. The side-effects of use of anabolic steroid in females are

(a) depression, decreased sperm production, deepening of voice, etc.
(b) mood swings, baldness, deepening of voice, etc.
(c) masculinisation, increased aggressiveness, enlargement of clitoris, etc.
(d) increased aggressiveness, mood swings enlargement of testicles, etc.

15. Which of the following drug is not obtained directly from plants?

(a) Cocaine (b) Atropine
(c) Morphine (d) Heroin

Response Index

01 ⓐ ⓑ ⓒ ⓓ	10 ⓐ ⓑ ⓒ ⓓ	19 ⓐ ⓑ ⓒ ⓓ
02 ⓐ ⓑ ⓒ ⓓ	11 ⓐ ⓑ ⓒ ⓓ	20 ⓐ ⓑ ⓒ ⓓ
03 ⓐ ⓑ ⓒ ⓓ	12 ⓐ ⓑ ⓒ ⓓ	21 ⓐ ⓑ ⓒ ⓓ
04 ⓐ ⓑ ⓒ ⓓ	13 ⓐ ⓑ ⓒ ⓓ	22 ⓐ ⓑ ⓒ ⓓ
05 ⓐ ⓑ ⓒ ⓓ	14 ⓐ ⓑ ⓒ ⓓ	23 ⓐ ⓑ ⓒ ⓓ
06 ⓐ ⓑ ⓒ ⓓ	15 ⓐ ⓑ ⓒ ⓓ	24 ⓐ ⓑ ⓒ ⓓ
07 ⓐ ⓑ ⓒ ⓓ	16 ⓐ ⓑ ⓒ ⓓ	25 ⓐ ⓑ ⓒ ⓓ
08 ⓐ ⓑ ⓒ ⓓ	17 ⓐ ⓑ ⓒ ⓓ	
09 ⓐ ⓑ ⓒ ⓓ	18 ⓐ ⓑ ⓒ ⓓ	

Performance Scanner

> 90% Excellent !	You have mastered these topics. The concepts of these topics are at your fingertips. Move on to the next test and maintain this momentum.
76-90% Very Good !	You have a good command over these topics. Revise these topics again after a few days and enhance your performance.
60-75% Good !	You have a wide scope to learn for these topics. Revise these topics again.
<60% Not Satisfactory!	You have a long way ahead of you to master these topics. Revise it thoroughly.

Chapter Break Thru

Syllabus

- Concept of health and disease; pathogens; parasites causing human diseases (malaria, filariasis, ascariasis, typhoid, pneumonia, common cold, amoebiasis, ringworm, dengue, chikungunya)
- Basic concepts of immunology
- Vaccines
- Cancer, HIV and AIDS
- Adolescence
- Drug and alcohol abuse
- Tobacco abuse

Important Instructions

- The test is of 1 hour duration and contains 30 Multiple-Choice Questions (Four options with a single correct answer).
- Choose the correct option and fill the OMR given on the last page of this test accordingly.
- At some instances, you may find more than 1 option to be correct. In such circumstances, you have to judge the most appropriate answer as per the conditions given in the question.

1. Identify the set of contagious diseases.

(a) Smallpox, ringworm, common flu
(b) Influenza, AIDS, cholera
(c) Leprosy, typhoid, AIDS
(d) AIDS, typhoid, ascariasis

2. What differentiates congenital diseases from acquired diseases?

(a) Congenital diseases occur after a certain age, while acquired diseases are present since birth.
(b) Congenital diseases are present since birth, while acquired diseases develop after birth.
(c) Congenital diseases remain present only during gestation time, while acquired disease appears immediately after the birth.
(d) Congenital diseases are curable, while acquired diseases are non-curable.

3. Read the statements carefully and identify the statements that qualify the attributes of non-communicable disease.

I. Malfunctioning of an organ or tissue can result in a reversible or non-reversible state of disease.
II. Overuse of alcohol causes reduced alertness of the brain.
III. AIDS is a curable disease like other non-communicable diseases.
IV. Cancer is the most common non-infectious disease existing in the world.

Choose the correct answer from the options given below.

(a) I, II and III
(b) Only I
(c) III and IV
(d) I, II and IV

4. Find the incorrect statement with respect to pneumonia.

(a) *Haemophilus influenzae* can contribute to the transmission of pneumonia.
(b) In severe cases of pneumonia, the lips and nails of the infected person turn blue or gray.
(c) Pneumonia is transmitted only by contaminated food and water.
(d) Pneumonia infects the lungs making them filled with several fluids which eventually toughens respiration.

5. Which of the following is used in the production of the recombinant hepatitis-B vaccine?

(a) *S. cerevisiae*
(b) *Microsporum* sp.
(c) *E. coli*
(d) *Streptococcus* sp.

6. Match the List I with List II.

	List I		List II
A.	Dengue	1.	*Mycobacterium*
B.	Plague	2.	*Flavivirus*
C.	Tuberculosis	3.	*Vibrio*
D.	Cholera	4.	*Yersinia*

Choose the correct answer from the options given below.

	A	B	C	D		A	B	C	D
(a)	3	2	4	1	(b)	2	4	1	3
(c)	4	1	3	2	(d)	1	2	4	3

7. Given below are two statements.

Statement I The overuse of antibiotics in treating viral infections like the common cold selects for resistant bacterial strains, making them less effective against future bacterial infections.

Statement II Since antibiotics target bacteria, they have no effect on viral infections like the common cold. Therefore, taking antibiotics for a cold is completely harmless.

In the light of the above statements, choose the correct answer from the options given below.

(a) Statement I is incorrect, but statement II is correct.

(b) Both statement I and statement II are correct.

(c) Both statement I and statement II are incorrect.

(d) Statement I is correct, but statement II is incorrect.

8. Given below are two statements; one is labelled as Assertion (A) and the other is labelled as Reason (R).

Assertion (A) Ascariasis, caused by the roundworm *Ascaris*, can be prevented by simply washing fruits and vegetables before consumption.

Reason (R) Eggs of *Ascaris* are only transmitted through contaminated water sources.

In the light of the above statements, choose the correct answer from the options given below.

(a) A is false, but R is true.

(b) Both A and R are true and R is the correct explanation of A.

(c) Both A and R are true but R is not the correct explanation of A.

(d) A is true, but R is false.

9. Given below is a picture of a human with a disease. Which of the following statement is incorrect w.r.t. the given disease?

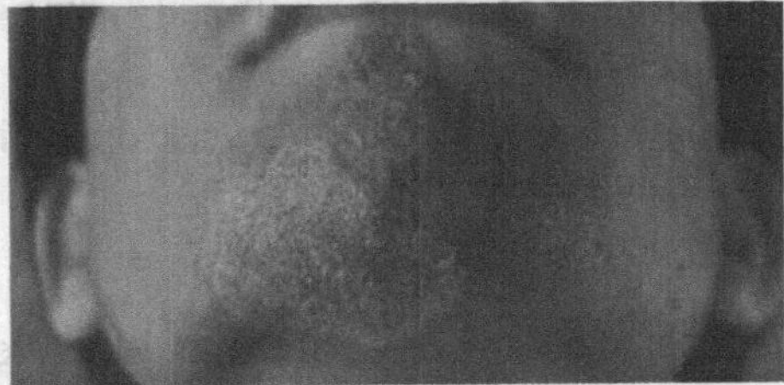

(a) It is caused by several different species of fungi belonging to genera like *Trichophyton* and *Epidermophyton*.

(b) The pathogen responsible for this infection can infect the skin, hair and nails, causing characteristic itchy and scaly lesions.

(c) The infection is primarily transmitted through direct contact with infected individuals or contaminated objects.

(d) The medications, either topical or oral, are not effective in treating these infections.

10. Consider the given features about amoebiasis.

I. Infection occurs in large intestine of humans

II. Transmitted primarily and only by houseflies

III. Symptoms include constipation, abdominal pain and bloody stools

IV. Contaminated food and water spread infection

V. Caused by the protozoan parasite

Choose the correct answer from of the options given below.

(a) I, II and III

(b) I, III, IV and V

(c) I, II, IV and V

(d) II, IV and V

11. Vaccines are most likely not effective in preventing

(a) tetanus (b) diphtheria

(c) malaria (d) pneumonia

12. Choose the option with disease mentioned in the following sentences.

There is always a time lag between the infection and appearance of .... symptoms. This period may vary from a few months to few years.

(a) pneumonia (b) AIDS

(c) common flu (d) ascariasis

13. Which of the following is not correct for antigens?
(a) Activate lymphocytes
(b) Differentiate between "self" and "non-self" molecules
(c) Initiates active immune response upon binding with antibodies
(d) Trapped by lymphatic vessels

14. The most standard HIV screening blood test
(a) predicts how fast one can develop AIDS
(b) measures the amount of virus in the blood
(c) detects antibodies against the virus
(d) can be done only after appearance of opportunistic infections

15. Match the List I with List II.

	List I		List II
A.	IgG	1.	First antibodies in response to an exposure to antigen
B.	IgA	2.	Crosses the placenta
C.	IgM	3.	Colostrum
D.	IgE	4.	Allergic reaction

Choose the correct answer from the options given below.

	A	B	C	D
(a)	3	4	1	2
(b)	2	3	1	4
(c)	4	1	3	2
(d)	3	2	1	4

16. How does the skin serve in the protection against the pathogens?
(a) Skin is the external tough layer which restricts the entry of bacteria and several other pathogens.
(b) Skin is a soft layer which allows the entry of virus, but restricts the entry of bacteria.
(c) Skin is the external tough layer and semi-permeable to bacteria, but not the virus.
(d) Skin is the external tough layer which allows the entry of both bacteria and viruses, but protects against other pathogens.

17. Cell-mediated immune response and humoral immune response can be distinguished by the action of different cells. Select the correct statement.
(a) Cell-mediated immune response is performed by B-cells, while humoral response is performed by T-cells.
(b) Cell-mediated immune response is performed by T-cells, while humoral response is performed by B-cells.
(c) Cell-mediated immune response is performed by natural killer cells, while humoral response is performed by cytokines.
(d) Macrophages are the primary players in both cell-mediated and humoral immune responses.

18. Given below are some statements regarding cancer.
I. Cancer can be induced by ionising radiations like UV rays.
II. Oncogenic viruses have genes called viral proto-oncogenes.
III. Several genes called *c*-onc have been found in normal cells and possess potential to convert into oncogenes.

Choose the incorrect statements from the following options.
(a) I and II (b) III and II
(c) I and III (d) I, II and III

19. Which of the following is not expected to be present significantly in the lymph?
(a) Macrophages
(b) Antigens
(c) Protein molecules
(d) RBCs

20. Given below are two statements.

Statement I Immunisation refers to the development of immunity in the body, either through natural infection or vaccination.

Statement II Vaccination always involves a single dose of a weakened or inactive pathogen to provide lifelong immunity.

In the light of the above statements, choose the correct answer from the options given below.

(a) Statement I is incorrect, but statement II is correct.
(b) Both statement I and statement II are correct.
(c) Both statement I and statement II are incorrect.
(d) Statement I is correct, but statement II is incorrect.

21. Given below are two statements; one is labelled as Assertion (A) and the other is labelled as Reason (R).

Assertion (A) Anti-venom injection and an infant receiving antibodies from breast milk are both examples of passive immunity.

Reason (R) Anti-venom injection and breast milk contain pre-formed antibodies that shows instant immunisation for short term.

In the light of the above statements, choose the correct answer from the options given below.

(a) A is false, but R is true.
(b) Both A and R are true and R is the correct explanation of A.
(c) Both A and R are true, but R is not the correct explanation of A.
(d) A is true, but R is false.

22. Primary and secondary lymphoid organs which are involved in the maturation of lymphocytes are

(a) spleen and liver
(b) bone marrow and thymus gland
(c) spleen and thymus gland
(d) liver and bone marrow

23. Prime constituent of *Cannabis sativa* is

(a) diacetylmorphine
(b) dimethyl amide
(c) tetrahydrocannabinol
(d) salicylic acid

24. Given below are two statements.

Statement I Excessive alcohol consumption can lead to liver cirrhosis.

Statement II Degraded nervous system function is a potential consequence of chronic alcohol abuse.

In the light of the above statements, choose the correct answer from the options given below.

(a) Statement I is incorrect, but statement II is correct.
(b) Both statement I and statement II are correct.
(c) Both statement I and statement II are incorrect.
(d) Statement I is correct, but statement II is incorrect.

25. Malignant tumours rapidly spread in the human body because of the property of

(a) slow proliferation
(b) metastasis
(c) contact inhibition
(d) damage the surrounding cells

26. Read the following statements about cocaine.

I. It interferes with the transport of neurotransmitter.
II. It is being abused by some sportspersons.
III. It increases risk of oral cancer.
IV. It causes hallucination.
V. It has stimulating action on CNS.

Choose the correct answer from the options given below.

(a) I, II and III (b) I, II and IV
(c) I, IV and V (d) I, II, III and IV

27. Choose the correct labelling of *A* and *B*.

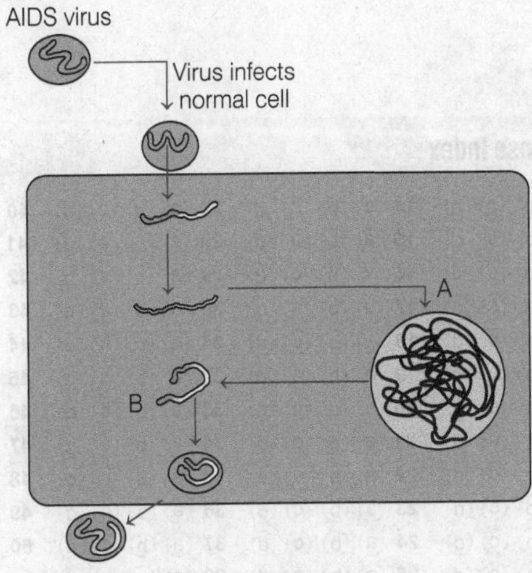

(a) *A*-Viral DNA incorporate into host, *B*-New viral DNA produced
(b) *A*-Viral RNA incorporate into host, *B*-New viral RNA produced

(c) *A*-Viral DNA incorporates into host, *B*-New viral RNA produced
(d) *A*-Viral RNA incorporates into host, *B*-New viral DNA produced

28. Which type of drug is derived from the plant shown in the image below?

(a) Hallucinogen
(b) Depressant
(c) Pain killer
(d) Stimulant

29. Given below are two statements; one is labelled as Assertion (A) and the other is labelled as Reason (R).

Assertion (A) Nicotine in cigarettes functions primarily as a calcium channel blocker in the heart, leading to decreased heart rate and a relaxation response.

Reason (R) Smokers often report feeling calmer and more relaxed shortly after smoking a cigarette.

In the light of the above statements, choose the correct answer from the options given below.
(a) A is false, but R is true.
(b) Both A and R are true and R is the correct explanation of A.
(c) Both A and R are true, but R is not the correct explanation of A.
(d) A is true, but R is false.

30. Read the following paragraph.

A is a vector-borne disease that is caused due to a virus. The fever and joint pain in this disease is much more than other vector-borne diseases. It can also disable people.

Choose the correct option w.r.t. *A*.
(a) *A* is chikungunya that is caused due to bite of *Anopheles aegypti*.
(b) *A* is dengue that is caused due to bite of male *Aedes aegypti*.
(c) *A* is chikungunya that is caused due to bite of female *Aedes aegypti*.
(d) *A* is dengue that is caused due to CHIKV virus from *Alphavirus* genes.

Scan for online chapter test

Response Index

01 ⓐ ⓑ ⓒ ⓓ	14 ⓐ ⓑ ⓒ ⓓ	27 ⓐ ⓑ ⓒ ⓓ	40 ⓐ ⓑ ⓒ ⓓ
02 ⓐ ⓑ ⓒ ⓓ	15 ⓐ ⓑ ⓒ ⓓ	28 ⓐ ⓑ ⓒ ⓓ	41 ⓐ ⓑ ⓒ ⓓ
03 ⓐ ⓑ ⓒ ⓓ	16 ⓐ ⓑ ⓒ ⓓ	29 ⓐ ⓑ ⓒ ⓓ	42 ⓐ ⓑ ⓒ ⓓ
04 ⓐ ⓑ ⓒ ⓓ	17 ⓐ ⓑ ⓒ ⓓ	30 ⓐ ⓑ ⓒ ⓓ	43 ⓐ ⓑ ⓒ ⓓ
05 ⓐ ⓑ ⓒ ⓓ	18 ⓐ ⓑ ⓒ ⓓ	31 ⓐ ⓑ ⓒ ⓓ	44 ⓐ ⓑ ⓒ ⓓ
06 ⓐ ⓑ ⓒ ⓓ	19 ⓐ ⓑ ⓒ ⓓ	32 ⓐ ⓑ ⓒ ⓓ	45 ⓐ ⓑ ⓒ ⓓ
07 ⓐ ⓑ ⓒ ⓓ	20 ⓐ ⓑ ⓒ ⓓ	33 ⓐ ⓑ ⓒ ⓓ	46 ⓐ ⓑ ⓒ ⓓ
08 ⓐ ⓑ ⓒ ⓓ	21 ⓐ ⓑ ⓒ ⓓ	34 ⓐ ⓑ ⓒ ⓓ	47 ⓐ ⓑ ⓒ ⓓ
09 ⓐ ⓑ ⓒ ⓓ	22 ⓐ ⓑ ⓒ ⓓ	35 ⓐ ⓑ ⓒ ⓓ	48 ⓐ ⓑ ⓒ ⓓ
10 ⓐ ⓑ ⓒ ⓓ	23 ⓐ ⓑ ⓒ ⓓ	36 ⓐ ⓑ ⓒ ⓓ	49 ⓐ ⓑ ⓒ ⓓ
11 ⓐ ⓑ ⓒ ⓓ	24 ⓐ ⓑ ⓒ ⓓ	37 ⓐ ⓑ ⓒ ⓓ	50 ⓐ ⓑ ⓒ ⓓ
12 ⓐ ⓑ ⓒ ⓓ	25 ⓐ ⓑ ⓒ ⓓ	38 ⓐ ⓑ ⓒ ⓓ	
13 ⓐ ⓑ ⓒ ⓓ	26 ⓐ ⓑ ⓒ ⓓ	39 ⓐ ⓑ ⓒ ⓓ	

Performance Scanner

> 90% Excellent !	You have mastered this chapter. The concepts of this chapter are at your fingertips. Move on to the next chapter and maintain this momentum.
76-90% Very Good !	You have a good command over this chapter. Revise the chapter again after a few days and enhance your performance.
60-75% Good !	You have a wide scope to learn for this chapter. Revise this chapter again.
<60% Not Satisfactory!	You have a long way ahead of you to master this chapter. Revise it thoroughly.

Test Booklet No. **3947358**

Test Booklet Code **CH8**

MEDACE
NEET (UG)
SELF ASSESSMENT KIT

Microbes in Human Welfare

Topics Covered

Microbes in Household and Industrial Products

Sewage-treatment, Biogas, Biocontrol Agents and Biofertilisers

Important Instructions

- This Booklet Contains – Two Topic Tests and One Test on Complete Chapter.
- Each question carries 4 marks.
- For each correct response, the candidate will get 4 marks. And for every incorrect response, 1 mark will be additionally deducted from total score.
- Use **Blue/Black** point pen only for filling the OMR.
- Rough work is to be done in the space provided for this purpose in the test booklet only.

Name of the Candidate (In Capitals) ______________

____

Candidate's Signature ______________

Invigilator's Signature ______________

Facsimile signature stamp of center superintendent ______________

Do not open this booklet until you start attempting the test

Topical Follow Thru

Test 1

Syllabus Microbes in household food processing and Industrial production

For deeper insight, **Scan the QR Code**

Important Instructions

- The test is of 30 minutes duration and contains 25 Multiple Choice Questions (four options with a single correct answer).
- Choose the correct option and fill the OMR given on the last page of this test accordingly.
- At some instances, you may find more than 1 option to be correct. In such circumstances, you have to judge the most appropriate answer as per the conditions given in the question.

1. Which of the following components within our stomach specifically contributes in controlling the growth of harmful microbes?

(a) *Streptococcus*
(b) Mucus lining
(c) Digestive enzymes
(d) Lactic acid bacteria

2. Select the pair of beverage produced without distillation.

(a) Whisky, brandy
(b) Rum, wine
(c) Wine, beer
(d) Whisky, beer

3. Bottled fruit juices bought from market are clearer as compared to those made at home. It is because of

(a) streptokinase
(b) yeast
(c) pectinases and proteases
(d) *Lactobacillus*

4. *Lactobacillus* mediated change of milk occurs due to

(a) coagulation and partial digestion of milk protein
(b) coagulation of milk fat and partial digestion of milk protein
(c) coagulation and full digestion of milk protein
(d) coagulation and partial digestion of milk fat

5. Given below are two statements.

Statement I Toddy is a traditional drink in some parts of Southern India. It is made by fermenting sap from bamboo shoots.

Statement II Cyclosporin-A, an immunosuppressant drug, is crucial to prevent organ rejection in transplants.

In the light of the above statements, choose the correct answer from the options given below.

(a) Statement I is incorrect, but statement II is correct
(b) Both statement I and statement II are correct
(c) Both statement I and statement II are incorrect
(d) Statement I is correct, but statement II is incorrect

6. Which of the following statement is correct with respect to the following diagram?

(a) It involves the industrial production of certain chemicals like organic acids, alcohols.
(b) It processes the distillation of the fermented broth.
(c) It includes the production of beverages and antibiotics on industrial scale.
(d) The production of antibiotics by using microbes occurs here.

7. The starter or inoculum is added to fresh milk in order to convert milk into curd. The inoculum or starter here refer to
(a) bacteria rich in protein
(b) liquid containing millions of LAB
(c) bacteria rich in vitamin-B_{12}
(d) liquid containing activated yeast

8. Match the List I with List II.

	List I		List II
A.	Fermenting malted cereals	1.	*Propionibacterium shermanii*
B.	Swiss cheese	2.	*Penicillium roqueforti*
C.	Roquefort cheese	3.	*Streptococcus*
D.	Clot buster	4.	*Saccharomyces cerevisiae*

Choose the correct answer from the options given below.

	A	B	C	D
(a)	1	4	2	3
(b)	3	1	4	2
(c)	4	1	2	3
(d)	4	2	3	1

9. The discovery of penicillin resulted from
(a) observing a mold's inhibitory effect on bacterial growth
(b) studying the chemical structure of *Staphylococcus*
(c) extensive use in treating wounds
(d) collaboration between Fleming, Chain and Florey

10. Given below are the two statements; one is labelled as Assertion (A) and the other is labelled as Reason (R).

Assertion (A) The puffed-up appearance of dough is caused by the production of carbon dioxide gas (CO_2) during fermentation.

Reason (R) Cheese is one of the oldest food items in which microbes were used.

In the light of the above statements, choose the correct answer from the options given below.
(a) A is false, but R is true
(b) Both A and R are true and R is the correct explanation of A
(c) Both A and R are true, but R is not the correct explanation of A
(d) A is true, but R is false

11. The modern day washing powders have some biological content. Which of the following will be mostly added to the powder as biocontrol content?
(a) DNA lipase
(b) Lactase
(c) Pectinase
(d) Lipase

12. Read the following statements (with respect to statin).
I. Statin are produced by the bacteria *Monascus purpureus*.
II. Statins have been commercialised as blood cholesterol lowering agent.
III. It acts by competitively inhibiting the enzyme responsible for the synthesis of cholesterol.
IV. Statin produced by the yeast.
V. Statin is not a bioactive enzyme.

Which of the above statements are correct?
(a) I, II and III
(b) II, III and IV
(c) III, IV and V
(d) I, III and V

13. Select the incorrect match pair.
(a) *Aspergillus niger* - Citric acid
(b) *Lactobacillus* - Lactic acid
(c) *Acetobacter aceti* - Butyric acid
(d) *Aspergillus niger* - Gluconic acid

14. Consider the following statements.

I. Antibiotics are chemical substances produced by some microbes which can kill or retard the growth of other disease causing microorganism.

II. The function of penicillin as an antibiotics was established by Alexander Fleming.

III. Bioactive molecules which inhibit cholesterol synthesis in blood is extracted from bacteria.

Choose the correct option having incorrect statement(s).

(a) I and III (b) Only II

(c) Only I (d) II and III

15. Microbes are the causal agents of most of the infections. But, they are useful in many important processes. Study the given table that enlist some microorganisms and their products.

Microorganisms	Products
A	Curd
Streptococcus	B
C	Ethanol
D	Statins

Identify A, B, C and D and choose the incorrect statement with respect to them.

(a) 'A' is involved in the partial digestion and coagulation of protein

(b) Statins is a bacterial product used to inhibit enzyme responsible for cholesterol synthesis

(c) Ethanol producing microbe 'C' involved in the production of toddy

(d) Project 'B' is help ful for patient with blocked arteries

16. All the following can be performed by LAB except,

(a) coagulation and partial digestion of milk protein

(b) increasing vitamin-B_{12} in curd

(c) can kill or retard growth of other microbes

(d) Check disease causing microbes

17. Consider the following statements.

I. Antibiotics are the attenuated microorganisms which in small concentration can kill or retard the growth of other harmful microorganisms.

II. Penicillin was the first antibiotic discovered by Alexander Fleming while working an bacterium *Staphylococci*.

III. The full potential of penicillin as an effective antibiotic was established by Ernest Chain and Howard Florey.

IV. Fleming, Chain and Florey were awarded the Nobel Prize in 1945.

Choose the incorrect options.

(a) I only (b) III only

(c) II and IV (d) I, III and IV

18. Match the List I with List II.

	List I		List II
A.	*Saccharomyces cerevisiae*	1.	Production of immunosuppressive agents
B.	*Monascus purpureus*	2.	Ripening of Swiss cheese
C.	*Trichoderma polysporum*	3.	Commercial production of ethanol.
D.	*Propionibacterium shermanii*	4.	Production of blood cholesterol lowering agents.

Choose the correct answer.

	A	B	C	D
(a)	3	4	1	2
(b)	4	3	2	1
(c)	4	2	1	3
(d)	3	1	4	2

19. Given below are the two statements; one is labelled as Assertion (A) and the other is labelled as Reason (R).

Assertion (A) Yeast such as *Saccharomyces cerevisiae* are used in baking industry.

Reason (R) Carbon dioxide produced during fermentation causes bread dough to rise by thermal expansion.

In the light of the above statements, choose the correct answer from the options given below.

(a) A is false, but R is true

(b) Both A and R are true and R is the correct explanation of A.

(c) Both A and R are true, but R is not the correct explanation of A.

(d) A is true, but R is false.

20. Big holes in Swiss cheese are formed as a result of

(a) machine used for making the cheese
(b) a bacterium producing a large amount of carbon dioxide
(c) a bacterium that is visible to naked eyes
(d) a fungus that produces large amount of carbon dioxide

21. Name the blank spaces A, B, C and D in the given table:

Type of microbes	Scientific names	Commercial products
A	*Monascus purpureus*	Statin
Fungus	*B*	Cyclosporin-A
Fungus	*C*	Citric acid
Bacteria	*Streptococcus*	*D*

Choose the correct option.

	A	*B*	*C*	*D*
(a)	Fungus	*Clostridium butylicum*	*Aspergillus niger*	Ethanol
(b)	Bacteria	*Acetobacter aceti*	*Clostridium butylicum*	Acetic acid
(c)	Yeast	*Trichoderma polysporum*	*Aspergillus niger*	Streptokinase
(d)	Fungus	*Penicillium*	*Trichoderma polysporum*	Protease

22. Brewer's yeast is used for A of malted cereals and fruit juices to produce B.

(a) A-distillation, B-CO_2
(b) A -distillation, B-organic acid
(c) A-fermentation, B – CO
(d) A-fermentation, B- alcohol

23. Which step is not involved in beer production?

(a) Malting and mashing
(b) Fermentation
(c) Clarification and carboxylation
(d) Distillation

24. Given below are two statements.

Statement I Pasteurisation alters the taste of food product.

Statement II The process of pasteurisation is named after Louis Pasteur.

In the light of the above statements, choose the correct answer from the options given below.

(a) Statement I is incorrect, but statement II is correct.
(b) Both statement I and statement II are correct.
(c) Both statement I and statement II are incorrect
(d) Statement I is correct, but statement II is incorrect

25. Consider the following statements and identify the incorrect one.

(a) Toddy a traditional drink made by fermenting sap from plams.
(b) Cheese is one of the oldest food items in which microbes were used.
(c) Production on an industrial scale requires growing microbes in small vessels.
(d) Wine and beer are produced without distillation.

Response Index

01	a	b	c	d	10	a	b	c	d	19	a	b	c	d
02	a	b	c	d	11	a	b	c	d	20	a	b	c	d
03	a	b	c	d	12	a	b	c	d	21	a	b	c	d
04	a	b	c	d	13	a	b	c	d	22	a	b	c	d
05	a	b	c	d	14	a	b	c	d	23	a	b	c	d
06	a	b	c	d	15	a	b	c	d	24	a	b	c	d
07	a	b	c	d	16	a	b	c	d	25	a	b	c	d
08	a	b	c	d	17	a	b	c	d					
09	a	b	c	d	18	a	b	c	d					

Performance Scanner

> 90% Excellent !	You have mastered these topics. The concepts of these topics are at your fingertips. Move on to the next test and maintain this momentum.
76-90% Very Good !	You have a good command over these topics. Revise these topics again after a few days and enhance your performance.
60-75% Good !	You have a wide scope to learn for these topics. Revise these topics again.
<60% Not Satisfactory!	You have a long way ahead of you to master these topics. Revise it thoroughly.

Test 2

Syllabus Microbes in sewage treatment, energy generation and as biocontrol agents and biofertilisers.

For deeper insight, **Scan the QR Code**

Important Instructions

- The test is of 30 minutes duration and contains 25 Multiple Choice Questions (four options with a single correct answer).
- Choose the correct option and fill the OMR given on the last page of this test accordingly.
- At some instances, you may find more than 1 option to be correct. In such circumstances, you have to judge the most appropriate answer as per the conditions given in the question.

1. In Sewage Treatment Plants (STPs), the breakdown of pollutants is primarily achieved by
(a) powerful chemical disinfectants
(b) artificial enzymes added to the sewage
(c) the natural activity of heterotrophic microbes present in the sewage.
(d) high-pressure filtration systems

2. What would happen if oxygen availability to activated sludge flocs is reduced?
(a) It will result in the growth of diatoms
(b) Flocs size will increase
(c) Flocs will break
(d) It will increase in the rate of degradation of organic matter.

3. The formation of biogas involves
(a) solubilisation — acidogenesis — methanogenesis
(b) sterilisation — fermentation — biosynthesis
(c) fermentation — purification — carbonification
(d) methanogenesis — fermentation — solubilisation

4. Read the following statements.
I. Methanogens are found in aerobic sludge during sewage treatment.
II. In the rumen of cattle, methanogens help in the breakdown of cellulose.
III. Cattle excreta is rich in these bacteria.
IV. Biogas produced is used for cooking and lightening.
V. Technology of biogas production was developed in India is due to the efforts of IARI and KVIC.

Which of the above statements are correct?
(a) I, II, III and V
(b) II, III and IV
(c) I, III and V
(d) II, III, IV and V

5. Given below are two statements.
Statement I In activated sludge method, the effluent from primary settling tank is passed into aeration tank where microbes form flocs.
Statement II Activated sludge is taken to aerobic sludge digester where, microbes act upon organic matter to produce monomers and organic acid.
In the light of the above statements, choose the correct answer from the options given below.
(a) Statement I is incorrect, but statement II is correct
(b) Both statement I and statement II are correct
(c) Both statement I and statement II are incorrect
(d) Statement I is correct, but statement II is incorrect

6. With respect to the given figure, select the correct statement.

(a) A treatment step involves physical removal of large and small particles
(b) A process of removal of floating debris by sequential filtration and then removal of grit by sedimentation
(c) Tank, involves primary sludge formation
(d) It is designed to substantially degrade the biological content of the waste through aerobic biological processes

7. The sediment of secondary treatment is pumped back into the aeration tank. This is because
(a) to serve as inoculum
(b) to measure BOD
(c) to decrease the growth of aerobic bacteria
(d) to treating millions of gallons of wastewater

8. Which of the following is the first step in sewage treatment?
(a) Sedimentation
(b) Filtration
(c) Both sedimentation and filtration
(d) Flocculation

9. Biological method of control of pests and disease relies on
(a) interspecific competition
(b) intraspecific competition
(c) natural predation
(d) introduced chemicals

10. Given below are two statements; one is labelled as Assertion (A) and the other one is labelled as Reason (R).
Assertion (A) Plants having mycorrhizae are more prone to diseases and drought.
Reason (R) Fungi absorbs phosphorus from the soil and passes it to the plant.
In the light of the above statements, choose the correct answer from the options given below.
(a) A is false, but R is true
(b) Both A and R are true and R is the correct explanation of A
(c) Both A and R are true, but R is not the correct explanation of A
(d) A is true, but R is false

11. Which of the following biofertilisers is responsible for 50% higher yields of rice?
(a) *Azolla pinnata*
(b) *Frankia*
(c) *Azospirillum*
(d) *Azotobacter*

12. Which of the following statement is incorrect?
(a) Ladybird is useful in controlling aphids
(b) Dragonfly is useful to get rid of mosquitoes
(c) Baculovirus is helpful against insects and other arthropods
(d) *Bacillus thuringiensis* is helpful in making the plant drought tolerant

13. Which of the following is used as a powerful agent in the integrated pest management programme?
(a) *Chlorella*
(b) *Anabaena*
(c) *Lactobacillus*
(d) *Nucleopolyhedrovirus*

14. Match the List I with List II.

	List I		List II
A.	*Trichoderma*	1.	Free-living fungi used as a biocontrol agent
B.	*Bacillus thuringiensis*	2.	Fix atmospheric nitrogen
C.	*Glomus*	3.	Biocontrol agents of lepidopteran plant pests
D.	*Anabaena*	4.	Add organic matter to the soil

Choose the correct answer from the options given below.

	A	B	C	D
(a)	3	2	4	1
(b)	2	1	3	4
(c)	2	3	4	1
(d)	1	3	4	2

15. Given below are two statements; one is labelled as Assestion (A) and other is labelled as Reason (R).

Assertion (A) The energy value of biogas is lower than that of organic matter, but the, energy output in roughly equal to the output in the burring of organic matter.

Reason (R) Biogas minimise the chance of spread of pathogen.

In the light of the above statements, choose the correct answer from the options given below.

(a) A is false, but R is true
(b) Both A and R are true and R is the correct explanation of A
(c) Both A and R are true, but R is not the correct explanation of A
(d) A is true, but R is false

16. Given below are two statements.

Statement I In a sewage treatment plant, the primary sludge is obtained by sequential filtration and sedimentation.

Statement II Methanogenic bacteria are found in anaerobic sludge digesters.

In the light of the above statements, choose the correct answer from the options given below.

(a) Statement I is incorrect, but statement II is correct.
(b) Both statement I and statement II are correct.
(c) Both statement I and statement II are incorrect
(d) Statement I is correct, but statement II is incorrect

17. Which of the following statement is correct?

(a) Cyanobacteria such as *Anabaena* and *Nostoc* are important mobilisers of phosphates and potassium for plant nutrition in soil
(b) At present it is not possible to grow maize without chemical fertilisers
(c) Runoff from agricultural areas rich in chemicals fertilisers may lead to eutrophication of nearby water bodies
(d) Both *Azotobacter* and *Rhizobium* fix atmospheric nitrogen in root nodules of plants

18. Which one of the following statements is incorrect about biogas?

(a) It contains 50-80% methane
(b) Agricultural wastes are utilised
(c) It is highly polluting
(d) Biogas plant is difficult to construct

19. For symbiotic nitrogen-fixation, the biofertiliser *Rhizobium* enters the leguminous partner through the

(a) root nodules
(b) stem tissues
(c) root hairs before nodule formation
(d) root hairs after nodule formation

20. Choose the incorrect statement about secondary sewage treatment.

(a) In settling tank, the bacterial flocs settle and the sediment is called activated sludge.
(b) A small part of the sludge is used as an inoculum. The remaining part is passed into anaerobic sludge digesters.
(c) On anaerobic digestion of bacteria and fungi, mixture of gases such as carbon dioxide, nitrogen and carbon monoxide are produced.
(d) Once the BOD of sewage is reduced significantly the effluent passed into settling tank where activated sludge allowed to sediment.

21. Given below are the two statements; one is labelled as Assertion (A) and the other is labelled as Reason (R).

Assertion (A) Biogas is used as fuel for cooking and lightning.

Reason (R) It is considered as ecofriendly and non-polluting source of energy.

In the light of the above statements, choose the correct answer from the options given below.

(a) A is false, but R is true
(b) Both A and R are true and R is the correct explanation of A.
(c) Both A and R are true, but R is not the correct explanation of A.
(d) A is true, but R is false.

22. Match the List I with List II

	List I		List II
A.	Biofertilisers	1.	Action of methane producing bacteria on component of microbial fermentation.
B.	Biocontrol agents	2.	Physical removal of particles
C.	Methanogenesis	3.	Organisms that enrich the nutrient quality of soil.
D.	Primary treatment	4.	Use of biological methods for pest control

Choose the correct option

	A	B	C	D
(a)	2	1	3	4
(b)	1	4	3	2
(c)	3	2	1	4
(d)	3	4	1	2

23. Consider the following statements.

I. Ladybirds and dragonflies are used to get rid of aphids and mosquitoes.

II. The bacteria *Bacillus_thuringiensis* (*Bt*) are used to control butterfly.

III. *Trichoderma* sp. is present in root ecosystems where they act against several plant pathogens.

IV. *Rhizobium* is a symbiotic bacterium that lives in the stem of legumes.

Which of the statements given above are correct?

(a) I, II and III (b) I, III and IV
(c) II, III and IV (d) II and IV

24. The free-living fungus *Trichoderma* can be used

(a) for killing insects
(b) as a biological control of plant diseases
(c) to control butterfly caterpillars
(d) for producing antibiotics

25. Primary treatment involves

(a) physical removal of large and small particles from sewage
(b) biological removal of large and small particles from sewage
(c) chemical removal of large and small particles from sewage
(d) physio-chemical removal of grit from sewage.

■ **Response Index**

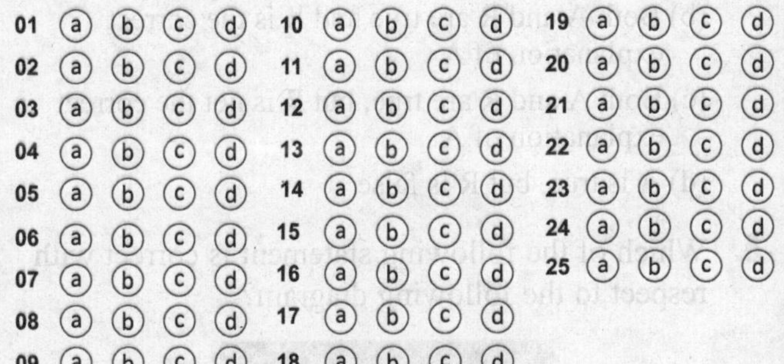

■ **Performance Scanner**

> 90% Excellent !	You have mastered these topics. The concepts of these topics are at your fingertips. Move on to the next test and maintain this momentum.
76-90% Very Good !	You have a good command over these topics. Revise these topics again after a few days and enhance your performance.
60-75% Good !	You have a wide scope to learn for these topics. Revise these topics again.
<60% Not Satisfactory!	You have a long way ahead of you to master these topics. Revise it thoroughly.

Chapter Break Thru

Syllabus	• In household food processing • Industrial production • Sewage treatment	• Energy generation and as biocontrol agents and biofertilisers.

Important Instructions

- The test is of 1 hour duration and contains 30 Multiple-Choice Questions (Four options with a single correct answer).
- Choose the correct option and fill the OMR given on the last page of this test accordingly.
- At some instances, you may find more than 1 option to be correct. In such circumstances, you have to judge the most appropriate answer as per the conditions given in the question.

1. The most abundant prokaryotes helpful to humans in making curd from milk and in the production of antibiotics are the ones characterised as
(a) chemosynthetic autotrophs
(b) heterotrophic bacteria
(c) cyanobacteria
(d) archaebacteria

2. Select the incorrect statement.
(a) Acetic acid is used in the preparation of vinegar
(b) Toddy is a traditional drink of Southern India, made by fermenting sap of palms
(c) Wine and beer are produced without distillation
(d) Large-holed Swiss cheese is ripened with *Penicillium roquefortii*

3. Dosa and idli are fermented preparation of rice and black gram, the puffed up appearance of dough is due to the
(a) production of ethanol
(b) production of CO_2
(c) production of O_2
(d) production of citric acid

4. Given below are two statements; one is labelled as Assertion (A) and other one is labelled as Reason (R).

Assertion (A) Cyclosporin-A is an immuno-stimulant.

Reason (R) A bioactive molecule which is given to organ-transplant patient is produced by bacterium *Trichoderma*.

In the light of the above statements, choose the correct answer from the options given below.
(a) A is false, but R is true
(b) Both A and R are true and R is the correct explanation of A
(c) Both A and R are true, but R is not the correct explanation of A
(d) A is true, but R is false

5. Which of the following statement is correct with respect to the following diagram?

(a) It encompasses the industrial production of various chemicals such as organic acids and alcohols
(b) It involves the distillation of fermented broth
(c) It includes the large-scale production of beverages and antibiotics in huge vessels
(d) The manufacturing of antibiotics using microbes takes place here

6. Primary treatment of wastewater is mainly a .... treatment while secondary treatment in .... treatment.
(a) chemical, physical
(b) physical, biological
(c) biological, physical
(d) physico-chemical, biological

7. Which of the following antibiotics was extensively used to treat American soldiers wounded in World War II?
(a) Penicillin (b) Streptomycin
(c) Neomycin (d) Tetracycline

8. Methanogens are commonly found in
(a) aerobic sludge and rumen of cattle
(b) anaerobic sludge and rumen of cattle
(c) gobar gas plant and saline water
(d) primary sludge and rumen of cattle

9. Which of the following is incorrectly matched in the given table?

	Products	Applications
A.	Pectinase	Clarification of fruit juice
B.	Methanogen	Production of biogas
C.	*Monascus purpureus*	Genetically modified to form clot buster
D.	*Bt* cotton	Resistance to attack by plants pests

(a) A (b) B
(c) C (d) D

10. Given below are two statements.
Statement I BOD represents the amount of dissolved oxygen that would be consumed, if all the organic matter in one litre of water were oxidised by microorganisms.
Statement II High value of BOD indicates that the water is highly polluted by organic matter.
In the light of above statements, choose the correct answer from the options given below.
(a) Statement I is incorrect, but statement II is correct
(b) Both statement I and statement II are correct
(c) Both statement I and statement II are incorrect
(d) Statement I is correct, but statement II is incorrect

11. In gobar gas, the maximum amount is that of
(a) butane (b) methane
(c) propane (d) carbon dioxide

12. After which of the following treatment, the effluent is generally released into natural water bodies like rivers and streams?
(a) Aerobic treatment
(b) Secondary treatment
(c) Primary treatment
(d) Sludge treatment

13. Match the List I with List II.

	List I		List II
A.	Primary treatment	1.	Aeration tanks
B.	Site of flocs growth	2.	Activated sludge
C.	Sediment in primary treatment	3.	Primary sludge
D.	Sediment in secondary treatment	4.	Physical process
		5.	Biological process

Choose the correct answer from the options given below.

	A	B	C	D
(a)	1	2	3	5
(b)	2	3	5	1
(c)	4	1	3	2
(d)	4	1	2	3

14. Which of the following is the main objective of Ganga action plan and Yamuna action plan proposed by the Ministry of Environment and Forest?

(a) Dumping of solid waste into landfills
(b) Reducing the biological oxygen demand of the river
(c) Constructing a large number of sewage treatment plants
(d) Introducing oil eating bacteria in the river

15. Which organisations were primarily responsible for the development of biogas production technology in India?

(a) Indian Council of Medical Research (ICMR) and Indian Agricultural Research Institute (IARI)
(b) Khadi and Village Industries Commission (KVIC) and Indian Agricultural Research Institute (IARI)
(c) Indian Council of Agricultural Research (ICAR) and Khadi and Village Industries Commission (KVIC)
(d) National Botanical Research Institute (NBRI)

16. Which of the following are free-living biofertilisers?

(a) *Anabaena* and *Frankia*
(b) *Azotobacter* and *Azospirillum*
(c) *Rhizobium* and *Rhizopus*
(d) VAM and mycorrhiza

17. Which of the following are bacteria, fungi and blue-green algae that help in improving the fertility of the soil?

(a) *Glomus, Alternaria* and *Anabaena*, respectively
(b) *Azotobacter*, *Glomus* and *Oscillatoria*, respectively
(c) *Clostridium*, *Rhizopus* and *Nostoc*, respectively
(d) *Nereis*, *Rhizopus* and *Anabaena*, respectively

18. Viruses belonging to genus-*Nucleopolyhedrovirus* that attack insects and other arthropods and is used to conserve beneficial insects are

(a) retrovirus
(b) rhinovirus
(c) baculovirus
(d) adenovirus

19. Which of the following group of microbes is used for controlling plant diseases and pests?

(a) *Trichoderma*, Baculovirus, *Bacillus thuringiensis*
(b) *Oscillatoria*, *Rhizobium*, *Trichoderma*
(c) *Plasmodium*, *Meloidegyne*, *Acetobacter*
(d) *Bacillius thuringiensis*, Tobacco mosaic virus, Aphids

20. Which of the following causes respiratory infections?

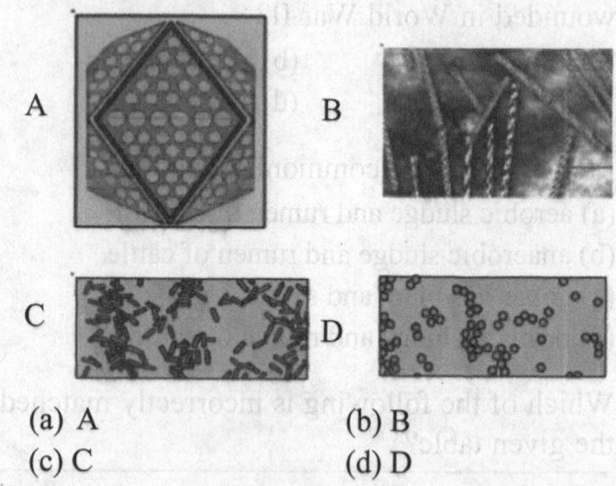

(a) A (b) B
(c) C (d) D

21. Identify the parts labelled as *A*, *B* and *C* with respect to biogas plant.

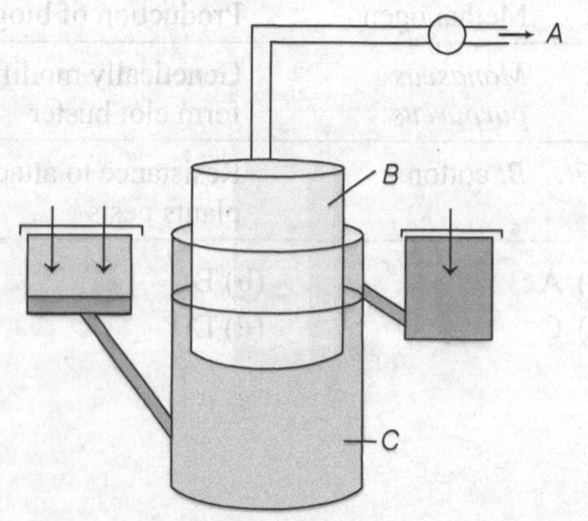

	A	*B*	*C*
I.	Gas	Sludge	Dung + Water
II.	Gas	Gas holder	Digester
III.	Gas holder	Sludge	Dung + Water
IV.	Gas holder	Digester	Dung + Water

(a) III (b) II
(c) I (d) IV

22. Match the List I with List II.

	List I		List II
A.	Lactic acid	1.	*Streptococcus*
B.	Streptokinase	2.	*Clostridium*
C.	Statins	3.	*Lactobacillus*
D.	Butyric acid	4.	*Monascus*

Choose the correct answer from the options given below.

	A	B	C	D
(a)	3	1	2	4
(b)	3	1	4	2
(c)	1	4	2	3
(d)	3	4	1	2

23. Given below are two statements; one is labelled as Assertion (A) and other is labelled as Reason (R).

Assertion (A) Whisky, brandy and rum are produced by distillation of a fermentation broth.
Reason (R) Distillation increases the alcohol content of beverages.
In the light of the above statements, choose the correct answer from the options given below.

(a) A is false, but R is true
(b) Both A and R are true and R is the correct explanation of A
(c) Both A and R are true, but R is not the correct explanation of A
(d) A is true, but R is false

24. Match the List I with List II.

	List I		List II
A.	Masses of bacteria associated with fungal filaments to form mesh	1.	High BOD
B.	Bacteria produce a mixture of gases such as CH_2, H_2S and CO_2	2.	Flocs
C.	Waterbodies with sewage waste	3.	Low BOD
D.	Fresh waterbody with petroleum waste	4.	Anaerobic sludge digester

Choose the correct answer from the options given below

	A	B	C	D
(a)	2	4	1	3
(b)	4	2	3	1
(c)	1	3	4	2
(d)	3	1	2	4

25. Given below is the flowchart of sewage treatment. Identify *A, B, C, D* and *E* and select the correct option.

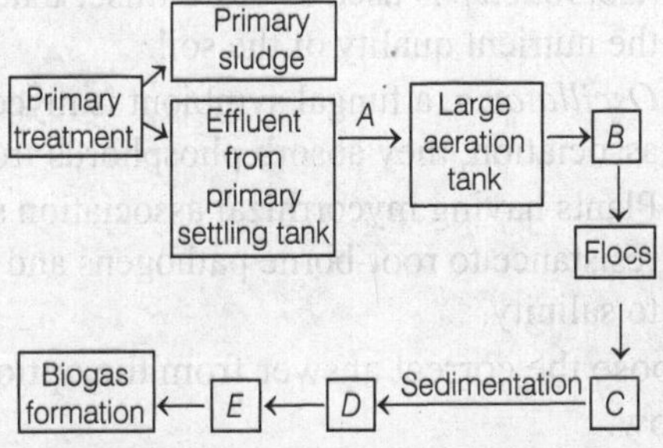

(a) *A*– Secondary treatment, *B*–Microbial digestion, *C*–High BOD, *D*–Activated sludge, *E*–Aerobic sludge digesters
(b) *A*–Aerobic treatment, *B*–Mechanical agitation, *C*–Low BOD, *D*–Deactivated sludge, *E*–Aerobic sludge digesters

(c) *A*–Small aeration tank, *B*–Microbial digestion, *C*–Low BOD, *D*–Activated sludge, *E*–Anaerobic sludge digesters

(d) *A*–Secondary treatment, *B*–Mechanical agitation, *C*–Reduced BOD, *D*–Activated sludge, *E*–Anaerobic sludge digesters

26. Read the following statements.

I. Citric acid is obtained from *Aspergillus niger*.
II. Lipases are used in detergent formulations.
III. Dragonflies are useful to get rid of aphids.
IV. Cyanobacteria increase alkalinity of soil.
V. The activated sludge is digested in an anaerobic sludge digester.

Choose the correct answer from the options given below.

(a) I, II and V (b) I, III and IV
(c) III and V (d) III and IV

27. Which of the following statements are correct.

I. Organic farmer works to create a environment which suits crops and pests are also not eradicated.
II. Conventional farming practices kept the insects at manageable levels by a complex system of checks and balances within a living ecosystem.
III. *Azotobacter* is used as biofertiliser that enrich the nutrient quality of the soil.
IV. *Oscillatoria*, a fungal symbiont is mycorrhizal association, they absorb phosphorus from soil.
V. Plants having mycorrhizal association show resistance to root-borne pathogens and tolerance to salinity.

Choose the correct answer from the options, given below.

(a) I, III and V
(b) III, IV and V
(c) II and IV
(d) I, II, III and IV

28. Read the following statements.

I. Lactic acid is produced by the process of fermentation.
II. Biofertilisers enrich the nutrient quality of the soil.
III. Yeast is a fungi which is used in the production of lipase and pectinase.
IV. *Anabaena* is a nitrogen fixing microbe associated with *Azolla* in rice field.
V. The domestic sewage in large cities, when treated in STPs does not really require the aeration step.

Choose the correct answer from the options given below.

(a) III and V are incorrect
(b) I, III and V are correct
(c) II, III and IV are correct
(d) I and II are incorrect

29. Given below are two statements; one is labelled as Assertion (A) and other one is labelled as Reason (R).

Assertion (A) *Bt* cotton plants are resistant to insect pests due to the introduction of *Bacillus thuringiensis* toxin genes into the plants.

Reason (R) The bacterial disease caused by *Bacillus thuringiensis* kills caterpillars by directly infecting their cells and multiplying within them, eventually causing the larvae to die.

In the light of the above statements, choose the correct answers from the options given below.

(a) A is false, but R is true
(b) Both A and R are true and R is the correct explanation of A
(c) Both A and R are true, but R is not the correct explanation of A
(d) A is true, but R is false

30. Given below are two statements.

Statement I Some beetles and dragonflies feed on butterfly caterpillers thus, help farmers in getting rid of them.

Statement II The biocontrol measures help us to avoid heavy use of toxic pesticides for controlling pests.

In the light of above statements, choose the correct answer from the options given below.

(a) Statement I is incorrect, but statement II is correct

(b) Both statement I and statement II are correct

(c) Both statement I and statement II are incorrect

(d) Statement I is correct, but statement II is incorrect

Response Index

01	ⓐ ⓑ ⓒ ⓓ	14	ⓐ ⓑ ⓒ ⓓ	27	ⓐ ⓑ ⓒ ⓓ	40	ⓐ ⓑ ⓒ ⓓ
02	ⓐ ⓑ ⓒ ⓓ	15	ⓐ ⓑ ⓒ ⓓ	28	ⓐ ⓑ ⓒ ⓓ	41	ⓐ ⓑ ⓒ ⓓ
03	ⓐ ⓑ ⓒ ⓓ	16	ⓐ ⓑ ⓒ ⓓ	29	ⓐ ⓑ ⓒ ⓓ	42	ⓐ ⓑ ⓒ ⓓ
04	ⓐ ⓑ ⓒ ⓓ	17	ⓐ ⓑ ⓒ ⓓ	30	ⓐ ⓑ ⓒ ⓓ	43	ⓐ ⓑ ⓒ ⓓ
05	ⓐ ⓑ ⓒ ⓓ	18	ⓐ ⓑ ⓒ ⓓ	31	ⓐ ⓑ ⓒ ⓓ	44	ⓐ ⓑ ⓒ ⓓ
06	ⓐ ⓑ ⓒ ⓓ	19	ⓐ ⓑ ⓒ ⓓ	32	ⓐ ⓑ ⓒ ⓓ	45	ⓐ ⓑ ⓒ ⓓ
07	ⓐ ⓑ ⓒ ⓓ	20	ⓐ ⓑ ⓒ ⓓ	33	ⓐ ⓑ ⓒ ⓓ	46	ⓐ ⓑ ⓒ ⓓ
08	ⓐ ⓑ ⓒ ⓓ	21	ⓐ ⓑ ⓒ ⓓ	34	ⓐ ⓑ ⓒ ⓓ	47	ⓐ ⓑ ⓒ ⓓ
09	ⓐ ⓑ ⓒ ⓓ	22	ⓐ ⓑ ⓒ ⓓ	35	ⓐ ⓑ ⓒ ⓓ	48	ⓐ ⓑ ⓒ ⓓ
10	ⓐ ⓑ ⓒ ⓓ	23	ⓐ ⓑ ⓒ ⓓ	36	ⓐ ⓑ ⓒ ⓓ	49	ⓐ ⓑ ⓒ ⓓ
11	ⓐ ⓑ ⓒ ⓓ	24	ⓐ ⓑ ⓒ ⓓ	37	ⓐ ⓑ ⓒ ⓓ	50	ⓐ ⓑ ⓒ ⓓ
12	ⓐ ⓑ ⓒ ⓓ	25	ⓐ ⓑ ⓒ ⓓ	38	ⓐ ⓑ ⓒ ⓓ		
13	ⓐ ⓑ ⓒ ⓓ	26	ⓐ ⓑ ⓒ ⓓ	39	ⓐ ⓑ ⓒ ⓓ		

Performance Scanner

> 90% Excellent !	You have mastered this chapter. The concepts of this chapter are at your fingertips. Move on to the next chapter and maintain this momentum.
76-90% Very Good !	You have a good command over this chapter. Revise the chapter again after a few days and enhance your performance.
60-75% Good !	You have a wide scope to learn for this chapter. Revise this chapter again.
<60% Not Satisfactory!	You have a long way ahead of you to master this chapter. Revise it thoroughly.

Scan for online chapter test

Scan for online unit test

Space for Rough Work

Test Booklet No. **3947359**

Test Booklet Code **CH9**

MEDACE
NEET (UG)
SELF ASSESSMENT KIT

Biotechnology : Principles and Processes

Topics Covered

Principles of Biotechnology

Tools of Recombinant DNA Technology

Process of Recombinant DNA Technology

Important Instructions

- This Booklet Contains – Three Topic Tests and One Test on Complete Chapter.
- Each question carries 4 marks.
- For each correct response, the candidate will get 4 marks. And for every incorrect response, 1 mark will be additionally deducted from total score.
- Use **Blue/Black** point pen only for filling the OMR.
- Rough work is to be done in the space provided for this purpose in the test booklet only.

Name of the Candidate (In Capitals)

____

Candidate's Signature __________

Invigilator's Signature __________

Facsimile signature stamp of center superintendent__________

Do not open this booklet until you start attempting the test

Topical Follow Thru

Test 1

Syllabus Principles of Biotechnology

For deeper insight, **Scan the QR Code** 

Important Instructions

- The test is of 30 minutes duration and contains 15 Multiple Choice Questions (four options with a single correct answer).
- Choose the correct option and fill the OMR given on the last page of this test accordingly.
- At some instances, you may find more than 1 option to be correct. In such circumstances, you have to judge the most appropriate answer as per the conditions given in the question.

1. Identify the incorrect statement.

(a) The definition of biotechnology by the EFB includes only the modern aspects.

(b) Humans have practiced biotechnology since ancient times.

(c) Biotechnology involves using living organisms or their enzymes to create useful products and processes.

(d) *In vitro* fertilisation is a technique included in biotechnology.

2. Which of the following is not the character of pBR322 vector?

(a) Most widely used, versatile and easily manipulative

(b) Has two antibiotic resistance genes, tet^R and amp^R

(c) First artificial cloning vector constructed in 1977 by Boliver and Rodriguez

(d) No restriction site for *Sal* I

3. The main aim of genetic engineering is to

I. Alter the structure of specific genes

II. Produce desired proteins

III. Change the phenotype of organisms

IV. Decipher the sequence of genes

V. Analyse the DNA profile of two individuals

Choose the correct answer.

(a) I and II (b) IV and V

(c) I, II and III (d) I, II and V

4. Given below are two statements.

Statement I As the genetic code is similar in all species, structural genes can be taken from one organism and incorporated into another.

Statement II The construction of first recombinant DNA emerged from the possibility of linking a gene encoding antibiotic resistance with a native plasmid of *Escherichia coli.*

In the light of the above statements, choose the correct answer from the options given below.

(a) Statement I is incorrect, but statement II is correct

(b) Both statement I and statement II are correct

(c) Both statement I and statement II are incorrect

(d) Statement I is correct, but statement II is incorrect

5. Select the incorrect statement with respect to the first construction of an artificial *r*DNA.

(a) Stanley Cohen and Herbert Boyer accomplished this in 1972.

(b) The recombinant DNA emerged from linking gene- encoding antibiotic resistance in the native plasmid of *E. coli.*

(c) The linking of antibiotic resistance gene with the plasmid vector becomes possible with the enzyme DNA ligase.

(d) The ability to multiply copies of antibiotic resistance gene in *E. coli* is called cloning of antibiotics gene in *E. coli.*

6. Given below are two statements; one is labelled as Assertion (A) and the other is labelled as Reason (R).

Assertion (A) Genetic engineering requires both nucleases and ligases.

Reason (R) Restriction enzymes serve as chemical knives to cut genes into defined fragments.

In the light of the above statements, choose the correct answer from the options given below.

(a) A is false, but R is true
(b) Both A and R are true and R is the correct explanation of A
(c) Both A and R are true, but R is not the correct explanation of A
(d) A is true, but R is false

7. ……… are obtained only from prokaryotes. It is their natural defence mechanism against bacteriophage infection.

(a) DNA ligases (b) Restriction enzymes
(c) Cloning vectors (d) Selectable markers

8. Select the incorrect match pair.

(a) DNA sequence for initiating replication - Primer
(b) Double-stranded circular vehicle DNA - Plasmid
(c) Vehicle with passenger DNA - Vector
(d) Multiplication of desired gene in host organism - Cloning

9. Sequence which is responsible for controlling the copy number of linked DNA is called

(a) origin of replication
(b) restriction site
(c) *rop*
(d) antibiotic resistance gene

10. The following is the role of restriction endonuclease in the construction of a recombinant DNA molecule, except

(a) formation of a phosphodiester bond between two DNA fragments
(b) recognition and cutting of specific DNA sequences
(c) creation of sticky or blunt ends on DNA fragments
(d) facilitating the insertion of DNA fragments into vectors

11. Cloning gene is a process where

(a) fragments of DNA are transferred from one organism to another, usually carried on a DNA vector
(b) gene is cloned in an animal
(c) DNA is cloned in plants
(d) fragments of DNA cloned in the same organism using carrier

12. Which pairs of enzymes are most commonly used in genetic engineering?

(a) Ligase and polymerase
(b) Endonuclease and ligase
(c) Restriction endonuclease and polymerase
(d) Restriction endonuclease and ligase

13. Why is *Salmonella typhimurium* not commonly used as a host organism to clone genes, despite its close relation to *Escherichia coli*?

(a) *Salmonella typhimurium* lacks the necessary genetic tools for cloning.
(b) *Escherichia coli* is more resistant to antibiotics.
(c) *Salmonella typhimurium* cannot replicate plasmids.
(d) *Salmonella typhimurium* is more pathogenic and possess higher biosafety risks compared to *Escherichia coli*.

14. Which statement is not correct regarding the basic steps in genetic modification?

(a) Identification of DNA with desirable genes is the first step.
(b) Introduction of the identified DNA into the host is the second step.
(c) Maintenance of the introduced DNA in the host and transfer of the DNA to its progeny is the third step.
(d) Sequencing the entire genome of the host is the fourth step.

15. Match the List I with List II.

List I	List II
A. Plasmid	1. Overhanging stretches at each end of DNA
B. First artificial recombinant molecule	2. Specific palindromic sequences
C. Restriction enzyme	3. Double-stranded circular DNA
D. Staggered end	4. Stanley Cohen and Herbert Boyer

Choose the correct answer from the options given below.

	A	B	C	D		A	B	C	D
(a)	3	1	4	2	(b)	3	4	2	1
(c)	2	3	4	1	(d)	4	2	3	1

Response Index

01	a	b	c	d	10	a	b	c	d	19	a	b	c	d
02	a	b	c	d	11	a	b	c	d	20	a	b	c	d
03	a	b	c	d	12	a	b	c	d	21	a	b	c	d
04	a	b	c	d	13	a	b	c	d	22	a	b	c	d
05	a	b	c	d	14	a	b	c	d	23	a	b	c	d
06	a	b	c	d	15	a	b	c	d	24	a	b	c	d
07	a	b	c	d	16	a	b	c	d	25	a	b	c	d
08	a	b	c	d	17	a	b	c	d					
09	a	b	c	d	18	a	b	c	d					

Performance Scanner

> 90% Excellent !	You have mastered these topics. The concepts of these topics are at your fingertips. Move on to the next test and maintain this momentum.
76-90% Very Good !	You have a good command over these topics. Revise these topics again after a few days and enhance your performance.
60-75% Good !	You have a wide scope to learn for these topics. Revise these topics again.
<60% Not Satisfactory!	You have a long way ahead of you to master these topics. Revise it thoroughly.

Test 2

Syllabus Tools of Recombinant DNA Technology

For deeper insight, **Scan the QR Code**

Important Instructions

- The test is of 30 minutes duration and contains 15 Multiple Choice Questions (four options with a single correct answer).
- Choose the correct option and fill the OMR given on the last page of this test accordingly.
- At some instances, you may find more than 1 option to be correct. In such circumstances, you have to judge the most appropriate answer as per the conditions given in the question.

1. During genetic engineering, the restriction endonucleases function is to

(a) transform the DNA into host cell

(b) ligate the foreign DNA into the host DNA

(c) produce cuts in the host DNA

(d) polymerise the vector molecule

2. Given below are two statements; one is labelled as Assertion (A) and the other is labelled as Reason (R).

Assertion (A) A bacterial cell with no restriction enzymes will be easily infected and lysed by bacteriophages.

Reason (R) Restriction enzymes cleaves DNA sequences at specific sites.

In the light of the above statements, choose the correct answer from the options given below.

(a) A is false, but R is true

(b) Both A and R are true and R is the correct explanation of A

(c) Both A and R are true, but R is not the correct explanation of A

(d) A is true, but R is false

3. Select the incorrect match w.r.t. restriction endonuclease.

(a) *Hin*dIII - The first restriction endonuclease

(b) *Eco*RI - Recognises a specific sequence of six base pairs

(c) Recognition site - Palindromic sequence

(d) *Bam*HI -Recognition site present in tetracycline resistance gene

4. Which of the following options best describes palindrome sequences in DNA?

(a) Read same on two strands when orientation of reading is opposite

(b) Read opposite on two strands when orientation of reading is same

(c) Read specific sequence in opposite direction

(d) Read opposite on two strands

5. Following diagram illustrates the action of restriction endonuclease enzyme.

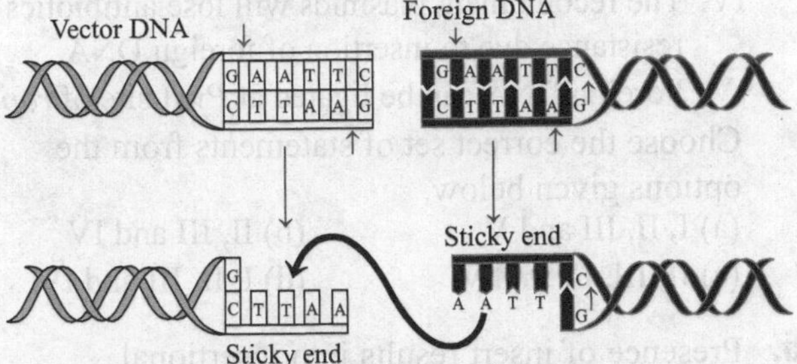

Which of the following enzyme is used to create such sticky end?

(a) *Eco*RII (b) *Eco*RI

(c) *Eco*RIII (d) *Sal*I

6. Given below are two statements.

Statement I The agarose matrix used in gel electrophoresis should have controllable pore size.

Statement II Agarose concentration can be changed to change pore size.

In the light of the above statements, choose the correct answer from the options given below.

(a) Statement I is incorrect, but statement II is correct

(b) Both statement I and statement II are correct

(c) Both statement I and statement II are incorrect

(d) Statement I is correct, but statement II is incorrect

7. Which of the following statements about cloning vectors are incorrect?

I. *ori* is a sequence responsible for controlling the copy number of linked DNA.

II. Selectable marker selectively permits the growth of the non-transformants.

III. To link the alien DNA, the vector needs to have single recognition site for the commonly used restriction enzymes.

IV. The ligation of alien DNA is carried out at a restriction site present in one of the two antibiotic resistance genes.

V. Multiple cloning site does not allow insertion of foreign DNA.

Choose the correct answer from the options given below.

(a) I and III (b) IV and V

(c) II and V (d) III and IV

8. Identify *A* and *B* in given diagram.

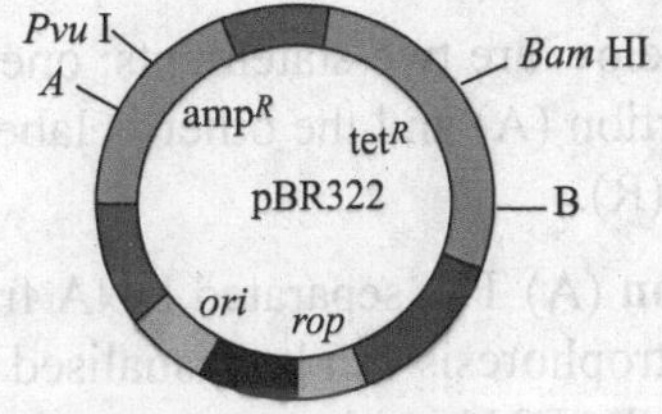

(a) *A*– *Pvu*II, *B* – *Cla*I

(b) *A*– *Hin*dII, *B* – *Sal*I

(c) *A*– *Pst*I, *B* – *Sal*I

(d) *A*– *Pst*I, *B* – *Bam*HI

9. Match the List I with List II.

List I	List II
A. Electroporation	1. Introduction of foreign genes using glass needles
B. Microinjection	2. Foreign DNA is bombarded into target cells
C. Gene gun	3. Enables the bacteria to take up the recombinant DNA
D. Heat shock	4. Creates transients pores in the plasma membrane

Choose the correct answer from the options given below.

	A	B	C	D		A	B	C	D
(a)	3	1	2	4	(b)	4	1	2	3
(c)	3	4	2	1	(d)	3	4	1	2

10. Which of the following statements is correct?

(a) *Eco*RI cuts the DNA between bases G and A only when the sequence GATTTC is present in the DNA.

(b) Today we know, more than 900 restriction enzymes that have been isolated from over 280 strains of bacteria, each of which recognise different recognition sequences.

(c) In *Eco*RI, the letter 'R' is derived from the name of restriction enzyme.

(d) Each restriction endonuclease functions by 'inspecting' the length of a DNA sequence.

11. Which of the following is not a characteristic of pBR322 vector?

(a) It is the first artificial cloning vector constructed in 1977 by Boliver and Rodriguez.

(b) It is the most widely used, versatile and easily manipulated vector.

(c) It has two antibiotic resistance genes, tet^R and amp^R.

(d) It does not have restriction site for *Sal* I.

12. Given below are two statements; one is labelled as Assertion (A) and the other is labelled as Reason (R).

Assertion (A) The separated DNA fragments by gel-electrophoresis can be visualised only after staining the DNA with a compound ethidium bromide followed by exposure to UV radiation.

Reason (R) Orange coloured bands of DNA are visible in an ethidium bromide stained gel exposed to UV light.

In the light of the above statements, choose the correct answer from the options given below.

(a) A is false, but R is true

(b) Both A and R are true and R is the correct explanation of A

(c) Both A and R are true, but R is not the correct explanation of A

(d) A is true, but R is false

13. Match the List with List II.

	List I		List II
A.	Exonuclease	1.	Cut at specific position within DNA
B.	Sticky ends	2.	Removes nucleotides from the ends of DNA
C.	Endonuclease	3.	Read the same sequence in both complementary strands
D.	Palindromic sequence	4.	Form hydrogen bonds with complementary cut counterparts

Choose the correct answer from the options given below.

(a) A-4, B-1, C-3, D-2 (b) A-2, B-4, C-1, D-3

(c) A-3, B-1, C-4, D-2 (d) A-1, B-3, C-4, D-2

14. Read the following statements.

I. In order to link the alien DNA, the vector needs to have very few, preferably single, recognition sites for the commonly used restriction enzymes.

II. Presence of more than one recognition sites within the vector will generate several fragments, which will complicate the gene cloning.

III. The ligation of alien DNA is carried out at a restriction site present in one of the two antibiotic resistance genes of pBR322.

IV. The recombinant plasmids will lose antibiotics resistance due to insertion of foreign DNA.

V. Foreign DNA can be ligated at *Pvu*I site of *rop*.

Choose the correct set of statements from the options given below.

(a) I, II, III and V (b) II, III and IV

(c) II, III, IV and V (d) I, II, III and IV

15. Presence of insert results into insertional inactivation of the β-galactosidase gene and the colonies do not produce any colour, these are identified as

(a) recombinant colonies

(b) transformant colonies

(c) non-recombinant colonies

(d) non-transformant colonies

Response Index

01	a	b	c	d	10	a	b	c	d	19	a	b	c	d
02	a	b	c	d	11	a	b	c	d	20	a	b	c	d
03	a	b	c	d	12	a	b	c	d	21	a	b	c	d
04	a	b	c	d	13	a	b	c	d	22	a	b	c	d
05	a	b	c	d	14	a	b	c	d	23	a	b	c	d
06	a	b	c	d	15	a	b	c	d	24	a	b	c	d
07	a	b	c	d	16	a	b	c	d	25	a	b	c	d
08	a	b	c	d	17	a	b	c	d					
09	a	b	c	d	18	a	b	c	d					

Performance Scanner

> 90% Excellent !	You have mastered these topics. The concepts of these topics are at your fingertips. Move on to the next test and maintain this momentum.
76-90% Very Good !	You have a good command over these topics. Revise these topics again after a few days and enhance your performance.
60-75% Good !	You have a wide scope to learn for these topics. Revise these topics again.
<60% Not Satisfactory!	You have a long way ahead of you to master these topics. Revise it thoroughly.

Test 3

Syllabus Processes of Recombinant DNA Technology

For deeper insight, **Scan the QR Code**

Important Instructions

- The test is of 30 minutes duration and contains 15 Multiple Choice Questions (four options with a single correct answer).
- Choose the correct option and fill the OMR given on the last page of this test accordingly.
- At some instances, you may find more than 1 option to be correct. In such circumstances, you have to judge the most appropriate answer as per the conditions given in the question.

1. Which of the following best explains why DNA precipitates out after the addition of chilled ethanol during DNA extraction?

(a) Ethanol forms covalent bonds with DNA, making it insoluble in water.

(b) Chilled ethanol causes DNA to denature, leading to precipitation.

(c) Ethanol reduces the solubility of DNA by decreasing the dielectric constant of the solution.

(d) Chilled ethanol causes DNA to hydrolyse, forming insoluble fragments.

2. Read the following statements w.r.t. PCR and select the incorrect statements.

I. PCR involves three temperature independent steps.

II. In the step III, DNA polymerase adds nucleotide to the primer.

III. It is possible to generate 2^n molecules after n number of cycles.

IV. PCR is a part of DNA fingerprinting.

V. Major limitation of PCR is that it cannot diagnose the specific mutation.

Choose the correct answer from the options given below.

(a) II and III (b) III and IV

(c) I and V (d) I and III

3. Given below are two statements.

Statement I A bioreactor provides the optimal conditions for achieving the desired product by providing optimum growth conditions.

Statement II Any protein encoding gene that is expressed in a homologous host is called a recombinant protein.

In the light of the above statements, choose the correct answer from the given options.

(a) Statement I is incorrect, but statement II is correct

(b) Both statement I and statement II are correct

(c) Both statement I and statement II are incorrect

(d) Statement I is correct, but statement II is incorrect

4. Following diagram depicts schematic representation of simple stirred-tank bioreactor.

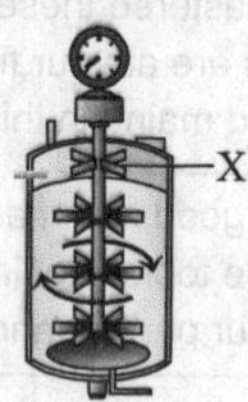

The structure designated as *X* is the part of
(a) agitator system
(b) oxygen delivery system
(c) foam control system
(d) temperature control system

5. Given below are two statements; one is labelled as Assertion (A) and the other is labelled as Reason (R).

Assertion (A) Agarose gel electrophoresis is employed to check the progression of a restriction enzyme digestion.

Reason (R) Agarose gel electrophoresis separates DNA fragments based on size, allowing visualisation of digestion results.

In the light of the above statements, choose the correct answer from the options given below.
(a) A is false, but R is true
(b) Both A and R are true and R is the correct explanation of A
(c) Both A and R are correct, but R is not the correct explanation of A
(d) A is true, but R is false

6. Given below are two statements; one is labelled as Assertion (A) and other is labelled as Reason (R).

Assertion (A) In recombinant DNA technology, human genes are often transferred into bacteria or yeast.

Reason (R) Both bacteria and yeast multiply very fast to form huge population which express the desired gene.

(a) A is false, but R is true
(b) Both A and R are true and R is the correct explanation of A
(c) Both A and R are true, but R is not the correct explanation of A
(d) A is true, but R is false

7. Identify *A*, *B* and *C* in given diagram.

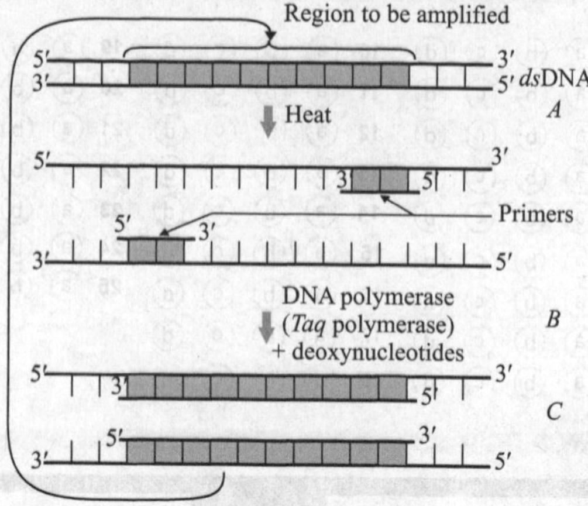

(a) *A*–Annealing, *B*–Denaturation, *C*–Extension
(b) *A*–Denaturation, *B*–Annealing, *C*–Extension
(c) *A*–Extension, *B*–Denaturation, *C*–Annealing
(d) *A*–Extension, *B*–Annealing, *C*–Denaturation

8. How thermostable DNA polymerases are obtained?
(a) By heating the bacteria manually over high temperature
(b) They are isolated from extremely stable thermophilic bacteria, which are often found growing in oceanic vents
(c) Can be found anywhere
(d) Obtained by genetically modifying the *E. coli* bacteria with thermal stability property

9. Given below are two statements.

Statement I After completion of the biosynthetic stage, the product has to be subjected through a series of processes before it is ready for marketing as finished product.

Statement II These processes include separation and purification and are collectively referred to as downstream processing.

In the light of the above statements, choose the correct answer from the options given below.
(a) Statement I is incorrect, but statement II is correct
(b) Both statement I and statement II are correct
(c) Both statement I and statement II are incorrect
(d) Statement I is correct, but statement II is incorrect

10. In which of the following types of fermentation, the used medium is drained out from one side of the bioreactor and the fresh medium is added from the other side to maintain the cells in their physiologically most active log exponential phase?
(a) Batch fermentation
(b) Continuous fermentation
(c) Downstream fermentation
(d) Anaerobic respiration

11. Arrange the following steps in the correct order for the process of recombinant DNA technology.
I. Extraction of the desired gene product.
II. Amplification of the gene of interest.
III. Isolation of a desired DNA fragment.
IV. Ligation of the DNA fragment into a vector.
V. Insertion of recombinant DNA into the host.
Choose the correct answer.
(a) I, II, III, IV and V
(b) III, II, IV, V and I
(c) III, IV, II, V and I
(d) I, IV, V, III and II

12. Match the List I with List II.

	List I		List II
A.	Plant cell	1.	Chitinase
B	Bacterial cell	2.	Cellulase
C.	Fungal cell	3.	Lysozyme
D.	Animal cell	4.	Detergent

Choose the correct answer from the options given below.

	A	B	C	D		A	B	C	D
(a)	1	2	3	4	(b)	2	3	1	4
(c)	3	4	2	1	(d)	2	4	1	3

13. Which of the following processes are involved in downstream processing?
I. Separation
II. Purification
III. Formulation
IV. Quality control
V. Culturing heterologous host
Choose the correct answer from the options given below.
(a) II, III and IV
(b) I, II, III and IV
(c) III, IV and V
(d) II, III and V

14. Match the List I with List II.

	List I		List II
A.	*Thermus aquaticus*	1.	Breakage of hydrogen bonds between DNA strands
B.	Ampicillin resistance gene	2.	Isolation of DNA
C.	Spooling	3.	Thermostable DNA polymerase
D.	Denaturation	4.	Selective marker

Choose the correct answer from the options given below.
(a) A-3, B-4, C-2, D-1
(b) A-1, B-4, C-3, D-2
(c) A-4, B-1, C-2, D-3
(d) A-4, B-2, C-1, D-3

15. Which of the following statements is incorrect?
(a) The cells harboring cloned genes of interest may be grown on a small scale in the laboratory.
(b) The downstream processing and quality control testing vary from product to product.
(c) Large scale production involves use of bioreactors.
(d) Primers are oligonucleotides that are complementary to self-replicating DNA.

Response Index

01	a	b	c	d	10	a	b	c	d	19	a	b	c	d
02	a	b	c	d	11	a	b	c	d	20	a	b	c	d
03	a	b	c	d	12	a	b	c	d	21	a	b	c	d
04	a	b	c	d	13	a	b	c	d	22	a	b	c	d
05	a	b	c	d	14	a	b	c	d	23	a	b	c	d
06	a	b	c	d	15	a	b	c	d	24	a	b	c	d
07	a	b	c	d	16	a	b	c	d	25	a	b	c	d
08	a	b	c	d	17	a	b	c	d					
09	a	b	c	d	18	a	b	c	d					

Performance Scanner

> 90% Excellent !	You have mastered these topics. The concepts of these topics are at your fingertips. Move on to the next test and maintain this momentum.
76-90% Very Good !	You have a good command over these topics. Revise these topics again after a few days and enhance your performance.
60-75% Good !	You have a wide scope to learn for these topics. Revise these topics again.
<60% Not Satisfactory!	You have a long way ahead of you to master these topics. Revise it thoroughly.

Chapter Break Thru

Syllabus • Principles and processes of biotechnology • Genetic engineering (recombinant DNA technology).

Important Instructions

- The test is of 1 hour duration and contains 50 Multiple Choice Questions (Four options with a single correct answer).
- Choose the correct option and fill the OMR given on the last page of this test accordingly.
- At some instances, you may find more than 1 option to be correct. In such circumstances, you have to judge the most appropriate answer as per the conditions given in the question.

1. Which function is performed by restriction endonucleases in molecular biology?

(a) Excise nucleotides from the ends of DNA molecules

(b) Recognise and bind to specific nucleotide sequences for DNA ligase activity

(c) Create a way to allow insertion of foreign DNA within the DNA vector

(d) Inhibit the activity of DNA polymerase

2. Read the following statements about cloning.

I. It is possible only in animals.

II. It is a technique to obtain copies of particular DNA molecule.

III. It results in exact replication of a cell, a living part or an organism.

IV. It results in large number of offsprings.

V. It does not require plasmid.

Choose the correct answer from the options given below.

(a) I, II and IV (b) II, III and V

(c) II, III and IV (d) III, IV and V

3. Which characteristic of plasmids makes them suitable vectors for genetic engineering?

(a) Presence of an antibiotic resistance gene

(b) Ability to integrate with eukaryotic DNA

(c) Capacity to replicate independently at both ends

(d) Capability to transfer between prokaryotic and eukaryotic cells

4. Select the correct match.

A.	Extrachromosomal genetic material	— Bacteria and yeast
B.	Restriction enzymes	— Defence mechanism of virus
C.	First artificial recombinant molecule	— Linus Pauling
D.	Group of cells with identical genotype	— Clone

5. A method uses ……… vectors, when they are allowed to infect the cell and transfer the recombinant DNA into the host.

(a) armed pathogen (b) disarmed pathogen

(c) phage (d) distorted

6. Given below are two statements.

Statement I Plasmids and bacteriophage have the ability to replicate within bacterial cells, which is dependent on the control of chromosomal DNA.

Statement II *ori* is a sequence responsible for controlling the copy number of the plasmid.

In the light of the above statements, choose the correct answer from the options given below.

(a) Statement I is incorrect, but statement II is correct

(b) Both statement I and statement II are correct

(c) Both statement I and statement II are incorrect

(d) Statement I is correct, but statement II is incorrect

7. If you discovered a bacterial cell that contained no restriction enzymes, which of the following would you, expect to happen?

I. Cell would be unable to replicate.
II. Cell would create incomplete plasmids.
III. Cell would easily infected and lysed by bacteriophages.
IV. The cell would become an obligate parasite.
V. The cell would develop resistance to infection.

Choose the correct answer from the options given below.

(a) I, IV and V (b) II and III
(c) Only III (d) Only V

8. Following are the selectable markers for *E. coli*, except

(a) ampicillin resistance genes
(b) tetracycline resistance genes
(c) β-galactosidase gene
(d) T-DNA segment

9. Which of the following characteristic about multiple cloning site is incorrect?

(a) It should have a restriction site for the insertion of the target DNA
(b) It should be small in size
(c) It should have a selectable marker with an antibiotic resistance gene
(d) It should have many copy of the restriction site per enzyme

10. Given below are two statements.

Statement I Phages have plasmid into which foreign DNA molecules can be inserted at several restriction sites.

Statement II When such foreign DNA fragments are introduced into appropriate host cells, such cells are said to be transformed.

In the light of the above statements, choose the correct answer from the options given below.

(a) Statement I is incorrect, but statement II is correct
(b) Both statement I and statement II are correct
(c) Both statement I and statement II are incorrect
(d) Statement I is correct, but statement II is incorrect

11. When a foreign gene is inserted between the gene coding for β-galactosidase, the recombinant cell does not produce the enzyme β-galactosidase due to inactivation of the gene. In the presence of a chromogenic substrate, non-recombinants and recombinants form

(a) colourless and blue colour colonies, respectively
(b) blue colour and dark purple colour colonies, respectively
(c) blue colour and colourless colonies, respectively
(d) Both form blue colour colonies

12. Which of the following statement is correct?

(a) *Agrobacterium tumefaciens*, a pathogen of several monocot plants is able to deliver a piece of DNA known as 'T-DNA'.
(b) The DNA containing retroviruses in animals have the ability to transform normal cells into cancerous cell.
(c) The Tumour inducing (Ti) plasmid of *Agrobacterium tumefaciens* is used as cloning vector in plants.
(d) The disarmed retroviruses that lose pathogenicity are used to deliver desirable genes into animal cells.

13. Provided diagram depicts the gel electrogram. In this electrogram, the thickness of bands provide the information primarily about

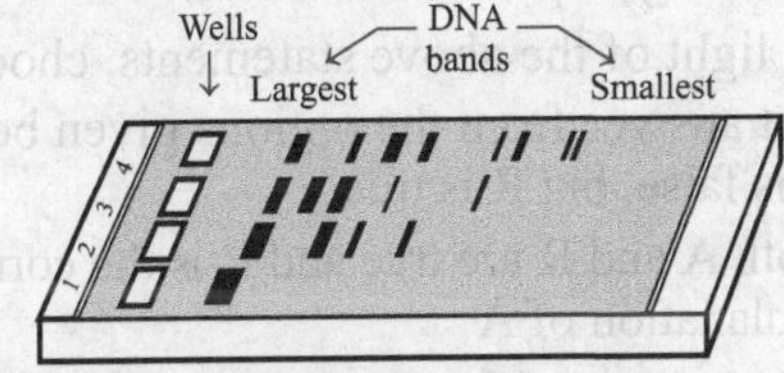

(a) the size of DNA segments
(b) the amount of DNA segments
(c) the nature of H-bonds between the nucleotides of two DNA strands
(d) the mass of DNA segments

14. Which technique is most appropriate for employing the gene gun method?

(a) Transformation of plant cells
(b) DNA fingerprinting
(c) Constructing recombinant DNA molecules
(d) Disarming pathogen vectors

15. A biologist intends to use polymerase chain reaction to perform a genetic task. The biologist probably is trying to
(a) discover new genes
(b) clone a gene
(c) cut DNA into many fragments
(d) isolate DNA from a living cell

16. What does the image most likely represent in the context of isolation of DNA?

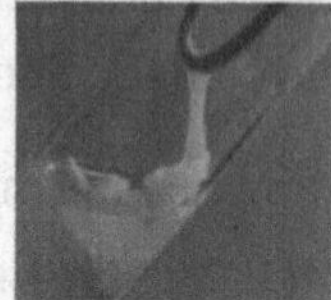

(a) The process of DNA replication
(b) The denaturation of proteins
(c) The precipitation of DNA
(d) The action of restriction enzymes on plasmid DNA

17. Given below are two statements; one is labelled as Assertion (A) and the other is labelled as Reason (R).

Assertion (A) In DNA electrophoresis, under the influence of electric field, DNA moves from anode to cathode.

Reason (R) It happens because of the presence of phosphate group found in DNA.

In the light of the above statements, choose the correct answer from the options given below.
(a) A is false, but R is true
(b) Both A and R are true and R is the correct explanation of A
(c) Both A and R are true, but R is not the correct explanation of A
(d) A is true, but R is false

18. If a recombinant DNA bearing gene for ampicillin resistance is transferred into *E. coli* cells and the host cells are spread on agar plates containing ampicillin, then
(a) Transformed recipient cells will grow and untransformed recipient cells will die
(b) Both transformed and untransformed recipient cells will die
(c) Both transformed and untransformed recipient cells will grow
(d) Transformed recipient cells will die and untransformed recipient cells will grow

19. Given below are two statements; one is labelled as Assertion (A) and the other is labelled as Reason (R).

Assertion (A) Traditional breeding technology to obtain crop of desired characters are not as good as recombinant DNA technology.

Reason (R) Traditional breeding technology very often leads to inclusion and multiplication of undesirable genes along with the desired genes.

In the light of the above statements, choose the correct answer from the options given below.
(a) A is false, but R is true
(b) Both A and R are true and R is the correct explanation of A
(c) Both A and R are correct, but R is not the correct explanation of A
(d) A is true, but R is false

20. Select the incorrect statement regarding PCR.
(a) The exposure of sample DNA to high temperature of about 94°C is aimed to disrupt sugar phosphate backbone of DNA strands.
(b) *Taq* polymerase used for polymerisation process is obtained from bacterium *Thermus aquaticus*.
(c) Each cycle of PCR has 3 steps- denaturation, annealing and extension.
(d) It is routinely being used to detect HIV in suspected AIDS patients.

21. Given below are two statements; one is labelled as Assertion (A) and the other is labelled as Reason (R).

Assertion (A) Recombinant DNA is forced into bacterial cells by incubating the cells with *r*DNA on ice, followed by heat shock.

Reason (R) DNA is hydrophobic molecule.

In the light of the above statements, choose the correct answer from the options given below.
(a) A is false, but R is true
(b) Both A and R are true and R is the correct explanation of A
(c) Both A and R are true, but R is not the correct explanation of A
(d) A is true, but R is false

22. Given below are two statements.

Statement I Among many, the two core techniques that enabled birth of modern biotechnology are genetic engineering and biomechanical engineering.

Statement II Biotechnology involve the genetic manipulation of an organism to get desired products and services.

In the light of the above statements, choose the correct answer from the options given below.

(a) Statement I is incorrect, but statement II is correct

(b) Both statement I and statement II are correct

(c) Both statement I and statement II are incorrect

(d) Statement I is correct, but statement II is incorrect

23. Which of the statement is correct about primers used in PCR?

(a) It is small segment of RNA extracted from host cell.

(b) It is small segment of RNA synthesised chemically.

(c) It is small segment of DNA extracted from *Thermus aquaticus*.

(d) It is small segment of DNA utilised to start elongation of new replica strand.

24. A bacterial cell was transformed with a recombinant DNA molecule that was generated using a human gene. However, the transformed cells did not produce the desired protein. Reasons could be

I. Human gene may have intron, which bacteria cannot process.

II. Amino acid codons for humans and bacteria are different.

III. Human protein is formed, but degraded by bacteria.

IV. Transformed cells produce inactive protein, which cannot be activated by bacteria.

V. Protein synthetic machinery of bacteria failed to cope with human gene.

Choose the correct answer.

(a) III and IV (b) I and IV
(c) II and V (d) Only I

25. Which statement accurately describes the method for visualising DNA molecules separated by agarose gel electrophoresis?

(a) Ethidium bromide stained DNA can be seen in visible light.

(b) DNA can be seen without staining in UV spectrophotometer.

(c) Ethidium bromide stained DNA can be seen under exposure to UV-light.

(d) DNA can be seen in visible spectrophotometer.

26. Match the List I with List II.

List I	List II
A. Cancerous cells	1. Plasmid
B. Selectable marker	2. Retrovirus
C. Chimeric DNA	3. *c*DNA and plasmid
D. Genophore	4. *Lac z*-gene

Choose the correct answer from the options given below.

	A	B	C	D		A	B	C	D
(a)	2	4	3	1	(b)	3	2	4	1
(c)	1	2	3	4	(d)	4	2	3	1

27. Given below are two statements.

Statement I If a recombinant DNA is inserted within the coding sequence of enzyme, β-galactosidase, if results into inactivation of that gene.

Statement II Presence of chromogenic substrate gives blue-coloured colonies, if the plasmid in the bacteria have an insert.

In the light of the above statements, choose the correct answer from the options given below.

(a) Statement I is incorrect, but statement II is correct

(b) Both statement I and statement II are correct

(c) Both statement I and statement II are incorrect

(d) Statement I is correct, but statement II is incorrect

28. Given below are two statements; one is labelled as Assertion (A) and the other is labelled as Reason (R).

Assertion (A) Cellulase is necessary for isolation of DNA from plant cells, but not required in animal cells.

Reason (R) Animal cell does not have cell wall.

In the light of the above statements, choose the correct answer from the options given below.

(a) A is false, but R is true

(b) Both A and R are true and R is the correct explanation of A

(c) Both A and R are true, but R is not the correct explanation of A

(d) A is true, but R is false

29. Select the incorrect match w.r.t. processes of recombinant DNA.

(a) Chitinase - Extracting DNA from fungal cell
(b) Gene of interest - Agarose gel electrophoresis
(c) PCR - Amplification of gene of interest
(d) Bioreactors -Production of foreign gene in large scale

30. Given below are two statements; one is labelled as Assertion (A) and the other is labelled as Reason (R).

Assertion (A) Downstream processing is the name given to the stage after fermentation when the desired product is recovered and purified.

Reason (R) After purification, the product has to be formulated with suitable preservatives.

In the light of the above statements, choose the correct answer from the options given below.

(a) A is false, but R is true
(b) Both A and R are true and R is the correct explanation of A
(c) Both A and R are true, but R is not the correct explanation of A
(d) A is true, but R is false

31. Identify the set of incorrect statements.

I. *Hin*d II always cut DNA molecules at a particular point by recognising a specific sequence of seven base pairs.
II. The convention for naming restriction enzymes that is the first letter of the name comes from the genus and the second two letters come from the species of the source prokaryote.
III. In *Hin*d II, the letter '*H*' is derived from the name of strain.
IV. Each restriction endonuclease recognises a specific palindromic nucleotide sequences in the DNA.
V. Exonucleases are used in genetic engineering to form recombinant molecules of DNA.

Choose the correct answer from the options given below.

(a) II, III, and IV (b) II, IV and V
(c) I, III and V (d) III and IV

32. Which of the following statements incorrectly explains the part of the normal process during the cloning of recombinant DNA in bacteria?

(a) Restriction enzymes are used to cut DNA fragments from cellular and plasmid DNA
(b) A copy of the required gene is inserted into a bacterial plasmid by using DNA ligase
(c) The Southern blotting technique is used to separate the recombinant DNA plasmids
(d) The bacterium is transformed by the recombinant DNA plasmids

33. Select the correct statements.

(a) If any protein encoding gene is expressed in a homologous host, it is called a recombinant protein.
(b) In PCR, the multiple copies of gene of interest is synthesised *in vitro* using one set of primers.
(c) A thermostable enzyme (*Taq* polymerase) is obtained from cyanobacterium, *Thermus aquaticus*.
(d) Restriction endonucleases are composed of DNA from different sources/genomes.

34. Identify the ones from following that are regarded as characteristic features of cloning vectors.

I. Origin of replication II. Selective markers
III. Exonucleases IV. Cloning sites
V. Gel electrophoresis

Choose the correct option.

(a) I, II and III (b) III, IV and V
(c) I, II and IV (d) III and V

35. Which of the following process make the bacterial cells able to take up the recombinant DNA?

(a) Treating them with a specific concentration of a divalent anion
(b) Treating them with a specific concentration of a monovalent cation
(c) By incubating the cells with recombinant DNA on ice, followed by placing them briefly at 42°C, and then putting them back on ice
(d) By incubating the cells with fragment of DNA on ice, followed by placing them briefly at 42°C, and then putting them back on ice

36. Given below are two statements.

Statement I Since DNA is a hydrophilic molecule, it can easily pass through cell membranes.

Statement II Retroviruses have also been disarmed and are used to deliver desirable genes into plant cells.

In the light of the above statements, choose the correct answer from the options given below.
(a) Statement I is incorrect, but statement II is correct
(b) Both statement I and statement II are correct
(c) Both statement I and statement II are incorrect
(d) Statement I is correct, but statement II is incorrect

37. Match the List I with List II.

	List I		List II
A.	Bioreactor	1.	Identification of transformants
B.	Ethidium bromide	2.	Bright orange bands of DNA
C.	Selectable marker	3.	Purification of DNA
D.	Chilled alcohol	4.	Growing microbes on large scale

Choose the correct answer from the options given below.
(a) A-4, B-2, C-3, D-1
(b) A-3, B-4, C-1, D-2
(c) A-4, B-2, C-1, D-3
(d) A-4, B-1, C-2, D-3

38. The construction of the first recombinant DNA emerged from the possibility of linking a gene encoding antibiotic resistance with a native plasmid of 'X' Which of the following option correctly identifies 'X' ?
(a) *Escherichia coli*
(b) *Salmonella typhimurium*
(c) *Agrobacterium tumefaciens*
(d) *Thermus aquaticus*

39. What has initiated the increase in usage of PCR (Polymerase Chain Reaction)?
(a) Easy availability of DNA template
(b) Availability of synthetic primers
(c) Availability of thermostable DNA polymerase
(d) Availability of cheap deoxyribonucleotides

40. The processes that include separation and purification of the recombinant proteins is collectively referred to as
(a) Polymerase chain reaction
(b) Transformation
(c) Gel electrophoresis
(d) Downstream processing

41. Match the List I with List II.

	List I		List II
A.	Restriction enzyme	1.	Ampicillin gene
B.	Sea weeds	2.	Gene of interest
C.	*ori*	3.	Matrix of agarose
D.	*Pst* I	4.	Initiates replication

Choose the correct answer from the options given below
(a) A-2, B-3, C-4, D-1
(b) A-3, B-4, C-1, D-2
(c) A-3, B-1, C-2, D-4
(d) A-1, B-4, C-3, D-2

42. Given below are two statements; one is labelled as Assertion (A) and the other is labelled as Reason (R)

Assertion (A) For isolation of DNA, enzyme DNAase is used.

Reason (R) Purified DNA precipitates out after the addition of chilled ethanol.

In the light of the above statements, choose the correct answer from the options given below.
(a) A is false, but R is true
(b) Both A and R are true and R is the correct explanation of A
(c) Both A and R are true but R is not the correct explanation of A
(d) A is true, but R is false

43. Identify the set of correct statements.
I. In PCR, repeated amplification is achieved by the use of a thermolabile DNA polymerase.
II. The amplified fragment of DNA is used to ligate with a vector for further cloning.
III. Recipient cells after making them 'competent' to receive, take up DNA present in its surrounding.
IV. If a recombinant DNA bearing gene for resistance to an antibiotic is transferred into *E. coli* cells, the host cells become transformed into ampicillin-resistant cells.
V. If the transformed cells are inoculated on agar plates containing ampicillin, only transformants will grow, untransformed recipient cells will die.

Choose the correct answer from the options given below.
(a) I, II, and III
(b) II, III, IV and V
(c) II and III
(d) I, IV and V

44. Match List I with List II.

List I	List II
A. *Thermus aquaticus*	1. Animal cells
B. pBR322	2. Blue coloured colonies
C. β-galactosidase	3. *E. coli*
D. Microinjection	4. Polymerisation

Choose the correct answer from the options given below.

(a) A-3, B-2, C-1, D-4 (b) A-2, B-3, C-1, D-4
(c) A-1, B-3, C-2, D-4 (d) A-4, B-3, C-2, D-1

45. In a continuous culture system, the used medium is drained out from one side, while fresh medium is added from the other to

(a) maintain the pH of the bioreactor
(b) maintain the cells in their physiologically most active phase
(c) maintain the temperature
(d) maintain the buffer

46. The maintenance of contamination-free medium in the engineering process is referred to as

(a) Genetic engineering
(b) Chemical engineering
(c) *r*DNA technology
(d) Biotechnology

47. Choose the incorrect statement.

(a) Transformation is a procedure through which a place of DNA is introduced in a host bacterium.
(b) Normally the genes encoding resistance to antibiotics like ampicillin, chloramphenicol, tetracycline, kanamycin, etc., are considered useful selectable markers for *E. coli*.
(c) The normal *E. coli* cells carry genes resistant against ampicillin, chloramphenicol, tetracycline and kanamycin.
(d) In order to link the alien DNA, the vector needs to have very few, preferably single, recognition site for the commonly used restriction enzymes.

48. *Agrobacterium tumefaciens*

(a) deliver a piece of DNA known as 'T-DNA' to transform normal plant cells into a tumor
(b) has the ability to transform cancerous cells into normal cells
(c) is disarmed and used to deliver desirable genes into animal cells
(d) causes tumour in monocot plants

49. Stirred-tank bioreactors have been designed for

(a) purification of the desired product
(b) availability of oxygen throughout the process
(c) addition of preservatives and enzymes to the product
(d) ensuring anaerobic conditions in the culture vessel

50. In a method, suitable for plants, cells are bombarded with high velocity micro-particles of gold or tungsten coated with DNA in a method known as

(a) microinjection
(b) biolistics or gene gun
(c) electroporation
(d) transformation

Scan for online chapter test

Response Index

01 ⓐ ⓑ ⓒ ⓓ	14 ⓐ ⓑ ⓒ ⓓ	27 ⓐ ⓑ ⓒ ⓓ	40 ⓐ ⓑ ⓒ ⓓ
02 ⓐ ⓑ ⓒ ⓓ	15 ⓐ ⓑ ⓒ ⓓ	28 ⓐ ⓑ ⓒ ⓓ	41 ⓐ ⓑ ⓒ ⓓ
03 ⓐ ⓑ ⓒ ⓓ	16 ⓐ ⓑ ⓒ ⓓ	29 ⓐ ⓑ ⓒ ⓓ	42 ⓐ ⓑ ⓒ ⓓ
04 ⓐ ⓑ ⓒ ⓓ	17 ⓐ ⓑ ⓒ ⓓ	30 ⓐ ⓑ ⓒ ⓓ	43 ⓐ ⓑ ⓒ ⓓ
05 ⓐ ⓑ ⓒ ⓓ	18 ⓐ ⓑ ⓒ ⓓ	31 ⓐ ⓑ ⓒ ⓓ	44 ⓐ ⓑ ⓒ ⓓ
06 ⓐ ⓑ ⓒ ⓓ	19 ⓐ ⓑ ⓒ ⓓ	32 ⓐ ⓑ ⓒ ⓓ	45 ⓐ ⓑ ⓒ ⓓ
07 ⓐ ⓑ ⓒ ⓓ	20 ⓐ ⓑ ⓒ ⓓ	33 ⓐ ⓑ ⓒ ⓓ	46 ⓐ ⓑ ⓒ ⓓ
08 ⓐ ⓑ ⓒ ⓓ	21 ⓐ ⓑ ⓒ ⓓ	34 ⓐ ⓑ ⓒ ⓓ	47 ⓐ ⓑ ⓒ ⓓ
09 ⓐ ⓑ ⓒ ⓓ	22 ⓐ ⓑ ⓒ ⓓ	35 ⓐ ⓑ ⓒ ⓓ	48 ⓐ ⓑ ⓒ ⓓ
10 ⓐ ⓑ ⓒ ⓓ	23 ⓐ ⓑ ⓒ ⓓ	36 ⓐ ⓑ ⓒ ⓓ	49 ⓐ ⓑ ⓒ ⓓ
11 ⓐ ⓑ ⓒ ⓓ	24 ⓐ ⓑ ⓒ ⓓ	37 ⓐ ⓑ ⓒ ⓓ	50 ⓐ ⓑ ⓒ ⓓ
12 ⓐ ⓑ ⓒ ⓓ	25 ⓐ ⓑ ⓒ ⓓ	38 ⓐ ⓑ ⓒ ⓓ	
13 ⓐ ⓑ ⓒ ⓓ	26 ⓐ ⓑ ⓒ ⓓ	39 ⓐ ⓑ ⓒ ⓓ	

Performance Scanner

> 90% Excellent !	You have mastered this chapter. The concepts of this chapter are at your fingertips. Move on to the next chapter and maintain this momentum.
76-90% Very Good !	You have a good command over this chapter. Revise the chapter again after a few days and enhance your performance.
60-75% Good !	You have a wide scope to learn for this chapter. Revise this chapter again.
<60% Not Satisfactory!	You have a long way ahead of you to master this chapter. Revise it thoroughly.

Test Booklet No. **3947360**

Test Booklet Code **CH10**

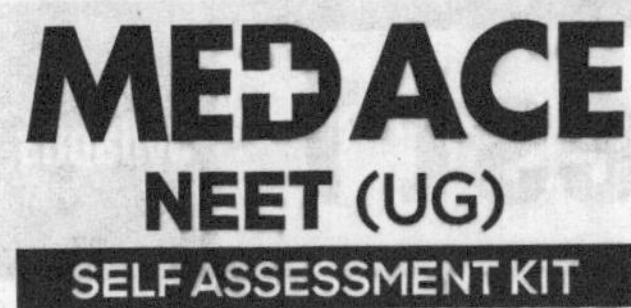

Biotechnology and Its Applications

Topics Covered

Application of Biotechnology in Agriculture

Application of Biotechnology in Medicine

Transgenic Animals and Ethical Issues

Important Instructions

- This Booklet Contains – Three Topic Tests and One Test on Complete Chapter.
- Each question carries 4 marks.
- For each correct response, the candidate will get 4 marks. And for every incorrect response, 1 mark will be additionally deducted from total score.
- Use **Blue/Black** point pen only for filling the OMR.
- Rough work is to be done in the space provided for this purpose in the test booklet only.

Name of the Candidate (In Capitals) ____________

Candidate's Signature ____________

Invigilator's Signature ____________

Facsimile signature stamp of center superintendent____________

Do not open this booklet until you start attempting the test

Topical Follow Thru

Test 1

Syllabus
- Application of biotechnology in agriculture
- Genetically modified organisms, *Bt* crop

For deeper insight, **Scan the QR Code** 

Important Instructions
- The test is of 30 minutes duration and contains 15 Multiple Choice Questions (four options with a single correct answer).
- Choose the correct option and fill the OMR given on the last page of this test accordingly.
- At some instances, you may find more than 1 option to be correct. In such circumstances, you have to judge the most appropriate answer as per the conditions given in the question.

1. Which of the following factors are responsible for the limited success of green revolution in developing countries?
(a) Expensive agrochemicals and harmful effect on environment
(b) Improved crop variety and irrigation
(c) Improved mechanisation and high yielding varieties
(d) Better pesticides and soil conservation technique

2. Given below are two statements.
Statement I Whole plants could be regenerated from explants, i.e., any part of a plant taken out could be grown in a test tube, under sterile conditions in special nutrient media.
Statement II The capacity to generate a whole plant from any cell/explant is called regeneration.
In the light of above statements, choose the correct answer from the options given below.
(a) Statement I is incorrect, but statement II is correct.
(b) Both statement I and statement II are correct.
(c) Both statement I and statement II are incorrect.
(d) Statement I is correct, but statement II is incorrect.

3. Which of the following is the best possible way to increase yield in developing countries?
(a) Use agrochemicals which increase yield at low cost
(b) Use of organic farming which improves yield
(c) Use of conventional breeding program as it is cost efficient
(d) Use of genetically modified crops which minimise the dependency on agrochemicals

4. The critical research areas of biotechnology are all, except
(a) providing the best catalyst in the form of improved organism or pure enzyme
(b) creating suitable environment for chemical reaction in space
(c) creating optimum conditions through engineering for a catalyst to perform its action
(d) enhancing downstream processing methods to purify the organic compounds

5. Select the incorrect match.

	GMOs	Transferred genes
(a)	Golden rice	β – carotene
(b)	*Flavr Savr* tomato	Polygalacturonase
(c)	Cotton bollworm	*cry* IAc
(d)	Tobacco	Nematode specific gene

6. Which of the following is incorrect about the significance of Genetically Modified Crops (GMOs)?
(a) Increased efficiency of mineral usage by plants
(b) Increased exhaustion of soil fertility
(c) Reduced post-harvest loss
(d) Enhanced nutritional value of food

7. A protoxin released by *Bacillus thuringiensis* becomes activated inside the gut of target insects. Which characteristic best describes this protoxin?
(a) A toxin requiring high pH for activation
(b) An enzymatically activated toxin
(c) A structurally immature toxin
(d) A toxin dependent on insect gut proteases

8. Match the List I with List II.

	List I		List II
A.	First commercial genetically engineered food	1.	RNAi
B.	Nematode resistant plants	2.	Insecticidal protein
C.	*Bt* cotton	3.	Antisense technology
D.	Pomato	4.	Somatic hybridisation

Choose the correct answer from the options given below.

	A	B	C	D		A	B	C	D
(a)	3	1	2	4	(b)	4	1	3	2
(c)	4	3	2	1	(d)	3	4	1	2

9. Application of *Bacillus thuringiensis* in agriculture could help with all of the following, except
(a) protection of the environment
(b) protection of biodiversity
(c) increase in productivity
(d) decrease in dependency on herbicides

10. The consumption of which one of the following foods can prevent the blindness in human suffering from vitamin-A deficiency?
(a) Golden rice
(b) Transgenic *Brassica napus*
(c) *Flavr Savr* tomato
(d) *Bt* soyabean

11. Which of the following statement is true about *Bt* toxin?
(a) Crystalline protein released by an unicellular eukaryote
(b) Crystalline protein that does not kill its own producing organism
(c) Intracellular neurotoxin activated in high pH
(d) Extracellular enzyme activated in low pH

12. Read the following statements carefully.
I. *cry IAb* gene controls both corn borer and cotton bollworm.
II. Nematode-specific genes were introduced into the host plant using *E. coli* vector.
III. RNAi technology is used in tobacco plant to get rid of a nematode, *Meloidegyne incognita*.
IV. Virus free plants can be obtained from both apical and axillary meristem.
V. The mechanism of RNAi started in eukaryotic cells when a single-stranded RNA is introduced either naturally or artificially in a cell.

Choose the correct answer from the options given below.
(a) Statements I, II and III are correct.
(b) Statements I and V are correct.
(c) Statements I, II and V are incorrect.
(d) Statements II, III and IV are correct.

13. Given below are two statements; one is labelled as Assertion (A) and other is labelled as Reason (R).

Assertion (A) Due to the speedy use of transgenic crops, the effectiveness of insecticidal proteins from *Bacillus thuringiensis* might be reduced.

Reason (R) Evolution of resistance in pests can reduce the effectiveness of insecticidal proteins.

In the light of the above statements, choose the correct answer from the options given below.
(a) A is false, but R true.
(b) Both A and R are true and R is the correct explanation of A.
(c) Both A and R are true, but R is not the correct explanation of A.
(d) A is true, but R is false.

14. Given below are two statements; one is labelled as Assertion (A) and the other is labelled as Reason (R).

Assertion (A) RNA interference (RNAi) takes place in all eukaryotic organisms as a method of cellular defence.

Reason (R) RNAi method involves silencing of a specific *m*RNA due to a complementary single stranded RNA molecule that binds to and prevents translation of the *m*RNA (silencing).

In the light of the above statements, choose the correct answer from the options given below.

(a) A is false, but R is true.

(b) Both A and R are true and R is the correct explanation of A.

(c) Both A and R are true, but R is not the correct explanation of A.

(d) A is true, but R is false.

15. Which of the following is not correct w.r.t. *Bacillus thuringiensis*?

(a) *B. thuringiensis* forms protein crystals during a particular phase of their growth.

(b) The *Bt* toxin protein exists as inactive protoxins, but once an insect ingests the inactive toxin, it is converted into an active form.

(c) The alkaline pH of the gut denatures the crystals, so the proteins become active.

(d) The activated proteins create pores in the midgut epithelial cells of gut lining that cause cell swelling and lysis and eventually cause death of the insect.

Response Index

01	a	b	c	d	10	a	b	c	d	19	a	b	c	d
02	a	b	c	d	11	a	b	c	d	20	a	b	c	d
03	a	b	c	d	12	a	b	c	d	21	a	b	c	d
04	a	b	c	d	13	a	b	c	d	22	a	b	c	d
05	a	b	c	d	14	a	b	c	d	23	a	b	c	d
06	a	b	c	d	15	a	b	c	d	24	a	b	c	d
07	a	b	c	d	16	a	b	c	d	25	a	b	c	d
08	a	b	c	d	17	a	b	c	d					
09	a	b	c	d	18	a	b	c	d					

Performance Scanner

> 90% Excellent !	You have mastered these topics. The concepts of these topics are at your fingertips. Move on to the next test and maintain this momentum.
76-90% Very Good !	You have a good command over these topics. Revise these topics again after a few days and enhance your performance.
60-75% Good !	You have a wide scope to learn for these topics. Revise these topics again.
<60% Not Satisfactory!	You have a long way ahead of you to master these topics. Revise it thoroughly.

Test 2

Syllabus

- Application of biotechnology in health
- Human insulin
- Vaccine production
- Gene therapy

For deeper insight, Scan the QR Code 

Important Instructions

- The test is of 30 minutes duration and contains 15 Multiple Choice Questions (four options with a single correct answer).
- Choose the correct option and fill the OMR given on the last page of this test accordingly.
- At some instances, you may find more than 1 option to be correct. In such circumstances, you have to judge the most appropriate answer as per the conditions given in the question.

1. Why do recombinant therapeutics not induce unwanted immunological responses as is common in case of similar products isolated from non-human sources?

(a) Recombinant therapeutics are usually administered with immune-suppressing drugs.

(b) Recombinant therapeutics are synthesised using human genes.

(c) Recombinant therapeutics have a special coating that makes them invisible to the immune system.

(d) Recombinant therapeutics are smaller in size compared to similar products isolated from non-human sources.

2. Why insulin cannot be introduced orally?

(a) Will not absorbed in blood

(b) Salivary amylase will digest it

(c) Acidic pH of stomach will denature it

(d) It will be digested by pancreatic enzymes

3. Given below are two statements; one is labelled as Assertion (A) and the other is labelled as Reason (R).

Assertion (A) When genes are altered, the encoded proteins are unable to carry out their normal functions resulting into genetic disorder.

Reason (R) An abnormal gene could be swapped for a normal gene through gene therapy.

In the light of the above statements, choose the correct answer from the options given below.

(a) A is false, but R is true.

(b) Both A and R are true and the R is the correct explanation of A.

(c) Both A and R are true, but the R is not the correct explanation of A.

(d) A is true, but R is false.

4. Prior to the production of insulin by using recombinant DNA technology, insulin was obtained from cows and pigs and was given to patients. One of the problems faced by this treatment was that

(a) there was a loss of functional pancreatic cells

(b) in some humans, it induced antibody production

(c) it reduced the weight of patients

(d) it caused the loss of memory power

5. Which of the following statement is incorrect with respect to gene therapy?

(a) It provides the scope to cure incurable diseases.

(b) A normal gene is inserted into the genome to replace an abnormal gene.

(c) Hematopoietic stem cells are ideal target for gene transfer due to the high potential for longevity.

(d) Gene therapy at childhood stage is much more successful than at embryonic stage.

6. Which of the following statement best describes the biochemical process illustrated in the diagram?

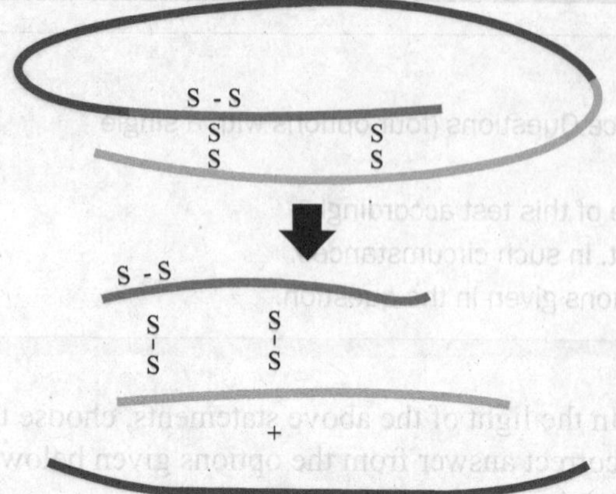

(a) The diagram depicts the process of protein folding, with disulfide bonds causing the protein to fold into its functional structure.
(b) The diagram illustrates the conversion of proinsulin into insulin and free A-peptide chain, with disulfide bonds being formed between chains B and C.
(c) The diagram illustrates the conversion of proinsulin into insulin and free C-peptide chain, with disulfide bonds being formed between chains A and B.
(d) The diagram illustrates the conversion of proinsulin into insulin and free B-peptide chain, with disulfide bonds being formed between chains A and C.

7. Which treatment method offers a permanent cure for the genetic defect known as Adenosine Deaminase (ADA) deficiency?
(a) Administering adenosine deaminase activators
(b) Enzyme replacement therapy
(c) Introducing bone marrow cells producing ADA into cells at early embryonic stages
(d) Periodic infusion of genetically engineered lymphocytes having functional ADA *c*DNA

8. Which gene does not appear in photographic film in autoradiography?
(a) Supplementary gene
(b) Polymeric gene
(c) Mutated genes
(d) Transcriptionally active gene

9. Given below are two statements.
Statement I ADA is an enzyme which is crucial for functioning of immune system.
Statement II The site of production of Adenosine Deaminase (ADA) in the body is primarily the erythrocyte.
In the light of the above statements, choose the correct answer from the options given below.
(a) Statement I is incorrect, but statement II is correct.
(b) Both statement I and statement II are correct.
(c) Both statement I and statement II are incorrect.
(d) Statement I is correct, but statement II is incorrect.

10. Read the following statements about insulin production and identify the correct ones.
I. Insulin is synthesised as a pro-hormone in mammals, including humans.
II. The C-peptide is present in mature insulin.
III. Bacteria are used to make human insulin.
IV. Eli Lilly prepared two DNA sequences corresponding to A and B chains of human insulin and introduced them in plasmids of *E. coli*.
V. Chains A and B were produced together, not separately.
Choose the correct set of statements from the options given below.
(a) I, III and IV (b) I, II and V
(c) II, III and V (d) III, IV and V

11. The Adenosine Deaminase deficiency occurs due to
(a) mutation of adenine nucleotide of adenosine deaminase
(b) deletion of adenosine deaminase gene
(c) duplication of adenosine deaminase gene
(d) mutation in poly-A sequence of adenosine deaminase gene

12. Select the incorrect statement from the following.
(a) PCR helps to detect very low concentration of pathogen at the time when the symptoms of the disease are clearly visible.
(b) PCR is used to detect HIV in suspected AIDS patient.

(c) PCR is used to detect mutations in genes.
(d) PCR is valuable in DNA fingerprinting and diagnosis of genetic disorders.

13. Match List I with List II.

List I	List II
A. PCR	1. Antigen-antibody interactions
B. ELISA	2. Detection of radioactive isotope
C. Autoradiography	3. *ss*DNA/RNA with radioactive molecule
D. Probe	4. Amplification of pathogenic DNA

Choose the correct answer from the options given below.

	A	B	C	D		A	B	C	D
(a)	2	1	4	3	(b)	3	4	2	1
(c)	4	1	2	3	(d)	4	2	3	1

14. Given below are two statements; one is labelled as Assertion (A) and the other is labelled as Reason (R).

Assertion (A) Molecular diagnosis, which includes *r*DNA technology, PCR and ELISA is better than conventional methods of diagnosis such as serum and urine analysis.

Reason (R) Serum and urine analysis are some of the techniques that serve the purpose of early diagnosis.

In the light of the above statements, choose the correct answer from the options given below.
(a) A is false, but R is true.
(b) Both A and R are true and R is the correct explanation of A.
(c) Both A and R are true, but R is not the correct explanation of A.
(d) A is true, but R is false.

15. Identify the correct statement w.r.t. molecular diagnosis.
(a) Full form of ELISA is Enzyme Linked Immuno-Solvent Assay
(b) PCR is used to detect infectious diseases only e.g. AIDS
(c) The first clinical gene therapy was given in 1980 to a 4-year old girl with adenosine deaminase (ADA) deficiency.
(d) In autoradiography technique, a single-stranded DNA or RNA, tagged with a radioactive molecule (probe) is used

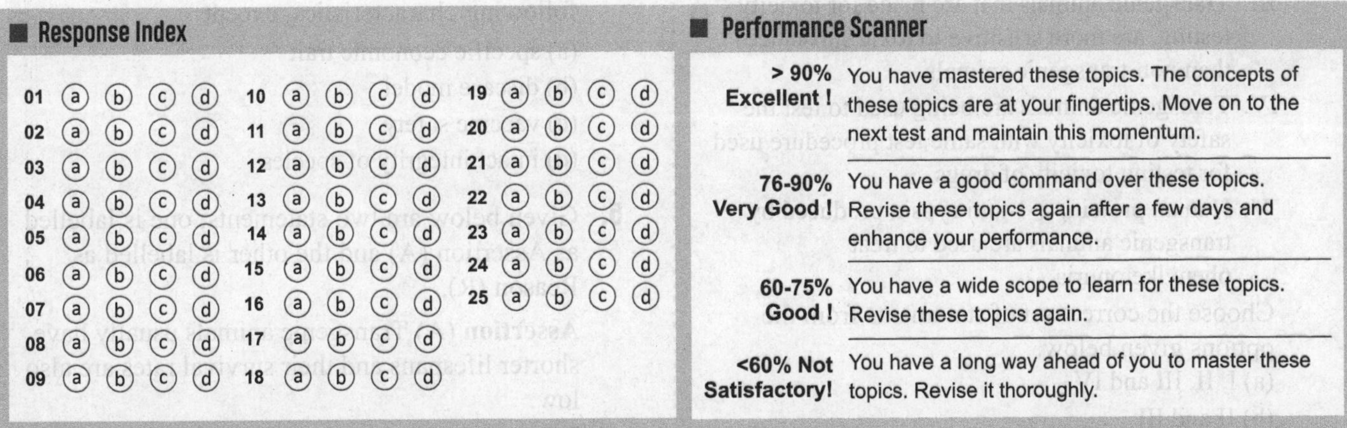

Test 3

Syllabus • Transgenic animals • Biosafety issues-biopiracy and patent.

For deeper insight, **Scan the QR Code**

Important Instructions

- The test is of 30 minutes duration and contains 15 Multiple Choice Questions (four options with a single correct answer).
- Choose the correct option and fill the OMR given on the last page of this test accordingly.
- At some instances, you may find more than 1 option to be correct. In such circumstances, you have to judge the most appropriate answer as per the conditions given in the question.

1. Genetically Modified Organisms (GMOs) are used for a variety of purposes, except

(a) for the study of complex factors involved in growth

(b) to know how genes contribute to the development of disease

(c) to produce better medical instruments

(d) for vaccine safety testing

2. Read the following statements.

I. Transgenic animals are used to the study of how genes are regulated and expressed.

II. Today transgenic models exist for many human diseases such as cancer, cystic fibrosis, rheumatoid arthritis and Alzheimer's.

III. Transgenic animals that are made for toxicity testing, are more sensitive to toxic substances than non-transgenic animals.

IV. Transgenic animals are being used to test the safety of toxicity with same test procedure used for testing toxicity of drugs.

V. Human protein, α-1-antitrypsin produced by transgenic animals are used to treat phenylketonuria.

Choose the correct set of statements from the options given below.

(a) I, II, III and IV

(b) II and III

(c) III, IV and V

(d) IV and V

3. Which of the following statement is not correct?

(a) First transgenic cow, Rosie came into existence in the year 1997.

(b) Rosie produced human protein-enriched milk, about 2.4 grams per litre.

(c) The milk produced by Rosie contained the human alpha-lactalbumin and was nutritionally a lesser balanced product for humans than natural cow-milk.

(d) Transgenic animals that produce useful biological products can be created by the introduction of the gene which codes for a particular product.

4. Animals that have had their DNA manipulated to possess and express an extra gene, have all the following characteristics, except

(a) specific economic trait

(b) disease model

(c) vaccine safety

(d) intact integrity of species

5. Given below are two statements; one is labelled as Assertion (A) and the other is labelled as Reason (R).

Assertion (A) Transgenic animals usually have shorter lifespans and their survival rates are also low.

Reason (R) During the production of transgenic animals, genetic mutation can occur which can end in disease and disorder.

In the light of the above statements, choose the correct answer from the options given below.
(a) A is false, but R is true.
(b) Both A and R are true and R is the correct explanation of A.
(c) Both A and R are true, but R is not the correct explanation of A.
(d) A is true, but R is false.

6. Given below are two statements; one is labelled as Assertion (A) and the other is labelled as Reason (R).

Assertion (A) Toxicity testing can be easily done in transgenic animals.

Reason (R) Transgenic animals are more resistant to toxic substances than non-transgenic animals.

In the light of the above statements, choose the correct answer from the options given below.
(a) A is false, but R is true.
(b) Both A and R are true and R is the correct explanation of A.
(c) Both A and R are true, but R is not the correct explanation of A.
(d) A is true, but R is false.

7. Given below are two statements.

Statement I Bioethics is the branch of ethics, philosophy and social commentary that deals with the biological sciences and their potential impact on society.

Statement II Introduction of a transgene from one species into another species goes against the integrity of species.

In the light of the above statements, choose the correct answer from the options given below.
(a) Statement I is incorrect, but statement II is correct.
(b) Both statement I and statement II are correct.
(c) Both statement I and statement II are incorrect.
(d) Statement I is correct, but statement II is incorrect.

8. Which of the following is correct regarding GEAC?
(a) GEAC is a private sector organisation.
(b) The full form of GEAC is Genetic Engineering Approval Council.
(c) It make decisions regarding the validity of Genetic Modification (GM) research.
(d) It concerns about the pricing of GMO introduced in public service.

9. Which of the following statement is incorrect?
(a) The US government has patented the Indian basmati rice as Rice Tech Inc.
(b) Biopatent system does not permit private monopoly rights over cells, genes, animals and plants.
(c) The important advantage of biopatents is that they are a direct incentive for genetic engineering.
(d) The arguments in favour of biopatents are primarily to increase economic growth.

10. Transgenic animals are those which have
(a) foreign DNA in some of its cells
(b) foreign DNA in all its cells
(c) foreign RNA in all its cells
(d) DNA and RNA both in the cells

11. Which of the following statements is not the major bioethical concern about biotechnology?
(a) Production of transgenic animals may lead to the origin of such species that are dangerous for humanity.
(b) It causes great suffering to the GMOs.
(c) Transfer of human genes into animals dilutes the concept of humanness.
(d) Biotechnology may pose unforeseen risks to the environment.

12. Match the List I with List II.

List I	List II
A. Bioethics	1. Unauthorised exploitation of bio-resources
B. Biopiracy	2. Ethical issues related to biology
C. Patent	3. Exclusive rights over an invention
D. Bio-resources	4. Biological materials used commercially

Choose the correct answer from the options given below.

	A	B	C	D		A	B	C	D
(a)	2	1	3	4	(b)	4	1	3	2
(c)	3	4	2	1	(d)	1	2	3	4

13. The use of bioresources by multinational companies and other organisations without proper authorisation from the countries and people concerned without compensatory payment is called

(a) bioethics (b) biopiracy

(c) bioterror (d) bioweapon

14. In 1997, an American company obtained patent rights on a 'new' variety of Basmati rice. Which of the following statements about this event is correct?

(a) The 'new' variety of Basmati was entirely developed by the American company without any external influence.

(b) The patent rights allowed the company to sell the 'new' variety of Basmati only within the United States.

(c) The 'new' variety of Basmati was derived by crossing Indian Basmati with semi-dwarf varieties and was claimed as an invention.

(d) The patent rights were granted by the Indian Patent Office.

15. The Indian Parliament has recently cleared the second amendment of the Indian Patents Bill (IPB), that takes following issues into consideration, except

(a) patent terms

(b) emergency provisions

(c) research and development initiative

(d) a method of agriculture

Response Index

01	a	b	c	d	10	a	b	c	d	19	a	b	c	d
02	a	b	c	d	11	a	b	c	d	20	a	b	c	d
03	a	b	c	d	12	a	b	c	d	21	a	b	c	d
04	a	b	c	d	13	a	b	c	d	22	a	b	c	d
05	a	b	c	d	14	a	b	c	d	23	a	b	c	d
06	a	b	c	d	15	a	b	c	d	24	a	b	c	d
07	a	b	c	d	16	a	b	c	d	25	a	b	c	d
08	a	b	c	d	17	a	b	c	d					
09	a	b	c	d	18	a	b	c	d					

Performance Scanner

> 90% Excellent !	You have mastered these topics. The concepts of these topics are at your fingertips. Move on to the next test and maintain this momentum.
76-90% Very Good !	You have a good command over these topics. Revise these topics again after a few days and enhance your performance.
60-75% Good !	You have a wide scope to learn for these topics. Revise these topics again.
<60% Not Satisfactory!	You have a long way ahead of you to master these topics. Revise it thoroughly.

Chapter Break Thru

Syllabus	• Application of biotechnology in health and agriculture: human insulin and vaccine production, gene therapy	• Genetically modified organisms-*Bt* crops	• Transgenic animals • Biosafety issues-biopiracy and patent

Important Instructions

- The test is of 1 hour duration and contains 30 Multiple-Choice Questions (Four options with a single correct answer).
- Choose the correct option and fill the OMR given on the last page of this test accordingly.
- At some instances, you may find more than 1 option to be correct. In such circumstances, you have to judge the most appropriate answer as per the conditions given in the question.

1. The pollen grains of *Bt* cotton caused

(a) allergic reaction in humans
(b) high mortality rates in bollworms
(c) low reproductive rates in certain dipterans
(d) high migratory rates in bollworms

2. Given below are two statements.

Statement I Vitamin-A deficiency is prevalent in countries with populations that are dependent on rice or other micronutrient-poor carbohydrate foods.

Statement II Vitamin-A deficiency can be overcome by the use of golden maize.

In the light of the above statements, choose the correct answer from the options given below.

(a) Statement I is incorrect, but statement II is correct.
(b) Both statement I and statement II are correct.
(c) Both statement I and statement II are incorrect.
(d) Statement I is correct, but statement II is incorrect.

3. Given below are two statements; one is labelled as Assertion (A) and the other is labelled as Reason (R).

Assertion (A) In agricultural biotechnology, changes are made directly to the plant's genome. Once the gene that determines a desirable trait is identified, it can be selected, extracted and transferred directly into another plant genome.

Reason (R) For the transformation of gene into plants, Ti-plasmid based vector and plant viral based vector are commonly used.

In the light of the above statements, choose the correct answer from the options given below.

(a) A is false, but R is true.
(b) Both A and R are true and R is the correct explanation of A.
(c) Both A and R are true, but R is not the correct explanation of A.
(d) A is true, but R is false.

4. Which of the following statements are correct regarding the process of RNA interference?

I. This is used to prevent the infestation of nematodes in tobacco.
II. It takes place in some eukaryotic and all prokaryotic organisms as a method of cellular defence.
III. The method involves silencing of a specific *m*RNA due to complementary *ds*RNA molecules.
IV. It is novel strategy to produce pest resistant plants.

Choose the correct answer from the options given below.

(a) I, III and IV
(b) I and III
(c) I, II and III
(d) II and III

5. The selection of a *Bt*-gene for an experiment depends on which of the following factors?

I. The host plant/crop
II. The targeted pest/insect
III. The *Bacillus* strain
IV. The environmental condition
V. The passenger DNA

Choose the correct set of answer.

(a) I, II and III (b) I and II
(c) II and III (d) IV and V

6. Which of the following statement is incorrect?

(a) The nematode-specific genes were injected into the host plant and these genes produced both sense and antisense RNA.
(b) RNAi involves silencing of a specific mRNA due to a complementary *ds*RNA.
(c) The source of the complementary RNA in host cell could be from an infection by viruses having RNA genomes.
(d) As a result of gene silencing due to double stranded DNA, both the parasite and the transgenic plants could not survive.

7. Following diagram depicts a disease in related to ......A...... family and is caused by ......B...... .

(a) *A*–Poaceae , *B*–Flies
(b) *A*–Fabaceae, *B*–Beetle
(c) *A*–Malvaceae, *B*–Bollworm
(d) *A*–Brassicaceae, *B*–*Albugo*

8. Which of the following statement is correct for insulin production?

(a) C-peptide chain of insulin is not produced by *r*DNA technology.
(b) The technique of insulin production was developed by Calgene company.
(c) Chains A and B were combined by creating hydrogen bonds to form human insulin.
(d) Chains A, B and C are part of mature human insulin.

9. In the context of the genetic disorder SCID, which enzyme deficiency disrupts the purine metabolism pathway?

(a) Arginine decarboxylase
(b) Adenosine deaminase
(c) Aspartate aminotransferase
(d) Adenosine deoxyaminase

10. Which statement is correct about the given diagram?

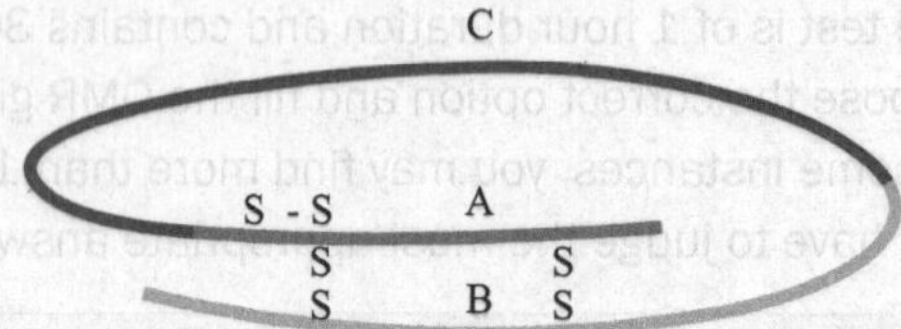

(a) The diagram depicts the mature insulin developed inside the transgenic bacteria.
(b) The C-peptide is responsible for formation of disulphide bond between chains A and B and is present in mature insulin.
(c) C-peptide is removed during maturation of pro-insulin to insulin.
(d) C-peptide is responsible for its biological activity, however removed during the process of maturation.

11. Enzyme Linked Immuno Sorbent Assay (ELISA) is carried out to detect and measure

(a) antibodies, carbohydrates and fats in the blood
(b) antibodies, hormones, peptides and proteins in the blood
(c) nucleic acid, carbohydrates and peptides in the urine
(d) antibodies, hormones, peptides in the urine

12. Proinsulin is made in bacteria and it is processed chemically out of bacteria because

(a) bacterial cell will burst due to hypertonic condition
(b) bacterial cell cannot perform post-translational modification
(c) bacterial cell is a prokaryotic organism
(d) processed insulin is very reactive, harmful to the bacterial cell

13. A probe, used to identify homologous sequences within a mixture of DNA or RNA molecules, could be

(a) a single-stranded RNA (*ss*RNA) only, because it pairs with DNA
(b) a single-stranded DNA (*ss*DNA) only, due to its stability
(c) either single-stranded RNA (*ss*RNA) or single-stranded DNA (*ss*DNA), as both can hybridise with complementary sequences
(d) can be single-stranded DNA (*ss*DNA), but not single-stranded RNA (*ss*RNA), since RNA is too unstable

14. The first step of gene therapy for ADA deficiency would be
(a) the culture of the lymphocytes from patient's blood, outside the body
(b) the use of vector for transmitting gene
(c) preparation of *c*DNA
(d) insertion of *c*DNA directly into the cells

15. Transgenic animals are specially made to serve as models for human diseases so that investigation of new treatments for diseases is made possible. The transgenic models exist for many human diseases such as
(a) Covid -19, cancer and arthritis
(b) Giardiasis, diphtheria and cancer
(c) Cancer, cystic fibrosis and rheumatoid arthritis
(d) Allergies, asthma, bipolar disorder

16. Which of the following statement is incorrect?
(a) Attempts have been done on transgenic animals to produce biological products to treat cystic fibrosis
(b) Emphysema can be treated by inhaling an aerosol spray containg α-1 Antitrypsin (AAT).
(c) The milk produced by the first transgenic cow contained human alpha-lactalbumin.
(d) Tracy was the first transgenic cow.

17. Which of the following statement is incorrect?
(a) The *Bt* toxins are thousands of times more powerful than the chemical insecticides.
(b) The transgene products may cause toxicity and produce allergies.
(c) Virus free plants can be obtained by culturing pollen grain of the infected plants, as gametes are free from viral infection
(d) The Ti-plasmid of *Agrobacterium* transfers a specific DNA segment called T-DNA into the plant genome

18. Attempts have been made to patent Indian plants by Western nations for their use. These plants are
I. Neem
II. Mango
III. Wheat
IV. Rice
V. Turmeric
Select the correct answer.
(a) I, II and IV
(b) I, IV and V
(c) III and IV
(d) I, II, III, IV and V

19. Nematode resistant tobacco plants have been developed through the introduction of DNA, which produces
(a) *m*RNA
(b) Both sense and antisense RNAs
(c) a particular hormone
(d) toxic protein

20. Given below are two statements.
Statement I Transgenes *cry*IAc and *cry*IIAb control the cotton bollworms in cotton plants.
Statement II Transgenes *cry*IAc and *cry*IAb control the corn borer in cotton plants.
In the light of the above statements, choose the correct answer from the options given below.
(a) Statement I is incorrect, but statement II is correct.
(b) Both statement I and statement II are correct.
(c) Both statement I and statement II are incorrect.
(d) Statement I is correct, but statement II is incorrect.

21. Some of the characteristics of *Bt* cotton are given below. Select the correct one.
(a) Long fibre and resistance to aphids
(b) Medium yield, long fibres and resistance to beetle pests

(c) High yield and production of toxic protein crystals which kill dipteran pests
(d) High yield and resistant to bollworms

22. Match List I with List II.

List I	List II
A. Golden rice	1. Enhanced nutritional value
B. *Flavr Savr* tomato	2. Kills lepidopterans
C. *Bt* cotton	3. Improved shelf life
D. RNAi	4. Novel strategy

Choose the correct answer from the options given below.

	A	B	C	D		A	B	C	D
(a)	1	3	2	4	(b)	1	3	4	2
(c)	2	4	1	3	(d)	3	1	4	2

23. Given below are two statements; one is labelled as Assertion (A) and the other is labelled as Reason (R).

Assertion (A) RNAi is used to inhibit the expression of the targeted gene.

Reason (R) RNAi can be initiated by a cell in response to pathogenic nucleic acids to bring about targeted degradation of genetic transcripts.

In the light of the above statements, choose the correct answer from the options given below.
(a) A is false, but R is true.
(b) Both A and R are true and R is the correct explanation of A.
(c) Both A and R are true, but R is not the correct explanation of A.
(d) A is true, but R is false.

24. Which of the following is not true regarding ADA deficiency?
(a) The first clinical gene therapy was given in 1990 to a 4-year old girl with Adenosine Deaminase (ADA) deficiency.
(b) ADA is an important coenzyme, which is crucial for the immune system to function.
(c) In some children, ADA deficiency can be cured by bone marrow transplantation, which is not completely curative.
(d) Retroviral vector is used to introduce a functional ADA *c*DNA into lymphocytes of patient.

25. Read the following statements.
I. Conventional method of diagnosis is not as good as molecular method as far as early detection of disease is concerned.
II. ELISA is an example of conventional diagnosis.
III. Molecular methods like PCR provide more accurate and quicker results.
IV. ELISA cannot detect diseases at a very early stage.
V. PCR can detect diseases even before symptoms appear.

Choose the correct statements from the options given below.
(a) I, II and III
(b) I, II and V
(c) II, III and IV
(d) I, III and V

26. Given below are two statements.

Statement I Transposons are immobile genetic elements that confers stability to it.

Statement II In gene therapy, the functional ADA *c*DNA is introduced into cultured lymphocytes using a retroviral vector.

In the light of the above statements, choose the correct answer from the options given below.
(a) Statement I is incorrect, but statement II is correct.
(b) Both statement I and statement II are correct.
(c) Both statement I and statement II are incorrect
(d) Statement I is correct, but statement II is incorrect

27. Given below are two statements.

Statement I There are an estimated 2 million varieties of rice in India. The diversity of rice in India is one of the richest in the world.

Statement II Basmati rice is distinct for its unique aroma and flavour and 27 documented varieties of Basmati are grown in India.

In the light of the above statements, choose the correct answer from the options given below.
(a) Statement I is incorrect, but statement II is correct.
(b) Both statement I and statement II are correct.
(c) Both statement I and statement II are incorrect.
(d) Statement I is correct, but statement II is incorrect.

28. Match the List I with List II.

	List I	List II
A.	Preparation of genetically engineered insulin	1. 1990
B.	The first clinical gene therapy	2. 1983
C.	The first transgenic cow	3. 1997
D.	An American company got patent rights on Basmati rice	4. 1997

Choose the correct answer from the options given below.

	A	B	C	D
(a)	3	2	4	1
(b)	1	2	3	4
(c)	1	4	2	3
(d)	2	1	3	4

29. Given below are few statements.

I. '*B*' in *Bt* cotton indicates that it is a genetically modified organism produced through biotechnology.

II. Transgenic mice constitute the highest ratio of all existing transgenic animals.

III. Transgenic animals can be used to study of complex factors involved in growth such as insulin-like growth factor.

IV. Transposons are source of complementary *ds*RNA involved, in the RNAi.

V. Nutrient medium for tissue culture must contain carbon source, inorganic salts and growth regulators like ethylene.

Choose the correct statements out of the given options.

(a) II, III and IV
(b) I, II, III and IV
(c) II, III and V
(d) I, II, III, IV and V

30. Given below are steps of somatic hybridisation in plant.

I. Digestion of cell wall
II. Isolation of naked protoplasts
III. Isolation of cells from plant tissues
IV. Fusion of protoplasts
V. Formation of somatic hybrids

Choose the correct order from the options given below.

(a) I $\rightarrow$ II $\rightarrow$ III $\rightarrow$ IV $\rightarrow$ V
(b) III $\rightarrow$ I $\rightarrow$ II $\rightarrow$ IV $\rightarrow$ V
(c) III $\rightarrow$ II $\rightarrow$ I $\rightarrow$ IV $\rightarrow$ V
(d) III $\rightarrow$ I $\rightarrow$ IV $\rightarrow$ III $\rightarrow$ V

Response Index

01 ⓐ ⓑ ⓒ ⓓ	14 ⓐ ⓑ ⓒ ⓓ	27 ⓐ ⓑ ⓒ ⓓ	40 ⓐ ⓑ ⓒ ⓓ
02 ⓐ ⓑ ⓒ ⓓ	15 ⓐ ⓑ ⓒ ⓓ	28 ⓐ ⓑ ⓒ ⓓ	41 ⓐ ⓑ ⓒ ⓓ
03 ⓐ ⓑ ⓒ ⓓ	16 ⓐ ⓑ ⓒ ⓓ	29 ⓐ ⓑ ⓒ ⓓ	42 ⓐ ⓑ ⓒ ⓓ
04 ⓐ ⓑ ⓒ ⓓ	17 ⓐ ⓑ ⓒ ⓓ	30 ⓐ ⓑ ⓒ ⓓ	43 ⓐ ⓑ ⓒ ⓓ
05 ⓐ ⓑ ⓒ ⓓ	18 ⓐ ⓑ ⓒ ⓓ	31 ⓐ ⓑ ⓒ ⓓ	44 ⓐ ⓑ ⓒ ⓓ
06 ⓐ ⓑ ⓒ ⓓ	19 ⓐ ⓑ ⓒ ⓓ	32 ⓐ ⓑ ⓒ ⓓ	45 ⓐ ⓑ ⓒ ⓓ
07 ⓐ ⓑ ⓒ ⓓ	20 ⓐ ⓑ ⓒ ⓓ	33 ⓐ ⓑ ⓒ ⓓ	46 ⓐ ⓑ ⓒ ⓓ
08 ⓐ ⓑ ⓒ ⓓ	21 ⓐ ⓑ ⓒ ⓓ	34 ⓐ ⓑ ⓒ ⓓ	47 ⓐ ⓑ ⓒ ⓓ
09 ⓐ ⓑ ⓒ ⓓ	22 ⓐ ⓑ ⓒ ⓓ	35 ⓐ ⓑ ⓒ ⓓ	48 ⓐ ⓑ ⓒ ⓓ
10 ⓐ ⓑ ⓒ ⓓ	23 ⓐ ⓑ ⓒ ⓓ	36 ⓐ ⓑ ⓒ ⓓ	49 ⓐ ⓑ ⓒ ⓓ
11 ⓐ ⓑ ⓒ ⓓ	24 ⓐ ⓑ ⓒ ⓓ	37 ⓐ ⓑ ⓒ ⓓ	50 ⓐ ⓑ ⓒ ⓓ
12 ⓐ ⓑ ⓒ ⓓ	25 ⓐ ⓑ ⓒ ⓓ	38 ⓐ ⓑ ⓒ ⓓ	
13 ⓐ ⓑ ⓒ ⓓ	26 ⓐ ⓑ ⓒ ⓓ	39 ⓐ ⓑ ⓒ ⓓ	

Performance Scanner

> 90% Excellent !	You have mastered this chapter. The concepts of this chapter are at your fingertips. Move on to the next chapter and maintain this momentum.
76-90% Very Good !	You have a good command over this chapter. Revise the chapter again after a few days and enhance your performance.
60-75% Good !	You have a wide scope to learn for this chapter. Revise this chapter again.
<60% Not Satisfactory!	You have a long way ahead of you to master this chapter. Revise it thoroughly.

Scan for online chapter test

Scan for online unit test

Space for Rough Work

Test Booklet No. **3947361**

Test Booklet Code **CH11**

MEDACE
NEET (UG)
SELF ASSESSMENT KIT

Organisms and Populations

Topics Covered
Organism and its Environment

Population

Important Instructions

- This Booklet Contains – Two Topic Tests and One Test on Complete Chapter.
- Each question carries 4 marks.
- For each correct response, the candidate will get 4 marks. And for every incorrect response, 1 mark will be additionally deducted from total score.
- Use **Blue/Black** point pen only for filling the OMR.
- Rough work is to be done in the space provided for this purpose in the test booklet only.

Name of the Candidate (In Capitals) ______________________

____

Candidate's Signature ______________

Invigilator's Signature ______________

Facsimile signature stamp of center superintendent ______________

Do not open this booklet until you start attempting the test

Topical Follow Thru

Test 1

Syllabus Organism and its environment

For deeper insight, **Scan the QR Code**

Important Instructions

- The test is of 30 minutes duration and contains 25 Multiple Choice Questions (four options with a single correct answer).
- Choose the correct option and fill the OMR given on the last page of this test accordingly.
- At some instances, you may find more than 1 option to be correct. In such circumstances, you have to judge the most appropriate answer as per the conditions given in the question.

1. Ecology is basically concerned with four levels of biological organisation. These are

(a) biome, communities, niche, organism
(b) biome, niche, organs, population
(c) organisms, population, communities, biomes
(d) cells, organs, ecosystem, atmosphere

2. Following graph illustrates the distribution of different biomes (designated as A - F) w.r.t. annual temperature and precipitation.

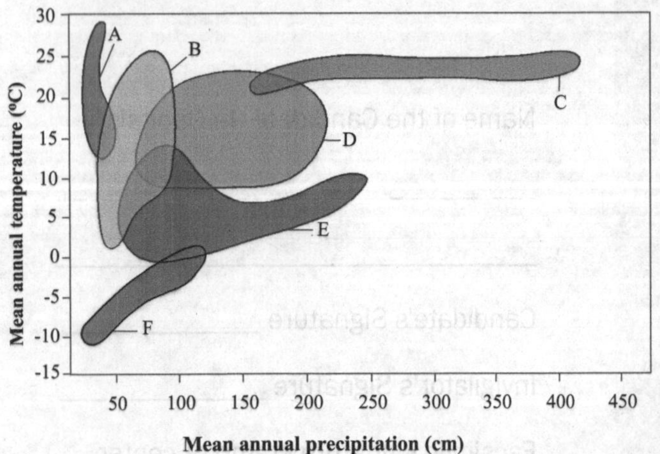

Which of the following biome has the highest level of biodiversity?

(a) C
(b) A
(c) D
(d) D and E

3. Given below are two statements.

Statement I The levels of thermal tolerance of different species determines to a large extent, their geographical distribution.

Statement II Organisms which can tolerate a wide range of salinities are stenohaline.

In the light of the above statements; choose the correct answer from the options given below.

(a) Statement I is incorrect, but statement II is correct.
(b) Both statement I and statement II are correct.
(c) Both statement I and statement II are incorrect.
(d) Statement I is correct, but statement II is incorrect.

4. Match the List I and List II.

	List I (Salt concentration)		List II (Example)
I.	<5 ppt	P.	Sea
II.	30-35 ppt	Q.	Hypersaline lagoons
III.	>100 %	R.	Inland water

Choose the correct option having the correct combination.

	I	II	III
(a)	P	Q	R
(b)	R	Q	P
(c)	R	P	Q
(d)	Q	P	R

5. Which of the abiotic factor is primarily responsible for the distribution of organisms?
(a) temperature (b) light
(c) water (d) soil

6. Select the incorrect match.
(a) Aestivation - Avoiding summer related problem
(b) Blubber - Acts as insulator
(c) Light - Horizontal distribution of organisms in water body
(d) Soil -determine the type of benthic animals

7. The success of mammals according to evolutionary biologists is largely due to their
(a) change in body temperature according to environment
(b) ability to maintain a constant body temperature
(c) adaptable organs
(d) phylogenetic evolution from synapsids

8. Consider the following diagrammatic representation of organismic response.

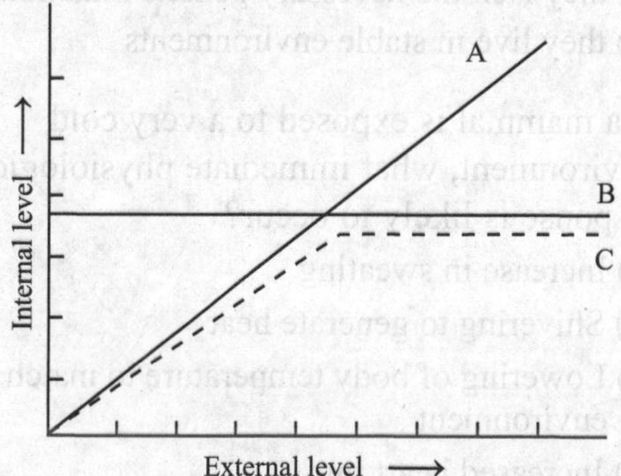

Which of the following statement is correct for 'C' ?
(a) They show only physiological adaptation.
(b) They have evolved mechanism for thermoregulation.
(c) These have limited ability to alter their body temperature.
(d) These organisms move away permanently from stressful habitat.

9. Given below are two statements; one is labelled as Assertion (A) and the other is labelled as Reason (R).

Assertion (A) A person goes to high altitude and experience altitude sickness with symptoms like breathing difficulty and heart palpitations.

Reason (R) Due to low atmospheric pressure at high altitude, the body does not get sufficient oxygen.

In the light of the above statements, choose the correct answer from the options given below.
(a) A is false, but R is true.
(b) Both A and R are true and R is the correct explanation of A.
(c) Both A and R are true, but R is not the correct explanation of A.
(d) A is true, but R is false.

10. Identify the incorrect statement from the following.
(a) During summer, humans sweat profusely when the outside temperature is more than the body temperature.
(b) In aquatic animals, the osmotic concentration of the body fluids change with that of the ambient water osmotic concentration.
(c) Small animals can generate heat energy easily due to their surface area to volume ratio.
(d) Most reptiles regulate their body temperature by staying in burrows during summer and by basking in the sun during winters.

11. Every winter, the famous ...*A*... (Bharatpur) in Rajasthan attracts thousands of migratory birds coming from ...*B*... and other extremely cold ...*C*... regions.
(a) *A*-Keoladeo National Park, *B*-America, *C*-Western
(b) *A*-Keoladeo National Park, *B*-Siberia, *C*-Northern
(c) *A*-Keoladeo National Park, *B*-Mexico, *C*-Eastern
(d) *A*-Keoladeo National Park, *B*-Siberia, *C*-Southern

12. Which characteristics of organisms enable them to survive and reproduce in their habitat?
(a) Mimicry
(b) Adaptations
(c) Acclimatisation
(d) Phenotypic plasticity

13. Following features are related to adaptations of plants found in different habitats.
I. Leaves are reduced to spines.
II. Roots hairs are absent or poorly developed.
III. Stem is long slender and spongy.

IV. Plant secretes excess salt through salt gland.
V. Stomata are sunken.

Identify the adaptations related to the xerophytes.

(a) III and V
(b) I and V
(c) II and III
(d) II and V

14. Temperature is considered as an ecologically relevant environmental factor affecting on organism. Which of the below given is not affected by temperature?

(a) Physiology of organism
(b) Morphology of organism
(c) Geographical distribution of organism
(d) Amount of organic matter present in the organism

15. Given below are two statements.

Statement I A habitat is the place where an organism lives, while a niche is the organism's role within that environment.

Statement II Acclimatisation is a long-term permanent adjustment of a group of organisms to a changing environment, whereas adaptation is a short-term rapid temporary adjustment of an organism to a changing environment.

In the light of the above statements, choose the correct answer from the options given below.

(a) Statement I is incorrect, but statement II is correct.
(b) Both statement I and statement II are correct.
(c) Both statement I and statement II are incorrect.
(d) Statement I is correct, but statement II is incorrect.

16. Which of the following strategies involves reducing the metabolic activity and entering a state of dormancy?

(a) Migration (b) Aestivation
(c) Hibernation (d) Diapause

17. Which of the following is an example of escape in time?

(a) Formation of thick-walled spores
(b) Birds migrating to Keoladeo national park
(c) Bears going into hibernation
(d) Mammals maintaining a constant body temperature

18. Conformation is an environmental adaptation in which

(a) an organism maintains a constant internal environment.
(b) organism's internal environment changes with external conditions
(c) an organism can regulate its body temperature in extreme conditions
(d) Organisms live only in polar regions

19. Conformers have not evolved into regulators because

(a) regulators are only found in polar regions
(b) thermoregulation is energetically expensive
(c) they lack the necessary genetic mutations
(d) they live in stable environments

20. If a mammal is exposed to a very cold environment, what immediate physiological response is likely to occur?

(a) Increase in sweating
(b) Shivering to generate heat
(c) Lowering of body temperature to match the environment
(d) Increased heart rate

21. Given below are two statements; one is labelled as Assertion (A) and the other is labelled as Reason (R).

Assertion (A) The blood of Antarctic fishes often freeze.

Reason (R) Fishes are poikilotherms with fluctuating body temperature.

In the light of the above statements, choose the correct answer from the options given below.
(a) A is false, but R is true.
(b) Both A and R are true and R is the correct explanation of A.
(c) Both A and R are true, but R is not the correct explanation of A.
(d) A is true, but R is false.

22. Given below are two statements.
Statement I Life on earth originated in water and cannot be sustained without it.
Statement II The productivity and distribution of plants are heavily dependent on water.
In the light of the above statements, choose the correct answer from the options given below.
(a) Statement I is incorrect, but statement II is correct.
(b) Both statement I and statement II are correct.
(c) Both statement I and statement II are incorrect.
(d) Statement I is correct, but statement II is incorrect.

23. Which one of the following is not an exclusive xerophytic adaptation?
(a) Presence of stunted stem
(b) Extensive roots with well developed root cap
(c) Presence of root pockets
(d) Waxy coating on stem and leaves

24. What role does sunlight play in the behaviour of animals?
(a) It provides them with food
(b) It regulates their body temperature directly
(c) It affects their ability to breathe
(d) It serves as a cue for timing their foraging, reproductive and migratory activities

25. How is the availability of light on land linked with temperature?
(a) Light has no effect on temperature
(b) The sun is the source of both light and temperature
(c) Temperature decreases as light intensity increases
(d) Light is produced by the heating of the earth's surface

Response Index

01	a	b	c	d	10	a	b	c	d	19	a	b	c	d
02	a	b	c	d	11	a	b	c	d	20	a	b	c	d
03	a	b	c	d	12	a	b	c	d	21	a	b	c	d
04	a	b	c	d	13	a	b	c	d	22	a	b	c	d
05	a	b	c	d	14	a	b	c	d	23	a	b	c	d
06	a	b	c	d	15	a	b	c	d	24	a	b	c	d
07	a	b	c	d	16	a	b	c	d	25	a	b	c	d
08	a	b	c	d	17	a	b	c	d					
09	a	b	c	d	18	a	b	c	d					

Performance Scanner

> 90% Excellent !	You have mastered these topics. The concepts of these topics are at your fingertips. Move on to the next test and maintain this momentum.
76-90% Very Good !	You have a good command over these topics. Revise these topics again after a few days and enhance your performance.
60-75% Good !	You have a wide scope to learn for these topics. Revise these topics again.
<60% Not Satisfactory!	You have a long way ahead of you to master these topics. Revise it thoroughly.

Test 2

Syllabus Population interactions-mutualism, competition, predation, parasitism | Population attributes-growth, birth rate, death rate and age distribution.

For deeper insight, **Scan the QR Code**

Important Instructions

- The test is of 30 minutes duration and contains 25 Multiple Choice Questions (four options with a single correct answer).
- Choose the correct option and fill the OMR given on the last page of this test accordingly.
- At some instances, you may find more than 1 option to be correct. In such circumstances, you have to judge the most appropriate answer as per the conditions given in the question.

1. Competition refers to a biological interaction where species compete with each other for different resources. This type of interaction will be serve between

(a) distantly related species growing in different habitat
(b) distantly related species growing in same habitat
(c) closely related species growing in different habitat
(d) closely related species observed in same habitat

2. Match the List I with List II.

List I	List II
A. Natality	1. Death rate
B. Mortality	2. Outflow of the individuals of same species
C. Immigration	3. Birth rate
D. Emigration	4. Inflow of the individuals of same species

Choose the correct answer from the options given below.

	A	B	C	D
(a)	1	3	2	4
(b)	3	1	4	2
(c)	4	3	2	1
(d)	3	4	1	2

3. A country with a high rate of population growth took measures to reduce it. Two age pyramids are given below. The pyramid 'A' represents present population growth while pyramid 'B' is the estimated age pyramid after twenty years.

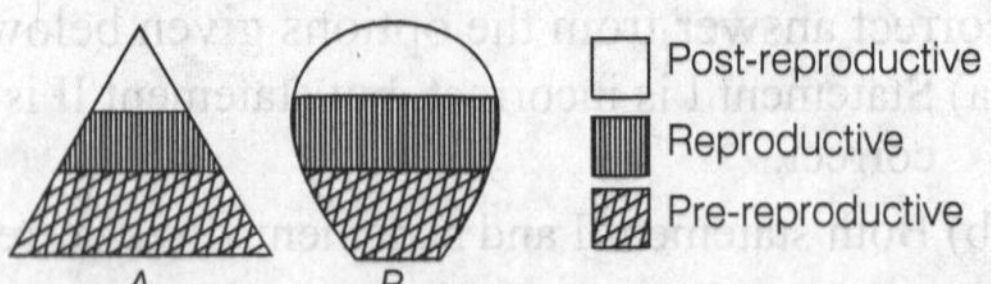

Select the correct interpretation about them.

(a) Pyramid '*A*' represents low rate of population growth.
(b) Number of adults is more than the number of children in pyramid '*B*'.
(c) The rate of growth is stable in '*B*'.
(d) '*B*' type pyramid is observed in India.

4. The figure depicts the significance of natality, mortality, immigration, and emigration for X.

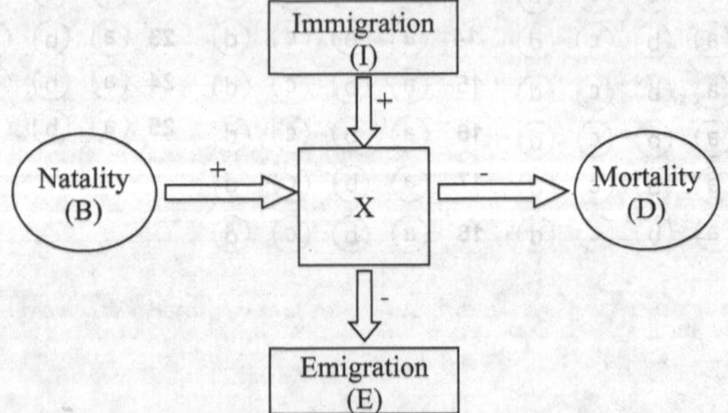

What does X stand for?

(a) Population abundance
(b) Species richness
(c) Species diversity
(d) Population density

5. Which of the following statement is incorrect?
(a) The population in which immigration or emigration occur is known as open population.
(b) Birth rate is generally expressed as number of births per 1000 individuals of a population per year.
(c) Absolute natality is the maximum production of new individuals under ideal conditions where there are no ecological limiting factors.
(d) Natality usually decreases with the period of maturity.

6. In a laboratory population of '80' *Drosophila* if '8' died during a week, the death rate in the population is .... individuals per *Drosophila* per week.
(a) 10 (b) 1.0
(c) Zero (d) 0.1

7. Which of the following would necessarily decrease the density of a population in a given habitat?
(a) Immigration
(b) Natality
(c) Mortality and emigration
(d) Natality and immigration

8. If in an ecosystem, the snake population is deleted and abundant crops are made available, which type of growth curve would be followed by the mice population in the area?
(a) Sigmoid curve
(b) J-shaped curve
(c) S-shaped curve
(d) Logistic

9. The logistic growth or Verhulst - Pearl logistic growth curve represents the population growing in a habitat with
(a) unlimited resources
(b) more competitive organisms
(c) limited resources
(d) unlimited space

10. In an area, if there are 200 *Calotropis* plants but only a single huge banyan tree with large canopy, then the population density will be measured in terms of
(a) number or biomass
(b) biomass or percentage cover
(c) number or percent cover
(d) number, biomass or percentage cover

11. Match List I with List II.

	List I		List II
A.	(–, –)	1.	Cuscuta and hedge plants
B.	(–, +)	2.	Moth and prickly pear cactus
C.	(+, +)	3.	Abingdon tortoise and goats
D.	(+, –)	4.	Fig and wasp

Choose the correct answer from the options given below.

	A	B	C	D
(a)	3	1	4	2
(b)	2	1	3	4
(c)	2	1	4	3
(d)	3	1	2	4

12. Given below are two statements; one is labelled as Assertion (A) and the other is labelled as Reason (R).
Assertion (A) The prickly pear cactus introduced into Australia in the early 1920s caused havoc by spreading rapidly into millions of hectares of rangeland.
Reason (R) When certain exotic species are introduced into a geographical area, they become invasive as the invaded land does not have its natural predators.
In the light of the above statements, choose the correct answer from the options given below.
(a) A is false, but R is true.
(b) Both A and R are true and R is the correct explanation of A.

(c) Both A and R are correct, but R is not the correct explanation of A.
(d) A is true, but R is false.

13. Given below are two statements.

Statement I The female mosquito is not considered as a parasite.
Statement II The female mosquito needs our blood for reproduction.
In the light of the above statements, choose the correct answer from the options given below.
(a) Statement I is incorrect, but statement II is correct.
(b) Both statement I and statement II are correct.
(c) Both statement I and statement II are incorrect.
(d) Statement I is correct, but statement II is incorrect.

14. Read the following adaptations in parasites.
I. Development of suckers to cling to the host
II. High reproductive capacity
III. Loss of organs
IV. Presence of adhesive organs
V. Loss of the digestive system
Choose the correct option:
(a) II, IV and V (b) I, III and IV
(c) I, II, IV and V (d) I, IV and V

15. Select the incorrect match pair.
(a) Fig flower and wasp - Parasitism
(b) *Balanus* and *Chathamalus* - Competition
(c) Mycorrhiza - Mutualism
(d) *Pisaster* and invertebrates - Predation

16. If a population has a natality rate of 50, an immigration rate of 20, a mortality rate of 30, and an emigration rate of 10, what will be the chance in population density?
(a) Increase by 30
(b) Increase by 40
(c) Increase by 20
(d) Increase by 50

17. Predation is an interaction that involves a predator and a prey. Which of the following does not denote the significance of predation?
(a) Prey population kept under check
(b) Increased reproductive capacity of predators
(c) Maintenance of species diversity in a community
(d) Biological control of weeds

18. Given below are two statements.

Statement I In a newly colonised habitat, immigration may have a more significant impact on population growth than natality.
Statement II Under normal conditions, mortality and emigration are the primary factors influencing population density.
In the light of the above statements, choose the correct answer from the options given below.
(a) Statement I is incorrect, but statement II is correct.
(b) Both statement I and statement II are correct.
(c) Both statement I and statement II are incorrect.
(d) Statement I is correct, but statement II is incorrect.

19. Given below are two statements; one is labelled as Assertion (A) and other is labelled as Reason (R).
Assertion (A) In predation, the predator benefits, while the prey is harmed.
Reason (R) Predation involves one species feeding on another, resulting in the death of the prey.
In the light of the above statements, choose the correct answer from the options given below.
(a) A is false, but R is true
(b) Both A and R are true and R is the correct explanation of A
(c) Both A and R are true, but R is not the correct explanation of A
(d) A is true, but R is false

20. Which type of reproductive strategy involves producing a large number of small-sized offsprings?
(a) *k*-strategy (b) *r*-strategy
(c) *s*-strategy (d) *b*-strategy

21. Which of the following statement explains 'competitive release'?
(a) The introduction of a new predator species into an ecosystem
(b) A species expanding its range after the removal of a competitively superior species
(c) Species utilising different food resources in the same habitat
(d) Two species evolving similar adaptations for the same resource

22. The Mediterranean orchid *Ophrys* uses .... to ensure pollination by mimicking the appearance of a female bee.
(a) sexual deceit (b) sexual dimorphism
(c) nectar (d) pheromones

23. Which mutualistic interaction involves a plant providing a reward of nectar to an insect in exchange for pollination services?
(a) Lichen symbiosis
(b) Mycorrhizal association
(c) Orchid-bee relationship
(d) Fig-wasp interaction

24. In the logistic growth model, which phase immediately follows the lag phase?
(a) Exponential phase
(b) Stationary phase
(c) Deceleration phase
(d) Decline phase

25. Which type of age pyramid would be formed in a population that is declining?
(a) Pyramid with a broad base
(b) Pyramid with a narrow base and broader top
(c) Rectangular pyramid
(d) Inverted pyramid

Response Index

01	a	b	c	d	10	a	b	c	d	19	a	b	c	d
02	a	b	c	d	11	a	b	c	d	20	a	b	c	d
03	a	b	c	d	12	a	b	c	d	21	a	b	c	d
04	a	b	c	d	13	a	b	c	d	22	a	b	c	d
05	a	b	c	d	14	a	b	c	d	23	a	b	c	d
06	a	b	c	d	15	a	b	c	d	24	a	b	c	d
07	a	b	c	d	16	a	b	c	d	25	a	b	c	d
08	a	b	c	d	17	a	b	c	d					
09	a	b	c	d	18	a	b	c	d					

Performance Scanner

> 90% Excellent !	You have mastered these topics. The concepts of these topics are at your fingertips. Move on to the next test and maintain this momentum.
76-90% Very Good !	You have a good command over these topics. Revise these topics again after a few days and enhance your performance.
60-75% Good !	You have a wide scope to learn for these topics. Revise these topics again.
<60% Not Satisfactory!	You have a long way ahead of you to master these topics. Revise it thoroughly.

Chapter Break Thru

Syllabus	• Organism and its environment • Population interactions-mutualism • Competition	• Predation • Parasitism • Population attributes-growth	• Birth rate and death rate • Age distribution

Important Instructions

- The test is of 1 hour duration and contains 30 Multiple-Choice Questions (Four options with a single correct answer).
- Choose the correct option and fill the OMR given on the last page of this test accordingly.
- At some instances, you may find more than 1 option to be correct. In such circumstances, you have to judge the most appropriate answer as per the conditions given in the question.

1. Which of the following statement is incorrect regarding tundra biome?

(a) It has long cold winter and very short summer.
(b) There is high humidity with heavy rainfall.
(c) It is the coldest region of all biomes.
(d) Permafrost remains frozen in this region.

2. Identify the basic levels of organisation of ecology.

I. Organisms
II. Species
III. Populations
IV. Communities
V. Human

Choose the correct option.

(a) I, II and III
(b) I, III and IV
(c) I, II, III and IV
(d) I, II, III and V

3. In the given graph, identify Desert, Grassland and Tropical forest, respectively.

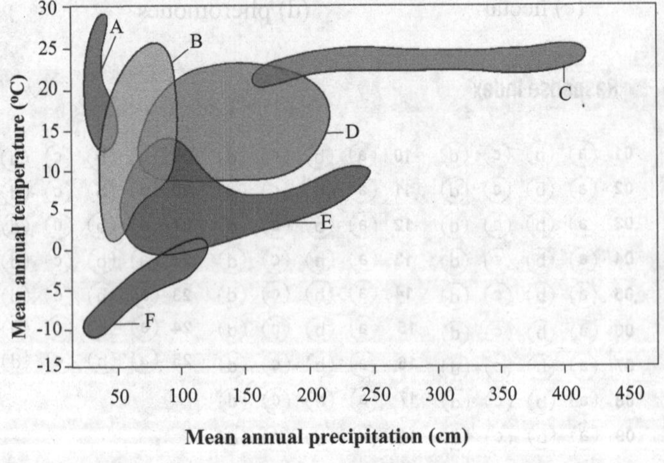

(a) A, C and D
(b) F, E and B
(c) D, B and A
(d) A, B and C

4. Microclimate can be defined as local variations of a climate that
(a) occurs on a high altitude
(b) occurs in an area of limited size
(c) occurs in temperate grassland
(d) occurs in tropical area

5. Which of the following correctly defines niche?
(a) The range of temperature that the organism need to live.
(b) The physical space where an organism lives.
(c) All the biological factors in the organism's environment.
(d) The functional role played by an organism where it lives.

6. The most accurate reason of why grasses predominate in the Savannah is
(a) there are few native herbivores in the biome
(b) grasses grow well in sandy soil, found in Savannah.
(c) grasses undergo a dual life cycle and these shows dominance in the first half of their cycle
(d) deep roots of the grasses can survive many months of droughts

7. Under unfavourable conditions, many zooplankton species in lakes and ponds enter a stage of diapause. This reaction to situation is an example of
(a) regulate (b) conform
(c) migrate (d) suspend

8. Given below are two statements.
Statement I Some organisms are able to maintain homeostasis by physiological and behavioural means to ensure a constant body temperature.
Statement II All birds, mammals, few lower vertebrates and invertebrates are ectotherms as they can adjust with external temperature.
In the light of the above statements, choose the correct answer from the options given below.
(a) Statement I is incorrect, but statement II is correct
(b) Both statement I and statement II are correct
(c) Both statements I and statements II are incorrect
(d) Statement I is correct, but statement II is incorrect

9. Some organisms like bear undergo ……A…… sleep called hibernation, and certain animals like snails and fish undergo ……B…… sleep known as aestivation.

	A	B
(a)	spring	winter
(b)	spring	Autumn
(c)	winter	summer
(d)	summer	Winter

10. Desert lizard can possibly survive high temperature of their habitat by some behavioual means. This is an example of
(a) regulation
(b) conformer
(c) adaptation
(d) migration

11. In a stable population of a country,
(a) reproductive and pre-reproductive individuals are nearly equal in number.
(b) reproductive individuals are less than post-reproductive individuals.
(c) pre-reproductive individuals are more than the reproductive individuals.
(d) pre-reproductive individuals are less than the reproductive individuals.

12. If a population of 50 *Paramoecium* present in a pool increases to 150 after an hour, what would be the growth rate, and the birth rate per individual per hour of the population?
(a) 50 per hour, and 100
(b) 200 per hour, and 300
(c) 5 per hour, and 50
(d) 100 per hour, and 2

13. The initial population of a bird species is N_0, during the time interval 't', B number of birds has been newly born and 'D'. number of birds have died due to ecological disturbances. I and E number of birds have been immigrated and emigrated, respectively. The population of bird after time 't' will be
(a) $N_0 + [(B+E) - (D+I)]$
(b) $N_0 + [(I+E) - (B+D)]$
(c) $N_0 + [(B+I) - (D+E)]$
(d) $N_0 + [(B-I) + (D-E)]$

14. If in a population of 2000 individuals, 80 births and 125 deaths were reported over a given period of time, which of the following graphs will correspond to it?

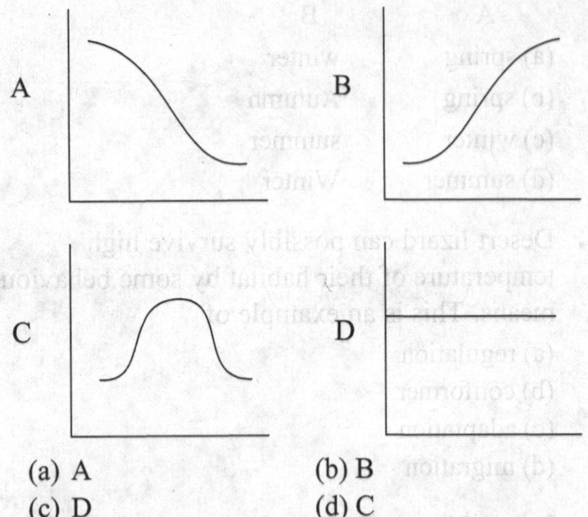

(a) A (b) B
(c) D (d) C

15. Which of the following statement is not correct with respect to predation?
(a) It might lead to extinction of a species.
(b) Both the interacting species are negatively impacted.
(c) It is necessitated by nature to maintain the ecological balance.
(d) It helps maintain species diversity in a community.

16. Match the List I with List II.

List I	List II
A. Ectoparasite	1. Virus
B. Endoparasite	2. *Cuscuta*
C. Brood parasitism	3. Liver fluke
D. Obligate parasite	4. Cuckoo-crow

Choose the correct answer from the options given below.

	A	B	C	D
(a)	2	3	4	1
(b)	2	1	3	4
(c)	3	4	2	1
(d)	3	1	4	2

17. Sea anemone and clown fish are two organisms that indulge in a relationship. In this, the sea anemone protects the clown fish from predators and in return, get protected from several parasites.
The above example will be observed under
(a) competition
(b) parasitism
(c) mutualism
(d) amensalism

18. Given below are two statements.

Statement I Resource partitioning may hold the answer to the coexistence of species that are ecologically similar

Statement II Competitive release is the expansion of the range of a species when a competitor for its niche is removed.

In the light of the above statements, choose the correct answer from the options given below.
(a) Statement I is incorrect, but statement II is correct.
(b) Both statement I and statement II are correct.
(c) Both statement I and statement II are incorrect.
(d) Statement I is correct, but statement II is incorrect.

19. Which of the following is true for two unrelated species feeding on the same food and living in the same area?
(a) one species is harmed and the other is benefitted
(b) one species is harmed and the other is unaffected
(c) one species is benefitted and the other is unaffected
(d) Both the species are harmed.

20. The introduction of goats resulted in the exclusion of Abingdon tortoise from Galapagos island. It is an example of
(a) Parasitism
(b) predations
(c) competitive exclusion
(d) competitive co-existence

21. The event depicted by the image is not characterised by

(a) sexual deceit
(b) pseudocopulation
(c) co-evolution
(d) sexual dimorphism

22. Given below are few statements.

I. A habitat of an organism is solely dependent on the physico-chemical components.
II. Gradually increasing average global temperatures will significantly affect the distributional range of some species to be affected.
III. Red algae is likely to be found in the deepest waters.
IV. A person can accomplish homeostasis through physiological means when she is using AC to cool herself/himself.

Choose the correct set of statements from the optons given below.

(a) II and III
(b) II, III and IV
(c) I, II and IV
(d) III and IV

23. Which of the following statement is incorrect regarding Allen's rule?

(a) Body surface area-volume ratio of exothermic animals tends to vary with the average temperature of their habitat.
(b) Mammals of colder climates have the shortest limbs.
(c) It is related to adaptation.
(d) It helps to explain the distribution of specific organism in polar region.

24. Select the incorrect match pair.

(a) Regulator - Endothermic
(b) Conformers - Ectothermic
(c) Migrate - Escape stressful space
(d) Suspend - Avoid stressful space

25. Which of the following is the main reason for the increase in human population?

(a) Availability of more space
(b) Better medical facility
(c) Green revolution
(d) High rate of immigration

26. Both niche and habitat are important for maintaining the biodiversity balance of an area by focussing on the impacts of organisms and ecosystem on each other. How niche is different from habitat?

(a) It is species specific.
(b) It comprises of different environmental factors.
(c) It is related to the competition between different species.
(d) It is a particular place where organisms live.

27. How does the age structure of a population affect its growth?

(a) Different age groups have equal reproductive abilities.
(b) A higher number of elderly individuals suggests population stability.
(c) A higher number of adults suggests a declining population.
(d) Different age groups have varying reproductive abilities.

28. Given below are two statements; one is labelled as the Assertion (A) and the other is labelled as the Reason (R).

Assertion (A) The logistic growth model is considered a more realistic graph.

Reason (R) The logistic growth model does not consider the limits of environmental responses.

In the light of the above statements, choose the correct answer from the options given below.

(a) A is false, but R is true.
(b) Both A and R are true and R is the correct explanation of A.

(c) Both A and R are true, but R is not the correct explanation of A.

(d) A is true, but R is false.

29. Given below are two statements.

Statement I Gause's principle of competitive exclusion states that more abundant species will exclude the less abundant species through competition.

Statement II Species with different food preferences in a given habitat avoid or overcome competitive exclusion.

In the light of the above statements, choose the correct answer from the options given below.

(a) Statement I is incorrect, but statement II is correct.

(b) Both statement I and statement II are correct.

(c) Both statement I and statement II are incorrect.

(d) Statement I is correct, but statement II is incorrect.

30. Identify the correct statement(s) from the following.

I. Intra-specific competition occurs between the members of the same population.

II. Predators are mostly carnivorous animals that eat up other animals and some plants.

III. Apparent competition occurs indirectly between individuals competing for the same resource.

IV. Cannibalism is an inter-specific competition quite common in both aquatic and terrestrial organisms.

V. Symbiosis is an interaction characterised by two or more species living purposefully in direct contact with each other.

Choose the correct answer from the options given below.

(a) I and II (b) I, II, III and V

(c) Only IV (d) IV and V

Scan for online chapter test

Response Index

01	ⓐ ⓑ ⓒ ⓓ	14	ⓐ ⓑ ⓒ ⓓ	27	ⓐ ⓑ ⓒ ⓓ	40	ⓐ ⓑ ⓒ ⓓ
02	ⓐ ⓑ ⓒ ⓓ	15	ⓐ ⓑ ⓒ ⓓ	28	ⓐ ⓑ ⓒ ⓓ	41	ⓐ ⓑ ⓒ ⓓ
03	ⓐ ⓑ ⓒ ⓓ	16	ⓐ ⓑ ⓒ ⓓ	29	ⓐ ⓑ ⓒ ⓓ	42	ⓐ ⓑ ⓒ ⓓ
04	ⓐ ⓑ ⓒ ⓓ	17	ⓐ ⓑ ⓒ ⓓ	30	ⓐ ⓑ ⓒ ⓓ	43	ⓐ ⓑ ⓒ ⓓ
05	ⓐ ⓑ ⓒ ⓓ	18	ⓐ ⓑ ⓒ ⓓ	31	ⓐ ⓑ ⓒ ⓓ	44	ⓐ ⓑ ⓒ ⓓ
06	ⓐ ⓑ ⓒ ⓓ	19	ⓐ ⓑ ⓒ ⓓ	32	ⓐ ⓑ ⓒ ⓓ	45	ⓐ ⓑ ⓒ ⓓ
07	ⓐ ⓑ ⓒ ⓓ	20	ⓐ ⓑ ⓒ ⓓ	33	ⓐ ⓑ ⓒ ⓓ	46	ⓐ ⓑ ⓒ ⓓ
08	ⓐ ⓑ ⓒ ⓓ	21	ⓐ ⓑ ⓒ ⓓ	34	ⓐ ⓑ ⓒ ⓓ	47	ⓐ ⓑ ⓒ ⓓ
09	ⓐ ⓑ ⓒ ⓓ	22	ⓐ ⓑ ⓒ ⓓ	35	ⓐ ⓑ ⓒ ⓓ	48	ⓐ ⓑ ⓒ ⓓ
10	ⓐ ⓑ ⓒ ⓓ	23	ⓐ ⓑ ⓒ ⓓ	36	ⓐ ⓑ ⓒ ⓓ	49	ⓐ ⓑ ⓒ ⓓ
11	ⓐ ⓑ ⓒ ⓓ	24	ⓐ ⓑ ⓒ ⓓ	37	ⓐ ⓑ ⓒ ⓓ	50	ⓐ ⓑ ⓒ ⓓ
12	ⓐ ⓑ ⓒ ⓓ	25	ⓐ ⓑ ⓒ ⓓ	38	ⓐ ⓑ ⓒ ⓓ		
13	ⓐ ⓑ ⓒ ⓓ	26	ⓐ ⓑ ⓒ ⓓ	39	ⓐ ⓑ ⓒ ⓓ		

Performance Scanner

> 90% Excellent !	You have mastered this chapter. The concepts of this chapter are at your fingertips. Move on to the next chapter and maintain this momentum.
76-90% Very Good !	You have a good command over this chapter. Revise the chapter again after a few days and enhance your performance.
60-75% Good !	You have a wide scope to learn for this chapter. Revise this chapter again.
<60% Not Satisfactory!	You have a long way ahead of you to master this chapter. Revise it thoroughly.

Space for Rough Work

Space for Rough Work

Test Booklet No. **3947362**

Test Booklet Code **CH12**

MEDACE

NEET (UG)

SELF ASSESSMENT KIT

Ecosystem

Topics Covered

Ecosystem : Structure and Function, Productivity and Decomposition

Energy Flow and Ecological Pyramids

Important Instructions

- This Booklet Contains – Two Topic Tests and One Test on Complete Chapter.
- Each question carries 4 marks.
- For each correct response, the candidate will get 4 marks. And for every incorrect response, 1 mark will be additionally deducted from total score.
- Use **Blue/Black** point pen only for filling the OMR.
- Rough work is to be done in the space provided for this purpose in the test booklet only.

Name of the Candidate (In Capitals) ____________

Candidate's Signature ____________

Invigilator's Signature ____________

Facsimile signature stamp of center superintendent____________

Do not open this booklet until you start attempting the test

Topical Follow Thru

Test 1

Syllabus

- Ecosystem : Patterns, Components
- Productivity
- Decomposition

For deeper insight, **Scan the QR Code** 

Important Instructions

- The test is of 30 minutes duration and contains 25 Multiple Choice Questions (four options with a single correct answer).
- Choose the correct option and fill the OMR given on the last page of this test accordingly.
- At some instances, you may find more than 1 option to be correct. In such circumstances, you have to judge the most appropriate answer as per the conditions given in the question.

1. The process of enzymatic conversion of the decomposing detritus into simpler compounds and inorganic substances is known as ...., which occurs simultaneously with .... and ...., operating on the detritus.

(a) leaching, fragmentation, mineralisation
(b) decomposition, fragmentation, leaching
(c) hydration, leaching, mineralisation
(d) catabolism, fragmentation, leaching

2. Identify the incorrect statement from the following.

(a) The annual net primary productivity of the whole biosphere is approximately 170 billion tons of organic matter.
(b) The productivity of the oceans is only 55 billion tons.
(c) The rate of gross primary productivity is estimated in terms of chlorophyll content.
(d) Secondary productivity increases with the rise of trophic level.

3. Given below are layers of vegetation found in a tropical rainforest.

I. Understorey
II. Canopy
III. Emergent
IV. Forest floor
V. Shrub

Rearrange them in the correct order from top to bottom layers.

(a) IV, V, II, I, III
(b) III, I, II, V, IV
(c) III, II, I, V, IV
(d) IV, V, I, II, III

4. Given below are two statements.

Statement I Detritus becomes pulverized as it passes through the digestive tract of animals.

Statement II Fragmentation increases the surface area of detritus.

In the light of the above statements, choose the correct answer from the options given below.

(a) Statement I is incorrect, but statement II is correct
(b) Both statement I and statement II are correct
(c) Both statement I and statement II are incorrect
(d) Statement I is correct, but statement II is incorrect

5. Given below are few statements.

I. Croplands possess less genetic diversity, but high productivity.
II. In deep sea hydrothermal vents, producers can be represented by chemosynthetic bacteria.
III. Species composition is maximum in tropical rain forests, while minimum in coral root system.

IV. Maximum stratification of plant species can be observed in grasslands followed by tropical rain forests.

Choose the incorrect statements from the options given below.
(a) I and II
(b) III and IV
(c) I, III and IV
(d) II, III and IV

6. Identify the incorrect statements about ecosystems from the following options.

I. Ecosystems are open systems that receive solar energy and matter inputs.
II. Pond, as an aquatic ecosystem is dependent on land ecosystem for its sustenance.
III. Structural components of ecosystems include material exchange, energy flow and nutrient cycling.
IV. The functional components of ecosystems encompass all living organisms and their interactions.
V. Flagellates represent the producers in pond ecosystem.

Choose the correct answer from the following options.
(a) I, II and V
(b) III and IV only
(c) III, IV and V
(d) II and V only

7. Which of the following option represents the correct order of decomposition process?
(a) Leaching → Mineralisation → Humification → Fragmentation
(b) Fragmentation → Leaching → Humification → Mineralisation
(c) Fragmentation → Leaching → Mineralisation → Humification
(d) Leaching → Mineralisation → Fragmentation → Humification

8. Given below are two statements, one is labelled as Assertion (A) and other one is labelled as Reason (R).

Assertion (A) Gross primary productivity (GPP) is always greater than net primary productivity (NPP) in ecosystems.

Reason (R) Net primary productivity (NPP) represents the amount of biomass or organic matter available for consumption by heterotrophs and is obtained by subtracting respiratory losses (R) from GPP.

In the light of the above statements, choose the correct answers from the options given below.
(a) A is false, but R is true
(b) Both A and R are true and R is the correct explanation of A
(c) Both A and R are ture, but R is not the correct explanation of A
(d) A is true, but R is false

9. Given below are two statements.

Statement I Net primary productivity (NPP) is directly consumed by herbivores only.

Statement II Secondary productivity represents the organic matter available for decomposers.

In light of the above statements, choose the correct answer from the options given below.
(a) Statement I is incorrect, but statement II is correct
(b) Both statement I and statement II are correct
(c) Both statement I and statement II are incorrect
(d) Statement I is correct, but statement II is incorrect

10. Leaching can negatively impact plant growth because it
(a) increases the availability of water in the soil.
(b) enhances the activity of soil microbes.
(c) creates a more acidic soil environment.
(d) removes essential mineral nutrients from the topsoil.

11. Which of the following statement about the decomposition of leaves is incorrect?
(a) Decomposers like fungi and bacteria break down partially consumed leaves.
(b) The breakdown process leads to the formation of litter, which loses its original structure.
(c) Litter is directly consumed as a food source by most plants.
(d) Decomposition is an essential step in nutrient cycling within an ecosystem.

12. The process of mineralisation by microorganisms helps in the release of
(a) inorganic nutrients from humus
(b) organic nutrients from humus
(c) both organic and inorganic nutrients from detritus
(d) inorganic nutrients from detritus and the formation of humus

13. Which of the following components in detritus slows down the rate of decomposition in a particular climatic condition?
(a) Nitrogen
(b) Sugars
(c) Lignin
(d) Water-soluble substances

14. Which of the following is not the correct statement?
(a) Many ecologists regard the entire biosphere as a global ecosystem as a composite of all local ecosystems on earth.
(b) Ecosystems with higher biodiversity tend to be more stable.
(c) Marine ecosystems cover less than 50% of the earth's surface.
(d) Natural ecosystems are balanced system.

15. Which of the following are considered abiotic components in an ecosystem?
(a) Flow of energy and cycling of materials
(b) Cycling of materials
(c) Consumers
(d) Flow of energy

16. Ravi is setting up an aquarium at home. He notices that the fish, plants, and other organisms in the aquarium seem to interact not only with each other but also with the water, rocks, and other non-living elements in the tank. Based on your understanding of ecosystems, how would you classify Ravi's aquarium?
(a) Natural aquatic ecosystem
(b) Man-made terrestrial ecosystem
(c) Man-made aquatic ecosystem
(d) Natural terrestrial ecosystem

17. Given below are two statements.
Statement I Primary productivity varies in different types of ecosystem.
Statement II Day-length is one of the factors regulating the rate of function of the entire pond.
In light of the above statements, choose the correct answer from the options given below.
(a) Statement I is incorrect, but statement II is correct
(b) Both statement I and statement II are correct
(c) Both statement I and statement II are incorrect
(d) Statement I is correct, but statement II is incorrect

18. In an aquatic ecosystem like a pond, which component is primarily responsible for converting inorganic materials into organic materials using sunlight?
(a) Consumers
(b) Decomposers
(c) Autotrophs
(d) Abiotic factors

19. Sara is studying a small pond ecosystem for her project. She observes that the pond has a variety of plants, fish, and microorganisms, all of which interact with one another and with the pond's physical environment. If Sara wants to analyse the role of organisms that break down dead matter in the pond, which group should she focus on?
(a) Phytoplankton (b) Zooplankton
(c) Fungi (d) Algae

20. In an ecosystem, if the gross primary productivity (GPP) is 6000 kcal m^{-2} yr^{-1} and the respiration losses (R) are 2000 kcal m^{-2} yr^{-1}. What is the net primary productivity (NPP)?

(a) 2000 kcal m^{-2} yr^{-1}
(b) 4000 kcal m^{-2} yr^{-1}
(c) 8000 kcal m^{-2} yr^{-1}
(d) 1000 kcal m^{-2} yr^{-1}

21. Match List I with List II.

List I	List II
A. Fragmentation	1. Degradation of detritus into simpler inorganic substances by bacterial and fungal enzymes.
B. Catabolism	2. Breakdown of detritus into smaller particles by detritivores.
C. Humification	3. Accumulation of a dark-coloured amorphous substance highly resistant to microbial action.
D. Mineralisation	4. Release of inorganic nutrients from humus by microbial action.

Choose the correct answer using the options given below.

	A	B	C	D
(a)	2	1	3	4
(b)	1	2	4	3
(c)	2	4	1	3
(d)	4	3	2	1

22. Which term refers to the amount of organic matter produced per unit area by plants during photosynthesis, before accounting for respiration losses?

(a) NPP
(b) Respiration
(c) Productivity
(d) GPP

23. In a forested area experiencing unusually low temperatures and high soil moisture, which of the following would you expect to occur regarding decomposition of organic matter?

(a) Accelerated decomposition
(b) Normal decomposition rate
(c) Slowed decomposition
(d) No effect on decomposition

24. Which region of the sea will have maximum productivity?

(a) Continental shelf water level
(b) Coastal
(c) Very deep sea
(d) Deep sea

25. In a compost bin, organic waste is decomposing into smaller particles and then into a dark, nutrient-rich substance. Which processes are primarily involved?

(a) Leaching and Catabolism
(b) Fragmentation and Humification
(c) Humification and Mineralisation
(d) Fragmentation and Mineralisation

Response Index

Performance Scanner

> 90% Excellent ! You have mastered these topics. The concepts of these topics are at your fingertips. Move on to the next test and maintain this momentum.

76-90% Very Good ! You have a good command over these topics. Revise these topics again after a few days and enhance your performance.

60-75% Good ! You have a wide scope to learn for these topics. Revise these topics again.

<60% Not Satisfactory! You have a long way ahead of you to master these topics. Revise it thoroughly.

Test 2

Syllabus
- Energy flow
- Pyramids of number, biomass and energy

For deeper insight, **Scan the QR Code** 

Important Instructions

- The test is of 30 minutes duration and contains 25 Multiple Choice Questions (four options with a single correct answer).
- Choose the correct option and fill the OMR given on the last page of this test accordingly.
- At some instances, you may find more than 1 option to be correct. In such circumstances, you have to judge the most appropriate answer as per the conditions given in the question.

1. An ecological pyramid may be
(a) upright, bell shaped and inverted
(b) always upright
(c) upright, inverted and spindle
(d) always inverted

2. Which of the following pyramid is inverted in shape?
(a) Pyramid of number in pond ecosystem
(b) Pyramid of biomass in tree ecosystem
(c) Pyramid of number in parasitic ecosystem
(d) Pyramid of biomass in grassland ecosystem

3. Given below are two statements.
Statement I In ecological pyramid, saprophytes are not given any place because they do not play any important role in ecosystem.
Statement II The base of each pyramid represents the producers or the first trophic level while the apex represent tertiary or top consumer level.
In the light of the above statements, choose the correct answer from the options given below.
(a) Statement I is incorrect, but statement II is correct
(b) Both statement I and statement II are correct
(c) Both statement I and statement II are incorrect
(d) Statement I is correct, but statement II is incorrect

4. Which of the following food chain represents the correct order of the organisms to their trophic level?
(a) Grass $(T_1) \rightarrow$ Frog $(T_2) \rightarrow$ Eagle $(T_3) \rightarrow$ Snake (T_4)
(b) Grass $(T_1) \rightarrow$ Grasshopper $(T_2) \rightarrow$ Frog $(T_3) \rightarrow$ Snake $(T_4) \rightarrow$ Eagle (T_5)
(c) Grass $(T_1) \rightarrow$ Grasshopper $(T_2) \rightarrow$ Eagle $(T_3) \rightarrow$ Frog $(T_4) \rightarrow$ Lion (T_5)
(d) Grass $(T_1) \rightarrow$ Cow $(T_2) \rightarrow$ Eagle $(T_3) \rightarrow$ Frog $(T_4) \rightarrow$ Lion (T_5)

5. Which of the following organisms have maximum biomass?
(a) Large group of phytoplanktons
(b) A large group of zooplanktons
(c) Large number of small fishes
(d) A blue whale

6. Plants capture only a small fraction of the Photosynthetically Active Radiation (PAR). What percentage of PAR is typically captured by plants to sustain the entire living world?
(a) 50-60%
(b) 40-80%
(c) 20-40%
(d) 2-10%

7. Ecosystems require a continuous supply of energy primarily for which of the following reasons?
(a) to synthesise molecules
(b) to counteract increasing disorderliness
(c) to counteract decreasing disorderliness
(d) to counteract increasing disorderliness and to synthesise molecules

8. Match List I with List II.

	List I		List II
A.	Producers	1.	Lion
B.	Carnivores	2.	Phytoplanktons
C.	Herbivores	3.	Wolf
D.	Top carnivores	4.	Cow

Choose the correct option.
(a) A-2, B-3, C-4, D-1
(b) A-3, B-4, C-2, D-1
(c) A-2, B-4, C-1, D-3
(d) A-4, B-2, C-1, D-3

9. Choose the correct answer from the given options.
A. Energy flow within an ecosystem can be described as ______
B. Transformation of solar energy from one form (light) to another (heat and food) is in complete sync with the ______ law of thermodynamics.
(a) cyclical, second
(b) unidirectional, first
(c) bidirectional, second
(d) multidirectional, third

10. Identify the type of pyramid.

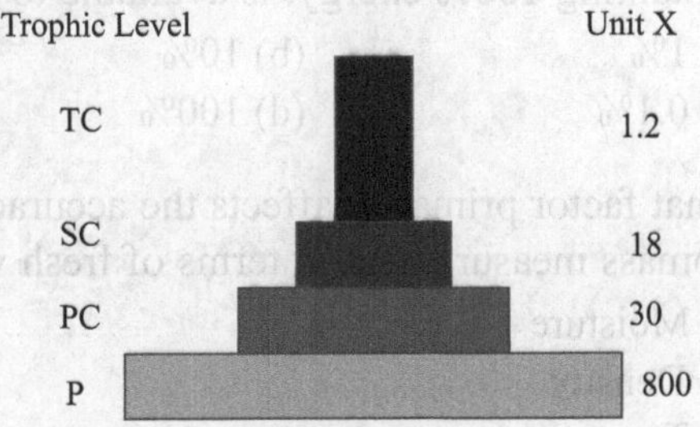

(a) Pyramid of energy
(b) Pyramid of number
(c) Pyramid of biomass
(d) Pyramid of weight

11. The food chain in which microorganisms breaks down the compounds synthesised by the producers is called .... food chain.
(a) parasitic (b) detritus
(c) grazing (d) predator

12. Match the trophic levels with their correct species examples in grassland ecosystem.

	List I		List II
A.	Fourth trophic level	1.	Crow
B.	Second trophic level	2.	Vulture
C.	First trophic level	3.	Rabbit
D.	Third trophic level	4.	Grass

Select the correct option.

	A	B	C	D
(a)	4	3	2	1
(b)	1	2	3	4
(c)	2	3	4	1
(d)	3	2	1	4

13. Energy pyramids are used to represent energy transfer in an ecosystem because energy is ______ between each trophic level.
(a) gained
(b) lost
(c) conserved
(d) either conserved or gained

14. Given below are two statements; one is labelled as Assertion (A) and other one is labelled as Reason (R).
Assertion (A) In a food chain, the number of organisms decrease at each successive trophic level.
Reason (R) The population size at any given trophic level is determined by the availability of food for organisms at the preceding level.
In the light of the above statements, choose the correct answers from the options given below.
(a) A is false, but R is true
(b) Both A and R are true and R is the correct explanation of A
(c) Both A and R are true, but R is not the correct explanation of A
(d) A is true, but R is false

15. In the context of its diet, a frog that primarily consumes insects is categorised as a

(a) primary consumer
(b) secondary consumer
(c) tertiary consumer
(d) decomposer

16. Given below are two statements.

Statement I Plants capture a meagre percent of the photosynthetically active radiation (PAR) from the sun, and this small amount of energy sustains the entire living world.

Statement II Ecosystems are not exempt from the First Law of Thermodynamics, which states that energy can neither be created or destroyed, only transformed.

In light of the above statements, choose the correct answer from the options given below.

(a) Statement I is correct, but statement II is incorrect
(b) Both Statement I and statement II are correct
(c) Both Statement I and statement II are incorrect
(d) Statement I is incorrect, but statement II is correct

17. Which of the following correctly identifies the role of producers in both terrestrial and aquatic ecosystems?

(a) Producers are the organisms that consume other organisms for energy.
(b) Producers are organisms that decompose dead matter and recycle nutrients.
(c) Producers are the green plants in terrestrial ecosystems and include phytoplankton, algae, and higher plants in aquatic ecosystems.
(d) Producers are organisms that are exclusively carnivores and feed on other animals.

18. If an environmental change causes a significant increase in the goat population, how might this affect the grass population?

(a) The grass population will increase due to less grazing pressure.
(b) The grass population will decrease due to increased grazing by goats.
(c) The grass population will remain the same.
(d) The grass will evolve to become a secondary consumer.

19. Which of the following statements correctly describes primary and secondary consumers?

(a) Primary consumers are always carnivores, while secondary consumers are herbivores.
(b) Primary consumers feed directly on producers, while secondary consumers feed on primary consumers.
(c) Secondary consumers feed on decomposers, while primary consumers feed on secondary consumers.
(d) Primary consumers are decomposers that recycle nutrients, while secondary consumers are plants.

20. Given below are two statements; one is labelled as Assertion (A) and the other is labelled as Reason (R).

Assertion (A) In an aquatic ecosystem, the grazing food chain (GFC) is the major conduit for energy flow.

Reason (R) In terrestrial ecosystems, a larger fraction of energy flows through the detritus food chain (DFC) than through the GFC.

(a) A is false, but R is true
(b) Both A and R are true and R is the correct explanation of A
(c) Both A and R are true, but R is not the correct explanation of A
(d) A is true, but R is false

21. In a simplified food chain (Grass → Rabbit → Fox), how much energy from the grass, containing 100% energy, is available to the fox?

(a) 1% (b) 10%
(c) 0.1% (d) 100%

22. What factor primarily affects the accuracy of biomass measurement in terms of fresh weight?

(a) Moisture
(b) Density
(c) Temperature
(d) Surface

23. In marine ecosystems, the pyramid of biomass is often inverted due to the higher biomass of

(a) phytoplankton (b) kelps
(c) fishes (d) algae

24. Neha was asked to draw a pyramid based on hypothetical data from an ecosystem. She created the pyramid as shown below. However, this pyramid is incorrect in term of

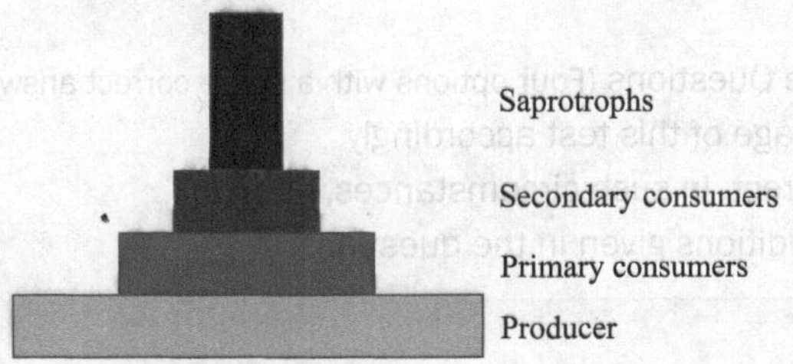

(a) consumers
(b) producers
(c) saprophytes
(d) herbivores

25. Heena was studying a forest ecosystem where the biomass of trees was significantly higher than the biomass of herbivores. What type of ecological pyramid would Heena most likely observe in this forest?

(a) Inverted Biomass Pyramid
(b) Upright Biomass Pyramid
(c) Inverted Energy Pyramid
(d) Upright Energy Pyramid

Response Index

01	(a)	(b)	(c)	(d)	10	(a)	(b)	(c)	(d)	19	(a)	(b)	(c)	(d)
02	(a)	(b)	(c)	(d)	11	(a)	(b)	(c)	(d)	20	(a)	(b)	(c)	(d)
03	(a)	(b)	(c)	(d)	12	(a)	(b)	(c)	(d)	21	(a)	(b)	(c)	(d)
04	(a)	(b)	(c)	(d)	13	(a)	(b)	(c)	(d)	22	(a)	(b)	(c)	(d)
05	(a)	(b)	(c)	(d)	14	(a)	(b)	(c)	(d)	23	(a)	(b)	(c)	(d)
06	(a)	(b)	(c)	(d)	15	(a)	(b)	(c)	(d)	24	(a)	(b)	(c)	(d)
07	(a)	(b)	(c)	(d)	16	(a)	(b)	(c)	(d)	25	(a)	(b)	(c)	(d)
08	(a)	(b)	(c)	(d)	17	(a)	(b)	(c)	(d)					
09	(a)	(b)	(c)	(d)	18	(a)	(b)	(c)	(d)					

Performance Scanner

> 90% Excellent !	You have mastered these topics. The concepts of these topics are at your fingertips. Move on to the next test and maintain this momentum.
76-90% Very Good !	You have a good command over these topics. Revise these topics again after a few days and enhance your performance.
60-75% Good !	You have a wide scope to learn for these topics. Revise these topics again.
<60% Not Satisfactory!	You have a long way ahead of you to master these topics. Revise it thoroughly.

Chapter Break Thru

Syllabus	• Ecosystem : Patterns, components • Productivity and decomposition Energy flow	• Pyramid of number • Pyramid of biomass • Pyramid of energy

Important Instructions

- The test is of 1 hour duration and contains 30 Multiple-Choice Questions (Four options with a single correct answer).
- Choose the correct option and fill the OMR given on the last page of this test accordingly.
- At some instances, you may find more than 1 option to be correct. In such circumstances, you have to judge the most appropriate answer as per the conditions given in the question.

1. Which of the following factors slows the process of decomposition?

(a) Detritus rich in sugars
(b) Low temperature
(c) More number of organic material in detritus
(d) Nitrogen-fixing bacteria

2. Which of these Eltonian pyramids are correctly described?

(a) (i) Pyramid of number → always erect
(ii) Pyamid of biomass → may be erect or inverted
(iii) Pyramid of energy → erect or inverted

(b) (i) Pyramid of number → may be erect or inverted
(ii) Pyramid of biomass → may be erect or inverted
(iii) Pyramid of energy → may be erect or inverted

(c) (i) Pyramid of number → may be erect or inverted
(ii) Pyramid of biomass → always erect
(iii) Pyramid of energy → may be erect or inverted

(d) (i) Pyramid of number → may be erect or inverted
(ii) Pyramid of biomass → may be erect or inverted
(iii) Pyramid of energy → always erect

3. Which of the following processes facilitates the movement of water-soluble inorganic nutrients down into the soil horizon, where they precipitate as unavailable salts?

(a) Humification
(b) Catabolism
(c) Fragmentation
(d) Leaching

4. Which of the following could not be considered as an ecosystem?

(a) A small drop of water containing bacteria
(b) All the fish in a coral reef
(c) Earth
(d) A pile of dung in a pasture

5. Which of the factor does not affect the primary productivity of a producer?

(a) Plant species inhabiting a particular area
(b) Rate of formation of new organic matter by consumers
(c) Availability of nutrients
(d) Photosynthetic capacity of plants

6. Identify the incorrect statement from the following with respect to Gross Primary Productivity (GPP).

(a) It is the rate of production of organic matter by producers during photosynthesis.
(b) It is measured in per unit time and area.

(c) Some amount of GPP is utilised by plants in cellular respiration.
(d) It is the available biomass for the consumption of heterotrophs.

7. Given below are two statements; one is labelled as Assertion (A) and other one is labelled as Reason (R).
Assertion (A) Biotic community is the assemblage of population of different species which live in particular area.
Reason (R) Biotic communities are mutually sustaining and interdependent and are constantly fixing and dissipating energy.
In the light of above statements, choose the correct answer from the options given below:
(a) A is false, but R is true
(b) Both A and R are true and R is the correct explanation of A
(c) Both A and R are true, but R is not the correct explanation of A
(d) A is true, but R is false

8. Which of the following best represents the pyramid of numbers in a single large tree ecosystem?

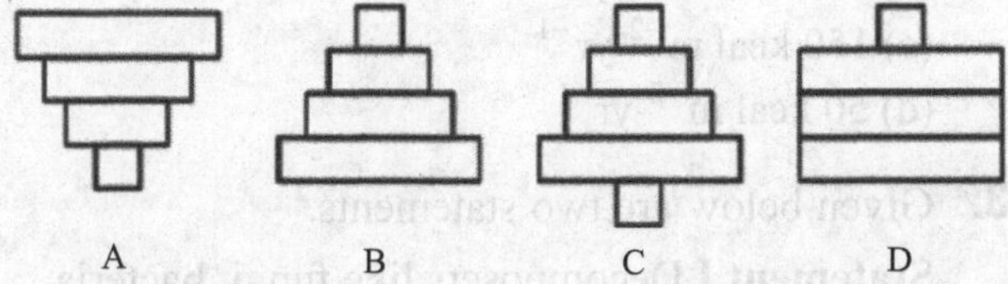

(a) A and B
(b) B and D
(c) A and C
(d) C and D

9. Which of the following statements is correct about decomposers?
(a) These organisms directly capture the sunlight for chemosynthesis.
(b) They release inorganic compounds from leaves litter only.
(c) These are the group of organisms found only in terrestrial ecosystem.
(d) They bring about a cyclic exchange of materials between biotic components in the environment.

10. The detritivore community includes
(a) maggots, millipedes, slugs and earthworms
(b) cockroaches, mosquitoes, lizards and slugs
(c) snails, springtails, salamanders and water strides
(d) molluscs, millipedes, slugs and lizards

11. The flow of energy in different trophic levels is as follows:
(a) Primary consumers → Secondary consumers → Producers → Decomposers
(b) Producers → Primary consumers → Secondary consumers → Tertiary consumers → Decomposers
(c) Producers → Decomposers → Primary consumers → Secondary consumers → Tertiary consumers
(d) Producers → Primary consumers → Tertiary consumers → Secondary consumers → Decomposers

12. Which of the following ecosystem has highest number of producers?
(a) Ocean ecosystem
(b) Tree ecosystem
(c) Pile of dead organic matter
(d) Shark carcass

13. In a cropland ecosystem, the earthworm is
(a) secondary consumer
(b) detritivores
(c) primary producer
(d) tertiary consumer

14. In which of the following regions, does the complete decomposition of detritus occur in about three to four months?
(a) Tundra region
(b) Humid tropical region
(c) Desert region
(d) Temperate region

15. If the energy produced at the level of the producers is 7000 J, the energy available for the secondary consumers is
(a) 7000 J (b) 700 J
(c) 70 J (d) 7 J

16. Given below are two statements.

Statement I The Food web lowers the adaptability and competitiveness of the organisms.

Statement II The structure of food webs suggests that the productivity and abundance of populations at any given trophic level are controlled by the productivity and abundance of populations at the trophic level below them.

In the light of above statements, choose the correct answer from the options given below.

(a) Statement I is incorrect, but statement II is correct

(b) Both statement I and statement II are correct

(c) Both statement I and statement II are incorrect

(d) Statement I is correct, but statement II is incorrect

17. The ______ is measured as the mass of a living organism or the number in a unit area at a specific time.

(a) biomass (b) ecosystem

(c) standing crop (d) productivity

18. Given below are two statements; one is labelled as Assertion (A) and other is labelled as Reason (R).

Assertion (A) Humus serves as a reservoir of nutrients.

Reason (R) Humus is colloidal in nature.

(a) A is false, but R is true

(b) Both A and R are true and R is the correct explanation of A

(c) Both A and R are true, but R is not the correct explanation of A

(d) A is true, but R is false

19. In the given food web, which organisms function as secondary consumers?

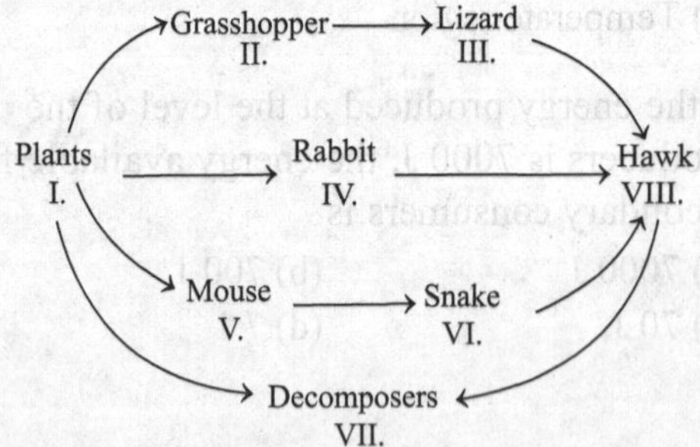

(a) III and VI

(b) IV and VII

(c) I and IV

(d) V and VI

20. Which of the following is incorrect w.r.t. energy flow?

(a) Detritus Food Chains (DFC) may be connected with the grazing food chain (GFC) at some levels.

(b) DFC is the major conduit for energy flow in the aquatic ecosystem.

(c) DFC is the major conduit for energy flow in the terrestrial ecosystem.

(d) The sources of energy flow in GFC and DFC are different.

21. The upright pyramid of number is absent in

(a) pond (b) forest

(c) lake (d) grassland

22. In an ecosystem, the Gross Primary Productivity (GPP) is 150 kcal m^{-2} yr^{-1}, and the Respiration (R) loss is 50 kcal $m^{-2}yr^{-1}$. What is the Net Primary Productivity (NPP) of the ecosystem?

(a) 200 kcal $m^{-2}yr^{-1}$

(b) 100 kcal m^{-2} yr^{-1}

(c) 150 kcal m^{-2} yr^{-1}

(d) 50 kcal m^{-2} yr^{-1}

23. Given below are two statements.

Statement I Decomposers like fungi, bacteria, and flagellates are abundant at the bottom of ponds and play a crucial role in nutrient cycling.

Statement II Ecosystems convert inorganic material to organic material, cycle nutrients through decomposition and involve energy transfer from autotrophs to heterotrophs.

In light of the above statements, choose the correct answer from the options given below.

(a) Statement I is incorrect, but statement II is correct

(b) Both statement I and statement II are correct

(c) Both statement I and statement II are incorrect

(d) Statement I is correct, but statement II is incorrect

24. Given below are two statements; one is labelled as Assertion (A) and other is labelled as Reason (R).

Assertion (A) The biomass pyramid in marine ecosystems is typically inverted.

Reason (R) In marine ecosystems, the total biomass of fish is much greater than that of phytoplankton.

In the light of above statements, choose the correct answer from the options given below.

(a) A is false, but R is true
(b) Both A and R are true and R is the correct explanation of A
(c) Both A and R are true, but R is not the correct explanation of A
(d) A is true, but R is false

25. Which of the following statements are correct?

I. The ecological pyramid of biomass is the most accurate as it provides the full information on the trophic structure of a system.
II. The biomass decreases with the rise of trophic levels, indicating wastage and biomass consumption at all trophic levels.
III. Pyramid of energy indicates the actual role of various organisms in energy transfer.
IV. The pyramid of energy is based on productivity instead of standing crops.
V. In the pyramid of biomass in the sea, the bar of the producer is generally narrower than the fishes.

Choose the correct answer from the options given below.

(a) I, II, III and V (b) I and V
(c) II, IV and V (d) I and II

26. Given below are two statements; one is labelled as Assertion (A) and other is labelled as Reason (R).

Assertion (A) There is a positive correlation between primary productivity and solar radiation.

Reason (R) Primary productivity decreases remarkably towards the poles.

In the light of above statements, choose the correct answer from the options given below.

(a) A is false, but R is true
(b) Both A and R are true and R is the correct explanation of A
(c) Both A and R are true, but R is not the correct explanation of A
(d) A is true, but R is false

27. Match List I with List II.

	List I		List II
A.	Ecological Pyramid	1.	Involves the degradation of human by microbes and release of inorganic nutrients.
B.	Food web	2.	Does not consider the existence of the same species at different levels.
C.	Mineralisation	3.	Defines the energy flow and predator prey relationship.
D.	Inverted pyramid	4.	Narrowed at the base and gradually broadens towards the tip.

Choose the correct answer from the options given below.

	A	B	C	D
(a)	2	3	1	4
(b)	2	1	4	3
(c)	1	2	3	4
(d)	4	1	2	3

28. Given below are two statements; one is labelled as Assertion (A) and other is labelled as Reason (R).

Assertion (A) The flow of energy in an ecosystem is unidirectional.

Reason (R) Energy enters the ecosystem through producers and exits through decomposers, forming a sequential pathway.

In the light of the above statements, choose the correct answer from the options given below.
(a) A is false, but R is true
(b) Both A and R are true and R is the correct explanation of A
(c) Both A and R are true, but R is not the correct explanation of A
(d) A is true, but R is false

29. Given below are two statements.
Statement I The flow of energy follows the second law of thermodynamics.
Statement II The transfer of energy from one organism to another is accompanied by degradation and loss of a major part of food energy as heat.
In the light of above statements, choose the correct answer from the options given below.
(a) Statement I is incorrect, but statement II is correct
(b) Both statement I and statement II are correct
(c) Both statement I and statement II are incorrect
(d) Statement I is correct, but statement II is incorrect

30. Given below are two statements.
Statement I Natural ecosystems are capable of operating and maintaining themselves without any major interference by human.
Statement II Natural ecosystems possess very little diversity of species.
In the light of above statements, choose the correct answer from the options given below.
(a) Statement I is incorrect, but statement II is correct
(b) Both statement I and statement II are correct
(c) Both statement I and statement II are incorrect
(d) Statement I is correct, but statement II is incorrect

Scan for online chapter test

Response Index

01 ⓐ ⓑ ⓒ ⓓ	14 ⓐ ⓑ ⓒ ⓓ	27 ⓐ ⓑ ⓒ ⓓ	40 ⓐ ⓑ ⓒ ⓓ
02 ⓐ ⓑ ⓒ ⓓ	15 ⓐ ⓑ ⓒ ⓓ	28 ⓐ ⓑ ⓒ ⓓ	41 ⓐ ⓑ ⓒ ⓓ
03 ⓐ ⓑ ⓒ ⓓ	16 ⓐ ⓑ ⓒ ⓓ	29 ⓐ ⓑ ⓒ ⓓ	42 ⓐ ⓑ ⓒ ⓓ
04 ⓐ ⓑ ⓒ ⓓ	17 ⓐ ⓑ ⓒ ⓓ	30 ⓐ ⓑ ⓒ ⓓ	43 ⓐ ⓑ ⓒ ⓓ
05 ⓐ ⓑ ⓒ ⓓ	18 ⓐ ⓑ ⓒ ⓓ	31 ⓐ ⓑ ⓒ ⓓ	44 ⓐ ⓑ ⓒ ⓓ
06 ⓐ ⓑ ⓒ ⓓ	19 ⓐ ⓑ ⓒ ⓓ	32 ⓐ ⓑ ⓒ ⓓ	45 ⓐ ⓑ ⓒ ⓓ
07 ⓐ ⓑ ⓒ ⓓ	20 ⓐ ⓑ ⓒ ⓓ	33 ⓐ ⓑ ⓒ ⓓ	46 ⓐ ⓑ ⓒ ⓓ
08 ⓐ ⓑ ⓒ ⓓ	21 ⓐ ⓑ ⓒ ⓓ	34 ⓐ ⓑ ⓒ ⓓ	47 ⓐ ⓑ ⓒ ⓓ
09 ⓐ ⓑ ⓒ ⓓ	22 ⓐ ⓑ ⓒ ⓓ	35 ⓐ ⓑ ⓒ ⓓ	48 ⓐ ⓑ ⓒ ⓓ
10 ⓐ ⓑ ⓒ ⓓ	23 ⓐ ⓑ ⓒ ⓓ	36 ⓐ ⓑ ⓒ ⓓ	49 ⓐ ⓑ ⓒ ⓓ
11 ⓐ ⓑ ⓒ ⓓ	24 ⓐ ⓑ ⓒ ⓓ	37 ⓐ ⓑ ⓒ ⓓ	50 ⓐ ⓑ ⓒ ⓓ
12 ⓐ ⓑ ⓒ ⓓ	25 ⓐ ⓑ ⓒ ⓓ	38 ⓐ ⓑ ⓒ ⓓ	
13 ⓐ ⓑ ⓒ ⓓ	26 ⓐ ⓑ ⓒ ⓓ	39 ⓐ ⓑ ⓒ ⓓ	

Performance Scanner

> 90% Excellent !	You have mastered this chapter. The concepts of this chapter are at your fingertips. Move on to the next chapter and maintain this momentum.
76-90% Very Good !	You have a good command over this chapter. Revise the chapter again after a few days and enhance your performance.
60-75% Good !	You have a wide scope to learn for this chapter. Revise this chapter again.
<60% Not Satisfactory!	You have a long way ahead of you to master this chapter. Revise it thoroughly.

Space for Rough Work

Space for Rough Work

Test Booklet No. 3947363

Test Booklet Code CH13

MEDACE
NEET (UG)
SELF ASSESSMENT KIT

Biodiversity and Conservation

Topics Covered

Biodiversity : Patterns and Importance

Loss of Biodiversity and Conservation

Important Instructions

- This Booklet Contains – Two Topic Tests and One Test on Complete Chapter.
- Each question carries 4 marks.
- For each correct response, the candidate will get 4 marks. And for every incorrect response, 1 mark will be additionally deducted from total score.
- Use **Blue/Black** point pen only for filling the OMR.
- Rough work is to be done in the space provided for this purpose in the test booklet only.

Name of the Candidate (In Capitals) ____________________

____

Candidate's Signature ____________________

Invigilator's Signature ____________________

Facsimile signature stamp of center superintendent____________________

Do not open this booklet until you start attempting the test

Topical Follow Thru

Test 1

Syllabus
- Concept of biodiversity
- Patterns of biodiversity
- Importance of biodiversity

For deeper insight, **Scan the QR Code**

Important Instructions

- The test is of 30 minutes duration and contains 25 Multiple Choice Questions (four options with a single correct answer).
- Choose the correct option and fill the OMR given on the last page of this test accordingly.
- At some instances, you may find more than 1 option to be correct. In such circumstances, you have to judge the most appropriate answer as per the conditions given in the question.

1. Which of the following is not the example of genetic diversity?

(a) More than 50,000 genetically different strains of rice
(b) Western Ghats having greater amphibian species than the Eastern Ghats
(c) More than thousand varieties of mangoes
(d) Different breeds of dogs

2. Identify the correct statement from the following.

(a) Because of possessing the rich biodiversity, India is considered as the mega diversity countries of the world.
(b) The number of animal species is more than 90%.
(c) The number of fish species in the world is more than the combined total of the species of other vertebrates.
(d) India has only 2.4% of the world's land area, but it possesses 25% species diversity of the world.

3. According to Robert May, the global species diversity is about

(a) 20 million
(b) 50 million
(c) 7 million
(d) 1.5 million

4. Match the List I with List II.

	List I (Regions)		List II (Number of bird species)
A.	Colombia	1.	56
B.	New York	2.	1200
C.	Greenland	3.	105
D.	India	4.	1400

Choose the correct answer from the options given below.

	A	B	C	D
(a)	4	1	2	3
(b)	4	3	1	2
(c)	3	4	2	1
(d)	1	4	3	2

5. Given below are two statements.

Statement I As per IUCN, the total number of global species described so far is slightly more than 1.5 million.

Statement II The completion rate of species inventories is higher in tropical regions than in the temperate regions.

In the light of above statements, choose the correct answers from the options given below.
(a) Statement I is incorrect, but statement II is correct
(b) Both statement I and statement II are correct
(c) Both statement I and statement II are incorrect
(d) Statement I is correct, but statement II is incorrect

6. According to Alexander von Humboldt,
(a) species richness decreases with increasing area of exploration
(b) species richness increases with increased area, but only up to a limit
(c) there is no relationship between species richness and area explored
(d) species richness goes on increasing with increasing area of exploration

7. Which type of graph curve is obtained for species richness of angiosperms, birds, bats and fresh water fishes, when drawn against the explored area?
(a) Straight line
(b) Rectangular hyperbola
(c) S-shaped
(d) Slide curve

8. Given below are two statements; one is labelled as Assertion (A) and the other is labelled as Reason (R).
Assertion (A) Biodiversity is normally greater in lower latitudes as compared to higher latitudes.
Reason (R) Along the mountain gradients, biodiversity is normally greater in lower altitudes as compared to higher altitudes.
In the light of the above statements, choose the correct answer from the options given below.
(a) A is false, but R is true.
(b) Both A and R are true and R is the correct explanation of A.
(c) Both A and R are true, but R is not the correct explanation of A.
(d) A is true, but R is false.

9. Which of the following best describes the impact of losing key species that drive major ecosystem functions?
(a) Co-extinction
(b) Darwin's fitness
(c) Rivet-popper hypothesis
(d) Species-area relationship

10. The following pie chart represents global diversity of invertebrates.

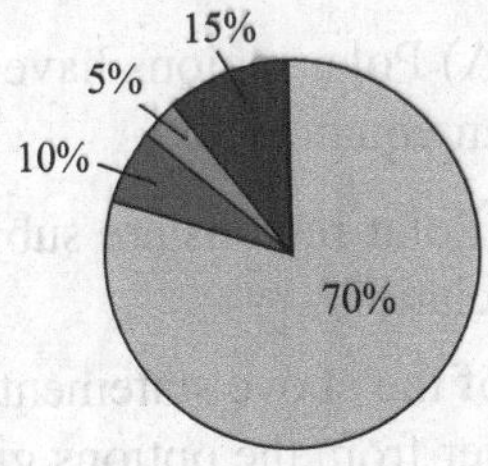

Identify the taxonomic groups which occupy the largest and the least area of the pie chart, respectively.
(a) Crustaceans and insects
(b) Insects and crustaceans
(c) Molluscs and insects
(d) Nematodes and molluscs

11. For frugivorous birds and mammals in the tropical forests of different continents, the slope of line is found to be
(a) 0.015 (b) 0.15
(c) 1.05 (d) 1.15

12. Which of the following is not related to the possible reason for having the greatest biodiversity in the tropics?
(a) Tropical latitudes have remained relatively undisturbed for millions of years and, thus had a long evolutionary time for species diversification.
(b) Tropical environments are less seasonal, relatively more constant, and predictable than that of other latitudes.
(c) More solar energy is available in the tropics, which contributes to higher productivity.
(d) Tropical regions have larger human populations, leading to more significant habitat modification and species conservation.

13. Which of the following is not a key characteristic of biodiversity hotspots?
(a) Mostly located in the tropics
(b) Abundance of endemic species
(c) Mostly located in the polar regions
(d) Large number of species

14. Given below are two statements; one is labelled as Assertion (A) and the other is labelled as Reason (R).

Assertion (A) Polar regions have more species diversity than equator.

Reason (R) Polar regions are subjected to frequent glaciation.

In the light of the above statements, choose the correct answer from the options given below.
(a) A is false, but R is true
(b) Both A and R are true and R is the correct explanation of A
(c) Both A and R are true, but R is not the correct explanation of A
(d) A is true, but R is false

15. Given below are few statements.
I. Amazonian forest is home to more species of birds than colombia.
II. Speciation is generally a function of time.
III. Number of prokaryotes are not yet estimated due to unsuitable conventional taxonomic methods.
IV. Various types of orchids in a tropical forest represent example of genetic diversity.
Choose the correct set of statements from the following options.
(a) I, II, III and IV
(b) II, III and IV
(c) II and III
(d) I and IV

16. Which of the following levels of biological organisation is not typically considered when discussing biodiversity?
(a) Molecular level
(b) Ecosystem level
(c) Social organisation level
(d) Individual organism level

17. Edward Wilson popularised the term biodiversity to specifically refer to
(a) combined diversity at all the levels of biological organisation.
(b) the number of species in a region
(c) genetic variation within a species
(d) species evenness in a particular habitat

18. Which of the following is a possible impact of global climate change on biodiversity?
(a) An increase in polar diversity due to warmer temperatures
(b) A decrease in tropical biodiversity due to more extreme weather conditions.
(c) A uniform increase in species diversity across all latitudes
(d) No significant change in biodiversity as species adapt to new climates.

19. The extraordinary biodiversity of the Amazonian rain forest is due to
(a) its proximity to the equator, resulting in stable and warm climatic conditions year-round
(b) high levels of pollution in these area, leading to natural selection and evolution of new species
(c) frequent natural disasters in the Amazon, which regularly clear the forest for new species to colonise
(d) the lack of evolutionary pressure in the Amazon, leading to more species surviving.

20. Given below are two statements.
Statement I India is one of the 12 mega diversity countries of the world, contributing 8.1% of the global species diversity.
Statement II According to May's global estimates, only 22% of the total species have been recorded so far.
In the light of above statements, choose the correct answer from the options given below.
(a) Statement I is incorrect, but statement II is correct
(b) Both statement I and statement II are correct
(c) Both statement I and statement II are incorrect
(d) Statement I is correct, but statement II is incorrect

21. David Tilman's experiments suggest that species richness might be linked to ecosystem stability. Which of the following statements is the correct interpretation of about the above information?

(a) More species always guarantee a more stable ecosystem.

(b) Ecosystems with fewer species are more stable.

(c) An ecosystem with high species richness may have a higher resilience to environmental disturbances.

(d) Productivity in ecosystem is unaffected by species richness.

22. There is a concern about species extinction leading to a less functional ecosystem because

(a) ecosystems have a fixed number of species that must be maintained for stability.

(b) every species has an irreplaceable role in the ecosystem.

(c) each ecosystem can function equally well with fewer species as long as key species remain as such.

(d) human activities have no impact on species extinction rates.

23. Which of the following statement is correct for the Z value closer to 1.2?

(a) It represents the species richness of birds in a small forest patch.

(b) It shows the species richness of plants in a British meadow.

(c) It represents species richness across multiple continents.

(d) It represents species richness in a freshwater lake.

24. India has a greater ecosystem diversity than a Scandivanian country like Norway. Which level of diversity does it represent?

(a) Species diversity

(b) Genetic diversity

(c) Molecular diversity

(d) Ecological diversity

25. Given below are two statements, one is labelled as Assertion (A) and other is labelled as Reason (R).

Assertion (A) More than 70% of all recorded species on Earth are animals.

Reason (R) Plants are less diverse than animals in terms of the number of species.

In the light of the above statements, choose the correct answer from the options given below.

(a) A is false, but R is true

(b) Both A and R are true and R is the correct explanation of A.

(c) Both A and R are true, but R is not the correct explanation of A.

(d) A is true, but R is false

Response Index

01	a	b	c	d	10	a	b	c	d	19	a	b	c	d
02	a	b	c	d	11	a	b	c	d	20	a	b	c	d
03	a	b	c	d	12	a	b	c	d	21	a	b	c	d
04	a	b	c	d	13	a	b	c	d	22	a	b	c	d
05	a	b	c	d	14	a	b	c	d	23	a	b	c	d
06	a	b	c	d	15	a	b	c	d	24	a	b	c	d
07	a	b	c	d	16	a	b	c	d	25	a	b	c	d
08	a	b	c	d	17	a	b	c	d					
09	a	b	c	d	18	a	b	c	d					

Performance Scanner

> 90% Excellent !	You have mastered these topics. The concepts of these topics are at your fingertips. Move on to the next test and maintain this momentum.
76-90% Very Good !	You have a good command over these topics. Revise these topics again after a few days and enhance your performance.
60-75% Good !	You have a wide scope to learn for these topics. Revise these topics again.
<60% Not Satisfactory!	You have a long way ahead of you to master these topics. Revise it thoroughly.

Test 2

Syllabus

- Loss of Biodiversity
- Biodiversity conservation
- Hotspots
- Endangered organisms
- Extinction
- Red Data Book
- Biosphere reserves
- National Parks and Sanctuaries
- Sacred Groves

For deeper insight, Scan the QR Code 

Important Instructions

- The test is of 30 minutes duration and contains 25 Multiple Choice Questions (four options with a single correct answer).
- Choose the correct option and fill the OMR given on the last page of this test accordingly.
- At some instances, you may find more than 1 option to be correct. In such circumstances, you have to judge the most appropriate answer as per the conditions given in the question.

1. Select the incorrect match w.r.t. recent extinction.
(a) Dodo - Mauritius
(b) Quagga - America
(c) Thylacine - Australia
(d) Steller's sea cow - Russia

2. The passenger pigeon, dodo, and steller's sea cow are extinct now. These were extinct due to
(a) their large body size
(b) over exploitation by human
(c) small population size
(d) habitat loss and fragmentation

3. Western Ghats have a large number of plants and animals species that are not found anywhere else. Which of the following is suitable term for such species?
(a) Endemic
(b) Vulnerable
(c) Threatened
(d) Keystone

4. Which statement is not correct regarding extinction of species?
(a) The IUCN Red List identifies and documents species' extinction risk to guide conservation actions.
(b) Currently, 12% of bird species, 23% of mammals species, 32% of amphibians species and 31% of gymnosperms species, worldwide are at risk of extinction.
(c) Over 15,500 species world-wide are facing the threat of extinction.
(d) Amphibians appear to be more impervious to extinction.

5. Which of the following statements about mass extinction of life on earth is incorrect?
(a) During the long period (> 3 billion years) since the origin and diversification of life on earth, there were five episodes of mass extinction of species.
(b) The current species extinction rates are estimated to be 100 to 1,000 times faster than in pre-human times.
(c) Human activities are responsible for the faster rates of the sixth mass extinction.
(d) If present trends continue, nearly half of all species on earth might be wiped out within the next 1,000 years.

6. The biodiversity hotspot which is not found in India is-
(a) Western Ghats and Sri Lanka
(b) Indo-Burma
(c) Himalaya
(d) Madagascar and the Indian Ocean Islands

7. Match the List I with List II.

	List I (Sacred groves region)		List II (States of India)
A.	Aravalli Hills	1.	Karnataka and Maharashtra
B.	Khasi and Jaintia Hills	2.	Madhya Pradesh
C.	Western Ghat regions	3.	Meghalaya
D.	Sarguja	4.	Rajasthan

Choose the correct answer from the options given below.

	A	B	C	D
(a)	1	3	2	4
(b)	4	1	3	2
(c)	3	1	2	4
(d)	4	3	1	2

8. Which of the following is not included in method of *ex-situ* conservation of biodiversity ?

(a) *In-vitro* fertilisation
(b) Micropropagation
(c) Cryopreservation
(d) National parks

9. The different advantages of *ex situ* conservation are all, except

(a) it gives longer life time and breeding activity to animals
(b) genetic techniques can be utilised in the process
(c) captive breeding species can again be reintroduced in the wild
(d) it creates competitiveness between the endangered species

10. 'The Evil Quartet' is the sobriquet used to describe causes of biodiversity losses. Following are the causes included in the quartet, except

(a) Habitat loss and fragmentation
(b) Population explosion
(c) Over exploitation
(d) Co-extinction

11. Which of the following is defined as exploration of molecular, genetic and species level diversity for novel products of economic importance?

(a) Biopiracy
(b) Bioenergetics
(c) Bioremediation
(d) Bioprospecting

12. Given below are two statements.

Statement I Biodiversity provides a lot of a pleasures of walking through thick woods, watching spring flowers in full bloom or waking to a bulbul's song in the morning.

Statement II The aesthetic pleasure provided by biodiversity comes under the narrowly utilitarian approach of biodiversity.

In the light of the above statements, choose the correct answer from the options given below.

(a) Statement I is incorrect, but statement II is correct
(b) Both statement I and statement II are correct
(c) Both statement I and statement II are incorrect
(d) Statement I is correct, but statement II is incorrect

13. Given below are two statements; one is labelled as Assertion (A) and the other is labelled as Reason (R).

Assertion (A) In National Parks, cultivation of land and grazing is not permitted.

Reason (R) National Park is meant for the protection of both flora and fauna under the Government.

In the light of the above statements, choose the correct answer from the options given below.

(a) A is false, but R is true
(b) Both A and R are true and R is the correct explanation of A
(c) Both A and R are true, but R is not the correct explanation of A
(d) A is true, but R is false

14. Select the incorrect statements from the following.

I. The Indian government has established biosphere reserves, national parks and wildlife sanctuaries for biodiversity conservation.

II. Sacred groves have been legally protected under community reserves in the Wildlife (Protection) Amendment act, 2002.
III. Sacred groves are dedicated to local deities or tree spirits.
IV. In Meghalaya, the sacred groves are the last refuges for a large number of rare and threatened plants.
V. The total number of biodiversity hotspots in the world is 24 .

Choose the correct answer from the options given below.
(a) Only V
(b) II, III and V
(c) II and V
(d) IV and V

15. The historic convention on biological diversity, the Earth Summit, held in Rio de Janeiro in 1992 was called
(a) for conservation of biodiversity and sustainable utilisation of its benefits
(b) to assess threats posed to native species by invasive weed species
(c) for immediate steps to discontinue the use of CFCs that were damaging the ozone layer
(d) to reduce CO_2 emissions and global warming

16. According to the IUCN Red List (2004), how many species have been documented as extinct in the last 500 years?
(a) 784 (b) 1,000
(c) 2,000 (d) 15,500

17. .... of all amphibian species in the world face the threat of extinction.
(a) 12% (b) 23%
(c) 32% (d) 31%

18. Which of the following statements is true about extinction rate of bird, mammals, amphibians and gymnosperms?
(a) Gymnosperms are less threatened than amphibians.
(b) Birds are more threatened than mammals
(c) Amphibians have the lowest extinction threat among the groups.
(d) All the species in the world have the same level of extinction threat.

19. By what percentage has the tropical rain forest cover decreased from its original extent?
(a) from 14% to 6%
(b) from 10% to 4%
(c) from 14% to 8%
(d) from 20% to 10%

20. Given below are two statements,
Statement I Co-extinctions occur when a species becomes extinct but does not affect any other species associated with it.
Statement II Co-extinction happens when the extinction of one species leads to the extinction of other species that depend on it.
In the light of the above statements, choose the correct answer from the options given below.
(a) Statement I is incorrect, but statement II is correct
(b) Both statement I and statement II are correct
(c) Both statement I and statement II are incorrect
(d) Statement I is correct, but statement II is incorrect

21. Which of the following is an example of a broadly utilitarian argument for conserving biodiversity?
(a) The ethical duty to protect endangered species
(b) The potential to discover new medicinal plants.
(c) The economic benefits derived from nature.
(d) The role of species in maintaining ecosystem services.

22. What are sacred groves primarily known for?
(a) Their use in large scale agricultural production
(b) Their protection and preservation due of biodiversity due to cultural and religious significance
(c) Their role in urban development
(d) Their function as major industrial zones.

23. The intangible benefit of biodiversity relates to the
(a) economic value of timber
(b) aesthetic pleasure of walking through a forest
(c) market price of fruits and vegetables
(d) cost savings from natural pest control.

24. According to the convention on Biological Diversity, who is responsible for the conservation of biodiversity?
(a) Individual countries alone
(b) Private organisations only
(c) All nations collectively
(d) Only developed nations

25. What is common feature of regions classified as biodiversity hotspots?
(a) They have low levels of species endemism
(b) They are areas with high human population density
(c) They experience accelerated habitat loss
(d) They are characterised by extensive urbanisation.

Response Index

01	a	b	c	d	10	a	b	c	d	19	a	b	c	d
02	a	b	c	d	11	a	b	c	d	20	a	b	c	d
03	a	b	c	d	12	a	b	c	d	21	a	b	c	d
04	a	b	c	d	13	a	b	c	d	22	a	b	c	d
05	a	b	c	d	14	a	b	c	d	23	a	b	c	d
06	a	b	c	d	15	a	b	c	d	24	a	b	c	d
07	a	b	c	d	16	a	b	c	d	25	a	b	c	d
08	a	b	c	d	17	a	b	c	d					
09	a	b	c	d	18	a	b	c	d					

Performance Scanner

> 90% Excellent !	You have mastered these topics. The concepts of these topics are at your fingertips. Move on to the next test and maintain this momentum.
76-90% Very Good !	You have a good command over these topics. Revise these topics again after a few days and enhance your performance.
60-75% Good !	You have a wide scope to learn for these topics. Revise these topics again.
<60% Not Satisfactory!	You have a long way ahead of you to master these topics. Revise it thoroughly.

Chapter Break Thru

Syllabus			
	• Concept of biodiversity • Patterns of biodiversity • Importance of biodiversity • Loss of biodiversity	• Biodiversity conservation • Hotspots • Endangered organisms • Extinction	• Red Data Book • Biosphere reserves • National Parks and Sanctuaries • Sacred Groves

Important Instructions

- The test is of 1 hour duration and contains 30 Multiple-Choice Questions (Four options with a single correct answer).
- Choose the correct option and fill the OMR given on the last page of this test accordingly.
- At some instances, you may find more than 1 option to be correct. In such circumstances, you have to judge the most appropriate answer as per the conditions given in the question.

1. Which of the following correctly describes the observation of Alexander von Humboldt?

(a) Species richness decreases with increasing area of exploration
(b) Species richness increases with increasing area of exploration, but upto a limit
(c) There is no relationship between species richness and area explored
(d) Species richness goes on increasing with increasing the area of exploration without any limit

2. The approximate number of species of ants, beetles and orchids in world are

(a) 20,000, 3,00,000 and 28,000 respectively
(b) 20,000, 3,00,000 and 20,000 respectively
(c) 15,000, 28,000 and 28,000 respectively
(d) 20,000, 30,0000 and 28,000 respectively

3. Select the incorrect statement w.r.t. biodiversity.

(a) More than 70 percent of all the species recorded are animals, while plants comprise approximately 22 percent of the total biodiversity.
(b) Insects are the most species-rich taxonomic group, making up more than 70 percent of the total biodiversity.
(c) The number of fungi species globally is more than the sum total of the species of fishes, amphibians, reptiles and mammals.
(d) Nearly 45,000 species of plants and twice as many species of animals have been recorded from India.

4. Which of the following explains the diverse number of niches, trophic levels and various ecological process that sustain energy flow, food webs and recycling of nutrients?

(a) Species diversity
(b) Ecosystem diversity
(c) Genetic diversity
(d) Kingdom diversity

5. The following graph shows Species-area relationship.

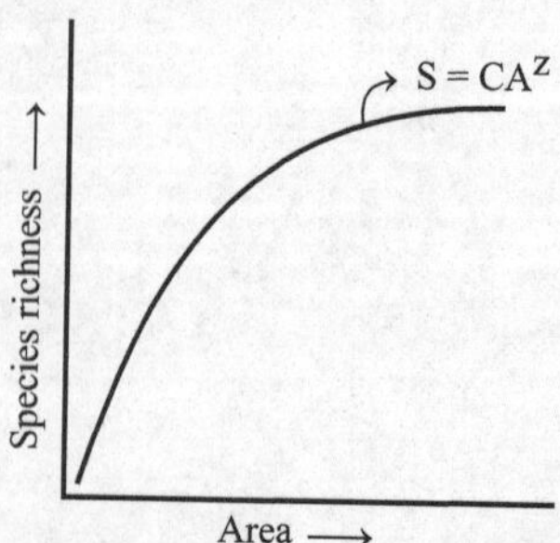

The S and C in this graph represent
(a) area and species richness, respectively
(b) y-intercept and area, respectively
(c) species richness and y-intercept, respectively
(d) species richness and regression coefficient, respectively

6. Where was the World Summit on Sustainable Development (2002) held?
(a) Brazil (b) Argentina
(c) Peru (d) South Africa

7. Given below are two statements.
Statement I The colonisation of tropical Pacific Islands by humans resulted in the extinction of more than 2000 species of native birds.
Statement II David Tilman showed that increased diversity contributed to higher productivity.
In light of the above statements, choose the correct answers from the options given below.
(a) Statement I is incorrect, but statement II is correct
(b) Both statement I and statement II are correct
(c) Both statement I and statement II are incorrect
(d) Statement I is correct, but statement II is incorrect

8. Given below are few statements.
I. Diversity of prokaryotes alone might run into millions if we accept biochemical or molecular criteria for their delineation.
II. The ratio of fungi to algae with respect to their proportionate number of species is lesser than the ratio of insects to crustaceans.
III. The large tropical region near the Nile basin in Africa has the greatest biodiversity on earth.
IV. Solar energy at the tropical and equatorial region is always more than the solar energy received at the temperate and polar region.
V. Stable community must be resistant to invasion by alien species.
Choose the correct set of statements from the options given below.
(a) I, II, III and IV
(b) I, II, III and V
(c) I, II, IV and V
(d) III and V

9. The most important cause for animals and plants being driven to extinction is
(a) drought and floods
(b) economic exploitation
(c) alien species invasion
(d) habitat loss and fragmentation

10. Communities with more species tend to be more stable than those with fewer species. This was concluded by
(a) Paul Ehrlich
(b) Edward Wilson
(c) David Tilman
(d) Alexander von Humboldt

11. Introduction of *Clarias gariepinus* in river Yamuna leads to decline in population of indian native fishes. This can be categorised as
(a) co-extinction
(b) habitat fragmentation
(c) over-exploitation
(d) alien species invasion

12. Decreasing population of honeybees is leading to a threat to the ecosystem. This can be explained by
(a) Keystone species hypothesis
(b) Rivet Popper hypothesis
(c) Trophic cascade hypothesis
(d) Red Queen hypothesis

13. Which of the following biodiversity product is not related to narrowly utilitarian argument of biodiversity conservation?
(a) Timber is obtained from pine trees
(b) Reserpine is a drug obtained from roots of *Rauwolfia serpentina*
(c) A number of organisms like bees, bumblebees, etc., are involved in pollination
(d) Natural fibers are obtained from some plants

14. All of the given are included in *ex situ* conservation, except
(a) Botanical gardens
(b) Sacred groves
(c) Wildlife safari parks
(d) Zoological parks

15. Which of the following species was introduced for ornamentation, but has become a troublesome weed in India?
(a) *Parthenium hysterophorus*
(b) *Eichhornia crassipes*
(c) *Prosopis juliflora*
(d) *Trapa bispinosa*

16. The protected areas are biogeographical regions where
(a) biological diversity alongwith natural and cultural resources is protected
(b) biological diversity is protected with the help of tribal communities
(c) domesticated species are protected
(d) recalcitrant seeds are grown and their varieties are maintained

17. Many species of plants and animals are on the verge of extinction. Such creatures are conserved in which of the following area?
(a) Zoos
(b) Botanical garden
(c) Wildlife sanctuary
(d) Sacred grove

18. The legally protected region of biosphere reserve where no human activity is allowed and an area of biosphere reserve where active coorporation between management and local people occur are known as
(a) core zone and transition zone, respectively
(b) buffer zone and core zone, respectively
(c) transition zone and buffer zone, respectively
(d) core zone and restoration zone, respectively

19. Which of the following is common to the techniques-(i) *In-vitro* fertilisation, (ii) cryopreservation, and (iii) tissue culture?
(a) All are *in-situ* conservation methods.
(b) All are *ex-situ* conservation methods.
(c) All require ultra-modern equipment and large space.
(d) All are methods of conservation of extinct organisms.

20. All are included in method of *in-situ* conservation of biodiversity, except
(a) wildlife sanctuary
(b) botanical garden
(c) sacred grove
(d) biosphere reserve

21. Biologically diverse communities are more likely to contain species that confer resilience to that ecosystem because as a community accumulates species,
(a) there is a higher chance of any one of them having traits that enable them to adapt to a changing environment
(b) there is a higher chance of competition between these species which leads to instability of community
(c) there is a chance of extinction of a species due to resource depletion
(d) there is a higher chance of genetic loss

22. Given below are two statements.

Statement I Species diversity decreases as we move away from the equator towards the poles, with very few exceptions.

Statement II Species diversity decreases with increasing altitude.

In the light of the above statements, choose the correct answer from the options given below.
(a) Statement I is incorrect, but statement II is correct
(b) Both statement I and statement II are correct
(c) Both statement I and statement II are incorrect
(d) Statement I is correct, but statement II is incorrect

23. A graph showing species-area relationship is given below.

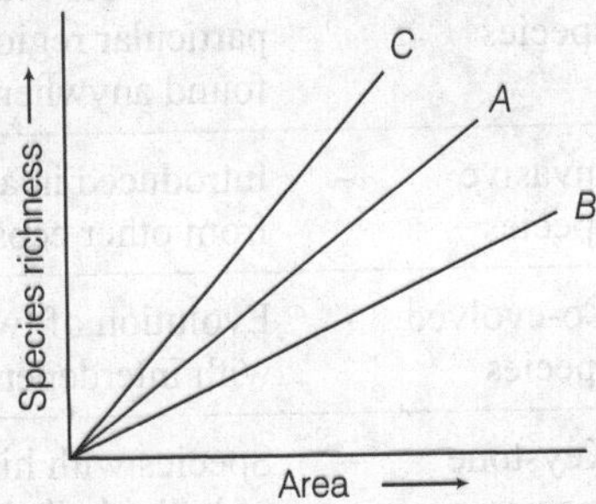

Choose the correct answer from the options given below which represents the correct interpretation of the given graph.
(a) The species richness of *B* is more than *A*.
(b) The species richness of *A* is more than *B*.
(c) A has more species richness than *C*.
(d) The value of *Z* for *B* could be in the range of 0.6 to 1.2.

24. Given below are two statements; one is labelled as the Assertion (A) and the other is labelled as the Reason (R).
Assertion (A) Endemic organisms with limited ranges are most affected by habitat destruction.
Reason (R) Endemic species are not found anywhere else in the world and thus have less chance of recovering.
In the light of the above statements choose the correct answer from the options given below.
(a) A is false, but R is true
(b) Both A and R are true and R is the correct explanation of A
(c) Both A and R are true, but R is not the correct explanation of A
(d) A is true, but R is false

25. Select the statements which are not true about sixth mass extinction of life on earth.
I. It is 100 - 1000 times faster than previous mass extinction.
II. Human greed and negligence are primarily responsible for the faster rate.
III. If the present trends continue, nearly half of all the species on earth might be perished within the next 1000 years.
IV. Earth faced mass extinction after appearance of human.
V. Mass extinction is a misleading concept which does not have any evidence.

Choose the correct answer out of the given options.
(a) I and III (b) III, IV, and V
(c) I, II, and III (d) IV and V

26. Which of the following scenario best illustrates the concept of coextinction?
(a) A predator species goes extinct due to habitat destruction, leading to an overpopulation of its prey
(b) The extinction of a *Pronuba* moth leads to the extinction of the *Yucca* plant
(c) A herbivorous mammal goes extinct, causing an increase in plant diversity due to reduced grazing pressure
(d) An invasive species outcompetes and replaces a native species, leading to a shift in the ecosystem's food web structure

27. Given below are two statements; one is labelled as the Assertion (A) and the other is labelled as the Reason (R).
Assertion (A) The relationship between species richness and area for a wide variety of taxa gives a rectangular hyperbola.
Reason (R) Within a region, species richness increases with increasing explored area, but only up to a limit.
In the light of the above statements, choose the correct answer from the options given below.
(a) A is false, but R is true
(b) Both A and R are true, and R is the correct explanation of A
(c) Both A and R are correct, but R is not the correct explanation of A
(d) A is true, but R is false

28. A species facing extremely high risk of extinction in the immediate future is called
(a) Endangered species
(b) Critically endangered species
(c) Vulnerable species
(d) Least Concerned species

29. What was the primary objective of the historic convention on Biological Diversity, also known as 'The Earth Summit,' held in Rio de Janeiro in 1992?

(a) To promote global trade and economic cooperation and to make farmers more aware of their rights

(b) To encourage the exploration and exploitation of natural resources and to make people aware of biopiracy

(c) To call upon all nations to take appropriate measures for the conservation of biodiversity and the sustainable utilization of its benefits

(d) To establish a unified global currency for environmental conservation

30. Select the incorrect match.

(a)	Endemic species	–	Species confined to particular region and not found anywhere else
(b)	Invasive species	–	Introduced in an ecosystem from other ecosystem
(c)	Co-evolved species	–	Evolution of two species with interdependency
(d)	Keystone species	–	Species with highest number of individuals in an ecosystem

Response Index

01 ⓐ ⓑ ⓒ ⓓ	14 ⓐ ⓑ ⓒ ⓓ	27 ⓐ ⓑ ⓒ ⓓ	40 ⓐ ⓑ ⓒ ⓓ
02 ⓐ ⓑ ⓒ ⓓ	15 ⓐ ⓑ ⓒ ⓓ	28 ⓐ ⓑ ⓒ ⓓ	41 ⓐ ⓑ ⓒ ⓓ
03 ⓐ ⓑ ⓒ ⓓ	16 ⓐ ⓑ ⓒ ⓓ	29 ⓐ ⓑ ⓒ ⓓ	42 ⓐ ⓑ ⓒ ⓓ
04 ⓐ ⓑ ⓒ ⓓ	17 ⓐ ⓑ ⓒ ⓓ	30 ⓐ ⓑ ⓒ ⓓ	43 ⓐ ⓑ ⓒ ⓓ
05 ⓐ ⓑ ⓒ ⓓ	18 ⓐ ⓑ ⓒ ⓓ	31 ⓐ ⓑ ⓒ ⓓ	44 ⓐ ⓑ ⓒ ⓓ
06 ⓐ ⓑ ⓒ ⓓ	19 ⓐ ⓑ ⓒ ⓓ	32 ⓐ ⓑ ⓒ ⓓ	45 ⓐ ⓑ ⓒ ⓓ
07 ⓐ ⓑ ⓒ ⓓ	20 ⓐ ⓑ ⓒ ⓓ	33 ⓐ ⓑ ⓒ ⓓ	46 ⓐ ⓑ ⓒ ⓓ
08 ⓐ ⓑ ⓒ ⓓ	21 ⓐ ⓑ ⓒ ⓓ	34 ⓐ ⓑ ⓒ ⓓ	47 ⓐ ⓑ ⓒ ⓓ
09 ⓐ ⓑ ⓒ ⓓ	22 ⓐ ⓑ ⓒ ⓓ	35 ⓐ ⓑ ⓒ ⓓ	48 ⓐ ⓑ ⓒ ⓓ
10 ⓐ ⓑ ⓒ ⓓ	23 ⓐ ⓑ ⓒ ⓓ	36 ⓐ ⓑ ⓒ ⓓ	49 ⓐ ⓑ ⓒ ⓓ
11 ⓐ ⓑ ⓒ ⓓ	24 ⓐ ⓑ ⓒ ⓓ	37 ⓐ ⓑ ⓒ ⓓ	50 ⓐ ⓑ ⓒ ⓓ
12 ⓐ ⓑ ⓒ ⓓ	25 ⓐ ⓑ ⓒ ⓓ	38 ⓐ ⓑ ⓒ ⓓ	
13 ⓐ ⓑ ⓒ ⓓ	26 ⓐ ⓑ ⓒ ⓓ	39 ⓐ ⓑ ⓒ ⓓ	

Performance Scanner

> 90% Excellent !	You have mastered this chapter. The concepts of this chapter are at your fingertips. Move on to the next chapter and maintain this momentum.
76-90% Very Good !	You have a good command over this chapter. Revise the chapter again after a few days and enhance your performance.
60-75% Good !	You have a wide scope to learn for this chapter. Revise this chapter again.
<60% Not Satisfactory!	You have a long way ahead of you to master this chapter. Revise it thoroughly.

Scan for online chapter test

Scan for online unit test

Space for Rough Work

Space for Rough Work

Test Booklet No. **3947364**

Test Booklet Code **SPT1**

MEDACE

NEET (UG)

SELF ASSESSMENT KIT

Syllabus Part Thru 1

(Half Syllabus Test)

Sexual Reproduction in Flowering Plants

Human Reproduction

Reproductive Health

Principles of Inheritance and Variation

Molecular Basis of Inheritance

Evolution

Human Health and Diseases

Important Instructions

- The test is of **1 hours 30 minutes** duration and the Test Booklet contains **90** multiple-choice questions (four options with a single correct answer) from biology.
- Candidates are advised to read all questions before they start attempting the question paper.
- Each questions carries 4 marks. For each correct response, the candidate will get 4 marks. For each incorrect response, one marks will be deducted from the total scores.
- In the event of candidate marking more than one option one mark will be deducted. The maximum marks are 180.
- Use **Blue/Black Point Pen only** for writing particular on this page/ marking response on Answer Sheet.

Name of the Candidate (In Capitals) ____________

____

Candidate's Signature ____________

Invigilator's Signature ____________

Facsimile signature stamp of center superintendent____________

Do not open this booklet until you start attempting the test

Biology

1. A man observed a plant in his garden. He hypothesized that the flower colour exhibited incomplete dominance.

To check for this, he created true-breeding lines of red flowered and white flowered plants. He then crossed these and sampled 1000 progeny of F_2 generations. Which of the following cases, matches his hypothesis?

(a) 500 red, flowered plants, 250 pink flowered plants, and 500 white flowered plants
(b) 250 red flowered plants, 500 pink flowered plants, and 250 white flowered plants
(c) 250 red flowered plants, 250 pink flowered plants, and 500 white flowered plants
(d) 125 red flowered plants, 750 pink flowered plants and 125 white flowered plants

2. Given below are two statements.

Statement I The microsporangium is surrounded by three wall layers, i.e. epidermis, endothecium and outer layer.

Statement II Tapetum is the outermost wall layer of microsporangium.

In the light of the above statements, choose the correct answer from the options given below

(a) Statement I is incorrect, but statement II is correct
(b) Both statements I and II are correct
(c) Both statements I and II are incorrect
(d) Statement I is correct, but statement II is incorrect

3. Given below are two statements.

Statement I Infundibulum helps in the collection of the ovum, without the need of any modification.

Statement II Each ovary is covered by a thin epithelium which encloses the ovarian stroma.

In the light of the above statements, choose the correct answer from the options given below.

(a) Statement I is incorrect, but statement II is correct
(b) Both statements I and II are correct
(c) Both statements I and II are incorrect
(d) Statement I is correct, but statement II is incorrect

4. Read the following statements regarding structure of polynucleotide chain (DNA) .

I. Thymine is common for both DNA and RNA.
II. Adenine and guanine are the purines.
III. A nitrogenous base is linked to the —CH of 5′C pentose sugar to form nucleoside.
IV. Two nucleotides are linked through 3′–5′ phosphodiester linkage to form dinucleotide.
V. It has three components, i.e. a nitrogenous base, a pentose sugar and a phosphate group.

Which of the following statements are correct from the options given below?

(a) I, II and IV only
(b) I, IV and V only
(c) II, IV and V only
(d) I, II and III only

5. Few accessory glands are listed below.

I. Seminal vesicles
II. Bulbourethral glands
III. Bartholin's gland

Select the correct option that consists of male accessory glands.

(a) I and II (b) II and III
(c) III (d) I, II and III

6. Which of the following statements regarding seed is incorrect?
(a) Apomictic seeds do not show segregation of characters
(b) Residue of integuments present in black paper is called perisperm.
(c) The micropyle remains as small pore in seed coat
(d) Seeds have better adaptive strategies for dispersal

7. Which of the following statements is correct regarding the mechanism and characteristics of hormonal contraceptive methods?
(a) Oral contraceptive pills-thickens cervical mucus, inhibits endometrial growth, and can be effective for up to 5 years.
(b) Contraceptive implants-release hormones into the bloodstream, which primarily work by thickening cervical mucus and preventing ovulation, and can be effective for up to 3 years.
(c) Hormonal IUD-work by preventing meeting of sperm and ovum.
(d) Emergency contraceptive pills-contain synthetic hormones that inhibit ovulation and is effective upto 72 days.

8. Given below are two statements; one is labelled as Assertion (A) and the other is labelled as Reason (R).

Assertion (A) Hilum represents the junction between ovule and funicle.
Reason (R) The ovule is a small structure attached to placenta by means of a stalk called funicle.
In the light of the above statements, choose the correct answer from the options given below
(a) A is false, but R is true
(b) Both A and R are true and R is the correct explanation of A
(c) Both A and R are true, but R is not the correct explanation of A
(d) A is true, but R is false

9. Given below are two statements; one is labelled as Assertion (A) and the other is labelled as Reason (R).

Assertion (A) Morphine is very useful in patients who have undergone surgery.

Reason (R) Morphine is obtained from *Erythroxylum coca*.

In the light of the above statements, choose the correct answer from the options given below.
(a) A is false, but R is true
(b) Both A and R are true and R is the correct explanation of A
(c) Both A and R are true, but R is not the correct explanation of A
(d) A is true, but R is false

10. What type of evolution is seen in the two examples given below?
(i) Thorn and tendrils of *Bougainvillea* and *Cucurbita*.
(ii) Food storage in potato and sweet potato.
Choose the correct option from the conclusions given below
(a) Both are divergent evolution
(b) Both are convergent evolution
(c) First is divergent and second is convergent
(d) First is convergent and second is divergent

11. Read the following statements.
I. The theca layer is organised into an inner theca interna and an outer theca externa.
II. Antrum is a fluid filled cavity.
III. The tertiary follicle is termed as the Graafian follicle.
IV. The tertiary oocyte retains bulk of the nutrient rich membrane and cytoplasm of the secondary oocyte.
V. The secondary oocyte form a new membrane called zona pellucida surrounding it.
Choose the correct set of statements from the options given below.
(a) I and II (b) II and III
(c) I, II and V (d) II, III and IV

12. Match List-I with List-II.

List-I		List-II
A. *m*RNA	1.	Reads the genetic code
B. *r*RNA	2.	Initiates transcription
C. RNA polymerase	3.	Provides template
D. *t*RNA	4.	Catalytic role during transcription

Choose the correct option.

	A	B	C	D		A	B	C	D
(a)	3	4	2	1	(b)	2	3	4	1
(c)	4	2	1	3	(d)	4	2	3	1

13. Which of the following statement is incorrect?

(a) AIDS has no cure as the virus attacks the T-lymphocytes
(b) Treatment of AIDS with anti retroviral drugs can cure it completely
(c) AIDS is diagnosed by ELISA test
(d) AIDS affects the immune system of the body

14. Below are few listed plants.

I. Ginkgos
II. Ferns
III. Progymnosperms
IV. Herbaceous lycopods

Choose the correct option that consists of the plants that evolved in Mesozoic era.

(a) I and IV (b) II
(c) III only (d) I, II and IV

15. Observe the diagram given below and identify the incorrect statement with respect to it.

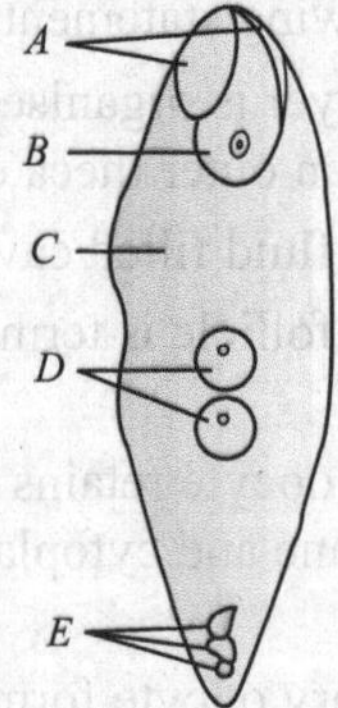

(a) 'A' have special cellular thickenings at the micropylar tip called filiform apparatus.
(b) Three cells that one labelled as structure 'E' are present at the micropylar end.
(c) 'A' and 'B' together constitute the egg apparatus and present at the micropylar end.
(d) 'C' posses two polar nuclei which are situated below the egg apparatus.

16. Spermiogenesis and spermiation are two processes taking place during the maturation of sperm cells. The major difference between both these processes is aptly explained by which of the following options?

(a) In spermiogenesis, spermatozoa from sertoli cells are released into the cavity of seminiferous tubles, whereas spermatozoa are formed in spermiation.
(b) Spermiogenesis involves formation of spermatozoa whereas spermiation involves release of spermatozoa from sertoli and into the cavity of seminiferous tubules.
(c) In spermiogenesis, spermatozoa are formed, while in spermiation, spermatids are formed
(d) In spermiogenesis, spermatozoa are formed.

17. Which of the following statement regarding pleiotropy is incorrect?

(a) A single gene can exhibit multiple phenotypic expression
(b) The gene that shows pleiotropy is called pleiotropic gene
(c) The underlying mechanism is that a gene contribute towards same kind of multiple phenotypes
(d) Phenylketonuria is one the good examples of pleiotropy

18. Match List-I with List-II.

List-I	List-II
A. GIFT	1. Transfer of zygote or early embryos with upto 8 blastomeres into the fallopian tube
B. ZIFT	2. Fertilisation outside the body
C. ICSI	3. Transfer of ovum from donor into the Fallopian tube of mother
D. IVF	4. Direct injection of sperm

Choose the correct option.

	A	B	C	D
(a)	3	1	4	2
(b)	3	2	4	1
(c)	1	4	3	2
(d)	1	3	2	4

19. Given below are two statements.

Statement I Pollen germination in flowers of *Vinca* can be easily studied using sugar solution (10%).

Statement II There is no need for emasculation in plants producing unisexual flowers.

In the light of the above statements, choose the correct answer from the options given below.

(a) Statement I is incorrect, but statement II is correct

(b) Both statements I and II are correct

(c) Both statements I and II are incorrect

(d) Statement I is correct, but statement II is incorrect

20. Given below are the two statements; one is labelled as the Assertion (A) and the other is labelled as the Reason (R).

Assertion (A) Person suffering from haemophilia will have non-stop bleeding in case of a minor cut.

Reason (R) Haemophilia is transmitted from father to daughter.

In the light of the above statements, choose the correct answer from the options given below.

(a) A is false, but R is true

(b) Both A and R are true and R is the correct explanation of A

(c) Both A and R are true, but R is not the correct explanation of A

(d) A is true, but R is false

21. Read the following statements.

I. A pure - breeding line is one that has undergone continuous self-pollination.

II. Gregor Mendel through his work, on pea plants, discovered the fundamental laws of inheritance.

III. Law of segregation explains the proportion of 3 : 1 obtained at F_2.

IV. Law of dominance is based on the fact that the alleles do not show any blending.

V. Punnett square was developed by a British geneticist, Reginald C. Punnett.

Which of the following set of statements is correct?

(a) I and II

(b) III, IV and V

(c) II and IV

(d) I, II and V

22. Given below are two statements.

Statement I A small stretch of DNA is repeated many times in satellite DNA.

Statement II DNA fingerprinting is a very lengthy and collaborated way to compare the DNA sequences of any two individuals.

In the light of the above statements, choose the correct answer from the options given below.

(a) Statement I is incorrect, but statement II is correct

(b) Both statement I and statement II are correct

(c) Both statements I and II are incorrect

(d) Statement I is correct, but statement II is incorrect

23. Given below are the two statements; one is labelled as the Assertion (A) and the other is labelled as Reason (R).

Assertion (A) The transcription and translation can be coupled in bacteria.

Reason (R) In bacteria, the *m*RNA does not require any processing to become active and also transcription and translation take place in the same compartment.

In the light of the above statements, choose the correct answer from the options given below.

(a) A is false, but R is true

(b) Both A and R are true and R is the correct explanation of A

(c) Both A and R are true, but R is not the correct explanation of A

(d) A is true, but R is false

24. Match List-I with List-II.

List-I		List-II
A. Amoebiasis	1.	*Plasmodium*
B. Ascariasis	2.	*Entamoeba histolytica*
C. Filariasis	3	*Ascaris* and *Wuchereria*
D. Malaria	4	*W.malayi*

Choose the correct option.

	A	B	C	D
(a)	2	4	3	1
(b)	2	3	4	1
(c)	3	4	1	2
(d)	3	1	4	2

25. The codons UCA, UGG and UGA codes for ...., ... and ...., respectively.
(a) Stop, Trp, Arg (b) Ser, Trp, Stop
(c) Stop, Arg, Lyr (d) Gly, Ala, Val

26. Observe the following diagram.

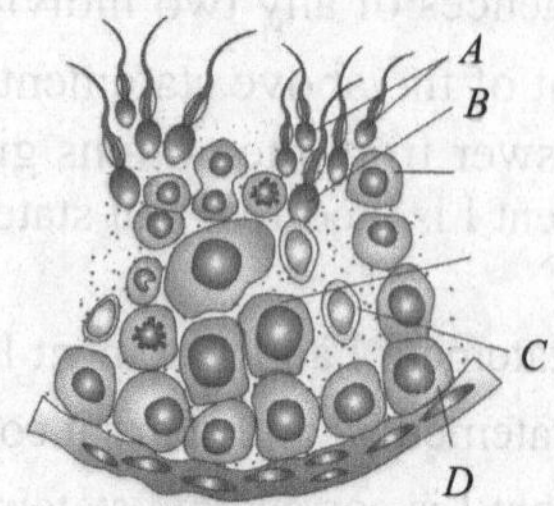

Which part harbour and nurture sperms as they mature?
(a) A (b) B
(c) C (d) D

27. Match List I with List II.

	List-I		List-II
A.	Syncarpous	1.	Orchid
B.	Apocarpous	2.	*Papaver*
C.	Single ovule	3.	Mango
D.	Multiple ovule	4.	*Michelia*

Choose the correct answer from the options given below.

	A	B	C	D
(a)	4	2	3	1
(b)	2	4	3	1
(c)	2	4	1	3
(d)	1	2	3	4

28. Which of the following statement regarding spleen is incorrect?
(a) It is a large bean shaped organ.
(b) It only consists of lymphocytes.
(c) It acts as a filter of the blood.
(d) It is a secondary lymphoid organ present just above the stomach.

29. The plant among the following that does not have any hallucinogenic properties is
(a) *Atropa belladonna* (b) *Datura*
(c) *Erythroxylum coca* (d) Poppy

30. Geitonogamy can be explained as
(a) Transfer of pollen grains from anther to the stigma of another flower of same plant
(b) Transfer of pollen grains from anther to the stigma of a different plant
(c) Transfer of pollen grains from anther to the stigma of same flower
(d) Transfer of pollen grains from anther to the stigma of a different breed of plant

31. Given below are the two statements; one is labelled as the Assertion (A) and the other is labelled as Reason (R).

Assertion (A) Oxytocin helps in parturition.
Reason (R) It stimulates vigorous contractions of the uterus at the time of child birth.

In the light of the above statements, choose the correct answer from the options given below.
(a) A is false, but R is true
(b) Both A and R are true and R is the correct explanation of A
(c) Both A and R are true, but R is not the correct explanation of A
(d) A is true, but R is false

32. .... are used by females as injections or implants under the skin.
A. Oestrogen alone
B. Progestogen and oestrogen
C. Progestogen alone
Choose the correct answer from the options given below.
(a) A and C
(b) B and C
(c) A and B
(d) B only

33. Two genes R and Y are located very close as seen on the chromosomal linkage map of a plant 'X' when RRYY and rryy genotypes are hybridised what conclusion can be drawn from the results obtained?
(a) higher number of recombinant types
(b) segregation expected in 9 : 3 : 3 :1 ratio
(c) segregation expected in 3 : 1 ratio
(d) higher number of parental types

34. Choose the wrong statement.
(a) Failure of segregation of chromatids during cell division results in aneuploidy.
(b) Additional copy of 'X' chromosomes in males results in klinefelter's syndrome.
(c) Closely located genes in a chromosomes always assort independently resulting in recombination.
(d) Failure of cytokinesis after replication results in polyploidy.

35. Which of the following statement regarding apomixis is incorrect?
(a) It produces seeds without fertilisation.
(b) It is a form of asexual reproduction.
(c) It is seen exclusively in Asteraceae family.
(d) Individual is directly developed from diploid eggs present in the embryo sac.

36. Read the following statements.
I. Nirodh is a popular brand of condom for the male.
II. Natural methods work on the principle of avoiding chances of meeting of ovum and sperms.
III. MTPs are considered safe during the second trimester of pregnancy.
IV. MTP was legalised in India in 1982.
V. STIs may lead to pelvic inflammatory diseases, abortions, infertility, etc.
Choose the correct set of statements from the options given below.
(a) I, III and IV (b) II and III
(c) I, II and V (d) III, IV and V

37. Given below are two statements.
Statement I Linkage is the physical association of genes on a chromosome.
Statement II ABO blood group system is an example of incomplete dominance and multiple allelism.
In the light of the above statements, choose the correct answer from the options given below.
(a) Statement I is incorrect, but statement II is correct
(b) Both statement I and statement II are correct
(c) Both statement I and statement II are incorrect
(d) Statement I is correct, but statement II is incorrect

38. A color blind man (X^cY) has a color blind sister (X^cX^c) and a normal brother (XY). What is the genotype of father and mother?
(a) X^cY, X^cX^c
(b) X^cY, X^cX
(c) XY, X^cX^c
(d) XY, X^cX

39. The satellite DNA is classified into many categories such as micro- satellite, mini-satellite, etc., depending on
(a) base composition
(b) width of the segment
(c) number of single gene
(d) quantity of genes

40. The primary transcript is subjected to a process called splicing in which
(a) adenylated residues are added
(b) an unusual nucleotide is added
(c) introns are removed and exons are joined
(d) exons are removed and introns are joined

41. The period that began 350 mya, which is the fifth interval of the paleozoic era and amphibians is called
(a) Permian (b) Carboniferous
(c) Cretaceous (d) Triassic

42. Given below are two statements.
Statement I The common cold is characterised by nasal congestion and discharge, sore throat cough, headache, etc.
Statement II Common cold being a viral infection is detected by widal test.
In the light of the above statements, choose the correct answer from the options given below.
(a) Statement I is incorrect, but statement II is correct
(b) Both statement I and statement II are correct
(c) Both statement I and statement II are incorrect
(d) Statement I is correct, but statement II is incorrect

43. Out of the following options, the gas which was not used in the experiment of Miller is
(a) CH_4 (b) CO_2
(c) H_2O (d) H_2

44. Match List-I with List-II.

List-I		List-II
A. Clitoris	1.	Cushion of fatty tissue
B. Hymen	2.	Opening of vagina
C. Mons pubis	3.	Paired folds of tissue
D. Labia minora	4.	Finger-like structure

Choose the correct option.

	A	B	C	D
(a)	4	2	1	3
(b)	2	4	3	1
(c)	2	1	3	4
(d)	3	2	1	4

45. Which salient feature of genetic code is incorrect?

(a) The codon is triplet in which 61 codons code for amino acids.

(b) Code is degenerate, e.g. serine is coded by UCU, UCC, UCA and UCG.

(c) UAA has dual functions.

(d) There are no punctuations in genetic code.

46. Given below are two statements.

Statement I Yellowish fluid colustrum is rich in IgG which is capable of crossing through placenta.

Statement II Immunisation given in response to snake venom is called active immunisation.

In the light of the above statements, choose the correct answer from the options given below.

(a) Statement I is incorrect, but statement II is correct

(b) Both statement I and statement II are correct

(c) Both statement I and statement II are incorrect

(d) Statement I is correct, but statement II is incorrect

47. Match List-I with List-II.

List-I		List-II
A. Exine	1.	Prominent aperture
B. Intine	2.	Sporopollenin
C. Germ pores	3.	Male gametophyte
D. Pollen grain	4.	Cellulose and pectin

Choose the correct option.

	A	B	C	D
(a)	2	3	4	1
(b)	2	4	1	3
(c)	2	1	4	3
(d)	1	2	3	4

48. Observe the following diagram.

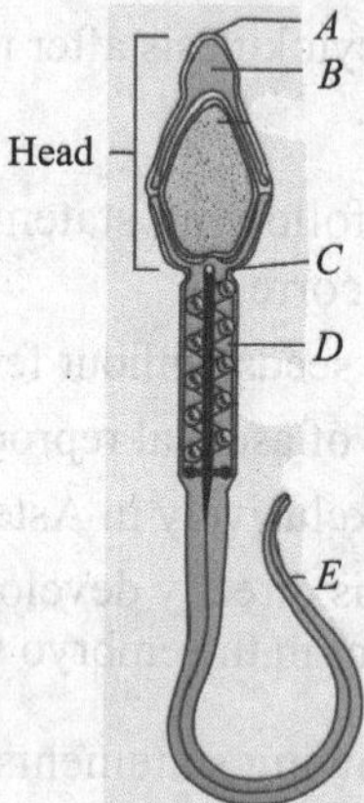

Which part consists of numerous mitochondria that produce energy for the movement of the tail?

(a) A (b) B
(c) D (d) E

49. Given below are certain characteristic features related to cross pollinated flowers.

I. Large and feathery stigma

II. Long and ribbon like pollen grains

III. Dull coloured flowers without scent

IV. Nectar less flowers.

Which of the above characters show similarity to both wind and water pollinated flowers?

(a) I Only (b) II and III
(c) III and IV (d) IV Only

50. Given below are the two statements; one is labelled as the Assertion (A) and the other is labelled as Reason (R).

Assertion (A) At the time of breast feeding, chances of conception are almost nil.

Reason (R) The contraception method of lactotional amenorrhea is reported to be effective only upto a maximum period of six months following parturition.

In the light of the above statements, choose the correct answer from the options given below.
(a) A is false, but R is true
(b) Both A and R are true and R is the correct explanation of A
(c) Both A and R are true, but R is not the correct explanation of A
(d) A is true, but R is false

51. Observe the following diagram.

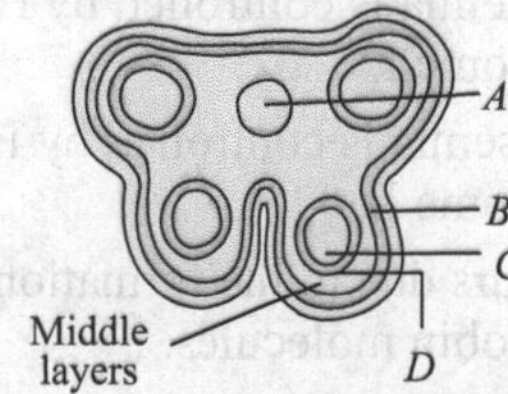

Which part is responsible for the nourishment of the pollen grains?
(a) A (b) B
(c) C (d) D

52. Which one of the following statements regarding Klinefelter's syndrome is incorrect?
(a) It is caused due to the absence of one of the X chromosomes.
(b) Such an individual has overall masculine development.
(c) It is a type of chromosomal disorder.
(d) Such individuals are sterile.

53. Given below are two statements.
Statement I Genes which code for a pair of contrasting traits are known as alleles.
Statement II Alleles are similar pair of genes.
In the light of the above statements, choose the correct answer from the option given below.
(a) Statement I is incorrect, but statement II is correct
(b) Both statement I and statement II are correct
(c) Both statement I and statement II are incorrect
(d) Statement I is correct, but statement II is incorrect

54. The RNA polymerase-I transcribes the following *r*RNAs except,
(a) 28S (b) 18S
(c) 5S (d) 5.8S

55. An autosome- linked recessive disease that is due to either mutation or deletion and affects the synthesis of one of the globin chains of haemoglobin is called
(a) Colourblindness
(b) Thalassemia
(c) Haemophilia
(d) Turner's syndrome

56. In a cross of two individuals both heterozygous for two traits (e.g., AaBb × AaBb), what proportion of the offspring are expected to be homozygous recessive for both traits?
(a) $\frac{1}{16}$ (b) $\frac{1}{4}$
(c) $\frac{3}{16}$ (d) $\frac{1}{8}$

57. Read the following statements.
I. Heroin is chemically diacetylmorphine and commonly called smat.
II. Heroin is obtained from *Datura* plant.
III. The flower tops, leaves and the resin of *Cannabis* plant are used in various combinations to produce marijuana.
IV. Cocaine is obtained from coca plant *Erythroxylum coca*.
V. Cannabinoids are also being used by some sportspersons.
Which of the following set of statements is correct?
(a) I and II
(b) III, IV and V
(c) II, III and IV
(d) IV and V

58. Read the following statements.
I. The cellular factory responsible for synthesising proteins is the ribosome.
II. The ribosome consists of structural RNAs and about 40 different proteins.
III. The ribosome exists as two subunits.
IV. For initiation of transcription, the ribosome binds to the *m*RNA at the start codon (AUG).
V. The ribosome also acts as a catalyst for the formation of peptide bond.

Which of the following statements are incorrect?
(a) I and II only
(b) II and III only
(c) II and IV only
(d) IV and V only

59. Given below are two statements.

Statement I *Ramapithecus* was more ape-like while *Dryopithecus* was more man-like.

Statement II *Australopithecus* lived nearly two mya.

In the light of the above statements, choose the correct answer from the options given below.
(a) Statement I is incorrect, but statement II is correct
(b) Both statement I and statement II are correct
(c) Both statement I and statement II are incorrect
(d) Statement I is correct, but statement II is incorrect

60. Which methodology is used for sequencing the total DNA that contains all the coding and non-coding sequence?
(a) Expressed sequence tags
(b) Sequence annotation
(c) Polymorphism
(d) DNA fingerprinting

61. The organism that causes a slowly developing chronic inflammation of the organs in which lymphatic vessels of the lower limb is commonly affected is
(a) *Entamoeba histolytica*
(b) *Wuchereria*
(c) *Ascaris*
(d) *Plasmodium*

62. Hardy-Weinberg principle explains the occurrence and consistency of gene frequency of a particular gene. Its expression can be written as
(a) $p^3 + 2p^2 + q^3 = 1$
(b) Binomial expansion of $(p+q)^2$
(c) Binomial expansion of $(p+q)^3$
(d) $p^2 + q^2 + qp = 1$

63. The regions outside the ……. called interstitial spaces, contain small blood vessels and ....
(a) Seminiferous tubules, Sertoli cells
(b) Seminal vesicle, Leydig cells
(c) Androgens, Interstitial cells
(d) Seminiferous tubules, Leydig cells

64. Which of the following statements regarding thalassemia is incorrect?
(a) α-thalassemia is controlled by HBA1 gene on chromosome I.
(b) β- thalassemia is controlled by HBB gene on chromosome II.
(c) This occurs due to the formation of abnormal haemoglobin molecules.
(d) It is a qualitative problem of synthesising an incorrectly functioning globin.

65. The recessive traits in pea plant according to Mendel include
I. White colour of flower
II. Axial position of flower.
III. Green colour of seed
IV. Inflated shape of pod

Choose the correct set from the options given below.
(a) I only
(b) I and IV only
(c) I and III only
(d) II and IV only

66. Below are few contraceptive methods.
A. Diaphragms B. Vaults
C. Saheli D. Tubectomy

Choose the correct set of options that consists of barrier methods.
(a) A and C
(b) A and B
(c) C and D
(d) B and D

67. Which of the following is a true statement about the genetic nature of apomictic seeds?
(a) Apomictic seeds have a higher genetic mutations compared to seeds produced through sexual reproduction.
(b) Apomictic seeds result in offsprings with a genetic composition different from the maternal plant due to recombination events.

(c) Apomictic seeds are genetically identical to the maternal plant because they are formed without fertilization.

(d) Apomictic seeds exhibit high genetic variability among offspring compared to sexually reproduced seeds.

68. Match List-I with List-II.

List-I	List-II
A. LH	1. Induces growth of ovarian follicles
B. FSH	2. Induce release of ovum
C. Relaxin	3. Maintains progesterone secretion
D. hCG	4. Helps in parturition

Choose the correct option.

	A	B	C	D
(a)	2	3	4	1
(b)	4	1	2	3
(c)	1	2	4	3
(d)	2	1	4	3

69. Read the following statements.

I. Only LH attains a peak level in the middle of the menstrual cycle.

II. Rapid secretion of FSH results in the release of ovum.

III. The corpus luteum secretes large amounts of progesterone which is essential for maintenance of endometrium.

IV. During fertilisation, sperm comes in contact with the zona pellucida layer of the ovum.

V. Menopause occurs around 50 years of age.

Choose the correct option with the incorrect set of statements.

(a) I and II (b) IV and V

(c) II and III (d) III and IV

70. Match List-I with List-II.

List-I	List-II
A. *y* gene	1. β - gal
B. *a* gene	2. Permease
C. *z* gene	3. Transacetylase
D. *i* - gene	4. Inhibitor

Choose the correct option.

	A	B	C	D
(a)	2	3	1	4
(b)	2	1	3	4
(c)	3	2	4	1
(d)	1	3	4	2

71. Given below are two statements.

Statement I Periodic abstinence is a natural method of contraception in which couples avoid or abstain from coitus from day 10 to 17 of the menstrual cycle.

Statement II The chances of fertilisation are very high during fertile period (i.e. 10-17 day).

In the light of the above statements, choose the correct answer from the options given below.

(a) Statement I is incorrect, but statement II is correct

(b) Both statement I and statement II are correct

(c) Both statement I and statement II are incorrect

(d) Statement I is correct, but statement II is incorrect

72. Match List-I with List-II.

List-I	List-II
A. XO type	1. Female heterogamety
B. XX-XY type	2. Honeybees
C. ZZ-ZW type	3. Grasshopper
D. Haplo-diploid type	4. Male heterogamety

Choose the correct option.

	A	B	C	D
(a)	3	4	1	2
(b)	3	1	4	2
(c)	2	4	1	3
(d)	4	1	2	3

73. Given below are the two statements; one is labelled as the Assertion (A) and the other is labelled as the Reason (R).

Assertion (A) Pollen consumption has been claimed to increase the performance of athletes and race horses.

Reason (R) Pollen grains are rich in sugar (nectar) only.

In the light of the above statements, choose the correct answer from the options given below.
(a) A is false, but R is true
(b) Both A and R are true and R is the correct explanation of A
(c) Both A and R are true, but R is not the correct explanation of A
(d) A is true, but R is false

74. What type of pollination occurs in *Vallisneria*?
(a) Pollination occurs in submerged condition by water.
(b) Flowers emerge above the water surface and pollination occurs by insects.
(c) Flowers emerge above water surface and pollen is carried by wind
(d) Male flowers are carried by water currents to female flowers at the water surface.

75. Given below are the two statements; one is labelled as the Assertion (A) and the other is labelled as Reason (R).

Assertion (A) CuT are very useful implants used as contraceptive device.

Reason (R) CuT increases phagocytosis of sperms within the uterus and Cu ions released suppress sperm motility.

In the light of the above statements, choose the correct answer from the options given below.
(a) A is false, but R is true
(b) Both A and R are true and R is the correct explanation of A
(c) Both A and R are true, but R is not the correct explanation of A
(d) A is true, but R is false

76. Given below are two statements.

Statement I Polymorphism is the variation at genetic level.

Statement II Jeffrey used the repetitive DNA as a probe in his technique of DNA fingerprinting.

In the light of the above statements, choose the correct answer from the options given below.
(a) Statement I is incorrect, but statement II is correct
(b) Both statement I and statement II are correct
(c) Both statement I and statement II are incorrect
(d) Statement I is correct, but statement II is incorrect

77. Read the following statements.
I. Opioids bind to specific opioid receptor present in our CNS and gastrointestinal tract.
II. Heroin is a depressant and slows body functions.
III. Amphotericin can produce a sense of euphoria.
IV. Smoking is associated with increased incidence of cancers of lung.
V. Tobacco chewing increases mainly the gastric ulcer.

Which of the following set of statements is incorrect?
(a) I and II (b) III and V
(c) II and IV (d) I and V

78. Given below are the two statements; one is labelled as the Assertion (A) and the other is labelled as Reason (R).

Assertion (A) *Lac* operon is a repressible operon.

Reason (R) The product of gene activity starts the activity of the gene itself.

In the light of the above statements, choose the correct answer from the options given below.
(a) A is false, but R is true
(b) Both A and R are true and R is the correct explanation of A
(c) Both A and R are true, but R is not the correct explanation of A
(d) A is true, but R is false

79. Given below are two statements.

Statement I A test cross determines whether the individual with dominant phenotype is homozygous dominant or heterozygous dominant.

Statement II A test cross is a cross between F_1 plant and the homozygous dominant plant.

In the light of the above statements, choose the correct answer from the options given below.
(a) Statement I is incorrect, but statement II is correct
(b) Both statements I and II are correct
(c) Both statements I and II are incorrect
(d) Statement I is correct, but statement II is incorrect

80. Immediately after implantation, the inner cell mass (embryo) differentiates into

(a) mesoderm and endoderm
(b) ectoderm (inner layer) and endoderm (outer layer)
(c) ectoderm (outer layer) and endoderm (inner layer)
(d) periderm and ectoderm

81. Given below are the two statements; one is labelled as the Assertion (A) and the other is labelled as Reason (R).

Assertion (A) Cancer patients are given α-interferon for destroying tumor.

Reason (R) α-interferon is a biological response modifier which activate the immune system and helps in destroying tumor.

In the light of the above statements, choose the correct answer from the options given below.

(a) A is false, but R is true
(b) Both A and R are true and R is the correct explanation of A
(c) Both A and R are true, but R is not the correct explanation of A
(d) A is true, but R is false

82. Continued self pollination results in inbreeding depression. Which of the following does not prevent inbreeding?

(a) Pollen release and stigma receptivity are not synchronised
(b) Anther and stigma are placed at different positions
(c) Self-incompatibility
(d) Anther and stigma are located close to each other

83. Read the following statements.

I. Oparin and Haldane proposed that the first form of life could be from pre-existing non-living organic molecules.
II. The universe is almost 20 billion years old.
III. Earth was supposed to have been formed about 2.3 billion years back.
IV. Embryological support for evolution was proposed by Von Baer.
V. Early Greek thinkers thought that units of life called spores were transferred to different planets.

Choose the incorrect set of statements from the options given below.

(a) I and II
(b) III, IV and V
(c) III and IV
(d) I and V

84. A sex-linked recessive disorder due to defect in either red or green cone of eye and mutation in certain genes present in the X chromosomes is called

(a) Colour blindness
(b) cataract
(c) Turner's syndrome
(d) Down's syndrome

85. Which of the following statement is incorrect?

(a) The wall of the ovary develops into the wall of fruit called pericarp.
(b) In the grass family, the cotyledon is called scutellum.
(c) The root tip is covered with a parenchymatous root cap.
(d) The cylindrical portion below the level of cotyledon is epicotyl.

86. Which of the following statement is incorrect?

(a) Antibody is represented as H_2L_2.
(b) Allergy is due to release of melatonin.
(c) Rheumatoid arthritis is an autoimmune disease.
(d) The primary lymphoid organs are bone marrow and thymus.

87. Read the following statements.

I. Stigma serves as a landing platform for pollen grains.
II. Ovary is the basal bulged part of the pistil.
III. Micropyle is the basal part of the ovule.
IV. Chalaza is the small opening in the integuments.
V. The number of ovules in an ovary may be one to many.

Choose the correct set of statements from the options given below.

(a) I, II and III (b) II and IV
(c) I, II and V (d) III and V

88. Which of the following statement is incorrect regarding co-dominance?

(a) The plasma membrane of the red blood cells has sugar polymers.

(b) ABO blood group are controlled by the gene I.

(c) Red blood cells have both A and B type of sugars.

(d) A total of four different types of genotype of human ABO blood types are observed.

89. Given below are two statements.

Statement I Most fruits develop only from ovary and are called false fruits.

Statements II Banana is a parthenocarpic fruit.

In the light of the above statements, choose the correct answer from the options given below.

(a) Statement I is incorrect, but statement II is correct

(b) Both statement I and statement II are correct

(c) Both statement I and statement II are incorrect

(d) Statement I is correct, but statement II is incorrect

90. If one parent has homozygous genotype for blood group I^A and other parent has homozygous genotype for blood group i, then the blood type of offspring will be?

(a) A (b) AB

(c) B (d) O

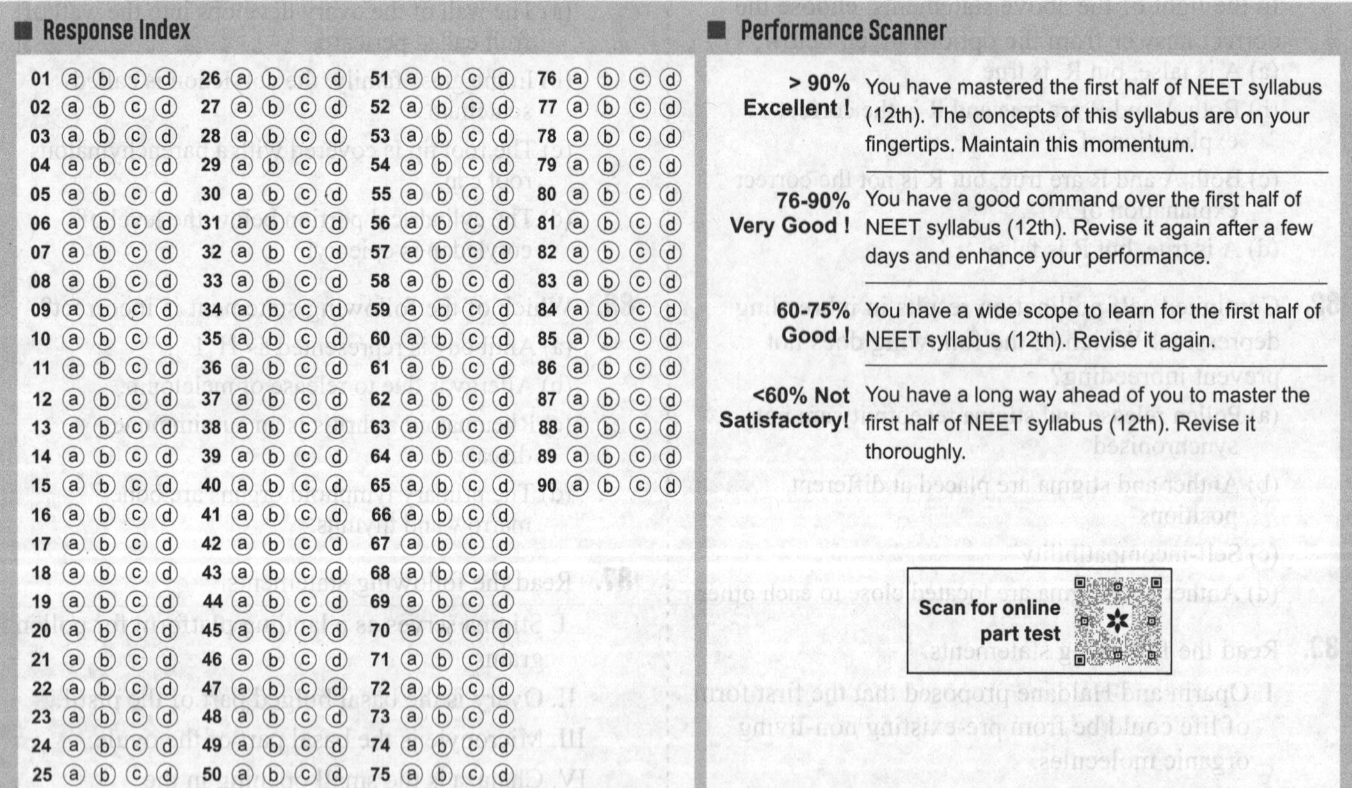

Space for Rough Work

Space for Rough Work

Test Booklet No. 3947365

Test Booklet Code SPT2

MEDACE
NEET (UG)
SELF ASSESSMENT KIT

Syllabus Part Thru 2
(Half Syllabus Test)

Chapters Covered

- Microbes in Human Welfare
- Biotechnology : Principles and Processes
- Biotechnology and its Applications
- Organisms and Populations
- Ecosystem
- Biodiversity and Conservation

Important Instructions

- The test is of **1 hours 30 minutes** duration and the Test Booklet contains **90** multiple-choice questions (four options with a single correct answer) from biology.
- Candidates are advised to read all questions before they start attempting the question paper.
- Each questions carries 4 marks. For each correct response, the candidate will get 4 marks. For each incorrect response, one marks will be deducted from the total scores.
- In the event of candidate marking more than one option one mark will be deducted. The maximum marks are 180.
- Use **Blue/Black Point Pen only** for writing particular on this page/ marking response on Answer Sheet.

Name of the Candidate (In Capitals) ______________________

____

Candidate's Signature ______________________

Invigilator's Signature ______________________

Facsimile signature stamp of center superintendent______________________

Do not open this booklet until you start attempting the test

Biology

1. There are three basic steps in genetically modifying an organism.

Which one of the following is not included in these steps?
(a) Identification of DNA with desirable genes
(b) Introduction of the identified DNA into the undesirable gene
(c) Maintenance of introduced DNA in the host
(d) Transfer of the DNA to its progeny

2. Read the following statements and choose the correct set of statements.

I. The example of African catfish and indigenous catfish in related to co-extinction.
II. Cryopreservation is a method of *in-situ* conservation.
III. There are 34 biodiversity hotspots in the world.
IV. Sacred groves are found in Khasi and Jaintia Hills in Meghalaya, Chanda and Bastar areas of Madhya Pradesh and many more.
V. Seeds of different genetic strains of commercially important plants can be kept for long periods in seed banks.

Choose the correct answer from the options given below.
(a) II, III and V (b) III, IV and V
(c) I, II and IV (d) II, III and IV

3. A collection of methods that allows correction of a gene defect in a child or embryo is termed as
(a) ELISA (b) gene silencing
(c) gene therapy (d) gene sequencing

4. Which of the following statement is incorrect?
(a) DNA template is the double-stranded DNA that needs to be amplified.
(b) Primers are chemically synthesised large segments of DNA.
(c) In extension step, the thermostable *Taq* DNA polymerase enzyme is used.
(d) Annealing is done at a temperature of 40°C to 60°C.

5. Given below are two statements.

Statement I Plasmid is an autonomously replicating linear DNA found majorly in prokaryotes.

Statement II In 1963, the two enzymes responsible for restricting the growth of bacteriophage in *E. coli* were isolated.

In the light of the above statements, choose the correct answer from the options given below.
(a) Statement I is incorrect, but statement II is correct
(b) Both statement I and statement II are correct
(c) Both statement I and statement II are incorrect
(d) Statement I is correct, but statement II is incorrect

6. The pyramid of number is

I. Upright
II. Inverted
III. Stable
IV. Tallest

Choose the correct answer from options given below.
(a) I and II (b) Only II
(c) Only III (d) Only IV

7. Consider the following cloning vector and choose the incorrect statement w.r.t it.

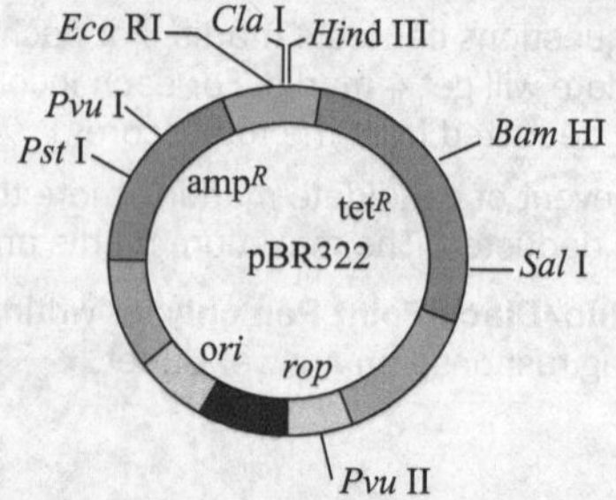

(a) Every cloning vector needs an *ori*
(b) *rop* codes for proteins involved in the replication of the plasmid
(c) amp^R and tet^R are important restriction sites.
(d) It is an *E. coli* cloning vector

8. The starfish *Pisaster* in the rocky intertidal communities of the American Pacific coast is an example of

(a) parasitism (b) predation
(c) mutualism (d) competition

9. The prickly pear cactus that caused havoc by spreading rapidly was brought under control after the introduction of a cactus feeding predator. This type of population interaction is termed as

(a) mutualism (b) parasitism
(c) predation (d) competition

10. Read the following statements and choose the incorrect set of statements.

I. '+', '–' sign determines mutualistic relationship.

II. Predation is a type of population interaction in which both are benefitted.

III. Parasitism in some birds is an example of brood parasitism.

IV. The Mediterranean orchid *Ophrys* employs sexual deceit to get pollination done.

V. Competition is an interaction in which one benefits and the other suffers.

Choose the correct answer from the options given below.

(a) I, II and V (b) II and V
(c) I, III and IV (d) III, IV and V

11. The relationship between species of fig trees and pollinator species of wasp shows the interaction of

(a) competition (b) mutualism
(c) parasitism (d) predation

12. Listed below are few organisms.

I. *Azospirillum*

II. *Azotobacter*

III. *Cycas*

IV. *Funaria*

Choose the correct option that contain nitrogen fixing free living bacteria in the soil.

(a) I and II (b) III and IV
(c) Only II (d) Only III

13. Which of the following statement is incorrect?

(a) Statins act by competitively inhibiting the enzyme reponsible for synthesising cholesterol.

(b) Microbes are also used to ferment fish, soyabean and bamboo shoots to make foods

(c) The Ministry of Environment and forests initiated GAP and YAP in the year 1993 and 1986 respectively.

(d) Solids that settle from the primary sludge and the supernatant forms the effluent

14. Read the following statements and choose the correct set of statements.

I. Transgenic mice are being developed for testing the safety of vaccines.

II. Toxicity testing in animals obtain results in longer time.

III. Almost 95 per cent of all existing transgenic animals are mice.

IV. Transgenic models exist for many human diseases such as cancer, Alzheimer's and colour blindness.

V. Transgenic animals are designed to allow the study about how genes are regulated.

Choose the correct answer from the options given below.

(a) I, II and III (b) I, III and V
(c) II, IV and V (d) I, II and V

15. Given below are two statements; one is labelled as Assertion (A) and the other is labelled as Reason (R).

Assertion (A) Restriction enzymes recognise palindromic sequence and cut at specific sites.

Reason (R) When a restriction enzyme acts on palindrome, it cleaves both the strands of DNA molecule.

In the light of the above statements, choose the correct answer from the options given below.

(a) A is false, but R is true

(b) Both A and R are true and R is the correct explanation of A

(c) Both A and R are true, but R is not the correct explanation of A

(d) A is true, but R is false

16. Given below are two statements.

Statement I In 1990, the first clinical gene therapy was given to a 4 year old girl suffering from ADA deficiency.

Statement II ADA deficiency can be treated completely by bone marrow transplantation only.

In the light of the above statements, choose the correct answer from the options given below.

(a) Statement I is incorrect, but statement II is correct
(b) Both statement I and statement II are correct
(c) Both statement I and statement II are incorrect
(d) Statement I is correct, but statement II is incorrect

17. In the given pie-chart representing proportionate number of species of major taxa of plants, choose the species that is globally more than combined total of the species of fishes, amphibians, reptiles and mammals.

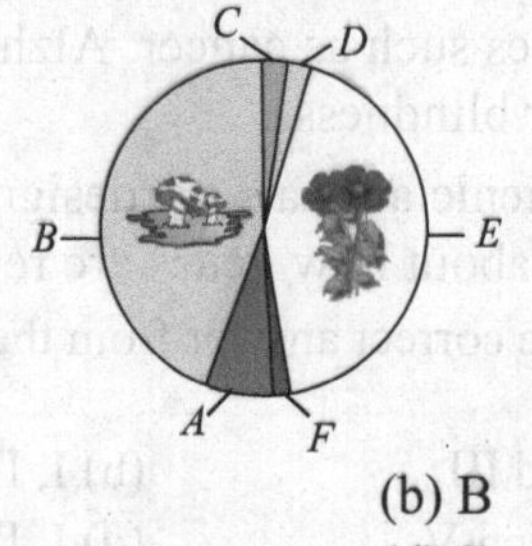

(a) A (b) B
(c) E (d) D

18. Match List I with List II.

List I	List II
A. Decomposers	I. Forest
B. Natural ecosystem	II. Fungi
C. Primary productivity	III. Consumers
D. Secondary productivity	IV. Producers

Choose the correct answer from the options given below.

(a) A-II, B-IV, C-I, D-III
(b) A-II, B-I, C-IV, D-III
(c) A-I, B-II, C-IV, D-III
(d) A-III, B-II, C-IV, D-I

19. Read the following statements and choose the correct set of statements.

I. *Bt* toxin is produced by a bacterium called *Bacillus thuringiensis*.
II. A nematode *Meloidegyne incognita* infects the roots of cotton plants.
III. The example of *Bt* crops are *Bt* corn, tomato, Basmati rice, soyabean, etc.
IV. GM crops have helped to reduce post-harvest losses.
V. GMO has made crops more tolerant to abiotic stresses like cold, drought, etc.

Choose the correct answer from the options given below.

(a) I, II and III (b) I, III and IV
(c) I, IV and V (d) II, III and IV

20. Given below are two statements.

Statement I Serum and urine analysis serve the purpose of early diagnosis.

Statement II Very low concentration of a bacteria or virus can be detected by amplification of their nucleic acid by the process of PCR.

In the light of the above statements, choose the correct answer from the options given below.

(a) Statement I is incorrect, but statement II is correct
(b) Both statement I and statement II are correct
(c) Both statement I and statement II are incorrect
(d) Statement I is correct, but statement II is incorrect

21. Given below are two statements.

Statement I Some strains of *Bacillus thuringiensis* produce proteins that kill certain insects such as coleopterans.

Statement II *Bt* cotton is resistant to pest lepidopteran such as flies and mosquitoes.

In the light of the above statements, choose the correct answer from the options given below

(a) Statement I is incorrect, but statement II is correct
(b) Both statement I and statement II are correct
(c) Both statement I and statement II are incorrect
(d) Statement I is correct, but statement II is incorrect

22. Given below are two statements; one is labelled as Assertion (A) and the other is labelled as Reason (R).

Assertion (A) Cyanobacteria serves as an important biofertiliser in paddy (rice) fields.

Reason (R) Cyanobacteria add the source of water to the soil.

In the light of the above statements, choose the correct answer from the options given below.

(a) A is false, but R is true
(b) Both A and R are true and R is the correct explanation of A.
(c) Both A and R are true, but R is not the correct explanation of A.
(d) A is true, but R is false

23. There were 20 plants last year in a pond and later 8 new plants were added through reproduction. The birth rate of the offspring per plant per year will be

(a) 0.1 (b) 0.2
(c) 0.4 (d) 0.8

24. ....is a bioactive molecule that is used as an immunosuppressive agent in organ transplant patients. It is produced by fungus ....

(a) Statins, *Clostridium butylicum*
(b) Cyclosporin-A, *Trichoderma polysporum*
(c) Streptokinase, *Streptococcus*
(d) Penicillin, *Monascus purpureus*

25. Read the following statements and choose the incorrect set of statements.

I. Each trophic level has a certain mass of living material at a particular time called as standing crop.
II. The standing crop is measured as the mass of living organisms or the quality of it.
III. The interconnection of food chain is called food web.
IV. Only 1.5 per cent of the energy is transferred to each trophic levels in food chain.
V. Grass is a producer in a simple grazing food chain.

Choose the correct answer from the options given below.

(a) I and II (b) II and IV
(c) III and V (d) III and IV

26. Match List I with List II.

List I	List II
A. Fragmentation	I. Formation of humus
B. Catabolism	II. Detritivores
C. Mineralisation	III. Fungal enzymes
D. Humification	IV. Release of inorganic nutrients from humus

Choose the correct answer from the options given below.

(a) A-II, B-III, C-IV, D-I
(b) A-I, B-II, C-III, D-IV
(c) A-II, B-IV, C-I, D-III
(d) A-III, B-II, C-IV, D-I

27. Observe the following figure.

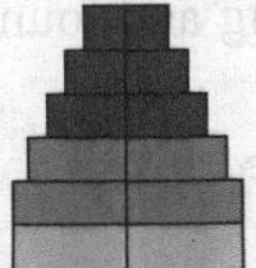

The above structure is formed when

(a) pre-reproductive individuals are more than reproductive individuals
(b) pre-reproductive and reproductive individuals are almost in equal number
(c) pre-reproductive individuals are less than reproductive individuals
(d) post reproductive individuals are higher than expected

28. Match List I with list II.

List I	List II
A. *In-situ*	I. Passenger pigeon
B. *Ex-situ*	II. Plant-pollinator mutualism
C. Over-exploitation	III. Zoological gardens
D. Co-extinction	IV. Wildlife sanctuaries

Choose the correct answer from the options given below.

(a) A-I, B-III, C-II, D-IV
(b) A-II, B-IV, C-III, D-I
(c) A-III, B-II, C-I, D-IV
(d) A-IV, B-III, C-I, D-II

29. Statins that are commercialised as blood cholesterol lowering agents prevent building up risks of heart attacks. These substances are produced by

(a) *Aspergillus niger*
(b) *Lactobacillus*
(c) *Monascus purpureus*
(d) *Streptococcus*

30. The equation of the population growth curve is given by $N_t = N_0 e^{rt}$. In this, r is

(a) rate of decline
(b) intrinsic rate of natural increase
(c) extrinsic rate of natural increase
(d) number of natural resources

31. The biocontrol agent of several plant pathogens that is free living and found in the root ecosystem is

(a) *Nucleopolyhedrovirus*
(b) *Trichoderma*
(c) *Bacillus thuringiensis*
(d) *Agrobacterium*

32. Which of the following statement is incorrect?

(a) More than 70 per cent of all the species recorded are algae.
(b) The term 'biodiversity' was popularised by Edward Wilson.
(c) India is one of the 12 mega diversity countries of the world.
(d) India's share of the global species diversity is 8.1 per cent.

33. Given below are two statements.

Statement I Vertical distribution of different species occupying different levels is called fragmentation.

Statement II Trees occupy top vertical strata or layer of a forest, shrubs occupy the second and herbs occupy the bottom layers.

In the light of the above statements, choose the correct answer from the options given below.

(a) Statement I is incorrect, but statement II is correct
(b) Both statement I and statement II are correct
(c) Both statement I and statement II are incorrect
(d) Statement I is correct, but statement II is incorrect

34. Which of the following statement is incorrect?

(a) ELISA is based on the principle of antigen-antibody interaction.
(b) Infection by pathogen can be detected by the presence of antigens.
(c) The antigens include proteins, vitamins, etc.
(d) Infection by pathogen can be detected by detecting the antibodies synthesised against the pathogen.

35. The ladybird and dragon flies are used to get rid of

(a) mosquitoes and aphids, respectively
(b) aphids and mosquitoes, respectively
(c) bollworms and corn borer, respectively
(d) bettles and centipedes, respectively

36. Match List I with List II.

List I	List II
A. Natality	I. Population per unit area
B. Mortality	II. Number of deaths in population
C. Population density	III. Population genetics and evolution
D. Population ecology	IV. Number of births in population

Choose the correct answer from the options given below.

(a) A-II, B-IV, C-I, D-III
(b) A-IV, B-II, C-I, D-III
(c) A-IV, B-III, C-I, D-II
(d) A-II, B-IV, C-III, D-I

37. The equation of species-area relationship is given below.

$\log S = \log C + Z \log A$

In this equation, 'S' is determined as

(a) Species decline
(b) Species richness
(c) Y-intercept
(d) Special area

38. Read the following statements and choose the correct set of statements.

I. Toddy is a drink made by fermenting soyabean.
II. The dough used for making dosa and idli is fermented by a yeast.
III. LAB is used to convert milk to curd to improve its nutritional quality by increasing vitamin-A.

IV. Production on an industrial scale, require growing microbes in very large vessel.

V. Microbes like bacteria and fungi can be grown on nutritive media to form colonies.

Choose the correct answer from the options given below.

(a) II, III and V
(b) II, IV and V
(c) I, III and IV
(d) I, II and V

39. Given below are two statements; one is labelled as Assertion (A) and the other is labelled as Reason (R).

Assertion (A) Human insulin can be produced in bacterial cells using biotechnology.

Reason (R) Insulin in humans is produced as a prohormone with polypeptides A, B and C. These polypeptides can be extracted from bacterial cells and combined by creating disulphide bonds.

In the light of the above statements, choose the correct answer from the options given below.

(a) A is false, but R is true
(b) Both A and R are true and R is the correct explanation of A
(c) Both A and R are true, but R is not the correct explanation of A
(d) A is true, but R is false

40. Match List I with List II.

List I		List II
A. Mutualism	I.	Orchids and bee
B. Competition	II.	*Balanus and Chathamalus*
C. Parasitism	III.	*Cuscuta* and hedge plants
D. Predation	IV.	Cactus and moth

Choose the correct answer from the options given below.

(a) A-I, B-III, C-II, D-IV
(b) A-I, B-II, C-III, D-IV
(c) A-II, B-III, C-I, D-IV
(d) A-III, B-IV, C-I, D-II

41. Given below are two statements; one is labelled as Assertion (A) and the other is labelled as Reason (R).

Assertion (A) Water pollution is generally measured in terms of BOD.

Reason (R) BOD measures the amount of oxygen that would be consumed if all the organic matter in one litre of water is oxidised by bacteria.

In the light of the above statements, choose the correct answer from the options given below.

(a) A is false, but R is true
(b) Both A and R are true and R is the correct explanation of A.
(c) Both A and R are true, but R is not the correct explanation of A.
(d) A is true, but R is false

42. Given below are two statements; one is labelled as Assertion (A) and the other is labelled as Reason (R).

Assertion (A) Golden rice is a genetically modified plant which has been made disease resistant.

Reason (R) It contains a precursor of vitamin-A, known as β-carotene and is golden yellow in colour.

In the light of the above statements, choose the correct answer from the options given below.

(a) A is false, but R is true
(b) Both A and R are true and R is the correct explanation of A
(c) Both A and R are true, but R is not the correct explanation of A
(d) A is true, but R is false

43. The bacteria which feed on dead animals are

(a) first link of the food chain and are known as primary producers.
(b) second link of the food chain and are herbivorous
(c) third link of the food chain and are tertiary consumers
(d) the end of food chain and are decomposers

44. Which of the following statement is incorrect?

(a) Fishes are most species rich taxonomic group among vertebrates.
(b) Algae are most species rich taxonomic group among plants.
(c) India has 14 biosphere reserves.
(d) In Meghalaya, the sacred groves are the last refuge for a large number of rare and threatened plants.

45. Match List I with List II.

List I	List II
A. Citric acid	I. *Lactobacillus*
B. Acetic acid	II. *Acetobacter aceti*
C. Butyric acid	III. *Aspergillus niger*
D. Lactic acid	IV. *Clostridium butylicum*

Choose the correct answer from the options given below.

(a) A-II, B-III, C-IV, D-I
(b) A-III, B-II, C-IV, D-I
(c) A-II, B-IV, C-I, D-III
(d) A-I, B-II, C-IV, D-III

46. Observe the following diagram.

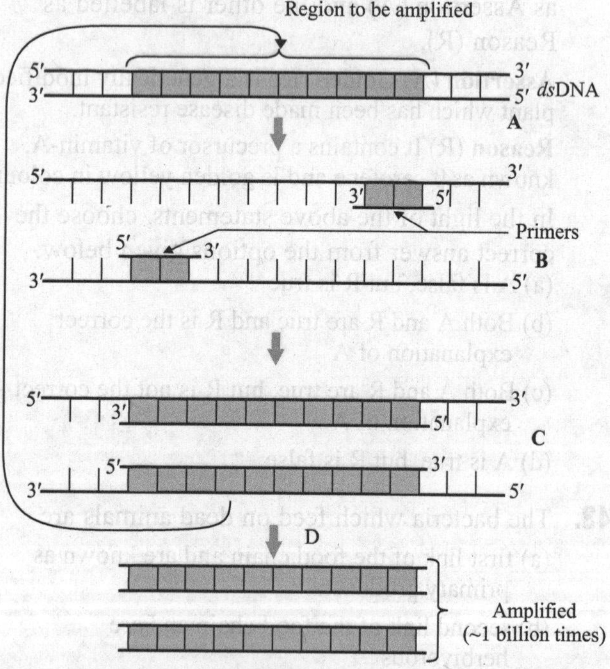

The DNA polymerase (*Taq* polymerase) is used in which step?

(a) A (b) B
(c) C (d) D

47. A researcher trying to extract out DNA from a sample under simulated conditions, fails even after following the correct sequence of steps from cell lysis to purifying desired DNA. However, he fails to extract DNA through the DNA elution technique what could be the possible reason of the failure?

(a) Use of alternate enzyme for cell lysis
(b) Chilled ethanol was not used
(c) Deterioration of sample
(d) Role of other factors like pH

48. The Amazon rainforest is being cut and cleared for soyabean cultivation or for conversion to grassland for raising beef cattle. This is an example of

(a) alien-species invasion
(b) over-exploitation
(c) co-extinction
(d) habitat loss and fragmentation

49. Listed below are the steps of Polymerase Chain Reaction (PCR).

I. Annealing
II. Denaturation
III. Extension

Arrange the steps in the right order and choose the correct answer.

(a) I → II → III (b) III → II → I
(c) II → I → III (d) III → I → II

50. Of the incident solar radiation, less than ... of it is PAR and plants are able to capture only ... of the PAR.

(a) 70%, 2 – 10 %
(b) 50%, 2 – 10%
(c) 40%, 5 – 15%
(d) 50%, 5 – 15%

51. Which one of the following palindromic base sequences in DNA can be easily cut at about the middle by some particular restriction enzyme?

(a) 5′– GATATC – 3′; 3′ – CTACTA – 5′
(b) 5′– CGCTTCG – 3′; 3′ – ATGGTA – 5′
(c) 5′– CACGTA – 3′; 3′ – CTCAGT – 5′
(d) 5′– GAATTC – 3′; 3′ – CTTAAG – 5′

52. Given below are two statements; one is labelled as Assertion (A) and the other is labelled as Reason (R).

Assertion (A) Cyclosporin-A is helpful in treating myocardial infarction.

Reason (R) It is used as a clot buster for removing clots from the blood vessels of patients who have undergone myocardial infarction.

In the light of the above statements, choose the correct answer from the options given below.

(a) A is false, but R is true
(b) Both A and R are true and R is the correct explanation of A
(c) Both A and R are true, but R is not the correct explanation of A
(d) A is true, but R is false

53. Given below are two statements.

Statement I Autoradiography is a method that serves the purpose of early diagnosis.

Statement II A single-stranded DNA or RNA tagged with a radiative molecule is allowed to hybridise to its complementary DNA in a clone of cells followed by detection using autoradiography.

In the light of the above statements, choose the correct answer from the options given below.

(a) Statement I is incorrect, but statement II is correct
(b) Both statement I and statement II are correct
(c) Both statement I and statement II are incorrect
(d) Statement I is correct, but statement II is incorrect

54. Given below are two statements.

Statement I The large holes in Roquefort cheese are due to production of a large amount of CO_2 by a bacterium.

Statement II The Roquefort cheese are ripened by growing a specific fungi which gives a particular flavour.

In the light of the above statements, choose the correct answer from the options given below.

(a) Statement I is incorrect, but statement II is correct
(b) Both statement I and statement II are correct
(c) Both statement I and statement II are incorrect
(d) Statement I is correct, but statement II is incorrect

55. Match List I with List II.

List I	List II
A. Organism	I. When responses are unlimited
B. Exponential growth	II. Basic unit of ecological hierarchy
C. Population	III. Same species in a geographical area
D. Logistic growth	IV. When responses are limiting the growth

Choose the correct answer from the options given below.

(a) A-II, B, III, C-I, D-III
(b) A-II, B-I, C-III, D-IV
(c) A-I, B-III, C-IV, D-II
(d) A-III, B-II, C-IV, D-I

56. In a terrestrial ecosystem, the base of the pyramid include trees. Herbivores like plants constitute a population more than the base and in turn, are fed upon by fewer carnivores.

The shape of pyramid obtained will be

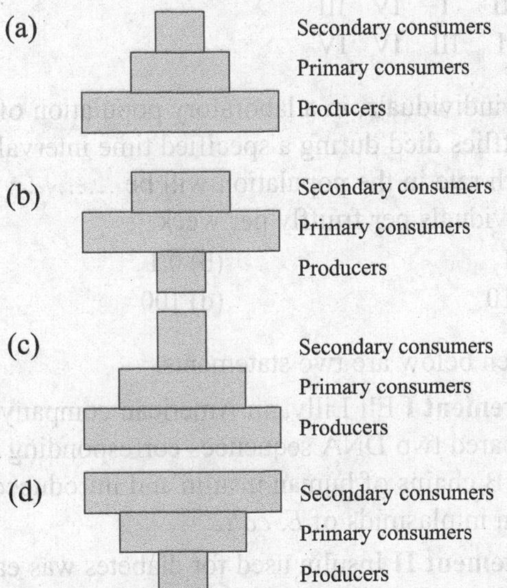

57. Observe the following diagram.

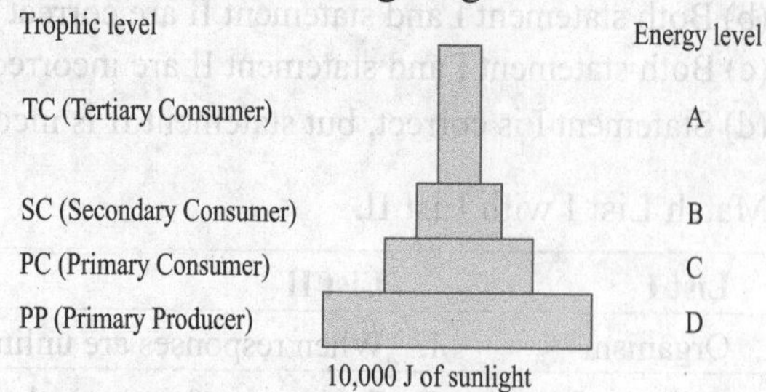

In which of the following trophic level, the available energy will be 1000J?

(a) A (b) B
(c) C (d) D

58. Match List I with List II.

List I	List II
A. Bread	I. Cellulosic material
B. Penicillin	II. *Methanobacterium*
C. Anaerobic sludge	III. *Saccharomyces cerevisiae*
D. Rumen	IV. *Penicillium notatum*

Choose the correct answer from the options given below.

	A	B	C	D
(a)	III	IV	II	I
(b)	II	III	II	IV
(c)	II	I	IV	III
(d)	I	III	IV	IV

59. If 4 individuals, in a laboratory population of 40 fruitflies died during a specified time interval, the death rate in the population will be .... individuals per fruitfly per week.

(a) 1 (b) 0.1
(c) 10 (d) 100

60. Given below are two statements.

Statement I Eli Lilly, an American company prepared two DNA sequences corresponding to A and B chains of human insulin and introduced them in plasmids of *E. coli*.

Statement II Insulin used for diabetes was earlier extracted from the gut of slaughtered cattle.

In the light of the above statements, choose the correct answer from the options given below.

(a) Statement I is incorrect, but statement II is correct
(b) Both statement I and statement II are correct
(c) Both statement I and statement II are incorrect
(d) Statement I is correct, but statement II is incorrect

61. Which of the following statement is incorrect?

(a) Around 200,000 varieties of rice are found in India.
(b) Basmati is distinct for its unique aroma and flavour.
(c) In India, 25 documented varieties of Basmati are grown.
(d) New variety of Basmati was actually derived from Indian farmer's varieties.

62. The majority of Baculoviruses used as biological control agents are in the genus

(a) Adenohypovirus
(b) *Nucleopolyhedrovirus*
(c) Ribonucleovirus
(d) Nucleohedrovirus

63. Which of the following statements is incorrect regarding RNA interference as a novel strategy?

(a) RNA interference takes place in only prokaryotic organisms
(b) RNA interference involves silencing of a specific *m*RNA due to a complementary *ds*RNA
(c) Transposons are mobile genetic elements
(d) Using *Agrobacterium* vectors, nematode specific genes were introduced into the host plant

64. If a big fish eats small fish which eats *Hydra* who in turns eats water fleas; water fleas in turn eat phytoplanktons. In this chain, water fleas will be

(a) producers (b) primary consumers
(c) secondary consumers (d) top consumers

65. Match List I with List II.

List I	List II
A. *Hind* III	I. Cloning vector
B. tet^R	II. Site of replication
C. pBR322	III. Restriction site
D. *ori*	IV. Antibiotic resistance gene

Choose the correct answer from the options given below.

(a) A-III, B-IV, C-I, D-II
(b) A-II, B-III, C-IV, D-I
(c) A-II, B-III, C-I, D-IV
(d) A-I, B-II, C-III, D-IV

66. A species population showed immediate decline after introduction of another species in the habitat. Identify the kind of interaction and the most appropriate example that represents the situation.

	Interaction	Example
(a)	Co-extinction	Plant pollinator
(b)	Predation	Nile perch, cichlid fish
(c)	Parasitism	Cow and grass
(d)	Competition	Steller's sea cow and passenger pigeon

67. The proteins encoded by the genes *cry*IAc and *cry*IIAb control whereas those encoded by *cry*IAb

(a) corn borer, cotton bollworm
(b) cotton bollworm, corn borer
(c) corn borer, corn borer
(d) tobacco virus

68. The graph shown below shows the BOD levels of a water sample taken from multiple sites (A-D).

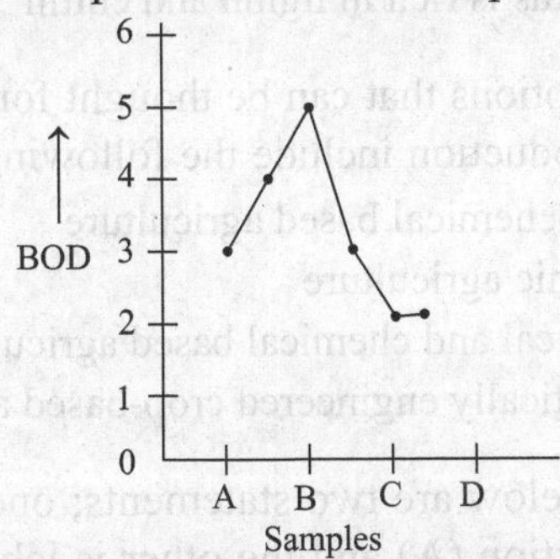

At which site will the bacteria be majorly deprived of the dissolved oxygen?

(a) Site A (b) Site C
(c) Site B (d) Site D

69. Read the following statements and choose the correct set of statements.

I. Plasmid DNA acts as vector to transfer the pieces of DNA attached to it.
II. The first restriction endonuclease was *Pvu* I.
III. The two enzymes responsible for restricting the growth of bacteriophage in *E. coli* were isolated in the year 1963.
IV. Exonuclease makes cuts at specific positions within the DNA.
V. Each restriction endonuclease function by inspecting the length of a DNA sequence.

Choose the correct answer from the options given below.

(a) I and II (b) I, III and V
(c) II and IV (d) II, IV and V

70. To make the bacterial cells competent for the transformation, the step that is required is

(a) treating them with divalent anion
(b) treating them with calcium
(c) washing them with detergent
(d) breaking the cell walls

71. Identify the incorrect statements.

I. Agarose matrix is a natural polymer extracted from sea weeds.
II. Recombinant vector molecule can be created even without the use of same restriction enzyme for cleaving vector and source DNA.
III. The ligation of alien DNA is carried out at a restriction site present in *rop* region.
IV. In insertional inactivation technique, the recombinant colonies produce blue colour.
V. The role of *Agrobacterium tumefaciens* is performed by adeno viruses in animal cells.

Choose the correct answer from the options given below

(a) II, III and IV (b) I, II and III
(c) I, II and IV (d) II, III, IV and V

72. Given below are two statements.

Statement I Population density is defined as number of individuals in a region or area by size of unit area in the region.

Statement II Death rate can be defined as number of individuals that are lost per unit time.

In the light of the above statements, choose the correct answer from the options given below.
(a) Statement I is incorrect, but statement II is correct
(b) Both statement I and statement II are correct
(c) Both statement I and statement II are incorrect
(d) Statement I is correct, but statement II is incorrect

73. Match List I with List II.

List I	List II
A. *Bacillus thuringiensis*	I. Cry proteins
B. *Thermus aquaticus*	II. Cloning vector
C. *Agrobacterium tumefaciens*	III. DNA polymerase
D. *Salmonella typhimurium*	IV. Construction of first recombinant DNA

Choose the correct answer from the options given below.
(a) A-I, B-II, C-III, D-IV
(b) A-I, B-III, C-II, D-IV
(c) A-II, B-IV, C-I, D-III
(d) A-III, B-II, C-I, D-IV

74. Which of the following statement is incorrect?
(a) Citric acid is used as a food preservative
(b) Biogas is used for cooking and acts as a source of lighting homes
(c) Penicillin is an antiviral product
(d) Many members of genus *Glomus* form mycorrhiza

75. Given below are two statements.

Statement I The Eastern ghats have a greater amphibian species diversity than the Western ghats.

Statement II India has a greater ecosystem diversity than Norway.

In the light of the above statements, choose the correct answer from the options given below.
(a) Statement I is incorrect, but statement II is correct
(b) Both statement I and statement II are correct
(c) Both statement I and statement II are incorrect
(d) Statement I is correct, but statement II is incorrect

76. Given below are two statements; one is labelled as Assertion (A) and the other is labelled as Reason (R).

Assertion (A) DNA ligase plays an important role in recombinant DNA technology.

Reason (R) The cutting of DNA at specific location became possible because of DNA ligase.

In the light of the given statements, choose the correct answer from the options given below.
(a) A is false, but R is true
(b) Both A and R are true and R is the correct explanation of A.
(c) Both A and R are true, but R is not the correct explanation of A.
(d) A is true, but R is false

77. The rate of decomposition is faster in the ecosystem. This is due to all of the following except,
(a) detritus is rich in sugars
(b) warm and moist environment
(c) presence of aerobic soil microbes
(d) detritus is rich in lignin and chitin

78. Three options that can be thought for increasing food production include the following, except
(a) agro-chemical based agriculture
(b) organic agriculture
(c) physical and chemical based agriculture
(d) genetically engineered crop-based agriculture

79. Given below are two statements; one is labelled as Assertion (A) and the other is labelled as Reason (R).

Assertion (A) The bottled fruit juices are much clearer than the ones made at homes.

Reason (R) The bottled juices are clarified by the use of lipase.

In the light of the above statements, choose the correct answer from the options given below.
(a) A is false, but R is true
(b) Both A and R are true and R is the correct explanation of A
(c) Both A and R are true, but R is not the correct explanation of A
(d) A is true, but R is false

80. .... which is also produced through transgenic organisms plays an important role in treatment of emphysema.
(a) α-2 antitrypsin
(b) α-1 antitrypsin
(c) β-1 antitrypsin
(d) α-2 trypsin

81. The organism among the following which do not belong to Lepidoptera.
(a) Tobacco budworm
(b) Army worm
(c) Butterflies
(d) Mosquitoes

82. Read the following statements and choose the correct set of statements.
I. Biogas is the mixture of gases such as methane, CO_2 and oxygen.
II. *Trichoderma* is excellent candidate for species- specific narrow spectrum insecticidal applications.
III. To control the butterfly caterpillars, the bacteria *Bacillus thuringiensis* is used.
IV. Cyanobacteria are autotrophic microbes widely distributed in aquatic and terrestrial environments.
V. Fungi are also known to form symbiotic associations with plants.

Choose the correct answer from the options given below.
(a) I and II
(b) III and V
(c) III, IV and V
(d) I, II and IV

83. The principle which states that two closely related species competing for the same resources cannot co-exist indefinitely and the competitively inferior one will be eliminated eventually, is called as
(a) resource partitioning
(b) gause's competitive exclusion principle
(c) competitive release principle
(d) co- existence principle

84. Given below are two statements.
Statement I The extinction of stellar's sea cow was due to co-extinction.
Statement II *In-situ* conservation is one of the factors of biodiversity loss.
In the light of the above statements, choose the correct answer from the options given below.
(a) Statement I is incorrect, but statement II is correct
(b) Both statement I and statement II are correct
(c) Both statement I and statement II are incorrect
(d) Statement I is correct, but statement II is incorrect

85. Given below are two statements; one is labelled as Assertion (A) and the other is labelled as Reason (R).
Assertion (A) In a marine aquatic ecosystem, pyramid of biomass is inverted.
Reason (R) Phytoplanktons exist in a higher number feeding on the zooplanktons.
In the light of the above statements, choose the correct answer from the options given below.
(a) A is false, but R is true
(b) Both A and R are true and R is the correct explanation of A
(c) Both A and R are true, but R is not the correct explanation of A.
(d) A is true, but R is false

86. The introduction of Nile perch in Lake Victoria leading to extinction of 200 species of cichlid fish is an example of
(a) fragmentation
(b) co-extinction
(c) over-exploitation
(d) alien species invasion

87. The first transgenic cow was named as ...X... whose milk has ...Y... to make it protein enriched.
(a) X-Dolly, Y-alpha-lactalbumin
(b) X-Rosie, Y-alpha-lactalbumin
(c) X-Dolly, Y- β-albumin
(d) X-Rosie, Y- β-albumin

88. *Ascaris* worm living in the intestine of human and tiger eating a deer are example of which of the following types of populatin interaction?

(a) Mutualism and competition, respectively
(b) Parasitism and predation, repectively
(c) Predation and competition, respectively
(d) Mutualism and parasitism, respectively

89. Given below are two statements.

Statement I Genetic engineering refers to the field of biotechnology that involve the use of technique to modify DNA and RNA.

Statement II Bioprocess engineering refers to the culturing of microbes in an open environment.

In the light of the above statements, choose the correct answer from the options given below.

(a) Statement I is incorrect, but statement II is correct
(b) Both statement I and statement II are correct
(c) Both statement I and statement II are incorrect
(d) Statement I is correct, but statement II is incorrect

90. The *ex-situ* conservation strategies includes all of the following except

(a) botanical garden, wildlife sanctuaries
(b) DNA bank, zoo
(c) national parks, biosphere reserves
(d) tissue culture, sacred groves

Response Index

01	ⓐ ⓑ ⓒ ⓓ	26	ⓐ ⓑ ⓒ ⓓ	51	ⓐ ⓑ ⓒ ⓓ	76	ⓐ ⓑ ⓒ ⓓ
02	ⓐ ⓑ ⓒ ⓓ	27	ⓐ ⓑ ⓒ ⓓ	52	ⓐ ⓑ ⓒ ⓓ	77	ⓐ ⓑ ⓒ ⓓ
03	ⓐ ⓑ ⓒ ⓓ	28	ⓐ ⓑ ⓒ ⓓ	53	ⓐ ⓑ ⓒ ⓓ	78	ⓐ ⓑ ⓒ ⓓ
04	ⓐ ⓑ ⓒ ⓓ	29	ⓐ ⓑ ⓒ ⓓ	54	ⓐ ⓑ ⓒ ⓓ	79	ⓐ ⓑ ⓒ ⓓ
05	ⓐ ⓑ ⓒ ⓓ	30	ⓐ ⓑ ⓒ ⓓ	55	ⓐ ⓑ ⓒ ⓓ	80	ⓐ ⓑ ⓒ ⓓ
06	ⓐ ⓑ ⓒ ⓓ	31	ⓐ ⓑ ⓒ ⓓ	56	ⓐ ⓑ ⓒ ⓓ	81	ⓐ ⓑ ⓒ ⓓ
07	ⓐ ⓑ ⓒ ⓓ	32	ⓐ ⓑ ⓒ ⓓ	57	ⓐ ⓑ ⓒ ⓓ	82	ⓐ ⓑ ⓒ ⓓ
08	ⓐ ⓑ ⓒ ⓓ	33	ⓐ ⓑ ⓒ ⓓ	58	ⓐ ⓑ ⓒ ⓓ	83	ⓐ ⓑ ⓒ ⓓ
09	ⓐ ⓑ ⓒ ⓓ	34	ⓐ ⓑ ⓒ ⓓ	59	ⓐ ⓑ ⓒ ⓓ	84	ⓐ ⓑ ⓒ ⓓ
10	ⓐ ⓑ ⓒ ⓓ	35	ⓐ ⓑ ⓒ ⓓ	60	ⓐ ⓑ ⓒ ⓓ	85	ⓐ ⓑ ⓒ ⓓ
11	ⓐ ⓑ ⓒ ⓓ	36	ⓐ ⓑ ⓒ ⓓ	61	ⓐ ⓑ ⓒ ⓓ	86	ⓐ ⓑ ⓒ ⓓ
12	ⓐ ⓑ ⓒ ⓓ	37	ⓐ ⓑ ⓒ ⓓ	62	ⓐ ⓑ ⓒ ⓓ	87	ⓐ ⓑ ⓒ ⓓ
13	ⓐ ⓑ ⓒ ⓓ	38	ⓐ ⓑ ⓒ ⓓ	63	ⓐ ⓑ ⓒ ⓓ	88	ⓐ ⓑ ⓒ ⓓ
14	ⓐ ⓑ ⓒ ⓓ	39	ⓐ ⓑ ⓒ ⓓ	64	ⓐ ⓑ ⓒ ⓓ	89	ⓐ ⓑ ⓒ ⓓ
15	ⓐ ⓑ ⓒ ⓓ	40	ⓐ ⓑ ⓒ ⓓ	65	ⓐ ⓑ ⓒ ⓓ	90	ⓐ ⓑ ⓒ ⓓ
16	ⓐ ⓑ ⓒ ⓓ	41	ⓐ ⓑ ⓒ ⓓ	66	ⓐ ⓑ ⓒ ⓓ		
17	ⓐ ⓑ ⓒ ⓓ	42	ⓐ ⓑ ⓒ ⓓ	67	ⓐ ⓑ ⓒ ⓓ		
18	ⓐ ⓑ ⓒ ⓓ	43	ⓐ ⓑ ⓒ ⓓ	68	ⓐ ⓑ ⓒ ⓓ		
19	ⓐ ⓑ ⓒ ⓓ	44	ⓐ ⓑ ⓒ ⓓ	69	ⓐ ⓑ ⓒ ⓓ		
20	ⓐ ⓑ ⓒ ⓓ	45	ⓐ ⓑ ⓒ ⓓ	70	ⓐ ⓑ ⓒ ⓓ		
21	ⓐ ⓑ ⓒ ⓓ	46	ⓐ ⓑ ⓒ ⓓ	71	ⓐ ⓑ ⓒ ⓓ		
22	ⓐ ⓑ ⓒ ⓓ	47	ⓐ ⓑ ⓒ ⓓ	72	ⓐ ⓑ ⓒ ⓓ		
23	ⓐ ⓑ ⓒ ⓓ	48	ⓐ ⓑ ⓒ ⓓ	73	ⓐ ⓑ ⓒ ⓓ		
24	ⓐ ⓑ ⓒ ⓓ	49	ⓐ ⓑ ⓒ ⓓ	74	ⓐ ⓑ ⓒ ⓓ		
25	ⓐ ⓑ ⓒ ⓓ	50	ⓐ ⓑ ⓒ ⓓ	75	ⓐ ⓑ ⓒ ⓓ		

Performance Scanner

> 90% Excellent !	You have mastered the second half of NEET syllabus (12th). The concepts of this syllabus are on your fingertips. Maintain this momentum.
76-90% Very Good !	You have a good command over the second half of NEET syllabus (12th). Revise it again after a few days and enhance your performance.
60-75% Good !	You have a wide scope to learn for the second half of NEET syllabus (12th). Revise it again.
<60% Not Satisfactory!	You have a long way ahead of you to master the second half of NEET syllabus (12th). Revise it thoroughly.

Scan for online part test

Space for Rough Work

Space for Rough Work

Test Booklet No. **3947366**

Test Booklet Code **NSS1**

NEET Stepping Stones 1

(Complete Syllabus Test 12th)

Name of the Candidate (In Capitals)

____

____

____

Candidate's Signature ____________

Invigilator's Signature ____________

Facsimile signature stamp of center superintendent____________

Important Instructions

- The test is of **1 hours 30 minutes** duration and the Test Booklet contains **90** multiple-choice questions (four options with a single correct answer) from biology.
- Candidates are advised to read all questions before they start attempting the question paper.
- Each questions carries 4 marks. For each correct response, the candidate will get 4 marks. For each incorrect response, one marks will be deducted from the total scores.
- In the event of candidate marking more than one option one mark will be deducted. The maximum marks are 180.
- Use **Blue/Black Point Pen only** for writing particular on this page/ marking response on Answer Sheet.

Do not open this booklet until you start attempting the test

Biology

1. The levels of diversity that can be observed in the biosphere are
   (a) genetic diversity, species diversity and ecological diversity.
   (b) genetic diversity, habitat diversity and ecological diversity.
   (c) geographical diversity, geological diversity, biological diversity
   (d) ecological diversity, species diversity, community diversity

2. In the production of test tube babies,
   (a) fertilisation and foetus formation is external
   (b) fertilisation and foetus formation is internal
   (c) fertilisation is internal and foetus formation is external
   (d) fertilisation is external and foetus formation is internal

3. In a dihybrid cross involving the genes R/r and Y/y, why does each gamete, i.e., RY, Ry, rY and ry have a frequency of 25% chance of gametes produced?
   (a) The presence of four different types of alleles in the F_1 generation guarantees that each gamete will have a 50% chance.
   (b) The genes segregate independently during meiosis, leading to equal probabilities for all possible combinations of alleles.
   (c) Each allele combination has equal probability of dominant and recessive alleles pairing together.
   (d) The presence of linked alleles during meiosis ensures that each combination has 25% chance.

4. Given below are two statements; one is labelled as Assertion (A) and other is labelled as Reason (R).

   Assertion (A) The process of splicing removes introns from the primary transcripts and joins the exons in a specific manner to produce a mature *m*RNA.

   Reason (R) Splicing along with capping and tailing, is necessary for the formation of mature *m*RNA.

   In the light of the above statements, choose the correct answer from the options given below.
   (a) A is false, but R is true
   (b) Both A and R are true, and R is the correct explanation of A
   (c) Both A and R are true, but R is not the correct explanation of A
   (d) A is true, but R is false

5. A man having Klinefelter's syndrome is
   (a) intersex with secondary sexual characters on the side of female
   (b) male with secondary sexual characters of female
   (c) female with secondary sexual characters of male
   (d) normal fertile male with secondary sexual characters of male.

6. Which of the following can be explained through law of dominance?
   (a) Expression of only one of the parental characters in a monohybrid cross.
   (b) Blending of both parental characters in F_1-generation in snapdragon.
   (c) Homozygous parents produce two kinds of gametes.
   (d) Heterozygous parents produce only one kind of gamete.

7. Among the following statement, which one is correct regarding tropical regions?
   (a) Tropical regions have experienced more recent speciation events due to their dynamic climates.
   (b) Tropical regions have remained climatically stable for millions of years, allowing continuous evolution and speciation.

(c) Tropical regions undergo rapid speciation because of their extreme and fluctuating environmental conditions.
(d) Topical regions have fewer competitions, allowing species to diversify rapidly.

8. Given below are two statements.

Statement I The underlying mechanism of pleiotropy in most cases is the effect of multiple genes on metabolic pathways which contribute towards a single phenotype.

Statement II Phenylketonuria is the best example of pleiotropy, as it is caused by mutation in the gene that codes for the enzyme phenylalanine hydroxylase leading to mental retardation and reduction in hair and skin pigmentation.

In the light of the above statements, choose the correct answer from the options given below.
(a) Statement I is incorrect, but statement II is correct
(b) Both statement I and statement II are correct
(c) Both statement I and statement II are incorrect
(d) Statement I is correct, but statement II is incorrect

9. A typical agarose gel electrophoresis showing migration of undigested and digested set of DNA fragments is given below.

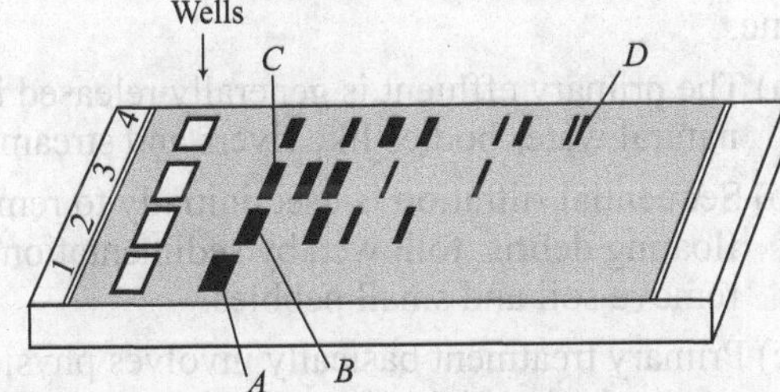

Identify the correct statement about the given figure.
(a) Fragment D migrates the fastest towards the cathode.
(b) Fragment A migrates the fastest towards the anode.
(c) Fragment B migrates the fastest towards the anode.
(d) Fragment D migrates the fastest towards the anode.

10. Given below are two statements; one is labelled as the Assertion (A) and other is labelled as the Reason (R)

Assertion (A) The presence of vestigial gill slits in the embryos of all vertebrates supports the concept of a common ancestor.

Reason (R) The embryos of all vertebrates including humans, develop a row of vestigial gill slit just behind the head, but it is a functional only in fish.

In the light of the above statements, choose the correct answer from the options given below.
(a) A is false, but R is true
(b) Both A and R are true and R is the correct explanation of A
(c) Both A and R are true, but R is the correct explanation of A
(d) A is true, but R is false

11. The somaclones are
(a) hybrid plants produced from tissue culture techniques
(b) genetically identical plants produced through micropropagation
(c) produced from somatic cells of plant through somatic hybridisation
(d) genetically modified plants produced through genetic engineering

12. The given figure represents ovum surrounded by few sperms. Identify the function of part 'A'.

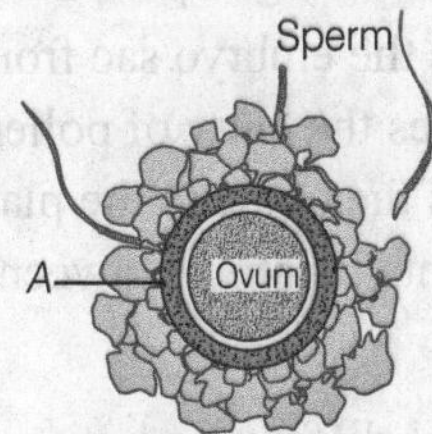

(a) It helps the sperm to enter into the cytoplasm of the ovum.
(b) It ensures that only one sperm can fertilise an ovum.
(c) It induces the completion of the meiotic division of the secondary oocyte.
(d) It secretes FSH and LH which increases the chance of fertilisation.

13. Identify the correct option containing features of genetic code.

(a) Inducer, Positive, Unspecific and Unambiguous
(b) Unambiguous, Specific, Contiguous and Degenerate
(c) Universal, Positive, Unspecific and Multipurpose
(d) Bifunctional, Universal, Degenerate and Unambiguous

14. Given below are two statements; one is labelled as Assertion (A) and other one is labelled as the Reason (R).

Assertion (A) Acquired immunity is pathogen specific and characterised by memory, leading to a highly intensified response upon subsequent encounters with the same pathogen.

Reason (R) The body remembers the first encounter with the pathogen, that results in strong primary response and a low intensity of secondary response.

In the light of the above statements, choose the correct answer from the options given below.

(a) A is false, but R is true
(b) Both A and R are true and R is the correct explanation of A
(c) Both A and R are true, but R is not the correct explanation of A
(d) A is true, but R is false

15. Which of the following is the primary function of the funicle in an angiospermic ovule?

(a) It protects the embryo sac from external shock.
(b) It facilitates the entry of pollen tube.
(c) It attaches the ovule to the placenta.
(d) It represents junction between ovule and nucellus.

16. The structural difference between a nucleoside and a nucleotide is that the

(a) former contains a pentose sugar only, while the latter contains a phosphate group.
(b) former contains pentose sugar and nitrogenous base, while the latter contains nucleoside with phosphate group.
(c) former contains a phosphate group, while the latter does not have this group.
(d) former contains a nitrogenous base and phosphate group, while the latter contains only uracil nitrogenous base.

17. Read the following statements carefully.

I. A pond is a shallow water body in which all the four basic components of an ecosystem are found.
II. Organisms occupy a place in the natural surrounding or in a community according to their feeding relationship with other organisms.
III. Each food chain has a certain mass of living material at a particular time called as the standing crop. It is measured as the mass of living organisms or the number in a unit area.
IV. The DFC begins with organic matter and is made up of decomposers which are heterotrophic organisms, mainly fungi and bacteria.
V. The number of trophic levels in the grazing food chain is restricted as the transfer of energy follows 10% law, i.e, only 10% percent of energy is used at each trophic level.

Choose the correct set of statements from the options given below.

(a) III and V
(b) I, II and V
(c) I, II and IV
(d) II, III and IV

18. Consider the following statements w.r.t. primary treatment of sewage and identify the incorrect one.

(a) The primary effluent is generally released into natural water bodies like rivers and streams.
(b) Sequential filtration is used initially to remove floating debris, followed by sedimentation to remove soil and small pebbles.
(c) Primary treatment basically involves physical removal of particles from the sewage through filtration and sedimentation.
(d) The primary effluent is passed into large aeration tanks for the biological treatment.

19. Given below are some stages of replication in retrovirus. Arrange them in the correct sequence.

I. New virus particles are produced.
II. Viral DNA incorporates into host genome.
III. New viral RNA is produced by the infected cell.
IV. Viral RNA is introduced into cell.
V. Viral DNA is produced by reverse transcriptase.

Choose the correct sequence from the options given below.
(a) I → II → III → IV → V
(b) IV → V → II → III → I
(c) IV → III → V → II → I
(d) III → IV → I → II → V

20. Given below are different codons and the amino acids coded by them.
I. ACG = Threonine II. GAG = Glycine
III. UAU = Tyrosine IV. CGU = Leucine
Choose the option containing the correct match pair.
(a) I and II (b) II and III
(c) II and IV (d) I and III

21. In a cross between true-breeding red-colour Snapdragon flower and true breeding white coloured Snapdragon flower, the F_1 offspring was pink. When the F_1 offspring was crossed with white flower, the F_2 resulted in the ratio
(a) 1 (Rr) Pink : 1 (rr) White
(b) 1 (RR) Red : 2 (Rr) Pink : 1 (rr) White
(c) 3 (RR) Red : 1 (rr) White
(d) 1 (RR) Red : 1 (Rr) Pink : 1 (rr) White

22. Which of the following statement is true regarding α-thalassemia?
(a) It is controlled by two closely linked genes HBA1 and HBA 2 on chromosome 16 of each parent.
(b) It is controlled by a single gene HBB on chromosome 11 of each parent.
(c) It affects the synthesis of β globin chains.
(d) It occurs due to mutation of one or both the genes.

23. Which step has been taken by Government of India to cater to the requirements of patent terms and other emergency provisions in this regards?
(a) Passing the Biopiracy Act
(b) Passing the Indian Patents Bill
(c) Forming the GEAC
(d) Passing the Bioethics Act

24. Observe the process of transcription in bacteria and choose the incorrect statement from the options given below.

Step 1 3′ 5′ 5′ 3′
Promoter σ DNA helix
RNA polymerase

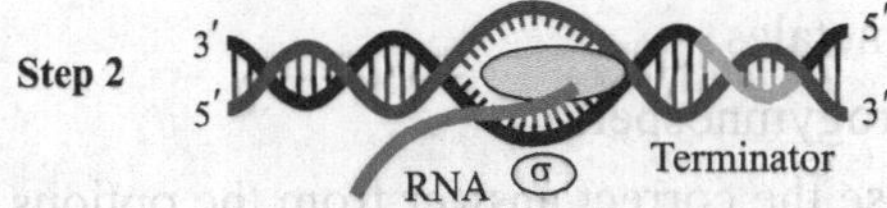

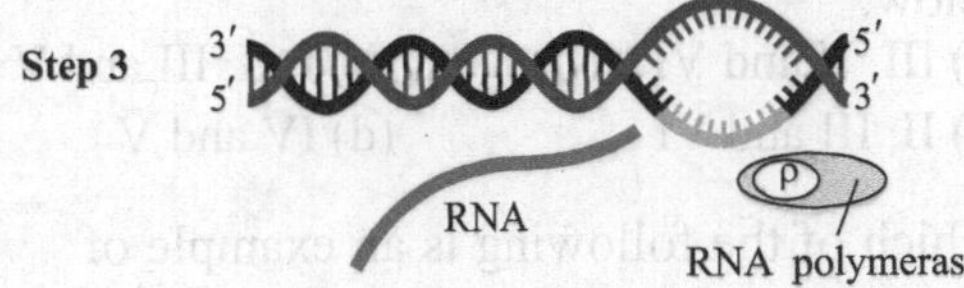

(a) In step 1, the RNA polymerase uses nucleoside triphosphate as substrate and polymerises in a template dependent fashion following the rule of complementarity.
(b) The RNA polymerase is only capable of catalysing the step 2.
(c) In step 3, polymerase reaches the terminator region and the nascent RNA falls off.
(d) Step 3 represents the association of sigma factor with RNA polymerase.

25. Identify the incorrect statements from the following.
(a) Aerobic microbes in the flocs consume the major part of the organic matter in the effluent, which significantly reduces the biological oxygen demand of the effluent.
(b) Streptokinase produced by the bacterium *Streptococcus* is modified by genetic engineering and is used as a clot buster for removing clots from the blood vessels.
(c) Cyclosporin-A is a thrombolytic medication used in organ-transplant patients and is produced by the fungus *Trichoderma polysporum*.
(d) Statins produced by the yeast *Monascus purpureus* have been commercialised as blood-cholesterol lowering agents.

26. Which of the following plant species originated in the Cretaceous period?

I. Bryophytes
II. Cycads
III. Ginkgos
IV. Monocotyledons
V. Dicotyledons
VI. Gnetales
VII. Progymnosperm

Choose the correct answer from the options given below.

(a) III, V and VI (b) I, II, III and V
(c) II, III and VI (d) IV and V

27. Which of the following is an example of convergent evolution?

(a) Different varieties of finches on the Galapagos island.
(b) Evolution of marsupials in Australia.
(c) Evolution of heart in vertebrates.
(d) Similarities between placental mammals and marsupials in Australia.

28. Consider the following and identify which one is incorrect regarding morphine.

(a) Very effective sedative and analgesic
(b) Very useful in patients who have undergone surgery
(c) Commonly known as smack
(d) Naturally occuring derivative of cocaine

29. Select the incorrect statement regarding ovum.

(a) Zona pellucida is secreted by the ovum itself
(b) Corona radiata is a primary egg membrane
(c) Hyaluronic acid which binds corona radiata cells is a mucopolysaccharide
(d) Zona pellucida is extracellular material that is composed of various glycoproteins

30. During DNA fingerprinting, the radioactive probes

(a) hybridise with DNA sample and form double-stranded structure
(b) degrade the DNA
(c) create positive charge on DNA
(d) produce cut in DNA sample at various site

31. The primary goal of gene therapy is

(a) to replace defective enzymes in patients with hereditary diseases through regular injections
(b) to permanently cure blood cancer by bone marrow transplantation
(c) to use stem cells for growing new tissues and organs in patients with genetic disorders
(d) to deliver normal genes into an individual's cells to correct defects and restore normal function

32. Given below are two statements; one is labelled as Assertion (A) and the other is labelled as Reason (R).

Assertion (A) The anaerobic digestion of sludge produces a mixture of gases such as methane, hydrogen sulphide and carbon dioxide.

Reason (R) Aerobic bacteria break down the organic matter of sludge in the presence of oxygen, producing biogas which is used as a source of energy due to its inflammable nature.

In the light of the above statements, choose the correct answer from the options given below.

(a) A is false, but R is true.
(b) Both A and R are true and R is the correct explanation of A.
(c) Both A and R are true, but R is not the correct explanation of A.
(d) A is true, but R is false.

33. Which statement is incorrect regarding plasmids as they are suitable vectors for genetic cloning?

(a) They have low molecule weight
(b) They have ability to combine readily with host cells
(c) They have several sites for a large number of restriction enzymes
(d) They have selectable markers which controls replication.

34. Given below are two statements; one is labelled as the Assertion (A) and other is labelled as the Reason (R).

Assertion (A) DNA fingerprinting involves identifying differences in some specific regions in DNA sequence called as repetitive DNA, because in these sequences, a small stretch of DNA is repeated many times.

Reason (R) DNA from different tissues of the same individual shows different degree of polymorphism.
In the light of the above statements, choose the correct answer from the options given below.
(a) A is false, but R is true.
(b) Both A and R are true and R is the correct explanation of A.
(c) Both A and R are true, but R is not the correct explanation of A
(d) A is true, but R is false.

35. Coca alkaloid or cocaine is obtained from coca plant, *Erythroxylum coca* native to South America. It produces its psychoactive effects primarily by
(a) interfering with the transport of the neuro transmitter dopamine
(b) interfering with the transport of serotonin
(c) binding with the receptors present in cardiovascular system
(d) binding with the receptors present in gastrointestinal tract

36. The specialised procedure to form an embryo in the laboratory in which a sperm is directly injected into the ovum is known as
(a) Intra Uterine Transfer
(b) Intra Uterine Insemination
(c) Intra Cytoplasmic Sperm Injection
(d) Gamete Intra Fallopian Transfer

37. Identify the correct description about the given diagram.

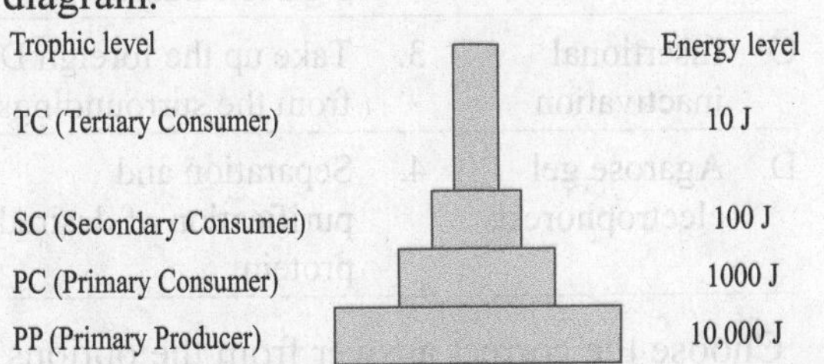

(a) Tertiary consumers are more in number because it shows greater vertical bar.
(b) Energy at a lower trophic level is always more than that of higher trophic level.
(c) Small standing crop of phytoplanktons supports large standing crop of zooplanktons.
(d) Each bar represents the amount of energy released at each trophic level at a given time.

38. Given below are two statements; one is labelled as Assertion (A) and other is labelled as Reason (R).
Assertion (A) In cloning vectors like pBR322, the presence of single recognition sites for restriction enzymes complicates the gene cloning process.
Reason (R) Presence of more than one recognition sites within the vector will generate several fragments.
In the light of the above statements, choose the correct answer from the options given below.
(a) A is false, but R is true
(b) Both A and R are true and R is the correct explanation of A
(c) Both A and R are true but R is not the correct explanation of A
(d) A is true, but R is false

39. Identify the incorrect statement from the following.
(a) After coitus, the motile sperms swim rapidly, pass through the cervix, enter into the uterus and finally reach the junction of the isthmus and ampulla of the Fallopian tube.
(b) The mitotic division starts as the zygote moves through the isthmus of the oviduct called cleavage and forms blastomeres.
(c) The embryo with 8 to 16 blastomeres is called morula and it continues to divide and transforms into trophoblast as it moves further into the Fallopian tubes.
(d) The trophoblast layer gets atlached to the endometrium and inner cell mass gets differentiated as the embryo and the uterine cells divide rapidly and covers the blastocyst.

40. Which of the following statement is correct about the pollen-pistil interaction?
(a) It guarantees the transfer of right type of pollen grains on the stigma.
(b) The pistil can distinguish between the compatible or incompatible pollen.
(c) The pistil accepts all types of pollens and promotes post-pollination events.
(d) Pollen from the same plant is always compatible and is accepted by the pistil.

41. Which of the following observation was obtained when Griffith injected mice with a mixture of heat-killed S-strain and live R-strain bacteria?

(a) The mice survived and S-strain bacteria were recovered from them.
(b) The mice died and live R-strain bacteria were recovered.
(c) The mice died and live S-strain bacteria were recovered.
(d) The mice survived and dead S-strain bacteria were recovered.

42. Read the following statements and choose the set of correct statements.

I. In a test cross, an organism showing recessive phenotype is crossed with dominant parent and their progeny can be analysed to predict the genotype of the test organism.
II. Dominance depends on the gene product and the particular phenotype chosen for examination, indicating that it is not an autonomous feature of a gene.
III. Experimental verification of the chromosomal theory of inheritance by Thomas Hunt Morgan and his colleagues, led to discovery of the basis for the variation produced during sexual reproduction.
IV. Walter Sutton and Theodore Boveri noted that the behaviour of chromosomes was parallel to the behaviour of genes and used chromosomal movement to explain Mendel's laws.

Choose the correct answer from the options given below.
(a) II and III
(b) II, III and IV
(c) III and IV
(d) I and III

43. Among the following, which one is a pair of homologous organs?

(a) Lungs of rabbit and gills of rohu
(b) Wing of bat and wing of butterfly
(c) Pectoral fin of rohu and the forelimb of horse
(d) Wing of grasshopper and wing of crow

44. Starch synthesis in pea seeds is controlled by one gene. It has two alleles viz. B and b. Which of the following statement correctly defines the nature of allele B?

(a) It shows incomplete dominance in both seed shape and starch grain size.
(b) It is recessive in seed shape and dominant in starch grain size.
(c) It is dominant in both seed shape and starch grain size.
(d) It shows complete dominance in seed shape, but incomplete dominance in starch grain size.

45. Which of the following option shows example of competition?

(a) The Abingdon tortoise in Galapagos islands became extinct within a decade after goats were introduced on the island.
(b) The coexistence between lions and hyenas for the access to dead animals.
(c) Nearly 25% of all insects are phytophagous.
(d) Cryptically coloured species of frogs and insects

46. Match List I with List II.

	List I		List II
A.	Downstream processing	1.	It is employed to check the progression of a restriction enzyme digestion
B.	Competent cell	2.	A recombinant DNA is inserted within the coding sequence of enzyme, β-galactosidase
C.	Insertional inactivation	3.	Take up the foreign DNA from the surroundings
D.	Agarose gel electrophoresis	4.	Separation and purification of desired protein

Choose the correct answer from the options given below.

	A	B	C	D
(a)	2	3	4	1
(b)	4	3	2	1
(c)	4	3	1	2
(d)	3	4	1	2

47. Given below are two statements; one is labelled as Assertion (A) and other is labelled as Reason (R).

Assertion (A) The rate of appearance of new forms is linked to the life cycle and reproductive rate of the organisms.

Reason (R) Microbes with shorter life spans can adapt and evolve into new forms much faster than fish or fowl with longer life spans.

In the light of the above statements, choose the correct answer from the options given below.

(a) A is false, but R is true

(b) Both A and R are true and R is the correct explanation of A

(c) Both A and R are true, but R is not the correct explanation of A

(d) A is true, but R is false

48. Given below are two statements; one is labelled as Assertion (A) and other one is labelled as Reason (R).

Assertion (A) Small volume cultures are essential for producing large volumes of recombinant proteins.

Reason (R) Bioreactor provides the optimal conditions for achieving the desired product by providing optimum growth conditions, i.e. temperature, pH, substrate, salts, vitamins, etc.

In the light of the above statements, choose the correct answer from the options given below.

(a) A is false, but R is true

(b) Both A and R are true and R is the correct explanation of A

(c) Both A and R are true, but R is not the correct explanation of A

(d) A is true, but R is false

49. The thymus is a lobed organ located near the heart and beneath the breastbone. It is quite large at the time of birth, but it keeps reducing in size with age. Thymus provides micro - environments for the

(a) proliferation of red blood cells

(b) development and maturation of T - lymphocytes

(c) reservoir of erthryocytes

(d) activation of lymphocytes

50. Among the given pairs of plant structures, which one has haploid number of chromosomes?

(a) Nucellus and antipodal cells

(b) Egg nucleus and secondary nucleus

(c) Megaspore mother cell and antipodal cells

(d) Egg cell and antipodal cells

51. Competition is best defined as a process in which the fitness of one species significantly

(a) increases in the presence of another species

(b) increases in the presence of certain abiotic factors

(c) gets lowered in the presence of another species

(d) gets lowered in the presence of certain abiotic factors

52. Which of the following statement is incorrect w.r.t. ABO blood group inheritance?

(a) The alleles I^A and I^B show co - dominance when present together.

(b) A person with ii genotype will have O blood group and no sugar on their red blood cells.

(c) The alleles I^A and I^B are completely dominant over i.

(d) Each person possesses any three of the four I gene allels.

53. The net primary productivity of ocean is low as compared to the terrestrial ecosystem. Identify the correct reason for it from following options.

(a) Terrestrial plants are huge in size as compared to aquatic plants.

(b) Oceans have lower light penetration and nutrient availability as compared to terrestrial environments.

(c) The total surface area of ocean is greater than land.

(d) Terrestrial ecosystems have more herbivores than aquatic ecosystems.

54. Given below are two statements.

Statement I α-interferons are biological response modifiers which are administered to cancer patients to destroy the tumour.

Statement II Those persons who take drugs intravenously are much more likely to acquire serious infections like AIDS and hepatitis-B.

In the light of the above statements, choose the correct answer from the options given below.
(a) Statement I is incorrect, but statement II is correct.
(b) Both statement I and statement II are correct.
(c) Both statement I and statement II are incorrect.
(d) Statement I is correct, but statement II is incorrect.

55. If the producers in an ecosystem capture 18000 kcal of energy per annum. How much energy will be available to secondary consumers according to the 10% law of energy?
(a) 1800 kcal (b) 180 kcal
(c) 18 kcal (d) 0.18 kcal

56. Which method is used to perpare *c*DNA in insulin preparation?
(a) Translation (b) Reverse transcription
(c) Transcription (d) Transversion

57. Which of the following role do predator- prey interactions play in the maintenance of stable ecosystem?
(a) It decreases biodiversity by allowing dominant prey species to proliferate uncontrollably.
(b) Predators remove or eat only weaker prey individuals, allowing stronger ones to dominate.
(c) Predators keep prey population under control and maintain ecosystem balance and biodiversity of that area.
(d) It has no significant effect on the maintenance of ecosystem.

58. Which of the following statement is true about the impact of invasive species on ecosystems?
(a) Invasive species typically increase biodiversity by providing new niches for native species.
(b) Nile perch introduced into lake Victoria in East Africa provides food to other small fishes.
(c) Co-evolved mutualistic relationships are strengthened by the introduction of alien-species.
(d) African catfish, *Clarias gariepinus* threatened the indigenous catfishes in Indian rivers.

59. Which of the following conservation method serve the purpose of *in-situ* conservation?
(a) Sacred groves of Meghalaya- The last refuges for a large number of rare and threatened plants.
(b) Cryopreservation-Gametes of threatened species can be preserved in viable and fertile condition for long periods.
(c) Seed banks- Seeds of different genetic strains of commercially important plants can be kept for long periods.
(d) Zoological parks-Many animals that have become extinct in the wild, but are found in zoological parks.

60. The transformation of the Graafian follicle into the corpus luteum is crucial for
(a) producing FSH hormone that induces the release of ovum
(b) maintaining the high level of FSH to support the development of multiple follicles
(c) producing large amount of progesterone which disintegrates the endometrium leading to menstruation
(d) secreting progesterone to prepare the endometrium for implantation

61. Recessive characters are expressed
(a) on any autosome
(b) when they are present on X-chromosomes of male
(c) on both the chromosomes of male
(d) when they are present on one X-chromosome of female

62. Identify the correct statement w.r.t. Meselson and Stahl experiment.
(a) They grew *E. coli* in a medium containing $^{15}NH_4Cl$ as the only nitrogen source for only one generation, because *E. coli* has shorter life span.
(b) The heavy DNA molecule could be distinguished from the normal DNA by centrifugation in a cesium chloride density gradient.
(c) The DNA that was extracted from the culture one generation after the transfer from N^{15} to N^{14} medium had heavy isotopes on both the strands.
(d) DNA extracted from the culture after second generation was composed of heavy and hybrid DNA.

63. The founder effect influences the genetic composition of a population by
(a) adding a new sample of population which become a different species
(b) introducing new alleles from large populations
(c) introducing selection pressure on old population
(d) continuous introduction and removal of genes due to migration

64. Read the following statements carefully.

I. Filament of a stamen is long and slender which supports the anther.

II. Pollen grains are generally hexagonal shaped, measuring about 25-50 μm in diameter and represents the male sporophytic generation.

III. The hard outer layer of pollen grain is known as exine, that is made up of sporopollenin.

IV. In a majority of flowering plants, one of the megaspores is functional, while the other three degenerate and only the functional megaspore develops into the embryo sac.

V. Majority of plants use biotic agents for pollination. Only a small proportion of plants use abiotic agents and about 30 genera, mostly dicotyledons are pollinated by water.

Choose the correct set of statements from the options given below.

(a) I, II and IV (b) II and V
(c) I, II and III (d) I, III and IV

65. All of the following are correct w.r.t. ascariasis, except

(a) it is caused by intestinal worm, *Ascaris*.
(b) symptoms of this disease include internal bleeding, muscular pain, fever and anaemia.
(c) appearance of dry, scaly lesions on various parts of the body is the main symptom.
(d) the eggs of the parasite are excreted along with faeces.

66. Match List I with List II.

List I	List II
A. *Trichoderma*	1. It forms symbiotic association with higher plant's root.
B. Ladybird	2. It is used to get rid of aphids.
C. *Nucleopolyhedrovirus*	3. These are very common in the root ecosystem.
D. *Glomus*	4. It attacks insect and other arthropods.

Choose the correct answer from the options given below.

	A	B	C	D		A	B	C	D
(a)	1	2	3	4	(b)	4	2	1	3
(c)	3	2	4	1	(d)	3	4	2	1

67. The Hardy-Weinberg principle cannot operate if

(a) the population is very large
(b) frequent mutations occur in the population
(c) the population has no chance of interaction with other populations
(d) free interbreeding, occurs among all members of the population

68. In PCR technique, polymerisation involves

(a) synthesis of DNA with the help of *Taq* polymerase, *d*NTPs and Mg^{2+} at 72°C
(b) hybridisation of primers to single stranded DNA at 55°C
(c) denaturation of double-stranded DNA at 72°C
(d) formation of single-stranded DNA

69. What would be the expected phenotypic ratio of the offspring when a female carrier of sickle-cell anaemia (Hb^AHb^S) marries with a non - carrier male showing genotype (Hb^AHb^A)?

(a) 100% normal
(b) 50% normal and 50% carriers
(c) 25% sickle-cell anaemic, 50% normal and 25% carriers
(d) 25% normal and 75% carriers

70. Which of the following statements is/are incorrect?

I. Chasmogamous flowers are invariably autogamous as there is no chance of cross pollen landing on the stigma and they produce assured seed-set.

II. Wind pollination requires that the pollen grains are light and non- sticky so that they can be transported in wind currents.

III. In some species, pollen release and stigma receptivity are not synchronised, either the pollen is released before the stigma becomes receptive or stigma becomes receptive much before the release of pollen.

IV. Self incompatibility is a genetic mechanism and prevents self-pollen from fertilising the ovules by inhibiting pollen germination or pollen tube growth in the pistil.

Choose the correct answer from the options given below.

(a) Only I (b) Only II
(c) III and IV (d) II and III

71. Given below are two statements; one is labelled as Assertion (A) and other one is labelled as Reason (R).

Assertion (A) The *Bt* toxin produced by bacterium *Bacillus thuringiensis* is inactive within the bacteria and does not harm the bacteria.

Reason (R) The *Bt* toxin protein exists as a inactive protoxin in *Bacillus thuringiensis* and requires activation by the alkaline pH to become toxic.

In the light of the above statements, choose the correct answer from the options given below.

(a) A is false, but R is true

(b) Both A and R are true and R is the correct explanation of A

(c) Both A and R are true, but R is not the correct explanation of A

(d) A is true, but R is false

72. Arrange the following events of translation in correct sequence and identify the correct answer from the options given below.

I. The ribosomes moves from codon to codon along the *m*RNA during elongation

II. Release factor binds to the stop codon.

III. The amino acids are joined by a peptide bond.

IV. Amino acids are activated in the presence of ATP and gets linked to their cognate *t*RNA.

(a) I → III → IV → II

(b) III → IV → II → I

(c) IV → III → I → II

(d) IV → I → III → II

73. The following are the statements about divergent evolution.

I. Homology indicates common ancestry.

II. Homologous structures are a result of divergent evolution.

III. Analogous structures are a result of divergent evolution.

IV. Forelimbs of whales, bats and cheetah show divergent evolution.

Choose the most appropriate answer showing correct statements from the options given below.

(a) I and IV (b) I, II and IV

(c) II and IV (d) II, III and IV

74. Math List I with List II.

List I (Components of vector pBR322)		List II (Role)
A. *Pst* I	1.	Foreign DNA is inserted
B. Recognition site	2.	Codes for the proteins involved in the replication of the plasmid
C. *rop*	3.	Helps in identifying and eliminating non-transformants
D. Selectable marker	4.	Restriction site within ampicillin resistance gene

Choose the correct answer from the options given below.

	A	B	C	D		A	B	C	D
(a)	4	1	2	3	(b)	1	4	2	3
(c)	1	2	4	3	(d)	3	2	1	4

75. Given below are two statements.

Statement I Blind approach of sequencing of the whole genome involves sequencing of all genomic regions that contained all the coding and non-coding sequence and later assigning different regions in the sequence with functions. It is referred to as sequence annotation.

Statement II Automated DNA sequencers are based on the principle of a method developed by Frederick Sanger.

In the light of the above statements, choose the correct answer from the options given below.

(a) Statement I is incorrect, but statement II is correct.

(b) Both statement I and statement II are correct.

(c) Both statement I and statement II are incorrect.

(d) Statement I is correct, but statement II is incorrect.

76. Which one of the following can be observed in population showing logistic growth?

I. Organisms show competition between individuals for limited resources.

II. The population grows in a geometric fashion.

III. The fittest individuals survive and reproduce.

IV. The population growth can be described by equation $dN/dt = rN\left(\frac{K-N}{K}\right)$.

V. The population growth can be described by equation $dN/dt = rN$.

Choose the correct answer from the options given below.

(a) I, II and III (b) I, III and IV
(c) III and IV (d) I and V

77. Which of the following example best illustrates the mutualistic relationship similar to that seen in lichens and mycorrhizae?

(a) A bird lays its eggs in the nest of other bird and let the other bird incubate them.
(b) The monarch butterfly is highly distasteful to certain birds because of a special chemical present in its body.
(c) The human liver fluke depends on snail and fish to complete its life cycle.
(d) The wasp pollinates the fig inflorescence while searching for suitable egg laying sites.

78. Given below are two statements.

Statement I Measuring the total number of individuals in a population is sometimes impractical or meaningless, especially when dealing with large populations or organisms, like the huge banyan tree with significant ecological roles.

Statement II For huge and large populations, the per cent cover or biomass is more meaningful measure for the population size.

In the light of the above statements, choose the correct answer from the options given below.

(a) Statement I is incorrect, but statement II is correct
(b) Both statement I and statement II are correct
(c) Both statement I and statement II are incorrect
(d) Statement I is correct, but statement II is incorrect

79. Identify the incorrect statements w.r.t. MTP from the following.

I. MTPs are considered relatively safe during the first trimester, i.e. upto 12 weeks of pregnancy as second trimester abortions are much more riskier.

II. MTP or induced abortion refers to the intentional termination of pregnancy before full gestation period and it accounts for nearly 1/5th of the total conceived pregnancies worldwide every year.

III. The primary purpose of legalising MTP in India was to determine the sex of the foetus to maintain equal balance between male and female.

IV. The use of MTP for terminating pregnancies based on the sex of the foetus through amniocentesis is legally permissible in India.

Choose the correct answer from the options given below.

(a) III and IV (b) I and II
(c) II and IV (d) I and III

80. Match the List I with List II.

List I	List II
A. Amniocentesis	1. Made up of rubber and inserted into the female reproductive tract
B. Cervical caps	2. Increase phagocytosis of sperms within the uterus
C. Lippes loop	3. Foetal sex determination test
D. Saheli	4. It is non- steroidal preparation

Choose the correct answer from the options given below.

	A	B	C	D		A	B	C	D
(a)	2	3	1	4	(b)	3	1	2	4
(c)	1	2	4	3	(d)	3	2	4	1

81. Match List I with List II.

List I	List II
A. Histones	1. Repeating unit of a structure called chromatin
B. Nucleosome	2. Set of positively charged, basic proteins
C. Euchromatin	3. Densely packed chromatin
D. Heterochromatin	4. Loosely packed chromatin

Choose the correct answer from the options given below.

	A	B	C	D		A	B	C	D
(a)	2	1	4	3	(b)	2	4	1	3
(c)	1	2	3	4	(d)	4	2	1	3

82. Arrange the following evolutionary history of vertebrates through geological periods.

I. Dinosaurs got extinct in the late tertiary period.

II. Early reptiles were extinct 350 mya.

III. Therapsids got extinct in the early triassic period.

IV. Thecodonts got extinct in the permian period.

Choose the correct answer from the options given below.

(a) II → IV → III → I
(b) II → I → IV → III
(c) II → I → III → IV
(d) IV → I → III → II

83. The use of *Cannabis* products (bhang, ganja, charas, marijuana or hashish) causes

(a) depression of brain activity and feeling of calmness
(b) alters thoughts, perceptions and feelings
(c) suppresses brain function and relieves pain
(d) stimulates the nervous system and increases alertness and activity

84. Consider the following statements and identify the incorrect statements.

I. Spleen is a large bean-shaped organ, mainly contains lymphocytes and phagocytes and acts as a filter of the blood by trapping blood-borne microorganisms.

II. The lymph nodes are small solid structures located at different point along the lymphatic system, and serves to trap the microorganisms.

III. The T-lymphocytes produce an army of proteins in response to pathogens into our blood to fight with them.

IV. Each antibody molecule has eight peptide chains, four smallers ones called light chains and four longer ones called heavy chains.

Choose the correct answer from the options given below.

(a) III and IV
(b) I and II
(c) II, III and IV
(d) I and III

85. Match List I with List II.

List I	List II
A. Down's syndrome	1. Masculine development with gynaecomastia; 47, XXY
B. Klinefelter's syndrome	2. Short statured with mental retardation; trisomy of 21
C. Turner's syndrome	3. Failure of segregation of chromatids during cell division
D. Aneuploidy	4. Females are sterile with rudimentary ovaries; 45, XO

Choose the correct answer from the options given below.

	A	B	C	D		A	B	C	D
(a)	2	1	4	3	(b)	2	3	1	4
(c)	4	3	2	1	(d)	2	4	3	1

86. Identify incorrect statement from the following regarding DNA.

(a) It is made up of two polynucleotide chains, where the backbone is constituted by sugar-phosphate and the nitrogenous bases project inside.
(b) Adenine forms two hydrogen bonds with thymine from opposite strand and guanine is bonded to cytosine with three H-bonds.
(c) In 1953, James Watson and Francis Crick, based on the X-ray diffraction data produced by Erwin Chargaff and Rosalin Franklin, proposed the theory of central dogma in molecular biology
(d) The pitch of the helix is 3.4nm and there are roughly 10bp in each turn and the distance between a bp in a helix is approximately equal to 0.34 nm.

87. Match List I with List II.

List I	List II
A. Saltation	1. Branching descent and natural selection as the two key concepts
B. Darwinian theory	2. It was about 20 feet in height and had huge fearsome dagger like teeth
C. *Coelacanth*	3. Sudden and significant change in the evolutionary development of an organism
D. *Tryannosaurus rex*	4. These were called lobefins and evolved into the first amphibians

Choose the correct answer from the options given below.

	A	B	C	D		A	B	C	D
(a)	3	2	4	1	(b)	1	2	4	3
(c)	4	3	2	1	(d)	3	1	4	2

88. Match List I with List II.

	List I		List II
A.	Active immunity	1.	Ready-made antibodies
B.	Passive immunity	2.	Slow and takes time
C.	Colostrum	3.	Generate memory B-and T-cells
D.	Vaccines	4.	Contains abundant IgA antibodies

Choose the correct answer from the options given below.

	A	B	C	D
(a)	2	1	4	3
(b)	1	2	4	3
(c)	2	4	3	1
(d)	2	3	1	4

89. Which of the following match pair is correct?

(a) Australian marsupial-Flying squirrel

(b) Homologous organs-Wings of butterfly and birds

(c) Analogous organs- Eye of the *Octopus* and mammal

(d) Placental mammal-Tasmanian tiger cat

90. Given below are two statements.

Statement I *Plasmodium* enters the human body as sporozoites through the bite of infected female *Anopheles* mosquito and these sporozoites multiply within the liver cells.

Statement II Bacteria like *Streptococcus pneumoniae* and *Haemophilus influenzae* are responsible for causing haemophilia in humans which infects the alveoli (air filled sacs) of the lungs.

In the light of the above statements, choose the correct answer from the options given below.

(a) Statement I is incorrect, but statement II is correct.

(b) Both statement I and statement II are correct.

(c) Both statement I and statement II are incorrect.

(d) Statement I is correct, but statement II is incorrect.

Response Index

01 ⓐ ⓑ ⓒ ⓓ	26 ⓐ ⓑ ⓒ ⓓ	51 ⓐ ⓑ ⓒ ⓓ	76 ⓐ ⓑ ⓒ ⓓ
02 ⓐ ⓑ ⓒ ⓓ	27 ⓐ ⓑ ⓒ ⓓ	52 ⓐ ⓑ ⓒ ⓓ	77 ⓐ ⓑ ⓒ ⓓ
03 ⓐ ⓑ ⓒ ⓓ	28 ⓐ ⓑ ⓒ ⓓ	53 ⓐ ⓑ ⓒ ⓓ	78 ⓐ ⓑ ⓒ ⓓ
04 ⓐ ⓑ ⓒ ⓓ	29 ⓐ ⓑ ⓒ ⓓ	54 ⓐ ⓑ ⓒ ⓓ	79 ⓐ ⓑ ⓒ ⓓ
05 ⓐ ⓑ ⓒ ⓓ	30 ⓐ ⓑ ⓒ ⓓ	55 ⓐ ⓑ ⓒ ⓓ	80 ⓐ ⓑ ⓒ ⓓ
06 ⓐ ⓑ ⓒ ⓓ	31 ⓐ ⓑ ⓒ ⓓ	56 ⓐ ⓑ ⓒ ⓓ	81 ⓐ ⓑ ⓒ ⓓ
07 ⓐ ⓑ ⓒ ⓓ	32 ⓐ ⓑ ⓒ ⓓ	57 ⓐ ⓑ ⓒ ⓓ	82 ⓐ ⓑ ⓒ ⓓ
08 ⓐ ⓑ ⓒ ⓓ	33 ⓐ ⓑ ⓒ ⓓ	58 ⓐ ⓑ ⓒ ⓓ	83 ⓐ ⓑ ⓒ ⓓ
09 ⓐ ⓑ ⓒ ⓓ	34 ⓐ ⓑ ⓒ ⓓ	59 ⓐ ⓑ ⓒ ⓓ	84 ⓐ ⓑ ⓒ ⓓ
10 ⓐ ⓑ ⓒ ⓓ	35 ⓐ ⓑ ⓒ ⓓ	60 ⓐ ⓑ ⓒ ⓓ	85 ⓐ ⓑ ⓒ ⓓ
11 ⓐ ⓑ ⓒ ⓓ	36 ⓐ ⓑ ⓒ ⓓ	61 ⓐ ⓑ ⓒ ⓓ	86 ⓐ ⓑ ⓒ ⓓ
12 ⓐ ⓑ ⓒ ⓓ	37 ⓐ ⓑ ⓒ ⓓ	62 ⓐ ⓑ ⓒ ⓓ	87 ⓐ ⓑ ⓒ ⓓ
13 ⓐ ⓑ ⓒ ⓓ	38 ⓐ ⓑ ⓒ ⓓ	63 ⓐ ⓑ ⓒ ⓓ	88 ⓐ ⓑ ⓒ ⓓ
14 ⓐ ⓑ ⓒ ⓓ	39 ⓐ ⓑ ⓒ ⓓ	64 ⓐ ⓑ ⓒ ⓓ	89 ⓐ ⓑ ⓒ ⓓ
15 ⓐ ⓑ ⓒ ⓓ	40 ⓐ ⓑ ⓒ ⓓ	65 ⓐ ⓑ ⓒ ⓓ	90 ⓐ ⓑ ⓒ ⓓ
16 ⓐ ⓑ ⓒ ⓓ	41 ⓐ ⓑ ⓒ ⓓ	66 ⓐ ⓑ ⓒ ⓓ	
17 ⓐ ⓑ ⓒ ⓓ	42 ⓐ ⓑ ⓒ ⓓ	67 ⓐ ⓑ ⓒ ⓓ	
18 ⓐ ⓑ ⓒ ⓓ	43 ⓐ ⓑ ⓒ ⓓ	68 ⓐ ⓑ ⓒ ⓓ	
19 ⓐ ⓑ ⓒ ⓓ	44 ⓐ ⓑ ⓒ ⓓ	69 ⓐ ⓑ ⓒ ⓓ	
20 ⓐ ⓑ ⓒ ⓓ	45 ⓐ ⓑ ⓒ ⓓ	70 ⓐ ⓑ ⓒ ⓓ	
21 ⓐ ⓑ ⓒ ⓓ	46 ⓐ ⓑ ⓒ ⓓ	71 ⓐ ⓑ ⓒ ⓓ	
22 ⓐ ⓑ ⓒ ⓓ	47 ⓐ ⓑ ⓒ ⓓ	72 ⓐ ⓑ ⓒ ⓓ	
23 ⓐ ⓑ ⓒ ⓓ	48 ⓐ ⓑ ⓒ ⓓ	73 ⓐ ⓑ ⓒ ⓓ	
24 ⓐ ⓑ ⓒ ⓓ	49 ⓐ ⓑ ⓒ ⓓ	74 ⓐ ⓑ ⓒ ⓓ	
25 ⓐ ⓑ ⓒ ⓓ	50 ⓐ ⓑ ⓒ ⓓ	75 ⓐ ⓑ ⓒ ⓓ	

Performance Scanner

> 90% Excellent !	You have mastered the NEET syllabus (12th). The concepts of this entire syllabus at your fingertips. Maintain this momentum.
76-90% Very Good !	You have a good command over the entire NEET syllabus (12th). Revise it again after a few days to enhance your performance.
60-75% Good !	You have a wide scope to learn for the entire NEET syllabus (12th). Revise it again.
<60% Not Satisfactory!	You have a long way ahead of you to master the NEET syllabus (12th). Revise it thoroughly.

Space for Rough Work

Test Booklet No. 3947367

Test Booklet Code NSS2

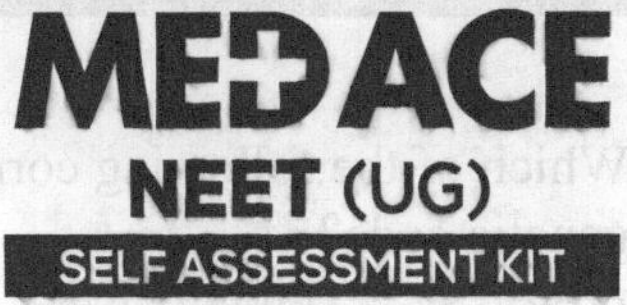

NEET Stepping Stones 2

(Complete Syllabus Test 12th)

Name of the Candidate (In Capitals)

____

____

____

Candidate's Signature ____________

Invigilator's Signature ____________

Facsimile signature stamp of center superintendent____________

Important Instructions

- The test is of **1 hours 30 minutes** duration and the Test Booklet contains **90** multiple-choice questions (four options with a single correct answer) from biology.
- Candidates are advised to read all questions before they start attempting the question paper.
- Each questions carries 4 marks. For each correct response, the candidate will get 4 marks. For each incorrect response, one marks will be deducted from the total scores.
- In the event of candidate marking more than one option one mark will be deducted. The maximum marks are 180.
- Use **Blue/Black Point Pen only** for writing particular on this page/ marking response on Answer Sheet.

Do not open this booklet until you start attempting the test

Biology

1. Which of the following correctly illustrates the genetic code?
   (a) It is a set of three - letter combinations of nucleotides, each of which corresponds to a specific amino acid.
   (b) It is a set of four - letter combinations of *m*RNA and each code is nearly universal.
   (c) These code overlap each other, meaning that each nucleotide is part of only one codon.
   (d) Total 64 codons are found in which 61 codes for amino acids and three are start codons.

2. Given below are two statements; one is labelled as Assertion (A) and other is labelled as Reason (R).

   Assertion (A) The cross between homozygous round yellow seeds and homozygous wrinkled green seeds produced only round yellow seeds in F_1-generation, while in F_2-generation, produced different types of phenotypic ratio.

   Reason (R) This type of cross can be explained through the Mendel's law of dominance in which only one of the parental character in dihybrid cross gets expressed in F_1, and in F_2, both are expressed.

   In the light of the above statements, choose the correct answer from the options given below.
   (a) A is false, but R is true.
   (b) Both A and R are true and R is the correct explanation of A.
   (c) Both A and R are true, but R is not the correct explanation of A.
   (d) A is true, but R is false.

3. Match the List I with List II.

List I	List II
A. Formation of sperms or ovum.	1. Implantation
B. Transfer of sperms into the female genital tract.	2. Gametogenesis
C. Development of blastocyst and its attachment to the uterine wall.	3. Parturition
D. Delivery of the baby.	4. Insemination

Choose the correct answer from the options given below.

	A	B	C	D
(a)	1	4	2	3
(b)	3	4	2	1
(c)	2	4	1	3
(d)	2	3	4	1

4. Identify the correct order of the Avery, MacLeod and Maclyn McCarty experiment.
   I. They identified the chemical nature of the transforming principle.
   II. They treated each tube with a specific enzyme that would degrade one single type of chemical compound.
   III. They took mixture of heat killed S-strain and live R-strain bacteria.

   Choose the correct answer form the options given below.
   (a) I → II → III
   (b) III → II → I
   (c) II → III → I
   (d) III → I → II

5. Given below are two statements.

   Statement I Periodic abstinence is a barrier method in which females use a latex sheath condom to cover vagina and cervix to prevent entry of semen into female genital tract.

   Statement II Withdrawal or coitus interruptus is a natural method of birth control in which the male partner withdraws his penis from the vagina just before ejaculation so as to avoid insemination.

   In the light of the above statements, choose the correct answer from the options given below.
   (a) Statement I is incorrect, but statement II is correct.
   (b) Both statement I and statement II are correct.
   (c) Both statement I and statement II are incorrect.
   (d) Statement I is correct, but statement II are incorrect.

6. Identify the incorrect statements from the following.

I. The Big-Bang theory explains the origin of universe which states that a single huge explosion led to the expansion of universe.

II. In the solar system of the Milky way galaxy, Earth was supposed to have been formed about 4.5 billion years back and there was no atmosphere on early earth.

III. Oparin of Russia and Haldane of England proposed that the first form of life could have come from pre-existing living cells or spores that have come from other planets.

VI. The theory that says that the first form of life arose slowly through evolutionary forces from non-living molecules is accepted by majority of the researchers.

V. Rocks form sediments and cross-section of earth's crust indicates the arrangement of sediments and fossils one over the other during the long history of earth and provides biochemical evidences for evolution.

Choose the correct answer from the options given below.

(a) III and V (b) I, II and III

(c) II, IV and V (d) II and III

7. Which of the following statement is correct about the mechanism of action of hashish in human body?

(a) It enhances the activity of transport of neuro-transmitter dopamine.

(b) It inhibits the synthesis of dopamine, leading to altered mood and sense of euphoria.

(c) It binds with opioid receptors present in central nervous system and gastrointestinal tract.

(d) It binds wiith cannabinoids receptors present in the brain.

8. Match the List I with List II.

	List I		List II
A.	Alfred Wallace	1.	All the existing life forms share similarities and share common ancestors
B.	Homologous organs	2.	Not anatomically similar, but perform similar functions
C.	Analogous organs	3.	Anatomically similar but perform different functions
D.	Evolution by anthropogenic action	4.	Drugs resistant microbes

Choose the correct answer from the options given below.

	A	B	C	D
(a)	1	3	2	4
(b)	3	4	1	2
(c)	2	4	3	1
(d)	1	4	2	3

9. Given below are two statements; one is labelled as Assertion (A) and other is labelled as Reason (R).

Assertion (A) In a typical human, half of the sperm produced by male carries the Y-chromosome.

Reason (R) During spermatogenesis, males produce two types of gametes, one carrying the *X*-chromosome and the other carrying the *Y*-chromosome.

In the light of the above statements, choose the correct answer from the options given below.

(a) A is false, but R is true.

(b) Both A and R are true and R is the correct explanation of A.

(c) Both A and R are true, but R is not the correct explanation of A.

(d) A is true, but R is false.

10. Identify the incorrect statement from the following options.

(a) The VNTR belongs to a class of satellite DNA referred to as micro- satellite.

(b) The DNA fingerprint differs from individual to individual in a population, except in the case of monozygotic twins.

(c) DNA fingerprinting involves identifying differences in some specific regions in DNA sequence.

(d) Repetitive sequences are stretches of DNA sequence that are repeated many times, sometimes hundred to thousand times.

11. Given below are two statements.

Statement I The step involving fragmentation of DNA by specific restriction endonuclease enzyme occurs after the isolation of a desired DNA fragment from agarose gel electrophoresis.

Statement II Culturing of host cells in a medium at large scale and extraction of the desired product is the last step of recombinant DNA technology.

In the light of the above statements, choose the correct answer from the options given below.

(a) Statement I is incorrect, but statement II is correct.

(b) Both statement I and statement II are correct.

(c) Both statement I and statement II are incorrect.

(d) Statement I is correct, but statement II is incorrect.

12. Identify the correct statements.

I. Pedigree analysis, the inheritance of a particular trait is represented in the family tree over generations which is utilised to trace the abnormality or disease.

II. DNA dependent DNA polymerases catalyse polymerisation only in one direction, i.e. $5' \rightarrow 3'$.

III. DNA dependent RNA polymerase catalyses the polymerisation in only one direction, i.e. $3' \rightarrow 5'$

IV. In bacteria, all three RNAs are transcribed by single DNA dependent RNA polymerase which binds to promoter and initiates transcription.

V. Marshall Nirenberg's cell free system for protein synthesis finally helped the genetic code to be deciphered.

Choose the correct answer from the following options.

(a) I, II, IV and V

(b) II, IV and V

(c) I, III and V

(d) I, II, III and IV

13. Given below are two statements.

Statement I The BOD test measures the rate of uptake of oxygen by micro-organisms in a sample of water.

Statement II When the BOD sewage or waste water is reduced significantly, the effluents from aeration tanks are then passed into natural water bodies like rivers and streams.

In the light of the above statements, choose the correct answer from the options given below.

(a) Statement I is incorrect, but statement II is correct.

(b) Both statement I and statement II are correct.

(c) Both statement I and statement II are incorrect.

(d) Statement I is correct, but statement II are incorrect.

14. Which of the following sequence correctly describes the flow of procedures in the Hershey Chase experiment?

A-The protein coat and DNA of bacteriophages are labelled with different radioactive isotopes.

B-The bacterial cells are agitated in a blender to remove the phage coats.

C- The bacterial cells and phage particles are separated by centrifugation.

D- Bacteria are infected with radioactive phages.

(a) $A \rightarrow B \rightarrow D \rightarrow C$ (b) $A \rightarrow D \rightarrow B \rightarrow C$

(c) $C \rightarrow A \rightarrow B \rightarrow D$ (d) $D \rightarrow C \rightarrow A \rightarrow B$

15. Identify the incorrect statement from the following options.

(a) Primary production is the amount of biomass or organic matter produced per unit area over a time period by plants during photosynthesis.

(b) Primary production is the amount of biomass or organic matter produced by primary consumer.

(c) The rate of biomass production is called productivity and is expressed in terms of $gm^{-2} yr^{-1}$ or $(kcal\ m^{-2}) yr^{-1}$.

(d) Primary productivity depends on the plant species inhabiting a particular area which also depends on a variety of environmental factors.

16. Given below are two statements.

Statement I Seeds collected from hybrid plants do not retain hybrid characteristics because the characters of progeny of hybrid plants segregate, leading to the loss of hybrid traits.

Statement II Production of hybrid seeds is expensive, making them costly for farmers to purchase every year.

In the light of the above statements, choose the correct answer from the options given below.

(a) Statement I is incorrect, but statement II is correct.
(b) Both statement I and statement II are correct.
(c) Both statement I and statement II are incorrect.
(d) Statement I is correct, but statement II is incorrect.

17. In a population of butterflies, individuals with larger wings have a higher chance of survival due to their ability to migrate longer distance. This scenario illustrates

(a) Disruptive selection
(b) Stabilizing selection
(c) Directional selection
(d) Genetic drift

18. Identify the correct statement about the given figure.

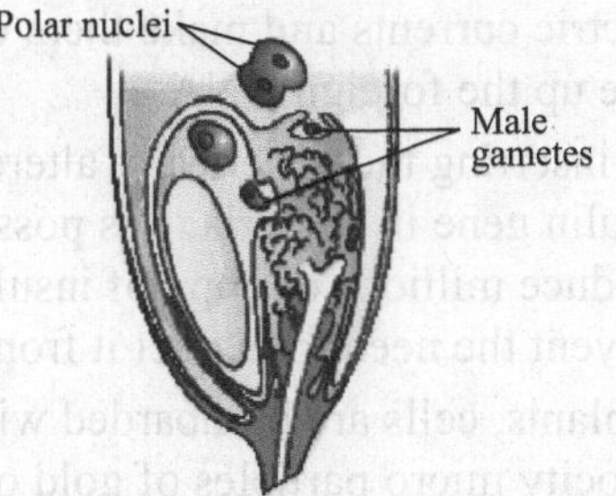

(a) It shows growth of pollen tube through the style.
(b) It shows the an egg apparatus and entry of pollen tube into synergid.
(c) It shows growth of synergid cells and fusion of polar nuclei with one of male gamete.
(d) It shows discharge of male gametes into a synergid and the movement of the sperms towards the egg and central cell.

19. Identify the narrowly utilitarian argument of biodiversity from the following.

I. Exploration of molecular, genetic and species-level diversity is done for products of economic importance.
II. More than 25 per cent of the drugs currently sold in the market worldwide are derived from plants.
III. Amazon forest is estimated to produce, through photosynthesis, 20 per cent of the total oxygen in the earth's atmosphere.
IV. The aesthetic pleasures of walking through thick woods, watching spring flowers in full bloom or waking up to bulbul's song in the morning.

Choose the correct answer from the following

(a) I and III (b) I and II
(c) III and IV (d) I, II and III

20. The diagram below shows the Miller-Urey experimental set up to test the Oparin-Haldane hypothesis about the origin of life on earth.

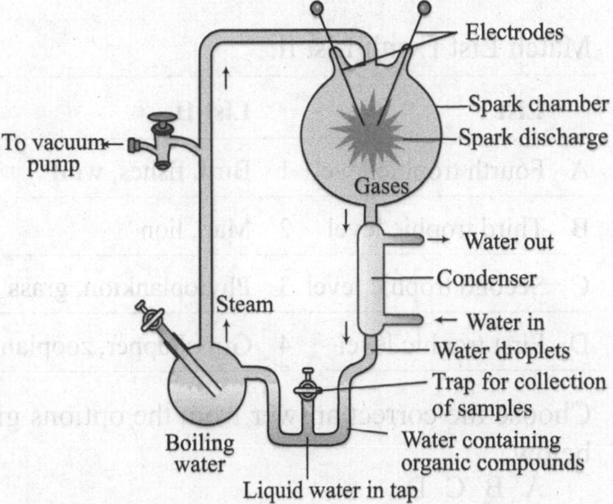

Which of the gases in the primitive atmosphere produced amino acids in the cooled water a week after the experiment had started?

(a) Carbon monoxide and methane
(b) Carbon monoxide and water vapour
(c) Methane and ammonia
(d) Hydrogen and carbon monoxide

21. What does a steeper slope in the species-area relationship indicate when analysing very large areas such as entire continents?

(a) A smaller increase in species richness with increasing area
(b) A decrease in species richness with increasing area
(c) A greater increase in species richness with increasing area
(d) A reduction in species richness with reducing area

22. Given below are two statements.

Statement I India has more than 50,000 genetically different strains of rice and over 1000 varieties of mango, representing high genetic diversity.

Statement II The Western ghats have a higher diversity of amphibian species compared to the Eastern ghats, indicating greater species diversity.

In the light of the above statements, choose the correct answer from the options given below.

(a) Statement I is incorrect, but statement II is correct.

(b) Both statement I and statement II are correct.

(c) Both statement I and statement II are incorrect.

(d) Statement I is correct, but statement II are incorrect.

23. Match List I with List II.

	List I		List II
A	Fourth trophic level	1	Bird, fishes, wolf
B	Third trophic level	2	Man, lion
C	Second trophic level	3	Phytoplankton, grass
D	First trophic level	4	Grasshopper, zooplankton

Choose the correct answer from the options given below.

	A	B	C	D
(a)	2	1	4	3
(b)	1	2	3	4
(c)	3	4	2	1
(d)	2	4	3	1

24. Given below are two statements; one is labelled as Assertion (A) and other is labelled as Reason (R).

Assertion (A) Humus is a dark coloured amorphous substance in the soil formed through the process of humification and serves as a reservoir of nutrients.

Reason (R) Humus is highly resistant to microbial action and undergoes decomposition at an extremely slow rate.

In the light of the above statements, choose the correct answer from the options given below.

(a) A is false, but R is true.

(b) Both A and R are true and R is the correct explanation of A.

(c) Both A and R are true, but R is not the correct explanation of A.

(d) A is true, but R is false.

25. Match List I with List II.

	List I		List II
A.	Fragmentation	1.	Precipitation of inorganic salts
B.	Leaching	2.	Break down of detritus into smaller particles
C.	Catabolism	3.	Degradation into detritus into simpler inorganic substances
D.	Humification	4.	Formation of humus

Choose the correct answer from the options given below.

	A	B	C	D		A	B	C	D
(a)	2	1	3	4	(b)	3	1	4	2
(c)	4	3	1	2	(d)	3	1	2	4

26. Identify the correct statements from the following.

I. Calcium ions and some proteins interact with the cell membrane of the host cell similar to electric currents and make them competent to take up the foreign DNA.

II. By inserting the genetically altered human insulin gene in bacteria, it is possible to produce millions of copy of insulin which prevent the need to extract it from animals.

III. In plants, cells are bombarded with high velocity micro particles of gold or tungsten coated with DNA through micro-injection gun.

IV. A stirred-tank reactor is usually cylindrical or with a curved base to factilitate the mixing of the reactor contents.

V. A nematode *Meloidegyne incognita* infects the roots of tobacco plants and causes a great reduction in yield.

Choose the correct answer from the options given below.

(a) I and III (b) II, III and IV

(c) II, IV and V (d) III and V

27. Identify the incorrect statement with respect to antibiotics.

(a) These are chemical substances produced by some microbes and can kill or retard the other microbes.

(b) Penicillin was extensively used to treat american soldiers wounded in world war II.

(c) These are effective against certain viral infections.
(d) Penicillin was the first antibiotic to be discovered.

28. Identify the incorrect statements from the following w.r.t malarial parasite.

I. *Plasmodium falciparum* is responsible for the most serious and potentially fatal form of malaria.
II. Haemozoin, released during the rupture of red blood cells, is responsible for the recurring chills and fever in malaria.
III. The parasite is transmitted to humans by the bite of infected female *Culex* mosquitoes.
IV. *Plasmodium* requires both human and mosquito hosts to complete its life cycle.
V. *Plasmodium* enters the human body as gametocytes through the bite of the infected female mosquitoes.

Choose the correct answer from the options given below.
(a) III and V (b) I, II and V
(c) II, III and V (d) I and II

29. The recombinant plasmids fail to produce colour on chromogenic substrate because
(a) they lack β-galactosidase activity due to gene inactivation
(b) they are resistant to chromogenic substrate
(c) they metabolise the substrate into a colorless compound
(d) they produce a different enzyme that suppresses colour formation

30. Which of the following are primary modes of HIV transmission?

I. Sexual contact with an infected person.
II. Blood transfusion with contaminated blood.
III. Sharing infected needles.
IV. Casual physical contact, like hugging or shaking hands.

Choose the correct answer from the options given below.
(a) I, II and III (b) II and IV
(c) I, II and IV (d) I and IV

31. The separated DNA fragments from ...*A*... can be visualised only after staining the DNA with a compound known as ...*B*... followed by exposure to UV radiation.

Choose the correct word for *A* and *B* from the options given below.

	A	*B*
(a)	PCR	X-gal
(b)	PCR	Ethidium bromide
(c)	Agarose gel electrophoresis	Ethidium bromide
(d)	Agarose gel electrophoresis	X-gal

32. Which of the following statement is incorrect about the given pyramid?

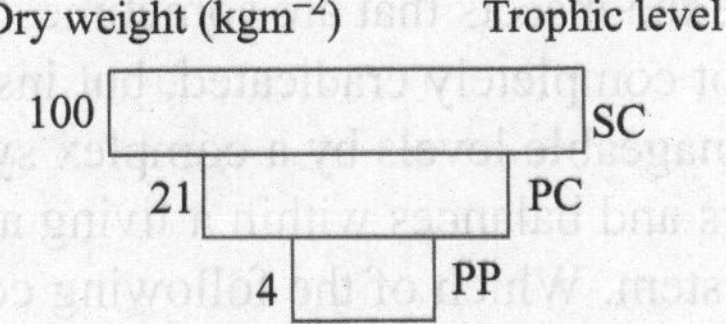

(a) It represents the inverted pyramid of biomass.
(b) The biomass of primary producers is smaller than the trophic levels above them.
(c) This type of pyramid can seen in pond ecosystem.
(d) This type of pyramid supports large number of secondary consumers.

33. What is the function of the untranslated regions (UTRs) in *m*RNA?
(a) They code for the initiation of translation.
(b) They catalyse the formation of peptide bonds.
(c) They are required for the efficient translation process.
(d) They provide the sequences for the formation of ribosomes.

34. Which of the following conditions does not result from the defective gene transmission in thalassemia?
(a) Anaemia due to abnormal haemoglobin molecules
(b) Reduced synthesis of one of the globin chain

(c) Increase in the number of functional red blood cells
(d) Possible formation of abnormal haemoglobin molecules

35. Consider the following pedigree analysis. Identify the correct statement.

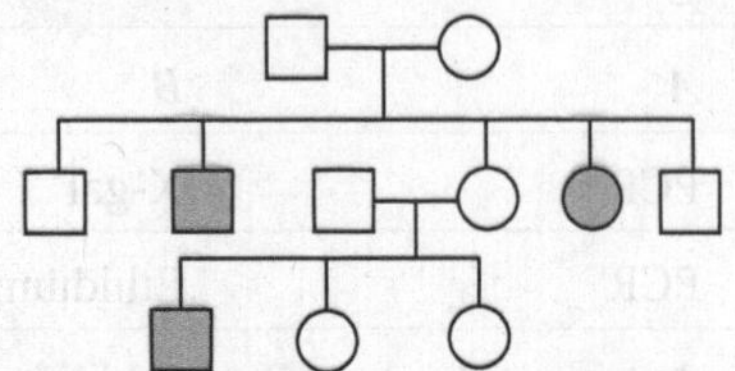

(a) It represents autosomal recessive trait.
(b) It represents autosomal dominant trait.
(c) It represents pedigree analysis of myotonic dystrophy.
(d) It represents sex- linked recessive disease.

36. The organic farmer works to create a system where the insects that are sometimes called pests, are not completely eradicated, but instead are kept at manageable levels by a complex system of checks and balances within a living and vibrant ecosystem. Which of the following concept is not related with organic farming?
(a) Developing an understanding of the webs of interaction between the myriad of organisms that constitute the field fauna and flora.
(b) Use of biocontrol measures greatly reduce the dependence on toxic chemicals and pesticides.
(c) Use of *Trichoderma* species as biocontrol agents for several plant pathogens.
(d) Use of pesticides and fertilisers, which increase the productivity of the crop and nutrition quality.

37. Match the List I with List II.

List I		List II
A. Operon	1.	Codes for the repressor of the *lac* operon
B. Operator	2.	Codes for β-galactosidase
C. i gene	3.	It is adjacent to the promoter region
D. z gene	4.	Groups of genes with a single promoter

Choose the correct answer from the options given below.

	A	B	C	D
(a)	1	3	4	2
(b)	4	3	1	2
(c)	3	4	2	1
(d)	2	1	3	4

38. Which of the following is the correct sequence of events during the first month of human pregnancy?
(a) Formation of heart → Differentiation into ectoderm and endoderm → Implantation → appearance of chorionic villi
(b) Implantation → Appearance of chorionic villi → Differentiation into ectoderm and endoderm → Formation of heart
(c) Appearance of chorionic villi → Implantation→ Formation of heart → Differentiation into ectoderm and endoderm
(d) Implantation → Differentiation into ectoderm and endoderm → Formation of heart → Appearance of chorionic villi

39. Match List I with List II.

List I		List II
A. Saheli	1.	Copper releasing IUD
B. Progestogens	2.	Non-steroidal
C. Multiload 375	3.	Hormone releasing IUD
D. LNG-20	4.	Used as injections

Choose the correct answer from the options given below.

	A	B	C	D
(a)	2	3	1	4
(b)	2	4	1	3
(c)	3	4	2	1
(d)	1	2	4	3

40. Identify the incorrect option from the following ones.
(a) Monocotyledons are primitive type of plants as compared to dicotyledons.
(b) Seed ferns evolved from progymnosperms.
(c) Chlorophytes are the ancestors of bryophytes.
(d) Conifers evolved from Psilophyton.

41. Identify the correct statements from the following ones.

I. Oogenesis starts just before birth when primary follicles are formed.

II. The primary oocyte completes the first meiotic division at puberty, forming a secondary oocyte and a first polar body.

III. The tertiary follicle is the stage where the primary oocyte completes its first meiotic division.

IV. The tertiary follicle is formed immediately after the primary follicle.

V. During ovulation, the Graafian follicle ruptures to release the secondary oocyte, which is then available for fertilisation..

Choose the correct answer from the options given below.

(a) I, II and III
(b) II, III and IV
(c) I, III and V
(d) II, III and V

42. A previously unknown virus has been isolated from the Eastern ghats of India. Analysis of its genome reveals that it is composed of a double stranded DNA molecules containing 18% T (thymine). Based on this information, what would you predict the % of C (cytosine) to be?

(a) 18% (b) 28%
(c) 32% (d) 36%

43. Female gametophyte contains only one egg nucleus, while pollen grain contains two male gametes. What is the best explanation about the above information?

(a) Pollen grains have to travel one place to another, to ensure pollination, thus they have two male gametes.
(b) One male gamete is diploid in nature and provide nourishment to the other male gamete.
(c) One male gamete fertilise egg nucleus, while other one undergoes triple fusion with polar nuclei.
(d) Egg nucleus requires presence of two male gametes.

44. Given below are two statements.

Statement I Presence of a pathogen in body is normally suspected only when the pathogen has produced a disease symptom.

Statement II Very low concentration of a bacteria or virus in body can be detected through the amplification of their nucleic acid by PCR at a time when the symptoms of the disease are not yet visible.

In the light of the above statements, choose the correct answer from the options given below.

(a) Statement I is incorrect, but statement II are correct
(b) Both statement I and statement II are correct.
(c) Both statement I and statement II are incorrect.
(d) Statement I is correct, but statement II is incorrect.

45. Gregor Mendel, conducted hybridisation experiments on garden peas for seven years. He conducted artificial pollination/cross pollination experiments using several true- breeding pea lines. He selected 14 true breeding pea plant varieties, as pairs which were

(a) heterozygous in F_1-generation and homozygous in F_2-generation
(b) recessive for all the 7 characters
(c) similar except for one character with contrasting traits
(d) similar for all the characters

46. Given below are two statements; one is labelled as Assertion (A) and other is labelled as Reason (R).

Assertion (A) The Hardy -Weinberg principle states that allele frequencies in a population remain constant from generation to generation under certain conditions.

Reason (R) Genetic equilibrium is maintained in a population only if there is presence of gene flow, genetic drift, mutation, genetic recombination or natural selection.

In the light of the above statements, choose the correct answer from the options given below.

(a) A is false, but R is true.
(b) Both A and R are true and R is the correct explanation of A.

(c) Both A and R are true, but R is not the correct explanation of A.

(d) A is true, but R is false.

47. Which of the following sequences correctly reflects the evolution of brain size of given human ancestral species (from smallest to largest)?

I. *Homo erectus*

II. *Homo habilis*

III. Neanderthal man

(a) II, I, III (b) III, I, II
(c) II, III, I (d) III, II, I

48. Given below are two statements.

Statement I *t*RNA has an anticodon loop that has bases complementary to the code and it also an amino acid acceptor end to which it binds to amino acids.

Statement II *t*RNAs are specific for each amino acid and for initiation of translation, there is another specific *t*RNA termed as initiator *t*RNA, and for termination stop codon, terminator *t*RNA are present.

In the light of the above statements, choose the correct answer from the options given below.

(a) Statement I is incorrect, statement II are correct.
(b) Both statement I and statement II are correct.
(c) Both statement I and statement II are incorrect.
(d) Statement I is correct, but statement II is incorrect.

49. When the population is small, there is a greater chances of

(a) mutations occurring
(b) natural selection
(c) gene flow
(d) genetic drift

50. Which transgenic animal was the first to produce human protein enriched milk and which type of protein did it contain?

(a) Dolly the sheep; insulin
(b) Rosie the cow; alpha- lactalbumin
(c) Rosie the cow; $\alpha - 1$ - antitrypsin
(d) Dolly the sheep; α – lactalbumin

51. Which of the following statements is incorrect regarding the early mammals?

(a) Continental drift allowed the pouched mammals of Australia to survive due to lack of competition from any other mammals.
(b) Mammals were viviparous and protected their unborn young ones inside the mother's body.
(c) The dominance of mammals on earth become apparent after the decline of reptiles.
(d) Due to continental drift, the South American mammals migrated to Australia and thrived there.

52. An individual heterozygous for two alleles (WwTt) produce two million sperms. How many of the sperms will have both the recessive alleles (in millions)?

(a) 1 (b) 2 (c) 0.5 (d) 0.25

53. Go through the figure and select the option for *C* and *D*. Here, *A* and *B* are taken as vector/plasmid DNA and foreign DNA, respectively.

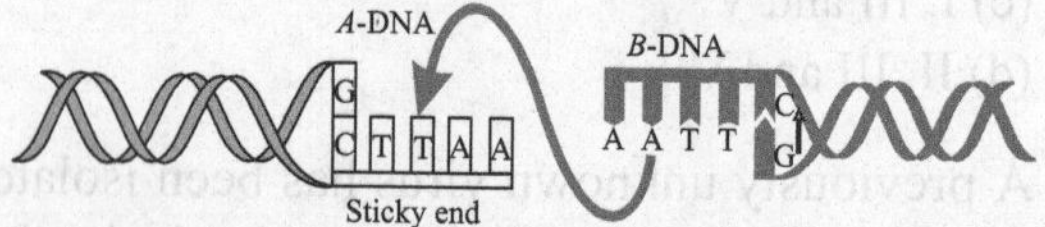

Restriction enzyme recognising palindrome $C \rightarrow$
Enzyme joining the sticky ends *D*

(a) *Eco* RI → DNA ligase
(b) DNA ligase → *Eco* RI
(c) Exonuclease → DNA ligase
(d) DNA ligase → Exonuclease

54. Given below are two statements; one is labelled as Assertion (A) and other is labelled as Reason (R).

Assertion (A) The nucleus of functional megaspore undergoes three rounds of mitotic division to produce an 8- nucleate and 7 celled embryo sac.

Reason (R) Each mitotic division of the functional megaspore is immediately followed by formation of a cell wall around the newly formed nuclei.

In the light of the above statements, choose the correct answer from the options given below

(a) A is false, but R is true
(b) Both A and R are true, and R is the correct explanation of A

(c) Both A and R are true, but R is not the correct explanation of A

(d) A is true, but R is false

55. The Monarch butterfly is highly distasteful to its predator bird because of a special chemical present in its body. The butterfly acquires this chemical

(a) during its caterpillar stage by feeding on a poisonous weed.

(b) through feeding on poisonous insect

(c) through some physiological process

(d) during its sexual stage alongwith the male butterfly

56. A novel strategy was adopted to prevent the nematode *Meloidegyne incognita* infection in the roots of tobacco plants. This strategy involves

(a) silencing of a DNA replication by the introduction of some chemical

(b) spraying of nematicide chemical extracted from transgenic bacteria

(c) silencing of a specific *m*RNA due to a complementary *ds* RNA

(d) spraying of insecticidal protein on the tobacco plant

57. Given below are two statements; one is labelled as Assertion (A) and other is labelled as Reason (R).

Assertion (A) Passive immunity involves the direct injection of ready made antibodies into an individual.

Reason (R) Passive immunity provides long-lasting immunity similar to active immunity.

In the light of the above statements, choose the correct answer from the options given below.

(a) A is false, but R is true.

(b) Both A and R are true and R is the correct explanation of A.

(c) Both A and R are true, but R is not the correct explanation of A.

(d) A is true, but R is false.

58. Which of the following characteristics is not related to agroecosystem?

(a) They are protected against pathogens and pests by the use of pesticides.

(b) They are more stable than natural ecosystem because they have more diversity.

(c) They are prone to destruction by drought, floods, pests and diseases.

(d) The physical condition of a cropland depends upon geographic location, climatic factors and soil conditions.

59. Consider the following figure and identify the correct explanation for 'A' from the options given below.

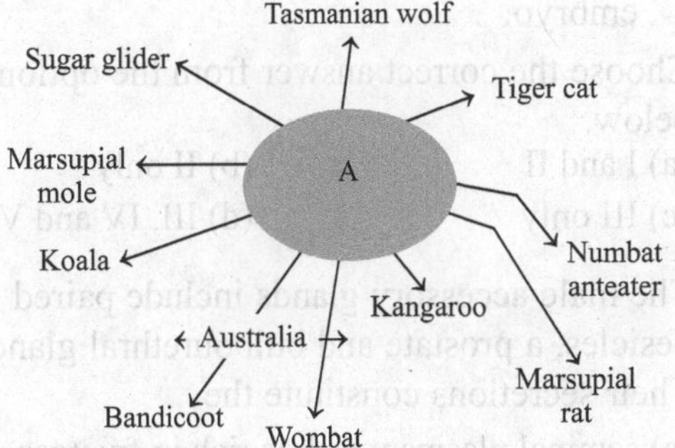

(a) Adaptive radiation of marsupials of Australia

(b) Convergent evolution of Australian marsupials

(c) Recombination between different Australian marsupials

(d) Different species of tiger by recombination

60. What are repeated DNA sequences?

(a) Repeated DNA sequences with direct coding functions

(b) DNA sequences with AT rich bases

(c) Repeated sequences with no direct coding functions

(d) Repeated sequences of DNA that do not play any role in the genome

61. Identify the incorrect statement(s) from the following.

I. Non-albuminous seeds have no residual endosperm as it completely consumed during embryo development, while albuminous seeds retain a part of endosperm as it is not completely used up during embryo development.

II. The perisperm of ovules harden as tough protective seed coat and it remains as a small pore in the seed coat and facilitates entry of oxygen and water into the seed during germination.

III. The primary endosperm cell divides repeatedly and forms a triploid endosperm tissue and these tissues are filled with reserve food material.

IV. The coconut water from tender coconut is nothing, but free- nuclear endosperm which is made up of thousands of nuclei and the surrounding, while kernel is the cellular endosperm.

V. The central cell after triple fusion becomes the primary endosperm cell and develops into the endosperm, while the zygote develops into an embryo.

Choose the correct answer from the options given below.

(a) I and II
(b) II only
(c) III only
(d) III, IV and V

62. The male accessory glands include paired seminal vesicles, a prostate and bulbourethral glands. Their secretions constitute the

(a) seminal plasma which is rich in fructose, calcium and certain enzymes
(b) androgens which stimulate the process of spermatogenesis
(c) androgens which help in fertilisation
(d) seminal plasma which increases the motility of sperms

63. Identify correct statement w.r.t HIV infection.

(a) HIV primarily infects macrophages and disrupts their ability to present antigens, leading to a breakdown in immune system communication.
(b) HIV directly destroys the bone marrow, preventing the production of all types of immune cells.
(c) HIV destroys helper T lymphocytes, leading to a critical reduction in their numbers and compromising the body's ability to mount an effective immune response.
(d) HIV infection leads to the overproduction of red blood cells.

64. According to Mendel's law of segregation, how are alleles distributed during gamete formation?

(a) Each gamete receives two copies of each allele.
(b) Each gamete receives one allele from each parent randomly.
(c) Each gamete receives one allele, with no influence from parental alleles.
(d) Each gamete receives all the alleles from the parents.

65. Identify the correct statement(s) from the following.

I. The finger-like projections of Fallopian tube and uterine tissue become interdigitated with each other and jointly form a structural and functional unit between embryo and maternal body called placenta.

II. The placenta facilitates the supply of oxygen and nutrients to the embryo and also removal of carbon dioxide and excretory materials produced by the embryo.

III. The placenta is connected to the embryo through chorionic villi which helps in the transport of substances to and from the embryo.

IV. Placenta acts as an endocrine tissue and produces several hormones like hCG, hPL, oestrogen, progestogen.

V. During pregnancy, the levels of other hormones like oestrogens, progestogens, cortisol, prolactin, thyroxine etc., are increased several folds in the maternal blood.

Choose the correct answer from the options given below.

(a) I, II, III and IV
(b) II, III and IV
(c) II, IV and V
(d) Only V

66. An age pyramid with a narrow base and a bulging middle section represents

(a) A population with a high birth rate and large elderly population
(b) A population undergoing rapid growth with many young dependents
(c) A population in decline with fewer birth rate and a large number of working age adults
(d) A stable population with equal distribution across age groups

67. Zygote Intra Fallopian transfer refers to the

(a) Transfer of embryos with more than 8 blastomeres into Fallopian tube
(b) Transfer of embryos upto 8 blastomeres into the Fallopian tube
(c) Transfer of ovum into a Fallopian tube
(d) Transfer of blastocyst into the uterus

68. If both parents are heterozygous for blood type A. what are the possible blood types of their children?

(a) Type A and Type O
(b) Type A and Type B
(c) Type O and Type B
(d) Type A, O and B

69. In a gene with two alleles where one produces a functional enzyme and the other produces a non-functional enzyme, which of the following is likely to be observed if the functional allele is dominant?

(a) The heterozygote will exhibit a phenotype similar to the homozygote for the functional allele.
(b) The heterozygote will show a blend of the phenotypes seen in both the homozygotes.
(c) The heterozygote will have a unique phenotype not seen in either homozygote.
(d) The homozygote will exhibit different phenotype from the heterozygote.

70. Match the List-I with List-II.

List-I		List-II	
A.	ELISA	1.	A single stranded DNA or RNA tagged with a radioactive molecule is allowed to hybridise and detect mutated gene.
B.	Autoradiography	2.	Amplification of even very low concentration of DNA.
C.	RNA interference	3.	Silencing of a specific *m*RNA due to a complementary *ds*RNA molecules.
D.	PCR	4.	Infection by pathogen can be detected by the presence of antigens

Choose the correct answer from the options given below.

	A	B	C	D		A	B	C	D
(a)	2	3	4	1	(b)	4	1	3	2
(c)	2	4	1	3	(d)	3	4	2	1

71. Which of the following is the characteristic feature of a recognition sequence that makes it suitable for a restriction endonuclease to bind and cut?

(a) It must be a random sequence of nucleotides.
(b) It must be a sequence with repeating nucleotides.
(c) It must be a palindromic sequence.
(d) It must be a sequence found at the ends of the DNA molecule.

72. The sex linked recessive disease which shows its transmission from unaffected carrier female to some of the male progeny has been observed in

(a) Sickle- cell anaemia
(b) Haemophilia
(c) Phenylketonuria
(d) Down's syndrome

73. Select the correct statement from the options given below.

(a) The occurrence of more than one adaptive radiation in an isolated geographical area results in divergent evolution.
(b) The adaptive radiation results in development of same character in different species.
(c) Factors like genetic drift, asexual reproduction and natural selection affect Hardy- Weinberg equilibrium.
(d) Natural selection is a process in which heritable variations enabling better survival are enabled to reproduce and leave greater number of progenies.

74. Given below are two statements.

Statement I Marijuana, commonly called smack, is chemically diacetylmorphine, which is a white, odourless, bitter crystalline compound.

Statement II Opioids are the drugs, which bind to specific opioid receptors present in central nervous system and gastrointestinal tract.

In the light of the above statements, choose the correct answer from the options given below.

(a) Statement I is incorrect, but statement II is correct.
(b) Both statement I and statement II are correct.
(c) Both statement I and statement II are incorrect.
(d) Statement I is correct, but statement II is incorrect.

75. Match the List I with List II.

List I	List II
A. Swiss cheese	1. *Lactobacillus*
B. Curd	2. *Aspergillus niger*
C. Butyric acid	3. *Clostridium butylicum*
D. Citric acid	4. *Propionibacterium shermanii*

Choose the correct answer from the options given below.

A B C D
(a) 2 3 1 4
(b) 4 1 3 2
(c) 3 1 4 2
(d) 2 4 1 3

76. Which of the following statement is incorrect?

(a) Globally, there are 25 biodiversity hotspots and protecting them can reduce mass extinctions by 20%.
(b) Globally, there are 34 biodiversity hotspots and protecting them can reduce mass extinctions by almost 30%.
(c) The ethical argument for conserving biodiversity relates to what we owe to millions of plant, animal and microbe species with whom we share this planet.
(d) The Amazon rainforest harbouring probably millions of species is being cut and cleared for cultivating soyabeans or for conversion to grasslands for raising beef cattles.

77. Given below are two statements.

Statement I Friedrich Meischer in 1869, identified DNA as an acidic substance present in nucleus and named it as nuclein.

Statement II The length of DNA double helix in a typical mammalian cell is calculated by dividing the total number of base pairs with distance between two consecutive base pairs.

In the light of the above statements, choose the correct answer from the options given below.
(a) Statement I is incorrect, but statement II is correct.
(b) Both statement I and statement II are correct.
(c) Both statement I and statement II are incorrect.
(d) Statement I is correct, but statement II are incorrect.

78. Match List I with List II.

List I	List II
A. Pyramid of numbers in grassland	1. Increase in population
B. Pyramid of biomass in pond	2. Decrease in population
C. Natality	3. Inverted
D. Mortality	4. Upright

Choose the correct answer from the options given below.

A B C D
(a) 4 3 1 2
(b) 3 4 2 1
(c) 1 2 4 3
(d) 2 1 3 4

79. Some of the examples are given below.

I. Eye of octopus and mammals
II. Flippers of penguins and dolphins
III. Wings of butterfly and birds

All of these represent
(a) Convergent evolution
(b) Divergent evolution
(c) Homologous organ
(d) Mutation in anatomical structure

80. Which of the following accurately describes the importance of the Earth Summit?

(a) It led to the identification of 50 new biodiversity hotspots.
(b) This Summit was on sustainable development, held in 2002 and aimed to reduce biodiversity loss by 20% by 2020.
(c) The Earth Summit in 1992 led to international commitments to conserve biodiversity and use it sustainably.
(d) It focused on climate change with minimal emphasis on biodiversity.

81. Given below are two statements; one is labelled as Assertion (A) and other is labelled as Reason (R).

Assertion (A) Interspecific competition is a significant driving force in organic evolution.

Reason (R) Darwin's concept of the survival of the fittest and the struggle for existence highlights the role of competition in natural selection.

In the light of the above statements, choose the correct answer from the options given below.
(a) A is false, but R is true.
(b) Both A and R are true, and R is the correct explanation of A.
(c) Both A and R are true but R is not the correct explanation of A.
(d) A is true, but R is false.

82. Identify the incorrect statements.
I. Jawless fish probably evolved around 350 mya.
II. The amphibians evolved into reptiles.
III. Turtles originated from synapsids.
IV. Lizards originated from synapsids.
V. Therapsids are the ancestors of mammals.
Choose the correct answer from the options given below.
(a) I, II and III (b) III and IV
(c) II and V (d) I, III and V

83. Given below are two statements.
Statement I Bamboo breeds only twice in their lifetime.
Statement II Logistic growth model is considered as the more realistic model as it takes the nature's carrying capacity in consideration.
In the light of the above statements, choose the correct answer from the options given below.
(a) Statement I is incorrect, but statement II is correct.
(b) Both statement I and statement II are correct.
(c) Both statement I and statement II are incorrect.
(d) Statement I is correct, but statement II is incorrect.

84. Many fungi belonging to the genera *Microsporum, Trichophyton* and *Epidermophyton* are responsible for.......which is one of the most common infectious diseases in man.
(a) ascariasis (b) ringworm
(c) roundworm (d) filariasis

85. Which of the following statements is true regarding *in situ* conservation in India?
(a) India has 20 biosphere reserves and 100 national parks.
(b) Sacred groves in India are located only in the Western ghats region.
(c) In-situ conservation includes the establishment of biosphere reserves, national parks and wildlife sanctuaries.
(d) Sacred groves in India have no relevance to conservation practices.

86. Which of the following correctly defines allergy?
(a) Excessive response of the immune system to certain antigens
(b) Reaction of mast cells to histamine
(c) Action of anti-histamine drugs on mast cells
(d) Normal response of the immune system to foreign substances

87. Which of the following defines a gene in terms of DNA sequence?
(a) A segment of DNA coding for a polypeptide
(b) A segment of DNA that codes for *t*RNA or *r*RNA
(c) A segment of DNA with introns and exons
(d) A segment of DNA containing regulatory sequences

88. What is elution in the context of DNA fragment analysis?
(a) Separating DNA fragments based on size
(b) Visualising DNA bands under UV light
(c) Cutting out and purifying DNA fragments from the gel
(d) Amplifying DNA fragments using PCR

89. The role of *r*RNAs during translation in cells is
(a) to provide the template for protein synthesis
(b) to bring amino acids near to ribosome
(c) to serve as the structural and catalytic components of the ribosome
(d) to initiate the transcription process

90. Consider the following figure and identify the anther walls which contribute(s) to the dehiscence of anther to release pollen grains.

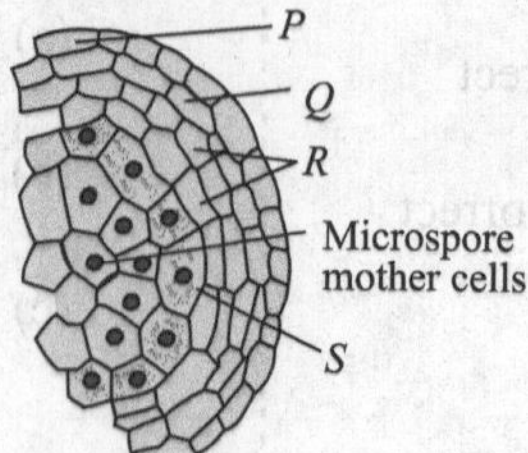

Choose the correct answer from the following options.
(a) *P*, *Q* and *R*
(b) *Q*, *R* and *S*
(c) *P* and *S*
(d) *R* and *S*

■ **Response Index**

01	ⓐ ⓑ ⓒ ⓓ	26	ⓐ ⓑ ⓒ ⓓ	51	ⓐ ⓑ ⓒ ⓓ	76	ⓐ ⓑ ⓒ ⓓ
02	ⓐ ⓑ ⓒ ⓓ	27	ⓐ ⓑ ⓒ ⓓ	52	ⓐ ⓑ ⓒ ⓓ	77	ⓐ ⓑ ⓒ ⓓ
03	ⓐ ⓑ ⓒ ⓓ	28	ⓐ ⓑ ⓒ ⓓ	53	ⓐ ⓑ ⓒ ⓓ	78	ⓐ ⓑ ⓒ ⓓ
04	ⓐ ⓑ ⓒ ⓓ	29	ⓐ ⓑ ⓒ ⓓ	54	ⓐ ⓑ ⓒ ⓓ	79	ⓐ ⓑ ⓒ ⓓ
05	ⓐ ⓑ ⓒ ⓓ	30	ⓐ ⓑ ⓒ ⓓ	55	ⓐ ⓑ ⓒ ⓓ	80	ⓐ ⓑ ⓒ ⓓ
06	ⓐ ⓑ ⓒ ⓓ	31	ⓐ ⓑ ⓒ ⓓ	56	ⓐ ⓑ ⓒ ⓓ	81	ⓐ ⓑ ⓒ ⓓ
07	ⓐ ⓑ ⓒ ⓓ	32	ⓐ ⓑ ⓒ ⓓ	57	ⓐ ⓑ ⓒ ⓓ	82	ⓐ ⓑ ⓒ ⓓ
08	ⓐ ⓑ ⓒ ⓓ	33	ⓐ ⓑ ⓒ ⓓ	58	ⓐ ⓑ ⓒ ⓓ	83	ⓐ ⓑ ⓒ ⓓ
09	ⓐ ⓑ ⓒ ⓓ	34	ⓐ ⓑ ⓒ ⓓ	59	ⓐ ⓑ ⓒ ⓓ	84	ⓐ ⓑ ⓒ ⓓ
10	ⓐ ⓑ ⓒ ⓓ	35	ⓐ ⓑ ⓒ ⓓ	60	ⓐ ⓑ ⓒ ⓓ	85	ⓐ ⓑ ⓒ ⓓ
11	ⓐ ⓑ ⓒ ⓓ	36	ⓐ ⓑ ⓒ ⓓ	61	ⓐ ⓑ ⓒ ⓓ	86	ⓐ ⓑ ⓒ ⓓ
12	ⓐ ⓑ ⓒ ⓓ	37	ⓐ ⓑ ⓒ ⓓ	62	ⓐ ⓑ ⓒ ⓓ	87	ⓐ ⓑ ⓒ ⓓ
13	ⓐ ⓑ ⓒ ⓓ	38	ⓐ ⓑ ⓒ ⓓ	63	ⓐ ⓑ ⓒ ⓓ	88	ⓐ ⓑ ⓒ ⓓ
14	ⓐ ⓑ ⓒ ⓓ	39	ⓐ ⓑ ⓒ ⓓ	64	ⓐ ⓑ ⓒ ⓓ	89	ⓐ ⓑ ⓒ ⓓ
15	ⓐ ⓑ ⓒ ⓓ	40	ⓐ ⓑ ⓒ ⓓ	65	ⓐ ⓑ ⓒ ⓓ	90	ⓐ ⓑ ⓒ ⓓ
16	ⓐ ⓑ ⓒ ⓓ	41	ⓐ ⓑ ⓒ ⓓ	66	ⓐ ⓑ ⓒ ⓓ		
17	ⓐ ⓑ ⓒ ⓓ	42	ⓐ ⓑ ⓒ ⓓ	67	ⓐ ⓑ ⓒ ⓓ		
18	ⓐ ⓑ ⓒ ⓓ	43	ⓐ ⓑ ⓒ ⓓ	68	ⓐ ⓑ ⓒ ⓓ		
19	ⓐ ⓑ ⓒ ⓓ	44	ⓐ ⓑ ⓒ ⓓ	69	ⓐ ⓑ ⓒ ⓓ		
20	ⓐ ⓑ ⓒ ⓓ	45	ⓐ ⓑ ⓒ ⓓ	70	ⓐ ⓑ ⓒ ⓓ		
21	ⓐ ⓑ ⓒ ⓓ	46	ⓐ ⓑ ⓒ ⓓ	71	ⓐ ⓑ ⓒ ⓓ		
22	ⓐ ⓑ ⓒ ⓓ	47	ⓐ ⓑ ⓒ ⓓ	72	ⓐ ⓑ ⓒ ⓓ		
23	ⓐ ⓑ ⓒ ⓓ	48	ⓐ ⓑ ⓒ ⓓ	73	ⓐ ⓑ ⓒ ⓓ		
24	ⓐ ⓑ ⓒ ⓓ	49	ⓐ ⓑ ⓒ ⓓ	74	ⓐ ⓑ ⓒ ⓓ		
25	ⓐ ⓑ ⓒ ⓓ	50	ⓐ ⓑ ⓒ ⓓ	75	ⓐ ⓑ ⓒ ⓓ		

■ **Performance Scanner**

> 90% Excellent !	You have mastered the NEET syllabus (12th). The concepts of this entire syllabus at your fingertips. Maintain this momentum.
76-90% Very Good !	You have a good command over the entire NEET syllabus (12th). Revise it again after a few days to enhance your performance.
60-75% Good !	You have a wide scope to learn for the entire NEET syllabus (12th). Revise it again.
<60% Not Satisfactory!	You have a long way ahead of you to master the NEET syllabus (12th). Revise it thoroughly.

Test Booklet No. 3947368

Test Booklet Code NSS3

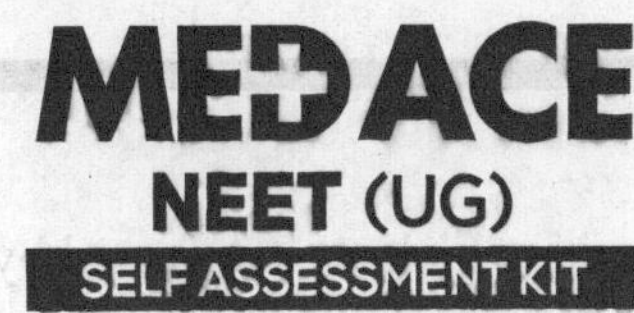

NEET Stepping Stones 3

(Complete Syllabus Test 12th)

Name of the Candidate (In Capitals)

____

____

____

Candidate's Signature ____________

Invigilator's Signature ____________

Facsimile signature stamp of center superintendent____________

Important Instructions

- The test is of **1 hours 30 minutes** duration and the Test Booklet contains **90** multiple-choice questions (four options with a single correct answer) from biology.
- Candidates are advised to read all questions before they start attempting the question paper.
- Each questions carries 4 marks. For each correct response, the candidate will get 4 marks. For each incorrect response, one marks will be deducted from the total scores.
- In the event of candidate marking more than one option one mark will be deducted. The maximum marks are 180.
- Use **Blue/Black Point Pen only** for writing particular on this page/ marking response on Answer Sheet.

Do not open this booklet until you start attempting the test

Biology

1. Traits which are expressed by the additive effect of multiple genes towards the quantitative phenotype of an organism are called
(a) Pleiotropic traits
(b) Multiallelic traits
(c) Polygenic traits
(d) Codominant traits

2. Read the following statements and choose the correct set of statements.
I. HIV belongs to a group of viruses called retrovirus.
II. HIV is transmitted through sexual contact with infected person.
III. Syndrome means a group of symptoms.
IV. HIV enters into erythrocytes and replicates.
V. AIDS can be treated and cured by anti-retroviral drugs.
Choose the correct answer from the options given below.
(a) I, III and IV (b) I, II and III
(c) II, IV and V (d) I, III and V

3. Given below are two statements.
Statement I In over 60 per cent of angiosperms pollen grains are shed at the 2 celled stage.
Statement II Pollen grains measure about 15-20 mm in diameter.
In the light of the above statements, choose the correct answer from the options given below.
(a) Statement I is incorrect, but statement II is correct
(b) Both statement I and statement II are correct
(c) Both statement I and statement II are incorrect
(d) Statement I is correct, but statement II is incorrect

4. Read the following statements and choose the correct set of statements.
I. MTP was enforced by the government in the year 2017.
II. MTP is not considered safe during the first trimester.
III. Hepatitis-B, genital herpes and HIV are curable.
IV. Hepatitis-B and HIV can be transmitted by sharing needles.
V. Nearly 45 to 50 million MTPs are performed in a year.
Choose the correct answer from the option given below
(a) I, II and III
(b) II and IV
(c) III, IV and V
(d) I, IV and V

5. Five factors are known to affect Hardy-Weinberg equilibrium. From the listed factors which factors are included in it?
I. Gene flow
II. Mutation
III. Random selection
IV. Genetic recombination
Choose the correct answer from the options given below.
(a) I and II
(b) I, II and IV
(c) II, III and IV
(d) Only I

6. An individual with characteristic palm crease can be affected with a genetic condition for which he has
(a) an additional pair of chromosome 21
(b) trisomy of chromosome 23
(c) deletion of a copy of chromosome 21
(d) a total of 47 chromosomes

7. Match list I with list II.

	List I		List II
A.	Chalaza	1.	Stalk
B.	Micropyle	2.	Small opening
C.	Integuments	3.	Protective envelope
D.	Funicle	4.	Basal part

Choose the correct answer from the options given below.

	A	B	C	D
(a)	4	2	3	1
(b)	3	1	2	4
(c)	1	2	4	3
(d)	2	3	4	1

8. Read the following statements and choose the correct set of statements.

I. There is a set of positively charged, basic proteins called histones.
II. Histones are rich in glycine and arginine.
III. Histones are organised to form a unit of six molecules.
IV. Nucleosome constitute the repeating unit of a structure in nucleus called chromatin.
V. Nucleosomes appear as the 'beads on string' structure.

Choose the correct answer form the options given below.

(a) I, II and III (b) II, IV and V
(c) I, IV and V (d) III, IV and V

9. Given below are two statements; one is labelled as Assertion (A) and the other is labelled as Reason (R).

Assertion (A) *Taq* polymerase does not help in the amplification of DNA segments.

Reason (R) *Taq* polymerase can remain active at high temperature present in some stages of PCR.

In the light of the above statements, choose the correct answer from the options given below.

(a) A is false, but R is true
(b) Both A and R are true and R is the correct explanation of A
(c) Both A and R are true but R is not the correct explanation of A
(d) A is true, but R is false

10. Choose the correct option that shows the correct pathway by which sperms move outside the body.

(a) Seminiferous tubules → Rete testes → Vasa efferentia → Epididymis → Vas deferens → Urethra → Ejaculatory duct
(b) Seminiferous tubules → Rete testes → Vas deferens → Epididymis → Vasa efferentia → Ejaculatory duct → Urethra
(c) Seminiferous tubules → Rete testes → Vasa efferentia → Epididymis → Vas deferens → Ejaculatory duct → Urethra
(d) Seminiferous tubules → Vas deferens → Vasa efferentia → Rete testes → Epididymis → Urethra → Ejaculatory duct

11. Match List I with List II.

	List I		List II
A.	*Ramapithecus*	1.	3-4 mya
B.	*Australopithecus*	2.	2 mya
C.	*Homo habilis*	3.	15 mya
D.	*Homo erectus*	4.	1.5 mya

Choose the correct answer from the options given below.

	A	B	C	D
(a)	1	3	4	2
(b)	3	1	2	4
(c)	3	2	4	1
(d)	2	3	1	4

12. Which one of the following statements is incorrect?

(a) GM has been used to create tailor-made plants to supply alternative resource to industries
(b) GM made crops tolerant to cold, drought, etc.
(c) GM decreased efficiency of mineral usage by plants
(d) GM helped to reduce post-harvest losses

13. Which of the following statement is incorrect?

(a) Swiss cheese is produced by a bacterium named *Propionibacterium shermanii*
(b) Toddy is made by fermenting sap from palm tree
(c) LAB plays very beneficial role in our stomach by checking disease causing microbes
(d) Microbes such as bacteria are needed for production of beverages

14. Observe the following diagram.

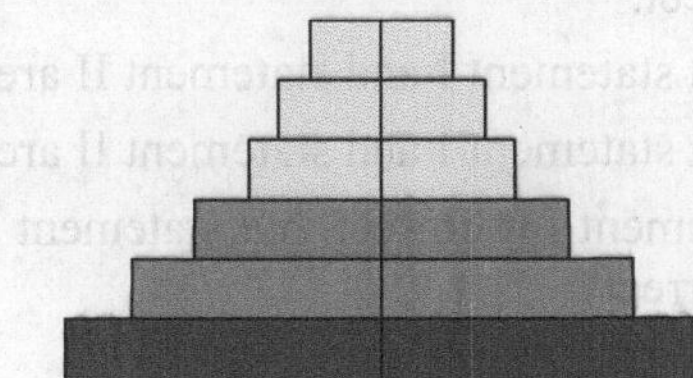

The above structure is formed when
(a) population of reproductive age group is least
(b) population of post-reproductive age group is very less
(c) population of pre-reproductive age group is lesser than post-reproductive age group
(d) population of reproductive age group is more than pre-reproductive age group.

15. Features that are required to facilitate cloning into a vector includes all of the following except,

I. *ori*
II. Selectable marker
III. Bacteriophage
IV. Cloning sites

Choose the correct answer from the options given below.
(a) I and II (b) II and III
(c) Only IV (d) Only III

16. Given below is a list of few organisms.

I. Zooplankton
II. Fishes
III. Phytoplankton
IV. Man

Arrange them in the increasing order of trophic levels and choose the correct answer from the options given below.
(a) I→ II → III → IV
(b) II→ I → IV → III
(c) III→ I → II → IV
(d) II→ III → IV → I

17. Given below are two statements.

Statement I Sexual deceit is not an act of true mutualism.

Statement II Mediterranean orchid cheats its bee to derive benefit out of it .

In the light of the above statements, choose the correct answer from the options given below.
(a) Statement I is incorrect, but statement II is correct.
(b) Both statement I and statement II are correct
(c) Both statement I and statement II are incorrect
(d) Statement I is correct, but statement II is incorrect

18. Given below are two statements.

Statement I Controlled bioprospecting is required for preventing over-exploitation.

Statement II Bioprospecting promotes conservation of biological diversity.

In the light of the above statements, choose the correct answer from the options given below.
(a) Statement I is incorrect, but statement II is correct
(b) Both statement I and statement II are correct
(c) Both statement I and statement II are incorrect
(d) Statement I is correct, but statement II is incorrect

19. Match List I with List II.

List I	List II
A. Ampulla	1. Birth canal
B. Infundibulum	2. womb
C. Uterus	3. wider part
D. Vagina	4. funnel-shaped

Choose the correct answer from the options given below.

	A	B	C	D
(a)	2	1	4	3
(b)	3	4	2	1
(c)	1	3	2	4
(d)	1	4	3	2

20. Match List I with List II.

List I	List II
A. Coleoptile	1. Cotyledon
B. Coleorrhiza	2. Undifferentiated sheath
C. Perisperm	3. Hollow foliar structure
D. Scutellum	4. Persistent nucellus

Choose the correct answer from the options given below.

	A	B	C	D
(a)	3	2	4	1
(b)	2	3	1	4
(c)	1	3	4	2
(d)	1	2	4	3

21. Which of the following statement is incorrect about haemophilia?

(a) Haemophilia is a sex-linked recessive disorder.
(b) Inheritance of haemophilic gene takes place from carrier male to male progeny
(c) The gene for haemophilia is located on X-chromosome
(d) The diseased individual has non-stop bleeding even after a simple cut

22. A typical dicotyledonous embryo consists of a/an ...... and ...... cotyledons.

(a) epicotyl, 2
(b) root cap, 2
(c) embryonal axis, 2
(d) globulary embryo, 3

23. Given below are two statements.

Statement I Scrotum is a pouch-like structure that keeps the temperature of testes lower than the normal internal body temperature.

Statement II Leydig cells produce testosterone and provide nutrition to the developing germ cells.

In the light of the above statements, choose the correct answer form the options given below.

(a) Statement I is incorrect, but statement II is correct
(b) Both statement I and statement II are correct
(c) Both statement I and statement II are incorrect
(d) Statement I is correct, but statement II is incorrect

24. Biofertilisers enrich the nutrient quality of soil and aid plants in mineral uptake. Which of the following bacteria is useful as a biofertiliser?

(a) Mycorrhiza (b) *Azotobacter*
(c) *Anabaena* (d) *Azolla*

25. Match List I with List II.

	List I		List II
A.	Interstitial cells	1.	Arise from rete testis
B.	Vas deferens	2.	Arise from epididymis
C.	Vasa efferentia	3.	Secrete androgens
D.	Spermatogonium	4.	Produced by male germ cells

Choose the correct answer from the option given below.

	A	B	C	D
(a)	3	2	1	4
(b)	3	1	2	4
(c)	2	3	4	1
(d)	1	2	4	3

26. Which of the following statement is incorrect?

(a) Chromosomes occur in pairs and can be easily seen during metaphase of the cell division.
(b) Dominance is not an autonomous feature of a gene
(c) The inheritane of flower colour of *Antirrhinum* sp. is a good example of multiple allele
(d) Gregor Mendel conducted hybridisation experiment for seven years

27. An infertile couple was advised GIFT. Which of the following stages occur in the woman after the transfer is completed in her?

I. Ovulation
II. Fertilisation
III. Cleavage
IV. Implantation

Choose the correct answer from the options given below.

(a) I, II and III (b) I and II
(c) II and III (d) II, III and IV

28. Identify the incorrect match pair.

(a) GUU, GUG - Valine
(b) CUU, UUA - Leucine
(c) CGU, GGG - Glycine
(d) UGA, UAG - No codon

29. Given below are two statements.

Statement I The essence of Darwinian theory about evolution is natural selection.

Statement II The rate of appearance of new forms is linked to the life line.

In the light of the above statements, choose the correct answer from the options given below.

(a) Statement I is incorrect, but statement II is correct
(b) Both statement I and statement II are correct
(c) Both statement I and statement II are incorrect
(d) Statement I is correct, but statement II is incorrect

30. Read the following statements and choose the correct set of statements.

I. After the completion of replication, each DNA molecule would have one parental and one newly synthesised strand.

II. *E. coli* has 3.6×10^5 bp and human has 6.6×10^6 bp.

III. Any mistake during replication would result into mutations.

IV. In prokaryotes the replication of DNA takes place at S-phase of the cell cycle.

V. A failure in cell division after DNA replication results into polyploidy.

Choose the correct answer from the options given below.

(a) I, II and IV
(b) II, IV and V
(c) I, III and V
(d) II, III and IV

31. Given below are two statements; one is labelled as Assertion (A) and other is labelled as Reason (R).

Assertion (A) Saheli is an exception to oral contraceptive pills having low contraceptive value and very high side effects.

Reason (R) It was developed by Central Drug Research Institute in Lucknow.

In the light of the above statements, choose the correct answer from the options given below.

(a) A is false, but R is true
(b) Both A and R are true and R is the correct explanation of A
(c) Both A and R are true but R is not the correct explanation of A
(d) A is true, but R is false

32. Given below are two statements; one is labelled as Assertion (A) and the other is labelled as Reason (R).

Assertion (A) DNA fragments can be separated by a technique called gel electrophoresis.

Reason (R) DNA is negatively charged, so it moves towards cathode under electric field.

In the light of the above statements, choose the correct answer from the options given below.

(a) A is false, but R is true
(b) Both A and R are true and R is the correct explanation of A
(c) Both A and R are true, but R is not the correct explanation of A
(d) A is true, but R is false

33. Three critical research areas of biotechnology includes all of the following, except

(a) providing best catalyst in the form of improved organism.
(b) creating optimal conditions through engineering
(c) downstream processing technologies to purify the protein
(d) chemical analysis of the product before the treatment process

34. Given below are two statements; one is labelled as Assertion (A) and the other is labelled as Reason (R).

Assertion (A) A colourblind father will always pass colourblind gene to the daughter.

Reason (R) Genes causing colour blindness are passed through sex-chromosome.

In the light of the above statements, choose the correct answer form the options given below.

(a) A is false, but R is true
(b) Both A and R are true and R is the correct explanation of A
(c) Both A and R are true but R is not the correct explanation of A
(d) A is true, but R is false

35. .... is native to South America and functions by interfering with the transport of dopamine, neurotransmitter.

(a) Cannabinoids (b) Heroine
(c) Opioids (d) Cocaine

36. The blood group of a child is O and that of his father is B. The genotype of the father can be represented as

(a) $I^O I^O$ (b) $I^O I^B$
(c) $I^A I^B$ (d) $I^B I^B$

37. Following are the steps involved in the infection caused by HIV.

I. Cell surface attachment
II. Formation of *ds* DNA
III. Formation of *m*RNA
IV. Release of capsid
V. Assembly of viral proteins

Choose the correct order from the options given below.

(a) I-IV-II-III-V
(b) I-II-III-IV-V
(c) I-II-IV-III-V
(d) I-III-II-IV-V

38. Given below are two statements.

Statement I The relationship between species of fig trees and pollinators species of wasp is called parasitism.

Statement II Mycorrhizae are associations between fungi and roots of higher plants which shows mutualism.

In the light of the above statements, choose the correct answer from the options given below

(a) Statement I is incorrect, but statement II is correct
(b) Both statement I and statement II are correct
(c) Both statement I and statement II are incorrect
(d) Statement I is correct, but statement II is incorrect

39. The new variety of rice that was created by an American company claimed a patent. This was actually made by

(a) crossing Indian Basmati with American rice
(b) crossing Indian Basmati with semi-dwarf variety
(c) crossing American rice with semi dwarf variety
(d) crossing dwarf plant with American rice

40. Given below are two statements.

Statements I The ethical argument for conserving biodiversity relates to what we owe to the millions of plant, animals and microbe species with whom we share this planet.

Statement II Biodiversity hotspots have high species richness and high degree of endemism.

In the light of the above statements, choose the correct anwer from the options given below.

(a) Statement I is incorrect, but statement II is correct
(b) Both statement I and statement II are correct
(c) Both statement I and statement II are incorrect
(d) Statement I is correct, but statement II is incorrect

41. Given below is an equation.

$N_{t+1}=N_t+[(B+I)-(D+E)]$

The above equation determines that population density will increase if

(a) number of deaths plus number of immigrants is more
(b) number of deaths plus number of immigrants is less
(c) number of births plus the number of immigrants is more
(d) number of births plus the number of emmigrants is less

42. Parturition is induced by the hormones

I. Oxytocin
II. Relaxin
III. Oestrogen
IV. HCG

Choose the correct answer from the options given below.

(a) I and II
(b) III and IV
(c) Only II
(d) Only IV

43. Given below are two statements; one is labelled as Assertion (A) and the other is labelled as Reason (R).

Assertion (A) Extinction of Abingdon tortoise was due to an intra-specific competition.

Reason (R) Even in the presence of surplus resources, competition might exist.

In the light of the above statements, choose the correct answer from the options given below.

(a) A is false, but R is true
(b) Both A and R are true and R is the correct explanation of A
(c) Both A and R are true, but R is not the correct explanation of A
(d) A is true, but R is false

44. Given below are two statements.

Statement I Primary productivity depends on the plant species inhabiting a particular area.

Statement II Secondary productivity is defined as the rate of formation of new organic matter by producers.

In the light of the above statements, choose the correct answer from the options given below.

(a) Statement I is incorrect, but statement II is correct
(b) Both statement I and statement II are correct
(c) Both statement I and statement II are incorrect
(d) Statement I is correct, but statement II is incorrect

45. The Mendelian disorder which is an autosome linked recessive disease transmitted from parents to the offspring when both the parents are heterozygous for the gene is

(a) colour blindness
(b) thalassemia
(c) haemophilia
(d) Down's syndrome

46. A particular plant species produces an important drug that serves different applications in the medical field. However, there are only 2-3 plants of that particular species is left all over the world. To preserve this plant which of the following conservation should be opted?

(a) *In situ* conservation
(b) Seed banks
(c) National parks
(d) Nurseries

47. Lactation delays the onset or return of menstruation and ovulation cycle due to interference of hormone

(a) prolactin (b) hCG
(c) oestrogen (d) progesterone

48. Match List I with List II.

List I	List II
A. Syncarpous	1. Slender stalk
B. Apocarpous	2. Homogenous cells
C. Filament	3. Free pistils
D. Sporogenous tissue	4. Pistils fused together

Choose the correct answer from the option given below.

	A	B	C	D
(a)	1	3	2	4
(b)	4	3	1	2
(c)	2	1	3	4
(d)	3	4	2	1

49. Read the following statements and choose the correct set of statements.

I. The mode of transmission of pneumonia is by inhaling droplets of infected person.
II. Dengue is transmitted by *Aedes aegypti* mosquito.
III. Typhoid is a viral disease.
IV. Common cold is diagnosed by widal test.
V. Malaria is a protozoan disease.

Choose the correct answer from the option given below.

(a) I, II and V
(b) II and III
(c) I and IV
(d) III and V

50. Observe the following diagram.

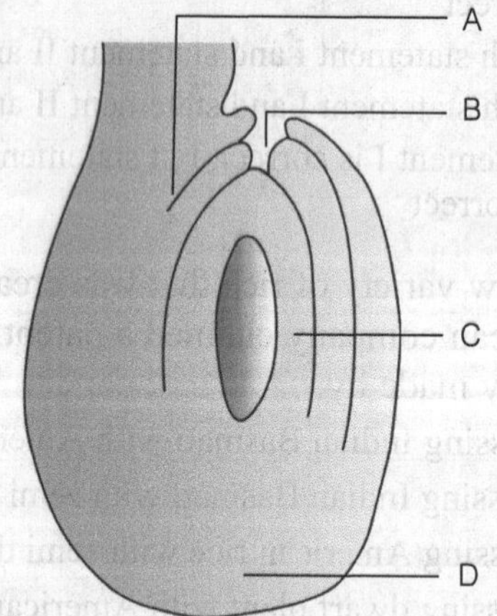

Which of the following part have abundant reserve food materials?

(a) A (b) B
(c) C (d) D

51. The turbidity of freshly squeezed oranges at home can be reduced by the action of

(a) pectinases and cellulase
(b) proteases and pectinases
(c) cellulase and chitinase
(d) lipases and proteases

52. Read the following statements and choose the correct set of statements.

I. Being colloidal in nature humus serves as a reservoir of nutrients.

II. Decomposition is largely an oxygen requring process.

III. Temperature and soil moisture regulate decomposition.

IV. Warm and moist environment inhibits decomposition.

V. Low temperature favours decomposition.

Choose the correct answer from the options given below.

(a) I, II and III (b) II and III
(c) II and IV (d) IV and V

53. Given below are two statements.

Statement I Brood parasitism is a type of parasitic relationship in which one organism, i.e. the parasitic bird lays its eggs in the next of another organism.

Statement II Competitive release is a mechanism evolved by two competing species for co-existence.

In the light of the above statements, choose the correct answer from the options given below.

(a) Statement I is incorrect, but statement II is correct
(b) Both statement I and statement II are correct
(c) Both statement I and statement II are incorrect
(d) Statement I is correct, but statement II is incorrect

54. In a given food chain there are four trophic levels. If the last trophic level has only 10 kJ of energy available for utilisation, calculate the amount of energy utilised by the second trophic level.

(a) 100 kJ (b) 1000 kJ
(c) 10,000 kJ (d) 1000 J

55. When a foreign DNA is ligated at the *Bam* HI site of tetracycline resistance gene in the vector pBR322, due to insertion of the foreign DNA, the recombinant plasmids will ...... tetracycline resistance.

(a) lose (b) gain
(c) increase (d) double

56. For frugivorous birds and mammals in the tropical forest of different continents the slope of the line is found to be

(a) 0.8 (b) 0.2
(c) 1.15 (d) 3.15

57. Match List I with List II.

	List I		List II
A.	Helminthic disease	1.	Pneumonia
B.	Fungal disease	2.	Dengue fewer
C.	Viral disease	3.	Elephantiasis
D.	Bacterial disease	4.	Ringworm

Choose the correct answer from the options given below.

(a) A-3, B-4, C-2, D-1
(b) A-2, B-3, C-1, D-4
(c) A-3, B-1, C-4, D-2
(d) A-1, B-4, C-3, D-2

58. Which one of the following statement is incorrect?

(a) Out of every 10 animals on this planet, 7 are insects
(b) Amazon forest is estimated to produce 20% of total oxygen in earth's atmosphere
(c) Environmental damage caused by *Lantana* and water hyacinth are examples of over-exploitation
(d) A single species might show high diversity at the genetic level over it distributional range

59. Match List I with List II.

	List I		List II
A.	*m*RNA	1.	Soluble RNA
B.	*t*RNA	2.	Carries codons
C.	*r*RNA	3.	Found in ribosomes
D.	*s*RNA	4.	Carry anticodons

Choose the correct answer from the options given below.

(a) A-2, B-4, C-3, D-1
(b) A-4, B-2, C-3, D-1
(c) A-1, B-2, C-4, D-3
(d) A-1, B-3, C-4, D-2

60. A fungus which is used as a biological control for the treatment of a plant disease is called

(a) *Bacillus thuringiensis*
(b) *Trichoderma*
(c) *Trichophyton*
(d) *Nucleopolyhedrovirus*

61. Match List I with List II.

	List I	List II
A.	Louis Pasteur	1. Spontaneous generation
B.	Miller Urey	2. Life came from pre-existing life
C.	Darwin	3. Chemical evolution
D.	Aristotle	4. Survival of the fittest

Choose the correct answer from the options given below.

(a) A-1, B-3, C-2, D-4
(b) A-2, B-3, C-4, D-1
(c) A-2, B-4, C-1, D-3
(d) A-4, B-3, C-1, D-2

62. Given below are two statements, one is labelled as Assertion (A) and the other is labelled as Reason (R).

Assertion (A) In morula stage, cells divide without increase in size.

Reason (R) Zona pellucida remain undivided till cleavage is complete.

In the light of the above statements, choose the correct answer from the options given below.

(a) A is false, but R is true
(b) Both A and R are true and R is the correct explanation of A
(c) Both A and R are true, but R is not the correct explanation of A
(d) A is true, but R is false

63. Forelimbs of mammals like whales, bats, cheetah and humans are called homologous organs because

(a) they perform similar functions
(b) they are similar in anatomical structure
(c) they are both used for hunting
(d) they are vestigial organs

64. Match List I with List II.

	List I	List II
A.	Statin	1. *Monascus purpureus*
B.	Cyclosporin-A	2. *Penicillium notatum*
C.	Streptokinase	3. *Trichoderma polysporum*
D.	*Penicillin*	4. *Streptococcus*

Choose the correct answer from the options given below.

	A	B	C	D
(a)	1	2	4	3
(b)	1	3	4	2
(c)	2	4	3	1
(d)	3	2	4	1

65. Given below are two statements; one is labelled as Assertion (A) and the other is labelled as Reason (R).

Assertion (A) All the pyramids of numbers and biomass are not always upright of the ecosystem.

Reason (R) In any food chain, the number and biomass of producers is more than that of herbivores which is in turn is more than that of carnivores.

In the light of the above statements, choose the correct answer from the options given below.

(a) A is false, but R is true
(b) Both A and R are true and R is the correct explanation of A
(c) Both A and R are true but R is not the correct explanation of A
(d) A is true, but R is false

66. Observe the following diagram.

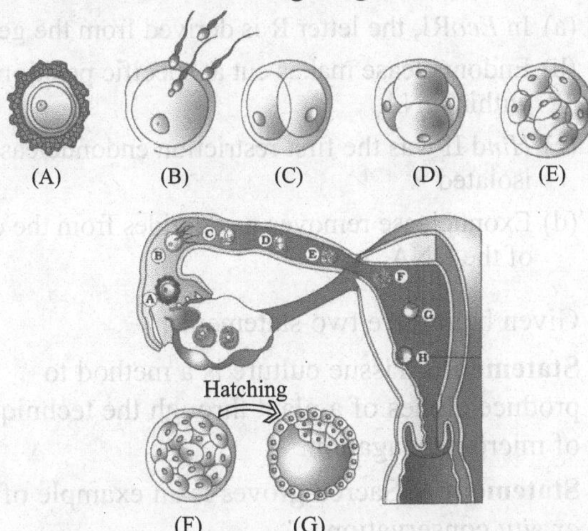

Which of the following part shows the stage preceeding a hollow bubble-like structure ready for implantation?

(a) A (b) B
(c) E (d) G

67. Identify the group that contains all the sexually transmitted diseases and/or infections.

(a) Hepatitis-B, Syphilis, Pneumonia
(b) Chlamydiasis, AIDS, Genital warts
(c) Tuberculosis, Hepatitis-B, Genital herpes
(d) Gonorrhoea, Syphilis, Hepatitis-E

68. The technique applied in hybridisation experiments to ensure the protection of stigma from any kind of unwanted interference unwanted pollen grains is called

(a) emasculation
(b) bagging
(c) polyspermy
(d) sterilisation

69. Given below are two statements; one is labelled as Assertion (A) and the other is labelled as Reason (R).

Assertion (A) Pollen grains are well preserved and can stay viable for long period of time.

Reason (R) The outer layer of pollen grains is made up of cellulose and pectin.

In the light of the above statements, choose the correct answer from the options given below.

(a) A is false, but R is true
(b) Both A and R are true and R is the correct explanation of A
(c) Both A and R are true but R is not the correct explanation of A
(d) A is true, but R is false

70. Which one of the following statements regarding sporopollenin is incorrect?

(a) It can withstand high temperature
(b) It can be degraded by an enzyme, cellulase
(c) Its presence lets the pollen grains to be preserved as fossils
(d) It is chemically inactive and can stay viable for longer period of time

71. Read the following statement and choose the correct set of statements.

I. Pea and groundnut are example of albuminous seeds.
II. Apple is an example of true fruit.
III. Banana is an example of parthenocarpic fruit.
IV. Apomixis is extensively used to produce hybrid varieties of seeds.
V. In some seeds, such as black pepper, remnants of nucellus are present.

Choose the correct answer from the options given below.

(a) I, II and IV (b) III, IV and V
(c) II and V (d) I and III

72. Read the following statements and choose the incorrect set of statements.

I. Implantation leads to pregnancy.
II. The trophoblast layer gets attached to the endometrium.
III. Colostrum contains several antibodies like IgG.
IV. Placenta supplies oxygen and nutrients to the embryo.
V. Placenta produces oxytocin and relaxin.

Choose the correct answer from the options given below.

(a) I and II (b) II and IV
(c) III and V (d) Only IV

73. Which of the following statement is incorrect regarding IUDs?

(a) They are inserted in the uterus of females through vagina
(b) Lippes loop is a copper releasing IUD
(c) Progestasert is a hormone releasing IUD
(d) They increase the phagocytosis of sperms

74. Listed below are few agents of pollination. Which of them are called biotic agents?

I. Wind　　II. Insects
III. Water　　IV. Birds

Choose the correct answer from the options given below.

(a) I and III　　(b) II and IV
(c) I and II　　(d) III and IV

75. Given below are two statements.

Statement I Variation is defined as the process of transmission of characters or traits from parents to their progeny.

Statement II Inheritance is defined as the degrees by which the offsprings differ from their parents.

In the light of the above statements, choose the correct answer from the options given below.

(a) Statement I is incorrect, but statement II is correct
(b) Both statement I and statement II are correct
(c) Both statement I and statement II are incorrect
(d) Statement I is correct, but statement II is incorrect

76. The transcription unit consists of

I. Promoter　　II. Terminator
III. Structural gene　　IV. UTR

Choose the correct answer from the options given below.

(a) Only I　　(b) II and III
(c) Only IV　　(d) I, II and III

77. The phase in which rapid secretion of LH leads to the rupture of Graffian follicle and lasts for 30-48 hours is called

(a) menstrual phase　　(b) proliferative phase
(c) ovulatory phase　　(d) luteal phase

78. Which of the following statement is incorrect regarding Turner's syndrome?

(a) It is caused due to the absence of one of the X chromosomes
(b) It results into a karyotyotype of 47 with XO
(c) The affected females are sterile with rudimentary ovaries
(d) Affected females lack secondary sexual characters.

79. Which of the following statement is incorrect?

(a) In *Eco*RI, the letter R is derived from the genus
(b) Endonuclease makes cut at specific position within DNA
(c) *Hind* II was the first restriction endonuclease isolated
(d) Exonuclease removes nucleotides from the ends of the DNA

80. Given below are two statements.

Statement I Tissue culture is a method to produce clones of a plant through the technique of micro-propagation.

Statement II Sacred groves is an example of *ex situ* conservation.

In the light of the above statements, choose the correct answer from the options given below.

(a) Statement I is incorrect, but statement II is correct
(b) Both statement I and statement II are correct
(c) Both statement I and statement II are incorrect
(d) Statement I is correct, but statement II is incorrect

81. Read the following statement and choose the correct set of statements.

I. Producers, consumers and decomposers act as biotic components of an ecosystem.
II. Gross primary productivity is the rate of production of organic matter during photosynthesis.
III. Mineralisation involves degradation of humus by microbe.
IV. Catabolism is the process of formation and accumulation of a dark-coloured amorphous substance.
V. Humification is the process by which detritus is degraded into simpler inorganic compounds by bacterial and fungal enzymes.

Choose the correct answer from the options given below.

(a) I, II and IV
(b) I, II and V
(c) I, II and III
(d) II, IV and V

82. A childless couple wherein the female partner fails to produce quality ovum but is capable of providing a suitable environment to the foetus should be advised with which of the following?

(a) IUT (b) ZIFT
(c) GIFT (d) ICSI

83. Given below are two statements.

Statement I Two closely linked genes HBA 1 and HBA2 on chromosome 18 of each parent controls α-thalassemia.

Statement II A single gene HBB on chromosome 11 of each contorls β-thalassemia.

In the light of the above statements, choose the correct answer from the options given below.

(a) Statement I is incorrect, but statement II is correct
(b) Both statement I and statement II are correct
(c) Both statement I and statement II are incorrect
(d) Statement I is correct, but statement II is incorrect

84. Methanogens are responsible for producing large amount of biogas. It includes

(a) CH_4 (30% – 40%), CO_2 (40%) and H_2
(b) CH_4 (50 – 70%), CO_2 (30% – 40%) and H_2
(c) CH_4 (50 – 70%), CO_2 and H_2 (13%)
(d) CH_4 (50 – 70%), NH_3 and H_2

85. Read the following statement and choose the incorrect set of statements.

I. FSH and LH levels reach highest in middle of the cycle.
II. Corpus luteum secretes large amount of progesterone in menstrual phase.
III. Proliferative phase lasts for 3-5 days.
IV. Endometrial regeneration takes place in proliferative phase.
V. Proliferative phase is where primary follicle change to Graafian follicle.

Choose the correct answer from the options given below

(a) I and II (b) II and III
(c) III and IV (d) IV and V

86. Given below are two statements, one is labelled as Assertion (A) and the other is labelled as Reason (R).

Assertion (A) Barriers like diaphragms, cervical caps and vaults are used and inserted into the female reproductive tract to prevent fertilisation.

Reason (R) Diaphragm, cervical caps and vaults help to kill the sperms.

In the light of the above statements, choose the correct answer form the options given below.

(a) A is false, but R is true
(b) Both A and R are true and R is the correct explanation of A
(c) Both A and R are true, but R is not the correct explanation of A
(d) A is true, but R is false

87. Observe the following diagram.

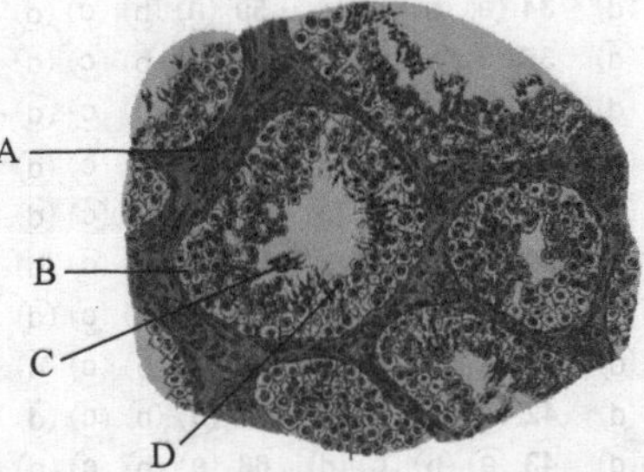

Which of the following part is responsible for synthesising androgens?

(a) A (b) B
(c) C (d) D

88. .... acts as a depressant and.........is an effective sedative and a painkiller.

(a) Cocaine, heroin
(b) Heroin, morphine
(c) Cannabinoid, hashish
(d) Tobacco, barbiturates

89. Hallucinogenic drugs are obtained from plants like

(a) *Atropa belladonna and Papaver somniferum*
(b) *Datura* sp. and daffodil
(c) *Atropa belladonna* and *Datura* sp.
(d) Daffodil and *Papaver somniferum*

90. Given below are two statements, one is labelled as Assertion (A) and the other is labelled as Reason (R).

Assertion (A) Infundibulum is responsible for the collection of ovum.

Reason (R) Fimbriae are finger-like projections which helps in collection of ovum.

In the light of the above statements, choose the correct answer from the options given below.
(a) A is false, but R is true
(b) Both A and R are true and R is the correct explanation of A
(c) Both A and R are true, but R is not the correct explanation of A
(d) A is true, but R is false

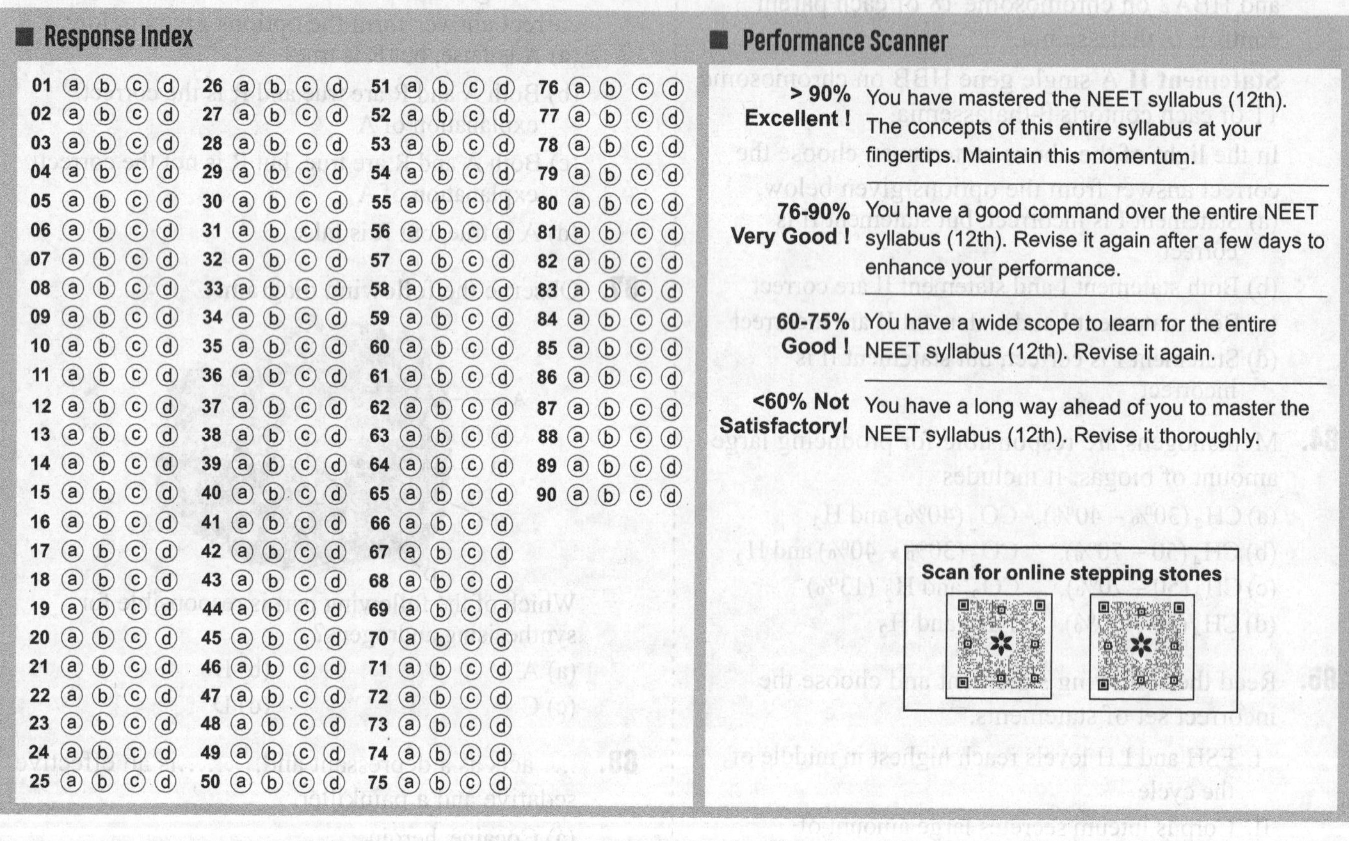

Space for Rough Work

Space for Rough Work

Test Booklet No. 3947369

Test Booklet Code NK01

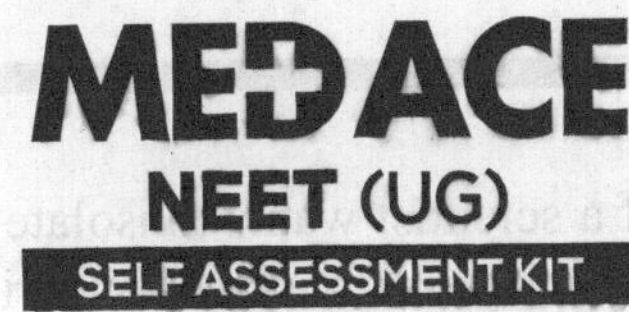

NEET Knock Offs 1

(NEET Simulator Test)

Name of the Candidate (In Capitals)

____

____

____

Candidate's Signature ____________

Invigilator's Signature ____________

Facsimile signature stamp of center superintendent____________

Important Instructions

- The test is of **1 hours 30 minutes** duration and the Test Booklet contains **90** multiple-choice questions (four options with a single correct answer) from biology.
- Candidates are advised to read all questions before they start attempting the question paper.
- Each questions carries 4 marks. For each correct response, the candidate will get 4 marks. For each incorrect response, one marks will be deducted from the total scores.
- In the event of candidate marking more than one option one mark will be deducted. The maximum marks are 180.
- Use **Blue/Black Point Pen only** for writing particular on this page/ marking response on Answer Sheet.

Do not open this booklet until you start attempting the test

Biology

1. If a scientist wants to isolate RNA from a tissue sample, which of the following nucleosides should they specifically look for to confirm the presence of RNA?

(a) Thymidine
(b) Deoxyguanosine
(c) Uridine
(d) Deoxyadenosine

2. Match List I with List II.

	List I		List II
A.	Parturition	1.	Signals for parturition
B.	Foetal ejection reflex	2.	Delivery of the foetus
C.	Lactation	3.	Milk produced during the initial few days of lactation
D.	Colostrum	4.	Production of milk through mammary gland

Choose the correct answer from the options given below.

	A	B	C	D
(a)	1	2	3	4
(b)	1	3	4	2
(c)	2	1	4	3
(d)	4	3	1	2

3. Given below are two statements; one is labelled as the Assertion (A) and the other is labelled as Reason (R).

Assertion (A) Vegetative reproduction usually takes place by fragmentation or by formation of different types of spores in Chlorophyceae.

Reason (R) Asexual reproduction in green algae is by flagellated zoospores produced in zoosporangia.

In the light of above statement, choose the correct answer from the options given below.

(a) A is false, but R is true
(b) Both A and R are true and R is the correct explanation of A
(c) Both A and R are true, but R is not the correct explanation of A
(d) A is true, but R is false

4. Given below are two statements.

Statement I Polygenic traits are controlled by multiple genes and can be influenced by environmental factors.

Statement II Polygenic traits result in only two distinct phenotypes.

In the light of the above statements, choose the correct answer form the options given below.

(a) Statement I is incorrect, but statement II is correct
(b) Both statement I and statement II are correct
(c) Both statement I and statement II are incorrect
(d) Statement I is correct, but statement II is incorrect

5. Which of the following statements is true about the cell walls in plants?

(a) The primary wall is non-flexible and does not grow
(b) The secondary cell wall is formed on the outer side of the primary cell wall
(c) The primary cell wall is capable of growth, and the secondary cell wall is formed on the inner side of the primary cell wall
(d) Both primary and secondary cell walls are formed simultaneously during cell growth

6. Which of the following statement is incorrect?

(a) Porifera includes multicellular animals which exhibit cellular level of organisation and have characteristic flagellated choanocytes
(b) The Platyhelminthes have flat body and exhibit bilateral symmetry and parasitic forms show distinct suckers and hooks
(c) The Urochordata is a large group of worm-like marine animals having cylindrical body with proboscis, collar and trunk
(d) Some of the vertebrates do not possess jaws

7. The zygote divide only after certain amount of endosperm is formed. It is an adaptation to provide

(a) assured nutrition to the developing embryo.
(b) suitable space for the endosperm development.
(c) enough time for the developing embryo.
(d) enough water to the developing embryo.

8. What did Morgan observe in his dihybrid crosses in *Drosophila* that led him to conclude that genes were linked?
(a) The F_2-generation followed a 9:3:3:1 ratio
(b) The genes segregated independently of each other
(c) The F_2-generation deviated significantly from the 9:3:3:1 ratio
(d) The genes were located on different chromosomes

9. The phenomena of co-dominance is observed in the situation when
(a) both alleles of a particular gene are expressed in only F_2-generation
(b) both allelels of a particular gene are expressed in dominant fashion in F_1 generation
(c) more than two genes are affecting a single character
(d) a single gene is affecting multiple phenotypic expression

10. Which of the following is an example of plasticity?
(a) Increase in the length of axis of grapes stalk
(b) Auxins being generally produced by the growing apices of the stems and roots.
(c) The leaves of the juvenile plant being different in shape from those in mature plant
(d) Production of some tissues in a woody dicotyledonous plant

11. Match List I with List II.

	List I		List II
A.	Physical barriers	1.	Saliva in the mouth
B.	Physiological barriers	2.	Mucus coating of the epithelium, lining the respiratory tract
C.	Cellular barriers	3.	Interferons
D.	Cytokine barriers	4.	Leucocytes

Choose the correct answer from the options given below.

	A	B	C	D
(a)	2	1	4	3
(b)	2	4	1	3
(c)	3	4	1	2
(d)	2	3	4	1

12. If the DNA plasmid is cut by same restriction enzyme, the resulting DNA fragments will have the same kind of .... and these can be joined together by using ....
(a) sticky ends, DNA ligases
(b) blunt ends, helicase
(c) blunt ends, DNA ligases
(d) sticky ends, helicase

13. Given below are two statements.

Statement I Removal of a co-factor from an enzyme results in loss of catalytic activity.

Statement II Co-factors are protein constituents that help the enzyme in substrate binding and catalysis.

In the light of the above statements, choose the correct answer from the options given below
(a) Statement I is incorrect, but statement II is correct
(b) Both statement I and statement II are correct
(c) Both statement I and statement II are incorrect
(d) Statement I is correct, but statement II is incorrect

14. Match List I with List II.

	List I		List II
A.	Myofibrils	1.	It forms light band
B.	Myosin	2.	It forms dark band
C.	Actin	3.	It forms skeletal muscle
D.	Fascicles	4.	It is parallely arranged filaments

Choose the correct answer from the options given below:

	A	B	C	D
(a)	2	3	4	1
(b)	4	3	1	2
(c)	4	2	1	3
(d)	2	3	1	4

15. Lipases of microbial origin are widely diversified in their enzymatic properties and substrate specificity which make them very attractive for industrial applications. These are used in
(a) detergent formulations which are helpful in removing oily stains from the laundry
(b) bottled juices for clarifying the juice
(c) medical formulation which are helpful in organ-transplant patients
(d) medicines as blood chloesterol lowering agents

16. Consider the following figure and identify the incorrect statement from the following.

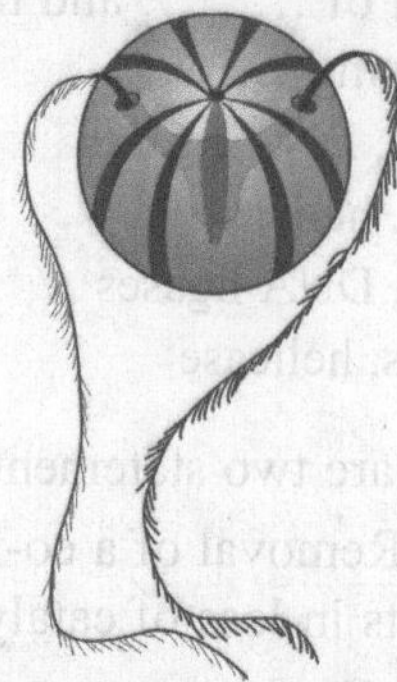

(a) These are exclusively marine, radially symmetrical and diploblastic
(b) Digestion is both extracellular and intracellular
(c) Sexes are not separate
(d) Reproduction takes place by both sexual and asexual means

17. Read the following events.

I. Chromosomes are decondensed and lose their individuality.
II. Chromosomes cluster at opposite spindle poles.
III. Nucleolus, Golgi compelex and ER reform.

All of these events are observed in which of the following phase of cell cycle?

(a) Anaphase I (b) Telophase II
(c) Telophase (d) Metaphase II

18. Given below are two statements.

Statement I Vital capacity is the maximum volume of air a person can breathe in after a forced expiration.

Statement II Vital capacity includes ERV, TV, RV and IRV or the total volume of air accomodated in the lungs at the end of a forced inspiration.

In the light of the above statements, choose the correct answer from the options given below.

(a) Statement I is incorrect, but statement II is correct
(b) Both statement I and statement II are correct
(c) Both statement I and statement II are incorrect
(d) Statement I is correct, but statement II is incorrect

19. Which of the following processes directly contributes to the decrease of proton concentration in the stroma during photosynthesis?

(a) The splitting of water molecules within the thylakoid lumen
(b) The direct transport of protons from the thylakoid lumen to the stroma
(c) The movement of electrons through CF_1 portion of the ATP synthase
(d) The transfer of protons to the $NADP^+$ to form $NADPH^+$ on the stroma side of the membrane

20. Match List I with List II.

	List I		List II
A.	High blood pressure	1.	It is caused by deposition of calcium, fat and cholesterol.
B.	Atherosclerosis	2.	It affects vital organs like brain and kidney
C.	Angina	3.	It's symptom is acute chest pain
D.	Heart failure	4.	Heart is not pumping blood effectively.

Choose the correct answer from the options given below.

	A	B	C	D
(a)	1	2	3	4
(b)	2	1	3	4
(c)	2	3	4	1
(d)	4	3	1	2

21. Which of the following statement is incorrect?

(a) Genetic modification of organisms can have unpredictable results when such organisms are introduced into the ecosystem.
(b) Very low concentration of a bacteria or virus can be detected by amplification of their nucleic acid by PCR.
(c) RNAi takes place in all eukaryotic organisms as a method of cellular defence.
(d) Transgenic monkeys are being used to test the safety of the polio vaccine.

22. Given below are two statements: one is labelled as Assertion (A) and the other is labelled as Reason (R).

Assertion (A) The pars intermedia region of pituitary, commonly called anterior pituitary, produces growth hormone, PRL, TSH ACTH, LH and FSH.

Reason (R) The adenohypophysis includes the pars distalis and pars intermedia, while the neurohypophysis stores and releases hormones synthesised by the hypothalamus.

In the light of above statements, choose the correct answer from the options given below:

(a) A is false, but R is true
(b) Both A and R are true and R is the correct explanation of A
(c) Both A and R are true, but R is not the correct explanation of A
(d) A is true, but R is false

23. During anaphase, what happens to the sister chromatids?

(a) They align along the metaphase plate
(b) They are pulled apart to opposite poles of the cell
(c) They condense and become attached to spindle fibres
(d) They form a new nuclear envelope

24. Arrange the following steps in the correct order as found in circulation of blood through the human body.

I. Blood is oxygenated in the lungs.
II. Deoxygenated blood is pumped by the right ventricle into the pulmonary artery.
III. Oxygenated blood is pumped by the left ventricle into the aorta.
IV. Blood travels through a network of arteries, arterioles and capillaries to the tissues.

(a) I, II, III and IV (b) II, I ,III and IV
(c) III, I, IV and II (d) IV, I, II and III

25. Which of the following hormones was identified by Cousins and was released as a volatile substance from ripened oranges that hastened the ripening of stored unripened bananas?

(a) Auxins (b) Gibberellins
(c) Cytokinins (d) Ethylene

26. Given below are two statements.

Statement I Divergent evolution is described as the independent evolution of similar features in different lineages due to similar environment conditions.

Statement II Both Australian marsupials and placental mammals in Australia have undergone adaptive radiation, evolving into various species that occupy different ecological niches.

In the light of the above statements, choose the correct answer from the options given below.

(a) Statement I is incorrect, but statement II is correct
(b) Both statement I and statement II are correct
(c) Both statement I and statement II are incorrect
(d) Statement I is correct, but statement II is incorrect

27. Which of the following is the common feature in all the three species - *Funaria*, *Dryopteris* and *Ginkgo*?

(a) Presence of archegonia
(b) Well-developed vascular tissue
(c) Independent gametophte
(d) Independent sporophyte

28. Identify the incorrect statements about gametogenesis in human.

I. The spermatogonia present on the inside wall of seminiferous tubules multiply by mitotic division.
II. Each spermatogonia is haploid and contains 26 chromosomes.
III. Spermatogenesis starts at the embryonic stage due to significant increase in the secretion of ganadotropin releasing hormone.
IV. The secondary spermatocytes undergo the second meiotic division to produce four equal, haploid spermatids.
V. The spermatids are transformed into spermatozoa by the process of spermiogenesis.

Choose the correct answer from the options given below.

(a) I, IV and V
(b) II and III
(c) I and II
(d) III and IV

29. Given below are two statements.

Statement I In contrast to mitosis, meiosis occurs in the diploid cells, which are destined to form gametes and is known as reduction division since it reduces the chromosome number by half, while making the gametes.

Statement II In both sexual and asexual reproduction, when the two gametes fuse, the chromosome number is restored to the value in the parent.

In the light of the above statements, choose the correct answer from the options given below.

(a) Statement I is incorrect, but statement II is correct
(b) Both statement I and statement II are correct
(c) Both statement I and statement II are incorrect
(d) Statement I is correct, but statement II is incorrect

30. How does the presence of Lactic Acid Bacteria (LAB) in the stomach benefit human health?

(a) It aids in the digestion of fats and spicy food.
(b) It competes with and inhibits the growth of disease causing microbes.
(c) It increases the synthesis of mucus from the stomach lining.
(d) It neutralises stomach acid, by producing some kinds of base.

31. In plants like mint and jasmine,

(a) lateral branch with short internodes and each node bearing a rosette of leaves originates from the base.
(b) a slender lateral branch arises from the base of the main axis and after growing aerially for some time, arch downwards to touch the ground.
(c) a lateral branch originates from the basal and underground portion of the main stem.
(d) underground stems spread to new niches and formed into new plants.

32. Read the following statements carefully and mark the incorrect statement.

(a) The proinsulin first undergoes post-translational modification to make the final functional insulin
(b) Previously, insulin was extracted from the pancreas of slaughtered animals like pigs and cattles
(c) In order to form human insulin, both chains A and C were produced separately, extracted and then combined by creating sulphide bonds
(d) A proinsulin can be distinguished from a mature insulin by the presence of an extra stretch

33. Bacteriophage labelled with S^{35} was allowed to attach to *E.coli*. After sometimes, the culture was agitated in a blender and then centrifuged. The radioactivity was noticed

(a) In supernatant
(b) In pellet
(c) In both supernatant and pellet
(d) More in pellet and less in supernatant

34. Which of the following statement is incorrect?

(a) Protonephridia or flame cells are the excretory structures in platyhelminthes.
(b) Nephridia are the tubular excretory structure of earthworms.
(c) Nephridia help to remove nitrogenous wastes and maintain a fluid and ionic balance.
(d) Malpighian tubules perform the excretory function in crustaceans.

35. Given below are two statements; one is labelled as Assertion (A) and other one is labelled as Reason (R).

Assertion (A) High rate of photosynthesis is found in red and blue regions of the spectrum.

Reason (R) Chlorophyll-*a* shows maximum absorption in the blue and red regions of white light.

In the light of above statements, choose the correct answer from the options given below.

(a) A is false, but R is true
(b) Both A and R are true and R is the correct explanation of A
(c) Both A and R are true, but R is not the correct explanation of A
(d) A is true, but R is false

36. Arrange the following steps in the correct sequence for secondary treatment of sewage.

I. Aeration of primary effluent in large tanks
II. Sedimentation of bacterial flocs
III. Reduction of BOD in effluent

IV. Formation of activated sludge
V. Transfer of activated sludge to anaerobic sludge digesters

(a) I, II, III, IV, V
(b) II, III, IV, I, V
(c) I, III, II, IV, V
(d) V, I, III, IV, II

37. Which of the following statement is not correct about prophase?

(a) Chromosomal material condenses to form compact mitotic chromosomes
(b) Chromosomes are seen to be composed of two chromatids together at the centromere
(c) Prophase is marked by the initiation of condensation of chromosomal material
(d) It is the first stage of karyokinesis of mitosis that just follows the G_1 and G_2 phase of interphase

38. Given below are two statements, one is labelled as Assertion (A) and other one is labelled as Reason (R).

Assertion (A) Competition is best defined as a process in which the fitness of one species is significantly lower in the presence of another species.

Reason (R) The feeding efficiency of one species might be reduced due to the interfering and inhibitory presence of the other species.

In the light of above statements, choose the correct answer from the options given below.

(a) A is false, but R is true
(b) Both A and R are true and R is the correct explanation of A
(c) Both A and R are true, but R is not the correct explanation of A
(d) A is true, but R is false

39. Given below are two statements: one is labelled as Assertion (A) and other one is labelled as Reason (R) .

Assertion (A) Aldosterone helps in the maintenance of electrolytes, body fluid volume, osmotic pressure and blood pressure.

Reason (R) Aldosterone acts mainly at the renal tubules and stimulates the reabsorption of Na^+ and water and excretion of K^+ and phosphate ions.

In the light of above statements, choose the correct answer from the options given below.

(a) A is false, but R is true
(b) Both A and R are true and R is the correct explanation of A
(c) Both A and R are true, but R is not the correct explanation of A
(d) A is true, but R is false

40. Which of the following statements are correct?

I. The begining of diakinesis is recognised by the dissolution of the synaptonemal complex and the tendency of the recombined homologous chromosomes of the bivalents to separate from each other except at the sites of crossovers.
II. During the diplotene phase, the chromosomes are fully condensed and the meiotic spindle is assembled to prepare the homologous chromosomes for separation.
III. The microtubules from the opposite poles of the spindle attach to the kinetochore of homologous chromosomes.
IV. The stage between the two meiotic divisions is called interkinesis and is generally short lived.
V. Diplotene can last for months or years in oocytes of some vertebrates.

Choose the correct answer from the options given below.

(a) I and II
(b) II, III and IV
(c) III, IV and V
(d) II and V

41. Which of the following statements are correct?

I. The neural system is better organised in insects as campared to *Hydra* where a brain is present along with a number of ganglia and neural tissues.
II. The afferent nerve fibres transmit impulses from the CNS to tissues/organs and the efferent fibres transmit regulatory impulses from the tissues to CNS.
III. The autonomic neural system relays impulses from the CNS to skeletal muscles, while the somatic neural system transmits impulses from the CNS to the involuntary organs.
IV. Visceral nervous system is the part of the peripheral nervous system that comprises the whole complex of nerve, fibres, ganglia and plexuses.
V. The cell body of neuron contains cytoplasm with typical cell organelles and certain granular bodies, i.e. Nissl's granules.

Choose the correct answer from the options given below.

(a) I, IV and V
(b) II and III
(c) I, II and III
(d) II, III and IV

42. Given below are two statements; one is labelled as Assertion (A) and the other is labelled as Reason (R).

Assertion (A) In a terrestrial ecosystem, the Detritus Food Chain (DFC) plays a more significant role in energy flow than the Grazing Food Chain (GFC).

Reason (R) Terrestrial ecosystems have a higher proportion of decomposers that break down dead organic matter compared to aquatic ecosystems.

In the light of above statements, choose the correct answer from the options given below.

(a) A is false, but R is true
(b) Both A and R are true and R is the correct explanation of A
(c) Both A and R are true, but R is not the correct explanation of A
(d) A is true, but R is false

43. The opening between the right atrium and the right ventricle is guarded by ...... , whereas a ...... guards the opening between the left atrium and left ventricle.

(a) Tricuspid valve, mitral valve
(b) Mitral valve, tricuspid valve
(c) Bicuspid valve, tricuspid valve
(d) Mitral valve, bicuspid valve

44. The Hatch and Slack pathway, also known as the C_4 pathway, is a cyclic process that plants in tropical deserts use for the dark reaction of photosynthesis. Some features are given below about this pathway.

Choose the correct answer from the options given below.

	Primary CO_2 acceptor	First CO_2 fixation product
(a)	RUBP	PEP
(b)	PEP	OAA
(c)	PuBP	PGA
(d)	PEP	PGA

45. In the given ecological pyramid, which of the following statement is true?

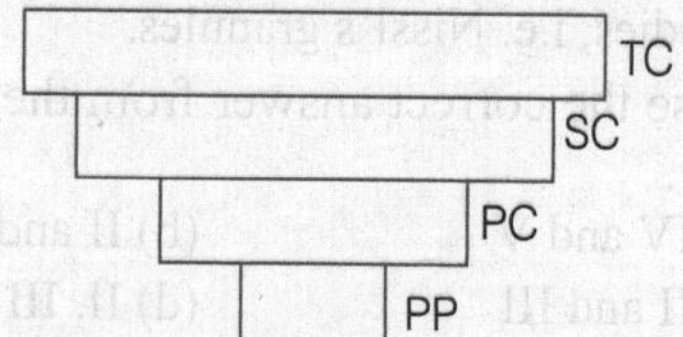

(a) The biomass of primary consumers is greater than the biomass of primary producers.
(b) The biomass of tertiary consumers is greater than secondary consumer, but lesser than primary consumer.
(c) The biomass of primary producers is the greatest.
(d) The biomass of secondary consumers is the greatest.

46. Identify the correct animal species in which protonephridia or flame cells are the excretory structures.

I. *Planaria*
II. Prawns
III. *Amphioxus*
IV. Rotifers
V. Earthworms
VI. Cockroach

Choose the correct set of answer from the options given below.

(a) I, III and IV
(b) II ,III and VI
(c) IV, V and VI
(d) I, II, III and IV

47. Arrange the following components required for PCR in the order they are added to the reaction mix.

I. DNA template
II. *Taq* polymerase
III. DNA primers
IV. Deoxynucleotides

Choose the correct answer from the options given below.

(a) I, II, IV, III
(b) I, III, IV, II
(c) III, IV, I, II
(d) II, I, IV, III

48. DNA polymerase uses a DNA template to catalyse the polymerisation of deoxynucleotides. In *E.coli*, that has 4.6×10^6 bp, DNA polymerase completes the process of replication within 38 minutes. The average rate of DNA polymerase's polymerisation is

(a) Approximately 200 bp per second
(b) Approximately 2000 bp per second
(c) Approximately 400 per second
(d) 400 bp per second

49. Match List I with List II.

	List-I		List-II
A.	Multiply more rapidly than the eukaryotic cells.	1.	Centrosome
B.	These are not bounded by any membrane and reserve food material.	2.	PPLO
C.	These are surrounded by amorphous pericentriolar materials.	3.	Microbodies
D.	These are found in both plants and animal cells.	4.	Inclusion bodies

Choose the correct answer from the options given below.

	A	B	C	D
(a)	2	3	4	1
(b)	2	4	1	3
(c)	4	2	3	1
(d)	3	1	2	4

50. What is the role of hexokinase in glycolysis?

(a) Conversion of glucose to glucose-6- phosphate

(b) Conversion of fructose-6- phosphate to fructose-1, 6- bisphosphate

(c) Conversion of 3- phosphoglyceraldehyde to 1,3-bisphosphoglycerate

(d) Conversion of phosphoenolpyruvate to pyruvate

51. A genetic disorder caused by the presence of an additional copy of the chromosome 21 is characterised by

(a) Tall stature with feminised character

(b) Short stature with underdeveloped feminine character

(c) Short stature with small round head, furrowed tongue and partially open mouth

(d) Tall structure with underdeveloped feminine character

52. Which of the following statement is true about the intermediate structural states between the substrate and product?

(a) All intermediate states are stable

(b) Only the transition state is stable

(c) All intermediate states are unstable

(d) The intermediate states are more stable than the substrate

53. Match List I with List II.

	List I		List II
A.	Unambiguous	1.	Some amino acids are coded by more than one codon
B.	Degenerate	2.	One codon codes for only one amino acid
C.	Contiguous fashion	3.	No punctuations in codon
D.	Universal	4.	From bacteria to human, UUU would code for phenylalanine

Choose the correct answer from the options given below.

	A	B	C	D		A	B	C	D
(a)	1	2	3	4	(b)	4	2	3	1
(c)	2	1	3	4	(d)	4	1	3	2

54. Given below are two statements.

Statement I The monocot stem has a sclerenchymatous hypodermis, a large number of scattered vascular bundles, each surrounded by a sclerenchymatous bundle sheath and a large, conspicuous parenchymatous ground tissue.

Statement II In monocot stem, peripheral vascular bundles are generally larger in size than the centrally located ones.

In the light of the above statements, choose the correct answer from the options given below.

(a) Statement I is incorrect, but statement II is correct

(b) Both statement I and statement II are correct

(c) Both statement I and statement II are incorrect

(d) Statement I is correct, but statement II is incorrect

55. Identify the incorrect statements from the following.

I. In diatoms, the cell walls form two thick overlapping shells, which fit together and form a ball-like structure.

II. *Euglena* has a protein layer called pellicle which makes their body indestructible and makes it energy rich source for protein consumers.

III. Slime moulds move their body along decaying twigs and leaves engulfing organic material.

IV. Slime mould, under suitable conditions, forms an aggregation called plasmodium which may grow and spread over several feet.

V. All protozoans are heterotrophs and live as predators or parasites and they are believed to be primitive relatives of animals.

Choose the correct answer from the options given below.

(a) I and IV
(b) IV and V
(c) I and II
(d) II, III and V

56. Match List I with List II.

List I	List II
A. Prions	1. It is smaller than viruses and cause potato spindle tuber disease.
B. Viroids	2. Infectious living fluid
C. Virus	3. Sexual phase is not known
D. Deuteromycetes	4. It consists of abnormally folded proteins.

Choose the correct answer from the options given below

	A	B	C	D
(a)	4	1	2	3
(b)	2	4	1	3
(c)	3	4	1	2
(d)	2	1	4	3

57. Given below are two statements : one is labelled as Assertion (A) and the other is labelled as Reason (R).

Assertion (A) During zygotene, homologous chromosomes start pairing together in a process called synapsis.

Reason (R) The complex formed by a pair of synapsed homologous chromosomes is called a bivalent or a tetrad.

In the light of above statements, choose the correct answer from the options given below.

(a) A is false, but R is true
(b) Both A and R are true and R is the correct explanation of A
(c) Both A and R are true, but R is not the correct explanation of A
(d) A is true, but R is false

58. Consider the following figure and choose the correct answer from the options given below.

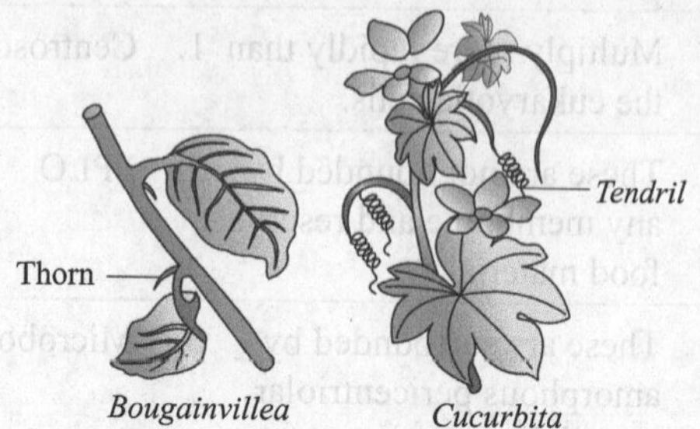

(a) Analogous organs; Convergent evolution
(b) Homologous organs; Divergent evolution
(c) Homologous organs; Adaptive radiation
(d) Analogous organs; Divergent evolution

59. Which of the following statements is incorrect?

I. Presently, 12 % of all bird species, 23 % of all mammal species, 32 % of all amphibian species and 31 % of all gymnosperm species in the world face the threat of extinction.

II. The current species extinction rates are slower than in pre-human times.

III. The Amazon rainforest is referred to as the 'lungs of the plant' and is being cleared for soyabean cultivation and grasslands for raising beef cattle.

IV. Ecologists warn that if the present trends of extinction continue, nearly half of all the species on earth might be wiped out within the next 100 years.

V. When larger habitats are broken up into small fragments due to various human activities, mammals and birds requiring large territories and certain animals with migratory habitats are badly affected.

Choose the correct answer from the options given below.

(a) Only II
(b) II and V
(c) I and IV
(d) II, IV and V

60. Given below are two statements, one is labelled as Assertion (A) and other is labelled as Reason (R)

Assertion (A) Pyruvate is formed by fermentation of carbohydrates in the cytosol and after this, it enters mitochondrial matrix and undergoes oxidative phosphorylation by a complex set of reactions.

Reason (R) This reaction is catalysed by pyruvate dehydrogenase that require the participation of several coenzymes, including NAD^+ and coenzyme-A.

In the light of above statements, choose the correct answer from the options given below.

(a) A is false, but R is true
(b) Both A and R are true and R is the correct explanation of A
(c) Both A and R are true, but R is not the correct explanation of A
(d) A is true, but R is false

61. In human which blood vessel would carry maximum amount of urea?

(a) Hepatic portal vein
(b) Renal vein
(c) Hepatic vein
(d) Femoral vein

62. Give below are two statements, one is labelled as Assertion (A) and the other is labelled as Reason (R).

Assertion (A) Pteridophytes are limited in their spread and are restricted to narrow geographical regions.

Reason (R) Pteridophyte gametophytes require cool, damp, shady places to grow and need water for fertilisation.

In the light of above statements, choose the correct answer form the options given below.

(a) A is false, but R is true
(b) Both A and R are true and R is the correct explanation of A
(c) Both A and R are true, but R is not the correct explanation of A
(d) A is true, but R is false

63. Given below are two statements, one is labelled as Assertion (A) and other is labelled as Reason (R).

Assertion (A) Incomplete dominance is observed in starch synthesis in pea seeds.

Reason (R) Heterozygotes (Bb) produce starch grains of intermediate size compared to homozygotes (BB and bb).

In the light of above statements, choose the correct answer from the options given below.

(a) A is false, but R is true
(b) Both A and R are true and R is the correct explanation of A
(c) Both A and R are true, but R is not the correct explanation of A
(d) A is true, but R is false

64. Identify the correct statements from the following.

I. The embryo differentiates after implantation into an outer layer called ectoderm and inner layer called endoderm, while the mesoderm soon appears between the ectoderm and the endoderm.
II. The first movement of the foetus and appearance of hair on the head are usually observed during the first trimester.
III. At the end of first trimester, most major organ systems are formed, and the limbs and external genital organs are well developed.
IV. In human beings, after one month of pregnancy, the embryo's heart is formed and its heartbeat can be heard using a stethoscope.
V. By the end of first trimester, the body is covered with fine hair, eyelids separate and eyelashes are formed.

Choose the correct answer from the options given below.

(a) I, III and IV
(b) II, III and IV
(c) I and II
(d) III and IV

65. Given below are two statements.

Statement I A chemosensitive area adjacent to the rhythm centre in the brain is sensitive to CO_2 and hydrogen ions.

Statement II Increase in CO_2 and hydrogen ions can activate the chemosensitive area, signaling the rhythm center to adjust the respiratory process.

In the light of the above statements, choose the correct answer from the options given below.

(a) Statement I is incorrect, but statement II is correct
(b) Both statement I and statement II are correct
(c) Both statement I and statement II are incorrect
(d) Statement I is correct, but statement II is incorrect

66. Which lymphoid organ provides site for interaction of lymphocytes with antigens?

(a) Primary lymphoid organs
(b) Secondary lymphoid organs
(c) Both primary and secondary lymphoid organs
(d) Mucosa-associated lymphoid tissue

67. Match List I with List II.

List I	List II
A. Predation	1. Plants need the help of animals for pollinating their flowers.
B. Competition	2. It helps in maintaining species diversity in a community.
C. Parasitism	3. It provides potent force in organic evolution.
D. Mutualism	4. Cuckoo and crow

Choose the correct answer from the options given below.

A B C D
(a) 1 2 3 4
(b) 2 3 4 1
(c) 3 2 4 1
(d) 1 4 3 2

68. Which of the following is not the feature of human genome?

(a) More than 2 per cent of the genome codes for proteins
(b) Chromosome 1 has most genes while chromosome Y has the fewest
(c) Repeated sequences make up very large portion of the human genome
(d) The human genome contains 3164.7 million nucleotide bases

69. Match List I with List II.

List I	List II
A. These are present in the gut of several ruminant animals such as cows and buffaloes.	1. Dinoflagellates
B. Their cell walls form two thin overlapping shells, which fit together.	2. Ciliated protozoans
C. They appear yellow, green, brown, blue or red depending on the main pigments present in their cell.	3. Chrysophytes
D. They have a cavity that opens to the outside of the cell surface.	4. Archaebacteria

Choose the correct answer from the option given below.

A B C D
(a) 2 3 1 4
(b) 1 2 4 3
(c) 4 3 1 2
(d) 3 4 2 1

70. Consider the following figure, and choose the incorrect statement from the following.

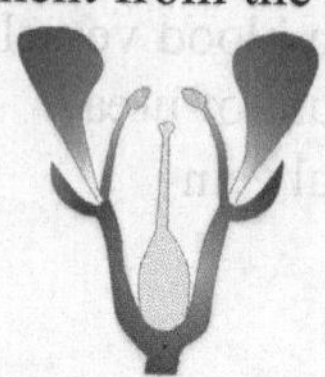

(a) Gynoecium is situated in the centre
(b) Ovary is half inferior
(c) It is observed in plum
(d) Flower is epigynous

71. Match List I with List II.

List I	List II
A. Dinosaurs suddenly disappeared	1. About 2000 mya
B. Dominance of reptiles of different shapes and sizes	2. About 350 mya
C. Jawless fish evolved	3. 65 mya
D. First cellular form of life appeared on earth	4. About 200 mya

Choose the correct answer from the options given below.

A B C D
(a) 3 4 2 1
(b) 2 4 1 3
(c) 1 2 3 4
(d) 2 4 3 1

72. Identify the correct statements from the following.

I. Plasma is a straw coloured, viscous fluid constituting nearly 55% of the blood and 90 – 92% of plasma is water and proteins contribute 6 – 8% of it.

II. Globulins are primarily involved in the defence mechanisms of the body and the albumins help in osmotic balance.

III. Basophils are the most abundant cells (60 – 65%) of the total WBCs and neutrophils are the least.

IV. Neutrophils and monocytes (6 – 8%) are phagocytic cells which destroy foreign organisms entering the body.

V. Basophils secrete histamine, serotonin, heparin etc., and are involved in inflammatory reactions.

Choose the correct answer from the options given below.

(a) I, II and III (b) I, III, IV and V
(c) III, IV and V (d) I, II, IV and V

73. Identify the incorrect statements about cell wall.

I. Non-living rigid structure
II. Living flexible structure
III. Present in all living organisms
IV. Protects the cell from mechanical damage and infection
V. Helps in cell-to-cell interaction

Choose the correct answer from the options given below.

(a) I, II and III (b) II and III
(c) I and II (d) III and IV

74. When an action potential arrives at the axon terminal, it stimulates

(a) the movement of the synaptic vesicles towards the membrane
(b) the formation of new neurons
(c) the closure of ion channels
(d) the breakdown of neurotransmitters

75. Identify the correct statements.

I. Sclerenchyma consists of long, narrow cells with thick and lignified cell walls having a few or numerous pits.

II. The meristem that occurs in the mature regions of roots and shoots of many plants, particularly those that produce woody axis and appear later than primary meristem is called lateral meristem.

III. Epidermis is usually multilayered and are parenchymatous with a large amount of cytoplasm and a small vacuole lined by the cell wall.

IV. The epidermis is often covered with a waxy thick layer celled the cuticle that prevents the loss of water.

V. The stomatal aperture, guard cells and the surrounding subsidiary cells are together called epidermal apparatus.

Choose the correct answer from the options given below.

(a) I, II and IV (b) III, IV and V
(c) I, II and III (d) II and V

76. Which of the following are the coverings of human brain?

I. Pericardium
II. Arachnoid
III. Pia mater
IV. Visceral peritoneum
V. Dura mater

Choose the correct answer from the options given below.

(a) I, II and III (b) II, III and V
(c) II, III and IV (d) I and II

77. Match List I with List II.

	List I		List II
A.	Glucose → Glucose-6 phosphate	1.	PEPcase
B.	Pyruvic acid → Acetyl Co-A	2.	Hexokinase
C.	CO_2 → 3-phosphoglycerate	3.	Pyruvate dehydrogenase
D.	CO_2 → Oxaloacetic acid	4.	RuBisCO

Choose the correct answer from the options given below.

	A	B	C	D
(a)	2	3	4	1
(b)	3	2	1	4
(c)	4	3	2	1
(d)	1	2	4	3

78. Which pair out of the following belongs to basidiomycetes?

(a) Mushroom, *Ustilago*
(b) *Claviceps, Neurospora*
(c) *Puccinia, Trichoderma*
(d) Mushroom, *Morels*

79. Given below are two statements.

Statement I *Trichoderma* species are available in sachets as dried spores which are mixed with water and sprayed onto vulnerable plants such as brassicas.

Statement II *Trichoderma* species are free-living fungi, very common in the root ecosystems.

In the light of the above statements, choose the correct answer from the options given below.

(a) Statement I is incorrect, but statement II is correct
(b) Both statement I and statement II are correct
(c) Both statement I and statement II are incorrect
(d) Statement I is correct, but statement II is incorrect

80. Malpighian tubules of insects have an analogous structure to the mammalian kidney which help in removal of excretory products from haemolymph. Which of the following excretory products is eliminated through Malpighian tubules?

(a) Urea (b) Uric acid
(c) Ammonia (d) CO_2

81. Select the correct statements from the following.

I. Prophase is marked by the movement of chromosomes to spindle equator and alignment along the prophase plate.
II. Kinetochores are small disc-shaped structures at the surface of the centromeres that serve as the sites of attachment of spindle fibres to the chromosomes.
III. At the onset of anaphase, each chromosome arranged at the metaphase plate is split simultaneously and two daughter chromatids begin their migration towards the two opposite poles.
IV. During diakinesis, the chromosomes are fully condensed and the meiotic spindle is assembled to prepare the non-homologous chromosome for separation.
V. Anaphase II begins with the simultaneous splitting of the centromere of each chromosome, allowing them to move towards opposite poles of the cell.

Choose the correct answer from the options given below.

(a) II and V (b) I and V
(c) II, III and IV (d) II, III and V

82. Which of the following statement is true about the coding strand in transcription?

(a) It is used by RNA polymerase as the template strand.
(b) It is also called as antisense strand.
(c) It binds to ribosomes during translation.
(d) It is identical to the RNA transcript except for the presence of thymine.

83. Given below are two statements.

Statement I A population has certain attributes as an individual organism does.

Statement II All the cormorants in a wetland, rats in an abondned dwelling and teakwood trees in a forest are some examples of a populations.

In the light of the above statements, choose the correct answer from the options given below

(a) Statement I is incorrect, but statement II is correct
(b) Both statement I and statement II are correct
(c) Both statement I and statement II are incorrect
(d) Statement I is correct, but statement II is incorrect

84. Which of the following statements is/are incorrect about blood?

I. It delivers nutrients to tissues.
II. It repair damage tissues.
III. It produces some hormones also, such as insulin.
IV. It provides defence against infectious disease.

Choose the correct answer from the options given below.

(a) Only III (b) Only II
(c) Only I (d) III and IV

85. Match List I with List II.

List I	List II
A. Opioids	1. *Papaver somniferum*
B. Cannabinoids	2. *Erythroxylum coca*
C. Cocaine	3. *Cannabis sativa*
D. Barbiturates	4. Depression

Choose the correct answer from the options given below.

	A	B	C	D
(a)	1	3	2	4
(b)	1	4	3	2
(c)	2	1	3	4
(d)	4	2	1	3

86. Given below are two statements.

Statement I The Indian Government has established the GEAC to oversee the validity of GM research and the safety of introducing GM organisms for public services.

Statement II Genetic modification of organisms is considered completely safe and has no-unpredictable results when introduced into the ecosystem.

In the light of the above statements, choose the correct answer from the options given below

(a) Statement I is incorrect, but statement II is correct
(b) Both statement I and statement II are correct
(c) Both statement I and statement II are incorrect
(d) Statement I is correct, but statement II is incorrect

87. Which of the following statement is incorrect?

(a) The antibiotic penicillin was extensively used to treat American soldiers wounded in World War II
(b) Cyclosporin-A used as an immunosuppressive agent in organ- transplant patients, is produced by the bacterium *Trichoderma polysporum*
(c) Lipases are used in detergent formulations and are helpful in removing oily stains from the laundry
(d) Streptokinase produced by bacterium *Streptococcus* is used as a clot buster for removing clots from the blood vessels

88. Which type of hormones usually generates second messengers like cycle AMP?

(a) Steriod hormones
(b) Idothyronines
(c) Peptide hormones
(d) Amino acid derivatives

89. Identify the incorrect statement from the following.

(a) Nearly 70% of CO_2 is transported as bicarbonate in the blood with help of the enzyme carbonic anhydrase
(b) Nearly 20 – 25% of carbon dioxide is carried by haemoglobin as carbaminohaemoglobin
(c) Exchange of O_2 and CO_2 at the alveoli and tissues occur by diffusion
(d) In the alveoli, where pO_2 is higher, O_2 gets dissociated from haemoglobin

90. Which of the following statements are correct about taxonomic categories?

I. Species is a group of individual organisms with fundamental similarities.
II. Genus comprises a group of related species which has more characters in common in comparison to species of other genera.
III. Potato and brinjal are two different species, but both belong to the genus–*Solanum*.
IV. Family is a group of related classes with still less number of similarities as compared to genus and species.
V. Genus is characterised on the basis of both vegetative and reproductive features of plant species.

Choose the correct answer from the options given below.

(a) I, II and III
(b) I, IV and V
(c) III and IV
(d) II and III

Response Index

01	(a) (b) (c) (d)	26	(a) (b) (c) (d)	51	(a) (b) (c) (d)	76	(a) (b) (c) (d)
02	(a) (b) (c) (d)	27	(a) (b) (c) (d)	52	(a) (b) (c) (d)	77	(a) (b) (c) (d)
03	(a) (b) (c) (d)	28	(a) (b) (c) (d)	53	(a) (b) (c) (d)	78	(a) (b) (c) (d)
04	(a) (b) (c) (d)	29	(a) (b) (c) (d)	54	(a) (b) (c) (d)	79	(a) (b) (c) (d)
05	(a) (b) (c) (d)	30	(a) (b) (c) (d)	55	(a) (b) (c) (d)	80	(a) (b) (c) (d)
06	(a) (b) (c) (d)	31	(a) (b) (c) (d)	56	(a) (b) (c) (d)	81	(a) (b) (c) (d)
07	(a) (b) (c) (d)	32	(a) (b) (c) (d)	57	(a) (b) (c) (d)	82	(a) (b) (c) (d)
08	(a) (b) (c) (d)	33	(a) (b) (c) (d)	58	(a) (b) (c) (d)	83	(a) (b) (c) (d)
09	(a) (b) (c) (d)	34	(a) (b) (c) (d)	59	(a) (b) (c) (d)	84	(a) (b) (c) (d)
10	(a) (b) (c) (d)	35	(a) (b) (c) (d)	60	(a) (b) (c) (d)	85	(a) (b) (c) (d)
11	(a) (b) (c) (d)	36	(a) (b) (c) (d)	61	(a) (b) (c) (d)	86	(a) (b) (c) (d)
12	(a) (b) (c) (d)	37	(a) (b) (c) (d)	62	(a) (b) (c) (d)	87	(a) (b) (c) (d)
13	(a) (b) (c) (d)	38	(a) (b) (c) (d)	63	(a) (b) (c) (d)	88	(a) (b) (c) (d)
14	(a) (b) (c) (d)	39	(a) (b) (c) (d)	64	(a) (b) (c) (d)	89	(a) (b) (c) (d)
15	(a) (b) (c) (d)	40	(a) (b) (c) (d)	65	(a) (b) (c) (d)	90	(a) (b) (c) (d)
16	(a) (b) (c) (d)	41	(a) (b) (c) (d)	66	(a) (b) (c) (d)		
17	(a) (b) (c) (d)	42	(a) (b) (c) (d)	67	(a) (b) (c) (d)		
18	(a) (b) (c) (d)	43	(a) (b) (c) (d)	68	(a) (b) (c) (d)		
19	(a) (b) (c) (d)	44	(a) (b) (c) (d)	69	(a) (b) (c) (d)		
20	(a) (b) (c) (d)	45	(a) (b) (c) (d)	70	(a) (b) (c) (d)		
21	(a) (b) (c) (d)	46	(a) (b) (c) (d)	71	(a) (b) (c) (d)		
22	(a) (b) (c) (d)	47	(a) (b) (c) (d)	72	(a) (b) (c) (d)		
23	(a) (b) (c) (d)	48	(a) (b) (c) (d)	73	(a) (b) (c) (d)		
24	(a) (b) (c) (d)	49	(a) (b) (c) (d)	74	(a) (b) (c) (d)		
25	(a) (b) (c) (d)	50	(a) (b) (c) (d)	75	(a) (b) (c) (d)		

Performance Scanner

> 90% Excellent !	You have mastered the NEET syllabus. The concepts of this syllabus are on your fingertips. Maintain this momentum.
76-90% Very Good !	You have a good command over the NEET syllabus. Revise it again after a few days and enhance your performance.
60-75% Good !	You have a wide scope to learn for the NEET syllabus. Revise it again.
<60% Not Satisfactory!	You have a long way ahead of you to master the NEET syllabus. Revise it thoroughly.

Scan to fill up online OMR and get AI based Rank prediction on performance

Test Booklet No. 3947370

Test Booklet Code NK02

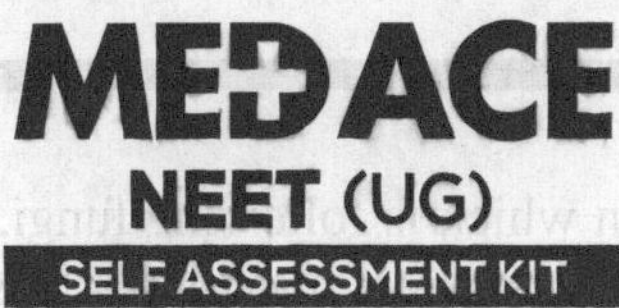

NEET Knock Offs 2

(NEET Simulator Test)

Name of the Candidate (In Capitals)

____

____

____

Candidate's Signature ____________

Invigilator's Signature ____________

Facsimile signature stamp of center superintendent____________

Important Instructions

- The test is of **1 hours 30 minutes** duration and the Test Booklet contains **90** multiple-choice questions (four options with a single correct answer) from biology.
- Candidates are advised to read all questions before they start attempting the question paper.
- Each questions carries 4 marks. For each correct response, the candidate will get 4 marks. For each incorrect response, one marks will be deducted from the total scores.
- In the event of candidate marking more than one option one mark will be deducted. The maximum marks are 180.
- Use **Blue/Black Point Pen only** for writing particular on this page/ marking response on Answer Sheet.

Do not open this booklet until you start attempting the test

Biology

1. In which is following fungi, karyogamy and meiosis take place in the basidium producing four basidiospores?
   (a) *Claviceps* and *Neurospora*
   (b) *Ustilago* and *Puccinia*
   (c) *Mucor* and *Rhizopus*
   (d) *Colletotrichum* and *Trichoderma*

2. Which of the following statement is correct among the following with reference to cardiac cycle?
   (a) During systole, the AVN generates an action potential.
   (b) Ventricular systole increases the ventricular pressure causing the closure of seminilunar valves.
   (c) The stroke volume multiplied by the heart rate gives the cardiac output.
   (d) The heart sound 'dub' is associated with the closure of the tricuspid and bicuspid valves.

3. Match the List I with List II.

List I	List II
A. Synaptonemal complex	1. Pachytene
B. Recombination nodules	2. Diakinesis
C. Terminalisation of chiasmata	3. Zygotene
D. Interkinesis	4. Prior to meiosis-II

Choose the correct answer from the options given below.

	A	B	C	D
(a)	3	1	2	4
(b)	2	1	4	3
(c)	2	1	3	4
(d)	1	4	3	2

4. Given below are two statements.

   Statement I The trichomes in the shoot system are invariably branched, soft and multicellular.

   Statement II The stomatal aperture, guard cells and the surrounding subsidiary cells are together called stomatal apparatus.

   In the light of the above statements, choose the correct answer from the option given below.
   (a) Statement I is incorrect, but statement II is correct.
   (b) Both statement I and statement II are correct.
   (c) Both statement I and statement II are incorrect.
   (d) Statement I is correct, but statement II is incorrect.

5. Observe the diagram carefully and identify the labelled diagram given below.

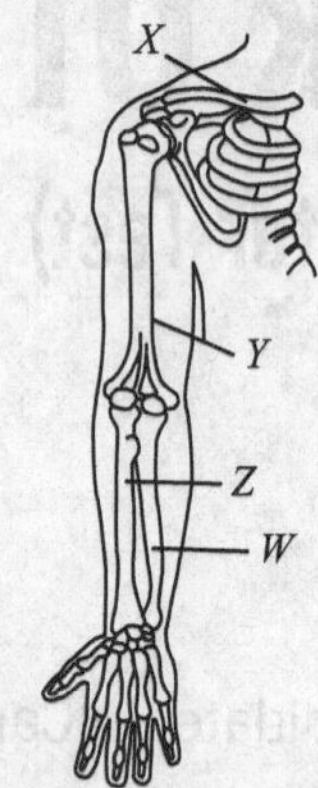

   (a) *X*-Scapula, *Y*-Humerus
   (b) *X*-Clavicle, *Z*-Ulna
   (c) *Z*- Radius, *W*-Ulna
   (d) *Y*- Humerus, *W*-Fibula

6. Which of the following is true for a eukaryotic cell?
   (a) Cell wall is made up of peptidoglycans.
   (b) 80S type of ribosomes are present in the mitochondria.
   (c) Mitochondria contains linear DNA.
   (d) Membrane bound organelles are present.

7. In plants like plum, rose and peach,
   (a) the margin of thalamus grows upward enclosing the ovary completely
   (b) gynoecium is situated in the centre and other parts of the flower are located on the rim of the thalamus
   (c) gynoecium occupies the highest position
   (d) calyx and corolla arise above the ovary

8. What makes our country one of the 12 mega diversity countries of the world?

(a) Its share of the global species diversity is an impressive 8.1 per cent.

(b) Its share of the global species diversity is an impressive 80.1 per cent.

(c) More than 70% of the all species are found in India.

(d) India has 2-4% of world land area.

9. Which of the following hormone stimulates the anterior lobe of pituitary to increase the secretion of a hormone that causes rupture of Graafian follicle?

(a) FSH (b) LH

(c) Oestrogen (d) Progesterone

10. Match the List I with List II.

List I	List II
A. Coconut	1. Middle fleshy edible mesocarp
B. Mango	2. Basal placentation
C. *Dianthus*	3. Fibrous mesocarp
D. Sunflower	4. Free central placentation

Choose the correct answer from the options given below.

	A	B	C	D
(a)	2	3	1	4
(b)	3	1	4	2
(c)	4	3	1	2
(d)	1	4	2	3

11. Match the List I with List II.

List I	List II
A. Haemophilia	1. RBCs become crescent-shaped
B. Sickle-cell anaemia	2. Phenylalanine is converted into phenylpyruvic acid and other derivatives
C. Phenylketonuria	3. Single gene HBB located on 11th chromosome
D. β- Thalassemia	4. Family pedigree of Queen Victoria

Choose the correct answer from the options given below.

	A	B	C	D		A	B	C	D
(a)	4	3	1	2	(b)	4	1	2	3
(c)	2	4	1	3	(d)		2	3	4

12. Which of the following statement is incorrect?

(a) Epidermis is the outermost wall layer of the anther.

(b) The pollen grain having the generative and vegetative cell marks the three-celled stage.

(c) Each cell of the sporogenous tissue is capable of giving rise to a microspore tetrad.

(d) Pollen grain exine has prominent apertures called germ pores where sporopollenin is absent.

13. Which of the following events associated with urine formation, makes the medullary interstium hypertonic?

(a) Reabsorption by renal tubules

(b) Secretion in PCT and DCT

(c) Counter current mechanism

(d) Reabsorption by collecting duct

14. Identify the correct statements.

I. The region of the stem where leaves are born are called nodes.

II. Leaves originate from shoot apical meristems and are arranged in a basipetal order.

III. Veins provide rigidity to the leaf blade and act as channels of transport for water, minerals and food materials.

IV. Root cap protects the tender apex of the root as it makes its way through the soil.

V. In some leguminous plants, the lamina may become swollen, which is called the pulvinus.

Choose the correct answer from the options given below.

(a) I, II, III and V only

(b) I, II and IV only

(c) II, III, IV and V only

(d) I, III and IV only

15. Given below are two statements; one is labelled as Assertion (A) and the other is labelled as Reason (R).

Assertion (A) Small mammals are not found in polar regions.

Reason (R) Their metabolic rate is higher than large mammals.

In the light of the above statements, choose the correct answer from the options given below.

(a) A is false, but R is true.

(b) Both A and R are true and R is the correct explanation of A.

(c) Both A and R are true, but R is not the correct explanation of A.

(d) A is true, but R is false.

16. Identify the correct statement w.r.t. filiform apparatus.

(a) Present at the micropylar tip and plays an important role in guiding the pollen tubes into the synergids

(b) Present at the chalazal end and plays important role in guiding pollen tube into antipodal cells

(c) Consists of eight nuclei and are surrounded by cell walls

(d) Consists of two synergids and one egg cell

17. Given below are two statements.

Statement I The vasa efferentia leave the testis and open into epididymis located along the anterior surface of each testis.

Statement II Immunologically competent cells are present in the interstitial space of testicular lobules.

In the light of the above statements, choose the correct answer from the options given below.

(a) Statement I is incorrect, but statement II is correct.

(b) Both statement I and statement II are correct.

(c) Both statement I and statement II are incorrect.

(d) Statement I is correct, but statement II is incorrect.

18. Match the List I with List II.

List I	List II
A. Archaebacteria	1. Heterocysts
B. Mycobiont	2. Production of methane
C. *Nostoc*	3. Survive without oxygen
D. Mycoplasma	4. Fungal component of lichen

Choose the correct answer from the options given below.

	A	B	C	D		A	B	C	D
(a)	1	3	2	4	(b)	2	4	1	3
(c)	3	2	4	1	(d)	4	3	1	2

19. Release of bile into the duodenum can be regarded as

(a) physical barrier

(b) physiological barrier

(c) cytokine barrier

(d) cellular barrier

20. Given below are two statements.

Statement I Cytotaxonomy is based on cytological information like chromosome number, structure, behaviour and the chemical constituents of the plant.

Statement II Phylogenetic classification system is based on evolutionary relationships between the various organisms.

In the light of the above statements, choose the correct answer from the options given.

(a) Statement I is incorrect, but statement II is correct.

(b) Both statement I and statement II are correct.

(c) Both statement I and statement II are incorrect.

(d) Statement I is correct, but statement II is incorrect.

21. Given below are two statements; one is labelled as Assertion (A) and the other is labelled as Reason (R).

Assertion (A) Administration of progestogens and progestogen-oestrogen combination is used as an emergency contraceptive pill.

Reason (R) Oral pills destroy the fertilising capacity of sperms.

In the light of the above statements, choose the correct answer from the options given below.

(a) A is false, but R is true.

(b) Both A and R are true and R is the correct explanation of A.

(c) Both A and R are true but R is not the correct explanation of A.

(d) A is true, but R is false.

22. In C_3 plants, when O_2 binds to RuBisCO,

(a) RuBP forms 2 molecules of 3PGA in the presence of RuBisCO

(b) RuBP forms one molecule of phosphoglycerate and phosphoglycolate in the presence of RuBisCO

(c) RuBP forms two molecules of phosphoglycolate

(d) PEP forms OAA in the presence of RuBisCO

23. A certain submerged plant is able to keep the photosynthetic organs, above the water surface due to production of which of the following phytohormone?

(a) Gibberellins (b) Ethylene
(c) Auxin (d) Cytokinin

24. Read the following statements.

I. In the solar system of the milkyway galaxy, earth was supposed to have been formed about 4.5 billion years back.

II. The first non-cellular forms of life could have originated 2 billion years back.

III. The fitness, according to Darwin, refers ultimately and only to reproductive fitness.

IV. The geological history of earth does not correlate with the biological history of earth.

V. The study showed that life forms varied over time and certain life forms are restricted to certain geological time spans.

Choose the correct set of statements from the options given below.

(a) I, II, IV and V (b) II, III and IV
(c) II, III and IV (d) I, III and V

25. Identify the correct description about the given figure w.r.t meiosis.

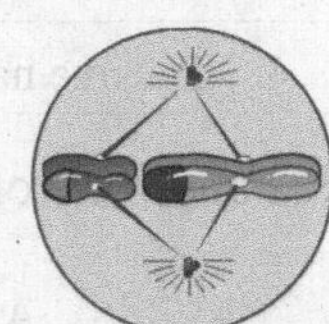

(a) The bivalent chromosomes align on the equatorial plate (metaphase plate)

(b) Nuclear envelope breaks down

(c) Microtubules from opposite poles of spindle get attached to the kinetochores of sister chromatids

(d) Centromere of the chromosomes splits

26. Following are the stages of C_4 pathway.

I. In bundle sheath cells, decarboxylation occurs and CO_2 is released which enters the Calvin cycle and the C_3 compound again goes back to the mesophyll cell.

II. Phosphoenolpyruvate (PEP) in the presence of enzyme PEP carboxylase forms Oxalo Acetic Acid(OAA).

III. The C_3 compound undergoes regeneration to form phosphoenolpyruvate.

IV. The four carbon compound is transferred from mesophyll cells to bundle sheath cells.

Choose the correct sequence of pathway from the options given below.

(a) II – III – IV – I
(b) II – IV – I – III
(c) IV – II – I – III
(d) I – III – IV – II

27. Match the List I with List II.

	List I		List II
A.	Predation	1.	Mycorrhizae
B.	Mutualism	2.	Lion and tiger
C.	Interspecific competition	3.	Loss of unnecessary sense organs
D.	Parasitism	4.	Starfish *Pisaster*

Choose the correct answer from the options given below.

	A	B	C	D
(a)	2	1	4	3
(b)	2	3	1	4
(c)	3	1	4	2
(d)	4	1	2	3

28. Which of the following option correctly identifies the labelled part of the graph?

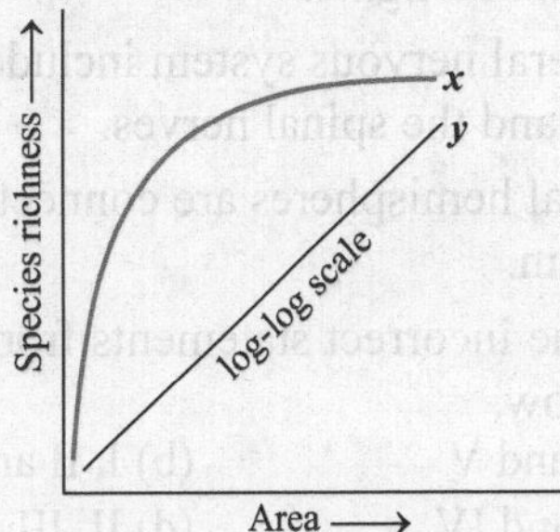

(a) x is the relation for species richness and explored area; $S = CA^Z$
(b) y is the regression coefficient
(c) x is the explored area, but only up to a limit
(d) y is represented as Z log A = log C + log S

29. Which of the following hormones interact with membrane bound receptors, normally do not enter the target cell, but generate secondary messengers which inturn regulate cellular metabolism?
(a) Glucocorticoid and glucagon
(b) Thyroxine and oestrogen
(c) Gonadotropin and prolactin
(d) Epinephrine and thyroxine

30. Match the List I with List II.

	List I		List II
A.	Collenchyma	1.	Parenchymatous cells
B.	Xylem vessels	2.	Secondary phloem
C.	Bast fibres	3.	Cellulose, hemicellulose and pectin
D.	Companion cells	4.	Lignified wall with large central cavity

Choose the correct answer from the options given below.

	A	B	C	D
(a)	3	2	4	1
(b)	2	3	4	1
(c)	1	2	4	3
(d)	3	4	2	1

31. Read the statements about the nervous system of frog.
I. There are 10 pairs of cranial nerves arising from the brain.
II. The mid brain is characterised by two pairs of optic lobes.
III. Hindbrain consist of cerebellum, pons and medulla oblongata.
IV. Peripheral nervous system includes cranial nerves and the spinal nerves.
V. Cerebral hemispheres are connected by corpus callosum.

Choose the incorrect statements from the options given below.
(a) II, IV and V (b) I, II and V
(c) II, III and IV (d) II, III and V

32 Read the following features of dark reaction.
I. Fixation of CO_2
II. Reduction of CO_2
III. Breakdown of water molecule
IV. Release of oxygen
V. Utilisation of ATP and NADPH

Choose the correct answer from the options given below.
(a) I, II and V (b) III and IV
(c) II, III, IV and V (d) I, III and IV

33. Which of the following are haploid structures formed during the spermatogenesis?
(a) Primary spermatocytes and secondary spermatocytes
(b) Spermatids and secondary spermatocytes
(c) Spermatozoa and primary spermatocytes
(d) Spermatogonia and secondary spermatocytes

34. The autotrophic components in a shallow water body are
(a) phytoplanktons, some algae and the floating, submerged and marginal plants found at the edges
(b) the fungi, bacteria and flagellates
(c) phytoplanktons and zooplanktons
(d) zooplanktons and the floating, submerged and marginal plants found at the edges

35. Match the List I with List II.

	List I		List II
A.	Hepatitis-B vaccine	1.	Organ transplant
B.	Antitoxin	2.	Recombinant DNA technology
C.	Colostrum	3.	Passive artificial immunity
D.	CMI	4.	Passive natural immunity

Choose the correct answer from the options given below.

	A	B	C	D
(a)	1	2	3	4
(b)	2	3	4	1
(c)	2	1	3	4
(d)	3	2	4	1

36. Which of the following are required for primary productivity?
I. Plant species inhabiting a particular area
II. Variety of environmental factors

III. Availability of nutrients
IV. Photosynthetic capacity of plants
V. Oxygen requirement

Choose the correct answer from the options given below.

(a) II, III, IV and V
(b) III, IV and V
(c) I, II, III and IV
(d) I, III and IV

37. Which of the following statement is incorrect about Gamete Intra Fallopian Transfer (GIFT)?

(a) It refers to the transfer of an ovum collected from the ovary of donor into the Fallopian tube of a female who cannot produce one, but can provide a suitable environment for fertilisation.
(b) This technique is employed for females with sterility conditions, but having at least one functional Fallopian tube and a normal uterus.
(c) It is an in-*vitro* fertilisation technique, in which the fertilisation is allowed inside the female body by natural coitus or artificial insemination.
(d) Fertilisation and cleavage take place in the Fallopian tube followed by implantation

38. Which of the following dinosaur is from the same lineage as that of *Tyrannosaurus*?

(a) *Triceratops*
(b) *Pteranodon*
(c) *Brachiosaurus*
(d) *Stegosaurus*

39. Match the List I with List II.

List I	List II
A. Staminode	1. Peas
B. Epipetalous	2. A sterile stamen
C. Epiphyllous	3. Stamens are attached to the petals
D. Diadelphous	4. Stamens attached to the perianth

Choose the correct answer from the options given below.

	A	B	C	D
(a)	1	2	4	3
(b)	2	3	4	1
(c)	1	3	4	2
(d)	4	3	2	1

40. Consider the following statements about Mendel's experiment.

I. The genotype of an organism showing a dominant phenotype, can be determined by self-crossing.
II. A true- breeding line is one that, having undergone continuous self-pollination, shows the stable trait inheritance and expression for several generations.
III. Mendel selected seven true-breeding pea plant varieties, as pairs which were similar except for one character with contrasting traits.
IV. The proportion of plants that were dwarf were 1/4th of the F_2 plants, while 3/4th of the F_2 plants were tall.
V. Punnett square is a graphical representation to calculate the probability of all possible phenotypes of offsprings in a genetic cross.

Choose the correct statements from the options given below.

(a) I, III and V
(b) II, III and IV
(c) II and IV
(c) III and V

41. The constituents of first filtrate formed in the lumen of Bowman's capsule is

(a) same as plasma
(b) same as plasma except proteins
(c) same as plasma except platelets
(d) same as serum

42. Match the List I with List II.

List I	List II
A. Heterocyclic rings	1. Purines and pyrimidines
B. Secondary metabolite	2. Transport protein
C. GLUT-4	3. Starch
D. Helical secondary structure	4. Cellulose

Choose the correct answer from the options given below.

	A	B	C	D
(a)	3	2	1	4
(b)	1	4	2	3
(c)	2	1	3	4
(d)	3	4	2	1

43. Following are steps involved in muscle contraction.

I. Acetylcholine (ACH) released into synapse
II. Action potential on sarcolemma
III. Myosin heads attach to actin
IV. Muscle contracts
V. Sodium ions (Na^+) rush into muscle cell

Which of the following option has correct sequence?

(a) II → IV → V → I → III
(b) I → II → V → III → IV
(c) III → II → I → IV → V
(d) IV → V → II → I → III

44. Choose the correct feature w.r.t. adenosine.

(a) Adenine is linked to the OH of 4' C of ribose sugar through a N-glycosidic linkage
(b) Adenine is linked to the OH of 3' C of ribose sugar through a N-glycosidic linkage
(c) Adenine is linked to the OH of 1' C of ribose sugar through a N-glycosidic linkage
(d) Adenine is linked to the OH of 2' C of ribose sugar through a N-glycosidic linkage

45. Match the List I with List II.

List I	List II
A. Hypothalamus	1. Highly convoluted
B. Corpora quadrigemina	2. Neuron cell bodies
C. Cerebral cortex	3. Neurosecretory cells
D. Cerebellum	4. Midbrain

Choose the correct answer from the options given below.

(a) A-4, B-1, C-2, D-3
(b) A-1, B-2, C-4, D-3
(c) A-3, B-4, C-2, D-1
(d) A-2, B-1, C-4, D-3

46. Match the List I with List II.

List I	List II
A. Origin of replication	1. Separating and purifying foreign gene products
B. Bioreactor	2. Controlling the copy of the number
C. Plasmid DNA	3. Large-scale production of biotechnological products
D. Down-streaming processing	4. Capable of replicating independent of chromosomal DNA

Choose the correct answer from the options given below.

	A	B	C	D
(a)	1	2	3	4
(b)	2	4	1	3
(c)	2	1	3	4
(d)	2	3	4	1

47. Given below are two statements.

Statement I Geographical barrier is a cause of divergent evolution.

Statement II Reproductive isolation leads to speciation.

In the light of the above statements, choose the correct answer from the options given below.

(a) Statement I is incorrect, but statement II is correct.
(b) Both statement I and statement II are correct
(c) Both statement I and statement II are incorrect
(d) Statement I is correct, but statement II is incorrect

48. The membrane-less structures in the cytoplasm that store the reserve material in prokaryotic cells are called

(a) inclusion bodies
(b) food vacuole
(c) gas vacuole
(d) polysome

49. Match the List I with List II.

List I	List II
A. Interphase	1. Chromosome duplication
B. M-phase	2. Period of preparation for cell division
C. G_2-phase	3. Period of cytoplasmic growth
D. S-phase	4. Actual period of cell division

Choose the correct answer from the options given below.

	A	B	C	D
(a)	3	4	1	2
(b)	2	4	3	1
(c)	1	3	4	2
(d)	4	1	2	3

50. When the F_1-generation of *Antirrhinum sp.* is self-pollinated, the F_2 resulted in the ratio 1 (RR) Red: 2 (Rr) Pink: 1 (rr) White. This is because of
(a) blending of the traits
(b) neither allele is completely dominant
(c) linkage between genes
(d) absence of segregation of alleles during gametes formation

51. Which of the following drugs normally used as medicine to help patients cope with mental illness like depression and insomnia, are often abused?
(a) *Atropa belladonna* and Morphine
(b) Barbiturates and Benzodiazepines
(c) *Cannabis* and Marijuana
(d) *Datura* and Amphetamine

52. Given below are two statements.
Statement I The IUCN Red List documents the extinction of 784 species (including 338 vertebrates, 359 invertebrates and 87 plants) in the last 500 years.
Statement II The last twenty years alone have witnessed the disappearance of 97 species.
In the light of the above statements, choose the correct answer from the options given below.
(a) Statement I is incorrect, but statement II is correct.
(b) Both statement I and statement II are correct.
(c) Both statement I and statement II are incorrect.
(d) Statement I is correct, but statement II is incorrect.

53. Following are the stages of foetal development, rearrange them in a sequencial order.
I. Development of limbs and digits
II. Heart formation and sound can be heard
III. Development of major organs
IV. Eye-lids separate and formation of eye lashes
V. Appearance of hair on head

Choose the correct option having the correct sequence of foetal development.
(a) I – II – IV – III – V
(b) II – I – III – V – IV
(c) II – V – IV – III – I
(d) II – III – I – IV – V

54. Which of the following is correct about Gause's competitive exclusion principle?
(a) Two closely related species competing for the same resources cannot coexist as competitively inferior one will be eliminated
(b) Two closely related species competing for the same resources can coexist as resources are unlimited
(c) Two unrelated species competing for the same resources can coexist as there is no intraspecific struggle
(d) Unrelated species competing for similar type of resources can coexist by sharing the resources

55. Match the List I with List II.

List I	List II
A. *Ancylostoma*	1. Parapodia
B. Mollusca	2. Balancing organs
C. Statocyst	3. Radula
D. *Nereis*	4. Muscular pharynx

Choose the correct answer from the options given below.

	A	B	C	D		A	B	C	D
(a)	4	2	1	3	(b)	4	3	2	1
(c)	2	4	3	1	(d)	1	2	4	3

56. Which of the following statement is correct?
(a) The process of formation of microspores from a pollen mother cell (PMC) through mitosis is called microsporogenesis.
(b) The microspores are arranged in a cluster of four cells, the microspore tetrad.
(c) As the anthers mature and rehydrate, the microspores dissociate from each other and develop into pollen grains.
(d) Inside each megasporangium, several thousands of microspores or pollen grains are formed that are released with the dehiscence of anther.

57. Which of the following option correctly identifies 'X' in the given diagram?

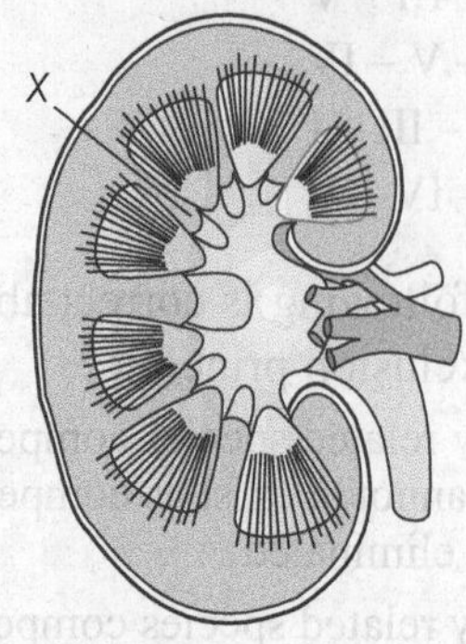

(a) Renal pyramids
(b) Part of renal pelvis
(c) Renal medulla between renal pyramids
(d) Extensions of the renal cortex

58. Who is/are responsible for purifying, concentrating and manufacturing the first antibiotic?
(a) Alexander Fleming
(b) Ernest Chain and Howard Florey
(c) Edward Jenner
(d) Louis Pasteur and Ernest Florey

59. An athlete with a resting heart rate of 70 beats/minute, performs an intensive cardio which raises the heart rate by 50%. The difference in strokes volume at rest and during intensive cardio is 15 mL. If the cardiac output during intensive exercise is 8925 mL, calculate the strokes volume at rest.
(a) 70 mL (b) 85 mL
(c) 75 mL (d) 105 mL

60. Match the List I with List II.

	List I		List II
A.	FW Went	1.	Cork cambium from fully differentiated parenchyma cells
B.	Plasticity	2.	Formation of tracheary elements
C.	Dedifferentiation	3.	Heterophylly in cotton
D.	Differentiation	4.	Isolation of auxin

Choose the correct answer from the options given below.

	A	B	C	D
(a)	4	1	2	3
(b)	2	4	3	1
(c)	1	3	4	2
(d)	4	3	1	2

61. When an animal is endangered or threatened and need urgent measures to save it from extinction, which of the following place will be desirable for its conservation?
(a) National park (b) Biosphere reserve
(c) Zoological park (d) Sacred grove

62. Match the List I with List II.

	List I		List II
A.	Acromegaly	1.	Hyposecretion of adrenal cortex hormone
B.	Diabetes insipidus	2.	Hypersecretion of thyroid hormone
C.	Grave's disease	3.	Hypersecretion of growth hormone
D.	Addison's disease	4.	Hyposecretion of ADH

Choose the correct answer from the options given below.

	A	B	C	D		A	B	C	D
(a)	4	2	1	3	(b)	4	1	2	3
(c)	3	2	4	1	(d)	3	4	2	1

63. Following biochemical reaction is mediated by which of the following enzymes?

$S - G + S' \rightarrow S + S'\text{-}G$

(a) Hydrolases (b) Lyases
(c) Ligases (d) Transferases

64. Given below are two statements.

Statement I Walter Sutton and Theodore Boveri noted that the behaviour of chromosomes was parallel to the behaviour of genes and used chromosome movement to explain Morgan's law.

Statement II In 1900, three Scientists (de Vries, Correns and von Tschermak) collectively rediscovered Mendel's results on the inheritance of characters.

In the light of the above statements, choose the correct answer from the options given below.
(a) Statement I is incorrect, but statement II is correct
(b) Both statement I and statement II are correct
(c) Both statement I and statement II are incorrect
(d) Statement I is correct, but statement II is incorrect

65. Which of the following statement is incorrect?
(a) Fibrinogens are needed for clotting or coagulation of blood.
(b) Globulins primarily are involved in defence mechanisms of the body.
(c) Albumins maintain osmolarity of blood.
(d) Factors for coagulation of blood are also present in the serum.

66. Match the List I with List II.

	List I		List II
A.	Adventitious roots	1.	Result of double fertilisation
B.	Monocot leaves	2.	Roots developed from parts of the plant other than radicle
C.	Hilum	3.	Parallel venation
D.	Endosperm	4.	Scar on the seed coat

Choose the correct answer from the options given below.

	A	B	C	D
(a)	3	4	2	1
(b)	2	3	4	1
(c)	2	1	4	3
(d)	4	1	3	2

67. Read the following statements.
I. Descending limb of Henle's loop is impermeable to water and the ascending limb is permeable to it.
II. Reabsorption of water from distal parts of the tubules is facilitated by hormone aldosterone.
III. Glomerulonephritis is inflammation of Malpighian corpuscles.
IV. A healthy adult human excretes 25 - 30 gm of urea/day
V. Amino acids are actively reabsorbed by PCT.

Choose the correct set of statements from the options given below.
(a) I, III, IV and V
(b) II, III, IV and V
(c) IV and V
(d) I, III and V

68. Match the List I with List II.

	List I		List II
A.	Chemosynthetic bacteria	1.	Convert light energy to chemical energy
B.	Photosystem-II	2.	NADP reductase
C.	Thylakoid	3.	Splitting of water molecule
D.	Chlorophyll-*a*	4.	Obtain energy from inorganic molecules

Choose the correct answer from the options given below.

	A	B	C	D
(a)	1	2	4	3
(b)	3	4	2	1
(c)	1	3	4	2
(d)	4	3	2	1

69. Given below are two statements; one is labelled as Assertion (A) and the other is labelled as Reason (R).
Assertion (A) When Griffith injected a mixture of heat-killed S and live R bacteria, the mice died.
Reason (R) Genetic material of the heat killed S-strain persisted.
In the light of the above statements, choose the correct answer from the options given below.
(a) A is false, but R is true.
(b) Both A and R are true and R is the correct explanation of A.
(c) Both A and R are true but R is not the correct explanation of A.
(d) A is true, but R is false.

70. Match the List I with List II.

	List I		List II
A.	Saheli	1.	Prevent STDs
B.	IUDs	2.	Non-steroidal oral contraceptive
C.	Condoms	3.	Suppress sperm motility
D.	Cervical caps	4.	Spermicidal cream

Choose the correct answer from the options given below.

	A	B	C	D		A	B	C	D
(a)	1	2	4	3	(b)	4	1	2	3
(c)	2	3	1	4	(d)	1	4	2	3

71. Apical dominance as expressed in dicotyledonous plants is due to the presence of more 'X' in the apical bud than in the lateral ones. 'X' is

(a) ethylene (b) auxin
(c) gibberellin (d) cytokines

72. Match the List I with List II.

List I	List II
A. Complex-I	1. Cytochrome-bc_1
B. Complex-II	2. NADH dehydrogenase
C. Complex-III	3. Succinic dehydrogenase
D. Complex-IV	4. Cytochrome-*c* oxidase

Choose the correct answer from the options given below.

	A	B	C	D
(a)	2	3	1	4
(b)	1	4	3	2
(c)	1	2	4	3
(d)	1	3	2	4

73. Which of the following diagnostic methods can be used to detect diseases before the appearance of symptoms?

(a) ELISA and blood test
(b) Blood test and X-ray
(c) ELISA and PCR
(d) Blood test and urine test

74. Given below are two statements.

Statement I Fossils discovered in Java in 1981 revealed *Homo habilis* probably did not eat meat

Statement II During ice age between 45,000 - 10,000 years ago, modern *Homo sapiens* arose.

In the light of the above statements, choose the correct answer from the options given below.

(a) Statement I is incorrect, but statement II is correct.
(b) Both statement I and statement II are correct.
(c) Both statement I and statement II are incorrect.
(d) Statement I is correct, but statement II is incorrect.

75. Match the List I with List II.

List I	List II
A. Ovulation	1. Corpus luteum
B. Menstruation	2. Increased oestrogen level
C. Follicular phase	3. LH surge
D. Luteal phase	4. No fertilisation

Choose the correct answer from the options given below.

	A	B	C	D		A	B	C	D
(a)	2	1	4	3	(b)	3	4	2	1
(c)	2	3	1	4	(d)	1	4	2	3

76. Read the following statements w.r.t transcription.

I. The promoter and terminator flank the structural gene in a transcription unit.
II. The promoter is said to be located towards 3'-end (upstream) of the structural gene.
III. The presence of a terminator in a transcription unit defines the template and coding strands.
IV. By switching position of promoter and terminator, the definition of coding and template strands could be reversed.
V. The terminator is located towards 5'-end of the coding strand and it usually defines the end of the process of transcription.

Choose the correct statements from the options given below.

(a) I, III and V (b) II, III and IV
(c) I and IV (d) III and V

77. How many animals given below have external fertilisation?

Euspongia, Fasciola, Asterias, Ascaris, Rana tigrina, Pristis, Labeo

(a) Two (b) Three
(c) Four (d) Six

78. Match the List I with List II.

List I	List II
A. Metagenesis	1. *Ctenoplana*
B. Bioluminescence	2. *Taenia*
C. Choanocytes	3. *Obelia*
D. Hooks and suckers	4. *Spongilla*

Choose the correct answer from the options given below.

A B C D
(a) 3 1 4 2
(b) 1 4 2 3
(c) 1 3 2 4
(d) 4 1 2 3

79. Match List I with List II.

List I	List II
A. Conjunctive tissue	1. Innermost layer of the cortex
B. Casparian strips	2. Parenchymatous cells which lie between the xylem and the phloem
C. Endodermis	3. Thick-walled parenchymatous cells
D. Pericycle	4. Waxy material suberin

Choose the correct answer from the options given below.

A B C D
(a) 3 2 1 4
(b) 3 4 1 2
(c) 1 2 3 4
(d) 2 4 1 3

80. Which of the following hormone pair stimulates the breakdown of glycogen resulting in an increased concentration of glucose in blood?

(a) Aldosterone and glucagon
(b) Glucagon and gonadotropin
(c) Thyroxine and vasopressin
(d) Epinephrine and norepinephrine

81. Given below are two statements.

Statement I Restriction endonucleases make single stranded cut in the phosphate backbone.

Statement II Phosphodiester bonds cut by restriction enzymes can be rejoined by ligase.

In the light of the above statements, choose the correct answer from the options given below.

(a) Statement I is incorrect, but statement II is correct
(b) Both statement I and statement II are correct
(c) Both statement I and statement II are incorrect
(d) Statement I is correct, but statement II is incorrect

82. Match the List I with List II.

List I	List II
A. Tidal volume	1. Additional volume of air exhaled
B. IRV	2. Volume of air inspired or expired
C. ERV	3. Additional volume of air inhaled
D. IC	4. IRV + TV

Choose the correct answer from the options given below.

A B C D
(a) 2 1 4 3
(b) 4 1 2 3
(c) 2 3 1 4
(d) 4 1 3 2

83. Which of the following statement is correct?

(a) Heartbeat is decreased by parasympathetic nerve by adrenaline.
(b) Fibrinogen is a carrier protein in blood.
(c) Lymph contains very small number of RBCs.
(d) Impulses generated at sinoatrial node initiates the contraction of heart.

84. Match the List I with List II.

List I	List II
A. Collagen	1. Homopolysaccharide
B. RuBisCO	2. Heteropolysaccharide
C. Chitin	3. Animal protein
D. Peptidoglycan	4. Most abundant in biosphere

Choose the correct answer from the options given below.

A B C D
(a) 3 2 4 1
(b) 3 4 1 2
(c) 2 1 3 4
(d) 2 1 4 3

85. Match the List I with List II.

List I	List II
A. Thermostable DNA polymerase	1. Spooling
B. Recombinant protein	2. PCR
C. Annealing	3. Heterologous host
D. DNA separation	4. Oligonucleotides

Choose the correct answer from the options given below.

A B C D
(a) 2 3 4 1
(b) 1 2 4 3
(c) 1 2 3 4
(d) 4 1 2 3

86. Match the List I with List II.

List I		List II	
A.	*cry*IAc	1.	Mobile genetic elements
B.	*cry*IAb	2.	Cotton bollworm
C.	Transposons	3.	Corn borer
D.	α-1-antitrypsin	4.	Emphysema

Choose the correct answer from the options given below.

A B C D
(a) 2 3 1 4
(b) 3 1 4 2
(c) 2 1 3 4
(d) 3 4 1 2

87. Given below are two statements; one is labelled as Assertion (A) and the other labelled as Reason (R).

Assertion (A) Increased reabsorption from DCT can lead to alkalosis of blood.

Reason (R) Ammonia is reabsorbed from the distal parts of the renal tubules.

In the light of the above statement, choose the correct answer from the options given below.

(a) A is false, but R is true
(b) Both A and R are true and R is the correct explanation of A.
(c) Both A and R are true, but R is not the correct explanation of A.
(d) A is true, but R is false.

88. Which of the following statement is correct?

(a) 23S *r*RNA is an enzyme for protein synthesis in eukaryotes.
(b) For initiation, the ribosome binds to *m*RNA at the AUU.
(c) There is a single *t*RNA for stop codon.
(d) The ribosome consists of structural RNAs and about 80 different proteins.

89. Given below are two statements.

Statement I The gastrointestinal tract secretes gastrin, secretin, cholecystokinin and thymosin to regulate secretion of digestive juices and help in digestion.

Statement II The atrial wall secrete atrial natriuretic factor which decreases blood pressure.

In the light of the above statements, choose the correct answer from the options given below.

(a) Statement I is incorrect, but statement II is correct.
(b) Both statement I and statement II are correct.
(c) Both statement I and statement II are incorrect.
(d) Statement I is correct, but statement II is incorrect.

90. Inserting a foreign gene at which of the following location, would make the plasmid lose its tetracycline resistance?

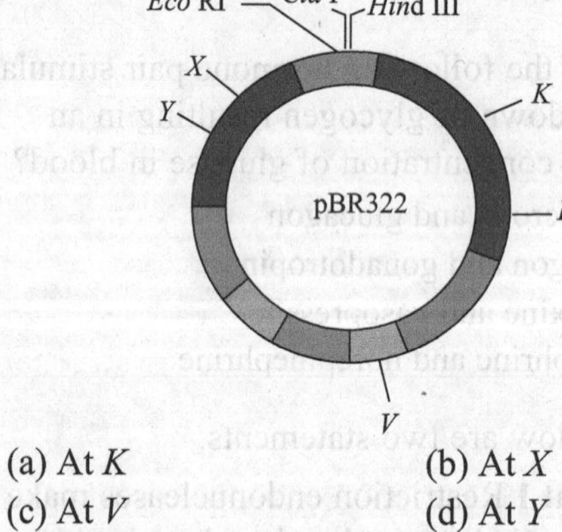

(a) At *K*
(b) At *X*
(c) At *V*
(d) At *Y*

Response Index

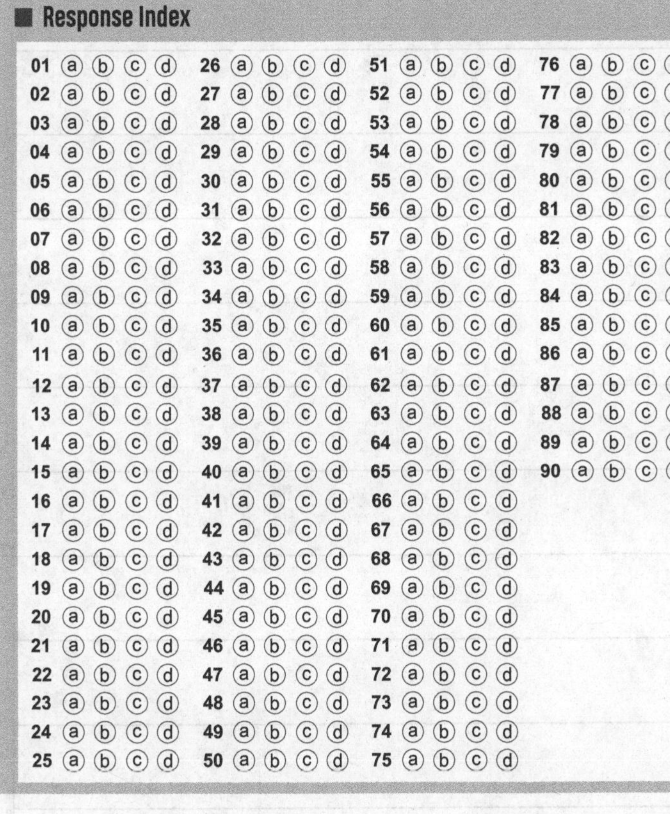

01	ⓐ ⓑ ⓒ ⓓ	26	ⓐ ⓑ ⓒ ⓓ	51	ⓐ ⓑ ⓒ ⓓ	76	ⓐ ⓑ ⓒ ⓓ
02	ⓐ ⓑ ⓒ ⓓ	27	ⓐ ⓑ ⓒ ⓓ	52	ⓐ ⓑ ⓒ ⓓ	77	ⓐ ⓑ ⓒ ⓓ
03	ⓐ ⓑ ⓒ ⓓ	28	ⓐ ⓑ ⓒ ⓓ	53	ⓐ ⓑ ⓒ ⓓ	78	ⓐ ⓑ ⓒ ⓓ
04	ⓐ ⓑ ⓒ ⓓ	29	ⓐ ⓑ ⓒ ⓓ	54	ⓐ ⓑ ⓒ ⓓ	79	ⓐ ⓑ ⓒ ⓓ
05	ⓐ ⓑ ⓒ ⓓ	30	ⓐ ⓑ ⓒ ⓓ	55	ⓐ ⓑ ⓒ ⓓ	80	ⓐ ⓑ ⓒ ⓓ
06	ⓐ ⓑ ⓒ ⓓ	31	ⓐ ⓑ ⓒ ⓓ	56	ⓐ ⓑ ⓒ ⓓ	81	ⓐ ⓑ ⓒ ⓓ
07	ⓐ ⓑ ⓒ ⓓ	32	ⓐ ⓑ ⓒ ⓓ	57	ⓐ ⓑ ⓒ ⓓ	82	ⓐ ⓑ ⓒ ⓓ
08	ⓐ ⓑ ⓒ ⓓ	33	ⓐ ⓑ ⓒ ⓓ	58	ⓐ ⓑ ⓒ ⓓ	83	ⓐ ⓑ ⓒ ⓓ
09	ⓐ ⓑ ⓒ ⓓ	34	ⓐ ⓑ ⓒ ⓓ	59	ⓐ ⓑ ⓒ ⓓ	84	ⓐ ⓑ ⓒ ⓓ
10	ⓐ ⓑ ⓒ ⓓ	35	ⓐ ⓑ ⓒ ⓓ	60	ⓐ ⓑ ⓒ ⓓ	85	ⓐ ⓑ ⓒ ⓓ
11	ⓐ ⓑ ⓒ ⓓ	36	ⓐ ⓑ ⓒ ⓓ	61	ⓐ ⓑ ⓒ ⓓ	86	ⓐ ⓑ ⓒ ⓓ
12	ⓐ ⓑ ⓒ ⓓ	37	ⓐ ⓑ ⓒ ⓓ	62	ⓐ ⓑ ⓒ ⓓ	87	ⓐ ⓑ ⓒ ⓓ
13	ⓐ ⓑ ⓒ ⓓ	38	ⓐ ⓑ ⓒ ⓓ	63	ⓐ ⓑ ⓒ ⓓ	88	ⓐ ⓑ ⓒ ⓓ
14	ⓐ ⓑ ⓒ ⓓ	39	ⓐ ⓑ ⓒ ⓓ	64	ⓐ ⓑ ⓒ ⓓ	89	ⓐ ⓑ ⓒ ⓓ
15	ⓐ ⓑ ⓒ ⓓ	40	ⓐ ⓑ ⓒ ⓓ	65	ⓐ ⓑ ⓒ ⓓ	90	ⓐ ⓑ ⓒ ⓓ
16	ⓐ ⓑ ⓒ ⓓ	41	ⓐ ⓑ ⓒ ⓓ	66	ⓐ ⓑ ⓒ ⓓ		
17	ⓐ ⓑ ⓒ ⓓ	42	ⓐ ⓑ ⓒ ⓓ	67	ⓐ ⓑ ⓒ ⓓ		
18	ⓐ ⓑ ⓒ ⓓ	43	ⓐ ⓑ ⓒ ⓓ	68	ⓐ ⓑ ⓒ ⓓ		
19	ⓐ ⓑ ⓒ ⓓ	44	ⓐ ⓑ ⓒ ⓓ	69	ⓐ ⓑ ⓒ ⓓ		
20	ⓐ ⓑ ⓒ ⓓ	45	ⓐ ⓑ ⓒ ⓓ	70	ⓐ ⓑ ⓒ ⓓ		
21	ⓐ ⓑ ⓒ ⓓ	46	ⓐ ⓑ ⓒ ⓓ	71	ⓐ ⓑ ⓒ ⓓ		
22	ⓐ ⓑ ⓒ ⓓ	47	ⓐ ⓑ ⓒ ⓓ	72	ⓐ ⓑ ⓒ ⓓ		
23	ⓐ ⓑ ⓒ ⓓ	48	ⓐ ⓑ ⓒ ⓓ	73	ⓐ ⓑ ⓒ ⓓ		
24	ⓐ ⓑ ⓒ ⓓ	49	ⓐ ⓑ ⓒ ⓓ	74	ⓐ ⓑ ⓒ ⓓ		
25	ⓐ ⓑ ⓒ ⓓ	50	ⓐ ⓑ ⓒ ⓓ	75	ⓐ ⓑ ⓒ ⓓ		

Performance Scanner

> 90% Excellent !	You have mastered the NEET syllabus. The concepts of this syllabus are on your fingertips. Maintain this momentum.
76-90% Very Good !	You have a good command over the NEET syllabus. Revise it again after a few days and enhance your performance.
60-75% Good !	You have a wide scope to learn for the NEET syllabus. Revise it again.
<60% Not Satisfactory!	You have a long way ahead of you to master the NEET syllabus. Revise it thoroughly.

Scan to fill up online OMR and get AI based Rank prediction on performance

Space for Rough Work

Test Booklet No. **3947371**

Test Booklet Code **NK03**

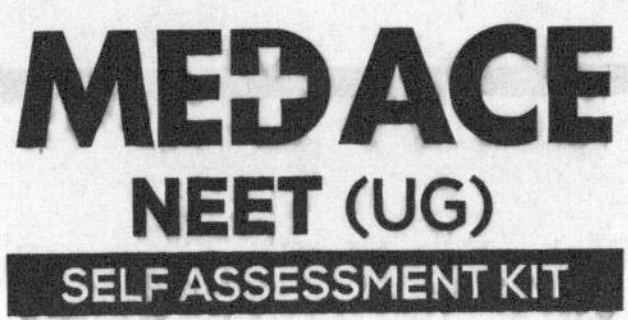

NEET Knock Offs 3

(NEET Simulator Test)

Name of the Candidate (In Capitals)

____

____

____

Candidate's Signature ______________

Invigilator's Signature ______________

Facsimile signature stamp of center superintendent______________.

Important Instructions

- The test is of **1 hours 30 minutes** duration and the Test Booklet contains **90** multiple-choice questions (four options with a single correct answer) from biology.
- Candidates are advised to read all questions before they start attempting the question paper.
- Each questions carries 4 marks. For each correct response, the candidate will get 4 marks. For each incorrect response, one marks will be deducted from the total scores.
- In the event of candidate marking more than one option one mark will be deducted. The maximum marks are 180.
- Use **Blue/Black Point Pen only** for writing particular on this page/ marking response on Answer Sheet.

Do not open this booklet until you start attempting the test

Biology

1. In the Worlds Summit on Sustainable Development held in 2002 in Johannesburg, South Africa, 190 countries pledged their commitment to achieve by 2010
   (a) 50 per cent increase in the number of biosphere reserves and National parks
   (b) a significant reduction in the current rate of biodiversity loss at global, regional and local levels
   (c) a significant reduction in the release of CFC gases in the atmosphere by developed countries
   (d) increase in the natural habitat by lion and tiger in developing countries

2. Mucosa-associated lymphoid tissue is located within the lining of the major tracts i.e., respiratory, digestive and urogenital tracts. It
   (a) provides micro-environments for the development and maturation of T-lymohocytes
   (b) acts as filter of the blood by trapping blood borne microorganisms
   (c) is a large reservoir of lymphocytes
   (d) constitutes about 50 percent of the lymphoid tissue in human body

3. Identify the correct set of statements.
   I. A flower is a modified shoot, where in the shoot apical meristem changes to floral meristem and internodes do not elongate.
   II. In racemose type of inflorescence, the main axis continues to grow, the flowers are borne laterally in an acropetal succession.
   III. In cymose type of inflorescence, the main axis terminates in a flower, the flower are borne in a basipetal order.
   IV. In twisted aestivation, margins of sepals or petals overlap one another, but not in any particular direction.
   V. In imbricate aestivation, the margins of the petals or sepals in a whorl just touch one another at the margin, without overlapping.

   Choose the correct answer from the options given below.
   (a) IV and V (b) I, II and III
   (c) II and IV (d) II, III and IV

4. If a cnidarian exhibits both polyp and medusa forms, what biological process does it demonstrate?
   (a) Metamorphosis (b) Metagenesis
   (c) Binary fission (d) Sporulation

5. Given below are two statements.
   Statement I In the solar system of the milky way galaxy, earth was supposed to have been formed about 4.5 billion years ago and there was no atmosphere on early earth.
   Statement II The surface of the early earth was covered by water vapour, methane, carbon dioxide and ammonia, which is released from the molten mass of earth.
   In the light of the above statements, choose the correct answer from the options given below.
   (a) Statement I is incorrect, but statement II is correct
   (b) Both statement I and statement II are correct
   (c) Both statement I and statement II are incorrect
   (d) Statement I is correct, but statement II is incorrect

6. The promoter is said to be located towards 5′-end of the structural gene, it
   (a) defines the end of transcription
   (b) provides a binding site for RNA polymerase
   (c) gets transcribed into RNA
   (d) defines the sequence of the RNA

7. Which of the following pair of species shows given below characteristics.
   I. Stored food - Cellulose and algin
   II. Number of flagella - two
   III. Major pigments - Chlorophyll *a*, *c* and fucoxanthin

Choose the correct answer from the options given below.
(a) *Chlorella, Gracilaria*
(b) *Ectocarpus, Fucus*
(c) *Volvox, Gelidium*
(d) *Fucus, Polysiphonia*

8. Given below are two statements.

Statement I A specialised cardiac musculature called the nodal tissue is present in the right upper corner of the right atrium called the Sino-Atrial Node (SAN).

Statement II A bundle of nodal fibres atrio-ventricular bundle (AV bundle) continues from the SAN which passes through the atrio-ventricular septa to emerge on the top of the inter-ventricular septum and immediately divides into a right and left bundle.

In the light of the above statements, choose the correct answer from the options given below.
(a) Statement I is incorrect, but statement II is correct
(b) Both statement I and statement II are correct
(c) Both statement I and statement II are incorrect
(d) Statement I is correct, but statement II is incorrect

9. Polypetalous, papilionaceous, diadelphous, dithecous anther, superior ovary and mono carpellary gynoecium conditions are observed in
(a) *Sesbania* (b) *Gloriosa*
(c) Tomato (d) *Petunia*

10. Identify the incorrect statement from the following.

I. Ovaries, oviducts, uterus, cervix, vagina and the mammary glands are integrated structurally and functionally to support the process of ovulation, fertilisation, pregnancy, birth and child care.
II. The shape of the uterus is like an inverted pear which is supported by ligaments attached to the pelvic wall.
III. The cavity of vagina is called cervical canal which along with cervix forms the birth canal.
IV. The external thick membranous perimetrium, middle thin layer of smooth muscle myometrium and inner glandular layer called endometrium lines the uterine cavity.
V. The endometrium undergoes cyclical changes during menstrual cycle while the myometrium exhibits strong contraction during delivery of the baby.

Choose the correct answer from the options given below.
(a) II, III and IV
(b) III and IV
(c) I and II
(d) IV and V

11. Which of the following is incorrect matched?
(a) *Funaria* - Gametophyte is the predominant stage of the life cycle.
(b) *Selaginella* - Sporophylls form compact strobili
(c) *Salvinia* - Produces two kinds of spores
(d) *Cedrus* - Stems are unbranched

12. Given below are two statements; one is labelled as Assertion (A) and other is labelled as Reason (R).

Assertion (A) During the resting state, the axonal membrane of a neuron is impermeable to negatively charged proteins present in the axoplasm.

Reason (R) The resting axonal membrane has a high concentration of Na^+ inside the axon and a high concentration of K^+ outside the axon.

In the light of above statements, choose the correct answer from the options given below.
(a) A is false, but R is true
(b) Both A and R are true and R is the correct explanation of A
(c) Both A and R are true, but R is not the correct explanation of A
(d) A is true, but R is false

13. How does transcription differ from DNA replication?
(a) Replication copies both strands of DNA, transcription copies only one strand
(b) Replication occurs in the cytoplasm, transcription occurs in the nucleus
(c) Replication involves RNA polymerase, transcription involves DNA polymerase
(d) Replication forms *m*RNA, transcription forms *t*RNA

14. Lactational amenorrhea method is based on the fact that
(a) conception could be prevented by withdrawal of penis just before ejaculation
(b) ovulation and menstrual cycle do not occur during the intense lactation following parturition
(c) conception could be prevent by using copper medicated medicines
(d) entry of sperms could be retarded by using some chemicals during lactation

15. Which of the following statements are correct, regarding binomial nomenclature?
I. In binomial nomenclature, first word denoting the genus starts with a small letter, while the specific epithet starts with a capital letter.
II. All the scientific names of organisms are usually Latin. Hence, they are written in italics.
III. Name of the author appears after the genus, i.e. at the end of the biological name and is written in italics.
IV. The first word in a biological name represents the specific epithet while the second component denotes the genus.
V. Both the words in a biological name, when handwritten, are separately underlined, or printed in italics to indicate their Latin orgin.

Choose the correct answer from the option given below.
(a) I and II (b) III, IV and V
(c) II and V (d) I, II and III

16. Given below are two statements; one is labelled as Assertion (A) and other one is labelled as Reason (R).
Assertion (A) Saheli is the oral contraceptive for the females and contains a non-steroidal preparation.
Reason (R) Saheli has to be taken daily for a period of 21 days starting preferably within the first five days of menstrual cycle.
In the light of above statements, choose the correct answer from the options given below.
(a) A is false, but R is true
(b) Both A and R are true and R is the correct explanation of A
(c) Both A and R are true, but R is not the correct explanation of A
(d) A is true, but R is false

17. Given below are two statements.
Statement I Carboxylation is the most crucial step of the Calvin cycle where CO_2 is utilised for the carboxylation of PEP and it is catalysed by enzyme PEPcase.
Statement II Reduction in Calvin cycle involves utilisation of 2 molecules of ATP for phosphorylation and two of NADPH for reduction per CO_2 molecule fixed.
In the light of the above statements, choose the correct answer from the options given below.
(a) Statement I is incorrect, but statement II is correct
(b) Both statement I and statement II are correct
(c) Both statement I and statement II are incorrect
(d) Statement I is correct, but statement II is incorrect

18. The Malpighian corpuscle, PCT and DCT of the nephron are situated in the cortical region of the kidney, whereas the loop of Henle dips into the medulla. In majority of nephrons, the loop of Henle is too short and extends only very little into medulla, such nephrons are called
(a) juxta medullary nephrons
(b) cortical nephrons
(c) convoluted nephrons
(d) Bertini nephrons

19. Select the incorrect statement regarding glycolysis.
(a) It is an anaerobic process
(b) Glucose undergoes partial oxidation to form 2 molecules of pyruvic acid
(c) It occurs outside mitochondria
(d) Glucose is phosphorylated to glucose-6-phosphate by isomerase enzyme

20. Consider the following events of muscle contraction and arrange them in correct order in which they occur.
I. Signal is sent by the central nervous system *via* a motor neuron.
II. The 'Z' line gets attached to the actin filaments, causing a shortening of the sarcomere.
III. Increase in Ca^{+2} level leads to the binding of calcium with a subunit of troponin on actin filaments.

IV. A neural signal reaching neuro- muscular junction and release of a neurotransmitter.

Choose the correct answer from the options given below.

(a) I, II, III, IV

(b) I, IV,III, II

(c) II, IV, III, I

(d) I, IV, III, II

21. Match List I with List II.

	List I		List II
A.	Standing crop	1.	Highly resistant to microbial action
B.	Trophic level	2.	Mass of living organisms
C.	Mineralisation	3.	Organisms occupy a specific space in the food web
D.	Humus	4.	Release of inorganic nutrients

Choose the correct answer form the options given below.

	A	B	C	D		A	B	C	D
(a)	2	3	4	1	(b)	3	2	1	4
(c)	4	1	3	2	(d)	3	4	1	2

22. Given below are two statements; one is labelled as the Assertion (A) and other is labelled as Reason (R).

Assertion (A) Haemophilia is sex- linked recessive disease and it is more common in males.

Reason (R) Males have only one X chromosome, so the presence of the haemophilia gene leads to the expression of the disease.

In the light of the above statements, choose the correct answer from the options given below.

(a) A is false, but R is true

(b) Both A and R are true and R is the correct explanation of A

(c) Both A and R are true, but R is not the correct explanation of A

(d) A is true, but R is false

23. Which of the following statement is correct about Archaebacteria?

(a) These bacteria differ from other bacteria in having a different cell wall structure

(b) They synthesise their own food from inorganic substrate

(c) They oxidise various inorganic substances

(d) They are mostly decomposers

24. *E. coli* cells with a mutated *z*-gene of the *lac* operon cannot grow in medium containing only lactose as the source of energy because

(a) in the presence of glucose, *E. coli* cells do not utilise lactose

(b) they cannot transport allolactose from the medium into the cell

(c) the *lac* operon is constitutively active in these cells

(d) they cannot synthesise functional beta galactosidase

25. Which of the following procedure is applied to kill or control dicot weeds in domestic lawns, commercial golf courses, field of corn, wheat and barley?

(a) Spraying of insecticidal protein

(b) Use of bicontrol agents such as leaf eating insects

(c) Spraying of 2,4-D on the whole field

(d) Spraying of Abscisic acid

26. The Mesozoic era was characterised by

(a) radiation of aves and origin of mammal-like reptiles

(b) dinosaurs become extinct and monocots appeared

(c) flowering plants and first shrew-like mammals appeared

(d) gymnosperms were dominant plants and first birds appeared

27. Identify incorrect statement regarding cytokinins.

(a) Natural cytokinins are synthesised in regions where rapid cell division occurs

(b) It helps in formation of lateral shoot growth

(c) They promote nutrient mobilisation

(d) It promotes apical dominance

28. Which of the following properties are related to malignant tumors?

I. Mass of proliferating cells

II. Actively dividing cells

III. Confined to their original location

IV. Starve the normal cell

V. Non- cancerous

Choose the correct answer from the options given below.

(a) I and II only

(b) I, II and IV only

(c) III, IV and V only

(d) II and IV only

29. Prophase of the first meiotic division is typically longer and more complex. It has been further subdivided into five phases and diakinesis is last stage. It is marked by
(a) dissolution of the synaptonemal complex
(b) the formation of recombination nodules
(c) terminalisation of chiasmata
(d) separation of chromatids from tetrad

30. Match List I with List II.

List-I	List-II
A. Oestrogen	1. Secreted by ovary
B. Progesterone	2. secreted by pituitary gland
C. Prolactin	3. Supports pregnancy by maintaining endometrium
D. Relaxin	4. Primary female sex organ needed for puberty

Choose the correct answer from the options given below.

	A	B	C	D		A	B	C	D
(a)	3	4	2	1	(b)	4	3	1	2
(c)	4	3	2	1	(d)	3	4	1	2

31. In the electron transport chain, the electrons pass from one carrier to another *via* complex I to IV, they are
(a) coupled to cytochrome *c* oxidase for the production of electron
(b) coupled to ATP synthase for the production of ATP
(c) coupled to complex II for the production of H_2O
(d) coupled to complex II for the production of ATP

32. Given below are two statements.
Statement I An increase in pulmonary volume increase the intra- pulmonary pressure to more than the atmospheric pressure which forces the air from outside to move into the lungs.
Statement II Relaxation of the diaphragm and the inter-costal muscles returns the diaphragm and sternum to their normal positions and reduce the thoracic volume and thereby the pulmonary volume.

In the light of the above statements, choose the correct answer from the options given below.
(a) Statement I is incorrect, but Statement II is correct
(b) Both statement I and statement II are correct
(c) Both statement I and statement II are incorrect
(d) Statement I is correct, but statement II is incorrect

33. Match the List I with List II.

List I	List II
A. Ethylene	1. Promotes flowering in pineapples
B. Abscisic acid	2. They are acidic in nature
C. Auxin	3. Promotes female flowers in cucumbers
D. Gibberellin	4. It acts as an antagonist to GAs

Choose the correct answer from the options given below.

	A	B	C	D		A	B	C	D
(a)	2	3	4	1	(b)	4	3	2	1
(c)	3	4	1	2	(d)	3	1	2	4

34. The major difference between inorganic catalysts and enzyme is
(a) inorganic catalysts work efficiently at high temperature, while enzymes get damaged at high temperature
(b) inorganic catalysts work efficiently in the presence of inhibitor, while enzymes do not work efficiently in the presence of inhibitor
(c) inorganic catalysts get damaged at high temperature, while enzymes work efficiently at high temperature
(d) inorganic catalysts get damaged at high pressure while enzymes work efficiently at high pressure

35. The axoneme possesses a number of microtubes running parallel to the long axis, it has usually
(a) two pairs of doublets radially arranged peripheral microtubules and a pair of centrally located microtubules
(b) two pairs of centrally located microtubules and a pair of doublets of radially arranged peripheral microtubules

(c) nine pairs of doublets of radially arranged peripheral microtubules and a pair of centrally located microtubules

(d) nine pairs of centrally located microtubules and a pair of radially arranged pheripheral microtubules

36. Identify the correct feature of the labelled part of the given below figure.

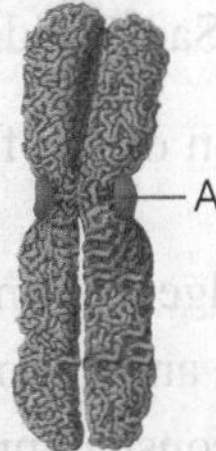

(a) It forms the body of cilia or flagella

(b) It is a disc shaped structure present on both centromere

(c) It forms two equal arms of the chromosome

(d) It contains DNA and some basic proeins

37. Given below are two statements.

Statement I The ability of the pistil to recognise the pollen followed by its acceptance or rejection is the result of a continuous dialogue between pollen grain and the pistil.

Statement II In all angiospermic plants, the generative cell divides and forms the two male gametes during the growth of pollen tube in the stigma.

In the light of the above statements, choose the correct answer form the options given below.

(a) Statement I is incorrect, but statement II is correct

(b) Both statement I and statement II are correct

(c) Both statement I and statement II are incorrect

(d) Statement I is correct, but statement II is incorrect

38. Pectoral and pelvic girdle bones help in the articulation of the upper and the lower limbs respectively with the axial skeleton. Each half of pectoral girdle consists of a

(a) ilium and ischium

(b) clavicle and scapula

(c) humerus and coxal bones

(d) acetabulum and ischium

39. Identify the correct sequence of events during mitosis.

I. Chromosomes are moved to spindle equator

II. Chromatids moves to opposite poles

III. Each centrosome radiates out microtubules.

IV. Chromosomes cluster at opposite spindle poles

Choose the correct answer from the options given below.

(a) I, II, III, IV (b) III, I, II, IV

(c) III, IV, I, II (d) IV, I, III, II

40. Given below are two statements.

Statement I Stirred tank bioreactors provide suitable environment is which an organism can efficiently produce a target product that may be cell biomass, a metabolite or bioconversion product.

Statement II The sparge ring located below the agitator is used to break the incoming air into small bubbles.

In the light of the above statements, choose the correct answer from the options given below.

(a) Statement I is incorrect, but Statement II is correct

(b) Both statement I and statement II are correct

(c) Both statement I and statement II are incorrect

(d) Statement I is correct, but statement II is incorrect

41. Identify the correct statement from the following.

I. Francis Crick suggested the existence of an adapter molecule that could read the code and bind to specific amino acid.

II. Amino acid are activated in the presence of ATP and linked to their cognate *t*RNA then amino acids are joined by peptide bonds.

III. Ribosomes are the cellular factory responsible for the synthesis of proteins and consists of structural RNAs and about 80 different proteins.

IV. The development and differentiation of embryo into adult organisms are also a result of the coordinated regulation of expression of several sets of genes.

V. In a translational unit, the activity of RNA polymerase at a given promoter is in turn regulated by interaction with accessory proteins, which affect its ability to recognise starts sites.

Choose the correct answer from the options given below.
(a) I, II, III and IV
(b) I, II and IV
(c) II, IV and V
(d) Only IV

42. Pineal gland is a small, whitish flattened gland situated at the tip of a small fibrous stalk that arises from dorsal wall of diencephalon. It is known to secrete one hormone , which
(a) cause dilation of blood vessels
(b) retards glucose conduction and protein synthesis
(c) cause demineralisation of bones
(d) helps in maintaining the normal rhythms of sleep wake cycle

43. Which of the following factor is not a consequence of loss of biodiversity in a region?
(a) Decline in plant production
(b) Increased variability in ecosystem processes
(c) Enhanced resistance to environmental perturbations
(d) Lowered resistance to environmental perturbations

44. If a population shows a directional change due to natural selection, what would be the expected outcome?
(a) More individuals will acquire the main character value
(b) More individuals will acquire a value other than the mean character value
(c) More individuals will acquire peripheral character values at both ends of the distribution curve
(d) There will be no change in the chracter value distribution

45. Which of the following factor determines the rate of exponential population growth according to the equation $dN / dt = rN$?
(a) The total number of birth in the population
(b) The difference between birth rate and death rate per capita
(c) The carrying capacity of the habitat
(d) The average age of individuals in the population

46. Which of the following is the correct chronological order of the evolutionary history of vertebrates from oldest to most recent ones?
(a) Early reptiles, Pelycosaurs, Thecodonts, Dinosaurs
(b) Early reptiles, Sauropsids, Synapsids, Therapsids
(c) Early reptiles, Therapsids, Thecodont, Turtles
(d) Early reptiles, Sauropsids, Synapsids, selycosaurs

47. The main function of the floating cover in a biogas plant is
(a) to prevent sludge to coming back to digestor
(b) to measure the amount of gas produced
(c) to maintain a constant pressure inside the tank
(d) to prevent gas from escaping

48. The presence of sporozoites in the salivary glands of the mosquito facilitate the spread of malaria because
(a) they can multiply rapidly within the mosquito salivary glands
(b) they are directly injected into humans when the mosquito bites
(c) they cause the mosquito to produce more saliva
(d) they provide the mosquito with nutrients

49. Identify the incorrect statements from the following.
I. Phloem in angiosperm is composed of sieve tube elements, companion cells, phloem parenchyma and phloem fibres.
II. Sieve tube elements are long, tube-like structures, arranged longitudinally and are associated with the companion cells, their end walls are perforated in a sieve-like manner to form the sieve plates.
III. A mature companion cell possesses a peripheral cytoplasm and a large vacuole but lacks a nucleus. The functions of companion cells are controlled by the sieve tubes.
IV. The sieve tube elements and companion cells are connected by pit fields present between their common longitudinal walls.
V. The phloem fibres are made up of sclerenchymatous cells and these are generally present in the primary phloem, but are absent in the secondary phloem.

Choose the correct answer from the options given below.
(a) III and V
(b) I, II and III
(c) II, III and V
(d) III and IV

50. Which of the following microbes are used for the production of cholesterol lowering medication and as an immunosuppressive agent, respectively?
(a) *Monascus purpureus* and *Trichoderma polysporum*
(b) *Trichoderma polysporum* and *saccharomyces cerevisiae*
(c) *Streptococcus* and *Aspergillus niger*
(d) *Acetobacter aceti* and *Clostridium butylicum*

51. Select the incorrect statement related to geitonogamy?
(a) They brings genetically different types of pollen grains to the stigma
(b) It is functionally cross - pollination
(c) It is genetically similar to autogamy
(d) It involves transfer of pollen grains from the anther to the stigma of another flower of the same plant

52. Match the List with List II.

List-I		List-II
A. ANF (Atrial Natriuretic Factor)	1.	It activates the JG cells to release renin
B. GFR (Glomerular Fitration Rate)	2.	Impermeable to electrolytes
C. Proximal Convoluted Tubule	3.	It maintain the pH
D. Descending limb of Henle's loop	4.	Vasodilation

Choose the correct answer from the option given below.

	A	B	C	D		A	B	C	D
(a)	4	1	3	2	(b)	3	4	1	2
(c)	2	4	1	3	(d)	3	2	4	1

53. Consider the following figure and choose the incorrect statement about it.

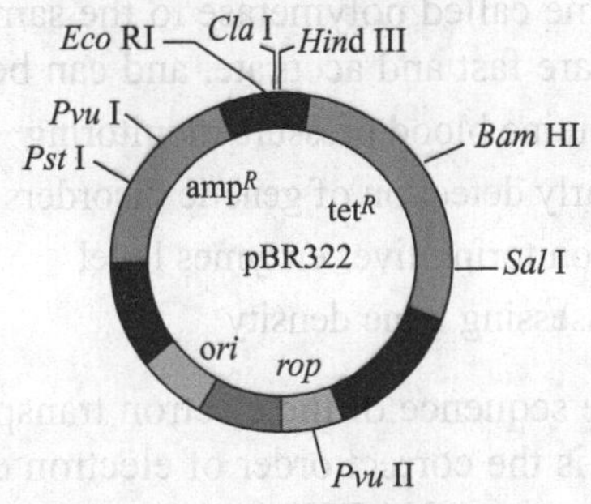

(a) It has total 8 restriction sites
(b) tet ^{R} resistance genes found at *Bam*HI restriction site
(c) *Pst* I restriction site is located closest to the amp ^{R} gene
(d) Site code for protein is located between *Pvu* I and *Pst* I sites

54. The placenta has several metabolic functions that are vital for the healthy growth of a foetus, it facilitate the
(a) supply of haemoglobin and blood clotting factor to the embryo
(b) supply of oxygen and nutrients to the embryo
(c) free movement of foetus in the womb
(d) production of elastin and phospholipids from mother's amino acid and fatty acids, respectively

55. How do *Agrobacterium* vectors facilitate the production of pest-resistant plants?
(a) These vector produce certain toxin which directly kill the nematodes
(b) Nematode specific genes are introduced into the host plant using these vectors, that produce sense and anti-sense RNA
(c) These vector enhance the natural resistance genes of the plant
(d) The vector increase the nutritional content of the plant

56. PCR tests work by taking a sample of blood, saliva, mucus or tissues and then adding an enzyme called polymerase to the sample. These tests are fast and accurate, and can be useful for

(a) routine blood pressure monitoring
(b) early detection of genetic disorders
(c) monitoring liver enzymes level
(d) assessing bone density

57. In the sequence of the electron transport system, what is the correct order of electron carriers starting from NADH?

(a) NADH $\rightarrow$ complex I $\rightarrow$ ubiquinone $\rightarrow$ complex III $\rightarrow$ cyt c $\rightarrow$ complex IV $\rightarrow O_2$
(b) NADH $\rightarrow$ complex II $\rightarrow$ ubiquinone $\rightarrow$ complex III $\rightarrow$ cyt c $\rightarrow$ complex IV $\rightarrow O_2$
(c) NADH $\rightarrow$ complex I $\rightarrow$ cyt c $\rightarrow$ ubiquinone $\rightarrow$ complex III $\rightarrow$ complex IV $\rightarrow O_2$
(d) NADH $\rightarrow$ complex I $\rightarrow$ complex III $\rightarrow$ ubiquinone $\rightarrow$ cyt c $\rightarrow$ complex IV $\rightarrow O_2$

58. Identify the correct statements from the following w.r.t. transmission of impulses.

I. A synapse is formed by the membranes of a pre-synaptic neuron and a post- synaptic neuron, which is always separated by synaptic cleft.
II. At electrical synapses, the membranes of pre and post- synaptic neurons are in very close proximity and electrical current can flow directly from one neuron into the other across these synapses.
III. At a chemical synapse, the membranes of the pre- and post-synaptic neurons are separated by a fluid filled space called synaptic cleft.
IV. Neurotransmitters are involved in the transmission of impulses, these are found at axon terminals in vesicles
V. Impulse transmission across a chemical synapse is always faster than that across an electrical synapse and electrical synapse are common in our body.

Choose the correct answer from the options given below.

(a) I, II and III
(b) II, IV and V
(c) II and V
(d) II, III and IV

59. Identify the incorrect statements from the following.

I. The members of chlorophyceae are usually green due to the dominance of pigments chlorophyll a and b, these pigments are localised in definite chloroplasts.
II. The chloroplasts in chlorophyceae may be discoid, plate-like, reticulate, cup-shaped, spiral or ribbon-shaped.
III. Most of the members of chlorophyceae have one or more storage bodies called pyrenoids located in the chloroplasts which contain protein only.
IV. Green algae usually have a soft cell wall made of an outer layer of cellulose and an inner layer of pectose.
V. Many species of *Porphyra*, *Laminaria* and *Sargassum* are among the 70 species of marine algae used as food.

Choose the correct answer from the options given below.

(a) I, II and V
(b) III and IV
(c) II, III and IV
(d) I, IV and V

60. Which of the following hormone stimulates reabsorption of Ca^{2+} by the renal tubules and increases Ca^{2+} absorption from the digested food?

(a) Thyroxine
(b) Thymosins
(c) Adrenaline
(d) PTH

61. During which phases of cell cycle, cell is metabolically active and continuously growing without replicating its DNA?

(a) G_1 and G_2-phases
(b) G_1 and S-phases
(c) M and G_2-phases
(d) G_1 and M-phases

62. How would the phenotype of an individual with the genotype AABBcc differ from that of an individual with aabbCC?

(a) AABBcc would have darker skin than aabbcc
(b) AABBcc would have lighter skin than aabbcc
(c) Both would have the same skin colour
(d) AABBcc would have mixed skin colour

63. Given below are two statements.

Statements I In Mendel's hybridisation experiments with pea plants, the F_1 -generation always ressembled either one of the parents.

Statement II In the F_2 -generation of Mendel's pea plant experiments, the ration of plants displaying the dominant trait to those displaying the recessive trait was observed to be 3;1, demostrating Mendel's law of segregation.

In the light of the above statements, choose the correct answer form the options given below.

(a) Statement I is incorrect, but statement II is correct
(b) Both statements I and statements II are correct
(c) Both statements I and statements II are incorrect
(d) Statement I is correct, but statement II is incorrect

64. Which of the following statement is incorrect ?

(a) Actin filament is made of two 'F' actins which are helically wound to each other and each F actin is a polymer of monomeric 'G' (Globular) actins
(b) A complex protein troponin is distributed at regular intervals on the tropomyosin
(c) Each myosin (thick) filament is a polymerised protein made up of meromyosins consists of two main parts, i.e. heavy meromyosin and light meromyosin
(d) The globular head of heavy meromyosin projects inward at regular intervals from the surface of the polymerised myosin filament forming cross-arms.

65. Match the List I with List II.

List I (Types of Placentation)		List II (Examples)
A. Marginal	1.	China rose, lemon
B. Axile	2.	Mustard, Argemone
C. Parietal	3.	Pea, moong
D. Basal	4.	Sunflower, marigold

Choose the correct answer from the option given below.

	A	B	C	D
(a)	3	1	2	4
(b)	3	4	2	1
(c)	2	4	1	3
(d)	4	3	2	1

66. Identify the incorrect match pair from the following options.

(a) Uremia- Accumalation of urea in blood
(b) Renal failures - kidney failure
(c) Renal calculi- Removal of nitrogenous waste from the convenient artery
(d) Glomerulonephritis- Inflammation of glomeruli of kidney

67. Given below are two statements.

Statement I Pyruvate formed by the glycolytic catabolism of carbohydrates in the cytosol, it undergoes photodecarboxylation by a complex set of reactions catalysed by succinate dehydrogenase in the mitochondrial matrix.

Statement II The condensation of acetyl group in the TCA cycle is catalysed by the enzyme citrate synthase and a molecule of Co-A is released.

In the light of the above statements, choose the correct answer from the options given below.

(a) Statement I is incorrect, but statement II is correct
(b) Both statement I and statement II are correct
(c) Both statement I and statement II are incorrect
(d) Statement I is correct, but statement II is incorrect

68. ....is a chronic disorder in which alveolar walls are damaged due to which respiratory surface is decreased. One of the major causes of this is cigarette smoking.

(a) Asthma
(b) Emphysema
(c) Angina
(d) Coronary Artery Disease

69. In plant, coleorrhiza is

(a) lower end of embryonal axis in potato family

(b) upper end of embryonal axis in monocot

(c) lower end of embryonal axis in monocot

(d) lower end of embryonal axis in dicots

70. A special neural centre in the medulla oblongata can moderate the cardiac function through autonomic nervous system. Neural signals through the sympathetic nerves

(a) can increase the rate of heart beat

(b) can decrease the rate of heart beat

(c) decrease the cardiac output

(d) decrease the speed of conduction of action potential

71. Match List I with List II.

List I	List II
A. Cytoskeleton	1. Small structures which works like oars
B. Cilia	2. Emerge from centriole-like structure
C. Flagella	3. Filamentous proteinaceous structure
D. Centrosome	4. Surrounded by amorphous pericentriolar materials

Choose the correct answer from the options given below.

	A	B	C	D
(a)	2	3	1	4
(b)	3	1	2	4
(c)	4	3	2	1
(d)	1	2	3	4

72. Match List I with List II.

List I	List II
A. P-wave	1. External layer of fibrous connective tissue with collagen fibres.
B. QRS complex	2. It leads to the contraction of both the atria.
C. Tunica intima	3. A layer of smooth muscle and elastic fibres.
D. Tunica externa	4. It initiates the ventricular contraction.

Choose the correct answer from the options given below.

	A	B	C	D
(a)	2	3	4	1
(b)	2	4	3	1
(c)	3	4	1	2
(d)	1	3	2	4

73. Match List I with List II.

List I	List II
A. Dehydrogenases	1. It calalyses oxido-reduction
B. Transferases	2. It catalyses hydrolysis of ester
C. Hydrolases	3. It catalyses the transfer of a group
D. Lyases	4. It catalyses the removal of groups from substrates.

Choose the correct answer from the options given below.

	A	B	C	D
(a)	3	2	1	4
(b)	1	3	2	4
(c)	1	2	4	3
(d)	4	2	1	3

74. Which of the following factor/feature is not related to allergies?

(a) The body is able to differentiate self and non-self and the cell- mediated immune response is responsible for the reaction of allergy

(b) Symptoms of allergic reactions are sneezing, watery eyes, running nose and difficulty is breathing

(c) It is due to the release of chemicals like histamine and serotonin from the mast cells

(d) It can be reduced by the use of anti-histamine, adrenalin and steroids

75. A nitrogenous base is linked to the

(a) pentose sugar through phosphodiester linkage to form a nucleoside

(b) pentose sugar through N-glycosidic linkage to form a nucleoside

(c) pentose sugar through N- glycosidic linkage to form a nucleotide

(d) pentose sugar through phosphodiester linkage to form a nucleotide

76. Match List I with List II.

List I		List II
A. Diptera	1.	Genus
B. Insecta	2.	Order
C. *Musca*	3.	Class
D. Arthropoda	4.	Phylum

Choose the correct answer from the options given below.

	A	B	C	D
(a)	2	3	1	4
(b)	3	2	1	4
(c)	2	1	3	4
(d)	4	1	3	2

77. The Abingdon tortoise in Galapagos islands became extinct within a decade after goats were introduced on the island, apparently due to greater browsing efficiency of the goats. This scenario explains,

(a) predation between two herbivores.

(b) competition between two herbivores.

(c) principle of resource partitioning between two species.

(d) parasitism between two species.

78. Which of the following pair of animals have tympanum in ear, heart is usually 3- chambered, poikilotherms, sexes are separate, fertilisation is internal and oviparous?

(a) *Corvus* and *Columba*

(b) *Testudo* and *Bungarus*

(c) Alligator and *Neophron*

(d) *Clarias* and *Betta*

79. Read the following statements about decomposition and find out the correct set of statements.

I. Decomposers breakdown complex organic matter into inorganic substances like CO_2, H_2O and nutrients.

II. Water soluble inorganic nutrients go down into the soil horizon and get precipitated as unavailable salts, by the process of leaching.

III. The rate of decomposition is controlled by chemical composition of detritus and climatic factors.

IV. The rate of decomposition is slower, if detritus is rich in nitrogen.

V. Cold and moist environment favour decomposition.

Choose the correct answer from the options given below.

(a) I, II and III

(b) IV and V

(c) II, IV and V

(d) I and II

80. What happens to enzymatic activity as substrate concentration increases?

(a) Activity increases linearly

(b) Activity increases until saturation, then levels off

(c) Activity decreases linearly

(d) Activity remains constant

81. Which of the following statement is incorrect?

(a) A true - breeding line is one that, having undergone continuous self - pollination, shows the stable trait inheritance and expression for several generations.

(b) The law of dominance is used to explain the expression of both the parental characters in a monohybrid cross in the F_1-generation in snapdrogon.

(c) Law of segregation states that alleles do not show any blending and both the characters are recovered in the F_2-generation, while one of the character is not seen in the F_1 stage.

(d) A homozygous parent produces all gametes that are similar while a heterozygous one produces two kinds of gametes each having one allele with equal proportion.

82. What is the role of the mesorchium in the male reproductive system of frogs?

(a) It secretes hormones

(b) It stores sperm

(c) It attaches the testes to the kidneys

(d) It produces eggs

83. Match List I with List II.

List I	List II
A. Fragments of *m*RNA sequences derived through single sequencing reaction performed on randomly selected clones from *c*DNA libraries.	1. Sequence annotation
B. Sequencing the whole set of genome that contained all the coding and non-coding sequence.	2. Expressed sequence tags
C. It contributes to the formation of crucial chromosome structures, heterochromatic establishment, genome stability and development.	3. Single nucleotide polymorphism
D. It represent a difference in a single DNA.	4. Satellite DNA

Choose the correct answer from the options given below.

	A	B	C	D
(a)	1	2	3	4
(b)	2	1	4	3
(c)	3	4	1	2
(d)	4	3	2	1

84. Match List I with List II.

List I	List II
A. Porifera	1. Flat body, suckers
B. Platyhelminthes	2. Worm shaped, elongated.
C. Aschelminthes	3. Body with pores and canals in walls.
D. Annelida	4. Body segmentation like rings

Choose the correct answer from the options given below.

	A	B	C	D
(a)	1	2	3	4
(b)	3	1	2	4
(c)	2	1	3	4
(d)	4	1	2	3

85. Which one of the following is the correct statement regarding the particular psychotropic drug specified?

(a) Hashish causes after thought perceptions and hallucinations

(b) Opium stimulates nervous system and causes hallucinations

(c) Morphine leads to delusions and disturbed emotions

(d) Barbiturates cause relaxation and temporary euphoria

86. Given below are two statements.

Statement I Ciliated protozoans are aquatic, actively moving organisms because of the presence of thousands of cilia.

Statement II *Trypanosoma* is a sporozoan, is most notorious, which causes malaria, a disease which has a staggering effect on human population.

In the light of the above statements, choose the correct answer from the options given below.

(a) Statement I is incorrect, but statement II is correct

(b) Both statement I and statement II are correct

(c) Both statement I and statement II are incorrect

(d) Statement I is correct, but statement II is incorrect

87. Given below are two statements; one is labelled as the Assertion (A) and other is labelled as Reason (R).

Assertion (A) Complex II of the electron transport chain does not directly pump protons across the inner mitochondrial membrane.

Reason (R) Complex II transfers electrons directly from $FADH_2$ to ubiquinone without contributing to the proton gradient.

In the light of above statements, choose the correct answer from the options given below.

(a) A is false, but R is true

(b) Both A and R are true, and R is the correct explanation of A

(c) Both A and R are true, but R is not the correct explanation of A

(d) A is true, but R is false

88. Match List I with List II.

List-I	List-II
A. Scrotum	1. Sperms are produced
B. Seminiferous tubules	2. It helps in maintaining the low temperature of the testes
C. Leydig cells	3. Provides nutrition to the germ cells
D. Sertoli cells	4. Secrete testicular hormones

Choose the correct answer from the options given below.

	A	B	C	D		A	B	C	D
(a)	2	1	4	3	(b)	4	2	1	3
(c)	3	2	1	4	(d)	1	4	3	2

89. Consider the following figure and identify the incorrect statements about it.

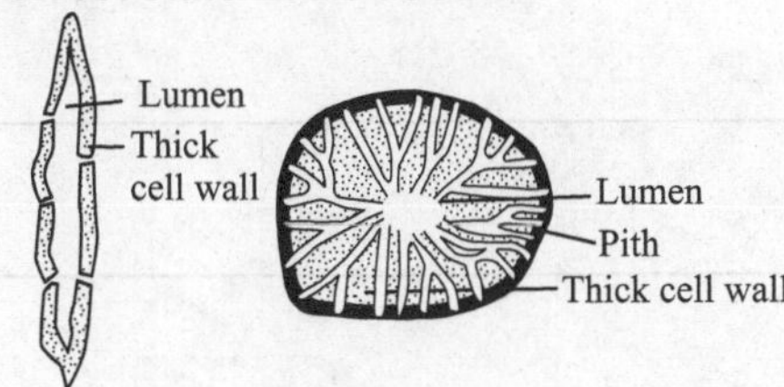

(a) They are usually dead and without protoplasts

(b) They are commonly found in the fruit walls of nuts

(c) It provides mechanical support to organs

(d) It occurs in layers below the epidermis in most of the dicot plants either as homogenous layer or in patches

90. Given below are two statements.

Statement I The first step in urine formation is reabsorption, the tubular epithelial cells in different segments of nephron perform reabsorption either by active or passive mechanisms.

Statement II The glomerular capillary blood pressure causes filtration of blood through 3 layers, i.e. the endothelium of glomerular blood vessels, the epithelium of Bowman's capsule and a basement membrane between these two layers.

In the light of the above statements, choose the correct answer from the options given below.

(a) Statement I is incorrect, but statement II is correct

(b) Both statement I and statement II are correct

(c) Both statement I and statement II are incorrect

(d) Statement I is correct but statement II is incorrect

Response Index

01 ⓐ ⓑ ⓒ ⓓ	26 ⓐ ⓑ ⓒ ⓓ	51 ⓐ ⓑ ⓒ ⓓ	76 ⓐ ⓑ ⓒ ⓓ
02 ⓐ ⓑ ⓒ ⓓ	27 ⓐ ⓑ ⓒ ⓓ	52 ⓐ ⓑ ⓒ ⓓ	77 ⓐ ⓑ ⓒ ⓓ
03 ⓐ ⓑ ⓒ ⓓ	28 ⓐ ⓑ ⓒ ⓓ	53 ⓐ ⓑ ⓒ ⓓ	78 ⓐ ⓑ ⓒ ⓓ
04 ⓐ ⓑ ⓒ ⓓ	29 ⓐ ⓑ ⓒ ⓓ	54 ⓐ ⓑ ⓒ ⓓ	79 ⓐ ⓑ ⓒ ⓓ
05 ⓐ ⓑ ⓒ ⓓ	30 ⓐ ⓑ ⓒ ⓓ	55 ⓐ ⓑ ⓒ ⓓ	80 ⓐ ⓑ ⓒ ⓓ
06 ⓐ ⓑ ⓒ ⓓ	31 ⓐ ⓑ ⓒ ⓓ	56 ⓐ ⓑ ⓒ ⓓ	81 ⓐ ⓑ ⓒ ⓓ
07 ⓐ ⓑ ⓒ ⓓ	32 ⓐ ⓑ ⓒ ⓓ	57 ⓐ ⓑ ⓒ ⓓ	82 ⓐ ⓑ ⓒ ⓓ
08 ⓐ ⓑ ⓒ ⓓ	33 ⓐ ⓑ ⓒ ⓓ	58 ⓐ ⓑ ⓒ ⓓ	83 ⓐ ⓑ ⓒ ⓓ
09 ⓐ ⓑ ⓒ ⓓ	34 ⓐ ⓑ ⓒ ⓓ	59 ⓐ ⓑ ⓒ ⓓ	84 ⓐ ⓑ ⓒ ⓓ
10 ⓐ ⓑ ⓒ ⓓ	35 ⓐ ⓑ ⓒ ⓓ	60 ⓐ ⓑ ⓒ ⓓ	85 ⓐ ⓑ ⓒ ⓓ
11 ⓐ ⓑ ⓒ ⓓ	36 ⓐ ⓑ ⓒ ⓓ	61 ⓐ ⓑ ⓒ ⓓ	86 ⓐ ⓑ ⓒ ⓓ
12 ⓐ ⓑ ⓒ ⓓ	37 ⓐ ⓑ ⓒ ⓓ	62 ⓐ ⓑ ⓒ ⓓ	87 ⓐ ⓑ ⓒ ⓓ
13 ⓐ ⓑ ⓒ ⓓ	38 ⓐ ⓑ ⓒ ⓓ	63 ⓐ ⓑ ⓒ ⓓ	88 ⓐ ⓑ ⓒ ⓓ
14 ⓐ ⓑ ⓒ ⓓ	39 ⓐ ⓑ ⓒ ⓓ	64 ⓐ ⓑ ⓒ ⓓ	89 ⓐ ⓑ ⓒ ⓓ
15 ⓐ ⓑ ⓒ ⓓ	40 ⓐ ⓑ ⓒ ⓓ	65 ⓐ ⓑ ⓒ ⓓ	90 ⓐ ⓑ ⓒ ⓓ
16 ⓐ ⓑ ⓒ ⓓ	41 ⓐ ⓑ ⓒ ⓓ	66 ⓐ ⓑ ⓒ ⓓ	
17 ⓐ ⓑ ⓒ ⓓ	42 ⓐ ⓑ ⓒ ⓓ	67 ⓐ ⓑ ⓒ ⓓ	
18 ⓐ ⓑ ⓒ ⓓ	43 ⓐ ⓑ ⓒ ⓓ	68 ⓐ ⓑ ⓒ ⓓ	
19 ⓐ ⓑ ⓒ ⓓ	44 ⓐ ⓑ ⓒ ⓓ	69 ⓐ ⓑ ⓒ ⓓ	
20 ⓐ ⓑ ⓒ ⓓ	45 ⓐ ⓑ ⓒ ⓓ	70 ⓐ ⓑ ⓒ ⓓ	
21 ⓐ ⓑ ⓒ ⓓ	46 ⓐ ⓑ ⓒ ⓓ	71 ⓐ ⓑ ⓒ ⓓ	
22 ⓐ ⓑ ⓒ ⓓ	47 ⓐ ⓑ ⓒ ⓓ	72 ⓐ ⓑ ⓒ ⓓ	
23 ⓐ ⓑ ⓒ ⓓ	48 ⓐ ⓑ ⓒ ⓓ	73 ⓐ ⓑ ⓒ ⓓ	
24 ⓐ ⓑ ⓒ ⓓ	49 ⓐ ⓑ ⓒ ⓓ	74 ⓐ ⓑ ⓒ ⓓ	
25 ⓐ ⓑ ⓒ ⓓ	50 ⓐ ⓑ ⓒ ⓓ	75 ⓐ ⓑ ⓒ ⓓ	

Performance Scanner

> 90% Excellent !	You have mastered the NEET syllabus. The concepts of this syllabus are on your fingertips. Maintain this momentum.
76-90% Very Good !	You have a good command over the NEET syllabus. Revise it again after a few days and enhance your performance.
60-75% Good !	You have a wide scope to learn for the NEET syllabus. Revise it again.
<60% Not Satisfactory!	You have a long way ahead of you to master the NEET syllabus. Revise it thoroughly.

Scan to fill up online OMR and get AI based Rank prediction on performance

Space for Rough Work

Test Booklet No. **3947372**

Test Booklet Code **NK04**

NEET Knock Offs 4

(NEET Simulator Test)

Name of the Candidate (In Capitals)

____

____

____

Candidate's Signature ________________

Invigilator's Signature ________________

Facsimile signature stamp of center superintendent________________

Important Instructions

- The test is of **1 hours 30 minutes** duration and the Test Booklet contains **90** multiple-choice questions (four options with a single correct answer) from biology.
- Candidates are advised to read all questions before they start attempting the question paper.
- Each questions carries 4 marks. For each correct response, the candidate will get 4 marks. For each incorrect response, one marks will be deducted from the total scores.
- In the event of candidate marking more than one option one mark will be deducted. The maximum marks are 180.
- Use **Blue/Black Point Pen only** for writing particular on this page/ marking response on Answer Sheet.

Do not open this booklet until you start attempting the test

Biology

1. Which of the following steps of plant cell transformation can promote a negative impact on the host?
(a) Increasing specificity towards host
(b) Retaining all the genes of Ti-plasmid
(c) Disarming the vector before transformation
(d) Inserting foreign gene of interest

2. A bacteria has a generation time of 25 minutes. After growing it in N^{14} medium for many generations, it was transferred to N^{15} medium. What will be the ratio of hybrid : heavy DNA after 75 minutes?
(a) 1:2 (b) 1:3
(c) 2:1 (d) 1:1

3. Given below are two statements.
Statement I O^+ person can donate blood safely to Rh^- people all the time.
Statement II People with O^+ blood groups are called universal donors.
In the light of the above statements, choose the correct answer from the options given below.
(a) Statement I is incorrect, but statement II is correct
(b) Both statement I and statement II are correct
(c) Both statement I and statement II are incorrect
(d) Statement I is correct, but statement II is incorrect

4. Which of the following is not a step involved in production of recombinant insulin?
(a) Expression of chain A, B and C peptides
(b) Ligation of gene A and B with plasmids
(c) Transformation in host *E. coli* cells
(d) Ligation by creating disulfide bridges

5. Following are the statements related to chromatin packaging.
I. Satellite DNAs are expressed more easily than other regions.
II. RNA polymerase cannot access heterochromatin regions.
III. Lysine provides covalent linkage between histone and DNA.
IV. Most genes are expressed from the euchromatin regions.
V. DNA binds to positive proteins in the nucleoid of prokaryotes.
Choose the correct statements from the options given below.
(a) I, IV and V (b) II and III
(c) II, IV and V (d) I, II and III

6. Match List I (placental mammals) with List II (marsupial mammals).

List I	List II
A. Anteater	1. Flying phalanger
B. Lemur	2. Tasmanian tiger cat
C. Bobcat	3. Numbat
D. Flying squirrel	4. Spotted cuscus

Choose the correct answer from the options given below.
(a) A-4, B-3, C-2, D-1
(b) A-3, B-4, C-2, D-1
(c) A-4, B-3, C-1, D-2
(d) A-3, B-4, C-1, D-2

7. Given below are two statements; one is labelled as Assertion (A) and the other is labelled as Reason (R).
Assertion (A) Two turns of Krebs' cycle occur per glucose molecule used.
Reason (R) Each turn of Krebs' cycle produces 3NADH, $1FADH_2$ and 1ATP molecules.
In the light of the above statements, choose the correct answer from the options given below.
(a) A is false, but R is true
(b) Both A and R are true and R is the correct explanation of A
(c) Both A and R are true, but R is not the correct explanation of A
(d) A is true, but R is false

8. Which of the following is correct about regulation of respiration by the body?
(a) Decrease in acidosis would activate the chemosensitive area.
(b) Oxygen levels regulate respiration by the rhythm centre.
(c) Increased CO_2 levels can be received by aortic arch.
(d) Pons play a limited role in the regulation of breathing rate.

9. Which of the following is the site of both sexual and asexual stage of *Plasmodium*?
(a) Salivary glands of mosquito
(b) Hepatocytes of human
(c) Intestinal cells of mosquito
(d) Red blood cells of human

10. On centrifuging eukaryotic ribosomes, which of the following would be present in the topmost fraction of the centrifuge tube?
(a) 60 S (b) 40 S
(c) 50 S (d) 30 S

11. Given below are two statements; one is labelled as Assertion (A) and the other is labelled as Reason (R).
Assertion (A) Urine analysis can confirm pregnancy.
Reason (R) Placental hormone relaxin is present in urine.
In the light of the above statements, choose the correct answer from the options given below.
(a) A is false, but R is true
(b) Both A and R are true and R is the correct explanation of A
(c) Both A and R are true, but R is not the correct explanation of A
(d) A is true, but R is false

12. Match List I with List II.

List I	List II
A. Lecithin	1. Concanavalin-A
B. Starch	2. Phosphate
C. Lectin	3. Cell membrane
D. Adenylic acid	4. Secondary structure

Choose the correct answer from the options given below.
(a) A-1, B-4, C-3, D-2
(b) A-3, B-4, C-2, D-1
(c) A-1, B-2, C-3, D-4
(d) A-3, B-4, C-1, D-2

13. Which of the following is the end product of turning the Calvin cycle 18 times?
(a) 3 glucose molecules, 54 ADP, 36 $NADP^+$
(b) 18 glucose molecules, 36 ADP, 18 NADPH
(c) 3 glucose molecules, 54 ATP, 36 NADPH
(d) 18 glucose molecules, 36 ATP, 18 $NADP^+$

14. Given below are two statements; one is labelled as Assertion (A) and the other is labelled as Reason (R).
Assertion (A) Most people find it difficult to sleep when lights are turned on.
Reason (R) There is over secretion of melatonin by the pineal glands under bright light.
In the light of the above statements, choose the correct answer from the options given below.
(a) A is false, but R is true
(b) Both A and R are true and R is the correct explanation of A
(c) Both A and R are true, but R is not the correct explanation of A
(d) A is true, but R is false

15. Following is the diagram of regulatory mechanism in bacteria. Which of the following can be concluded from the diagram?

(a) Glucose is present in the media.
(b) Inducer is added to the media.
(c) Structural genes can be expressed.
(d) RNA polymerase can access operator.

16. Given below are two statements.
Statement I Subsequent encounter from a virus, promotes secretion of antibodies by T-cells.
Statement II T-cells promote self and non-self differentiation by the immune system.

In the light of the above statements, choose the correct answer from the options given below.
(a) Statement I is incorrect, but statement II is correct
(b) Both statement I and statement II are correct
(c) Both statement I and statement II are incorrect
(d) Statement I is correct, but statement II is incorrect

17. Match List I with List II.

	List I		List II
A.	Auxin	1.	Salt tolerance
B.	Gibberellins	2.	Seedless fruits
C.	Abscisic acid	3.	Photosynthesis
D.	Cytokinin	4.	Malting

Choose the correct answer from the options given below.
(a) A-3, B-4, C-1, D-2
(b) A-2, B-4, C-1, D-3
(c) A-3, B-1, C-4, D-2
(d) A-2, B-1, C-4, D-3

18. Which of the following would result in assured genetic variability in offsprings?
(a) Chasmogamy (b) Cleistogamy
(c) Xenogamy (d) Geitonogamy

19. Consider the following conditions.
I. Heat killed S-strain + Heat killed R-strain
II. Heat killed S-strain + Live R-strain
III. Live S-strain + Heat killed R-strain
IV. Live S-strain + Live R-strain
Under which of the following conditions will the mice die?
(a) I and III (b) II only
(c) II, III and IV (d) III and IV

20. A cell becomes committed to division, if it passes
(a) G_1 phase
(b) S-phase
(c) M-phase
(d) G_0-phase

21. Given below are two statements.
Statement I Location of NADP reductase is important in driving ATP synthesis across thylakoid.
Statement II Flow of electrons across CF_1 of ATP synthase causes the gradient to break down.
In the light of the above statements, choose the correct answer from the options given below.
(a) Statement I is incorrect, but statement II is correct
(b) Both statement I and statement II are correct
(c) Both statement I and statement II are incorrect
(d) Statement I is correct, but statement II is incorrect

22. The following diagram shows the functional unit of filtration organs. Which of the following correctly represents the concentration of filtrate with respect to blood?

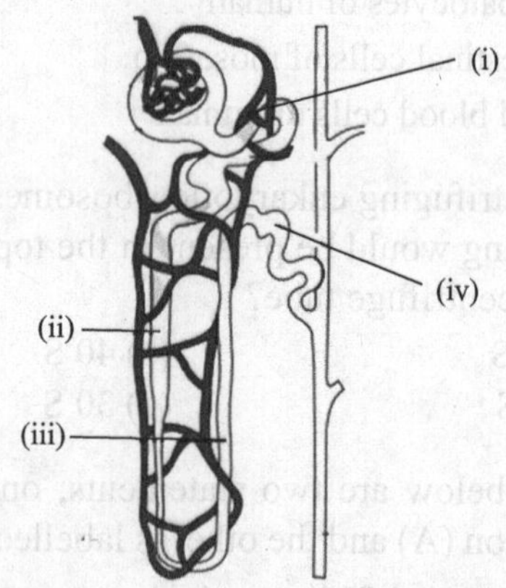

(a) (i) – Isotonic, (ii) – Hypertonic, (iii) – Hypotonic, (iv) – Hypotonic
(b) (i) – Isotonic, (ii) – Hypotonic, (iii) – Hypertonic, (iv) – Hypotonic
(c) (i) – Isotonic, (ii) – Hypertonic, (iii) – Hypotonic, (iv) – Isotonic
(d) (i) – Hypotonic, (ii) – Hypertonic, (iii) – Hypotonic, (iv) – Isotonic

23. Consider the following statements.
I. *Adamsia* has an undifferentiated layer between ectoderm and endoderm.
II. In *Obelia*, polyps produce medusae sexually.
III. Water is drawn into the spongocoel by osculum in sponges.
IV. *Asterias* have a ventrally located mouth and dorsally located anus.
V. No coelom is found in platyhelminthes.
Choose the correct answer from the options given below.
(a) II and III (b) I, IV and V
(c) II, III and IV (d) I, II and III

24. What is the probability of getting a red snapdragon flower, from a cross involving a pink snapdragon with a white snapdragon?

(a) 1/4 (b) 1/2
(c) 3/4 (d) 0

25. Match List I with List II.

	List I	List II
A.	44 + XXY	1. Plants
B.	44 + XO	2. Gynaecomastia
C.	Lack of cytokinesis	3. Palm crease
D.	Aneuploidy	4. Sterile individuals

Choose the correct answer from the options given below.

(a) A-2, B-4, C-3, D-1
(b) A-4, B-2, C-1, D-3
(c) A-4, B-2, C-3, D-1
(d) A-2, B-4, C-1, D-3

26. The following image represents the conduction of action potential through the axon. Consider the steps involved in the process and arrange them in the correct order.

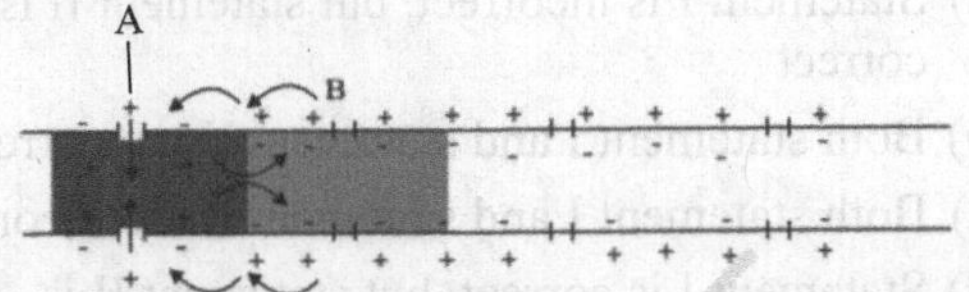

I. Impermeability to Na^+ at A
II. Depolarisation at A
III. Influx of sodium ions
IV. Increased permeability of K^+ at A
V. Repolarisation at A

Choose the correct order from the options given below.

(a) III – I – V – II – IV
(b) III – I – II – V – IV
(c) III – I – II – IV – V
(d) I – III – II – IV – V

27. Which of the following is the correct pathway of sperm movements?

(a) Rete testis, vas deferens, epididymis, vasa efferentia, urethra, urethral meatus
(b) Rete testis, vasa efferentia, epididymis, vas deferens, urethra, ejaculatory duct
(c) Rete testis, vasa efferentia, epididymis, vas deferens, ejaculatory duct, urethra
(d) Rete testis, vas deferens, epididymis, vasa efferentia, urethra, ejaculatory duct

28. What would be the genotype of a person with blood group A, if he marries a woman with B blood group and has a child with blood group O?

(a) I^AI^B (b) I^AI^A
(c) I^AI^A or I^Ai (d) I^Ai

29. Given below are two statements; one is labelled as Assertion (A) and the other is labelled as Reason (R).

Assertion (A) Gene therapy done to early embryos can cure genetic diseases permanently.

Reason (R) Most cells of the human body like B and T-lymphocytes are not immortal.

In the light of the above statements, choose the correct answer from the options given below.

(a) A is false, but R is true
(b) Both A and R are true and R is the correct explanation of A
(c) Both A and R are true, but R is not the correct explanation of A
(d) A is true, but R is false

30. Following is the diagram of a female gametophyte of an angiosperm. Which of the following correctly represents the fate of the labelled parts after fertilisation?

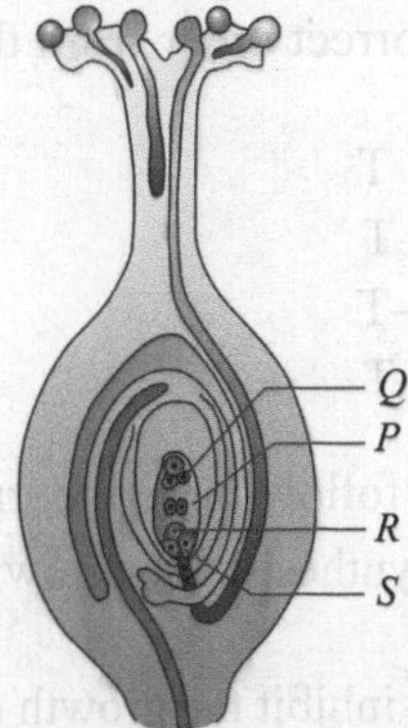

(a) *P* – Endosperm nuclei, *Q* – Disintegrate, *R* – Zygote, *S* – Disintegrate
(b) *P* – Disintegrates, *Q* – Disintegrates, *R* – Zygote, *S* – Endosperm
(c) *P* – Endosperm nuclei, *Q* – Zygote, *R* – Disintegrates, *S* – Disintegrates
(d) *P* – Zygote, *Q* – Disintegrates, *R* – Endosperm nuclei, *S* – Disintegrates

31. In a given food chain, primary consumers have 1000 J of energy for their utilisation. If plants can use only 1% of the solar radiation, then calculate the energy available to the producers.

(a) 10^3 J (b) 10^4 J
(c) 10^6J (d) 100 J

32. Given below are two statements; one is labelled as Assertion (A) and the other is labelled as Reason (R).

Assertion (A) Plasma from recovered patients can provide active immunity to a person.

Reason (R) Plasma contains antibodies which effectively counters antigens.

In the light of the above statements, choose the correct answer from the options given below.

(a) A is false, but R is true
(b) Both A and R are true and R is the correct explanation of A
(c) Both A and R are true, but R is not the correct explanation of A
(d) A is true, but R is false

33. Following are the steps involved in HIV multiplication in the host.

P. Release of naked genome
Q. Fusion of envelope with host cell
R. Integration in host genome
S. Reverse transcription
T. Packing of progeny particles

Choose the correct order from the options given below.

(a) P–Q–S–R–T
(b) Q–P–R–S–T
(c) Q–P–S–R–T
(d) P–Q–R–S–T

34. Which of the following is incorrect about auxin?

(a) Auxin is synthesised by growing roots and shoots
(b) Auxin can inhibit the growth of lateral buds
(c) Auxin causes cell elongation in illuminated side of stem
(d) Auxins promote rooting in cut stems for vegetative propagation

35. Following are the statements related to enzyme action on a substrate.

I. Transition state is characterised by E-P complex formation.
II. In an exothermic process, free energy of P is more than S.
III. Release of enzyme from E-P makes E available for reuse.
IV. Saturation of enzymes brings a stop to the reaction.
V. Enzymes increase the energy barrier between S and P.

Choose the correct statements from the options given below.

(a) III and IV (b) I, II and V
(c) II, III and IV (d) I, IV and V

36. Given below are two statements.

Statement I Successful sewage treatment requires BOD to be increased significantly.

Statement II Flocs growing in secondary treatment, contains bacterial and fungal aggregates.

In the light of the above statements, choose the correct answer from the options given below.

(a) Statement I is incorrect, but statement II is correct
(b) Both statement I and statement II are correct
(c) Both statement I and statement II are incorrect
(d) Statement I is correct, but statement II is incorrect

37. Which of the following happens when a person has been fasting for a prolonged time?

(a) Glycogenesis in liver
(b) Glycogenolysis in blood
(c) Gluconeogenesis in liver
(d) Glycogenesis in adipocytes

38. Consider the following statements with respect to ART.

I. Women who undergo GIFT, develop embryos by *in vitro* fertilisation.
II. IUT is effective for women who does not have a healthy uterus.

III. Males with low sperm count, can use AI for impregnating female partners.
IV. ICSI is just an *in vivo* technique of ART to form blastomeres.

Choose the correct statement from the options given below.
(a) II only (b) I only
(c) IV only (d) III only

39. Given below are two statements.
Statement I Cell plate is the precursor of middle lamella in plant cells.
Statement II Cell division in plant cells proceeds centripetally.
In the light of the above statements, choose the correct answer from the options given below.
(a) Statement I is incorrect, but statement II is correct
(b) Both statement I and statement II are correct
(c) Both statement I and statement II are incorrect
(d) Statement I is correct, but statement II is incorrect

40. Given below are two statements; one is labelled as Assertion (A) and the other is labelled as Reason (R).
Assertion (A) Genes on the same chromosome have higher recombination frequency.
Reason (R) Distance between genes can be calculated by their recombination frequency.
In the light of the above statements, choose the correct answer from the options given below.
(a) A is false, but R is true
(b) Both A and R are true and R is the correct explanation of A
(c) Both A and R are true, but R is not the correct explanation of A
(d) A is true, but R is false

41. Consider the following statements.
I. Grasshopper is an example of female heterogamety.
II. In haplo-diploid sex-determination, males are formed by parthenogenesis.
III. Birds and humans share the same sex-determination mechanism.
IV. *Drosophila* and birds have male homogametic system.

Choose the correct statement from the options given below.
(a) Only II (b) Only I
(c) Only IV (d) Only III

42. Match List I with List II.

List I	List II
A. Lactational amenorrhoea	1. Space child birth
B. Multiload 375	2. No side effects
C. Vaults	3. Spermicidal creams
D. Saheli	4. Non-steroidal

Choose the correct answer from the options given below.
(a) A-1, B-3, C-2, D-4
(b) A-1, B-2, C-3, D-4
(c) A-2, B-1, C-3, D-4
(d) A-2, B-3, C-1, D-4

43. Given below are two statements; one is labelled as Assertion (A) and the other is labelled as Reason (R).
Assertion (A) Competitive exclusion principle does not always hold true in nature.
Reason (R) Fitness of organism is the basis for the competitive exclusion principle.
In the light of the above statements, choose the correct answer from the options given below.
(a) A is false, but R is true
(b) Both A and R are true and R is the correct explanation of A
(c) Both A and R are true, but R is not the correct explanation of A
(d) A is true, but R is false

44. Following are the processes that occurs during gaseous transport within the body
I. Formation of CO_2 from bicarbonates
II. Association of oxygen with haemoglobin
III. Dissociation of carbamino haemoglobin
IV. Right ward shift of dissociation curve
Which of the following conditions are favoured at the tissues?
(a) II and III (b) I, II and III
(c) II and IV (d) Only IV

45. Given below are two statements.

Statement I PCR primers are short, double stranded oligonucleotide sequences.

Statement II The A-T bond is more stable during denaturation step of PCR than G-C.

In the light of the above statements, choose the correct answer from the options given below.

(a) Statement I is incorrect, but statement II is correct
(b) Both statement I and statement II are correct
(c) Both statement I and statement II are incorrect
(d) Statement I is correct, but statement II is incorrect

46. Which of the following techniques can produce genetically different offsprings?

(a) Tissue culture
(b) Explant culture
(c) Micropropagation
(d) Somatic hybridisation

47. Following is the diagram of pBR322 vector of *E. coli.* A foreign gene is cut by *Pst* I restriction enzyme followed by ligation into this vector. Which of the following will happen if the products of transformation are grown in tetracycline containing media?

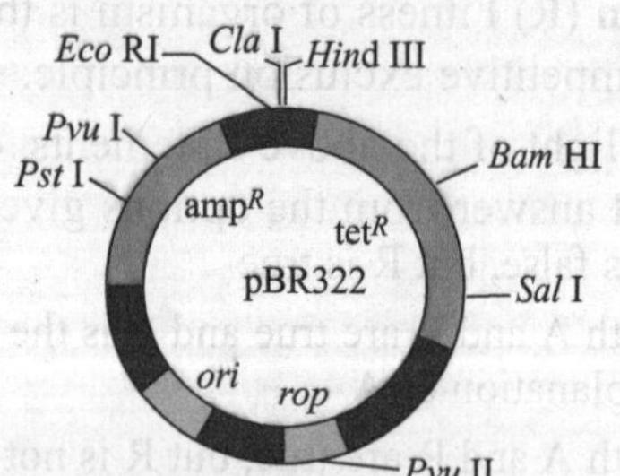

(a) Selection of recombinants from non-transformants
(b) Selection of recombinants from non-recombinants
(c) Selection of transformants from non-transformants
(d) Selection of transformants from non-recombinants

48. Match List I with List II.

List I	List II
A. Pachytene	1. Tetrad
B. Diakinesis	2. Chiasma
C. Diplotene	3. Synapsis
D. Zygotene	4. Terminalisation

Choose the correct answer from the options given below.

(a) A-3, B-4, C-2, D-1
(b) A-3, B-2, C-4, D-1
(c) A-2, B-4, C-1, D-3
(d) A-1, B-4, C-2, D-3

49. Given below are two statements.

Statement I A sparrow eating a seed and an insect is part of more than one trophic level.

Statement II Ecological pyramids do not consider the operation of interlinked food chains.

In the light of the above statements, choose the correct answer from the options given below.

(a) Statement I is incorrect, but statement II is correct
(b) Both statement I and statement II are correct
(c) Both statement I and statement II are incorrect
(d) Statement I is correct, but statement II is incorrect

50. Fungi can be distinguished from algae on the basis of

(a) cellulosic cell wall and heterotrophic nature
(b) chitinous cell wall and no chloroplast
(c) heterotrophic food habit and have chloroplast
(d) autotrophic and have chloroplast

51. Given below are two statements.

Statement I Stability of a community depends on its resilience to disturbances.

Statement II Paul Ehrlich's analogy states rivets of the plane represents ecosystem.

In the light of the above statements, choose the correct answer from the options given below.
(a) Statement I is incorrect, but statement II is correct
(b) Both statement I and statement II are correct
(c) Both statement I and statement II are incorrect
(d) Statement I is correct, but statement II is incorrect

52. Which of the following cannot be done in a simple stirred tank bioreactor?
(a) Addition of acid to maintain pH
(b) Removal of used culture broth
(c) Injecting sterile air from time to time
(d) Adding cells from their stationary phase

53. Match List I with List II.

List I	List II
A. *Propionibacterium*	1. Fungus
B. *Streptococcus*	2. Large holes in cheese
C. Immunosuppressant	3. Clot remover
D. Cholesterol reducing agent	4. Yeast

Choose the correct answer from the options given below.
(a) A-2, B-3, C-1, D-4
(b) A-3, B-2, C-4, D-1
(c) A-3, B-2, C-1, D-4
(d) A-2, B-3, C-4, D-1

54. Which of the following are analogous structures?
(a) Wings of bats and human hand
(b) Wings of birds and flippers of dolphin
(c) Wings of insects and wings of birds
(d) Wings of birds and flipper of whale

55. The ploidy of the nucellus and female gametophyte, respectively are
(a) $2n$ and n (b) $2n$ and $2n$
(c) n and $2n$ (d) n and n

56. Which of the following species are protected by *in situ* conservation?
A. Endemic
B. Endangered
C. Extinct
D. Vulnerable

Choose the correct answer from the options given below.
(a) A and C (b) Only B
(c) A, B and D (d) B and D

57. Priya has blue eyes, while her brother has black eyes. She marries a man with black eyes and give birth to a child having blue eyes. Similarly Priya's brother marries a girl with black eyes. But their son has blue eyes. Based on the above information identify the genotype of Priya's husband and Priya's brother's wife.
(a) BB and bb
(b) Bb and Bb
(c) bb and Bb
(d) Bb and bb

58. Given below are two statements.
Statement I *P. americana* passes through a larval stage during development.
Statement II 13 moulting events lead to successful transition into adults in *P. americana.*
In the light of the above statements, choose the correct answer from the options given below.
(a) Statement I is incorrect, but statement II is correct
(b) Both statement I and statement II are correct
(c) Both statement I and statement II are incorrect
(d) Statement I is correct, but statement II is incorrect

59. Given below are two statements; one is labelled as Assertion (A) and the other is labelled as Reason (R).
Assertion (A) Fluidity of membrane allows transport of substances.
Reason (R) Endocytosis of materials is needed for cell functioning.
In the light of the above statements, choose the correct answer from the options given below.
(a) A is false, but R is true
(b) Both A and R are true and R is the correct explanation of A
(c) Both A and R are true, but R is not the correct explanation of A
(d) A is true, but R is false

60. Match List I with List II.

	List I	List II
A.	Mesosomes	1. Protein synthesis
B.	Polysomes	2. Adherence to surface
C.	Pili	3. DNA replication
D.	Fimbriae	4. Reproduction

Choose the correct answer from the options given below.

(a) A-1, B-3, C-2, D-4
(b) A-1, B-2, C-3, D-4
(c) A-3, B-1, C-4, D-2
(d) A-3, B-1, C-2, D-4

61. Which of the following equations holds true for a population of beetles surviving in an island where they feed on tree leaves and are predated on by a specific bird species?

(a) $dN/dT = rN$
(b) $Nt = N_0e^{rt}$
(c) $dN/dT = (b-d)N$
(d) $dN/dT = rN(K-N/K)$

62. Given below are two statements; one is labelled as Assertion (A) and the other is labelled as Reason (R).

Assertion (A) Association between flatworms and humans is a negative-zero interaction.

Reason (R) Platyhelminthes like *Taenia* are often provided with hooks and suckers.

In the light of the above statements, choose the correct answer from the options given below.

(a) A is false, but R is true
(b) Both A and R are true and R is the correct explanation of A
(c) Both A and R are true, but R is not the correct explanation of A
(d) A is true, but R is false

63. Following are the steps involved in a female for successful fertilisation.

I. Secretion by corpus luteum
II. Stimulation by anterior pituitary
III. Rupture of Graafian follicle
IV. Increased FSH and LH
V. Completion of meiosis-II

Choose the correct order from the options given below.

(a) II-IV-III-V-I
(b) IV-II-III-I-V
(c) IV-II-III-V-I
(d) II-IV-III-I-V

64. Match List I with List II.

	List I	List II
A.	*Gracilaria*	1. Space food
B.	*Chlorella*	2. Agar
C.	*Laminaria*	3. Algin
D.	Phaeophycae	4. Food

Choose the correct answer from the options given below.

(a) A-3, B-4, C-1, D-2
(b) A-2, B-4, C-1, D-3
(c) A-2, B-1, C-4, D-3
(d) A-3, B-1, C-4, D-2

65. Consider the following statements.

I. Gritty texture of diatomaceous earth finds application in filtration.
II. Most red tides are splendid to the eyes, but are usually dead waters.
III. *Euglena* are both partial and conditional heterotrophs of freshwater.
IV. Spores of slime moulds are formed during favourable conditions.

Choose the incorrect statement from the following options.

(a) I only
(b) II only
(c) III only
(d) IV only

66. Given below are two statements; one is labelled as Assertion (A) and the other is labelled as Reason (R).

Assertion (A) A cockroach may survive for few days after chopping off its head.

Reason (R) Most part of nervous system in a cockroach is located in dorsal part of body.

In the light of the above statements, choose the correct answer from the options given below.

(a) A is false, but R is true
(b) Both A and R are true and R is the correct explanation of A
(c) Both A and R are true, but R is not the correct explanation of A
(d) A is true, but R is false

67. Match List I with List II.

List I	List II
A. Nicotine	1. Stimulation of CNS
B. Crack	2. Immuno-stimulant
C. α-interferon	3. Increased epinephrine
D. Serotonin	4. Mast cells

Choose the correct answer from the options given below.
(a) A-3, B-1, C-4, D-2
(b) A-1, B-3, C-4, D-2
(c) A-1, B-3, C-2, D-4
(d) A-3, B-1, C-2, D-4

68. Given below are two statements.
Statement I Karyogamy always succeeds plasmogamy in fungi.
Statement II Karyogamy forms zygospores with a $2n$ ploidy.
In the light of the above statements, choose the correct answer from the options given below.
(a) Statement I is incorrect, but statement II is correct.
(b) Both statement I and statement II are correct.
(c) Both statement I and statement II are incorrect.
(d) Statement I is correct, but statement II is incorrect.

69. Match List I with List II.

List I	List II
A. Hypothalamus	1. Anger and aggression
B. Amygdala	2. Speech
C. Cerebral cortex	3. Hunger
D. Cerebellum	4. Posture

Choose the correct answer from the options given below.
(a) A-2, B-1, C-3, D-4
(b) A-3, B-1, C-2, D-4
(c) A-2, B-4, C-3, D-1
(d) A-1, B-3, C-2, D-4

70. Following are the statements related to expression of genes.
I. Lagging strand synthesis starts after completion of leading strand.
II. RNA polymerase requires elongation factor for adding nucleotides.
III. In *m*RNA, a 5′-modified GTP and 3′-poly A tail, are added post transcription.
IV. ATP hydrolysis provides energy for peptide bond formation in translation.
V. Binding of release factor is homologous to binding of rho in transcription.
Choose the correct statements from the options given below.
(a) IV and V
(b) I, IV and V
(c) I, II and III
(d) III, IV and V

71. Given below are two statements.
Statement I The peripheral arrangement is same in both centrioles and flagella.
Statement II Centrioles arise from the basal bodies formed by cilia or flagella.
In the light of the above statements, choose the correct answer from the options given below.
(a) Statement I is incorrect, but statement II is correct
(b) Both statement I and statement II are correct
(c) Both statement I and statement II are incorrect
(d) Statement I is correct, but statement II is incorrect

72. Following are certain techniques used in molecular biology.
A. PCR
B. Gel electrophoresis
C. Southern blot
D. ELISA
Which of the following can be used to detect a genetic mutation for a congenital disease?
(a) B and C
(b) A and D
(c) C only
(d) A and C

73. Match List I with List II.

List I	List II
A. *Salpa*	1. Notochord persistent in adult
B. *Saccoglossus*	2. Rudimentary stomochord
C. *Branchiostoma*	3. Notochord present only in larvae
D. *Myxine*	4. Jawless fish with circular mouth

Choose the correct answer from the options given below.
(a) A-3, B-4, C-1, D-2
(b) A-1, B-2, C-3, D-4
(c) A-1, B-4, C-3, D-2
(d) A-3, B-2, C-1, D-4

74. Given below are two statements; one is labelled as Assertion (A) and the other is labelled as Reason (R).

Assertion (A) Female gametophyte in *Pinus* cannot exist freely.

Reason (R) Female gametophyte in gymnosperms stays within sporophyte.

In the light of the above statements, choose the correct answer from the options given below.
(a) A is false, but R is true
(b) Both A and R are true and R is the correct explanation of A
(c) Both A and R are true, but R is not the correct explanation of A
(d) A is true, but R is false

75. Following are the statements related to biosynthetic phase of photosynthesis.

I. Biosynthesis occurs through C_3 pathway in maize plants.
II. First stable product of C_4 pathway is a oxaloacetate.
III. $CO_2 : O_2$ ratio is high in the mesophyll cells of C_4 plants.
IV. PEP carboxylase operates in the bundle sheath cells.
V. RuBisCO behaves as a carboxylase in bundle sheath.

Choose the correct statements from the options given below.
(a) I, II and III
(b) I, III and IV
(c) II and V
(d) I, III and V

76. What would be the effect of lowering pH of a medium, on amino acids?

I. Amino acids would behave like a base.
II. NH_3^+ would be formed by protonation.
III. COO^- would be formed by deprotonation.
IV. Amino acids would behave like an acid.

Which of the following is correct from the options given below?
(a) I and III
(b) I and II
(c) II only
(d) IV only

77. Consider the following statements.

I. Detritus is decomposed by anaerobic microorganisms.
II. Release of nutrients from humus restores soil fertility.
III. Moist and warm conditions accelerate decomposition.
IV. For percolation, nutrients should be water soluble.

Choose the incorrect statement from the options given below.
(a) II only
(b) I only
(c) III only
(d) IV only

78. Following is the diagram of a section of a plant. Identify the structure and choose the correct statement w.r.t. them.

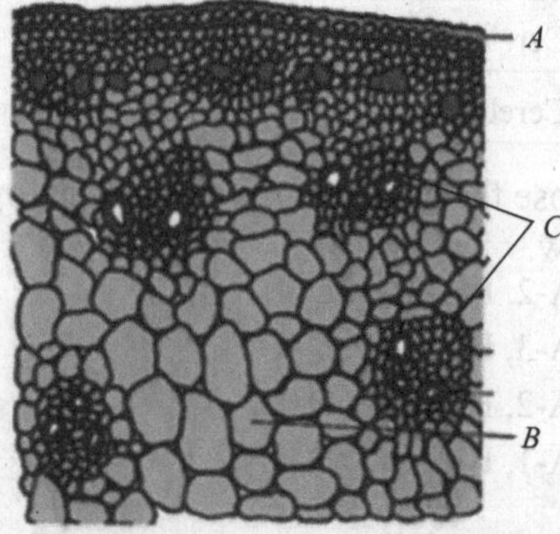

(a) *A* is a collenchymatous hypodermis found in dicot stem.
(b) *C* represents the large number of scattered vascular bundles.
(c) *B* represents pith which has parenchymatous cells with large intercellular spaces.
(d) In between C, medullary rays are present.

79. Match List I with List II.

List I	List II
A. DCT	1. Opposes ANF
B. JGA	2. Increases blood pH
C. Aldosterone	3. Resistance to blood flow
D. Angiotensin-II	4. Increased osmolarity

Choose the correct answer from the options given below.
(a) A-4, B-1, C-2, D-3
(b) A-2, B-1, C-4, D-3
(c) A-4, B-3, C-2, D-1
(d) A-2, B-1, C-3, D-4

80. Which of the following is incorrect about dicot roots?
(a) Cells lying between the vascular bundles are actively dividing.
(b) Casparian strips resist the movement of water through them.
(c) The stele makes up for the tissues lying interior to endodermis.
(d) Epiblema layer extends in the form of unicellular root hair.

81. Following shows the arrangement of ovules in an ovary. Which of the following is correct about the placentation being represented?

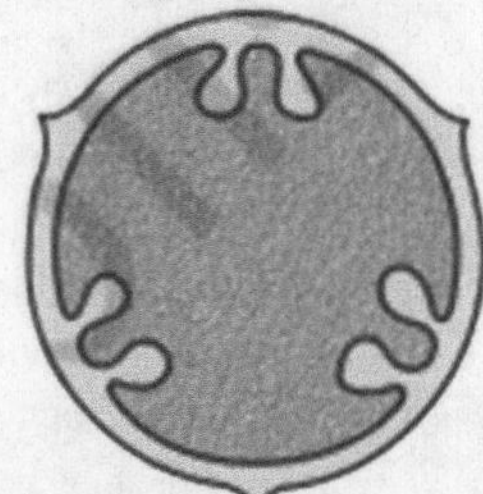

(a) Absence of septum
(b) Multilocular ovary
(c) Ovules borne on ridge
(d) Presence of false septum

82. Match List I with List II.

List I	List II
A. Tympanum	1. Smell
B. Sensory papillae	2. Reproduction
C. Nasal epithelium	3. Touch
D. Copulatory pads	4. Balance

Choose the correct answer from the options given below.
(a) A-4, B-2, C-3, D-1
(b) A-4, B-3, C-1, D-2
(c) A-2, B-4, C-3, D-1
(d) A-2, B-4, C-1, D-3

83. Which of the following evolutionary theory represents the idea of common ancestry?
(a) Saltation theory
(b) Natural selection
(c) Theory of use and disuse
(d) Branching descent

84. Given below are two statements; one is labelled as Assertion (A) and the other is labelled as Reason (R).

Assertion (A) While rotating the thumb, we use our wrist as well.

Reason (R) Free rotation of thumb is allowed by the fluid between the bones.

In the light of the above statements, choose the correct answer from the options given below.
(a) A is false, but R is true
(b) Both A and R are true and R is the correct explanation of A
(c) Both A and R are true, but R is not the correct explanation of A
(d) A is true, but R is false

85. Following are statements related to generation of heart beat.

I. Atria are the first chambers to be contracted by SAN.
II. Contraction of ventricles require impulse conduction through SAN.
III. Increase in ventricular pressure is related to generation of sound 'lub'.
IV. Pumping of blood out of the ventricles produces the sound 'dub'.

V. Ventricular diastole is marked as a short positive wave on ECG.

Choose the correct statements from the options given below.
(a) II and III
(b) I, III and V
(c) I, II and IV
(d) I, IV and V

86. Which of the following happens in the common cockroach?
(a) Malpighian tubules are excretory organs projecting out from the colon
(b) Carbon dioxide is transported by haemoglobin in plasma
(c) Nitrogenous excretory product is urea
(d) The food is grinded by mandibles and gizzard

87. Match List I with List II.

	List I	List II
A.	*Pheretima*	1. Proboscis
B.	*Pinctada*	2. Parapodia
C.	*Nereis*	3. Radula
D.	*Balanoglossus*	4. Nephridia

Choose the correct answer from the options given below.
(a) A-4, B-3, C-2, D-1
(b) A-2, B-1, C-4, D-3
(c) A-2, B-3, C-4, D-1
(d) A-4, B-1, C-2, D-3

88. Breakdown of proteins by carboxypeptidase requires
(a) Zn as a prosthetic group
(b) Zn as a coordination metal
(c) Zn as an apoenzyme
(d) Zn as a co-enzyme

89. Given below are two statements; one is labelled as Assertion (A) and the other is labelled as Reason (R).

Assertion (A) Competitive inhibition is reversible in nature.

Reason (R) Competition is independent of substrate levels.

In the light of the above statements, choose the correct answer from the options given below.
(a) A is false, but R is true
(b) Both A and R are true and R is the correct explanation of A
(c) Both A and R are true, but R is not the correct explanation of A
(d) A is true, but R is false

90. Consider the following statements.

I. Auxin and cytokinin promotes cell growth in the same way.
II. Gibberellins and abscisic acid promote seed germination.
III. Respiratory climactic promotes senescence process.
IV. Gibberellins are widely used in micropropagation techniques.

Choose the correct statement from the options given below.
(a) II only (b) I only (c) IV only (d) III only

Response Index

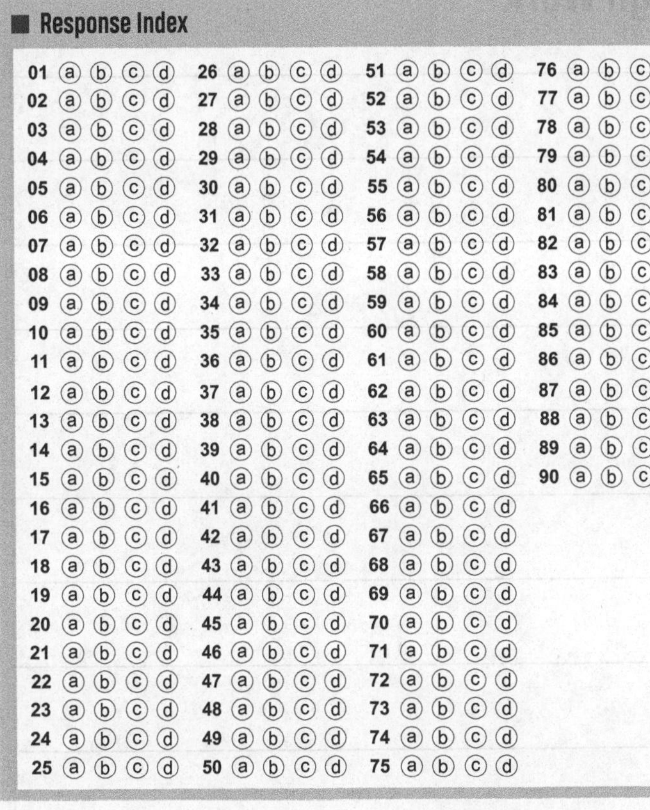

Performance Scanner

> 90% Excellent ! You have mastered the NEET syllabus. The concepts of this syllabus are on your fingertips. Maintain this momentum.

76-90% Very Good ! You have a good command over the NEET syllabus. Revise it again after a few days and enhance your performance.

60-75% Good ! You have a wide scope to learn for the NEET syllabus. Revise it again.

<60% Not Satisfactory! You have a long way ahead of you to master the NEET syllabus. Revise it thoroughly.

Scan to fill up online OMR and get AI based Rank prediction on performance

Space for Rough Work

Test Booklet No. **3947373**

Test Booklet Code **NK05**

NEET Knock Offs 5

(NEET Simulator Test)

Name of the Candidate (In Capitals)

____

____

____

Candidate's Signature ____________

Invigilator's Signature ____________

Facsimile signature stamp of center superintendent____________

Important Instructions

- The test is of **1 hours 30 minutes** duration and the Test Booklet contains **90** multiple-choice questions (four options with a single correct answer) from biology.
- Candidates are advised to read all questions before they start attempting the question paper.
- Each questions carries 4 marks. For each correct response, the candidate will get 4 marks. For each incorrect response, one marks will be deducted from the total scores.
- In the event of candidate marking more than one option one mark will be deducted. The maximum marks are 180.
- Use **Blue/Black Point Pen only** for writing particular on this page/ marking response on Answer Sheet.

Do not open this booklet until you start attempting the test

Biology

1. An organism has 18×10^6 base pairs and completes the process of replication within 300 minutes then the average rate of polymerisation is
(a) 3000 bp/s
(b) 1000 bp/s
(c) 30000 bp/s
(d) 10000 bp/s

2. Which of the following is correct about the inhibition of succinic dehydrogenase?
(a) Malonate resembles the active site of succinic dehydrogenase
(b) Succinate concentration does not affect malonate inhibition
(c) Binding of malonate to succinate, makes it unavailable
(d) Presence of malonate, decreases the rate of the reaction

3. Given below are two statements.
Statement I *Cry* gene cloned in a plant protects it from all insect pests.
Statement II *Bt* toxins can cause intestinal perforations and lysis in insects.
In the light of the above statements, choose the correct answer from the options given below.
(a) Statement I is incorrect, but statement II is correct
(b) Both statement I and statement II are correct
(c) Both statement I and statement II are incorrect
(d) Statement I is correct, but statement II is incorrect

4. What is the probability of having a colourblind child, if an unaffected woman with a colour blind father, marries a colourblind man?
(a) 1/2
(b) 1/4
(c) 3/4
(d) 1

5. Following is the diagrammatic representation of gene expression. Which of the following is correct with respect to the given process?

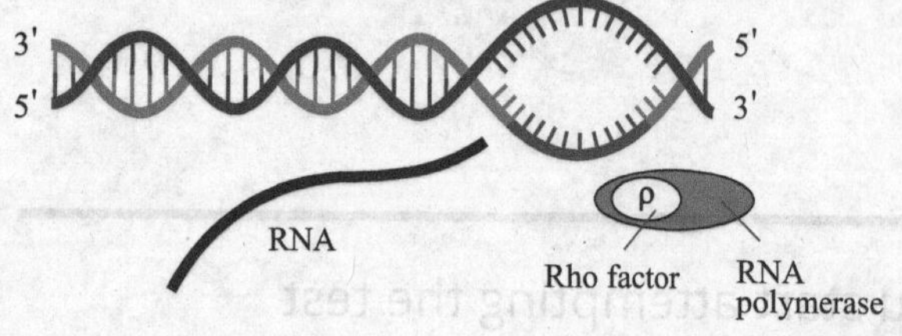

(a) RNA polymerase II initiates transcription at the promoter.
(b) Release factor causes termination of transcription.
(c) Transcription proceeds along with translation in bacteria.
(d) *m*RNA undergoes polyadenylation after termination.

6. A typical bilobed anther of an angiosperm has
(a) 2 thecae, 2 sporangia
(b) 2 thecae, 4 sporangia
(c) 4 thecae, 4 sporangia
(d) 4 thecae, 2 sporangia

7. Given below are two statements; one is labelled as Assertion (A) and the other is labelled as Reason (R).
Assertion (A) Organ implants often face immune rejection.
Reason (R) CMI by the B-cells causes graft rejection reactions.
In the light of the above statements, choose the correct answer from the options given below.
(a) A is false, but R is true
(b) Both A and R are true and R is the correct explanation of A
(c) Both A and R are true, but R is not the correct explanation of A
(d) A is true, but R is false

8. Match List I with List II.

	List I	List II
A.	Mesorchium	1. Aids reproduction
B.	Copulatory pad	2. Attaches testes
C.	Bidder's canal	3. Tactile organ
D.	Papillae	4. Contains Vasa efferentia

Choose the correct answer from the options given below.

	A	B	C	D
(a)	4	2	1	3
(b)	4	1	2	3
(c)	2	1	4	3
(d)	2	3	4	1

9. CGU, CGC, CGA and CGG coding for the same amino acid Arginine, proves that the genetic code is

(a) Universal (b) Degenerate
(c) Contiguous (d) Triplet

10. Following are the statements related to translation of *m*RNA.

I. 3-D structure of *t*RNA appear like clover leaf.
II. Aminoacylation provides energy for peptide bond formation.
III. In prokaryotes, 50S subunit binds to the *m*RNA first.
IV. For every codon of genetic code, there is a cognate *t*RNA.
V. H-bonds stabilise the codon-anticodon interaction.

Choose the correct set of statements from the options given below.

(a) II and V (b) I, III and IV
(c) II, IV and V (d) I, II and IV

11. How can plants growing in extreme hot weather be protected?

(a) By adding synthetic auxin to their roots to initiate rooting.
(b) By spraying them with gibberellins to delay senescence.
(c) By administering them with abscisic acid.
(d) By spraying them with cytokinin or zeatin.

12. Which of the following statement about blood coagulation is incorrect?

(a) Injured site releases factors essential for activating enzyme cascade.
(b) Thrombokinase activity is dependent on presence of calcium ions.
(c) Inactive fibrinogen in plasma is an insoluble protein component.
(d) Fibrin threads form the meshwork that trap red blood cells.

13. Given below are two statements; one is labelled as Assertion (A) and the other is labelled as Reason (R).

Assertion (A) Head sitting on the vertebral column shows considerable rotation.

Reason (R) Cartilaginous joints between adjacent vertebrae allows limited movement.

In the light of the above statements, choose the correct answer from the options given below.

(a) A is false, but R is true
(b) Both A and R are true and R is the correct explanation of A
(c) Both A and R are true, but R is not the correct explanation of A
(d) A is true, but R is false

14. Which of the following is correct about mechanism of enzyme action?

(a) There is no conformational change associated with an enzyme.
(b) Active site of an enzyme catalyses bond alteration in substrate.
(c) Substrate concentration and reaction kinetics increase exponentially.
(d) Formation of E-P complex is more permanent than formation of E-S.

15. Given below are two statements.

Statement I Competition can be considered to be a negative zero interaction.

Statement II Competitive exclusion principle works in case of unlimited resources.

In the light of the above statements, choose the the correct answer from the options given below.

(a) Statement I is incorrect, but statement II is correct
(b) Both statement I and statement II are correct
(c) Both statement I and statement II are incorrect
(d) Statement I is correct, but statement II is incorrect

16. How does $FADH_2$ produced during TCA cycle contribute towards energy generation?

(a) Reduction of $FADH_2$ by NADH dehydrogenase
(b) Oxidation of $FADH_2$ by Ubiquinone
(c) Reduction of $FADH_2$ to FAD^+
(d) Oxidation of FAD^+ by Ubiquinol

17. Match List I with List II.

List I	List II
A. Secondary constriction	1. Centromere
B. Nucleolus	2. NOR
C. Primary constriction	3. Ribosomes
D. Kinetochores	4. Attachment of spindle fibres

Choose the correct answer from the options given below.
(a) A-1, B-3, C-2, D-4
(b) A-2, B-3, C-1, D-4
(c) A-1, B-4, C-2, D-3
(d) A-2, B-4, C-1, D-3

18. Consider the following statements about a biomacromolecule. Identify the correct one.
(a) The primary structure of proteins starts with a C-terminal amino acid.
(b) Hydrogen bonds stabilise the β-helices and β-sheets of primary structure.
(c) Disulfide bonds stabilise tertiary structure, having functional importance.
(d) Appearance of subunits of a protein is apparent in tertiary structure

19. Consider the following conditions.
I. High pO_2
II. Acidosis
III. Low temperature
IV. High pCO_2
Which of the following condition(s) would be ideal for the reversal of oxyhaemoglobin dissociation?
(a) II and IV
(b) I and III
(c) I only
(d) I, III and IV

20. Match List I with List II.

List I	List II
A. Choanocytes	1. *Obelia*
B. Stomochord	2. *Sepia*
C. Nematocyst	3. *Sycon*
D. Radula	4. *Saccoglossus*

Choose the correct answer from the options given below.

	A	B	C	D
(a)	3	4	1	2
(b)	3	4	2	1
(c)	3	1	4	2
(d)	3	2	1	4

21. Which of the following is not a contributory factor for extinction of species caused by introduction of an alien species?
(a) Competition between the invasive and local species
(b) Predatory effect of the invasive species on the local ones
(c) Absence of possible predator of the invasive species
(d) Reduced reproductive ability of the native species

22. If the gross primary productivity in a grassland ecosystem is 2500 (k cal m^{-2}) yr^{-1} and the available biomass to the heterotrophs is 1100 (k cal m^{-2}) yr^{-1}, then calculate the loss suffered due to respiration.
(a) 600 (k cal m^{-2}) yr^{-1}
(b) 3600 (k cal m^{-2}) yr^{-1}
(c) 400 (k cal m^{-2}) yr^{-1}
(d)1400 (k cal m^{-2}) yr^{-1}

23. Given below are two statements.

Statement I Amino acids behave as acids in alkaline media.

Statement II pH affects the protonation ability of amino acids.

In the light of the above statements, choose the correct answer from the options given below:
(a) Statement I is incorrect, but statement II is correct
(b) Both statement I and statement II are correct
(c) Both statement I and statement II are incorrect
(d) Statement I is correct, but statement II is incorrect

24. If allolactose is added in absence of glucose, which of the following genes products ensure activation of the *lac* operon?
(a) *i* gene
(b) *z* gene
(c) *a* gene
(d) *y* gene

25. Consider the following statements

I. Carpel in angiosperms is equivalent to megasporangium in gymnosperms and pteridophytes.

II. Most of the angiosperms possess orthotropous ovule.

III. The functional megaspore that develops into the embryo sac is located at the chalazal end.

IV. Antipodals and synergids are haploid cells that degenerate after fertilisation.

Choose the correct set of statements from the options given below.

(a) III and IV (b) I and II
(c) I, III and IV (d) I, II and III

26. Given below are two statements.

Statement I There are four energy generating steps in partial oxidation of glucose.

Statement II Four ATP molecules are produced, while two are consumed in glycolysis.

In the light of the above statements, choose the most appropriate answer from the options given below.

(a) Statement I is incorrect, but statement II is correct
(b) Both statement I and statement II are correct
(c) Both statement I and statement II are incorrect
(d) Statement I is correct, but statement II is incorrect

27. Which of the following is not a possible reason for maintaining a higher proton concentration in the thylakoid lumen?

(a) Photolysis of water
(b) Electron transport by plastoquinone
(c) ATP synthesis by ATP synthase
(d) Activity of NADP reductase

28. Which of the following is correct about C_3 plants?

(a) RuBP behaves as oxygenase when $O_2 : CO_2$ is less.
(b) Primary carbon acceptor is 3-C molecule.
(c) RuBP forms a 2-C compound as an carboxygenase.
(d) First stable product in C_3 is a 3-C compound.

29. Following is the diagrammatic representation of an anatropous ovule. Which of the following is the correct about the parts labelled as P to S?

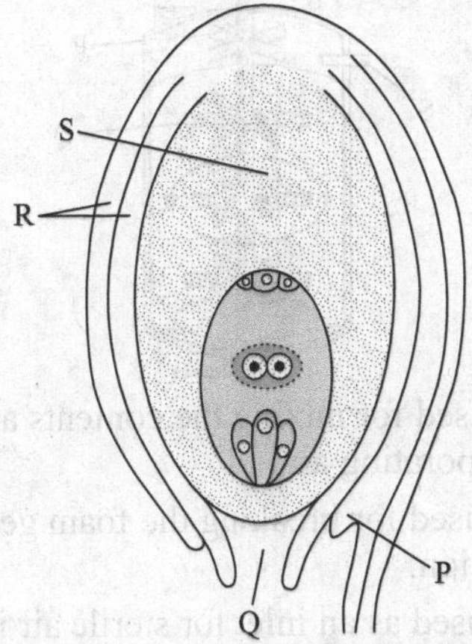

(a) P is the point of attachment of ovule to the placenta.
(b) Q represents the end where antipodals are located.
(c) R develops into protective seed coat post fertilisation.
(d) S develops into the endosperm and provides nourishment.

30. Match List I with List II.

List I	List II
A. *Australopithecus*	1. Man-like being
B. *Homo erectus*	2. Use of weapons
C. *Ramapithecus*	3. Non-vegetarian
D *Homo habilis*	4. Vegetarian

Choose the correct answer from the options given below.

	A	B	C	D
(a)	1	3	2	4
(b)	2	1	3	4
(c)	1	3	4	2
(d)	2	3	1	4

31. Following is the image of a stirred tank bioreactor. Which of the following is the correct function of the marked label?

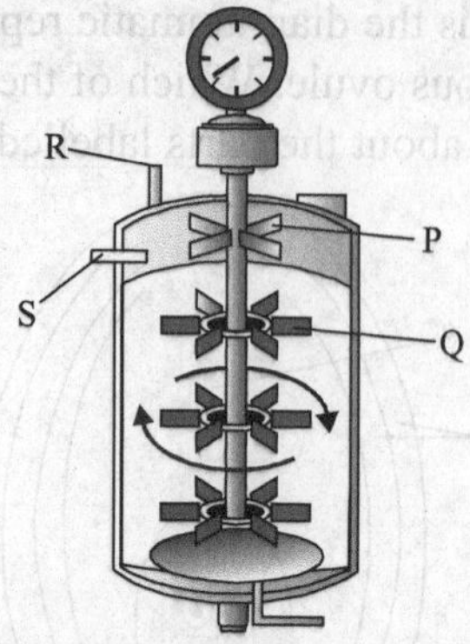

(a) P is used for mixing the contents and incorporating air.

(b) Q is used for breaking the foam generated agitation.

(c) R is used as an inlet for sterile air into the reactor.

(d) S is used for high temperature mediated sterilisation.

32. Which of the following is incorrect about sea urchin?

(a) They have an endoskeleton supported mostly by calcium salts.

(b) They have a body cavity or coelom lined by mesoderm.

(c) Respiration is taken care of by water vascular system.

(d) Water enters their body through opening called osculum.

33. Given below are two statements; one is labelled as Assertion (A) and the other is labelled as Reason (R).

Assertion (A) Bulliform cells help in water conservation in plants.

Reason (R) In monocot leaves, turgidity is maintained by bulliform cells.

In the light of the above statements, choose the correct answer from the options given below.

(a) A is false, but R is true

(b) Both A and R are true and R is the correct explanation of A

(c) Both A and R are true, but R is not the correct explanation of A

(d) A is true, but R is false

34. If a scientist discovers a drug from a plant, using the information received from locals of a forest, he cannot file patent on grounds of

(a) Bioprospecting (b) Biopiracy

(c) Lack of novelty (d) Plagiarism

35. Which of the following is not an ex-situ conservation technique?

(a) Cryopreservation of gametes

(b) *In vivo* fertilisation of gametes

(c) Micropropagation techniques

(d) Storage in seed banks

36. Which of the following cannot be concluded from the Law of dominance?

I. Discrete units called factors control characters of an organism.

II. Alleles of a pair separate from each other during gametogenesis.

III. In a dissimilar pair of factors, one member of the pair dominates.

IV. The dominant allele masks the expression of its recessive counterpart.

Choose the correct answer from the options given below.

(a) Only II (b) Only I

(c) Only III (d) Only IV

37. Consider the following food chain, and choose the correct statement from the following.

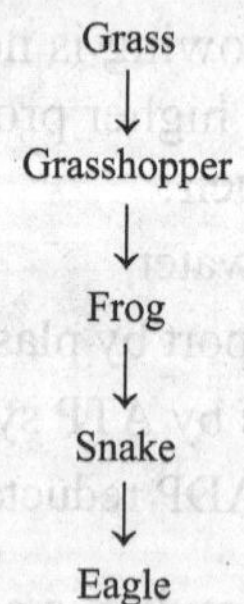

I. Snakes, at a given point, cannot be a part of more than one food chain.

II. The frogs are the tertiary consumers in the given food chain.

III. The detritus food chain is not operative in this terrestrial network.

IV. The major flow of energy takes place through DFC and not by GFC.

Choose the correct answer from the options given below.
(a) Only II (b) Only I
(c) Only III (d) Only IV

38. Consider the following statements.
A. Genetically engineered insulin does not trigger immune reaction in the host.
B. C-peptide is present only in proinsulin and is absent in the mature insulin forms.
C. Insulin synthesised by genetic engineering lacks disulfide bridges.
D. Assembly of insulin peptide was the main challenge in rDNA technology.
Choose the incorrect statement from the options given below.
(a) B only (b) A only
(c) D only (d) C only

39. Given below are two statements.
Statement I Collecting spices is the narrowly utilitarian argument for biodiversity conservation.
Statement II A plant with no direct benefit to humans, is protected under ethical argument.
In the light of the above statements, choose the the correct answer from the options given below
(a) Statement I is incorrect, but statement II is correct
(b) Both statement I and statement II are correct
(c) Both statement I and statement II are incorrect
(d) Statement I is correct, but statement II is incorrect

40. Following is the graphical representation of sigmoid growth curve observed in plants in culture. Which of the following accounts for the initial lag in the growth curve?

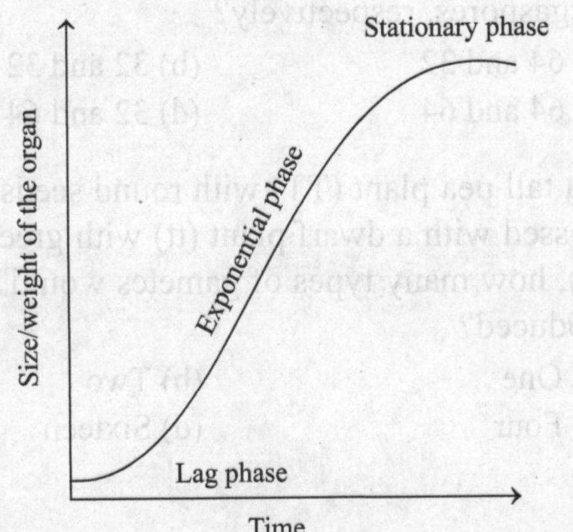

(a) Depletion of nutrients in the media
(b) Release of secondary metabolites
(c) Acclimatisation to new conditions
(d) Competition for same resources

41. Consider the following statements and choose the incorrect statement.
(a) Multiple adaptive radiation taking place in one area leads to convergent evolution.
(b) Branching descent theory of evolution speaks about common ancestral connections.
(c) Natural selection theory by Darwin states that variations occur due to random mutations.
(d) Theory of use and disuse proposed by Lamarck is based on acquired traits.

42. Which of the following is responsible for the development of Rheumatoid arthritis?
(a) Failure of T-cell maturation in the thymus
(b) Failure of self-nonself cell differentiation by T-cells
(c) Reactivity to self-antigens mediated by B-cells
(d) Production of antibodies against self cells by T cells

43. Following are the steps involved in cloning a gene.
I. Restriction digestion of gene and vector
II. Competent cell and heat shock treatment
III. Selection on antibiotic containing media
IV. Ligation between foreign gene and vector
V. PCR amplification of gene of interest
Choose the correct order from the options given below.
(a) V-I-IV-III-II (b) V-I-IV-II-III
(c) I-V-IV-III-II (d) I-V-IV-II-III

44. Consider the following statements.
I. Middle lamella is the precursor of cell plate.
II New cell walls are deposited at the periphery.
III. Plasmodesmata cannot cross middle lamella.
IV. Algae and plants have different wall composition.
Choose the correct statement from the options given below.
(a) Only II (b) Only I
(c) Only IV (d) Only III

45. Which of the following transport processes would be used in transporting lysine and arginine amino acids across the cell membrane?
(a) Active transport
(b) Osmosis
(c) Facilitated diffusion
(d) Simple diffusion

46. Given below are two statements.
Statement I Notochord is persistent through out the lives of all chordates.
Statement II Chordates have a dorsal heart in contrast to non-chordates.
In the light of the above statements, choose the the correct answer from the options given below.
(a) Statement I is incorrect, but statement II is correct
(b) Both statement I and statement II are correct
(c) Both statement I and statement II are incorrect
(d) Statement I is correct, but statement II is incorrect

47. Choose the correct statement about cockroaches.
(a) Spiracles circulate air within the body of the cockroach.
(b) Spermatophores are collection of sperms in male testes.
(c) Oothecae are coverings that encapsulate unfertilised eggs.
(d) Spermatheca are reproductive structures in female cockroaches.

48. Which of the following is incorrect about Hardy-Weinberg equilibrium?
(a) It is resilient to environmental stress.
(b) Natural selection favours change in allelic frequency.
(c) Genetic drift is operational in case of a sudden natural disaster.
(d) Genetics of founders change significantly from initial population.

49. Given below are two statements; one is labelled as Assertion (A) and the other is labelled as Reason (R).
Assertion (A) Annealing temperature is lesser than denaturation during PCR.
Reason (R) Single stranded primers anneal to complementary strands of DNA.
In the light of the above statement, choose the correct answer from the options given below.
(a) A is false, but R is true
(b) Both A and R are true and R is the correct explanation of A
(c) Both A and R are true, but R is not the correct explanation of A
(d) A is true, but R is false

50. How can we ensure that bushy appearance of tea plantations are maintained?
(a) Spraying with indole-3-acetic acid
(b) Trimming the lateral branches
(c) Chopping off shoot tips
(d) Adding auxin along with manure

51. Given below are two statements; one is labelled as Assertion (A) and the other is labelled as Reason (R).
Assertion (A) Cells with DNA damage often exit G_1-phase.
Reason (R) DNA damage or mutation can be lethal, if accumulated.
In the light of the above statement, choose the correct answer from the options given below.
(a) A is false, but R is true
(b) Both A and R are true and R is the correct explanation of A
(c) Both A and R are true, but R is not the correct explanation of A
(d) A is true, but R is false

52. If the megaspore mother cell has 64 chromosomes in a gymnosperm, what would be the chromosome number of the nucellus and megaspores, respectively?
(a) 64 and 32
(b) 32 and 32
(c) 64 and 64
(d) 32 and 64

53. If a tall pea plant (TT) with round seeds (RR) is crossed with a dwarf plant (tt) with green seeds (rr), how many types of gametes would be produced?
(a) One
(b) Two
(c) Four
(d) Sixteen

54. Given below are two statements.

Statement I Autoimmune disorder is a condition where the body defense mechanism recognises its own cells as foreign bodies.

Statement II Rheumatoid arthritis is a condition where the body rejects self-cells causing degeneration of skeletal muscles.

In the light of the above statements, choose the correct answer from the options given below.

(a) Statement I is incorrect, but statement II is correct

(b) Both statement I and statement II are correct

(c) Both statement I and statement II are incorrect

(d) Statement I is correct, but statement II is incorrect

55. Which of the following is not a feature of *Labeo rohita*?

(a) Oviparity is observed in this organism.

(b) Operculum covers the respiratory organ.

(c) Skin covered with placoid scales.

(d) Absence of larval stage in development.

56. Following are the statements related to conduction of action potential.

I. Inner membrane of axon remains negative at rest.

II. Depolarisation occurs due to influx of sodium ions.

III. Repolarisation is linked to sodium ion permeability.

IV. Repolarisation returns excitability of the membrane.

V. Na-K pump uses ATP to pump two Na^+ outside.

Choose the correct answer from the options given below.

(a) II and III (b) I, III and V

(c) I, II and IV (d) II, III and V

57. Which of the following events of prophase are reversed in telophase?

I. Duplication of centrosomes

II. Disappearance of nucleolus

III. Condensation of chromatin

IV. Splitting of centromere

Choose the correct answer from the options given below.

(a) Only II (b) II and III

(c) Only IV (d) I and III

58. The increased strength during an emergency is associated with

(a) Glycogenolysis stimulated by Glucagon

(b) Glycogenesis stimulated by insulin

(c) Glycogenolysis stimulated by epinephrine

(d) Gluconeogenesis stimulated by Cortisol

59. A person who met with an accident, sometimes shows breathing difficulty due to injury in the

(a) Hypothalamus of forebrain.

(b) Association area of cerebral cortex.

(c) Medulla of hind brain.

(d) Medulla or pons of hind brain.

60. Consider the following statements.

I. Products of photolysis are accumulated in the lumen of thylakoid.

II. Photolysis replaces the electrons removed from PS-I through PS-II.

III. In the absence of 680 nm light, cyclic flow of e^- drives ATP synthesis.

IV. PS-I and PS-II are both operational in the stroma lamellae.

Choose the incorrect statement from the options given below.

(a) Only II (b) Only I

(c) Only III (d) Only IV

61. Following are the statements related to dicot stems.

I. Vascular bundles are situated in different radii.

II. They cannot form secondary xylem and phloem.

III. Pericycle forms semilunar patches of sclerenchyma.

IV. Protoxylem lies inner to the metaxylem.

V. Pith harbours large intercellular spaces.

Choose the correct answer from the options given below.

(a) Only II and III (b) Only I, IV and V

(c) Only III, IV and V (d) Only I, II and III

62. Which of the following hormone secretion is steadily increased if remnant of Graafian follicle does not degenerate?
(a) Oestrogen
(b) Relaxin
(c) Progesterone
(d) HCG

63. Given below are two statements.
Statement I Smooth muscles of endometrium contracts to induce labor during pregnancy.
Statement II Fusion of egg and sperm releases the cell cycle arrest of secondary oocyte.
In the light of the above statements, choose the correct answer from the options given below.
(a) Statement I is incorrect, but statement II is correct
(b) Both statement I and statement II are correct
(c) Both statement I and statement II are incorrect
(d) Statement I is correct, but statement II is incorrect

64. Which of the following statements regarding human respiratory system are true?
I. Oxygen diffuses from alveoli to blood.
II. CO_2 diffuses from blood to alveoli.
III. Diaphragm relaxes as the air is entering the lungs.
IV. Vital capacity is the maximum volume of air that can be exhaled after maximum inhalation.
V. Respiration involves utilisation of oxygen by the cells for catabolic reactions and resultant release of CO_2.
Choose the correct answer from the options given below.
(a) Statements I, II, IV and V are correct.
(b) Statements I, III, IV and V are correct.
(c) Statements II, III, IV and V are correct.
(d) Only statement II is true, rest are incorrect.

65. Following diagram shows a stage in the breathing process. Which of the following is correct with respect to the diagram?

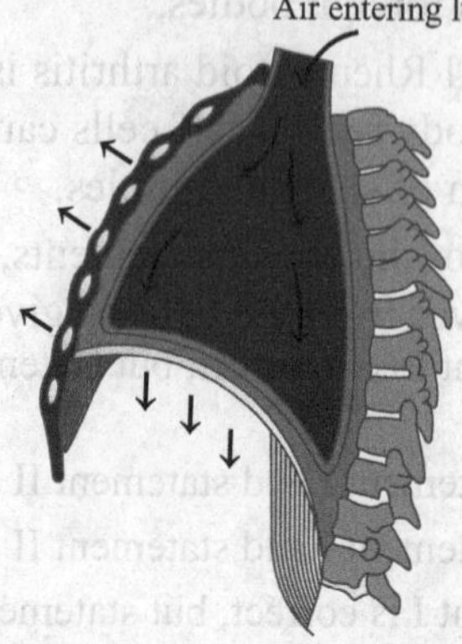

(a) Contraction of external intercostal muscles which causes an increase in the antero-posterior axis
(b) Contraction of diaphragm muscles which causes an increase in the volume of dorso-ventral axis
(c) An overall increase in thoracic volume which causes a decrease in the pulmonary volume
(d) The pressure in the lungs is negative compared to the outside atmospheric pressure

66. Which of the following does not show coevolution of prey species to employ defensive strategies against predators?
(a) *Calotropis* secreting poisonous glycosides
(b) Thorns of Cactus or *Acacia*
(c) Cactus feeding moth in Australia
(d) Distasteful Monarch butterflies

67. Euglenoids have more flexibility in their structures due to presence of
(a) Cellulose
(b) Glycans
(c) Proteins
(d) Starch

68. Given below are two statements; one is labelled as Assertion (A) and the other is labelled as Reason (R).

Assertion (A) Hepatocytes have abundant smooth ER.

Reason (R) Smooth ER is involved in synthesis of lipids.

In the light of the above statements, choose the correct answer from the options given below.
(a) A is false, but R is true
(b) Both A and R are true and R is the correct explanation of A
(c) Both A and R are true, but R is not the correct explanation of A
(d) A is true, but R is false

69. Following are the steps that are operational when there is a fall in GFR.

I. Activation and secretion from JG cells
II. Release of aldosterone
III. Stimulation of adrenal cortex
IV. Conversion of angiotensinogen
V. Reabsorption of Na^+ from renal tubules

Choose the correct order from the options given below.
(a) I-II-IV-III-V (b) II-I-III-IV-V
(c) I-IV-II-III-V (d) I-IV-III-II-V

70. Given below are two statements.

Statement I Larger areas will have much steeper slope in species-area curve.

Statement II Steeper slope shows that species richness and area increases at same rate, in case of larger continents.

In the light of the above statements, choose the the correct answer from the options given below.
(a) Statement I is incorrect, but statement II is correct
(b) Both statement I and statement II are correct.
(c) Both statement I and statement II are incorrect
(d) Statement I is correct, but statement II is incorrect

71. How is metaphase I different from metaphase II?
(a) Microtubules attach to kinetochores of sister chromatids in metaphase-I.
(b) Bivalent chromosomes arrange at the equatorial plate in metaphase-II.
(c) Spindle fibres attach to the kinetochores of homologues in metaphase-I.
(d) Homologues are separated from each other in the stage following metaphase-II.

72. Match List I with List II.

List I	List II
A. Alternate	1. Neem
B. Pinnate	2. Silk cotton
C. Opposite	3. China rose
D. Palmate	4. Guava

Choose the correct answer from the options given below.

	A	B	C	D
(a)	3	4	1	2
(b)	3	1	4	2
(c)	2	1	3	4
(d)	3	1	2	4

73. Given below are two statements; one is labelled as Assertion (A) and the other labelled as Reason (R).

Assertion (A) Lichens accumulate in areas with a high AQI.

Reason (R) Lichens are indicators of pollution in an area.

In the light of the above statement, choose the correct answer from the options given below.
(a) A is false, but R is true.
(b) Both A and R are true and R is the correct explanation of A.
(c) Both A and R are true, but R is not the correct explanation of A
(d) A is true, but R is false

74. Given below are two statements.

Statement I Zygotene is the best stage to observe bivalents.

Statement II Synapsis is assisted by the synaptonemal complex.

In the light of the above statements, choose the correct answer from the options given below.
(a) Statement I is incorrect, but statement II is correct
(b) Both statement I and statement II are correct
(c) Both statement I and statement II are incorrect
(d) Statement I is correct, but statement II is incorrect

75. Which of the following is the correct reason for appearance of blue coloration on adding iodine to a bread loaf?
(a) Unbranched structure of cellulose
(b) Presence of homopolymer glycogen
(c) Presence of secondary helices
(d) Formation of cellulose-I_2 complex

76. Following is the diagrammatic representation of ECG wave pattern. Which of the following is the correct match of the labelled parts?

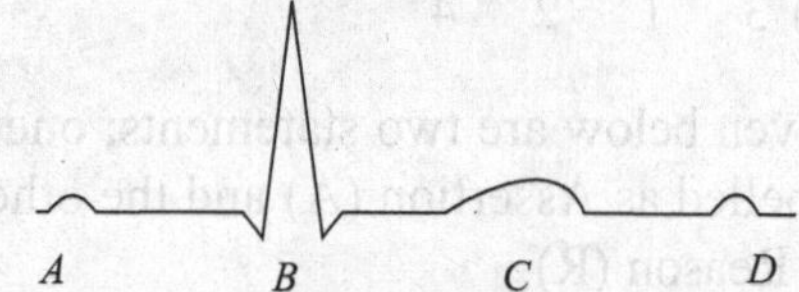

(a) A= Action potential at SAN, B = Generation of Dub, C = Closure of semilunar valves
(b) A= Action potential at SAN, B = Generation of Lub, C = Closure of semilunar valves
(c) A= Action potential at SAN, B = Generation of Dub, C = Closure of atrioventricular valves
(d) A= Action potential at SAN, B = Generation of Lub, C = Closure of atrioventricular valves

77. Match List I with List II.

	List I		List II
A.	Pectinases	1.	Prevention of heart attacks
B.	Lipases	2.	Suppression of immune system
C.	Streptokinase	3.	Processing of bottle fruit juices
D.	Cyclosporin A	4.	Removal of grease from laundry

Choose the correct answer from the options given below.

	A	B	C	D
(a)	4	3	2	1
(b)	3	2	1	4
(c)	3	4	2	1
(d)	3	4	1	2

78. Given below are two statements.
Statement I Sporophyte has independent existence in mosses.
Statement II Capsule and seta have a ploidy of n in bryophytes.
In the light of the above statements, choose the the correct answer from the options given below.
(a) Statement I is incorrect, but statement II is correct
(b) Both statement I and statement II are correct
(c) Both statement I and statement II are incorrect
(d) Statement I is correct, but statement II is incorrect

79. Given below are two statements; one is labelled as Assertion (A) and the other is labelled as Reason (R).
Assertion (A) Enzyme catalysed reactions slow down at higher temperatures.
Reason (R) Enzymes catalyse a reaction by lowering the activation energy.
In the light of the above statements, choose the correct answer from the options given below.
(a) A is false, but R is true
(b) Both A and R are true and R is the correct explanation of A
(c) Both A and R are true, but R is not the correct explanation of A
(d) A is true, but R is false

80. Which of the following statement about Gramineae is incorrect?
(a) Flowers have 3-6 androecium and are polyandrous.
(b) Ovary is superior and hypogynous.
(c) Flowers contain a stalk or pedicel.
(d) Ovaries show basal placentation.

81. Following are the steps involved in matching DNA sample from crime scene with possible suspect.

I. Isolation of DNA from blood/tissue
II. Hybridisation with radiolabelled probe
III. Blotting on nitrocellulose/nylon
IV. Agarose gel electrophoresis
V. Restriction digestion

Choose the correct order from the options given below.

(a) I-III-V-IV-II (b) I-III-IV-V-II
(c) I-III-V-II-IV (d) I-V-IV-III-II

82. Given below are two statements.

Statement I PCT and DCT secrete more H^+ ions, if blood becomes too alkaline.

Statement II Active transport of urea maintains osmotic gradient for concentration of filtrate.

In the light of the above statements, choose the correct answer from the options given below.

(a) Statement I is incorrect, but statement II is correct
(b) Both statement I and statement II are correct
(c) Both statement I and statement II are incorrect
(d) Statement I is correct, but statement II is incorrect

83. Following diagram shows the sliding model for muscle contraction. Which of the following is correct about the diagram being represented?

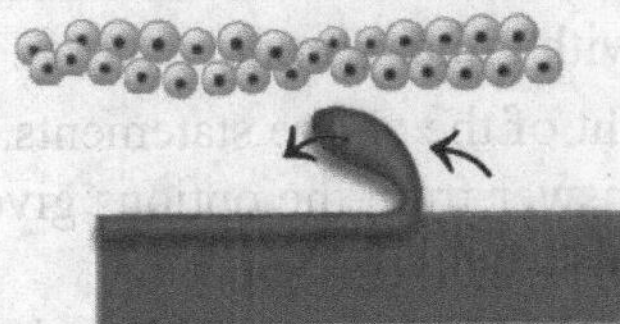

(a) Sequestration of Ca^{2+} in the sarcoplasmic reticulum
(b) Unmasking of the actin binding sites by troponin
(c) Contraction of I-band and disappearance of H-zone
(d) Decrease in the length of A-band and Z lines

84. Carefully examine the given figure.

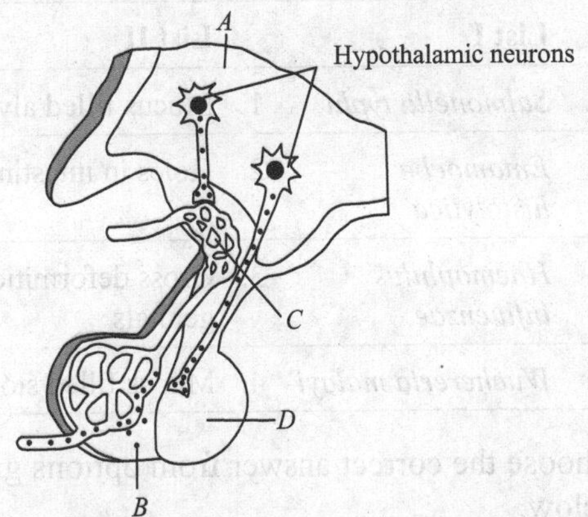

Which of the following option correctly identifies structures labelled as A, B, C, and D in the figure above, along with their corresponding functions.

(a) C-Hypothalamus – Produces prolactin hormone
(b) D-Posterior pituitary – Releases oxytocin and vasopressin
(c) B-Portal circulation – Supplies blood from hypothalamus to posterior pituitary
(d) A-Anterior pituitary – Releases FSH and LH

85. Given below are some situations.

I. A person who recovered from chicken pox.
II. Sucking breast milk of mother by an infant.
III. Receiving plasma from a recently recovered patient.
IV. Injection received after a venomous snake bite.
V. Pulse polio drops received by children.

Based on your understanding, identify which of the following situations are examples of passive immunity?

(a) II and III
(b) II, III and IV
(c) I, III and V
(d) I and IV

86. Match List I with List II.

List I	List II
A. *Salmonella typhi*	1. Mucus filled alveoli
B. *Entamoeba histolytica*	2. Holes in intestine
C. *Haemophilus influenzae*	3. Gross deformities of genitals
D. *Wuchereria malayi*	4. Mucus filled stool

Choose the correct answer from options given below.

(a) A-2, B-4, C-1, D-3
(b) A-2, B-1, C-4, D-3
(c) A-3, B-1, C-4, D-2
(d) A-3, B-4, C-1, D-2

87. Following are the statements related to different worms of the kingdom Animalia.

I. Sexual dimorphism is apparent in pseudocoelomates.
II. Metamerism are characteristics of annelids.
III. Only flatworms are endoparasites in nature.
IV. All the three types of worms have three germ layers.
V. Mesoderm is present in pouches in *Fasciola*.

Choose the correct answer from the options given below.

(a) II and III only
(b) I, II and IV
(c) II, III and V
(d) I, IV and V

88. Match List I with List II.

List I	List II
A. Oxytocin	1. Milk secretion
B. Melatonin	2. Milk ejection
C. Prolactin	3. Thermoregulation
D. Epinephrine	4. Piloerection

Choose the correct answer from the options given below.

	A	B	C	D
(a)	1	3	2	4
(b)	2	3	1	4
(c)	1	4	2	3
(d)	2	4	1	3

89. Given below are two statements.

Statement I Neoplastic cells metastasise to form secondary tumours.

Statement II Biological agents can also trigger neoplastic transformation.

In the light of the above statements, choose the correct answer from the options given below.

(a) Statement I is incorrect, but statement II is correct
(b) Both statement I and statement II are correct
(c) Both statement I and statement II are incorrect
(d) Statement I is correct, but statement II is incorrect

90. Given below are two statements; one is labelled as Assertion (A) and the other is labelled as Reason (R).

Assertion (A) A test cross is used to determine the genotype of a dominant phenotype.

Reason (R) In a test cross, dominant individual is crossed with either parent.

In the light of the above statements, choose the correct answer from the options given below.

(a) A is false, but R is true
(b) Both A and R are true and R is the correct explanation of A
(c) Both A and R are true, but R is not the correct explanation of A
(d) A is true, but R is false

Scan to fill up online OMR and get AI based Rank prediction on performance

Response Index

01 (a) (b) (c) (d)	26 (a) (b) (c) (d)	51 (a) (b) (c) (d)	76 (a) (b) (c) (d)
02 (a) (b) (c) (d)	27 (a) (b) (c) (d)	52 (a) (b) (c) (d)	77 (a) (b) (c) (d)
03 (a) (b) (c) (d)	28 (a) (b) (c) (d)	53 (a) (b) (c) (d)	78 (a) (b) (c) (d)
04 (a) (b) (c) (d)	29 (a) (b) (c) (d)	54 (a) (b) (c) (d)	79 (a) (b) (c) (d)
05 (a) (b) (c) (d)	30 (a) (b) (c) (d)	55 (a) (b) (c) (d)	80 (a) (b) (c) (d)
06 (a) (b) (c) (d)	31 (a) (b) (c) (d)	56 (a) (b) (c) (d)	81 (a) (b) (c) (d)
07 (a) (b) (c) (d)	32 (a) (b) (c) (d)	57 (a) (b) (c) (d)	82 (a) (b) (c) (d)
08 (a) (b) (c) (d)	33 (a) (b) (c) (d)	58 (a) (b) (c) (d)	83 (a) (b) (c) (d)
09 (a) (b) (c) (d)	34 (a) (b) (c) (d)	59 (a) (b) (c) (d)	84 (a) (b) (c) (d)
10 (a) (b) (c) (d)	35 (a) (b) (c) (d)	60 (a) (b) (c) (d)	85 (a) (b) (c) (d)
11 (a) (b) (c) (d)	36 (a) (b) (c) (d)	61 (a) (b) (c) (d)	86 (a) (b) (c) (d)
12 (a) (b) (c) (d)	37 (a) (b) (c) (d)	62 (a) (b) (c) (d)	87 (a) (b) (c) (d)
13 (a) (b) (c) (d)	38 (a) (b) (c) (d)	63 (a) (b) (c) (d)	88 (a) (b) (c) (d)
14 (a) (b) (c) (d)	39 (a) (b) (c) (d)	64 (a) (b) (c) (d)	89 (a) (b) (c) (d)
15 (a) (b) (c) (d)	40 (a) (b) (c) (d)	65 (a) (b) (c) (d)	90 (a) (b) (c) (d)
16 (a) (b) (c) (d)	41 (a) (b) (c) (d)	66 (a) (b) (c) (d)	
17 (a) (b) (c) (d)	42 (a) (b) (c) (d)	67 (a) (b) (c) (d)	
18 (a) (b) (c) (d)	43 (a) (b) (c) (d)	68 (a) (b) (c) (d)	
19 (a) (b) (c) (d)	44 (a) (b) (c) (d)	69 (a) (b) (c) (d)	
20 (a) (b) (c) (d)	45 (a) (b) (c) (d)	70 (a) (b) (c) (d)	
21 (a) (b) (c) (d)	46 (a) (b) (c) (d)	71 (a) (b) (c) (d)	
22 (a) (b) (c) (d)	47 (a) (b) (c) (d)	72 (a) (b) (c) (d)	
23 (a) (b) (c) (d)	48 (a) (b) (c) (d)	73 (a) (b) (c) (d)	
24 (a) (b) (c) (d)	49 (a) (b) (c) (d)	74 (a) (b) (c) (d)	
25 (a) (b) (c) (d)	50 (a) (b) (c) (d)	75 (a) (b) (c) (d)	

Performance Scanner

> 90% Excellent !	You have mastered the NEET syllabus. The concepts of this syllabus are on your fingertips. Maintain this momentum.
76-90% Very Good !	You have a good command over the NEET syllabus. Revise it again after a few days and enhance your performance.
60-75% Good !	You have a wide scope to learn for the NEET syllabus. Revise it again.
<60% Not Satisfactory!	You have a long way ahead of you to master the NEET syllabus. Revise it thoroughly.

Scan for online NEET knock offs

Space for Rough Work

Test Booklet No. **3947374**

Test Booklet Code **NC1**

MEDACE
NEET (UG)
SELF ASSESSMENT KIT

NEET Chronicles 1

(2023 Paper)

Name of the Candidate (In Capitals)

____

____

____

Candidate's Signature ____________

Invigilator's Signature ____________

Facsimile signature stamp of center superintendent________________

Important Instructions

- The test is of **1 hours 40 minutes** duration and the Test Booklet contains **100** multiple-choice questions (four options with a single correct answer) from Botany and Zoology. 50 questions in each subject are divided into two sections (A and B) as per the details given below.
  - **Section A** shall consist of **35 (Thirty-five)** questions in each subject (Questions Nos - 1 to 35, 51 to 85). All questions are compulsory.
  - **Section B** shall consist of **15 (Fifteen)** questions in each subject (Question Nos- 36 to 50, 86 to 100). In Section B, a candidate needs to attempt any 10 (Ten) questions out of 15 (Fifteen) in each subject. **Candidates are advised to read all 15 questions in each subject of Section B** before they start attempting the question paper. In the event of a candidate attempting more than ten questions. **The first ten questions answered by the candidate shall be evaluated.**
- Each question carries 4 marks. For each correct response, the candidate will get 4 marks. For each incorrect response, one mark will be deducted from the total scores.
- Use **Blue/Black Point Pen only** for writing particulars on this page/ marking response on Answer Sheet.

Do not open this booklet until you start attempting the test

Botany (Q. No. 1-50)

Section-A

1. Among eukaryotes, replication of DNA takes place in

(a) S-phase (b) G_1-phase
(c) G_2-phase (d) M-phase

2. Cellulose does not form blue colour with iodine because

(a) it is a helical molecule
(b) it does not contain complex helices and hence cannot hold iodine molecules
(c) it breaks down when iodine reacts with it
(d) it is a disaccharide

3. In gene gun method used to introduce alien DNA into host cells, microparticles of .... metal are used.

(a) zinc (b) tungsten and gold
(c) silver (d) copper

4. What is the function of tassels in the corn cob?

(a) To trap pollen grains
(b) To disperse pollen grains
(c) To protect seeds
(d) To attract insects

5. Given below are two statements; one is labelled as Assertion (A) and the other is labelled as Reason (R).

Assertion (A) Late wood has fewer xylary elements with narrow vessels.

Reason (R) Cambium is less active in winters.

In the light of the above statements, choose the correct answer from the options given below.

(a) Both A and R are true, but R is not the correct explanation of A
(b) A is true, but R is false
(c) A is false, but R is true
(d) Both A and R are true and R is the correct explanation of A

6. The historic convention on biological diversity, 'The Earth Summit' was held in Rio de Janeiro in the year

(a) 1992 (b) 1986
(c) 2002 (d) 1985

7. What is the role of RNA polymerase-III in the process of transcription in eukaryotes?

(a) Transcription of *t*RNA, 5 *sr*RNA and *sn*RNA
(b) Transcription of precursor of *m*RNA
(c) Transcription of only *sn*RNAs
(d) Transcription of *r*RNAs (28S, 18S and 5.8S)

8. Identify the pair of heterosporous pteridophytes among the following

(a) *Selaginella* and *Salvinia*
(b) *Psilotum* and *Salvinia*
(c) *Equisetum* and *Salvinia*
(d) *Lycopodium* and *Selaginella*

9. Given below are two statements.

Statement I The forces generated by transpiration can lift a xylem-sized column of water over 130 metres height.

Statement II Transpiration cools leaf surfaces sometimes 10 to 15 degrees, by evaporative cooling.

In the light of the above statements, choose the most appropriate answer from the options given below.

(a) Both statement I and statement II are incorrect
(b) Statement I is correct, but statement II is incorrect
(c) Statement I is incorrect, but statement II is correct
(d) Both statement I and statement II are correct

10. The reaction centre in PS-II has an absorption maxima at

(a) 700 nm (b) 660 nm
(c) 780 nm (d) 680 nm

11. Among 'The Evil Quartet', which one is considered the most important cause driving extinction of species?
(a) Over exploitation for economic gain
(b) Alien species invasions
(c) Co-extinctions
(d) Habitat loss and fragmentation

12. Which of the following stages of meiosis involves division of centromere?
(a) Metaphase-II (b) Anaphase-II
(c) Telophase (d) Metaphase-I

13. Spraying of which of the following phytohormone on juvenile conifers helps in hastening the maturity period, that leads to early seed production?
(a) Gibberellic acid
(b) Zeatin
(c) Abscisic acid
(d) Indole-3-butyric acid

14. Identify the correct statements.
A. Detritivores perform fragmentation.
B. The humus is further degraded by some microbes during mineralisation.
C. Water soluble inorganic nutrients go down into the soil and get precipitated by a process called leaching.
D. The detritus food chain begins with living organisms.
E. Earthworms breakdown detritus into smaller particles by a process called catabolism.
Choose the correct answer from the options given below.
(a) B, C and D (b) C, D and E
(c) D, E and A (d) A, B and C

15. Which micro-nutrient is required for splitting of water molecule during photosynthesis?
(a) Molybdenum (b) Magnesium
(c) Copper (d) Manganese

16. Large, colourful, fragrant flowers with nectar are seen in
(a) bird pollinated plants
(b) bat pollinated plants
(c) wind pollinated plants
(d) insect pollinated plants

17. Movement and accumulation of ions across a membrane against their concentration gradient can be explained by
(a) facilitated diffusion
(b) passive transport
(c) active transport
(d) osmosis

18. The thickness of ozone in a column of air in the atmosphere is measured in terms of
(a) decibels (b) decameter
(c) kilobase (d) Dobson units

19. Upon exposure to UV radiation, DNA stained with ethidium bromide will show
(a) bright blue colour
(b) bright yellow colour
(c) bright orange colour
(d) bright red colour

20. Unequivocal proof that DNA is the genetic material was first proposed by
(a) Alfred Hershey and Martha Chase
(b) Avery, MacLeod and McCarty
(c) Wilkins and Franklin
(d) Frederick Griffith

21. In tissue culture experiments, leaf mesophyll cells are put in a culture medium to form callus. This phenomenon may be called as
(a) dedifferentiation
(b) development
(c) senescence
(d) differentiation

22. Given below are two statements; one is labelled as Assertion (A) and the other is labelled as Reason (R).

Assertion (A) ATP is used at two steps in glycolysis.

Reason (R) First ATP is used in converting glucose into glucose-6-phosphate and second ATP is used in conversion of fructose-6-phosphate into fructose-1,6- bisphosphate.

In the light of the above statements, choose the correct answer from the options given below.

(a) Both A and R are true, R is not the correct explanation of A
(b) A is true, but R is false
(c) A is false, but R is true
(d) Both A and R are true and R is the correct explanation of A

23. The process of appearance of recombination nodules occurs at which sub-stage of prophase-I in meiosis?

(a) Pachytene (b) Diplotene
(c) Diakinesis (d) Zygotene

24. In the equation, GPP – R = NPP
GPP is Gross Primary Productivity.
NPP is Net Primary Productivity. R here is ....

(a) Respiratory quotient
(b) Respiratory loss
(c) Reproductive allocation
(d) Photosynthetically active radiation

25. The phenomenon of pleiotropism refers to

(a) presence of two alleles, each of two genes controlling a single trait
(b) a single gene affecting multiple phenotypic expression
(c) more than two genes affecting a single character
(d) presence of several alleles of a single gene controlling a single cross-over

26. During the purification process for recombinant DNA technology, addition of chilled ethanol precipitates out

(a) DNA
(b) histones
(c) polysaccharides
(d) RNA

27. In angiosperm, the haploid, diploid and triploid structures of a fertilised embryo sac sequentially are

(a) antipodals, synergids and primary endosperm nucleus
(b) synergids, zygote and primary endosperm nucleus
(c) synergids, antipodals and polar nuclei
(d) synergids, primary endosperm nucleus and zygote

28. Axile placentation is observed in

(a) China rose, Beans and Lupin
(b) Tomato, *Dianthus* and Pea
(c) China rose, *Petunia* and Lemon
(d) Mustard, Cucumber and Primrose

29. Which hormone promotes internode/petiole elongation in deep water rice?

(a) Kinetin (b) Ethylene
(c) 2, 4-D (d) GA_3

30. Given below are two statements; one is labelled as Assertion (A) and the other is labelled as Reason (R).

Assertion (A) The first stage of gametophyte in the life cycle of moss is protonema stage.

Reason (R) Protonema develops directly from spores produced in capsule.

In the light of the above statements, choose the most appropriate answer from the options given below.

(a) Both A and R are true, but R is not the correct explanation of A
(b) A is correct, but R is not correct
(c) A is not correct, but R is correct
(d) Both A and R are correct and R is the correct explanation of A

31. Frequency of recombination between gene pairs on same chromosome as a measure of the distance between genes to map their position on chromosome, was used for the first time by

(a) Sutton and Boveri
(b) Alfred Sturtevant
(c) Henking
(d) Thomas Hunt Morgan

32. Family-Fabaceae differs from Solanaceae and Liliaceae. With respect to the stamens, pick out the characteristics specific to family-Fabaceae, but not found in Solanaceae or Liliaceae.

(a) Polyadelphous and epipetalous stamens
(b) Monoadelphous and monothecous anthers
(c) Epiphyllous and dithecous anthers
(d) Diadelphous and dithecous anthers

33. How many ATP and $NADPH_2$ are required for the synthesis of one molecule of glucose during Calvin cycle?

(a) 18 ATP and 12 $NADPH_2$
(b) 12 ATP and 16 $NADPH_2$
(c) 18 ATP and 16 $NADPH_2$
(d) 12 ATP and 12 $NADPH_2$

34. Expressed Sequence Tags (ESTs) refers to

(a) All genes that are expressed as proteins
(b) All genes whether expressed or unexpressed
(c) Certain important expressed genes
(d) All genes that are expressed as RNA

35. Given below are two statements.

Statement I Endarch and exarch are the terms often used for describing the position of secondary xylem in the plant body.

Statement II Exarch condition is the most common feature of the root system.

In the light of the above statements, choose the most appropriate answer from the options given below.

(a) Both statement I and statement II are false
(b) Statement I is correct, but statement II is false
(c) Statement I is incorrect, but statement II is true
(d) Both statement I and statement II are true

Section-B

36. Which of the following combination is required for chemiosmosis?

(a) Membrane, proton pump, proton gradient, NADP synthase
(b) Proton pump, electron gradient, ATP synthase
(c) Proton pump, electron gradient, NADP synthase
(d) Membrane, proton pump, proton gradient, ATP synthase

37. How many different proteins does the ribosome consist of?

(a) 60 (b) 40
(c) 20 (d) 80

38. Given below are two statements; one is labelled as Assertion (A) and the other is labelled as Reason (R).

Assertion (A) A flower is defined as modified shoot wherein the shoot apical meristem changes to floral meristem.

Reason (R) Internode of the shoot gets condensed to produce different floral appendages laterally at successive nodes instead of leaves.

In the light of the above statements, choose the correct answer from the options given below:

(a) Both A and R are true, but R is not the correct explanation of A
(b) A is true, but R is false
(c) A is false, but R is true
(d) Both A and R are true and R is the correct explanation of A

39. Match List I with List II.

List I		List II
A. M-Phase	I.	Proteins are synthesised
B. G_2-Phase	II.	Inactive phase
C. Quiescent stage	III.	Interval between mitosis and initiation of DNA replication
D. G_1-Phase	IV.	Equational division

Choose the correct answer from the options given below.

(a) A-IV, B-II, C-I, D-III
(b) A-IV, B-I, C-II, D-III
(c) A-II, B-IV, C-I, D-III
(d) A-III, B-II, C-IV, D-I

40. Main steps in the formation of recombinant DNA are given below. Arrange these steps in a correct sequence.

A. Insertion of recombinant DNA into the host cell.
B. Cutting of DNA at specific location by restriction enzyme.
C. Isolation of desired DNA fragment.

D. Amplification of gene of interest using PCR.

Choose the correct answer from the options given below.

(a) C, A, B, D (b) C, B, D, A
(c) B, D, A, C (d) B, C, D, A

41. Given below are two statements.

Statement I Gause's 'Competitive exclusion principle' states that two closely related species competing for the same resources cannot co-exist indefinitely and competitively inferior one will be eliminated eventually.

Statement II In general, carnivores are more adversely affected by competition than herbivores.

In the light of the above statements, choose the correct answer from the options given below.

(a) Both statement I and statement II are false
(b) Statement I is true, but statement II is false
(c) Statement I is false, but Statement II is true
(d) Both statement I and statement II are true

42. Match List-I with List-II.

List-I		List-II
A. Cohesion	I.	More attraction in liquid phase
B. Adhesion	II.	Mutual attraction among water molecules
C. Surface tension	III.	Water loss in liquid phase
D. Guttation	IV.	Attraction towards polar surfaces

Choose the correct answer from the options given below.

(a) A-IV, B-III, C-II, D-I
(b) A-III, B-I, C-IV, D-II
(c) A-II, B-I, C-IV, D-III
(d) A-II, B-IV, C-I, D-III

43. Malonate inhibits the growth of pathogenic bacteria by inhibiting the activity of

(a) amylase
(b) lipase
(c) dinitrogenase
(d) succinic dehydrogenase

44. Match List I with List II.

List I	List II
A. Oxidative decarboxylation	I. Citrate synthase
B. Glycolysis	II. Pyruvate dehydrogenase
C. Oxidative phosphorylation	III. Electron transport system
D. Tricarboxylic acid cycle	IV. EMP pathway

Choose the correct answer from the options given below.

(a) A-II, B-IV, C-I, D-III
(b) A-III, B-I, C-II, D-IV
(c) A-II, B-IV, C-III, D-I
(d) A-III, B-IV, C-II, D-I

45. Which of the following statements are correct about Klinefelter's syndrome?

A. This disorder was first described by Langdon Down (1866).
B. Such an individual has overall masculine development. However, the feminine development is also expressed.
C. The affected individual is short statured.
D. Physical, psychomotor and mental development is retarded.
E. Such individuals are sterile.

Choose the correct answer from the options given below.

(a) C and D only (b) B and E only
(c) A and E only (d) A and B only

46. Which one of the following statement is 'not' correct?

(a) Algal blooms caused by excess of organic matter in water improve water quality and promote fisheries
(b) Water hyacinth grows abundantly in eutrophic water bodies and leads to an imbalance in the ecosystem dynamics of the water body
(c) The amount of some toxic substances of industrial wastewater increases in the organisms at successive trophic levels
(d) The microorganisms involved in biodegradation of organic matter in a sewage polluted water body consume a lot of oxygen causing the death of aquatic organisms

47. Given below are two statements; one is labelled as Assertion (A) and the other is labelled as Reason (R).

Assertion (A) In gymnosperms, the pollen grains are released from the microsporangium and carried by air currents.

Reason (R) Air currents carry the pollen grains to the mouth of the archegonia where the male gametes are discharged and pollen tube is not formed.

In the light of the above statements, choose the correct answer from the options given below.

(a) Both A and R are true, R is not the correct explanation of A
(b) A is true, but R is false
(c) A is false, but R is true
(d) Both A and R are true and R is the correct explanation of A

48. Match List I with List II.

List-I	List-II
A. Iron	I. Synthesis of auxin
B. Zinc	II. Component of nitrate reductase
C. Boron	III. Activator of catalase
D. Molybdenum	IV. Cell elongation and differentiation

Choose the correct answer from the options given below.

(a) A-II, B-III, C-IV, D-I
(b) A-III, B-I, C-IV, D-II
(c) A-II, B-IV, C-I, D-III
(d) A-III, B-II, C-I, D-IV

49. Match List I with List II.

List-I (Interaction)	List-II (Species *A* and *B*)
A. Mutualism	I. +(*A*), 0(*B*)
B. Commensalism	II. –(*A*), 0(*B*)
C. Amensalism	III. +(*A*), –(*B*)
D. Parasitism	IV. +(*A*), +(*B*)

Choose the correct answer from the options given below.

(a) A-IV, B-I, C-II, D-III
(b) A-IV, B-III, C-I, D-II
(c) A-III, B-I, C-IV, D-II
(d) A-IV, B-II, C-I, D-III

50. Identify the correct statements.

A. Lenticels are the lens-shaped openings permitting the exchange of gases.
B. Bark formed early in the season is called hard bark.
C. Bark is a technical term that refers to all tissues exterior to vascular cambium.
D. Bark refers to periderm and secondary phloem.
E. Phellogen is single-layered in thickness.

Choose the correct answer from the options given below.

(a) A and D only
(b) A, B and D only
(c) B and C only
(d) B, C and E only

Zoology (Q. No. 51–100)

Section-A

51. Once the undigested and unabsorbed substances enter the caecum, their backflow is prevented by

(a) ileo-caecal valve
(b) gastro - oesophageal sphincter
(c) pyloric sphincter
(d) sphincter of Oddi

52. In which blood corpuscles, the HIV undergoes replication and produces progeny viruses?

(a) B-lymphocytes (b) Basophils
(c) Eosinophils (d) T_H-cells

53. Broad palm with single palm crease is visible in a person suffering from

(a) Turner's syndrome
(b) Klinefelter's syndrome
(c) Thalassemia
(d) Down's syndrome

54. Which one of the following common sexually transmitted diseases is completely curable when detected early and treated properly?

(a) Gonorrhoea (b) Hepatitis-B
(c) HIV infection (d) Genital herpes

55. Match List-I with List-II.

List-I (Interacting species)	List-II (Name of interaction)
A. A leopard and a lion in a forest/grassland	I. Competition
B. A cuckoo laying egg in a crow's nest	II. Brood parasitism
C. Fungi and root of a higher plant in mycorrhizae	III. Mutualism
D. A cattle egret and a cattle in a field	IV. Commensalism

Choose the correct answer from the options given below.

(a) A-I, B-II, C-IV, D-III
(b) A-III, B-IV, C-I, D-II
(c) A-II, B-III, C-I, D-IV
(d) A-I, B-II, C-III, D-IV

56. Match List-I with List-II.

	List-I (Cells)		List-II (Secretion)
A.	Peptic cells	I.	Mucus
B.	Goblet cells	II.	Bile juice
C.	Oxyntic cells	III.	Proenzyme pepsinogen
D.	Hepatic cells	IV.	HCl and intrinsic factor for absorption of vitamin-B_{12}

Choose the correct answer from the options given below.

(a) A-II, B-I, C-III, D-IV
(b) A-III, B-I, C-IV, D-II
(c) A-II, B-IV, C-I, D-III
(d) A-IV, B-III, C-II, D-I

57. Given below are two statements.

Statement I If a protein is imagined as a line, the left end is represented by first amino acid (C-terminal) and the right end is represented by last amino acid (N-terminal).

Statement II Adult human haemoglobin, consists of 4 subunits (two subunits of α type and two subunits of β type).

In the light of the above statements, choose the correct answer from the options given below.

(a) Both statement I and statement II are false
(b) Statement I is true, but statement II is false
(c) Statement I is false, but statement II is true
(d) Both statement I and statement II are true

58. Given below are two statements.

Statement I RNA mutates at a faster rate.

Statement II Viruses having RNA genome and shorter lifespan mutate and evolve faster.

In the light of the above statements, choose the correct answer from the options given below.

(a) Both statement I and statement II are false
(b) Statement I is true, but statement II is false
(c) Statement I is false, but statement II is true
(d) Both statement I and statement II are true

59. Match List-I with List-II.

List-I	List-II
A. Vasectomy	I. Oral method
B. Coitus interruptus	II. Barrier method
C. Cervical caps	III. Surgical method
D. Saheli	IV. Natural method

Choose the correct answer from the options given below.

(a) A-III, B-IV, C-II, D-I
(b) A-II, B-III, C-I, D-IV
(c) A-IV, B-II, C-I, D-III
(d) A-III, B-I, C-IV, D-II

60. Match List-I with List-II.

List-I	List-II
A. Ringworm	I. *Haemophilus influenzae*
B. Filariasis	II. *Trichophyton*
C. Malaria	III. *Wuchereria bancrofti*
D. Pneumonia	IV. *Plasmodium vivax*

Choose the correct answer from the options given below.

(a) A-II, B-III, C-I, D-IV
(b) A-III, B-II, C-I, D-IV
(c) A-III, B-II, C-IV, D-I
(d) A-II, B-III, C-IV, D-I

61. Match List-I with List-II.

List-I	List-II
A. CCK	I. Kidney
B. GIP	II. Heart
C. ANF	III. Gastric gland
D. ADH	IV. Pancreas

Choose the correct answer from the options given below.

(a) A-III, B-II, C-IV, D-I
(b) A-II, B-IV, C-I, D-III
(c) A-IV, B-II, C-III, D-I
(d) A-IV, B-III, C-II, D-I

62. Given below are two statements.

Statement I Vas deferens receives a duct from seminal vesicle and opens into urethra as the ejaculatory duct.

Statement II The cavity of the cervix is called cervical canal which along with vagina forms birth canal.

In the light of the above statements, choose the correct answer from the options given below.

(a) Both statement I and statement II are false
(b) Statement I is true, but statement II is false
(c) Statement I is false, but statement II is true
(d) Both statement I and statement II are true

63. Which one of the following techniques does not serve the purpose of early diagnosis of a disease for its early treatment?

(a) Serum and urine analysis
(b) Polymerase Chain Reaction (PCR) technique
(c) Enzyme Linked Immuno-Sorbent Assay (ELISA) technique
(d) Recombinant DNA technology

64. Which of the following are not considered as the part of endomembrane system?

A. Mitochondria B. Endoplasmic reticulum
C. Chloroplast D. Golgi complex
E. Peroxisomes

Choose the most appropriate answer from the options given below.

(a) A, C and E only (b) A and D only
(c) A, D and E only (d) B and D only

65. Match List-I with List-II.

List-I	List-II
A. Heroin	I. Effect on cardiovascular system
B. Marijuana	II. Slow down body function
C. Cocaine	III. Painkiller
D. Morphine	IV. Interfere with transport of dopamine

Choose the correct answer from the options given below.
(a) A-I, B-II, C-III, D-IV
(b) A-IV, B-III, C-II, D-I
(c) A-III, B-IV, C-I, D-II
(d) A-II, B-I, C-IV, D-III

66. Given below are two statements.

Statement I Low temperature preserves the enzyme in a temporarily inactive state whereas high temperature destroys enzymatic activity because proteins are denatured by heat.

Statement II When the inhibitor closely resembles the substrate in its molecular structure and inhibits the activity of the enzyme, it is known as competitive inhibitor.

In the light of the above statements, choose the correct answer from the options given below.
(a) Both statement I and statement II are false
(b) Statement I is true, but statement II is false
(c) Statement I is false, but statement II is true
(d) Both statement I and statement II are true

67. Which of the following functions is carried out by cytoskeleton in a cell?
(a) Protein synthesis
(b) Motility
(c) Transportation
(d) Nuclear division

68. Given below are two statements.

Statement I Ligaments are dense irregular tissue.

Statement II Cartilage is dense regular tissue.

In the light of the above statements, choose the correct answer from the options given below.
(a) Both statement I and statement II are false
(b) Statement I is true, but statement II is false
(c) Statement I is false, but statement II is true
(d) Both statement I and statement II are true

69. Match List-I with List-II

List-I	List-II
A. Cartilaginous joint	I. Between flat skull bones
B. Ball and socket joint	II. Between adjacent vertebrae in vertebral column
C. Fibrous joint	III. Between carpal and metacarpal of thumb
D. Saddle joint	IV. Between humerus and pectoral girdle

Choose the correct answer from the options given below.
(a) A-II, B-IV, C-I, D-III
(b) A-I, B-IV, C-III, D-II
(c) A-II, B-IV, C-III, D-I
(d) A-III, B-I, C-II, D-IV

70. Match List-I with List-II.

List-I	List-II
A. Gene '*a*'	I. β-galactosidase
B. Gene '*y*'	II. Transacetylase
C. Gene '*i*'	III. Permease
D. Gene '*z*'	IV. Repressor protein

Choose the correct answer from the options given below.
(a) A-II, B-III, C-IV, D-I
(b) A-III, B-IV, C-I, D-II
(c) A-III, B-I, C-IV, D-II
(d) A-II, B-I, C-IV, D-III

71. Which one of the following symbols represents mating between relative in human pedigree analysis?

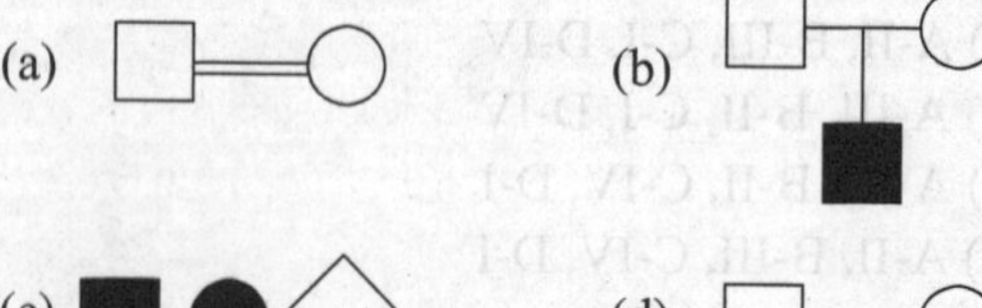

72. Given below are two statements; one is labelled as Assertion (A) and the other is labelled as Reason (R).

Assertion (A) Endometrium is necessary for implantation of blastocyst.

Reason (R) In the absence of fertilisation, the corpus luteum degenerates that causes disintegration of endometrium.

In the light of the above statements, choose the correct answer from the options given below.

(a) Both A and R are true, but R is not the correct explanation of A
(b) A is true, but R is false
(c) A is false, but R is true
(d) Both A and R are true and R is the correct explanation of A

73. Given below are two statements; one is labelled as Assertion (A) and the other is labelled as Reason (R).

Assertion (A) Nephrons are of two types: Cortical and juxta medullary, based on their relative position in cortex and medulla.

Reason (R) Juxta medullary nephrons have short loop of Henle whereas, cortical nephrons have longer loop of Henle.

In the light of the above statements, choose the correct answer from the options given below.

(a) Both A and R are true, but R is not the correct explanation of A
(b) A is true, but R is false
(c) A is false, but R is true
(d) Both A and R are true and R is the correct explanation of A

74. Radial symmetry is not found in adults of phylum

(a) Hemichordata
(b) Coelenterata
(c) Echinodermata
(d) Ctenophora

75. Match List-I with List-II.

List-I		List-II	
A.	Fovea	I.	Visible coloured portion of eye that regulates diameter of pupil.
B.	Iris	II.	External layer of eye formed of dense connective tissue.
C.	Blind spot	III.	Point of greatest visual acuity or resolution.
D.	Sclera	IV.	Point where optic nerve leaves the eyeball and photoreceptor cells are absent.

Choose the correct answer from the options given below.

(a) A-IV, B-III, C-II, D-I
(b) A-I, B-IV, C-III, D-II
(c) A-II, B-I, C-III, D-IV
(d) A-III, B-I, C-IV, D-II

76. Which of the following statement is correct?

(a) Biomagnification refers to increase in concentration of the toxicant at successive trophic levels
(b) Presence of large amount of nutrients in water restricts 'algal bloom'
(c) Algal bloom decreases fish mortality
(d) Eutrophication refers to increase in domestic sewage and wastewater in lakes

77. Which of the following statements are correct regarding female reproductive cycle?

A. In non-primate mammals, cyclical changes during reproduction are called oestrus cycle.
B. First menstrual cycle begins at puberty and is called menopause.
C. Lack of menstruation may be indicative of pregnancy.
D. Cyclic menstruation extends between menarche and menopause.

Choose the most appropriate answer from the options given below.

(a) A and B only
(b) A, B and C only
(c) A, C and D only
(d) A and D only

78. Given below are two statements.

Statement I In prokaryotes, the positively charged DNA is held with some negatively charged proteins in a region called nucleoid.

Statement II In eukaryotes, the negatively charged DNA is wrapped around the positively charged histone octamer to form nucleosome.

In the light of the above statements, choose the correct answer from the options given below.

(a) Both statement I and statement II are false
(b) Statement I is true, but statement II is false
(c) Statement I is false, but statement II is true
(d) Both statement I and statement II are true

79. Select the correct group/set of Australian Marsupials exhibiting adaptive radiation.

(a) Numbat, spotted cuscus, flying phalanger
(b) Mole, flying squirrel, tasmanian tiger cat
(c) Lemur, anteater, wolf
(d) Tasmanian wolf, bobcat, marsupial mole

80. Match List-I with List-II.

	List-I		List-II
A.	*Taenia*	I.	Nephridia
B.	*Paramecium*	II.	Contractile vacuole
C.	*Periplaneta*	III.	Flame cells
D.	*Pheretima*	IV.	Urecose gland

Choose the correct answer from the options given below.

(a) A-I, B-II, C-IV, D-III
(b) A-III, B-II, C-IV, D-I
(c) A-II, B-I, C-IV, D-III
(d) A-I, B-II, C-III, D-IV

81. Given below are two statements; one is labelled as Assertion (A) and the other is labelled as Reason (R).

Assertion (A) Amniocentesis for sex determination is one of the strategies of reproductive and child healthcare programme.

Reason (R) Ban on amniocentesis checks increasing menace of female foeticide.

In the light of the above statements, choose the correct answer from the options given below.

(a) Both A and R are true, but R is not the correct explanation of A
(b) A is true, but R is false
(c) A is false, but R is true
(d) Both A and R are true and R is the correct explanation of A

82. Which of the following is not a cloning vector?

(a) YAC (b) pBR322
(c) Probe (d) BAC

83. Given below are two statements.

Statement I Electrostatic precipitator is most widely used in thermal power plant.

Statement II Electrostatic precipitator in thermal power plant removes ionising radiations.

In the light of the above statements, choose the correct answer from the options given below.

(a) Both statement I and statement II are false
(b) Statement I is true, but statement II is incorrect
(c) Statement I is false, but statement II is correct
(d) Both statement I and statement II are true

84. Match List-I with List-II.

	List-I		List-II
A.	P-wave	I.	Beginning of systole
B.	Q-wave	II.	Repolarisation of ventricles
C.	QRS complex	III.	Depolarisation of atria
D.	T-wave	IV.	Depolarisation of ventricles

Choose the correct answer from the options given below.

(a) A-IV, B-III, C-II, D-I
(b) A-II, B-IV, C-I, D-III
(c) A-I, B-II, C-III, D-IV
(d) A-III, B-I, C-IV, D-II

85. Vital capacity of lung is
(a) IRV + ERV + TV + RV
(b) IRV + ERV + TV − RV
(c) IRV + ERV +TV
(d) IRV + ERV

Section-B

86. Given below are two statements.

Statement I During G_0-phase of cell cycle, the cell is metabolically inactive.

Statement II The centrosome undergoes duplication during S-phase of interphase.

In the light of the above statements, choose the most appropriate answer from the options given below.

(a) Both statement I and statement II are false
(b) Statement I is true, but statement II is false
(c) Statement I is false, but statement II is true
(d) Both statement I and statement II are true

87. The parts of human brain that helps in regulation of sexual behaviour, expression of excitement, pleasure, rage, fear, etc., are
(a) corpora quadrigemina and hippocampus
(b) brain stem and epithalamus
(c) corpus callosum and thalamus
(d) limbic system and hypothalamus

88. In cockroach, excretion is brought about by –

A. Phallic gland B. Urecose gland
C. Nephrocytes D. Fat body
E. Collaterial glands

Choose the correct answer from the options given below.

(a) A, B and E only (b) B, C and D only
(c) B and D only (d) A and E only

89. Which of the following statements are correct?

A. An excessive loss of body fluid from the body switches off osmoreceptors.
B. ADH facilitates water reabsorption to prevent diuresis.
C. ANF causes vasodilation.
D. ADH causes increase in blood pressure.
E. ADH is responsible for decrease in GFR.

Choose the correct answer from the options given below.

(a) B, C and D only
(b) A, B and E only
(c) C, D and E only
(d) A and B only

90. Which one of the following is not an advantage of inbreeding?
(a) It exposes harmful recessive genes that are eliminated by selection
(b) Elimination of less desirable genes and accumulation of superior genes takes place due to it
(c) It decreases the productivity of inbreed population, after continuous inbreeding
(d) It decreases homozygosity

91. Which of the following statements are correct regarding skeletal muscle?

A. Muscle bundles are held together by collagenous connective tissue layer called fascicle.
B. Sarcoplasmic reticulum of muscle fibre is a store house of calcium ions.
C. Striated appearance of skeletal muscle fibre is due to distribution pattern of actin and myosin proteins.
D. M-line is considered as functional unit of contraction called sarcomere.

Choose the most appropriate answer from the options given below.

(a) B and C only
(b) A, C and D only
(c) C and D only
(d) A, B and C only

92. Match List-I with List-II.

	List-I		List-II
A.	Logistic growth	I.	Unlimited resource availability condition
B.	Exponential growth	II.	Limited resource availability condition
C.	Expanding age pyramid	III.	The per cent individuals of pre-reproductive age is largest followed by reproductive and post-reproductive age groups
D.	Stable age pyramid	IV.	The per cent individuals of pre-reproductive and reproductive age group are same

Choose the correct answer from the options given below.
(a) A-II, B-III, C-I, D-IV
(b) A-II, B-IV, C-I, D-III
(c) A-II, B-IV, C-III, D-I
(d) A-II, B-I, C-III, D-IV

93. Which one of the following is the sequence on corresponding coding strand, if the sequence on *m*RNA formed is as follows
5' AUCGAUCGAUCGAUCGAUCGAUCG AUCG 3'?
(a) 3' UAGCUAGCUAGCUAGCUAGCUAGCUAGC 5'
(b) 5' ATCGATCGATCGATCGATCGATCGATCG 3'
(c) 3' ATCGATCGATCGATCGATCGATCGATCG 5'
(d) 5' UAGCUAGCUAGCUAGCUAGCUAGCUAGC 3'

94. Which of the following statements are correct.
A. Basophils are most abundant cells of the total WBCs.
B. Basophils secrete histamine, serotonin and heparin.
C. Basophils are involved in inflammatory response.
D. Basophils have kidney shaped nucleus.
E. Basophils are agranulocytes.

Choose the correct answer from the options given below.
(a) C and E only
(b) B and C only
(c) A and B only
(d) D and E only

95. Match List-I with List-II.

	List-I		List-II
A.	Mast cells	I.	Ciliated epithelium
B.	Inner surface of bronchiole	II.	Areolar connective tissue
C.	Blood	III.	Cuboidal epithelium
D.	Tubular parts of nephron	IV.	Specialised connective tissue

Choose the correct answer from the options given below.
(a) A-II, B-III, C-I, D-IV
(b) A-II, B-I, C-IV, D-III
(c) A-III, B-IV, C-II, D-I
(d) A-I, B-II, C-IV, D-III

96. Which of the following is characteristic feature of cockroach regarding sexual dimorphism?
(a) Presence of anal styles
(b) Presence of sclerites
(c) Presence of anal cerci
(d) Dark brown body colour and anal cerci

97. Which one of the following are not under the control of thyroid hormone?
A. Maintenance of water and electrolyte balance.
B. Regulation of basal metabolic rate.
C. Normal rhythm of sleep-wake cycle.
D. Development of immune system.
E. Support the process of RBCs formation.

Choose the correct answer from the options given below.
(a) B and C only
(b) C and D only
(c) D and E only
(d) A and D only

98. Select the correct statements.

A. Tetrad formation is seen during leptotene.

B. During anaphase, the centromeres split and chromatids separate.

C. Terminalisation takes place during pachytene.

D. Nucleolus, Golgi complex and ER are reformed during telophase.

E. Crossing over takes place between sister chromatids of homologous chromosome.

Choose the correct answer from the options given below.

(a) B and D only (b) A, C and E only
(c) B and E only (d) A and C only

99. The unique mammalian characteristics are

(a) hairs, pinna and mammary glands
(b) hairs, pinna and indirect development
(c) pinna, monocondylic skull and mammary glands
(d) hairs, tympanic membrane and mammary glands

100. Select the correct statements with reference to chordates.

A. Presence of a mid-dorsal, solid and double nerve cord.

B. Presence of closed circulatory system.

C. Presence of paired pharyngeal gill slits.

D. Presence of dorsal heart.

E. Triploblastic pseudocoelomate animals.

Choose the correct answer from the options given below.

(a) B and C only
(b) B, D and E only
(c) C, D and E only
(d) A, C and D only

Response Index

01	ⓐ ⓑ ⓒ ⓓ	26	ⓐ ⓑ ⓒ ⓓ	51	ⓐ ⓑ ⓒ ⓓ	76	ⓐ ⓑ ⓒ ⓓ
02	ⓐ ⓑ ⓒ ⓓ	27	ⓐ ⓑ ⓒ ⓓ	52	ⓐ ⓑ ⓒ ⓓ	77	ⓐ ⓑ ⓒ ⓓ
03	ⓐ ⓑ ⓒ ⓓ	28	ⓐ ⓑ ⓒ ⓓ	53	ⓐ ⓑ ⓒ ⓓ	78	ⓐ ⓑ ⓒ ⓓ
04	ⓐ ⓑ ⓒ ⓓ	29	ⓐ ⓑ ⓒ ⓓ	54	ⓐ ⓑ ⓒ ⓓ	79	ⓐ ⓑ ⓒ ⓓ
05	ⓐ ⓑ ⓒ ⓓ	30	ⓐ ⓑ ⓒ ⓓ	55	ⓐ ⓑ ⓒ ⓓ	80	ⓐ ⓑ ⓒ ⓓ
06	ⓐ ⓑ ⓒ ⓓ	31	ⓐ ⓑ ⓒ ⓓ	56	ⓐ ⓑ ⓒ ⓓ	81	ⓐ ⓑ ⓒ ⓓ
07	ⓐ ⓑ ⓒ ⓓ	32	ⓐ ⓑ ⓒ ⓓ	57	ⓐ ⓑ ⓒ ⓓ	82	ⓐ ⓑ ⓒ ⓓ
08	ⓐ ⓑ ⓒ ⓓ	33	ⓐ ⓑ ⓒ ⓓ	58	ⓐ ⓑ ⓒ ⓓ	83	ⓐ ⓑ ⓒ ⓓ
09	ⓐ ⓑ ⓒ ⓓ	34	ⓐ ⓑ ⓒ ⓓ	59	ⓐ ⓑ ⓒ ⓓ	84	ⓐ ⓑ ⓒ ⓓ
10	ⓐ ⓑ ⓒ ⓓ	35	ⓐ ⓑ ⓒ ⓓ	60	ⓐ ⓑ ⓒ ⓓ	85	ⓐ ⓑ ⓒ ⓓ
11	ⓐ ⓑ ⓒ ⓓ	36	ⓐ ⓑ ⓒ ⓓ	61	ⓐ ⓑ ⓒ ⓓ	86	ⓐ ⓑ ⓒ ⓓ
12	ⓐ ⓑ ⓒ ⓓ	37	ⓐ ⓑ ⓒ ⓓ	62	ⓐ ⓑ ⓒ ⓓ	87	ⓐ ⓑ ⓒ ⓓ
13	ⓐ ⓑ ⓒ ⓓ	38	ⓐ ⓑ ⓒ ⓓ	63	ⓐ ⓑ ⓒ ⓓ	88	ⓐ ⓑ ⓒ ⓓ
14	ⓐ ⓑ ⓒ ⓓ	39	ⓐ ⓑ ⓒ ⓓ	64	ⓐ ⓑ ⓒ ⓓ	89	ⓐ ⓑ ⓒ ⓓ
15	ⓐ ⓑ ⓒ ⓓ	40	ⓐ ⓑ ⓒ ⓓ	65	ⓐ ⓑ ⓒ ⓓ	90	ⓐ ⓑ ⓒ ⓓ
16	ⓐ ⓑ ⓒ ⓓ	41	ⓐ ⓑ ⓒ ⓓ	66	ⓐ ⓑ ⓒ ⓓ	91	ⓐ ⓑ ⓒ ⓓ
17	ⓐ ⓑ ⓒ ⓓ	42	ⓐ ⓑ ⓒ ⓓ	67	ⓐ ⓑ ⓒ ⓓ	92	ⓐ ⓑ ⓒ ⓓ
18	ⓐ ⓑ ⓒ ⓓ	43	ⓐ ⓑ ⓒ ⓓ	68	ⓐ ⓑ ⓒ ⓓ	93	ⓐ ⓑ ⓒ ⓓ
19	ⓐ ⓑ ⓒ ⓓ	44	ⓐ ⓑ ⓒ ⓓ	69	ⓐ ⓑ ⓒ ⓓ	94	ⓐ ⓑ ⓒ ⓓ
20	ⓐ ⓑ ⓒ ⓓ	45	ⓐ ⓑ ⓒ ⓓ	70	ⓐ ⓑ ⓒ ⓓ	95	ⓐ ⓑ ⓒ ⓓ
21	ⓐ ⓑ ⓒ ⓓ	46	ⓐ ⓑ ⓒ ⓓ	71	ⓐ ⓑ ⓒ ⓓ	96	ⓐ ⓑ ⓒ ⓓ
22	ⓐ ⓑ ⓒ ⓓ	47	ⓐ ⓑ ⓒ ⓓ	72	ⓐ ⓑ ⓒ ⓓ	97	ⓐ ⓑ ⓒ ⓓ
23	ⓐ ⓑ ⓒ ⓓ	48	ⓐ ⓑ ⓒ ⓓ	73	ⓐ ⓑ ⓒ ⓓ	98	ⓐ ⓑ ⓒ ⓓ
24	ⓐ ⓑ ⓒ ⓓ	49	ⓐ ⓑ ⓒ ⓓ	74	ⓐ ⓑ ⓒ ⓓ	99	ⓐ ⓑ ⓒ ⓓ
25	ⓐ ⓑ ⓒ ⓓ	50	ⓐ ⓑ ⓒ ⓓ	75	ⓐ ⓑ ⓒ ⓓ	100	ⓐ ⓑ ⓒ ⓓ

Performance Scanner

> 90% Excellent !	You have mastered the NEET syllabus. The concepts of this syllabus are on your fingertips. Maintain this momentum.
76-90% Very Good !	You have a good command over the NEET syllabus. Revise it again after a few days and enhance your performance.
60-75% Good !	You have a wide scope to learn for the NEET syllabus. Revise it again.
<60% Not Satisfactory!	You have a long way ahead of you to master the NEET syllabus. Revise it thoroughly.

Space for Rough Work

Test Booklet No. 3947375

Test Booklet Code NC2

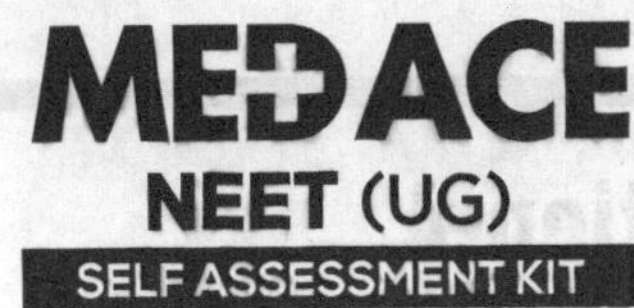

NEET Chronicles 2

(2024 Paper)

Name of the Candidate (In Capitals)

____

____

____

Candidate's Signature ____________

Invigilator's Signature ____________

Facsimile signature stamp of center superintendent______________

Important Instructions

- The test is of **1 hours 40 minutes** duration and the Test Booklet contains **100** multiple-choice questions (four options with a single correct answer) from Botany and Zoology. 50 questions in each subject are divided into two sections (A and B) as per the details given below.
  - **Section A** shall consist of **35 (Thirty-five)** questions in each subject (Questions Nos - 1 to 35, 51 to 85).
    All questions are compulsory.
  - **Section B** shall consist of **15 (Fifteen)** questions in each subject (Question Nos- 36 to 50, 86 to 100).
    In Section B, a candidate needs to attempt any 10 (Ten) questions out of 15 (Fifteen) in each subject. **Candidates are advised to read all 15 questions in each subject of Section B** before they start attempting the question paper. In the event of a candidate attempting more than ten questions. **The first ten questions answered by the candidate shall be evaluated.**
- Each question carries 4 marks. For each correct response, the candidate will get 4 marks. For each incorrect response, one mark will be deducted from the total scores.
- Use **Blue/Black Point Pen only** for writing particulars on this page/ marking response on Answer Sheet.

Do not open this booklet until you start attempting the test

Botany (Q. No. 1-50)

Section-A

1. Lecithin, a small molecular weight organic compound found in living tissues, is an example of

(a) amino acids (b) phospholipids
(c) glycerides (d) carbohydrates

2. Which of the following are required for the dark reaction of photosynthesis?

A. Light B. Chlorophyll
C. CO_2 D. ATP
E. NADPH

Choose the correct answer from the options given below.

(a) A, B and C only (b) B, C and D only
(c) C, D and E only (d) D and E only

3. Spindle fibres attach to kinetochores of chromosomes during

(a) prophase (b) metaphase
(c) anaphase (d) telophase

4. Bulliform cells are responsible for

(a) inward curling of leaves in monocots
(b) protecting the plant from salt stress
(c) increased photosynthesis in monocots
(d) providing large spaces for storage of sugars

5. In the given figure, which component has thin outer walls and highly thickened inner walls?

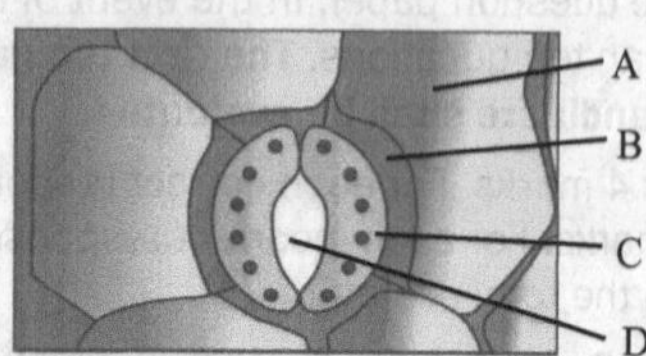

(a) C (b) D
(c) A (d) B

6. What is the fate of a piece of DNA carrying only gene of interest which is transferred into an alien organism?

A. The piece of DNA would be able to multiply itself independently in the progeny cells of the organism.
B. It may get integrated into the genome of the recipient.
C. It may multiply and be inherited along with the host DNA.
D. The alien piece of DNA is not an integral part of chromosome.
E. It shows ability to replicate.

Choose the correct answer from the options given below.

(a) A and B only
(b) D and E only
(c) B and C only
(d) A and E only

7. Given below are two statements.

Statement I *Bt* toxins are insect group specific and coded by a gene *cry* IAc.

Statement II *Bt* toxin exists as inactive protoxin in *B. thuringiensis*. However, after ingestion by the insect, that inactive protoxin gets converted into active form due to acidic pH of the insect gut.

In the light of the above statements, choose the correct answer from the options given below.

(a) Both statement I and statement II are true
(b) Both statement I and statement II are false
(c) Statement I is true, but statement II is false
(d) Statement I is false, but statement II is true

8. List of endangered species was released by

(a) GEAC (b) WWF
(c) FOAM (d) IUCN

9. Identify the part of the seed from the given figure which is destined to form root when the seed germinates.

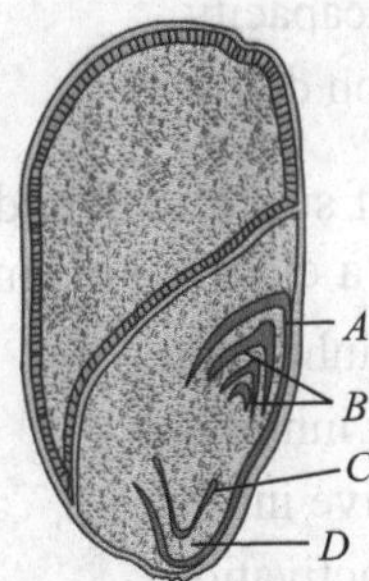

(a) A (b) B
(c) C (d) D

10. Match List I with List II.

List I	List II
A. *Clostridium butylicum*	I. Ethanol
B. *Saccharomyces cerevisiae*	II. Streptokinase
C. *Trichoderma polysporum*	III. Butyric acid
D. *Streptococcus* sp.	IV. Cyclosporin-A

Choose the correct answer from the options given below:
(a) A-III, B-I, C-II, D-IV
(b) A-II, B-IV, C-III, D-I
(c) A-III, B-I, C-IV, D-II
(d) A-IV, B-I, C-III, D-II

11. Identify the type of flowers based on the position of calyx, corolla and androecium with respect to the ovary from the given figures (*A*) and (*B*).

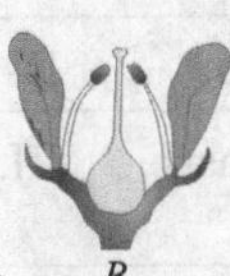
A *B*

(a) (*A*) Epigynous; (*B*) Hypogynous
(b) (*A*) Hypogynous; (*B*) Epigynous
(c) (*A*) Perigynous; (*B*) Epigynous
(d) (*A*) Perigynous; (*B*) Perigynous

12. Auxin is used by gardeners to prepare weed-free lawns. But no damage is caused to grass as auxin
(a) promotes apical dominance
(b) promotes abscission of mature leaves only
(c) does not affect mature monocotyledonous plants
(d) can help in cell division in grasses, to produce growth

13. A pink flowered snapdragon plant was crossed with a red flowered snapdragon plant. What type of phenotype(s) is/are expected in the progeny?
(a) Only red flowered plants
(b) Red flowered as well as pink flowered plants
(c) Only pink flowered plants
(d) Red, pink as well as white flowered plants

14. Which one of the following is not a criterion for classification of fungi?
(a) Morphology of mycelium
(b) Mode of nutrition
(c) Mode of spore formation
(d) Fruiting body

15. The lactose present in the growth medium of bacteria is transported to the cell by the action of
(a) beta-galactosidase
(b) acetylase
(c) permease
(d) polymerase

16. In a plant, black seed colour (BB/Bb) is dominant over white seed colour (bb). In order to find out the genotype of the black seed plant, with which of the following genotype will you cross it?
(a) BB (b) bb
(c) Bb (d) BB/Bb

17. Given below are two statements.

Statement I Parenchyma is living, but collenchyma is dead tissue.

Statement II Gymnosperms lack xylem vessels, but presence of xylem vessels is the characteristic of angiosperms.

In the light of the above statements, choose the correct answer from the options given below.
(a) Both statement I and statement II are true
(b) Both statement I and statement II are false
(c) Statement I is true, but statement II is false
(d) Statement I is false, but statement II is true

18. How many molecules of ATP and NADPH are required for every molecule of CO_2 fixed in the Calvin cycle?
(a) 2 molecules of ATP and 3 molecules of NADPH
(b) 2 molecules of ATP and 2 molecules of NADPH
(c) 3 molecules of ATP and 3 molecules of NADPH
(d) 3 molecules of ATP and 2 molecules of NADPH

19. A transcription unit in DNA is defined primarily by the three regions in DNA and these are with respect to upstream and downstream end
(a) Repressor, operator gene, structural gene
(b) Structural gene, transposons, operator gene
(c) Inducer, repressor, structural gene
(d) Promoter, structural gene, terminator

20. Tropical regions show greatest level of species richness because
A. tropical latitudes have remained relatively undisturbed for millions of years, hence more time was available for species diversification.
B. tropical environments are more seasonal.
C. more solar energy is available in tropics.
D. constant environments promote niche specialisation.
E. tropical environments are constant and predictable.

Choose the correct answer from the options given below.
(a) A, C, D and E only
(b) A and B only
(c) A, B and E only
(d) A, B and D only

21. The equation of Verhulst-Pearl logistic growth is $\frac{dN}{dt} = rN\left[\frac{K-N}{K}\right]$.
From this equation, K indicates
(a) intrinsic rate of natural increase
(b) biotic potential
(c) carrying capacity
(d) population density

22. Inhibition of succinic dehydrogenase enzyme by malonate is a classical example of
(a) cofactor inhibition
(b) feedback inhibition
(c) competitive inhibition
(d) enzyme activation

23. Which one of the following can be explained on the basis of Mendel's law of dominance?
A. Out of one pair of factors, one is dominant and the other is recessive.
B. Alleles do not show any expression and both the characters appear as such in F_2-generation.
C. Factors occur in pairs in normal diploid plants.
D. The discrete unit controlling a particular character is called factor.
E. The expression of only one of the parental characters is found in a monohybrid cross.

Choose the correct answer from the options given below.
(a) A, B and C only
(b) A, C, D and E only
(c) B, C and D only
(d) A, B, C, D and E

24. Match List I with List II.

List I	List II
A. Nucleolus	I. Site of formation of glycolipid
B. Centriole	II. Organisation like the cartwheel
C. Leucoplasts	III. Site for active ribosomal RNA synthesis
D. Golgi apparatus	IV. For storing nutrients

Choose the correct answer from the options given below.
(a) A-III, B-II, C-IV, D-I
(b) A-II, B-III, C-I, D-IV
(c) A-III, B-IV, C-II, D-I
(d) A-I, B-II, C-III, D-IV

25. Identify the set of correct statements.

A. The flowers of *Vallisneria* are colourful and produce nectar.
B. The flowers of water lily are not pollinated by water.
C. In most of water-pollinated species, the pollen grains are protected from wetting.
D. Pollen grains of some hydrophytes are long and ribbon like.
E. In some hydrophytes, the pollen grains are carried passively inside water.

Choose the correct answer from the options given below.

(a) C, D and E only
(b) A, B, C and D only
(c) A, C, D and E only
(d) B, C, D and E only

26. Match List I with List II.

	List-I		List-II
A.	*Rhizopus*	I.	Mushroom
B.	*Ustilago*	II.	Smut fungus
C.	*Puccinia*	III.	Bread mould
D.	*Agaricus*	IV.	Rust fungus

Choose the correct answer from the options given below.

(a) A-III, B-II, C-IV, D-I
(b) A-I, B-III, C-II, D-IV
(c) A-III, B-II, C-I, D-IV
(d) A-IV, B-III, C-II, D-I

27. *Hind* II always cuts DNA molecules at a particular point called recognition sequence and it consists of

(a) 8 bp (b) 6 bp
(c) 4 bp (d) 10 bp

28. Which of the following is an example of actinomorphic flower?

(a) *Datura* (b) *Cassia*
(c) *Pisum* (d) *Sesbania*

29. The type of conservation in which the threatened species are taken out from their natural habitat and placed in special setting where they can be protected and given special care is called

(a) *in-situ* conservation
(b) biodiversity conservation
(c) semi-conservative method
(d) sustainable development

30. Given below are two statements.

Statement I Chromosomes become gradually visible under light microscope during leptotene stage.

Statement II The beginning of diplotene stage is recognised by dissolution of synaptonemal complex.

In the light of the above statements, choose the correct answer from the options given below.

(a) Both statement I and statement II are true
(b) Both statement I and statement II are false
(c) Statement I is true, but statement II is false
(d) Statement I is false, but statement II is true

31. Formation of interfascicular cambium from fully developed parenchyma cells is an example for

(a) differentiation
(b) redifferentiation
(c) dedifferentiation
(d) maturation

32. The capacity to generate a whole plant from any cell of the plant is called

(a) totipotency
(b) micropropagation
(c) differentiation
(d) somatic hybridisation

33. Match List I with List II.

List I	List II
A. Two or more alternative forms of a gene	I. Back cross
B. Cross of F_1 progeny with homozygous recessive parent	II. Ploidy
C. Cross of F_1 progeny with any of the parents	III. Allele
D. Number of chromosome sets in plant	IV. Test cross

Choose the correct answer from the options given below.

(a) A-I, B-II, C-III, D-IV
(b) A-II, B-I, C-III, D-IV
(c) A-III, B-IV, C-I, D-II
(d) A-IV, B-III, C-II, D-I

34. The cofactor of the enzyme carboxypeptidase is
(a) zinc (b) niacin
(c) flavin (d) haem

35. These are regarded as major causes of biodiversity loss:
A. Overexploitation
B. Co-extinction
C. Mutation
D. Habitat loss and fragmentation
E. Migration
Choose the correct option:
(a) A, C and D only
(b) A, B, C and D only
(c) A, B and E only
(d) A, B and D only

Section-B

36. Match List I with List II.

List I (Types of Stamens)		List II (Example)
A. Monoadelphous	I.	Citrus
B. Diadelphous	II.	Pea
C. Polyadelphous	III.	Lily
D. Epiphyllous	IV.	China rose

Choose the correct answer from the options given below.
(a) A-IV, B-II, C-I, D-III
(b) A-IV, B-I, C-II, D-III
(c) A-I, B-II, C-IV, D-III
(d) A-III, B-I, C-IV, D-II

37. Match List I with List II.

	List I		List II
A.	GLUT-4	I.	Hormone
B.	Insulin	II.	Enzyme
C.	Trypsin	III.	Intercellular ground substance
D.	Collagen	IV.	Enables glucose transport into cells

Choose the correct answer from the options given below.
(a) A-IV, B-I, C-II, D-III
(b) A-I, B-II, C-III, D-IV
(c) A-II, B-III, C-IV, D-I
(d) A-III, B-IV, C-I, D-II

38. Identify the step in tricarboxylic acid cycle, which does not involve oxidation of substrate.
(a) Malic acid → Oxaloacetic acid
(b) Succinic acid → Malic acid
(c) Succinyl-Co-A → Succinic acid
(d) Isocitrate → Ñ-ketoglutaric acid

39. Match List I with List II.

List I		List II
A. Citric acid cycle	I.	Cytoplasm
B. Glycolysis	II.	Mitochondrial matrix
C. Electron transport system	III.	Intermembrane space of mitochondria
D. Proton gradient	IV.	Inner mitochondrial membrane

Choose the correct answer from the options given below.
(a) A-I, B-II, C-III, D-IV
(b) A-II, B-I, C-IV, D-III
(c) A-III, B-IV, C-I, D-II
(d) A-IV, B-III, C-II, D-I

40. Match List I with List II.

List I		List II
A. Frederick Griffith	I.	Genetic code
B. Francois Jacob and Jacque Monod	II.	Semi-conservative mode of DNA replication
C. Har Gobind Khorana	III.	Transformation
D. Meselson and Stahl	IV.	*Lac* operon

Choose the correct answer from the options given below.
(a) A-III, B-II, C-I, D-IV
(b) A-III, B-IV, C-I, D-II
(c) A-II, B-III, C-IV, D-I
(d) A-IV, B-I, C-II, D-III

41. Given below are two statements.

Statement I In C_3 plants, some O_2 binds to RuBisCO, hence CO_2 fixation is decreased.

Statement II In C_4 plants, mesophyll cells show very little photorespiration, while bundle sheath cells do not show photorespiration.

In the light of the above statements, choose the correct answer from the options given below.

(a) Both statement I and statement II are true
(b) Both statement I and statement II are false
(c) Statement I is true, but statement II is false
(d) Statement I is false, but statement II is true

42. Identify the correct description about the given figure.

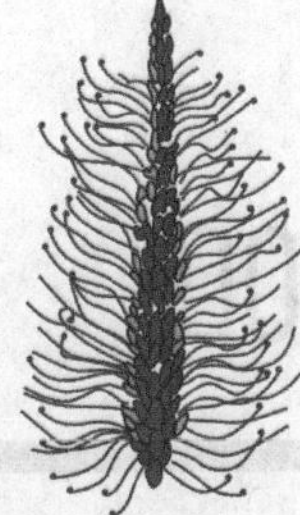

(a) Wind pollinated plant inflorescence showing flowers with well exposed stamens
(b) Water pollinated flowers showing stamens with mucilaginous covering
(c) Cleistogamous flowers showing autogamy
(d) Compact inflorescence showing complete autogamy

43. Match List I with List II.

List I	List II
A. Rose	I. Twisted aestivation
B. Pea	II. Perigynous flower
C. Cotton	III. Drupe
D. Mango	IV. Marginal placentation

Choose the correct answer from the options given below.

(a) A-II, B-IV, C-I, D-III
(b) A-I, B-II, C-III, D-IV
(c) A-IV, B-III, C-II, D-I
(d) A-II, B-III, C-IV, D-I

44. Read the following statements and choose the set of correct statements.

In the members of Phaeophyceae,

A. asexual reproduction occurs usually by biflagellated zoospores.
B. sexual reproduction is by oogamous method only.
C. stored food is in the form of carbohydrates which is either mannitol or laminarin.
D. the major pigments found are chlorophyll-*a*, *c*, carotenoids and xanthophyll.
E. vegetative cells have a cellulosic wall, usually covered on the outside by gelatinous coating of algin.

Choose the correct answer from the options given below.

(a) A, B, C and D only
(b) B, C, D and E only
(c) A, C, D and E only
(d) A, B, C and E only

45. In an ecosystem, if the Net Primary Productivity (NPP) of first trophic level is $100 \times (\text{kcal m}^{-2})\text{yr}^{-1}$. What will be the GPP (Gross Primary Productivity) of the third trophic level of the same ecosystem

(a) $\frac{x}{10}(\text{kcal m}^{-2})\text{yr}^{-1}$
(b) $x\,(\text{kcal m}^{-2})\text{yr}^{-1}$
(c) $10x\,(\text{kcal m}^{-2})\text{yr}^{-1}$
(d) $\frac{100x}{3x}(\text{kcal m}^{-2})\text{yr}^{-1}$

46. Which of the following statement is correct regarding the process of replication in *E. coli*?

(a) The DNA-dependent DNA polymerase catalyses polymerisation in one direction that is $3' \rightarrow 5'$
(b) The DNA-dependent RNA polymerase catalyses polymerisation in one direction, that is $5' \rightarrow 3'$
(c) The DNA-dependent DNA polymerase catalyses polymerisation in $5' \rightarrow 3'$ as well as $3' \rightarrow 5'$ direction
(d) The DNA-dependent DNA polymerase catalyses polymerisation in $5' \rightarrow 3'$ direction

47. Which of the following are fused in somatic hybridisation involving two varieties of plants?

(a) Callus (b) Somatic embryos
(c) Protoplasts (d) Pollens

48. Spraying sugarcane crop with which of the following plant growth regulators, increases the length of stem, thus increasing the yield?

(a) Auxin (b) Gibberellin
(c) Cytokinin (d) Abscisic acid

49. Match List I with List II.

List I		List II
A.	Robert May	I. Species-area relationship
B.	Alexander von Humboldt	II. Long term ecosystem experiment using outdoor plots
C.	Paul Ehrlich	III. Global species diversity at about 7 million
D.	David Tilman	IV. Rivet popper hypothesis

Choose the correct answer from the options given below.

(a) A-II, B-III, C-I, D-IV
(b) A-III, B-I, C-IV, D-II
(c) A-I, B-III, C-II, D-IV
(d) A-III, B-IV, C-II, D-I

50. The DNA present in chloroplast is

(a) linear, double-stranded
(b) circular, double-stranded
(c) linear, single-stranded
(d) circular, single-stranded

Zoology (Q. No. 51-100)

Section-A

51. Match List I with List II.

List I	List II
A. Common cold	I. *Plasmodium*
B. Haemozoin	II. Typhoid
C. Widal test	III. Rhinoviruses
D. Allergy	IV. Dust, mites

Choose the correct answer from the options given below.

(a) A-II, B-IV, C-III, D-I
(b) A-I, B-III, C-II, D-IV
(c) A-III, B-I, C-II, D-IV
(d) A-IV, B-II, C-III, D-I

52. Match List I with List II.

List I	List II
A. Cocaine	I. Effective sedative in surgery
B. Heroin	II. *Cannabis sativa*
C. Morphine	III. *Erythroxylum*
D. Marijuana	IV. *Papaver somniferum*

Choose the correct answer from the options given below.

(a) A-IV, B-III, C-I, D-II
(b) A-I, B-III, C-II, D-IV
(c) A-II, B-I, C-III, D-IV
(d) A-III, B-IV, C-I, D-II

53. Match List I with List II.

List I	List II
A. Fibrous joints	I. Adjacent vertebrae, limited movement
B. Cartilaginous joints	II. Humerus and pectoral girdle, rotational movement
C. Hinge joints	III. Skull, do not allow any movement
D. Ball and socket joints	IV. Knee, help in locomotion

Choose the correct answer from the options given below.
(a) A-IV, B-II, C-III, D-I
(b) A-I, B-III, C-II, D-IV
(c) A-II, B-III, C-I, D-IV
(d) A-III, B-I, C-IV, D-II

54. Which of the following are autoimmune disorders?
A. Myasthenia gravis
B. Rheumatoid arthritis
C. Gout
D. Muscular dystrophy
E. Systemic Lupus Erythematosus (SLE)
Choose the most appropriate answer from the options given below.
(a) A, B and D only
(b) A, B and E only
(c) B, C and E only
(d) C, D and E only

55. Which of the following is not a component of Fallopian tube?
(a) Uterine fundus (b) Isthmus
(c) Infundibulum (d) Ampulla

56. The flippers of the penguins and dolphins are the example of the
(a) adaptive radiation
(b) natural selection
(c) convergent evolution
(d) divergent evolution

57. Match List I with List II.

List I	List II
A. $\alpha-1$ antitrypsin	I. Cotton bollworm
B. *cry* IAb	II. ADA deficiency
C. *cry* IAc	III. Emphysema
D. Enzyme replacement therapy	IV. Corn borer

Choose the correct answer from the options given below.
(a) A-II, B-I, C-IV, D-III
(b) A-III, B-I, C-II, D-IV
(c) A-III, B-IV, C-I, D-II
(d) A-II, B-IV, C-I, D-III

58. The following diagram showing restriction sites in *E. coli* cloning vector pBR322. Find the role of 'X' and 'Y' genes.

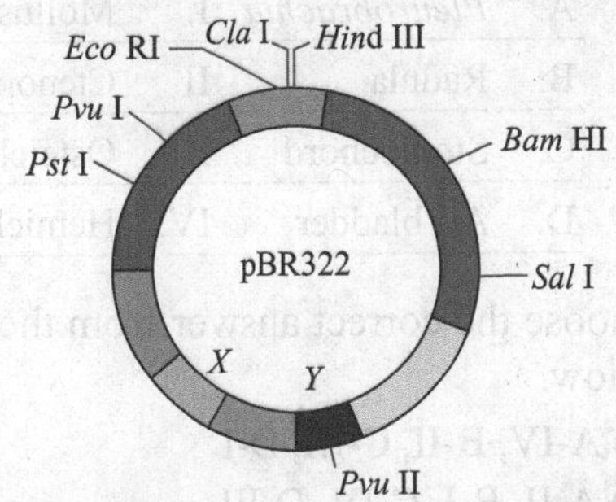

(a) The gene 'X' is responsible for resistance to antibiotics and 'Y' for protein involved in the replication of plasmid
(b) The gene 'X' is responsible for controlling the copy number of the linked DNA and 'Y' for protein involved in the replication of plasmid
(c) The gene 'X' is for protein involved in replication of plasmid and 'Y' for resistance to antibiotics
(d) Gene 'X' is responsible for recognitions sites and 'Y' is responsible for antibiotic resistance

59. Given below are two statements; one is labelled as Assertion (A) and the other is labelled as Reason (R).
Assertion (A) Breast-feeding during initial period of infant growth is recommended by doctors for bringing a healthy baby.
Reason (R) Colostrum contains several antibodies absolutely essential to develop resistance for the new born baby.
In the light of the above statements, choose the most appropriate answer from the options given below.
(a) Both A and R are correct and R is the correct explanation of A
(b) Both A and R are correct, but R is not the correct explanation of A
(c) A is correct, but R is not correct
(d) A is not correct, but R is correct

60. The Ti-plasmid of *Agrobacterium tumefaciens* stands for
(a) Tumour inhibiting plasmid
(b) Tumour independent plasmid
(c) Tumour inducing plasmid
(d) Temperature independent plasmid

61. Match List I with List II.

	List I		List II
A.	*Pleurobrachia*	I.	Mollusca
B.	Radula	II.	Ctenophora
C.	Stomochord	III.	Osteichthyes
D.	Air bladder	IV.	Hemichordata

Choose the correct answer from the options given below.

(a) A-IV, B-II, C-III, D-I
(b) A-II, B-I, C-IV, D-III
(c) A-II, B-IV, C-I, D-III
(d) A-IV, B-III, C-II, D-I

62. Given below are some stages of human evolution. Arrange them in correct sequence. (Past to Recent)

A. *Homo habilis* B. *Homo sapiens*
C. *Homo neanderthalensis* D. *Homo erectus*

Choose the correct sequence of human evolution from the options given below.

(a) D-A-C-B (b) B-A-D-C
(c) C-B-D-A (d) A-D-C-B

63. Which of the following is not a steroid hormone?

(a) Cortisol (b) Testosterone
(c) Progesterone (d) Glucagon

64. In both sexes of cockroach, a pair of jointed filamentous structures called anal cerci are present on

(a) 5th segment
(b) 10th segment
(c) 8th and 9th segment
(d) 11th segment

65. Which one of the following factors will not affect the Hardy-Weinberg equilibrium?

(a) Genetic recombination
(b) Genetic drift
(c) Gene migration
(d) Constant gene pool

66. Match List I with List II.

	List I		List II
A.	Pons	I.	Provides additional space for neurons, regulates posture and balance
B.	Hypothalamus	II.	Controls respiration and gastric secretions
C.	Medulla	III.	Connects different regions of the brain
D.	Cerebellum	IV.	Neuro secretory cells

Choose the correct answer from the options given below.

(a) A-II, B-III, C-I, D-IV
(b) A-III, B-IV, C-II, D-I
(c) A-I, B-III, C-II, D-IV
(d) A-II, B-I, C-III, D-IV

67. Match List I with List II.

	List I		List II
A.	Down's syndrome	I.	11th chromosome
B.	α –thalassemia	II.	X-chromosome
C.	β –thalassemia	III.	21st chromosome
D.	Klinefelter's syndrome	IV.	16th chromosome

Choose the correct answer from the options given below.

(a) A-I, B-II, C-III, D-IV
(b) A-II, B-III, C-IV, D-I
(c) A-III, B-IV, C-I, D-II
(d) A-IV, B-I, C-II, D-III

68. Which one is the correct product of DNA dependent RNA polymerase to the given template?

3′TACATGGCAAATATCCATTCA5′

(a) 5′AUGUACCGUUUAUAGGUAAGU3′
(b) 5′AUGUAAAGUUUAUAGGUAAGU3′
(c) 5′AUGUACCGUUUAAGGGAAGU3′
(d) 5′ATGTACCGTTTATAGGTAAGT3′

69. Given below are two statements; one is labelled as Assertion A and the other is labelled as Reason (R).

Assertion (A) FSH acts upon ovarian follicles in female and Leydig cells in male.

Reason (R) Growing ovarian follicles secrete oestrogen in female, while interstitial cells secrete androgen in male human being.

In the light of the above statements, choose the correct answer from the options given below.

(a) Both A and R are true and R is the correct explanation of A
(b) Both A and R are true, but R is not the correct explanation of A
(c) A is true, but R is false
(d) A is false, but R is true

70. Which of the following is not a natural/traditional contraceptive method?

(a) Coitus interruptus
(b) Periodic abstinence
(c) Lactational amenorrhea
(d) Vaults

71. Match List I with List II.

	List I		List II
A.	Non-medicated IUD	I.	Multiload 375
B.	Copper releasing IUD	II.	Progestogens
C.	Hormone-releasing IUD	III.	Lippes loop
D.	Implants	IV.	LNG-20

Choose the correct answer from the options given below.

(a) A-III, B-I, C-II, D-IV
(b) A-I, B-III, C-IV, D-II
(c) A-IV, B-I, C-II, D-III
(d) A-III, B-I, C-IV, D-II

72. Consider the following statements.

A. Annelids are true coelomates.
B. Poriferans are pseudocoelomates.
C. Aschelminthes are acoelomates.
D. Platyhelminthes are pseudocoelomates.

Choose the correct answer from the options given below.

(a) B only (b) A only
(c) C only (d) D only

73. Three types of muscles are given as (i), (ii) and (iii). Identify the correct matching pair along with their location in human body:

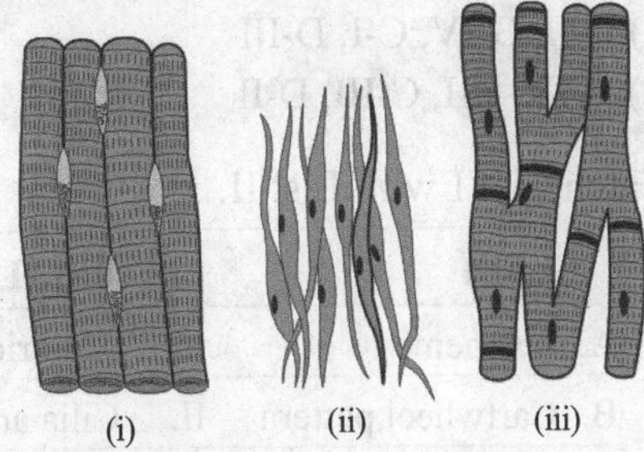

Name of muscle/location

(a) (i) Smooth - Toes
(ii) Skeletal - Legs
(iii) Cardiac - Heart

(b) (i) Skeletal - Triceps
(ii) Smooth - Stomach
(iii) Cardiac - Heart

(c) (i) Skeletal - Biceps
(ii) Involuntary-Intestine
(iii) Smooth - Heart

(d) (i) Involuntary - Nose tip
(ii) Skeletal - Bone
(iii) Cardiac - Heart

74. Following are the stages of pathway for conduction of an action potential through the heart.

A. AV bundle
B. Purkinje fibres
C. AV node
D. Bundle branches
E. SA node

Choose the correct sequence of pathway from the options given below.

(a) E-C-A-D-B (b) A-E-C-B-D
(c) B-D-E-C-A (d) E-A-D-B-C

75. Match List I with List II.

	List I		List II
A.	Lipase	I.	Peptide bond
B.	Nuclease	II.	Ester bond
C.	Protease	III.	Glycosidic bond
D.	Amylase	IV.	Phosphodiester bond

Choose the correct answer from the options given below.
(a) A-IV, B-II, C-III, D-I
(b) A-III, B-II, C-I, D-IV
(c) A-II, B-IV, C-I, D-III
(d) A-IV, B-I, C-III, D-II

76. Match List I with List II.

List I	List II
A. Axoneme	I. Centriole
B. Cartwheel pattern	II. Cilia and flagella
C. Crista	III. Chromosome
D. Satellite	IV. Mitochondria

Choose the correct answer from the options given below.
(a) A-IV, B-III, C-II, D-I
(b) A-IV, B-II, C-III, D-I
(c) A-II, B-IV, C-I, D-III
(d) A-II, B-I, C-IV, D-III

77. Match List I with List II.

List I (Sub-phases of Prophase-I)	List II (Specific Characters)
A. Diakinesis	I. Synaptonemal complex formation
B. Pachytene	II. Completion of terminalisation of chiasmata
C. Zygotene	III. Chromosomes look like thin threads
D. Leptotene	IV. Appearance of recombination nodules

Choose the correct answer from the options given below.
(a) A-IV, B-II, C-III, D-I
(b) A-I, B-II, C-IV, D-III
(c) A-II, B-IV, C-I, D-III
(d) A-IV, B-III, C-II, D-I

78. Which of the following factors are favourable for the formation of oxyhaemoglobin in alveoli?
(a) High pO_2 and high pCO_2
(b) High pO_2 and lesser H^+ concentration
(c) Low pCO_2 and high H^+ concentration
(d) Low pCO_2 and High temperature

79. Match List I with List II.

List I	List II
A. *Pterophyllum*	I. Hag fish
B. *Myxine*	II. Saw fish
C. *Pristis*	III. Angel fish
D. *Exocoetus*	IV. Flying fish

Choose the correct answer from the options given below.
(a) A-II, B-I, C-III, D-IV
(b) A-III, B-I, C-II, D-IV
(c) A-IV, B-I, C-II, D-III
(d) A-III, B-II, C-I, D-IV

80. Match List I with List II.

List I	List II
A. Typhoid	I. Fungus
B. Leishmaniasis	II. Nematode
C. Ringworm	III. Protozoa
D. Filariasis	IV. Bacteria

Choose the correct answer from the options given below.
(a) A-I, B-III, C-II, D-IV
(b) A-IV, B-III, C-I, D-II
(c) A-III, B-I, C-IV, D-II
(d) A-II, B-IV, C-III, D-I

81. Which of the following statement is incorrect?
(a) A bio-reactor provides optimal growth conditions for achieving the desired product
(b) Most commonly used bio-reactors are of stirring type
(c) Bio-reactors are used to produce small scale bacterial cultures
(d) Bio-reactors have an agitator system, an oxygen delivery system and foam control system

82. Given below are two statements.

Statement I In the nephron, the descending limb of loop of Henle is impermeable to water and permeable to electrolytes.

Statement II The proximal convoluted tubule is lined by simple columnar brush border epithelium and increases the surface area for reabsorption.

In the light of the above statements, choose the correct answer from the option given below.
(a) Both statement I and statement II are true
(b) Both statement I and statement II are false
(c) Statement I is true, but statement II is false
(d) Statement I is false, but statement II is true

83. Given below are two statements.

Statement I The presence or absence of hymen is not a reliable indicator of virginity.

Statement II The hymen is torn during the first coitus only.

In the light of the above statements, choose the correct answer from the options given below.
(a) Both statement I and statement II are true
(b) Both statement I and statement II are false
(c) Statement I is true, but statement II is false
(d) Statement I is false, but statement II is true

84. Match List I with List II.

List I	List II
A. Expiratory capacity	I. Expiratory reserve volume + Tidal volume + Inspiratory reserve volume
B. Functional residual capacity	II. Tidal volume + Expiratory reserve volume
C. Vital capacity	III. Tidal volume + Inspiratory reserve volume
D. Inspiratory capacity	IV. Expiratory reserve volume + Residual volume

Choose the correct answer from the options given below.
(a) A-II, B-IV, C-I, D-III
(b) A-III, B-II, C-IV, D-I
(c) A-II, B-I, C-IV, D-III
(d) A-I, B-III, C-II, D-IV

85. Following are the stages of cell division

A. Gap 2 phase B. Cytokinesis
C. Synthesis phase D. Karyokinesis
E. Gap 1 phase

Choose the correct sequence of stages from the options given below.
(a) C-E-D-A-B (b) E-B-D-A-C
(c) B-D-E-A-C (d) E-C-A-D-B

Section-B

86. Given below are two statements.

Statement I Mitochondria and chloroplasts both are double membraned bound organelles.

Statement II Inner membrane of mitochondria is relatively less permeable, as compared to chloroplast.

In the light of the above statements, choose the most appropriate answer from the options given below.
(a) Both statement I and statement II are true
(b) Both statement I and statement II are false
(c) Statement I is true, but statement II is false
(d) Statement I is false, but statement II is true

87. Match List I with List II.

List I	List II
A. Mesozoic Era	I. Lower invertebrates
B. Proterozoic Era	II. Fish and Amphibia
C. Cenozoic Era	III. Birds and reptiles
D. Paleozoic Era	IV. Mammals

Choose the correct answer from the options given below.
(a) A-II, B-I, C-III, D-IV
(b) A-III, B-I, C-II, D-IV
(c) A-I, B-II, C-IV, D-III
(d) A-III, B-I, C-IV, D-II

88. Given below are two statements.

Statement I Gause's competitive exclusion principle states that two closely related species competing for different resources cannot exist indefinitely.

Statement II According to Gause's principle, during competition, the inferior will be eliminated. This may be true, if resources are limiting.

In the light of the above statements, choose the correct answer from the options given below.
(a) Both statement I and statement II are true
(b) Both statement I and statement II are false
(c) Statement I is true, but statement II is false
(d) Statement I is false, but statement II is true

89. Match List I with List II.

List I	List II
A. Unicellular glandular epithelium	I. Salivary glands
B. Compound epithelium	II. Pancreas
C. Multicellular glandular epithelium	III. Goblet cells of alimentary canal
D. Endocrine glandular epithelium	IV. Moist surface of buccal cavity

Choose the correct answer from the options given below.

(a) A-II, B-I, C-III, D-IV
(b) A-IV, B-III, C-I, D-II
(c) A-III, B-IV, C-I, D-II
(d) A-II, B-I, C-IV, D-III

90. Match List I with List II related to digestive system of cockroach.

List I	List II
A. The structures used for storing of food	I. Gizzard
B. Ring of 6-8 blind tubules at junction of foregut and midgut.	II. Gastric caeca
C. Ring of 100-150 yellow coloured thin filaments at junction of midgut and hindgut.	III. Malpighian tubules
D The structures used for grinding the food.	IV. Crop

Choose the correct answer from the options given below.

(a) A-IV, B-II, C-III, D-I
(b) A-I, B-II, C-III, D-IV
(c) A-IV, B-III, C-II, D-I
(d) A-III, B-II, C-IV, D-I

91. Choose the correct statement given below regarding juxta medullary nephron.

(a) Juxta medullary nephrons are located in the columns of Bertini
(b) Renal corpuscle of juxta medullary nephron lies in the outer portion of the renal medulla
(c) Loop of Henle of juxta medullary nephron runs deep into medulla
(d) Juxta medullary nephrons out number the cortical nephrons

92. Match List I with List II.

List I	List II
A. RNA polymerase	I. *sn*RNPs
B. Termination of transcription	II. Promotor
C. Splicing of exons	III. *rho* factor
D. TATA box	IV. *sn*RNAs, *t*RNA

Choose the correct answer from the options given below.

(a) A-II, B-IV, C-I, D-III
(b) A-III, B-II, C-IV, D-I
(c) A-III, B-IV, C-I, D-II
(d) A-IV, B-III, C-I, D-II

93. Given below are two statements.

Statement I The cerebral hemispheres are connected by nerve tract known as corpus callosum.

Statement II The brain stem consists of the medulla oblongata, pons and cerebrum.

In the light of the above statements, choose the most appropriate answer from the options given below.

(a) Both statement I and statement II are true
(b) Both statement I and statement II are false
(c) Statement I is true, but statement II is false
(d) Statement I is false, but statement II is true

94. Identify the correct option (*A*), (*B*), (*C*), (*D*) with respect to spermatogenesis.

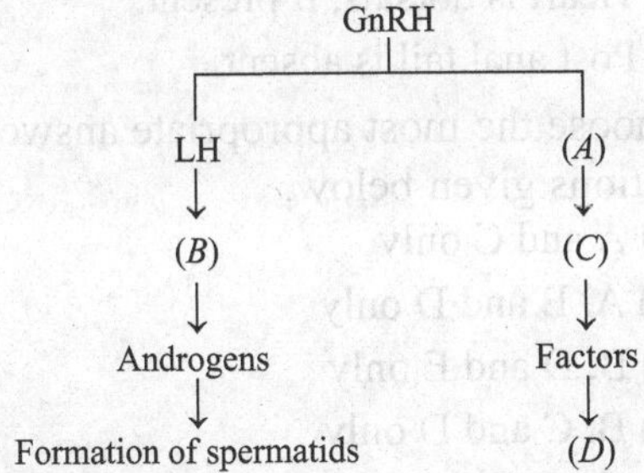

(a) FSH, Leydig cells, Sertoli cells, Spermiogenesis
(b) ICSH, Interstitial cells, Leydig cells, spermiogenesis
(c) FSH, Sertoli cells, Leydig cells, Spermatogenesis
(d) ICSH, Leydig cells, Sertoli cells, Spermatogenesis

95. As per the ABO blood grouping system, the blood group of father is B^+, mother is A^+ and child is O^+. Their respective genotype can be

A. $I^Bi / I^Ai / ii$
B. $I^BI^B / I^AI^A / ii$
C. $iI^B / iI^A / I^AI^B$
D. $I^Ai / I^Bi / I^Ai$
E. $iI^B / iI^A / I^AI^B$

Choose the most appropriate answer from the options given below.

(a) A only (b) B only
(c) C and B only (d) D and E only

96. Given below are two statements.

Statement I Bone marrow is the main lymphoid organ where all blood cells including lymphocytes are produced.

Statement II Both bone marrow and thymus provide micro-environments for the development and maturation of T-lymphocytes.

In the light of above statements, choose the most appropriate answer from the options given below.

(a) Both statement I and statement II are true
(b) Both statement I and statement II are false
(c) Statement I is true, but statement II is false
(d) Statement I is false, but statement II is true

97. Regarding catalytic cycle of an enzyme action, select the correct sequential steps.

A. Substrate enzyme complex formation
B. Free enzyme ready to bind with another substrate
C. Release of products
D. Chemical bonds of the substrate broken
E. Substrate binding to active site

Choose the correct answer from the options given below.

(a) E, A, D, C, B (b) A, E, B, D, C
(c) B, A, C, D, E (d) E, D, C, B, A

98. Match List I with List II.

	List I		List II
A.	P-wave	I.	Heart muscles are electrically silent
B.	QRS-complex	II.	Depolarisation of ventricles
C.	T-wave	III.	Depolarisation of atria
D.	T-P gap	IV.	Repolarisation of ventricles

Choose the correct answer from the options given below.

(a) A-I, B-III, C-IV, D-II
(b) A-III, B-II, C-IV, D-I
(c) A-II, B-III, C-I, D-IV
(d) A-IV, B-II, C-I, D-III

99. Match List I with List II.

	List I		List II
A.	Exophthalmic goitre	I.	Excess secretion of cortisol, moon face and hypergylcemia
B.	Acromegaly	II.	Hyposecretion of thyroid hormone and stunted growth
C.	Cushing's syndrome	III.	Hypersecretion of thyroid hormone and protruding eye balls
D.	Cretinism	IV.	Excessive secretion of growth hormone

Choose the correct answer from the options given below.

(a) A-I, B-III, C-II, D-IV

(b) A-IV, B-II, C-I, D-III

(c) A-III, B-IV, C-II, D-I

(d) A-III, B-IV, C-I, D-II

100. The following are the statements about non-chordates.

A. Pharynx is perforated by gill slits.

B. Notochord is absent.

C. Central nervous system is dorsal.

D. Heart is dorsals, if present.

E. Post anal tail is absent.

Choose the most appropriate answer from the options given below.

(a) A and C only

(b) A, B and D only

(c) B, D and E only

(d) B, C and D only

Response Index

Q	Options	Q	Options	Q	Options	Q	Options
01	(a) (b) (c) (d)	26	(a) (b) (c) (d)	51	(a) (b) (c) (d)	76	(a) (b) (c) (d)
02	(a) (b) (c) (d)	27	(a) (b) (c) (d)	52	(a) (b) (c) (d)	77	(a) (b) (c) (d)
03	(a) (b) (c) (d)	28	(a) (b) (c) (d)	53	(a) (b) (c) (d)	78	(a) (b) (c) (d)
04	(a) (b) (c) (d)	29	(a) (b) (c) (d)	54	(a) (b) (c) (d)	79	(a) (b) (c) (d)
05	(a) (b) (c) (d)	30	(a) (b) (c) (d)	55	(a) (b) (c) (d)	80	(a) (b) (c) (d)
06	(a) (b) (c) (d)	31	(a) (b) (c) (d)	56	(a) (b) (c) (d)	81	(a) (b) (c) (d)
07	(a) (b) (c) (d)	32	(a) (b) (c) (d)	57	(a) (b) (c) (d)	82	(a) (b) (c) (d)
08	(a) (b) (c) (d)	33	(a) (b) (c) (d)	58	(a) (b) (c) (d)	83	(a) (b) (c) (d)
09	(a) (b) (c) (d)	34	(a) (b) (c) (d)	59	(a) (b) (c) (d)	84	(a) (b) (c) (d)
10	(a) (b) (c) (d)	35	(a) (b) (c) (d)	60	(a) (b) (c) (d)	85	(a) (b) (c) (d)
11	(a) (b) (c) (d)	36	(a) (b) (c) (d)	61	(a) (b) (c) (d)	86	(a) (b) (c) (d)
12	(a) (b) (c) (d)	37	(a) (b) (c) (d)	62	(a) (b) (c) (d)	87	(a) (b) (c) (d)
13	(a) (b) (c) (d)	38	(a) (b) (c) (d)	63	(a) (b) (c) (d)	88	(a) (b) (c) (d)
14	(a) (b) (c) (d)	39	(a) (b) (c) (d)	64	(a) (b) (c) (d)	89	(a) (b) (c) (d)
15	(a) (b) (c) (d)	40	(a) (b) (c) (d)	65	(a) (b) (c) (d)	90	(a) (b) (c) (d)
16	(a) (b) (c) (d)	41	(a) (b) (c) (d)	66	(a) (b) (c) (d)	91	(a) (b) (c) (d)
17	(a) (b) (c) (d)	42	(a) (b) (c) (d)	67	(a) (b) (c) (d)	92	(a) (b) (c) (d)
18	(a) (b) (c) (d)	43	(a) (b) (c) (d)	68	(a) (b) (c) (d)	93	(a) (b) (c) (d)
19	(a) (b) (c) (d)	44	(a) (b) (c) (d)	69	(a) (b) (c) (d)	94	(a) (b) (c) (d)
20	(a) (b) (c) (d)	45	(a) (b) (c) (d)	70	(a) (b) (c) (d)	95	(a) (b) (c) (d)
21	(a) (b) (c) (d)	46	(a) (b) (c) (d)	71	(a) (b) (c) (d)	96	(a) (b) (c) (d)
22	(a) (b) (c) (d)	47	(a) (b) (c) (d)	72	(a) (b) (c) (d)	97	(a) (b) (c) (d)
23	(a) (b) (c) (d)	48	(a) (b) (c) (d)	73	(a) (b) (c) (d)	98	(a) (b) (c) (d)
24	(a) (b) (c) (d)	49	(a) (b) (c) (d)	74	(a) (b) (c) (d)	99	(a) (b) (c) (d)
25	(a) (b) (c) (d)	50	(a) (b) (c) (d)	75	(a) (b) (c) (d)	100	(a) (b) (c) (d)

Performance Scanner

Score	Remark
> 90% Excellent !	You have mastered the NEET syllabus. The concepts of this syllabus are on your fingertips. Maintain this momentum.
76-90% Very Good !	You have a good command over the NEET syllabus. Revise it again after a few days and enhance your performance.
60-75% Good !	You have a wide scope to learn for the NEET syllabus. Revise it again.
<60% Not Satisfactory!	You have a long way ahead of you to master the NEET syllabus. Revise it thoroughly.

MED+ACE

NEET (UG)

SELF ASSESSMENT KIT

Exactly as per the Latest pattern of NTA

BIOLOGY - XIIth

Hints, Explanations & Mind Maps Booklet

MEDACE

NEET (UG)

SELF ASSESSMENT KIT

Exactly as per the Latest pattern of NTA

BIOLOGY - XIIth

Hints, Explanations & Mind Maps Booklet

Authors

Rakhi Bisht, Kashvi & Anita

ARIHANT PRAKASHAN (SERIES), MEERUT

卐 **Administrative & Production Offices**

Regd. Office

'Ramchhaya' 4577/15, Agarwal Road, Darya Ganj, New Delhi -110002
Tele: 011- 47630600, 43518550

卐 **Head Office**

Kalindi, TP Nagar, Meerut (UP) - 250002
Tel: 0121-7156203, 7156204

卐 **Sales & Support Offices**

Agra, Ahmedabad, Bengaluru, Bareilly, Chennai, Delhi, Guwahati, Hyderabad, Jaipur, Jhansi, Kolkata, Lucknow, Nagpur & Pune.

卐 **PRICE** ₹1200.00

卐 **PO No :** TXT-59-T063620-03-25

Published by Arihant Publications (India) Ltd.

For further information about the books published by Arihant, log on to www.arihantbooks.com or e-mail at info@arihantbooks.com

CONTENT LIST

MEDACE

MEDACE

NEET (UG)

SELF ASSESSMENT KIT

HINTS & EXPLANATIONS

Ch-1 Sexual Reproduction in Flowering Plants

Topical Follow Thru

Test 1

1. (*b*) The incorrect statement can be corrected as
The endothecium does not provide nourishment to the developing pollen grains. Instead, the tapetum, another layer within the microsporangium, is responsible for nourishing the pollen grains.

2. (*c*) Amphitropous ovule involves presence of a horse-shoe shaped nucellus. It is found in family– Alismataceae. Other options can be explained as
Anatropous ovule- Micropyle lie close to funicle, e.g. in most angiosperms.
Orthotropous ovule - Micropyle and funicle lie in one line, e.g. Polygonaceae.
Circinotropous ovule- Inverted ovule; e.g. Cactaceae.

3. (*c*) The sequence of microsporogenesis with correct ploidy level is-sporogenous tissue-$2n$, PMC-$2n$, microspore tetrad-n.

4. (*c*) The structure '*C*' represents the tapetum which is distinguished by its dense cytoplasm, teaming with organelles for vital metabolic activities to support pollen maturation.
Other options can be explained as
Structure *A* represents the middle layers which are involved in protection of anther.
Structure *B* represents the microspore mother cells. They have a single nucleus with a moderate amount of cytoplasm.
Structure *D* represents the pollen grains that typically possess two cells, the vegetative cell and the generative cell, in its mature state.

5. (*c*) The four layers of microsporangia from outer to inner side are
Epidermis - endothecium - middle layers - tapetum.
Epidermis is the outermost layers of the microsporangium, providing protection.
Endothecium located just beneath the epidermis, plays a role in the dehiscence of the anther.
Middle layer situated below the endothecium, often degenerate as the anther matures.
Tapetum is the innermost layer and is crucial for nourishing the developing pollen grains.

6. (*b*) A- 2, B- 4, C- 1, D- 3.
The microspore undergoes mitotic division to give rise to two unequal cells. The vegetative cell is a larger one and gives rise to a pollen tube.
The generative cell is the smaller one which further divides to form two male gametes.
The wall of pollen grain is called sporoderm. It consists of inner intine and outer exine.
The exine consists of sporopollenin. Intine is a thin and continuous layer consisting of cellulose and pectin.

7. (*b*) Both statement I and statement II are correct and can be explained as
The pollen grains are spherical in shape. Their diameter is measured at about 20-50 μm. As the anther matures and dehydrates, the microspores dissociate from each other and develop into pollen grains.

8. (*a*) A is false, but R is true. A can be corrected as
The megaspore mother cell divides meiotically, but only once, to form four megaspores. Out of these, only one megaspore remains functional.
This functional megaspore undergoes three successive mitotic divisions, resulting in an eight-nucleate embryo sac.

9. (*d*) Statements I and IV are correct. The other incorrect statements can be corrected as
Integuments are the protective envelopes around the ovule.
The ovule body fuses with the funicle in the region called hilum.
Integuments encircle the nucellus, leaving a small opening at the tip, known as micropyle.

10. (*a*) Incorrectly matched pair can be corrected as
The filiform apparatus guides the pollen tubes and not the pollen grains into synergids.

11. (*b*) Both statement I and statement II are correct.
Pollen grains are microscopic and are easily blown by wind. Many species of pollen grains cause allergies and bronchial infections as they impact the mucous membranes of the eyes, nose, etc. *Parthenium* or carrot grass is one such species.

12. (*c*) In about 40% of angiosperms, the generative cell (A) divides mitotically to give rise to two male gametes (B) before pollen grains are shed at 3-celled state. In about 60% of species, pollen grains (C) are shed at 2-celled stage.

13. (*c*) The funicle is the stalk that attaches the ovule to the placenta. The point where the funicle attaches to the ovule itself (which includes the nucellus) is called the hilum.

14. (*d*) Callose is a plant polysaccharide that surrounds the microspore mother cell. It acts as a temporary wall to prevent the product of meiosis from cohesion and fusion and its dissolution results in the release of pollen grains.

15. (*d*) The incorrect statement can be corrected as

A single microsporangium produces several thousands, and not millions of pollen grains.

Test 2

1. (*b*) Stamens positioned above the pistil make it likely for pollen to fall directly on the stigma. This promotes self-pollination.
2. (*a*) Statements I and IV are correct. Statements II, III and V can be corrected as

Geitonogamy provides no genetic variation as the pollen comes from the same plant.

Bright colours, fragrance and sticky pollen are adaptations for attracting animal pollinators, not for wind pollination.

In species like *Viola, Oxalis* and *Commelina*, two types of flowers, i.e. chasmogamous and cleistogamous flowers are found.

3. (*d*) The incorrect statement can be corrected as

The type of pollination that brings the genetically different types of pollen grains to the stigma is xenogamy, not cleistogamy.

4. (*a*) Xenogamy does not produce similar types of offsprings. This is because, in xenogamy, hybrid type of offsprings are formed as it takes place between two genetically different plants.
5. (*a*) A–4, B–3, C–2, D–1.
   - The chasmogamous flowers have exposed anther and stigma like other flowers.
   - In cleistogamous flowers, the anthers and stigma lie close to each other.
   - The transfer of pollen grains from anther to the stigma of a different plant is called xenogamy.
   - The transfer of pollen grains from the anther to the stigma of another flower of the same plant is called geitonogamy.
6. (*d*) Statement I is correct, but statement II is incorrect. The incorrect statement can be corrected as

The wind pollination is more common amongst abiotic pollinations.

7. (*a*) Incorrect statement is in option (a) and it can be corrected as

Pollination by water is quite rare in flowering plants and is limited to about 30 genera, mostly monocotyledons.

8. (*d*) Outbreeding is the mechanism in which the plants adapt to prevent self-pollination. The reason behind the adoption of such techniques by plants is due to continued inbreeding. One of the device from outbreeding is to prevent inbreeding is self-incompatibility. It prevents self-pollen from fertilising the ovules by inhibiting germination or pollen tube growth in the pistil.
9. (*b*) Statements II and IV are incorrect. These can be corrected as

The biotic agent comes in contact with stigma as well as anther for harvesting the nectar.

The flowers pollinated by flies and beetles secrete foul odours to attract these animals.

10. (*a*) In papaya, the unisexual (dioecious) flowers are produced which help in preventing both autogamy and geitonogamy.
11. (*b*) Statements I, II and III are correct. The incorrect statement can be corrected as

Not all plants exhibit mechanism to prevent self-pollination. Other options can be explained as

Self-incompatibility specifically targets self-pollen, preventing inbreeding.

Monoecious plants with separate male and female flowers cannot self-pollinate (autogamy), but can still exchange pollen between flowers on the same plant (geitonogamy).

Self-incompatibility is highly effective as compared to have monoecious plants, and less effective than to have dioecious plants.

12. (*c*) The ability of pistil to recognise the pollen followed by its acceptance or rejection is the result of a continuous dialogue between pollen grain and pistil.
13. (*b*) Sugar solution is the most suitable solution for the given experiment as it provides essential nutrients (mainly carbohydrates) for the pollen grain to initiate germination and support pollen tube growth. A 10% concentration is commonly used as it balances providing energy without hindering the process through high osmotic pressure.
14. (*a*) A-4,1, B-3, C-2, D-5.

Syngamy is also known as amphimixis which gives rise to zygote.

The fusion of a male gamete with the central cell is known as triple fusion as it involves three nuclei, two polar nuclei and one male gamete. It gives rise to triploid Primary Endosperm Nucleus (PEN) and Cell (PEC).

Emasculation and bagging are done during artificial hybridisation.

Emasculation is removal of anther, while bagging is covering of emasculated flower.

15. (*c*) Both A and R are true, but R is not the correct explanation of A.

Majority of angiosperms bear chasmogamous flowers, means the flower expose their mature anthers and stigma to the pollinating agents. There is another group of plants which set seeds without exposing their sex organs, such flowers are called cleistogamous and the phenomenon is known as cleistogamy.

Test 3

1. (*b*) The free nuclear endosperm is the liquid portion in a young coconut, containing free nuclei suspended in a nutrient-rich solution.
2. (*a*) Statements I, II and III are correct. The incorrect statements can be corrected as

While free nuclear endosperm is the most common type, some flowering plants exhibit cellular endosperm development, where cell walls form after each nuclear division.

Seed coats develop from tissues surrounding the ovule, not the endosperm itself.

3. (*d*) The correct match pairs are given in 2 and 4.

Proembryo is the initial stage of cell division after the zygote divides. It marks the beginning of the embryonic development.

Mature embryo is the final stage of embryo development, where the embryo has formed all its essential organs and structures, ready for germination or birth (depending on the plant species).

4. (*a*) Statements I, III, IV and V are correct. Only statement II is incorrect and can be corrected as

Dicot embryo is initially undifferentiated and globular in shape. An early embryo with radial symmetry is termed a pro-embryo. Eventually, pro-embryo becomes heart-shaped.

5. (*d*) The correct options are B and D.

B is the hypocotyl which is the stalk-like part below the cotyledons. It ends in the root tip (radicle).

D is the scutellum, which is the cotyledon of grass family and is located on the side of the embryonic axis.

6. (*c*) In the grain of maize, the cotyledon is modified into an organ called scutellum. The scutellum absorbs the food of endosperm and supplies it to the developing embryo.

7. (*a*) The part A is the edible one. It represents the thalamus as apple is a false fruit. Other parts are: B is the seed, C is endocarp, while D shows the mesocarp.

8. (*b*) A-4, B-3, C-2, D-1.

In favourable conditions, ovules mature into seeds and ovary into fruits, simultaneously.

The wall of ovary develops into the wall of fruit, pericarp. The fruits may be fleshy as in guava, orange, mango, etc. or may be dry, as in groundnut and mustard, etc.

9. (*b*) Both statement I and statement II are correct. Seeds have better adaptive strategies for dispersal to new habitats and help plants to colonise in other areas due to sufficient food reserves.

Hard seed coat provides protection to the young embryo.

10. (*c*) A-1, B-2, C-4, D-3.

Cashew is a false fruit.

Corolla falls off after fertilisation.

Perisperm (residual/persistent nucellus) can be found in some seeds such as black pepper and beet.

Persistent endosperm is found in case of castor and coconut.

11. (*a*) A record of 2000 years old viable seed is of date palm.

12. (*d*) The incorrect statement can be corrected as

Polyembryony is suitable for large-scale production of uniform plants.

13. (*c*) Endosperm is triploid ($3n$). Thus, if it has 36 number of chromosomes, then haploid number is 12.

So, number of chromosomes in the given part of embryo sac will be

Nucellus ($2n$) $= 2 \times 12 = 24$

Male gamete (n) $= 12$

Synergids (n) $= 12$

Antipodals (n) $= 12$

Female gamete (n) $= 12$

Integument ($2n$) $= 2 \times 12 = 24$

14. (*b*) Both A and R are true and R is the correct explanation of A.

Endosperm provides nourishment to the developing embryo. Thus, embryo development starts after the endosperm is formed.

15. (*b*) Thalamus contributes to fruit formation in apple, strawberry and cashewnut. In such plant species where the thalamus contributes to the fruit formation along with ovary, the fruits are called false fruit.

On the other hand, fruit formed directly from ovary are called true fruits, e.g. mango. Banana is a parthenocarpic fruit.

Chapter Break Thru

1. (*c*) The tapetal layer of the microsporangial wall does not help in the dehiscence of anther. The endothecium layer helps in the dehiscence of anther. The rest of the options are correct about the functions of the tapetal layer.

2. (*a*) Only statements I and III are correct. Rest statements are incorrect and can be corrected as

Microspores undergo further mitosis and differentiation to become mature pollen grains.

The pollen sac wall becomes multilayered during development, providing protection and support.

3. (*b*) Both A and R are true and R is the correct explanation of A.

The exine is a hard layer made of sporopollenin, a resistant organic material.

This hardness provides protection for the pollen grains during several crucial stages such as dispersal and germination.

4. (*d*) The development of microsporangia leads to the formation of pollen sacs. These pollen sacs are labelled as D. These are the cavities that produce pollen grains.

5. (*d*) Statement I is correct, but statement II is incorrect. The incorrect statement can be corrected as

The generative cell is small and floats in the cytoplasm of the vegetative cell. It is spindle-shaped with dense cytoplasm and a nucleus.

6. (*b*) Some plants can cause allergic reactions because the body's immune system mistakenly identifies certain elements in pollen as a threat, leading to an allergic reaction.

The allergic reactions are typically caused by the body's immune system overreacting to specific proteins in a foreign substance, such as pollen.

While pollen has other components, proteins are the most likely culprit in triggering allergies.

7. (*a*) Statements III and V are incorrect and can be corrected as

Pollen grains increase the performance of athletes and race horses.

Carrot grass came to India with imported wheat (not rice) as a contaminant and caused pollen allergy.

8. (*b*) The papaya, watermelon and orchids have more than one ovule located inside their ovary.

9. (*b*) A-3, B-4, C-1, D-2.

Funicle is a stalk that attaches ovule to the placenta.

Integuments (one or two) encircles the ovules as protective envelops.

Chalaza is the basal part of ovule present opposite to the micropyle.

Nucellus is a mass of cell enclosed within integument and possesses abundant food reserves.

10. (*d*) The chalazal pole represented by 'D', acts as the attachment point of ovule where three antipodal cell lie. It is present opposite to the micropylar end.

11. (*d*) Statement I is correct, but statement II is incorrect. Incorrect statement can be corrected as

The nucleus of a functional megaspore divides mitotically to form two nuclei which move to the opposite poles, forming the 2-nucleate embryo sac.

12. (*c*) Statements I, III and IV are incorrect and can be corrected as

There occur 3 sequential mitotic nuclear divisions that results in, respectively 2-nucleate, 4-nucleate and 8-nucleate stages of embryo sac.

Instead of four, six of the eight nuclei are surrounded by the cell walls and organised into cells. Two polar nuclei are situated below the egg apparatus in the large central cell when chalazal end is considered at top.

13. (*c*) Both statement I and statement II are incorrect. These can be corrected as

At the micropylar end, three cells are grouped together to form the egg apparatus.

The egg apparatus comprises two synergids and one egg cell.

14. (*b*) During megagametogenesis, the functional megaspore divides three times by mitotic division. As a result, eight haploid nuclei and seven cells are formed.

15. (*a*) The cleistogamous flowers are the ones that ensure seed production in the absence of pollinators. It is because, in these flowers, pollination occurs in the bud stage of the flower.

16. (*b*) Both A and R are true and R is the correct explanation of A.

Honeybee visit flowers to gather nectar and turn it into honey.

Visiting of insects for nectar helps in pollination.

17. (*a*) Statement I is incorrect, but statement II is correct. Incorrect statement can be corrected as

Wind-pollinated flowers typically rely on wind for pollen dispersal and do not require the visual or olfactory cues needed to attract insects.

18. (*c*) A-4, B-1, C-2, D-3.

Zoophily is the pollination that occurs by animals.

Ornithophily is the pollination that occurs by birds.

Entomophily is the pollination that occurs by insects.

Chiropterophily is the pollination that occurs by bats.

19. (*b*) *Vallisneria* is a specific example of a freshwater plant that relies on water pollination. Its female flowers reach the water surface by long stalks, and male flowers release pollen grains that float on the water, potentially reaching the female stigma for pollination.

20. (*d*) All statements are correct except statement I. The incorrect statement can be corrected as

Self-incompatibility is a mechanism to prevent inbreeding. It allows a plant to perform outbreeding.

21. (*d*) Statement I is correct, but statement II is incorrect.

The incorrect statement can be corrected as

Self-pollination can be advantageous in some situations, such as ensuring seed production in environments with limited pollinators. Not all flowering plants need to prevent it completely.

22. (*d*) Statement in option (d) is incorrect. It can be corrected as

Emasculation is the removal of anthers from the flower bud before the anther dehisces in bisexual flowers.

23. (*b*) In the given figure, A, B and C represent geitonogamy, xenogamy and autogamy, respectively.

Continued autogamy results in inbreeding depression.

24. (*a*) Non-albuminous seeds have no residual endosperm and rely on thickened cotyledons for stored food reserves.

25. (*b*) Both statement I and statement II are correct.

Endosperm is formed by the fusion of one male gamete and secondary nucleus.

It is known as triple fusion as three nuclei are involved in the process. It is responsible for providing nutrition to the developing embryo.

26. (*b*) Both A and R are true and R is the correct explanation of A.

Pea is known as ex-albuminous or non-endospermic seed because its seed lacks endosperm. The endosperm is completely used by the developing embryo.

27. (*d*) Option (d) is incorrect and can be corrected as

It is the seeds, not the fruit whose water content gets reduced and they get dried on maturation.

28. (*c*) The cotyledons (C) serve as the food storage structures in some seeds, and the diagram shows relatively thick cotyledons compared to other parts. Endosperm (A) also helps in providing nutrition.

29. (*a*) Statement I is incorrect, but statement II is correct.

The incorrect statement can be corrected as

Apomixis acts as an alternative strategy, implying these plant

families might also have sexual reproduction.
In apomixis, an embryo forms from an unfertilised egg cell, mimicing asexual reproduction with seeds.

30. (*c*) Option (c) directly addresses the problem of need to buy new hybrid seeds every year.
Apomixis would allow farmers to reuse seeds from the hybrid crop, maintaining the desired traits.

31. (*a*) In cereals such as wheat, rice and maize, the endosperm typically persists in the mature seed. This is because the endosperm serves as a crucial source of nutrients for the seeding during germination.

32. (*c*) In the process of endosperm development, the Primary Endosperm Nucleus (PEN) undergoes successive nuclear divisions without the formation of cell walls between the nuclei initially. This stage is known as the free-nuclear endosperm stage.

33. (*b*) Given figure shows pollination by water in *Vallisneria*, where pollen travels through water to reach the female flower.

34. (*a*) Statement I is incorrect, but statement II is correct. Statement I can be corrected as
The primary role of endosperm development is to provide nutritional support, not structural support to the developing embryo.

35. (*b*) The primary disadvantage of cleistogamous flowers is that they only allow for self-pollination. Self-pollination involves the transfer of pollen from the anther to the stigma of the same flower on another flower on the same plant. This means that the genetic material being exchanged is very similar or identical, resulting in limited genetic variation.

36. (*c*) All statements are correct, except II, it can be corrected as
The bilobed nature of an anther is very distinct in the transverse section of the anther.

37. (*b*) *Viola*, *Oxalis* and *Commelina* are the plants that produce both chasmogamous and cleistogamous flowers. This dual strategy allows them to maximise their chances of successful pollination and seed set under varying environmental conditions.

38. (*c*) The vegetative cell is responsible for forming the pollen tube, which grows through the style and into the ovule, allowing the male gametes to reach and fertilise the egg cell and central cell.

39. (*a*) The given figure represents pollen tetrad. The tetrad stage is a key step in the formation of pollen grains, as each microspore in the tetrad will develop into an individual pollen grain.

40. (*d*) A is true, but R is false, it can be corrected as
In flowers with exposed anther and stigma, autogamy is rare to occur because for autogamy to occur, there must be synchrony in pollen release and stigma receptivity and the anthers and stigma must lie close to each other.

41. (*b*) The correct order is as follows : II $\rightarrow$ IV $\rightarrow$ I $\rightarrow$ III.
The protoplast of pollen grain divides mitotically to form two unequal cell - a small thin walled generative cell and a large vegetative cell.

42. (*b*) The endothecium is involved in the dehiscence of the anther, which is crucial for releasing pollen grains. If it cannot function properly, the anther would not be able to open and release the pollen.

43. (*a*) The given figure I represents multicarpellary, syncarpous pistil of *Papaver* and figure II represents multicarpellary, apocarpous gynoecium of *Michelia*.

44. (*b*) The dense cytoplasm and multiple nuclei in tapetal cells enhance their metabolic activity, allowing them to produce and transport nutrients efficiently to the developing pollen grains.

45. (*d*) Statement I is correct, but statement II is incorrect, it can be corrected as
Sporogenous tissue is a group of compactly arranged homogenous cells that occupy the center of a microsporangium in a young anther. Each sporogenous cell is also known as a pollen mother cell or microspore mother cell.

46. (*c*) A-3, B-4, C-1, D-2.
- Pollen grains represents the male gametophytic generation.
- Embryo sac represents the female gametophytic generation.
- At the micropylar end, synergid cells are present and at the chalazal end, three antipodal cells are present.

47. (*b*) During the formation of the embryo sac, the initial nuclear divisions occur without immediate cell wall formation. This process is crucial for the development of the embryo sac.

48. (*b*) Both A and R are true and R is the correct explanation of A.
In a majority of flowering plants, one of the megaspores is functional, while the other three degenerate. Only the functional megaspore develops into the embryo sac. This method is termed monosporic development.

49. (*a*) In flowering plants (with $n = 8$), integuments are diploid structure, hence their chromosomes number will be 16. Antipodals and synergid cells are haploid entities consisting of 8 chromosomes, while endosperm is triploid structure consisting of 24 chromosomes.

50. (*b*) Each pollen grains divides mitotically to form two cells,a large vegetative cell and small generative cell. The generative cell divides by mitosis and produces two male gametes.

Ch-2 Human Reproduction

Topical Follow Thru

Test 1

1. (*c*) Each seminiferous tubule is lined on its inside by two types of cells called male germ cells (spermatogonia) and sertoli cells. Interstitial cells or Leydig cells are present in the region outside the seminiferous tubules.

2. (*b*) Seminal plasma is contributed by the seminal vesicles which provide the majority of the fluid, the prostate gland, which adds enzymes and nutrients, and the bulbourethral glands, which secrete a lubricating mucus.

3. (*d*) The clitoris is a tiny finger-like structure which lies at the upper junction of the two labia minora above the urethral opening.

4. (*a*) The correct path of milk production to its suction out of the body by the baby is

Mammary alveoli- Mammary tubules- Mammary ducts- Mammary ampulla- Lactiferous duct- Nipples.

5. (*a*) Statement I is incorrect, but statement II is correct. Incorrect statement can be corrected as

Male sex accessory ducts includes rete testis, vasa efferentia, epididymis and vas deferens.

6. (*b*) Tunica vasculosa, tunica albuginea and tunica vaginalis is the correct sequence of layers of testis from inside to outside.

Testis remains covered with three coats. Tunica vasculosa is the innermost layer, tunica albuginea is the middle layer and tunica vaginalis is the outermost coat of the testis.

7. (*b*) Statements I, III, and IV are correct. Statements II and V are incorrect and can be corrected as

The uterus is supported by ligaments attached to the pelvic wall.

The myometrium exhibits strong contractions during the delivery of the baby.

8. (*c*) The correct match is A–2, B–4, C–5, D–3, E–1.

Interstitial cells or Leydig cells synthesise and secrete androgen (testicular hormone). Prostate gland is unpaired and enhances motility of spermatozoa. Sertoli cells provides nutrition to the male germ cells or spermatogonia. Seminal vesicles are paired and club-shaped gland located posteriorly to prostate gland.

Testicular lobules are the functional unit of paired male organ, testis.

9. (*a*) A is false, but R is true. A can be corrected as

The ampulla is the longest and widest part of the Fallopian tube, however it connects isthmus to the uterus.

10. (*b*) *A*–Seminal vesicle, *B*–Prostate gland and *C*–Bulbourethral gland.

In the given diagram of the male reproductive system, the Seminal vesicle is located near the bladder, the Prostate gland is situated just below the bladder surrounding the urethra, and the Bulbourethral gland is found below the prostate, along the urethra.

11. (*a*) The epididymis is a long, coiled tube that connects the testes to the vas deferens. After sperm cells are produced in the testes, they move to the epididymis, where they mature and gain the ability to move and fertilize an egg. The mature sperms are then stored in the epididymis until ejaculation.

12. (*c*) The cavity of the cervix, cervical canal which alongwith vagina forms the birth canal.

13. (*d*) The bulbourethral gland, also known as Cowper's gland, secretes a pre-ejaculate fluid that lubricates the penis and neutralises any acidity, providing a smoother passage for sperm during ejaculation. Removing the gland would primarily affect this lubrication process.

14. (*d*) The correct flow chart for the pathway of sperm transportation in human males is as follows

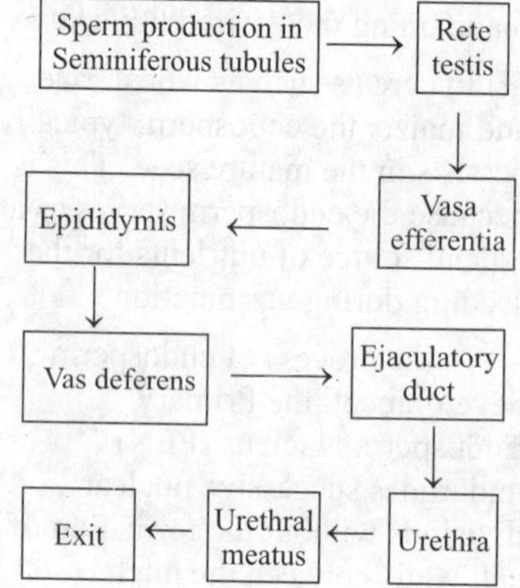

15. (*c*) Statement in option (c) is incorrect. Secretions of seminal gland are alkaline in nature. These neutralise acidity of male urethra and vagina to facilitate the survival of spermatozoa.

Test 2

1. (*d*) A human female has the maximum number of primary oocytes in her ovaries at birth, with approximately 1-2 million oocytes within each fetal ovary. This number declines over time and by puberty, around 60,000 - 80,000 oocytes remain. Throughout a female's reproductive years, the number of oocytes continues to decrease due to ovulation and atresia (natural cell death). By menopause, very few, if any, functional primary oocytes are left.

2. (*b*) Spermatogenesis is the process of sperm production. Sertoli cells contribute to spermatogenesis by releasing testosterone. It also regulate excess spermatogenesis by releasing inhibin hormone. Inhibin sends negative feedback to hypothalamus to stop FSH which eventually restricts further spermatogenesis.

3. (*c*) The correct match is A-4, B-3, C-2 and D-1.
Menstrual cycle occurs in four major phases namely,
- Follicular phase in which Graafian follicle is formed from primary oocyte by the regulation of FSH hormone.
- Ovulatory phase in which Graafian follicle gets ruptured to release the secondary oocyte or ovum due to increased secretion of LH.
- Luteal phase is marked by the presence of corpus luteum which regress to corpus albicans in the absence of fertilisation.
- Menstrual phase occurs due to breakdown of endometrium lining of uterus and blood vessels. It lasts for 3-5 days.

4. (*a*) Each spermatid undergoes a maturation process called spermiogenesis to transform into a single sperm cell. Therefore, 100 spermatids will produce 100 sperm.

5. (*c*) In given diagram of sperm *A* is mitochondria, energy source for motility. These are present in numerous amount in middle piece, which provide energy for the movement of tail to facilitate sperm motility and maintains the structure of sperm.
B is acrosome, a cap-like structure present on sperm head after an elongated nucleus. It is filled with enzymes that help fertilisation of the ovum.

6. (*b*) I–Interstitial cells, II–Sertoli cells and III–Spermiogenesis.
LH acts on Leydig cells or interstitial cells, while FSH acts on Sertoli cells. LH stimulates spermatogenesis by synthesis and secretion of androgen, while the FSH is important to stimulate spermiogenesis.

7. (*c*) The correct flowchart for spermatogenesis is as follow

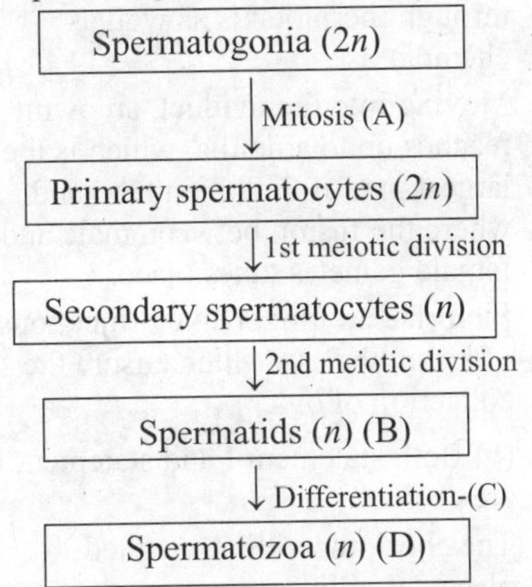

8. (*c*) A haploid set of chromosomes means having 23 chromosomes, which is the characteristic of gametes or cells involved in sexual reproduction.
The secondary oocyte, produced after the first meiotic division of the primary oocyte, has 23 chromosomes and is thus haploid. In contrast, oogonia and primary oocytes are diploid, each with 46 chromosomes, while a zygote, formed by the fusion of a sperm and an ovum, is also diploid with 46 chromosomes.

9. (*d*) A is true, but R is false. R can be corrected as
Rapid secretion of LH peaks during the mid-cycle and causes LH surge and thereby the release of ovum (ovulation).

10. (*a*) The degenerative process of follicles or eggs in the ovary is correctly termed "atresia," not "regression". Atresia refers to the natural degeneration and resorption of immature ovarian follicles that do not reach ovulation.

11. (*c*) Both A and R are true, but R is not the correct explanation of A.
The menstrual cycle typically lasts about 28 days and the luteal phase is consistently around 14 days, the reason the menstrual cycle is approximately 28 days long also involves the variable length of the follicular phase, not just the consistent duration of the luteal phase.

12. (*c*) The role of Gonadotropin Releasing Hormone (GnRH) is to stimulate the production of gonadotropins, LH (Luteinizing Hormone) and FSH (Follicle Stimulating Hormone.
Both LH and FSH attain a peak level in the middle of cycle (about 14th day). FSH stimulates the growth of ovarian follicles, while LH helps in the process of rupture of graafian follicle, and release of ovum, i.e., ovulation.

13. (*a*) During the luteal phase, the corpus luteum forms and secretes high levels of progesterone and some estrogen. These elevated hormone levels provide negative feedback to the hypothalamus and pituitary gland, reducing the secretion of Luteinizing Hormone (LH). As a result, LH levels decline during this phase.

14. (*a*) Statement I is incorrect, but statement II is correct. Incorrect statement can be corrected as
There is no similarity between estrous cycle and menstrual cycle except the ovulation. Estrous cycle occurs only in the breeding season, while in the menstrual cycle, breeding season is not specified.

15. (*c*) Statements I, III and IV are correct, whereas statements II and V are incorrect. The incorrect statements can be corrected as
The difference in the process of spermatogenesis and oogenesis results in a significant difference in the size of sperm and ova and thus sperms are much smaller than ova.
Spermiogenesis results in four sperms, while, oogenesis results in one ovum and a tiny polar body.

Test 3

1. (*c*) Spermatozoa (sperm) ejaculated by male follows the following pathway
Vagina → Cervix → Uterus → Isthmus → Ampulla (fertilisation of ovum and sperm)
Thus, the spermatozoa does not pass through infundibulum during fertilisation.

2. (*c*) Both A and R are true, but R is not the correct explanation of A. The correct reason is as follows
Fertilisation can only occur if the ovum and sperms are transported simultaneously to the ampullary region. This is the reason why not all copulations lead to fertilisation and pregnancy.

3. (*a*) The correct order of events of fertilisation is
III → I → V → II → IV
The process of fertilisation begins with the acrosomal reaction (III), where the sperm's acrosome releases enzymes to penetrate the egg. This allows the entry of the sperm into the egg cytoplasm (I). The egg then completes meiosis-II (V), followed by karyogamy (II) and then, the fusion of the sperm and egg nuclei. Finally, a zygote (IV) is formed, marking the end of fertilisation.

4. (*b*) During blastulation, the blastula forms, eventually developing into a blastocyst. The trophoblast, an outer layer of cells in the blastocyst, adheres to the uterine wall during implantation.
This structure plays a crucial role in establishing contact with the maternal tissues and facilitating the exchange of nutrients and waste, supporting pregnancy.

5. (*b*) The correct match is A-2, B-4, C-1 and D-3.
Endometrium forms a lining within the uterus to provide support to the implantation of zygote after fertilisation. Endometrium plays a key role in the formation of placenta.
Oviduct releases ova after ovulation as well as guides the path of sperm through thermotaxis as well as chemotaxis.
Moving into the oviduct, an ovum reaches up to ampulla, which is the largest part of Fallopian tube and where the fusion between male and female gametes takes place.
Fimbriae are finger-like projections of infundibulum which ensure the collection of ova.

6. (*b*) Both statement I and statement II are correct.
The chorionic villi also called placental villi, sprout from the area of chorion in order to ensure that the area of contact with maternal blood is maximised.
Placenta is formed by the interdigitation of chorionic villi and uterine tissue.

7. (*a*) The correct order of development of embryo is Zygote, Morula, Blastula and Gastrula. Development begins with the zygote, the fertilised egg cell formed by the union of sperm and egg. The zygote undergoes several divisions to become a morula, a solid ball of cells. The morula then develops into a blastula, characterised by a hollow ball of cells. Finally, the blastula undergoes gastrulation to form the gastrula.

8. (*a*) Oxytocin is said to be a main parturition hormone as well as it induces the milk ejection reflex.

9. (*a*) In human beings, after one month of pregnancy, the embryo's heart is formed. The first sign of growing foetus may be noticed by listening to the heart sound carefully through the stethoscope.

10. (*c*) The production of germ layers from the inner cell mass occurs during the process of gastrulation in embryonic development. The inner cell mass differentiates into three primary germ layers: ectoderm, mesoderm, and endoderm. The ectoderm forms the outer layer, giving rise to the skin and nervous system. The mesoderm forms the middle layer, developing into muscles, bones, and the circulatory system. The endoderm forms the inner layer, creating the digestive and respiratory systems. These germ layers are the foundation for all tissues and organs in the body.

11. (*c*) Option (c) is incorrect. It can be corrected as
The first movements of the foetus and appearance of hair on the head are usually observed during the fifth month.

12. (*d*) The foetal ejection reflex is triggered by signals originating from the fully developed foetus and the placenta. These signals initiate mild uterine contractions, which are part of the complex neuroendocrine mechanism leading to parturition.

13. (*b*) Option (b) is correct.
The corpus luteum, a temporary endocrine structure in the ovary, secretes progesterone, which prepares the uterus for pregnancy and supports early pregnancy by maintaining the uterine lining.
Incorrect matches can be corrected as
Placenta acts as an endocrine gland and synthesise hCG, oestrogen and progesterone. The pituitary gland produces oxytocin, which stimulates uterine contractions during childbirth and milk ejection during breastfeeding.
The ovary produces relaxin, a hormone that helps relax the ligaments in the pelvis and soften and widen the cervix during pregnancy.

14. (*a*) Statement I is incorrect, but Statement II is correct. The incorrect statement can be corrected as
The term gastrulation period is not used to refer to the duration of human pregnancy. The correct term is gestation period.

15. (*a*) Statement (a) is incorrect. It can be corrected as
Meiotic division of the secondary oocyte is completed at the time of fusion of a sperm with an ovum.

Chapter Break Thru

1. (*b*) Sperm consists of head, neck, middle part and tail. Middle part of sperm contains several mitochondria which produce energy to enhance the sperm motility.
2. (*c*) The correct sequence is III, IV, II, I and V.
   Rete testis are the minute tubules of testis which collect sperm produced in testis. Rete testis fuse to give rise to a ductule called vasa efferentia. It further opens into epididymis where functional maturation of sperms take place. Epididymis transfers sperms to vas deferens. Ejaculatory ducts are the site of ejaculation of sperm outside of body.
3. (*b*) In the diagram, H, I and J represents seminal vesicles, prostate and bulbourethral glands respectively. Secretions of male accessory glands, which include paired seminal vesicles, unpaired prostate gland and paired bulbourethral glands constitute the seminal plasma. This fluid is rich in fructose, calcium and certain enzymes.
4. (*a*) Statement (a) is incorrect and can be corrected as
   The scrotum helps in maintaining the low temperature of the testes (2–2.5°C lower than the normal internal body temperature), which is necessary for spermatogenesis, not specifically for the longevity of sperm.
5. (*c*) Placenta plays a vital role in fulfilment of respirational needs of foetus *via* diffusion of gases.
   Oxygen flows through the blood of mother and *via* placenta it reaches upto the growing foetus, simultaneously carbon dioxide molecule is also diffused into the mother's blood *via* placenta.
6. (*a*) After first trimester (12 weeks of pregnancy), the external genitals of the foetus are completely developed. Hence, doctor can determine the gender at this stage. However it is important to know that gender revelation is illegal in India.
7. (*c*) The uterus, also called womb, is the inverted pear-shaped structure where the embryo or foetus develops. In given diagram, C represents uterus, whereas A, B and D are pubic symphysis, urinary bladder and cervix respectively.
8. (*d*) Secondary spermatocytes and secondary oocytes are the correct set involving haploid cells.
   Spermatogonia and oogonia are diploid cells that undergo mitosis to produce primary spermatocytes and primary oocytes, respectively.
   Primary spermatocytes and primary oocytes are also diploid and undergo the first meiotic division to produce secondary spermatocytes and secondary oocytes respectively.
9. (*c*) The correct order of spermatogenesis is: Spermatogonia, Primary Spermatocytes, Secondary Spermatocytes, Spermatid.
   Spermatogenesis starts with spermatogonia, which are stem cells that divide mitotically.
   These cells differentiate into primary spermatocytes, which undergo the first meiotic division to form secondary spermatocytes. Secondary spermatocytes, then undergo the second meiotic division to produce spermatids. These spermatids are then transformed into spermatozoa (sperms).
10. (*d*) Tertiary mature follicle stage is also called as Graafian follicle stage.
    Graafian follicles surround the ovum to protect them, stromal cells give rise to Graafian folicle by the events of follicular development.
    The onset of formation of primary follicle is called primordial follicle which develops into primary follicle, which leads to formation of secondary follicle followed by formation of tertiary follicle.
    Fundamental development in tertiary follicle results in the maturation of tertiary follicle.
11. (*c*) The menstrual cycle encompasses the follicular/proliferative phase, characterized by follicular development and uterine lining growth. It also includes the luteal/secretory phase, marked by corpus luteum formation and hormone secretion. Lastly, the cycle involves the menses or menstruation phase, where the uterine lining sheds. Maturation phase is not part of the menstrual cycle.
12. (*c*) Statement (c) is incorrect and can be corrected as
    The female body loses about 30 to 50 mL blood during one menstrual cycle.
    Rest all other statements are correct about menstrual flow.
13. (*b*) The correct option is (b). The incorrect matches can be corrected as
    In proliferative phase, rapid regeneration of endometrium and maturation of Graafian follicle occur.
    Menstruation involves the breakdown of endometrium when ovum is not fertilised. Progesterone increases after ovulation due to its secretion by the corpus luteum.
14. (*c*) The onset of puberty in male is characterised by process of spermatogenesis that occurs due to significant increase in the secretion of gonadotropin releasing hormone (GnRH).
15. (*a*) Ampulla of Fallopian tube is the widest portion of tube where the fertilisation process of ova and sperm takes place. After fertilisation, the formed zygote reaches upto uterus to develop into pregnancy. When pregnancy happens, cervix gets closed to keep foetus inside the uterus.
16. (*b*) Both A and R are true and R is the correct explanation of A.
    Prevention from polyspermy is mandatory for the proper growth of the fertilised eggs otherwise polyspermy can show defective growth of the fertilised egg. Zona pellucida is the outer covering of oocyte which becomes impermeable to sperms immediately after encountering one sperm.
17. (*d*) Incorrect statement can be corrected as
    During cleavage, a single-celled zygote divides into many smaller

blastomeres, without increasing in mass. This means that each daughter cell has roughly half the cytoplasm of the original zygote and the ratio of nuclear to cytoplasmic material increases.

18. (*d*) Statement (d) is incorrect. It can be corrected as
The presence or absence of hymen is not a reliable indicator of virginity or sexual experience. The hymen is often torn during the first coitus (intercourse). However, it can also be broken by a sudden fall or jolt, insertion of a vaginal tampon, active participation in some sports like horseback riding, cycling, etc. In some women, the hymen persists even after coitus.

19. (*b*) After parturition (childbirth), the levels of progesterone and oestrogen decrease. This drop in hormone levels removes the inhibition on the hormone prolactin, allowing it to stimulate milk production. Meanwhile, oxytocin promotes the ejection of this milk. So, it's the lowering of progesterone and oestrogen that indirectly promotes milk ejection.

20. (*d*) During pregnancy, the urine of females contains Human Chorionic Gonadotropin (HCG), which is produced by the placenta after implantation. LH, Progesterone, and FSH are incorrect as they are not typically found in significant levels in the urine during pregnancy.

21. (*d*) The correct matches are A-1, B-3, C-2 and D-4.
- Leydig's cells, found in the testes, produce testosterone, which is crucial for the development and maintenance of male reproductive tissues and secondary sexual characteristics.
- During the proliferative phase of the menstrual cycle, estrogen levels rise, stimulating the growth and thickening of the uterine lining in preparation for potential implantation of a fertilised egg.
- The secretory phase occurs after ovulation, and it is characterised by increased progesterone production by the corpus luteum. Progesterone prepares the uterine lining for possible implantation and helps maintain pregnancy if fertilisation occurs.
- Spermatogenesis is regulated by hormones, including Gonadotropin Releasing Hormone (GnRH), which stimulates the release of Follicle-Stimulating Hormone (FSH) and Luteinizing Hormone (LH), necessary for spermatogenesis.

22. (*c*) The paired bulbourethral (Cowper's) glands are located near base of the penis. In response to sexual stimulation, the bulbourethral glands secrete an alkaline mucus-like fluid. This fluid helps in the neutralisation of acidity of urine and provides lubrication to the penis during intercourse.

23. (*a*) Statement I is incorrect, but statement II is correct. The incorrect statement can be corrected as
A secondary oocyte is formed after meiosis I of an oocyte, which occurs before fertilisation.

24. (*b*) Both A and R are true and R is the correct explanation of A.
The development of the Graafian follicle is essential for ovulation, as it produces estrogen. This estrogen triggers a surge in Luteinizing Hormone (LH), which is necessary for ovulation.

25. (*b*) Both statement I and statement II are correct.
Breasts enlargement starts at the time of puberty when prolactin hormone becomes active. Menarche refers to the first menstrual flow of a female which marks the onset of puberty. Therefore, it can be said that menarche indicates prolactin activation.

26. (*d*) Statements II, III and V are correct. Statements I and IV are incorrect and can be corrected as
Breakdown of endometrial lining and blood vessels causes menstrual flow. Therefore, there are no chances of pregnancy. Menstruation occurs at the end of menstrual cycle due to sudden decline in progesterone levels because of degeneration of corpus luteum.

27. (*b*) During fertilisation, a sperm comes in contact with the zona pellucida layer of the ovum) and induces changes in the membrane that block the entry of additional sperms. Thus, it ensures that only one sperm can fertilise an ovum.

28. (*d*) Statements I, IV, and V are correct. Statements II and III are incorrect. These can be corrected as
Limbs and digits develop by the end of the second month of pregnancy. By the end of 12 weeks (first trimester), most of the major organ systems are formed.

29. (*b*) Both statement I and statement II are correct.
Parturition is the process of giving birth. It is the delivery of full grown foetus on the completion of the normal pregnancy period.
During parturition, the cervix dilates and relaxes. Oxytocin helps in contraction of smooth muscles of myometrium of uterus which helps to direct the foetus towards birth canal. On the other hand, relaxin causes relaxation of the pelvic ligaments to prepare uterus for child birth.

30. (*c*) The correct matches are A-4, B-1, C-2 and D-3.
- The opening of the vagina is often covered partially by a membrane called hymen.
- The uterus opens into vagina through a narrow cervix. The cavity of the cervix is called cervical canal, which alongwith vagina forms the birth canal.
- The oviducts (Fallopian tubes), uterus and vagina constitute the female accessory ducts.
- The labia majora are fleshy folds of tissue, which extend down from the mons pubis and surround the vaginal opening.

31. (*c*) Both A and R are true, but R is not the correct explanation of A.
Low pH in the vaginal tract is essential to maintain vaginal health. This is because acidic conditions

protect against infectious microorganism.

32. (*a*) The correct order is A-D-E-B-C.
- The sperm binds to the zona pellucida layer of the secondary oocyte.
- The hydrolytic enzymes of the acrosome facilitate penetration of the layers of the secondary oocyte.
- The vitelline membrane of the secondary oocyte fuses with the plasma membrane of the sperm.
- These events trigger the completion of meiosis II of secondary oocyte thus forming second polar body and ootid.
- The nuclei of sperm and ovum fuses to form a diploid nucleus of the zygote.

33. (*d*) *X* is FSH and *Y* is LH. At around the mid of the cycle, LH surge causes ovulation. Following this, the Graafian follicle is converted to corpus luteum which secretes progesterone. Progesterone stimulates endometrial thickening for a possible implantation in case of successful fertilisation. Progesterone also inhibits the secretion of FSH and LH to prevent follicle development and ovulation of the next cycle to maintain and support the pregnancy.

34. (*c*) Statements I and II are correct. The structure is a product of mitotic division of the diploid zygote. Individual cells of the structure are called blastomeres.
The incorrect statements can be corrected as
Implantation into the endometrium occurs in the blastocyst stage which occurs after this stage.
Blastocoel appears in the stage following this. In the next stage called blastocyst, fluid filled cavity called blastocoel develops.
Germinal layers separate in the following stage (Blastocyst). The blastomeres of the blastocyst separate into trophoblast and inner cell mass. Inner cell mass forms the germinal layers ectoderm, mesoderm and endoderm.

35. (*b*) Statement in option (b) is incorrect and can be corrected as Corona radiata is a secondary egg membrane because it is not secreted by ovum itself. Zona pellucida is the primary egg membrane.
Rest all options are correct.

36. (*b*) Both A and R are true and R is the correct explanation of A.
Polyploidy is the condition when more than two sets of chromosomes are present. Humans, are diploid containing 23 pairs of chromosomes. When a sperm and ovum fuses, their nuclei fuses to restore the 46 chromosome condition. However, if multiple sperms fuse with a single ovum, multiple copies of chromosomes can exist which leads to the condition of polyploidy.

37. (*a*) B is the seminal vesicle. Seminal vesicles add fructose or sugar to the seminal fluid. This sugar is broken down by the mitochondria in the midpiece of the sperm to release energy for sperm motility.
A is urinary bladder that stores the urine.
C is prostate gland which makes the semen alkaline.
D is Bulbourethral gland that provides lubrication.

38. (*c*) Whatever be the number of primary spermatocyte, only one spermatozoa is able to fertilise an ovum and hence form a zygote.

39. (*a*) The correct match is A-2, B-3, C-4 and D-1.
- Seminiferous tubules open into vasa efferentia through rete testis. Rete testis is involved in transporting sperm to the vas deferens.
- Alveoli are the milk secreting cells present in the mammary glands.
- Urethral meatus is the opening of the urethra through which semen and urine are released.
- Clitoris is a finger-like structure located above the urethral opening and is richly supplied with blood vessels and nerves.

40. (*b*) Both A and R are true and R is the correct explanation of A.
Pregnant mother can transfer viral pathogens to the growing foetus through the placenta. Nutrients and oxygen are supplied to the foetus through the placenta, while excretory wastes are returned back to the maternal circulation. However, if mother is infected with a viral pathogen, in some cases viruses can cross the placental barrier to reach the developing foetus.

41. (*d*) Gonadotropins secreted by anterior pituitary are FSH and LH. FSH acts on Sertoli cells and stimulate the production of factors that help in spermiogenesis. LH acts on Leydig cells and stimulate the release of male hormones androgens like testosterone. Androgens control secondary sexual features in males like low pitched heavy voice, muscle development, growth of pubic hair etc. Androgens also regulate sperm production by spermatogenesis.
Hence, if there is under secretion of gonadotropins then there would be a low sperm count, under developed testes and low testosterone levels.

42. (*c*) *A* – Head, *B* – Neck, *C* – Middle piece and *D* – Tail. During fertilisation, the acrosomes release enzymes that digest zona pellucida of the secondary oocyte. The sperm plasma membrane fuses with the vitelline membrane of the secondary oocyte. Only the head of the sperm (A) enters the cytoplasm of the secondary oocyte for fusion, while the remaining parts are left outside.

43. (*c*) Increased secretion of FSH and LH are observed in the follicular or the proliferative phase. This leads to growth and development of the ovarian follicles into Graafian follicles followed by ovulation. The growing follicles also secrete estrogen during this period.

44. (*b*) The zona pellucida, a thick membrane that surrounds mammalian eggs, prevents polyspermy and becomes impermeable, preventing more sperms from entering.

45. (*c*) The correct pathway is Alveoli $\rightarrow$ mammary tubules $\rightarrow$ mammary duct $\rightarrow$ lactiferous duct.
The glandular tissue of each breast is divided into 15-20 mammary lobes containing cluster of milk secreting cells called alveoli. The alveoli open into mammary tubules. The tubules

of each lobe join to form mammary duct. Several mammary ducts join to form a wider ampulla that connects to the lactiferous duct through which milk is sucked out.

46. (*b*) Oxytocin causes uterine contractions at the end of gestation period to initiate parturition. Thus, the doctor will inject the synthetic, version of oxytocin to induce contraction.

47. (*d*) The primary oocyte surrounds itself with granulosa cells to form primary follicle. The primary follicle produces more granulosa cells and a new theca to form secondary follicle. Fluid filled antrum develops in the tertiary follicle.

It is at the stage of tertiary follicle when meiosis II completes in the primary oocyte resulting in an unequal division which forms the secondary oocyte and a tiny first polar body.

48. (*d*) The correct matches are A-2, B-4, C-1, D-3.

- Progesterone secreted by corpus luteum inhibits the secretion of FSH which prevents development of ovarian follicles and release of ovum. Also progesterone maintains the endometrial wall during the course of pregnancy and hence prevent their breakdown and menstruation.
- Relaxin secreted by the ovaries in pregnant females relaxes and loosens the muscles of the pelvis.
- hCG or human chorionic gonadotropin is secreted by the placenta and stimulates the secretion of progesterone by the corpus luteum.
- Oestrogen secreted by the ovaries control secondary sexual features in females like breast development.

49. (*d*) Statement I is correct, but statement II is incorrect and can be corrected as

Foetal ejection reflex stimulates the posterior pituitary of the pregnant female.

Mild uterine contractions called foetal ejection reflex triggers the release of oxytocin from the posterior pituitary of pregnant females.

Oxytocin in turn causes stronger contraction. Hence, uterine contractions and oxytocin hormone have stimulatory effect on one another.

50. (*a*) The outer layer of the blastocyst forms trophoblast. Trophoblast cells form chorionic villi which gets interdigitated with uterine tissue to form placenta.

The inner layer of blastocyst is organised into inner cell mass. Inner cell mass differentiates into the three germ layers which form different cell types of the body.

Ch-3 Reproductive Health

Topical Follow Thru

Test 1

1. (*a*) Intense lactation causes the suppression of GnRH, which in turn, reduces the secretion of LH and FSH. These hormones are crucial for ovulation, and their reduced levels prevent conception during the period of intense lactation.

2. (*a*) Gender equality, women empowerment, foeticide prevention is not the part of reproductive health problem and its strategies run by Indian government.

3. (*b*) Emergency contraceptive pills and implants contain either progestogens or oestrogen- progestogen hormones together in combination.

They inhibit ovulation and implantation as well as alter the quality of cervical mucus to prevent/retard entry of sperms.

4. (*b*) An increase in the population growth of an area is possible due to both low MMR (Maternal Mortality Rate) and IMR (Infant Mortality Rate). The proportion of reproductively active males and females in a population also influences population growth.

5. (*b*) Amniocentesis involves a procedure where a thin needle is inserted into the pregnant women's abdomen to extract a small sample of amniotic fluid. This fluid contains fetal cells that can be analysed for genetic disorders and other abnormalities.

6. (*a*) Statements I, II and III are correct, while statements IV and V are incorrect and can be corrected as

Phagocytosis of sperms does not happen during lactational amenorrhea. Instead, phagocytosis of sperm takes place at the time of fertilisation when sperm completely enters in the cytoplasm of ovum.

Natural fertility rate does not decrease as this is a temporary phase. As soon as ovulation restarts, the mother can conceive.

7. (*a*) A is false, but R is true. A can be corrected as

Periodic abstinence involves abstaining from intercourse during the fertile window, typically around ovulation, to prevent pregnancy. Periodic abstinence is avoiding intercourse when ovulation is expected, usually from day 10 to 17 of a typical menstrual cycle.

8. (*d*) While condoms are highly effective in preventing pregnancy and reducing the risk of STDs when used correctly, But they are not 100% reliable, there is a small chance of breakage or slippage which can lead to unintended pregnancy or transmission of STDs.

9. (*a*) In lactational amenorrhea, due to high prolactin level, ganadotropin level decreases.

Oral pills are either progestogens or progestogen-oestrogen combinations used by the females.

Emergency contraceptive includes the administration of progestogens combination or IUDS within 72 hours of coitus.

So, lactational amenorrhea, oral pills and emergency contraceptive involve a role of hormone.

10. (*d*) Statement I is correct, but statement II is incorrect and can be corrected as

Early sex education or reproductive education in schools or at home will never pollute the young brains, although it will help them to maintain their life free from reproductive pollution.

11. (c) Norplant contain progestin as its active ingredient. Progestin is a synthetic hormone that mimics the effects of progesterone. It prevents ovulation by suppressing the production of hormone that trigger it. It is effective for upto 5 years.

12. (*c*) The given diagram depicts implants, which contain steroidal hormones like progestogens alone or in combination with oestrogen. Their mode of action is similar to that of pills, i.e. they inhibit ovulation and implantation, as well as alter the quality of cervical mucus to prevent or retard the entry of sperm.

Additionally, their effective periods are much longer than that of oral pills.

13. (*c*) Features given in statements I, II and V are correct with respect to copper –T device.

The Copper-T device primarily prevents fertilisation by releasing copper ions that are toxic to sperm, suppressing sperm motility, and thereby preventing them from reaching the egg.

These IUDs does not enhance luteal activities. These are inserted by doctors or expert nurses in the uterus through vagina.

14. (*d*) The correct matches are A-1, B-3, C-2, D-4.

- Coitus interruptus or Withdrawal is the natural method in which the male partner withdraws his penis from the vagina just before ejaculation so as to avoid insemination.
- Lactational amenorrhea (absence of menstruation) method is based on the fact that ovulation does not occur during the period of intense lactation following parturition.
- Pills inhibit ovulation and implantation as well as alter the quality of cervical mucus to prevent/retard entry of sperms.
- Sterilisation is a surgical method that blocks gamete transport and thereby prevents conception.

15. (*b*) The incorrect match pair can be corrected as

Multiload 375 is an intrauterine device (IUD) that does not contain steroids. It is a copper-containing IUD (Intra Uterine Device).

16. (*d*) India is in the phase of population growth, which is caused due to high birth rate (natality) and low death rate (mortality).

17. (*a*) RU486 (Mifepristone) is a synthetic steroid that works by blocking the progesterone hormone receptor. This action prevents the body from producing progesterone, a hormone necessary to maintain a pregnancy.

18. (*d*) A is true, but R is false. R can be corrected as

In order to attain zero population growth, couples need to have less than two children. But in large democratic country like India, it will take many years for population growth to attain this level.

19. (*c*) Spermicidal creams contain chemicals which kill the sperms. There use along with barrier contraceptives will increase its effect of contraception.

20. (*c*) Statements II and III are correct. Rest of the statements are incorrect.

The incorrect statement can be corrected as

- India has become the largest populated country in the world surpassing china
- RCH programmes led to decrease in population growth rate but it was only marginal.

21. (*b*) Incorrect statement can be corrected as

Vaults are reusable and can be self inserted.

22. (*b*) The graph (b) correctly represents progesterone level of female 'X'. As the women consuming Mala-D as birth control thus, the progesterone level will remain high resulting in pervention of ovulation.

23. (*d*) The success rate of sterilisation method is very high as compared to the other techniques and the number of complications are also very less. So, sterilisation technique is the safest and best.

24. (*b*) The vaginal diaphragm covers the cervix and physically prevents sperm from entering the uterus.

25. (*a*) Due to the release of prolactin in lactating womens ovulation does not takes place. Prolactin suppresses the release of Follicle Stimulating Hormone (FSH) resulting in absence of ovulation.

Test 2

1. (c) Statement in option (c) is correct regarding HIV.

HIV is a retrovirus that causes AIDs, whereas hepatitis-B, gonorrhoea and trichamoniasis are categorised as STDs.

Other options are incorrect regarding HIV, hepatitis-B, gonorrhoea, trichomoniasis.

Ganorrhoea is a bacterial disease, hepatitis-B still affects chronically and can only be eradicated with vaccination.

2. (*b*) The statement (b) is incorrect w.r.t. MTP can be corrected as

Government of India legalised MTP in 1971, with some strict conditions to avoid its misuse.

3. (*c*) The high incidence of infections among 15-24 year-olds is primarily due to increased engagement in risky sexual behaviors. This age group often lacks adequate knowledge about safe sex practices and the consistent use of protection, leading to a higher susceptibility to sexually transmitted infections (STIs). Their exploratory behavior and peer influences also contribute to this vulnerability.

4. (*c*) Nearly 45 to 50 million medical terminations of pregnancies (MTPs) occur globally, constituting one-fifth of the total number of conceived pregnancies each year. This highlights the significant prevalence of MTPs worldwide, often deemed essential due to various factors such as maternal health risks, foetal abnormalities, or socio-economic considerations.

5. (*d*) The claim that people exploit abortion laws does not explain the prevalence of unsafe abortions. Unsafe abortions are still frequently reported in India despite multiple laws because of following reasons.

- Many women are unaware of government-provided information.
- Government hospitals are often inadequately equipped.
- Societal stigma deters people from seeking legal abortions in cases of rape or extramarital relations.

6. (*c*) Both statement I and statement II are incorrect and can be corrected as

- Except for hepatitis -B, genital herpes and HIV infection, all other reproductive tract diseases are completely curable if detected early and treated properly.
- Cancer is not a potential cause of STDs. Rather, some constant sexually transmitted infection and their symptoms can cause cancer in reproductive tract.

7. (*b*) Both A and R are true and R is the correct explanation of A.
MTP Act, 2017 allows termination of pregnancy under certain conditions, like in the case, if the continuation of pregnancy has potential risk of mental or physical injury to pregnant woman.
Additionally, if the foetus is developing some life threatening or mental abnormality risk, in this case also, MTP is allowed.

8. (*c*) Early symptoms of STIs are usually mild, and the social stigma associated with these infections prevents individuals from seeking prompt diagnosis and treatment. The fear of judgment and discrimination often discourages individuals from discussing or addressing STIs, leading to delayed diagnosis and treatment. This delay can worsen health issues and increase the chances of spreading the infection to others.

9. (*c*) The correct matches are A-3, B-4, C-1, D-2.

- Trichomoniasis is a sexually transmitted infection (STI) caused by a protozoan parasite called *Trichomonas vaginalis*. It primarily affects the urogenital tract including vagina in females and urethra in both male and female.
- Gonorrhoea is a STI caused by bacterium *Neisseria gonorrhoeae*. It can infect both men and women and is typically transmitted through sexual contact with an infected person.
- Genital warts, also known as *Condyloma acuminata*, are a common STI caused by certain strains of HPV (Human papilloma Virus).
- AIDS is a condition caused by HIV. It is a retrovirus that attacks the immune system, specifically target CD4+ T cells which are crucial for body's defence against infection.

10. (*c*) Both statement I and statement II are incorrect. These can be corrected as
Embryo with more than 8 blastomeres are introduced into the uterus to complete their further development is called IUT (Intra Uterine Transfer).
The semen collected either from the husband or a healthy donor is artificially transferred into the uterus by a process called IUI (Intra-Uterine Insemination).

11. (*a*) The correct set with odd one out of series is Hepatitis B, syphilis and ZIFT.

- Hepatitis-B is the only STDs out of the four which is not curable.
- Syphililis is not a consequence of STDs unlike the other three. It is a STD itself.
- ZIFT is an IVF procedure while the other three are *in-vivo* procedure.

12. (*c*) A test tube baby refers to a baby conceived through *in-vitro* fertilisation (IVF), where fertilisation happens outside the female body in a laboratory setting. This is distinct from fertilisation occurring inside the body (*in-vivo* fertilisation).

13. (*c*) Uterus is the site of implantation of embryo with 16 blastomeres. Implantations of the embryo into the uterine lining typically occurs at the blastocyst stage, which is a few days after fertilisation when the embryo has developed further.

14. (*d*) The correct matches are A-4, B-2, C-1, D-3.

- GIFT (Gamete Intra Fallopian Transfer) is the process in which ovum is extracted from one female and transferred into the reproductive environment of another female who cannot produce one, but can provide suitable environment for fertilisation.
- IVF (*In vitro* Fertilisation) is the process in which sperms are fused with ovum in the lab environment followed by embryo transfer.
- Intra Cytoplasmic Sperm Injection (ICSI) is a specialised procedure to form an embryo in the laboratory in which a sperm is directly injected into the ovum.
- In Artificial Insemination (AI) technique, the semen collected either from the husband or a healthy donor is artificially introduced either into the vagina or into the uterus of a female.

15. (*a*) Statement I is incorrect, but statement II is correct. The incorrect statement can be corrected as MTP is not mandatory to keep the sex ratio upright or to maintain the population growth rate. MTP is never necessary unless and until the pregnancy is complicated enough to risk mother's or foetus's life.

16. (*c*) Statement III is incorrect about STD and can be corrected as

Abstinence means abstain from sexual intercourse thus, it can help in preventing STD infection.

17. (*d*) Statement I is correct but statement II is incorrect it can be corrected as

In ZIFT early embryo or zygote with 8 blastomeres in transferred into Fallopian tube but in IUT embryo with more than 8 blastomere is transferred into the uterus.

18. (*b*) Statement I, II and III are correct with respect to GIFT.

The procedure of GIFT is useful for woman's with atleast one potent fallopian tube or whose fimbriae does not function effectively. It is also helpful for those females whose cervics produce antibodies against sperm.

19. (*c*) If the male or husband has very low sperm count than in that case Artificial insemination technique is beneficial. In this procedure a sperm from healthy donor or husband is injected either into the vagina or uterus of female which further lead to fertilisation.

20. (a) The correct sequence of events in development of test tube baby are as follows

Removal of unfertilised ovum → *in vitro* fusion of sperm and ovum → Development of zygote up to 32 cell stage → Embryo transfer into the uterus mother.

21. (*c*) Both A and R are true, but R is not the correct explanation of A.

Though test tube baby has been a miracle in the life of infective couples but on the other hand it has raised several legal problems such as right on child.

Surrogacy is one such method of this procedure where a healthy women or carrier nourishes zygote of other couple who cannot concive. This sometime result in legal issues such as right on child.

22. (*d*) Abortion does not impart any utilitarian value to a woman because a sharp distinction exists between those who support a woman's right to choose abortion and those who oppose abortion on the grounds of foetal rights to life.

23. (*d*) The Medical Termination Pregnancy Act, 1971 is responsible for the legalisation of abortion. However legally, it can only be performed up to 20 weeks of conception.

24. (*b*) The incorrectly matches pair can be corrected as

GIFT or Gamete Intra Fallopian Transfer is a method of transfer of an ovum collected from a donor female into the Fallopian tube. Rest options are correctly matched pairs.

25. (*b*) Both statements I and II are correct.

Infertility is the inability of a couple to conceive even after 2 years of unprotected sexual co-habitation. This could be of various reasons such as immunological, physical, psychological, etc.

Chapter Break Thru

1. (*b*) Saheli is a non-hormonal pill that acts by inhibiting oestrogen activity. This alters uterus lining and thus, prevent implantation.

2. (*d*) Statement I is correct, but statement II is incorrect. The incorrect statement can be corrected as

The primary concern of RCH programmes is to create awareness among people about various reproduction related aspects and providing facilities and support for building up a reproductively healthy society.

3. (*d*) Incorrect statement can be corrected as

Amniocentesis is an invasive prenatal test that involves the insertion of a needle into the amniotic sac to obtain a sample of amniotic fluid. This procedure carries a small risk of complications, such as miscarriage, and is considered invasive due to its direct intervention in the pregnancy.

4. (*a*) The correct statements are I, II, IV, and V. Only statement III is incorrect and it can be corrected as

By 2000, the world population was about 6 billion, not 7.2 billion. The world population reached 7.2 billion in 2011.

5. (*c*) As per the methods of contraception, saheli and Lippes loop are odd pairs. Saheli is oral contraceptive for females containing a non-steroidal preparation, while Lippes loop is a non-medicated intra uterine device. Other options can be explained as

Cervical cap and fem shield are barrier methods of contraception. Coitus interruptus and Lactational amenorrhea are natural methods of contraception. Condom and diaphragm are barrier methods of contraception.

6. (*b*) The method of IVF involve three procedures which are as follows

- ICSI (Intra Cytoplasmic Sperm Injection): - This procedure involves injecting a single sperm directly into an egg during the IVF process.
- ZIFT (Zygote Intrafallopian Transfer): -This procedure involves fertilizing an egg outside the body and then transfering the zygote or early embryo upto 8 blastomeres into the Fallopian tube.
- IUT (Intrauterine Transfer): - This typically refers to transferring embryos with more than 8 blastomeres directly into the uterus after external fertilisation.
- IUI and GIFT are not the part of IVF because both the procedues in volve fertilisation inside the female body.

7. (*c*) Incorrect statement can be corrected as

Cu-T is a copper releasing IUDs, which supresses sperm mortality and the fertilising capacity of sperm.

8. (*c*) The incorrectly matched pair can be corrected as
Saheli is not a barrier method. It is a non-steroidal oral contraceptive pill.

9. (*c*) Both A and R are true, but R is not the correct explanation of A.
Amniocentesis can determine the gender of the developing embryo and check the paternity. It is also used to identify potential disorders in the baby, such as chromosomal abnormalities. As it involve the study of amniotic fluid present around the developing foetus.

10. (*b*) The incorrect statement can be corrected as
For termination of pregnancies between 12 and 24 weeks, the law requires the opinion of two registered medical practitioners.

11. (*c*) Trichomoniasis is caused by a protozoan parasite called *Trichomonas vaginalis*. It infects reproductive parts of women body. Rest all other diseases are caused by bacteria.

12. (*a*) Gonorrhoea is caused by *Neisseria gonorrhoea*.
This bacterium can grow and multiply easily in the warm, moist areas of the reproductive tract and mainly affects cervix, uterus and Fallopian tube.

13. (*a*) An ectopic pregnancy is a medical condition where the fertilised egg implants and develops outside the uterus, most commonly in the Fallopian tube.
This condition is serious and can be life-threatening if not treated promptly because the Fallopian tube cannot support the growing embryo, leading to potential rupture and severe internal bleeding.

14. (*d*) STDs typically possess symptoms like itching, fluid discharge, pain, swelling, and complications such as ectopic pregnancies and stillbirths. But high blood pressure and frequent urination are not common symptoms of STDs.

15. (*a*) The correct matches are A-3, B-4, C-1, D-2.
The correct year of the following programmes or acts are as follows.
MTP amendment - 2017
Family planning program activation in India-1951
India's population reached 7.2 billion - 2011
MTP legalization in India - 1971

16. (*b*) In Gamete Intra Fallopian Transfer (GIFT), ovum is transferred from a donor into the Fallopian tube of the female who cannot conceive one but can provide suitable conditions or environment for fertilisation and and then further development occurs inside her body only.

17. (*a*) The correct sequence for ZIFT (Zygote Intra Fallopian Transfer) is (a) B, C, D, A. These can be explained as

- Hormonal treatments stimulate the ovaries to produce multiple eggs, which are then retrieved surgically.
- Fertilisation in the laboratory The retrieved eggs are fertilised with sperm in the laboratory to create zygotes.
- Zygote culture The fertilised eggs are cultured briefly to ensure successful fertilisation and early development.
- Transfer to the Fallopian tubes The zygotes are transferred into the woman's Fallopian tubes for natural implantation in the uterus.

18. (*c*) *In vitro* Fertilisation (IVF) involves fertilising an egg outside the body and then transferring it into the fallopian tube or uterus. The transfer can be done at the zygote stage (a fertilized egg) or when the embryo has developed up to the 8-cell stage (ZIFT). This flexibility allows for the best timing based on individual medical circumstances. The transfer of an embryo at the 32-cell stage is not typically transferred into fallopian tube in standard IVF procedures. It is done in the uterus (IUT).

19. (*b*) The term "Test-tube Baby" typically refers to a baby conceived through *In Vitro* Fertilisation (IVF). In the IVF process, eggs are fertilised outside the body to create zygotes. These zygotes can then be transferred to the Fallopian tubes by, a procedure known as Zygote Intra Fallopian Transfer (ZIFT). This technique is specifically used in the Test-tube baby program.

20. (*a*) Artificial insemination (AI) is the method of ART suggested due to inability of the male partner to inseminate the female or due to very low sperm count in the ejaculate.

21. (*b*) Both A and R are true and R is the correct explanation of A.
Sex education in schools should be encouraged to dispel myths and misconceptions, which aligns with the reason that providing proper information about various reproductive health topics helps adolescents lead a reproductively healthy life.

22. (*a*) The incorrectly matched pair can be corrected as
Condom is a barrier method it prevents insemination like coitus interruptus does. While, in case of vasectomy, sperms are not found in semen.

23. (*b*) The sterilisation technique, such as tubectomy for females or vasectomy for males, is considered one of the safest and most effective forms of birth control. These methods are very effective and have a very low failure rate compared to other contraceptive methods.

24. (*b*) Only statement II is incorrect, it can be corrected as
Miscarriages are not the part of contraception as miscarriages happen spontaneously. It is not induced through some external source.

25. (*a*) Infertility is when couple is unable to produce children inspite of unprotected sexual cohabitation. This definition accurately reflects the general understanding of infertility, which can be due to factors affecting either partner.

26. (*a*) The correct matches are A-3, B-1, C-4, D-2.

- Several techniques are performed to cure the infertility of a couple. Artificial insemination is the procedure for infertile males who are unable to inseminate their partners. Semen is artificially injected in the vagina and uterus of the female.
- Amniocentesis is not Assisted Reproductive Technologies (ARTs), but it is used to determine several abnormalities in the foetus and the chromosomes are observed to determine the gender of the baby.
- ICSI, i.e. Intra Cytoplasmic Sperm Injection is also a fertility procedure in which sperms are directly injected into the cytoplasm of ovum to allow the fertilisation.
- Test-tube babies are produced by *in vitro* fertilisation of embryo and their transplant into uterus of mother or surrogate mother.

27. (*d*) Statement I is correct, but statement II is incorrect and it can be corrected as
For surrogacy, it is not mandatory that surrogate mother has to give her ovum. Mostly in surrogacy, a fertilised embryo is transferred to the womb of surrogate mother which contain gametes of biological parents.

28. (*a*) The correct matches are A-3, B-1, C-4, D-2.

- Cervical caps are rubber made barrier used by female to cover their cervix during coitus and block the sperm entry.
- Vaults is a barrier method which is hemispherical cup made up of plastic or rubber, it gets fixed over the vaginal vault near cervix to restrict the path of sperms.
- Sponge is a small, round, soft piece of plastic foam that's coated with spermicides, chemical method of contraception. It involves role of spermicide to kill sperms by rupturing their membranes.
- Cu-T is an intra uterine device which secretes harmful cytokines to denature gametes and suppress the sperm motility.

29. (*c*) Both A and R are true, but R is not the correct explanation of A.
Intra cytoplasmic sperm injection is an effective assisted reproductive technology used to address male infertility. It involve injecting a sperm directly into an egg to fertilise it in laboratory condition.

30. (*b*) Venereal diseases, or sexually transmitted infections (STIs) can spread through

- Infected needles
- Unprotected sex
- Blood transfusion from infected individual
- Infected mother to foetus
- Inheritance from parents

STIs do not spread by kissing hand shaking or eating with infected person.

Ch-4 Principles of Inheritance and Variation

Topical Follow Thru

Test 1

1. (*c*) In snapdragons, incomplete dominance results in pink flowers (Rr), when red (RR) and white (rr) are crossed. Back-crossing a pink (Rr) flower with its dominant red parent (RR) produces the following genotypes: 50% RR (red) and 50% Rr (pink). Thus, the phenotypic ratio of the offspring is 50% red flowers and 50% pink flowers.

2. (*c*) The incorrect statement can be corrected as
The law of dominance is used to explain the expression of only one of the parental traits in a monohybrid cross in the F_1 and the expression of both in the F_2 generation.

3. (*a*) The correct matches are A-4, B-2, C-1 and D-3.

- A monohybrid cross involves breeding individuals that differ in only one trait and the F_2 -ratio is 3:1.
- In a test cross, a known dominant phenotype is crossed with a homozygous recessive parent to determine the genotype. The F_2 generation ratio is 1:1, indicating that the genotype of dominant phenotype is heterozygous.
- Dihybrid cross involves two characters and the F_2 -generation ratio is 9:3:3:1.
- Incomplete dominance is a type of allelic interaction where neither of the allele is completely dominant, resulting in an intermediate phenotype. The ratio of the F_2-generation is 1:2:1 for the three possible phenotypes.

4. (*b*) The incorrect statement can be corrected as
Reciprocal cross is made to eliminate maternal effects. The reciprocal crosses are used to distinguish between genetic and maternal effects. By swapping the parental roles in two crosses, any differences in offspring can be attributed to maternal influences, not genetics. This helps in eliminate maternal effect.

5. (*b*) The Mendel's laws of inheritance, apply primarily to plants that reproduce sexually. Sexual reproduction involves the fusion of gametes from two parents, leading to genetic variation in offspring.

Mendel's laws elucidate the patterns of inheritance of traits passed from one generation to the next through the combination and segregation of alleles during sexual reproduction.

6. (*d*) Mendel's classic experiments on pea plants focused on several key traits, including the arrangement of flowers (axial or terminal), the pigmentation of seeds (yellow or green) and the round or wrinkled morphology of seeds. However, he did not study the anatomy of pods. Instead, he examined traits such as the shape (inflated or constricted) and color (green or yellow) of pods.

7. (*d*) Mendel's self-pollination of F_1 offspring led him to propose the law of segregation. This law states that the two alleles for each trait segregate (separate) during gamete formation and then unite at random, one from each parent, at fertilisation. Thus, each trait is controlled by discrete, independent factors, now known as genes.

8. (*c*) Incorrect statement can be corrected.as

Mendel conducted extensive experiments with a large sample size of pea plants. This meticulous approach contributed significantly to the reliability and accuracy of his findings. His careful statistical analysis of the data was groundbreaking.

9. (*a*) Statements I, III and IV are correct with respect to law of dominance. Statements II and V are incorrect w.r.t law of dominance but are correct with respect to law of segregation.

10. (*d*) Statement I is correct, but statement II is incorrect. The incorrect statement can be corrected as:

The law of dominance is not universal because in certain cases, such as in the case of incomplete dominance, neither allele is dominant over other, and in codominance, both the alleles are expressed.

11. (*a*) The ABO blood group system is determined by the presence of specific antigens on the surface of red blood cells. These antigens are produced by enzymes encoded by the ABO gene, which exists in three main alleles: I^A, I^B and I^O / i. These alleles determine which antigens are present. For example, individuals with the I^A allele express A antigens, while those with the I^B allele express B antigens. The I^O allele produces no antigens. The expression of these antigens is critical for blood compatibility and transfusion safety.

12. (*b*) In ABO blood group inheritance, the A and B alleles exhibit co-dominance, where both antigens are expressed in individuals with the AB genotype. Both A and B alleles are dominant to the O allele. Additionally, multiple alleles (A, B and O) exist for this trait, with the expression of antigens determined by specific combinations of these alleles.

13. (*d*) Option (d) is correctly matched. Remaining options can be corrected as:

Multiple alleles – Presence of more than one allele for a gene at same gene locus of homologous chromosomes.

Co-dominance – Alleles for I^A and I^B for blood group AB in humans.

Incomplete Dominance – F_1 hybrids resembling neither parental phenotype but rather exhibiting an intermediate phenotype.

14. (*c*) The correct matches are A-2, B-3, C-4 and D-1.

- In Dominance, only one allele expresses itself in a heterozygous organism.
- Both alleles in a heterozygous organism express themselves fully in co-dominance.
- Intermediate characteristic appears in heterozygous organism in incomplete dominance.
- Multiple alleles present at the same locus of homologous chromosomes.

15. (*b*) Both A and R are true and R is the correct explanation of A.

The law of segregation state that, during gamete formation, two alleles for a particular trait separate from each other, with only one allele passing to each gamete. Alleles are alternative forms of a gene that occupy the same locus on homologous chromosomes.

Test 2

1. (*b*) The cross between AABb and aaBb is as follows

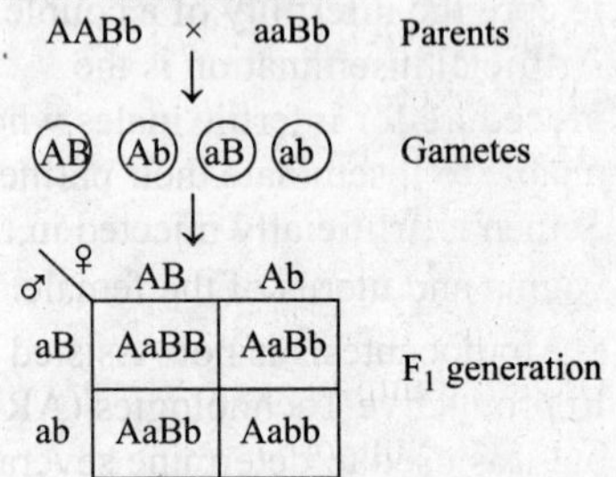

The obtained ratio is AaBB : AaBb : Aabb : aabb :: 1 : 2 : 1 : 0.

2. (*d*) In Mendel's experiments, crossing RRYY (round, yellow) with rryy (wrinkled, green) produces F_1 hybrids (RrYy), all round and yellow. Self-crossing F_1 hybrids (RrYy × RrYy) yields an F_2 generation with a 9:3:3:1 phenotypic ratio for round yellow, round green, wrinkled yellow, and wrinkled green, respectively. Therefore, the F_2 generation includes multiple phenotypes including round seeds with yellow colour and wrinkeled seeds with yellow colour and not just a single combination.

3. (*c*) In the F_2 generation from self-pollination of a dihybrid F_1 (RrYy), 9 different genotypes are produced. These genotypes are: RRYY, RRYy, RrYY, RrYy, RRyy, Rryy, rrYY, rrYy, and rryy. Each combination results from independent assortment of alleles during gamete formation.

4. (*c*) In the F_1-generation, all individuals will be heterozygous for both traits (TtVv).

When two heterozygous individuals (TtVv x TtVv) are crossed, the phenotypic ratio in the F_2 generation will typically follows 9:3:3:1 ratio according to Mendel's principles.

So, out of 16 plants:

9/16 would be tall with violet flowers (1TtVv, 2TTVv, 2TtVV, 4TTVV)

3/16 would be tall with white flowers (2Ttvv, 1TTvv)
3/16 would be short with violet flowers (1ttVV, 2TtVv)
1/16 would be short with white flowers (1ttvv)
So, out of 16 plants in the F_2 generation, 4 plants would be short.

5. (*b*) In the given cross, the F_1 progeny will be heterozygous for all three traits: AaBbCc.
To determine the number of different types of gametes that can be formed, we can use the formula = 2^n, here n is equal to number of heterozygosity. In this case the number of heterozygosity is 3 (AaBbCc) so, the no. of possible gametes will be 2^3 = 8.
Therefore, the F_1 progeny can produce 8 different types of gametes.

6. (*d*) In a dihybrid cross, a 9:3:3:1 ratio signifies independent assortment of two genes. Each parent contributes two alleles, which segregate independently during gamete formation. This results in four types of gametes. When crossed, they form 16 combinations, giving rise to four phenotypes in a 9:3:3:1 ratio, demonstrating Mendel's law of independent assortment.

7. (*b*) Sutton and Boveri noted that the behavior of chromosomes paralleled the behaviour of genes and proposed the chromosome theory of inheritance, which stated that chromosomes carry genes. They observed chromosome movement during cell division and correlated it with Mendel's laws.
Other incorrect options can be explained as:
Hugo de Vries is known for his work on mutation theory. Beadle and Tatum formulated the one gene-one enzyme hypothesis. T.H. Morgan conducted pioneering research on fruit flies, contributing to the understanding of inheritance.

8. (*d*) The given diagram explains independent assortment by chromosomal segregation during meiosis where homologous chromosomes align randomly at the metaphase plate, resulting in the independent assortment of alleles located on different chromosomes. This process occurs during the first division of meiosis, known as metaphase I, where homologous pairs line up independently of each other. As a result, the combinations of alleles from different genes become randomised, leading to the creation of genetically diverse gametes and supporting the principles of Mendelian genetics.

9. (*b*) Independent assortment refers to the random distribution of alleles for different genes during gamete formation. However, when genes are located on the same chromosome, they tend to be inherited together, a phenomenon called linkage. During meiosis, crossover events can separate linked genes, but they are usually inherited together as a unit. Therefore, independent assortment is absent for genes on the same chromosome, impacting genetic variability and inheritance patterns.

10. (*c*) Both A and R are true but R is not the correct explanation of A.
The discovery of non-Mendelian inheritance patterns, such as linked genes, did support the chromosomal theory. Linked genes are genes that are located close together on the same chromosome and tend to be inherited together. This discovery provided evidence that genes reside on the chromosomes.

11. (*b*) Linkage restricts genetic variation among siblings by causing linked genes on the same chromosome to be inherited together. Although crossing over during meiosis can separate them, it occurs infrequently. Thus, siblings inheriting linked genes are likely to share similar genetic compositions, reducing overall genetic diversity among them.

12. (*b*) Statements I, III, IV, and V are correct. While statement II is incorrect, it can be corrected as They complete their life-cycle in about 2 weeks.

13. (*a*) In bacteria like *E. coli*, the number of linkage groups corresponds to the number of chromosome copies, which is usually one for bacteria. Therefore, *E. coli* typically has one linkage group. Genes on the bacterial chromosome are generally considered to be linked due to their proximity and lack of independent assortment.

14. (*d*) Genes of a linkage group demonstrate co-inheritance due to their physical proximity on the same chromosome.
Genes exhibiting linkage behaviour, they are physically close together on the same chromosome, resulting in their tendency to be inherited as together. This phenomenon, termed co-inheritance. This occurs due to the limited opportunity for genetic recombination between linked genes during meiosis.

15. (*b*) When two genes in a dihybrid cross are situated on the same chromosome, the proportion of the parental gene combinations are much higher than the non-parental or recombinant type as linked genes are inherited together in offspring.

16. (*b*) The law of independent assortment is applicable to only those genes which are either located distantly on the same chromosome or occur on different chromosomes.
During linkage, two genes of a chromosome that are closely related are frequently inherited together. Thus, the independent assortment is violated in case of linkage.

17. (*c*) A test cross is used to determine the genotype of an individual with a dominant phenotype and unknown genotype. This is done by crossing that individual with another individual who is homozygous recessive for the trait in question. In the context of genetic mapping, test crosses are often used to determine the distance between genes (the map distance) on a chromosome.

18. (*d*) Crossing over is a process that occurs during meiosis where two chromosomes pair up and exchange segments of their genetic material. This leads to the production of chromosomes that are a mixture of

both parents, increasing genetic diversity. The longer the chromosome, the more chance there is for crossing over to occur, leading to greater genetic variability.
Other options can be explained as independent assortment, mutation and linkage can lead to genetic variability but this does not increase with the length of chromosome.

19. (*b*) Chromosome map is important to know the strength of linkage between two genes and the chance of recombination. A linkage or genetic or chromosomal map is a linear graphical representation of the sequence and relative distances of various genes present in a chromosome. It is the strength of linkage, that is inversely proportional to the distance between the genes. On the other hand, recombination frequency is directly proportional to the distance between the genes. Linkage or chromosome map does not exactly depict the physical distance amongst the genes because of crossing over.

20. (*c*) Sturtevant, a disciple of Morgan, used the frequency of recombination between gene pairs on the same chromosome to assess gene distance, measured in centimorgans (cM). Increased recombination indicated greater physical separation between genes. By correlating recombination frequencies with gene positions, typically measured in centimorgans, Sturtevant constructed chromosome maps, revolutionising genetics and advancing our understanding of inheritance patterns and genetic mapping techniques.

21. (*c*) A genetic map unit, also known as a centimorgan (cM), is a unit of measurement used to describe the relative distance between genes on a chromosome. One map unit corresponds to a 1% chance of recombination occurring between two genes during meiosis. It is used in genetic mapping to quantify the frequency of recombination events and determine the relative positions of genes along a chromosome.

22. (*a*) The distance between genes on a chromosome and the percentage of recombination between them exhibit a direct relationship. As the physical distance between genes increases, the likelihood of recombination events during meiosis also increases. Consequently, a higher percentage of recombination is observed between genes that are farther apart, reflecting the linear relationship between genetic distance and recombination frequency along the chromosome.

23. (*c*) The possible value of X is 15. In a polygenic trait controlled by three genes, the phenotypic ratio follows a pattern of 1:6:15:20:15:6:1 due to the distribution of different combinations of alleles. Each gene contributes independently to the phenotype, resulting in a higher frequency of intermediate phenotypes and a peak at the mean value.

24. (*b*) Both statement I and statement II are correct.
Polygenic inheritance involves multiple genes, each contributing to a trait, with each gene having two alleles. Traits like height, skin color, and intelligence are examples. Unlike single-gene traits with discrete phenotypes, polygenic traits display continuous variation due to the cumulative effect of multiple genes. This inheritance pattern often results in a wide range of phenotypic variation within a population, forming a bell-shaped curve when plotted, known as a polygenic distribution or quantitative trait distribution.

25. (*c*) The correct match is A-2, B-1, C-4, D-3.
- Linkage: Genes located closely on the same chromosome tend to be inherited together, impacting genetic inheritance patterns.
- Polygenic inheritance: Multiple genes collectively influence a single trait, resulting in a continuum of phenotypic variation.
- Recombinant : New combination of gene occur in pachytene stage.
- Independent assortment: Alleles for different genes segregate independently during gamete formation, enhancing genetic diversity in offspring.

Test 3

1. (*d*) In birds, female heterogamety is observed. Rest of the organisms, i.e., grasshopper, *Drosophila* and human beings show male heterogamety.

2. (*d*) Incorrect match can be corrected as
Substitution mutation - Involves the replacement of one nucleotide with another in the DNA sequence.

3. (*b*) Statements II and IV are incorrect. These statements can be correct as
Male drones are developed by the unfertilised eggs by means of parthenogenesis. Female bees (queens or workers) are developed by union of a sperm and an egg. In XO type of sex-determination, males have only one X chromosome and lack a Y chromosome.

4. (*a*) Diabetes mellitus type 1 is a metabolic disorder characterised by high blood sugar levels resulting from the body's inability to produce insulin. It is not directly related to disorders of blood composition or clotting, unlike the other options. Haemophilia A, sickle-cell anaemia, and beta-thalassemia major are all blood disorders characterised by abnormalities in the composition or function of blood components.

5. (*c*) In domesticated fowls, offspring sex is determined by the type of egg. In birds, including domesticated fowls, females are heterogametic (ZW), while males are homogametic (ZZ). Therefore, the sex of the offspring is determined by the type of egg (Z or W) that the female contributes.

6. (*c*) Mutagens are substances which induce mutations. Acridine is a chemical mutagen, while X-rays, β-rays and UV rays are physical mutagens.

7. (*a*) Statements I, II and V are correct, while statements III and IV are incorrect and can be corrected as

Nitrous acid is mutagenic to both replicating and non-replicating DNA.
Aneuploidy occurs due to a change in the number of chromosomes due to the non-disjunction of two homologous chromosomes.

8. (*c*) Incorrect match pair can be corrected as
In grasshoppers, XX-XO sex determination mechanism is found in which females carry two X chromosomes (XX), while males possess only one X chromosome (XO). The absence of a second sex chromosome (Y) in males leads to their XO genotype. This system determines sex through the presence or absence of the second sex chromosome, i.e. XX individuals develop as females, while XO individuals develop as males.

9. (*b*) The incorrect statement can be corrected as
Pedigree analysis is used to study the inheritance of human traits, not for plant traits.

10. (*b*) Pedigree analysis in human genetics primarily focuses on studying the inheritance pattern of Mendelian traits. These traits are controlled by a single gene with clear dominant or recessive inheritance patterns, following Mendel's laws of segregation and independent assortment. Through pedigree analysis, researchers track the transmission of these traits across generations within families to understand their genetic basis and inheritance patterns.

11. (*b*) The pedigree represented in the given figure is of siblings. Individuals are connected together with a horizontal line between them.

12. (*a*) In the first generation, both parents are non-affected. However, they have offsprings in the second generation who are affected (shaded). This suggests that both parents are carriers of the disease, meaning they are heterozygous (Aa) for the trait.

13. (*d*) Sterile condition in man associated with sex chromosomal abnormality is usually due to increase in X complement.
This syndrome in called Klinefelter's syndrome.
This increase in X-complement result into a karyotype of 47, XXY.

14. (*d*) Holandric genes are located exclusively on the Y chromosome. These genes are passed from fathers to their sons, as only males possess the Y chromosome. Unlike autosomes, which are inherited equally from both parents, holandric genes are inherited solely through the paternal line.

15. (*b*) The husband's father was colour blind (X^CY), but the husband is not Colourblind (XY) because he received his X chromosome from his mother, who is neither colourblind nor a carrier (XX). The wife's mother was colourblind (X^CX^C), so the wife is a carrier (X^CX) because she received one X^C chromosome from her mother. Each male child will receive his X chromosome from his mother (who is a carrier) and his Y chromosome from his father. There's a 50% chance that the X chromosome from the mother carries the colour blind gene (X^C). So, 50% or 1/2 of their male children are expected to be colourblind (X^CY).

16. (*d*) Statement I is correct, but statement II is incorrect and can be corrected as
The progeny of a colourblind woman and a normal man will consist of 100% colourblind boys (X^hY) and 100% carrier girls (X^hX). This is because all the eggs of the female shall carry the trait of colour blindness. All the male babies will become colourblind as they obtain the alleles for colour blindness from their mother. However, in case of girl babies, the dominant allele for normal vision is present. It does not allow recessive allele to express itself. Hence, they will be carrier for the disease.

17. (*d*) In sickle cell anaemia, a point mutation replaces the nucleotide adenine (A) with thymine (T) in the DNA sequence, altering the codon from GAG (which codes for glutamic acid) to GUG (coding for valine). During protein synthesis, this mutation causes the incorporation of valine instead of glutamic acid in the haemoglobin protein.
Consequently, the altered haemoglobin structure leads to the characteristic sickle-shaped red blood cells observed in individuals with sickle cell anaemia.

18. (*a*) Statements I, III and V are correct, while other statements are incorrect and can be corrected as
Tyrosine hydroxylase converts tyrosine to L-DOPA, a precursor for neurotransmitters such as dopamine, norepinephrine and epinephrine and is not related to phenylketonuria. The phenylketonuria is an example of pleiotropy, not polygenic inheritance.

19. (*d*) The incorrect statement can be corrected as
β-globin chains are formed from the beta-globin gene, which is encoded by a single gene located on chromosome 11 in humans. Mutations in this gene can lead to disorders, such as beta-thalassemia or sickle cell disease. So, only one gene is necessary to make beta-globin chains.

20. (*b*) The correct matches are A-2, B-4, C-1, D-3.

- Grasshopper females have a pair of X-chromosomes (XX) and males have only one. X-chromosome (XO).
- Both human and *Drosophila* have the female with a pair of XX chromosome (homogametic) and the male with XY (heterogametic) composition.
- Female bird has a pair of ZW and the male has ZZ type of chromosome composition besides the autosomes.
- Butterflies have same sex chromosome like birds, but in female butterflies, one of the chromosome is lost, i.e. in ZO, O denotes the absence of sex chromosome.

21. (*b*) Chromosomal aberrations involve a change in a single gene to a segment of a chromosome. It typically involve changes in the structure or number of chromosomes, not just alterations in single genes.

Chromosomal aberrations can indeed be caused by mutagens, leading to genetic disorders like Down's syndrome and can be detected through techniques like karyotyping, which visualises an individual's chromosomes.

22. (*c*) Females have two X-chromosomes, whereas males have one X and one Y-chromosome. Genes on the X-chromosome can be recessive or dominant. Their expression in females and males is not the same. Genes on the Y- chromosome do not exactly pair up with the genes on the X chromosome. X-linked recessive genes are expressed in females only if there are two copies of the gene (one on each X-chromosome). However, for males, there needs to be only one copy of an X-linked recessive gene in order for the trait or disorder to be expressed.

23. (*a*) The incorrect statement about the Klinefelter's syndrome can be corrected as

The affected individual has 47 chromosomes. Such an individual has overall masculine development, however, the feminine development (Gynaecomastia) is also expressed.

24. (*b*) Individuals affected with Turner's syndrome possess 44 + X0 chromosomes. Thus, affected female individual possesses 45 chromosomes instead of 46 (one X-chromosome is missing).

25. (*d*) Down's syndrome, also known as trisomy 21, is characterised by specific physical features such as a flat facial profile, a simian crease (a single crease across the palm), poor muscle tone (hypotonia) poor physical, psychomotor and mental development which lead to poor reflexes. Polydactyly, the presence of extra fingers or toes, is not typically associated with Down syndrome.

Chapter Break Thru

1. (*d*) All of the children will be healthy since none of them can be homozygous recessive (aa).

However, there will be a 50% chance at each birth that the child will be a carrier (Aa), but they will also be healthy.

The remaining 50% will be healthy homozygous dominant.

2. (*d*) Incorrect match pair can be corrected as

The term genetics was also coined by William Bateson, while Reginald Punnett introduced the graphical method in the early 20th century as a way to predict the outcomes of genetic crosses, called punnett square.

3. (*b*) The incorrect statement can be corrected as

The wild type allele is not necessarily the dominant allele; it can either be dominant or recessive.

4. (*d*) Statement I is correct, but statement II is incorrect. The incorrect statement can be corrected as

Alleles are alternative form of a gene that govern contrasting characters of single traits.

5. (*c*) The genes A and B represent genetic disorders which affect 'X' chromosome (the larger chromosome), while the Y-chromosome is unaffected. This shows sex-linked disease, thus the genetic disorder could be haemophilia and colour blindness.

6. (*c*) Both A and R are true but R is not the correct explanation of A.

Mendel's law of segregation does not directly explain the 3:1 phenotypic ratio observed in the F_2 generation of a monohybrid cross. This ratio is actually a result of the combination of alleles during fertilisation. The law of segregation is more about the separation of alleles during gamete formation.

7. (*c*) The child from her first husband had-blood group type O, i.e. genotype ii. This means that the child recieved two recessive alleles, one from each of his parents.

The child from second husband had blood group type AB, i.e. genotype $I^A I^B$. This indicate that the child recieved I^B allele from father and I^A from mother. Thus, it can be concluded that the genotype of women is I^A i and the blood group type is 'A'.

8. (*b*) Statements I and V are incorrect, and can be corrected as

Mendel discovered the fundamental laws of inheritance. He tracked the segregation of parental genes and their reappearance is the offspring as dominant or recessive traits. Sutton and Boveri discovered that chromosomes are responsible for the inheritance.

The seven characters studied by Mendel is plant height, pod shape, pod colour, flower position, flower colour, seed shape, seed colour. Leaf shape was not studied by Mendel because it does not show any contrasting features.

9. (*c*) When green plant was self-fertilised, appearance of white seedling in progeny indicate parents were heterozygous for one allele, e.g. Gg × Gg. Where G represent dominant green allele and g is recessive white allele.

10. (*d*) Statement I is correct, but statement II is incorrect. The incorrect statement can be corrected as

The outcome ratio of test cross is 1:1 if the unknown genotype is heterozygous.

11. (*d*) In a monohybrid cross, if the F_1 generation (heterozygous, Aa) is crossed with a homozygous dominant parent (AA), all offspring will inherit at least one dominant allele (A). The possible genotypes of the offspring are AA and Aa, both of which exhibit the dominant phenotype. Therefore, no recessive phenotypes will be observed among the offspring.

12. (*a*) Principle of segregation is also called as the law of purity of gametes. According to this law, a gamete may carry either the dominant or the recessive factor, but not both, as we find in F_1 individuals. The gametes which are formed are always pure for a particular character.

13. (*d*) Unlike zygotes, somatic cells and embryos, gametes are haploid, i.e., contain a single set of chromosomes, or genes. Thus, do not possess genes occurring in pairs. During fertilisation, the sperm and egg combine their genetic material, resulting in a zygote with paired genes. This ensures the offspring has the correct number of chromosomes.

14. (*d*) Gibberellin treatment increases the height of the dwarf plant, but it does not change its genetic makeup. Thus, when crossed with another dwarf plant, all offsprings in the F_1 generation will also be dwarf.

15. (*d*) The incorrect match pair can be corrected as
Intermediate size of starch grain in pea seed is an example of Incomplete dominance, while human blood group is an example of Multiple allelism.

16. (*d*) The man has blood group 'AB', meaning his genotype could be $I^A I^B$. The woman has blood group 'O', meaning her genotype is ii. When we cross these genotypes, we get offspring with genotypes I^Ai and I^Bi, resulting in blood groups A and B, respectively. Thus, the offspring will not have blood group AB and O.

17. (*a*) Mendel crossed round and wrinkled seed varieties of garden peas. The round seeds were obtained in F_1 generation and wrinkled trait had dissappeared in F_1 progeny. When round seed hybrids were selfed, about 3/4th round and 1/4th wrinkled seeds were obtained in F_2 progeny. In total, 1064 seeds were obtained in F_2 generation out of which 787 seeds were round and 277 were wrinkled, a nearly perfect 3 : 1 ratio obtained.

18. (*b*) Both A and R are true and R is the correct explanation of A.
When genes are very far apart on the same chromosome, crossing over occurs in nearly every meiotic event, leading to 100 percent recombination between them. This results in 50 percent of offsprings exhibiting non-parental combinations, making the genes behave as if they are unlinked and assorting independently.

19. (*b*) When two genes are located very close on the chromosome, they tend to be inherited together, exhibiting linkage. In this scenario, the genes R and Y are located very close, so they are likely to be inherited together more often. Therefore, the F_2 generation will show a higher number of the parental types (RRYY and rryy) and a lower number of the non-parental types.

20. (*c*) The pea plant with genotype RrYy will produce RY, rY, Ry and ry gametes. We can see through the Punnett Square.

	R	r
Y	RY	rY
y	Ry	ry

21. (*c*) In a dihybrid cross, the ratio 9:3:3:1 represents that 9 individual out of 16 would contain dominant allele for both characters, 6 (3+3) individual out of 16 contain dominant allele of a character and recessive allele of another character. Only one individual out of 16 contains recessive allele for both the characters.

22. (*b*) In a dihybrid cross (AaBb x AaBb), each gene pair (A and a, B and b) segregates independently according to Mendel's law of independent assortment. To find the probability of an offspring being homozygous recessive for both traits (AABB or aabb), we calculate the probability for each gene pair separately and then multiply them.
- The probability of being homozygous recessive for the first trait (aa) is 1/4.
- The probability of being homozygous recessive for the second trait (bb) is also 1/4.

So, the combined probability is: ¼ × ¼ = 1/16
Therefore, the probability of obtaining an offspring that is homozygous recessive for both traits is 1/16.

23. (*c*) The correct matches are A-1, B-2, C-4, D-3.
- Independent assortment refers to the random distribution of alleles for different genes into gametes during meiosis.
- Chromosomal theory of inheritance proposes that genes are located on chromosomes.
- Mendel's law of segregation describes the random distribution of alleles for a single gene into gametes during meiosis.
- Mendel's law of dominance states that in a heterozygote, one allele may conceal the presence of another allele for the same characteristic.

24. (*d*) Statement I is correct, but statement II is incorrect. It can be corrected as:
Drosophila melanogaster were found suitable for genetic studies because they could be grown on a simple synthetic medium and had clearly distinguishable sexes.

25. (*a*) Statements I and II are correct while statements III and IV are incorrect. These can be corrected as Mendel could not find out linkage because all of his experimental characters of pea were not linked. They were present far apart from each other on four different chromosomes.

26. (*c*) B cannot lie on the same side of C because the distance between B and C would then become (8-5) = 3 unit against 13 unit. Therefore, it must lie on the opposite side of C with A present between the two, at a distance of 5 units from B and 8 units from C.

13 units
C ⟷ A ⟷ B
8 units 5 units

27. (*d*) A is true, but R is false and can be corrected as

Thalassemia is indeed caused by mutations in the genes that produce haemoglobin. However, increasing dietary iron intake is not an effective treatment for thalassemia, as this condition is related to haemoglobin production, not iron deficiency. In fact, excessive iron can be harmful to individuals with thalassemia.

28. (*b*) Genes which are involved in quantitative inheritance are called polygenes. Skin color in humans is controlled by at least three genes.

29. (*c*) In polygenic inheritance, when two heterozygous individuals (AaBb) are crossed, the phenotypic ratio of their offspring depends on the number of additive alleles. So, the resulting phenotypic ratio is 1:4:6:4:1.. This means for every 1 individual with extreme phenotype (AABB), there are 4 individuals with slightly less extreme phenotype (2 AABb and 2 AaBB), 6 with intermediate phenotype (4 AaBb, 1 AAbb, and 1 aaBB), and 4 with slightly more extreme phenotype (2 aabB and 2 Aabb), and again 1 with another extreme phenotype (aabb).

30. (*a*) In grasshoppers, males are heterogametic (XO) and females are homogametic (XX), meaning females have one more chromosome than males. In birds, males are homogametic (ZZ) and females are heterogametic (ZW), both having the same number of chromosomes. In humans, males are heterogametic (XY) and females are homogametic (XX), also with the same number of chromosomes. Honey bees use haplodiploidy, with males being haploid and females diploid, differing from standard heterogametic sex-determination.

31. (*b*) In the haplo-diploid sex-determination system of honey bees, females (queens and workers) are diploid, meaning they have two sets of chromosomes (32 chromosomes). Males (drones) are haploid, having only one set of chromosomes (16 chromosomes). Workers, being females, are also diploid.

32. (*b*) Incorrect statement can be corrected in the following way

Deletions can be detected during pairing of homologous chromosomes.

33. (*a*) In sickle-cell anaemia, a mutation in the β-globin gene leads to a substitution of valine (Val) for glutamic acid (Glu) at the sixth position of the β-chain of haemoglobin. This change alters the structure of haemoglobin, resulting in the characteristic sickle shape of red blood cells, leading to various complications associated with the condition.

34. (*c*) In pedigree analysis, different symbols are used to represent different genders. A circle represents females and a square represents males. When the sex is unspecified or unknown, a diamond is used. This standard formatting helps in understanding the inheritance patterns of genetic traits and disorders.

35. (*b*) Suppose heterozygous for albinism is represented by Aa. If heterozygous for albinism tobacco plant is self- pollinated, 1200 seeds are germinated.

The genotypic ratio is 1AA : 2Aa : 1aa. This shows that 50% seedlings have the parental genotype. Thus, out of 1200 seeds, 50% or 600 seedlings would have the parental genotype.

36. (*a*) The given pedigree chart indicates dominant X-linked trait. Since only 50% of the second generation has inherited the trait, it cannot be homozygous dominant. Hence, father is homozygous recessive while mother is heterozygous.

One of four children marries an affected individual. The couple produce two affected daughters and two normal sons. This is possible only when one partner is homozygous recessive and other is heterozygous dominant. X-linked character cannot pass to the sons. Hence, it is X-linked dominant trait.

37. (*c*) The disease is likely to be colour blindness. This condition of disease is X-linked recessive, meaning the gene causing the disease is located on the X chromosome. A carrier female has one normal and one affected X chromosome. She can pass the affected X chromosome to her male offspring, who have only one X chromosome. If they inherit the affected X, they will express the disease. In contrast, Phenylketonuria and sickle cell anaemia are autosomal recessive dirorder, and myotonic dystrophy is autosomal dominant disorder.

38. (*a*) In an autosomal dominant disorder like myotonic dystrophy, affected individuals (Mm) must have at least one affected parent. If affected individuals have unaffected siblings, it means the parent must be heterozygous (Mm). Here, parent 1 is affected (Mm) and must pass on the dominant (M) and recessive (m) alleles to the progeny. So, the affected progeny must be heterozygous (Mm), and the unaffected one must be homozygous recessive (mm), as seen in individuals 3 and 2, respectively.

39. (*b*) Sickle-cell anaemia is an autosomal recessive Mendelian disorder. If both parents are carriers (genotype AS), there is 25% chance, their child will have the disease (SS), 50% chance the child will be a carrier (AS), and 25% chance that the child will be unaffected (AA). Therefore, the probability that their child will be a carrier is 50%.

40. (*d*) Statement I is correct, but statement II is incorrect. It can be corrected as

The males have only one X chromosome, so if they inherit the defective gene, they will be colour blind.

41. (*d*) Incorrect statement can be corrected as

Haemophilia is a sex-linked recessive disorder.

42. (*c*) Phenylketonuria (PKU) in humans results from the deficiency of phenylalanine hydroxylase. This enzyme is vital for converting phenylalanine to tyrosine. Without it, phenylalanine accumulates, in the body. Elevated phenylalanine levels can cause intellectual disabilities, behavioral problems, and other health issues. The other enzymes are unrelated to PKU and function in different pathways.

43. (*b*) Thalassemia is an autosomal recessive disorder, meaning it is transmitted when both parents are unaffected carriers (heterozygous for the gene). Each parent carries one normal allele and one mutated allele. When two carriers have children, there is a 25% chance their child will inherit both mutated alleles and have thalassemia.

44. (*d*) Statements I, IV and V are correct. While incorrect statement are II and III. These can be corrected as Turner's syndrome is characterised by the absence of one X chromosome in females, leading to short stature and infertility. Klinefelter's syndrome results from the presence of an extra X chromosome in males, causing underdeveloped testes and infertility.

45. (*c*) In a trisomic condition (2n+1), an extra chromosome is added to the normal diploid set. So, if the haploid number is 23, the diploid number will be 46 (23x2). In trisomy, one more chromosome is added, making the total 47. Hence, the trisomic number will be 47.

46. (*b*) The incorrect match can be corrected as
Turner's syndrome is caused due to monosomy ($2n$ - 1). It is formed by the union of allosome-free egg (22 + 0) and a normal X sperm or normal egg and an allosome-free sperm (22 + 0). The individual has($2n - 1$) = 45 chromosomes (44 + X0) instead of 46. Rest of the options are correct match pairs.

47. (*d*) The correct matches are A–4, B–1, C–2, D–3.
Alleles are different or alternate form of a gene, e.g. T and t for height.
Recessive allele are expressed only when they are present in homozygous state as in heterozygous state, they are masked by dominant allele.
Pleiotropy involves instances where a single gene can exhibit multiple phenotypic expression.
Polygenic inheritance involves traits that are generally controlled by three or more genes, i.e. Human skin colour.

48. (*d*) Incorrect statement can be corrected as
The principle of independent assortment describes how different genes independently separate from one another where reproductive cells develop. The independent assortment of genes occurs during meiosis in eukaryotes. During meiosis, the pairs of homologous chromosomes are divided in half to form haploid cells and this separation, or assortment of homologous chromosomes is random.

49. (*b*) The correct matches are A-2, B-4, C-1 and D-3.
- Wild type phenotype is found most commonly in nature.
- Phenotype is the appearance of an individual.
- Punnett square was developed by a British geneticist, Reginald C. Punnett.
- Dihybrid test cross ratio is 1:1:1:1.

50. (*d*) Statements II, III, IV and V are incorrect. They can be corrected as:
Mutant traits are mostly recessive, not dominant, in a population.
Emasculation is a technique used by Mendel to ensure cross-pollination by removing the male parts of the flower to prevent self-pollination, not to prevent cross-pollination.
In pea plants, wrinkled seeds have small sized starch grains, not intermediate-sized.
The law of purity of gametes, also known as the law of segregation, is the only law of inheritance without exceptions. Other laws, like the law of dominance (e.g., incomplete dominance), and independent assortment (e.g., linked genes) , have exceptions.

Ch-5 Molecular Basis of Inheritance

Topical Follow Thru

Test 1

1. (*a*) Only $\phi\times 174$ - 5386 nucleotides shows the correct match. The other incorrect matches can be corrected as
Bacteriophage lambda - 48502 bp
Escherichia coli - 4.6×10^{6} bp
Human (haploid content) –3.3×10^{9} bp.

2. (*c*) Both A and R are true, but R is not the correct explanation of A.
In DNA, adenine forms two hydrogen bonds with thymine from opposite strand and *vice-versa*. Similarly, guanine form three hydrogen bonds with cytosine. As a result, always a purine comes opposite to a pyrimidine. This generates approximately uniform distance between the two strands of the helix.

3. (*a*) In the given figure *A*, *B* and *C* represents the pitch (a complete turn) of helix, distance between a base pair in a helix and distance between two strand of DNA molecule which are 3.4 nm, 0.34 nm and 2 nm, respectively.

4. (*d*) Statement I is correct, but statement II is incorrect. The incorrect statement can be corrected as
Chromosomes, not the centromeres, are condensed structures of DNA and proteins that are visible during cell division. This organisation facilitates the accurate segregation of genetic material into daughter cells.

5. (*d*) In the given diagram, the histone octamer (*C*) is positively charged, while the negatively charged DNA (*A*) is wrapped around it.

6. (*c*) The correct matches are A–4, B–1, C–3 and D–2.

- Heat killed S-type bacteria–Demonstrated the necessity of a specific bacterial structure for virulence.
- Live R-type bacteria–Showed that hereditary material could transform bacteria.
- Mixture of heat killed S-type bacteria and live R-type bacteria–Provided evidence, that transformation required direct interaction between cells.
- Smooth colonies observed in mice–Confirmed that genetic information could be transferred between bacteria.

7. (*b*) The correct order of organisation is Genome-Chromosome-Gene-Nucleotide.
The genome is described as the genetic information repository of an organism.
The genetic material, i.e. DNA is packaged into thread-like structures called chromosome.
Gene is the segment of DNA that codes for the protein.
Nucleotide is the building block of genetic material.

8. (*d*) The incorrect statement can be corrected as
The RNA world hypothesis proposes that RNA, was the initial genetic material and also had catalytic functions (ribozymes). Proteins are believed to have emerged later in evolution, after the RNA world era, to perform more diverse and specialised functions.

9. (*b*) Taylor and his colleagues while working on faba beans (*Vicia faba*) in 1958 proved that DNA in chromosomes also replicates semi-conservatively.

10. (*a*) Hershey and Chase found that when bacteriophages containing ^{32}P or radioactive DNA, were allowed to infect non-radioactive bacteria, all the infected cells became radioactive and in fact, much of the radioactivity was passed on to the next generation of *E. coli* bacteria. Similarly when the bacteriophage containing ^{35}S or radioactive protein were allowed to infect non-radioactive bacteria, thus neither of the bacteria get infected nor the ^{35}S or radioactive protein was passed to the next generations.

11. (*a*) Statement I is incorrect, but statement II is correct. Incorrect statement can be corrected as
Synthesis of new DNA strand takes place by the addition of DNA nucleotides to the 3′ – OH group of the last ribonucleotide of the RNA primer. This synthesis takes place in the 5′ and 3′ direction and is catalysed by DNA polymerase.

12. (*b*) Helicase is an enzyme that binds to DNA and travels along the double helix, separating the two strands by breaking hydrogen bonds between complementary base pairs. This unwinding of the DNA helix creates the replication fork where DNA polymerase and other enzymes can then synthesise new DNA strands.

13. (*b*) Both statement I and statement II are correct. These can be explained as
Enzyme DNA-dependent DNA polymerase is essential for DNA replication, as it reads the original DNA strand and helps to form a new complementary strand by linking together the appropriate deoxynucleotides.
Replication is semiconservative because each new DNA molecule consists of one parental strand and one newly synthesised complementary strand. It is semi-discontinuous because DNA polymerase can only add nucleotides to the 3' end, leading to continuous synthesis on the leading strand and discontinuous synthesis on the lagging strand.
DNA replication is bi-directional because the two strands of DNA are antiparallel, with one running 3'-5' and the other 5'-3'.

14. (*b*) Statements I, III, IV and V are correct. Statement II is incorrect and can be corrected as
Genetic material should be both chemically and structurally stable. It should be chemically stable to maintain integrity over generations, but it should not be structurally unstable, as this would lead to frequent errors and mutations.

15. (*c*) According to Chargaff's rule, the amount of adenine is always equal to that of thymine and similarly the amount of guanine is always equal to that of cytosine.
So, if A = T and A = 120, then T = 120.
Similarly, if G = C and C = 120, then G = 120.
So, the total number of nucleotids in the segment = $120 \times 4 = 480$.

Test 2

1. (*c*) Heterogeneous nuclear RNA (*hn*RNA) is the primary transcript, synthesised from DNA during transcription in eukaryotic cells, which includes both introns and exons and undergoes processing to become mature *m*RNA.

2. (*d*) As the reading frame is determined by the triplet codons (groups of three nucleotides) that encode amino acids in a protein sequence.
So, insertion or deletion of a single or two nucleotides can disrupt the reading frame of a gene from the points of insertion or deletion.

3. (*b*) The promoter (P) serves as the "landing pad" for RNA polymerase, the enzyme responsible for transcribing DNA into RNA. It also defines the template and coding strands.

4. (*b*) *Sigma* (*A*) and *rho* (*C*) factors transiently associate with RNA polymerase (*D*), altering its specificity for initiation and termination, respectively.

5. (*a*) The correct matches are A–3, B–1, C–4 and D–2.
Activation of amino acid occurs in the presence of ATP and linked

cognate *t*RNA. This process is called changing of *t*RNA or aminoacylation of *t*RNA.

Transfer of activated amino acid to *t*RNA takes place under the direction of an enzyme aminoacyl *t*RNA synthetase.

Initiation of polypeptide chain synthesis typically starts with methionine.

Untranslated regions are the additional sequences present at both 5' -end (before start codon) and at 3' -end (after stop codon) and are required for an efficient translation process.

6. (*b*) The incorrect statement can be corrected as

The entire DNA molecule do not participate in transcription, instead a segment of DNA and only one of the strands is copied in RNA. This is because if both strands of DNA will act as template then they would code for RNA molecules with different sequence and if they code for proteins, the sequence of amino acids in the protein would be different. And, secondly if two RNA molecules is produced simultaneously, it would be complemantary to each other resulting in formation of a double stranded RNA.

7. (*a*) Statement I is incorrect, but statement II is correct. Incorrect statement can be corrected as

Introns are non-coding DNA sequences that get removed from RNA during processing (splicing). Thus, they do not appear in mature RNA. Instead exons are said to be those sequences that appear in mature or processed RNA.

8. (*b*) The correct matches are A–4, B–3, C–1 and D–2.

Sigma factor is required for transcription initiation in bacteria by RNA polymerase.

The *t*RNA is also called *s*RNA (soluble RNA).

RNA polymerase-II transcribes precursor of *m*RNA, i.e. heterogenous RNA (*hn*RNA).

RNA polmerase-I transcribes *r*RNA.

9. (*a*) The enzyme polynucleotide phosphorylase was given by Severo Ochoa thus, it is also known as Severo Ochoa enzyme. It was helpful in polymerising RNA with defined sequences in a template independent manner (enzymatic synthesis of RNA).

10. (*c*) Both statement I and statement II are incorrect. These incorrect statements can be corrected as

The anticodon loop of *t*RNA binds to the codon on *m*RNA based on its complementary sequence. The amino acid is attached to the 3'-end of the *t*RNA by the enzyme aminoacyl-*t*RNA synthetase.

The amino acid attachment site of *t*RNA is located at the 3'-end of the acceptor arm, not the 5'-end.

11. (*a*) The large deletions and rearrangements involve bigger DNA changes, making them easier to identify.

12. (*d*) The post-transcriptional modification involve tailing where adenylate residues are added at 3′-end in a template independent manner.

Other statements are incorrect and can be corrected as

- The post-transcriptional modification involve conversion of *hn*RNA into *m*RNA.
- In capping, methyl-guanosine triphosphate is added to the 5′-end.
- It result in removal of intron and joining of exons in a definite order.

13. (*c*) Statements II, III and V are correct, whereas statements I and IV are incorrect. These can be corrected as

*m*RNA provides template for protein synthesis.

A DNA segment that codes for proteins is called cistron.

14. (*b*) Statements I, III and IV are correct. While statements II and V are incorrect. The incorrect statement can be corrected as

Three consecutive nucleotides form a codon and there are 64 codons in total. Out of these, 61 codons code for amino acids, while 3 codons (UAA, UAG and UGA) are stop codons that do not code for any amino acids and instead signal the termination of translation.

Stop codons (UAA, UAG, UGA) do not specify any amino acid. Instead, they signal the termination of translation.

15. (*c*) 999 bases in RNA codes for a protein with 333 amino acids.

If base at 901 position is deleted the first 900 bases will be normal while bases after 901th position will be altered that is 99 bases will be altered

3 bases = 1 codon

So, 99 bases = 33 codons

Thus, 33 codons will be altered due to deletion of one base at 901 position.

Test 3

1. (*d*) The promotor region in the *lac* operon contains the specific sequence where RNA polymerase binds to initiate transcription of the *lac* operon genes.

2. (*a*) The *Lac* operon of *E. coli* contains three structural genes, i.e. z, y and A.

- Gene-z codes for the enzyme β-galactosidase which hydrolyses lactose into glucose and galactose.
- Gene-y codes for β-galactose permease, a membrane bound carrier protein which helps in the transfer of metabolites.
- Gene-a codes for enzyme β-galactose transacetylase, an enzyme that tranfers an acetyl group from acetyl co-A to β-galactosidase.

3. (*a*) The correct match is given in option (a) i.e. Sequence annotation-Assigning functions to different regions of a sequenced genome.

Incorrect match pairs can be corrected as

Expressed Sequence Tags (ESTs) focused on identifying all the genes that are expressed.

Bacterial Artificial Chromosomes (BACs) and Yeast Artificial

Chromosomes (YACs) are the cloning vector for small DNA fragments.

4. (*d*) Statement (d) is correct. Rest other statements are incorrect and can be corrected as

An operon has its specific operator and repressor.

A common promotor and regulatory genes can regulate a polycistronic and not the monocistronic structural genes.

Allolactose inactivates the functioning of the repressor by interacting it.

5. (*c*) The control of gene expression can take place at transcription, splicing regulation and translation levels.

6. (*c*) The incorrect statement can be corrected as

Southern blotting is the accurate technique used to separate DNA fragments based on size after restriction enzyme digestion.

Rest statements are correct.

7. (*d*) The *lac-z* codes for the enzyme β-galactosidase which breaks lactose into glucose and galactose to be utilised in the cell.

Therefore, *E.coli* cells with a mutated *z*-genes cannot grow in medium containing only lactose as the source of energy because they cannot synthesise functional β-gatactosidase.

8. (*b*) The human genome project, a landmark international initiative spanning 13 years, was coordinated by the US Department of Energy and the National Institute of Health. During the early years of the HGP, the Wellcome Trust (UK) become a major partner. This project was completed in 2003.

9. (*c*) All the given statements are correct except one which can be corrected as

Though, HGP primarily foused on sequencing the human genome but one of the important goal of HGP was also, the addiers the Ethical, Legal and Social Issues (ELSI) that may arise from the project.

10. (*b*) Expressed Sequence Tags (ESTs) is used to identify all the given expressed as RNA.

As, this technique involves isolating and sequencing short *c*DNA fragments (copies of *m*RNA) from a cell. Since, *m*RNA represents the transcribed portion of the genome that codes for proteins, ESTs provide a snapshot of the genes actively being expressed in a particular cell or tissue.

11. (*c*) While repetitive DNA sequences do make up a large portion of the human genome, most of these sequences do not code for proteins. They can influence genomic structure, stability and the regulation of gene expression.

12. (*d*) Statement I is correct, but statement II is incorrect.

Statement II can be corrected as

The primary usefulness of SNP information lies in finding chromosomal locations for disease-associated sequences and tracing human history, rather than merely identifying protein-coding genes.

13. (*b*) Both A and R are true and R is the correct explanation of A.

VNTR analysis is a powerful technique for DNA fingerprinting because of its high degree of polymorphism.

The core reason behind VNTR's polymorphism lies in the variation of tandem repeat numbers between individuals. This variation directly leads to the generation of distinct banding patterns on autoradiograms, allowing for individual identification.

14. (*d*) Statement I is correct, but statement II is incorrect. Incorrect statement can be corrected as

Enzyme beta-galactosidase is synthesised by bacteria *E. coli*. It responsible for the hydrolysis of lactose into galactose and glucose.

15. (*a*) A is false, but R is true. A can be corrected as

The *C. elegans* and other model organisms share a significant portion of genes with humans. Studying DNA variations in these organisms can provide valuable insights into genes potentially relevant to human health, even if there are also differences.

The information about shared genes between *C. elegans* and humans will supports the use of these organisms as models for understanding human health at the genetic level.

Chapter Break Thru

1. (*c*) Total number of bases present in RNA = 666

Number of bases after insertion

$= 667 - 600 = 67$

Number of codons present in 67 bases = 22 approx.

Hence, approximately 22 codons will be altered as then codons code for one amino acid.

2. (*c*) The observation of a significant increase in lightly stained regions (euchromatin) in a cell undergoing rapid protein synthesis suggests that genes in these regions are being actively transcribed to produce the necessary proteins.

The other options are incorrect because

- Inactive genes are typically located in heterochromatin, not euchromatin.
- DNA replication involves unwinding of both euchromatin and heterochromatin, not just euchromatin.
- Condensation primarily occurs in heterochromatin during cell division, not euchromatin.

3. (*b*) Statements II, III and IV are correct, while rest of the statements are incorrect. The incorrect statements can be corrected as

DNA was first identified by Friedrich Miescher in 1869.

The daughter DNA molecules produced during replication are identical to the parental DNA molecule.

4. (*d*) Statements I, II and III are correct.

The incorrect statements can be corrected as

- Anticondon loop of *t*RNA possess condons complementary to the condons on *m*RNA.
- RNA is more unstable than DNA because of the presence of reaction 2'–OH group at every nucleotide in RNA.

5. (c) Both A and R are true, but R is not the correct explanations of A.

Repeated or repetitive sequences make up a large portion of human genome. These sequences are nucleotide sequences that are repeated many times, sometimes hundreds to thousand times.

They have no direct coding function but provide informations to chromosome structure, dynamics and evolution.

6. (*c*) The process of flow of information in viruses is called reverse transcriptase represented by 'D'. Some viruses, like retroviruses carry their genetic information as RNA.

When they infect a host cell, an enzyme called reverse transcriptase converts the viral RNA into complementary DNA (*c*DNA).

7. (*a*) A is false, but R is true. A can be corrected as

While RNA is the genetic material in some viruses like retroviruses, DNA is the predominant genetic material in most living organisms.

8. (*b*) The first generation would have a mixture of parental heavy DNA and newly synthesised light DNA, resulting in two bands of equal intensity. This represents the semi-conservative model of replication.

9. (*d*) Statement I is correct, but statement II is incorrect and can be corrected as

The positive charge of lysine and arginine residues in histones arises from the side chains (*R* groups) of these amino acids, not the main chain. The main chain of amino acids has a similar structure across all amino acids and does not contribute significantly to the overall charge.

10. (*b*) The correct matches are A- 2, B- 4, C- 1 and D- 3.

RNA polymerase catalyses the process of elongation.

RNA polymerase-III transcribes *t*RNA, *hn*RNA and *sn*RNAs.

DNA-dependent DNA polymerase catalyses polymerisation.

DNA ligase joins the ends of DNA.

11. (*b*) Both statement I and statement II are correct.

In eukaryotes, a specific DNA sequence called the promotor, located upstream of the gene, acts as the binding site for RNA polymerase-II. This is where transcription initiation occurs. The promotor contains specific sequences such as the TATA box, which are crucial for the binding of transcription factors and RNA polymerase-II.

The specific DNA sequences located downstream of the coding region of a gene signal the termination of transcription. These sequences are recognised by various proteins and factors that help to stop RNA synthesis and release the newly synthesised RNA molecule.

12. (*b*) Statements I, II, III and IV correctly describe the observations from Griffith's experiment.

13. (*d*) A is true, but R is false. R can be corrected as

Amino acids in a polypeptide chain are joined by peptide bonds, which are covalent bonds formed between the carboxyl group of one amino acid and the amino group of another. Hydrogen bonds do play a role in the secondary and tertiary structures of proteins, but they are not responsible for the primary linkage of amino acids in a protein chain.

14. (*c*) In prokaryotes, the transcription enzyme for *m*RNA synthesis is DNA-dependent RNA polymerase. In eukaryotes, there are three types of transcription enzymes. RNA polymerase-II catalyses the synthesis of messenger RNA, RNA polymerase-I, which transcribes *r*RNA and RNA polymerase-III, which transcribes *t*RNA.

15. (*d*) A is true, but R is false. R can be corrected as

Griffith's experiment did not conclusively identify DNA as the genetic material. This was later determined by Avery, MacLeod and McCarty in their experiments. Griffith's experiment showed that genetic material from the heat-killed S strain bacteria could transform the R strain bacteria, changing their phenotype.

16. (*d*) At the 5' end, a cap structure (a 7-methylguanosine cap) is added, and at the 3' end, a poly-A tail is added. Both of these additions occur without the use of a template.

17. (*b*) Both statements I and II are correct.

The initial steps of the Hershey-Chase experiment, where radioactive bacteriophages are attached to *E. coli* and then their coats are removed using a blender. Radioactivity detected in the bacteria after coat removal indicates that the radioactive DNA (not protein) from the virus entered and remained within the bacteria.

18. (*b*) The correct matches are A–2, B–4, C–1 and D–3.

- *m*RNA (messenger RNA) carries genetic information from DNA to the ribosome, where it is translated into a protein. It is often referred to as "genetic RNA."
- *r*RNA (ribosomal RNA) is a structural component of ribosomes, which are the sites of protein synthesis. It is known to be stable.
- *t*RNA (transfer RNA) is involved in translation, where it brings amino acids to the ribosome during protein synthesis. It is soluble.
- *hn*RNA (heterogeneous nuclear RNA) is the precursor to *m*RNA and includes introns and exons before RNA splicing.

19. (*c*) Statement in option (c) is correct, whereas options (a), (b) and (d) are incorrect. These can be corrected as Coding strand has opposite polarity (5' to 3') compared to *m*RNA.

RNA polymerase transcribes only from the template strand (3' to 5').

Terminator marks the end of transcription on both strands, not just the coding strand.

20. (*b*) The correct matches are A-2, B-1, C-1 and 2.

Elongation continues with incorrect amino acids incorporated. Insertion of a single nucleotide disrupts the reading frame, leading to misinterpretations of codons from that point onwards.

Chain termination immediately after the mutation site. Deletion of a single nucleotide alters the reading frame, but a stop codon might be created immediately after the deletion due to the shift, causing termination.

Altered amino acid sequence from the mutation point onwards. Both insertion and deletion of a single nucleotide disrupt the reading frame, resulting in a new sequence of codons being read and different amino acids incorporated downstream.

21. (*b*) DNA fingerprinting is the technique used to identify highly variable regions of DNA that are unique to each individual (except identical twins). These unique sequences are used for various applications, including forensic identification, paternity testing, genetic disorders.

22. (*d*) Statement in option (d) is incorrect regarding the goals of HGP.

It can be corrected as

Mapping all the functional proteins encoded by human genome is not then goal of HGP.

23. (*b*) Both statement I and statement II are correct.

In prokaryotes, gene expression is primarily regulated at the level of transcription initiation. This regulation is often achieved by controlling the binding of RNA polymerase to the promotor regions of genes, which can be influenced by activators and repressors.

In many prokaryotic operons, repressors bind to operator regions, which are typically located downstream or overlapping the promotor region. When a repressor binds to the operator, it can physically block RNA polymerase from binding to the promotor, thereby preventing the initiation of transcription.

24. (*d*) In order the provide valuable insights into human biology the DNA-sequence of non-human models such as *C. elegans*, bacteria, yeast, *Drosophila*, rice and *Arbidopsis* have been sequenced.

25. (*b*) Lagging strand is synthesised discontinuously in short fragments called Okazaki fragments, also in the 5' to 3' direction. These fragments are later joined by an enzyme called DNA ligase.

26. (*c*) Histones are not gene repressors themselves, but can play a role in both repressing and activating gene expression depending on their modifications and the context within the chromatin.

27. (*b*) Cytidine is a nucleoside, which means it consists of two components

- A nitrogenous base- Cytosine
- A pentose sugar- Ribose

28. (*b*) Both A and R are true and R is the correct explanation of A. According to Chargaff's rule, the base ratio A + T / C+ G is specific for a species. This is therefore, used for the identification of species.

29. (*a*) The incorrect statement can be corrected as

DNA does not have a 2'-OH group; this group is present in RNA. The presence of the 2'-OH group in RNA makes it more reactive and less stable compared to DNA, which lacks this group and is therefore more stable.

30. (*d*) A particular *m*RNA codon codes for a particular amino acids. As there are 64 codons and only 20 amino acids thus more than one codon can code for single amino acids.

	Amino acids	Codons
(i)	Leucine	CUU, CUC, CUA, CUG, UUA, UUG
(ii)	Threonine	ACU, ACC, ACA, ACG
(iii)	Proline	CCU, CCC, CCA, CCG

31. (*b*) A poly-A tail, consisting of 200-300 adenylate residues, is added to the 3' end of the RNA molecule in a process that does not rely on a complementary DNA sequence.

32. (*c*) Both A and R are correct, but R is not the correct explanation of A.

Aminoacyl *t*RNA synthetases are indeed enzymes that catalyse the attachment of amino acids to their corresponding *t*RNA molecules, a crucial step in protein synthesis.

*t*RNA molecules are transcribed by RNA polymerase-III in eukaryotic cells.

33. (*c*) The humans share an incredibly high degree of genetic similarity. Their DNA base sequences are almost identical, with only about 0.1% variation between two random individuals.

This means that 99.9% of the base pairs in our DNA are the same.

34. (*a*) An inducer binds with the repressor protein and prevents the repressor protein to bind with operator. Glucose and galactose cannot act as an inducer because they do not have the binding sites for attaching to the repressor protein.

35. (*a*) The Human Genome Project (HGP) completed in the year 2003. It was a mega project that took 13 years to complete.

36. (*d*) Statement I is correct, but statement II is incorrect. Incorrect statement can be corrected as

Analysing large data sets requires expertise from various disciplines, including public and private sectors.

37. (*d*) Incorrect statement can be corrected as

The untranslated region (UTR) are present at both 5′ end (before start codon) and 3′ end (after stop codon).

38. (*a*) Polymorphism is the general term for the presence of multiple variants of a gene or DNA sequence in a population.

39. (*c*) Statements II and IV are incorrect and can be corrected as

One codon codes for only one amino acid, hence it is unambiguous and specific. There is no ambiguity in the coding of amino acids by codons.

There are no punctuation marks separating codons in *m*RNA. The codons are read continuously without any 'stop' signals between them.

40. (*d*) The correct matches are A-3, B-4, C-1 and D-2.

The *z* gene codes for beta-galactosidase (β-gal) which is primarily responsible for the hydrolysis of disaccharide. The *y* gene codes for permease which increase the permeability of the cell to β-galactosidase. The *a* gene encodes a transacetylase. The *i* gene codes for the repressor of the *lac* operon.

41. (*b*) Both statement I and statement II are correct

DNA fingerprinting employes the principle of polymorphism in DNA sequences as the polymorphism are inheritable from parent to children.

The DNA sample hybridised with DNA probe when kept in contact with X-ray film results into photographic image of DNA bands due to redactive probe.

42. (*b*) Both A and R are true and R is the correct explanation of A.

DNA replication begins at a specific region called the origin of replication, not randomly.

Vectors used in recombinant DNA technology provide the origin of replication necessary for the replication and propagation of the inserted DNA fragment.

43. (*a*) Statements in option (b), (c) and (d) are correct. Other incorrect statement can be corrected as

Ribosomal RNA (*r*RNA) is a structural component of ribosomes, the cellular machinery for protein synthesis. It does not act as a template for protein synthesis.

44. (*b*) The ribosomal unit that attaches to *m*RNA to form *m*RNA-subunit complex is the smaller subunit (30S or 40S) of the ribosome. The larger subunit joins the smaller subunit to form a complete translation initiation complex.

45. (*b*) Length of *E. coli* DNA is 1.36 mm.

1 mm = 10,00,000 nanometers

So, 1.36 mm = 13,60,000 nanometers.

Now, we use the fact that there are approximately 0.34 nanometers between each base pair in DNA.

Number of base pairs = Length / Distance between base pairs

Number of base pairs = 13,60,000 nm / 0.34 nm/base pair

Number of base pairs = 40,00,000 base pairs

Therefore, there are approximately 40,00,000 base pairs in *E. coli* DNA.

46. (*a*) Both DNA and RNA are able to mutate. RNA being unstable mutates at a faster rate. Consequently, virus having RNA genome and having shorter lifespan mutate and evolve at faster rate.

47. (*a*) Helix-destabilising proteins is any protein that binds to single-stranded regions of duplex DNA and thereby cause unwinding of the helix, e.g. helicase.

Thus, it helps to keep uncoiled DNA strands far apart.

48. (*b*) Both statements I and II are correct.

Structural genes code for the synthesis of specific polypeptides such as enzymes and structural proteins. Operator genes contain the code to begin transcribing the DNA message of structural genes into *m*RNA.

By defining the direction of transcription and indicating which strand will be described, promoter gene base sequence determines which strand of DNA acts as a template for transpiration.

49. (*c*) The end product is often utilised in some reactions so, it rarely accumulates. However, in *lac* operon, it accumulates and stops the operon system. It is called as feedback inhibition or repression.

50. (*b*) All given characters are required for protein synthesis except III. Incorrect character can be corrected as

Genetic RNAs do not play any role in protein synthesis.

Ch-6 Evolution

Topical Follow Thru

Test 1

1. (*b*) Theory of spontaneous generation was disapproved by Louis Pasteur. The theory of spontaneous generation hypothesised that life could emerge solely from inanimate matter and suggested a mysterious, independent process by which life could originate, without the involvement of living organisms or specific conditions. This theory was later disapproved by scientific experiments done by Pasteur.

2. (*c*) Both A and R are true, but R is not the correct explanation of A. Early earth was formed by the leftover dust of sun and had no atmosphere or gaseous envelope. It was in the form of solidified red hot cloud containing free atoms. The surface of earth was in molten state.

3. (*d*) Statements I, II, III and V are correct. Statement IV is incorrect. This can be corrected as
Fossils of all organisms, whether modern or extinct, are not found in every geological layer. Certain life forms are confined to specific geological time spans.

4. (*c*) Theory of chemical evolution was proposed by Oparin and Haldane and stated that the first form of life could have come from pre-existing non-living organic molecules, such as RNA, protein, etc. SL Miller in 1953, performed an experiment by creating a simulated condition of primitive earth in laboratory and provided a limited evidence in favour of chemical evolution.

5. (*a*) Miller's experiment simulated early Earth's conditions, which were believed to be hot, stormy, and had a reducing atmosphere rich in methane (CH_4), ammonia (NH_3), and other similar gases. This environment was conducive for the formation of complex organic molecules, leading to the origin of life.

6. (*d*) The earliest life forms originated in aquatic environments, specifically oceans. Over time, some species adapted to live in terrestrial environments, a transition marked by significant evolutionary developments, for example, the development of lungs and legs in amphibians, and development of vascular tissue in pteridophyte. This trend is evident in the fossil record.

7. (*d*) Darwin's evidence for evolution included fossils, geographical distribution and species diversity on oceanic islands. However, anthropogenic selection, which refers to human-induced changes in species (such as those seen in domesticated plants and animals), was not a primary evidence. Darwin used to support natural evolution. Darwin focused on natural selection - the process by which species adapt to their environment and evolve over time without human intervention.

8. (*d*) The atmosphere of early earth probably had no O_2 until the emergence of organisms that used water as an electron source for photosynthesis. These organisms are known as cyanobacteria, which evolved from earlier phototrophic prokaryotes.
It led to the gradual increase of atmospheric oxygen and the transformation of earth's anaerobic environment into one that could support aerobic life.

9. (*c*) Both statement I and statement II are incorrect. They can be corrected as:
Darwin's theory of evolution was based on his observations during the voyage of the HMS Beagle and was influenced by contemporary works. Wallace independently formulated the theory of natural selection after extensive studies in the Amazon and Malay Archipelago and observed that the geological history of earth closely correlates with the biological history of earth.

10. (*d*) The correct matches are A-3, B-2, C-4, D-1.
In a reducing atmosphere, a lesser amount of energy is required to form carbon rich molecules and therefore, it helped in the origin of life.
The surface of earth was in molten state and received UV rays.
Hydrogen, being lighter, escaped, while oxygen combined with ammonia and methane to form water, CO_2 and others.

11. (*a*) The given figure shows homologous organs, thorn of *Bougainvillea* and tendrils of *Cucurbita*, respectively. Organs having similar embryonic origin and basic structure, but which may or may not perform the similar function, are known as homologous organs. Relationship between the structure of different groups of organism is called homology or divergent evolution.

12. (*b*) In whales, bats, cheetahs and humans, the same structure is developed along different directions due to adaptations to different needs. This is divergent evolution and these structures are homologous.

13. (*d*) The incorrect statement about theories of origin of life can be corrected as
Theory of biogenesis states that life has originated slowly and automatically through evolutionary forces from the living materials.

14. (*d*) Ernst Haeckel proposed the biogenetic law or recapitulation theory. Embryological support for evolution given by Ernst Haeckel includes the presence of gill slits in the embryos of all vertebrates, including humans. These gill slits develop into different structures in different animals, their presence in the embryonic stage suggests a shared evolutionary history.

15. (*a*) Paleontological evidence, which includes fossils, provides direct evidence of evolution as it shows the physical remains of organisms from the past. These fossils demonstrate the progression of evolution over millions of years, showing changes in structure and the emergence of new species over time. Other options like embryological evidence, comparative anatomy, and adaptive radiation provide indirect evidence, as they infer evolutionary relationships, but do not show the actual process of evolution over time.

Test 2

1. (*d*) Weismann's experiment directly challenged Lamarck's theory, which proposed that acquired traits could be passed onto offspring. Since the mice continued to be born with tails despite generations of tail removal, it disproved the idea of inheritance of acquired characteristics.

2. (*c*) Antibiotic-resistant bacteria arise due to pre-existing genetic variations within bacterial populations. When exposed to antibiotics, bacteria with resistance traits survive and reproduce, leading to an increase in resistant strains. This process illustrates natural selection acting on existing genetic diversity, rather than the emergence of entirely new traits through other mechanisms like adaptive radiation or transduction.

3. (*a*) Lamarck's theory proposed that acquired characteristic could be inherited by its offspring. Statement (a) directly aligns with this concept by suggesting that environmental influences can lead to genetic changes that are passed on.

4. (*a*) Due to continental drift, Australia became isolated, resulting in unique ecosystems. Pouched mammals, like kangaroos and koalas, evolved in isolation without competition from other mammals.

5. (*a*) Statements I, II, III and IV are key concepts of Darwin's theory of evolution, which include overproduction, variation, survival of the fittest, and inheritance. Statement V, i.e. "New traits arise spontaneously in each generation," is incorrect and not a part of Darwin's theory, as it suggests random, inheritable changes.

6. (*c*) The two key concepts of Darwinian theory of evolution are natural selection and branching descent. Natural selection is a mechanism of evolution which states that the organisms that are more likely to survive and pass on the genes to their offsprings are reproductively fit. Branching descent refers to the process of evolving a new species from a single common ancestor.

7. (*d*) In reality, natural selection, mutation, gene flow, genetic drift, and non-random mating can all cause changes in allelic frequencies, which is contrary to the conditions required for Hardy-Weinberg equilibrium.

8. (*b*) According to Hugo de Vries, evolution occurs due to mutations, which are random and directionless changes in genes. This is different from option (a) and (d), which are more aligned with Darwin's theory of natural selection, option (c) is generally not a driving force of evolution, as undesired characters would not typically be preserved and passed onto future generations.

9. (*d*) Directional selection typically involves environmental pressures that consistently favor individuals with specific traits, causing the frequency of those traits to increase over time. Covid-19 is caused by a virus and does not involve the evolutionary process of directional selection. Instead, it is related to mutation.

10. (*b*) Hardy-Weinberg principle does not operate in a population, if frequent mutations occur in the population. Mutation is one of the factors that can affect Hardy-Weinberg principle.

11. (*d*) A is true, but R is false. R can be corrected as

Speciation occurs due to preservation and accumulation of beneficial adaptations.

12. (*c*) The incorrect match is (c) Frequency of heterozygous genotype (Aa) - pq.

According to the Hardy-Weinberg principle, the frequency of the heterozygous genotype (Aa) is represented by $2pq$, not pq. The frequencies of the recessive allele (a) and dominant allele (A) are represented by q and p respectively, and the frequency of the homozygous dominant (AA) and homozygous recessive genotype (aa) are represented by p^2 and q^2, respectively.

13. (*b*) The frequency of the recessive allele (q) is given as 0.3.

The frequency of the dominant allele (p) is : $p = 1 - q = 0.7$.

Carriers are heterozygous individuals (Aa), and their frequency is represented by 2pq in the Hardy-Weinberg equation.

So, the frequency of carriers, $2pq = 2 \times 0.7 \times 0.3 = 0.42$.

In a population of 1000 individuals, the number of carriers would be $0.42 \times 1000 = 420$.

14. (*d*) Statement I is correct, but statement II is incorrect. It can be corrected as follows

Changes or disturbances in Hardy-Weinberg equilibrium can be considered as an indicator of evolution.

15. (*b*) The correct matches are A-2, B-1, C-4 and D-3

- Genetic drift is a random change in allele frequencies in a population, significantly in small populations, reducing genetic variation.
- Gene flow is the transfer of alleles or genes from one population to another.
- Sometimes, the change in allele frequency is so different in the new sample of population that they become a different species. The original drifted population becomes founders and the effect is called founder effect.
- Hugo de Vries believed mutation caused speciation and hence called it saltation (single step large mutation).

Test 3

1. (*c*) Sphenopsids (horsetails) and *Ginkgos* evolved during Cretaceous period of Mesozoic era.
2. (*b*) Devonian epoch, part of Paleozoic era is also known by name the 'age of fishes'.
3. (*a*) Scientists studying mitochondrial DNA from living human all over the world have argued that their research shows that all human races originated from one *Homo sapiens* ancestor in Africa. The divergence of mitochondrial DNA of Africans from common source began just some years back which was late for *Homo erectus* to split in Asia.
   Thus, there is greater DNA variation in Asia than in Africa.
4. (*b*) Both statements I and statement II are correct.
   Australopithecus is the connecting link between ape and human. They appeared around 5 million years ago. They had erect posture and showed bipedal movement.
5. (*a*) Lobe-finned fishes are believed to be the ancestors of amphibians because they exhibit structural adaptations, such as fleshy, lobed fins, that are similar to amphibian limbs. These adaptations likely facilitated the transition from aquatic to terrestrial environments, allowing them to live both in water and on land, as amphibians.
6. (*d*) Continental drift did not cause mammals to thrive due to a lack of competition from marsupials.
   Instead, the diversification of mammals occurred after the decline of dinosaurs, allowing them to occupy various ecological niches. It was marsupials that continued to exist and thrive in regions like Australia due to same continental drift and lack of competition from any other mammals.
7. (*b*) Both statement I and statement II are correct.
   Both statements accurately reflect the timeline of evolutionary events.
   Invertebrates were active by 500 mya, and jawless fish evolved around 350 mya.
8. (*a*) Statement (a) is correct. Rest all statements are incorrect. Incorrect statements can be corrected as
   Tyrannosaurus rex was about 20 feet in height and had huge fearsome dagger-like teeth.
   About 65 mya, in Cretaceous period, the dinosaurs suddenly disappeared from the earth.
   When reptiles came down, mammals took over this earth.
9. (*b*) The most accepted sequence of human evolution is *Ramapithecus* → *Homo habilis* → *Homo erectus* → *Homo sapiens*.
   Ramapithecus, one of the earliest hominids, marks the beginning of this lineage. *Homo habilis*, known for tool usage, follows. *Homo erectus*, with a larger brain and more sophisticated tools, comes next. Finally, *Homo sapiens*, modern humans, represent the peak of this evolutionary path. This sequence reflects significant developments in brain size, tool-making abilities, and overall adaptability.
10. (*a*) *Ramapithecus* is known for exhibiting more human-like features compared to its predecessors, having jaws and teeth similar to humans. Their diet was likely more plant-based. They existed about 15 mya. They were hairy and walked like chimpanzee and gorillas.
11. (*c*) Bipedal locomotion was not a characteristic feature of *Dryopithecus*. They were more ape like.
12. (*b*) Statements I, II, III and V are correct, whereas statement IV is incorrect. It can be corrected as
    Jawless fish probably evolved around 350 mya.
13. (*d*) A is true, but R is false. R can be corrected as
    Homo habilis hunted with stone weapons, but essentially ate fruit. They probably did not eat meat.
14. (*d*) Statements I and III are correct regarding *Homo erectus*. Statements II and IV are incorrect regarding *Homo erectus* and can be corrected as
    - *Homo erectus* survived about 1.7 million years ago in the Pleistocene.
    - *Homo erectus* resembled modern man, not monkey.
15. (*d*) The Neanderthal man with a brain size of 1400 cc lived in near east and central asia between 1,00,000-40,000 years back. They used hides to protect their body and buried their dead.

Chapter Break Thru

1. (*b*) According to the chemical theory of the origin of life, the synthesis of organic monomers is believed to have occurred first. This process involves simple molecules combining to form more complex ones, such as amino acids and nucleotides.
   These monomers are the building blocks for the subsequent formation of polymers, protobionts, and eventually DNA-based genetic systems.
2. (*b*) Miller's experiment involved a reducing atmosphere containing CH_4, NH_3, etc., under high temperature and volcanic storm conditions.
   This environment was believed to be conducive for the formation of complex organic molecules from simpler ones, providing a possible pathway for the origin of life.
3. (*c*) Evolution encompasses not just physical changes and adaptations, but also genetic variations and biodiversity over generations. It is a broad and comprehensive process that explains the diversity of life on earth.
4. (*b*) Statements I, II, IV and V are correct. Statement III is incorrect and can be corrected as
   The earth was formed in the solar system of the Milky Way Galaxy, not the Andromeda Galaxy.

5. (*b*) The correct order of geological period from older to recent time is Triassic → Jurassic → Cretaceous → Tertiary.

6. (*c*) The theory of organic evolution, primarily associated with Charles Darwin, is based on the concept that species change over generations through descent with modification. This involves the gradual accumulation of genetic changes that enhance survival and reproduction.

7. (*c*) Statements I and IV are incorrect. These can be corrected as

The skull of baby chimpanzee is more like adult human than adult chimpanzee skull.

Dryopithecus was more ape-like.

8. (*b*) Both A and R are true and R is the correct explanation of A.

Convergent evolution occurs when different species independently evolve similar traits to adapt to similar environments, despite having different evolutionary origins. This process creates analogous organs—structures with similar functions, but different anatomical origins.

9. (*a*) The correct matches are A-4, B-1, C-2 and D-3.

- Darwin is associated with evolution by natural selection.
- Oparin is known for the abiogenesis theory, explaining the origin of life from non-living matter.
- Lamarck proposed the theory of use and disuse of organs.
- Due to continental theory Australian marsupials survived as a result of no competition from other mammals.

10. (*c*) The type of natural selection observed in moth *Biston betularia* is directional.

This is because the diagram illustrates how a change in the environment (industrial pollution darkening the bark of trees) led to an increase in the frequency of a particular trait (dark coloration) that provided a survival advantage.

11. (*c*) According to Hugo de Vries, the mutation is large and causes speciation, named saltation (Single step large mutation). He introduced the term mutation. He conducted his study on the evening primrose plant and stated that mutation is a large change arising suddenly in the population.

12. (*b*) The correct matches are A-3, B-1, C-4 and D-2.

- Homologous organs are those that have a similar embryonic origin, but may perform different functions in different species.
- Analogous organs are those that perform similar functions in different species but may have different embryonic origins.
- Divergent evolution refers to the process where species with a common ancestry evolve and diversify differently based on different environmental factors.
- Convergent evolution refers to the process where different species independently evolve similar traits as a result of having to adapt to similar environments or ecological niches.

13. (*d*) The incorrect match pair can be corrected as

Synapsids evolved in Carboniferous period (before permian period). Permian period showed presence of thecodont.

14. (*a*) Eon, Era, Period, Epoch is the correct order of geological time period.

15. (*b*) Criteria III and IV are correct w.r.t. Darwinian fitness.

The ability to survive and reproduce and successful passing of genes to the next generation are aligned with Darwin's concept of fitness, while other criteria are potentially beneficial, but not the primary criteria of Darwinian fitness.

16. (*b*) The similarities between placental mammals and Australian marsupials arise because they evolved independently under similar environmental conditions, leading to analogous structures despite not being closely related. This is a classic example of convergent evolution.

17. (*b*) *Tyrannosaurus rex*, represented by 'B' was a large, bipedal carnivorous dinosaur that lived during the Late Cretaceous period. It is known for its immense size, powerful jaws with huge fearsome dagger-like teeth, and status as one of the most formidable predators of Late Cretaceous period.

18. (*d*) All depicted limbs are examples of homologous structures with common ancestory that have developed along different directions due to adaptations to different needs. They show divergent evolution.

19. (*d*) Statement I is correct, but statement II is incorrect. Incorrect statement can be corrected as

Hardy-Weinberg principle actually states that allele frequencies in a population remain constant from generation to generation in the absence of disturbing factors. It is the deviation from Hardy-Weinberg equilibrium that indicates evolution.

20. (*c*) Viviparity is considered as more evolved reproduction strategy because it ensures that the young ones are protected within the mother's body during development, and often receive parental care after birth. Thus they remain protected from predator. This increases their chances of survival compared to those in external environment or with less parental care.

21. (*d*) A is true, but R is false. R can be corrected as

Not all the angiosperms developed in the Cretacious period. Dicotyledons evolved in Cretaceous period, while monocotyledons, being more advanced evolved in tertiary period.

22. (*d*) Neanderthals had a cranial capacity that often reached 1400 cc, which is larger than the average modern human. In contrast, *Australopithecus, Dryopithecus,* and *Ramapithecus* are earlier hominids with significantly smaller cranial capacities. These species represent earlier stages in human evolution, with brain sizes more comparable to those of modern non-human primates.

23. (*b*) According to Hardy-Weinberg equilibrium, the original population is said to be in genetic equilibrium when population size is very large, random mating is occurring, no natural selection occurs and no immigration takes place.

24. (*a*) Coelacanth are considered as the ancestors of modem day frogs and salmanders. They evolved into the primary amphibians that in particular lived on land and water, clearly contrary to popular notion.

25. (*d*) Darwin observed and proposed the concepts of variation within species, over production of offspring, and survival of the fittest. However, he did not understand the mechanism of inheritance. The understanding of genes and inheritance came later with the work of Gregor Mendel and the development of genetics.

26. (*c*) The primary driving force behind adaptive radiation is natural selection. Adaptive radiation occurs when a single species diversifies into multiple distinct species, each adapted to different ecological niches. Natural selection drives this process by favoring traits that enhance survival and reproduction in various environments.

27. (*b*) The incorrect statement can be corrected as
Homo sapiens sapiens, the modern man appeared during ice age between 75,000 – 10000 years ago.

28. (*d*) The incorrect statement can be corrected as
After a single huge explosion, the universe expanded in volume and the temperature of space came down.

29. (*a*) The correct matches are A-3, B-4, C-2, D-1.
- Mutation is a sudden inheritable change in DNA.
- Genetic drift takes place when the occurrence of variant forms of a gene, called alleles, increases and decreases by chance over time.
- Gene flow is any movement of individual, and/or the genetic material they carry, from one population to another.
- Genetic drift describes random fluctuations in the number of gene variants in a population. It can be magnified by natural calamities such as natural disaster leading to drastic reduction in the population.

30. (*d*) Hardy-Weinberg equation, i.e. $(p+q)^2 = p^2 + 2pq + q^2 = 1$ is used in population genetics, specifically to describe the genetic variation in a population under ideal conditions where allele and genotype frequencies remain constant from generation to generation.

Ch-7 Human Health and Diseases

Topical Follow Thru

Test 1

1. (*a*) Presence of gray to bluish coloured lips and nails are characteristic of severe pneumonia in humans.

2. (*d*) *Streptococcus pneumoniae* is pathogen for pneumonia. It affects the alveoli of lungs which eventually causes several breathing problems.

3. (*d*) The incorrect statement can be corrected as
Many pathogens highly affect internal vital organs, causing various diseases and health complications. Pathogens can infect and damage organs such as the heart, liver, lungs and kidneys, leading to serious health issues.

4. (*a*) The correct set of diseases spread by bacterial agents is : Tetanus, diphtheria, cholera.
Smallpox, AIDS and dengue are viral diseases, while ascariasis and malaria are caused by protozoan.

5. (*a*) A is false, but R is true. A can be corrected as
Filarial worms (such as *Wuchereria bancrofti* and *W. malayi*) transmitted by mosquito bites do not reach the spine or block nerves. Instead, they typically reside in the lymphatic system, where they cause blockages.

6. (*b*) A-4, B-1, C-2, D-3
- Ascariasis is caused due to filarial worm (*Wuchereria*) and common roundworms, that are pathogenic helminths.
- Malaria is caused due to different species of protozoan called *Plasmodium* (*P. vivax*, *P. malaria* and *P. falciparum*).
- Ringworm is caused due to many fungi belonging to the genera–*Microsporum*, *Trichophyton* and *Epidermophyton*.
- Polio is caused due to virus called Poliovirus.

7. (*d*) Statement I is correct, but statement II is incorrect. Statement II can be corrected as
The absence of symptoms alone does not guarantee complete well-being. Mental and social factors also play a role in complete well-being of a person.

8. (*d*) Common cold is not characterised by consistent fever and chills. Common cold infects the nose and the respiratory passage, but not the lungs.

The common cold is characterised by nasal congestion and discharge, sore throat, hoarseness, cough, headache, tiredness, etc. which usually lasts for 3-7 days. It may also include fever and chills but their consistent occurrence signify a bigger problem.

9. (*c*) Haemozoin is a byproduct of haemoglobin breakdown by the *Plasmodium* parasite within infected red blood cells. This breakdown triggers the chills and fever associated with malaria.

10. (*c*) The presence of constipation and stools with mucus and blood clots is observed in a person suffering from amoebiasis (amoebic dysentery) caused by protozoan parasite, *Entamoeba histolytica*. It is transmitted by drinking water and food contaminated by the faecal matter of the patient.

11. (*a*) The incorrect statement can be corrected as

Gametocytes develop from sporozoites, but are formed in the human host's blood (RBCs), not in the mosquito's salivary gland. Sporozoites are the form of the parasite that is injected by the mosquito and initially infect the liver cells in humans.

12. (*b*) Ringworm is a fungal infection caused by dermatophytes, commonly from the genera *Trichophyton*, *Microsporum* and *Epidermophyton*.

13. (*d*) Houseflies do not harbor the parasite within them (reservoir or definitive). They pick up cysts on their legs from contaminated areas and then deposit them on food, acting as mechanical vectors for transmission.

14. (*d*) Educational workshops on proper cough etiquette and respiratory hygiene would be least effective in case of reduction of incidence of typhoid in a community because it is spread by a bacteria, not a virus.

It is not spread by inhaling the droplets/aerosols released by infected person. Instead, it is caused due to contaminanted food and water.

15. (*d*) Typhoid fever is caused by bacteria *Salmonella typhi* and the widal test is used as a confirmatory test for typhoid.

16. (*b*) The discovery of blood circulation by William Harvey using experimental method and the demonstration of normal body temperature in persons with blackbile using thermometer disproved the good humor hypothesis of health.

17. (*b*) Modern biology recognizes that the mind and mental state can have significant impact on physical health. The mind and mental state affect the neural and endocrine systems, which in turn influence the immune system.

18. (*b*) The option that shows the correct sequence of life cycle of malaria is II $\rightarrow$ VI $\rightarrow$ V $\rightarrow$ III $\rightarrow$ I $\rightarrow$ IV.

- The female *Anopheles* mosquito (through its saliva) transmits the malarial sporozoites into the hosts.
- The sporozoites enter liver and multiply asexually.
- Liver cells get damaged and parasite gets released (merozoites) into blood.
- Parasites reproduce asexually in RBCs, bursting them and causing cycles of fever and other symptoms. Released parasites infect new RBCs (intraerythrocytic cycle).
- Sexual stage (gametocytes) develop in RBCs.
- Female mosquito takes up gametocytes with boood meal.

19. (*d*) Statement I is correct, but statement II is incorrect. Statement II can be corrected as

There is currently no vaccine for the common cold. The common cold is caused by many different viruses, and the large variety of these viruses makes it challenging to develop a single effective vaccine.

20. (*d*) The most effective public health strategy to prevent the spread of chikungunya is mosquito control and reduction of breeding sites. The chikungunya virus is transmitted by mosquitoes. Thus, controlling their population can significantly reduce the risk of transmission.

21. (*c*) Statements I, II, III and V are correct, while statement IV is incorrect and it can be corrected as

Controlling insect vectors is not a preventive measure for diseases transmitted through food and water. Diseases like typhoid and amoebiasis are primarily transmitted through contaminated food and water. The effective preventive measures for these diseases focus on maintaining good personal and public hygiene.

22. (*a*) Mosquito control measures would reduce the incidence of filariasis as well as ascariasis. The worms of filariasis are transmitted to a healthy person through the bite by the female mosquito vectors. Sanitation improvements would help control ascariasis. The eggs of the *Ascaris* are excreted along with the faeces of infected persons which contaminate soil, water, plants, etc.

23. (*c*) Mechanical carriers, or mechanical vectors, are organisms that carry pathogens on their bodies without being infected themselves. Houseflies pick up the cysts of *Entamoeba histolytica* from faeces or other contaminated materials and physically transfer them to food or water.

24. (*b*) Both A and R are true and R is the correct explanation of A.

Pathogens have to adopt life within the environment of the host. For example, the pathogens that enter the gut must know a way of surviving in the stomach at low pH and resisting the various digestive enzymes.

25. (*a*) A–2, B–1, C–3, D–4.

Malaria-*Plasmodium*

Typhoid-*Salmonella typhi*

Pneumonia - *Haemophilus influenzae*

Amoebiasis - *Entamoeba histolytica*

Test 2

1. (*c*) Acquired immunity is pathogen specific and involves the adaptive immune system, which can specifically recognise and remember pathogens, leading to a targeted and efficient response upon subsequent exposures. The production of specific antibodies is a hallmark of this process.

2. (*d*) A-1, B-3, C-4, D-2.

- PMNL-neutrophils (polymorpho-nuclear leukocytes) along with monocytes, natural killer cells and macrophages are cellular barriers of immunity.
- Mucus coating of epithelium lining the respiratory, gastrointestinal and urogenital tracts along with skin on our body constitute the physical barrier of immunity.
- Interferons (proteins secreted by viral-infected cells) protect non-infected cells from infection and constitute the cytokine barriers of immunity.
- Acid in the stomach, saliva in the mouth, tears from eyes are examples of physiological barriers of immunity.

3. (*d*) Statement I is correct, but statement II is incorrect. Statement II can be corrected as
The cell-mediated immunity is mediated by T-lymphocytes, not B-lymphocytes. B-lymphocytes mediate humoral immune response.

4. (*b*) Statements I, III and IV are correct, while statement II is incorrect. Incorrect statement can be corrected as
Spleen is a secondary lymphoid organ. It possesses large reservoir of erythrocytes and is called as 'graveyard of RBCs'.

5. (*a*) The exaggerated response of immune system to certain antigens present in the environment is called allergy. It mainly involves IgE antibodies and chemicals like histamine and serotonin released from mast cells.

6. (*d*) A is true, but R is false. R can be corrected as
Colostrum, rich in abundant antibodies (IgA), provides passive immunity to the newborn, to protect the infant from various infections.

7. (*a*) Statements I, III and V are correct. Statements II and IV are incorrect and can be corrected as
Vaccines generate both memory B-cells and memory T-cells.
Passive immunisation provides immediate, but short-term protection. Long-term protection is provided by active immunisation.

8. (*d*) The thymus (*C*) is the primary lymphoid organ where immature lymphocytes differentiate into antigen-sensitive lymphocytes.
The lymph nodes (*B*) are specialised sites where lymphocytes encounter antigens and mature into immune cells.

9. (*d*) A-1, B-3, C-4, D-2.

- The antibodies produced against allergens are IgE type.
- Spleen has a large reservoir of erythrocytes.
- The bone marrow is the primary lymphoid organ where all blood cells including lymphocytes are produced.
- Lymph nodes serve to trap the microorganisms or other antigens, which happen to get into the lymph and tissue fluid.

10. (*c*) Antihistamines work by blocking histamine receptors, which helps reduce the allergic symptoms such as sneezing, watery eyes and a runny nose.

11. (*d*) Interferons are proteins released by host cells in response to the presence of viruses.
They help to inhibit viral replication within host cells by activating enzymes that degrade viral RNA and inhibit protein synthesis.

12. (*b*) Transplantation of tissues/organs often fails due to Cell-Mediated Immunity (CMI). It may result in the rejection of transplanted organs. The immune system recognises the protein in the transplanted tissues or organs as foreign and initiates cellular immunity. To suppress the immune response during transplantation, immunosuppressant drugs are given.

13. (*c*) Rheumatoid arthritis is an autoimmune disease where the immune system attacks the body's own tissues, particularly the joints.

14. (*d*) The production of antibodies involves the immune system recognising specific antigens (non-self molecules) and generating a targeted response against them, highlighting its ability to differentiate between the body's own cells and foreign invaders.

15. (*c*) The MALT (Mucosa-Associated Lymphoid Tissue) constitutes about 50% of the lymphoid tissue in the human body.

16. (*b*) Immunity refers to the body's overall ability to protect itself from infections and disease causing organisms such as bacteria, viruses, fungi and parasites. This defense system involves a complex network of cells, tissues and organs that work together to identify and neutralise harmful pathogens.

17. (*b*) Innate Immunity is the body's first line of defense against infections. These responses are non-specific. Virus-infected cells secrete proteins called interferons which protect non-infected cells from further viral infection. These are the type of innate immunity.

18. (*c*) Innate immunity is non-specific type of defence. It is present at the time of birth. Innate immunity is accomplished by providing different types of barriers to the entry of the foreign agents into our body. These consist of skin and mucous membranes, saliva and leukocytes.

19. (*c*) Statements I, III, IV and V are correct, while statement II is incorrect and it can be corrected as
The hepatitis B vaccine is not an example of passive immunisation. It is an example of active immunisation produced using RDT.

20. (*a*) Antigen binding site is present on the N-terminal of peptide chain in antibodies. These antigen binding sites are unique in each antibody that is compatible with specific antigens and forms an antigen antibody complex upon binding.

21. (*b*) Both statement I and statement II are correct. Higher vertebrates have developed a complex immune system capable of distinguishing self from non-self. However, due to genetic and other factors, this system sometimes, malfunctions, leading to auto-immune diseases.

22. (*b*) Epitope refers to the specific sites or regions of an allergen molecule that interact with immune cells such as T-cells and B-cells. These sites are recognised by the antibody molecule on B-cells or presented to T-cell by Antigen Presenting Cells (APCs).

23. (*b*) Modern urban life styles involve increased cleanliness and reduced exposure to natural environmental factors, such as diverse microbes and allergens. As a result, the immune system may become more reactive to common allergens.

24. (*c*) The spleen is a large bean-shaped organ. It mainly contains lymphocytes and phagocytes. It acts as a filter of the blood by trapping blood-borne micro-organisms.

25. (*a*) The thymus is largest and most active during childhood and pre-adolescence, but begins to decrease in size and activity in early teens. By adulthood, the thymus is gradually replaced by fatty tissue, though some T-cell development continues.

Test 3

1. (*d*) The transmission of HIV from infected mother to her child occurs through placenta.

2. (*d*) Individuals with HIV infection are more susceptible to opportunistic infections due to a weakened immune system. Thus, they can co-exist with other infections.

3. (*c*) HIV or Human Immunodeficiency Virus, is a group of retrovirus which has an envelope enclosing a *ss*RNA genome.

4. (*a*) Statements II, III and IV are correct. Statements I and V are incorrect and can be corrected as

Metastasis is the most feared property of malignant tumours, not benign tumours.

Analgesics are used to manage pain. They are ineffective on cancer.

5. (*c*) Normal cells show the property of contact inhibition. Contact inhibition is a regulatory mechanism that enables non-cancerous cells to cease proliferation and growth when they contact each other. This characteristic is lost in cancerous cells.

6. (*c*) Flower tops and leaves of *Cannabis sativa* are known to be used in combination for psychoactive substances.

7. (*b*) The illegal drug that most likely disrupts the movement of a feel-good brain chemical (neurotransmitter) is cocaine. Cocaine or coca alkaloid blocks the reuptake of dopamine, a neurotransmitter associated with pleasure and reward, leading to an accumulation of dopamine in the synaptic cleft and prolonged stimulation of the post-synaptic neuron.

8. (*b*) The incorrect statement can be corrected as

Opioid receptors are primarily located in the Central Nervous System (CNS), not in the Peripheral Nervous System (PNS).

9. (*a*) A-4, B-1, C-2, D-3.

- Heroin, commonly called smack, is chemically diacetylmorphine.
- *Datura* possesses hallucinogenic properties.
- *Erythroxylum coca* plant is used to obtaine cocaine commonly called as coke or crack.
- Morphine is a very effective sedative and painkiller and is very useful in surgery.

10. (*b*) Nicotine stimulates adrenal (I) gland to release adrenaline and nor-adrenaline (II) into blood circulation, both of which raise blood pressure and increase (III) heart rate.

11. (*c*) Amphetamines are normally used as medicines to help patients cope with mental illnesses like depression and insomnia. Other drugs performing same function are barbiturate and benzodiazepines.

12. (*a*) Statement I is incorrect, but statement II is correct. Incorrect statement can be corrected as

Cancerous cells spread to distant site by a property called metastasis. Contact inhibition is a property shown by non-cancerous cells.

13. (*d*) The structure of morphine is shown in the given diagram. It is an opioid and is used as a depressant that slows down body functions.

14. (*c*) The side-effects of the use of anabolic steroids in females include masculinisation, increased aggressiveness, mood swings, depression, abnormal menstrual cycles, excessive hair growth on the face and body, enlargement of clitoris and deepening of voice.

15. (*d*) Heroin, commonly called as smack, is chemically diacetylmorphine and is obtained by acetylation of morphine. Other drugs are directly obtained from flowering plants, e.g. cocaine from *Erythroxylum coca*, Atropine from *Atropa belladona* and morphine from *Papaver somniferum* (poppy).

Chapter Break Thru

1. (*a*) Smallpox, ringworm and common flu are the contagious diseases.

2. (b) Congenital diseases are present in infants since birth, while acquired diseases develop after birth. Congenital diseases are either passed on by the parents or develop during gestation period.

3. (*d*) Statements I, II and IV qualify the attributes of non-communicable diseases.

Statement III is incorrect and it can be corrected as

Neither AIDS is a curable disease, Nor some of the other non-communicable diseases are curable, such as dwarfism.

4. (*c*) The incorrect statement can be corrected as

Pneumonia spreads by coming in direct contact with aerosols or droplets liberated by the infected person. Reusing the utensils or glasses used by the infected person can transmit pathogens of pneumonia.

5. (*a*) Vaccine of hepatitis-B is produced from yeast, *Saccharomyces cerevisiae*.

6. (*b*) A-2, B-4, C-1, D-3.

• Dengue is a viral disease caused due to *Flavivirus* and is transmitted by the female *Aedes* mosquito.

• Plague, also called black death, is caused by *Yersinia pestis*.

• Tuberculosis is caused by *Mycobacterium tuberculosis*.

• Cholera is an acute infectious disease caused by *Vibrio cholerae*.

7. (*d*) Statement I is correct, but statement II is incorrect. Statement II can be corrected as

Antibiotics are ineffective against viruses and taking them for a cold would not help and might contribute to resistance, which will be harmful for humans.

8. (*d*) A is true, but R is false. R can be corrected as

Contaminated water is a primary source of transmission of Ascariasis, but it is not the only one. *Ascaris* eggs can also contaminate soil, which can then come into contact with unwashed vegetables or hands, leading to accidental ingestion.

9. (*d*) The incorrect statement can be corrected as

Antifungal medications (topical or oral) are the standard treatment for ringworm.

10. (*b*) Features I, III, IV and V are correct w.r.t. amoebiasis. The incorrect feature can be corrected as

Houseflies can play a role in mechanical transmission by carrying cysts on their surfaces, but they are not a primary vector for amoebiasis. The primary mode of transmission is through ingestion of food or water contaminated with *Entamoeba histolytica* cysts.

11. (*c*) Vaccines for malaria are not yet widely effective or available.

12. (b) Disease like AIDS and hepatitis-B may go asymptomatic for a long time. There is always a time lag between the infection and appearance of symptoms. This period may vary from a few months to few years.

13. (*d*) The antigens are trapped by lymph nodes, not the lymphatic vessels and get into the lymph fluid.

14. (*c*) The standard HIV screening blood test works on the principle of antibody-antigen interaction. So, it detects antibodies formed against the virus antigen in the body.

15. (*b*) A-2, B-3, C-1, D-4.

Amount of immunoglobulins in blood depends upon their requirement in different mechanisms to fight with pathogens.

IgG is able to cross the placenta and is the main blood antibody for secondary response.

IgA is secreted into mucus, saliva, tears, colostrum and tags pathogens for destruction.

IgM is the main antibody of primary response.

IgE binds to mast cells and basophils and is involved in responses due to allergy.

16. (*a*) Skin is the outermost tough layer of the body which forms a lining and restriction for the direct entry of virus and bacteria. Although any cut or minute opening can expose skin to virus and bacteria.

17. (*b*) Cell-mediated immune response is performed by T-cells, where no production of antibodies take place, while humoral response is performed by B-cells by the production of antibodies, specifically immunoglobulins.

18. (*a*) Statements I and II are incorrect and can be corrected as

• Cancer can be induced by ionising radiations like X-rays and non-ionising rays like UV rays.

• Oncogenic viruses have genes called viral oncogenes.

19. (*d*) Red Blood Cells (RBCs) primarily function within the bloodstream for oxygen and carbon dioxide transport. While some RBCs might rupture and release their contents into the lymph fluid, their presence is not expected in significant amounts. The lymphatic system has its own mechanisms for fluid movement and does not rely heavily on RBCs.

20. (*d*) Statement I is correct, but statement II is incorrect. Incorrect statement can be corrected as

Vaccines may provide long-term immunity with a single dose, but many require a series of vaccinations to ensure sufficient and lasting protection. The number of doses and the timing between them depends on the specific vaccine and immune response required.

21. (*b*) Both A and R are true and R is the correct explanation of A.

Antivenom injection provides antibodies to neutralise snake venom, offering immediate passive immunity. The antibodies from the mother provide immediate protection to the newborn. Passive immunity involves acquiring antibodies produced by another organism, offering short-term protection.

22. (*b*) Bone marrow and thymus glands are primary lymphoid organs that are involved in the production and maturation site of B-lymphocytes and T-lymphocytes.

After maturation, the lymphocytes migrate to secondary lymphoid organs like spleen, lymph nodes, tonsils, Peyer's patches of small intestine and appendix.

23. (*c*) Tetrahydrocannabinol is the main constituent of *Cannabis sativa*.

24. (*b*) Both statement I and statement II are correct.

Excessive alcohol consumption can damage the liver and lead to cirrhosis, a serious condition characterised by scarring and impaired function.
Chronic alcohol abuse can harm the nervous system, leading to problems with coordination, memory and cognitive function.

25. (*b*) Malignant tumours exhibit metastasis property, which make them highly spreadable. Slow proliferation and contact inhibition are the properties of normal cells. Tumour cells do not damage surrounding cells, but compete with them for nutrients.

26. (*c*) Statements I, IV and V are related to cocaine. Cocaine is obtained from coca plant, *Erythroxylum coca*. It is usually snorted. It interferes with the transport of neurotransmitter, dopamine. It has potent stimulating action on central nervous system producing sense of euphoria and increases energy. Excessive doses of cocaine causes hallucination.

27. (*c*) The given figure shows replication of retroviruses in the host cell. The correct labelling of *A* and *B* are
A-Viral DNA incorporates into host,
B-New viral RNA produced.

28. (*b*) The given image shows the flower of opium poppy. It is chemically diacetylmorphine, which is taken by snorting and injection. Heroin is a depressant and slows down body functions.

29. (*a*) A is false, but R is true. A can be corrected as
Nicotine is a stimulant, not a calcium channel blocker. It actually increases heart rate and blood pressure.

30. (*c*) Chikungunya is a vector-borne disease that is caused due to CHIKV virus, belonging to genus-*Alphavirus* and is transmitted *via* female *Aedes aegypti* mosquito. Its fever and joint pain is much more severe than in case of dengue. It can even cause disability.

Ch-8 Microbes in Human Welfare

Topical Follow Thru

Test 1

1. (*d*) Lactic Acid Bacteria (LAB) are a group of beneficial bacteria that reside in the gastrointestinal tract and contribute to control harmful microbes. They produce lactic acid and other antimicrobial substances that inhibit the growth of pathogenic bacteria.

2. (*c*) Wine and beer are produced without distillation whereas whisky, brandy and rum are produced with distillation.

3. (*c*) Bottled juices bought from market are clearer as compared to those made at home this is because the bottled juices are clarified by the use of pectinases and proteases.

4. (*a*) LAB converts lactose sugar of milk into lactic acid, which causes coagulation and partial digestion of milk protein, i.e. casein.

5. (*a*) Statement I is incorrect, but statement II is correct. Incorrect statement can be corrected as
Toddy is indeed a traditional drink in some parts of Southern India. However, it is not made by fermenting sap from bamboo shoots instead it is typically made from the sap of palm trees.

6. (*b*) The given diagram is of the fermentation plant. The distillation of the fermented broth occurs in it.

7. (*b*) The starter or inoculum added to fresh milk is a liquid which contain millions of LAB (*Lactobacillus*) bacteria.

8. (*c*) The correct matches are A-4, B-1, C-2 and D-3.
Saccharomyces cerevisiae is used for fermenting malted cereals to produce ethanol.
Swiss cheese has large holes due to production of CO_2 given out by a bacterium known as *Propionibacterium sharmanii*.
Roquefort cheese are ripened by growing a specific fungi on them known as *Penicillium roqueforti*.
Streptokinase produced by bacterium *Streptococcus* and is genetically modified in order to use it as clot buster for removing clots from the blood vessels of patients.

9. (*a*) The discovery of penicillin is famously attributed to Alexander Fleming. He observed that a mold (*Penicillium notatum*) inhibited the growth of *Staphylococcus* bacteria in a petri dish.
This serendipitous observation led to the realisation that the mold was producing a substance capable of killing bacteria, which Fleming named penicillin.

10. (*c*) Both A and R are true, but R is not the correct explanation of A.
During fermentation, microorganisms like yeast break down sugars (primarily glucose) present in the dough. This process releases CO_2 gas, which gets trapped within the dough, causing it to expand and become puffy.

11. (*d*) Lipase are used in detergents formulations and are helpful in removing oily stains from the laundary.

12. (*b*) Statements II, III and IV are correct. Statements I and V are incorrect and can be corrected as
Statins are produced by the yeast *Monascus purpureus*.
Statin is a bioactive molecule.

13. (*c*) Incorrect match pair can be corrected as
The bacterium *Acetobacter aceti* produces acetic acid.

14. (*d*) Statements II and III are incorrect and can be corrected as

• The function of penicillin as an antibiotics was established by Ernest Chain and Howard Florey.

• Bioactive molecules which inhibits cholesterol synthesis in blood is extracted from yeast *Monascus purpureus*.

15. (*b*) Statins is produced by yeast *monascus purpureus*. It inhibits the enzyme responsible for synthesis of chlolesterol. Thus, act as blood cholesterol lowering agent.

16. (*c*) Antibiotics are chemical substances, which are produced by some microbes and can kill or retard the growth of other (disease-causing) microbes.

17. (*a*) Only statement I is incorrect. It can be corrected as

Antibiotics are chemical substances secreted by certain microbes which can kill or inhibit the growth and development of harmful microbes. Most of them produced by Actinomycetes and fungi, e.g., tetracyline, chloramphenicol, streptomycin, etc.

18. (*a*) The correct matches are A-3, B-4, C-1 and D-2.

Saccharomyces cerevisiae also known as Brewer's yeast used for fermenting malted cereals and fruit juices to produce ethanol.

Statins produced by the yeast *Monascus purpureus* have been commercialised as blood-cholesterol lowering agents.

A fungus, *Trichoderma polysporum* used as an immunosuppressive agent in organ-transplant patients.

Ripening in Swiss cheese by a bacterium, *Propionibacterium sharmanii* by production of large amount CO_2.

19. (*b*) Both A and R are true and R is the correct explanation of A.

The dough used for making bread is fermented by *Saccharomyces cerevisiae* or commonly called Baker's yeast. CO_2 released during the process of fermentation gives the puffy appearance to dough. It is used to make foods like idli, dosa, bread, etc.

20. (*b*) Swiss cheese is characterised by large holes and it is ripened by the bacteria, *Propionibacterium sharmanii*. *Penicillium roqueforti* is involved in ripening of roquefort cheese. Camemberti cheese is ripened by *Penicillium camemberti*.

21. (*c*) Statin produced by the yeast *Monascus purpureus*. Cyclosporin-A is produced by the fungus *Trichoderma polysporum*.

Aspergillus niger produces acetic acid is a fungus.

Streptokinase produced by the bacterium *Streptococcus*.

22. (*d*) Fermentation is the process of converting sugars into alcohol through the action of microorganisms, primarily yeast. The primary product of fermentation by brewer's yeast is ethanol, which is commonly referred to as alcohol. This is the basis for alcoholic beverages like beer and wine.

23. (*d*) Distillation is not involved in beer production. Brewing is the process of production of malt beverages, e.g., beer. It is a complex fermentation process. It differ from other industrial fermentation because flavour, aroma, clarity, colour, foam production, foam stability and percentage of alcohol are the factors associated with finished product.

24. (*a*) Statement I is incorrect, but statement II is correct.

Statement I can be corrected as

Pasteurisation is a process whereby fluids such as wine and milk are heated for a predetermined time at a temperature that is below the boiling point of the liquid. The treatment kills any microorganisms that are in the fluid, but does not alter the taste, appearance, or nutritive value of the fluid.

25. (*c*) Statement given in option (*c*) is incorrect and can be corrected as Production on an industrial scale, requires growing microbes in very large vessels called fermentors.

Test 2

1. (*c*) Heterotrophic microbes naturally present in sewage are the primary decomposers that break down organic pollutants. This process is facilitated by creating an environment that promotes their growth and activity.

2. (*c*) If oxygen availability to activated sludge is reduced, the center of flocs will become anoxic, which could cause the death of bacteria and eventually breakage of flocs.

3. (*a*) The formation of biogas involves solubilisation – acidogenesis– methanogenesis.

Solubilisation involves the digestion of organic matter to monomers by enzymes, such as cellulase, amylase, proteases, etc. In acidogenesis, fermentative microbes convert monomers to organic acids, e.g. acetic acid. Methanogenesis is utilisation of hydrogen, carbon dioxide and acetic acid to form methane and carbon dioxide by methanogens.

4. (*d*) Statements II, III, IV and V are correct, while statement I is incorrect and it can be corrected as

Methanogens are found in anaerobic sludge during sewage treatment and not the aerobic sludge.

5. (*d*) Statement I is correct, but statement II is incorrect. The incorrect statement can be corrected as

Activated sludge is taken to anaerobic sludge digesters along with the primary sludge. Here, anaerobic microbes act upon organic matter to first produce monomer and then organic acids.

6. (*d*) The figure represents secondary treatment. Here, the primary effluent is passed through large aeration tank with constant mechanical agitation and air supply. Useful microbes grow and form flocs. The growing microbes use organic matter and thereby reduce the BOD of the effluent.

7. (*a*) The sediment of secondary treatment, i.e. activated sludge is pumped back into aeration tank to serve as inoculum. The inoculum supplies to the medium which degrade the organic substrates.

8. (*a*) The first step in sewage treatment is sedimentation. This process ensures that all solid material in the sewage is removed before further processing is done.

9. (*c*) One of the common methods used as biological control is natural predation, e.g. dragonflies are used in certain areas to get rid of mosquitoes because dragonflies naturally feed on mosquitoes and help to reduce their population.

10. (*a*) A is false, but R is true. A can be corrected as

Mycorrhizae form symbiotic associations with the roots of higher plants.

Plants with such association show resistance to root-borne pathogens, tolerance to salinity and drought and an overall increase in plant growth and development.

11. (*a*) *Azolla pinnata* is used as an excellent fertiliser in rice field and by using this farmers have reported over 50% higher yield of rice.

12. (*d*) *Bacillus thuringiensis*, a microbial biocontrol agent can be introduced to control butterfly, caterpillars, etc. Such plants are resistant to attack by insect pests, e.g. *Bt* cotton.

13. (*d*) *Nucleopolyhedrovirus* is a genus containing most baculoviruses. These are pathogens that attack insects and other pathogen. These viruses are excellent candidates for species-specific, narrow-spectrum insecticidal applications. It is mainly used in integrated pest management programme where beneficial insects are being conserved.

14. (*d*) The correct matches are A-1, B-3, C-4 and D-2.

Trichoderma species are free-living fungi. They are effective biocontrol agents for several plant pathogens.

Bacillus thuringiensis acts as biocontrol agent for lepidopteran and plant pests.

Glomus is a fungus that forms mycorrhiza to absorb phosphorus from soil and add organic matter to it.

Anabaena fixes the atmospheric nitrogen.

15. (*c*) Both A and R are true, but R is not the correct explanation of A.

The energy value of biogas is lower than that of organic matter, but the energy output is roughly equal to the net energy output obtained by during organic matter. This is due to handling process and more over the energy release from biogas depends upon the amount of methane present in it.

16. (*b*) Both statement I and statement II are correct.

Primary treatment basically involve physical removal of particles large and small from the sewage through filtration and sedimentation.

Initially floating debris is removed by sequential filtration. Then the grit are removed by sedimentation.

Methanogenic bacteria are commonly found in anaerobic sludge digesters during sewage treatment, live without oxygen.

17. (*c*) Statement in option (*c*) is correct.

Excess fertiliser in the environment, especially nitrogen and phosphorus can pollute local groundwater as well as lakes and streams resulting in eutrophication. Other statements are incorrect and can be corrected as

• Cyanobacteria such as *Anabaena* and *Nostoc* have heterocyst which help in nitrogen-fixation. Hence, these are important mobilisers of nitrogen.

• Maize can be grown without chemical fertilisers, by using organic farming.

• *Azotobacter* is a free-living bacteria that fix nitrogen but do not occur in root nodules like *Rhizobium*.

18. (*c*) Statement in option (*c*) is incorrect and can be corrected as

Biogas mostly consists of 50-80% methane. It burns with a blue flame and does not produce smoke. Thus, it is not polluting.

Rest statements are correct about biogas.

19. (*c*) The *Rhizobium* bacteria help leguminous plants by converting atmospheric nitrogen to soluble form for the plant to make proteins and in return the plant provides the bacteria with sugars or food. To develop symbiotic relation with legume crop, *Rhizobium* enter into the root hair before the formation of root nodules.

20. (*c*) Statement in option (*c*) is incorrect and can be corrected as

Methane, hydrogen sulphide and CO_2 are main gases produced in the digesters by the anaerobic digestion by heterotrophic bacteria and fungi. Carbon monoxide is not produced during this process.

Rest statements are correct about secondary sewage treatements.

21. (*c*) Both A and R are true, but R is not the correct explanation of A.

Biogas is a mixture of inflammable gases due to which it is used as fuel for cooking, lightening, generating power for irrigation and other purposes, as an alternative of firewood, kerosene, dung cakes or even electricity. It is ecofriendly and pollution free source of energy.

22. (*d*) The correct matches are A-3, B-4, C-1 and D-2.

Biofertiliser are organism that enrich the nutrient quality of the soil. The main sources are bacteria, fungi and cyanobacteria.

Biocontrol agents refer to the use of biological methods for controlling plant diseases and pests.

Methanogenesis is a process by which microbes methanogens, produce methane on component of microbial fermentation.

Primary treatment involve physical removal of particles-large and small through filtration and sedimentation.

23. (*a*) All given statements are correct except statement IV.
Incorrect statement can be corrected as
Rhizobium is a symbiotic bacterium that lives in the root nodules of legumes and fixes atmospheric nitrogen into organic compounds.
Thus, option (a) is correct.

24. (*b*) *Trichoderma* is a free-living saprophytic fungi that most commonly lives on dead organic matter in the soil and rhizosphere. It acts as a biopesticide for biological control of many soil borne plant diseases.

25. (*a*) Primary treatment of sewage is the process of removal of small and large, floating and suspended solid from sewage through filtration and sedimentation.

Chapter Break Thru

1. (*b*) Heterotrophic bacteria are the most abundant prokaryotes. These are helpful to human in making curd from milk, e.g. LAB and in the production of antibiotics, e.g. penicillin.

2. (*d*) The incorrect statement can be corrected as
Large-holed Swiss cheese is ripened with *Propionibacterium sharmanii*.
The rest of the statements are correct.

3. (*b*) The bacteria helps in the fermentation of dough. The puffed up appearance of dough is due to the production of CO_2 gas. The dough, which is used for making foods such as dosa and idli is fermented by bacteria. Some predominant bacterial species include *Leuconostoc mesenteroides* and *Streptococcus faecalis*.

4. (*a*) A is false, but R is true. A can be corrected as
Cyclosporin-A is an immuno-suppressant used to prevent organ rejection in transplant patients.

5. (*c*) Fermentors are specialised bioreactors that provide a controlled environment for large-scale cultivation of microorganisms. They facilitate the efficient production of various products like beverages, antibiotics, enzymes and organic acids through fermentation.

6. (*b*) Primary treatment of wastewater involves physical processes such as screening, sedimentation and flotation to remove large solids and debris from the wastewater. This initial step aims to reduce the load of solids and organic matter before further treatment processes like biological and chemical treatments are applied.
The secondary treatment is also known as biological treatment as it include involvement of microbes.

7. (*a*) Penicillin was extensively used to treat American soldiers wounded in World War II. It was successfully used to treat infections. Without it many injuries would get infected, which would lead to rotting, amputation or even death.

8. (*b*) A group of anaerobic bacteria which produces methane in large amount are called as methanogens. These bacteria are commonly found in the anaerobic sludge during sewage treatment and in the rumen of cattle.

9. (*c*) The incorrect matched pair. It can be corrected as
The yeast *Monascus purpureus* produces statins, which act as blood-cholesterol lowering agents.

10. (*b*) Both statement I and statement II are correct.
BOD is applied to determine the aerobic destructibility of organic substances. It measures the amount of oxygen consumed by microorganisms for the process of decomposition of organic matters in water bodies.

11. (*b*) Gobar gas contains maximum amount of methane. Biogas is an environmental-friendly renewable energy source produced by the breakdown of organic matter. Raw biogas typically consists of methane (50-75%), carbon dioxide 25-50% and smaller amounts of nitrogen.

12. (*b*) The effluent from the secondary treatment plant is generally released into natural waterbodies like river and streams. It uses biological methods to purify water.

13. (*c*) The correct matches are A-4, B-1, C-3 and D-2.
Primary treatment is the physical process which involves removal of large and solid particles from sewage through filtration and sedimentation.
During secondary treatment primary effluent are passed into aeration tanks and constantly agitated which favours the vigrous growth of useful aerobic heterotrophic microbes into flocs. In primary treatment all solid that settle forms primary sludge. Thus, the sediment in primary treatment is called primary sludge. Sediment in secondary treatment is called activated sludge.

14. (*c*) The Ministry of Environment and Forests has initiated Ganga action plan and Yamuna action plan to save these major rivers of our country from pollution. Under these plans, it is proposed to build a large number of sewage treatment plants, so that only treated sewage may be discharged in the rivers.

15. (*b*) The primary organisations responsible for developing biogas production technology in India are the Khadi and Village Industries Commission (KVIC) and the Indian Agricultural Research Institute (IARI). These institutions played significant roles in promoting and refining biogas technology, which is used extensively for energy production in rural areas.

16. (*b*) *Azotobacter* and *Azospirillum* are free-living biofertilisers. These bacteria can fix atmospheric nitrogen, while free-living in the soil. Thus, enriching the nitrogen content of soil.

17. (*b*) *Azotobacter* (bacteria), *Glomus* (fungi) and *Oscillatoria* (blue-green algae) help in improving the fertility of the soil. They are used as biofertilisers as they enrich the nutrient quality of soil. Biofertilisers are used in organic farming.

18. (*c*) Viruses belonging to genus–*Nucleopolyhedrovirus* that attack insects and other arthropods are Baculoviruses. They are known to control pests like potato beetles, aphids and corn borers.

19. (*a*) The correct group of biocontrol agents is *Trichoderma*, Baculovirus and *Bacillus thuringiensis*.

Trichoderma is extensively used against pathogenic fungi which causes soil borne diseases.

Baculovirus are pathogens that attack insects and other arthropods. Most of baculoviruses used as biocontrol agent belong to the genus–*Nucleopolyhedrovirus*.

Bacillus thuringiensis secretes toxin crystals which kill the insect larvae.

20. (*a*) The respiratory infections are caused by adenovirus. It is shown in diagram (A).

21. (*b*) The correct labelling of parts *A*, *B* and *C* in a biogas plant is gas, gas holder and digester, respectively.

22. (*b*) The correct matches are A-3, B-1, C-4 and D-2.

Lactic acid bacteria (*Lactobacillus*) grow in milk and convert it into curd.

Streptokinase produced by the bacterium *Streptococcus* and modified by genetic engineering is used as a clot buster for removing clots from the blood vessels of patients.

Statins produced by the yeast *Monascus purpureus* have been commercialised as blood-cholesterol lowering agents.

Clostridium butylicum (a bacterium) produces butyric acid.

23. (*b*) Both A and R true and R is the correct explanation of A. Whisky, brandy and rum are produced by the process of distillation, so as to increase the alcohol content in these drinks. On the other hand, wine and beer contain less concentration of alcohol as distillation is not carried out for these drinks.

24. (*a*) The correct matches are A-2, B-4, C-1 and D-3.

Flocs is masses of bacteria associated with fungal filaments to form mesh like structure.

In anaerobic sludge digester, bacteria produces a mixture of gases such as CH_4, CO_2 and H_2S. These gases form biogas. Waterbodies with sewage waste discharge has high BOD. It is the measure of the organic matter of the water.

Petroleum is non-biodegradable pollutant. Water body with petroleum does not show any fluctuation in BOD. Hence, the freshwater body have low BOD.

25. (*d*) *A*–Secondary treatment, *B*–Mechanical agitation, *C*–Reduced BOD, *D*–Activated sludge and *E*–Anaerobic sludge digesters

26. (*a*) Statements I, II and V are correct. Other statements are incorrect and can be corrected as

Dragonflies are useful to get rid of mosquitoes.

Cyanobacteria reduce alkalinity of soil.

27. (*a*) Statements I, III and V are correct, but statements II and IV are incorrect. These can be corrected as

The organic farmer create a system where the insects are not eradicated, instead, are kept at manageable levels by a complex system of checks and balances within a living ecosystem.

The conventional farming practices use chemical methods to kill both useful and harmful life forms.

Oscillatoria is a cyanobacterial species that does not form the mycorrhizal association, but fix atmospheric nitrogen. Instead, *Glomus* is a genus of arbuscular mycorrhizal fungi which forms mycorrhizal association with plants.

28. (*a*) Statements III and V are incorrect. These can be corrected as

Yeast is used to manufacture alcoholic beverages like wine and beer. It is also used in production of breads.

The domestic sewage in large cities is processed by aerobic and then anaerobic bacteria is the secondary treatment in STPs.

Rest statements are correct.

29. (*d*) A is true, but R is false. R can be corrected as

Bt cotton plants are resistant to insect pests because they have been genetically engineered to express the *Bacillus thuringiensis* (*Bt*) toxin genes.

The actual mechanism by which *Bacillus thuringiensis* kills caterpillars involves the release of a toxin in the gut of the larvae after ingestion, not by directly infecting their cells and multiplying within them.

30. (*a*) Statement I is incorrect, but statement II is correct. Incorrect statement can be corrected as

The beetles like ladybird and dragonflies are useful to get rid to aphids and mosquitoes. They donot feed on butterfly caterpillars.

Biocontrol measures, such as using *Bt*, indeed help reduce the heavy use of toxic pesticides by providing a natural method of pest control.

Ch-9 Biotechnology : Principles and Processes

Topical Follow Thru

Test 1

1. (*a*) Statement (a) is incorrect and can be corrected as
The EFB's definition of biotechnology encompasses both traditional and modern aspects.
2. (*d*) The vector pBR322 contains a recognition site for *Sal* I within its tetracycline resistance gene.
3. (*c*) Statements I, II and III are correct. Incorrect statements can be corrected as
Deciphering gene sequences and analysing DNA profiles are important in genomics and forensic science, but are not the main goals of genetic engineering.
4. (*d*) Statement I is correct, but statement II is incorrect. Incorrect statement can be corrected as
The construction of first recombinant DNA emerged from the possibility of linking a gene encoding antibiotic resistance with a native plasmid of *Salmonella typhimurium.*
5. (*b*) The first recombinant DNA was formed by linking a gene-encoding antibiotic resistance with native plasmid of *Salmonella typhimurium*.
6. (*c*) Both A and R are true, but R is not the correct explanation of A.
Genetic engineering indeed requires both nucleases and ligases, because the former can cut DNA, into specific fragments, while the latter can join DNA fragments, enabling the assembly of new genetic constructs.
7. (*b*) Restriction enzymes are obtained only from prokaryotes as it is their natural defence mechanism against bacteriophage infection. Later, *Eco*RI became a fundamental tool in recombinant DNA technology and genetic engineering.
8. (*a*) The incorrect match pair given in option (a). It can be corrected as DNA sequence initiating replication is the 'origin of replication' (*ori*) because a primer is a short nucleic acid sequence that provides a starting point for DNA synthesis and not a DNA sequence specifically for initiating replication.
9. (*a*) Origin of replication (*ori*) is a sequence responsible for controlling the copy number of linked DNA.
10. (*a*) Restriction endonucleases recognise and cut specific DNA sequences, creating sticky or blunt ends that facilitate the insertion of DNA fragments into vectors. However, the formation of a phosphodiester bond between two DNA fragments is the role of DNA ligase, not restriction endonucleases.
11. (*a*) Cloning is the process where fragment of DNA from the donor cell is transferred to recipient organism or cell with the help of vector DNA. Dolly sheep was the first cloned animal formed in 1997.
12. (*d*) In genetic engineering, restriction endonucleases are crucial for cutting DNA at specific sites, while DNA ligases are essential for joining DNA fragments together. This combination allows for the precise insertion of genes into vectors, enabling various genetic manipulations and cloning procedures.
13. (*d*) *Salmonella typhimurium* is more pathogenic than *Escherichia coli*, presenting higher biosafety risks when used in laboratory settings. This increased pathogenicity necessitates stricter containment and safety protocols, making *Salmonella typhimurium* less practical and more hazardous for gene cloning purposes compared to the well-established and safer *E. coli*.
14. (*d*) The essential steps typically involve identifying DNA with desirable genes, introducing this DNA into the host organism and ensuring the stable integration and inheritance of the introduced DNA. While sequencing the genome can provide valuable information, it is not necessary in the basic steps of genetic modification.
Genome sequencing may be conducted for further characterisation or to confirm the genetic changes, but it is not a mandatory step in every genetic modification process.
15. (*b*) The correct matches are A-3, B-4, C-2, D-1.
   - Plasmid is an extrachromosomal double-stranded circular DNA.
   - First artificial recombinant molecule was constructed by Stanley Cohen and Herbert Boyer.
   - Restriction enzyme acts on specific palindromic sequences.
   - Staggered end is overhanging stretches at each end of DNA.

Test 2

1. (*c*) Restriction endonucleases are a very important tool used in genetic engineering. These are the enzymes which make cuts at specific positions within the double-stranded DNA molecule.
They recognise the palindromic base sequence in DNA duplex and form nicks in its strands. For example, restriction endonuclease *Eco*RI recognises the base sequence GAATTC in DNA duplex and cuts the strands between G and A.
2. (*c*) Both A and R are true, but R is not the correct explanation of A.
Restriction enzymes produced in a bacterial cell, recognise and cleave foreign DNA introduced (such as bacteriophage) into the cell.
Thus, bacterial cell cannot be infected and lysed by bacteriophage, and hence, bacterial cell lacking restriction enzyme is very susceptible to infection of phages.

3. (*a*) *Hind* III - The first restriction endonuclease is incorrectly matched. It can be corrected as
The first restriction endonuclease is *Hind* II.

4. (*b*) Palindromic sequences in DNA are those sequences that read the same forward on one strand and backwards on the complementary strand (5' to 3' on one strand and 3' to 5' on the other). This feature is vital for the recognition by restriction enzymes, which cut DNA at specific sites.

5. (*b*) *Eco*RI is a restriction endonuclease enzyme that recognises the palindromic sequence GAATTC and cuts between the G and A, creating sticky ends. These sticky ends facilitate the annealing of complementary DNA fragments, enabling the insertion of foreign DNA into the vector DNA.

6. (*b*) Both statement I and statement II are correct.
The agarose matrix used in gel electrophoresis can have controllable pore size depending upon concentration of agarose used in gel preparation. This controllable pore size is essential for efficaciously separating and analysing DNA molecules of different size during electrophoresis.
Agarose concentration can be changed to change pore size. Higher agarose concentration results in smaller pores which are suitable for separating smaller DNA fragments, while lower agarose concentration results in larger pores, allowing separation of larger DNA fragments.

7. (*c*) Statements II and V are incorrect. These can be corrected as
- The selectable marker helps in identifying and elimination of non-transformants and selectively permitting the growth of transformants.
- Multiple cloning site allows for the insertion of foreign DNA without disrupting rest of the plasmid.

8. (*c*) In the pBR322 plasmid map, the restriction site labelled *A* corresponds to *Pst* I and the restriction site labelled *B* corresponds to *Sal* I. These restriction sites are used for cloning and insertion of foreign DNA into the plasmid, which carries antibiotic resistance genes (amp^R and tet^R) for selection.

9. (*b*) The correct matches are A-4, B-1, C-2, D-3.
- Electroporation creates transient pores in the plasma membrane.
- Microinjection involves the introduction of foreign genes using glass needles.
- Gene gun technology bombards foreign DNA into target cells.
- Heat shock enables bacteria to take up the recombinant DNA.

10. (*d*) Statement (d) is correct. Other incorrect statements can be corrected as
- *Eco*RI cuts the DNA between bases G and A only when the sequence GAATTC is present in the DNA.
- Today, we know more than 900 restriction enzymes that have been isolated from over 230 strains of bacteria, each of which recognise different recognition sequences.
- In *Eco*RI, the letter 'R' is derived from the name of strain.

11. (*d*) Option (d) is not a characteristic of pBR322 vector. It can be corrected as
pBR322 has a restriction site for *Sal*I present in the tet^R antibiotic resistance gene.

12. (*c*) Both A and R are true, but R is not the correct explanation of A.
The separated DNA fragments can be visualised only after staining the DNA with a compound known as ethidium bromide followed by exposure to UV radiation. Pure DNA fragments cannot be visualised in the visible light spectrum and without staining.

13. (*b*) The correct matches are A-II, B-IV, C-I, D-III.
- Exonuclease removes nucleotides from the ends of DNA whereas, endonucleases make cuts at specific position within DNA.
- Sticky ends form hydrogen bonds with their complementary cuts counterparts.
- Palindromic is a sequence of base pairs that read the same sequence in both complementary cut counterparts.

14. (*d*) Statement V is incorrect and can be corrected as
Foreign DNA can be ligated at *Pvu*II site of rop. rop codes for the proteins involved in the replication of the plasmid.

15. (*a*) Presence of insert results into insertional inactivation of the β-galactosidase and the colonies do not produce any colour, these are identified as recombinant colonies. A recombinant DNA is inserted within the coding sequence of an enzyme, β-galactosidase. This results into inactivation of the gene for synthesis of the enzyme, which is referred to as insertional inactivation.

Test 3

1. (*c*) Ethanol reduces the solubility of DNA by decreasing the dielectric constant of the solution. Chilled ethanol promotes DNA precipitation by reducing the solution's dielectric constant, which diminishes the solubility of DNA in water and causes it to aggregate and precipitate out of the solution.

2. (*c*) Statements I and V are incorrect. These can be corrected as
PCR involves three temperature dependent steps.
1. Denaturation- 94°C
2. Annealing- 50°-60°C
3. Primer extension or polymerisation-72°C

PCR can be used to detect the presence of specific mutation that is responsible for causing particular genetic disease such as AIDS, sickle-cell anaemia.

3. (*d*) Statement I is correct, but statement II is incorrect. Incorrect statement can be corrected as
Any protein encoding gene that is expressed in a heterologous host is called a recombinant protein.

4. (*c*) The structure designated as *X* in the diagram is part of the foam control system. In bioreactors, foam formation can occur due to the agitation and aeration of the culture medium. Foam control systems typically include sensors and anti-foam addition mechanisms to manage and minimise foam. The *X* structure likely represents such a component, ensuring efficient and uninterrupted bioprocessing.

5. (*b*) Both A and R are true and R is the correct explanation of A.
Agarose gel electrophoresis separates DNA fragments by size, enabling the visualisation of fragments produced by restriction enzyme digestion, thereby confirming the progression and completion of the digestion process.

6. (*b*) Both A and R are true and R is the correct explanation of A.
Recombinant DNA is the DNA whose nucleotide sequence has undergone alteration as a result of incorporation or exchange with another DNA strand.
In recombinant DNA technology, human genes are often transferred into bacteria or yeast because both bacteria and yeast multiply very fast to form huge population, which express the desired gene.

7. (*b*) In the diagram, *A* represents the denaturation step, where double-stranded DNA is heated to separate into two single strands. *B* represents the annealing step, where primers bind to the single-stranded DNA. *C* represents the extension step, where DNA polymerase synthesises the new DNA strand by adding nucleotides. This cycle repeats approx. 30 times to amplify the target DNA region.

8. (*b*) Thermostable DNA polymerases are found naturally in thermophilic bacteria, which can be found growing in oceanic vents. They have high stability and their DNA polymerase can function effectively even at high temperature *in vivo*.

9. (*b*) Both statement I and statement II are correct.
After the two synthetic stages of producing a biological or pharmaceutical product, there are typically several downstream processes that the product must go through before it is ready for marketing as a finished product. These downstream processes can vary depending on the specific product and its intended use. Downstream processing encompasses the steps involved in isolating and purifying a bioproduct such as protein after its production in a bioreactor or fermenters.

10. (*b*) A continuous culture system is maintained in a bioreactor by continuously and regularly feeding with culture medium steadily and by providing optimum growth conditions like pH, temperature, vitamins, salts, and oxygen.
It is also necessary to drain out the used medium from the other side. In short, the used medium is drained out from one side of the bioreactor and the fresh medium is added from the other side.

11. (*b*) The correct order for the process of *r*DNA technology is III, II, IV, V and I.
The process of recombinant DNA technology involves isolating the desired DNA fragment (III), amplifying the gene of interest (II), ligating the DNA fragment into a vector (IV), inserting the recombinant DNA into the host (V) and finally extracting the desired gene product (I).

12. (*b*) The correct matches are A-2, B-3, C-1, D-4.
- To obtain DNA from plant cells, they are treated with cellulase.
- The bacterial cell wall is digested by lysozyme.
- The fungal cell wall contains chitin and it is treated with chitinase to dissolve its cell wall and obtain its fungal DNA.
- The animal cell is treated with detergent to dissolve cell membrane and nuclear membrane.

13. (*b*) All the processes are involved in downstream processing except V. Step of culturing heterologous host is not involved in downstream processing. It is a part of upstream processing.

14. (*a*) The correct matches are A-3, B-4, C-2, D-1
- A thermostable DNA polymerase is isolated from a bacterium, *Thermus aquaticus*.
- The ampicillin resistance gene is called a selectable marker.
- DNA that separates during isolation can be removed by spooling.
- During denaturation, double stranded DNA form single stranded DNA due to breakage of hydrogen bonds.

15. (*d*) Statement given in option (d) is incorrect. Incorrect statement can be corrected as
Primers are small chemically synthesised oligonucleotides of about 10-30 nucleotides, that are complementary to two DNA strands at the 3'-end.

Chapter Break Thru

1. (*c*) Restriction endonucleases create specific cuts within DNA molecules, allowing foreign DNA to be inserted into vectors.
These enzymes recognise particular nucleotide sequences and cleave the DNA at these sites, facilitating the introduction of new genetic material.
This precise cutting mechanism is essential for recombinant DNA technology, enabling genetic manipulation and cloning by creating openings for foreign DNA integration.

2. (*c*) The correct statements are II, III and IV. Other statements are incorrect and can be corrected as

- Cloning is possible in both plant and animal cells, although the specific methods may vary.
- Cloning involves breaking the desired piece of DNA and through *r*DNA technology, inserting it in the plasmid.

3. (*a*) Plasmids are ideal vectors in genetic engineering primarily due to the presence of antibiotic resistance genes, which facilitate the selection of successfully transformed cells. These circular DNA molecules can integrate with eukaryotic DNA, but their primary utility lies in conferring resistance to antibiotics, thus allowing researchers to identify and isolate modified cells easily.

4. (*d*) Group of cells with identical genotype are called clones. These are a group of morphological and genetically similar copies of their parents.

Other options are incorrect and can be corrected as

Extrachromosomal genetic material is present only in bacteria.

Restriction enzymes are present in prokaryotes and protect them against bacteriophage.

The first artificial recombinant molecule was constructed by Cohen and Boyer.

5. (*b*) Disarmed pathogen vectors are used in a method when they are allowed to infect the cell and transfer the recombinant DNA into the host. The basic process involves allowing these disarmed vectors to infect host cells, where they transfer the recombinant DNA which can carry specific genes of interest into hosts genome.

6. (*a*) Statement I is incorrect, but statement II is correct. Statement I can be corrected as

Plasmids and bacteriophage have the ability to replicate within bacterial cells, independent of the control of chromosomal DNA.

7. (*c*) If a bacterial cell contained no restriction enzyme, then the cell would be easily infected and lysed by bacteriophage. The DNA of the host bacterial cell is protected from its own restricted endonuclease by methylation within their recognition site.

8. (*d*) T-DNA is found in the Ti-plasmid of *Agrobacterium*, which can induce tumours in higher plants. Hence, it cannot be used as a selectable marker for *E. coli*. Rest all others are selectable marker for *E. coli*.

9. (*d*) Statement given in option (d) is incorrect and can be corrected as

Only a single copy of the restriction site per enzyme should be present, ideally. This is because more than one copy of the same recognition site within the vector will generate several fragments, which will make gene cloning complicated.

10. (*a*) Statement I is incorrect, but statement II is correct. Incorrect statement can be corrected as

Phages usually have linear DNA molecules into which foreign DNA can be inserted at several restriction site. This property can be useful for genetic engineering and the creation of *r*DNA for various research purposes.

11. (*c*) When a foreign gene is inserted into the gene coding for β-galactosidase, the recombinant cells do not produce the enzyme due to gene inactivation. In the presence of a chromogenic substrate (such as X-gal), non-recombinant cells produce β-galactosidase, leading to blue colonies, while recombinant cells do not produce the enzyme, resulting in colourless colonies. This differentiation helps in identifying recombinants.

12. (*d*) Statements given in option (d) is correct. Other statements can be corrected as

Agrobacterium tumefaciens, a pathogen of several dicot plants is able to deliver a piece of DNA known as 'T-DNA'.

The RNA containing retroviruses in animals have the ability to transform normal cells into cancerous cells.

The Tumour inducing (Ti) plasmid of *Agrobacterium tumefaciens* has now been modified into a cloning vector, which is no more pathogenic to the plants, but is still able to use the mechanisms to deliver genes of our interest into a variety of plants.

13. (*b*) In gel electrophoresis, the thickness of bands indicates the quantity of DNA present in each band, not the size of DNA segments. Thicker bands represent a greater amount of DNA at that specific fragment size. The position of bands from top to bottom reflects the size, with smaller fragments migrating further down the gel.

14. (*a*) The gene gun method is ideal for transforming plant cells, as it allows direct DNA delivery into plant tissues. This technique is particularly useful for plants that are resistant to other transformation methods. Other applications like DNA fingerprinting, pathogen vector disarming and constructing recombinant DNA molecules typically use different specialised techniques.

15. (*b*) PCR is a method to dramatically increase the number of particular sequences of DNA. This technique is the most useful while cloning DNA.

16. (*c*) This process involves isolating DNA from a sample by adding a precipitation agent such as chilled ethanol to the solution. The DNA then forms a visible precipitate, which can be collected and further processed.

17. (*a*) A is false, but R is true. A can be corrected as

In DNA electrophoresis, DNA actually moves from the cathode to the anode under the influence of an electric field. This movement occurs because the phosphate groups in DNA are negatively charged, which causes DNA to migrate towards the positively charged anode.

18. (*a*) Transformation is a procedure through which a piece of DNA is introduced in a host bacterium. DNA bearing ampicillin resistance gene (transformed recipient cells) when introduced into the plate containing ampicillin, will grow. In contrast, DNA not bearing ampicillin resistance gene (untransformed recipient cells) will die.

19. (*b*) Both A and R are true and R is the correct explanation of A.

Traditional breeding often results in the inclusion and multiplication of undesirable genes along with the desired ones, making it less precise than recombinant DNA technology. Recombinant DNA technology allows for the specific insertion of desired genes, avoiding unwanted genetic material and resulting in more efficient and targeted improvements.

20. (*a*) Statement given in option (a) is incorrect and it can be corrected as

The high temperature breaks the hydrogen bonds between the two strands of the original DNA double-helix, thus providing the necessary single-stranded template.

21. (*d*) A is true, but R is false. R can be corrected as

DNA is a hydrophilic molecule. This hydrophilic property of DNA is essential for its biological functions such as replication and transcription which occurs in aqueous cellular environment. It cannot enter into the cell. Recombinant DNA is forced into bacterial cells with *r*DNA on ice, followed by heat shock.

22. (*a*) Statement I is incorrect, but statement II is correct. Incorrect statement can be corrected as

Among many, the two core techniques that enabled birth of modern biotechnology are genetic engineering and bioprocess engineering or chemical engineering.

23. (*d*) It is a small segment of DNA utilised for starting the elongation of a new replica strand. In PCR, primers are short DNA sequences that anneal to the target DNA, providing a starting point for DNA polymerase to begin synthesis. They are synthesised chemically and designed to match the flanking regions of the target sequence, ensuring specific amplification.

24. (*b*) The failure of bacterial cells to produce the desired protein from a human gene can be due to human genes often contain introns, which bacterial cells cannot process because they lack the necessary splicing machinery. This can prevent proper transcription and translation of the gene into functional protein. Additionally, the transformed bacterial cells may produce an inactive protein that cannot be properly processed or activated within the bacterial environment, leading to non-functional protein production.

25. (*c*) Ethidium bromide stained DNA can be seen under exposure to UV-light. Ethidium bromide intercalates with DNA and illuminates under UV light, enabling the visualisation of DNA bands. Without staining or UV exposure, DNA remains invisible to the naked eye in visible light.

26. (*a*) The correct match is A-2, B-4, C-3, D-1.

- Normal cells are transformed into cancerous cells by retrovirus infection.
- *Lac z*-gene is the selectable marker used for selection of transformants and non-transformants.
- Chimeric DNA is a combination of *c*DNA and plasmid.
- Genophore is called plasmid.

27. (*d*) Statement I is correct, but statement II is incorrect. Incorrect statement can be corrected as

Presence of chromogenic substrate gives blue coloured colonies, if the plasmid in the bacteria does not have an insert.

28. (*c*) Both A and R are true, but R is not the correct explanation of A.

The presence or absence of a cell wall is just one factor that determines the need for cellulose in DNA isolation. The main reason is that plant cells have a cellulose cell wall that needs to be broken down, whereas animal cells do not.

29. (*d*) The incorrect match is in option (d).

Bioreactors are actually used for the large-scale production of proteins or other products expressed by the foreign gene, not for producing the foreign gene itself. The foreign gene is typically cloned and amplified in microorganisms or cell cultures before being introduced into bioreactors for mass production of its expressed product.

30. (*c*) Both A and R are true, but R is not the correct explanation of A.

Downstream processing is the stage after fermentation when the desired product is recovered and purified. After completion of biosynthetic phase, the product has to be subjected through a series of process before it is ready for marketing as a finished product. After purification the product has to be formulated with suitable preservatives.

31. (*c*) Statements I, III and V are incorrect and can be corrected as

*Hin*d II always cut DNA molecules at a particular point by recognising a specific sequence of six base pairs. In *Hin*d II, the letter '*H*' is derived from the name of genus. Restriction endonucleases are used in genetic engineering to form 'recombinant' molecules of DNA.

32. (*c*) Statement in option (c) incorrectly explains the part of the normal process during the cloning of recombinant DNA in bacteria and can be corrected as

Southern blotting is not used for separation of recombinant DNA plasmids. Southern technique is used to confirm the presence of specific DNA in sample.

33. (*d*) All statements are incorrect except option (d) and incorrect statements can be corrected as

- If any protein encoding gene is expressed in a heterologous host, it is called a recombinant protein.
- In PCR, the multiple copies of gene of interest is synthesised *in vitro* using two sets of primers.

• A thermostable enzyme (*Taq* polymerase) is obtained from bacterium, *Thermus aquaticus*.

34. (*c*) A cloning vector should possess an origin of replication so that it can self-replicate inside the host cell. It should have a restriction site for the insertion of the target DNA. It should also have a selectable marker with an antibiotic resistance gene that facilitates screening of the recombinant organism.

35. (*c*) The process that makes the bacterial cells to take up the recombinant DNA is by incubating the cells with recombinant DNA on ice, followed by placing them briefly at 42°C (heat shock), and then putting them back on ice.

36. (*c*) Both statement I and statement II are incorrect and can be corrected as

Since, DNA is a hydrophilic molecule, it cannot pass through cell membranes. Retroviruses have also been disarmed and are used to deliver desirable genes into animal cells.

37. (*c*) The correct matches are A-4, B-2, C-1, D-3.

• Bioreactors are required to grow microbes on large scale.

• DNA strands appear bright orange bands on staining with ethidium bromide.

• Selectable markers help to identify transformed cells.

• Chilled alcohol precipitates the DNA during purification.

38. (*b*) The construction of the first recombinant DNA emerged from the possibility of linking a gene encoding antibiotic resistance with a native plasmid (autonomously replicating circular extra-chromosomal DNA) of *Salmonella typhimurium*.

Stanley Cohen and Herbert Boyer accomplished this in 1972 by isolating the antibiotic resistance gene by cutting out a piece of DNA from a plasmid which was responsible for conferring antibiotic resistance.

39. (*c*) Availability of thermostable DNA polymerase has initiated the increase in usage of PCR. It is highly efficient and remain enzymatically active after each cycle.

40. (*d*) The processes include separation and purification, which are collectively referred to as downstream processing. The product has to be formulated with suitable preservatives. Such formulation has to undergo through clinical trials, as in case of drugs.

41. (*a*) The correct matches are A-2, B-3, C-4, D-1.

• Restriction enzymes cut the strands of DNA at specific palindromic sequence.

• Now-a-days, the most commonly used matrix is agarose which is a natural polymer extracted from sea weeds.

• *ori* is a sequence where replication starts.

• *Pst* I is a cloning site at ampicillin gene.

42. (*a*) A is false, but R is true. A can be corrected as

For isolation of pure DNA, DNAase enzyme is not used because it will digest the DNA.

43. (*b*) Statements II, III, IV and V are correct. Statement I is incorrect and can be corrected as

In PCR, repeated amplification is achieved by the use of a thermostable DNA polymerase. It is isolated from a bacterium, *Thermus aquaticus*, which remain active during the high temperature induced denaturation of double-stranded DNA.

44. (*d*) The correct matches are A-4, B-3, C-2, D-1.

• Thermostable DNA polymerase is isolated from a bacterium *Thermus aquaticus*.

• pBR322 is vector used for introduction of *r*DNA into *E. coli*.

• β-galactosidase is presence of a chromogenic substrate gives blue coloured colonies.

• Microinjection is used for transfer of *r*DNA into animal cells.

45. (*b*) In a continuous culture system, the used medium is drained out from one side, while fresh medium is added from the other to maintain the cells in their physiologically most active log/exponential phase. This type of culturing method produces a larger biomass leading to higher yields of desired protein.

46. (*b*) The maintenance of contamination-free medium in the engineering process is referred to as chemical engineering. This process enables the growth of desired microbes in mass to manufacture enzymes, drugs, vaccines, etc.

47. (*c*) The incorrect statement given in option (c). It can be corrected as

The normal *E. coli* cell does not carry genes resistant against ampicillin, chloramphenicol, tetracycline and kanamycin. These antibiotic resistance genes are often introduced into *E. coli* cells through genetic engineering techniques to create strain that are resistant to specific antibiotics.

48. (*a*) *Agrobacterium tumifaciens* delivers a piece of DNA known as 'T-DNA' to transform normal plant cells into a tumor. It is pathogen of several dicot plants.

49. (*b*) A stirred-tank bioreactor is usually cylindrical and provided with rotating shafts and blades to facilitate the mixing of the reaction contents.

The stirrer provides facility of mixing the contents as well as the availability of oxygen throughout the process. Alternatively, air can be bubbled through the reactor.

50. (*b*) In a method, suitable for plants, cells are bombarded with high velocity micro-particles of gold or tungsten coated with DNA in a method known as biolistics or gene gun.

Ch-10 Biotechnology and Its Applications

Topical Follow Thru

Test 1

1. (*a*) The high cost of agrochemicals made it difficult for small farmers to afford them, limiting the spread of the green revolution. Additionally, the extensive use of these chemicals had a detrimental impact on the environment, leading to soil degradation and loss of biodiversity.

2. (*d*) Statement I is correct, but statement II is incorrect. The incorrect statement can be corrected as
The capacity to generate a whole plant from any cell/explant is called totipotency.

3. (*d*) The best possible way to increase yield in developing countries is use of genetically modified crops which minimise dependency on agrochemicals. GM crops can significantly enhance yield and resilience to pests and diseases, reducing the need for expensive and harmful agrochemicals. While agrochemicals can increase yield at lower cost, they may have environmental and health drawbacks. Organic farming can improve yield sustainably, but often requires more labour and expertise. Conventional breeding is cost-efficient, but is slower in achieving significant yield improvements compared to GM technology.

4. (*b*) While biotechnology involves the manipulation of biological systems, organisms or derivatives to produce products, it does not typically involve creating environment for chemical reactions in space.

5. (*b*) The incorrect match is given in option (b). *Flavr Savr* tomato was developed to delay ripening and increase shelf life by suppressing the polygalacturonase gene, which breaks down pectin in cell walls and causes softening. Therefore, the transferred gene should be an antisense-polygalacturonase gene, not polygalacturonase itself.

6. (*b*) Statement given in option (b) is incorrect. It can be corrected as Genetically Modified Crops (GMOs) increases the efficiency of mineral usage by plants, i.e. prevents early exhaustion of the fertility of soil. It also reduces post-harvest losses.

7. (*a*) The protoxin from *Bacillus thuringiensis* is an inactive form that requires the alkaline (high pH) environment of the insect's gut for activation. In this environment, gut proteases cleave the protoxin into its active form, making it toxic to the insect.

8. (*a*) The correct matches are A-3, B-1, C-2, D-4.
   - *Flavr Savr* tomato was the first commercial genetically engineered food developed using antisense technology.
   - Nematode resistant plants are created through RNA interference (RNAi).
   - *Bt* cotton contains insecticidal protein genes.
   - Pomato involves somatic hybridisation by fusion of protoplast of tomato and potato.

9. (*d*) *Bacillus thuringiensis* (*Bt*) is primarily used as a biological pesticide to target specific insect pests, thereby reducing the need for chemical insecticides. It helps protect the environment, conserve biodiversity by targeting specific pests and can increase crop productivity by reducing pest damage. However, it does not affect the use of herbicides, which are used to control weeds, not insects.

10. (*a*) Golden rice is a variety of rice produced through genetic engineering to biosynthesise β-carotene. It is a precursor of vitamin-A whose deficiency causes xerophthalmia and a range of eye conditions from night blindness to more severe clinical outcomes.

11. (*b*) *Bt* toxin, produced by *Bacillus thuringiensis*, is a crystalline protein that acts as an insecticide. It does not harm the bacteria that produce it because it is synthesised in an inactive form. The toxin becomes active only in the alkaline environment of the insect's gut, where it is then able to exert its toxic effects.

12. (*c*) Statements I, II and V are incorrect. These can be corrected as *cry* IAc and *cry* IIAb genes control the cotton bollworms, while *cry* IAb gene controls corn borer.
Nematode specific genes were introduced into the host plant using *Agrobacterium tumefaciens* vector.
Mechanism of RNAi started in eukaryotic cells when a double stranded RNA is introduced either naturally or artificially in a cell. This method involves silencing of a specific *m*RNA due to complementary *ds*RNA molecule that binds to and prevents translation of the *m*RNA (silencing).

13. (*b*) Both A and R are true and R is the correct explanation of A.
Crop plants, genetically engineered to produce insecticidal toxins derived from the bacterium *Bacillus thuringiensis* are being grown on millions of hectares, but their success will be short-lived if pests adapt to them quickly.

14. (*d*) A is true, but R is false. R can be corrected as
RNAi involves double-stranded RNA (not single-stranded RNA) that triggers the silencing mechanism by binding to the target *m*RNA, leading to its degradation and preventing translation.

15. (*c*) The alkaline pH of the insect gut does not denature the crystals.

Instead, it solubilises the protein crystals, allowing the protoxin to be activated by proteases. This active toxin then binds to gut cell membranes, creating pores, leading to cell lysis and insect death.

Test 2

1. (*b*) Recombinant therapeutics are synthesised using human genes. As a result, they are recognised as 'self' by the immune system and do not induce unwanted immunological responses. This is unlike the products isolated from non-human sources, which can trigger such responses.
2. (*c*) Insulin, a protein hormone, cannot be taken orally due to the harsh environment of the digestive system. The acidic pH in the stomach denatures it, altering its structure and rendering it ineffective. While option (d), i.e. insulin will be digested by pancreatic enzymes, is technically true, it is not the primary reason that insulin cannot be taken orally. The denaturation happens before the insulin would even reach the stage where it could be broken down by pancreatic enzymes.
3. (*c*) Both A and R are true, but R is not the correct explanation of A.
When a mutation renders a gene altered and the encoded protein is unable to function properly this is called as a loss-of-function mutation. This affects the overall function of body. Gene therapy is designed to introduce genetic materials into cells to compensate for abnormal genes or to make a beneficial protein.
4. (*b*) Insulin used for diabetes was earlier extracted from pancreas of slaughtered cattle and pigs. Insulin from an animal source caused some patients to develop allergy or other types of reactions to the foreign protein, by which production of antibody gets induced.
5. (*d*) Statement given in option (d) is incorrect. It can be corrected as
Gene therapy is more successful at the embryonic stage than at the childhood stage.
6. (*c*) The diagram illustrates the conversion of pro-insulin into insulin and free C-peptide chain.
During this process, disulfide bonds are formed between the A and B chains of insulin, stabilising its structure. This conversion is crucial for insulin's biological activity, as the C peptide is removed to yield the functional hormone.
7. (*c*) Introducing bone marrow cells that produce ADA into cells at early embryonic stages offers a permanent cure for ADA deficiency. This method ensures that the functional ADA gene is incorporated into the patient's cells, providing a long-term solution. Other options provide temporary relief, but do not address the root cause at the genetic level.
8. (*c*) The clone having the mutated gene will not appear on the photographic film because the probe will not have complementarity with the mutated gene.
A single stranded DNA or RNA, tagged with a radioactive molecule (probe) is allowed to hybridise to its complementary DNA in a clone of cells followed by detection using autoradiography.
9. (*d*) Statement I is correct, but statement II is incorrect. The incorrect statement can be corrected as
The site of production of Adenosine Deaminase (ADA) in the body is primarily the lymphocytes. While erythrocytes also contain some ADA, its activity is significantly higher in lymphocytes.
10. (*a*) Statements I, III and IV are correct. Statements II and V are incorrect. These can be corrected as
The C-peptide is not present in mature insulin. It is removed during maturation.
Chains A and B were produced separately, not together.
11. (*b*) ADA deficiency occurs due to deletion of adenosine deaminase. It can be cured by bone marrow transplantation. It can also be treated by enzyme replacement therapy.
12. (*a*) PCR is a technique to amplify small segments of DNA. It helps to detect very low concentration of bacteria or virus by amplification of their nucleic acid at the time when the symptoms of the disease are not even visible.
13. (*c*) The correct matches are A-4, B-1, C-2, D-3.
    - The Polymerase Chain Reaction (PCR) technique amplifies pathogenic DNA, making the early diagnosis of disease easier.
    - Enzyme-Linked Immuno Sorbent Assay (ELISA) is used for detecting antigen-antibody interactions, crucial in diagnosing various diseases.
    - Autoradiography is a technique that detects radioactive isotopes, often used in biological and chemical research.
    - A probe is a single stranded DNA or RNA tagged with a radioactive molecule.
14. (*d*) A is true, but R is false. R can be corrected as
Molecular diagnostic techniques, e.g. PCR, ELISA serve to the purpose of early diagnosis.
15. (*d*) The correct statement is give in option (d), i.e. in autoradiography technique, a single stranded DNA or RNA, tagged with a radioactive molecule (probe) is used.
Incorrect statements can be corrected as
Full form of ELISA is Enzyme Linked Immuno-Sorbent Assay.
PCR is used to detect both infectious as well as non-infectious diseases.
The first clinical gene therapy was given in 1990 to a 4-year old girl with Adenosine Deaminase (ADA) deficiency.

Test 3

1. (*c*) Genetically Modified Organisms (GMOs) are used for various purposes, such as studying complex factors involved in growth, understanding how genes contribute to the development of diseases, and ensuring vaccine safety through testing. However, GMOs are not

used to produce better medical instruments. The development and improvement of medical instruments involve engineering and material science rather than genetical modification techniques.

2. (*a*) Statements I, II, III and IV are correct. Statement V is incorrect. It can be corrected as

Human protein, α-1-antitrypsin produced by transgenic animals is used to treat emphysema.

3. (*c*) Statement given in option (c) is not correct. It can be corrected as

The milk produced by Rosie contained the human alpha-lactalbumin and was nutritionally a more balanced product for human babies than natural cow-milk.

4. (*d*) Animals that have had their DNA manipulated to possess and express an extra gene may result into loss of the integrity of species because of the introduction of a transgene from other species.

5. (*b*) Both A and R are true and R is the correct explanation of A.

Transgenic animals often have shorter lifespans and lower survival rates. This is because genetic mutations can occur during the production of transgenic animals, leading to diseases and disorders.

6. (*d*) A is true, but R is false. R can be corrected as

Transgenic animals carry genes which make them more sensitive to toxic substances than non-transgenic animals. Thus, they are exposed to toxins to study the effect of toxicity (Toxicity testing).

7. (*b*) Both statement I and statement II are correct.

Bioethics is commonly referred to the ethical implications and applications of the health-related life sciences.

The major bioethical concern pertaining to genetic modification of organisms is the transfer of gene from one species to another as it goes against the integrity of species.

8. (*c*) Statement given in option (c) is correct. Rest of the statements can be corrected as

GEAC is established by government of India.

The full form of GEAC is Genetic Engineering Approval Committee.

It concerns about the safety of introducing GM-organisms for public services.

9. (*b*) Statement given in option (b) is incorrect and it can be corrected as

Biopatent allows private monopoly rights over plants and animals. This includes the plants and animals that are not formed naturally, but are produced using biotechnological means.

10. (*b*) Transgenic animals are developed by introducing foreign genes into the fertilised egg, which give rise to all the cell lines in the body. So, all the cells of the trangenic animals have foreign genes (DNA).

11. (*a*) While production of a dangerous species as a result of production by transgenic animals, is a concern, it is not a primary bioethical issue compared to the others listed. The major bioethical concerns typically focus on the ethical implications of genetic integrity, the concept of humanness and the potential unforeseen environmental risks posed by biotechnology.

12. (*a*) The correct match is A-2, B-1, C-3, D-4.

- Bioethics involves the ethical issues related to biology.
- Biopiracy refers to the unauthorised extraction and commercialisation of biological resources, such as medicinal plants, without providing fair compensation.
- A patent is a legal document that gives the inventor exclusive rights to profit from an invention for a certain period of time.
- Bio-resources are biological materials like plants, animals and microorganisms that are used for various commercial and scientific purposes. They are crucial for biodiversity.

13. (*b*) Biopiracy is a term used to refer to the use of bio-resources by MNCs and other organisations without proper authorisation from countries and people concerned without compensatory payment.

14. (*c*) The patent rights allowed the company to sell the 'new' variety of Basmati only within the United States. The American company did not develop the 'new' Basmati variety entirely on its own. They derived it by crossing Indian Basmati with semi-dwarf varieties, claiming it as an invention. The patent rights, allowed the company to sell this 'new' variety not only in the US, but also abroad. The patent rights were granted by the US Patent and Trademark Office, not the Indian Patent Office.

15. (*d*) The Indian Parliament has recently cleared the second amendment of the Indian Patents Bill (IPB), that takes various issues into consideration, except a method of agriculture. It is non-patentable. The discoveries/inventions which are fully or partially related to the natural laws/principles are not patentable.

Chapter Break Thru

1. (*b*) *Bt* cotton is genetically modified to produce *Bt* toxin, which is lethal to specific insect pests like bollworms. When these pests ingest *Bt* toxin from the pollen or other parts of the plant, it disrupts their digestive system, leading to their death.

2. (*d*) Statement I is correct, but statement II is incorrect, it can corrected as

Golden rice is the realistic solution for vitamin-A deficiency. It is a variety of rice produced through genetic engineering to biosynthesise β - carotene, a precursor of vitamin-A.

3. (*c*) Both A and R are true, but R is not the correct explanation of A.

In agricultural biotechnology, changes are made directly to the plant's genome. Once the gene that determines a desirable trait is identified, it can be selectively extracted and transferred directly into another plant genome through vector. The most commonly used vectors are Ti-piasmid and viral-based vectors.

4. (*a*) Statements I, III and IV are correct. Statement II is incorrect and can be corrected as

RNA takes place in all eukaryotic organisms as a method of cellular defence.

5. (*a*) The correct set of factors is I, II and III. The choice of a *Bt* gene for an experiment depends on the host plant/crop, the targeted pest/insect and the *Bacillus* strain. These factors ensure that the *Bt*-gene is compatible with the plant, effective against the specific pest, and derived from an appropriate bacterial strain to maximise efficacy and safety.

6. (*d*) Statement given in option (d) is incorrect. It can be corrected as

As a result of gene silencing due to RNAi, the parasite could not survive, but the transgenic plant remains unharmed.

7. (*c*) The image shows two cotton bolls, one is damaged and other is healthy. Cotton belongs to the Malvaceae family (*A*). The damage seen in plant is indicative of bollworm (*B*) infestation. Bollworms are common pests of cotton, boring into the cotton bolls and causing significant damage, as seen in the diagram.

8. (*a*) Statement given in option (a) is correct. Rest statements are incorrect. They can be corrected as

The technique of insulin production *via r*DNA technology was developed by Eli Lilly, an American company.

Chains A and B were combined by creating disulphide bonds to form human insulin.

Only chains A and B are present in mature insulin.

9. (*b*) Severe Combined Immuno Deficiency (SCID) involves a defect in the immune system due to the deficiency of the enzyme Adenosine Deaminase (ADA). ADA plays a critical role in purine metabolism and its deficiency results in the accumulation of toxic deoxyadenosine and deoxyadenosine triphosphate. These metabolites inhibit the development and function of lymphocytes, leading to severe immunodeficiency.

10. (*c*) The diagram shows the structure of pro-insulin, which consists of three parts: the A chain, the B chain, and the connecting C-peptide. The C peptide is crucial for the correct folding and formation of disulphide bonds between the A and B chains during the synthesis of pro-insulin. However, it is removed during the maturation process to produce active insulin, which consists only of the A and B chains linked by disulphide bonds.

11. (*b*) ELISA is a basic assay technique. It is carried out to detect and measure antibodies, hormones, peptides and proteins in the blood. ELISA is a distinguished analysis compared to other antibody assays as it yields quantitative results.

12. (*b*) Proinsulin contains an extra stretch, i.e. C-peptide. It undergoes post-translational modification to make the functional insulin by removing C-peptide. The post-translational conversion to insulin has been carried out chemically because bacterial cells cannot perform post-translational modification.

13. (*c*) A probe can be either single-stranded RNA (*ss*RNA) or single-stranded DNA (*ss*DNA) because both types of molecules are capable of hybridising with complementary sequences in a target DNA or RNA mixture. The ability of a probe to hybridise with its target depends on the sequence complementarity, not on the specific type of nucleic acid used as the probe. Therefore, both ssRNA and *ss*DNA can serve as effective probes in molecular biology techniques.

14. (*a*) The first step of gene therapy for ADA deficiency involves growing cultures of lymphocytes from the patient's blood outside the patient's body.

15. (*c*) Many transgenic animals are designed to increase the understanding of how genes contribute to the development of diseases.

These are specially made to serve as the models for human disease, so that investigation of new treatments for many disease can be made possible. Today, transgenic models exist for many human diseases such as cancer, cystic fibrosis, rheumatoid arthritis and Alzheimer's.

16. (*d*) Statement given in option (d) is incorrect and it can be corrected as

In 1997, the first transgenic cow, Rosie produced human protein enriched milk.

17. (*c*) Statement given in option (c) is incorrect and it can be corrected as

Virus free plants can be obtained by culturing meristem (apical and axillary), as the fast dividing meristematic cells are free from viral infection.

18. (*b*) Several attempts have been made to patent uses, products, processes based on Indian traditional herbal medicines like turmeric, neem and cereals like rice.

These attempts have raised issues of biopiracy and the need for protecting traditional knowledge.

19. (*b*) Nematode-resistant tobacco plants have been developed by introducing DNA that produces both sense and antisense RNAs. This results in the formation of double-stranded RNA (*ds*RNA), which triggers RNA interference (RNAi) to silence specific genes essential for nematode survival. This biotechnological approach effectively reduces nematode infestation in the plants without the need for chemical treatment.

20. (*d*) Statement I is correct, but statement II is incorrect. The incorrect statement can be corrected as

The proteins encoded by the genes *cry*IAc and *cry*IIAb control cotton bollworms, whereas the gene *cry*IAb specifically targets corn borers. These genes are part of the *Bt* (*Bacillus thuringiensis*) toxin, which confers pest resistance in genetically modified cotton plants. The *Bt* toxin causes pore formation in the gut of insects, leading to their demise.

21. (*d*) *Bt* cotton is produced by integrating a *cry* gene from *Bacillus thuringiensis* to form insecticidal protein or *Bt* toxin. This toxin can kill lepidopterans like bollworms and thus make it resistance from the same and results in high yield.

22. (*a*) The correct matches are A-1, B-3, C-2, D-4.

- Golden rice is used to enhance nutritional value (vitamin A).
- The *Flavr Savr* tomato has an improved shelf life.
- *Bt* cotton is engineered to kill lepidopterans such as bollworms.
- The RNAi technique is a novel strategy of pest control.

23. (*b*) Both A and R are true and R is the correct explanation of A.

RNAi is used to inhibit the expression of the targeted gene. RNAi can be triggered by cells in response to pathogenic nucleic acids, leading to targeted degradation of genetic transcripts.

24. (*b*) Statement given in option (b) is incorrect. It can be corrected as ADA (Adenosine Deaminase) is an important enzyme, which is crucial for the immune system to function.

25. (*d*) Statements I, III and V are correct. Statements II and IV are incorrect and can be corrected as

ELISA is an example of molecular diagnosis. Serum and urine analysis are conventional diagnostic procedures. ELISA can detect diseases at a very early stage.

26. (*a*) Statement I is incorrect, but Statement II is correct. Statement I can be corrected as

Transposons are mobile genetic elements that conifers stability to it.

27. (*a*) Statement I is incorrect, but statement II is correct. The incorrect statement can be corrected as

There are an estimated 2,00,000 (2 lakh) varieties of rice in India. The diversity of rice in India is one of the richest in the world.

28. (*d*) The correct matches are A-2, B-1, C-3, D-4.

- In 1983 Eli Lilly, an American company prepared genetically engineered insulin.
- The first clinical gene therapy, was successfully conducted in the year 1990 on a 4 years old girl suffering from ADA deficiency.
- The first transgenic cow, Rosie, was created in the year 1997.
- In 1997, an American company got patent rights on Basmati rice through the US Patent and Trademark Office.

29. (*a*) Statements II, III and IV are correct. Statements I and V are incorrect and can be corrected as

- '*B*' in *Bt* stands for *Bacillus*, a bacterial genus.
- Nutrient medium for tissue culture must contain carbon source such as sucrose, inorganic salts, vitamins, amino acids and growth regulators like auxin, cytokinins, etc. Usually plant tissue culture does not employ use of ethylene.

30. (*b*) The correct order of somatic hybridisation in plant is

- Isolation of single cell from plant tissues (III)
- Digestion of cell wall of these cells (I).
- Isolation of naked protoplasts (surrounded by plasma membranes) (II)
- Fusion of protoplasts isolated from two diferent varieties of plants (IV)
- Formation of somatic hybrids (V).

Ch-11 Organisms and Populations

Topical Follow Thru

Test 1

1. (*c*) Ecology is the interaction among organisms and between the organism and its physical environment. Ecology is basically concerned with four levels of biological organisation, e.g. organisms, population, communities and biomes.

2. (*a*) In the provided graph, 'C' is designated as tropical forest. The tropical forest biome has the highest level of biodiversity. This richness is due to its stable, warm climate, high levels of rainfall, and complex structure, providing numerous niches for diverse species. The constant availability of resources support a wide variety of plants, animals, and microorganisms, making it the most biologically diverse biome on earth.

3. (*d*) Statement I is correct, but statement II is incorrect. The incorrect statement can be corrected as:

Organisms which can tolerate a wide range of salinities are called euryhaline, while the organisms which are restricted to a narrow range of salinities are called stenohaline.

4. (*c*) The correct matches are I–R, II–P, III–Q.

The salt concentration is less than 5 parts per thousand (ppt) in inland waters, 30-35 ppt in sea and more than 100 percent in hypersaline lagoons.

5. (*a*) Temperature is the primary abiotic factor, influencing the distribution of organisms because it affects metabolic rates, enzyme activity, and overall physiological processes. Different species have specific temperature ranges for optimal survival and reproduction. Extreme temperatures can limit the distribution of organisms, making temperature a critical determinant of where life can thrive.

6. (*c*) The incorrect match pair can be corrected as

Light primarily affects the vertical distribution of organisms in water bodies, with photosynthetic organisms limited to well-lit upper layers.

Some animals, undergo aestivation in order to avoid summer related problems such as heat and dessication. Blubber is a thick layer of fat below the skin of some polar aquatic animals like seal which acts as insulator and prevents heat loss. Soil (Sediment- characteristics) determines the type of benthic animals.

7. (*b*) Evolutionary biologists believe that the success of mammals is largely due to their ability to maintain a constant body temperature and thrive, whether they live in Antarctica or in the Sahara desert.

8. (*c*) In the given graph, 'C' represents partial regulators. These organisms have evolved only a limited ability to alter their body temperature, in accordance with the environment in which they live in.

9. (*b*) Both A and R are true and R is the correct explanation of A.

If a person goes to the high altitude and experiences altitude sickness like heavy breathing and heart palpitation, it is due to low atmospheric pressure at high altitude that the body does not get sufficient oxygen.

10. (*c*) Statement in option (c) is incorrect, it can be corrected as:

Small animals have a large surface area relative to their volume, so they tend to lose body heat very fast when it is cold outside. Because of that, they have to expend much energy to generate body heat through metabolism.

11. (*b*) The correct answer is (b) A-Keoladeo National Park, B-Siberia, C–Northern.

Every winter, Keoladeo National Park in Bharatpur, Rajasthan, becomes a host for thousands of migratory birds from Siberia and other cold northern regions. These birds travel vast distances to escape the harsh winter conditions and find a more suitable environment.

12. (*b*) Adaptations are morphological, physiological, and behavioural traits that enhance an organism's ability to survive and reproduce in its specific habitat. These attributes evolve over generations, enabling organisms to cope with environmental challenges, find food, evade predators, and reproduce successfully.The other options refer to the specific survival strategies but do not encompass the broad range of traits like adaptations do.

13. (*b*) Statements I and V are related to xerophytes or desert plant. The xerophytic plants are those which develop adaptations in order to survive in conditions where water availability is very low such as in desert.

The plants modify their leaves into spines and their stomata become sunken in order to reduce water loss.

14. (*d*) Temperature as an external environmental factor affects the physiology, morphology as well as geographical distribution of individuals. However, if does not affect the amount of organic matter present in the individual.

15. (*d*) Statement I is correct, but statement II is incorrect. The incorrect statement can be corrected as

Adaptation is a long-term permanent adjustment of a group of organisms to a changing environment, whereas acclimatisation is a short-term rapid temporary adjustment of an organism to a changing environment.

16. (*d*) Diapause is a specific type of dormancy seen in animals like zooplanktons, insects and other species. During diapause, the organism enters a state of suspended development, essentially pausing its life cycle until environmental conditions improve.

17. (*c*) Escape in time refers to the strategy where organisms avoid stressful conditions by entering a dormant or inactive state before the conditions become extreme. Hibernation is a classic example of escape in time. Bears, for instance, hibernate during winter, which allows them to avoid the cold and the scarcity of food.

18. (*b*) Conformers are organisms that do not maintain a constant internal environment. Instead, their internal environment changes in response to the external environment.

19. (*b*) Thermoregulation is the process by which an organism maintains a constant internal body temperature despite changes in the external environment. This process requires significant energy because the organisms must continuously produce or lose heat to maintain a stable temperature. As a result, many organisms have not evolved into regulators because the energy cost of maintaining a constant internal environment is high.

20. (*b*) Shivering is an involuntary muscle activity that generates heat. The rapid contractions of muscles' during shivering produce heat, which helps raise the body's temperature back to a stable level. This is the body's way of counteracting the cold and maintaining homeostasis.

21. (*a*) A is false, but R is true. A can be corrected as

The blood of Antarctic fishes does not freeze despite the dropping temperatures. This is because they have evolved over time to express certain antifreeze compounds in them which prevents their body fluids from freezing.

22. (*b*) Both statement I and statement II are correct.

Water is the most important factor influencing the life of organisms. Infact, life on earth originated in water and is unsustainable without water. Its availability is so limited in deserts. The productivity and distribution of plants is also heavily dependent on water.

23. (*c*) Xerophytes include plants adapted to dry conditions. Such plants possess stunted stems and an extensive root system with well developed root cap. These gave waxy coating on stem and leaves. However, presence of root pockets is a feature of hydrophytes.

24. (*d*) Sunlight plays a crucial role in regulating the biological rhythms of animals. For many animals, light is important, as they use the diurnal and seasonal variations in light intensity and duration as cues for timing their foraging, reproductive and migratory activities.

25. (*b*) The relationship between light and temperature on land is fundamentally linked to the sun, which provides both energy in the form of light and heat. The availability of light on land is naturally connected to temperature. During daylight hours, especially when the sun is at its peak, temperatures rise due to the heat energy provided by sunlight.

Test 2

1. (*d*) Competition is severely observed between closely related species that share the same habitat.

2. (*b*) The correct matches are A-3, B-1, C-4, D-2.

- Natality refers to the number of births during a given period in the population that are added to the initial density.
- Mortality is the number of deaths in the population during a given period.
- Immigration is the number of individuals of the same species that have come into the habitat from elsewhere during the time period under consideration.
- Emigration is the number of individuals of the population who left the habitat and gone elsewhere during the time period under consideration.

3. (*b*) Pyramid 'B' represents the bell-shaped declining pyramid. In this pyramid, the numbers of pre-reproductive individuals or children are lower than the number of reproductive individuals or adults. Pyramid 'A' represents triangular, expanding age pyramid. It shows high rate of population growth.

4. (*d*) The density of a population in a given habitat during a given period, fluctuates due to changes in four basic processes, two of which (natality and immigration) contribute to an increase in population density and two of them (mortality and emigration) contribute to a decrease in population density.

5. (*d*) Statement in option (d) is incorrect and can be corrected as Natality is the rate of production of new individuals per unit of population per unit time. It usually increases with the period of maturity and then falls again as the organisms gets older.

6. (*d*) Number of *Drosophila* in laboratory = 80
Number of *Drosophila* that died in a week = 08
Death rate

$$= \frac{\text{Number of individuals died}}{\text{Total number of individuals}}$$

$$= \frac{8}{80} = 0.1$$

The death rate in the population is 0.1 individuals per *Drosophila* per week.

7. (*c*) Increased mortality reduces the number of individuals, and emigration results in individuals leaving the habitat. Together, they decrease the population density. Natality is the birth rate, and immigration is the inflow of individual, both of these are responsible for the increase in population.

8. (*b*) In the absence of limiting factor and presence of abundant resources, the mice population would grow unchecked and would follow exponential growth or geometric growth. Such growth curves are J-shaped.

9. (*c*) The logistic growth or Verhulst-Pearl Logistic growth curve represents the population growing in a habitat with limited resources. In nature, a given habitat has enough resources to support a maximum possible number, beyond which no further growth is possible.

10. (*b*) Area having 200 *Calotropis* plants and a single huge banyan tree with large canopy shows low population density of banyan tree relative to that of *Calotropis*. In this case, the population density will be measured in terms of biomass or percent cover.

11. (*a*) The correct matches are A-3, B-1, C-4, D-2.

(–, –) interaction is observed in competition. The Abingdon tortoise in Galapagos Islands became extinct within a decade after goats were introduced on the island, apparently due to the greater browsing efficiency of the goats.

(+, –) interaction is observed in parasitism where one species is harmed and the other is benefitted. The *Cuscuta* plant (+) is parasitic to hedge plants (–) and derives nourishment from them.

(+, +) interaction is observed in mutualism where both interacting species are mutually benefitted. The fig and its pollinator shares this interaction. The female wasp uses the fruit not only as an oviposition (egg-laying) site, but uses the developing seeds within the fruit for nourishing its larvae. The wasp pollinates the fig inflorescence, while searching for suitable egg-laying sites. In return for the favour of pollination, the fig offers the wasp some of its developing seeds, as food for the developing wasp larvae.

(+, –) interaction is observed in case of moth (+) and prickly pear cactus

(–). Prickly pear cactus is an invasive species which can be controlled by its predator moth. This shows predation interaction.

12. (*b*) Both A and R are true and R is the correct explanation of A.
The prickly pear cactus did indeed cause extensive damage in Australia by spreading rapidly. This spread occurred because, the introduced species lacked natural predators in the new environment, allowing it to proliferate uncontrollably.

13. (*b*) Both statement I and statement II are correct.
The parasite is an organism that depends on other organisms for its growth and survival. A female mosquito though feeds on blood, is still not considered as a parasite since it does not require or live on the host, it only feeds on the blood. The female mosquito feeds on human blood for reproduction to get the nourishment for their egg development.

14. (*c*) All the given are the adaptions observed in parasite except loss of organs. The presence of adhesive organs, the development of suckers to cling to their hosts, the loss of digestive systems, and a high reproductive capacity are features that enhance their survival and reproduction within host organisms.

15. (*a*) The incorrect match pair can be corrected as
The relationship between fig flowers and wasps is actually mutualism. In this mutualistic relationship, wasps pollinate the fig flowers while laying their eggs inside them, benefitting both the fig (through pollination) and the wasps (providing a habitat for their larvae). Rest of the match pairs are correct.

16. (*a*) Change in population density
$N_t + [(B+I) - (D+E)]$
B – 50
I – 20
D – 30
E – 10
$N_{6+1} = N_t + [(50+20) - (30+10)]$
$N_t + (70-40)$
$N_t + 30$
So, there will be increase by 30 in population.

17. (*b*) Predation involves the interaction between a prey and a predator in which the former eats the latter. The interaction holds the following significance
- Prey population is kept under control.
- Maintenance of species diversity in community.
- Biological control of weeds.

However, increased reproductive capacity is an adaptation related to parasites.

18. (*d*) Statement I is correct, but statement II is incorrect. Statement II can be corrected as
Under normal conditions, natality and mortality are typically the most important factors influencing population density. Immigration and emigration become significant in a newly colonised habitats.

19. (*b*) Both A and R are true and R is the correct explanation of A.
Predation involves one species feeding on another leading to the death of the prey.
It can be classified into different types based on the relationship between the predator and the prey. The most common type of predation is carnivory.

20. (*b*) *r*-strategy of reproduction is a strategy that is characterised by a high reproductive rate, early reproduction and small sized offsprings. They tend to thrive in unpredictable environments and follow exponential growth.

21. (*b*) Competitive release refers to the phenomenon where a species expands its distributional range and potentially increases in abundance when a competitively superior species is removed from the environment.

22. (*a*) The Mediterranean orchid *Ophrys* employs a unique strategy known as sexual deceit to achieve pollination. One of its petals mimics the appearance of a female bee in terms of size, colour and markings. This resemblance tricks male bees into attempting to mate (pseudocopulate) with the flower, while flower gets pollinated during this period.

23. (*c*) Many orchids have evolved to attract bees by offering nectar as a reward. This mutualistic interaction benefits both the orchid and the bee. The orchid gets pollinated, ensuring its reproduction, while the bee collects nectar, which it uses as a food source.

24. (*a*) The logistic growth model describes how a population grows in an environment with limited resources. A population growing in these habitats show initially a lag phase, followed by phases of acceleration (exponential) and deceleration and finally an asymptote.

25. (*b*) A declining population pyramid is a population age pyramid that is narrowed at the bottom and wider at the top. A narrow base and broader top indicate fewer young individuals and more older individuals, respectively.

Chapter Break Thru

1. (*b*) Statement in option (b) is incorrect. It can be corrected as
Tundra include treeless regions found in the Arctic and the tops of mountains. It is cold and windy and rainfall is scanty. Tundra lands are covered with snow for most of the year, but summer brings bursts of wildflower.

2. (*b*) The correct levels of organisation of ecology is I, III, and IV.
The basic levels of organisation in ecology include organisms (individual living entities), populations (groups of individuals of the same species living in an area), and communities (different species living together in an area). The incorrect ones can be corrected as
Species is a taxonomical classification level, not an organisational level, and humans are not a separate level in ecological organisation.

3. (*d*) A, B and C denote desert grassland and tropical forest respectively.
In the given graph, the biomes are identified based on their mean annual temperature and mean annual precipitation.
Here are the identifications.
Desert (A) is characterised by low precipitation (typically less than 50 cm annually) and can have a wide range of temperatures.
Grassland (B) Moderate precipitation and temperature.
Tropical forest (C) High precipitation (usually more than 200 cm annually) and high temperature.

4. (*b*) Microclimate can be defined as local variations of a climate that occurs in an area of limited size.
Microclimate is the effective climate upon which life of an organism depends. An interesting example of microclimate is the desert animal's burrows, in which the physical conditions are very much different from those of the region as a whole.

5. (*d*) Niche is an ecological component of habitat which is delimited by functioning of an organism. A species may live in more than one niche at different stages of its life cycle.

6. (*b*) Grasses predominate in the Savannah due to the presence of fewer number of herbivores there. Overgrazing that occurs due to herbivores gets minimised and growth of grasses increases.

7. (*d*) Under unfavorable conditions, many zooplankton species in lakes and ponds enter a stage of diapause. This response to the situation is an example of suspend. Other options can be explained as:
Diapause is a suspension of development and metabolic activity to survive adverse conditions.
Regulate refers to maintaining the internal stability despite external changes. Conform means adjusting to external conditions, and migrate involves moving to a different location.

8. (*d*) Statement I is correct, but statement II is incorrect. The incorrect statement II can be corrected as
All birds, mammals, few lower vertebrates and invertebrates are endotherms as they maintain constant inner body temperature.

9. (*c*) Some organisms are unable to migrate so they avoid stress by escaping in time. These organisms suspend their metabolic functions during the stressful period and resume their functions at the return of favourable conditions. For example, bear undergoes winter sleep called hibernation and certain animals like snails and fish undergo summer sleep known as aestivation.

10. (*c*) Desert lizard lack the physiological ability that mammals have to deal with the high temperatures of their habitat, but they manage to keep body temperature fairly constant.
They bask in sun and absorb heat when the temperature drops below comfort zone, but move into shade when the ambient temperature starts increasing. This is an example of adaptation.

11. (*a*) In a stable population, younger population (or pre-reproductive individuals) and reproductive individuals are nearly equal in number. Reproductive individuals are less than post-reproductive in declining population.
Pre-reproductive individuals are more than the reproductive individuals in expanding population.

12. (*d*) The initial population of *Paramoecium* is 50, and it increases to 150 after an hour. The growth in population is 150 - 50 = 100 individuals per hour. So, the growth rate is 100 per hour. The birth rate per individual per hour is calculated as: 100/50 = 2. Therefore, the growth rate will be 100 per individual per hour, and the birth rate is 2 per individual per hours.

13. (*c*) N_0 is the initial population of the bird, B is the total births. D is the total death, I is the immigration of birds and E is the emigration of birds. B and I increase the population and D and E are responsible for decrease in population.
Hence, the population after time 't' will be
$N_t = N_0 + [(B+I)-(D+E)]$

14. (*a*) Based on the given situation, it can be concluded that the number of deaths is more than the number of birth. Hence, this condition shows declining population as shown in graph (a).

15. (*b*) All the statements are connected to predation except option (b). It can be corrected as
In predation, one species is negatively impacted and other is completely benefitted. Predators also help to maintain species diversity in a community, by reducing the intensity of competition among competing prey species.

16. (*a*) The correct matches are A-2, B-3, C-4, D-1.
- *Cuscuta*, an ectoparasitic plant that is commonly found growing on hedge plants.
- Endoparasites live inside the host body at different sites (liver, kidney, lungs, red blood cells, etc.). Liver fluke is an example of endoparasite.
- Brood parasitism is found in some birds in which the parasitic bird lays its eggs in the nest of its host and lets the host incubate them. Cuckoo lays its egg in crow's nest.

- In obligate parasites, parasitism is the only way of nutrition and multiplication. Virus is the intracellular obligate parasite.

17. (*c*) The given example is observed under mutualism. In such an interaction, both the species involved, mutually benefit each other. As seen in this case, sea anemone protects the clown fish from predators by hiding it under its tentacles and in return, the clown fish keeps the anemone free of parasite and also helps to oxygenate the anemone.

18. (*b*) Both statement I and statement II are correct. Resource partitioning is a mechanism to avoid competition between the species competing for the same resource under which they choose different times for feeding or different foraging pattern.
Competitive release occurs when a species whose distribution is restricted to a small geographical area because of the presence of a competitively superior species, is found to expand its distributional range dramatically when the competing species is experimentally removed.

19. (*d*) In competition, both the species are harmed. Two species which depend on the same resource and live in the same area, would be competing with one another.

20. (*c*) The introduction of goats that resulted in the exclusion of Abingdon tortoise from Galapagos islands is an example of competition exclusion. It states two closely related species competing for the same resources cannot co-exist indefinitely and the competitively inferior one will be essentially eliminated.

21. (*d*) The image depicts a bee and an orchid, highlighting sexual deceit and pseudocopulation, where the orchid mimics a female bee to attract male bees for pollination, illustrating coevolution. Sexual dimorphism is not related to this interaction.

22. (*a*) Statements II and III are correct. Statements I and IV are incorrect and can be corrected as

- A habitat of an organism is dependent on the physico-chemical (abiotic) as well as the biotic components.
- A person can accompolish homeostasis through artificial means, not physiological means when she is using AC to cool herself/himself.

23. (*a*) Option (a) is incorrect regarding Allen's rule. Allen's rule states that mammals in colder climates have shorter limbs to minimize heat loss, which is related to adaptation and helps explain the distribution of organisms in polar regions.
The rule states that the body surface area-volume ratio of endothermic animals tends to vary with the average temperature of their habitat.

24. (*d*) The incorrect match pair can be corrected as
"Suspend" typically refers to organisms entering a state like hibernation or dormancy to escape stressful times, not space. Other Matches are correct as they align with the definitions of thermoregulation and behavioural adaptations.

25. (*b*) Enhanced medical care reduces mortality rates and improves life expectancy, directly increasing the population.
Availability of more space is less impactful alone. The Green Revolution increases food supply, indirectly supporting population growth. High immigration rates boost up population but depend on the receiving region's capacity.

26. (*a*) Niche is different from habitat because it is species specific, i.e. Niche is specific to a particular species which may overlap with a similar niche, but must have distinct differences.

27. (*d*) Population growth is influenced by the age structure because different age groups have varying reproductive capabilities. Younger and middle-aged individuals are typically more reproductive than older ones, significantly affecting the overall growth rate.

28. (*d*) A is true, but R is false. R can be corrected as
The logistic growth model is more realistic because it considers the environmental limits, i.e. density, food, resting place, sickness, parasites, competition, etc. It represents that resources are finite and become limiting sooner or later.

29. (*a*) Statement I is incorrect, but statement II is correct. Statement I can be corrected as
Gause's principle of competitive exclusion states that no two species can occupy the same niche indefinitely for the same limiting resources.

30. (*b*) Statements I, II, III and V are correct, statement IV is not correct, it can be corrected as
Cannibalism is competition within a species, i.e. intra-specific. It is actually quite common in both aquatic and terrestrial food webs. It often occurs when food resources is scarce, forcing organisms of the same species to feed on each other.

Ch-12 Ecosystem

Topical Follow Thru

Test 1

1. (*d*) Catabolism refers to the enzymatic breakdown of complex organic molecules into simpler ones, releasing energy and resulting in simpler compounds and inorganic substances. This is the correct term for the enzymatic conversion process during decomposition. It occurs simultaneously with the processes such as fragmentation and teaching occurring on the detritus.

2. (*d*) The incorrect statement can be corrected as

Secondary productivity is the rate of synthesis of new organic matter by consumers. It is small and decreases with rise of trophic level. Secondary productivity is due to assimilation of food energy at consumer's trophic level.

3. (*c*) The correct order of strata from top to bottom in a tropical rainforest is:

Emergent (III) → Canopy (II) → Understorey (I) → Shrub (V) → Forest floor (IV)

4. (*a*) Statement I is incorrect, but statement II is correct. The incorrect statement can be corrected as

Detritus (organic matter) typically undergoes fragmentation (physical breakdown into smaller pieces) by mechanical actions of organisms like detritivores (e.g. earthworms), rather than becoming pulverized in the digestive tract of animals.

5. (*b*) Statement III and IV are incorrect and can be corrected as:

- Maximum species composition is seen in the tropical rain forests and coral reef, whereas minimum occurs in desert.
- Maximum stratification of plant species can be seen in tropical rain forests. Grasslands possess lesser strata of plant species.

6. (*d*) Statements II and V are incorrect and can be corrected as

- Pond, as an aquatic ecosystem is fairly a self-sustainable unit.
- Flagellates represent the decomposers in pond ecosystem along with bacteria and fungi and are especially abundant at the bottom of the pond.

7. (*b*) The correct order of decomposition process is

Fragmentation → Leaching → Humification → Mineralisation

Fragmentation : This is the physical breakdown of organic matter into smaller pieces by organisms like detritivores (e.g. earthworms) or through physical processes.

Leaching : This involves the loss of soluble nutrients from the decomposing material due to the percolation of water through the soil or organic matter.

Mineralisation : This is the breakdown of organic matter into inorganic forms (minerals) by microbial action, releasing nutrients like nitrogen, phosphorus and potassium into the soil.

Humification : This is the formation of humus, a dark, organic substance remaining after decomposition, which enriches the soil and improves its structure.

8. (*c*) Both A and R are true, but R is not the correct explanation of A. A can be explained as

Some of the energy expended by plants in respiration (R) reduces the amount of biomass available for higher trophic levels. Hence, Gross Primary Productivity (GPP) is always greater than Net Primary Productivity (NPP) in ecosystems.

9. (*c*) Both statement I and statement II are incorrect. They can be corrected as

While herbivores are the primary consumers of NPP, decomposers can also access some NPP indirectly through dead plant material and litter. Secondary productivity refers to the production of new organic matter by consumers (herbivores and carnivores), not the available organic matter for decomposers. Decomposers primarily utilise NPP and the remains of consumers (dead organic matter).

10. (*d*) Leaching removes water-soluble inorganic nutrients (essential for plants) from the topsoil, making them unavailable for plant uptake.

11. (*c*) The incorrect statement can be corrected as

Litter can decompose further into usable nutrients for plants. It is not directly consumable as food by most plants. They rely on decomposers to break it down first.

12. (*a*) The humus is further degraded by some microbes and release of inorganic nutrients occurs by the process known as mineralisation.

13. (*c*) The rate of decomposition is slower if detritus is rich in lignin. Lignin is a complex organic polymer found in the cell walls of plants, making it more resistant to breakdown.

14. (*c*) The incorrect statement can be corrected as

Marine ecosystems actually cover about 70% of the Earth's surface, not less than 50%.

15. (*a*) Abiotic components in an ecosystem refer to non-living factors that influence the environment. They include physical and chemical factors such as sunlight, temperature, water, soil, air, and nutrients.

16. (*c*) An ecosystem is a functional unit of nature where living organisms interact with each other and their physical environment. Aquariums are examples of man-made ecosystems where both living organisms (fish, plants) and non-living components (water, rocks) interact. Since an aquarium involves water as its primary medium, it is classified as an aquatic ecosystem. However, because it is constructed and maintained by humans, it is categorised as a man-made aquatic ecosystem.

17. (*b*) Both statement I and statement II are correct.

Primary productivity depends on variety of environmental factors, availability of nutrients and photosynthetic capacity of plants along with plant species inhabiting a particular area. Therefore, it varies in different types of ecosystems.

18. (*c*) Autotrophs, such as phytoplankton, algae, and aquatic plants, are responsible for converting inorganic materials into organic materials using sunlight through the process of photosynthesis. Consumers feed on autotrophs, while decomposers break down organic matter, and abiotic components refer to non-living factors like water and soil.

19. (*c*) Fungi, along with bacteria and certain flagellates, are the decomposers in the pond ecosystem. They break down dead organic matter, which is crucial for nutrient cycling and the overall functioning of the ecosystem.

20. (*b*) Net Primary Productivity (NPP) is calculated using the formula, NPP = GPP – R, where GPP is the gross primary productivity and R is the respiration losses.

So, NPP = 6000 kcal m^{-2} yr^{-1} – 2000 kcal m^{-2} yr^{-1} = 4000 kcal m^{-2} yr^{-1}

21. (*a*) The correct matches are A- 2, B- 1, C- 3, D- 4.

- Fragmentation involves breaking down detritus into smaller particles by detritivores.
- Catabolism is the process where bacterial and fungal enzymes degrade detritus into simpler inorganic substances.
- Humification leads to the accumulation of humus, a dark-coloured amorphous substance resistant to microbial action.
- Mineralisation is the release of inorganic nutrients from humus by microbial action.

22. (*d*) Gross Primary Productivity (GPP) refers to the total amount of organic matter produced by plants during photosynthesis, before accounting for the energy used in respiration. Net Primary Productivity (NPP) is derived from GPP by subtracting respiration losses (R). Productivity generally refers to the rate of biomass production, but is not specific to gross or net measures.

23. (*c*) Decomposition is favoured by warm and moist conditions, but inhibited by low temperatures and anaerobiosis. In a forest area with low temperatures and high soil moisture, the low temperatures would inhibit decomposition despite the high moisture. Therefore, you would expect slowed decomposition in these conditions.

24. (*a*) Continental shelf is the seabed from the shore to the edge of the continental slope, covered by relatively shallow seas and gulfs. Generally, it is one of the most productive parts of the ocean due to presence of benthic coastal animals, kelp forests and the light availability.

25. (*b*) Fragmentation breaks down the waste into smaller particles. Humification converts these particles into dark, nutrient-rich humus.

Test 2

1. (*c*) An ecological pyramid may be upright, inverted and spindle-shaped. Producers occupy the base of the pyramid, consumers in the middle and top position is occupied by top consumers in all pyramids, except in parasitic food chain where parasites are at the apex. The term "spindle-shaped" is used to describe pyramids where the middle trophic levels are wider than the base or top. This accurately describes the possible shapes of ecological pyramids.

2. (*c*) In a parasitic ecosystem, the pyramid of number is typically inverted because a single host organism can support many parasites, and each parasite can support numerous hyperparasites.

Other pyramids are erect.

3. (*a*) Statement I is incorrect, but statement II is correct. The incorrect statement can be corrected as

In ecological pyramids, saprophytes are not given any place even though they play a vital role in the ecosystem.

4. (*b*) The correct sequence of organism in a food chain according to their trophic level is : Grass (T_1) → Grasshopper (T_2) → Frog (T_3) → Snake (T_4) → Eagle (T_5). Grass represents the first trophic level, which is eaten by 2nd trophic level organisms, e.g. grasshopper, followed by 3rd trophic level organisms, e.g. frog, then snake represents the fourth trophic level and eagle represents the fifth trophic level.

5. (*a*) Phytoplanktons are primary producers in aquatic ecosystems. They convert solar energy into biomass through photosynthesis and form the base of the food web. Due to their primary producer role and their high reproduction rates, they generally have a high total biomass.

6. (*d*) Plants capture only a small fraction of the Photosynthetically Active Radiation (PAR). This small fraction is the energy is used by plants for photosynthesis. Typically, this percentage ranges from 2-10%.

7. (*d*) Energy flow through ecosystems helps maintain organisation and order, counteracting the natural tendency of systems to increase entropy (disorder). Energy is essential for various biochemical processes within organisms, including the synthesis of complex molecules such as proteins, carbohydrates, and lipids.

Therefore, ecosystems require a continuous supply of energy, primarily both to maintain order and to support biochemical processes such as molecule synthesis.

8. (*a*) The correct matches are A-2, B-3, C-4, D-1.

Phytoplanktons are producers and are types of plants or plant-like organisms.

Wolf is a secondary consumer and a typical carnivore.

Cow is a primary consumer and a typical herbivore.

Lion is at the top of the food chain as a tertiary consumer.

9. (*b*) Energy flow in an ecosystem is unidirectional. While there are cycles of nutrients within an ecosystem, where energy is not recycled. It enters as sunlight and flows through the food chain, with some lost as heat at each transfer between trophic levels. Energy flow follows the first law of thermodynamics as the solar energy is transformed from one form to another.

10. (*c*) The given pyramid is the pyramid of biomass that shows a sharp decrease in biomass at higher trophic levels.

11. (*b*) The food chain in which microorganism breaks down the compounds synthesised by the producers is called detritus food chain.

12. (*c*) The correct matching of both the lists is A-ii, B-iii, C-iv, D-i.

- Vulture is a top carnivore and thus occupies fourth trophic level.
- Rabbit is a herbivore and thus occupies second trophic level.
- Grass is producer and thus occupies the first trophic level.
- Crow is a carnivore and thus occupies third trophic level.

13. (*b*) Energy pyramids are used to represent the energy transfer in an ecosystem to illustrate how energy flows through different trophic levels. At each trophic level, a significant portion of energy is lost, primarily as heat due to metabolic processes, and only a small fraction of energy is transferred to the next level.

14. (*b*) Both A and R are true and R is the correct explanation of A.

The primary reason why the number of organisms decreases at higher trophic levels is due to the limited transfer of energy from lower to higher trophic levels. This limited transfer is directly related to the availability of biomass and energy at each level.

15. (*b*) The frog, which feeds on insects, does not consume plants (producers) directly. Instead, it consumes organisms (insects) that are primary consumers (herbivores), as insects typically feed on plants. Therefore, the frog occupies the secondary consumer trophic level in this food chain.

16. (*b*) Both statement I and statement II are correct.

Plants indeed capture only a small fraction (2-10%) of PAR, which is crucial for sustaining life on Earth. Ecosystems follow First Law of Thermodynamics, where energy transformations occur, but total energy is conserved.

17. (*c*) Producers, also known as autotrophs, are organisms that produce their own food through processes like photosynthesis. In terrestrial ecosystems, these are primarily herbaceous and woody plants, while in aquatic ecosystems, they include phytoplanktons, algae, and higher plants.

18. (*b*) An increase in the goat population means more grazing on grass, which would likely lead to a decrease in the grass population due to higher consumption rates.

19. (*b*) Primary consumers are herbivores that directly consume producers (plants). Secondary consumers feed on primary consumers, thus they are carnivores or omnivores that get their energy by eating animals that have already eaten plants.

20. (*c*) Both A and R are true, but R is not the correct explanation of A.

It can be explained as

In aquatic ecosystems, the GFC is the major conduit for energy flow because in an aquatic ecosystem, decomposition is very less.

21. (*a*) If only 10 percent of the energy is transferred at each trophic level, the energy available to the fox (secondary consumer) from the grass (producer) is 1% of the initial energy (100%).

22. (*a*) Fresh weight measurements are affected by the moisture content of organisms, which can vary and lead to inaccuracies. Dry weight measurements are more reliable as they account for this variability.

23. (*c*) In marine ecosystems, the pyramid of biomass is inverted because the biomass of fishes is much higher than that of phytoplanktons.

24. (*c*) Ecological pyramids do not include saprophytes, despite their crucial role in decomposing organic matter and recycling nutrients in ecosystems.

25. (*b*) In a forest ecosystem where trees have higher biomass than herbivores, the pyramid of biomass would be upright, with producers (trees) having more biomass than the herbivores.

Chapter Break Thru

1. (*b*) Low temperature slows down the process of decomposition. If detritus is rich in nitrogen and water-soluble substances like sugars, the process of decomposition become quick.

2. (*d*) The pyramid of number and biomass can be erect or inverted, but the pyramid of energy is always erect.

3. (*d*) Leaching is the process where water-soluble nutrients are washed down through the soil layers by rainfall or irrigation, eventually accumulating in lower soil horizons where they can precipitate as less soluble salts, becoming unavailable for plants.

4. (*c*) Earth comprises multiple ecosystems (terrestrial, aquatic, etc.) interacting globally, but the entire planet itself is not considered an ecosystem due to its scale and complexity. Therefore, Earth could not be considered as an ecosystem.

5. (*b*) Primary productivity is the rate at which producers (plants, algae, etc.) convert solar energy into chemical energy in the form of organic matter. Factors like plant species inhabiting that area, nutrient availability and photosynthetic capacity, directly affect this process. However, the rate at which consumers (herbivores, carnivores) form new organic matter does not directly affect the primary productivity of producers.

6. (*d*) Gross Primary Productivity (GPP) represents the total amount of energy captured via photosynthesis by producers. However, not all of this energy is available to heterotrophs (consumers). The producers themselves use a portion of the GPP for respiration. The energy or biomass that remains after subtracting the energy used for respiration is called Net Primary Productivity (NPP), which is the actual available biomass for consumption by heterotrophs.

7. (*c*) Both A and R are true, but R is not the correct explanation of A. It can be explained as:

A biotic community consists of populations of various species living in a specific area and interacting with each other. In a biotic community, species interact in a way that sustains the community, and there is a continuous flow of energy as organisms consume food and release energy through metabolic processes.

8. (*c*) Pyramids shown in A and C figures represent the pyramid of numbers in a single large tree ecosystem. It occurs in ecosystems where a single large producer supports a larger number of consumers. One large tree (producer) can provide food for many insects, birds and small mammals (consumers) at various trophic levels.

9. (*d*) Decomposers, such as bacteria and fungi, are essential for the recycling of nutrients in ecosystems. They break down dead organisms and organic waste, converting complex organic compounds into simpler inorganic compounds. This process releases nutrients back into the soil or water, making them available for uptake by producers (plants and other autotrophs), thus maintaining the cycle of matter in the ecosystem.

10. (*a*) Maggots, millipedes, slugs and earthworms comprise organisms that are all known to feed on dead organic matter and play a role in the decomposition process, making them detritivores. The other options include organisms that do not fit the definition of detritivores.

11. (*b*) The order -Producers → Primary consumers → Secondary consumers□ → Tertiary consumers → Decomposers correctly follows the typical flow of energy through an ecosystem, from producers to various levels of consumers and finally to decomposers.

12. (*a*) The ocean ecosystem, particularly areas with high sunlight penetration, supports an immense number of phytoplanktons, which are the primary producers. These tiny organisms form the foundation of the marine food web and are present in vast quantities, far surpassing the number of producers found in the other ecosystems listed.

13. (*b*) In a cropland ecosystem, earthworms are detritivores. They play a crucial role in decomposing dead organic matter, enriching the soil with nutrients and aiding in the process of nutrient cycling.

14. (*b*) In humid tropical regions, the warm temperatures and high humidity create optimal conditions for decomposers to break down detritus rapidly. This results in the complete decomposition of detritus within about three to four months, which is significantly faster than in tundra, desert, or temperate regions.

15. (*c*) According to ten per cent law of energy (given by Lindemann, 1942), only 10% of energy is transferred from one trophic level to the next. If producer has an energy value of 7000J, then the energy available for secondary consumers will be 70J as explained as follows

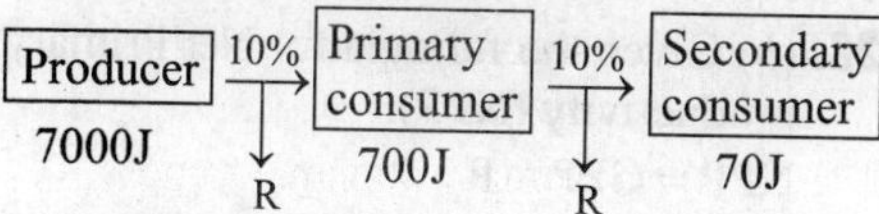

16. (*a*) Statement I is incorrect, but statement II is correct. The incorrect statement can be corrected as

In fact, a food web increases the adaptability and competitiveness of organisms because it provides multiple pathways for energy flow and nutrient cycling. This diversity in food sources and interactions allows organisms to adapt to changes in their environment more effectively and enhances their ability to compete for resources.

17. (*c*) The standing crop specifically refers to the total biomass or the number of organisms in a particular area at a specific time. It represents the current amount of living material present in the ecosystem, which aligns with the given definition.

18. (*b*) Both A and R are true and R is the correct explaination of A. Being colloidal in nature, humus serves as reservoir of nutrients.

19. (*a*) Species III and VI represents the secondary consumers.

Snake and lizard are considered as secondary consumers as they depend on the mouse and grasshopper respectively, for their food requirements. Hawk (VIII) can be considered either secondary or tertiary consumer depending the food chain.

20. (*b*) The incorrect statement can be corrected as

It is not DFC, but GFC that is the major conduit for energy flow in the aquatic ecosystem.

21. (*b*) In a forest, few trees support many primary consumers, mostly insects. Thus, the pyramid of number is inverted or spindle shaped i.e. upright pyramid is absent in forest ecosystem. Other cases of inverted pyramids of number can be seen in the case of a single tree or a parasitic food chain.

22. (*b*) Given the formula for Net Primary productivity (NPP),
NPP = GPP – R
Substituting the given values
NPP =
150 kcal $m^{-2} yr^{-1}$ – 50 kcal m^{-2} yr^{-1}
NPP = 100 kcal m^{-2} yr^{-1}
Therefore, the correct answer is 100 kcal m^{-2} yr^{-1}.

23. (*b*) Both Statement I and statement II are correct.
Decomposers are indeed abundant in aquatic environments like ponds and are essential for breaking down dead organic matter, which releases nutrients back into the ecosystem.
Ecosystems function through processes that include the conversion of inorganic to organic material *via* photosynthesis by autotrophs, consumption of these autotrophs by heterotrophs and the decomposition of organic matter by decomposers, which recycles nutrients back into the system.

24. (*b*) Both A and R are true and R is the correct explanation of A.
The pyramid of biomass in marine ecosystems is generally inverted, with a smaller biomass of producers (phytoplankton) supporting a larger biomass of consumers (fish). Thus, the biomass of fish often exceeds the biomass of phytoplankton.

25. (*a*) Statements I, II, III and V are correct. Statement IV is incorrect and can be corrected as
The pyramid of energy is based on the flow of energy through trophic levels over time, not on productivity (which refers to the rate of biomass production).

26. (*c*) Both A and R are true, but R is not the correct explanation of A. A can be explained as:
There is a generally a positive correlation between primary productivity (amount of organic matter produced by producers) and solar radiation. Plants need sunlight for photosynthesis. Higher levels of solar radiation provide more energy for photosynthesis, leading to potentially greater primary productivity.

27. (*a*) The correct matches are A-2, B-3, C-1, D-4.
Ecological pyramids do not consider the existence of the same species at different levels.
Food web defines the energy flow and predator-prey relationship.
Mineralisation involves degradation of humus by microbes and release of inorganic nutrients.
Inverted pyramid has narrowed base which gradually broadens towards the tip.

28. (*b*) Both A and R are true and R is the correct explanation of A.
The flow of energy in an ecosystem is indeed unidirectional, moving from producers forming a sequential pathway through the ecosystem to consumers and then to the decomposers.

29. (*b*) Both statement I and statement II are correct.
The second law of thermodynamics states that in any energy transfer or transformation, some energy is lost as unusable heat. This applies to the flow of energy in ecosystems as well, where energy is transferred from one organism to another and eventually lost as heat during metabolism and other processes.
When energy is transferred between trophic levels in an ecosystem, a significant amount of energy is lost at each transfer as heat due to metabolic processes and other inefficiencies. This phenomenon is a direct consequence of the second law of thermodynamics.

30. (*d*) Statement I is correct, but statement II is incorrect. The incorrect statement can be corrected as
Natural ecosystems typically exhibit high biodiversity, meaning they contain a wide variety of species occupying different niches and roles within the ecosystem. Biodiversity is a hallmark of natural ecosystems, contributing to their stability, resilience and overall functioning.

Ch-13 Biodiversity and Conservation

Topical Follow Thru

Test 1

1. (b) All of the options related to genetic diversity are correct except (b) which can be explained as
The Western Ghats having a greater amphibian species diversity than the Eastern Ghats, represent the species diversity. The genetic diversity is the product of recombination of genetic material in the process of inheritance. It changes with time and space.

2. (a) India is one of the 12 mega diversity countries recognized globally for its rich biodiversity.
The other options are incorrect and can be corrected as
Animal species constitute more than 70% of total species.
Fish species do not outnumber all the other vertebrates combined.
India possesses about 8% of global species diversity, while covering 2.4% of the world's land area.

3. (c) Robert May estimated global species diversity at about 7 million. Although some other scientists estimate its range from 20-50 million.

4. (b) The correct matches are A-4, B-3, C-1, D-2.
   - In general, species diversity decreases as we move away from the equator towards the poles. Colombia, located near the equator, has nearly 1,400 species of birds.
   - New York at 41° N has 105 bird species.
   - Greenland at 71° N has only 56 species of birds.
   - India, with much of its land area in the tropical latitudes, has more than 1,200 species of birds.

5. (d) Statement I is correct, but statement II is incorrect. The incorrect statement can be corrected as
   The completion rate of species inventories is higher in temperate regions than in the tropical. This is due to the presence of higher biodiversity in tropical regions than in temperate regions.

6. (b) Alexander von Humboldt was a German naturalist and geographer. He proposed that within a region, species richness increases with increasing explored area, but only up to a limit.
   Accordingly, the relation between species richness and area for a wide variety of taxa turns out to be rectangular hyperbola. The relationship appears as a straight line on logarithmic scale and is described by the given equation
   $\log S = \log C + Z \log A$
   Where, S–Species richness,
   A–Area,
   Z–Regression coefficient,
   C–Y-Intercept.

7. (b) The relation between species richness and area, for a wide variety of taxa, i.e. angiosperms, birds, bats, fresh water fishes turns out to be rectangular hyperbola as shown in the following graph.

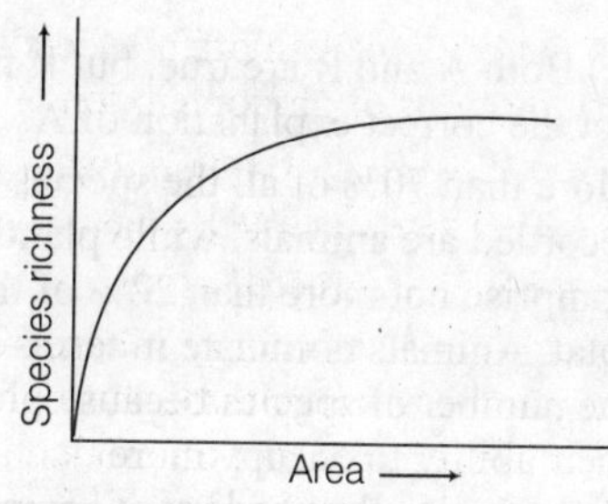

8. (c) Both A and R are true, but R is not the correct explanation of A. A can be explained as
   Biodiversity is indeed greater in lower latitudes compared to higher latitudes due to more favourable climatic conditions in the lower latitudes.

9. (c) The rivet-popper hypothesis suggests that losing key species is like removing rivets from the wings of an airplane causing serious threat to the ecosystem. This highlights the critical role of key species in maintaining ecosystem functions.

10. (b) The taxonomic groups that occupies the largest and the least area of the pie chart representing the global diversity of invertebrates comprises insects and crustaceans respectively.
   This is consistent with general biological knowledge, as insects are the most diverse group of animals on Earth, comprising a significant portion of invertebrate species.

11. (d) For Frugivorous birds and mammals in the tropical forests of different continents, the slope of line is found to be 1.15.

12. (d) Tropical regions have larger human populations, leading to more significant habitat modification and species conservation. This option is unrelated to the reasons for high biodiversity in the tropics. While the other options highlight factors that promote biodiversity.

13. (c) Biodiversity hotspots are typically characterised by a large number of species, including many endemic species, and are mostly located in the tropical regions.
   The polar regions, which have harsh climates and lower species diversity, do not fit this description.

14. (a) A is false, but R is true. A can be corrected as
   Polar regions have lesser species diversity than equator. Species diversity decreases as we move away from the equator towards the poles.

15. (c) Statements II and III are correct. The incorrect statements can be corrected as
   - Amazonian forest is home to lesser species of birds (1300) than Colombia (1400).
   - Various types of orchids in a tropical forest represent species diversity.

16. (c) Biological organisation of biodiversity includes molecular level, ecosystem level and individual organism level. The social organisation pertains more to social organisation and behaviour within species rather than the biological diversity.

17. (a) Edward Wilson popularised the term biodiversity at multiple levels of biological organisation. This includes diversity within species, between species and across ecosystems. Biodiversity covers the entire spectrum of biological diversity from the smallest genetic variations to the complex ecosystems.

18. (b) Global climate change is expected to have significant impacts on biodiversity, particularly in tropical regions. The extreme weather conditions such as more droughts and temperature fluctuations are likely to disrupt stable conditions that have allowed tropical regions to maintain high diversity.
   These conditions lead to habitat loss, reduced food causing a decrease in biodiversity.

19. (*a*) The Amazonian rainforest is known for its extraordinary biodiversity, which is largely due to its location near the equator. This proximity to the equator provides the Amazon with stable, warm temperatures and high levels of sunlight throughout the year, which are crucial factors for high primary productivity.

20. (*b*) Both statement I and statement II are correct.
India accounts for only 2.4% of the world's land area, it holds an impressive 8.1% global species diversity. May's global estimates suggest that only 22% of the world's species have been documented so far.

21. (*c*) David Tilman's experiments indicate that ecosystem with greater species richness tend to have less year to year variation in total biomass, implying more stability. This suggests that ecosystems with more species are better able to maintain consistent productivity.

22. (*b*) The concern about species extinction leading to a less functional ecosystem is based on the idea that each species plays a unique and important role in the ecosystem. This role could involve contributing to biodiversity, maintaining balance among species, aiding in nutrient cycling, pollination etc.

23. (*c*) The slope (Z) in the species-area relationship equation indicates how species richness increases as the area being studied increases. For smaller regions or areas, the Z value typically ranges from 0.1 to 0.2. For larger areas, such as entire continents, the Z value is much steeper, ranging from 0.6 to 1.2.

24. (*d*) India with its deserts, rainforests, mangroves, coral reefs, wetlands, estuaries and alpine meadows has a greater ecosystem diversity than a Scandinavian country like Norway. This type of diversity, present at the ecosystem level, represents ecological diversity.

25. (*c*) Both A and R are true, but R is not the correct explanation of A.
More than 70% of all the species recorded are animals, while plants comprise not more than 22% of the total. Animals dominate in terms of the number of species because of their ability to occupy more ecological niches and more complex evolutionary pathways.

Test 2

1. (b) Quagga – America is mismatched.
Quagga belonged to Africa not America.

2. (b) The extinction of the passenger pigeon, dodo, and Steller's sea cow was primarily due to over-exploitation by humans. Intense hunting and exploitation for food, feathers, and other resources led to their rapid decline. Although habitat loss and fragmentation also contributed to it, human activities were the main driving force behind their extinction, overshadowing factors like body size or population size.

3. (a) Endemic species are those species which are confined to a particular region and not found anywhere else. For example, species of Western Ghats.
Vulnerable and threatened species are the species which face high risk of extinction.
Keystone species are the species whose presence or absence significantly affects other species in an ecosystem.

4. (d) Option (d) is incorrect statement and can be corrected as
Amphibians appear to be more vulnerable to extinction.

5. (d) Option (d) is incorrect can be corrected as
If present trends continue, nearly half of all the species on earth might be wiped out within the next 100 years. The rapid acceleration of extinction rates due to human activities suggests a much shorter timeline for this drastic loss of biodiversity.

6. (d) Madagascar and the Indian Ocean Islands are not found in India. The Western Ghats and Sri Lanka, Indo-Burma, and the Himalayas are all the recognized biodiversity hotspots that include regions within India. Madagascar and the Indian Ocean Islands, however, are geographically separated and located off the southeastern coast of Africa, making them distinct from India's hotspots.

7. (d) The correct matches are A-4, B-3, C-1, D -2.
In many cultures, tracts of forest were set aside, and all the trees and wildlife within were venerated and given total protection. Such sacred groves are found in
- Aravalli Hills of Rajasthan
- Khasi and Jaintia Hills in Meghalaya,
- Western Ghat regions of Karnataka and Maharashtra, and
- Sarguja, Chanda and Bastar areas of Madhya Pradesh.

8. (d) National parks are not a method of *ex situ* conservation. These are sites of protecting an endangered plant or animal species in its natural habitat, i.e. *in situ* method. *Ex situ* conservation literally means, "off-site conservation" which is the process of protecting an endangered species, variety or breed, of plant or animal outside its natural habitat. For example, by removing part of the population from a threatened habitat and placing it in a new location, which may be a wild area or within the care of humans. For example, cryopreservation, micropropagation, *in-vitro* fertilisation, zoological parks, etc.

9. (d) *Ex situ* conservation involves maintenance and breeding of endangered plants and animals under partially or wholly controlled conditions in specific area. The different advantages of *ex-situ* conservation are

- It gives longer life time and breeding activity to animals.
- Genetic techniques can be utilised in the process.
- Captive breeding species can again be reintroduced in the wild.

It does not create competitiveness between the endangered species. On the other hand, *ex-situ* conservation provides less competition for food, water and space among the organisms.

10. (b) The "Evil Quartet" refers to the main causes of biodiversity loss: habitat loss and fragmentation, overexploitation, co-extinction, and alien species invasions. Population explosion is not included in this quartet. While population explosion contributes indirectly to biodiversity loss, it is not specifically a part of the "Evil Quartet."

11. (d) Bioprospecting is the exploration of molecular, genetic, and species-level diversity for novel products of economic importance. Other options can be corrected as

Biopiracy involves the unethical exploitation of biological resources. Bioenergetics studies energy flow in biological systems.

Bioremediation uses organisms to clean up pollutants.

12. (d) Statement I is correct, but statement II is incorrect. Statement II can be corrected as

The broadly utilitarian argument says that the biodiversity plays a major role in many ecosystem services that nature provides, e.g. oxygen supply, pollination, aesthetic pleasure, flood and erosion control. The aesthetic pleasure provided by biodiversity comes under the broadly utilisation.

13. (b) Both A and R are true and R is the correct explanation of A.

In National park, cultivation of land and grazing is not permitted. It is maintained by government and helps in betterment of wildlife. It includes protection of both flora and fauna.

14. (a) Statements I, II, III, and IV are correct. While statement V is incorrect and can be corrected as

The total number of biodiversity hotspots in the world is 34.

'Biodiversity hotspots' regions have very high levels of species richness and high degree of endemism (that is, species confined to that region and not found anywhere else).

15. (a) The Earth summit held in Rio de Janeiro in 1992 was called for the conservation of biodiversity and sustainable utilisation of its benefits. In this summit, more than 130 nations signed a convention on biodiversity and climate change.

16. (*a*) The IUCN Red List (2004) reports that 784 species have been documented as extinct over the past 500 years. This total includes a diverse range of species, encompassing 338 vertebrates, 359 invertebrates and 87 plants.

17. (*c*) Amphibians are a unique group of animals that live on every continent except for Antarctica.

Loads of amphibian species are threatened by extinction, and many of them are listed as endangered by IUCN. 32% of all amphibian species in the world face the threat of extinction.

18. (*a*) Statement (a) is correct. Rest statements are incorrect. They can be corrected as

The extinction threats vary across the different species groups. They do not all have the same level of threat.

Mammals are more threatened than birds.

Amphibians have the highest extinction threat.

19. (*a*) Habitat loss and fragmentation is the most important cause driving animals and plants to extinction. The most dramatic examples of habitat loss come from tropical rainforests. Once covering more than 14% of the earth's land surface, these rainforests now cover no more than 6%.

20. (*a*) Statement I is incorrect, but statement II is correct. Incorrect statement can be corrected as

Co-extinctions refer to the phenomenon where the extinction of a species leads to the extinction of other species that are closely associated with it, such as parasites or mutalistic partners.

21. (*d*) Broadly utilitarian arguments consider the importance of biodiversity for maintaining ecosystem services, which provide indirect benefits to humans beyond immediate economic uses.

22. (*b*) Sacred groves are forest areas that are protected and preserved primarily due to the cultural, religious or spiritual significance. These areas are often considered sacred by the local communities and are managed with great care to maintain their cultural value.

23. (*b*) The intangible benefits that we derive from nature is the aesthetic pleasures of walking through thick woods, watching spring flowers in full bloom or waking up to a bulbul's song in the morning.

24. (*c*) The convention on Biological Diversity, established at the Earth Summit in Rio de Janeiro in 1992, emphasises that biodiversity conservation is a global responsibility. This collective responsibility recognises that biodiversity transcends national borders and requires coordinated efforts from all countries to address the challenges of biodiversity.

25. (*c*) Biodiversity hotspots are characterised by two main features i.e., high levels of species richness and high degrees of endemism. Additionally, these areas often experience significant habitat loss, which threatens their biodiversity.

Chapter Break Thru

1. (c) Alexander von Humboldt was a great German naturalist and geographer. He did extensive explorations in the wilderness of South American forests. He established species-area relationship. He observed that within a region, species richness increases with increasing explored area, but upto a certain limit. Infact, the relationship between species richness and area for a variety of taxa turns out to be a rectangular hyperbola as shown in the figure below.

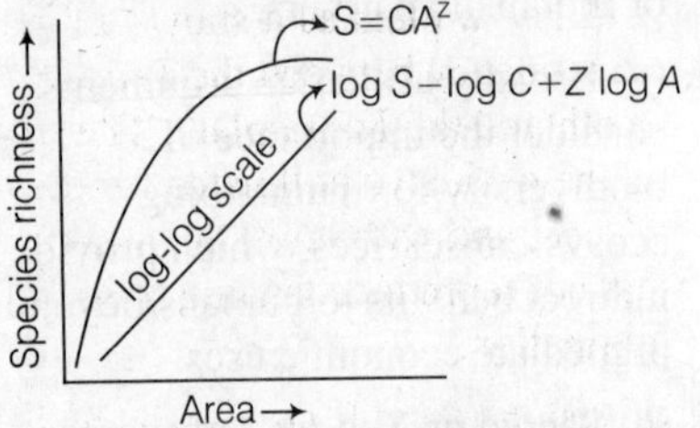

2. (b) The approximate number of species of ants, beetles and orchids are 20,000, 3,00,000 and 20,000 respectively. The planet earth is the home of millions of species.

3. (b) Statement of option (b) is incorrect. It can be corrected as: Among animals, insects are the most species-rich taxonomic group, making up more than 70 per cent of the total animal diversity. That means, out of every 10 animals on this planet, 7 are insects.

4. (b) Ecosystem diversity explains the diverse number of niches, trophic levels and various ecological processes that sustain energy flow, . food webs and recycling of nutrients within the geographical area. There may be variable number of ecosystems. The number of ecosystems or habitats present in a region is also a measure of biodiversity.

5. (c) The species-area relationship given by Alexander von Humboldt is represented by the equation $S = CA^z$ where,

S = species richness

Z = slope of regression (regression coefficient)

C = Y-intercept

A = Area

6. (d) The World Summit on Sustainable Development (WSSD) in 2002 was held in Johannesburg, South Africa. This significant event brought together world leaders, NGOs, and other stakeholders to discuss and promote sustainable development goals. The summit focused on various issues, including poverty eradication, sustainable consumption and production patterns, and the management of natural resources for economic and social development.

7. (b) Both statement I and II are correct. The colonisation of tropical Pacific Islands by humans resulted in the extinction of more than 2000 species of native birds.
David Tilman in his experiments showed that increased diversity contributed to higher productivity.

8. (c) Statements I, II, IV and V are correct. Statement III is incorrect and can be corrected as
The large tropical Amazonian rain forest in South America has the greatest biodiversity on earth.

9. (d) Habitat loss and fragmentation is the most important cause for animals and plants being driven to extinction. Due to habitat fragmentation and loss, around 14% of the earth land surface, rainforest has shrunk to only 6% in last few years. Fragmentation and loss of large habitats due to various human activities has badly affected mammals and birds requiring large territories. Certain animals with migratory habits are also affected by habitat loss and fragmentation.

10. (c) David Tilman conducted extensive research on biodiversity and ecosystem stability. His experiments demonstrated that communities with higher species diversity tend to be more resilient and stable, as they can better withstand environmental fluctuations and disturbances. This finding emphasizes the importance of biodiversity for maintaining ecosystem health and functionality.

11. (d) Decline in the population of Indian native fishes due to introduction of *Clarias gariepinus* in river Yamuna can be categorised as alien species invasions. It is posing a threat to the indigenous catfishes in our rivers and causing a loss of biodiversity.

12. (b) The Rivet Popper hypothesis, proposed by Paul Ehrlich, compares an ecosystem to an airplane held together by rivets (species). Just as removing too many rivets can cause an airplane to fail, the loss of key species, like honeybees, can lead to the collapse of ecosystem stability and function. Honeybees are vital pollinators, and their decline affects many plants and animals, illustrating this hypothesis.

13. (c) Pollination is not narrowly utilitarian argument based, but an ecosystem service benefitting broader ecological processes (broader utilitarian argument of biodiversity conservation) and supporting the entire ecosystem's health and productivity.
Other options represent narrowly utilitarian products as they are specific resources directly used by humans.

14. (b) Sacred groves is a mode of *in-situ* conservation in which forest fragments of varying size are protected by religious communities. It helps to protect the biota of that area on site.
On the other hand, botanical gardens, seed banks and wildlife safari parks are the examples of *ex situ* conservation in which the biota is protected outside its natural habitat.

15. (b) *Eichhornia crassipes*, (water hyacinth) was introduced in several tropical countries including India for ornamentation. But later, this exotic species became a troublesome aquatic weed. This free floating weed clogged rivers and lakes and threatened the survival of many native species to the point of extinction. This species was also called the 'Terror of Bengal' in India.

16. (a) The protected areas are biogeographical regions where biological diversity along with natural and cultural resources is protected, maintained and managed through legal or other effective measure. India has largest network of protected areas in the world.

17. (c) Many species of plants and animals are on the verge of extinction. Such creatures are conserved in the wildlife sanctuaries. Various sanctuaries have been developed, such as Bharatpur Bird Sanctuary, Rajasthan, established in 1956 to protect the indigenous and migratory bird species that frequently visited the region.

18. (a) Biosphere reserve consists of three zones, i.e., core, buffer and transition zone. Core zone comprises an undisturbed and legally protected ecosystem, where no human activity is allowed. Buffer zone surrounds the core area. Transition zone is the outermost area of the biosphere reserve, where active cooperation between reserve management and the local people occur.

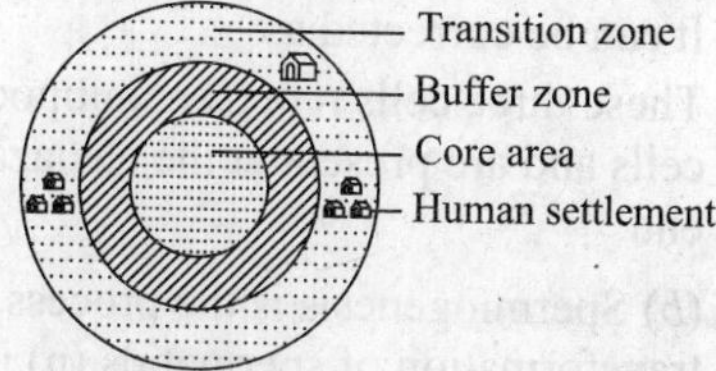

Zonation in terrestrial biosphere reserve

19. (b) *In-vitro* fertilisation, cryopreservation, and tissue culture are all *ex-situ* conservation methods, i.e. they involve conserving biological material outside their natural habitats. These techniques are used to preserve genetic material, propagate plants and animals, and assist in species survival and reproduction, often in controlled environments like laboratories and gene banks.

20. (b) Botanical garden is not a method of *in-situ* conservation of biodiversity. It is a type of *ex-situ* or off-site conservation in which rare plants are conserved in places outside their natural habitat.

Rest all are methods of *in-situ* conservation of biodiversity.

21. (a) Biologically diverse communities are also more likely to contain species that confer resilience to that ecosystem because as a community accumulates species, there is a higher chance of any one of them having traits that enable them to adapt to a changing environment. Such species could buffer the system against the loss of other species.

22. (b) Both statement I and statement II are correct.

Species diversity generally decreases as one moves from the equator towards the poles, with tropical regions hosting more species than temperate or polar areas.

Additionally, species diversity tends to decrease with increasing altitude, i.e. plains typically have higher species richness compared to hills.

23. (b) The slope of regression (Z) indicates that species richness increases with the increase in area. As shown in the graph, A is steeper than B, thus A shows more species richness than B. C shows the maximum species richness among A, B and C.

24. (b) Both A and R are true and R is the correct explanation of A.

A species may be considered endemic when a species is confined to only a single geographical area and not found anywhere else. Endemic species are unique to a particular geographical region. So, they are more vulnerable to extinction.

25. (b) Statements III, IV and V are incorrect and can be corrected as

- If the present trends continue, nearly half of all the species on earth might perish within the next 100 years.
- Earth faced mass extinctions long before humans appeared.
- Mass extinction is a well-documented concept with substantial evidence from the fossil record.

26. (b) The scenario that illustrates the concept of co-extinction is the relationship between *Pronuba* moth and *Yucca* plant as it shows a direct dependency between the *Pronuba* moth and the *Yucca* plant. The moth is the exclusive pollinator for the *Yucca*, and without it, the plant cannot reproduce leading to its extinction.

27. (b) Both A and R are correct and R is the correct explanation of A.

The species-area relationship is often described as a rectangular hyperbola. Species richness increases with increasing explored area, but upto a point.

28. (b) A species facing extremely high risk of extinction in the immediate future is called critically endangered (CR) species, e.g., Great Indian Bustard.

29. (c) The Earth Summit in Rio de Janeiro in 1992 aimed to address global environmental issues, specifically focusing on the conservation of biodiversity and the sustainable use of its benefits.

The summit resulted in the Convention on Biological Diversity, which urged nations to implement strategies for preserving biodiversity and ensuring that its use is sustainable, benefitting both the current and future generations.

30. (d) The incorrect match pair can be corrected as

Keystone species are typically those that have a disproportionately large effect on their environment relative to their abundance, often influencing the structure and function of an ecosystem, e.g. Tiger, elephant.

SPT1 Syllabus Part Thru 1

1. (*b*) The phenotypic and genotypic ratio of the progenies that exhibit incomplete dominance is 1 : 2 : 1. Therefore, of 1000 plants sampled from the progeny, 250 should be red flowered plants, 500 should be plant with flowers of intermediate colour, e.g. pink and 250 should be white flowered plants (1 : 2 : 1).

2. (*c*) Both statements I and II are incorrect. They can be corrected as:
The microsporangium is surrounded by four layer, i.e., the epidermis, endothecium, middle layer and tapetum.
Tapetum is the innermost wall layer of microsporangium.

3. (*a*) Statement I is incorrect, while statement II is correct. Incorrect statement can be corrected as
Infundibulum possesses finger-like projections called fimbriae which help in collection of the ovum after ovulation.

4. (*c*) Statements II, IV and V are correct. Statements I and III are incorrect. They can be corrected as
- Thymine is present only in DNA, not in RNA. In RNA, uracil is present instead of thymine.
- A nitrogenous base is linked to the —OH of 5′ C pentose sugar through a N-glycosidic linkage to form a nucleoside.

5. (*a*) The male accessory glands include paired seminal vesicles, a prostate and paired bulbourethral glands.
Bartholin's gland is a part of female accessory gland.

6. (*b*) Statement in option (b) is incorrect. It can be corrected as
In seeds such as blackpepper and beet, remnants of nucellus are peristent and called as perisperm.

7. (*b*) Contraceptive implants release hormones (usually progestin) into the bloodstream. These hormones work by thickening cervical mucus to block sperm entry and prevent ovulation. Implants are effective for up to 3 years, depending on the specific type.

8. (*c*) Both A and R are true, but R is not the correct explanation of A.
- The body of the ovule fuses with funicle in the region called hilum.
- Funicle is the stalk that attaches an ovule to the placenta in the ovary of a flowering plant.

9. (*d*) A is true, but R is false. R can be corrected as
Morphine is a very effective sedative and painkiller. Obtained from latex from *Papaver somniferum* (poppy plant).

10. (*c*) Thorns and tendrils of *Bougainvillea* and *Cucurbita* are homologous structures showing divergent evolution. Potato (stem modification) and sweet potato (root modification) are analogous structures showing convergent evolution.

11. (*c*) Statements I, II and V are correct, while statements III and IV are incorrect. They can be corrected as
- The tertiary follicle changes into mature follicle which is termed as the Graafian follicle.
- The secondary oocyte retains bulk of the nutrient rich cytoplasm of the primary oocyte.

12. (*a*) The correct matches are A-3, B-4, C-2, D-1.
- *m*RNA, i.e., messenger RNA provide the template for protein synthesis.
- *r*RNA, i.e., ribosomal RNA, play structural and catalytic role during transcription.
- RNA polymerase binds to promoter and initiates transcription.
- *t*RNA molecules are adaptor. They bring amino acid and read the genetic code.

13. (*b*) Statement in option (b) is incorrect and can be corrected as
Treatment of AIDS with anti-retroviral drugs is only partially effective. They can only prolong the life of a patient, but cannot prevent death.

14. (*d*) Ginkgos, Ferns and Herbaceous lycopods evolved during the Mesozoic era. Progymnosperms evolved during Paleozoic era.

15. (*b*) Statement given in option (b) is incorrect.
It can be corrected as
These three cells represent antipodal cells and are present at the chalazal end.

16. (*b*) Spermiogenesis is the process of transformation of spermatids (n) into sperms or spermatozoa. It involves a differentiation phase in which a spermatid develops into spermatozoan.
Spermiation involves the release of sperm from the seminiferous tubules through sertoli cells.

17. (*c*) The incorrect statement is given in option (c). It can be corrected as
The underlying mechanism of pleiotropy is the effect of a gene on metabolic pathways which contribute towards different phenotypes.

18. (*a*) The correct matches are A-3, B-1, C-4, D-2.
- Zygote Intra Fallopian Transfer (ZIFT) is the transfer of zygote or early embryos (with upto 8 blastomere) into the Fallopian tube.
- Gamete Intra Fallopian transfer (GIFT) is the transfer of an ovum collected from a donor into the Fallopian tube of another female who cannot produce one, but can provide suitable environment for fertilisation and further development.
- In Intra Cytoplasmic Sperm Injection (ICSI), the sperms are

directly injected into the ovum in laboratory.

• *In-vitro* Fertilisation (IVF) is the ferlilisation outside the body.

19. (*b*) Both statements I and II are correct.

Pollen germination can be easily studied by dusting some pollens from flowers such as pea, chickpea, *Crotolaria*, balsam and *Vinca* on a glass slide containing a drop of sugar solution (about 10 percent). After 15–30 minutes, slide can be observed under the low power lens of microscope, to see the pollen tubes coming out of the pollen grains.

If the female parent produces unisexual flowers, there is no need for emasculation.

20. (*c*) Both A and R are true but R is not the correct explanation of A.

• In haemophilia, a single protein that is a part of the cascade of proteins involved in the clotting of blood is affected.

• Due to this, in an affected individual, a simple cut will result is non-stop bleeding. This disease exhibits, criss-cross pattern for transmission of disease.

21. (*d*) Statements I, II and V are correct, while statements III and IV are incorrect. These can be corrected as

• Law of Dominance explains the proportion of 3 : 1 obtained at the F_2.

• Law of segregation is based on the fact that the alleles do not show any blending.

22. (*a*) Statement I is incorrect, but statement II is correct. It can be corrected as

A small stretch of DNA is repeated many times in repeated DNA.

23. (*b*) Both A and R true and R is the correct explanation of A.

In bacteria, since the *m*RNA does not require any processing to become active, and also since transcription and translation take place in the same compartment (there is no separation of cytosol and nucleus in bacteria), many times the translation can begin much before the mRNA is fully transcribed.

Consequently, the transcription and translation becomes coupled in bacteria.

24. (*b*) The correct matches are A-2, B-3, C-4, D-1.

• Amoebiasis (amoebic dysentry) is cased by *Entamoeba histolytica,* which is a protozoan parasite present in the large intestine of humans.

• Ascariasis is caused by *Ascaris* which is an intestinal parasite.

• Filariasis is caused by *Wuchereria malayi*, which is a filarial worm and causes elephantiasis.

• Parasites like *Plasmodium vivax*, *P. malaria* and *P. falciparum* are responsible for different types of malaria.

25. (*b*) The codon, UCA codes for serine, UGG codes for tryptophan and UGA is a stop codon.

26. (*c*) After spermiogenesis, sperm heads become embedded in the Sertoli, cells where they get nurture and care.

27. (*b*) The correct match is A-2, B-4, C-3, D-1.

• *Papaver somniferum* has multicarpellary synacrpous pistil.

• Flower of *Michelia* has multicarpellary, apocarpous pistil.

• Wheat, paddy, mango have single ovule in ovary.

• Papaya, watermelon, orchids have multiple ovules in ovary.

28. (*b*) The incorrect statement (b) can be corrected as

Spleen mainly consists of lymphocytes and phagocytes. It also has large reservoir of erythrocytes.

29. (*d*) Opioids that are extracted from latex of *Papaver somniferum* bind to the receptor in the body and act as depressants. They do not cause hallucinations.

30. (*a*) Geitonogamy is the transfer of pollen grains from the anther to the stigma of another flower of the same plant.

31. (*b*) Both A and R are true and R is the correct explanation of A.

Oxytocin helps in parturition and is known as birth hormone. It stimulates uterus muscles and causes stronger uterine contractions during child birth.

32. (*b*) Progestogens alone or in combination with oestrogen can be used by females as injection or implants under the skin as contraceptive device.

33. (*d*) F_2 generation will show higher number of parental type as when the genes are tightly linked, the recombination frequency is less and there is greater chances of obtaining parental types.

34. (*c*) The incorrect statement can be corrected as

Distantly located genes in a chromosome always assort independently resulting in recombinations.

35. (*c*) The incorrect statement is given in option (c). It can be corrected as

Apomixis is seen in a few flowering plants such as some species of Asteraceae and grasses.

36. (*c*) The correct set of statements are I, II and V, while statements III and IV can be corrected as

• MTPs are considered safe during the first trimester, i.e upto 12 weeks of pregnancy. Second trimester abortions are much more riskier.

• MTP was legalised in India in 1971.

37. (*d*) Statement I is correct, but statement II is incorrect. The incorrect statement can be corrected as

ABO blood group system is an example of co-dominance. It occurs when both the alleles of a gene lack dominant and recessive relationship and both are observed phenotypically to the same degrees. It also shows multiple alleles due to presence of three genes-I^A , I^B and i.

38. (*b*) The genotype of the father and mother of colourblind man will be X^CY, X^CX.

From the given data, it is confirmed that the daughter is affected which means both the 'X' chromosomes carry genes for the disease and one of the son is unaffected, i.e. normal. This indicatess that the other chromosome of mother is normal. This concludes that both parents are heterozygous for the disease. It can be explained as

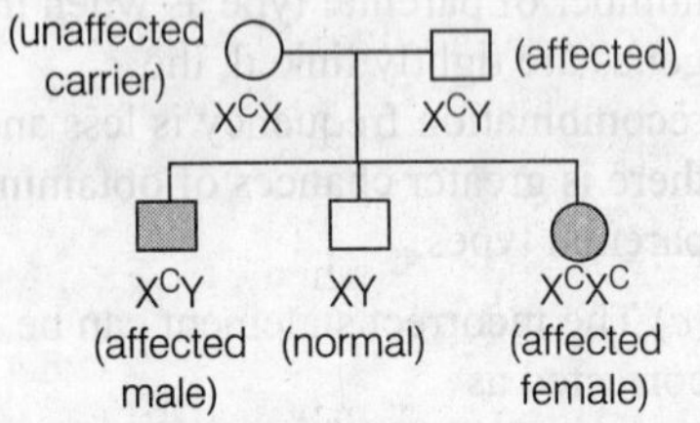

39. (*a*) Depending on base composition A : T. rich or G : C rich, length of segment and number of repetitive units, the satellite DNA is classified into many categories.

40. (*c*) The primary transcripts contain both exons and introns and are non-functional. Hence, splicing is done in order to remove the introns and join the exons in a defined order.

41. (*b*) Carboniferous period is succeeded by the permian period and began approximately 350 mya and is also known as the age of amphibians.

42. (*d*) Statement I is correct, but statement II is incorrect. It can be corrected as

Typhoid fever would be confirmed by widal test.

43. (*b*) The Miller-Urey experiment was proof that the building block of life could be synthesised abiotically from gases like CH_4, NH_3 , H_2O and H_2.

44. (*a*) The correct matches are A-4, B-2, C-1, D-3.

- Clitoris is a tiny finger-like structure which lies at the upper junction of the two labia minora.
- Hymen is the opening of the vagina which is covered partially by a membrane.
- Mons pubis is a cushion of fatty tissue covered by skin and pubic hair.
- Labia minora are paired folds of tissue under the labia majora.

45. (*c*) AUG has dual functions. It codes for Methionine (met) and it also acts as initiator codon. On the other hand, UAA is a stop codon.

46. (*c*) Both statements I and II are incorrect. Yellowish fluid colustrum is rich in IgA which is capable of crossing placenta.

Immunisation given in response to snake venom is passive immunisation since it involves preformed antibodies.

47. (*b*) The correct matches are A-2, B-4, C-1, D-3.

- Exine is the outer hard layer of pollen grain which is made up of sporopollenin.
- Intine is the inner wall of pollen grain, which is made up of cellulose and pectin.
- Germ pores are prominent aperture of pollen grain exine.
- Pollen grains represent the male gemetophytes.

48. (*c*) Middle piece possesses numerous mitochondria, which produce energy for the movement of tail that facilitates sperm motility essential for fertilisation.

49. (*c*) Feature III and IV are common to both wind and water pollinated flowers. In such flowers that get pollinated by water and wind, the flowers are not brightly coloured and also lack nectar since they do not attract insects.

50. (*c*) Both A and R are true, but R is not the correct explanation of A. It can be explained as

Lactational amenorrhea (absence of menstruation) method is based on the fact that ovulation and therefore, the cycle do not occur during the period of intense lactation following parturition.

51. (*d*) Tapetum is the innermost wall layer of the microsporangium. It nourishes the developing pollen grains. Cells of tapetum possess dense cytoplasm and generally have more than one nucleus.

52. (*a*) Statement in option (a) is incorrect and can be corrected as Klinefelter's syndrome is caused due to the presence of an additional copy of X chromosome resulting into a karyotype of 47, XXY.

53. (*d*) Statement I is correct, but statement II is incorrect. It can be corrected as

Alleles are slightly different forms of the same gene.

54. (*c*) The RNA polymerase I transcribes *r*RNA (28*S*, 18*S* and 5.8*S*) whereas 5*S r*RNA is transcribed by RNA polymerase III.

55. (*b*) Thalassemia is an autosome-linked recessive blood disease transmitted from parents to the offspring when both the partners are unaffected carrier for the gene. This defect is due to mutation or deletion which ultimately results in reduced rate of synthesis of one of the globin chains (α – and β chains) that make up haemoglobin.

56. (*a*) For trait A (dominant allele A, recessive allele a)

Probability of being homozygous recessive (*aa*) = $\frac{1}{4}$ (from a Punnett square of Aa × Aa).

For trait B (dominate allele B, recessive allele b)

Probability of being homozygous recessive (bb) $= \frac{1}{4}$ (from a Punnett square of Bb × Bb).
Probability of being homozygous recessive for both traits (aa and bb) $= \frac{1}{4} \times \frac{1}{4} = \frac{1}{16}$.

57. (*b*) Statements III, IV and V are correct, while statements I and II are incorrect. They can be corrected as
Heroin is chemically diacetylmorphine and commonly called smack. It is obtained by acetylation of morphine, which is extracted from the latex of poppy plant, *Papaver somniferum*.

58. (*c*) Statements II and IV are incorrect and can be corrected as
The ribosome consists of structural RNAs and about 80 different proteins. For initiation of translation, the ribosome binds to the *m*RNA at the start codon (AUG).

59. (*a*) Statement I is incorrect, but statement II is correct. Incorrect statement can be corrected as
Ramapithecus was more man-like while *Dryopithecus* was more ape-like.

60. (*b*) Sequence Annotation is the process of sequencing the whole set of genome that contains all the coding and non-coding sequence and later assigning different regions in the sequence with functions.

61. (*b*) *Wuchereria* (*W. bancrofti* and *W. malayi*) are the filarial worms that cause a slowly developing chronic inflammation of the organs in which they live for many years affecting the lymphatic vessels of the lower limbs.

62. (*b*) Hardy-Weinberg principle can be represented by the binomial expansion of $(p+q)^2$, i.e.
$p^2 + 2pq + q^2 = 1$.

63. (*d*) Outside the seminiferous tubule, there are interstitial spaces that contain small blood vessels and interstitial cells or Leydig cells.

64. (*a*) Statement in option (a) is incorrect. It can be corrected as
α- thalassemia is controlled by HBA1 and HBA2 genes on chromosomes 16.

65. (*c*) White flower colour and green seed color are the recessive traits of Mendel's hybridization experiments conducted on pea plants.

66. (*b*) Diaphragms and vaults are the barrier methods of contraception while, Saheli is an oral contraceptive method and tubectomy is a surgical method.

67. (*c*) In apomixis, seeds are produced without the need for fertilization, and thus the resulting offsprings are genetically identical to the maternal plant. This is because apomictic seeds develop from the maternal tissue without undergoing meiosis or recombination, resulting in no genetic variation between the parent and the offspring.

68. (*d*) The correct match is A-2. B-1, C-4, D-3.
- LH induces release of ovum (ovulation) and progesterone secretion by corpus luteum.
- FSH induces the growth of ovarian follicles and oestrogen secretion
- Relaxin helps in dilation of cervix, during parturition.
- hCG maintains progesterone secretion from corpus luteum.

69. (*a*) Statements I and II are incorrect. They can be corrected as
Both LH and FSH attains a peak level in the middle of the menstrual cycle. Rapid secretion of LH leading to its maximum level during the mid-cycle called LH surge induces rupture of Graafian follicle and thus, release the ovum.

70. (*a*) The correct matches are A-2, B-3, C-1, D-4.
- *y*-gene in *lac* operon codes for permease which increases permeability of use of β-gal.
- *a* - gene codes for transacetylase.
- *z*-gene codes for betagalactosidase (β-gal), which is primarily responsible for hydrolysis of disaccharide, lactose into its monomeric units, galactose and glucose.
- *i*-gene is the regulatory gene that is derived from the word inhibitor.

71. (*b*) Both statements I and II are correct
Periodic abstinence is one of the natural methods of contraception which work on the principle of avoiding the chance of ova and sperm meeting. In this, the couple abstains from coitus from day 10 to 17 of the menstual cycle when ovulation could be expected.

72. (*a*) The correct matches are A-3, B-4, C-1, D-2.
- XO type of sex-determination is seen in grasshopper.
- Human have XX-XY chromosomes in which male heterogamety is observed (XY).
- The mechanism of sex determination, ZZ-ZW is seen in birds in which female heterogamety is observed (ZW).
- Honey bees have haplo-diploid type of sex-determination.

73. (*d*) A is true, but R is false. R can be corrected as
Pollen grains are rich in nutrients and are used as tablets or food supplements.

74. (*d*) *Vallisneria* is a water pollinated plant. In it the female flowers reach the water surface by the long stalk and the male flowers or pollens are released on to the water surface and are carried to female flowers passively by water currents.

75. (*a*) A is false, but R is true. A can be corrected as

CuT is an Intra-Uterine Device (IUD) that is inserted by doctors in the uterus through vagina.

76. (*d*) Statement I is correct, but statement II is incorrect. It can be corrected as

Alec Jeffrey used satellite DNA as probe that shows very high degree of polymorphism in his technique of DNA fingerprinting.

77. (*b*) Statements III and V are incorrect. They can be corrected as

- Cocaine has a potent stimulating action on central nervous system, producing a sense of euphoria and increased energy. Amphotericin is a anti-fungal drug, not a euphoric drug.
- Tobacco chewing is associated with increased risk of cancer of the oral cavity.

78. (*a*) A is false, but R is true. A can be corrected as

Lac operon is an inducible operon. It is a regulatory unit of genetic material which is switched on in response to the presence of an inducer.

79. (*d*) Statement I is correct, but statement II is incorrect. It can be corrected as

Test cross is done between F_1-plant and homozygous recessive plant.

80. (*c*) Immediately after implantation, embryo differentiates into ectoderm (outer layer) and endoderm (inner layer). Mesoderm appears later on.

81. (*b*) Both A and R are true and R is the correct explanation of A.

Cancer patients are given substances called biological response modifiers such as α-interferon which activates their immune system and helps in destroying the tumor.

82. (*d*) Flowering plants have developed many devices to discourage self pollination and to encourage cross-pollination. Anther and stigma, being located at close proximity, does not help in preventing inbreeding.

83. (*c*) The incorrect set of statements are III and IV. They can be corrected as Earth was supposed to have formed about 4.5 million years back. Embryological support for evolution was proposed by Ernst Haeckel.

84. (*a*) Colourblindness is due to defect in either red or green cone of eye resulting in failure to discriminate between red and green colour. This defect is due to mutation in certain genes present in the X-chromosome.

85. (*d*) Statement in option (d) is incorrect. It can be corrected as

The cylindrical portion below the level of cotyledons is hypocotyl that terminates at its lower end in the radicle or root tip.

86. (*b*) The statement in option (b) is incorrect. It can be corrected as

Allergy is due to the release of chemicals like histamine and serotonin from the mast cells.

87. (*c*) Statements I, II and V are correct, while statements III and IV are incorrect. They can be corrected as

- Micropyle is a small opening in the integuments.
- Chalaza is found at the opposite of the micropylar end which represents the basal part of the ovule.

88. (*d*) The incorrect statement is in option (d). It can be corrected as

There are three different alleles and six different combination of these three alleles. So, a total of six different genotypes of the human ABO blood types can be seen.

89. (*a*) Statement I is incorrect, but statement II is correct. Incorrect statement can be corrected as

- Most fruits develop only from the ovary and are called true fruits.
- In a few species such as apple strawberry, cashew, etc., the thalamus also contributes to fruit formation such fruits are called false fruits.

90. (*a*) Alleles from parent 1 is I^A and parent 2 is i, then the cross will be

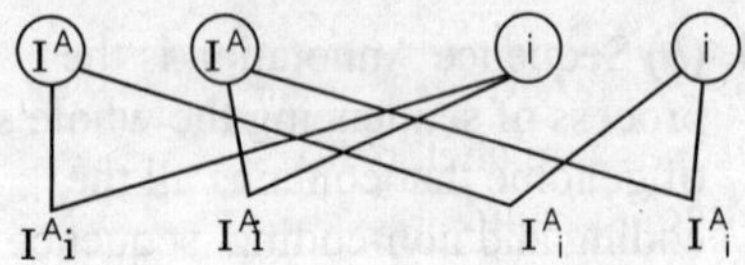

The genotype of all offsprings will be I^A i and the blood group will be type A.

SPT 2 Syllabus Part Thru 2

1. (*b*) The steps included in genetically modifying an organism are
   - identification of DNA with desirable gene.
   - introduction of the identified DNA into the host.
   - maintenance of introduced DNA in the host.
   - transfer of DNA to its progeny.

2. (*b*) The correct set of statements is III, IV and V, whereas statements I and II are incorrect. These can be corrected as
   - The introduction of African catfish for agriculture purposes posing threat to the indigenous catfishes in river, is an example of alien species invasion.
   - Cryopreservation is an *ex-situ* conservation method in which gametes of threatened species can be preserved in viable and fertile condition for long periods.

3. (*c*) Gene therapy is a collection of methods that allows correction of a gene defect in a child or embryo.

4. (*b*) The incorrect statement is option (b). It can be corrected as
   Primers are chemically synthesised oligonucleotide (short segment of DNA) that are complementary to the regions of DNA template.

5. (*a*) Statement I is incorrect, but statement II is correct. Incorrect statement can be corrected as
   Plasmid is an autonomously replicating circular extra-chromosomal DNA molecule.

6. (*a*) The pyramid of number is either upright or inverted. An upright pyramid of number is found in grassland ecosystem and inverted number pyramid is seen in cases like parasitic food chains.

7. (c) Statement (c) is incorrect and can be corrected as the cloning vector amp^R and tet^R are the antibiotic resistance genes of the vector, not restriction sites (i.e., *Hind* III, *Eco*Rl, *Bam* HI, *Pvu* II, *Pst* I, *Cla* I).

8. (*b*) Predation is an interaction between two different species where one is called predator and other is prey. Here, the starfish *Pisaster* is an important predator in the rocky intertidal communities of the American pacific coast which feed on invertebrates.

9. (*c*) Predation plays an important role in checking prey population and transferring energy across trophic levels. The cactus feeding predator (moth) was introduced to control the spread of prickly pear cactus.

10. (*a*) Statements I, II and V are incorrect and can be corrected as
    '+', '+' sign determines mutualism in which both species are benefitted.
    Predation is a type of population interaction in which one benefits and the other suffers. In competition (–, –), both the species are harmed in same way.

11. (*b*) Mutualism is an interaction in which both the interacting species are benefitted. In this, a particular fig species can be pollinated only by its partner wasp species and not from any other species.

12. (*a*) *Azospirillum* and *Azotobacter* are nitrogen fixing free living bacteria found in the soil that fix atmospheric nitrogen. They help in enriching the nitrogen content of the soil.

13. (*c*) The incorrect statement is option (c). It can be corrected as
    The ministry of Environment and Forests has initiated the GAP and YAP in the year 1986 and 1993 respectively.

14. (*b*) The correct set of statements are I, III and V, whereas statements II and IV are incorrect. These can be corrected as
    - Toxicity testing in animals obtain results in much lesser time.
    - Transgenic models exist for many human diseases such as cancer, cystic fibrosis, Alzheimer's and rheumatoid arthritis.

15. (*c*) Both A and R are true and R is not the correct explanation of A. It can be explained as
    The restriction endonuclease cut the DNA sequences at specific site and produce DNA strands with the sticky ends. It cuts both the strand of DNA at the palindromic site.

16. (*d*) Statement I is correct, but statement II is incorrect. It can be corrected as
    Adenosine Deaminase (ADA) deficiency can be treated partially by bone marrow transplantation and enzyme replacement therapy.

17. (*b*) B, i.e., Fungi is globally more than the combined total of the species of fishes, amphibians, reptiles, and mammals.

18. (*b*) A-II, B-I, C-IV, D-III.
    Decomposers are also called saprotrophs, e.g. bacteria, fungi, etc.
    Natural ecosystem is a community of living and non-living entities in nature, e.g., forest, lakes, etc.
    The production of organic matter by the producers is called primary productivity.

The production of organic matter by the consumers is called secondary productivity.

19. (*c*) Statements I, IV and V are correct, whereas statements II and III are incorrect. These can be corrected as

A nematode *Meloidegyne incognita* infects the roots of tobacco plants and causes a great reduction in yield. The example of *Bt* crops are *Bt* cotton, *Bt* corn, tomato, rice, etc. Basmati rice is not *Bt* crop.

20. (*a*) Statement I is incorrect, but statement II is correct. Incorrect statement can be corrected as

Techniques like recombinant DNA technology, Polymerase Chain Reaction (PCR) and ELISA (Enzyme Linked Immuno Sorbent Assay) serve the purpose of early diagnosis.

21. (*d*) Statement I is correct, but Statement II is incorrect. It can be corrected as

Bt cotton is resistant to pest lepidopterans such as tobacco budworm and armyworm.

22. (*d*) A is true, but R is false. R can be corrected as

Cyanobacteria is also known as blue green algae. They serve as an important biofertiliser in paddy (rice) fields as it adds organic matter to the soil and hence, increases its fertility.

23. (*c*) The current population of the pond is 28 and the birth rate will be 8/20, i.e. 0.4, offspring per plants per year.

24. (*b*) Cyclosporin-A is a bioactive molecule that is used as an immunosupressive agent in organ-transplant patients. It is produced by the fungus *Trichoderma polysporum*.

25. (*b*) The incorrect set of statements II and IV and can be corrected as

The standing crop is measured as the mass of living organism (biomass) or the number in a unit area.

Only 10 per cent of the energy is transferred to each trophic level from the lower trophic level.

26. (*a*) A-II, B-III, C-IV, D-I.

- Detritivores, e.g. earthworms break down detritus into smaller particles by the process of fragmentation.
- Bacterial and fungal enzymes degrade detritus into simple inorganic substances by the process of catabolism.
- Humus is degraded by microbes by the process of mineralisation.
- Humification leads to accumulation of a dark coloured amorphous substance called humus.

27. (*b*) The diagram shows a stable pyramid or bell-shaped age pyramid. In this, the pre-reproductive and reproductive individuals are almost in equal number and the post reproductive individuals are relatively fewer.

28. (*d*) A-IV, B-III, C-I, D-II.

- *In-situ* conservation is a method of conserving all the living species in their natural habitats, e.g. wildlife sanctuaries.
- *Ex-situ* conservation means conserving all the living species in artificial habitats, e.g. zoological gardens.
- Passenger pigeon became extinct in the last 500 years due to over-exploitation.
- Co-evolved plant-pollinator shows mutualism where extinction of one invariable leads to the extinction of the other is an example of co-extinction.

29. (*c*) *Monascus purpureus* is an yeast that produce statins which have been commercialised as blood cholesterol lowering agents.

30. (*b*) In the given exponential growth equation, *r* is determined by intrinsic rate of natural increase.

31. (*b*) *Trichoderma* is a fungus which is used as biocontrol agent for the treatment of plant diseases. It is free-living and found commonly in the root ecosystem.

32. (*a*) Statement in option (a) is incorrect. It can be corrected as

More than 70 percent of all the species recorded are animals, while plants (including algae, fungi, bryophytes, gymnosperms and angiosperms) comprise 22 per cent of the total species.

33. (*a*) Statement I is incorrect, but statement II is correct. Statement I can be corrected as

Vertical distribution of different species occupying different levels is called stratification. Fragmentation is the breakdown of detritus into smaller particles by detritivores.

34. (*c*) Statement in option (c) is incorrect. It can be corrected as

In ELISA, the antigen includes proteins, glycoproteins, etc. It is the glycoprotein or proteins by which the presence of infection by pathogen can be detected.

35. (*b*) The ladybird and dragon flies act as biocontrol agents. They are useful to get rid of aphids and mosquitoes, respectively.

36. (*b*) A-IV, B-II, C-I, D-III.

Natality refers to the number of birth during a given period in the population.

Mortality is the number of deaths in the population during a given period. Population density is the population size, which is designated as *N* and is calculated as population per unit area.

Population ecology links ecology to population genetics and evolution.

37. (*b*) In the given equation, '*S*' is the species richness, *A* is the Area, *Z* is the slope of the line and *C* is the *y*-intercept.

38. (*b*) The correct statements are II, IV and V. Incorrect statements I and III can be corrected as

Toddy is a traditional drink that is made by fermenting sap from palms. Lactic Acid Bacteria (LAB) is used to convert milk to curd to improve its nutritional quality by increasing vitamin-B_{12}.

39. (*b*) Both A and R are true, and R is the correct explanation of A. It can be explained as

Transgenic bacteria have been produced that translate the constituting polypeptide chains of human insulin.

40. (*b*) A-I, B-II, C-III, D-IV.

• In mutualism, both the species involved are benefitted, e.g. Orchids and bees.

• *Balanus* and *Chathamalus* show competition within the species.

• *Cuscuta* and hedge plants are an example of parasitism in which one species is benefitted and the other one suffers.

• Interaction of cactus and moth represents an example of predation where moth is the predator of cactus.

41. (*b*) Both A and R are true and R is the correct explanation of A.

BOD is the measure of the amount of oxygen required to remove waste organic matter from water in the process of decomposition by aerobic microbes. Thus, it provides a measure of the amount of waste in receiving water body.

42. (*a*) A is false, but R is true. A can be corrected as

Golden rice is a genetically modified plant which has been made to overcome the shortage of dietary vitamin A that is important for healthy eyes.

43. (d) Bacteria and fungi are the decomposers in the food chain and represents the end of the food chain.

44. (*b*) The incorrect statement (b) can be corrected as

Angiosperms are the most species rich taxonomic group among plants.

45. (*b*) A-III, B-II, C-IV, D-I.

• Citric acid is produced by a fungus, *Aspergillus niger*.

• Acetic acid is produced by a bacterium, *Acetobacter aceti*.

• Butyric acid is produced by a bacterium, *Clostridium butylicum*.

• Lactic acid is produced by a bacterium, *Lactobacillus*.

46. (*c*) The DNA polymerase (*Taq* polymerase) + dinucleotides is used in step C. *Taq* DNA polymerase is used to amplify or synthesise DNA or gene of interest during extension phase.

47. (*b*) In order to extract out DNA, use of chilled ethanol is necessary as the ethanol eliminates the solvation shell that envelops the DNA, thus, allowing it to precipitate.

Since the use of chilled ethanol was not made, DNA couldnot be precipitated out.

48. (*d*) Habitat loss and fragmentation are the most common factors for extinction. The large habitats are broken into small fragments due to various human activities leading to population decline.

49. (*c*) Polymerase Chain Reaction (PCR) is technique to make many copies of a specific DNA region *in-vitro*. The steps included are :

Denaturation $\rightarrow$ Annealing $\rightarrow$ Extension

50. (*b*) Of the incident solar radiation, less than 50 per cent of it is photo. synthetically active radiation (PAR). Plants capture only 2 – 10% of the PAR and this small amount of energy sustains the entire living world.

51. (d) The palindromic base sequence in DNA that can be easily cut at about the middle by some particular restriction enzymes is

5′– GAATTC – 3′

3′ – CTTAAG – 5′

Here, it is the correct palindromic DNA sequence of base pairs that reads the same on the two strands, when the orientation of reading is kept the same.

52. (*a*) A is not correct, but R is correct. A can be corrected as

Streptokinase produced by the bacterium *Streptococcus* is helpful in treating blood clots from patients who have undergone myocardial infarction leading to heart attack.

53. (*a*) Statement I is incorrect, but statement II is correct. The incorrect statement can be corrected as

Autoradiography is a method allowing the detection of radioactive molecule (probe) within a biological sample. It is often preferred due to lower cost and high speed.

54. (*a*) Statement I is incorrect, but statement II is correct. Statement I can be corrected as

The large holes in Swiss cheese are due to production of a large amount of CO_2 by a bacterium named *Propionibacterium shermanii*.

55. (*b*) A-II, B-I, C-III, D-IV.

• Organism is defined as the basic unit of ecological hierarchy.

• Exponential growth is seen under unlimited resource availability in a habitat.

• Population is the term given to same species in a geographical area.

• Logistic growth is seen under limited resource availability in a habitat.

56. (*b*) The correct shape of the pyramid obtained in the given scenario is represented by option (b) the ecosystem depicts a forest ecosystem wherein the trees constitute the base of the pyramid. The primary consumers are insects that are numerous than trees. The number of small birds feeding upon insects is even fewer. This gives the pyramid a spindle shape.

57. (*c*) The diagram shows an ideal pyramid of energy. The bottom and largest level of the pyramid is the producers and contains the largest amount of energy. It will go from below to above as 10,000 J $\rightarrow$ 1000 J $\rightarrow$ 100J $\rightarrow$ 10 J.

So, C will have 1000 J.

58. (a) A-III, B-IV, C-II, D-I.

• The dough used for making bread is fermented using Baker' yeast (*Saccharomyces cerevisiae*).

• Penicillin was produced by *Penicillum notatum*.

• *Methanobacterium* are commonly found in the anaerobic sludge during sewage treatment.

• A lot of cellulosic material present in the food of cattle is also present in the rumen.

59. (*b*) If 4 individuals, in a laboratory population of 40 fruitflies died during a specified time interval, the death rate in the population during that period will be 4/40 = 0.1 individuals per fruitflies per weeks.

60. (*d*) Statement I is correct, while statement II is incorrect. Statement II can be corrected as

Insulin used for diabetes was earlier extracted from pancreas of slaughtered cattles and pigs.

61. (*c*) The statement in option (c) is incorrect. It can be corrected as

In India, 27 documented varieties of Barmati rice are grown.

62. (*b*) *Nucleopolyhedrovirus* is a Baculovirus that infects insects and is utilised as a bio-insecticide.

63. (*a*) Statement in option (a) is incorrect. It can be corrected as

RNA interference (RNAi) takes place in all eukaryotic organanisms as a method of cellular defence.

64. (*b*) In the given scenerio

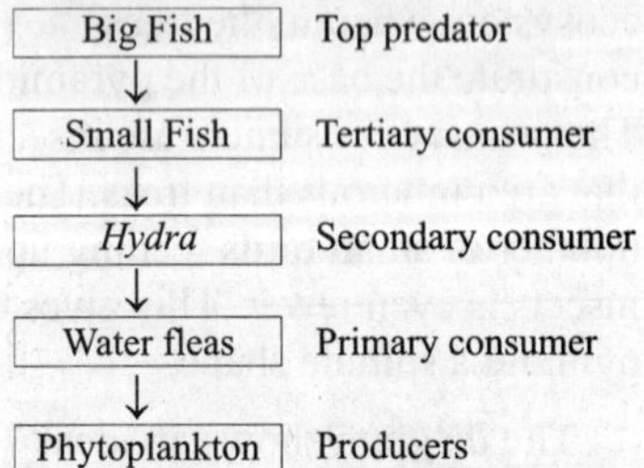

So, the water fleas, that feeds on the phytoplankton or producers are primary consumers.

65. (*a*) A-III, B-IV, C-I, D-II.

• *Hind* III is restriction site which binds to a given restriction enzyme.

• Tet^R is an antibiotic resistance gene present in a cloning vector, pBR322.

• pBR322 is a plasmid and one of the first widely used *E. coli* cloning vector.

• *ori* (origin of replication) is a sequence from where replication starts.

66. (*b*) The interaction shown here is predation in which alien species (Nile perch), when introduced into the habitat of cichlid fish, thus making the latter disappear.

67. (*b*) The proteins encoded by the genes *cry*IAc and *cry* II Ab control the cotton bollworms.

*cry*IAb gene is used to control corn borers.

68. (*c*) Bacteria will be majorly deprived of dissolved oxygen in the sample collected from site B. This is because the level of BOD is shown maximum at the site B. BOD value indicates more polluted water and a higher oxygen demand.

69. (*b*) The correct statements are I, III and V. Statements II and IV are incorrect. These can be corrected as

The first restriction endonuclease found was *Hind* III.

Endonuclease makes cuts at the specific position within the DNA.

70. (*b*) For the transformation process to take place, the bacterial cells are first made competent to take up DNA. This is done by treating them with specific concentration of a divalent cation such as calcium. It increases the efficiency with which DNA enters the bacterium.

71. (*d*) Statements II, III, IV and V are incorrect and can be corrected as

• Unless one cuts the vector and the source DNA with the same restriction enzyme, the recombinant vector molecule cannot be created.

• The ligation of alien DNA is carried out at a restriction site present in one of the two antibiotic resistance genes.

• In insertional inactivation technique, the recombinant colonies do not produce any colour.

• The role of *Agrobacterium tumefaciens* is performed by retroviruses in the animal cells.

72. (*d*) Statement I is correct, but statement II is incorrect. Statement II can be corrected as

Death rate can be defined as number of individuals that are lost per unit of population per unit time.

73. (*b*) A-I, B-III, C-II, D-IV.

• *Bacillus thuringiensis* produce Cry proteins, which are *Bt* toxins and have insecticidal properties.

• *Thermus aquaticus* is highly thermostable DNA polymerase.

• The tumor-inducing (Ti) plasmid of *Agrobacterium tumefaciens* has been modified into a cloning vector.

• The construction of the first recombinant DNA emerged from the possibility of linking a gene encoding antibiotic resistance with a native plasmid of *Salmonella typhimurium*.

74. (*c*) Statement in option (c) is incorrect and can be corrected

Penicillin is an antibiotic that kill pathogens that cause harmful disease and infections.

75. (*a*) Statement I is incorrect, but Statement II is correct. Statement I can be corrected as

The Western ghats have a greater amphibian species diversity than the Eastern ghats.

76. (*d*) A is true, but R is false. R can be corrected as

• The linking of antibiotic resistance gene with the plasmid vector became possible with the enzyme DNA ligase.

• The cutting of DNA at specific locations became possible because of restriction enzymes.

77. (*d*) The rate of decomposition is faster in the ecosystem in all of the given conditions except when detritus is rich in lignin and chitin. In such a condition, the rate of decomposition get slower.

78. (*c*) All the options except physical chemical base agriculture are thought for increasing food production.

79. (*d*) A is true, but R is false. R can be corrected as

The bottled fruit juices are clarified by the use of pectinase and protease.

80. (*b*) α-1 antitrypsin is a protein that is helpful in treatment of emphysema. It is also produced through transgenic organisms.

81. (*d*) Mosquitoes do not belong to the order-Lepidoptera, rather it belongs to order-Diptera.

82. (*c*) The correct set of statements are III, IV and V. Statements I and II are incorrect and can be corrected as

Biogas is the mixture of gases such as methane, CO_2 and hydrogen sulphide.

Nucleopolyhedrovirus is an excellent candidate for species-specific narrow spectrum insecticidal application.

83. (*b*) Gause's competitive exclusion principle states that two closely related species competing for the same resources cannot co-exist indefinitely and the competitively inferior one will be eliminated eventually.

84. (*c*) Both statement I and statement II are incorrect. They can be corrected as

The extinction of stellar's sea cow was due to over- exploitation by humans. The factors of biodiversity loss include over exploitation, alien species invasion, co- extinction and habitat loss and fragmentation.

In-situ conservation helps in the biodiversity conservation.

85. (*d*) A is true, but R is false. R can be corrected as

Phytoplanktons are consumed by zooplanktons, almost as rapidly as they are formed and have shorter life spans. They are smaller than zooplanktons and thus, possesses lesser biomass.

86. (*d*) The example of alien species invasion includes the introduction of Nile perch into Lake Victoria in East Africa, which led to the extinction of more than 200 species of cichlid fish in the lake.

87. (*b*) The first transgenic cow was Rosie, which was produced in 1997. It is helpful in the production of human protein-enriched milk. The milk has alpha-lactalbumin and is balanced food for human babies.

88. (*b*) Endoparasites are the parasites that live inside the host body at different locations like liver, kidney, etc., for obtaining food. Predation is a form of interspecific interaction in which tiger (predator) kills and consumes the weaker animal deer (prey).

89. (*d*) Statement I is correct, but statement II is incorrect. It can be corrected as

Bioprocess engineering is the method that involves the maintenance of sterile, i.e. microbial contamination -free environment in chemical engineering process to enable growth of only desired microbe.

90. (*c*) The *ex-situ* conservation includes the conservation of components of biological diversity outside their natural habitats, e.g., botanical gardens, zoological garden, DNA banks, etc.

National parks and biosphere reserves are *in-situ* conservation methods.

NSS1 NEET Stepping Stones 1

1. (*a*) The levels of diversity that can be observed in the biosphere are genetic diversity, species diversity and ecological diversity.

2. (*d*) In the production of test tube babies, an ovum is taken out from a woman's Fallopian tube and fertilised with preserved sperm in a test tube. After that zygote is formed that is implanted in the woman's uterus for further embryonic development. Thus, fertilisation is external and foetus formation is internal in test tube babies.

3. (*b*) The principle of independent assortment states that the segregation of one pair of alleles (R/r) is independent of the segregation of another pair (Y/y). This leads to an equal probability (25%) of occurrence for each combination in the gametes.

4. (*c*) Both A and R are true, but R is not the correct explanation of A.
The primary transcripts contain both the coding and non-coding sequences. Non-coding sequences, i.e., introns, are removed and exons are joined together, through splicing and then *hn*RNA undergoes additional processing called as capping and tailing.

5. (*b*) Phenotypically, Klinefelter's individuals are males, but they can show some female secondary sexual characteristics and are usually sterile.

6. (*a*) The law of dominance is used to explain the expression of only one of the parental characters in a monohybrid cross in the F_1-generation and the expression of both the parental characters in F_2-generation.

7. (*b*) Speciation is the process by which new species are formed and it generally takes a long time. It requires sustained periods without major disruptions to allow species to gradually adapt, differentiate, and evolve into new species. In the tropics, the prolonged periods of stable climate provide uninterrupted time for evolutionary processes to occur. This allows species to evolve continuously and fill various ecological niches.

8. (*a*) Statement I is incorrect, but statement II is correct. Incorrect statement can be corrected as:
The underlying mechanism of pleiotropy in most cases is the effect of a gene on metabolic pathways which contribute towards different phenotypes.

9. (*d*) Agarose gel electrophoresis is a technique used to separate DNA fragments based on their size through sieving effect provided by the agarose gel. DNA is negatively charged molecule. They can be separated by forcing them to move towards the anode under an electric field. Fragment D is smallest among the four and it can move fastest through the gel towards the anode.

10. (*b*) Both A and R are true and R is the correct explanation of A. The presence of common structures in the embryos of all vertebrates suggest that they have evolved from a common origin.

11. (*b*) Somaclones are genetically identical to the original plant from which they were grown. These plants are produced through micro-propagation.

12. (*b*) Label '*A*' represents zona pellucida layer of the ovum. It blocks the entry of additional sperms. It ensures that only one sperms can fertilise the ovum.

13. (*b*) The genetic code is a set of rules defining how the four letter genetic code of DNA is translated into the twenty amino acid. Properties of genetic code are as follows

- Triplet code
- Non-ambiguous and universal
- Degenerate
- Specific
- Contiguous fashion

14. (*d*) A is true, but R is false. R can be corrected as
The body encounters a pathogen for the first time and produces a response called primary response which is of low intensity. Subsequent encounters with the same pathogen elicits a highly intensified secondary response.

15. (*c*) The ovule is a small structure attached to the placenta by means of a stalk called funicle. Thus, funicle serves as an attachment of the ovule to the placenta.

16. (*b*) A nucleoside consists of a nitrogenous base linked to a pentose sugar through a N-glycosidic linkage. A nucleotide includes a phosphate group linked to the 5' carbon of the pentose sugar in addition to the base and sugar.

17. (*c*) Statements I, II and IV are correct. Rest other statements are incorrect and these can be corrected as

- Each trophic level has a certain mass of living material at a particular time called as the standing crop.
- The number of trophic levels in the grazing good chain is restricted as the transfer of energy follows 10% law, i.e. only 10% of the energy is transferred to each trophic level from the lower trophic level.

18. (*a*) The incorrect statement can be corrected as

The effluent from the primary settling tank is taken for secondary treatment. It is not directly released into natural water bodies.

19. (*b*) The correct sequence of stages of replication in reterovirus is as follows:

- Viral RNA is introduced into cell.
- Viral DNA is produced by reverse transcriptase.
- Viral DNA incorporates into host genome.
- New viral RNA is produced by the infected cell.
- New virus particles are produced.

20. (*d*) The correct match pair is I and III, whereas II and IV are incorrectly matched and can be corrected as

GAG = Glutamic acid

CGU = Arginine

21. (*a*) Cross between true breeding red coloured flower and white coloured flower will give rise to pink coloured flower (Rr).

The cross between pink (F_1) and white flower (rr) is as follows.

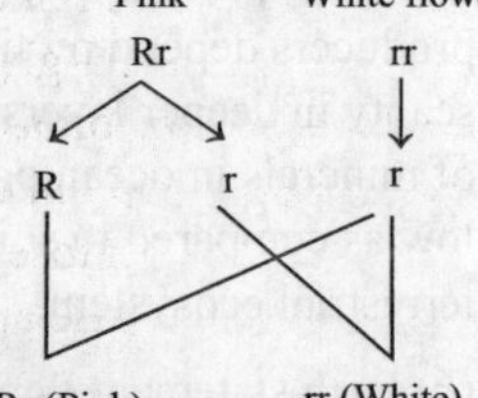

The F_2 resulted in the ratio 1 (Rr) Pink : 1 (rr) White.

22. (*a*) In α-thalassemia, production of α globin chain is affected. It is controlled by two closely related linked genes HBA1 and HBA2 on chromosome 16 of each parent. It is observed due to mutation or deletion of one or more of the four genes.

23. (*b*) Some nations are developing laws to prevent unauthorised exploitation of their bioresearch and traditional knowledge.

Indian parliament has recently cleared the second amendment of the Indian Patents Bill that takes such issues into consideration.

24. (*d*) Statement (d) is incorrect and can be corrected as

Step 3 represents termination of transcription. When RNA polymerase encounters rho factor (ρ), it terminates the transcription.

25. (*c*) Incorrect statement can be corrected as

Cyclosporin-A is used as an immunosuppressive agent in organ - transplant patients and is produced by the fungus *Trichoderma polysporum.*

26. (*a*) The Cretaceous period was the last and longest segment of the Mesozoic era. It saw the first appearance and initial diversification of flowering plants and was dominated by sphenopsids (horsetails), Ginkgos and Gnetales.

27. (*d*) Convergent evolution occurs in different species that have evolved similar traits independently of each other. Placental mammals and marsupials in Australia have evolved separately by exhibiting similar physical forms.

28. (*d*) Incorrect statement regarding morphine can be corrected as

It is a naturally occurring derivative of opium.

29. (*b*) Corona radiata is a secondary egg membrane because it is not secreted by ovum itself. Zona pellucida is the primary egg membrane.

Rest all options are correct.

30. (*a*) In DNA fingerprinting, DNA probes are hybridised with DNA sample and form a double-stranded structure. Thus, these single-stranded DNA fragments are used to detect the presence of complementary nucleic acid sequence by hybridisation.

31. (*d*) Gene therapy is a therapeutic approach which is used to treat genetic defects. It involves the introduction of normal genes into a patient's cells to replace or compensate for abnormal genes causing the disorder.

32. (*d*) A is true, but R is false. R can be corrected as

Anaerobic bacteria break down the organic matter of sludge in the absence of oxygen. During this digestion, bacteria produce a mixture of gases known as biogas that can be used as source of energy as it is inflammable.

33. (*d*) Incorrect statement regarding plasmid can be corrected as

Ori is the sequence from where the replication starts and any piece of DNA when linked to this sequence, can be made to replicate within the host cell. This sequence provides the ability to replicate autonomously, so as to generate its multiple copies within the host itself.

34. (*d*) A is true, but R is false. R can be corrected as

DNA from different tissues of the same individual shows same degree of polymorphism.

35. (*a*) Coca alkaloid or cocaine is obtained from coca plant *Erythroxylum coca*. It interferes with the transport of the neurotransmitter dopamine. It has a potent stimulating effect on central nervous system, producing a sense of euphoria and increases energy.

36. (*c*) Intra Cytoplasmic Sperm Injection (ICSI) is a specialised form of *in vitro* fertilisation. It involves directly injecting a single sperm into the cytoplasm of ovum. This technique is primarily used in case of male infertility.

37. (*b*) The given diagram shows the ideal pyramid of energy. Pyramid of energy is always upright and can never be inverted because when energy flows from a particular trophic level to the next trophic level, some energy is always lost. Also energy at lower trophic level is always more than that of higher trophic level.

38. (*a*) A is false, but R is true. A can be corrected as

In pBR322, there are single recognition sites for several commonly used restriction enzymes, such as *Eco*RI, *Bam*HI, *Pst*I and others, which are used in molecular cloning. Each of these enzymes cuts at a specific site within the plasmid, allowing for the insertion or removal of DNA fragments.

39. (*c*) Incorrect statement can be corrected as

The embryo with 8 to 16 blastomeres is called morula and it continues to divide and transforms into blastocysts as it moves further into the uterus.

40. (*b*) Statement (b) is correct w.r.t the pollen-pistil interaction. Rest of the statements are incorrect and can be corrected as

- It guarantees the gamination of right type of pollen grains on the stigma.
- The pistil rejects the incompatible pollen grains.
- Pollen grains from the same plant may not be always compatible.

41. (*c*) Griffith observed that mixture of heat killed S-strain and live R-strain bacteria killed the mice.

He recovered living S-strain bacteria from the dead mice.

It demonstrated that the genetic material could be transferred from dead bacteria to live bacteria.

42. (*b*) All of the given statements are correct except statement I. It can be corrected as

In a test cross, an organism showing dominant phenotype is crossed with the recessive parent and their progeny can be analysed to predict the genotype (homozygous/ heterozygous nature) of the test organism.

43. (*c*) Pectoral fins of rohu and forelimbs of horse have similar origin and basic structure, hence these are homologous organs.

44. (*d*) The expression of the allele B depends on the specific trait being examined. BB seeds are round and bb seeds are wrinkled. Heterozygotes (Bb) produce round seeds, but the starch grains are of intermediate size. Thus, for seed shape, it shows complete dominance, but for starch grain size, it shows incomplete dominance.

45. (*a*) Competition is a process in which the fitness of one species is lowered in the presence of another species. For example, due to greater browsing efficiency of goats, Abingdon tortoise became extinct.

46. (*b*) A-4, B-3, C-2, D-1.

- Downstream processing refers to the recovery and the purification of desired proteins or products from recombinant cell.
- Competent cells are able to take up foreign DNA from their surroundings.
- In insertional inactivation process, a recombinant DNA is inserted within the coding sequence of an enzyme, β-galactosidase. This results into enzyme inactivation. This is used as 'Blue-White' screening method.
- Agarose gel electrophoresis is employed to check the progression of restriction enzyme digestion.

47. (*b*) Both A and R are true and R is the correct explanation of A.

Microbes or other organisms with short life spans and rapid reproduction rates evolve into new forms quickly due to genetic variation and selection pressures acting in short time frames.

48. (*a*) A is false, but R is true. A can be corrected as

Small volume cultures cannot yield appreciable quantities of products. To produce large quantities of desired protein, bioreactors are used.

49. (*b*) The thymus gland is the primary lymphoid organ for T - lymphocyte development and maturation that mediates immune defense against foreign antigens.

It also produces and secretes thymosin, a hormone necessary for T-cell development and production.

50. (*d*) Egg cell and antipodal cells have haploid number of chromosomes. In angiosperms, a single diploid megaspore mother cell matures. Through meiosis, it gives rise to four haploid megaspores.

51. (*c*) Competition is a fundamental ecological interaction where organisms competes for the same limited resources. It is best defined as a process in which the fitness of one species significantly gets lowered in the presence of another species.

52. (*d*) Incorrect statement can be corrected as

ABO blood group is controlled by the gene I.

The gene I has three alleles, i.e. I^A, I^B and i. Humans are diploid organisms, and each person possesses any two of the three I gene alleles.

53. (*b*) In aquatic ecosystem, the limiting factor for productivity is light as the producers depend on light which is scanty in deeper layers. The amount of minerals in oceanic water is also low as compared to soil in the terrestrial ecosystem.

54. (*b*) Both statement I and statement II are true.

Tumours cells are often undetectable and undestroyable by immune system. Therefore, patients are given biological response modifiers such as α-interferons which activate their immune system and help in destroying the tumour.

Taking drugs intravenously can cause serious infections like AIDS and Hepatitis B.

55. (*b*) According to 10% law of energy transfer, primary consumers would receive only 10% of the energy of producers, i.e 1800 kcal and secondary consumers would then receive 10% of 1800 kcal, i.e 180 kcal of energy.

$$\underset{\text{Producers}}{18000\,\text{kcal}} \xrightarrow{10\%} \underset{\text{Primary consumer}}{1800\,\text{kcal}} \xrightarrow{10\%} \underset{\text{Secondary consumer}}{180\text{ kcal}}$$

56. (*b*) To prepare insulin from cDNA, the method used is reversed transcription.

In this process, complementary DNA copy is made from the mRNA of the insulin genes in order to create a synthetic version of the insulin gene that can be inserted into a bacterial plasmid to produce insulin protein.

57. (*c*) Predator-prey interactions are crucial in maintaining stable ecosystems by regulating prey populations and preventing them from overgrazing resources. This top- down control has a cascading effect on the entire ecosystem that influence biodiversity and nutrient cycling.

58. (*d*) Alien invasive species such as water hyacinth are known to significantly impact native ecosystems negatively. Similarly, introduction of African catfish, *Clarias gariepinus* for aquacultural purposes posed threat to the indigenous catfishes in Indian rivers. These invasive species can outcompete native species for resources such as light, space, water and nutrients.

59. (*a*) *In situ* conservation mainly focuses on protecting the organism in its natural habitat, e.g. biosphere reserves, national parks, wildlife sanctuaries and sacred groves. Cryopreservation, seed banks and zoological parks are the examples of *ex-situ* conservation.

60. (*d*) The Graafian follicle is a mature ovarian follicle that releases an egg during ovulation. After ovulation, the Graafian follicle transforms into the corpus luteum. These corpus luteum secrete large amounts of progesterone which is essential for maintenance of the endometrium for implantation.

61. (*b*) Recessive characters are expressed when they are present in homozygous condition or when other chromosome of the chromosome pair does not possess that character, e.g. in male, the sex chromosomes are XY, as Y does not possess any recessive gene, only X is enough to express that recessive characters.

62. (*b*) Statement (b) is correct. Rest statements are incorrect and can be corrected as

- They grew *E. coli* in a medium containing $^{15}NH_4Cl$ as the only nitrogen source for many generations.
- The DNA that was extracted from the culture one generation after the transfer from N^{15} to N^{14} medium had a hybrid density.
- DNA extracted from the culture after second generation was composed of equal amounts of hybrid DNA and light DNA.

63. (*a*) The founder effect occurs when a small group of individuals establishes a new population and the allele frequencies in this new population can be quite different from those in the original population that they become a different species.

64. (*d*) Statements I, III and IV are correct while statements II and V are incorrect, these statements can be corrected as

- The pollen grains represent the male gametophytes. It is generally spherical measuring about 25-50 μm in diameter.
- Pollination by water is quite rare in flowering plants and is limited to about 30 genera, mostly in monocotyledons.

65. (*c*) The appearance of dry, scaly lesions on various parts of the body such as skin, nails and scalp are the main symptoms of the ringworm. Rest other statements are correct w.r.t. ascariasis.

66. (*c*) A-3, B-2, C-4, D-1.

Trichoderma species are free- living fungi that are very common in the root ecosystems.

The ladybirds are useful to get rid of aphids.

Nucleopolyhedrovirus are pathogens that attack insects and other arthropods.

Many members of the genus *Glomus* (fungi) form symbiotic association with roots of higher plants (mycorrhiza).

67. (*b*) Hardy-Weinberg principle does not operate in a population, if frequent mutation occurs in that population.

68. (*a*) In PCR technique, polymerisation involves *Taq* polymerase DNA polymerase-I named after the thermophilic bacterium, *Thermus aquaticus*.

Deoxynucleoside triphosphates (*d*NTPs) consist of four basic nucleotides, *d*ATP, *d*CTP, *d*GTP and *d*TTP, as building blocks of new DNA strands. Magnesium is a required cofactor for thermostable DNA polymerases. Mg^{2+} in the PCR mixture stabilises *ds*DNA.

69. (*b*) The cross between carrier and non-carrier parent is as follows

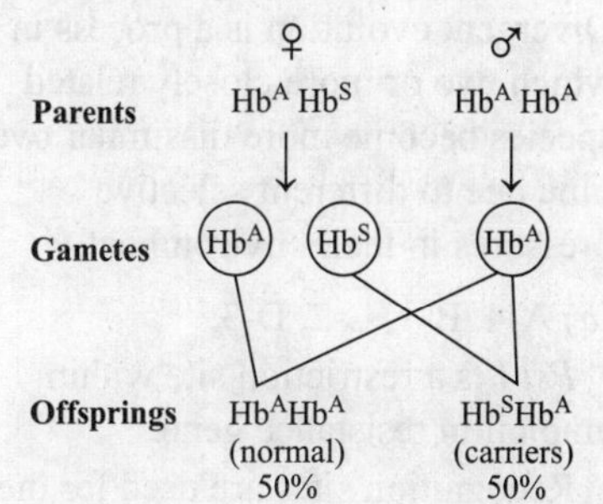

70. (*a*) Statement I is incorrect and can be corrected as

In cleistogamous flowers, the anthers and stigma lie close to each other. They are self-pollinated flowers as there is no chance of cross-pollination. They produce assured seed sets, even in the absence of pollinators.

71. (*b*) Both A and R are correct, and R is the correct explanation of A.

B. thuringiensis forms protein crystals during a particular phase of their growth. These crystals contain a toxin insecticidal protein. It exists as inactive protoxin but once an insect ingests the inactive toxin, it gets converted into an active form of toxin due to the alkaline pH of the insect's gut.

72. (*c*) The correct sequence of translation is IV $\rightarrow$ III $\rightarrow$ I $\rightarrow$ II

- In the first phase of translation, amino acids are activated in the presence of ATP and gets linked to their cognate *t*RNA.
- After the charging of *t*RNA, amino acids are joined by a peptide bond.
- During elongation phase, the ribosome move from codon to codon along the *m*RNA.
- At the end, a release factor binds to the stop codon and terminates translation.

73. (*b*) Statements I, II and IV are related to divergent evolution, whereas statement III is related to convergent evolution, i.e. analogous structures are a result of convergent evolution.

Divergent evolution is a process in which two or more closely related species become more dissimilar over time due to different selective pressures in their environment.

74. (*a*) A-4, B-1, C-2, D-3.

- *Pst* I is a restriction site within ampicillin resistance gene.
- Recognition sites are used for the the insertion of foreign DNA.
- rop codes for the proteins involved in the replication of the plasmid.
- Selectable markers help in identifying and eliminating non-transformants.

75. (*b*) Both statement I and statement II are correct.

The DNA fragments are sequenced using automated DNA sequencers that work on the principle of a method developed by Frederick Sanger. These sequences are arranged based on some overlapping regions present in them.

76. (*b*) The logistic growth model is a model that describes the growth of a population in an environment with limited resources. Following situations can be observed in logistic growth.

- Due to limited resources, organisms show competition.
- Fittest individuals survive and reproduce.
- Population growth is calculated through equation: $dN/dt = rN\left(\frac{K-N}{K}\right)$

Statements II and V corresponds to the geometric or exponential population growth model.

77. (*d*) The mutualistic relationship is seen in fig inflorescence and wasp. The wasp pollintes the fig inflorescence while searching for suitable egg-laying sites. In return for the favour of pollination, the fig offers the wasp some of its developing seeds, as food for the developing wasp larvae.

78. (*b*) Both statement I and statement II are correct. Population size, more technically called population density, need not necessarily be measured in numbers only. Although, total number is generally the most appropriate measure of population density. The percent cover or biomass is a more meaningful measure of the population size where counting is not possible.

79. (*a*) Statements III are IV are incorrect. These can be corrected as

- The primary purpose of legalising MTP in India was reducing the incidence of illegal abortion and consequent maternal mortality and morbidity.
- The misuse of amniocentesis to determine the sex of the foetus, leading to MTP in case of a female foetus is an illegal practice in India.

80. (*b*) A-3, B-1, C-2, D-4.

- Amniocentesis is used for foetal sex determination based on the chromosomal pattern in the amniotic fluid.
- Cervical caps are barriers made of rubber that are inserted into the female reproductive tract.
- Lippes loop are IUDs used to increase phagocytosis of sperms.
- Saheli is non- steroidal preparation.

81. (*a*) A-2, B-1, C-4, D-3.

- Histones are positively charged, basic proteins.
- Nucleosomes consitute the repeating unit of a structure called chromatin.
- Euchromatin is loosely packed region of chromatin.
- Heterochromatin is densely packed chromatin.

82. (*a*) The correct sequence of evolutionary history of vertebrates is as follows

- Early reptiles were extinct 350 mya.
- Thecodonts got extinct in the permian period.
- Therapsids got extinct in the early triassic period.
- Dinosaurs got extinct in the late tertiary period.

83. (*b*) Hallucinogens are chemical substances that causes psychological effects, like *Cannabis* products alters thoughts, perceptions and feelings.

84. (*a*) Statements III and IV are incorrect. These statements can be corrected as

- The B-lymphocytes produce an army of proteins in response to pathogen into our blood to fight with them. These proteins are called antibodies or immunoglobulins.
- Each antibody molecule has four peptide chains, two smaller called light chains and two longer called heavy chains. It is represented as H_2L_2.

85. (*a*) A-2, B-1, C-4, D-3.

- Down's syndrome-Short statured females with mental retardation; trisomy of 21.
- Klinefelter's syndrome-Masculine development in males with gynaecomastia; 47, XXY.
- Turner's syndrome-Females are sterile with rudimentary ovaries; 45, XO.
- Aneuploidy- Failure of segregation of chromatids during cell division.

86. (*c*) Statement in option (c) is incorrect and it can be corrected as

In 1953, James Watson and Francis Crick, based on the X-ray diffraction data produced by Maurice Wilkins and Rosalind Franklin, proposed a double helix model for the structure of DNA. Francis Crick proposed the central dogma in molecular biology.

87. (*d*) A-3, B-1, C-4, D-2.

- Saltation is the sudden and significant change in the evolutionary development of an organism.
- Branching descent and natural selection are the two key concepts of Darwinian Theory of Evolution
- *Coelacanth* were called lobefins and evolved into the first amphibians.
- *Tyrannosaurs rex* was about 20 feet in height and had huge fearsome dagger-like teeth.

88. (*a*) A-2, B-1, C-4, D-3.

- Active immunity is slow and takes time for its full effective response.
- Ready-made antibodies induce passive immunity. These are quick in action but their effect is short-termed.
- Colostrum has abundant IgA antibodies which gives immunity to the newborns.
- Vaccines generate memory B- and T-cells in our body.

89. (*c*) Match pair (c) is correct. Rest are incorrect and can be corrected as

- Wings of butterfly and birds are analogous organs.
- Tasmanian tiger cat is an Australian marsupial.
- Flying squirrel is a placental mammal.

90. (*d*) Statement I is correct, but statement II is incorrect. It can be corrected as

Bacteria like *Streptococcus pneumoniae* and *Haemophilus influenzae* are responsible for causing pneumonia in humans which infects the alveoli (air filled sacs) of the lungs.

NSS2 NEET Stepping Stones 2

1. (*a*) The genetic code is a set of three-letter combinations of nucleotide called codons, each of which corresponds to a specific amino acid or stop signal. The concept of codons was first described by Francis crick and his colleagues.

2. (*d*) A is true, but R is false. R can be corrected as

Dihybrid cross can be explained through the Mendel's law of independent assortment. The law states that when two pairs of traits are combined in a hybrid, segregation of one pair of characters is independent of the other pair of characters.

3. (*c*) The correct matches are A-2, B-4, C-1, D-3.

- Gametogenesis refers to the formation of gametes, i.e. sperms or ovum in male and female, respectively.
- Insemination is the process of transfer of sperms into the female genital tract.
- Implantation is the attachment of blastocyst to the uterine wall.
- Parturition refers to the delivery of the baby.

4. (*b*) The correct order of the Avery, MacLeod and Maclyn McCarty experiment is III $\rightarrow$ II $\rightarrow$ I

- They took mixture of heat - killed S-strain and live R-strain bacteria in different tubes.
- They treated each tube with a specific enzyme that would degrade one single type of chemical compound.
- They identified the chemical nature of the transforming principle.

5. (*a*) Statement I incorrect, but statement II is correct. Incorrect statement can be corrected as

Periodic abstinence is a natural method of birth control in which the couples avoid or abstain from coitus from day 10 to 17 of the menstrual cycle when ovulation could be expected.

6. (*a*) Statements III and V are incorrect. These can be corrected as

• Oparin of Russia and Haldane of England proposed that the first form of life could have come from pre-existing non-living organic molecules (e.g. RNA, protein, etc.) and that formation of life was preceded by chemical evolution.

• Fossils are remains of hard parts of life forms found in rocks. Different aged rock sediments contain fossil of different life forms who probably died during the formation of the particular sediment. These fossils provide paleontological evidence for evolution.

7. (*d*) Hashish is a cannabinoid, obtained from the plant *Cannabis sativa*. It interacts with cannabinoid receptors present principally in the brain.

8. (*a*) The correct match is A-1, B-3, C-2, D-4.

• Alfred Wallace highlights the common ancestry and evolutionary relationship among different species.

• Homologous organs are anatomically similar, but perform different functions.

• Analogous organs are not anatomically similar, but perform similar functions.

• Human actions significantly contributes to the evolution of drug-resistant microbes.

9. (*b*) Both A and R are true, and R is the correct explanation of A.

The chromosomal patern in human male is X-Y, therefore, in the male, the sex chromosomes could be either X or Y. Hence, 50% of sperms carry the X chromosome, while the other 50% carry the Y.

10. (*a*) The incorrect statement can be corrected as

The VNTR (Variable Number of Tandem Repeats) belongs to a class of satellite DNA referred to as mini-satellite.

11. (*a*) Statement I is incorrect, but statement II is correct. Incorrect statement can be corrected as

In RDT, fragmentation of DNA by specific restriction endonuclease enzyme is followed by the isolation of a desired DNA fragment from agarose gel electrophoresis.

12. (*a*) All of the statements are correct, except statement III, it can be corrected as

The DNA dependent RNA polymerases catalyse the transcription in only one direction, i.e. $5' \rightarrow 3'$.

13. (*d*) Statement I is correct, but statement II is incorrect. Statement II can be corrected as

When the BOD of sewage or waste water is reduced significantly, the effluent from aeration tanks is then passed into a settling tank where the bacterial flocs are allowed to sediment.

14. (*b*) The correct flow of procedures of Hershey Chase experiment is as follows.

• The protein coat and DNA of bacteriophages are labelled with different radioactive isotopes.

• The bacteria are infected with radioactive phages.

• The bacterial cells are agitated in a blender to remove the phage coats.

• The bacterial cells and phage particles are separated by centrifugation.

15. (*b*) Incorrect statement can be corrected as

Secondary productivity is defined as the rate of formation of new organic matter by consumers.

16. (*b*) Both statement I and statement II are correct.

Hybrid plants have been proven helpful in order to improve yield. But preserving and retaining hybrid characteristics is not easy. This is because the characters in progeny of hybrid plants segregate. Moreover, the production of hybrid seeds is expensive, which makes them costly for farmers to purchase them every year.

17. (*c*) The given scenario is related to directional selection. This means that there is a selective pressure favoring butterflies with larger wings, leading to an increase in the frequency of this trait within the population over time. As a result, the average wing size of the population shifts towards larger sizes, reflecting the directional change in the trait under selection.

18. (*d*) The given figure represents the discharge of male gametes into the synergid and the movements of the sperms, one into the egg and the other one into the central cell.

19. (*b*) Statements I and II are related to narrowly utilitarian argument of biodiversity, that includes conservation of biodiversity for direct economic benefits from nature. Statements III and IV are related to broadly utilitarian argument which involves biodiversity conservation for the ecosystem services that nature provides.

20. (*c*) In the Miller-Urey experiment, the researchers used a mixture of gases that were thought to resemble the composition of earth's primitive atmosphere. The specific gases they used were methane, ammonia, water vapour and hydrogen.

21. (*c*) In a species-area relationship graph, a steeper slope means that the number of species increases faster as the area explored increases. For example, for frugivorous fruit eating birds and mammals in the tropical forests of different continents, the slope is found to be 1.15.

22. (*b*) Both statement I and statement II are correct.

• India has more than 50,000 genetically different strains of rice and over 1000 varieties of mango represents that a single species show high diversity at the genetic level over its distributional range.

• Species diversity is defined as the number of different species present in an ecosystem and relative abundance of each of those species, e.g. higher amphibian species diversity in Western ghats compared to Eastern ghats.

23. (*a*) The correct matches are A-2, B-1, C-4, D-3.

First trophic level-Phytoplankton grass (Producers).

Second trophic level-zooplankton, grasshopper (Primary consumers).

Third trophic level-Birds, fishes, wolf (Secondary consumers).

Fourth trophic level-Man, lion (Tertiary consumers).

24. (*c*) Both A and R are true, but R is not the correct explanation of A.

Humification leads to accumulation of a dark coloured amorphous substance called humus. It is highly resistant to microbial action and undergoes decomposition at an extremely slow rate. Being colloidal in nature, it serves as a reservoir of nutrients.

25. (*a*) The correct matches are A-2, B-1, C-3, D-4.

• Fragmentation is breaking down of detritus into smaller particles.

• Leaching involves the precipitation of inorganic salts.

• Catabolism is the degradation of detritus into simpler substances.

• Humification is the formation of humus.

26. (*c*) Statements II, IV and V are correct, whereas statements I and III are incorrect and can be corrected as

• Bacterial cells are made competent by treating them with a specific concentration of a diavalent cation, such as calcium, which increases the efficiency with which DNA enters the bacterium through pores in its cell wall.

• In plants, cells are bombarded with high velocity micro-particles of gold or tungsten coated with DNA in a method known as gene gun.

27. (*c*) Incorrect statement can be corrected as

Antibiotics are not effective against viral infections because they target bacteria.

28. (*a*) Statements III and V are incorrect. These can be corrected as

The *Plasmodium* enters the human body as sporozoite (infectious form) through the bite of infected female *Anopheles* mosquito.

29. (*a*) To identify recombinant colonies, a piece of DNA is introduced into the β-galactosidase gene. As a result, the inactivated gene cannot produce functional β-galactosidase. Since, β-galactosidase is responsible for breaking down chromogenic substrate to produce a blue colour, its inactivation result into white recombinant colonies.

30. (*a*) Trasmission of HIV infection generally occurs by sexual contact with the infected person, by transfusion of contaminated blood and blood products, by sharing infected needles as in the case of intravenous drug abusers and from infected mother to her child through placenta.

31. (*c*) The separated DNA fragments from agarose gel electrophoresis (*A*) can be visualised only after staining the DNA with a compound known as ethidium bromide (*B*) followed by exposure to UV radiation.

32. (*d*) The incorrect statement can be corrected as

Inverted pyramid of biomass supports less number of secondary consumers, but their biomass is higher than the producers.

33. (*c*) UTRs are non- coding sequences present at both ends of the *m*RNA (5′ and 3′). It plays a crucial role in the regulation and efficiency of the translation process.

34. (*c*) Thalassemia causes a reduction in the synthesis of globin chains, leading to anaemia and the formation of abnormal haemoglobin molecules, not an increase in functional red blood cells.

35.(*a*) In the given pedigree, the trait skips a generation but reappears in subsequent generation. This suggests a recessive pattern. It is equally distributed in males and females, thus autosomal trait. So, the disease is autosomal recessive.

36. (*d*) The incorrect statement can be corrected as

Organic farming represents a holistic approach. It instead of relying on synthetic pesticides, employs natural pedators, pest-resistant crops, etc.

37. (*b*) The correct matches are A-4, B-3, C-1, D-2.

• Operon is a group of genes with a single promoter that encodes genes for the transport and metabolism of lactose in *E. coli* and other bacteria.

• The operator region is adjacent to the promoter elements in the most operons.

• The *i* gene codes for the repressor of the *lac* operon.

• z-gene codes for the β-galactosidase.

38. (*b*) After implantation, the trophoblast develops chorionic villi, subsequently, the inner cell mass differentiates into ectoderm and endoderm, with the heart forming by the end of the first month.

39. (*b*) The correct matches are A-2, B-4, C-1, D-3.

• Saheli is non-steroidal preparation for contraception.

• Multiload 375 is a copper releasing IUD, while LNG 20 is a hormone releasing IUD.

• Progestogens can be used as injection for contraception.

40. (*a*) Incorrect statement can be corrected as

Monocots are not more primitive than dicots; they are both highly evolved groups of plants.

41. (*d*) Statements II, III and Vare correct. Statements I and IV are incorrect. They can be corrected as

• Oogenesis begins during embryonic development when oogonia are formed in the foetal ovaries.

• The tertiary follicle is the stage where the primary oocyte completes its first meiotic division to form a secondary oocyte and a first polar body.

42. (*c*) According to Chargaff's rule in a DNA molecule, adenine is paired with thymine and cytosine is paired with guanine and their total proportion is

$A+G+C+T=100\%$

If $T=18\%$

So, Adenine is also 18%

$G+C+18+18=100\%$

$G+C=(100-36)\%$

$G+C=64\%$ $[\%G=\%C]$

$C=32\%$

43. (*c*) In angiosperms, pollen grains have two male gametes. One of the male gametes moves towards the egg cell and fuses with its nucleus forming zygote. The other male gamete moves towards the two polar nuclei located in the central cell and fuses with them to produce a triploid primary endosperm nucleus (PEN).

44. (*b*) Both statement I and statement II are correct.

PCR is incredibly sensitive and can detect even a single molecule of DNA in a sample. This sensitivity makes it possible to detect bacterial DNA or virus at very low concentration, even when the bacteria are present in minimal amount.

45. (*c*) Mendel investigated characters in the garden pea plant that were manifested as two opposing traits, e.g. tall or dwarf plants. He conducted artificial pollination experiments using several true breeding pea line. A true breeding line, one that, having undergone continuous self-pollination, shows the stable trait inheritance and expression for several generations. Mendel selected 14 true-breeding pea plant varieties, as pairs which were similar except for one character with contrasting traits.

46. (*d*) A is true, but R is false. R can be corrected as

Genetic equilibrium is maintained in a population only if there is no gene flow, genetic drift, mutation, genetic recombination or natural selection.

47. (*a*) The correct order is II, I, III. *Homo habilis* had a brain size of 650-800cc. *Homo erectus* had a brain size of about 900cc, and Neanderthal man had a brain capacity of approximately 1400cc.

48. (*d*) Statement I is correct, but statement II is incorrect. Incorrect statement can be corrected as

For initiation of translation, initiator tRNA are found in the cell, but there are no *t*RNAs for stop codons.

49. (*d*) In small population, there is a greater chance of genetic drift due to a limited gene pool, which can cause changes in allele frequencies more quickly than in larger population.

50. (*b*) In 1997, the first transgenic cow, Rosie produced human protein - enriched milk (2.4 g/ltr). The milk contained the human alpha-lactalbumin and was nutritionally a more balanced product for human babies than natural cow-milk.

51. (*d*) The incorrect statement can be corrected as

Due to continental drift, when South America joined North America, the local mammals in South America (which resembled animals like horses and rabbits) were overridden by fauna from North America.

52. (*c*) The given heterozygous individual will produce sperms having following genotype WT, Wt, wT, wt in the ratio 1:1:1:1. Thus, out of 2 million sperms, sperms having both the recessive alleles are 0.25×2 million = 0.5 million sperms.

So, the correct answer is option (c).

53. (*a*) The restriction enzyme that recognises this palindrome is EcoRI (C).

The enzyme that can link these two DNA fragments DNA ligase (D).

54. (*d*) A is true, but R is false. R can be corrected as

The first three mitotic divisions in the formation of embryo sac are free nuclear, meaning they are not immediately followed by cell wall formation.

55. (*a*) The monarch butterfly is highly distasteful to its predator bird because of a special chemical present in its body. The butterfly acquires this chemical during its caterpillar stage by feeding on a poisonous weed.

56. (*c*) A nematode *Meloidegyne incognita* infects the roots of tobacco plants and causes a great reduction in yield. A novel strategy was adopted to prevent this infestation which was based on the process of RNA interference (RNAi). RNAi takes place in all eukaryotes as a method of cellular defence. This method involves silencing of a specific *m*RNA due to a complementary *ds*RNA molecule that binds to and prevents translation of the *m*RNA (silencing).

57. (*d*) A is true, but R is false. R can be corrected as

Passive immunity offers immediate protection, but is typically short-lived as the injected antibodies are eventually degraded.

58. (*b*) Incorrect statement can be corrected as

Agroecosystem or croplands lack stability because these are mostly monocultures and do not have diversity.

59. (*a*) The label A in the given figure represents adaptive radiation of marsupials of Australia. The marsupials diversified into numerous species with distant adaptations and represents the adaptive radiation.

60. (*c*) Repetitive sequences are stretches of DNA sequences that are repeated many times. They have no direct coding functions, but they shed light on chromosome structure, dynamics and evolution.

61. (*b*) Statement II is incorrect and it can be corrected as

Integuments of ovules harden as tough protective seed coats. The micropyle remains as a small pore in the seed coat. This facilitates entry of oxygen and water into the seed during germination.

62. (*a*) The male accessory glands include paired seminal vesicles, a prostate and paired bulbourethral glands. Secretions of these glands constitute the seminal plasma which is rich in fructose, calcium and certain enzymes. The secretions of bulbourethral glands also help in the lubrication of the penis.

63. (*c*) The progressive destruction of helper T-cells by HIV is a key factor in the development of immunodeficiency in the infected individuals.

64. (*b*) Mendel's law of segregation states that during the formation of gametes through meiosis, the two alleles for a given gene separate so that each gamete receives only one allele.

65. (*c*) Statements II, IV and V are correct. Statements I and III are incorrect. They can be corrected as

- The chorionic villi and uterine tissue become interdigitated with each other and jointly form placenta.
- The placenta is connected to the embryo through an umbilical cord which helps in the transport of substances.

66. (*c*) A narrow base indicates fewer births and a bulging middle suggests a significant number of adults. This type of pyramid is observed is declining population.

67. (*b*) Zygote Intra- Fallopian Transfer (ZIFT) is an assisted reproductive technology used to treat infertility. In ZIFT, the zygote or early embryos with upto 8 blastomeres are transferred into the Fallopian tube for further development.

68. (*a*) The cross between the parents is as follows

P I^Ai × I^Ai

Gametes (I^A) (i) (I^A) (i)

Offspring I^AI^A I^Ai I^Ai ii

Hence, the offspring can only inherit type A or type O blood group.

69. (*a*) In typical dominance, the presence of one functional allele is often sufficient to produce enough enzyme for a normal phenotype, making the heterozygote appear like the homozygote for the functional allele.

70. (*b*) The correct matches are A-4, B-1, C-3, D-2.

- ELISA is based on the principle of antigen-antibody interaction. Infection by pathogen can be detected by the presence of antigens or antibodies.
- A single stranded DNA or RNA, tagged with a radioactive molecules is allowed to hybridise to its complementary DNA in a clone of cells followed by detection using autoradiography.
- Very low concentration of a DNA can be detected by amplification of their nucleic acid by PCR.
- RNA interference involves silencing of a specific mRNA due to a complementary dsRNA molecule that binds to and prevents translation of the *m*RNA.

71. (*c*) Restriction endonucleases inspect the DNA to find and bind to their specific palindromic recognition sequences, which allows them to cut the DNA precisely at these sites.

72. (*b*) The example of sex linked recessive disease, which shows its transmission from unaffected carrier female to some of the male progeny has been widely studied in haemophilia. In this disease, a single protein that is a part of the cascade of proteins involved in the clotting of blood is affected.

73. (*d*) Natural selection is a process in which heritable variations enabling better survival are enabled to reproduce and leave greater number of progenies. The incorrect statements can be corrected as

- The occurrence of more than one adaptive radiation in an isolated geographical area results in convergent evolution.
- The adaptive radiation results in development of different species from a same species.
- Factors like genetic drift, gene flow, mutation, genetic recombination and natural selection affect the Hardy-Weinberg equilibrium.

74. (*a*) Statement I is incorrect, but statement II is correct. Incorrect statement can be corrected as

Heroin, commonly called smack, is chemically diacetylmorphine, which is a white, odourless, bitter crystalline compound.

75. (*a*) The correct match is A-4, B-1, C-3, D-2.

• The large holes in Swiss cheese are due to production of a large amount of CO_2 by a bacterium named *Propionibacterium shermanii*.

• *Lactobacillus* and others commonly called lactic acid bacteria grow in milk and convert it to curd.

• *Clostridium butylicum* is used to produce butyric acid.

• *Aspergillus niger* is used to produce acetic acid commercially.

76. (*a*) Incorrect statement can be corrected as

Currently 34 biodiversity hotspots have been identified worldwide. Protecting these areas is significant as they have a high number of endemic species and can reduce the ongoing mass extinctions by almost 30%.

77. (*d*) Statement I is correct, but statement II is incorrect. It can corrected as

The length of DNA double helix in a typical mammalian cell is calculated by multiplying the total number of base pairs with distance between two consecutive base pairs.

78. (*a*) The correct matches are A-4, B-3, C-1, D-2.

• Pyramid of numbers in grassland is always upright.

• Pyramid of biomass in pond ecosystem is inverted.

• Natality (number of births) leads to increase in population density.

• Mortality (number of deaths) leads to decrease in population density.

79. (*a*) All the given examples represent convergent evolution. These structures are not anatomically similar, though they perform similar functions and are called analogous structures.

80. (*c*) The Earth Summit (Rio) was held in 1992. In the summit, the nations agreed to take appropriate measures for conservation of biodiversity and sustainable utilisation of its benefits.

81. (*b*) Both A and R are true and R is the correct explanation of A.

Charles Darwin believed that interspecific competition, which occurs between different species competing for the same resources is a driving force in organic evolution. In competition, not all organisms will succeed.

Only those best adapted to their environment will survive and reproduce and evolve over the time to survive.

82. (*b*) Statements III and IV are incorrect. These can be corrected as

Both turtles and lizards originated from sauropsids.

83. (*a*) Statement I is incorrect, but statement II is correct. Statement I can be corrected as

Bamboo breeds only once in their lifetime and then dies, i.e. monocarpic.

84. (*b*) Ringworms are caused by many fungi belonging to the genera *Microsporum*, *Trichophyton* and *Epidermophyton*. Ringworms are generally acquired from soil or by using towels, clothes of infected persons.

85. (*c*) The in-situ conservation includes the establishment of biosphere reserves, national parks and wild life sanctuaries. Rest statements are incorrect. These can be corrected as

• India has 18 biosphere reserves, 106 national parks and around 573 wildlife sanctuaries.

• Sacred groves also contribute to *in situ* conservation by preserving rare and threatened plants. It is also present in Eastern ghats.

86. (*a*) The exaggerated response of the immune system to certain antigens present in the environment is called allergy. The substance to which such an immune response is produced are called allergens.

87. (*c*) In eukaryotes, genes often have split coding sequences known as exons interrupted by non-coding introns, complicating the definition of gene based solely on a continuous DNA segment.

88. (*c*) Elution refers to the process of cutting out and purifying specific DNA fragments from the agarose gel after gel electrophoresis.

89. (*c*) The *r*RNA is responsible for linking the animo acid in a pre-determined order to form proteins. It serves as the primary building block for both ribosomes and the assembly line on which protein synthesis occur.

Thus, the role of *r*RNAs during translation in cells is to serve as the structural and catalytic components of the ribosome.

90. (*a*) In the given figure, *P*-Epidermis, *Q*-Endothecium, *R*- Middle layer and *S*-Tapetum.

The epidermis, endothecium and middle layers (outer three wall layers) of the anther wall contribute to the mechanical strength and dehiscence process, which facilitates the release of pollen grains.

NSS3 NEET Stepping Stones 3

1. (*c*) Polygenic inheritance is the inheritance where multiple genes control a specific phenotype of an organism. It has a net additive effect on the expression of the character. For example, the human skin colour gene.

2. (*b*) Statements I, II and III are correct, while statements IV and V are incorrect and can be corrected as
   - HIV enters into helper T-lymphocytes (T_H) and replicates and produce progeny virus.
   - Treatment of AIDS with anti-retroviral drugs is only partially effective. They can only prolong the life of the patient, but cannot prevent death.

3. (*d*) Statement I is correct, but statement II is incorrect. The incorrect statement can be corrected as
   Pollen grains are spherical shaped measuring about 25-50 micrometers in diameter. It has a prominent two-layered wall.

4. (*d*) Statement I, IV and V are correct while Statement II and III are incorrect and can be corrected as
   - MTP is considered safe during the first trimester, i.e. upto 12 weeks of pregnancy.
   - Except hepatitis-B, genital herpes and HIV other disease are completely curable.

5. (*b*) The factors that are known to affect Hardy-Weinberg equilibrium are gene flow or gene migration, genetic drift, mutation, genetic recombination and natural selection.

6. (*d*) Characteristic palm crease is observed in people with Down's syndrome where there is an additional copy of chromosome 21 (21st trisomy) and hence they have a total of 47 chromosomes in their nucleus.

7. (*a*) The correct matches are A-4, B-2, C-3, D-1.
   - Chalaza is located opposite to the micropylar end representing the basal part of the ovule.
   - Micropyle is a small opening where the integuments encircle the nucellus.
   - Each ovule has one or two protective envelopes called integuments.
   - Ovule is attached to the placenta by means of a stalk called funicle.

8. (*c*) The correct set of statements are I, IV and V, while statements II and III are incorrect and can be corrected as
   Histones are rich in the basic amino acid residues, i.e. lysine and arginine. Histones are organised to form a unit of eight molecules called histone octamer.

9. (*a*) A is false, but R is true. A can be corrected as
   Taq DNA polymerase is an enzyme used for DNA amplification in PCR reactions.

10. (*c*) The pathway by which sperm move outside the body is shown below.
    Seminiferous tubules → Rete testes → Vasa efferentia → Epididymis → Vas deferens → Ejaculatory duct → Urethra.

11. (*b*) The correct matches are A-3, B-1, C-2, D-4.
    - *Ramapithecus* were more man like and existed 15 mya.
    - *Australopithecus* were man like primates that existed 3-4 mya.
    - *Homo habilis* were the first human like beings who existed 2 mya.
    - *Home erectus* were the Java man and existed 1.5 mya.

12. (*c*) The incorrect statement can be corrected as
    Genetic Modification (GM) increased efficiency of mineral usage by plants and prevents early exhaustion of fertility of soil.

13. (*d*) The incorrect statement can be corrected as
    Microbes such as yeasts have been used for the production of beverages like wine, bear, whisky, brandy or rum.

14. (*b*) The above structure shows an expanding pyramid or triangle shaped pyramid. In this, population of pre-reproductive and reproductive age group is larger and population of post-reproductive age group is very less.

15. (*d*) The features that are required to facilitate cloning into a vector are origin of replication (*ori*), selectable marker and cloning sites.
    Bacteriophages are a group of viruses that infect bacteria. These do not facilitate cloning in a vector.

16. (*c*) Phytoplanktons belong to first trophic level (Primary producer), zooplankton belongs to second trophic level (primary consumer), Fishes belong to third trophic level (secondary consumer) and Man belongs to fourth trophic level (tertiary consumer).

17. (*b*) Both statement I and statement II are correct. The mediterranean orchid cheats its pollinator bee and tricks it into believing that one of its petal is the female partner of the bee. The bee tries to pseudocopulate with the petal while the flower gets pollinated in the process.

18. (*b*) Both statement I and statement II are correct. Bioprospecting is the exploration of molecular, genetic and species level diversity to derive products of economic importance. However, if not done in controlled manner it could lead to over

exploitation and thus harm the nature.

19. (*b*) The correct matches are A-3, B-4, C-2, D-1.

• Ampulla is the wider part of the oviduct.

• Infundibulum is the funnel-shaped part, possessing finger-like projections.

• Uterus is also called womb where the development of foetus takes place.

• Vagina is also known as birth canal as during parturition the fully developed foetus passes through it.

20. (*a*) The correct matches are A-3, B-2, C-4, D-1.

• Epicotyl has a shoot apex and few leaf primordia included in a hollow foliar structure called coleoptile.

• The embryonal axis has radical and root cap enclosed in an undifferentiated sheath called coleorhiza.

• Perisperm is the persistent nucellus after fertilisation, observed in plants like black pepper.

• In the grass family the cotyledon is called scutellum.

21. (*b*) Statement in option (b) is incorrect about haemophilia and can be corrected as

Haemophilia is the disorder transmitted from unaffected carrier female to some of the male progeny.

22. (*c*) A typical dicotyledonous embryo consists of an embryonal axis and two cotyledons.

23. (*d*) Statement I is correct, but statement II is incorrect. It can be corrected as

Sertoli cells are the cells that provide nutrition to the developing germ cells in the testes.

24. (*b*) *Azotobacter* is one such free living bacteria that fixes nitrogen for plants in order to increase their mineral uptake capacity. *Azotobacter* is non-pathogenic and does not have the plant in any way.

25. (*a*) The correct match is A-3, B-2, C-1, D-4.

• Interstitial cells synthesise and secretes testicular hormones called androgens.

• Vas deferens arise from epididymis.

• Vasa efferentia arise from rete testis.

• Spermatogonium is produced by male germ cells by mitotic division.

26. (*c*) The incorrect statement can be corrected as

The inheritance of flower colour of *Antirrhinum sp.* is a good example of incomplete dominance. It is a form of intermediate inheritance.

27. (*d*) If the woman undergoes GIFT or Gamete Intra Fallopian Transfer, it means that she is unable to produce a healthy egg, but has a healthy uterus for the baby to develop. Thus, a donor woman would ovulate to release a healthy ovum which would be transferred into the Fallopian tube of female. This could be followed by fertilisation by a sperm to form the zygote. The zygote undergoes mitotic divisions to form the embryo which finally gets embedded into the endometrium.

28. (*c*) CGU-Glycine represents the incorrect match pair CGU as codons, code for Arginine and not Glycine.

29. (*d*) Statement I is correct, but statement II is incorrect. The incorrect statement can be corrected as

The rate of appearance of new form is linked to the life cycle or the lifespan.

30. (*c*) The correct statements are I, III and V, while statements II and IV are incorrect and can be corrected as

E.coli has 4.6×10^6 bp while human has 6.6×10^9 bP. In eukaryotes, the replication of DNA takes place at S-phase of the cell cycle.

31. (*a*) A is false, but R is true. A can be corrected as

Saheli is an oral contraceptive pills which has high contraceptive value and very few side effects.

32. (*d*) A is true, but R is false. R can be corrected as

DNA is negatively charged, so the fragments can be separated by forcing them to move towards the anode under an electric field through a medium.

33. (*d*) The three critical research areas of biotechnology are

• Providing best catalyst in the form of improved organism,usually a pure enzyme.

• Creating optimal conditions through engineering for a catalyst to act.

• Downstream processing technologies to purify the organic compound.

34. (*b*) Both A and R are true and R is the correct explanation of A. It can be explained as

A father can only pass on the X-chromosome to his daughter and the Y chromosome to his son. The X chromosome contains the genes that might cause colourblindness.

35. (*d*) Cocaine or coca alkaloids is obtained from coca plant *Erythroxylum coca*. It acts on central nervous system and produces a sense of euphoria and increased energy.

36. (*b*) Genotype of father is I^OI^B. A person with blood group B may be homozygous (I^BI^B) or heterozygous (I^BI^O) for that trait.

A person with genotype I^BI^B cannot produce an offspring with blood group O. Whereas that with genotype I^BI^O can as shown below.

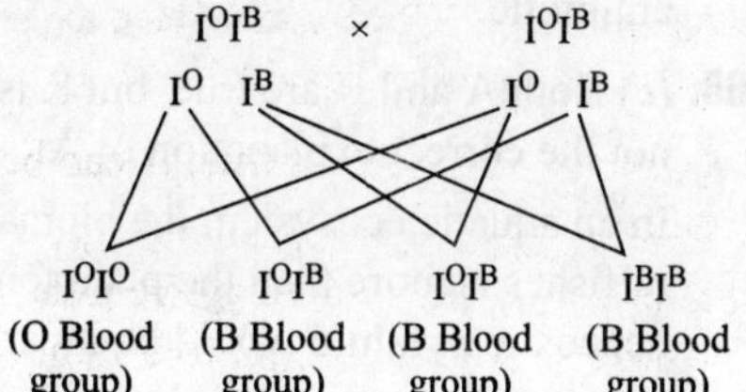

37. (*a*) The correct order is I-IV-II-III-V.

• At the very first step the HIV attaches to the surface of the host cell.

• It then releases its nucleoprotein layer or capsid into the host cell's cytoplasm.

• This is followed by reverse transcription of the RNA into DNA. The DNA gets integrated into the host cell's genome and is replicated.

• DNA is next transcribed to form *m*RNA that is translated into viral proteins.

• Viral proteins are assembled into viral particles that exocytose out of the host cell.

38. (*a*) Statement I is incorrect, but statement II is correct. Incorrect statement can be corrected as

The relationship between species of fig trees and pollinator species of wasp is called mutualism where both species are benefitted.

39. (*b*) In 1997, an American company got patent right on Basmati rice through the US patent. This new variety of rice was made by crossing Indian Basmati with semi-dwarf variety.

40. (*b*) Both statement I and statement II are correct. They can be explained as

All species are interdependent so the loss of one species may affect the other. This was the ethical argument for conserving biodiversity. Hotspots are regions with high species richness and endemism.

41. (*c*) The population density will increase if the number of births plus the number of immigrants is more than the number of deaths plus the number of emmigrants.

42. (*a*) Parturition is induced by oxytocin and relaxin. Oxytocin directs the fully grown foetus towards birth canal and relaxin helps to widen the pelvis.

43. (a) A is false, but R is true. A can be corrected as

Extinction of Abingdon tortoise was due to an inter-specific competition. The competition existed between two different species that is Abingdon tortoise and goats. As goats had a better browsing efficiency, they out competed the tortoises.

44. (*d*) Statement I is correct, but statement II is incorrect. The incorrect statement can be corrected as

Secondary productivity is defined as the rate of formation of new organic matter by consumers.

45. (*b*) Thalassemia is an autosome-linked recessive blood disease transmitted from parents to the offsprings when both the partners are heterozygous. The cause of this disease can be either mutation or deletion.

46. (b) Seed banks are an example of *ex situ* conservation where plants and animals are taken out in their natural habitat and placed in a protected setting. In this case since only 2-3 plants are remaining, the best way to preserve them is to get the seeds and store them in a seed bank.

47. (*a*) Increased prolactin levels inhibit the secretion of FSH which is the hormone known for triggering ovulation, so, if prolaction levels are high ovulation may be suppressed.

48. (*b*) The correct matches are A-4, B-3, C-1, D-2.

• More than one pistils may be fused together in an ovary. Such ovary is known as syncarpous ovary.

• When pistils are free, they are called apocarpous.

• Filament is the long and slender stalk found in stamen.

• A group of compactly arranged homogenous cells is called sporogenous tissue.

49. (*a*) Statements I, II and V are correct, while statements III and IV are incorrect. They can be corrected as

Typhoid is a bacterial disease caused by *Salmonella typhi*

Widal test is used to diagnose typhoid fever and not common cold.

50. (*c*) C denotes nucellus. It is a mass of cells that have abundant reserve food materials.

51. (*b*) Freshly squeezed juices have fibres and pulps that make them more turbid. Proteases and pectinases are used in bottled juices to clarify the turbidity.

52. (*a*) The correct set of statements are I, II and III, while statements IV and V are incorrect and they can be corrected as

Warm and moist environment favour decomposition whereas low temperature and anaerobiosis inhibit decomposition.

53. (*d*) Statement I is correct, but statement II is incorrect. It can be corrected as

Resource partitioning is a mechanism evolved by two species for co-existence. If two species compete for the same resource, they could avoid competition by choosing for example different times for feeding or different foraging patterns.

54. (b) According to the 10 % law, only 10 % of available energy is used up a trophic level. Let the amount of energy be Y for trophic level III, so energy used by trophic level IV is

$10/100 \times Y = 10$ kJ ; Y = 100 kJ

In similar way, let the energy be A for trophic level II, thus $10/100 \times A = 100$; A = 1000 kJ

55. (*a*) Due to insertion of the foreign DNA, the recombinant plasmids will lose tetracycline resistance.

56. (*c*) For frugivorous or fruit eating birds and mammals in tropical forests the slope of the line showing species area relationship becomes much steaper , i.e. 1.15.

57. (*a*) The correct match is A-3, B-4, C-2, D-1.

- Elephantiasis is a helminthic disease caused by *W. malayi* and *W. bancrofti*.
- Ringworm is a fungal disease caused by *Microsporum*.
- Dengue fever is a viral disease caused by *Flavivirus*.
- Pneumonia is a bacterial disease caused by *Streptococcus pneuamoniae*.

58. (*c*) The incorrect statement can be corrected as

Environmental damage caused by invasive weeds like *Lantana* and water hyacinth is example of alien species invasion.

59. (*a*) The correct matches are A-2, B-4, C-3, D-1.

- *m*RNA or messenger *r*RNA carries codons for the translation process.
- *t*RNA or transfer RNA carries anticodons specific to particular amino acids.
- *r*RNA or ribosomal RNA are found in ribosomes.
- *s*RNA or soluble RNA was the former name of *t*RNA.

60. (*b*) *Trichoderma* are free living fungi, found commonly in the root ecosystems. They act as effective biocontrol agents of several plant pathogens.

61. (*b*) The correct matches are A-2, B-3, C-4, D-1.

- Miller and Urey performed an experiment to prove the chemical evolution.
- Louis pasteur concluded that life come from pre-existing life.
- The term survival of the fittest was coined by Darwin.
- The Greek philosopher Aristotle gave the theory of spontaneous generation.

62. (*c*) Both A and R are true, but R is not the correct explanation of A.

Zygote divides vertically to form two blastomeres. This is followed by a vertical division and a horizontal division.

Now, several divisions occur forming equal sized blastomeres called morula. There is no increase in size of cells. Zona pellucida is a transparent non-cellular layer surrounding egg cell. It remains undivided till the cleavage is complete.

63. (*b*) Forelimbs of mammals like whale, bats, cheetah and humans are called homologous organs because they are similar in anatomical structure, but perform different functions.

64. (*b*) The correct matches are A-1, B-3, C-4, D-2.

- Statin is produced by *Monascus purpureus*. It is used as blood cholesterol lowering agents.
- Cyclosporin-A is produced by *Trichoderma polysporum* and used as an immunosupperessive agent.
- Streptokinase is produced by *Streptococcus* and is used as a clot buster.
- Penicillin is produced by *Penicillium* notatum. It is an antibiotic.

65. (*c*) Both A and R are true, but R is not the correct explanation of A.

In an aquatic ecosystem the biomass of fishes is more than the planktons, hence the pyramid would be inverted.

66. (*c*) E is the morula, which is the embryo with 8-16 blastomeres. It continues to divide and transform into blastocyst (that is bubble-like structure ready for implantation).

67. (*b*) All the sexually transmitted diseases and/or infections are represented by option (b)

Chlamydiasis is caused by *Chlamydia trachomatis* and results in scrotal pain and swelling.

AIDS is caused by the Human Immunodeficiency Virus (HIV) and is transmitted *via* blood, semen and infected mother's milk.

Genital warts is caused by the Human Papilloma Virus (HPV) and results in small bumps on genitals.

68. (*b*) Bagging is a technique in which the flowers are covered with a bag of suitable size.

69. (*d*) A is true, but R is false. R can be corrected as

The outer layer of pollen grains is called exine which is made-up of sporopollenin, one of the most resistant organic material.

70. (*b*) The incorrect statement regarding sporopollenin can be corrected as

Sporopollenin is present in pollen grains and it cannot be degraded by any known enzyme.

71. (*b*) The correct statements are III, IV and V, while statements I and II are incorrect. These can be corrected as

- Pea and groundnut are examples of non- albuminous seeds and wheat is an example of albuminous seeds.

• Apple is an example of false fruit, while Mango is an example of true fruit.

72. (*c*) The incorrect statements are III and V. They can be corrected as

Colostrum is the milk which is produced during the initial few days of lactation. It contains antibodies like IgA.

Placenta produces hormones like hCG, oestrogens, progestrogens, etc.

73. (*b*) The incorrect statement is in option (b). It can be corrected as

CuT, Cu7, Mulitload 375 are copper releasing IUD's while lippes loop is non-medicated IUD.

74. (*b*) The biotic agents of pollination are insects and birds, while wind and water are abiotic agents of pollination.

75. (*c*) Both statements I and II are incorrect they can be corrected as

• Inheritance is defined as the process of transmission of characters or traits from parents to their progenies

• Variation is defined as the degrees by which the offsprings differ from their parents.

76. (*d*) The transcription unit has three regions such as promoter, structural gene and terminator.

77. (*c*) Ovulatory phase is determined by rapid secretion of LH that leads to the rupture of Graafian follicle. It lasts for 30-48 hours.

78. (*b*) Statement in option b is incorrect and can be corrected as

Turner's syndrome results into a karyotype of 45 with XO. Individuals with this syndrome have short stature, small uterus, webbed neck, etc.

79. (*a*) The incorrect statement can be corrected as

In *Eco*RI, the letter R is derived from the name of strain of organism from which enzyme has been isolated.

80. (*d*) Statement I is correct, but statement II is incorrect. It can be corrected as

Sacred grove is an example of *in situ* conservation. These are tracts of forests with special religious and cultural importance.

81. (*c*) Statements I, II and III are correct while statements IV and V are incorrect. They can be corrected as

• Catabolism is the process by which detritus is degraded into simpler inorganic compounds by bacterial and fungal enzymes.

• Humification is the process of formation and accumulation of a dark coloured amorphous substance called humus.

82. (*c*) A childless couple wherein the female partner fails to produce quality ovum but can provide suitable environment to the foetus should be advised with Gamete Intra Fallopian Transfer (GIFT). In this, the Ovum collected from a donor is transfered into the fallopian tube of another female, who cannot produce one, but can provide suitable environment to it.

83. (*a*) Statement I is incorrect, but statement II is correct. Incorrect statement can be corrected as

Two closely linked genes HBA 1 and HBA2 on chromosome 16 of each parent controls α- thalassemia.

84. (*b*) Methanogens produce large amount of biogas consisting of CH_4 (50–70%), CO_2 (30–40%) and H_2.

85. (*b*) Statements II and III are incorrect and can be corrected as

• Corpus luteum secretes large amount of progesterone for endometrium maintenance in luteal phase.

• Menstrual phase lasts for 3-5 days while proliferative phase lasts for 10-14 days.

86. (*d*) A is true, but R is false. R can be corrected as

Diaphragms, cervical caps and vaults block the entry of sperms through the cervix and thus prevent conception.

87. (*a*) A is the Interstitial cells or leydig cells. They synthesise and secrete testicular hormones called androgens.

88.(*b*) Heroin acts as a depressant and slows down body functions.

Morphine is an effective sedative and painkiller taken by patients who have undergone surgery.

89. (*c*) Hallucinogenic drugs change mood, behaviour, thoughts and perceptions. Hallucinogenic drug are obtained from *Atropa belladonna* and *Datura* sp.

90. (*a*) A is false, but R is true. A can be corrected as

Infundibulum is a funnel-shaped organ that possess finger-like projections called fimbriae, which helps in collection of ovum after ovulation.

NK01 NEET Knock Offs 1

1. (*c*) Uridine is a nucleoside specific to RNA. In RNA, uracil replaces thymine. So, one can find uridine in RNA and thymidine in DNA.

2. (*c*) The correct matches are A-2, B-1, C-4, D-3.

- Delivery of the foetus is known as parturition.
- The signals for parturition originate from the fully developed foetus and placenta which induce mild uterine contractions called foetal ejection reflex.
- The mammary glands of the female starts producing milk towards the end of pregnancy by the process called lactation.
- The milk produced during the initial few days of lactation is called colostrum.

3. (*c*) Both A and R are true, but R is not the correct explanation of A. It can be explained as

Vegetative reproduction typically involves parts of the algae breaking off or splitting and growing into new organisms or forming specific types of non-motile spores directly from the parent body. Asexual reproduction involves production of new individual through specialised reproductive structures like zoospores.

4. (*d*) Statement I is correct, but statement II is incorrect and it can be corrected as

Polygenic traits, such as human skin colour are controlled by multiple genes and can result in a range of phenotypes rather than just two distinct forms.

5. (*c*) Cell wall is a non-living rigid structure, which forms an outer covering for the plasma membrane of fungi and plants. In the cell wall of a young plant cell, the primary wall is capable of growth, which gradually diminishes as the cell matures and the secondary wall is formed on the inner side of the cell.

6. (*c*) Statement given in option (c) is incorrect. It can be corrected as

The hemichordates are small group of worm-like marine animals. They have a cylindrical body with proboscis, collar and trunk. Urochorodates are protochordates, which are exclusively marine and have notochord only in their larval tail.

7. (*a*) The division of the zygote is delayed until sufficient endosperm has been formed to ensure that there are enough nutrients, energy and support available for the embryo. This strategy maximises the chances of successful seed development and plant production.

8. (*c*) Morgan hybridised yellow bodied, white eyed females to brown-bodied, red eyed males and intercrossed their F_1 progeny. He observed that the two genes did not segregate independently of each other and F_2 ratio deviated very significantly from the 9:3:3:1 ratio.

9. (*b*) Sometimes both alleles of a particular gene are expressed in a dominant fashion even in F_1 generation, meaning both alleles for the same characteristics are simultaneously expressed in the heterozygote. This is called codominance, e.g. ABO blood grouping.

10. (*c*) Plants follow different pathways (in response to environments) or phase of life to form different kinds of structures. This ability is called plasticity, e.g. heterophylly in cotton. In these plants, the leaves of the juvenile plants are different in shapes from those in mature plants, e.g. *Larkspur*. It can also be seen as the difference in shapes of leaves produced in air and those produced in water, e.g. in buttercup.

11. (*a*) The correct matches are A-2, B-1, C-4, D-3.

- Mucus coating of the epithelium lining the respiratory tract is an example of physical barriers.
- Saliva in the mouth an example of physiological barriers.
- Cellular barriers include certain types leucocytes.
- Cytokine barriers include interferons protect non-infected cells from further viral infection.

12. (*a*) When DNA is cut by the same restriction enzyme,the resultant DNA fragments have the same kind of sticky ends and these can be joined together (end to end) using DNA ligases.

13. (*d*) Statement I is correct, but statement II is incorrect, it can be corrected as

Co-factors are non-protein constituents, bound to the enzyme to make the enzyme catalytically active.

14. (*c*) The correct matches are A-4, B-2, C-1, D-3.

- Presence of myofibrils is the characteristic feature of the muscle fibre. They are parallely arranged filaments.
- The light bands contain actin and the dark band contains myosin
- Each organised skeletal muscle is made up of a number of fascicles.

15. (*a*) Lipase is an additive to detergents. This enzyme breaks down the oily stain, then surfactants in the detergent attach to the remnants of the stain to remove it from the clothing.

16. (*d*) The incorrect statement can be corrected as
The given figure is of *Pleurobrachia* that belongs to phylum Ctenophora. In these organisms, reproduction takes place only by sexual means.

17. (*c*) At the beginning of the final stage of karyokinesis, i.e. telophase, the chromosomes that have reached their respective poles decondense and lose their individuality. Nucleus envelope develops around the chromosome clustered at each pole forming two daughter nuclei. Nucleolus, Golgi complex and ER reform.

18. (*d*) Statement I is correct, but statement II is incorrect and it can be corrected as
Vital capacity includes ERV, TV and IRV or the maximum volume of air a person can breathe out after a forced inspiration. Whereas, the total volume of air accomodated in the lungs at the end of a forced inspiration is called total lung capacity.

19. (*d*) The NADP reductase enzyme is located on the stroma side of the membrane. Along with electrons that come from the acceptor of electrons of PS I, protons are necessary for the reduction of $NADP^+$ to $NADPH^+$. These protons are removed from stroma. Hence, within the chloroplast, protons in the stroma decrease in number.

20. (*b*) The correct matches are A-2, B-1, C-3, D-4.

- High blood pressure affects vital organs like brain and kidney.
- Atherosclerosis is caused by deposition of calcium, fat and cholesterol.
- Angina is also called angina pectoris. A symptom of acute chest pain appears when no enough oxygen is reaching the heart.
- Heart failure means the state of heart when it is not pumping blood effectively.

21. (*d*) The incorrect statement can be corrected as
Transgenic mice are being developed for use in testing the safety of vaccines before they are used on humans. Transgenic mice are being used to test the safety of the polio vaccine.

22. (*a*) A is false, but R is true. A can be corrected as
The pars distalis region of pituitary is commonly called the anterior pituitary which secretes GH, PRL, TSH, ACTH, LH and FSH. Pars intermedia secretes only one hormone called MSH.

23. (*b*) In anaphase, the sister chromatids are pulled apart by the spindle fibres towards opposite poles of the cell, ensuring each daughter cell receives an identical set of chromosomes.

24. (*b*) The correct order of circulation of blood through the human body is as follows:

- Deoxygenated blood is pumped by the right ventricle into the pulmonary artery.
- Blood is oxygenated in the lungs.
- Oxygenated blood is pumped by the left ventricle into the aorta.
- Blood travels through a network of arteries, arterioles and capillaries to the tissues.

25. (*d*) Cousins confirmed the release of a volatile substance from ripened oranges that hastened the ripening of stored unriped bananas. Later, this volatile substance was identified as ethylene.

26. (*a*) Statement I is incorrect, but statement II is correct. Statement I can be corrected as
Convergent evolution is described as the independent evolution of similar features in different lineages due to similar environment conditions.

27. (*a*) *Funaria* is a bryophyte, *Dryopteris* is a pteridophyte and *Ginkgo* is a gymnosperm. All of these possess archegonia. It is a female reproductive structure where eggs are produced.

28. (*a*) Statements I, IV and V are correct. Statements II and III are incorrect. The incorrect statements can be corrected as:

- Each spermatogonia is diploid and contains 46 chromosomes.
- Spermatogenesis starts at the age of puberty due to significant increase in the secretion of gonadotropin releasing hormone.

29. (*d*) Statement I is correct, but statement II is incorrect. Statement II can be corrected as
In only sexual reproduction, when the two gametes fuse, the chromosome number is restored to the value in the parent.

30. (*b*) Microbes such as *Lactobacillus* and others commonly called Lactic Acid Bacteria (LAB) grow in milk and convert it to curd. In our stomach, it plays very beneficial role in checking disease causing microbes.

31. (*b*) In plants like mint and jasmine, a slender lateral branch arises from the base of the main axis and after growing aerially for sometime, arch downwards to touch the ground.

32. (*c*) The incorrect statement (c) can be corrected as:
In order to form human insulin, both chains A and B were produced separately, extracted and then combined by creating di-sulphide bonds.

33. (*a*) S^{35} is a radioactive isotope, commonly used to label proteins because sulphur is found in some amino acids. In the case of S^{35} labelled bacteriophages, radioactivity was detected primarily in the phage coats (the supernatant portion).

34. (*d*) The incorrect statement (d), it can be corrected as:

The animal kingdom represents a variety of excretory structures. In most of the invertebrates, these structures are simple tubular forms whereas, vertebrates have complex tubular organs called kidney. Malpighian tubules help in the removal of nitrogenous wastes in most of the insects. While antennal glands perform the excretory function in crustaceans like prawns.

35. (*b*) Both A and R are true and R is the correct explanation of A.

Chlorophyll-*a* is the major pigment responsible for trapping light. Other thylakoids pigments like chl-*b*, xanthophylls and carotenoids act as accessory pigments, by absorbing light and transferring the energy to chl-*a*. Maximum absorption by chl-*a* is in the blue and the red regions, also shows higher rate of photosynthesis.

36. (*c*) The correct sequence for secondary treatment of sewage is as follows

- Aeration of primary effluent in large tanks.
- Reduction of BOD in effluent.
- Sedimentation of bacterial flocs.
- Formation of activated sludge.
- Transfer of activated sludge to anaerobic sludge digesters.

37. (*d*) Statement (d) is not correct, it can be corrected as:

Prophase is the first stage of karyokinesis of mitosis that follows the S and G_2 phases of interphase. In the S and G_2 phases, the new DNA molecules formed are not distinct, but intertwined. The chromosomal material becomes untangled during the process of prophase.

38. (*c*) Both A and R are true, but R is not the correct explanation of A. It can be explained as:

Competition occurs when closely related species compete for the same resources that are limiting. The feeding efficiency of one species is also affected by the competition.

39. (*b*) Both A and the R are true and the R is the correct explanation of A.

Aldosterone is a steroid hormone synthesised in and secreted from the outer layer of the adrenal cortex. It is responsible for regulating sodium homeostasis, thereby helping to control blood volume and blood pressure.

40. (*c*) Statements III, IV and V are correct, and statements I and II are incorrect. The incorrect statements can be corrected as:

The beginning of diplotene is recognised by the dissolution of the synaptonemal complex and the tendency of the recombined homologous chromosomes of the bivalents to separate from each other, except at the sites of crossovers.

The final stage of meiotic prophase-I is diakinesis. During this phase, the chromosomes are fully condensed and meiotic spindle is assembled to prepare the homologous chromosomes for separation.

41. (*a*) Statements I, IV and V are correct. Statements II and III are incorrect. The incorrect statements can be corrected as:

The afferent nerve fibres transmit impulses from tissues/organs to the CNS and the efferent fibres transmit regulatory impulses from the CNS to the concerned peripheral tissues/organs.

The somatic neural system relays impulses from the CNS to skeletal muscles, while the autonomic neural system transmits impulses from the CNS to the involuntary organs and smooth muscles of the body.

42. (*c*) Both A and R are true, but R is not the correct explanation of A. It can be explained as:

The DFC is more significant in energy flow in terrestrial ecosystems because a large amount of energy is stored in dead organic matter. Decomposers are highly efficient at breaking down this matter and the DFC plays a critical role in nutrient recycling.

43. (*a*) The tricuspid valve allows blood flow between the right atrium and right ventricle. The bicuspid valve or mitral valve allows blood flow between the left atrium and the left ventricle.

44. (*b*) The primary CO_2 acceptor molecule in C_4 pathway is a 3-carbon molecule, Phosphoenol Pyruvate (PEP) and is present in the mesophyll cell. It converted into C_4 acid, i.e Oxalo Acetic Acid (OAA).

45. (*a*) An inverted pyramid is typically observed in pyramid of biomass of the aquatic ecosystem. This pyramid occurs when the biomass of the consumers at a certain trophic level is greater than the biomass of the producers.

46. (*a*) Flame cells are specialised excretory cells that function like kidneys, removing waste materials from *Planaria*, rotifers and *Amphioxus*. Bundles of flame cells are called protonephridia.

47. (*b*) In PCR, the components are typically added to the reaction mix in a specific order to ensure that the reaction works efficiently. The correct order is as follows

- DNA template
- DNA primers
- Deoxynucleotides
- *Taq* polymerase

48. (*b*) DNA dependent DNA polymerase uses a DNA template to catalyse the polymerisation of deoxynucleotides.

These enzymes are highly efficient enzymes as they have to catalyse polymerisation of a large number of nucleotides in a very short time. *E.coli*, that has only 4.6×10^6 bp, completes the process of replication within 38 minutes; that means the average rate of polymerisation has to be approximately 2000 bp/second.

49. (*b*) The correct matches are A-2, B-4, C-1, D-3.

- Pleuro Pneumonia Like Organisms (PPLO) are generally smaller and multiply more rapidly than the eukaryotic cells.
- In prokaryotic cells, reserve food material is stored in the form of inclusion bodies, not bounded by any membrane.
- Centrosomes are surrounded by amorphous pericentriolar materials.
- Microbodies are membrane- bound minute vesicles that contain various enzymes and are present in both plants and animal cells.

50. (*a*) In glycolysis, glucose and fructose are phosphorylated to give rise to glucose 6- phosphate by the activity of the enzyme hexokinase. This phosphorylated form of glucose isomerises to produce fructose 6-phosphate.

51. (*c*) Down's syndrome is a condition in which a person has an extra copy of chromosome 21. The affected individual is short statured with small round head, furrowed tongue and partially open mouth.

52. (*c*) The transition state represents the highest energy state that the substrate must achieve to be converted into the product because it is the peak of the energy barrier. It is unstable. Once the transition state is achieved, the reaction proceeds rapidly to form a more stable product.

53. (*c*) The correct matches are A-2, B-1, C-3, D-4

- In unambiguous condition one codon codes for only one amino acid.
- Some amino acids are coded by more than one codon, hence the code is degenerate.
- The codon is read in *m*RNA in a contiguous fashion. There are no punctuations.
- The code is nearly universal; e.g. , from bacteria to human, UUU would code for phenylalanine.

54. (*d*) Statement I is correct, but statement II is incorrect. It can be corrected as:

In monocot stem, vascular bundles are conjoint and closed. Peripheral vascular bundles are generally smaller than the centrally located ones.

55. (*c*) Statements I and II are incorrect, the incorrect statements can be corrected as:

- In diatoms, the cell walls form two thin overlapping shells, which fit together as a soap box. The walls are embedded with silica and thus the walls are indestructible.
- *Euglena* has a protein rich layer called pellicle which makes their body flexible.

56. (*a*) The correct matches are A-4, B-1, C-2, D-3.

- Viroids were discovered by T.O Diener and were smaller than viruses and caused potato spindle tuber disease.
- Prions consist of abnormally folded protein.
- MW Beijerinek called the virus as infectious living fluid.
- Deuteromycetes are known as the imperfect fungi because only the asexual or vegetative phase are known and sexual phase is not known.

57. (*c*) Both A and R are true, but R is not the correct explanation of A. It can be explained as

During the zygotene stage of prophase I in meiosis I, homologous chromosomes begin to pair up closely in a process known as synapsis. The chromosome synapsis is accompanied by the formation of complex structure called synaptonemal complex. These paired chromosomes are known as bivalent or tetrad as they consist of four chromatids.

58. (*b*) The thorn and tendrils of *Bougainvillea* and *Cucurbita,* respectively represent homology. Homology is based on divergent evolution, where same anatomical structures are developed along different directions due to adaptations.

59. (*a*) Statement II is incorrect, it can be corrected as

The current species extinction rates are estimated to be 100 to 1000 times faster than in pre-human times.

Rest statements are correct.

60. (*a*) A is false, but R is true. A can be corrected as

Pyruvate is formed by the glycolytic catabolism of carbohydrates in the cytosol, and after this it enters mitochondrial matrix and undergoes oxidative decarboxylation by a complex set of reactions catalysed by pyruvate dehydrogenase that requires participation of several coenzymes, including NAD^+ and coenzyme-A.

61. (*c*) Urea is synthesised in liver and excreted through kidneys. So, the maximum amount of urea is present in the hepatic vein and minimum in renal vein.

62. (*b*) Both A and R are true, and R is the correct explanation of A.

Pteridophytes are the first terrestrial plants to possess vascular tissues, i.e. xylem and phloem. The restricted distribution of pteridophytes is due to the specific requirements of their gametophytes related to water for growth and fertilisation.

63. (*b*) Both A and R are true, and R is the correct explanation of A.
The heterozygotes (Bb) show intermediate phenotypes, i.e. starch grain of intermediate size, while homozygotes (BB) produce large grain size and bb produce small grain size. It demonstrates incomplete dominance.

64. (*a*) Statements I, III and IV are correct, statements II and V are incorrect, these can be corrected as
- The first movements of the foetus and appearance of hair on the head are usually observed during the fifth month.
- By the end of second trimester, the body is covered with fine hair, eye-lids separate and eyelashes are formed.

65. (*b*) Both statement I and statement II are correct.
Human beings have a significant ability to maintain and moderate the respiratory rhythm to suit the demands of the body tissues. A chemosensitive area is situated adjacent to the rhythm centre which is highly sensitive to CO_2 and hydrogen ions. Increase in these substance can activate this center, which in turn, can signal the rhythm center to make necessory adjustments in the respiratory process by which these substance can be eliminated.

66. (*b*) In primary lymphoid organs, lymphocytes are proliferated and matured into antigen-sensitive lymphocytes. After maturation, these lymphocytes migrate to secondary lymphoid organs like spleen, lymph nodes, tonsils, etc. These organs provide the site for interaction of lymphocytes with the antigen, which then proliferate to become effector cells.

67. (*b*) The correct matches are A-2, B-3, C-4, D-1.
- Predation helps in maintaining species diversity in a community.
- Competition provides potent force in organic evolution.
- The interaction between cuckoo and crow represent brood parasitism.
- Plants need the help of animals for pollinating their flowers, and in turn, rewards pollen and nectar for pollinators. This is an example of mutualism.

68. (*a*) Incorrect statement can be corrected as
Research has shown that less than 2 per cent of human genome consists of protein coding genes.

69. (*c*) The correct matches are A-4, B-3, C-1, D-2.
- Arachebacteria : (Methanogens) - are present in the gut of several ruminant animals such as cows and buffaloes.
- The cell walls of chrysophytes form two thin overlapping shells which fit together as in a soap box.
- Dinoflagellates appear yellow, green, brown, blue or red depending on the main pigments presents in their cells.
- Ciliated protozoans have a cavity that opens to the outside of the cell surface.

70. (*d*) The given figure shows a perigynous flower. In this flower, gynoecium is situated in the centre and other parts of the flower are located on the rim of the thalamus, almost at the same level. Ovary is half inferior.

71. (*a*) The correct matches are A-3, B-4, C-2, D-1.
- About 65 mya, dinosaurs suddenly disappeared from the earth.
- About 200 mya, reptiles of different shapes and size dominated on earth.
- Jawless fish probably evolved around 350 mya.
- About 2000 mya, the first cellular forms of life appeared on earth.

72. (*d*) Statements I, II, IV and V are correct. Statement III is incorrect and can be corrected as
Neutrophils are the most abundant cells (60 – 65%) of the total WBCs and basophils are the least (0.5 – 1%) among them.

73. (*b*) Statements II and III are incorrect. Rest are correct. The incorrect statements can be corrected as:
Cell wall is a non-living rigid structure. It forms an outer covering for the plasma membrane of fungi and plants. It is absent in animal cells.

74. (*a*) The axon terminals contain vesicles filled with neurotransmitters. When an impulse arrives at the axon terminal, it stimulates the movement of the synaptic vesicles towards the membrane where they fuse with the plasma membrane and release their neurotransmitters in the synaptic cleft.

75. (*a*) Statements I, II and IV are correct and statements III and V are incorrect. The incorrect statements can be correct as
- Epidermis is usually single layered. Its cells are parenchymatous with a small amount of cytoplasm lined by the cell wall.
- The stomatal apperture, guard cells and the surrounding subsidiary cells are together called stomatal apparatus.

76. (*b*) The human brain is well protected by the skull. Inside the skull, the brain is covered by cranial meninges consisting of an outer layer called dura mater, very thin middle layer called arachnoid and an inner layer called pia mater.

77. (*a*) The correct matches are A-2, B-3, C-4, D-1.
- Glucose is phosphorylated to give rise to glucose-6-phosphate by the activity of hexokinase.
- Pyruvate undergoes oxidative decarboxylation to form acetyl Co-A

by a complex set of reactions catalysed by pyruvic dehydrogenase.

- CO_2 is utilised for the carboxylation of RuBP to produce 3-phosphoglycerate with the help of RuBisCO enzyme.
- In C_4 cycle, CO_2 reacts with PEP to produce OAA with the help of PEPcase.

78. (*a*) The commonly known forms of Basidiomycetes are mushrooms, bracket fungi, puffballs, *Ustilago* (smut) etc. They grow in soil, on logs and tree stumps and in living plant bodies as parasites.

79. (*a*) Statement I is incorrect, but statement II is correct. Statement I can be corrected as

Bacillus thuringiensis are available in sachets as dried spores which are mixed with water and sprayed onto vulnerable plants.

80. (*b*) The excretory system in insects is comprised of malpighian tubules. They release their waste in the form of uric acid. They have glandular and ciliated cells that absorb nitrogenous waste products. The waste products are converted into uric acid inside the hindgut of the insects like cockroach.

81. (*d*) Statements II, III and V are correct. While statements I and IV are incorrect. The incorrect statements can be corrected as

- Prophase is marked by the initiation of condensation of chromosomal material. The chromosomal material becomes untangled during the process of chromatin condensation.
- During diakinesis, the chromosomes are fully condensed and the meiotic spindle is assembled to prepare the homologous chromosomes for separation.

82. (*d*) In transcription, the template DNA strand is one that RNA polymerase reads to synthesise the RNA transcript. The coding strand, also known as the sense strand, has the same nucleotide sequence as the RNA transcript, except that it contains thymine instead of uracil.

83. (*a*) Statement I is incorrect, but statement II is correct. Incorrect statement can be corrected as

A population has certain attributes whereas, an individual organism does not. An individual may have birth and deaths, but a population has birth rates and death rates.

84. (*a*) Statements I, II and IV are correct. Statement III is incorrect. Incorrect statement can be corrected as:

Blood is a special connective tissue consisting of a fluid matrix, plasma and formed elements. Blood only transports hormones secreted by the endocrine glands, but does not produce them.

85. (*a*) The correct matches are A-1, B-3, C-2, D-4.

- Opioids are extracted from the latex of *Papaver somniferum*.
- Cannabinoids are obtained from the *Cannabis sativa*.
- Cocaine is obtained from *Erythroxylum coca*.
- Drugs like barbiturates are normally used to help patients cope wi.ı depression.

86. (*d*) Statement I is correct, but statement II is incorrect, it can be corrected as

Genetic modifications of organisms can have unpredictable results when such organisms are introduced into the ecosystem.

87. (*b*) Statement given in option (b) is incorrect. The incorrect statement can be corrected as

Cyclosporin-A is used as an immunosupppressive agent in organ-transplant patients and is produced the fungus *Trichoderma polysporum*.

88. (*c*) Peptide hormones interact with membrane bound receptors and normally do not enter the target cell, but generate secondary messengers, which in turn, regulate cellular metabolism.

89. (*d*) Statement given in option (d) is incorrect. The incorrect statement can be corrected as

In the alveoli, where pO_2 is higher, O_2 gets bound to haemoglobin whereas it is easily dissociated at the tissues where pO_2 is low and pCO_2 and H^+ concentration are high.

90. (*a*) Statements I, II and III are correct, while statements IV and V are incorrect. The incorrect statements can be corrected as

Family has a group of related genera with still less number of similarities as compared to genus and species. Families are characterised on the basis of both vegetative and reproductive features of plant species.

NK02 NEET Knock Offs 2

1. (*b*) In *Ustilago* and *Puccinia*, karyogamy and meiosis take place in the basidium producing four basidiospores. The basidiospores are exogenously produced on the basidium (pl.: basidia). The basidia are arranged in fruiting bodies called basidiocarps.

2. (*c*) Option (c) is correct regarding cardiac cycle. Incorrect statements can be corrected as

During systole, the SAN generates an action potential. Ventricular systole increases the ventricular pressure causing the closure of tricuspid and bicuspid valves. The heart sound 'lub' is associated with the closure of the tricuspid and bicuspid valves.

3. (*a*) The correct matches are A–3, B–1, C–2 and D–4.

Synaptonemal complex is formed during zygotene.

Recombination nodule is formed during pachytene. Terminalisation of chiasmata occurs in diakinesis.

Interkinesis is a stage before meiosis II.

4. (*a*) Statement I is incorrect, but statement II is correct.

Statement I can be corrected as

The trichomes in the shoot system are usually multicellular. They may be branched or unbranched and soft or stiff. They may even be secretory. They help in preventing water loss due to transpiration.

5. (*c*) In the given diagram X, Y, Z and W represents clavicle, humerus, radius and ulna, respectively.

6. (*d*) Membrane bound organelles are present in eukaryotic cells. Eukaryotic cells have definite nuclear membrane.

Other incorrect statements can be corrected as

- In eukaryotes, plants have cell wall made up of cellulose.
- In fungi, it is made up of chitin and in animal cells, cell wall is absent.
- The ribosome of mitochondria is of 70S type.
- Mitochondria possess single circular DNA.

7. (*b*) In plants like plum, rose and peach, gynoecium is situated in the centre and other parts of the flower are located on the rim of the thalamus almost at the same level. Flower in this case is called perigynous. The ovary in this case is half-inferior.

8. (*a*) India's share of the global species diversity is an impressive 8.1 per cent, which makes our country one of the 12 mega diversity countries of the world.

9. (*c*) Oestrogen stimulates the anterior lobe of pituitary to increase the secretion of LH that causes rupture of Graafian follicle. Oestrogen has positive feedback on anterior lobe of pituitary for the secretion of LH, which causes the LH surge.

10. (*b*) The correct matches are A–3, B–1, C–4 and D–2.

- In mango, middle fleshy edible part is mesocarp and an inner stony hard endocarp.
- In coconut, the mesocarp is fibrous.
- In *Dianthus*, the placentation is called free central, where the ovules are borne on central axis with no septa.
- In sunflower, basal placentation is present where the placenta develops at the base of ovary and a single ovule is attached to it.

11. (*b*) The correct matches are A–4, B–1, C–2 and D–3.

- The family pedigree of Queen Victoria shows a number of haemophilic descendents as she was a carrier of the haemophilia.
- In sickle-cell anaemia, the mutant haemoglobin molecule undergoes polymerisation under low oxygen tension causing the change in the shape of the RBC from biconcave disc to elongated sickle like-structure.
- In phenylketonuria, phenylalanine is accumulated and converted into phenylpyruvic acid and other derivatives.
- β-thalassemia is controlled by a single gene HBB on chromosome 11 of each parent and occurs due to mutation of one or both the genes.

12. (*b*) The incorrect statement can be corrected as

The pollen grain having the generative and vegetative cell marks the two-celled stage. The generative cell lies in the cytoplasm of the vegetative cell. The generative cell is elongated that helps it to move through the pollen tube. The vegetative cell has most of the cytoplasm and is needed to provide nutrition to the pollen grain.

13. (*c*) Counter current mechanism helps in maintaining an increased osmolarity towards the inner medullary interstitium, i.e., from 300 mOsmol/L in the cortex to about 1200 mOsmol/L in the inner medulla.

This makes the interstitum hypertonic. This gradient is mainly caused by NaCl and urea.

14. (*d*) Statements I, III and IV are correct. Incorrect statements II and V can be corrected as

Leaves originate from shoot apical meristems and are arranged in an acropetal order.

In some leguminous plants, the leaf base may become swollen, which is called the pulvinus.

15. (*c*) Both A and R are true, but R is not the correct explanation of A.

Small mammals are not found in polar regions as they have large surface area compared to the volume so they lose heat easily in cold and have to expend energy to generate body heat.

16. (*a*) Filiform apparatus is present at the micropylar tip which plays an important role in guiding the pollen tubes into the synergids. The synergids have special cellular thickenings at the micropylar tip called filiform apparatus.

Statements given in option (c) and (d) are correct with respect to the female gametophyte or embryo sac.

17. (*a*) Statement I is incorrect, but statement II is correct. Incorrect statement can be corrected as

The vasa efferentia leave the testis and open into epididymis located along the posterior surface of each testis.

18. (*b*) The correct match is A–2, B–4, C–1 and D–3.

- Methanogens are archaebacteria, which are responsible for the production of methane (biogas) from the dung of herbivorous animals.
- *Nostoc* can fix atmospheric nitrogen in specialised cells called heterocysts.
- The algal component is known as phycobiont and fungal component as mycobiont, which are autotrophic and heterotrophic, respectively.
- The mycoplasma are anaerobic organisms that completely lack a cell wall.

19. (*b*) Secretion of bile into the duodenum part of small intestine is regarded as physiological barrier due to the germicidal nature of bile.

20. (*a*) Statement I is incorrect, but statement II is correct. Statement I can be corrected as

Cytotaxonomy is based on cytological information like chromosome number, structure, behaviour and chemotaxonomy considers the chemical constituents of the plants.

21. (*d*) A is true, but R is false. R can be corrected as

Administration of progestogens or progestogen-oestrogen combination is used as an emergency contraceptive pill. These pills prevent pregnancy by delaying ovulation.

22. (*b*) In C_3 plants, some O_2 does bind to RuBisCO, and hence CO_2 fixation is decreased. Here, the RuBP instead of being converted to 2 molecules of PGA, binds with O_2 to form one molecule of phosphoglycerate (3 carbon) and phosphoglycolate (2 Carbon) in a pathway called photorespiration.

23. (*b*) In deep water rice plants, ethylene stimulates internode elongation allowing the photosynthetic organs to remain afloat.

24. (*d*) Statements I, III and V are correct, but statement II and IV are incorrect.

The incorrect statements can be corrected as

The first non-cellular forms of life could have originated 3 billion years back. The geological history of earth closely correlates with the biological history of earth.

25. (*c*) The given diagram represents stage of metaphase II. At this stage, the chromosomes align at the equator and the microtubules from opposite poles of the spindle get attached to the kinetochores of sister chromatids.

26. (*b*) Phosphoenolpyruvate (PEP), in the presence of enzyme PEP carboxylase forms Oxalo Acetic Acid (OAA) $\rightarrow$ The compound containing four carbon is transferred from mesophyll cells to bundle sheath cells $\rightarrow$ In bundle sheath cells, decarboxylation occurs and a CO_2 is released which enters the Calvin cycle and the C_3 compound again goes back to the mesophyll cell $\rightarrow$ The C_3 compound undergoes regeneration to form phosphoenolpyruvate.

27. (*d*) The correct matches are A-4, B-1, C-2 and D-3.

In the rocky intertidal communities of the American Pacific coast, the *Pisaster* starfish is an important predator.

Mycorrhizae is an example of mutualism; it is an association between fungi and roots of higher plants.

Parasites have special adaptation, i.e. they lose their sense organs.

Lions and tigers hunt the same prey and compete with each other.

28. (*a*) X is the relation between species richness and explored area: $S = CA^Z$. The relation between species richness and area for a wide variety of taxa (angiosperm plants, birds, bats, freshwater fishes) was given by Alexander Humboldt and turns out to be a rectangular hyperbola.

On a logarithmic scale, the relationship is a straight line described by the equation

log S = log C + Z log A

where,

S= Species richness, A= Area,

Z = Slope of the line (regression coefficient) and C = Y-intercept

29. (*c*) Gonadotropin and prolactin interact with membrane bound receptors normally do not enter the target cell, but generate secondary messengers which inturn regulate cellular metabolism. These hormones use secondary messenger like cyclic AMP, IP_3, Ca^{++}, etc.

30. (*d*) The correct matches are A–3, B–4, C–2 and D–1.

- Collenchyma consists of cells which are much thickened at the corner due to deposition of cellulose, hemicellulose and pectin.
- Xylem vessel is cylindrical tube-like structure with lignified wall and a large central cavity.
- Bast fibres are phloem fibres, present only in secondary phloem.
- The companion cells are specialized parenchymatous cells, which are closely associated with sieve tube elements.

31. (*d*) Statements II, III and V are incorrect and can be corrected as-

The midbrain is characterised by one pair of optic lobes. Hindbrain consist of cerebellum and medulla oblongata. Corpus callosum is absent in amphibians. It is present only in mammals.

32. (*a*) Options I, II and V are correct features of dark reaction.

The dark reaction involves fixation of CO_2, reduction of CO_2, synthesis of compounds from glucose. It is independent of light.

Breakdown of water molecule or photolysis, and evolution of oxygen occurs in light reaction.

33. (*b*) The secondary spermatocytes and spermatids are haploid structures formed during spermatogenesis. During the process of spermatogenesis, the primary spermatocytes (2n) undergo meiosis. after completing the first meiotic division, it result in the formation of two equal haploid cells (*n*) called secondary spamatocytes. These further undergo the second meiotic division to produce four equal haploid (*n*) spermatids.

34. (*a*) The autotrophic components in a shallow water body are phytoplanktons, some algae and the floating, submerged and marginal plants found at the edges. The consumers are represented by the zooplanktons, the free swimming and bottom dwelling forms. The decomposers are the fungi, bacteria and flagellates especially abundant in the bottom of the pond.

35. (*b*) The correct matches are A-2, B-3, C-4 and D-1.

Hepatitis-B vaccine is produced by recombinant DNA technology. Antitoxin provides passive artificial immunity. Colostrum provides natural passive immunity to young ones (infant). Cell mediated immunity provides immune responses against organ transplant.

36. (*c*) Option (c) shows correct requirements for primary productivity.

Primary productivity depends on the plant species inhabiting a particular area. It also depends on a variety of environmental factors, availability of nutrients and photosynthetic capacity of plants. Therefore, it varies in different types of ecosystems.

37. (*c*) The incorrect statement can be corrected as

GIFT is an *in vivo* fertilisation technique, in which the fertilisation is allowed inside the female body by natural coitus or artificial insemination.

38. (*c*) *Brachiosaurus* is from the same lineage as that of *Tyrannosaurus rex*. *T. rex* was about 20 ft. in height (biggest dinosaur) and had huge dagger like teeth.

39. (*b*) The correct match is A-2, B-3, C-4 and D-1.

- A sterile stamen is called staminode.
- When stamens are attached to the petals, they are epipetalous.
- Stamens are epiphyllous when attached to the perianth, as in the flowers of lily.
- In diadelphous condition as in pea, stamens are present in two bundles.

40. (*c*) Statements II and IV are correct about Mendel's experiment.

Statements I, III and V are incorrect. These can be corrected as

Mendel crossed the tall plant from F_2 with a dwarf plant to know the genetype of dominant phenotype. This is called a test cross. In a typical test cross, an organism (pea plants here) showing a dominant phenotype (and whose genotype is to be determined) is crossed with the recessive parent, instead of self-crossing.

Mendel selected fourteen true-breeding pea plant varieties, as seven pairs which were similar except for one character with contrasting traits.

Punnett square is a graphical representation to calculate the probability of all possible genotypes of offsprings in a genetic cross.

41. (*b*) The constituents of first filtrate formed in the lumen of Bowman's capsule is same as plasma except proteins. The high pressure causes the liquid part of the blood to filter out from the glomerulus into the renal tubule.

This filtrate is known as 'glomerular filtrate'. Glomerular filtrate consists of water, urea, salts, glucose and other plasma solutes.

42. (*b*) The correct matches are A–1, B–4, C–2 and D–3.

Purines and pyrimidines have heterocyclic ring.

Cellulose is an example of secondary metabolite. GLUT-4 is a transport protein, which enables glucose transport into cells. Starch is a polysaccharide consisting of numerous glucose units jointed by glycosidic bond. It forms helical secondary structure.

43. (*b*) Action potential travels down motor neuron → Acetylcholine (ACH) released into synapse → Action potential on sarcolemma → Sodium ions (Na^+) rush into muscle cell → Calcium (Ca^+) released from cisternae which causes Myosin heads attach to actin → Muscle contracts.

44. (*c*) In adenosine, adenine is linked to the OH of 1' C of ribose sugar through a N-glycosidic linkage. Adenosine is a nucleoside. A nucleoside consists of a nitrogenous base covalently attached to a sugar (ribose or deoxyribose) but without the phosphate group, it is the precursor of nucleotide.

45. (*c*) The correct matches are A-3, B-4, C-2 and D-1.

Hypothalamus contains several groups of neurosecretory cells which secrete hormones called hypothalamic hormones. Corpora quadrigemina is present on dorsal portion of mid brain consisting of four round swellings. Cerebral cortex is referred to as grey matter. Grey appearance is due to neuron cell bodies that are concentrated there giving the colour. Cerebellum has very convoluted surface in order to provide additional surface for many more neurons.

46. (*d*) The correct matches are A–2, B–3, C–4 and D–1.

Ori is responsible for controlling the copy of the number of the linked DNA.

Bioreactors are large vessels that are used for the large-scale production of biotechnological products from raw resources. Plasmid DNA are capable of replicating independent of chromosomal DNA. Downstream processing is a method of separating and purifying foreign gene products once the biosynthetic stage is completed.

47. (*b*) Both statement I and statement II are correct.

Divergent evolution leads to development of homologous organs in different species which traces them back to a common ancestor. Geographical barrier can cause distinct population group to separate and evolve independently.

Speciation is the formation of new species. One of the major contributing factor towards speciation is reproductive separation or isolation of a defined population.

48. (a) Reserve material in prokaryotic cells are stored in the cytoplasm in the form of inclusion bodies. These are not bound by any membrane system and lie freely in the cytoplasm, e.g., phosphate granules, cyanophycean granules and glycogen granules. Gas vacuoles are found in blue green and purple and green photosynthetic bacteria.

Food vacuoles are membrane-bound sacs. Polysomes are multiple ribosomes bound to an *m*RNA.

49. (*b*) The correct matches are A-2, B-4, C-3 and D-1.

- Interphase is a period of preparation for cell division.
- Mitosis (M phase) is the actual period of cell division.
- G_2-phase is the period of cytoplasmic growth.
- S-phase marks the phase of DNA replication and chromosome duplication.

50. (*b*) When the F_1 was self-pollinated, the F_2 resulted in the following ratio: 1 (RR) Red: 2 (Rr) Pink: 1 (rr) White. This is because of one allele which is incompletely dominant over the other allele. This is called incomplete dominance.

51. (*b*) Barbiturates and benzodiazepines are normally used as medicine to cure mental illness like depression, and insomnia, but are often abused.

52. (*d*) Statement I is correct, but statement II is incorrect.

Incorrect statement II can be corrected as

The last twenty years alone have witnessed the disappearance of 27 species.

53. (*b*) Option (b) shows the correct order.

In human beings, after one month of pregnancy, the embryo heart is formed. The first sign of growing foetus may be noticed by listening to the heart sound carefully through the stethoscope.

Thus, by the end of second month of pregnancy, the foetus develops limbs and digit. Then, by the end of first trimester, most of the major organs systems are formed.

The first movement and the appearance of hair on the head are usually observed during fifth month. By the end of about 24 weeks, the body is covered with fine hair, eye-lids separate, and eyelashes are formed.

54. (*a*) According to Gause's competitive exclusion principle, two closely related species competing for the same resources cannot coexist as competitively inferior one will be eliminated.

55. (*b*) The correct matches are A-4, B-3, C-2 and D-1.

In *Ancylostomata*, alimentary canal is complete with a well-developed muscular pharynx. Molluscs have radula in mouth, which is file-like rasping organ for feeding. Statocyst is balancing organ present in invertebrates. *Nereis* possesses lateral appendages, parapodia which help in swimming.

56. (*b*) Statement (b) is correct. Incorrect statements can be corrected as

The process of formation of microspores from a pollen mother cell (PMC) through meiosis is called microsporogenesis. As the anthers mature and dehydrate, the microspores dissociate from each other and develop into pollen grains. Inside each microsporangium, several thousands of microspores or pollen grains are formed that are released with the dehiscence of anther.

57. (*d*) 'X' is columns of Bertini. They are the extensions of the renal cortex into the renal medulla between the renal pyramids.

58. (*b*) Full potential of penicillin as an effective antibiotics was established by Ernest Chain and Howard Florey. Fleming, Chain and Florey were awarded the Nobel Prize in 1945, for the discovery of penicillin.

59. (*a*) At rest, heart rate is 70 beats/minute, during exercise it increases by 50 %,

Heart rate during cardio

$= 70 + (50/100) \times 70$

$= 70 + 35 = 105$ beats/minute

Cardiac output

= Strokes volume × Heart rate

Strokes volume at exercise

= Cardiac output/heart rate

= 8925/105 = 85mL

Stroke volume at rest

= 85 - 15 = 70 mL

60. (*d*) The correct matches are A-4, B-3, C-1 and D-2.

- Auxin was isolated by F.W. Went from tips of coleoptiles of oat seedlings.
- Plants follow different pathways in response to environment or phases of life to form different kinds of structures. This ability is called plasticity, e.g., heterophylly in cotton.
- Formation of cork cambium from fully differentiated parenchyma cells is an example of dedifferentiation.
- Formation of a tracheary element, where the cells lose their protoplasm is an example of differentiation.

61. (*c*) When an animal is endangered or threatened and need urgent measures to save it from extinction, zoological park will be desirable for its conservation. In zoological park, it can be protected and given special care.

62. (*d*) The correct matches are A–3, B–4, C–2 and D–1.

Excess secretion of growth hormone in adults especially in middle age can result in severe disfigurement (especially of the face) called acromegaly, which may lead to serious complications, and premature death if unchecked. An impairment affecting synthesis or release of ADH results in a diminished ability of the kidney to conserve water leading to water loss and dehydration. This condition is known as diabetes insipidus.

Grave's disease is caused due to hypersecretion of thyroid hormone. Underproduction of hormones by the adrenal cortex alters carbohydrate metabolism causing acute weakness and fatigue leading to a disease called Addison's disease.

63. (*d*) In reaction, $S - G + S' \rightarrow S + S' - G$, enzymes catalyses a transfer of a group, G (other than hydrogen) between a pair of substrate S and S'. Such enzymes are called transferases.

64. (*c*) Both statement I and statement II are incorrect. These can be corrected as

Walter Sutton and Theodore Boveri noted that the behaviour of chromosomes was parallel to the behaviour of genes and used chromosome movement to explain Mendel's law.

In 1900, three Scientists (de Vries, Correns and von Tschermak) independently rediscovered Mendel's results on the inheritance of characters.

65. (*d*) Incorrect statement can be corrected as

Factors for coagulation or clotting of blood are also present in the plasma in an inactive form. Plasma without the clotting factors is called serum.

66. (*b*) The correct matches are A-2, B-3, C-4 and D-1.

- Adventitious roots are developed from parts of the plant other than radicle.
- Parallel venation is present in monocot leaves.
- Hilum is a scar on the seed coat through which the developing seed is attached to the fruit.
- Endosperm is formed after double fertilisation.

67. (*c*) Statements IV and V are correct. Incorrect statements are I, II and III and can be corrected as

Descending limb of Henle's loop is permeable to water and the ascending limb is impermeable to it.

Reabsorption of water from distal parts of the tubules is facilitated by hormone ADH.

Glomerulonephritis is inflammation of glomeruli.

68. (*d*) The correct matches are A-4, B-3, C-2 and D-1.

Chemosynthetic bacteria obtain energy from inorganic molecules. Water molecules split in photosystem II.

NADP reductase enzyme is present in the outer surface of thylakoid of chloroplast. Chlorophyll-*a* converts light energy to chemical energy.

69. (*b*) Both A and R are true and R is the correct explanation of A.

The R strain bacteria had somehow been transformed by the heat-killed S strain bacteria. Some 'transforming principle (genetic material)', transferred from the heat-killed S strain, had enabled the R strain to synthesise a smooth polysaccharide coat and become virulent. This must be due to the transfer of the genetic material.

70. (*c*) The correct match is A–2, B–3, C–1 and D–4.

Saheli is non-steroidal oral contraceptive, prepared by CDRI, Lucknow. IUDs prevent pregnancy by suppressing sperm motility. Condoms prevent STDs. Cervical caps are reusable and used with spermicidal creams.

71. (*b*) 'X' is PGR auxin. Apical dominance as expressed in dicotyledonous plants is due to the presence of more auxin in the apical bud than in the lateral ones.

72. (*a*) The correct matches are A-2, B-3, C-1 and D-4.

- Complex I is NADH dehydrogenase.
- Complex II is succinic dehydrogenase.
- Complex III is cytochrome bc_1.
- Complex IV is cytochrome *c* oxidase.

73. (*c*) Both ELISA and PCR diagnostic methods can be used to detect diseases before the appearance of symptoms. Molecular diagnosis refers to the identification of genetic mutations or variations in an individual's DNA that contributes to the development of a disease. This is achieved by ELISA and PCR.

74. (*c*) Both statement I and statement II are incorrect and can be corrected as Fossils discovered in Java in 1981 revealed *Homo erectus* probably ate meat. During ice age between 75,000 . -10,000 years ago, modern *Homo sapiens* arose.

75. (*b*) The correct matches are A–3, B–4, C–2 and D–1.

LH surge causes rupture of Graafian follicle, thereby causing ovulation. Menstruation only occurs if the released ovum is not fertilised. Oestrogen level is elevated during follicular phase. Luteal phase is characterised by secretion of progesterone by corpus luteum.

76. (*c*) Statements I and IV are correct. Incorrect statements II, III and V can be corrected as

The promoter is said to be located towards 5'-end (upstream) of the structural gene (the reference is made with respect to the polarity of coding strand).

It is a DNA sequence that provides binding site for RNA polymerase, and it is the presence of a promoter in a transcription unit that also defines the template and coding strands.

The terminator is located towards 3'-end (downstream) of the coding strand and it usually defines the end of the process of transcription.

77. (*b*) In *Asterias*, *Rana tigrina* and *Labeo*, fertilisation is external, i.e., fertilisation takes place outside the body.

78. (*a*) The correct match is A-3, B-1, C-4 and D-2.

Obelia exists in both forms and thus exhibits alternation of generation, called metagenesis. Bioluminescence (the property of a living organism to emit light) is well-marked in *Ctenoplana*. Choanocytes or collar cells line the spongocoel and the canals in *Spongilla*. Hooks and suckers are parasitic adaptation present in the parasitic forms of Platyhelminthes, e.g., *Taenia*.

79. (*d*) The correct matches are A–2, B–4, C–1 and D–3.

- The parenchymatous cells which lie between the xylem and the phloem are called conjuctive tissue.
- The tangential as well as radial walls of the endodermal cells have a deposition of water-impermeable, waxy material suberin in the form of Casparian strips.
- The innermost layer of the cortex is called endodermis.
- Next to endodermis, lies a few layers of thick-walled parenchymatous cells referred to as pericycle.

80. (*d*) Epinephrine and norepinephrine stimulate the breakdown of glycogen resulting in an increased concentration of glucose in blood. They are secreted by adrenal medulla.

81. (*a*) Statement I is incorrect, but statement II is correct. Statement I can be corrected as

Restriction endonucleases make double stranded cut in the phosphate backbone.

82. (*c*) The correct match is A-2, B-3, C-1 and D-4.

Volume of air inspired or expired during a normal respiration is called tidal volume (500mL). IRV (2500 -3000) is additional volume of air a person can inhale.

Additional volume of air a person can exhale after normal expiration is called ERV (1000 -1100 mL). IC is total volume of air a person can inhale after normal expiration.

83. (*d*) Option (d) is correct. Rest all statements are incorrect and can be corrected as

Heartbeat is decreased by parasympathetic nerve by acetylcholine. Fibrinogen is involved in clotting of blood. Lymph does not contain RBCs.

84. (*b*) The correct matches are A-3, B-4, C-1 and D-2.

- Collagen is most abundant protein in the animal world.
- RuBisCO is most abundant protein in the whole biosphere.
- Chitin is a homopolysaccharide, a polymer of N-acetyl glucosamine.
- Peptidoglycan is a heteropolysaccharide, a polymer of N-acetyl glucosamine (NAG) and N-acetyl muramic acid (NAM).

85. (*a*) The correct matches are A–2, B-3, C-4 and D-1.

Taq polymerase is thermostable DNA polymerase, used in PCR. If any protein encoding gene is expressed in a heterologous host, it is called recombinant protein.

Annealing is attachment of oligonucleotides (primer at the 3' end of the DNA fragment. DNA is separated by spooling method.

86. (*a*) The correct matches are A-2, B-3, C-1 and D-4.

. The protein encoded by *cry*IAc and *cry*IIAb control the cotton bollworm and that of *cry*IAb controls corn borer.

Transposons are mobile genetic elements used in genetic engineering.

α-1-antitrypsin is used for treating emphysema.

87. (*d*) A is true, but R is false. R can be corrected as

Bicarbonate is reabsorbed from the distal parts of the renal tubules. Reabsorption of bicarbonates from the DCT to the blood makes the blood more alkaline.

88. (*d*) Statement in option (d) is correct. Incorrect statements can be corrected as

23S *r*RNA is an enzyme for protein synthesis in prokaryotes. For initiation, the ribosome binds to *m*RNA at the AUG. There is no *t*RNA for stop codon.

89. (*a*) Statement I is incorrect, but statements II is correct.Incorrect statement can be corrected as

The gastrointestinal tract secrete gastrin, secretin, cholecystokinin and gastric inhibitory peptide to regulate secretion of digestive juices and help in digestion.

90. (*a*) In the given plasmid,

X = *Pvu*I, *y* = *Pst*I,

K = *Bam* HI, *L* = *Sal*I, *V* = *Pvu*II

if gene of interest is introduced at *Bam*HI and *sal*I, plasmid will lose its tetracycline resistance.

NK03 NEET Knock Offs 3

1. (*b*) In the World Summit on Sustainable Development held in 2002 in Johannesburg, South Africa, 190 countries pledged their commitment to achieve by 2010, a significant reduction in the current rate of biodiversity loss at global, regional and local levels.

2. (*d*) The mucosa-associated lymphoid tissue initiates immune responses to specific antigen encountered along all mucosal surfaces. It constitutes about 50 percent of the lymphoid tissue in human body. MALT inductive sites are secondary immune tissues where antigen sampling occurs and immune responses are intiated.

3. (*b*) Statements I, II and III are correct while, statements IV and V are incorrect and can be corrected as
   - In imbricate aestivation, sepals or petals overlap one another, but not in any particular direction.
   - In valvate aestivation, sepals or petals in a whorl just touch one another at the margin without overlapping.

4. (*b*) Metagenesis is a biological phenomenon observed in some cnidarians where they exhibit an alternation of generation between two distinct body forms, i.e. polyp and medusa.

5. (*b*) Both statement I and statement II are correct.

   Evolution of Earth is old phenomenon but some believes that evolution of earth is a continuous phenomenon. In the solar system of the milky way galaxy, earth was supposed to have been formed about 4.5 billion years ago.

   There was no atmosphere on early earth. The UV rays from the sun brokeup water into hydrogen and oxygen and the lighter H_2 escaped. Oxygen combined with ammonia and methane to form water, CO_2 and others. The ozone layer was formed.

6. (*b*) The promoter is a specific DNA sequence located towards the 5′- end of the structural gene on the coding strand. Its primary role is to provide a binding site for RNA polymerase. The enzyme polymerase is responsible for synthesising RNA from the DNA template.

7. (*b*) Both *Ectocarpus* and *Fucus* are the members of phaeophyceae or brown algae. The vegetative cells have a cellulosic wall usually covered on the outside by a gelatinous coating of algin. Food is stored as complex carbohydrates, which may be in the form of laminarin or mannitol. The major pigment in brown algae are chlorophyll a, c and fucoxanthin.

8. (*d*) Statement I is correct, but statement II is incorrect. Statement II can be corrected as

   A bundle of nodal fibres, atrio-ventricular bundle (AV bundle) continues from the AVN which passes through the atrio - ventricular septa to emerge on the top of the inter- ventricular septum and immediately divides into a right and left bundle.

9. (*a*) All of these features belong to family–Leguminosae. *Sesbania* belong to family Leguminosae.

10. (*b*) Statements III and IV are incorrect, these statements can be corrected as
    - The cavity of the cervix is called cervical canal which alongwith vagina forms the birth canal.
    - The external thin membranes perimetrium, middle thick layer of smooth muscle, myometrium and inner glandular layer called endometrium that the uterine cavity.

11. (*d*) Incorrect match pair can be corrected as

    Cedrus is a gymnosperm. Stems in cases of *Pinus* and *Cedrus* are branched in structure.

12. (*d*) A is true, but R is false. R can be explained as

    The axoplasm inside the axon contains high concentration of K^+ and negatively charge proteins and low concentration of Na^+.

13. (*a*) The process of copying genetic information from one strand of the DNA into RNA is termed as transcription. Unlike, in the process of replication, which once set in, the total DNA of an organism gets duplicated, in transcription only a segment of DNA and only one of the strands copied into RNA.

14. (*b*) Lactational amenorrhea method is based on the fact, that ovulation and menstruation cycle do not occur during the period of intense lactation following parturition. Therefore, as long as the mother breast-feeds the child fully, chances of conception are nil.

15. (*c*) Statements II and V are correct. Rest all statements are incorrect and can be corrected as
    - In binomial nomenclature, first word denoting the genus starts

with a capital letter, while the specific epithet starts with a small letter.

- Name of the author appears after the specific epithet, i.e., at the end of the biological name and is written in an abbreviated form, e.g. *Mangifera indica* Linn.
- The first word in a biological name represents the genus, while the second component denotes the specific epithet.

16. (*c*) A is true, but R is false. R can be corrected as:
Saheli is a once a week pill with very few side effects and high contraceptive value.

17. (*a*) Statement I is incorrect, but statement II is correct. Incorrect statement can be corrected as
Carboxylation is the most crucial step of the Calvin cycle where CO_2 is utilised for the carboxylation of RuBP. This reaction is catalysed by the enzyme RuBisCO.

18. (*b*) Each kidney is made up of over one million nephrons. There are two types of nephrons, i.e. cortical nephrons, which are deep in the renal cortex and juxtamedullary nephrons, which lie in the renal cortex close to the renal medulla.

19. (*d*) Statement in option (d) is incorrect and can be corrected as
Glucose is phosphorylated to glucose-6-phosphate by using ATP in the presence of isomerase enzyme, i.e. hexokinase or glucokinase.
Rest options are correct statements.

20. (*b*) The correct order of events of muscle contraction is as follows:

- Signal is sent by the central nervous system *via* a motor neuron.
- A neural signal reaching neuro-muscular junction and release of a neurotransmitter.
- Increase in Ca^{2+} level leads to the binding of calcium with a subunit of troponin on actin filaments.
- The 'Z' line gets attached to the actin filaments, causing a shortening of the sarcomere.

21. (*a*) The correct matches are A-2, B-3, C-4, D-1.

- Each trophic level has a certain mass of living material at a particular time called as the standing crop.
- Organisms occupy a specific place in the food chain that is known as trophic level.
- Humus is highly resistant to microbial action and undergoes decomposition at an extremely slow rate.
- The humus is degraded by some microbes and released of inorganic nutrients occur by the process known as mineralisation.

22. (*b*) Both A and R are true and R is the correct explanation of A.
Males have only one X chromosome. Therefore, if they inherit an X chromosome carrying the haemophilia gene, they will express the disease because they do not have a second X chromosome to potentially mask the effect of the defective gene.

23. (*a*) Statement (a) is correct.
Archaebacteria are special since they live in some of the most harsh habitats such as extreme salty areas, hot spring and marshy areas. These differ from other bacteria in having a different cell wall structure and this feature is responsible for their survival in extreme conditions.

24. (*d*) *Lac* z codes for the enzyme β-galactosidase which breaks lactose into glucose and galactose to be utilised in the cell.
Therefore, *E. coli* cells with a mutated *z*-genes cannot grow in medium containing only lactose as the source of energy because they cannot synthesise functional β-galactosidase.

25. (*c*) Weedicide is a chemical substance used to kill or remove a weed. It is used to build weed-free lawns by gardeners. Several synthetic auxins are extensively applied for the removal of weeds in agriculture. 2,4-D is commonly used as selective weedicide to remove the unwanted dicot weeds. It is non-toxic to monocot plants and is thus, the basis of killing weeds in rice, corn, wheat and barley fields.

26. (*d*) Jurassic period of Mesozoic era existed about 19-20 crore years ago and lasted for about 5.5- 6 crore years ago. The climate was hot and damp. It is called the age of dinosaurs. First primitive bird *Archaeopteryx* evolved from reptiles. First angiosperm appeared as a dicotyledon, but gymnosperms were dominant in this era.

27. (*d*) Statement (d) is incorrect statement and can be corrected as:
Cytokinin helps to overcome the apical dominance. Cytokinins have specific effects on cytokinesis and were discovered as kinetin from the autoclaved herring sperm DNA.

28. (*b*) Malignant tumour means that the tumour is made of cancer cells and it can invade the nearby tissues. These tumours are the mass of proliferating cells called neoplastic or tumour cells. These cells grow very rapidly, invading and damaging the surrounding normal tissues. As these cells actively divide and grow, they also starve the normal cells by competing for vital nutrients.

29. (*c*) Diakinesis is marked by terminalisation of chiasmata. During this phase the chromosomes are fully condensed and the meiotic spindle is assembled to prepare the homologous chromosomes for separation.

30. (*c*) The correct matches are A-4, B-3, C-2, D-1.

- Oestrogen is one of the main female sex hormone involved in changes in puberty and regulating the menstrual cycle.

- The main function of progesterone is to prepare the endometrium for a fertilised egg to implant and grow.
- Prolactin is secreted by pituitary gland and is involved in the lactation, certain breast tissue development and milk production.
- Relaxin is secreted by corpus luteum ovary. It relaxes the pelvic ligaments and widens the cervix for helping in child birth.

31. (*b*) When the electrons pass from one carrier to another *via* complex I to IV in the electron transport chain, they are coupled to ATP synthase (Complex V) for the production of ATP from ADP and inorganic phosphate. The number of ATP molecules synthesised depends on the nature of the electron donor.

32. (*a*) Statement I is incorrect, but statement II is correct. Incorrect statement can be corrected as

An increase in pulmonary volume decreases the intra pulmonary pressure to less than the atmosphereric pressure which forces the air from outside to move into the lungs.

33. (*c*) The correct matches are A-3, B-4, C-1, D-2.

- Ethylene promotes female flowers in cucumbers.
- Abscisic acid acts as an antagonist to GAs.
- Auxins promote flowering in pineapples.
- All gibberellins (Giberellic acid) are acidic in nature.

34. (*a*) Enzyme catalysts differ from inorganic catalysts in many ways, but one major difference is the inorganic catalysts work efficiently at high temperatures and high pressures, while enzymes get damaged at high temperature.

35. (*c*) The electron microscopic study of a cilium or the flagellum show that they are covered with plasma membrane. Their core called the axoneme, possesses a number of microtubules running parallel to the long axis. The axoneme usually has nine doublets of radially arranged peripheral microtubules, and a pair of centrally located microtubules. Such an arrangement of axonemal microtubules is referred to as the 9+2 array.

36. (*b*) The given figure represents chromosome with kinetochore. Kinetochore is a small disc shaped structure at the surface of the centromeres.

37. (*d*) Statement I is correct, but statement II is incorrect. Incorrect statement can be corrected as

In some angiospermic plants, pollen grains are shed at two-celled conditions. In such plants, the generative cell divides and forms the two male gametes during the growth of pollen tube in the stigma.

38. (*b*) Each half of pectoral girdle consists of a clavicle and a scapula. Scapula is a large triangular flat bone situated in the dorsal part of the thorax between the second and the seventh ribs.

39. (*b*) The correct sequence of events during mitosis is as follows:

- Each centrosome radiates out microtubules (Prophase).
- Chromosomes are moved to spindle equator (metaphase).
- Chromatids moves to opposite poles (Anaphase).
- Chromosomes cluster at opposite spindle poles (Telophase).

40. (*b*) Both statement I and statement II are correct.

A bioreactors provide the optimal conditions for achieving the desired product by providing optimum growth conditions (temperature, pH, substrate, salts, vitamins, oxygen). The air sparges is used to break the incoming air into small bubbles. Thus bubbles rise directly into the impeller blades, facilitating bubble break up. The sparger along with impellers create a uniform and homogenous environment through the bioreactor.

41. (*a*) Statements I, II, III and IV are correct. Statement V is incorrect and can be corrected as:

In a transcription unit, the activity of RNA polymerase at a given promoter is in turn regulated by interaction with accessory proteins, which affect its ability to recognise start sites.

42. (*d*) The pineal gland is located on the dorsal side of forebrain. It secretes a hormone called melatonin. Melatonin plays a very important role in the regulation of a 24 hour rhythm of our body. In addition, it also influences metabolism, pigmentation, the menstrual cycle a well as our defense capability.

43. (*c*) Loss of biodiversity in a region may lead to decline in plant production, lowered resistance to environmental perturbations such as drought and increased variability in certain ecosystem processes such as plant productivity, water use, pest and disease cycles.

Enhanced resistance to environmental perturbation is generally a positive outcome and is associated with higher biodivesity.

44. (*b*) Natural selection can lead to different patterns of evolutionary change in a population, one of which is directional selection. It occurs when environmental pressures favor individuals with traits that are at one extreme end of the spectrum.

45. (*b*) In the equation $dN/dt = rN$, r represents the intrinsic rate of natural increase, which is the difference between birth rate and death rate per capita. This difference determines how fast the population will grow under ideal conditions with unlimited resources.

46. (*a*) The correct sequence of evolutionary history of vertebrates is as follows

- The early reptiles appeared during the carboniferous.
- Following early reptiles, Pelycosarus appeared in Permian peroid.
- Thecodont were archosaur reptiles that lived during the Triassic period.
- Dinosaurs emerged after thecodonts and dominated during the Jurassic period and got extinct around the tertiary period.

47. (*d*) A floating cover is placed over the slurry, which keeps on rising as the gas is produced in the tank due to the microbial activity. The biogas plant has on outlet, which is connected to a pipe to supply biogas to nearby houses.

48. (*b*) The sporozoites are the infectious form of the *Plasmodium* parasite. The presence of sporozoites in the salivary glands of the mosquito is critical for the spread of malaria because it ensures that each mosquito bites has the potential to inject a new human host with the *Plasmodium* parasite.

49. (*a*) Statements III and V are incorrect. These statements can be corrected as:

- A mature sieve element posseses a peripheral cytoplasm and a large vacuole, but lacks a nucleus. The functions of sieve tubes are controlled by the nucleus of companion cells.
- Phloem fibres are made up of sclerenchymatous cells. These are generally absent in the primary phloem but are found in the secondary phloem.

50. (*a*) Statins produced by the yeast *Monascus purpureus* have been commercialised as blood- cholesterol lowering agents. Cyclosporin A is used as an immunosuppresive agent, is produced by the fungus *Trichoderma polysporum*.

51. (*a*) Incorrect statement about geitonogamy can be corrected as

Geitonogamy is functionally similar to cross-pollination as it involves a pollinating agent, genetically similar to autogamy.

Xenogamy is the only type of pollination which during pollination brings genetically different types of pollen grains to the stigma.

52. (*a*) The correct matches are A-4, B-1, C-3, D-2.

- ANF can cause vasodilation i.e., dilation of blood vessels and thereby decrease the blood pressure.
- GFR can activate the JG cells to release renin which converts angiotensinogen in blood to angiotensin I and further to angiotensin II.
- Proximal Convoluted Tubule (PCT) helps to maintain the pH and ionic balance of the body fluids.
- Descending limb of loop of Henle's is permeable to water, but almost impermeable to electrolytes.

53. (*d*) Incorrect statement can be corrected as

The rop gene codes for proteins involved in the replication of the plasmid. *Pvu* I and *Pst* I sites are away from the *rop*, i.e. the amp^R gene in the *E.coli* vector pBR322 *Pvu* II site is present in the *rop*.

54. (*b*) Embryo gets attached to the mother's uterine wall with the help of the placenta. It is a disc-like structure and is embedded in the uterine wall. It provides nutrition and oxygen to the foetus from the mother's blood and carries out foetal waste removal.

It also acts as an endocrine tissue and produces several hormones like hCG, hPL, oestrogen, progestogen, etc.

55. (*b*) *Agrobacterium* vectors are used to introduce nematode specific genes into the plant, which produce both sense and anti-sense RNA, leading to the formation of *ds*RNA and subsequent RNAi-mediated gene silencing.

56. (*b*) A polymerase chain reaction (PCR) test is a diagnostic test that can be used to identify genetic disorders and infectious diseases. PCR tests are fast and accurate, and can detect small amounts of cancer cells that might be missed by other tests.

57. (*a*) The metabolic pathway through which the electron passes from one carrier to another is called the Electron Transport System (ETS). The correct sequence of electron carriers starting from NADH is as follows

NADH $\rightarrow$ complex I $\rightarrow$ ubiquinone $\rightarrow$ complex III $\rightarrow$ cyt c $\rightarrow$ complex IV $\rightarrow O_2$.

58. (*d*) Statements II, III and IV are correct, while statements I and V are incorrect, these statements can be corrected as

- A synapse is formed by the membranes of a pre- synaptic neuron and a post- synaptic neuron, which may or may not be separated by a gap called synaptic cleft.
- Impulse transmission across an electrical synapse is always faster than that across a chemical synapse. Electrical synapses are rare in our system.

59. (*b*) Statements III and IV are incorrect, these can be corrected as

- Most of the members have one or more storage bodies called pyrenoids located in the chloroplast. Pyrenoids contain protein besides starch.
- Green algae usually have a rigid cell wall made of an inner layer of cellulose and an outer layer of pectose.

60. (*d*) Parathyroid Hormone (PTH) stimulates reabsorption of calcium ions by the renal tubules and increases Ca^{2+} absorption from the digested food. It is a hypercalcemic hormone, i.e. it increases the blood calcium ions levels.

61. (*a*) The G_1-phase corresponds to the interval between mitosis and the initiation of DNA replication, where the cell is metabolically active and continuously growing with no DNA replication taking place in this phase. The G_2-phase is characterised by protein synthesis in preparation of mitosis while cell growth continues. Here, also the DNA replication is not occurring. DNA replication and centriole duplication in the cytoplasm occurs in the S-phase. M phase is the phase of cell division.

62. (*a*) In polygenic inheritance, such as with human skin colour controlled by three genes (A, B and C), each gene contributes additively to the overall phenotype. AABBcc has two dominant alleles for genes A and B and two recessive alleles for gene C. It would have darker skin because it has two dominant alleles for genes A and B, and a recessive alleles for gene C. aabbCC would have lighter skin because it has two recessive allele for genes A and B and a dominant allele for gene C.

63. (*b*) Both statement I and statement II are correct.

When Mendel self pollinated the F_1-tall plants he found that the F_2-generation included both tall and dwarf plants. The F_2-generation had a consistent ratio of 3:1. This ratio confirmed Mendel's law of segregation.

64. (*d*) Statement (d) is incorrect and can be corrected as

The globular head of heavy meromyosin projects outward at regular intervals from the surface of the polymerised myosin filament, forming cross-arms.

65. (*a*) The correct matches are A-3, B-1, C-2, D-4.

Marginal placentation is mainly found in Pea, Moong, etc.

Axile placentation is mainly found in china rose , lemon, etc.

Parietal placentation is found in mustard, *Argemone*, etc.

Basal placentation is found in sunflower, marigold, etc.

66. (*c*) Incorrect match pair is option (c) and it can be corrected as:

Renal calculi is referred to the formation of stone or insoluble mass of crystallised salts within the kidney.

67. (*a*) Statement I is incorrect, but statement II is correct. Incorrect statement can be corrected as:

The final product of glycolysis i.e., pyruvate is transported from the cytoplasm into the mitochondria. Inside the mitochondrial matrix, it undergoes oxidative decarboxylation by a complex set of reactions catalysed by pyruvic dehydrogenase. The reactions catalysed by pyruvic dehydrogenase require the participation of several coenzymes, including NAD^+ and coenzyme A.

68. (*b*) Emphysema is a lung condition that causes shortness of breath. In people with emphysema, the air sacs in the lungs are damged. This reduces the surface area of the lungs.

69. (*c*) At the lower end of monocotyledonous embryo, the embryonal axis has the radicle and root cap enclosed in an undifferentiated sheath called coleorrhiza.

70. (*a*) Neural signals through the sympathetic nerves (part of ANS) can increase the rate of heart beat, the strength of ventricular contraction and thereby the cardiac output.

71. (*b*) The correct matches are A-3, B-1, C-2, D-4.

- Filamentous proteinaceous structures present in the cytoplasm is collectively referred to as cytoskeleton.
- Cilia are small structures which work like oars.
- Flagella emerge from centriole-like structure called the basal bodies.
- Centrosome is an organelle containing centrioles. They are surrounded by amorphous pericentriolar materials.

72. (*d*) The correct matches are A-2, B-4, C-3, D-1.

P-wave represents the electrical excitation of the atria which leads to the contraction of both the atria.

QRS complex represents the depolarisation of the ventricles, which leads to the ventricular contraction.

Tunica intima is the middle layer of blood vessels which constitutes of smooth muscle and elastic fibres.

Tunica externa is the external layer of blood vessels, having fibrous connective tissues with longitudinally arranged white and yellow fibres.

73. (*b*) The correct matches are A-1, B-3, C-2, D-4.

- Oxido-reductases catalyse the oxido-reduction between two substrates.
- Transferases catalyse the transfer of a group between a pair of substrate.
- Hydrolases catalyse the hydrolysis of ester, ether, etc.
- Lyases catalyse removal of groups from substrates.

74. (*a*) The exaggerated response of the immune system to certain antigens present in the environment is called allergy. The substances to which such an immune response is produced are called allergers. A person becomes allergic when their body develops antigens against a substance, upon repeated exposure the severity of the reaction may increase. Hay fever, eczema, hives, asthma are some common types of allergic diseases. The body is able to differentiate self and non- self and the cell mediated response is responsible for the graft rejection.

75. (*b*) A nitrogenous base is linked to the pentose sugar through a N-glycosidic linkage to form a nucleoside, such as deoxycytidine adenosine, etc.

76. (*a*) The correct matches are A-2, B-3, C-1, D-4.

For housefly, the taxonomic categories are as follows:

Species - *domestica*

Genus - *Musca*

Family - Muscidae

Order - Diptera

Class - Insect

Phylum - Arthropoda

77. (*b*) The Abingdon tortoise in Galapagos islands became extinct within a decade after goats were introduced on the island, apparently due to the greater browsing efficiency of the goats. This explain the competition between goat and tortoise for the same resource e.g., grass.

78. (*b*) *Testudo* (Tortoise) and *Bangarus* (Krait) belongs to class Reptilia. They are mostly terrestrial animals and their body is covered by dry and cornified skin, epidermal scales. They do not have external ear openings.

Tympanum represents ear. Heart is usually 3- chambered, but four-chambered in crocodiles. They are poikilotherms, sexes are separate, fertilisation is internal.

79. (*a*) Statements I, II and III are correct. Statements IV and V are incorrect, it can be corrected as:

- The rate of decomposition is slower if detritus is rich in lignin and chitin and quicker, if detritus is rich is nitrogen & water - soluble substances like sugars.
- Warm and moist environment favours decomposition.

80. (*b*) Enzymatic activity increases with substrate concentration until the enzyme becomes saturated. Once saturation is reached, the activity levels off as the enzyme cannot work any faster regardless of additional substrate.

81. (*b*) Statement (b) is incorrect and can be corrected as

The law of dominance is used to explain the expression of only one of the parental characters in a monohybrid cross in the F_1 and the expression of both in the F_2. Snapdragon follow the law of incomplete dominance.

82. (*c*) Frogs have well organised male and female reproductive systems. Male reproductive organs consist of a pair of yellowish ovoid testes, which are found adhered to the upper part of kidneys by a double fold of peritoneum called mesorchium.

83. (*b*) The correct matches are A-2, B-1, C-4, D-3.

- Sequence annotation - Sequencing the whole set of genome that contained all the coding and non-coding sequence.
- Expressed sequence tags - Fragments of *m*RNA sequences derived through single sequencing reaction performed on randomly selected clones form *c*DNA libraries.
- Satellite DNA - It contributes to the formation of crucial chromosome structures, heterochromatic establishment, genome stability and development.
- Single nucleotide polymorphism - It represents a difference in a single DNA.

84. (*b*) The correct matches are A-3, B-1, C-2, D-4.

Porifera - Body with pores and canals in walls.

Platyhelminthes- They have flat body with hooks and suckers.

Aschelminthes- They are worm shaped, elongated.

Annelida- Their body are metamerically segmented.

85. (*a*) Hashish causes after thought perceptions and hallucinations. Hashish is a preparation of *Cannabis* composed of the compressed trichomes collected from the *Cannabis* plant.

86. (*d*) Statement I is correct, but statement II is incorrect. It can be corrected as:

Plasmodium is a sporozoan. It is most notorious species which causes malaria, a disease which has a staggening effect on human population. *Trypanosoma* is a flagellated protozoans.

87. (*b*) Both A and R are true, and R is correct explanation of A.

Complex II does not pump protons. It passes electrons, from $FADH_2$ to ubiquinone, contributing electrons, but not to the proton gradient.

88. (*a*) The correct matches are A-2, B-1, C-4, D-3.

- The scrotum helps in maintaining the low temperature of the testes.
- In seminiferous tubules, sperms are produced.
- Leydig cell synthesise and secrete testicular hormones.
- Sertoli cells provide nutrition to the germ cells.

89. (*d*) The given figures are of sclerenchyma. It consists of long, narrow cells with thick and lignified cell walls. They are usually dead and without protoplasts.

Incorrect statement is regarding collenchyma. The collenchyma occurs in layers below the epidermis in most of the dicot plants or either as a homogenous layer or in patches.

90. (*a*) Statement I is incorrect, but statement II is correct. Incorrect statement can be corrected as

The first step in urine formation is the filtration of blood, which is carried out by the glomerulus and is called glomerular filtration.

NK04 NEET Knock Offs 4

1. (*b*) A Ti-plasmid of *Agrobacterium* has T-DNA that can transform normal plant cells into a tumour and direct these tumour cells to produce the chemicals required by the pathogen. If these genes of pathogens are not deleted, then the host would develop tumours. So, retaining all the genes, and not deleting the pathogenic ones would have a negative impact on host.

2. (*b*) After transferring to N^{15} media, the heavy DNA would be made according to semiconservative replication. After 25 minutes, there would be two hybrid DNAs. After 50 minutes there would be 2 hybrid and 2 heavy DNA molecules. After 75 minutes, there would be 2 hybrid and 6 heavy DNAs. Thus, ratio would be 2/6 or 1:3.

3. (*c*) Both statement I and statement II are incorrect. These can be corrected as
   - O^+ person can donate blood safely to Rh^- people only once. This is because after first donation, Rh^- person would develop antibodies against Rh antigen from O^+ person. In subsequent transfusion, the antibodies would attack Rh antigens and cause agglutination reactions.
   - People with O^- blood groups are called universal donors. This is because in blood transfusion Rh antigens should also be considered. O^- blood groups lack antigen-a, b as well as Rh antigen, while O^+ people have Rh antigens on their RBC surface. Hence, O^+ people can trigger antigen-antibody agglutination in recipient.

4. (*a*) For creating recombinant insulin, the two DNA sequences corresponding to A and B chains of human insulin are introduced in plasmids of *E. coli* to produce insulin chains. Chains A and B are produced separately, extracted and combined by creating disulfide bonds to form human insulin.

   Only chains A and B are expressed. C peptide is the extra stretch which is absent from mature protein product and is present only in pro insulin. Hence, C peptide is not expressed in this *r*DNA technology.

5. (*c*) Statements II, IV and V are correct, while statements I and III are incorrect and can be corrected as
   - Satellite DNAs are mostly the non-coding regions of the DNA and do not code for any protein.
   - Lysine provides electrostatic interaction between histone and DNA.

6. (*b*) The correct matches are A-3, B-4, C-2, D-1.

   Placental mammals in Australia exhibit adaptive radiation in evolving into varieties of such placental mammals, each of which appears to be 'similar' to a corresponding marsupial. Thus, anteater is similar to numbat, lemur is similar to spotted cuscus, bobcat is similar to Tasmanian tiger cat and flying squirrel is similar to flying phalanger.

7. (*c*) Both A and R are true, but R is not the correct explanation of A. It can be explained as

   Two turns of krebs cycles are needed per glucose molecule because glycolysis results in the formation of 2 pyruvate by breakdown of one molecule of glucose.

8. (*c*) Increased CO_2 and H^+ concentration would activate the chemosensitive area and would be received by the receptors of the aortic arch and carotid artery.

   The other incorrect statements can be corrected as:
   - Increase in H^+ causes acidosis of blood which would activate the chemosensitive area.
   - The role of oxygen in the regulation of respiratory rhythm is quite insignificant.
   - Pneumotaxic centre of the pons moderate the function of rhythm centres. Neural signal from this centre can reduce the duration of inspiration and thereby alter the respiratory rate.

9. (*d*) The human RBCs are the sites where both sexual and asexual stage occurs. The parasites reproduce asexually in RBCs, causing their rupture. Gametocytes are also formed in the RBCs. In the liver, the parasite reproduces only asexually. In mosquito's intestine, fertilisation takes place, which is the sexual stage. Sporozoites formed, migrate to the mosquito's salivary glands.

10. (*b*) Eukaryotic ribosomes are 80S where the large subunit is 60S and the smaller subunit is 40S. Centrifugation of the ribosomes would separate the subunits, where the lighter fragments would collect at the top due to lower density, while the denser fractions would be settled at the bottom. Hence, the top section would contain the smaller 40S ribosomal subunit.

11. (*d*) A is true, but R is false. R can be corrected as:

Placental hormone hCG is present in urine. Placenta of pregnant women secretes certain hormones like human chorionic gonadotropins that is not secreted in normal females. Presence of such hormone in urine, can confirm pregnancy. Relaxin is secreted by the ovaries in pregnant women during parturition.

12. (*d*) The correct matches are A-3, B-4, C-1, D-2.

- Lecithin is a phospholipid present in the cell membrane.
- Starch forms helical secondary structures.
- Lectin like concanavilin-A is an example of secondary metabolite.
- Adenylic acid is a nucleotide that contains a phosphate group.

13. (*a*) 6 turns of the cycle forms 1 glucose molecule, so 18 turns would form 3 glucose molecules. In one turn of the cycle, 3 ATP is hydrolysed to form 3 ADP and Pi and 2 NADPH is oxidised to form 2 $NADP^+$. Therefore, in 18 turns, 18 x 2 = 36 $NADP^+$ would be formed, and 18 x 3 = 54 ADP would be formed.

14. (*d*) A is true, but R is false. R can be corrected as

There is under secretion of melatonin by the pineal glands under bright light. Melatonin from the pineal gland is synthesised under low light conditions or dark. Melatonin promotes sleep and maintains the sleep wake cycle, hence in bright light, the synthesis stops. Thus, a person finds it difficult to fall asleep when lights are turned on.

15. (*a*) The diagram shows *lac* operon. In the diagram, it is clear that repressor protein binds to the operator, which is possible when glucose is present and lactose is absent. Thus, structural genes cannot be expressed as operator is blocked and RNA polymerase cannot access the operator and promoter segments.

16. (*a*) Statement I is incorrect, but statement II is correct. Statement I can be corrected as

Subsequent encounter from a virus, promotes secretion of antibodies by B-cells.

17. (*b*) The correct matches are A-2, B-4, C-1, D-3

- Auxins promote parthenocarpy and production of seedless fruits.
- Gibberellins are used in brewing industry to fasten the malting process.
- Abscisic hormone induces tolerance to abiotic stresses in plants.
- Cytokinin promotes chloroplast formation and hence help in photosynthesis.

18. (*c*) Xenogamy is the transfer of pollens from anther to stigma of different flowers borne on different plants. Hence, there is genetic variability. In other types of pollination the plant body remains the same, hence chances of variability are less.

19. (*c*) S-strain of bacteria can cause pneumonia in mice and the mice would die. R-strain is non-virulent. In condition I, since both strains are heat killed, none would be able to cause the disease and the mice would live. In condition II, DNA from heat killed S-strain would transform the live R-strain and hence, mice would die of pneumonia. In conditions III and IV, presence of live S-strain would cause the disease and the mice would die.

20. (*b*) S-phase is the stage when a cell replicates its DNA. Thus, after crossing S-phase successfully, a cell becomes irreversibly committed to division.

21. (*d*) Statement I is correct, but statement II is incorrect. Statement II can be corrected as

Flow of electrons across CF_0 of ATP synthase causes the gradient to break down.

22. (*a*) (i) is PCT, here the filtrate is isotonic. (ii) is the descending limb of Henle's loop and the filtrate gets concentrated here as it is permeable to water, but impermeable to electrolytes. (iii) is the ascending limb of Henle's loop and the filtrate gets diluted here since it is impermeable to water, but permeable to electrolytes. (iv) is DCT which receives diluted hypotonic filtrate from descending limb. Here, filtrate remains hypotonic.

23. (*b*) Statements I, IV and V are correct, whereas statements II and III are incorrect and can be corrected as

- In *Obelia*, polyps produce medusae asexually.
- Water in drawn into the spongocoel by ostia in sponges.

24. (*d*) A red snapdragon is homozygous dominant (RR), while a white snapdragon is homozygous recessive (rr). In the heterozygous condition, Rr, pink flowers are formed. So, when a homozygous recessive (white) and heterozygous parents (pink) cross with each other, the result will be 50 per cent heterozygous offsprings (Rr) and 50% homozygous recessive (rr) offsprings.

This can be best explained by cross shown below.

Rr × rr

	R	r
r	Rr (pink)	rr (white)
r	Rr (pink)	rr (white)

Hence , the probability of getting red snapdragon, (RR) is 0.

25. (*d*) The correct matches are A-2, B-4, C-1, D-3.

- 44 + XXY refers to Klinefelter's syndrome, where there is an additional X-chromosome in males. Such males show feminine characters like development of breasts or gynaecomastia.

- 44 + XO denotes Turner's syndrome and is the absence of one X chromosome in females. Such females are sterile.
- Lack of cytokinesis, leads to an increase in whole set of chromosome, a condition called polyploidy, that is common in plants.
- Aneuploidy occurs due to failure of segregation of chromatids. 21 trisomy is Down's syndrome, where there is an additional copy of 21st chromosome. Such individuals have mental retardation and characteristic palm crease.

26. (*d*) The correct order is I–III–II–IV–V.

- At *A*, membrane is impermeable to Na^+ and permeable to K^+. Thus, sodium concentration is more outside in the fluid than axoplasm. This sets up a concentration gradient, further maintained by Na-K pump.
- At *A*, when there is influx of sodium ions, an action potential is generated in response to a stimulus.
- This causes reversal of polarity at *A*, i.e. *A* becomes depolarised.
- At site *B*, membrane has a positive charge on the outer surface and a negative charge on its inner surface. As a result, a current flows on the inner surface from site *A* to site *B*. On the outer surface, current flows from site *B* to site *A* to complete the circuit of current flow. Hence, the polarity at the site is reversed, and an action potential is generated at site *B*.
- A becomes repolarised by increased permeability of potassium ions. Within a fraction of a second, K^+ diffuses outside the membrane and restores the resting potential of the membrane at the site of excitation.

27. (*c*) The correct pathway of sperm movement after its formation in the seminiferous tubules is rete testis, vasa efferentia, epididymis, vas deferens, ejaculatory duct, urethra and urethral meatus.

28. (*d*) A person with blood group A can have a child with blood group O, upon marrying a woman with B blood group, only in one condition, that is the parents are I^Ai and I^Bi. This is because for the child to have O blood type, the child must be inheriting genotype, one allele from the father and one allele from the mother.

29. (*c*) Both A and R are true, but R is not the correct explanation of A. A can be explained as

Gene therapy done to early embryos can cure genetic diseases permanently as embryonic cells undergo cell division and differentiation into germ layers. These germ layer cells are totipotent and can give rise to different cell types of the body. Hence, the corrected gene is delivered to all the cells that constitute the organism.

30. (*a*) Here, *P* – Polar nuclei, *Q* – Antipodals, *R* – Egg cell and *S* – Synergids.

After fertilisation, synergids and antipodals disintegrate. One of the male gamete fuses with egg to form zygote. Other male gamete fuses with the two polar nuclei to form triploid endosperm nuclei.

31. (*c*) Let the solar energy received by plants be y.

Plants can use 1%, thus energy utilised by plants is 1/100 × y

Primary consumers can use 10 % of the energy from the producers, that is 10/100 × (1/100)y

$$\Rightarrow \frac{10}{100} \times \frac{y}{100}$$

$$\Rightarrow \frac{y}{1000}$$

$$\Rightarrow \frac{y}{1000} = 1000 \text{ J}$$

$$\Rightarrow y = 1000 \times 1000$$

$$\Rightarrow 10^6 \text{ J}$$

32. (*a*) A is false, but R is true. A can be corrected as

Plasma from recovered patients can provide passive immunity to a person. People who have recovered from an infection, would contain antibodies against the pathogen in their plasma. Thus, pre-made antibodies of plasma, when injected to a patient, would provide passive immunisation to them.

33. (*c*) The correct order is Q–P–S–R–T.

- In the very first step, the envelope of HIV fuses with the cell membrane of host, thus envelope remains behind.
- The RNA genome is released into the cytoplasm of the host.
- This is followed by reverse transcription of RNA to DNA.
- The viral DNA integrates into the host genome. This is further replicated and translated to form viral proteins.
- Viral proteins are assembled to form new viral particles.

34. (*c*) Statement in option (c) is incorrect and can be corrected as:

Auxin causes cell elongation in dark side of stem. This phytohormone is synthesised in the illuminated side and then diffuses to the shaded side and promotes cell elongation there.

35. (*a*) Statements III and IV are correct. Statements I, II and V can be corrected as

- Transition state is characterised by E-S complex formation.
- In an exothermic process, free energy of S is more than P.
- Enzymes decrease the energy barrier between S and P.

36. (*a*) Statement I is incorrect, but statement II is correct. Statement I can be corrected as

Successful sewage treatment requires BOD to be reduced significantly. This is because, lower the BOD value, the lesser the organic matter present in the water.

37. (*c*) Prolonged fasting will decrease the blood glucose levels. Hence, the body compensates this with gluconeogenesis or production of glucose in the liver.

- Glycogenolysis is breakdown of glycogen into glucose and it occurs in the liver cells or hepatocytes.
- Glycogenesis is synthesis of glycogen from glucose which occurs in liver cells and fat cells or adipocytes. However, it occurs when there is rise in blood glucose levels.

38. (*d*) Statement III is correct, while all other statements are incorrect and can be corrected as

- Women who undergo GIFT, develop embryos by *in vivo* fertilisation. Here, the gametes are transferred to the female's Fallopian tube where fertilisation takes place. Hence, embryos are formed by *in vivo* fertilisation.
- IUT is not effective for women who does not have a healthy uterus. In intra uterine transfer, embryos are transferred for their development into foetus into the uterus. In the absence of healthy uterus, embryos would fail to develop, leading to miscarriage.
- ICSI is just an *in vitro* technique of ART to form blastomeres. ICSI is intra cytoplasmic sperm injection, where an embryo is formed in the laboratory by injecting a sperm directly into the ovum. Hence, it is an *in vitro* technique.

39. (*d*) Statement I is correct, but statement II is incorrect. Statement II can be corrected as

Cell division in plant cells proceeds centrifugally. In animal cells, cytokinesis occurs centripetally.

40. (*a*) A is false, but R is true. A can be corrected as

Genes on the same chromosome has lower recombination frequency than genes located on different chromosomes. This is because closer the genes, higher are their chances of being linked. Linked genes have lower chances of crossing over and hence lower recombination frequency.

41. (*a*) Statement II is correct. Statements I, III and IV are incorrect and can be corrected as:

- Grasshopper is an example of male heterogamety because they produce two different types of sperm cells with or without X chromosome.
- Birds and humans share different sex-determination mechanism. Birds have ZZ/ZW, while humans have XX/XY system. Birds have female heterogamety while humans have male heterogamety.
- Birds have male homogametic system, while *Drosophila* has male heterogametic system.

42. (*c*) The correct matches are A-2, B-1, C-3, D-4.

- Lactational amenorrhoea is a natural contraceptive method, with no side effects. During intense lactation period following parturition, there is no menstruation and hence, chances of fertilisation is nil.
- Multiload 375 is an IUD that is often used by couples who want to delay pregnancy and space children.
- Vaults are barriers inserted into female vagina and are often used along with spermicidal jellies and creams to increase their contraceptive efficiency.
- Saheli is a once a week pill with no side effects that is made out of non-steroidal preparation.

43. (*c*) Both A and R are true, but R is not the correct explanation of A. It can be explained as

Competitive exclusion principle does not always hold true in nature because species facing competition might evolve mechanisms that promote co-existence rather than exclusion by mechanism known as 'resource partitioning'.

44. (*d*) At the alveoli, the pO_2 is more than pCO_2. This favours more association of oxygen with haemoglobin and will cause a left ward shift of the curve. Also, there would be dissociation of CO_2 from haemoglobin at the alveoli, so that they are expelled from the body. Likewise, CO_2 is transported as bicarbonates in plasma by the action of carbonic anhydrase and the reaction would proceed in the reverse direction leading to formation of CO_2 and H_2O at alveoli.

At the tissues, when pCO_2 is more than pO_2, the curve shifts to the right due to decreased affinity of haemoglobin for oxygen that results in their dissociation.

45. (*c*) Both statement I and statement II are incorrect. These can be corrected as

- PCR primers are short single-stranded oligonucleotide sequences. Primers have to anneal to form base pair with complementary sequence of the region of DNA to be amplified.

- The G-C bond is more stable during denaturation step of PCR than A-T. This is because A pairs with T with two H-bonds, while G pairs with C with three H-bonds.

46. (*d*) Somatic hybridisation involves fusion of protoplast of two parents. Hence, the offspring has novel features and combined genetics of both parents. Tissue culture or explant culture or micropropagation produces somaclones which are genetically identical to one another and the parent.

47. (*c*) If foreign gene is cut by *Pst* I enzyme, then it should be ligated to the vector at the *Pst* I site. This causes insertional inactivation of ampicillin resistance gene.
After transformation, the cells grown on tetracycline containing media would select the transformants, which would be able to grow in that media, from non-transformants.
Non-transformants would fail to grow as they lack tetracycline resistance gene. However, this does not provide selection of recombinants and non-recombinants. For this, transformed cells from tetracycline plate should be grown in ampicillin containing media. This would allow growth of non-recombinants that have functional ampicillin gene and prevent growth of recombinants whose ampicillin resistance gene is inactivated.

48. (*d*) The correct matches are A-1, B-4, C-2, D-3.
- Tetrad or bivalents appear distinctly in pachytene stage.
- Diakinesis is the stage where terminalisation of chiasma occurs.
- Diplotene stage shows certain distinct X-shaped regions called chiasma, where crossing over has taken place.
- Zygotene stage shows pairing of homologous chromosomes or synapsis.

49. (*b*) Both statement I and statement II are correct.
A species may occupy more than one trophic level in the same ecosystem at the same time. A sparrow is a primary consumer when it eats seeds, fruits, peas and a secondary consumer when it eats insects and worms. Ecological pyramids does not accomodate a food web.

50. (*b*) Fungi are non-chlorophyllous heterotrophic organisms. They do not contain chloroplast, but possess chitin cell wall. Whereas, algae are grouped under Thallophyta division of plant kingdom. They possess cellulosic cell wall and chloroplast.

51. (*d*) Statement I is correct, but statement II is incorrect. Statement II can be corrected as
Paul Ehrlich's analogy states rivets of the plane represents species of an ecosystem.

52. (*d*) Cells used in a bioreactor normally produce a product of importance, like alcohol, etc. The cells are taken from their active phase of growth which is the log phase, where cells are actively dividing. If they are taken from stationary phase, then rate of cell formation and rate of cell death is same, which means that no new cells are added, and this could decrease the production capacity of the cells.

53. (*a*) The correct matches are A-2, B-3, C-1, D-4.
- *Propionibacterium shermanii* is responsible for production of large holes in Swiss cheese due to CO_2 production.
- Streptokinase produced by the bacterium *Streptococcus* and modified by genetic engineering is used as a 'clot buster' for removing clots from the blood vessels of patients.
- Cyclosporin-A is used as an immunosuppressive agent in organ-transplant patients and is produced by the fungus *Trichoderma polysporum*.
- Statins produced by the yeast *Monascus purpureus* have been commercialised as blood-cholesterol lowering agents.

54. (*c*) Analogous structures have different anatomy but share similar function. Such as wings of insects and birds have different anatomy, but serve the same purpose of flying. Ramaining all are the example of homologous structures.

55. (*a*) The ploidy of nucellus tissues is $2n$ meaning that they are diploid. Female gametophyte arises from megaspores formed by meiotic division of megaspore mother cell. Hence, they are haploid with a ploidy of n.

56. (*c*) *In situ* conservation protects the organism in its natural habitat, like national parks, wildlife sanctuaries, etc. This helps in protecting organisms in biodiversity hotspots where endemic organisms are conserved. Also, this results in conservation of endangered and vulnerable species. Extinct species are already wiped out and hence, cannot be protected.

57. (*b*) The blue eyes are recessive, while black eyes are dominant in nature. Thus, blue eyes will be expressed only when present in homozygous condition. So, here Priya has blue eyes, i.e. genotype will be bb (homozygous recessive). She marries a man with black eyes so the genotype of man can be BB (homozygous dominant) or Bb (heterozygous). But because their child has blue eyes this shows that the genotype of man is Bb (heterozygous) as shown in cross below.

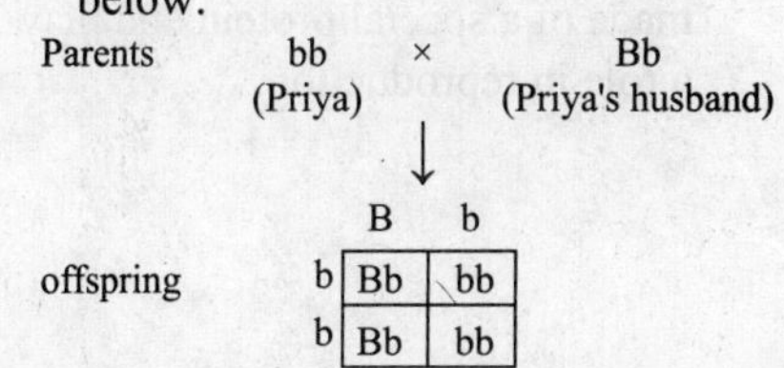

In case II, where Priya's brother marry a girl with black eyes their son also have blue eyes. This concludes that both Priya's brother and her brother's wife are heterozygous for the trait as shown in cross below.

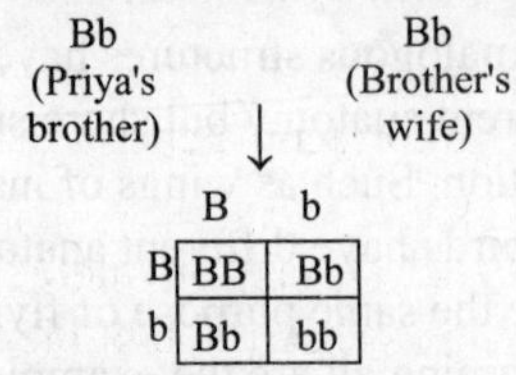

58. (*a*) Statement I is incorrect, but statement II is correct. Statement I can be corrected as

P. americana passes through a nymphal stage during development.

59. (*c*) Both A and R are true, but R is not the correct explanation of A. It can be explained as

Fluidity of membrane allows transport of substances as the fluidity due to phospholipids allow lateral movement of proteins within the membrane, which in turn allows molecules to enter and exit from the cell.

60. (*c*) The correct matches are A-3, B-1, C-4, D-2.

- Mesosomes are formed by the extensions of plasma membrane into the cell. They help in cell wall formation, DNA replication and distribution to daughter cells. They also help in respiration, secretion processes, to increase the surface area of the plasma membrane and enzymatic content.
- Several ribosomes may attach to a single *m*RNA and form a chain called polyribosomes or polysomes. The ribosomes of a polysome translate the *m*RNA into proteins.
- Pili are elongated tubular structures made of a special protein and play a role in reproduction.
- Fimbriae are small bristle-like fibres sprouting out of the cell and help in attaching the bacteria to the surface.

61. (*d*) The conditions given in the question paint a real life situation with limited food availability, competition and predation. Hence, logistic growth curve would be predominant. Hence, the equation would be $dN/dT = rN(K-N/K)$, where K is carrying capacity.

62. (*a*) A is false, but R is true. A can be corrected as

Association between flatworms and humans is a positive-negative interaction. This is because they have hooks and suckers that they use to suck nutrition from human host. This causes a negative impact on the host, but brings about a positive effect on the parasitic flatworm.

63. (*a*) The correct option is II-IV-III-V-I

- Stimulation of anterior pituitary releases the gonadotrophins.
- FSH and LH secretion increases.
- LH surge causes rupture of Graafian follicle to release the ovum (ovulation).
- Ovum fuses with the sperm at ampulla, which completes meiosis-II.
- Following fertilisation, Graafian follicle persists and is converted to corpus luteum which secretes progesterone that maintains pregnancy.

64. (*c*) The correct matches are A-2, B-1, C-4, D-3.

- Agar, one of the commercial products obtained from *Gelidium* and *Gracilaria* are used to grow microbes and in preparations of ice-creams and jellies.
- *Chlorella*, a unicellular alga rich in proteins, is used as food supplement even by space travellers.
- Many species of *Porphyra, Laminaria* and *Sargassum* are among the 70 species of marine algae used as food.
- Certain marine brown and red algae produce large amounts of hydrocolloids (water holding substances), e.g. algin (brown algae or Phaeophyceae).

65. (*d*) The incorrect statement can be corrected as:

Spores of slime moulds are formed during unfavourable conditions.

66. (*d*) A is true, but R is false. R can be corrected as

Most part of nervous system in a cockroach is located in ventral part of body.

67. (*d*) The correct match is A-3, B-1, C-2, D-4.

- Nicotine increases the epinephrine or adrenaline levels in the blood, which affect heart rate and blood pressure.
- Crack is cocaine which stimulates the CNS since it interferes with the transport of the neuro-transmitter dopamine.
- α-interferon is a biological response modifier that activates the immune system to destroy tumour cells.
- Serotonin and histamine are released by mast cells in response to allergic reactions in a person.

68. (*a*) Statement I is incorrect, but statement II is correct. Statement I can be corrected as:

Karyogamy does not always succeed plasmogamy in fungi. In some fungi (Ascomycetes and Basidiomycetes), an intervening dikaryotic stage ($n + n$, i.e. two nuclei per cell) occurs; such a condition is called a dikaryon and the phase is called dikaryophase of fungus.

69. (*b*) The correct matches are A-3, B-1, C-2, D-4.

- Hypothalamus of forebrain controls body temperature and hunger.
- Amygdala forms a part of limbic system and along with hypothalamus controls emotions in a person like anger, aggression, etc.
- Cerebral cortex, the largest part of the brain contains association area which controls speech in a person.
- Cerebellum is a part of hindbrain and controls balance, posture and coordination in a person.

70. (*a*) Statements IV and V are correct, while statements I, II and III are incorrect and can be corrected as

- Lagging strand synthesis and leading strand synthesis occur simultaneously.
- RNA polymerase can catalyse only the elongation step. For initiation and termination, it requires sigma and rho factors, respectively.
- To *hn*RNA, a 5'modified GTP and a 3' poly-A tail are added post transcription.

71. (*c*) Both statement I and statement II are incorrect. These can be corrected as

- The peripheral arrangement is different in centrioles and flagella. Cilia or flagella contain nine peripheral doublets of microtubules, while centrioles contain nine triplets of peripheral fibrils.
- Centrioles form the basal body of cilia or flagella.

72. (*d*) PCR can be used to amplify the mutated gene in a population of cells. Southern blot followed by autoradiography can also be used to find the mutated gene using radioactive probe.

Gel electrophoresis can be only used to separate DNA, while ELISA works on protein products.

73. (*d*) The correct matches are A-3, B-2, C-1, D-4.

- *Salpa* is a Urochordate where notochord is present only in larval tail.
- *Saccoglossus* is a hemichordate that has a rudimentary structure in the collar called stomochord.
- *Branchiostoma* is a cephalochordate that has persistent notochord from head to tail, all throughout the life.
- *Myxine* belongs to cyclostomata, and has a circular mouth without jaws.

74. (*b*) Both A and R are true and R is the correct explanation of A.

In gymnosperms like *Pinus*, male and female gametophytes do not have independent existence. They are present within the sporangia that are retained on sporophytes.

75. (*c*) Statements II and V are correct, while statements I, III and IV can be corrected as:

- Biosynthesis occurs through C_4 pathway in maize plants.
- CO_2:O_2 ratio is high in the bundle sheath cells of C_4 plants.
- PEP carboxylase operates in the mesophyll cells.

76. (*b*) Amino acids behave as zwitter ions. In acidic pH, the amino group ($-NH_2$) would behave as a base and accept protons or H^+ ions to form NH_3^+.

77. (*b*) Statement I is incorrect. Statement I can be corrected as Detritus is decomposed by aerobic microorganisms. Anaerobiosis inhibits decomposition, thus oxygen is essential for decomposing the detritus.

78. (*b*) The labelled parts *A*, *B* and *C* are hypodermis, ground tissue and vascular bundles, respectively.

The vascular bundles found in monocot stem are scattered which are surrounded by parenchymatous ground tissue.

79. (*b*) The correct matches are A-2, B-1, C-4, D-3.

- DCT or Distal Convoluted Tubule causes reabsorption of bicarbonate ions and secretion of H^+ into the filtrate, which increases blood pH to alkaline.
- JGA releases renin in response to fall in glomerular blood flow. The renin-angiotensin pathway works antagonistic to the ANF pathways.
- Aldosterone causes reabsorption of sodium ions from the filtrate which raises the osmolarity of blood.
- Angiotensin-II constricts blood vessel and possesses a resistance to blood flow. This increases blood pressure.

80. (*a*) Cells lying between the vascular bundles do not divide. These cells are parenchymatous in nature and form the conjunctive tissue.

81. (*d*) The given placentation is that of parietal type. Here, ovary is one-chambered, but it becomes two chambered due to the formation of the false septum. It is found in mustard and *Argemone*.

82. (*b*) The correct matches are A-4, B-3, C-1, D-2.

- Tympanum is the membranous structure that helps in receiving sound and maintains balance.
- Sensory papillae are the organs for the sensation of touch in a frog.
- Nasal epithelium is used to perceive smell.
- Copulatory pads help male frogs to attach with a female and aids in the reproduction process.

83. (*d*) The branching descent put forward by Darwin, explains that all organisms have a common ancestor from which they have descended.

- Natural selection is another driving force of evolution, which states that nature selects the fittest individuals from the population.
- Hugo de Vries stated that mutation caused speciation and hence, called it saltation (single step large mutation). This was the mutational theory or saltation theory of evolution.
- Lamarck proposed the theory of use and disuse. He stated that evolution of life forms had occurred, but was driven by use and disuse of organs.

84. (*c*) Both A and R are true, but R is not the correct explanation of A. A can be explained as

While rotating the thumb, we use our wrist as well because of the saddle joint which connects the carpals of the wrist bone to the metacarpal of thumb.

85. (*b*) Statements I, III and V are correct, while statements II and IV are incorrect and can be corrected as

- Contraction of ventricles require impulse conduction through AVN, AV bundle and bundle of His.
- Pumping of blood out of the ventricles does not produce the sound 'dub'. 'Dub' is the second heart sound produced by closure of semilunar valves. The semilunar valves close when ventricular pressure falls during relaxation or diastole of ventricles.

86. (*d*) Mouth part of cockroach contains two mandibles, which bear teeth. If both the mandibles work simultaneously in a horizontal plane, the food matter is cut and masticated into fine and smaller pieces.

Gizzard is another part of alimentary canal. It possesses six muscular folds which are covered by chitinous conical plates called the teeth. These are used for grinding the food. Thus, the food is grinded by mandibles and gizzard in common cockroach.

87. (*a*) The correct matches are A-4, B-3, C-2, D-1.

- *Pheretima* is an annelid that uses nephridia as an excretory organ.
- *Pinctada* is a mollusc whose mouth contains a file-like rasping organ for feeding, called radula.
- Aquatic annelids like *Nereis* possess lateral appendages, parapodia, which help in swimming.
- *Balanoglossus* is a hemichordate whose excretory organ is proboscis gland.

88. (*b*) Zn is a metal ion cofactor for carboxypeptidase that forms coordinate bond with side chains at the active site and at the same time form one or more coordination bonds with the substrate.

89. (*d*) A is true, but R is false. R can be corrected as

Competition (as in competitive inhibition) depends on substrate concentration. If concentration of substrate far exceeds concentration of inhibitor, then inhibition can be reversed and normal substrate can replace inhibitor.

90. (*d*) Statement III is correct, while statements I, II and IV are incorrect. Incorrect statements can be corrected as

- Auxin and cytokinin promotes cell growth in different ways. Auxin promotes cell elongation, while cytokinin stimulates cell division.
- Gibberellins promote seed germination while abscisic acid promotes seed dormancy.
- Auxins are widely used in micro-propagation techniques.

NK05 NEET Knock Offs 5

1. (*b*) No. of base pairs in the organism $= 18 \times 10^6$ bp

Time taken for replication

$= 300$ minutes

$= (300 \times 60)$ s

$= 18000$ s

$\therefore$ Rate of polymerisation

$= \frac{18 \times 10^6}{18000\text{s}}$ bp

$= 1000$ bp/s

2. (*d*) Option (d) is correct about inhibition of succinic dehydrogenase. Other statements can be corrected as
   - Malonate resembles the substrate succinate.
   - Succinate concentration can affect malonate inhibition. Increasing succinate or substrate concentration can reverse the competitive inhibition.
   - Binding of malonate to the active site of succinic dehydrogenase, makes it unavailable for succinate.

3. (*a*) Statement I is incorrect, but statement II is correct. Statement I can be corrected as

cry gene cloned in a plant protects it from some specific groups of insects. *cry* gene product can protect the plant against insects of lepidopterans (tobacco, budworm, armyworm) coleopterans (beetles) and dipterans (flies, mosquitoes) group, but not all kinds of pests.

4. (*a*) An unaffected woman with a colourblind father would be carrier of the disease, X^cX. She marries a colourblind man, X^cY.

	X^C	X
X^C	X^CX^C	X^CX
Y	X^CY	XY

X^cX^c is a colour blind daughter. X^cY is a colour blind son. X^cX is a carrier daughter and XY is a normal son. Thus 2/4 of the children are colourblind. Hence probability of having a colourblind child is 2/4 or 1/2.

5. (*c*) In prokaryotes, post transcriptional modifications are not needed and hence, transcription and translation can proceed simultaneously. The incorrect statements can be corrected as
   - Sigma factor initiates transcription at the promoter. RNA polymerase-II can elongate by adding nucleoside triphosphates.
   - *rho* factor causes termination of transcription.
   - *hn*RNA undergoes polyadenylation after termination.

6. (*c*) A bilobed anther is dithecous, with each lobe having two thecae. Thus, two lobes have 4 thecae. Anther is a tetragonal structure consisting of four microsporangia located at the corners, two in each lobe.

7. (*d*) A is true, but R is false. R can be corrected as

CMI (cell-mediated Immunity) by the T-cells causes graft rejection reactions.

8. (*c*) The correct match is A-2, B-1, C-4, D-3.
   - Male reproductive organs consist of a pair of yellowish ovoid testes, which are found adhered to the upper part of kidneys by a double fold of peritoneum called mesorchium.
   - Copulatory pads in males are used during the process of copulation or mating.
   - Vasa efferentia arise from testes and enter the kidneys on their side and open into Bidder's canal.
   - Sensory papillae are the organs of touch in frogs.

9. (*b*) Some amino acids are coded by more than one codon, hence the genetic code is degenerate.

Other terms can be explained as
   - The code is nearly universal for example, from bacteria to human, UUU would code for Phenylalanine.
   - The codon is read in *m*RNA in a contiguous fashion, i.e. there are no punctuations.
   - The codon is triplet. Each codon is made up of three nucleotides.

10. (*a*) Statements II and V are correct, while statements I, III and IV are incorrect and can be corrected as
   - 2-D structure of *t*-RNA appears like clover leaf. 3-D structure appears as an inverted L.
   - In prokaryotes, 30S subunit binds to the *m*RNA first. Smaller subunit of ribosome binds the *m*RNA first and initiate translation.
   - Not every codon of genetic code has a cognate *t*RNA. There are no *t*RNAs for stop codons.

11. (*c*) Abscisic acid is the stress hormone which can protect them from excess heat. ABA will promote the closure of stomata, thereby conserving water and preventing water loss by transpiration.

12. (*c*) The incorrect statement can be corrected as

Inactive fibrinogen in plasma is a soluble protein component.

13. (*c*) Both A and R are true, but R is not the correct explanation of A. Head sitting on the vertebral column shows considerable rotation because the joint between atlas and axis vertebra is pivot synovial joint. The remaining vertebrae are joined by cartilaginous joints between them.

14. (*b*) Active site is the part of an enzyme to which substrate bind and where a reaction is catalysed. The incorrect statements can be corrected as

- There is conformational change associated with an enzyme. The binding of the substrate induces the enzyme to alter its shape, fitting more tightly around the substrate.
- Substrate concentration and reaction kinetics increase initially. However, with saturation of enzymes with substrates, the rate of the reaction becomes stationary.
- Formation of E-P complex is more transient than formation of E-S. This is because E-P complex soon breaks to release the product and the free enzyme.

15. (*c*) Both statement I and statement II are incorrect. They can be corrected as

Competition can be considered to be a negative-negative interaction. Competitive exclusion principle works in case of limited resources.

16. (*b*) $FADH_2$ is generated from FAD^+ during conversion of succinate to fumarate. In the electron transport chain, reduced $FADH_2$ transfers electrons to ubiquinone which gets reduced to ubiquinol. $FADH_2$ in the process gets oxidised to FAD^+. For every molecule of $FADH_2$ that gets oxidised in the ETC, 2 ATP molecules are synthesised by ATP synthase enzyme.

17. (*b*) The correct matches are A-2, B-3, C-1, D-4.

- Secondary constriction is also called Nucleolar Organising Region or NOR as it is involved in synthesis of nucleolus of the cell.
- Nucleolus is involved in ribosome synthesis.
- Primary constriction is the region of centromere. Centromeres in a chromosome holds the sister chromatids together.
- Kinetochores are the protein discs at the centromere where spindle fibres attach during cell division.

18. (*c*) Statement (c) is correct. The incorrect statements can be corrected as

- The primary structure of proteins end with a C-terminal amino acid.
- Hydrogen bonds stabilise the β-helices and β-sheets of secondary structure.
- Appearance of subunits of a protein is apparent in quarternary structure.

19. (*b*) The reverse of oxyhaemoglobin dissociation is formation of oxyhaemoglobin complex. This complex formation occurs in the alveoli where there is high pO_2, low pCO_2, lesser H^+ concentration and lower temperature.

20. (*a*) The correct matches are A-3, B-4, C-1, D-2.

- Choanocytes or collar cells are present in Porifera like *Sycon*.
- Stomochord is similar to notochord present in the collar of hemichordates like *Saccoglossus*.
- Nematocysts are stinging capsules used to immobilise prey by coelenterates like *Obelia*.
- The mouth of molluscs contain a file-like rasping organ for feeding, called radula.

21. (*d*) Invasive species does not affect the reproductive ability of local species. However, when an invasive species is introduced, it causes an increase in competition among the local ones for same resources. Invasive species could be a predator of local species. Also, invasive species can outcompete local ones if they do not have any possible predator in the new habitat.

22. (*d*) Gross primary productivity (GPP) - Respiratory losses (R) = Net primary productivity (NPP).

NPP = 1100 (kcal m^{-2}) yr^{-1}; GPP = 2500 (kcal m^{-2}) yr^{-1}

Respiratory losses = GPP - NPP

= 2500 - 1100 (kcal m^{-2}) yr^{-1}

= 1400 (kcal m^{-2}) yr^{-1}.

23. (*b*) Both statement I and statement II are correct.

In alkaline media, COOH group can donate its hydrogen ion and form COO^-, hence behaving as an acid. When the pH is decreased, the amino groups are protonated,and *vice versa*.

24. (*d*) *y* gene codes for the enzyme permease which increases permeability of the cell to allolactose, which acts as the inducer. Thus, the product of gene y would allow entry of the inducer, which would further interact with repressor molecule and inhibit its action. This would lead to activation of the operon, as the operator could be accessed by RNA polymerase. Other options can be explained as

- *i* gene though expressed constitutively, codes for repressor protein that can bind to the operator and inhibit the operon.
- *z* gene codes for β-galactosidase, which catalyses the breakdown of lactose into glucose and galactose.
- *a* gene encodes for a transacetylase.

25. (*a*) Statements III and IV are correct. The incorrect statements can be corrected as

- Carpels in angiosperms is equivalent/homologous to megasporophylls in gymnosperms and pteriolophytes
- Most of the angiosperms possess anatropous ovule.

26. (*a*) Statement I is incorrect, but statement II is correct. Statement I can be corrected as

There are two energy generating steps in partial oxidation of glucose. Partial oxidation of glucose occurs in cytoplasm by glycolysis. In converting two molecules of BPGA to 2 molecules of 3-phosphoglyceric acid, two ATP molecules are produced. Also, during conversion of two molecules of phosphoenol pyruvate to two molecules of pyruvate, two ATPs are generated. Hence, there are two energy generating steps.

27. (*c*) ATP synthesis occurs due to the break down of the proton gradient as protons flow down their concentration gradient through the ATP synthase enzyme.
The thylakoid lumen has higher proton concentration due to the three following reasons.
- Splitting of the water molecule or photolysis takes place on the inner side of the membrane, hence the protons or hydrogen ions that are produced by the splitting of water accumulate within the lumen of the thylakoids.
- Primary accepter of electron, located towards the outer side of the membrane transfers its electron to a H carrier plastoquinone. Hence, this molecule removes a proton from the stroma while transporting an electron. When this molecule passes on its electron to the electron carrier on the inner side of the membrane, the proton is released into the inner side or the lumen side of the membrane
- NADP reductase enzyme reduces $NADP^+$ to NADPH and H^+ using protons removed from the stroma. This lowers proton concentration in stroma and increases its concentration in the thylakoid lumen.

28. (*d*) The first stable product in C_3 pathway is 3-Phosphoglycerate which is a 3-carbon compound.
Other incorrect statements can be corrected as
- RuBP behaves as carboxygenase when $O_2 : CO_2$ is less or $CO_2 : O_2$ is more.
- Primary carbon acceptor is 5-C molecule, Ribulose-1, 5-bisphosphate.
- RuBP forms a 2-C compound phosphoglycolate as an oxygenase.

29. (*c*) R represents the integuments. Integuments are protective coverings of ovule and following fertilisation, they form seed coat.
Other incorrect statements can be corrected as
- P is hilum which represents the junction between funicle and ovule. The point of attachment of ovule to the placenta is funicle.
- Q is the micropyle present at the micropylar end which contains the egg apparatus bearing the egg cell and synergids. Antipodals are present at the opposite chalazal end.
- S is the nucellus that contains reserve food. However, endosperm develops from the fusion of male gamete with two polar nuclei.

30. (*d*) The correct matches are A-2, B-3, C-1, D-4.
- *Australopithecines* probably lived in East African grasslands. Evidence shows they hunted with stone weapons, but essentially ate fruit.
- *Homo erectus* probably ate meat.
- *Ramapithecus* were man-like being that existed at about 15 mya.
- *Homo habilis* were the first human-like being that did not eat meat.

31. (*d*) 'P' is foam breaker to break the excess foam. Q is flat blade impeller to mix the contents and increase oxygen availability. R is an inlet of acid/base for pH control of the media. S is inlet of steam for sterilisation.

32. (*d*) Osculum is the opening to eliminate water from the body of poriferans. In echinoderms like sea urchin and starfish, water leaves the body through a structure called madreporite.

33. (*c*) Both A and R are correct, but R is not the correct explanation of A. A can be explained as
Bulliform cells help in water conservation in plants because they can make the leaves curl inwards to minimise water loss by transpiration.

34. (*b*) As the scientist has used traditional knowledge of locals without compensating them, he cannot file a patent. This would be unethical and would be considered as an act of biopiracy.

35. (*b*) *In vivo* fertilisation takes place within the body of the organism.
In *ex situ* methods, gametes of threatened species can be preserved in viable and fertile condition for long periods using cryopreservation techniques, eggs can be fertilised in vitro, and plants can be propagated using tissue culture methods. Seeds of different genetic strains of commercially important plants can be kept for long periods in seed banks.

36. (*a*) Statement II can be derived from the Law of segregation and not from Law of dominance. According to the law of segregation, alleles of a pair segregate from each other such that a gamete receives only one of the two factors.

37. (*d*) The given food chain is operational in a terrestrial ecosystem, where the major conduit of energy occurs through detritus food chain or DFC. Grazing food chain of GFC is the major conduit for energy flow in aquatic ecosystem.
Incorrect statements can be corrected as
- Snakes, at a given point, can be a part of more than one food chain.
- The frogs are the secondary consumers in the given food chain. Eagle is the tertiary consumer.
- The detritus food chain is operative in this terrestrial network.

38. (*d*) Incorrect statement can be corrected as
Insulin synthesised by genetic engineering also contains disulfide bonds that link chain A and chain B of the hormone.

39. (*b*) Both statement I and statement II are correct.

Collecting spices from forest is a direct economic benefit received by humans and hence, are classified under the narrowly utilitarian argument of biodiversity conservation. Even if a plant or any other organism shows no direct benefit to human, they should be protected based on the ethical argument that every organism has an intrinsic value.

40. (*c*) The initial lag phase observed in most realistic growth curve (S-curve) accounts for the slow and steady growth rate. This occurs as the cells take some time to adjust to new conditions of the media.
Secondary metabolites if toxic would kill many cells, but that usually happens in the stationary phase.
Decrease in growth rate due to increased competition on limitation of nutrients and space, is often observed in stationary phase.

41. (*c*) The incorrect statement can be corrected as
Saltation theory by Hugo de Vries states that variations occur due to random mutations.

42. (*b*) Rheumatoid arthritis is an autoimmune disorder where the body cannot recognise self from non-self cells. This is mediated normally by T-cells in the thymus.

43. (*b*) The correct order is V-I-IV-II-III
- Gene of interest isolated from a definite source is amplified using polymerase chain reaction.
- Digestion of gene of interest and vector using the same restriction enzyme to generate same sticky ends
- Ligation of gene of interest with vector using DNA ligase
- Calcium chloride treatment to make host cells competent followed by heat shock treatment to allow entry of recombinant plasmids into the host cells.
- Selection of recombinants from non-recombinants using selectable markers.

44. (*c*) Statement IV is correct, while statements I, II and III are incorrect and can be corrected as
- Cell plate formed during cell division in plants, is the precursor of middle lamella.
- New cell walls are deposited to the interior of primary cell wall. Secondary cell wall lies inner to primary cell wall.
- Plasmodesmata can traverse both cell wall and middle lamella. These are cytoplasmic connections between adjacent plant cells that allow transport of substances between them.

45. (*c*) Lysine and arginine are positively charged amino acids. Being polar in nature, they cannot cross the non-polar core of the membrane, and hence, are transported by carrier proteins through facilitated diffusion.

46. (*c*) Both statement I and statement II are incorrect. These can be corrected as
- Notochord is not persistent throughout the lives of all chordates. For example, vertebrates have a notochord present in embryonic stages, which is replaced by vertebral column.
- Chordates have a ventral heart in contrast to non-chordates.

47. (*d*) Spermatheca present in female cockroaches are responsible for receiving the sperms.
Other statements can be corrected as
- Trachea circulates air within the body of the cockroach. Spiracles are openings in their exoskeleton through which air enters and leaves their body.
- Spermatophores are collection of sperms in male seminal vesicles.
- Oothecae are coverings that encapsulate fertilised eggs.

48. (*a*) Hardy-Weinberg equilibrium is not resilient to environmental stress as nature can put selection pressure, which might cause changes in population and allelic frequencies.

49. (*c*) Both A and R are true, but R is not the correct explanation of A. It can be corrected as
Annealing temperature is lesser than denaturation during PCR, since complementary base pairing occurs during annealing and strand separation takes place during denaturation. Denaturation temperatures are higher to allow the two DNA strands to separate.

50. (*c*) Auxin or its synthetic derivative Indole-3-acetic acid promotes apical dominance. Apical dominance allows growth of apical buds which promote a vertical growth of plants and prevent development of lateral buds. Thus, chopping off shoot tips, will allow lateral buds and branches to grow, which would give the plants, a bushy appearance.

51. (*b*) Both A and R are true and R is the correct explanation of A.
Some cells exit G_1-phase and get temporarily arrested in the G_0-phase. This is done so that DNA damage can be repaired. If they are left to accumulate, they can cause lethal mutations that could cause diseases or cancer.

52. (*a*) The megaspore mother cell as well as the nucellar tissue are diploid. Hence, if MMC has 64 chromosomes, the nucellus would also contain 64 chromosomes. The spores are formed from MMC by meiosis, hence spores would have half the number of chromosomes as in MMC. Number of chromosomes in spores is 32.

53. (*b*) Two types of gametes, RT and rt will be produced.
- RRTT can produce one type of gamete, RT.

- rrtt can also produce one type of gamete, rt.

54. (*d*) Statement I is correct but Statement II is incorrect. Incorrect statement can be corrected as Rheumatoid arthritis is an example where the body attacks self-cells (synovial membrane) causing inflammation of joints.

55. (*c*) Incorrect statement (c) can be corrected as
Labeo rohita is a bony fish or a member of class-Osteichthyes. They have skin covered with cycloid or ctenoid scales.

56. (*c*) Statements I, II and IV are correct, while statements III and V are incorrect. They can be corrected as
- Repolarisation is linked to potassium ion permeability.
- Na-K pump uses ATP to pump three Na^+ outside the cell.

57. (*b*) Event II and III correctly explains the reversed stage of prophase in telophase.
- Nucleolus disappears at prophase, but reappears again in telophase.
- Chromatin condenses to form discrete chromosomes in prophase. In telophase, they decondense back and lose their discrete identity.

Other options can be explained as
- In prophase, centrosomes start moving towards opposite pole and they reach the opposite poles at telophase. Centrosomes had already duplicated during interphase.
- Splitting of centromere happens in anaphase due to contraction of spindle.

58. (*c*) Under emergency, the adrenal medulla is stimulated to secrete epinephrine or adrenaline. The adrenaline stimulates breakdown of glycogen by glycogenolysis to increase blood glucose levels.

59. (*d*) Medulla and Pons both contain respiratory centres. Hence, if either of them are damaged, it can alter the respiratory rate or breathing patterns in an individual.

60. (*d*) Statement IV can be corrected as Only PS-I is operational in stroma lamellae. The membrane or lamellae of the grana have both PS-I and PS-II, but the stroma lamellae membranes lack PS-II as well as NADP reductase enzyme.

61. (*c*) Statements III, IV and V are correct, w.r.t. dicot stems, but statements I and II are incorrect and can be corrected as
- Vascular bundles are situated jointly in the same radius.
- They can form secondary xylem and phloem. This is because they have open type of vascular bundle which means they have cambium between xylem and phloem. This allows growth of secondary xylem and phloem.

62. (*c*) Remnant of Graafian follicle after ovulation is corpus luteum. If fertilisation occurs, corpus luteum does not degenerate and secretes progesterone that helps in maintaining the blood lining of endometrium and maintains pregnancy.

63. (*a*) Statement I is incorrect, but statement II is correct. Statement I can be corrected as
Smooth muscles of myometrium contracts to induce labor during pregnancy.

64. (*a*) Statements I, II, IV and V are correct, but statements III is incorrect. Statement III can be corrected as
Diaphragm contracts during inspiration, when air is entering the lungs and relaxes during expiration, when air is expelled from the lungs.

65. (*d*) The diagram shows the process of inspiration. During inspiration
- Pressure within the lungs (intra-pulmonary pressure) is less than the atmospheric pressure, i.e. there is a negative pressure in the lungs w.r.t. atmospheric pressure
- Contraction of external intercostal muscles causes an increase in the dorso-ventral axis
- Contraction of diaphragm muscles causes an increase in the volume of antero-posterior axis
- An overall increase in thoracic volume causes an increase in the pulmonary volume

66. (*c*) The prickly pear *Cactus* introduced into Australia was an invasive species, that was brought under control only after a Cactus-feeding predator (a moth) from its natural habitat was introduced into the country.
Remaining all are defensive strategies used by organisms to avoid predation.

67. (*c*) In euglenoids, instead of a cell wall, they have a protein rich layer called pellicle which makes their body flexible.

68. (*c*) Both A and R are true, but R is not the correct explanation of A. A can be explained as
Hepatocytes have abundant smooth ER since SER is involved in detoxification process. The smooth ER in the liver cells or hepatocytes can detoxify and solubilise lipid soluble drugs.

69. (*d*) The correct order of steps during fall in GFR is I-IV-III-II-V
- A fall in GFR stimulates the JG cells to secrete Renin.
- Renin converts angiotensinogen to angiotensin I which is further converted to angiotensin II.
- Angiotensin II stimulates the adrenal cortex.
- Adrenal cortex secretes the mineralocorticoid aldosterone.
- Aldosterone causes reabsorption of sodium ions and water from the distal tubules.

70. (*d*) Statement I is correct, but statement II is incorrect. Incorrect statement can be corrected as

Steeper slope shows that species richness increases faster than area being explored, in case of large areas like continents.

71. (*c*) Spindle fibres from opposite poles attach the kinetochore of homologous chromosomes in metaphase-I.

The incorrect statements can be corrected as

- In metaphase-II, they attach to the kinetochores of sister chromatids.
- Bivalent chromosomes arrange at the equatorial plate in metaphase-I.
- Homologues are separated from each other in the stage following metaphase-I. Following metaphase-II, there is anaphase-II, where sister chromatids get separated.

72. (*b*) The correct matches are A-3, B-1, C-4, D-2.

- In alternate type of phyllotaxy, a single leaf arises at each node in alternate manner, as in China rose.
- In pinnately compound leaves, a number of leaflets are present on a common axis, the rachis, which represents the midrib of the leaf, as in neem.
- In opposite type, a pair of leaves arise at each node and lie opposite to each other as in *Calotropis* and guava plants.
- In palmately compound leaves, the leaflets are attached at a common point, i.e. at the tip of petiole, as in silk cotton.

73. (*a*) A is false, but R is true. A can be corrected as

Lichens accumulate in areas with a low AQI (Lower the AQI, better the air quality). Lichens are symbiotic associations between algae and fungi. They are indicators of pollution and accumulate in regions of low pollution levels.

74. (*a*) Statement I is incorrect, but statement II is correct. Statement I can be corrected as

Pachytene is the best stage to observe bivalents.

75. (*c*) Blue colouration observed on adding Iodine to bread loaf is a positive starch test. This happens because starch present in bread, can form starch-I_2 complex in its secondary helical structure.

76. (*b*) In the diagrammatic representation of ECG, A represents P wave, B represents QRS complex and C represents T wave. The P wave represents atrial depolarisation caused by generation of action potential by SAN. QRS represents ventricular contraction when the AV valves are closed shut which leads to generation of first heart sound which is lub. T wave represents ventricular repolarisation where ventricles relax leading to closure of semilunar valves and opening of AV valves.

77. (*d*) The correct matches are A-3, B-4, C-1, D-2.

- Pectinases and proteases are used to clarify and make bottled juices clearer.
- Lipases are used in detergent formulation to remove oily stains.
- Streptokinase produced by *Streptococcus*, is used as a 'clot buster' for removing clots from the blood vessels of patients who have undergone myocardial infarction, leading to heart attack.
- Cyclosporin-A, that is used as an immunosuppressive agent in organ-transplant patients, is produced by the fungus *Trichoderma polysporum*.

78. (*c*) Both statement I and statement II are incorrect. These can be corrected as

- Sporophyte does not have an independent existence in mosses. The sporophyte is not free-living, but attached to the photosynthetic gametophyte and derives nourishment from it.
- Capsule and seta have a ploidy of $2n$ in bryophytes. Capsule and seta belong to sporophyte which undergoes meiosis to produce haploid spores. Hence, capsule and seta are diploid ($2n$).

79. (*c*) Both A and R are true, but R is not the correct explanation of A. A can be explained as

Enzyme catalysed reactions slow down at higher temperatures because enzymes are proteins which get denatured at higher temperatures.

80. (*c*) Flowers of Gramineae are sessile, meaning they do not contain a stalk or pedicel.

81. (*d*) The correct order is I-V-IV-III-II

- DNA is isolated from the tissue sample from a crime scene.
- Isolated DNA is digested by restriction endonuclease to generate smaller fragments.
- DNA is separated based on their size on agarose gel.
- Separated DNA fragments are blotted or transferred to a nitrocellulose/nylon membrane.
- Fragments are allowed to hybridise with complementary radiolabelled VNTR probes. This is followed by detection using autoradiography.

82. (*c*) Both statement I and statement II are incorrect. These statements can be corrected as

- PCT and DCT secrete more NH_3 if blood becomes too alkaline.
- Passive transport of urea maintains osmotic gradient for concentration of filtrate.

83. (*c*) The diagram represents contraction of the muscle fibres. Other incorrect statements can be corrected as

- Release of Ca^{2+} from the sarcoplasmic reticulum
- Unmasking of myosin binding sites by troponin
- No change in the length of A-band, decrease in the length of sarcomere

84. (*b*) The labelling in option (b) is correct which represents Neurohypophysis, also known as posterior pituitary (D). which stores and releases two hormones called oxytocin and vasopressin.

The rest of the labellings can be explained as

- A is hypothalamus that produces releasing hormones that stimulate the anterior pituitary gland to produce prolactin hormone.
- B is anterior pituitary, responsible for releasing Follicle-Stimulating Hormone (FSH) and Luteinizing Hormone (LH).
- C is portal circulation and supplies blood from the hypothalamus to the posterior pituitary gland. This specialised blood vessel system allows hormones produced by the hypothalamus to be transported directly to the posterior pituitary for storage and subsequent release into the bloodstream when needed.

85. (*b*) Passive immunisation is the act of receiving pre-made antibodies. This is done in situation II, III and IV. Breast milk contains antibody IgA. Plasma of a recovered patient has antibodies against the particular antigen. Antivenom contains pre-made antibodies to counter the snake venom.

- Whereas, A person who recovered from chicken pox depended on the body's natural ability to fight of the germs by activating the B-lymphocytes, which not only produced antibodies but also kept memory of the infection.
- Pulse polio drops are vaccines that contain live attenuated or killed pathogens that can trigger an immune response in the body.

86. (*a*) The correct matches are A-2, B-4, C-1, D-3.

- *Salmonella typhi* causes typhoid diseases, which in severe cases, causes intestinal perforation and even death.
- *Entamoeba histolytica* causes amoebiasis where there is discharge of mucus in stool.
- *Haemophilus influenzae* causes pneumonia where air sacs or alveoli of lungs get filled with fluid or mucus.
- *Wuchereria malayi* causes filariasis that causes gross deformities of genital organs.

87. (*b*) Statements I, II and IV are correct. Statements III and V are incorrect and can be corrected as

- Both flatworms and round worms can be endoparasites.
- Mesoderm is present in pouches in aschelminthes, like *Ascaris, i.e. pseudocoelomate. Fasciola*, a flatworm is acoelomate, i.e. without mesoderm.

88. (*b*) The correct matches are A-2, B-3, C-1, D-4.

- Oxytocin secreted by posterior pituitary controls ejection of milk from the mammary gland.
- Melatonin, apart from regulating the sleep wake cycle, also controls body temperature.
- Prolactin secreted by anterior pituitary stimulates milk secretion in mammary glands.
- Epinephrine secreted by adrenal medulla prepares the body for 'fight or flight' response.

89. (*b*) Both statement I and statement II are correct.

- Neoplastic cells of a primary tumour can breach the basement membrane and travel by blood to reach new locations. Wherever they get dislodged, they form a secondary tumour.
- Biological agents like cancer causing viruses called oncogenic viruses have genes called viral oncogenes that causes neoplastic transformation.

90. (*d*) A is true, but R is false. R can be corrected as

In a test cross, dominant individual is crossed with the recessive parent. A dominant individual can be either homozygous or heterozygous for the dominant allele. Crossing with the recessive parent will help to understand the genotype.

NC1 NEET Chronicles 1

Botany

Section A

1. (*a*) Among eukaryotes, replication of DNA occurs during the synthetic or S- phase of the cell cycle. During this phase, the cell synthesises an exact copy of its DNA. After DNA replication is complete, the cell proceeds to the G_2-phase, during which it checks the replicated DNA for errors and prepares for mitosis (M-phase), i.e. the process of cell division.

2. (*b*) Cellulose does not form blue colour with iodine solution because it does not contain the helical structure which is present in starch.
Starch forms an iodine-starch complex with iodine, which results in a blue-black colour. If iodine molecules come into contact with cellulose, they cannot penetrate the tightly packed and rigid structure of cellulose chains to form a complex.

3. (*b*) In this method, small microparticles made of tungsten or gold are coated with the DNA of interest and then accelerated to high velocities using a device called a gene gun. This technique is also called biolistic method.

4. (*a*) In a corn cob, tassels are used to trap pollen grains. The tassels on a corn cob are the stigma and style which wave in the wind to trap pollen grains.

5. (*d*) Both A and R are true and R is the correct explanation of A.
Latewood or autumn wood is the part of a tree's growth ring that is produced later in the growing season. It has fewer xylary elements and narrower vessels than the earlywood. The latter is produced earlier in the growing season.
The cambium is the layer of cells between the bark and wood of a tree that is responsible for producing new xylem and phloem cells.
During the growing season, the cambium produces a large number of new xylem cells which result in the formation of wide vessels in the earlywood or spring wood.
Later in the growing season, as the cambium slows down its production of xylem cells, the vessels become narrower and fewer in number, resulting in the formation of latewood.

6. (*a*) The historic Convention on Biological Diversity. "The Earth Summit" was held in Rio de Janeiro, Brazil in the year 1992. The summit was organised by the United Nations and was attended by representatives from over 170 countries. The goal of the convention was to promote the conservation of biodiversity, the sustainable use of its components, etc.

7. (*a*) The role of RNA polymerase-III (Pol-III) in eukaryotes is the transcription of several types of small non-coding RNAs, including transfer RNAs (*t*RNAs), 5S ribosomal RNA (5S rRNA), and some small nuclear RNAs (*sn*RNAs). *t*RNAs are involved in protein synthesis, 5S *r*RNA is a component of the ribosome and *sn*RNAs play a role in RNA splicing. Pol-III binds to specific DNA sequences called promoters and synthesises RNA using the DNA strand as a template.

8. (*a*) Among the given options, *Selaginella* and *Salvinia* represent the pair of heterosporous pteridophytes. Heterosporous pteridophytes are plants that produce two types of spores namely, megaspores and microspores. These spores develop into female and male gametophytes, respectively.

9. (*d*) Both statement I and statement II are correct. Transpiration is the process by which plants lose water vapour through their leaves. This loss of water creates a negative pressure in the xylem vessels that extends from the roots to the leaves. It in turn, generates a force known as the transpiration pull, that can lift water upward over 130 meters in height. Additionally, transpiration can have a cooling effect on the leaf surface due to evaporative cooling. As water is lost through the stomata on the leaf surface, heat is absorbed from the surrounding tissues and the leaf surface can be cooled by as much as 10-15 degrees celsius.

10. (*d*) The reaction centre in photosystem-II (PS-II) has an absorption peak at around 680 nanometers (nm) in the visible light spectrum. PS-II is one of the two photosystems found in the thylakoid membranes of chloroplasts and is responsible for generating the oxygen released into the atmosphere as a by-product of photosynthesis. The other photosystem, photosystem-I (PS-I), has an absorption peak at around 700 nm and is responsible for producing NADPH.

11. (*d*) Among "The Evil Quartet", habitat loss and fragmentation are the most important cause of driving extinction of species. As habitats are destroyed or broken up into smaller

and more isolated fragments, species become more vulnerable to other threats such as predation, disease, and climate change. Habitat loss and fragmentation can have direct and indirect impacts on species, including loss of resources, increased isolation, and reduced genetic diversity.

12. (*b*) The division of the centromere occurs during the anaphase-II stage of meiosis. During this stage, the sister chromatids of each chromosome separate and are pulled toward opposite poles of the cell by spindle fibers. The separation of the sister chromatids is facilitated by the division of the centromere, which is the specialised region of the chromosome that links the sister chromatids together.

13. (*a*) The spraying of Gibberellic Acid (GA) on juvenile conifers can help in hastening the maturity period, leading to early seed production. Gibberellic acid is a plant hormone that plays a key role in promoting stem and leaf growth, seed germination, and flowering. In conifers, GA can help to promote growth and hasten the maturity period thus, leading to early seed production.

14. (*d*) Among the given statements A, B and C are correct, whereas statements D and E are incorrect. The incorrect statements can be corrected as

The detritus food chain begins with the breakdown of dead organic matter, also known as detritus. It includes dead plant and animal material, as well as waste products like faeces and fallen leaves. The process by which earthworms breakdown the complex detritus into smaller particles is called fragmentation.

15. (*d*) The micronutrient required for splitting water molecules during photosynthesis is manganese (Mn). In the light-dependent reactions of photosynthesis, light energy is used in the photolysis of water molecules into oxygen, protons, and electrons. This process occurs in the thylakoid membranes of chloroplasts and is facilitated by a complex of proteins called Photosystem-II (PS-II). Manganese is a critical co-factor for the PS-II complex, as it plays a key role in binding and stabilising the water molecules during the photolysis reaction.

16. (*d*) Large, colourful, fragrant flowers with nectar are often seen in plants that are pollinated by animals, particularly insects. These flowers have evolved to attract pollinators, which transfer pollen from the anthers of one flower to the stigma of another flower of the same species. Some examples of plants that produce large, colourful, fragrant flowers with nectar include roses, lilies, *Hibiscus*, and magnolias.

17. (*c*) The movement and accumulation of ions across a membrane against their concentration gradient can be explained by active transport. It is a process by which ions or molecules are moved across a cell membrane against their concentration gradient, from a region of lower concentration to a region of higher concentration. This requires energy in the form of ATP and the use of specific transport proteins or pumps.

18. (*d*) The thickness of ozone in a column of air in the atmosphere is measured in the terms of Dobson unit. This unit is commonly used by atmospheric scientists to monitor changes in the thickness and distribution of the ozone layer over time.

19. (*c*) Upon exposure to UV radiation, DNA stained with ethidium bromide will show bright orange colour. Ethidium bromide is a fluorescent dye that binds to DNA and becomes brightly coloured under ultraviolet (UV) light. When exposed to UV radiation, the dye intercalates into the double helix structure of DNA and emits a bright orange-red colour. This property is often used in molecular biology and genetics research to visualise and analyse DNA fragments in agarose gel.

20. (*a*) Unequivocal proof that DNA is the genetic material was first proposed by Alfred Hershey and Martha Chase. In 1952, Alfred Hershey and Martha Chase conducted a series of experiments using a virus called bacteriophage T_2 to infect bacteria. They demonstrated that only the DNA of the virus, and not its protein coat, was transferred into the bacterial cell. This experiment, known as the Hershey-Chase experiment, provided strong evidence that DNA, and not protein, was the genetic materials responsible for passing on the traits from one generation to the next.

21. (*a*) In tissue culture experiments, leaf mesophyll cells are put in a culture medium to form a callus. This phenomenon may be called dedifferentiation. It refers to the process by which mature cells lose their particular characteristics and they closely resemble embryonic cells. In tissue culture experiments, leaf mesophyll cells can be induced to undergo dedifferentiation and form callus when placed in a culture medium that contains the right combination of nutrients, hormones, and growth factors. The cells in the callus can then be induced to differentiate and form new tissues or organs.

22. (*d*) Both A and R are true and R is the correct explanation of A.
In glycolysis, glucose is converted into pyruvate through a series of

enzymatic reactions, and ATP is used in two steps. First, it is used when glucose is phosphorylated to glucose-6-phosphate by hexokinase, using one ATP molecule. Second, when fructose-6-phosphate is phosphorylated to fructose-1,6-bisphosphate by phosphofructokinase, using another ATP molecule.

23. (*a*) The appearance of recombination nodules occurs during the pachytene substage of prophase-I in meiosis. During this stage, the homologous chromosomes continue to undergo synapsis and become fully paired, forming structures known as bivalents or tetrads. At this point, the recombination nodules become more visible along the paired chromosomes.

24. (*b*) In the given equation, R represents respiratory loss. The rate at which organic matter is produced during photosynthesis is referred to as the ecosystem's Gross Primary Productivity (GPP). When we subtract respiratory losses (R) from GPP, we get Net Primary Productivity (NPP). The available biomass for heterotrophic consumption is defined as net primary productivity.

25. (*b*) Pleiotropism refers to a phenomenon where a single gene can affect multiple traits or phenotypic expressions. In other words, a single gene has multiple effects on the organism's phenotype. For example, in phenylketonuria, a single mutation in the gene responsible for the production of an enzyme causes hypopigmentation of the hair and skin, as well as mental retardation.

26. (*a*) In *r*DNA technology, the addition of chilled ethanol precipitates out DNA. The chilled ethanol causes the DNA molecules to lose their solubility by disrupting the hydrogen bonds between the bases and the water molecules. The precipitated DNA can then be separated from the mixture.

27. (*b*) In angiosperms, the haploid structure is synergids, the diploid structure is zygote and the triploid structure is the primary endosperm nucleus. The synergids are two small, haploid cells that are present adjacent to the egg cell in the female gametophyte of the angiosperm. The diploid structure is the zygote, which is formed when the sperm cell fuses with the egg cell during fertilisation. The triploid structure is the endosperm, which is a tissue that nourishes the developing embryo.

28. (*c*) Axile placentation is observed in china rose, *Petunia*, and lemon. Axile placentation is a type of placentation where the ovules are attached to the central axis or the centre of the ovary, and the septa (walls) of the ovary divide it into two or more locules.

29. (*b*) In deep water rice, Ethylene promotes internode or petiole elongation. Ethylene is a plant hormone that regulates various physiological processes, including growth and development. In deep water rice, it promotes the elongation of internodes and petioles, which helps the plant to grow taller and maintain its leaves above the water surface to access air and sunlight.

30. (*d*) Both A and R are correct and R is the correct explanation of A.
The first stage of the gametophyte generation of mass is the protonema, which is a thread-like structure. It develops directly from the spores that are produced in the capsule of the sporophyte through meiosis.
The spores are released from the capsule and they germinate and grow into a protonema. The protonema is usually green and photosynthetic, and it may develop into a thalloid or leafy gametophore depending on the species of moss. The gametophore is the mature gametophyte plant and produces the gametes (sperm and eggs).

31. (*b*) Frequency of recombination between gene pairs on same chromosome as a measure of the distance between genes to map their position on the chromosome was used for the first time by Alfred Sturtevant. His work paved the way for the development of genetic mapping techniques based on recombination frequencies, which are still widely used in modern genetics and genomics.

32. (*d*) Diadelphous and dithecous anthers are characteristics of the family Fabaceae, which includes many species of legumes such as beans, peas, and lentils. These anthers are composed of two fused pairs of pollen sacs, with one pair shorter than the other. In contrast, the families Solanaceae and Liliaceae have different types of anther arrangements. For example, in Solanaceae, anthers open by small pores to release the pollen, while Liliaceae have basifixed or dorsifixed anthers, meaning they are attached at the base or back of the anther.

33. (*a*) The synthesis of one molecule of glucose during Calvin cycle requires 18 ATP and 12 $NADPH_2$.The Calvin cycle is a series of biochemical reactions that takes place in the stroma of chloroplasts during photosynthesis, where atmospheric CO_2 is converted into glucose. The synthesis of one molecule of glucose requires energy in the form of ATP and reducing power in the form of $NADPH_2$.

34. (*d*) Expressed Sequence Tags (ESTs) refer to all the genes that are expressed as RNA. ESTs are short DNA sequences that are generated by sequencing the transcribed regions of genes, specifically the complementary DNA (cDNA) produced from mRNA molecules. ESTs represent the expressed portion of a genome.

35. (*c*) Statement I is incorrect but statement II is true. Incorrect statement can be corrected as Endarch, exarch and mesarch are primary xylem while secondary xylem refers to the formation that occurs after the vascular cambium's secondary growth. It consists of larger-sized vessels and tracheids. Exarch is a characteristic feature of the root system of plants.

Section B

36. (*d*) Chemiosmosis requires a membrane, proton pump, proton gradient and ATP synthase enzyme. During cellular respiration and photosynthesis, a proton pump actively transports protons (H^+) through proton pump across a selectively permeable membrane. It leads to the generation of a proton gradient. This gradient is used by the ATP synthase enzyme to produce ATP through the process of chemiosmosis.

37. (*d*) Ribosome consists of 80 proteins. The ribosomal proteins can be divided into two groups those present in the small ribosomal subunit and those present in the large subunit. The small ribosomal subunit has around 35 proteins, whereas the large subunit has 53 proteins. In total, the ribosome consists of about 80 proteins, which help to stabilise the structure of the ribosome and facilitate its function in protein synthesis.

38. (*d*) Both A and R are correct and R is the correct explanation of A.

A flower is a modified shoot in which the shoot apical meristem changes to a floral meristem. The floral meristem produces floral appendages such as sepals, petals, stamens, and carpels. The internode of the shoot gets condensed to produce different floral appendages laterally at successive nodes instead of leaves. The floral appendages are arranged in a whorl-like pattern, and their number and arrangement vary among different plant species.

39. (*b*) The correct match is A-IV, B-I, C-II and D-III.

M- phase is equational division as a parent cell divides to give rise to two equal- sized daughter cells. G_2-phase is characterised by the synthesis of proteins required for mitotic division. The quiescent phase is an inactive phase of the cell cycle wherein cells remain metabolically active and the G_1-phase represents an interval between mitosis and initiation of DNA replication.

40. (*d*) The correct sequence of the main steps in the formation of recombinant DNA is B, C, D, A.

First, the DNA is cut at specific locations using restriction enzymes in order to produce fragments of the desired size. The desired DNA fragment is then isolated and amplified using PCR.

The recombinant DNA is then inserted into the host cell using various techniques such as transformation or electroporation. The insertion of recombinant DNA into the host cell results in the production of a genetically modified organism (GMO).

41. (*b*) Statement I is true, but statement II is false. Incorrect statement can be corrected as

The effects of competition on different organisms depend on several factors such as the types of resources being competed for the availability of those resources and the adaptations of the competing species. In some cases, carnivores may have an advantage over herbivores in competition because they are at a higher trophic level and require fewer resources to survive.

42. (*d*) The correct match is A-II, B- IV, C- I and D- III.

Cohesion represents mutual attraction among the water molecules and adhesion is attraction of water molecules towards polar surfaces.

These forces are responsible for capillary action, which allows water to move up a narrow tube, such as the xylem vessel in plants. Surface tension is due to more attraction in the liquid phase. It is measure of the cohesive forces between the molecules at the surface of a liquid, which creates a surface layer that resists external forces. Guttation is loss of water from the margins of the leaf in the form of liquid droplets.

43. (*d*) Malonate is a competitive inhibitor of succinate dehydrogenase, which is a key enzyme in the tricarboxylic acid (TCA) cycle or Krebs' cycle. TCA cycle plays an essential role in the cellular respiration process of aerobic organisms, including bacteria. By inhibiting the activity of succinate dehydrogenase, malonate can disrupt the energy metabolism of pathogenic bacteria, leading to their growth inhibition.

44. (*c*) The correct matches are A- II, B- IV, C-III and D- I.

Oxidative decarboxylation involves the conversion of pyruvate into acetyl-CoA. Pyruvate is first decarboxylated by pyruvate dehydrogenase, releasing carbon dioxide and then oxidized to form acetyl-CoA. Glycolysis is also known as the Embden-Meyerhof-Parnas (EMP) pathway. Oxidative photophosphorylation occurs during the electron transport chain. In this process, energy is produced by the transfer of electrons from NADH and $FADH_2$ to oxygen.

Tricarboxylic acid cycle requires citrate synthase, which catalyses the formation of citrate from acetyl-CoA and oxaloacetate.

45. (*b*) Statements B and E are correct whereas A, C and D are incorrect. The incorrect statements can be corrected as

- Klinefelter's syndrome was first described by Harry Klinefelter in 1942, not by Langdon Down.
- It is not typically associated with short stature.
- Physical, psychomotor and mental development may be affected in individuals with Klinefelter's syndrome, but this can vary widely and is not necessarily always present. It is a usual symptom of Down's syndrome.

46. (*a*) Statement in option (a) is incorrect and can be corrected as Algal blooms caused by excess organic matter in water can lead to eutrophication, which can reduce water quality by depleting oxygen levels and producing toxins harmful to aquatic organisms, including fish. Eutrophication can also cause the loss of biodiversity and alter the ecological balance of the water body. So, algal blooms caused by excess organic matter do not improve water quality and promote fisheries.

47. (*b*) A is true, but R is false. R can be corrected as

In gymnosperms, the pollen grains are produced in the microsporangia, which are located in the male cones. The pollen grains are released from the microsporangium and are carried by air currents to the female cones, where they may land on the ovule. However, the male gametes are not discharged at the mouth of the archegonia. Instead, the pollen grain germinates on the surface of the ovule, and a pollen tube grows into the ovule to deliver the male gametes. The male gametes are then released from the pollen tube to fertilise the female gamete in the ovule.

48. (*b*) The correct matches are A- III, B- I, C- IV and D- II.

Iron is an activator of catalase, which is involved in the breakdown of hydrogen peroxide, a toxic byproduct of cellular metabolism. Zinc is required for the activity of enzymes involved in auxin biosynthesis, and its deficiency can result in reduced auxin levels and stunted growth. Boron is essential for cell elongation and differentiation, which are key processes in plant growth and development. Molybdenum is an essential component of the enzyme nitrate reductase, which is involved in the reduction of nitrate to nitrite during nitrogen assimilation in plants.

49. (*a*) The correct matches are A- IV, B- I, C- II and D- III.

In mutualism, both species *A* and *B* are benefited. In commensalism, species *A* is benefited whereas species *B* does not get any benefit. In amensalism, species *A* is negatively impacted whereas the other species *B* do not get any benefit. In parasitism, species *A* is benefitted whereas the species *B* is negatively impacted.

50. (*a*) Statements A and D are correct, whereas statements B, C and E are incorrect. These can be corrected as

- Bark formed early in the season is called soft bark.
- Bark is the non- technical term that reflects all tissues lying outside the vascular cambium.
- Phellogen is multi- layered in thickness.

Zoology

Section A

51. (*a*) The ileo-caecal valve is a sphincter that separates the ileum from the caecum. The valve prevents the backflow of the contents of the colon into the small intestine.

Once the undigested and unabsorbed substances enter the caecum, they are further acted upon by bacteria present in the colon.

The colon absorbs water and electrolytes from the undigested material and moves it forward for elimination. The ileo-caecal valve ensures that this material moves forward in the digestive tract and is eventually eliminated from the body.

52. (*d*) The HIV (Human Immunodeficiency Virus) undergoes replication and produces progeny viruses in the T helper cells. HIV targets the immune system T helper cells, which are a type of white blood cell that play a critical role in the body's defence against infection. The virus enters the T cells and takes over their machinery to replicate itself, leading to the destruction of the T cells.

53. (*d*) A broad palm with a single palm crease is a common physical feature seen in individuals with Down's syndrome.

Normally, most people have two palm creases on their palms, but in individuals with Down's syndrome, there is only one crease. This feature is also known as a "simian crease or line".

It is a genetic disorder caused by the presence of an extra copy of chromosome 21. It is characterised by a range of physical and intellectual disabilities.

54. (*a*) Gonorrhoea is a common sexually transmitted disease that is completely curable when detected early and treated properly. It is caused by the bacterium *Neisseria gonorrhoeae* and can infect both men and women. The infection is transmitted through sexual contact with an infected partner. Symptoms can include painful urination, discharge from the penis or vagina, and pain or swelling in the testicles. If detected early, gonorrhoea can be easily treated with antibiotics.

55. (*d*) The correct matches are A-I, B-II, C-III and D-IV.

Leopard and lion in the same forest or grassland exhibit competition as they are both large carnivores occupying similar niches. Cuckoo laying eggs in a crow, nest is an example of brood parasitism as it lays its eggs in the nest of another bird species for them to raise the cuckoo chicks. Fungi and roots of higher plants in mycorrhiza is an example of mutualism as both organisms benefit from the association. Cattle egrets and cattle in a field show commensalism as the cattle egret benefits by feeding on insects found on the cattle, while the cattle are unaffected.

56. (*b*) The correct matches are A- III, B- I, C-IV and D-II.

Peptic cells are located in the gastric glands of the stomach and secrete pepsinogen, a precursor to the enzyme pepsin which helps in the breakdown of proteins. Goblet cells are also present in the stomach lining and produce mucus, which helps to protect the stomach wall from the corrosive action of gastric acid. Oxyntic cells are found in the lining of the stomach and secrete hydrochloric acid (HCl) and intrinsic factor, which is required for the absorption of vitamin-B_{12}. Hepatic cells are found in the liver and produce bile juice, which is stored in the gall bladder and released into the small intestine to help in the digestion of fats.

57. (*c*) Statement I is false, but statement II is true. Statement I can be corrected as

The N-terminal is the first amino acid in the protein sequence, and the C-terminal is the last amino acid. So, the left end of the protein would be the N-terminal and the right end would be the C-terminal.

58. (*d*) Both statement I and statement II are true.

RNA mutates at a faster rate because RNA polymerases lack proofreading ability and RNA viruses have high error rates during replication. Also, RNA viruses have shorter generation times, larger population sizes, and higher mutation rates as compared to DNA viruses.

It results in rapid evolution and adaptation in RNA viruses to changing environments.

59. (*a*) The correct matches are A- III, B- IV, C- II and D- I.

Vasectomy is the surgical method of contraception in males. Coitus interruptus is the natural method of contraception in which the penis is withdrawn just before the ejaculation. Cervical caps are used as the barrier method of contraception by females. Saheli is an oral non-hormonal contraceptive pill.

60. (*d*) The correct matches are A- II, B- III, C- IV and D- I.

Ringworm is caused by fungi of the genus *Trichophyton*, filariasis is caused by the parasite *Wuchereria bancrofti*, malaria is caused by parasites of the genus *Plasmodium vivax* and pneumonia can be caused by bacteria such as *Haemophilus influenzae*.

61. (*d*) The correct matches are A-IV, B- III, C- II and D- I.

CCK (cholecystokinin) acts on both gall bladder and pancreas and stimulates the secretion of pancreatic and bile juice respectively.

GIP (Gastric Inhibitory Peptide) is a hormone secreted by the gastric gland that inhibits gastric secretion and motility. ANF (Atrial Natriuretic Factor) is a hormone secreted by the heart that regulates blood pressure and fluid balance. ADH (Antidiuretic Hormone) is a hormone secreted by the kidney that regulates water balance in the body.

62. (*d*) Both statement I and statement II are true.

Vas deferens is a muscular duct that receives sperm from the epididymis and also receives a duct from seminal vesicle. The vas deferens opens into the urethra as the ejaculatory duct. The cervical canal is the cavity of the cervix that connects the uterus to the vagina. The vagina and the cervical canal together form the birth canal.

63. (*a*) Early diagnosis and understanding of a disease's pathogenesis are critical for efficient treatment. Early detection is not achievable by traditional diagnostic approaches (e.g. serum and urine analysis).

Some of the procedures used for early diagnosis include recombinant DNA technology, Polymerase Chain Reaction (PCR), and Enzyme Linked Immunosorbent Assay (ELISA).

64. (*a*) A, C and E are not considered as the part of endomembrane system. Mitochondria, chloroplasts and peroxisomes are not considered part of the endomembrane system while endoplasmic reticulum and Golgi complex are part of the endomembrane system.

65. (*d*) The correct matches are A- II, B- I, C- IV and D- III.

Heroin is an opioid that slows down the central nervous system and can cause respiratory depression. Marijuana can affect the cardiovascular system by increasing heart rate and blood pressure. Cocaine interferes with the transport of dopamine, a neurotransmitter associated with pleasure and reward, and can lead to addiction. Morphine is a powerful painkiller that works by binding to opioid receptors in the brain and spinal cord.

66. (*d*) Both statement I and statement II are true.

Low temperature slows down the enzyme activity and high temperature denatures the enzyme. Competitive inhibitor closely resembles the substrate and competes with it to bind to the active site of the enzyme, reducing the enzyme's activity.

67. (*b*) The cytoskeleton is a complex network of protein filaments that provides structural support, helps maintain cell shape and facilitates various cellular functions. One of the key functions of the cytoskeleton is to enable cell movement or motility, both within the cell and through the environment. It is achieved through the interaction of its different components, including microfilaments, intermediate filaments, and microtubules, which work together to generate and transmit forces that produce movement.

68. (*a*) Both statement I and statement II are false. It can be corrected as

Ligaments are dense regular connective tissue that connects bones to other bones or cartilages. Cartilage is a type of supportive connective tissue that is avascular and has no nerves. It is not classified as dense regular or dense irregular tissue. It is a specialised connective tissue along with bones and blood.

69. (*a*) The correct match is A- II, B- IV, C- I and D- III.

- Cartilaginous joints are present between the adjacent vertebrae in the vertebral column. They allow for limited movement and provide support to the spine.
- Ball and socket joint is present between humerus and pectoral girdle. This type of joint allows for a wide range of movements in multiple planes, such as rotation.
- Fibrous joint is present between the flat skull bones. These joints are immovable and provide stability and protection to the brain.
- Saddle joint is present between carpal and metacarpal of thumb. This type of joint allows for a wide range of movements, including flexion, extension, abduction, adduction, etc.

70. (*a*) The correct matches are A- II, B- III, C- IV and D- I.

Gene '*a*' is associated with the function of transacetylase, which transfers an acetyl group from acetyl-CoA to various compounds, including lactose.

Gene '*y*' is associated with the function of permease, which is a membrane protein that facilitates the transport of lactose into the cell.

Gene '*i*' is associated with the function of repressor protein, which binds to the operator site of the lac operon to prevent transcription of the genes involved in lactose metabolism.

Gene '*z*' is associated with the function of β-galactosidase, which is an enzyme that breaks down lactose into glucose and galactose.

71. (*a*) Among the given options, (a) is correct.

This symbol shows consanguineous mating (marriage of blood relatives).

72. (*a*) Both A and R are true but R is not the correct explanation of A.

Endometrium is necessary for the implantation of blastocyst.

It is the inner lining of the uterus that prepares every month to receive a fertilised egg. It is richly supplied with blood vessels and glands, which provides nourishment and support to the developing embryo. It also secretes hormones and other substances that are essential for the growth and development of the embryo.

If there is no fertilisation, the corpus luteum simply regresses or degenerates. This leads to menstruation whereby the endometrial linining sheds.

73. (*b*) A is true, but R is false. R can be corrected as

The juxtamedullary nephrons have a long Henle's loop that extends deep into the renal medulla, whereas the cortical nephrons have a shorter Henle's loop that only extends into the outer section of the renal medulla.

74. (*a*) Radial symmetry is a type of symmetry found in many animals, in which the body is arranged in a circular pattern around a central axis. This means that any plane passing through the centre of the animal divides it into two identical halves. Coelenterata (Cnidarians) and Ctenophora (Comb jellies) are two phyla that exhibit radial symmetry in their adult stages. Echinodermata (Starfish, sea urchins, etc.) exhibits bilateral symmetry in larval stage and radial symmetry in adult stage. Hemichordata (acorn worms) exhibits bilateral symmetry in their adult stages.

75. (*d*) The correct matches are A-III, B-I, C- IV and D- II.

Fovea is the point of greatest visual activity or resolution. It is a small depression in the retina of the eye where visual acuity is highest. Iris is the visible coloured portion that regulates diameter of pupil, allowing more or less light to enter the eye. Blind spot is the point where optic nerve leaves the eyeball and photoreceptor cells are absent. Sclera is the external layer of eye formed of dense connective tissue. The sclera is the tough, white outer layer of the eye that protects and supports the eyeball, and provides attachment points for the muscles that move the eye.

76. (*a*) Statement option (a) is correct, while other statements are incorrect. These can be corrected as
Algal blooms are caused by an excess of nutrients in the water, particularly nitrogen and phosphorus. Algal blooms can cause a variety of problems for fish, including depleting oxygen levels in the water and producing toxins that can harm or kill fish. Eutrophication is the process by which a body of water becomes enriched with nutrients, often due to runoff from land. This enrichment can come from a variety of sources, including sewage and waste water, agricultural runoff, etc.

77. (*c*) Statements A, C and D are correct. Statement B is incorrect and can be corrected as
The first menstrual cycle in human females typically begins at puberty and is called menarche. Menopause marks the end of menstrual cycles, not the beginning of it.

78. (*c*) Statement I is false, but statement II is true. The incorrect statement can be corrected as
DNA is a negatively charged molecule, whereas proteins are positively charged molecules. In prokaryotes, the DNA is not enclosed within a membrane-bound nucleus, and it is present in the nucleoid region.

79. (*a*) The correct group/set of Australian Marsupials exhibiting adaptive radiation is- Numbat, spotted cuscus, flying phalanger. Adaptive radiation is the evolutionary divergence of members of a single group into a variety of forms, each adapted to a specific environment or mode of life. The three marsupials mentioned in option (a) have diversified into different forms that are adapted to different habitats and feeding strategies, such as arboreal (tree-dwelling) and terrestrial (ground-dwelling). The other options do not contain marsupials that have undergone significant adaptive radiation.

80. (*b*) The correct matches are A- III, B- II, C- IV and D- I.
Taenia is a parasitic flatworm that lacks a specialised excretory system. Instead, it has specialised flame cells which help in excretion. *Paramecium* is a unicellular organism with a contractile vacuole that helps in the regulation of water content by collecting and expelling excess water from the body. *Periplaneta* is a species of cockroach that has specialised uric acid-secreting glands called urecose glands, which help in the excretion of nitrogenous waste products. *Pheretima* or earthworms possess nephridia as excretory structures.

81. (*c*) A is false, but R is true. A can be corrected as
Amniocentesis for sex determination is not a strategy of Reproductive and Child Health Care Programme. In fact, sex determination tests are banned in many countries, including India, due to the increasing menace of female foeticide. Amniocentesis is a medical procedure that involves the collection of a small amount of amniotic fluid from the amniotic sac surrounding the developing foetus. This procedure is primarily used to diagnose genetic disorders and chromosomal abnormalities in the foetus and not for determining the sex of the foetus.

82. (*c*) Probe is not a cloning vector. A cloning vector is a DNA molecule used to carry foreign genetic material into a host cell for the purpose of replicating or expressing it. A probe, on the other hand, is a short, single-stranded DNA or RNA fragment that is used to detect the presence of a specific target sequence in a complex mixture of nucleic acids, such as in a Southern or Northern blot.

83. (*b*) Statement I is true, but statement II is incorrect. The incorrect statement can be corrected as
An electrostatic precipitator is an efficient dust collection device that is widely used in thermal power plants and other industries to remove particulate matter from exhaust gas streams. However, in a thermal power plant, it does not help to remove ionising radiations. Ionising radiation is a type of radiation that has enough energy to ionise atoms or molecules, causing them to become charged.

84. (*d*) The correct matches are A- III, B- I, C- IV and D- II.
The P-wave in an electrocardiogram (ECG) represents the depolarisation (contraction) of the atria. The Q-wave is the first negative deflection in the QRS complex and marks the beginning of ventricular depolarisation and the onset of systole. The QRS complex in an ECG represents the depolarisation of the ventricles, which leads to the contraction of the ventricles.The T-wave in an ECG represents the repolarisation (relaxation) of the ventricles after contraction.

85. (*c*) Vital capacity (VC) is the maximum amount of air that a person can exhale after taking a deep breath. It is a measure of lung function and is commonly used to assess respiratory health. It is calculated by summing tidal volume, inspiratory reserve volume, and expiratory reserve volume; VC = TV + IRV + ERV.

Section B

86. (*c*) Statement I is false, but statement II is true. The incorrect statement can be corrected as

During the G_0-phase of cell cycle, cell is metabolically active. The G_0-phase of the cell cycle is a period of quiescence, where cells are not actively dividing. Some cells in the G_0-phase, such as nerve cells, muscle cells and some immune cells are highly metabolically active and perform their specialised functions even though they are not actively dividing.

87. (*d*) Limbic system and hypothalamus helps in the regulation of sexual behaviour, expression of excitement, pleasure, rage and fear. The limbic system is a complex network of brain structures that are involved in the processing and regulation of emotions, motivation, and memory. The hypothalamus is a small but important structure located in the brain that is involved in the regulation of many bodily functions, including temperature control, hunger and thirst, and the release of hormones.

88. (*b*) Among the given options, B, C and D are correct.

In cockroach, excretion is brought about by urecose gland, nephrocytes and fat body. The urecose gland, also known as the urinary bladder, is involved in the storage and elimination of urine in cockroaches. The nephrocytes, which are specialised cells found in the fat body, are also involved in the removal of nitrogenous waste products. The phallic gland and collaterial glands are not involved in excretion in cockroaches. The phallic gland is a gland associated with the male reproductive system, while the collateral glands are involved in the production of accessory gland secretions that are important for sperm storage and transfer.

89. (*a*) Statements B, C and D are correct. Statements A and E are incorrect and can be corrected as Excessive loss of body fluid, such as through sweating, vomiting or diarrhoea, can lead to dehydration and an increase in the concentration of solutes in the blood. This can activate the osmoreceptors and stimulate the release of ADH to help restore the body's fluid balance. ADH is antidiuretic hormone which prevents diuresis but it also causes constriction of blood vessels thus increasing the glomerular filtrate rate (GFR).

90. (*c*) Among given statements, option (c) does not represent the advantage of inbreeding. When inbreeding occurs, the genetic diversity within the population decreases, which can increase the expression of harmful recessive traits and decrease the overall productivity of the population. Hence, it is a drawback of inbreeding.

91. (*a*) Statements B and C are correct while statement A and D are incorrect and can be corrected as

- Skeletal muscle fibers are bundled together into fascicles by a connective tissue layer called the perimysium. The perimysium is a collagenous connective tissue layer that surrounds each fascicle and helps to protect and support the muscle fibers within it.
- The sarcomere is the basic functional unit of muscle contraction. It is a highly organised structure that is composed of actin and myosin filaments, as well as other proteins that regulate muscle contraction. The M-line is a region in the center of the sarcomere that anchors the myosin filaments and helps to maintain the structural integrity of the sarcomere during muscle contraction.

92. (*d*) The correct matches are A-II, B-I, C- III and D- IV.

- Logistic growth occurs when a population grows rapidly initially, but then levels off due to limited resources such as food, water or space. The growth rate slows down and eventually reaches a carrying capacity where the population size stabilises.
- Exponential growth occurs when a population grows at a constant rate, without any constraints on resources. This type of growth is rarely observed in natural populations.
- An expanding age pyramid occurs when a population has a large proportion of young individuals who are not yet reproductive, and a smaller proportion of older individuals who have already passed their reproductive years.
- A stable age pyramid occurs when a population has roughly equal proportions of individuals in each age group, with similar numbers of pre-reproductive, reproductive, and post-reproductive individuals.

93. (*b*) The coding strand is the DNA strand that has the same nucleotide sequence as the *m*RNA transcript, except that thymine (T) is replaced with uracil (U) in the RNA molecule. Hence, the sequence of given coding strand will be as follows
5' ATCGATCGATCGATCGATCG ATCGATCG 3'

94. (*b*) Statements B and C are correct, whereas statements A, D and E are incorrect.These statements can be corrected as

- Basophils are the least abundant cells of total WBCs.

• Basophils have a bilobed nucleus, which gives them an S-shaped or irregularly shaped appearance.

• Basophils are granulocytes, not agranulocytes.

95. (*b*) The correct matches are A-II, B-I, C- IV and D- III.

• Mast cells are a type of white blood cell that are found in connective tissue throughout the body. They plays a role in the immune response and the development of allergies. Areolar tissue is a loose connective tissue that contains a variety of cell types, including mast cells.

• The bronchioles are small tubes that branch off from the bronchi in the lungs. The inner surface of the bronchioles is lined with a layer of ciliated epithelial cells that have hair-like projections called cilia.

• Blood is a type of specialised connective tissue that circulates throughout the body, delivering oxygen and nutrients to cells and tissues and removing waste products.

• The tubular part of the nephron is lined with a layer of cuboidal epithelial cells. These cells play a role in reabsorbing water and other substances from the filtrate that is produced by the glomerulus.

96. (*a*) The anal style is a modified structure on the last abdominal segment of male cockroaches that is absent in females. The anal style is used by male cockroaches during mating to help grip the female during copulation.

97. (*b*) Statements C and D represents the activities which are not under the control of thyroid hormone. The normal rhythm of sleep-wake cycles is under the control of the pineal gland. It is responsible for regulating the production and secretion of the hormone melatonin, which is involved in the timing of the sleep-wake cycle. On the other hand, the development and regulation of the immune system is under the control of the endocrine system, particularly the thymus gland.

98. (a) Statements B and D are correct, whereas statements A, C and E are incorrect. These can be corrected as

• Tetrad formation is seen during pachytene stage of prophase-I, of meiosis.

• Terminalisation of chiasmata occur during diakinesis stage of prophase-I, of meiosis.

• Crossing over takes place between non- sister chromatids of homologous chromosomes.

99. (*a*) The unique mammalian characters are hair, pinna and mammary glands. Hair provides insulation and protection, pinna (external ear) is used for hearing, and mammary glands produce milk for nourishing young ones. These features are exclusive to mammals and play important roles in their survival and reproduction.

100.(*a*) Statements B and C are correct, whereas statement A, D and E are incorrect.These can be corrected as

• Chordates possess a hollow, dorsal nerve cord. The nerve cord is not double but is a single tube-like structure located dorsal to the notochord.

• Chordates possess a ventral heart. The heart is located on the ventral side of the body, not the dorsal side.

• Chordates are triploblastic coelomate animals. They possess three germ layers (endoderm, mesoderm and ectoderm) and a true coelom, i.e. a body cavity completely lined by mesoderm.

NC2 NEET Chronicles 2

Botany

Section A

1. (*b*) Lecithin is a type of phospholipid which is a class of lipids. It is the major component of cell membranes. Lecithin specifically contains a phosphate group, a glycerol backbone, two fatty acid chains and a choline molecule.

2. (*c*) The dark reaction of photosynthesis, also known as biosynthetic phase, occurs in the stroma of chloroplasts. It does not require direct light, instead it utilises the products of the light dependent reaction, i.e. ATP (D) and NADPH (E), along with CO_2 (C), to produce glucose. These molecules provide the necessary energy and carbon source for the synthesis of glucose during the dark reaction of photosynthesis.

3. (*b*) During metaphase, the chromosomes are aligned at the metaphase plate, which is the equitorial plane of the cell. At this stage, spindle fibres, also known as microtubules, attach to the kinetochores, which are specialised protein structures located at the centromeres of the chromosomes.

   These spindle fibres help to align the chromosomes properly along the metaphase plate. It also ensures that each chromatid will be pulled to opposite poles of the cell during anaphase.

4. (*a*) In grasses (monocots), certain adaxial epidermal cells along the veins modify themselves into large, empty, colourless cells. These are called bulliform cells. When the bulliform cells in the leaves have absorbed water and become turgid, the leaf surface is exposed. When they are flaccid due to water stress, they make the leaves curl inwards to minimise water loss.

5. (*a*) Component *C* represents guard cells.

   Guard cells are kidney-shaped, specialised cells in plants that control the opening and closing of the stomata. The outer walls of guard cells are thin and inner walls are highly thickened.

   Rest components can be identified as

   A-Epidermal cells are parenchymatous with a small amount of cytoplasm lining the cell wall and a large vacuole.

   B-Subsidiary cells are specialised epidermal cell, in the vicinity of the guard cells.

   D-Stomatal pores is tiny opening on the surface of leaves that controls gaseous exchange in plants.

6. (*c*) Statements B and C are correct regarding the piece of DNA carrying only gene of interest, transferred into an alien organism.

   Rest statements are incorrect and these can be corrected as

   - DNA typically requires host cellular machinery to replicate. It cannot multiply independently in progeny cells without the help of the host organism.
   - When the DNA integrates into the host genome, it becomes an integral part of the chromosome.
   - While the transferred DNA indeed have the ability to replicate if it contains appropriate regulatory sequences, replication alone does not guarantee its inheritance or integration into the host genome.

7. (*c*) Statement I is true, but statement II is false. The incorrect statement can be corrected as

   The *Bt* toxin protein exists as inactive protoxins in *B. thuringiensis*, but once an insect ingests the inactive toxin, it is converted into an active form of toxin due to the alkaline pH of the gut.

8. (*d*) The International Union for Conservation of Nature and Natural Resources (IUCN) is a global organisation dedicated to assessing the conservation status of species and ecosystems. It releases lists of endangered species in Red Data Book. The IUCN Red List of threatened species is the most comprehensive source of information on the list of extinction for animal, plant and fungal species.

   As of 2023, the IUCN Red List includes more than 157,100 species, with more than 44,000 threatened with extinction.

9. (*c*) Based on the given figure of a seed, the part destined to form the root when the seed germinates is the embryonic root or radicle *(C)*.

   It is the first part of the embryo to develop into the plant's root system. The radicle grows downward into the soil, anchoring the seedling and allowing it to absorb water and nutrients.

   Rest parts can be identified as

   A-Coleoptile is a cylindrical, rigid, protective sheath that covers the first leaf and shoot apex of a grass seedling.

B-Plumule is the embryonic shoot of a plant.

D-Coleorhiza is a protective layer of tissue that surrounds the embryonic root or radicle of monocot seeds.

10. (*c*) The correct matches are A-III, B-I, C-IV, D-II.

• *Clostridium butylicum* is a bacterium known for its ability to produce butyric acid through fermentation.

• *S. cerevisiae* is a yeast commonly used in fermentation process, such as brewing and baking, where it produces ethanol as a metabolic byproduct.

• *Trichoderma polysporum* is a fungus that produces cyclosporin-A, a potent immunosuppressive agent.

• *Streptococcus* sp. produces streptokinase, a thrombolytic agent.

11. (*d*) Both of the given figures *A* and *B* represent perigynous condition. In this condition, gynoecium is situated in the centre and other parts of the flower are located on the rim of the thalamus, almost at the same level. The ovary in these flowers is said to be half inferior, e.g. plum, rose, peach, etc.

12. (*c*) Auxin is a plant hormone that regulates various aspects of plant development. They are commonly used by gardeners to prepare weed free lawns, it does not affect mature monocotyledonous plants (grass). Auxin primarily promotes the abscission of mature leaves, particularly, in broad leaf weeds, i.e. dictoyledonous weeds.

Rest other options are correct regarding auxin, but not relevant to the scenario described.

13. (*b*) The inheritance of flower colour in snapdragon shows incomplete dominance.

The cross between pink flower and red flower is as follows

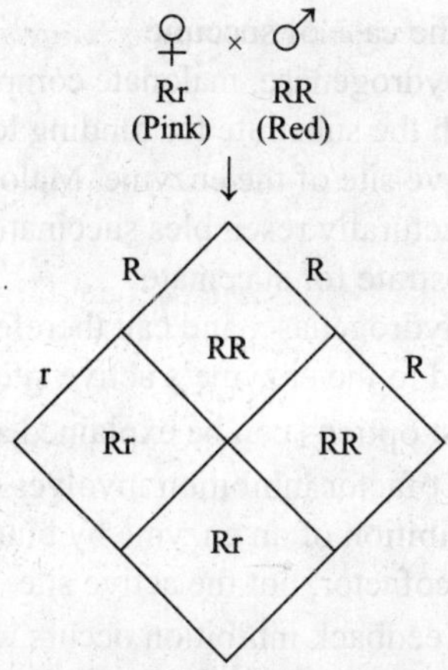

Genotypic ratio—(Red) : Pink = 1 : 1
Phenotypic ratio—RR : Rr = 1 : 1

Thus, the expected progeny will have red as well as pink flowered plants.

14. (*b*) The morphology of the mycelium, mode of spore formation and fruiting bodies form the basis for the division of the kingdom into various classes. It does not depend on the mode of nutrition. Fungi are heterotrophs, they can not make their own food.

15. (*c*) Permease is a type of transporter protein that facilitates the movement of molecules such as lactose, across the cell membrane.

Other options can be explained as

• In *E. coli*, it is coded by gene *Y*. Inside the bacterial cell, the enzyme β-galactosidase catalyses the hydrolysis of lactose into its constituent monosaccharides, i.e., glucose and galactose.

This enzymatic reaction enables the bacterium to utilise lactose as a carbon source for energy and growth.

• Acetylase is involved in acetylation reactions. It speeds up the production of acetic acid esters.

• Polymerase is an enzyme involved in DNA replication and RNA transcription.

16. (*b*) To determine the genotype of the black seed plant, one needs to perform a test cross by crossing it with a plant that has the homozygous recessive genotype (bb).

It can be explained through the following crosses

Case I If parent is homozygous dominant.

Gametes from homozygous dominant parent (BB).

Gametes from recessive parent (bb)		B	B
	b	Bb	Bb
	b	Bb	Bb

All of the progenies will be of dominant phenotype.

Case II If parent is heterozygous dominant.

Gametes from heterozygous parent (Bb)

Gametes from recessive parent (bb)		B	b
	b	Bb	bb
	b	Bb	bb

It will results into 1 : 1 ratio of black and white seed.

17. (*d*) Statement I is false, but Statement II is true. Incorrect statement can be corrected as

Both parenchyma and collenchyma cells are living tissue. The collenchyma occurs in layers below the epidermis in most of the dicotyledonous plants. It consists of cells which are more thickened at the corners due to the deposition of cellulose, hemicellulose and pectin.

18. (*d*) Each turn of Calvin cycle requires a certain number of molecules of ATP and NADPH to provide energy and reducing power, respectively, for the various chemical reactions involved.

For every CO_2 molecule entering the Calvin cycle, 3 molecules of ATP and 2 molecules of NADPH are required.

19. (*d*) A transcription unit is a segment of DNA that takes part in transcription. It has three components.

(i) Promoter : It is located towards 5′ end of the structural gene and provides binding site for RNA polymerase.

(ii) Structural gene : It codes for an RNA which may be *m*RNA, *t*RNA or *r*RNA

(iii) Terminator : It is located towards 3′-end of the coding strand and usually defines the end of the process of transcription.

20. (*a*) Statements A, C, D and E are the correct explanation for the species richness in tropical regions because

• tropical latitudes have remained relatively undisturbed for millions of years and thus had a long evolutionary time for species diversification.

• these environments are less seasonal, relatively more constant and predictable. Such constant environments promote niche specialisation. It leads to a greater species diversity.

• more solar energy is available in the tropics, which contributes to higher productivity. This, in turn might contribute indirectly to greater diversity.

21. (*c*) In the Verhulst-Pearl logistic growth equation, K represents the carrying capacity of the environment for a particular species. Carrying capacity is the maximum population size that the environment can sustainably support over the long term. It is determined by factors such as the availability of resources, space and other environmental conditions.

22. (*c*) Competitive inhibition occurs when a molecule, known as the inhibitor, competes with the substrate for binding to the active site of the enzyme.

In the case of succinic dehydrogenase, malonate competes with the substrate for binding to the active site of the enzyme. Malonate structurally resembles succinate, the substrate for succinate dehydrogenase, and can therefore bind to the enzyme's active site.

Rest options can be explained as

• Cofactor inhibition involves the inhibition of an enzyme by binding to its cofactor, not the active site.

• Feedback inhibition occurs when the end product of a metabolic pathway inhibits an enzyme earlier in the pathway.

• Enzyme activation refers to processe that increases the activity of an enzyme.

23. (*b*) Statements A, C, D and E can be explained on the basis of Mendel's law of dominance.

Statement B contradicts Mendel's law of dominance because, in the F_2-generation, the recessive alleles can still be expressed if present in the genotype, although they may be masked in the F_1-generation due to dominance.

24. (*a*) The correct matches are A-III, B-II, C-IV, D-I.

• Nucleolus is the site for active ribosomal RNA synthesis.

• Centrioles are the two cylindrical structures in the centrosome. Each centriole appears like a cartwheel.

• Leucoplasts are colourless plastids of various shape and size that perform function for storing nutrients.

• Golgi apparatus is the important site for the formation of glycoproteins and glycolipids in eukaryotic cells.

25. (*d*) Statements B, C, D and E are correct. Statement A is not correct, it can be corrected as

Vallisneria flowers are not very colourful and do not produce nectar because they are water-pollinated flowers. These flowers do not need to attract insects for pollination.

26. (*a*) The correct match is A-III, B-II, C-IV, D-I.

• *Rhizopus* is commonly known as bread mould. It belongs to Class-Phycomycetes.

• *Ustilago* is commonly known as smut. It belongs to Class-Basidiomycetes.

• *Puccinia* is commonly known as rust fungi. It belongs to Class-Basidiomycetes.

• *Agaricus* is commonly called mushroom. It belongs to Class-Basidiomycetes.

27. (*b*) *Hind* II is a restriction endonuclease that cuts DNA molecules at a specific point by recognising a sequence of 6 base pairs. This specific base sequence is known as the recognition sequence. *Hind* II specifically recognises 5′–AAGCTT–3′ sequence.

28. (*a*) An actinomorphic flower is one that can be divided into symmetrical halves in any plane, typically through the center, resulting in multiple lines of symmetry. In the given example, *Datura* flower shows actinomorphic symmetry.

In *Cassia*, *Pisum* and *Sesbania*, zygomorphic flowers are seen.

29. (*b*) The type of conservation in which threatened animals and plants are taken out from their natural habitat and placed in special setting where they can be protected and given special care is called *ex-situ* conservation. It is a type of biodiversity conservation.

The biodiversity conservation is a broad term that encompasses various conservation strategies, including both *in-situ* and *ex-situ* conservations.

30. (*a*) Both statement I and statement II are true.

• During leptotene stage (First stage of meiosis I) chromosomes begin to condense and attain a composite structure that become visible under light microscope.

• The beginning of diplotene (fourth stage of meiosis-I) is charaterised by dissolution of synaptonemal complex and separation of homologous chromosomes except at the site of crossing over. The formation of chiasmata (X-like structure takes place at this stage only).

31. (*c*) Dedifferentiation is a cellular process in plants where differentiated cells revert to a less differentiated or stem cell-like state. This process allows the cells to regain their ability to divide and re-enter the cell cycle.
In the case of the formation of interfascicular cambium from fully developed parenchyma cells, these parenchyma cells undergo dedifferentiation to become meristematic cells that are capable of division. These meristematic cells then differentiate into cambial cells, which give rise to secondary growth in plants.
Other options can be explained as

• Differentiation refers to the process by which undifferentiated cells become specialised into specific cell types.

• Redifferentiation is a process by which dedifferentiated cells regain their specialised characteristics.

• Maturation is usually reached just prior to the end of growth and may include physical and biochemical changes in a plant.

32. (*a*) Totipotency refers to the capacity of a single plant cell to give rise to an entire new plant. Totipotent cells have the ability to regenerate into all types of cell and tissues.
It plays crucial role in various aspects of plant biology, including regeneration, tissue culture and plant propagation.
Rest options can be explained as

• Micropropagation is a technique used to produce large numbers of genetically identical plants from a single parent plant using tissue culture methods.

• Differentiation is the process by which a cell becomes specialised to perform a specific function, but it does not involve generating a whole plant from a single cell.

• Somatic hybridisation involves the fusion of protoplasts from different plant species to produce hybrids with combined traits.

33. (*c*) The correct matches are A-III, B-IV, C-I, D-II.

• Two or more alternative forms of a gene are called alleles.

• Cross of F_1-progeny with homozygous recessive parent is a test cross.

• Cross of F_1-progeny with any of the parents is a back cross.

• Number of chromosome sets in a plant or an animal is called ploidy.

34. (*a*) Zinc is a cofactor for the proteolytic enzyme carboxypeptidase. A cofactor is a non-protein part of an enzyme that is made up of metal ions.
In carboxypeptidase, the zinc cofactor is located in the active site of the enzyme and is essential for its catalytic ativity.

• Niacin is associated with coenzyme NAD and NADP.

• Haem is the prosthetic group in peroxidase and catalase.

• Flavin as a cofactor catalyses the oxidation of nucleophilic nitrogen, sulphur and phosphate.

35. (*d*) The accelerated rates of species extinctions that the world is facing now are largely due to human activities.
There are four major causes of biodiversity loss. 'The Evil Quartet' is the sobriquet used to describe them
(i) Habitat loss and fragmentation
(ii) Overexploitation
(iii) Alien-species invasions
(iv) Co-extinctions

Section B

36. (*a*) The correct matches are A-IV, B-II, C-I, D-III.

• In China rose, monoadelphous androecium is present.

• Diadelophous androecium is found in pea plant.

• Polyadelphous androecium is found is citrus.

• Epiphyllous stamen is found in lily.

37. (*a*) The correct matches are A-IV, B-I, C-II, D-III.

• GLUT-4 is a glucose transporter protein found in the membrane of certain cells.

• Insulin is a hormone produced by the pancreas that regulates glucose metabolism.

• Trypsin is an enzyme involved in the digestion of proteins.

• Collagen is a structural protein found in the extracellular matrix of various tissues.

38. (*c*) In the tricarboxylic acid cycle, most of the steps involve the oxidation of substrates, leading to the generation of reducing equivalents, i.e., NADH and $FADH_2$ and ATP.
However, the conversion of succinyl Co-A to succinic acid by the enzyme succinyl Co-A synthetase, does not directly involve oxidation.
Rest other conversions involve oxidation.

39. (*b*) The correct matches are A-II, B-I, C-IV, D-III.

• The citric acid, cycle occurs in the mitochondrial matrix.

• The glycolysis occurs in the cytoplasm of the cell.

• The electron transport system takes place in the inner mitochondrial membrane.

- The proton gradient is established across the intermembrane space of mitochondria.

40. (*b*) The correct matches are A-III, B-IV, C-I, D-II.

- Frederick Griffith's in a series of experiment with *Streptococcus pneumoniae* witnessed miraculous transformation in the bacteria.
- The elucidation of *lac* operon was a result of a close association between geneticist, Francois Jacob and a biochemist, Jacque Monod.
- Har Gobind Khorana developed chemical method to define combination of bases in genetic code.
- Meselson and Stahl provided proof of the semi-conservative mode of DNA replication.

41. (*c*) Statement I is true, but statement II is false. It can be corrected as

Photorespiration does not occur in C_4 plants as they lack RuBisCO in mesophyll cells. Additionally, bundle sheath cells in C_4-plants do not show photorespiration due to the Kranz anatomy.

42. (*a*) Wind pollinated flowers possess well exposed stamens. This is an adaptation to maximise pollen dispersal by wind. Having well-exposed stamens ensures that the pollen is readily available for dispersal.

43. (*a*) The correct matches are A-II, B-IV, C-I, D-III.

- In rose, gynoecium is said to be perigynous.
- In pea, placenta forms a ridge along the ventral suture of the ovary and the ovules are borne on this ridge forming two rows. This type of placentation is known as marginal.
- In twisted aestivation, margin of the appendage overlaps that of the next one, e.g. cotton.
- In mango, fruit is drupe.

44. (*c*) Statements A, C, D and E are correct w.r.t the members of Phaeophyceae. Statement B is not correct, it can be corrected as

In members of Phaeophyceae, sexual reproduction can be isogamous, anisogamous and oogamous. They produce motile gametes that are biflagellated, with two laterally attached flagella.

45. (*c*) The NPP of the first trophic level is the GPP of the second trophic level and the NPP of the second trophic level is GPP of the third trohpic level.

According to the 10% law, 90% is the respiratory loss at each trophic level.

$NPP = GPP - R$

At the first trophic level, NPP is $100x$ which is GPP of second trophic level.

At second trophic level, NPP is 10% of GPP = $10x$. Since, the GPP of the 3rd trophic level is the same as the NPP of the second trophic level, it is equal to $10x$.

46. (*d*) Statement in option (d) is correct regarding the process of replication in *E. coli*. It can be explained as

In living cells, such as *E. coli*, the process of replication requires a set of catalysts or enzymes. The main enzyme is referred to as DNA-dependent DNA polymerase. These enzymes use a DNA template to catalyse the polymerisation of deoxynucleotides. The enzyme DNA-dependent DNA polymerase catalyses polymerisation only in one direction, i.e. $5' \rightarrow 3'$.

47. (*c*) In somatic hybridisation, protoplasts of two varieties of plants are fused. During this process, protoplasts are isolated and brought together and fused using techniques such as chemical treatment or electric fields. This fusion combines the genetic material from the two parent plants, leading to the formation of somatic hybrids.

48. (*b*) Spraying sugarcane crop with gibberellin increases the length of the stem, thus increasing the yield by as much as 20 tonnes per acre.

Gibberellins are plant hormones that promote stem elongation, cell division and cell expansion. Applying gibberellin to sugarcane crops, stimulate the elongation of the internodes. This increased stem length allows for more space for sugar accumulation and ultimately leads to higher yields.

Other options can be explained as

- Auxin primarily regulates plant growth by promoting cell elongation and is not responsible for stem elongation in sugarcane.
- Cytokinin is involved in cell division and lateral bud development, whereas abscisic acid acts as stress hormone.

49. (*b*) The correct matches are A-III, B-I, C-IV, D-II.

- Robert May places the global species diversity at about 7 million.
- Alexander von Humboldt provided species-area relationship.
- Paul Ehrlich used an analogy "rivet popper hypothesis" to explain the role of species in the ecosystem.
- David Tilman performed long term ecosystem experiments using outdoor plots.

50. (*b*) Chloroplasts are organelles found in plant cells, responsible for photosynthesis. They contain their own genome, which is typically a circular molecule of DNA. This DNA is double stranded.

The circular nature of chloroplast DNA is a characteristic feature shared with bacterial DNA, reflecting the endosymbiotic theory.

Zoology

Section A

51. (*c*) The correct matches are A-III, B-I, C-II, D-IV.

- Common cold is caused by rhinoviruses.
- Haemozoin is a chemical released due to the rupturing of RBCs by *Plasmodium*.
- Widal test is used to diagnose typhoid.
- Allergy is caused by allergens like dust, mites.

52. (*d*) The correct matches are A-III, B-IV, C-I, D-II.

- Cocaine is derived from coca plant, i.e. *Erythroxylum*.
- Heroin is an opioid obtained from latex of poppy plant, *Papaver somniferum*.
- Morphine is an effective sedative used for treating patients who have undergone surgery.
- Marijuana is a cannabinoid obtained from the plant *Cannabis sativa*.

53. (*d*) The correct matches are A-III, B-I, C-IV, D-II.

- Fibrous joints are present in skull. They do not allow any movement.
- Cartilaginous joints are present in adjacent vertebrae. They provide limited movement.
- Hinge joint is present in knee and helps in locomotion.
- Ball and socket joints are present between humerus and pectoral girdle and provide rotational movement.

54. (*b*) Among the given options, Myasthenia gravis, Rheumatoid arthritis and Systemic Lupus Erythematosus (SLE) are autoimmune disorders.

The autoimmune disease is a type of disease in which the body's immune system attacks healthy tissues of the body. Other options can be explained as

Gout is an inflammatory disorder and muscular dystrophy is a progressive degeneration of skeletal muscles in which mutated genes interfere with healthy muscle function.

55. (*a*) Uterine fundus is not a component of Fallopian tube. It is the part of uterus that is farthest away from its opening, the cervix. On the other hand, isthmus, infundibulum and ampulla are the parts of Fallopian tube.

56. (*c*) The flippers of the penguins and dolphins are the examples of convergent evolution. The convergent evolution can be defined as a process in which unrelated organisms evolve similar body forms, colourations and adaptations. However, they do not belong to a common ancestor.

57. (*c*) The correct matches are A-III, B-IV, C-I, D-II.

- α-1 antitrypsin is used for treatment of emphysema.
- *cry* I Ab gene controls corn borer.
- *cry* I Ac controls cotton bollworm.
- Enzyme replacement therapy can be used as treatment in ADA deficiency.

58. (*b*) In the given figure of pBR322, *X* represents '*ori*' region, while *Y* represent '*rop*' region. The '*ori*' site is the origin of replication that controls the copy number of the linked DNA. Whereas *rop* codes for proteins which are involved in the process of replication of the plasmid.

59. (*a*) Both A and R are correct and R is the correct explanation of A.

Doctors recommend breast-feeding during initial period of infant growth because it contains IgA antibodies that provide passive immunity to the newborn baby.

60. (*c*) The 'Ti-plasmid' of *Agrobacterium tumefaciens* stands for tumour inducing plasmid. It induces crown gall disease in plants by transferring crucial regions from the plasmid.

61. (*b*) The correct matches are A-II, B-I, C-IV, D-III.

- *Pleurobrachia* is a member of phylum- Ctenophora.
- Radula is a rasping or feeding organ present in phylum-Mollusca.
- Stomochord is rudimentary structure similar to notochord found in collar region of members of phylum-Hemichordata.
- Air bladder is found in Osteichthyes, which regulates buoyancy.

62. (*d*) The correct sequence of human evolution from past to recent is as follows

Homo habilis $\rightarrow$ *Homo erectus* $\rightarrow$ *Homo neanderthalensis* $\rightarrow$ *Homo sapiens*

Homo habilis appeared around 3.2 mya. They were capable of making sharpened tools and their cranial capacity was 650-800 cc.

Homo erectus appeared around 1.5 mya. They had erect body posture and cranial capacity was 900 cc.

Homo neanderthalensis appeared around 40,000 to 1,00,000 years ago. They had cranial capacity of 1400 cc.

Homo sapiens is the modern man evolved somewhere between 75,000 to 10,000 years ago. Their cranial capacity is 1450 cc.

63. (*d*) Glucagon is a peptide hormone. It is produced by α-cells of the pancreas. It raises the concentration of glucose and fatty acids in the blood stream. On the other hand, cortisol, testosterone and progesterone are the examples of steroid hormones.

64. (*b*) Anal cerci, a pair of jointed filamentous structures are present on 10th segment in both sexes of cockroach. These are sense organs that are sensitive to wind and also detect vibration.

65. (*d*) Among the given options, a constant gene pool will not affect the Hardy-Weinberg equilibrium. It was proposed by GH Hardy and W Weinberg independently in 1908. According to this, a stable population has constant allelic frequencies in sexually reproducing organisms from generations to generations. The factors which cause change in allelic frequencies in a population are recombination, mutation, gene migration, genetic drift and natural selection.

66. (*b*) The correct matches are A-III, B-IV, C-II, D-I.

- Pons connects different regions of the brain.
- Hypothalamus also have neuro secretory cells which secrete hormone.
- Medulla controls respiration and gastric secretion.
- Cerebellum provides additional space for neurons, regulates posture and balance.

67. (*c*) The correct matches are A-III, B-IV, C-I, D-II.

- Down's syndrome is caused due to trisomy of 21st chromosome.
- α-thalassemia is controlled by two closely linked genes HBA1 and HBA2 on chromosome 16 of each parent and occurs due to mutation or deletion of one or more of the four genes.
- β-thalassemia is controlled by a single gene HBB on chromosome 11 of each parent and occurs due to mutation of one or both genes.
- Klinefelter's syndrome is caused due to the presence of an additional copy of X chromosome resulting into a karyotype of 47, XXY.

68. (*a*) The strand of DNA which is copied into *m*RNA and subsequently translated, possesses complementary sequence to the *m*RNA. It is called as template strand. During transcription, RNA polymerase binds to the template strand and synthesis RNA. However, due to the complementarity rule, in RNA, uracil is present in place of thymine. Therefore, the correct product will be determined as follows:
3′
TACATGGCAAATATCCATTCA5'
5'AUGUACCGUUUAUAGGUAAG
U3′

69. (*d*) A is false, but R is true. A can be corrected as
LH and FSH both are secreted by anterior pituitary. In females, FSH acts upon ovarian follicles; while LH stimulates Leydig's cells of testis to secrete androgen.

70. (*d*) Among the given options, vaults are not the natural contraceptive methods. Instead, they are barrier methods. The vaults are disposable cup-like structures made of rubber that are inserted into the vaginal tract to cover the cervix before coitus. They prevent the entry of sperms through cervix to prevent fertilisation.

71. (*d*) The correct matches are A-III, B-I, C-IV, D-II.

- Example of non-medicated IUD is lippes loop.
- Example of copper releasing IUD is Multiload 375.
- Example of hormone releasing IUD is LNG-20.
- Progestogens alone or in combination with estrogen can be used by females as injections or implants under the skin.

72. (*b*) Among the given statements, only statement A is correct. Rest of the statements are incorrect and can be corrected as follows

- Poriferans and Platyhelminthes are acoelomate as they lack coelom.
- Aschelminthes are pseudocoelomates.

73. (*b*) (i) represents skeletal muscles which are present in triceps. These are voluntary muscles and show striations.
(ii) represents smooth muscles which are involuntary in action and are present in stomach, whereas (iii) represents cardiac muscles which are exclusively found in heart.

74. (*a*) The correct sequence of pathway for conduction of an action potential through the heart is as follows
SA node → AV node → AV bundle → Bundle branches → Purkinje fibres

75. (*c*) The correct matches are A-II, B-IV, C-I, D-III.

- Lipase helps in digestion of ester bond.
- Nuclease helps in digestion of phosphodiester bond.
- Protease helps in digestion of peptide bond.
- Amylase helps in digestion of glycosidic bond.

76. (*d*) The correct match is A-II, B-I, C-IV, D-III.

- Axoneme is seen in cilia and flagella.
- Centriole shows cartwheel appearance.
- Crista is found in mitochondria.
- Few chromosomes have secondary constrictions at a constant location. This gives the appearance of a small fragment called satellite.

77. (*c*) The correct matches are A-II, B-IV, C-I, D-III.

- In diakinesis, completion of terminalisation of chiasmata takes place.

• In pachytene, appearance of recombination nodule takes place.
• In zygotene, synaptonemal complex formation takes place.
• In leptotene, chromosomes look like thin threads.

78. (*b*) Among the given factors, high pO_2 and lesser H^+ concentration are favourable for the formation of oxyhaemoglobin in alveoli. The higher the partial pressure of oxygen, the more efficiently haemoglobin binds to O_2.

79. (b) The correct matches are A-III, B-I, C-II, D-IV.
• *Pterophyllum* is the scientific name for angel fish.
• *Myxine* is the scientific name for hag fish.
• *Pristis* is the scientific name for saw fish.
• *Exocoetus* is the scientific name for flying fish.

80. (*b*) The correct matches are A-IV, B-III, C-I, D-II.
• Typhoid is caused by *Salmonella typhimurium* (Bacteria).
• Leishmaniasis is caused by protozoan, i.e. *Leishmania donovani*.
• Ringworm is caused by fungi belonging to genera-*Microsporum*.
• Filariasis is caused by *Wuchereria bancrofti* (Nematode).

81. (*c*) All the statements are correct except (c), which can be corrected as Bio-reactors are used to produce large scale bacterial cultures.

82. (*b*) Both statement I and II are false. These can be corrected as
• In the nephron, the decending limb of loop of Henle is permeable to water, but almost impermeable to electrolytes.
• The PCT is lined by simple cuboidal brush border epithelium which increases the surface area for reabsorption.

83. (*c*) Statement I is true, but statement II is false. Statement II can be corrected as

The hymen is often torn during first coitus. However, it may get torn due to a sudden fall or a jolt during horse-riding, cycling, gymnastics and dance movements, etc.

84. (*a*) The correct matches are A-II, B-IV, C-I, D-III.

Expiratory capacity	Tidal volume + Expiratory reserve volume.
Functional residual capacity	Expiratory reserve volume + Residual volume
Vital capacity	Expiratory reserve volume + Tidal volume + Inspiratory reserve volume
Inspiratory capacity	Tidal volume + Inspiratory reserve volume

85. (*d*) The correct sequence of different stages of cell division is as follows
Gap$_1$ phase → Synthesis phase → Gap$_2$ phase → Karyokinesis → Cytokinesis
In Gap$_1$ and Gap$_2$ phases, cell prepares itself for cell division; while actual division occurs in synthesis (S) phase. Karyokinesis is division of nucleus that is followed by cytokinesis.

Section B

86. (*c*) Statement I is true, but Statement II is false. The incorrect statement can be corrected as
The inner membrane of chloroplast is relatively less permeable, as compared to mitochondria.

87. (*d*) The correct matches are A-III, B-I, C-IV, D-II.
• Birds and reptiles evolved in mesozoic era.
• Lower invertebrates evolved in Proterozoic era.
• Mammals evolved in Cenozoic era.
• Fish and amphibians evolved in Paleozoic era.

88. (*d*) Statement I is false, but statement II is true. Statement I can be corrected as

Gause's competitive exclusion theory states that two closely related species competing for the same resources cannot co-exist indefinitely.

89. (*c*) The correct matches are A-III, B-IV, C-I, D-II.
• Unicellular glandular epithelium is present in goblet cells of alimentary canal.
• Compound epithelium is present in moist surface of buccal cavity.
• Multicellular glandular epithelium is present in salivary glands.
• Endocrine glandular epithelium is present in pancreas.

90. (*a*) The correct matches are A-IV, B-II, C-III, D-I.
• In cockroach, the structures used for storing of food is called crop.
• In cockroach a ring of 6-8 blind tubules at junction of foregut and midgut is gastric caeca.
• Ring of 100-150 yellow coloured thin filaments at the junction of midgut and hindgut are called Malpighian tubules.
• The structures used for grinding the food is called gizzard.

91. (*c*) Statement (c) is correct, while rest of the statements are incorrect. These can be corrected as follows.
• Juxta medullary nephrons are not present in columns of Bertini.
• Renal corpuscle of juxta medullary nephron lies in the inner cortical region.
• Juxta medullary nephrons are lesser in number than cortical nephrons.

92. (*d*) The correct matches are A-IV, B-III, C-I, D-II.
• In eukaryotes, RNA polymerase-III is responsible for transcription of *sn*RNAs, *t*RNA and 5*sr*RNA.
• rho-factor is responsible for termination of transcription.

- Splicing of exons is performed by snRNPs.
- TATA box is present in promoter region of transcription unit.

93. (*c*) Statement I is true, but statement II is false. Statement II can be corrected as
The brain stem consist of the medulla oblongata, pons and midbrain.

94. (*a*) In the given flow chart, A, B, C and D are, FSH, Leydig cells, Sertoli cells and spermiogenesis, respectively. LH and FSH both are secreted by anterior pituitary. LH stimulates Leydig's cells to secrete androgens. FSH stimulates Sertoli cells that release some factors which help in spermiogenesis.

95. (*a*) If the blood group of father is B^+, mother is A^+ and child is O^+ their respective genotypes will be
$I^B i$ / $I^A i$ / ii

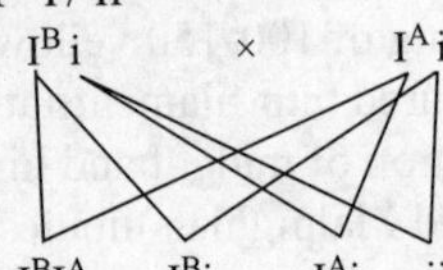

96. (*a*) Both statement I and statement II are true.
Bone marrow is the main lymphoid organ where all the blood cells including lymphocytes are produced. Both bone marrow and thymus provide micro-environments for the development and maturation of T-lymphocytes.

97. (*a*) The catalytic cycle of an enzyme action occurs in the following steps
Substrate binding to active site (E)
↓
Substrate enzyme complex formation (A)
↓
Chemical bonds of the substrate broken (D)
↓
Release of products (C)
↓
Free enzyme ready to bind with another substrate (B)

98. (*b*) The correct matches are A-III, B-II, C-IV, D-I.

- P-wave–Depolarisation of atria.
- QRS complex–Depolarisation of ventricles.
- T-wave–Repolarisation of ventricles.
- T-P gap–Heart muscles are electrically silent.

99. (*d*) The correct matches are A-III, B-IV, C-I, D-II.

- Exophthalmic goitre – Hypersecretion of thyroid hormone and protruding eye balls.
- Acromegaly – Excessive secretion of growth hormone.
- Cushing's syndrome – Excess secretion of cortisol, moon face and hyperglycemia.
- Cretinism – Hyposecretion of thyroid hormone and stunted growth.

100. (*c*) Statements B, D and E are true for non-chordates, while statements A and C are incorrect. These can be corrected as

- Pharynx is not perforated by gill slits in non-chordates.
- In non-chordates, the central nervous system is ventral and solid.

BIOLOGY-XIIth

MIND MAP

- Sexual Reproduction in Flowering Plants
- Human Reproduction
- Reproductive Health
- Principles of Inheritance and Variation
- Molecular Basis of Inheritance
- Evolution
- Human Health and Diseases
- Microbes in Human Welfare
- Biotechnology : Principles and Processes
- Biotechnology and Its Applications
- Organisms and Populations
- Ecosystem
- Biodiversity and Conservation

MEDACE

Test 1

Syllabus Flower structure; Development of male and female gametophytes

NCERT Page 03 to 11

For deeper insight, **Scan the QR Code**

Flower

Amphimixis/Sexual reproduction : Formation of new individual through meiosis.

Non-essential Whorls

- Outermost whorl called **calyx** — Unit: **Sepals** — Function: To protect inner whorls in bud condition.
- Inner to calyx is **corolla** — Unit: **Petals** — Function: To help in pollination and protection of inner whorls.

Essential Whorls

- **Androecium** — Unit: **Stamens** (Anther, Connective, Filament) — Function: In reproduction, as male reproductive organ
- **Gynoecium** — Unit: **Carpels** (Ovary, Style, Stigma) — Function: In reproduction, as female reproductive organ

Pollen Viability

The capability of pollen to get mature and then fertilise.

- Depends on prevailing temperature and humidity.
- Rice and wheat pollen grains lose viability within 30 minutes.
- Leguminosae, Rosaceae and Solanaceae families can remain viable for months.
- Pollen can act as a nutritional source, e.g. tablets and syrups.
- **Pollen bank** (storage of pollen) : Liquid N_2 (–196°C)
- Pollen can also trigger severe allergies and bronchial afflictions, e.g. *Parthenium*.

Pre-Fertilisation Events

Vacuole
Exine (Wall covering; Sporopollenin)
Intine (Helps in the germination of the pollen tube)
Germ pore (Exine absent and pollen tube formation)
Tube cell
Tube nucleus/Vegetative nucleus (controls and directs the growth or pollen tube)
Generative cell (Reproductive cell of pollen)

Epidermis: Outermost layer, thickened fibrous matter and protects the pollen sacs.

Endothecium Inner epidermis; develops cellulose with pectin and lignin; prevent it from splitting.

Middle layer Three to four layers; nourishes the microspore to facilitate pollen production.

Tapetum Innermost layer; provides nutrients and enzymes to the microspore mother cell; secretes **ubisch** bodies and **callase** enzyme.

1 — **Anther** (Bilobed and dithecous); PMC (2*n*)
2 — Ovary; MMC (Megaspore Mother Cell); Meiosis
3 — Microspore (*n*) (united by callose); Megaspore (*n*); Surviving/Functional megaspore
4 — Microspore (*n*); Mitosis; Generative; Each microspore develops into a pollen grain; Pollen grain (immature male gametophyte); Pollination
5 — Developing pollen tube of mature male gametophyte
6 — **Embryo sac** (mature female gametophyte); 3 antipodals (*n*); Polar nuclei; 2 synergids (*n*); Egg nucleus; Pollen tube; Two sperm cells
7 — Double fertilisation; Endosperm (3*n*); Zygote (2*n*); 2 synergids (*n*); Fruit; Embryo, Seed coat — Seed; Seedling

HAPLOID (*n*) GAMETOPHYTE GENERATION

DIPLOID (2*n*) SPOROPHYTE GENERATION

Types of Ovules

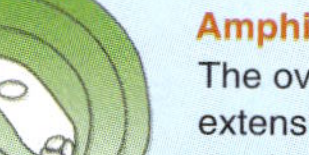

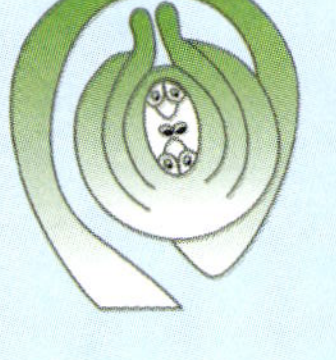

Orthotropous or Atropous
Here, the body of the ovules is straight, allowing the micropyle, the funicle connecting the ovule to the placenta and the chalaza, where the integuments and nucellus combine, to be in alignment, e.g. *Piper nigrum*, *Polygonum*, etc.

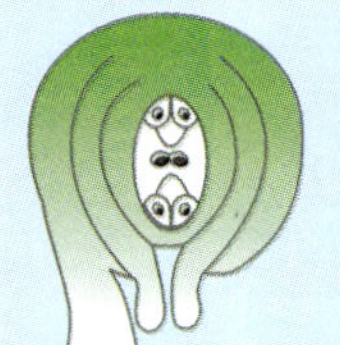

Circinotropous
In this instance, the funicle is particularly long, forming a nearly complete circle around the ovule, whose micropyle eventually points upward, e.g. *Opuntia*.

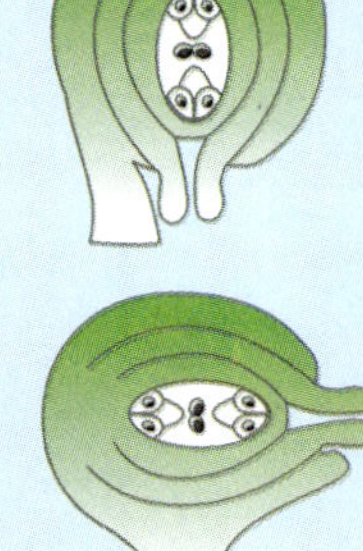

Anatropous
The ovules in this scenario is inverted during development, causing the micropyle to be located near the hilum.
A hilum scar denotes the spot where the funicle connects the seed to the fruit wall, e.g. lilies, beans, etc.

Hemi-anatropous
These ovules appear lying on their side because their bodies develop at right angles to the funicle, e.g. *Ranunculus*.

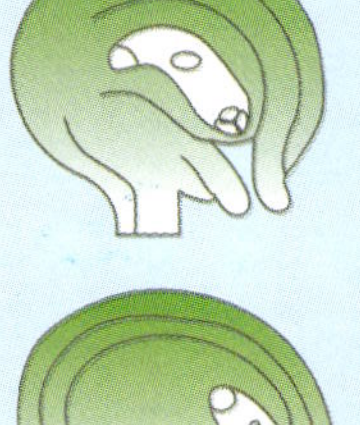

Amphitropous
The ovule's body is so extensively curved that the ovule itself and the embryo sac resembles a horseshoe, e.g. *Lemna*, poppy, etc.

Campylotropous
The coordination between the micropyle and chalaza is broken, and the body is bent. The nucellus is bent only along the lower side, e.g. Pea.

Test 2

Syllabus: Pollination-types, agencies and examples; Outbreeding devices; Pollen-Pistil interaction; Double fertilisation

NCERT Page 11 to 18

For deeper insight, **Scan the QR Code**

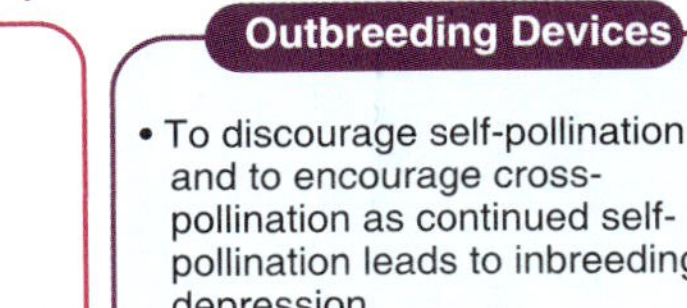

Pollination

(Transfer of pollen from anther to sigma)

Self-pollination
A single plant is involved

- **Autogamy** (Pollen grains fall on the stigma of the same flower) e.g. pea, rice, wheat
  - In plants like *Viola*, *Oxalis* and *Commelina*
    - **Chasmogamous flower**
      - These open at maturity and expose their stigma(s) and stamen(s).
      - They may be cross pollinated or self-pollinated.
    - **Cleistogamous flower**
      - These are bisexual flowers which do not open at all even in maturity.
      - Self-pollinated only.
- **Geitonogamy** (Pollen grains fall on the stigma of different flowers of the same plant)

Cross-pollination (Allogamy) or **Xenogamy**
It involves two different plants. Pollen grains reach the other plant with the help of pollinating agents.

Agents

- **Biotic agencies**
  - Entomophily (insects)
  - Ornithophily (birds)
  - Chiropterophily (bats)
  - Malacophily (Molluscs)
- **Abiotic agencies**
  - Anemophily (wind)
  - Hydrophily (water)
    - Epihydrophily (at water's surface) e.g. *Vallisneria*
    - Hypohydrophily (beneath water's surface) e.g. *Ceratophyllum*.

Outbreeding Devices

- To discourage self-pollination and to encourage cross-pollination as continued self-pollination leads to inbreeding depression.
- **Devices**
  (i) Non-synchronisation of pollen release and stigma receptivity (**Dichogamy** - Protandry/ Protogyny)
  (ii) Position of anthers and stigma in such a way that pollens cannot come in contact of stigma of same flower (Heterostyly, Herkogamy).
  (iii) **Self incompatibility**
  (iv) Production of unisexual flower (**Dicliny**).

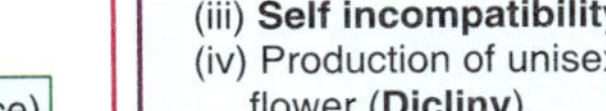

Artificial Hybridisation

- **Emasculation*** - Removal of anther from the bisexual flower.
- **Bagging** The emasculated flower is bagged. It is covered to prevent the contamination of the stigma with unwanted pollen grains.
- **Pollination** When the stigma attains maturity, pollination is carried out with the selected pollens. Pollen grains are dusted on the stigma in this step.
- **Rebagging** The flower is then rebagged to avoid any interference or contamination from undesired pollens.

* Emasculation is done to prevent self-pollination. Plants with unisexual flowers do not require this process.

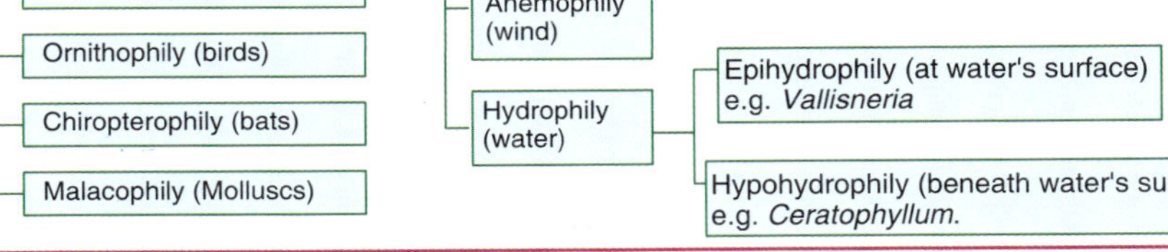

Pollen-pistil Interaction

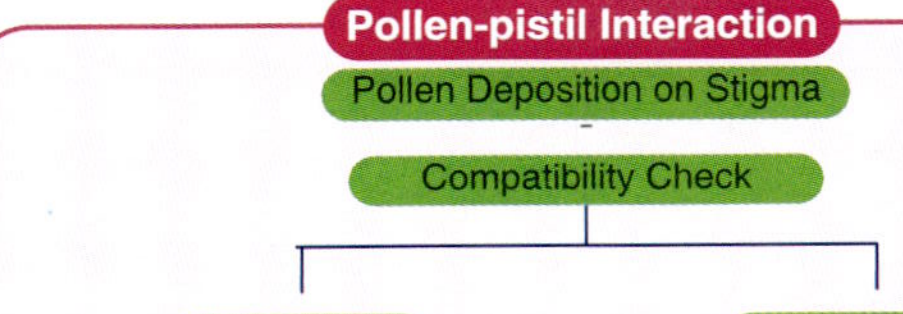

Pollen Deposition on Stigma
↓
Compatibility Check

- **If compatible**
  → Pollen grain **accepted**
  → Pollen germinates to form **pollen tube**
  → Content of generative cells or male gametes transfers into pollen tube
  → **Growth** of pollen tube due to Calcium-boron inositol sugar complex through stigma and style by secreting enzymes
  → Entry into ovule through **micropyle** (generally) *via* synergids with filiform apparatus guiding the entry of pollen tube
  - Pollen tube entry can be through micropyle **(Porogamy)** or chalaza **(Chalazogamy)**.
- **If incompatible**
  → Pollen grain **rejected**
  → No pollen germination

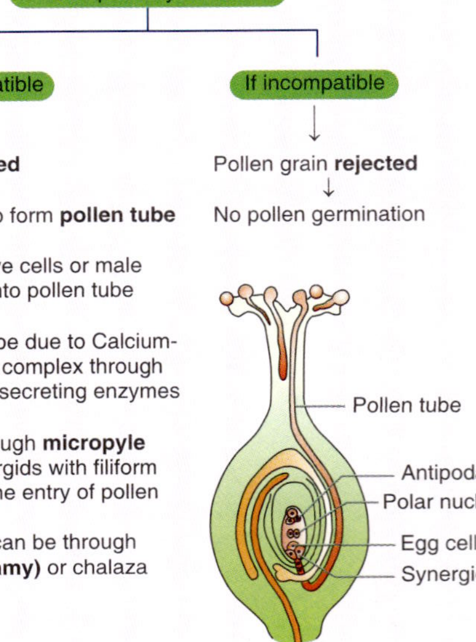

Double Fertilisation

- Characteristic feature of angiosperms discovered by **Nawaschin**.
- Pollen tube releases two male gametes into the cytoplasm of synergids.

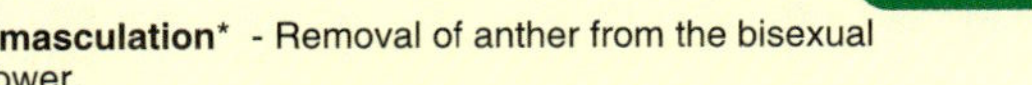

One male gamete + Egg → Zygote($2n$) — **Syngamy**

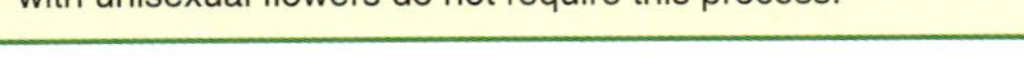

Other male gamete + 2 polar nuclei → Primary endosperm nucleus ($3n$) — **Triple fusion**

↓

Double fertilisation

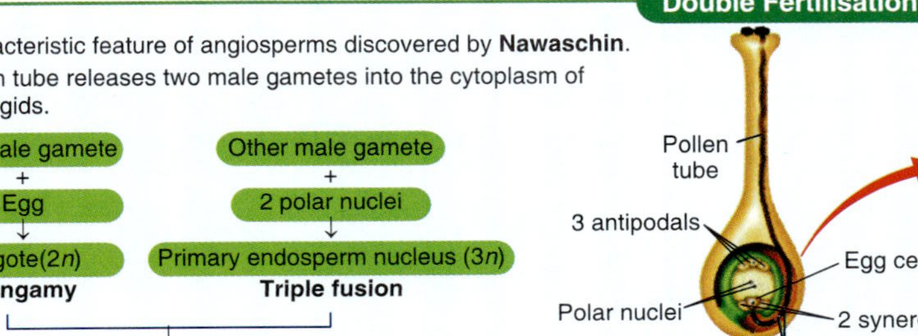

Test 3

Syllabus

Post-fertilisation events- Development of endosperm and embryo; Development of seed and formation of fruit; Special modes-apomixis, parthenocarpy, polyembryony; Significance of seed and fruit formation

NCERT Page 18 to 23

For deeper insight, **Scan the QR Code**

Post-Fertilisation Events

Fate of Floral Parts

Ovary ($2n$)	→ Fruit	PEN ($3n$) → Endosperm	
Ovary wall ($2n$)	→ Pericarp	Sepal ($2n$), Petal ($2n$)	Wither away, fall down
Ovule ($2n$)	→ Seed	Stigma ($2n$), Style ($2n$)	Wither away, fall down
Outer integument ($2n$)	→ Testa	Nucellus ($2n$) → Consumed/ Present as perisperm	
Inner integument ($2n$)	→ Tegmen	Synergids (n)	Degenerate
Zygote ($2n$)	→ Embryo	Antipodals (n)	Degenerate

- **Development of Endosperm**
  - The primary endosperm nucleus or cell (PEN/PEC) in embryo sac divides repeatedly to form triploid endosperm.
- **Development of Embryo**
  - Embryo formation starts after certain amount of endosperm is formed.
  - Different stages of development of a dicot embryo are: zygote, pro-embryo, globular embryo, heart shaped embryo, mature embryo.

Monocot Embryo

- One cotyledon, called **scutellum**.
- The embryonal axis has radicle/root tip with root cap enclosed by coleorhiza.
- Upper end (epicotyl) has plumule/shoot tip covered by **coleoptile.** e.g. rice, maize, etc.

Dicot Embryo

- Consists of an embryonal axis and two cotyledons.
- Portion of embryonal axis above the level of cotyledon is epicotyl which terminates into plumule shoot tip.
- Portion of embryonal axis below the level of cotyledon is hypocotyl which terminates with radicle (covered with calyptra).

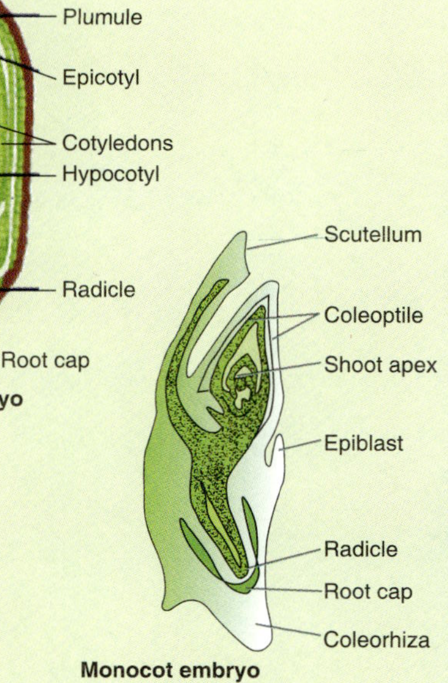

Dicot embryo

Monocot embryo

Polyembryony

The phenomenon of having more than one embryo is called polyembryony, e.g. onion or groundnut.

- It is of the following types:

- **Simple polyembryony** Occurrence of polyembryony due to fertilisation of more than one egg, e.g. *Pinus.*
- **Adventive polyembryony** Formation of extra embryos through sporophytic budding, e.g. *Cycas.*
- **False polyembryony** More than one embryos arise in different embryo sacs in the ovule, e.g. *Saxifraga* and *Bergenia.*
- **True polyembryony** More than one embryos are formed in the same embryo sac in the ovule, e.g. *Citrus* plant.

Parthenocarpy vs Parthenogenesis

Parthenocarpy is about seedless fruit production that occur without fertilisation, often seen in horticulture. On the other hand, **Parthenogenesis** is a form of asexual reproduction in which certain plants develop offspring from an unfertilised egg.

Seed and Fruit

Seed (Fertilised ovule)

- Seed Coat
  - **Testa** (Outer)
  - **Tegmen** (Inner)
- Kernel
  - Perisperm
  - Endosperm
  - Embryo
    - Embryonal axis
      - Plumule
      - Radicle
    - Cotyledons

- Seeds may be **albuminous** (endosperm present, e.g. wheat and maize) or non-albuminous (endosperm absent, e.g. pea, bean).
- Seeds of black pepper and beet show remnants of nucellus called perisperm.

Fruit (Mature ovary)

- Fruit may be fleshy (e.g., mango and orange) or dry (e.g., groundnut and mustard).

True Fruit	False Fruit
- Fruit formation by ovary. - e.g. mango Endocarp (Seed/Stone) Mesocarp (Pulp) Epicarp/Exocarp (Peel)	- Fruit formation by other floral parts along with ovary. - e.g. apple (from thalamus) Thalamus Seed

- **Parthenocarpic fruit** : e.g. Banana ; seedless.

Apomixis

It is a form of asexual reproduction that mimics sexual reproduction where seeds are formed without fertilisation.

Types of Apomixis	Description
Parthenogenesis	The embryo develops from an egg cell.
Apogamy	The embryo originates from synergids or antipodal cells. It may be haploid or diploid.
Diplospory	The unreduced embryo sac is derived from megaspore mother cell by aborted meiotic division or a direct mitotic division. Major types include *Taraxacum, Ixeris,* and *Antennaria.*
Apospory	Nucellar cells known as aposporous initials differentiate and produce an apomictic embryo sac.

Benefits of Apomixis

- It helps in hybrid seed production.
- It is one of the most cost-effective methods to produce seeds.
- Apomixis prevents the loss of specific characters in the hybrid.

Test 1

Syllabus: Male and female reproductive systems; Microscopic anatomy of testis.

NCERT Page 26-31,32

For deeper insight, **Scan the QR Code**

Reproductive System

Humans are sexually reproducing and viviparous; includes following steps in reproduction :
Gametogenesis → Insemination → Fertilisation → Implantation → Gestation → Parturition

Male Reproductive System

Testes
Seminiferous tubule : Male germ cell (sperm formation) and Sertoli cell (nutrition); Outside- blood vessels and Leydig cells.

Accessory Duct
- Rete testis
- Vasa efferentia
- Epididymis
- Vas deferens

Glands
- Seminal vesicle
- Prostate gland
- Bulbourethral gland

External Genitalia
Penis covered by foreskin; Copulatory organ

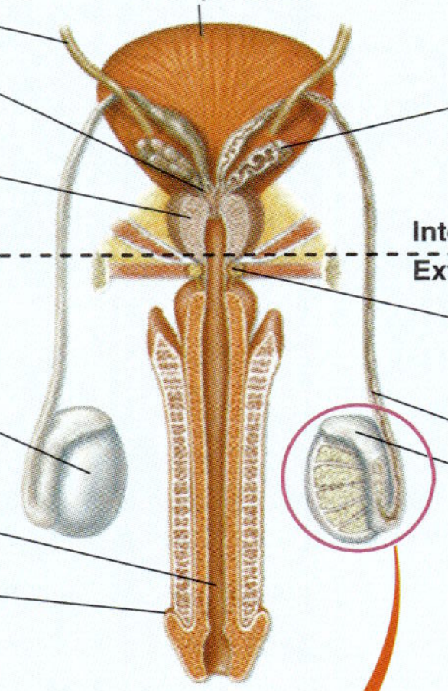

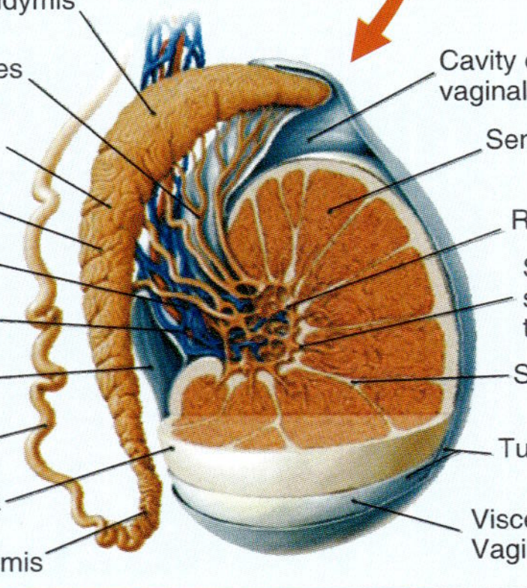

Sperm Pathway
Seminiferous duct → Rete testis → Vasa efferentia → Epididymis → Vas deferens → Ejaculatory duct → Urethra

- **Semen** Sperm + Secretion of prostate gland, seminal vesicle and bulbourethral gland.
- **Gubernaculum** Fibrous cord, connects testis to scrotum
- **Castration** Removal of testes
- **Inguinal Canal** Passage through which the testes descend into the scrotum and contain the spermatic cord
- **Cryptorchidism** Testes fail to descend

Female Reproductive System

Ovaries
- Paired primary sex organ
- Produces gamete (ovum) and hormones
- Covered by germinal epithelium
- Two zones: cortex and medulla

Accessory Ducts

Oviduct
- Infundibulum
- Ampulla
- Isthmus

Uterus
- Perimetrium
- Myometrium
- Endometrium

Vagina

Cervix
Cervical canal + Vagina ⇓ Birth canal

External Genitalia
- Mons pubis
- Labia majora
- Labia minora
- Hymen
- Clitoris

Vestibular Glands
Bartholin's Glands: Pea-sized glands; located on either side of the vaginal opening.
Skene's Glands: Tiny ducts; situated in the vestibule, the triangular area between clitoris and the vaginal opening.

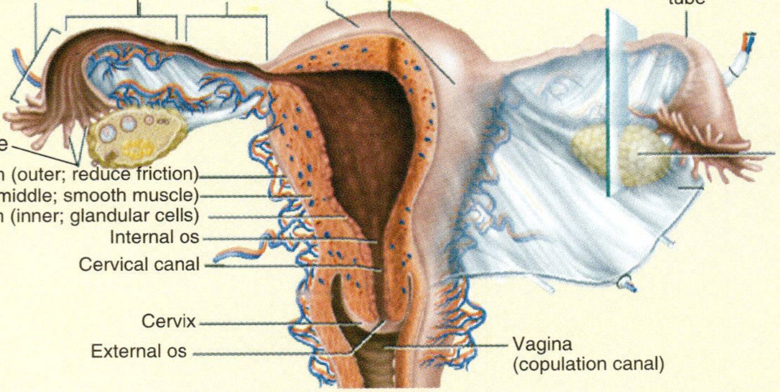

Mammary Glands

Supported by strands of connective tissue (suspensory ligaments).
- Modified sudoriferous (sweat) gland.
- Breast= Glandular tissue + Fibrous tissue + Fatty tissue
- Secrete and eject milk (lactation).

Milk pathway
Mammary alveoli → Mammary tubule → Mammary duct → Mammary ampulla → Lactiferous duct → Nipple

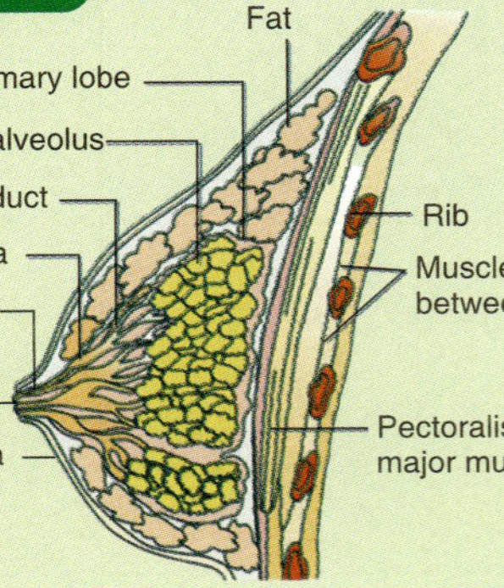

Test 2

Syllabus: Gametogenesis-Spermatogenesis and Oogenesis; Microscopic anatomy of ovary; Menstrual cycle

NCERT Page 31 to 35

For deeper insight, **Scan the QR Code**

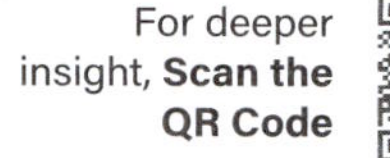
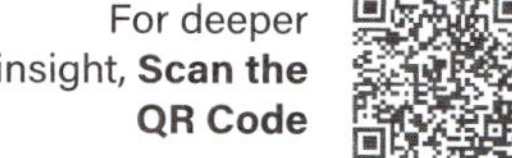

Chapter 02

Gametogenesis

Spermatogenesis
Formation of sperm

- Multiplication Phase: **Spermatogonia** (2n) → Mitotic division
- Growth Phase: **Primary spermatocyte** (2n) → Meiosis-I → **Secondary spermatocyte** (n) → Meiosis-II
- Maturation Phase: **Spermatid** (n) → Spermiogenesis → **Spermatozoa**

Oogenesis
Formation of ovum

- **Foetal life**: (2n) **Oogonia** → Mitotic division → (2n) **Primary oocyte** (Arrest at diplotene, prophase-I)
- **Birth**, **Childhood**, **Puberty**: First polar body (n); **Secondary oocyte** (n)
- **Adult reproductive life**: Completion of meiosis-II → Second polar body (n); **Ovum** (n) (Arrest at metaphase-II)

* Sperm gets embedded in Sertoli cell and released from seminiferous tubule by process called **spermiation**.

Sperm

- **60%** normal shape and size, at least **40%** show rigorous motility.
- Ejaculations: 200 to 300 million sperm per ejaculation.

Menstrual Cycle

Menarch
- First menstruation
- Begins at puberty

Menstrual Phase
- Menstruation
- Follicular phase
- Ovulation
- Luteal phase
- Next cycle

Menopause
- Menstrual cycle ceases around 50 years of age

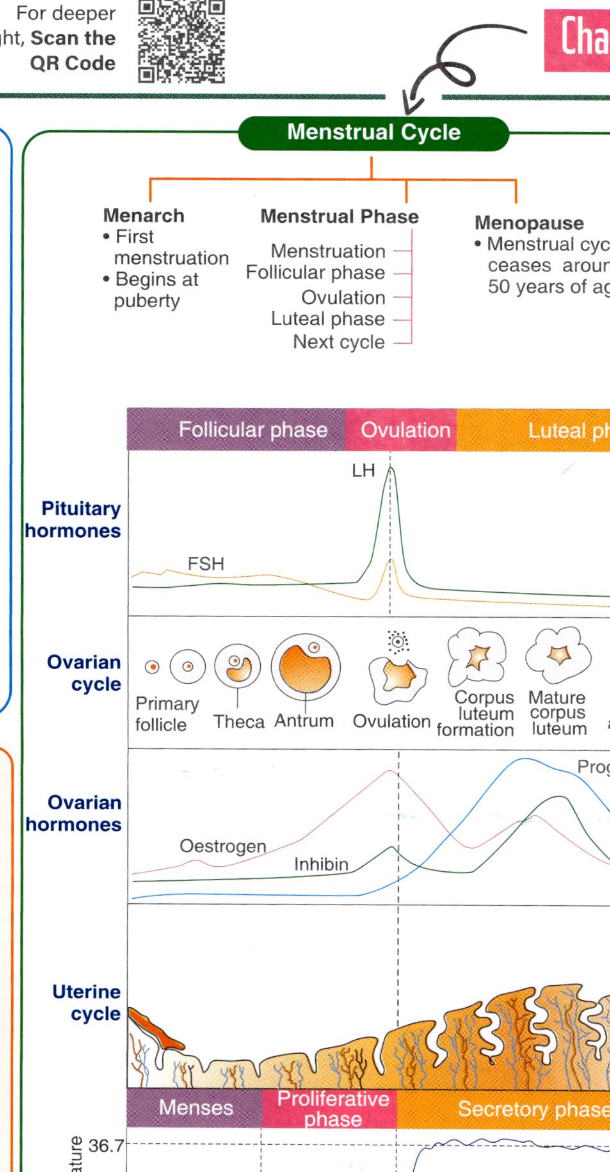

Ovary

- **Primary follicle:** 60,000 to 80,000 per ovary (surrounded by granulosa cells).
- **Secondary follicle:** More granulosa layer and new theca layer.
- **Tertiary follicle:** Characterised by antrum (fluid filled cavity) differentiates into theca interna and theca externa.
- **Graafian follicle:** Zona pellucida

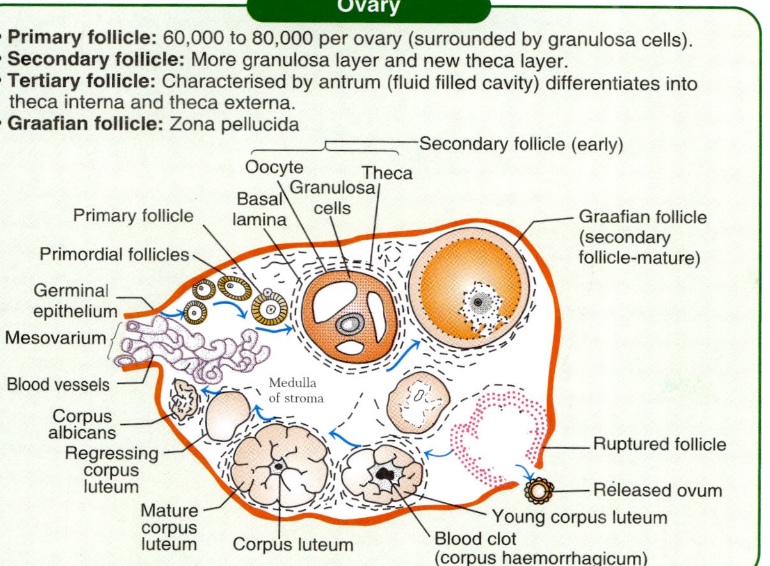

Hormonal Regulation

At puberty: Hypothalamus → GnRH → Anterior pituitary

- **FSH**
  - Male: Sertoli cell → Helps in spermiogenesis
  - Female: Graafian follicle → Oestrogen
- **LH**
  - Male: Leydig cell → Androgen → Stimulates spermatogenesis
  - Female: Corpus luteum → Progesterone

Test 3

Syllabus Fertilisation; Embryo development up to blastocyst formation; Implantation: Pregnancy and placenta formation; Parturition; Lactation

NCERT Page 35 to 38

For deeper insight, **Scan the QR Code**

Fertilisation and Implantation

Fertilisation

- Only occur if the ovum and sperm are transported simultaneously to the ampullary region.
- Formation of second polar body and haploid ovum (ootid).

Implantation

- Mitotic division starts
- Cleavage : Zygote → Morula (8-16 cells)
- The embedding of blastocyst (Trophoblast and inner cell mass) in the endometrium is called **implantation**.
- The side containing the inner mass is positioned against the uterine wall.
- The trophoblast cells erode endometrial lining. It allows the blastocyst to penetrate into the thick endometrium.
- Chorionic villi help in the fixation of blastocyst and absorption of nutrients.

Fertilisation

1. Sperm makes contact with egg
2. Acrosome reacts with zona pellucida
3. Acrosome reacts with perivitelline space
4. Plasma membranes of sperm and egg fuse
5. Sperm nucleus enters egg
6. Cortical granules fuse with egg plasma membrane, which renders the vitelline layer impenetrable to sperm

Sperm
Acrosome
Hydrolytic enzymes
Protein receptors
Zona pellucida
Perivitelline space
Egg plasma membrane
Cortical granule
Sperm nucleus

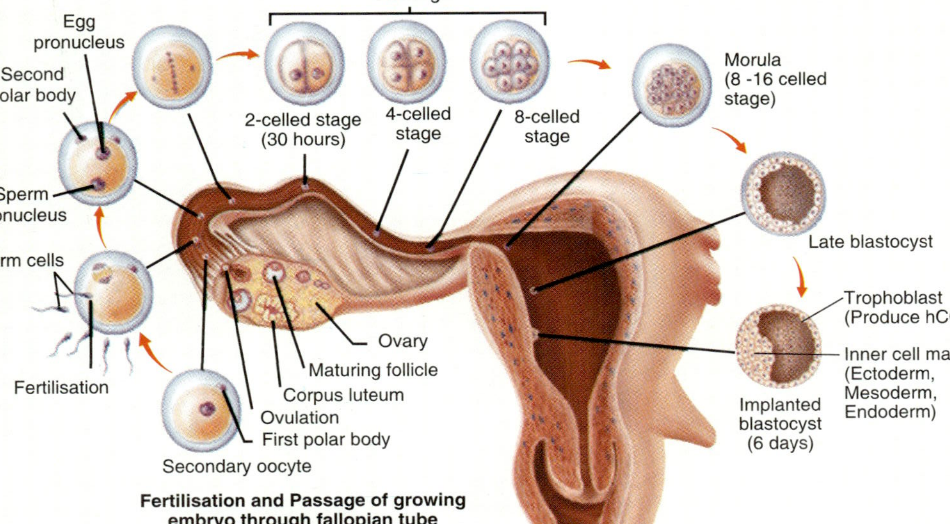

Fertilisation and Passage of growing embryo through fallopian tube

Pregnancy and Embryonic Development

Pregnancy

- Chorionic villi appears on trophoblast.
- Chorionic villi and uterine tissue become interdigitated to form placenta which supply O_2 and nutrients; remove CO_2 and excretory material *via* umbilical cord.
- Placenta acts as endocrine tissue; produces hCG, oestrogen, progesterone; relaxin secreted by ovary.
- Other hormones: cortisol, prolactin, thyroxine, etc.

Embryonic Development

- One month : Heart formed
- Second month end : Developed limbs and digits.
- First trimester : Major organ system formed.
- Fifth month : First movement and hair on head.
- Second trimester end : Fine hair, separate eye lid and eye lashes formed.
- Nine months : Foetus fully developed.

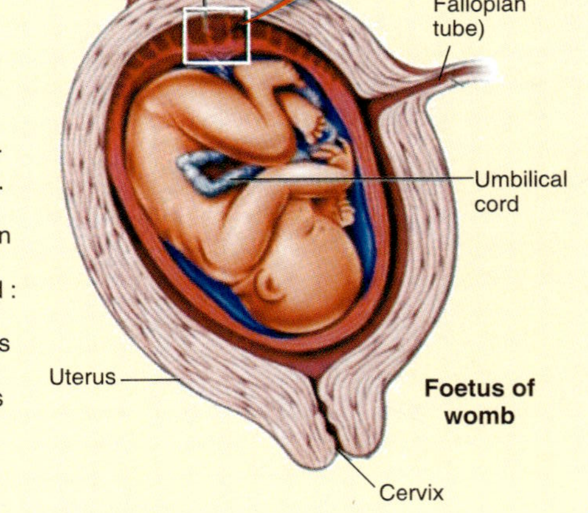

Parturition and Lactation

- **Parturition** Delivery of foetus.
- **Gestation period** About 9 months.
- **Induced** by a complex neuroendocrine mechanism.
- **Foetal-ejection reflex** Parturition signal from fully developed foetus and the placenta (triggers release of oxytocin to induce contractions) which leads to expulsion of baby out of uterus through birth canal.
- **Lactation** Production and release of milk from mammary glands.
- Initial few days of lactation is called **colostrum** that contains several antibodies.

Test 1

Syllabus: Need for Reproductive Health, Birth Control-Need and Methods; Contraception; Amniocentesis

NCERT Page 41 to 46

For deeper insight, **Scan the QR Code**

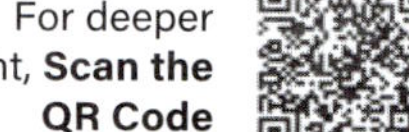

Chapter 03

Reproductive Strategies

According to WHO, reproductive health = Total well being (physical, emotional, behavioural and social aspect of reproduction).

- India was amongst the first countries in the world to initiate action plans and programmes at a national level to attain total reproductive health.
- Earlier called Family Planning (1951), now Reproductive and Child Healthcare (RCH) programme.
- **Main aim** : Awareness of reproductive organs, accessory organs of reproduction, secondary sexual characters, adolescence and associated changes, safe and hygienic sexual practices, STDs.

- Few programmes undertaken by the government:

- Massive child immunisation
- Statutory ban on **amniocentesis** for sex-determination of the foetus.
- In May 1947, WHO launched programme to immunise the children of entire world against six communicable diseases.

- Diphtheria	- Polio
- Pertussis	- Tuberculosis
- Tetanus	- Measles

Amniocentesis

Ultrasound transducer

Foetus

Amniotic fluid

Amniocentesis

Prenatal diagnosis of chromosomal abnormalities and fetal infections.

1. Amniocentesis is performed when a woman is 16 to 22 weeks pregnant.
2. A sample of amniotic fluid is taken from the amniotic sac.
3. Amniotic fluid has cells of the skin of the developing baby.
4. Each cell has complete set of chromosomes.
5. Karyotype is prepared and analysed for chromosomal abnormalities.

Population Explosion

- Better health facilities and better living conditions has led to increase in number of people of reproducible age.
- India has overtaken China as the most populous country in the world as on April, 2023.
- Reduction in birth rate by:

- Education	- Incentives
- Awareness	- Birth control
- Increase marriageable age	- Family planning

Causes

- Rapid decline in death rate, i.e. Maternal Mortality Rate (MMR) and Infant Mortality Rate (IMR).
- Increase in number of people in reproductive age group.
- Better medical facilities.
- Better sanitation.

Birth Control

- The regulation of conception by prevention methods or devices to limit the number of offsprings; prevent unwanted pregnancies.
- Prevent fertilisation by blocking : Sperm transport to ovum, ovulation and implantation of early embryo; wide range of contraceptive methods are presently available and these could be broadly classified into the following categories:

Methods

Temporary

Natural Method

- **Periodic Abstinence**
  – Avoiding coitus during fertile period (from 10-17 days of menstrual cycle).
- **Coitus Interruptus**
  – Withdrawal of penis from vagina just before ejaculation.
- **Lactational Amenorrhea**
  – Absence of menstruation during period of intense lactation following parturition.

Barrier Method

- **Condoms**
  – For both males and females.
- **Diaphragms, Cervical caps and Vaults.**
  – Inserted into female reproductive tract.
- **Spermicidal creams, jellies and foams.**

Intra-Uterine Devices

- Inserted into the uterus through vagina.

– **Non-medicated IUDs**
Increase phagocytosis of sperms within uterus, e.g. Lippes loop.

– **Copper Releasing IUDs**
(Copper) Suppresses sperm motility, e.g. CuT, Multiload 375.

– **Hormone Releasing IUDs**
Make uterus unsuitable for conception, e.g. Progestasert, LNG - 20.

Chemical Method

- To prevent ovulation

Oral Contraceptives

– Progestogen or Progestogen + Oestrogen combination pill (e.g. Mala-D).
– Non-steroidal pill (e.g. Saheli).

Emergency Pills

– Within 72 hrs of coitus.

Injections

– Progestogen/Progestogen-oestrogen (every 3 month).

Implants

– Progestogen
– Progestogen-oestrogen patches (under skin).

Permanent

Surgical/Sterilisation Method

- Highly effective, but poor reversibility
- **Tubectomy**
  – A small part of Fallopian tube is removed or tied.
- **Vasectomy**
  – A small part of vas deferens is removed or tied.

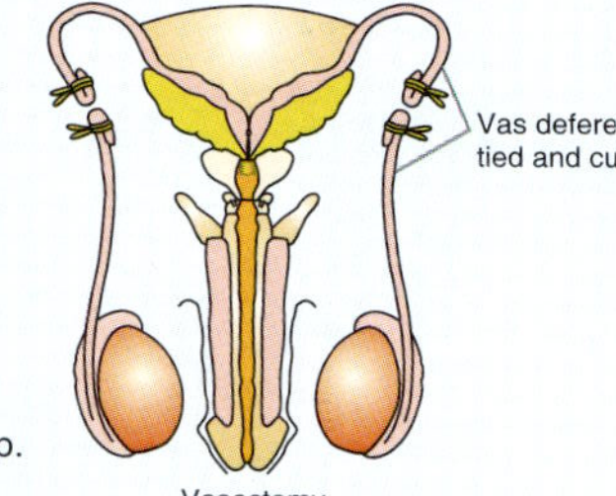

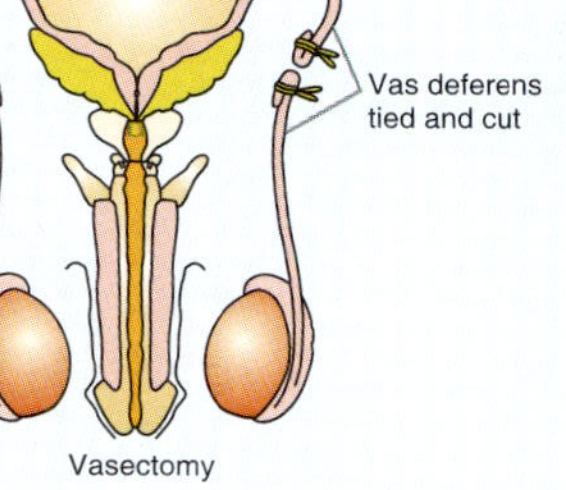

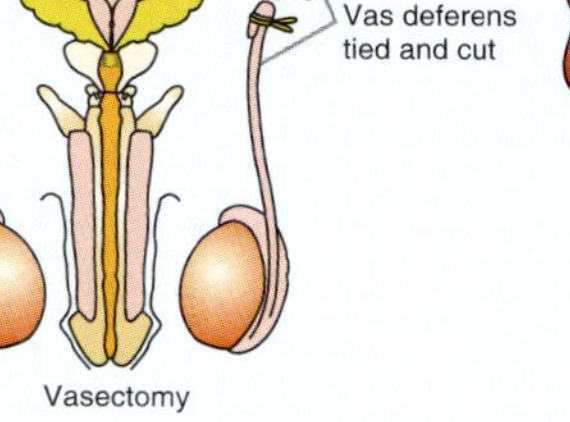

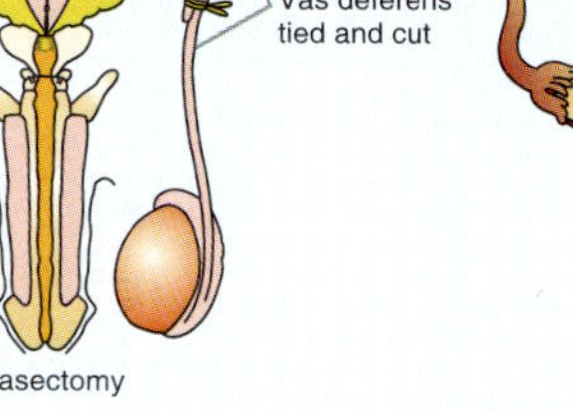

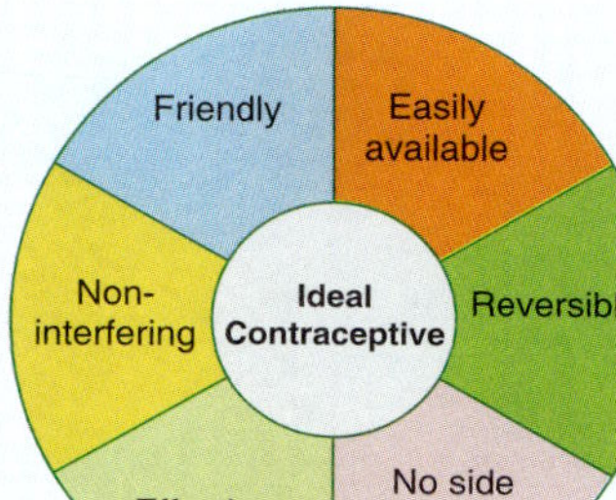

Saheli It is a mini pill that contains a non-steroidal preparation called centchroman which is taken once in a week after an initial intake of twice a week dose for 3 months. It blocks oestrogen receptors in the uterus and hence, alters the uterine lining and prevents fertilised egg from being implanted.

Test 2

Syllabus Prevention of Sexually Transmitted Diseases; MTP; Infertility and Assisted Reproductive Technologies - IVF, ZIFT, GIFT.

NCERT Page 46 to 48

For deeper insight **Scan the QR Code**

Medical Termination of Pregnancy (MTP)

- Voluntary or intentional abortion performed to terminate pregnancy before completion of full term.
- Legalised by Indian government in 1971.
- **Need for Legalisation**

1. To abort unwanted pregnancies.
2. If pregnancy is likely to produce a congenitally malformed child.
3. Pregnancy due to the failed contraceptives or result of rape.

- **Safer during the first trimester of pregnancy;** legally allowed up to 24th week of pregnancy.
  – Illegal use of MTP - After misuse of amniocentesis for female foeticide.
- MTPs are performed in a year all over the world. It accounts to 1/5th of the total number of conceived pregnancies in a year.

Significance of MTP

- MTP has a significant role in decreasing the population though it is not meant for that purpose.
- MTPs are essential in certain cases where the continuation of the pregnancy could be harmful to the mother, foetus or both.

Disadvantages of MTP

- Performed illegally by unqualified persons (unsafe); could be fatal too.
- Misused to abort female foetus.
- Raises many emotional, ethical, religious and social issues.

Infertility and ARTs

- **Infertility** - Inability to produce children, inspite of unprotected sexual cohabitation of a couple.

Reasons for Infertility

Physical | Congenital disease | Drugs | Immunological | Psychological

- Infertile couples can be assisted to have children through certain special techniques called as **Assisted Reproductive Technologies** (ARTs).

Techniques of ARTs

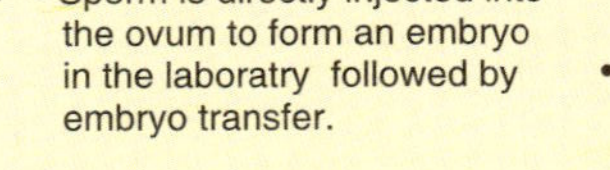

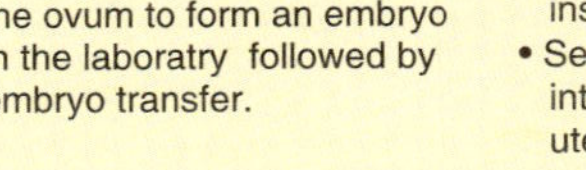

In - Vitro (IVF) Fertilisation

- Fertilisation outside the body in simulated conditions followed by embryo transfer.
- **Test Tube Baby Program**
  – Collection of ova (♀) and sperm (♂)

Gamete - Intra Fallopian Transfer (GIFT)

- Transfer of an ovum collected from a donor to Fallopian tube of another female who cannot produce ova, but can provide suitable conditions for fertilisation and further development of foetus.

Intra Cytoplasmic Sperm Injection (ICSI)

- Sperm is directly injected into the ovum to form an embryo in the laboratry followed by embryo transfer.

Artificial Insemination (AI)

- Used in case of low sperm count and inability of male to inseminate the females.
- Semen → artificially introduced into vagina or uterus **(IUI).**

IVF
↓
Embryo Transfer

Upto 8 blastomeres → **ZIFT** (Zygote Intra Fallopian Transfer)

More than 8 blastomeres → **IUT** (Intra Uterine Transfer)

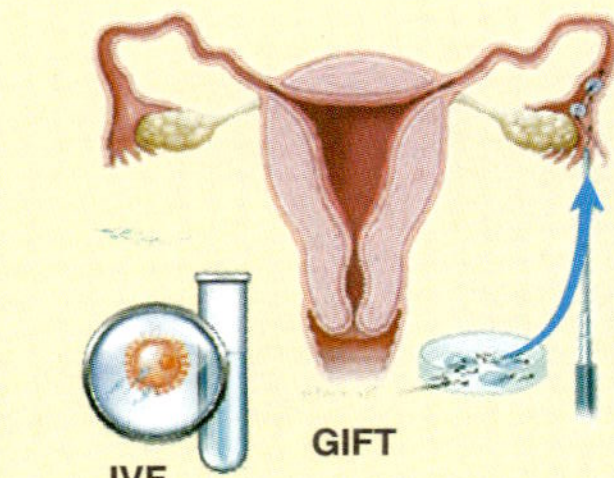

IVF

GIFT

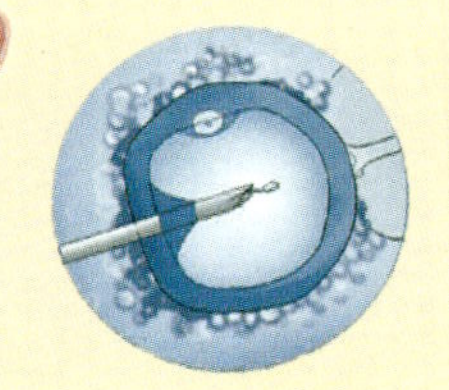

ICSI

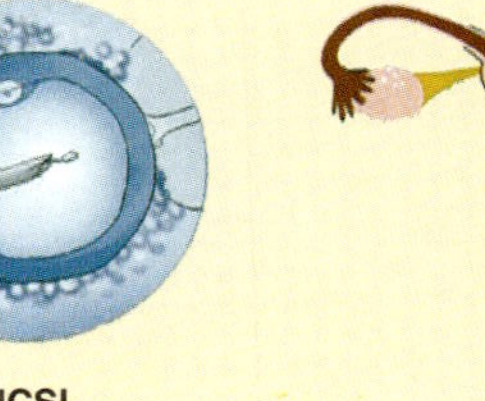

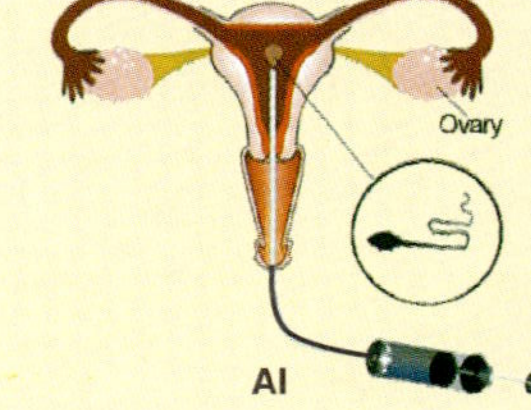

AI

Sexually Transmitted Infections (STIs)

- Also called Venereal Disease (VD) or Reproductive Tract Infection (RTI); transmitted through sexual intercourse.
- STIs are caused by bacteria, viruses, protozoan, ectoparasite and fungi.

Diseases	Causative agents	Symptoms
Syphilis (bacteria)	*Treponema pallidum*	Sores and lesions in genital tract, painful urination, etc.
Gonorrhoea (bacteria)	*Neisseria gonorrhoeae*	14 days infections of urinogenital tract genital discharge, etc.
AIDS (virus)	Human immunodeficiency virus	Fever, lethargy, nausea, head ache, etc.
Hepatitis-B (virus)	Hepatitis-B virus	Yellowing of skin, jaundice, dark urine, etc.
Genital herpes (virus)	Herpes simplex virus	Painful genital blisters, fever, itching, etc.
Genital warts (virus)	Human papilloma virus	Hard outgrowth with horny surface over skin.
Chlamydiasis (bacteria)	*Chlamydia trachomatis*	Infertility and damage of reproductive organs.
Trichomoniasis (protozoan)	*Trichomonas vaginalis*	Infection (vulva, vagina and urethra), itching, discharge, etc.

- Except for hepatitis-B, genital herpes and HIV infection, other diseases are completely curable, if treated early and properly.

- These diseases are reported high among individuals of age group of 15-24 years.
- The early general symptoms of STDs include the following in the genital region:
  - Itching
  - Fluid discharge
  - Slight pain
  - Swellings
- These infections could be avoided or prevented by the following practices:
  - Avoiding sex with unknown or many partners.
  - Use of condoms every time while engaging in coitus.
  - Seeking medical help in case of any doubt and getting it completely cured.

Test 1

Syllabus: Mendelian Inheritance- I; Deviations from Mendelism- Incomplete dominance, Co-dominance, Multiple alleles and Inheritance of blood groups, Pleiotropy.

NCERT Page 53-62, 69

For deeper insight, **Scan the QR Code**

Principle of Inheritance and Variation

- **Heredity**-Transfer of characters from parents to their offspring. **Inheritance** controlled by factors, now called genes.
- **Variation** is the degree by which progeny differs from their parents.

Genetic Terms

- **Gene**- Unit of DNA responsible for the appearance and inheritance of character.
- **Allelomorph or allele** A pair of genes that control the two alternatives of the same character.
- **Heterozygous** Two different alleles for a particular character, e.g. Tt.
- **Homozygous** Two similar alleles for a particular character, e.g. TT or tt.
- **Gene locus** Region on chromosome representing a single gene.
- **Dominant** Two contrasting genes or alleles, but only one of the two is able to express itself.
- **Recessive** Two contrasting genes or alleles but another remain hidden.
- **Genotype** Sum total of genes inherited from both the parents.
- **Phenotype** The appearance of an individual.
- **Genome** Total set of genes in the haploid set of chromosomes.
- **Gene pool** The genotypes of all organisms in a population.
- **Back cross** The breeding of F_1-generation with one of its parent plants. **Reciprocal cross** Cross in which sex of parents are reversed.
- **Test cross** Cross between an individual (with dominant phenotype) of unknown genotypes and recessive parent.

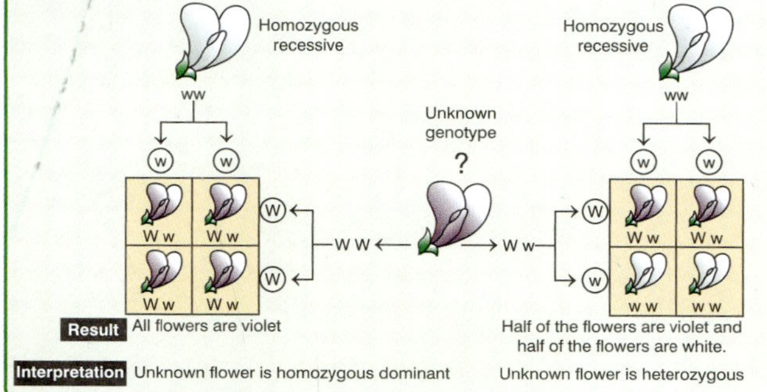

Monohybrid Cross

Cross in which single pair of contrasting traits of a character is involved.

Parental Generation: TT × tt; Gametes: T, t

F_1 Generation

Genotype	All are Tt.
Phenotype	All are tall

Tt X (Mating) Tt; Gametes: T t, T t → TT, Tt, Tt, tt

F_2 Generation

Genotype	TT : Tt : tt = 1 : 2 : 1
Phenotype	Tall:Dwarf = 3:1

TT, Tt, Tt, tt

Incomplete Dominance

Red Flower RR × White Flower rr → Pink Flower (Rr) (F_1)

1Red : 2Pink : 1White (F_2)

Pink Flower Rr × Pink Flower Rr

	R	r
R	RR	Rr Pink Flower
r	Rr Pink Flower	rr White Flower

Mendel's Law

Law of Dominance
- Expression of only one of parental character in F_1.
- Occurrence of **3 : 1** ratio in F_2 individual.

Law of Segregation (Law of purity of gametes)
- Alleles of a pair segregate from each other such that gamete receives only one of the two factors.

Law of Independent Assortment
- Two pairs of traits are combined in a hybrid.
- Segregation of one pair of character is independent of the other pair of characters.

Deviation from Mendelism

Incomplete Dominance
- Both alleles are partially expressed, resulting in intermediate or distinct phenotype; Dog flower (Snapdragon or *Antirrhinum* sp).
- 1:2:1 for Red : Pink : White.

Co-dominance
- Both alleles express simultaneously, i.e. AB blood group.
- I gene controls sugar polymer of RBCs.
- Multiple alleles : ABO blood grouping.
- Genotype-6
- Phenotype-4

Pleiotropy
- A single gene can exhibit multiple phenotypic expression.
- In garden pea, pleiotropic gene controls-flower colour, seed coat.

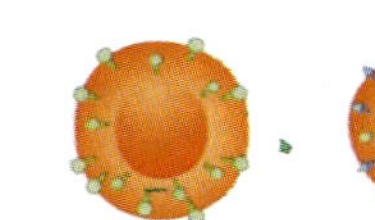
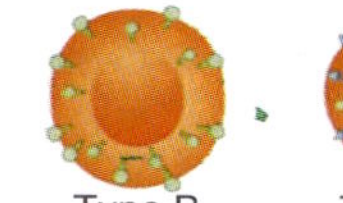
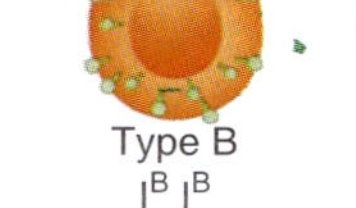
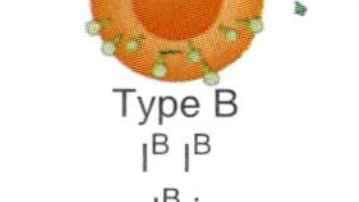
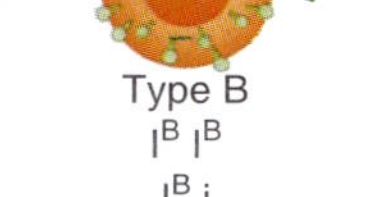
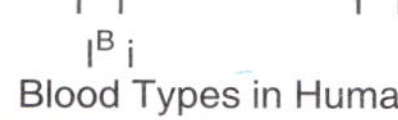

Type A: $I^A I^A$, $I^A i$ | Type B: $I^B I^B$, $I^B i$ | Type AB: $I^A I^B$ | Type O: i i

Blood Types in Humans

Mendel's Experiment

Character	Seed form	Seed colour	Pod form	Pod colour	Flower color	Flower position	Stem length
Dominant	Round	Yellow	Inflated	Green	Violet	Axial	Tall
Recessive	Wrinkled	Green	Constricted	Yellow	White	Terminal	Short

- Gregor Johann Mendel is known as the Father of Genetics. He conducted hybridisation experiments on garden peas for seven years (1856-1863) and proposed the laws of inheritance.
- Mendel conducted artificial pollination/cross pollination experiments using several true-breeding pea lines (plants that show the stable trait inheritance and expression for several generations).
- He chose seven different **alleles** (pair of contrasting characters).
- The flowers here in this plant were bisexual.
- Cross-pollination can be effortlessly conducted in this plant.
- They follow the self-pollination process.
- This plant has a briefer lifespan.

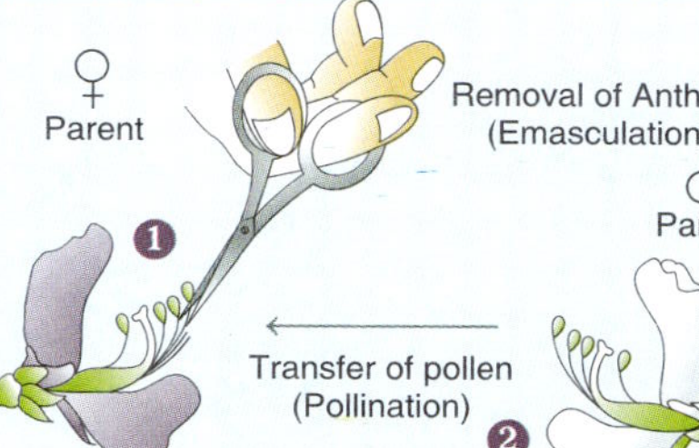

Cross-pollination

Test 2

Syllabus: Mendelian Inheritance- II; Elementary idea of polygenic inheritance; Chromosomal theory of inheritance; Chromosomes and genes; Linkage and crossing over

NCERT Page 62 to 69

For deeper insight, **Scan the QR Code**

Chapter 04

Dihybrid Cross

- A cross in which two pure breeding plants, differing in two characters or two pairs of contrasting traits are crossed.
- A typical dihybrid: seed shape and seed colour.

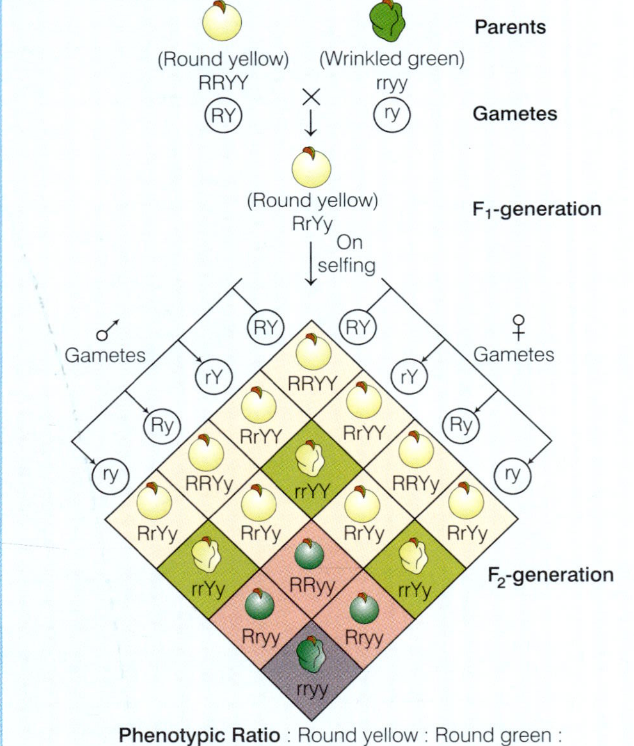

Phenotypic Ratio : Round yellow : Round green : Wrinkled yellow : Wrinkled green = 9 : 3 : 3 : 1

Gene Interaction

- Modification of normal phenotypic expression of a gene due to either its alleles or non-allelic genes.

Interactions	F_2-phenotypic ratio
Dominant epistasis	12 : 3 : 1
Recessive epistasis	9 : 3 : 4
Complementary genes	9 : 7
Supplementary genes	9 : 3 : 4
Duplicate genes	15 : 1
Inhibitor genes	13 : 3

Variation

(Difference found in morphological, physiological, cytological and behavioural traits)

Somatic variations (During life time; somatic cells) due to
- Environmental factors
- Use and disuse of organ
- Conscious effort

Germinal variations (Inheritable variation; germinal cells) due to
- Continuous variation (Recombination)
- Discontinuous variations (Saltation)

Chromosomal Theory

- **Sutton and Boveri** noted that the behaviour of chromosome was parallel to the behaviour of genes.
- **Chromosomal segregation + Mendelian principle**
- Verification of theory done by **Thomas Hunt Morgan** and his colleague.
- Morgan worked on fruit flies, *Drosophila melanogaster*.

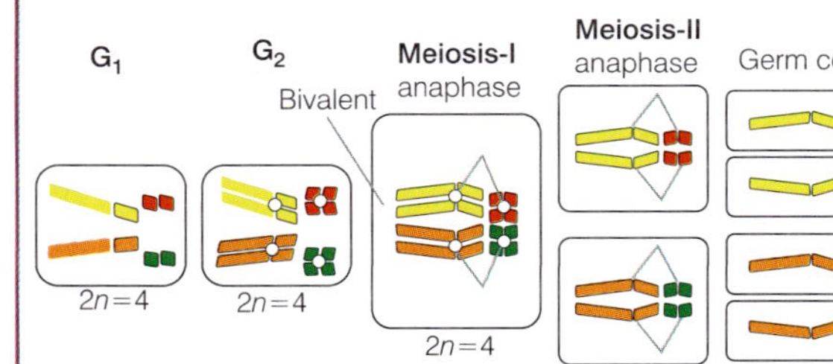

Segregation of homologous chromosomes

- Comparison between the behaviour of chromosome and gene.

Chromosomes	Genes
Occur in pairs.	Occur in pairs.
Segregate at the time of gamete formation such that only one of each pair is transmitted to a gamete.	Segregate at gamete formation and only one of each pairs is transmitted to a gamete.
Independent pairs segregate independently of each other.	One pair segregates independently of another pair.

Polygenic Inheritance

Inheritance controlled by three or more genes is called **polygenic inheritance,** i.e. skin colour, kernel colour in wheat, etc.

Parent: aabbcc (very light) × AABBCC (very dark)

F_1 - generation: AaBbCc × AaBbCc

F_2 - generation: aabbcc 1/64, 6/64, 15/64, 20/64 AaBbCc, ... AABBCC

Skin color

Linkage and Recombination

- **Linkage** Tendency of genes staying together (parental combination)

Types of linkage

Complete linkage
Genes located closely; No separation during crossing over

Incomplete linkage
Genes separate during crossing over

- **Recombination/ Crossing over** : Non- parental combination
- **Alfred Sturtevant** used frequency of recombination
  1 map unit = 1% of crossing over
- 1 **map unit** is now referred as cM (**Centi Morgan**)

Wild type ♀ × Black vestigial ♂

Parental genotypes — Recombinant genotypes

Black vestigial 944 | Wild type 965 | Gray vestigial 206 | Black normal 185

Parental genotypes — Recombinant genotypes

Test 3

Syllabus Sex determination-In humans, birds, honey bee; Sex linked inheritance-Haemophilia colour blindness; Mendelian disorders in humans-Thalassemia; Chromosomal disorders in humans-Down's syndrome, Turner's and Klinefelter's syndromes

NCERT Page 69 to 76

For deeper insight, **Scan the QR Code**

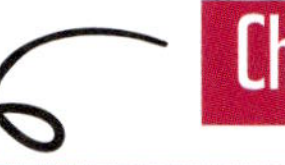

Chapter 04

Mutation

Alternation of DNA sequence: results change in genotype and phenotype.

- **Chromosomal mutation** (Change in number or sequence without any change of ploidy)
  - addition
  - deletion
  - duplication
  - inversion
  - translocation
- **Gene mutation** (Sudden stable change due to change in nucleotide sequence)
  - **Point mutation** (Change in nucleotide sequence)
  - **Frameshift mutation** (Shift in reading frame)

Sex-determination

Method by which distinction between males and female is established.

- In 1891, Henking observed X-body.
- The X and Y-chromosomes are named as **allosome** or sex **chromosomes** and other chromosomes, which determine the somatic characters as **autosomes** (AA).
- Thus, on the basis of the type of allosome present in the gamete, the parents can be of two types
  - Homogametic, i.e. producing similar gametes.
  - Heterogametic, i.e. producing different gametes.
- Genetic sex-determination
  - **XX - XY** type in humans and *Drosophila*.
  - **XX - XO** type in insects.
  - **ZW - ZZ** type in birds
  - **ZO - ZZ** type in moths and butterfly.
  - Haploid diploid method in honeybees.

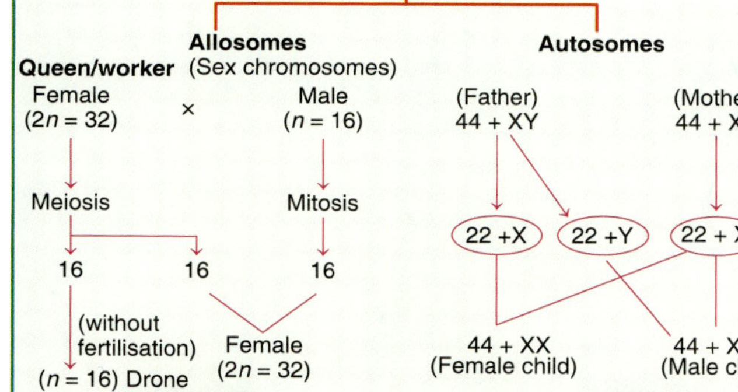

Genetic Disorders

These are disorders or illnesses which are caused by one or more abnormalities in the autosomes or sex chromosomes of the person. Thus, referred to as autosomal disorders or sex-linked disorders, respectively.

Mendelian Disorders

- It is caused due to alteration or mutation in a single gene.
- These are transmitted to offspring following the principles of inheritance. So, these can be traced by pedigree analysis.
- Mendelian disorders may be dominant or recessive.

Disorders	Patterns	Symptoms	Effects
Colour blindness	Sex-linked recessive	Failure to discriminate between red and green colour.	Defect in either red or/and green cone cells of retina.
Haemophilia	Sex-linked recessive	Failure of blood to clot.	Defective form of blood clotting factor VIII/IX.
Sickle-cell anaemia (Substitution of Glu by Val)	Autosomal recessive	Aggregation of erythrocytes, more rapid destruction of erythrocytes leading to anaemia.	Abnormal haemoglobin in RBC's.
Phenylketonuria	Autosomal recessive	Failure of brain to develop in infancy, mental retardation.	Defective form of enzyme phenylalanine hydroxylase.
Thalassemia (α/β)	Autosomal recessive	Leads to anaemia	Abnormal formation of haemoglobin.
Cystic fibrosis	Autosomal recessive	Pulmonary disease, pancreatic malfunction	Failure of chloride ion transport mechanism.

Chromosomal Disorder

- It is caused due to excess, or absence or abnormal arrangement of one or more chromosomes.
- **Aneuploidy** Loss or gain of a chromosome.
- **Polyploidy** Increase in a whole set of chromosome (plants).

Down's syndrome	Autosomal, aneuploidy **(Trisomy+21)**	Retarded mental development, IQ below 40.
Turner's syndrome	Sex chromosomal monosomy, **44+XO**	Sterile, hearing problem.
Klinefelter's syndrome	Sex chromosomal aneuploidy, trisomy of X chromosomes, **44+XXY**	Gynaecomastia, azospermia, sterile
Patau's syndrome	Trisomy at 13	Multiple defects; death by age of 4 months
Edward's syndrome	Trisomy at 18	Ears deformed, heart defect, cleft palate, mental retardation
Cri-du-chat syndrome	Deletion of p arm of chromosome 5	Microcephaly; widely spaced eyes, moon like face, heart disease, cry resemble mewing of a cat

Test 1

Syllabus

Search for genetic material and DNA as genetic material; Structure of DNA and RNA; DNA packaging; DNA replication; Central Dogma

NCERT Page 79 to 91

For deeper insight, **Scan the QR Code**

The Search for Genetic Material

Genetic material: Substance that controls the inheritance of traits from one generation to next generation.

Frederick Griffith	1928	Provide first clear cut evidence that the DNA is the hereditary material while working on *Streptococcus pneumoniae*. Biochemical nature of genetic material was not defined.
Avery, MacLeod and McCarty	1944	Discovered that transforming principle of DNA not a protein or RNA. First identification that DNA is the hereditary material.
Hershey and Chase	1952	Performed experiment with *Escherichia coli* and bacteriophage and showed that it is the viral DNA and not protein that passed from virus to bacteria and therefore DNA serves as the genetic material.

DNA and RNA Structure

There are two types of genetic material:RNA and DNA.

RNA (Some viruses)
- Long polymer of ribonucleotides.
- First genetic material as well as catalyst.

DNA (Most of the organisms)
- Long polymer of deoxyribonucleotides.
- Double helix structure.
- Nucleotide = Nucleoside + Phosphate group

- Type of RNA: Depends on molecular size and function
  - *m*RNA: Messenger Ribonucleic Acid
  - *t*RNA: Transfer Ribonucleic Acid
  - *r*RNA: Ribosomal Ribonucleic Acid

Nitrogenous base
- Purines
  - Adenine
  - Guanine
- Pyrimidines
  - Cytosine
  - Thymine
  - Uracil (only in RNA)

Pentose sugar
- Ribose (RNA)
- Deoxyribose (DNA)

- RNA: A, U, G and C
- DNA: A, T, G and C
- 1 base pair = 2 nucleotides.
- Right handed coiling
- **Pitch** of DNA = 3.4 nm/ 34 Å
- **Chargaff's rule**; Erwin Chargaff (1950) A+T/G+C=1; A=T and G≡C (Hydrogen bond)
- Sugar phosphate backbone.
- **Glycosidic linkage**:Sugar and nitrogenous base
- 3' - 5' phosphodiester linkage : Sugar and phosphate group

- There are many types of DNA, including:
  - A-DNA: Right-handed double helix DNA
  - B-DNA: Right-handed double helix DNA; that is common in most cells
  - C-DNA: Right-handed double helix DNA
  - D-DNA: Lacks the Guanine (G) base unit
  - E-DNA: Eccentric and extended form of DNA
  - Z-DNA: Left-handed double helix DNA with a *zig-zag* pattern

Central Dogma

Francis Crick proposed central dogma; DNA → RNA → Protein
- Replication and transcription occur in the nucleus of eukaryotic cells, or cells with a nucleus, while translation occurs in the cytoplasm outside of the nucleus. Prokaryotic cells, or cells without a nucleus, undergo all three processes in their cytoplasm.

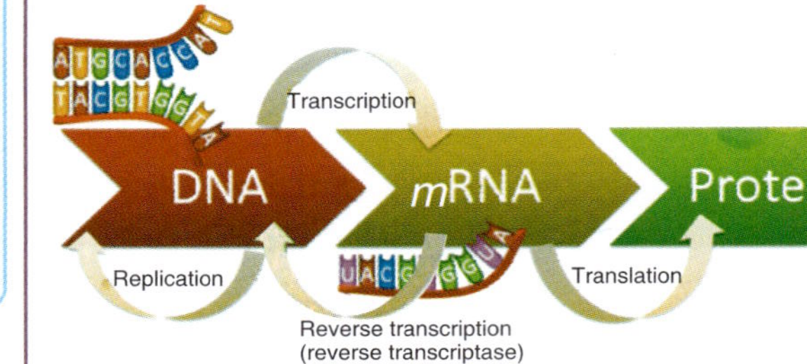

- It displays how information stored in DNA is passed to *m*RNA by the process of transcription and how *m*RNA forms proteins by the method of translation.

Packaging of DNA

DNA length : 2.2 metres (Mammalian cell) ; 1.36 mm (*E. coli*)
- Prokaryotes : DNA + proteins (positively charged)
- Eukaryotes : DNA + Histone (positively charged)
- Histone octamer: H_2A, H_2B, H_3, H_4; linker histone-H_1
- Histones gain hydrophobicity when a methyl group is added to them. This results in DNA packaging that is very tight.
- Acetylation and phosphorylation loosen DNA packing by making it more negatively charged.
- Histone methyltransferases are enzymes that add methyl groups to histones.
- Histone acetyltransferases add acetyl groups to histones, while histone deacetylases remove them.

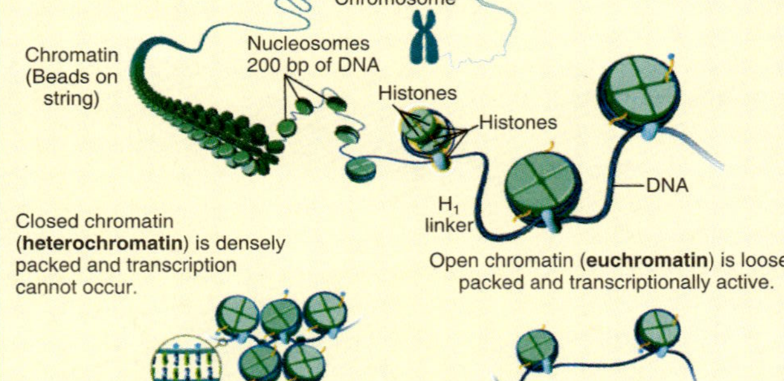

Replication

The mechanism by which exact copies of genetic material are formed.
- Semi-conservative mode of DNA replication proved by **Meselson** and **Stahl** on *E. coli* and **Taylor** on *Vicia faba*.
- DNA replication is a highly enzyme-dependent process. There are many enzymes involved in DNA replication.
- The **DNA-dependent** DNA synthesis; occurs in S-phase of cell cycle.
- **DNA helicase**: at the Replication fork, helicase divides the two DNA strands.
- **DNA polymerase**: During DNA replication, this enzyme catalyses the addition of nucleotide substrates to DNA in the 5' to 3' orientation.
- **Single-stranded binding proteins**: Bind to *ss*DNA to inhibit the DNA double helix from re-annealing after DNA helicase unwinds it.
- **Topoisomerase**: Relaxes the DNA, which is normally super-coiled.
- **Primase:** Synthesises short RNA sequences called primers.
- **DNA Ligase**: Joins okazaki fragments during discontinuous lagging strand synthesis in DNA.

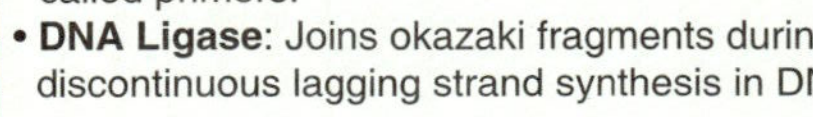

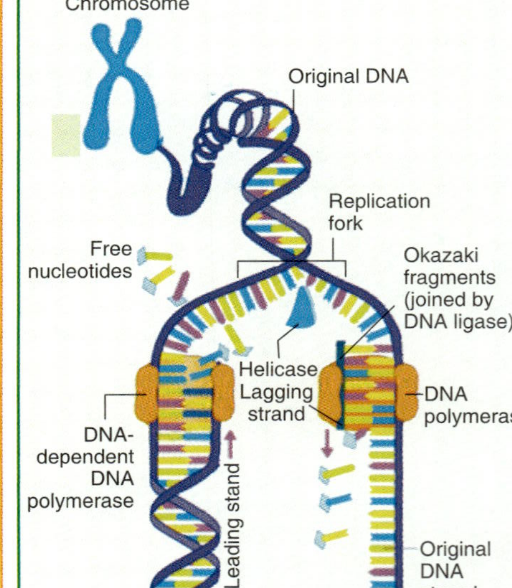

Test 2

Syllabus: Transcription, Genetic code, Translation; Protein biosynthesis

NCERT Page 91 to 99

For deeper insight, **Scan the QR Code**

Chapter 05

Transcription

- Transfer of information from DNA strand to RNA.
- Transcription unit : Promoter, structural gene and terminator.

Promoter | RNA-coding sequence | Terminator

DNA 5′ — 3′ Non-template strand; 3′ — 5′ Template strand

Transcription initiation site | Transcription termination site

Upstream of gene ← | → Downstream of gene

-Eukaryotic RNA polymerase, each with a distinct core structure and specific functions:

- **RNA polymerase-I** transcribes *r*RNAs (28S, 18S and 5.8S)
- **RNA polymerase-II** transcribes *hn*RNA
- **RNA polymerase-III** transcribes *t*RNA, 5*sr*RNA and *sn*RNAs
- **Cistron** : A segment of DNA coding for a polypeptide; Monocistronic (Eukaryotes) and Polycistronic (Prokaryotes or bacteria).

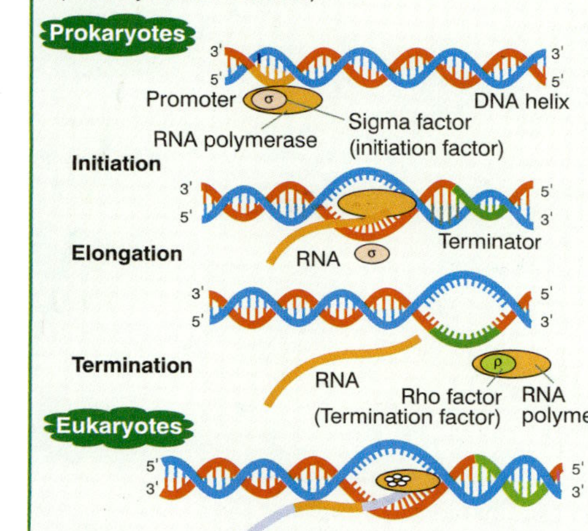

Genetic Code

- The genetic code comprises the complete information of the protein manufactured from RNA.
- The sequence of base pairs of amino acids codes for protein to be synthesised.
- George Gamow (1954) proposed triplet code.
- Marshall Nirenberg, Severo Ochoa, Har Gobind Khorana, Francis Crick and Matthaei deciphered the genetic code.

Salient features

- 61 out of 64 codons code for amino acid with a start codon.
- The genetic code is nearly universal. Minor exceptions exist in protozoans or in mitochondria of mammals, yeast and several other.
- The code is degenerate, i.e. a given amino acid can be specified by more than one codon, e.g. both UUU and UUC codes for phenylalanine.
- **Initiator codon** : AUG (Methionine)
- **Terminator codon** : UAG, UAA, UGA

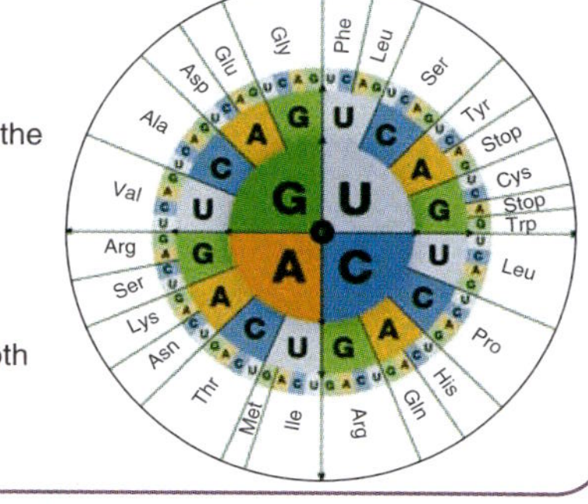

Translation

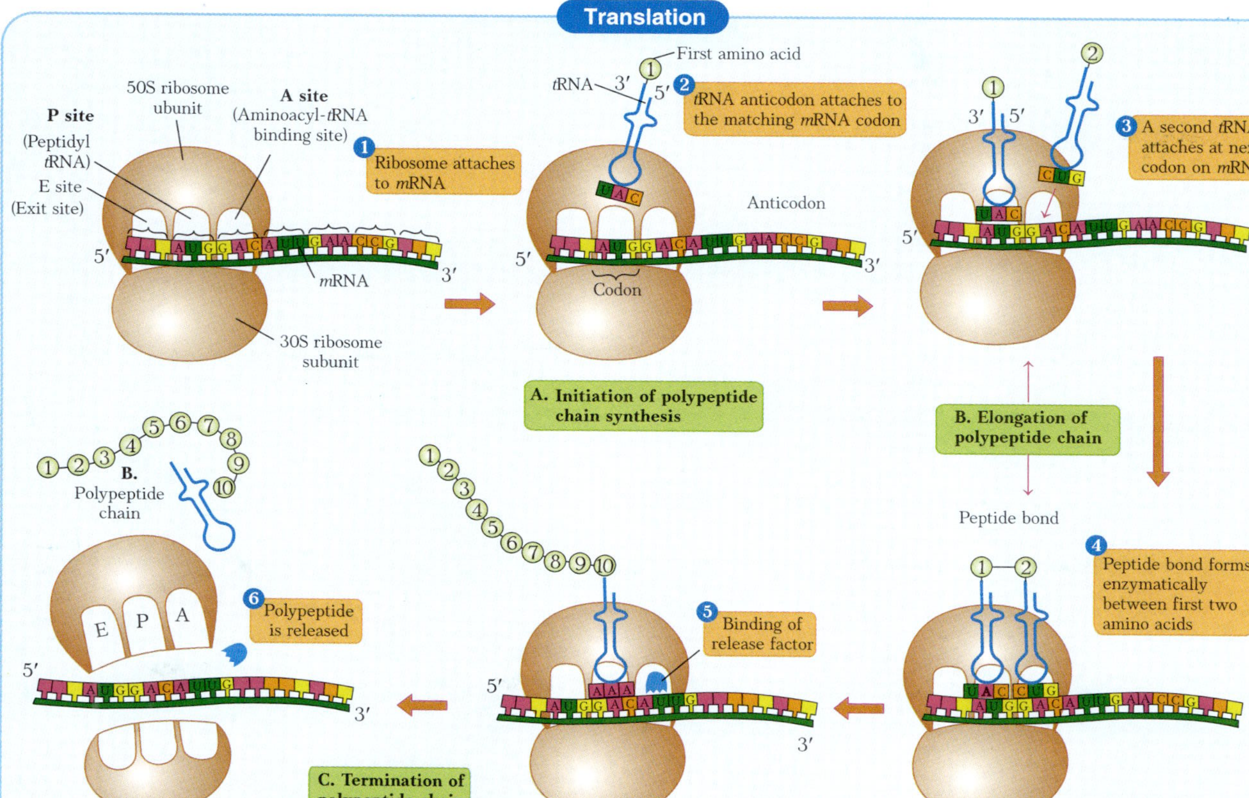

Test 3

Syllabus: Gene expression and regulation- *Lac* operon; Genome and human genome project; DNA fingerprinting

NCERT Page 99 to 107

For deeper insight, **Scan the QR Code**

Chapter 05

Regulation of Gene Expression

- **Gene expression**: Mechanism at the molecular level by which a gene can express itself in the phenotype of an organism.
- **Gene regulation**: Mechanism of switching off and on of the genes depending upon the requirement of the cells and the state of development.
- Two types of regulation: Positive and Negative.
- Gene regulation is exerted at four levels:
  - -Transcriptional level (formation of primary transcript)
  - -Processing level (regulation of splicing)
  - -Transport of *m*RNA (nucleus to cytoplasm)
  - -Translational level

Human Genome Project

- Mega project launched in 1990 and completed in 2003 (13 years).

Goals

- Optimisation of data analysis.
- Sequencing the whole genome.
- Identification of the whole human genome.
- Creating genomic sequence databases for storing the data.
- Taking care of any legal, ethical or social difficulties that the project may raise.

Methodologies

Expressed Sequence Tag (EST; identify gene that expressed as RNA) and sequencing whole set of genome and then assigning different regions with functions (sequence annotation).

- **Commonly used host** Bacteria (BAC) and yeast (YAC).

Features

- Complete genome: 3164.7 million base pairs.
- A gene has an average of 3000 nucleotides.
- More than half of the genes' functions remain unknown.
- Proteins are encoded by less than 2% of the genome.
- The majority of the genome is made up of repeated sequences (satellite DNA).
- 99% of DNA of human population is identical.
- **Longest gene** of human body, Duchenne muscular dystrophy on X-chromosome.
- **Smallest gene** of human body is Testis Determining Factor (TDF).

Applications

- Treatments for both hereditary and acquired diseases.
- Understanding the biological basis of complex disorders.
- Identification of mutations.
- Helps in advancing research in forensic sciences.
- Agriculture, environment and biotechnology.

Lac Operon

- **Prokaryotes : *Lac* Operon**
- Francis Jacob and Jacques Monod; elucidated transcriptionally regulated system.
- **Consist** of Regulatory gene (*i* gene repressor), promoter gene, operator, 3 structural gene (*z, y, a*: polycistronic gene), inducer (lactose or allolactose).

In the absence of inducer

Repressor binds with operator → operator turns OFF → RNA polymerase stops the transcription → structural genes do not produce *lac* *m*RNA and enzymes.

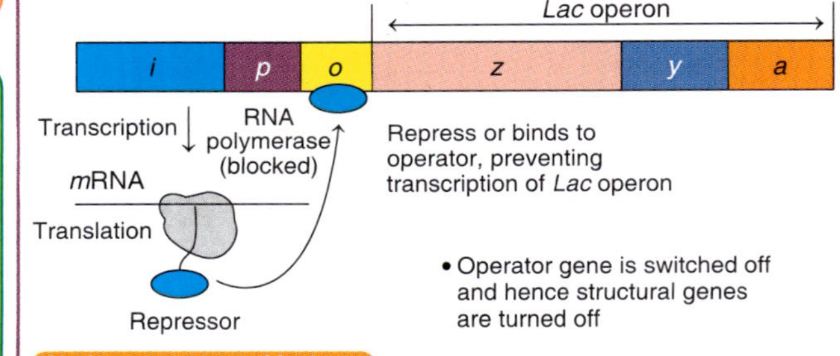

- Operator gene is switched off and hence structural genes are turned off

In the presence of inducer

Repressor binds to inducer → operator turns ON → RNA polymerase starts the transcription.

i p o z y a
Transcription
RNA polymerase (unblocked)
*m*RNA
Translation
lac *m*RNA (polycistron)
Inducer
Inducer-repressor complex does not binds to operator
β-galactosidase (breaks lactose into glucose and galactose)
Permease (helps in transport of metabolites)
Trans-acetylase (transfer acetyl group)

Tryptophan operon

- In this operon, three enzymes are necessary for the synthesis of amino acid, tryptophan. These enzymes are synthesised by the activity of five different genes, i.e. trpA, trpB, trpC, trpD and trpE in coordinated manner.
- The addition of tryptophan, however stops the production of these enzymes.

DNA Fingerprinting

- A chemical test that can be used to determine the genetic makeup of an individual or other living organisms.
- Developed by **Alec Jeffreys**.
- **Principle**: Based on the polymorphism of satellite DNAs; two groups based on the size of the repeats-Variable Number Tandem Repeats (VNTRs) and Short Tandem Repeats (STRs).
- **Application**: Forensic science, paternity testing, insurance claims, research disease remedies, agricultural science and phylogeny.

Process

Extraction of DNA → Amplification → Restriction digestion → Separation of DNA fragments → Southern blotting → Hybridisation → Autoradiography.

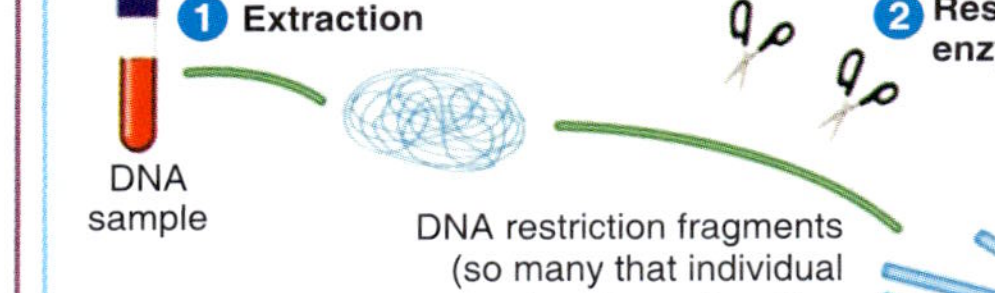

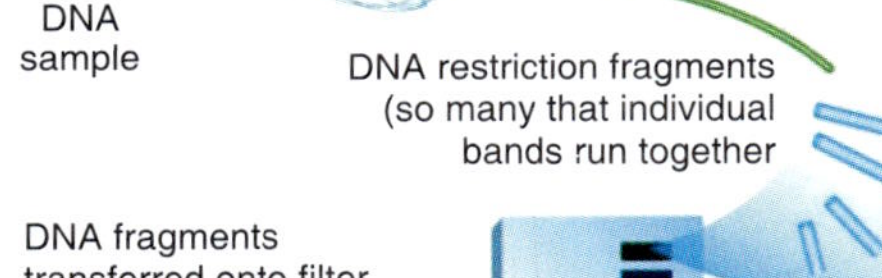

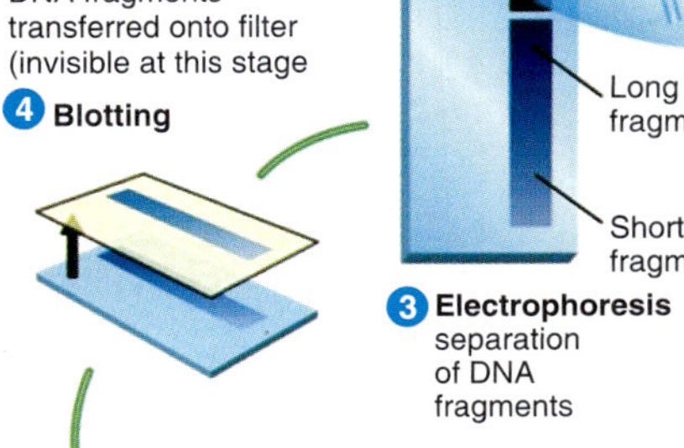

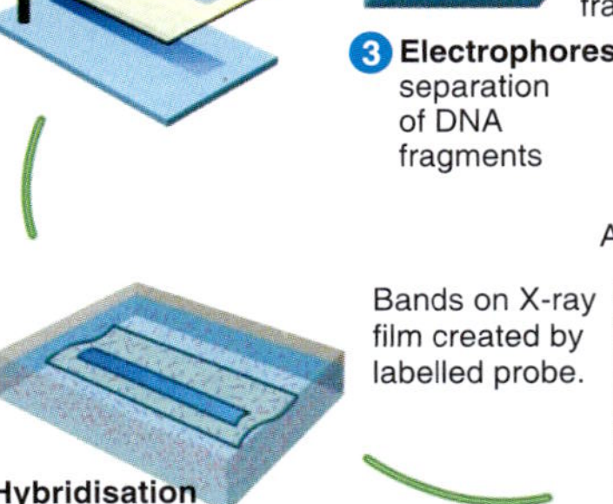

Test 1

Syllabus: Origin of life; Biological evolution and evidences for biological evolution (from Paleontology, comparative anatomy, embryology and molecular biology)

NCERT Page 110 to 115

For deeper insight, **Scan the QR Code**

Theory of Evolution

Ancient

- **Theory of Special Creation**
  These are mythological theories, which believes that the life was created by supernatural powers.
- **Theory of Panspermia**
  Arrhenius (1908) proposed this theory. It also supports the process of living material coming from other planet.
- **Theory of Spontaneous Generation**
  Life originated spontaneously from the non-living decaying and rotting matter like straw and mud.
- **Theory of Biogenesis**
  Life came from pre-existing life. **Louis Pasteur's experiment** disproved the theory of spontaneous generation by performing a well-designed experiment called **Swan-necked flask experiment**.

Modern

- **Theory of Chemical Origin: Oparin** and **Haldane** proposed that first form of life could have come from pre-existing non-living organic molecule.
- **Urey and Miller Experiment Condition :**
  - High temperature
  - Volcanic storms
  - Reducing atmosphere

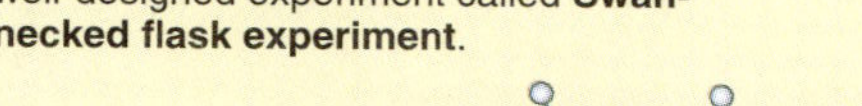

Miller's Experiment

Protocol of Miller's Experiment

Electric discharge and water vapour at 800°C
↓
Spark
↓
Hot gas cooled; dissolved soluble molecule
↓
Organic molecule presence
↓
Artificial atmosphere

Origin of Life

- **Universe** : Big Bang theory (20 bya); huge explosion, hydrogen and helium formed, gas condensed.
- **Milky way** : 14 bya
- **Earth** : 4.5 bya, Primitive earth (no atmosphere); water vapours, CH_4, CO_2, NH_3, released from molten mass.

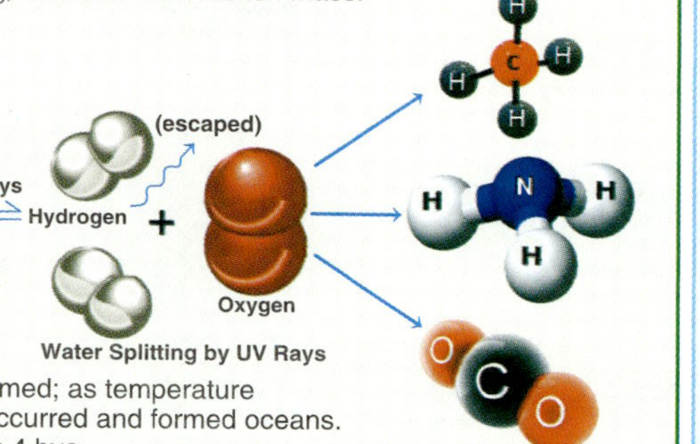

- Ozone layer formed; as temperature dropped, rain occurred and formed oceans.
- **Life appeared** : 4 bya

Evolution of Life Forms

- **Charles Darwin**, during sea voyage (HMS Beagle), concluded that existing living forms share similarities to varying degrees, not only among themselves but also with life forms that existed million of years ago.
- There has been gradual evolution of life forms.
- There were variation in characteristics.
- He referred to fitness as reproductive fitness.
- He implied natural selection as mechanism of evolution.
- **Alfred Wallace** concluded the same; new life forms also came into existence and the existing life forms shows similarities and share common ancestors.
- Geological history of earth closely correlates with the biological history of earth.

Evidences

Palaeontological

- Study of fossil
- Rock arrangement
- Geological time (Eras, Periods and Epochs)
- Radioactive carbon dating; (Concentration of C-14; radioactive content is 50% than living matter).

Embryological Support

'Ontogeny recapitulates phylogeny'

Gill slits, Tail — Fish, Reptile, Bird, Human

Atavism

- It occurs when an ancestral genetic trait reappears in species after being lost.
- E.g. power of moving pinna, larger canine teeth, etc.

Vestigial Organ

- No apparent function and is considered to be residual parts from past ancestors; e.g. coccyx, wisdom tooth, nictitating membrane, appendix, tonsils, etc.

Morphology and Comparative Anatomy

Homologous Organs	Analogous Organs
They have same embryonic origin.	They have different developmental origin.
These are the organs which differ in appearance and function in different organisms but, they have similar basic structure and indicate common ancestry.	These are the organs which are similar in appearance in different organisms but, they develop as different structures in different organisms.
Homology is based on divergent evolution.	Analogy is based on convergent evolution.
e.g. Flipper of seal, wings of a bat, legs of horse and arms of man.	e.g. Insect and bird wings are different in their basic structures and origin.

Test 2

Syllabus: Darwin's contribution, Modern Synthetic theory of Evolution; Mechanism of evolution- Variation (Mutation and Recombination) and Natural Selection with examples, Types of natural selection; Gene flow and genetic drift; Hardy-Weinberg's principle; Adaptive Radiation

NCERT Page 115 to 121

For deeper insight, **Scan the QR Code**

Natural Selection

- The way by which nature selects suitable and the fittest organism for evolution.

Industrial Melanism

Before Industrialisation (unpolluted) more white winged moths

After industrialisation (polluted) more dark winged moths

- **Drug Resistance**
  The drugs that eliminate pathogens become ineffective over time because pathogenic species can tolerate them, survive and flourish to produce tolerant population.
- **Variations** in organisms are caused by mutations or sexual reproduction.

- **Causes of Variation**
  - The mutation is the ultimate source of variation
  - Recombination.
  - The intermingling of two widely separated populations.
  - Due to variations, some individuals would be better adjusted in the surroundings than the others

Property	Lamarckism	Darwinism	Mutation Theory
Natural selection	• The theory does not take into account natural selection or survival of the fittest. • Based on use and disuse of organs	Darwinism is based on natural selection or survival of the fittest. **Two key concept**: Branching descent and natural selection	• Mutations theory believes in natural selection or survival of the fittest. • Based on discontinuous variations or mutations.

Mechanism of Evolution

Hugo de Vries proposed **mutation** theory of evolution, experimented on evening primrose; believed mutation caused **speciation** and called it **Saltation** (Single step large mutation).

Darwinian Evolution	de Vries Mutation
Minor variation	Large variation
Slow and directional	Random, sudden and directionless
Gradual evolution	Speciation by saltation (single step, large mutation)

Synthetic Theory

- Evolution as gene variants in a population that results in the establishment of a new species.
- According to synthetic theory; there are five basic factors involved in the process of organic evolution, these are:
  - Gene mutations
  - Changes in the chromosome structure and number
  - Genetic recombinations
  - Natural selection
  - Reproductive isolation

Hardy-Weinberg Principle

- The frequency of occurrence of alleles of a gene on a locus using algebraic expression.
- Principle states that allele frequencies in a population are stable and is constant from generation to generation.
- Gene pool remains constant (Genetic equilibrium).

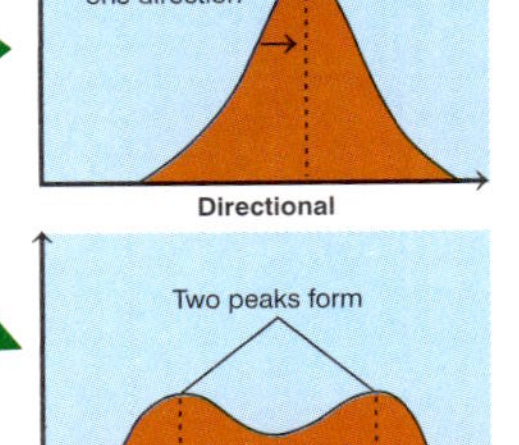

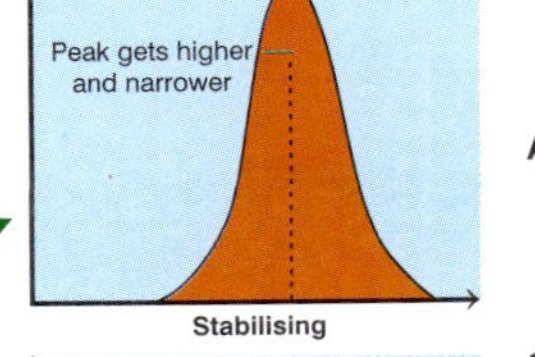

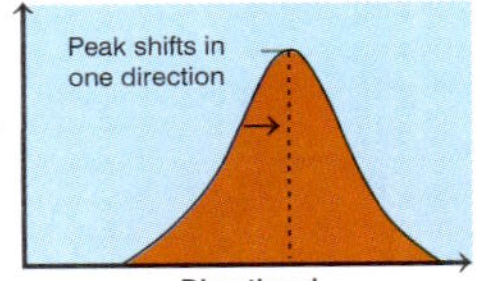

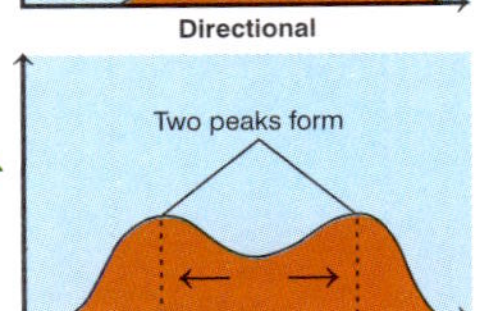

$(p+q)^2=p^2+2pq+q^2=1$

Frequency of allele 'A' = p
Frequency of allele 'a' = q
Frequency of population with 'AA' = p^2
Frequency of population with 'Aa' = $2pq$
Frequency of population with 'aa' = q^2

Principle: A large population where individuals mate randomly, the frequencies of genotypes and alleles remain stable from one generation to the next unless evolutionary forces act upon them.

Assumptions
- Large population size
- Random mating
- No selection
- No migration

Significance
- The genetic composition of a population remains stable through generations under certain conditions.
- Key aspects of the Hardy-Weinberg principle
  - Predicting genetic variation
  - understanding evolution

Applications
- Estimating genetic variation
- Understanding disease prevalence
- Conservation genetics
- Studying migration patterns
- Testing population structure

Adaptive Radiation

Evolution of different species in a given geographical area starting from a point and literally radiating to other areas of geography.

Darwin Finches
(Small black bird)
- Darwin realised there were many varieties of finches in Galapagos Island.
- Original seed eating beak.

(Altered beak arose)
- Insectivorous
- Vegetarian

Warbler Finch, Woodpecker Finch, Small Insectivorous Tree Finch, Large Insectivorous Tree Finch, Vegetarian Tree Finch, Cactus Ground Finch, Sharp-Beaked Ground Finch, Small Ground Finch, Medium Ground Finch, Large Ground Finch

Placental Mammals
- In Australia, placental mammals also exhibit adaptive radiation in evolving into varieties; similar to marsupials.
- e.g. Tasmanian wolf and placental wolf.

Australian Marsupials
- Within Australian island continent.
- Marsupials different from each other and from an ancestral stock.

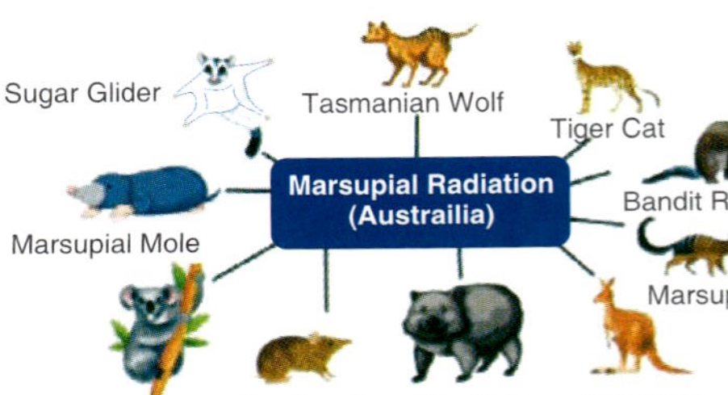

Test 3

Syllabus

- Evolution of Plants and Animals
- Human Evolution

NCERT Page 121 to 125

For deeper insight, **Scan the QR Code**

Chapter 06

Brief Account of Evolution

1st cellular life : 2 bya
Invertebrates : 500 mya
Jawless fishes : 350 mya
Sea weeds and few plants : 320 mya
Reptiles : 200 mya (*Ichthyosaurus*)
Dinosaur disappeared : 65 mya

- Lobe fins evolved into first amphibians.
- Amphibians evolved into reptiles, Giant ferns forms coal deposits slowly.
- *Tyrannosaurus rex* : 20 feet height and dagger like teeth.
- First mammals were like shrews.
- Mammals were viviparous.

Evolution of Plants

Cenozoic
Quaternary
Tertiary
Mesozoic
Cretaceous
Jurassic
Triassic
Paleozoic
Permian
Carboniferous
Devonian
Silurian
Bryophytes
Herbaceous lycopods
Arborescent lycopods
Sphenopsids (horsetails)
Ferns
Ginkgos
Conifers
Gnetales
Cycads
Dicotyledons
Angiosperms (flowering plants)
Monocotyledons
Seed ferns
Progymnosperms
Zosterophyllum
Psilophyton
Rhynia-type plants
Tracheophyte ancestors
Chlorophyte ancestors

Evolution of Animals

- Invertebrates or lower animals had formed around 500 million years ago and were active. These invertebrates evolved into vertebrates with the course of time in the following ways
Fish → Amphibians → Reptiles → Mammals

Quaternary 0
Tertiary 50
Cretaceous 100
Jurassic 150
Triassic 200
Permian 250
Carboniferous 300
350
Turtles
Lizards
Snakes
Tuataras
Crocodiles
Birds
Mammals
Dinosaurs (extinct)
Therapsids (extinct)
Thecodonts (extinct)
Pelycosaurs (extinct)
Sauropsids
Synapsids
Early reptiles (extinct)

Origin of Eukaryotes

Invagination-Cell organelles were formed by the invagination of the membranes of primitive prokaryotic cell.

Symbiotic-Prokaryotic bacteria established themselves as host into a cell, thus later become first eukaryotic cell.

Origin of Prokaryotes

Organic molecules
↓
Coacervates
↓
Eobionts or protocells
↓
First Living cell

Evolution of modes of Nutrition

↓
Heterotrophs
↓
Autotrophs
↓
Chemoautotrophs
↓
Photoautorophs

Evolution of Man

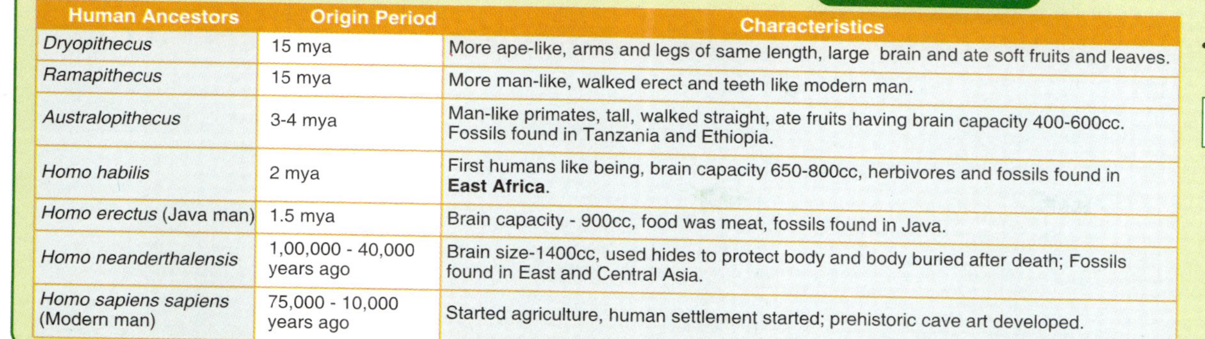

Human Ancestors	Origin Period	Characteristics
Dryopithecus	15 mya	More ape-like, arms and legs of same length, large brain and ate soft fruits and leaves.
Ramapithecus	15 mya	More man-like, walked erect and teeth like modern man.
Australopithecus	3-4 mya	Man-like primates, tall, walked straight, ate fruits having brain capacity 400-600cc. Fossils found in Tanzania and Ethiopia.
Homo habilis	2 mya	First humans like being, brain capacity 650-800cc, herbivores and fossils found in **East Africa**.
Homo erectus (Java man)	1.5 mya	Brain capacity - 900cc, food was meat, fossils found in Java.
Homo neanderthalensis	1,00,000 - 40,000 years ago	Brain size-1400cc, used hides to protect body and body buried after death; Fossils found in East and Central Asia.
Homo sapiens sapiens (Modern man)	75,000 - 10,000 years ago	Started agriculture, human settlement started; prehistoric cave art developed.

- The chronological order of human evolution (from early to the recent) is

Dryopithecus (Ape-like) → *Ramapithecus* (Man-like) → *Australopithecus* → *Homo habilis* (Human like) → *Homo erectus* (Java man) → *Homo neanderthalensis* (Neanderthal man - Primitive man) → *Homo sapiens sapiens* (Modern man)

- Cro-Magnon man had highest cranial capacity, i.e. 1650 cc.

Test 1

Syllabus Health and Diseases; Pathogens; Parasites causing human diseases (Malaria, Filariasis, Ascariasis, Typhoid, Pneumonia, Common Cold, Amoebiasis, Ring Worm, Dengue, Chikungunya)

NCERT Page 129 to 134

For deeper insight, **Scan the QR Code**

Human Health

Health: A state of complete physical, mental and social well-being.

Affected by
- **Genetic disorders** (Inborn disease and inherited from parents)
- **Infection**
- **Life style**

Both health and disease together contribute to the state of entire well-being. Diseases can be classified into these types:

-**Congenital diseases** (diseases present by birth) e.g. haemophilia, colour blindness, down's syndrome, Turner's syndrome, etc.

-**Acquired diseases** (diseases acquired during a lifetime)

-**Infectious or contagious diseases** (transmitted from one person to another)

-**Non-communicable diseases** (diseases do not spread by infection)

-**Deficiency disease** (diseases are caused by deficiency of an important nutrient, enzyme or hormone) e.g. anaemia, kwashiorkor, beri-beri, diabetes, etc.

Viral Diseases

Diseases	Causative Agents
Mumps	Mumps virus
Common Cold*	Rhinovirus (and various other viruses)
Rabies	Rabies virus
Encephalitis	Various viruses, including herpes simplex virus, West Nile virus, etc.
Dengue fever	Dengue virus
Smallpox	Variola virus (now eradicated)
Chickenpox	Varicella zoster virus
AIDS	Human Immunodeficiency Virus (HIV)
Measles	Measles virus
Chikungunya	Chikungunya virus

* Common cold does not infect lungs.

Protozoan Diseases

Malaria	*Plasmodium* parasite (e.g. *Plasmodium falciparum*)
Amoebic dysentery	*Entamoeba histolytica* (*Amoeba*)
Sleeping sickness	*Trypanosoma brucei* (parasitic protozoan)
Kala azar	*Leishmania donovani* (parasitic protozoan)

Fungal Diseases

Ringworm	*Trichophyton, Micosporum* and *Epidermophyton*
Candidiasis	*Candida oesophagitis*

Mode of Transmission

- **Air** (droplet/aerosol) or object borne : Pneumonia, diphtheria, common cold, small pox.
- **Direct contact** : Tetanus, small pox
- **Contaminated food and water** : Typhoid, dysentery, polio, amoebiasis, ascariasis.
- **Insect/vector* borne** : Plague, chikungunya, dengue, malaria, filariasis
- **Body fluids** : Syphilis, AIDS, Trichomoniasis.

* **Vector** : Transmits disease from one organisms to another e.g. female *Aedes* mosquito is the vector for dengue and chikungunya, while *Anopheles* spreads malaria.

Bacterial Diseases

Diseases	Causative agents
Cholera	*Vibrio* (*Vibrio cholerae*)
Pneumonia	*Diplococcus pneumoniae*
Typhoid* **Diagnostic test:** Widal test	*Salmonella typhi*
Tetanus **Treatment:**Antitetanus serum	*Clostridium tetani*
Diphtheria **Treatment:**DPT vaccine	*Corynebacterium diphtheriae*
Whooping cough	*Bordetella pertussis*
Tuberculosis **Treatment:**Bacillus Calmette-Guerin (BCG)	*Mycobacterium tuberculosis*
Plague	*Pasteurella pestis*
Leprosy	*Mycobacterium leprae*
Syphilis	*Treponema pallidum*
Gonorrhoea	*Neisseria gonorrhoeae*
Diarrhoeal Diseases	*Escherichia coli, Shigella dysenteriae, Campylobacter*
Anthrax	*Bacillus anthracis*
Dysentery (Shigellosis)	*Shigella dysenteriae*

*Mary Mallon-typhoid carrier

Helminthic Diseases

Ascariasis	*Ascaris lumbricoides*
Filariasis or Elephantiasis	*W. bancrofti* and *W. malayi*

The Life Cycle of *Plasmodium* (Malarial Parasite)

Malaria: It is caused by a tiny protozoan, called *Plasmodium*. Female *Anopheles* mosquito is the vector of this protozoan. Four different species of *Plasmodium viz. P. vivax, P. ovale, P. malariae* and *P. falciparum* are responsible for causing different types of malaria.

The Life Cycle of *Plasmodium*

- *Plasmodium* enters the body by the bite of female *Anopheles* mosquitoes.
- The infectious form is sporozoites, which come from the saliva of female *Anopheles* when they bite.
- It multiplies in the liver cells and then attacks RBCs resulting in RBCs rupture.
- Haemozoin, a toxic substance gets released.
- The gametocyte produced in the human blood gets transferred to the mosquito when it bites an infected person.
- Macro and micro-gametocytes undergo fertilisation, transformation and sporogenesis in the mosquito's intestine and sporozoites are formed.
- Sporozoites migrate to the salivary gland of mosquitoes and the cycle is repeated.
- *Plasmodium* sp. needs human and female *Anopheles* mosquitoes to complete their life cycle.

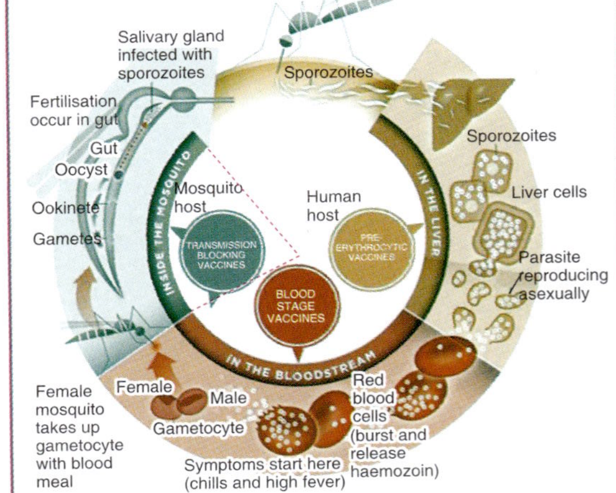

Malarial Cycle

Treatment: Chloroquine is the most commonly used drug to treat malaria. Artemisinin based combination therapy is recommended for treatment of *P. falciparum* malaria.

Test 2

Syllabus Basic Concepts of Immunology; Vaccines

NCERT Page 134 to 138

For deeper insight, **Scan the QR Code**

Immunity

- Ability of host to fight the disease causing organisms, conferred by the immune system

-**Father of Immunology**: Edward Jenner

Innate Immunity
- Non-specific
- An individual is born with all the barriers.
- Protect the individual.

Physical barriers	Skin, mucous coating of the epithelium lining the respiratory, gastrointestinal and urogenital tract.
Physiological barriers	Acid in the stomach, saliva in the mouth, tears from eyes.
Cellular barriers	Leucocytes such as PMNL, neutrophils; monocytes; macrophages and natural killer cells.
Cytokine barriers	e.g. interferons.

Acquired Immunity
- The immunity a person acquires after birth.
- It can be acquired by either suffering from the disease or artificially, i.e, by vaccination.
- It is specific (pathogen specific).

Cells of the Immune System
- Lymphocytes are agranulocytes in the foetus; they are produced by the liver and spleen and in the adults; they are produced by the bone marrow and lymph nodes.
- There are two types of lymphocytes:
  - B-lymphocytes
  - T-lymphocytes
- Both the lymphocytes need stimulation by specific antigens to trigger them to respond.

Allergies

Exaggerated response of immune system to certain antigens present in the environment.

The responses to the foreign substance are of two types:

(i) Immediate allergic responses: Cold like symptoms, due to the activity of antibodies.

(ii) Delayed allergic responses: Produced due to the activity of T-cells such as contact dermatitis.

Allergens – Substances to which exaggerated immune response is produced, e.g. pollens, mites in dust, animal dander, etc.

Antibodies – IgE type

Symptoms – Sneezing, watery eyes, running nose, difficulty in breathing

Chemical released Histamine and serotonin from mast cell.

Treatment Anti-histamine, adrenaline and steroids quickly reduce the symptoms of allergy.

Lymphocytes

B cells → **Humoral immune response** → Antibodies or Immunoglobulins e.g. IgA, IgM, IgE, IgG, IgD

T cells → **Cell-mediated immunity** → Responsible for graft rejection.

Antigen binding site
Variable region
Antigen
Disulphide bond
Light chain
Constant region
Hinge region
Heavy chain

- Two chains exist in antibodies - a Variable Chain and a Constant Chain.

Immunoglobulins/ Antibodies
- Antibodies are made up of four different polypeptides (Polymer of Amino Acids) chains.
- Two Heavy Chain (H) and Two Light Chain (L), collectively called H_2L_2.
- These two chains are joined by disulfide chains, which form a Y-shaped structure.

Immune Response

Primary Response
- Body encounters pathogen for first time
- Slow response

Secondary/Anamnestic Response
- Encounters same pathogen again
- Fast response

Blood Antibody Level
Primary Immune Response
Immunological Memory
Secondary Immune Response
IgG
IgM
0
14
28
42
56
Days →
First Ag exposure
Second Ag exposure
(Ag-antigen)

Vaccine & Immunisation

Vaccine Introduction of vaccine into an individual to provide protection against a disease; extract of dead/attenuated pathogen.

Immunisation Body produces antibodies against the vaccine preventable disease through administration of specific vaccines.

Active Immunity	Passive Immunity
Host exposed to antigens (dead or living microbes or protein).	Ready made antibodies directly given.
Slow and long lasting.	Fast and lasts only for few weeks or months
e.g. vaccination	Colostrum (yellowish fluid ; IgA rich).

Auto-immunity

These diseases occur when immune system fails to recognise 'self' molecules and starts destroying body's own proteins. This condition may cause chronic and serious diseases.

For examples, insulin-dependent diabetes, multiple sclerosis, rheumatoid arthritis, etc.

Immune System in the Body

Human immune system consists lymphoid organs, tissues, cells and antibodies.

Lymphoid organs Organs where origin and/or maturation and proliferation of lymphocyte occur.

Primary Lymphoid Organ

Bone Marrow Main lymphoid organs : Blood cells and lymphocytes are produced.

Thymus Lobed organ; near heart beneath breast bone, reduce in size with age.

Secondary Lymphoid Organ
- Spleen (Large reservior of erythrocytes)
- Lymph nodes (trap micro organisms)
- Peyer's patches of small intestine, appendix.

Thymus

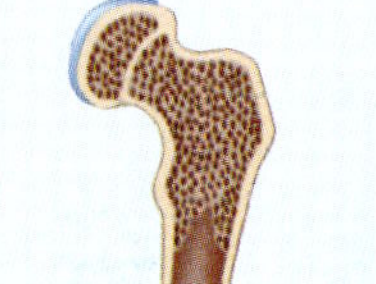
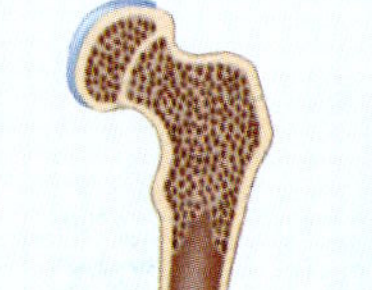
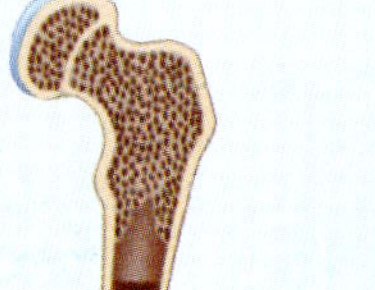

Bone Marrow

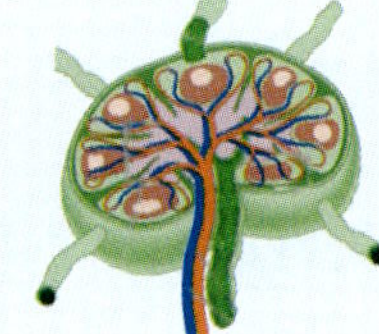

Lymphatic Lobe

- **Lymphoid tissue** Within the lining of the major tracts (respiratory, digestive and urogenital tract) called **MALT** (Mucosa Associated Lymphoid Tissue; 50% of lymphoid tissue).

Test 3

Syllabus Cancer; HIV-AIDS; Adolescence, Drug and Alcohol abuse, Tobacco abuse.

NCERT Page 138 to 147

For deeper insight, **Scan the QR Code**

Cancer

An uncontrolled proliferation of cells without any differentiation; shows no contact inhibition.

Tumour (Masses of Cell)

Benign Tumour
Remains confined to their location, cause little damage.

Malignant Tumour
Neoplastic cell, grows very rapidly, invading and damaging surrounding normal tissue (metastasis).

Proliferating cancer cells
Normal cells
Basement layer
Metastasis

Causes of cancer agent Carcinogens
- Ionizing radiation (X-rays and gamma rays)
- Non-ionizing radiation (UV rays)
- Oncogenic virus
- Cellular oncogenes
- Tobacco smoke

Detection
- Biopsy
- Histopathological studies

Treatment
- Immunotherapy
- Biological modifiers (α-interferon)
- Chemotherapy
- Radiation therapy

Drugs

Addictive substances or habituating substances.

Drugs	Source	Examples
Opioids	Latex of poppy plant, *Papaver somniferum*	Morphine, heroin/smack (Diacetylmorphine)
Cannabinoids	Inflorescence, flower tops, leaves and resin of *Cannabis* plant	Charas, hashish, ganja, marijuana
Stimulants	Coca plant, *Erythroxylum coca* (Native of South America)	Cocaine, coka, alkaloid, commonly called coke/crack
Hallucinogens	*Atropa belladonna*	Atropine
Other drugs	Synthetic	Barbiturates, benzodiazepines, amphetamines

Smoking

Tobacco is smoked, chewed or used as a snuff.

Nicotine $\xrightarrow{\text{stimulates}}$ Adrenal gland $\xrightarrow{\text{releases}}$ Adrenaline and nor-adrenaline
↓
Raise blood pressure and heart rate.

AIDS

- AIDS (Acquired Immuno Deficiency Syndrome) is caused by Human Immunodeficiency Virus (HIV; retrovirus).
- Incubation period : 6 months to 10 years.

1. The glycoproteins spike enables the virus to attach the specific receptors on certain WBCs.
2. The virus infiltrates the macrophages and releases viral proteins and RNA inside the cell.
3. Reverse transcriptase facilitates the production of a DNA strand that is complementary to the viral RNA.
4. Reverse transcriptase initiates the synthesis of a second DNA strand complementary to the first one.
5. The viral DNA gets incorporated as a provirus into the host cell's DNA.
6. Proviral genes are transcribed into RNA molecules, serving as both genomes for progeny viruses and as template for translation into viral protein.
7. The capsid proteins and reverse transcriptase are synthesised (made in the cytosol and envelope glycoproteins are produced in the ER).
8. The glycoproteins are transported to the cell's plasma membrane by vesicles.
9. Capsids are formed around viral genomes and reverse transcriptase enzymes.
10. New viruses, containing viral envelope glycoproteins, bud from the host cell.

Viral envelope
Capsid
RNA (two identical strands)
HIV
Glycoprotein
Reverse transcriptase
Host cell
Viral capsid proteins
Reverse transcriptase
Viral RNA
RNA-DNA hybrid
DNA
Nucleus
Provirus
Chromosomal DNA
RNA genome for the progeny viruses
mRNA

Adolescence and Drug/Alcohol Abuse

Adolescence period : 12-18 years
Addiction : Physiological attachment to certain effects such as euphoria.
Withdrawal syndrome : If regular dose of drugs/alcohol is abruptly discontinued.
Effects : More likely to acquire serious infections; damages nervous system and liver **(cirrhosis).**
Prevention : Avoid undue peer pressure, education and counselling, seek help from parents and peers, looking for danger signs.

Test 1

Syllabus: Microbes in household food processing and Industrial production

NCERT Page 149 to 153

For deeper insight, **Scan the QR Code**

Microorganisms

- All organisms that are microscopic, and cannot be seen with the naked eye are referred to as **microorganisms**.
- Microbes are cosmopolitan; present even in thermal vents (100°C), deep within the soil, below the layers of snow and in extremely acidic environments.
- Microbes are diverse-protozoa, bacteria, fungi, microscopic animal and plant viruses, viroids and additionally prions that are proteinaceous infectious agents.
- Microbes like bacteria and various fungi can be grown on nutritive media to make custom colonies directly or in fermented form.

Microbes in Household Products

- **LAB (Lactic Acid Bacteria)** grows in milk and converts it into curd; partially digest milk protein at sustainable temperature; increases vitamin-B_{12} and improve the nutritional quality of curd. It also plays beneficial role in checking pathogenic microbes.
- **Baker's Yeast** (*Saccharomyces cerevisiae*) causes fermentation and produces carbon dioxide.

Dough

- Foods like **idli** and **dosa** are prepared using dough fermented by bacteria like *Leuconostoc* and *Streptococcus* species.
- The puffed up appearance of the dough is due to the production of CO_2 gas during fermentation.
- **Toddy**
  A traditional drink prepared by fermenting palm sap using microbes.
- **Swiss Cheese**
  Large holes due to CO_2 production by bacterium, *Propionibacterium shermanii*.
- Roquefort cheese (greenish blue mottling) ripened by *Penicillium roqueforti*.
- Camembert cheese employs *Penicillium camemberti* for ripening.
- Microbes are also used to ferment fish, soybean and bamboo shoots to make food items.
- Soy sauce is brown flavored salty sauce fermented from soybean and wheat.
- Tender bamboo shoots are used as vegetables directly or in fermented form.

Microbes in Industries

Microbes are used in industries to form fermented beverages, antibiotics and other chemicals, enzymes and bioactive molecules.

Microbes	Products	Roles
Aspergillus niger (fungus)	Citric acid	In beverages
Acetobacter (bacterium)	Acetic acid	Preservatives
Lactobacillus (bacterium)	Lactic acid	In making curd
Clostridium butylicum (bacterium)	Butyric acid	Protective role in inflammatory bowel disease
Saccharomyces cerevisiae (fungus)	Ethanol	Disinfectant, fuel
Streptococcus (bacteria)	Streptokinase	Clot buster
Pseudomonas (bacteria)	Lipases	In detergent formulation
Bacillus subtilis	Proteases	Bottle juice
Aspergillus niger	Pectinases	Fruit pulp juice
Monascus purpureus	Statins	Blood cholesterol lowering agent
Trichoderma polysporum (Fungus)	Cyclosporin-A	Immunosuppressive agent

Microbes in Antibiotic Production

- Antibiotics are the chemical substances, produced by some microbes that can kill or retard the growth of other disease causing microbes.
- The first antibiotic was **Penicillin** discovered by **Alexander Fleming**.
- It was commercially extracted by the efforts of Chain and Florey.
- The chemical was extensively used in treating wounded American soldiers in World War II.
- Fleming, Chain and Florey were awarded with Nobel Prize in 1945.
- Antibiotics are obtained from lichens, bacteria, fungi (mostly actinomycetes).

Antibiotics	Sources	Action
Chloramphenicol	*Streptomyces venezuelae*	Typhoid, Whooping cough
Erythromycin	*Streptomyces erythreus*	Diptheria
Chloromycetin	*Streptomyces lavendulae*	Pneumonia
Streptomycin	*Streptomyces griseus*	Meningitis, Pneumonia, TB
Bacitracin	*Bacillus licheniformis*	Syphilis
Terramycin	*Streptomyces rimosus*	Intestinal and urinary infections

Fermentation

Some fermented beverages, their sources and alcohol content.

Beverages	Substrate used	Alcohol concentration
Beer	Barley malt	4-8%
Wine	Fruit juices	10-20%
Whisky	Fermented cereals	50%
Brandy	Fruit juices	60-70%
Rum	Molasses	40%
Gin	Rye malt	30%
Vodka	Potato	60-80%

- It is the oldest microbiological process.
- Fermented beverages including wine, whisky, and brandy, are as old as civilization.
- The most prevalent microbe to use for fermentation is *Saccharomyces cerevisiae* (brewer's yeast).
- Used to manufacture ethanol by fermenting malt-based food products and fruit juices.
- Depending on the fermentation type and raw material used, various alcoholic beverages are produced.
- Whisky, brandy, and rum are manufactured by distillation of fermented broth.
- While, both wine and beer are manufactured by fermentation of plant-based food products.

The steps in alcohol production are as follows:

- Yeast is grown in very large vessels called **fermenters**.
- The fermenter is filled with a nutrient solution such as sugars (e.g. sugarcane, sugarbeets), starches (e.g. grains, potatoes) and cellulose (e.g. wood and paper mill).
- It is then inoculated with a pure culture of yeast.
- Temperature and pH of the media are adjusted and alcohol is produced along with and energy.
- The whole process of breakdown of carbohydrates by yeast into carbon dioxide and alcohol in the absence of oxygen is summarised as follows

$C_6H_{12}O_6$ + Yeast $\rightarrow 2CO_2 + 2C_2H_5OH$ + Energy

Test 2

Syllabus: Microbes in Sewage treatment, energy generation and as biocontrol agents and biofertilizers.

NCERT Page 153 to 158

For deeper insight, **Scan the QR Code**

Chapter 08

Microbes in Sewage Water Treatment

- Sewage contains a huge amount of toxic organic matter.
- Heterotrophic bacteria, which are generally present in wastewater, are required to treat the sewage.
- The sewage treatment procedure is divided into three phases: primary treatment, secondary treatment land tertiary treatment.
- Primary treatment: Manual elimination of small and large particulates via filtration and sedimentation.
- Sequential filtration eliminates debris and then removes the soil and small pebbles.
- The remainder is known as **effluent**.
- Secondary Treatment- Effluent is moved through aeration tanks using continuous aeration.
- Aerobic microbes combine to form flocs.
- **Flocs** (mesh-like structures); association of fungal filaments with masses of bacteria.
- This lowers biological oxygen demand (BOD).
- The higher the BOD, the faster oxygen is exhausted in the stream.
- After the BOD of the sewage is lowered, it is carried to sediment in activated sludge.
- A small portion of activated sludge is pumped back into the aeration tank to serve as inoculum.
- The remaining sludge is poured into large tanks known as anaerobic sludge digesters.
- Tertiary treatment- Final stage; effluent treated for best quality before being discharged to the environment.
- Ensure very high standards of treating the effluents; It reduces the phosphorous and ammoniacal nitrogen.

Primary treatment | Secondary treatment | Tertiary treatment

Coarse Debris Screen

Sewage

Removal of floating debris by sequential filtration

Sand and grit removal by sedimentation

Primary clarification

Primary effluent sludge

Aeration

Formation of flocs; BOD↓

Secondary clarification

Secondary effluent sludge

Activated sludge

Sludge digester

Anaerobic digestion of bacteria and fungi in sludge

Disinfection

Chlorine (Cl_2) or Ultraviolet (UV) light treatment

Nutrient removal

Nitrogen and phosphorus removal

Effluent released into natural water bodies

Sewage Treatment Plant

Microbes in Biogas Production

- Some bacteria growing anaerobically on cellulose material produce large amount of methane (CH_4), along with carbon dioxide and hydrogen. These bacteria are methanogens.
- Methanogens are naturally found in rumen of cattles, cow dung and sewage.

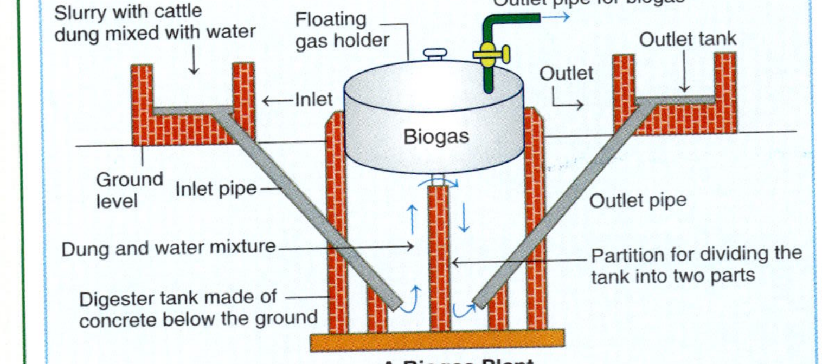

A Biogas Plant

- The technology of biogas production was developed in India by the Indian Agricultural Research Institute (IARI) and the Khadi and Village Industries Commission (KVIC).
- Two types of Biogas plants are present:
  - Fixed dome-shaped Biogas Plant
  - Floating gas-holding Biogas Plant
- **Advantages of Biogas**
  - Biogas can be used as fuel.
  - Biogas burns without smoke, thus preventing air pollution.
  - Biogas can be used to light street lights and driving engines.
  - The spent slurry can be used as manure.

Cellulose, Hemicellulose, Storage polysaccharide, Fats, Proteins

↓ **Solubilisation** — **Decomposer microbes**

Monomers

↓ **Acidogenesis** — **Fermentative microbes**

Organic acids

↓ **Methanogenesis** — **Methanogens** (*Methanococcus*)

Biogas (CH_4, CO_2, H_2, N_2, H_2S)

Stages in Biogas Formation

Microbes as Biocontrol Agents

- **Biocontrol** refers to the use of biological methods for controlling plant diseases and pests.
- **Integrated Pest Management**: Need to not eradicate the pests of the crops but limit them to a number.
- The pests are kept at a manageable level by a complex system of checks and balances within the ecosystem.
- Some insects may be pests for one crop but maybe helpful in pollination and seed sets of the other crops.
- If all the pests are eradicated, then the crops for which they are useful may not be pollinated and would die.
- Ladybird beetle is useful to get rid of aphids and dragonflies to control mosquitoes.
- **Fungus** e.g. *Trichoderma* sp. → Kills root borne pathogens, *Beauveria bassiana* → Controlling insect pests.
- **Bacteria** e.g. *Bacillus thuringiensis* → Kills the pink bollworm attacking *Bt*-cotton by producing an insecticidal 'cry' protein.
- **Viruses** e.g. *Nucleopolyhedrovirus* (Baculoviruses) → attacks specific insects and other arthropods.

Microbes as Biofertilisers

Bacteria
- Fix atmospheric N_2 and enrich soil nutrients

Cyanobacteria
- Enrich organic matter of soil through nitrogen fixation.
- e.g., *Nostoc*, *Anabaena* and *Oscillatoria*.

Fungi
- Form mycorrhizal association to provide better absorption of phosphorus from soil; provides resistance.
- e.g., *Glomus*.

By forming symbiotic relationships
e.g., *Rhizobium* with legumes (nodules)

By free-living existence
e.g., *Azospirillum*

Microbes in the human body
- Different microbes colonize various parts of the human body,
  –*Streptococcus*, *Staphylococcus* → Stomach
  –*Enterobacteriaceae*→Intestine
- Viruses are also microbes that are used as a vector in recombinant DNA technology to transmit a required gene.

Test 1

Syllabus: Principles of Biotechnology

NCERT Page 163 to 165

For deeper insight, **Scan the QR Code**

Chapter 09

Biotechnology

- Biotechnology deals with the technique of using live organisms/ enzymes producing products and processes useful to human.

Parameters	Traditional biotechnology	Modern biotechnology
Organisms involved	Microbes	Genetically modified organisms
Production	Small scale	Large scale
Examples/ Techniques	Curd, bread or wine making	• *In-vitro* fertilisation leading to a test-tube baby • Synthesising a gene • DNA vaccine • Correcting a defective gene

- According to **European Federation of Biotechnology** (EFB), Biotechnology is the integration of natural science and organisms, cells, parts thereof, and molecular analogue for products and services.

Principles of Biotechnology

2 core techniques gave birth to modern biotechnology

Genetic Engineering
Techniques to alter the chemistry of DNA / RNA to introduce them into host organisms and change the phenotype of the host.

Bioprocess Engineering
Maintenance of sterile conditions to enable growth of only the desired microbes.

Genetic Engineering

The techniques of genetic engineering such as recombinant DNA technology, gene cloning, etc. Genetically modifying an organism has the following basic steps

- Identification of DNA containing desired genes.
- Introduction of desired DNA into the host organism.
- Maintenance of the introduced DNA in the host genome and transfer of the DNA to its progeny.

Technique for Genetic Engineering

- A piece of DNA multiplies and is inherited along with the host DNA, which can replicate.
- In a chromosome, there is a specific DNA sequence called the origin of replication, responsible for initiating replication.
- An alien DNA is linked with the origin of replication and can replicate and multiply itself in the host organism called cloning or making multiple identical copies of any template DNA.

Construction of First Artificial Recombinant DNA

- **Plasmids** are extra-chromosomal materials present in bacteria.
- It can be physically separated and can replicate independently of the bacterial chromosome.
- It provides resistance to the bacteria against certain antibiotics.
- The **first artificial recombinant** DNA molecule was constructed by Stanley Cohen and Herbert Boyer in 1972.
- They isolated an antibiotic-resistant gene by cutting a fragment of DNA from a plasmid. This antibiotic-resistant gene fragment was then integrated with the plasmid DNA.
- They cut the antibiotic resistance gene from a plasmid with the help of a restriction enzyme.
- They joined it to the plasmid of *Salmonella typhimurium* with the help of DNA ligase.
- The cutting of DNA at specific locations by '**molecular scissors**'- restriction enzymes.

- The cut piece of DNA was then linked with the plasmid DNA.
- These plasmid DNA act as **vectors** to transfer the piece of DNA attached to it.
- A plasmid can be used as a vector to deliver an alien piece of DNA into the host organism.
- The linking of the antibiotic resistance gene with the plasmid vector by **DNA ligase** acts on cut DNA molecules and join their ends.
- Circular autonomously replicating DNA- **Recombinant DNA**.
- When *r*DNA is transferred into *Escherichia coli*, it replicates using the new host's DNA polymerase enzyme and makes multiple copies.
- The ability to multiply copies of antibiotic resistance genes in *E. coli* were called cloning of antibiotic resistance genes in *E. coli*.

Basic Steps in Biotechnology

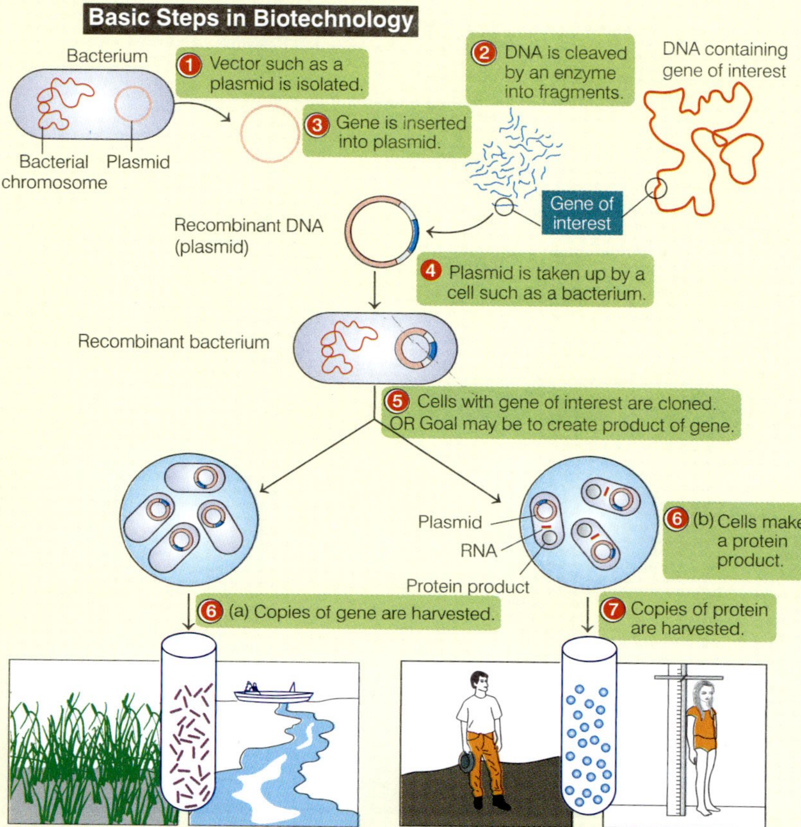

For deeper insight, **Scan the QR Code**

Tools of Recombinant DNA Technology

Restriction Enzyme | Cloning Vector | Competent Host

Restriction Enzymes (RE) → Endonuclease, → Exonuclease

- 900 restriction enzymes isolated from 230 strains till now.
- 1st restriction enzyme *Hind* II, isolated from *Haemophilus influenzae.*
- *Hind* II cuts by recognising specific sequence of 6 bp.
- **Recognised sequence** → Palindromic sequence*

The enzyme cuts both DNA strands at the same site

EcoRI cuts the DNA between bases G and A only when the sequence GAATTC is present in the DNA

Vector DNA (Plasmid)

Foreign DNA

Eco RI

Sticky end

Sticky end

DNA fragments join at sticky ends

DNA ligase

Recombinant DNA

Steps in the formation of recombinant DNA by action of restriction endonuclease enzyme - *Eco* RI

Nomenclature of Restriction Enzyme

E co R I

Genus *Escherichia* | Species *coli* | Strain RY13 | Order of isolation

- **Blunt ends** : *Sma* I, *Eco* RV, *Pvu* II, *Hind* II
- **Sticky ends** : *Eco* RI, *Bam* HI, *Hind* III, *Pst* I

- In the year 1963, the two enzymes responsible for restricting the growth of bacteriophage in *E. coli* were isolated.

- **Methylase** - Add methyl groups to bacterial DNA
- **Restriction endonuclease**

- **Ligase** When foreign DNA and vector DNA are cut by the same restriction enzyme, the resultant DNA fragments have the same kind of 'sticky-ends' which facilitates joining of fragments by ligase.
- **Sticky ends** are named so because they form hydrogen bonds with their complementary cut counterparts.

* **Palindromic seqence** reads same on the two strands (from any direction) when orientation of reading is kept same.

Competent Host

A competent host allows easy insertion of the cloning vector inside it and, on the other hand, produces positive results as required by the scientist.

- DNA is a hydrophilic molecule; that cannot pass through a cell membrane.
- **Method of Transformation**
  - **For Bacterial Cell**
    – Treat with Ca^{2+} → Ice → Heat shock → Ice again
  - **For Plant Cell**
    – Biolistics / Gene Gun: Plant cells are bombarded with high velocity micro particles of gold or tungsten coated with DNA.
  - **For Animal Cell**
    – Micro-injection: DNA is directly injected in the nucleus of animal host cell.

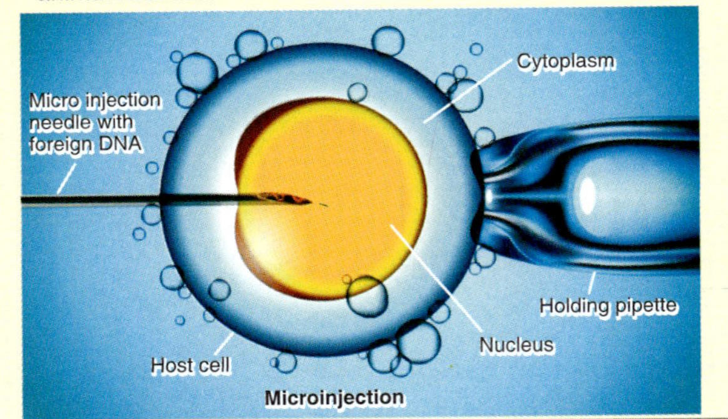

Electrophoresis

- Fragments are separated by gel electrophoresis; molecules carry charged groups that cause them to migrate under an electric field through a matrix.
- The fragments move across the pores according to their size.
- The most commonly used matrix is agarose, a natural polymer extracted from seaweeds.
- The separated DNA fragments can be visualised only after staining the DNA with ethidium bromide followed by exposure to UV radiation.
- The separated bands of DNA are cut out from agarose gel and extracted from the gel piece (elution).

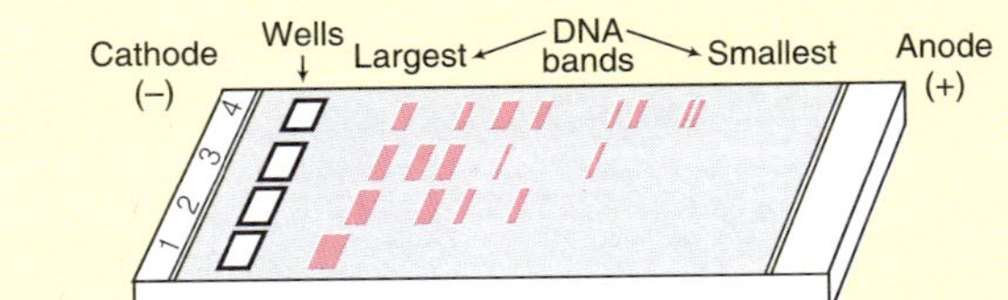

Cloning Vectors

1. Origin of replication (*ori*)
2. Cloning sites (ideally should have single cloning site)
3. Selectable marker (for selection of transformed cells)

- Vectors (for cloning genes in plants and animals)
  e.g. Plant vector → Ti-plasmid; Animal vector → Retroviruses

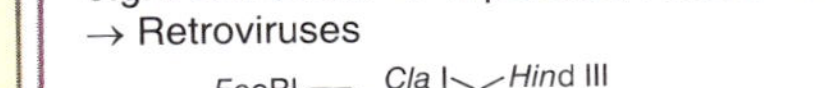
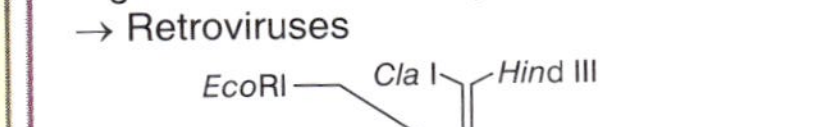
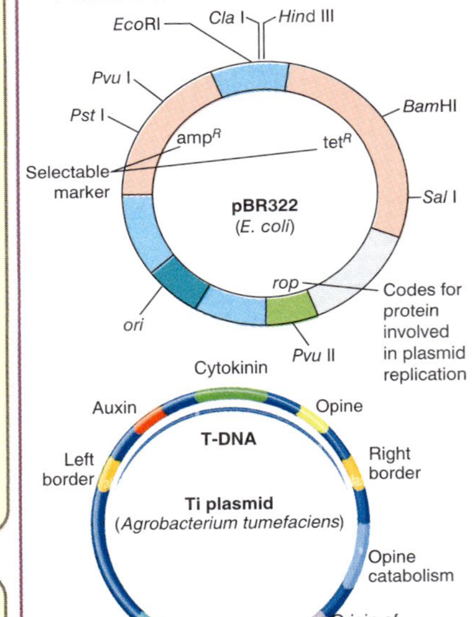

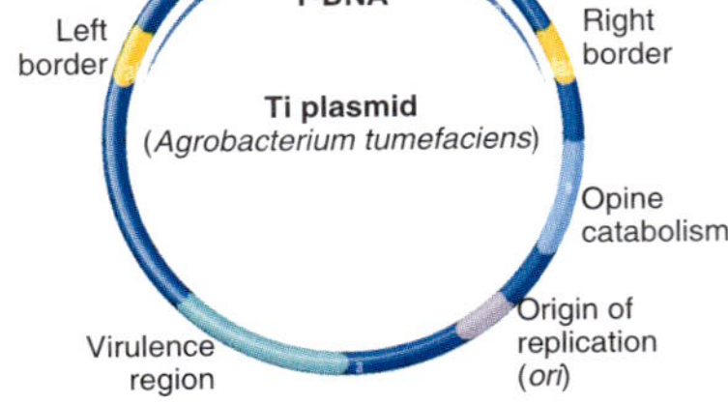

- Selection of recombinants due to inactivation of antibiotics is a cumbersome procedure.
- Alternative selectable markers have been developed to differentiate recombinants from non-recombinants based on their ability to produce colour in the presence of a chromogenic substrate.
- In this, recombinant DNA is inserted within the coding sequence of an enzyme, which is referred to as **insertional inactivation**.
- The presence of a chromogenic substrate β-galactosidase gives blue-coloured colonies (no insertion).
- The presence of insert results in insertional inactivation of the β-galactosidase (no colour).

Processes of Recombinant DNA Technology

- Recombinant DNA molecule is produced by joining together of two or more DNA segments usually originating from different organisms.
- A recombinant DNA molecule is a vector (e.g. a plasmid, phage or virus) into which the desired DNA fragment has been inserted to enable its cloning in an appropriate host.

1 Isolation of genetic material (cell digestion)

- Bacterial cells → Lysozyme
- Plant cell → Cellulase
- Fungal cell → Chitinase

DNA that separates out can be removed by **spooling.**

Spooling : Method to extract DNA from remains of the cell by treating it with chilled ethanol.

2 Cutting of DNA at specific location by restriction enzyme

3 Separation and isolation of DNA by Gel Electrophoresis (GE)

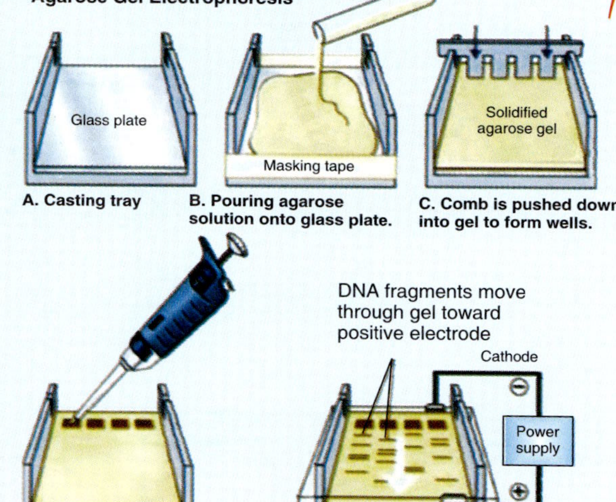

4 Amplification of gene of interest using **Polymerase Chain Reaction** (PCR) by **Kary Mullis**

Amplification Mechanism Polymerase Chain Reaction

Denaturation initiates following cycles (mostly 25 to 40)

Denaturation >90°C
PCR cycle
50°-72°C Annealing
68°-72°C Elongation

The repetition of these three essential steps are the basis for exponential DNA amplification

Initial denaturing leads to melting of double stranded DNA into single strands

Lowered temperature allows special **annealing** of primers

Thermostable DNA. Polymerase (Pol) elongates primers (Elongation/Extension)

After **elongation,** the target DNA-strands are duplicated

Exponential amplification allows accumulation of the specific PCR-product.

5 Insertion of *r*DNA into host cell.

It may take place in two ways, which are as follows

- **Indirect gene transfer** When the *r*DNA is inserted into host cell by the use of a vector, the method of gene transfer is called indirect gene transfer.
- **Direct gene transfer** The method of gene transfer in which *r*DNA is inserted directly into host cell is called direct gene transfer.

6 Obtaining the foreign gene product.

- Recombinant DNA is transferred into a bacterial, plant or animal cell, the foreign DNA is multiplied; aim to produce desirable protein.
- **Recombinant protein -** Protein encoding gene is expressed in a heterologous host.
- After cloning of gene of interest, one has to maintain the optimum condition to induce the expression of the target gene.
- Cloned gene of interest is grown on small scale in the laboratory. The culture may be used for extracting and purifying the desired protein.
- Culturing method produces a larger biomass to get higher yield of desired protein in bio-reactors or fermentors.

Bioreactors

- Raw materials are biologically converted into specific products by microbes, plant and animal cell or their enzymes.
- Large culture vessels (100- 1000 litres) for biosynthesis.
- Provides the optimal conditions for obtaining the desired product by providing optimum growth conditions such as temperature, pH, substrate, vitamins, oxygen and salts.
- Most commonly used bioreactor-stirring type which is usually cylindrical or with curved base, stirrer, agitator system, oxygen delivery system, pH control system, foam-control system, sampling port.

Acid/Base for pH control
Steam for sterilisation
Motor
Foam breaker
Flat bladed impeller
Culture broth
Sterile air

Simple stirred tank bioreactor

Increased surface area for oxygen transfer
Gas entrainment
Bubbles dramatically increase the oxygen transfer area

Sparged stirred tank bioreactor

Downstream Processing

- After completion of the biosynthetic stage, the product has to be subjected through a series of processes before it is ready for marketing as a finished product.
- The processes include separation and purification, which are collectively referred to as **downstream processing.**
- The product has to be formulated with suitable preservatives.
- Such formulation has to undergo through clinical trials as in case of drugs. Strict quality control testing for each product is also required.
- The downstream processing and quality control testing vary from product to product.

Test 1

Syllabus: Application of Biotechnology in Agriculture; Genetically Modified Organism-*Bt* crops.

NCERT Page 177 to 181

For deeper insight, **Scan the QR Code**

Biotechnology

- **Biotechnology** deals with industrial scale production of bio-pharmaceuticals and biological products using genetically modified microbes, fungi, plants and animals.
- Three research areas of biotechnology are:
  - Improving an organism through the process of biotechnology to act as the best catalyst.
  - Creating optimum conditions for a catalyst to act.
  - Downstream technologies to purify the compounds being formed.

Biotechnology Application in Agriculture

- Agro-chemical based agriculture
- Organic agriculture
- Genetically engineered crop based agriculture
- **Green Revolution** Introduction of High Yielding Variety (HYVs) seeds for increasing the food supply three times.

Somatic Hybridisation

Tomato protoplast → Potato protoplast → Fuse → Hybrid protoplast → Somatic hybrid (Pomato)

Tissue Culture

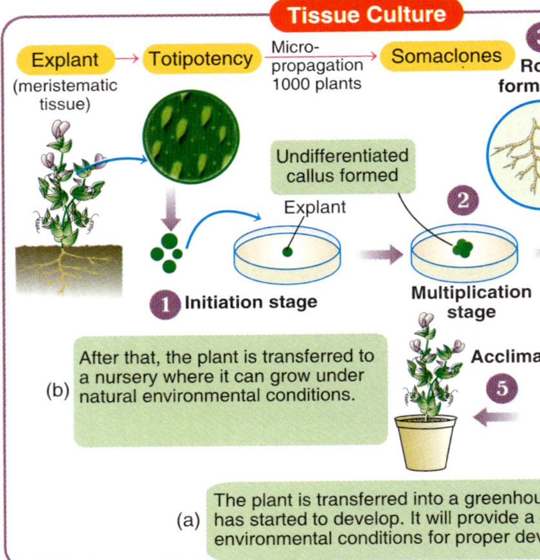

(b) After that, the plant is transferred to a nursery where it can grow under natural environmental conditions.

(a) The plant is transferred into a greenhouses when the plant has started to develop. It will provide a controlled environmental conditions for proper development.

Genetically Modified Organisms (GMOs)

The organisms like plants, bacteria, fungi and animals which have their genes altered by manipulation are called Genetically Modified Organisms or GMOs.

- Tolerant to abiotic stresses
- Pest resistant crops
- Reduce post harvest losses
- Increase efficiency of mineral usage by plants
- Enhanced nutritional value of food

Bt Cotton

- **Cotton bollworms** : *cry* IAc and *cry* IIAb
- **Corn borer** : *cry* IAb

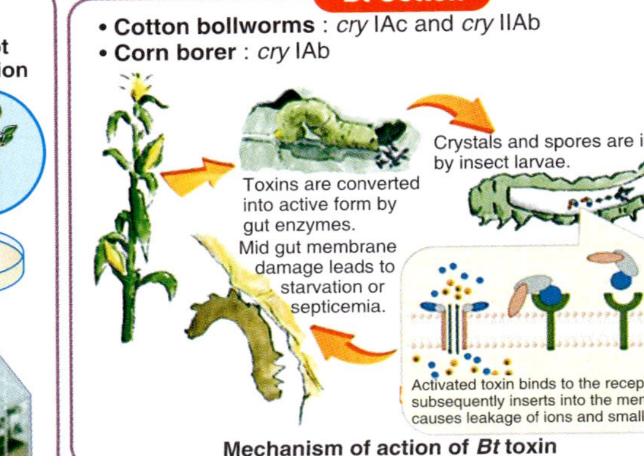

Mechanism of action of *Bt* toxin

Pest Resistance in Tobacco Plant

RNA interference (RNAi) strategy is used to prevent the infestation of tobacco plants by nematode *Meloidegyne incognita*.

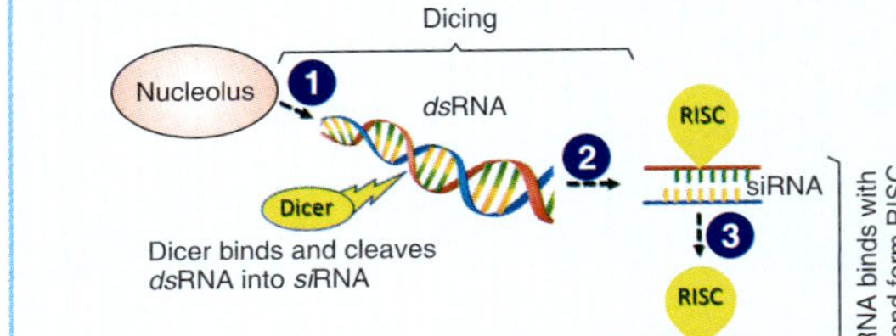

Production of Transgenic Plants

Agrobacterium tumefaciens → Ti plasmid (T-DNA, Restriction site); DNA containing gene for desired trait

1. Insertion of gene into plasmid using restriction enzyme and DNA ligase → Recombinant Ti-plasmid
2. Introduction into plant cells in culture → Plant cell; T-DNA carrying new gene within plant chromosome
3. Regeneration of plant → Plant with new traits

Some Other Agricultural Applications

- **Hirudin** (protein) present in leech prevents blood clotting; chemically synthesised in *Brassica napus;* extracted by downstream process.
- ***Flavr Savr***- first transgenic variety of tomato; inactivation of polygalacturonase enzyme to prevent over-ripening.
- **Golden rice**- a transgenic variety of rice (*Oryza sativa*) contains beta carotene (provitamin-A).

Test 2

Syllabus: Application of Biotechnology in Health: Human insulin and Vaccine production; Gene therapy

NCERT Page 181 to 185

For deeper insight, **Scan the QR Code**

Biotechnological Application in Medicine

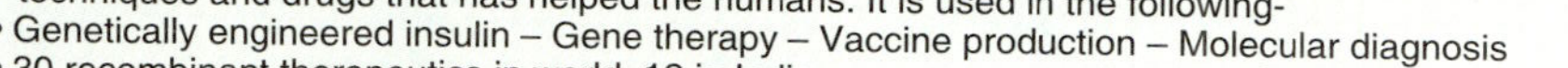

- Recombinant DNA technology is used in the field of healthcare and has led to the development of many techniques and drugs that has helped the humans. It is used in the following-
- Genetically engineered insulin – Gene therapy – Vaccine production – Molecular diagnosis
- 30 recombinant therapeutics in world, 12 in India.

Humulin

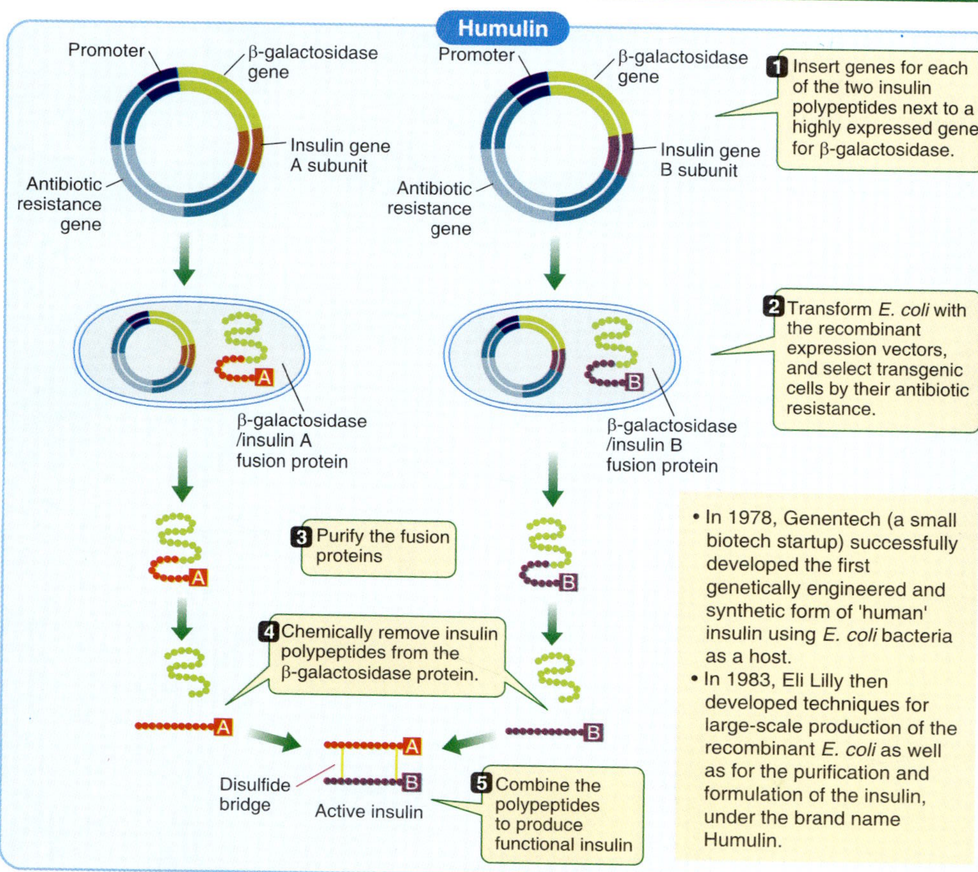

- In 1978, Genentech (a small biotech startup) successfully developed the first genetically engineered and synthetic form of 'human' insulin using *E. coli* bacteria as a host.
- In 1983, Eli Lilly then developed techniques for large-scale production of the recombinant *E. coli* as well as for the purification and formulation of the insulin, under the brand name Humulin.

Vaccine Production

Vaccination is protection for people against various types of diseases; prevents sickness or illness.

- Generation of vaccines based on its production.
  - **First Generation:** Inactivated pathogens, most effective approach to immunisation, e.g. smallpox, polio, etc.
  - **Second Generation:** Prepared by genetic engineering and contains toxoids, e.g. hepatitis, diphtheria, etc.
  - **Third generation:** Artificially synthesised, made up of a small circular piece of bacterial DNA, e.g. leukemia and ebola virus.

Gene Therapy

Gene therapy is a set of ways through which gene defects in the embryo or child can be corrected after diagnosis.

- The first clinical gene therapy was given in 1990, to a 4-year old girl with **Adenosine Deaminase** (ADA) deficiency.
- This enzyme is very important for the immune system to function. SCID is caused due to defect in the gene for the enzyme adenosine deaminase.

Bone marrow transplantation
Enzyme replacement therapy } Both are not completely curative

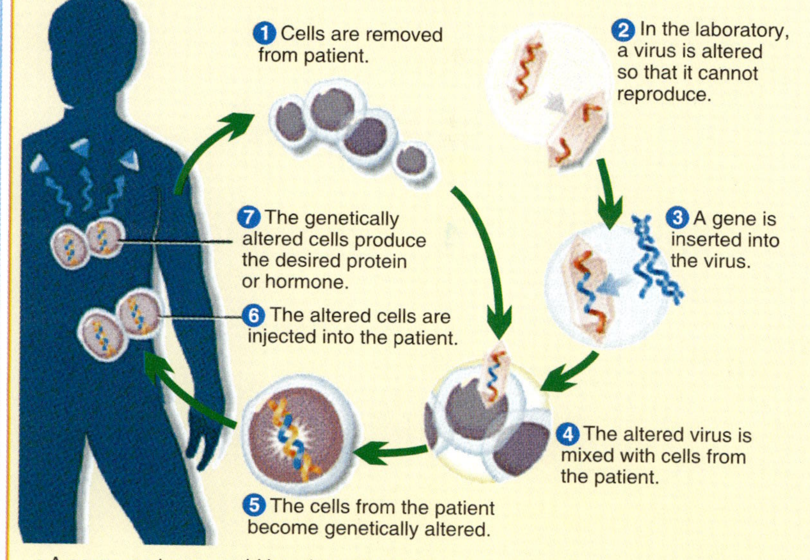

- A permanent cure could be when genes are isolated from the bone marrow and introduced into the developing embryo.

Molecular Diagnosis

- To detect infection of pathogens in the body in the early days as its cure becomes easy and possible.
- However, with the traditional ways in which the serum, blood, or urine is analysed, it becomes difficult to detect in the early stages of infection.
- The early detection of an infection is possible by:
  - **Recombinant DNA Technology:** Cells are cloned from the patient; Probe, a single-stranded DNA or RNA is tagged with a radioactive molecule which is allowed to hybridise with the complementary DNA in the cloned cells, followed by detection using autoradiograph.
  - **Polymerase Chain Reaction:** Amplify the DNA or RNA of the pathogen detected in the body in low quantity and once the genome is amplified, the detection of the pathogen in the early stages becomes easy.
  - **Enzyme-Linked Immuno-Sorbent Assay (ELISA)** The principle of antigen-antibody interaction; detects even a small amount of the protein with the help of the enzyme.

Test 3

Syllabus Transgenic Animals; Biosafety Issues-Biopiracy and Patents.

NCERT Page 183 to 185

For deeper insight, **Scan the QR Code**

Chapter 10

Transgenic Animals

Animal whose genome has been altered.
e.g. transgenic cattle, transgenic mice (95%), etc.
The modification of the animals has been done to study-

(i) **Normal Physiology and Development** Transgenic animals are used to study the normal working of the genes in the normal growth and development of the animals.
-Also used to study the effect of complex factors like insulin-like growth factors, etc. on the growth of the organism.
-Genes from other species can be introduced and the effects of the introduced gene can be studied in the animals.

(ii) **Study of Disease** Transgenic animals help us to study the diseases.
-They serve as models for human diseases.
-Today, transgenic animals are used to find cures for cancer, cystic fibrosis, rheumatoid arthritis and Alzheimer's.

(iii) **Biological Products** Transgenic animals are made to produce useful biological products such as human protein (α-1-antitrypsin) used to treat emphysema.
-Attempts are being made for the treatment of phenylketonuria (PKU) and cystic fibrosis.
-In 1997, the first transgenic cow, Rosie, produced human protein-enriched milk (2.4 gm/litre). The milk contained human α-lactalbumin and was nutritionally a balanced product for human babies than natural cow milk.

(vi) **Vaccine Safety** Animals are being developed for use in testing the safety of vaccines before they are used on humans.
-Transgenic mice are being used to test the safety of the polio vaccine, and presently even monkeys are being used.
-If the mice proven to be safe, then in the years to come they will replace the use of monkeys.

(v) **Chemical Safety Testing** This is known as toxicity/safety testing.
-Some transgenic animals carry genes that make them more sensitive to toxic substances than non-transgenic animals.
-They are then exposed to toxic substances and the effects are studied. It will help us to save time and obtain results fast.

Transgenic Microorganisms

Various microorganisms, particularly bacteria have been modified through genetic engineering to meet specific needs. For example,

- *Pseudomonas putida* - degradation of oil spills.
- *nif* gene-N_2 fixing ability of bacteria (crop improvement).
- *E. coli* - Medicine.

Production of Transgenic Animals

1. Identification and isolation of the desirable gene →
2. Selection of the vector →
3. Insertion of desirable gene into the vector with the help of enzyme ligase →
4. Introduction of vector into the cell, tissue, or embryo →
5. Expression of the foreign gene in the transgenic animal

Method 1

Recombinant DNA

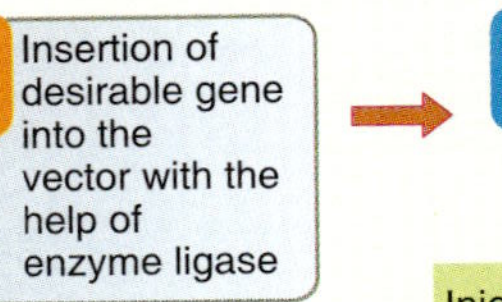

Select transformed embryonic stem cells* containing desired gene

Inject transformed ES cells into inner cell mass of blastocyst

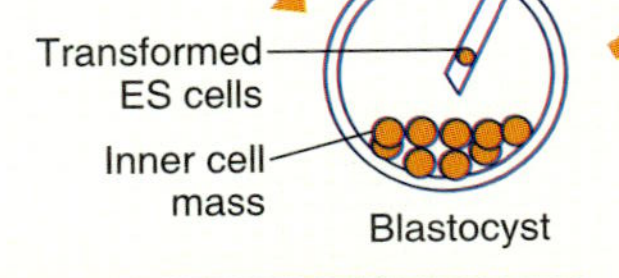

Implant in uterus

Method 2

Injecting DNA into the oocytes or 1-2 celled embryos taken from female mice. After injecting the DNA, the embryo is implanted into the uterus of receptive females.

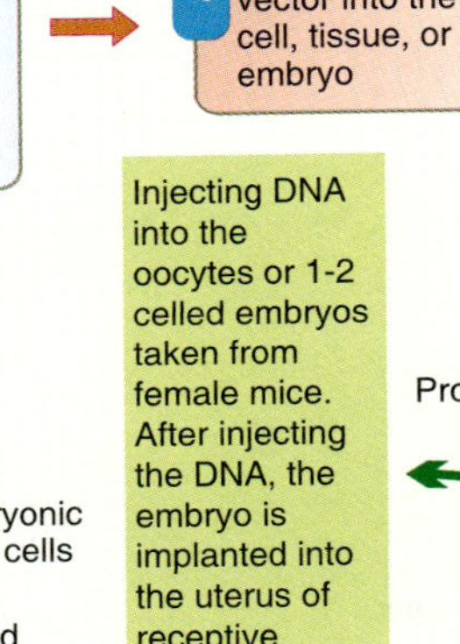

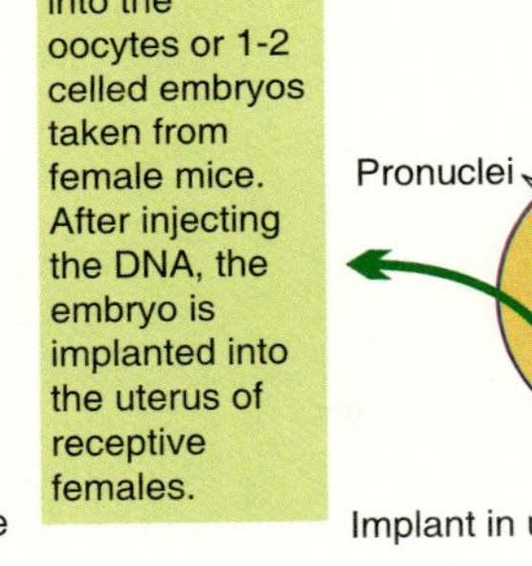

Implant in uterus

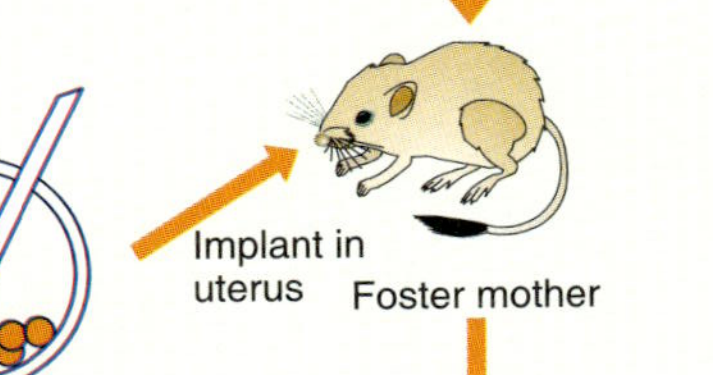

Offspring testing for transgene

Mate two heterozygous offsprings and screen their offsprings for homozygous transgenic strain (that will have 1/4 probability)

* **Stem cells:** These are undifferentiated cells that can develop into any type of tissue and perform a specialised function. Stem cells can be obtained from bone marrow, umbilical cord, inner cell mass of embryos and amniotic fluid.

Ethical Issues

The modification of the living organisms needs to be monitored otherwise it can cause havoc.

GEAC Make decisions regarding the validity of GM research and the safety of introducing GMO for public services.

Biopatent

A patent is the right granted by the government to an inventor which prevent others to make commercial use of one's invention. Different countries have different patent laws, which are changed with the advent of time.

- A patent is granted for
  - An invention (including a product).
  - An improvement in an earlier invention.
  - The process of generating a product.
  - A concept or a design.

Controversies in India regarding patent

- Turmeric
- Neem
- Basmati rice

Biopiracy

Use of bioresources by multinational companies and other organisation without proper authorisation from the countries and people concerned without compensatory payment.

- Industrialised countries are poor in bio-resources and traditional knowledge while developing countries are rich in bio-resources.
- There have been many cases of no proper compensation and benefit-sharing between developed and developing countries.
- Now, nations are developing laws to prevent unauthorised exploitation of their bio-resources and traditional knowledge.
- The Indian Parliament has recently cleared the second amendment of the Indian Patents Bill, which considers such issues and tries to prevent such exploitation.

Bio-war The war, which is fought with the help of biological organism using them as weapons against humans, their crops and animals is called as **biowar** or **biological war**. In biowar, viruses, bacteria and some other harmful organisms are used and are called as **Bioweapons** (BW).

Test 1

Syllabus: Levels of Ecology; Major Abiotic Factors; Responses to Abiotic Factors; Adaptations in Organisms

NCERT Old Page 219 to 226

For deeper insight, **Scan the QR Code**

Chapter 11

Levels of Ecology

PROTONS, NEUTRONS, ELECTRONS → ATOM → MOLECULE → COMPOUND → COMPLEXES OF COMPOUND (PHYSICAL HIERARCHY; NON-LIVING)

CELL → TISSUE → ORGAN → ORGAN-SYSTEM → ORGANISM (CELLULAR COLONY; BIOLOGICAL HIERARCHY; LIVING)

POPULATION → BIOTIC COMMUNITY + ABIOTIC COMPONENTS → ECOSYSTEM (BIOGEOCOENOSIS) → BIOME → BIOSPHERE (ECOSPHERE) (ECOLOGICAL HIERARCHY)

SIZE AND COMPLEXITY OF UNITS INCREASE

SIZE AND COMPLEXITY OF UNITS DECREASE

Major Abiotic Factors

Abiotic components characterising habitat of an organism

Temperature
- **Stenothermal** (Can tolerate narrow range of temperature)
- **Eurythermal** (Can tolerate wide range of temperature)
  - **Ectotherms**: Body temperature changes and matches with that of the environment.
  - **Endotherms**: Body temperature is maintained relatively constant by physiological regulations.

Water
- **Euryhaline** (Can tolerate wide range of salinities)
- **Stenohaline** (Restricted to narrow range of salinities)
  - A vertebrate, Molly fish.
  - An invertebrate, Green crab, Oyster and blue crabs.
  - Mangrove trees and most of the sea grasses.

Soil
- pH
- Soil composition
- Grain size
- Aggregation
- Topography

Light
- **Sciophytes** : Herbaceous plants and shrubs that live under the canopy (low light intensities).
- **Animals** : Diurnal and seasonal variation in the light intensity and photoperiod (duration of light) are important for their foraging, reproductive and migratory activities.
- The UV component of light is harmful for many organisms.
- **Red**, **brown** and **green alga**: Found thriving in different zones in the ocean (depends on the light, reaching the different depths); the red algae can live in very deep waters.

Organismic Responses to Abiotic Factors

- **Regulate** (To control their internal environment)
  - **Partial Regulator:** Regulate internal environment; but beyond a certain limit, conform to the external environmental conditions for survival.
- **Conform** (Depending on changes in external environment)
- **Migrate** (Seasonal movement of animals from one habitat to another) e.g., Siberian crane reach Keoladeo Ghana (Bharatpur) National Park.
- **Suspend** (A period of dormancy)
  - **Aestivation** (Summer sleep, e.g. snail)
  - **Hibernation** (Winter sleep, e.g. bear)
  - **Diapause** (e.g. Zooplankton sp.)

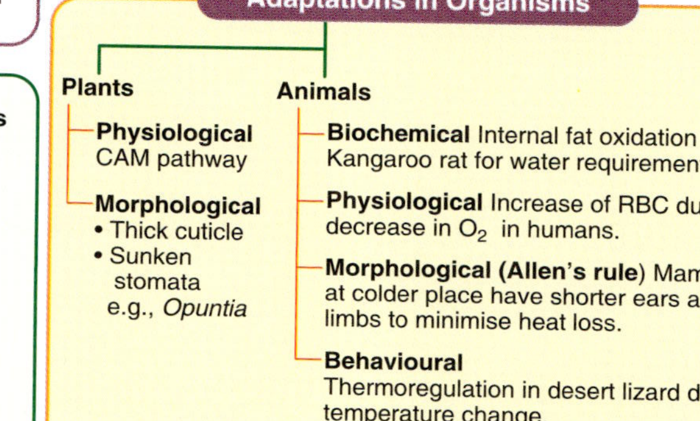

Biomes

Mean annual temperature (°C): 30, 25, 20, 15, 10, 5, 0, -5, -10, -15

Mean annual precipitation (cm): 50, 100, 150, 200, 250, 300, 350, 400, 450

Desert; Grassland; Tropical forest; Temperate forest; Coniferous forest; Arctic and Alpine tundra

Major Biomes in India
- Tropical rainforest
- Deciduous forest
- Desert
- Sea coast

- The **habitat** of an organism is characterised by physico-chemical components and biotic components.
- **Niche** of an organism has an invariably defined range of conditions that it can tolerate, diversity in the resources it utilises and a distinct functional role in the ecological system.

Adaptations in Organisms

Plants
- **Physiological** CAM pathway
- **Morphological**
  - Thick cuticle
  - Sunken stomata e.g., *Opuntia*

Animals
- **Biochemical** Internal fat oxidation in Kangaroo rat for water requirement.
- **Physiological** Increase of RBC during decrease in O_2 in humans.
- **Morphological (Allen's rule)** Mammals at colder place have shorter ears and limbs to minimise heat loss.
- **Behavioural** Thermoregulation in desert lizard during temperature change.

- **Aquatic mammals:** Seals in the polar seas have blubber below their skin; acts as an insulator and prevents loss of body heat.
- Some animals are capable of burrowing into the soil and hide to escape the ground heat.
- Tribes living at high altitudes of mountain (like Himalayas) have a higher count of red blood cells and total haemoglobin and also high vital capacity than people living in plains.

Test 2

Syllabus

Population Attributes-Growth, Birth rate and death rate, Age distribution
Population Interactions-Mutualism, Competition, Predation, Parasitism.

NCERT New Page 191 to 202

For deeper insight, **Scan the QR Code**

Chapter 11

Populations and its Attributes

- Population ecology is a link between ecology with population genetics and evolution.
- **Natural selection** is a process for the survival of the fittest and it operates at the level of population.

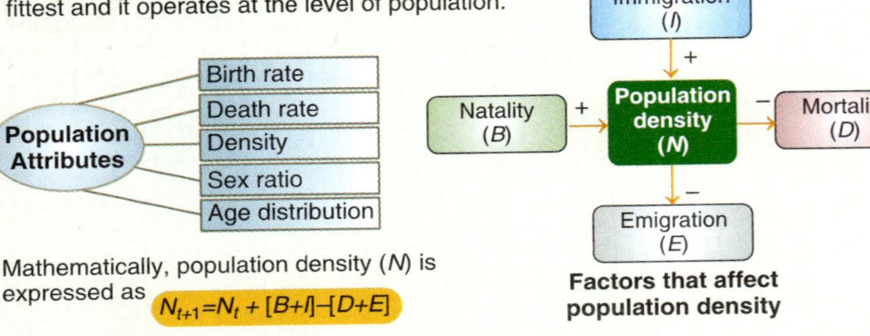

Factors that affect population density

Mathematically, population density (N) is expressed as $N_{t+1} = N_t + [B+I] - [D+E]$

- Natality and immigration always contribute to an increase in the size and density of a population.
- Mortality and emigration always contribute to a decrease in the population.

Age Pyramids

- Population is composed of individuals that belong to different ages/age groups at a specific time.

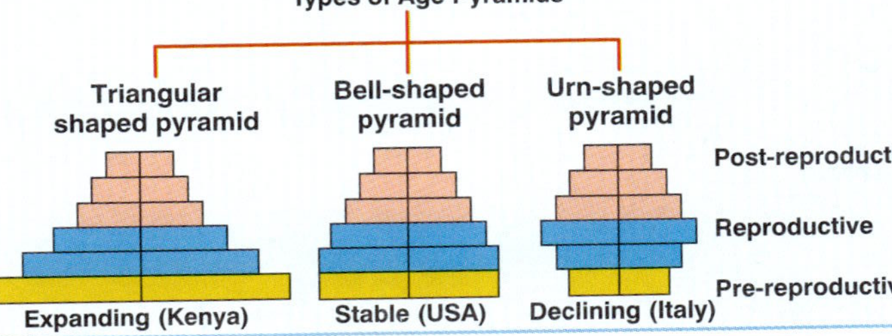

- The size of any population is never the same, it keeps changing with time depending on the factors like:
  - Food availability
  - Weather
  - Predation pressure
  - Competition among individuals

Population Growth Models

Exponential (unrestricted) Growth	Logistic (restricted) Growth
• Unlimited resources • Population passes well beyond the carrying capacity of the ecosystem. • An inflection in phase of diminishing growth is not reached.	• Limited resources • Population seldom grows beyond the carrying capacity of ecosystem • Prior to reaching the equilibrium phase, population growth shows a phase of declining growth.
Population size; The growth rate of the population accelerates; 0; Time	Population size; Carrying capacity of environment; The growth rate accelerates initially; The growth rate slows down later; Point of maximum growth (before it begins to slow); 0; Time
• Mathematically, expressed as $N_t = N_0 e^{rt}$ • **J- shaped Curve**	• Mathematically, expressed as $dN/dt = rN\,(K-N/K)$ • **Sigmoid Curve**

- **r-species**: Intrinsic rate of increase or biotic potential is very high; multiply rapidly; mortality rate high, e.g. fishes or insects.
- **K-species** : Rate of reproduction is very slow; low number of offsprings; heavy parental care and nurturing; low mortality, e.g. humans.

Life History Variation

- Evolution of population aims at improving the reproductive fitness.
- According to ecologists, organisms have developed life history traits to cope with various biotic and abiotic factors in their habitats, in order to strengthen their survival and continuity of species.

Reproductive strategies in organisms

- Breed only once in their lifetime, e.g. Pacific salmon fish, bamboo, produce large number of small sized offsprings, e.g. oysters, Pelagic fishes.
- Breed many times during lifetime, e.g. most birds and mammals, produce a small number of large sized offsprings, e.g. birds and mammals.

Population Interactions

TYPES OF INTERACTIONS	SPECIES 1	SPECIES 2	EXAMPLES
Amensalism	–	0	*Penicillium* and bacteria; Black walnut root (Juglone toxin) and herbaceous plant.
Mutualism	+	+	Roots of higher plants and mycorrhiza; fig and wasp (coevolution); Mediterranean orchid *Ophrys* and bee (sexual deceit).
Commensalism	+	0	Cattle egret and grazing cattle; sea anemone and clown fish.
Competition	–	–	Abingdon tortoise and goats.
Parasitism	+	–	*Ascaris* and tapeworm in human digestive tract; Liver fluke and host; Koel and crow (Brood parasitism).
Predation	+	–	Prickly pear cactus and cactus feeding moth *Calotropis* (poisonous) and goat or cattle (cardiac glycosides).

Protocooperation : Association is not obligatory in nature but both the partners get benefitted, e.g. anemone (*Adamsia*) and hermit's crab, oxpecker and rhinoceros.

Test 1

Syllabus: Ecosystem-Structure (Patterns, Components) and Function; Productivity and Decomposition

NCERT Page 205 to 208

For deeper insight, **Scan the QR Code**

Chapter 12

Ecology

- **Ecology** involves the study of inter-relationships of organisms with one another and with their environment for survival.
- **Biotic community** An environment which fulfills its material and energy requirements.
- Living organisms and their physical environment are in an inseparable relationship.
- This relationship constitutes different ecosystems.
- **Ecosystem** is the functional unit of nature.

Ecosystem

- **Arthur Tansley** coined the term ecosystem.
- Ecosystem is a self-sustained unit in which living and non-living components interact with each other.

Classification of Ecosystem

- Terrestrial
  - Natural e.g. forest
  - Man-made e.g. crop fields
- Aquatic
  - Natural e.g. pond
  - Man-made e.g. aquarium

Structure of Ecosystem

- **Biotic**
  - Producers (autotrophs)
  - Consumers (heterotrophs)
  - Decomposers (reducers)
- **Abiotic**
  - Light
  - Wind
  - Soil
  - Temperature
  - Water

Patterns of Ecosystem

- **Species composition**
- **Stratification**

- The two important structural features of an ecosystem are:
- **Species composition**- It refers to the total number of different living organisms within a given biome or ecosystem and includes identification and enumeration of species.
  It is generally expressed as percentage; maximum species composition is seen in tropical rainforests and coral reef, whereas minimum occurs in deserts.
- **Stratification**- It refers to the vertical distribution of various species at different strata/levels in the ecosystem, e.g. trees occupy top vertical strata or layer of a forest followed by shrubs, herbs and grasses.

-**Tropical forest** : Tall trees, a dense canopy, understorey trees, a layer of short trees, a shrub layer and bottom layers of herbs or ground vegetation.

-**Pond** : Euphotic zone, Metalimnion, Profundal zone and Benthic zone.

Functions of Ecosystem

Productivity | **Decomposition** | **Energy flow** | **Nutrient cycling**

Productivity

- A constant input of solar energy is the basic requirement of any ecosystem to function and sustain.
- Expressed in terms of $gm^{-2}\ yr^{-1}$ or $(kcal\ m^{-2})\ yr^{-1}$.

Types of Productivity

Primary Productivity
Rate at which radiant energy of the sun is stored by producers.

Secondary Productivity
Rate of assimilation and formation of new organic matter by consumers.

Gross Primary Productivity (GPP)
It is the rate of production or synthesis of organic matter by producers during photosynthesis in a given unit area. The rate of gross primary productivity is estimated, in terms of chlorophyll content as chlorophyll/gm dry weight/unit area.

Net Primary Productivity (NPP)
It is the total amount of GPP minus energy lost by plant during respiration. Thus, NPP is equal to the rate of organic matter stored by photosynthesis minus the rate of respiration and other losses.

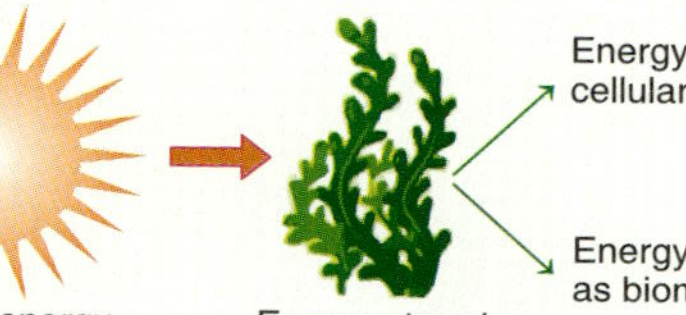

NPP = GPP - R

(Net Primary Productivity) = (Gross Primary Productivity) - (Respiratory loss)

- **Factors affecting primary productivity**
  - The plant species in a particular area
  - Availability of nutrients
  - Photosynthetic capacity of plants
  - Environmental factors

Decomposition

- Breakdown of complex organic matter into inorganic substances like water and nutrients is decomposition.
- Steps in the process of decomposition
  - **Fragmentation:** Breaking of the detritus into smaller particles by detritivores.
  - **Leaching:** Water-soluble inorganic substances run down into soil horizon and get precipitated as unavailable salts.
  - **Catabolism**: Enzymatic conversion of the detritus into simple organic compounds and then into inorganic compounds, secreted by the decomposers like bacteria and fungi.
  - Fragmentation, leaching and catabolism operate simultaneously on the detritus.
  - **Humification:** Accumulation of dark coloured amorphous substances (humus).
  - **Mineralisation:** Humus is degraded by certain microbes and the inorganic nutrients are released.
  - Decomposition is largely an aerobic process.

A tree grows in the soil.
A green leaf falls to the ground.
Some are eaten by insects and other animals. Nutrients and energy enter food web.
Leaves partially consumed by decomposers such as fungi and bacteria. They begin to lose form and become litter.
Some nutrients leach into soil by chemical action.
Further decomposition by earthworms, bacteria, soil mites, fungi, etc.
Organic rich soil

- **Factors affecting decomposition:**
  - The chemical composition of detritus and the climatic factors.
  - Decomposition is slow, if detritus is rich in lignin and chitin.
  - Decomposition is faster if detritus is rich in nitrogen and water-soluble substances (e.g., sugars).
  - Temperature and soil moisture also affect it.
  - Warm and moist environment and aerobic conditions favour decomposition.
  - A dry environment, low temperature and anaerobic conditions inhibit decomposition.

Syllabus Energy Flow; Pyramids of Number, Biomass, Energy

NCERT Page 209 to 214

For deeper insight, **Scan the QR Code**

Food Chain

Sequence of transfer of nutrients and energy in the form of food from organism to organism.

- **Unidirectional flow** of energy from sun to producers and then to various consumers.
- Shorter food chains provide greater amount of energy to the top level consumers.

Types of food chain

Characters	Grazing Food Chain	Detritus Food Chain
Primary source of energy	Solar radiations	Detritus
First trophic level	All herbivores	Detritivores (a mixed group in terms of trophic levels and may be herbivores, omnivores and primary carnivores)
Size	Long-sized chains	Small-sized chains
Examples	Predatory food chains on land and in water	Mangrove leaf litter bed in brackish zone of South Florida

Trophic level

- Specific place of an organism in a food chain characterised by their source of nutrition.

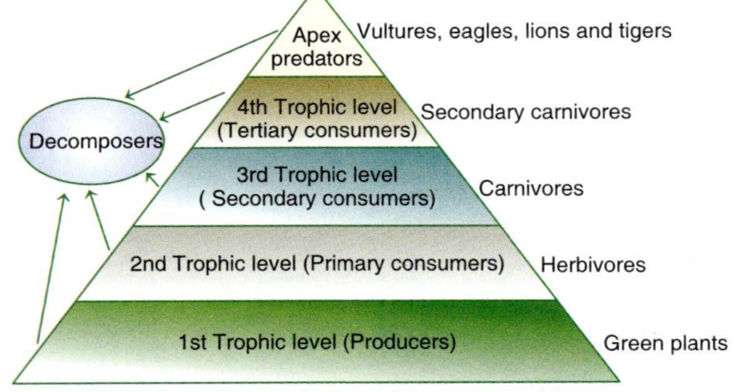

Trophic levels constituting a pyramid

- The amount of energy decreases at successive trophic levels.
- The number of trophic levels in a grazing food chain is restricted to four or five.
- **Standing crop:** Mass of living material at a particular time; measured as the mass of living organisms (biomass) or the number in a unit area.

Ecological Pyramids

- The food or energy relationship among organisms at different trophic levels can be expressed in terms of number, biomass or energy.
- The expression assumes the shape of a pyramid, where the base represents the producers or first trophic level, while the apex represents the tertiary or top level consumer.
- Each trophic level represents a functional level and not any one species in particular.

Pyramid of Number It shows the relationship between producers and consumers in an ecosystem in terms of numbers.

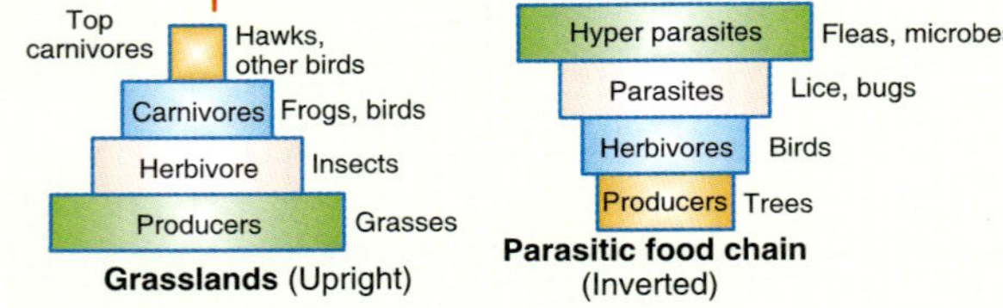

Pyramid of Energy It shows the relationship between producers and consumers in any ecosystem in terms of flow of energy.

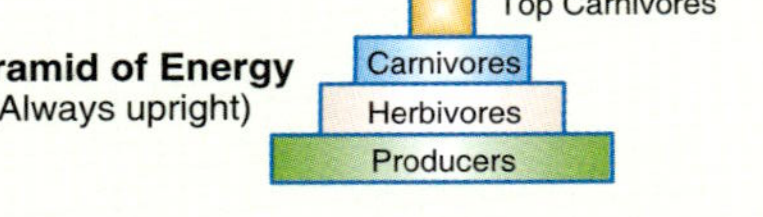

Pyramid of Biomass It shows the relationship between producers and consumers in an ecosystem in terms of biomass.

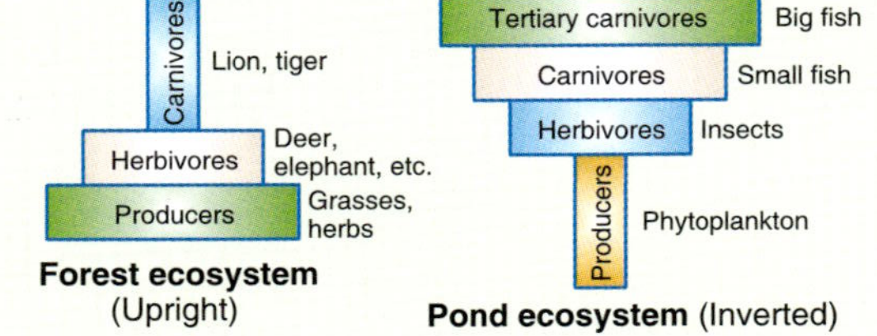

Limitations of Ecological Pyramids

- It includes a simple food chain which never exists in nature.
- It never keeps an account of the same species belonging to two or more trophic levels.
- Inspite of the vital role played by saprophytes/decomposers, they are not given any position in ecological pyramids.

Energy flow

- It is a sequential process of the movement of energy in an ecosystem through a series of organisms. It is always unidirectional.
- The source of energy in an ecosystem is solar energy. Approximately 50% of the solar energy incident on the earth is Photosynthetically Active Radiation (PAR).
- Incident radiation on plants is about 1×10^6 kJ/m²/yr. Of this, as much as 95-99% is immediately lost from the plants by reflection, radiation or heat of evaporation.
- The remaining 1-5% of incoming radiation is absorbed by the chlorophyll and used in the production of organic molecules.

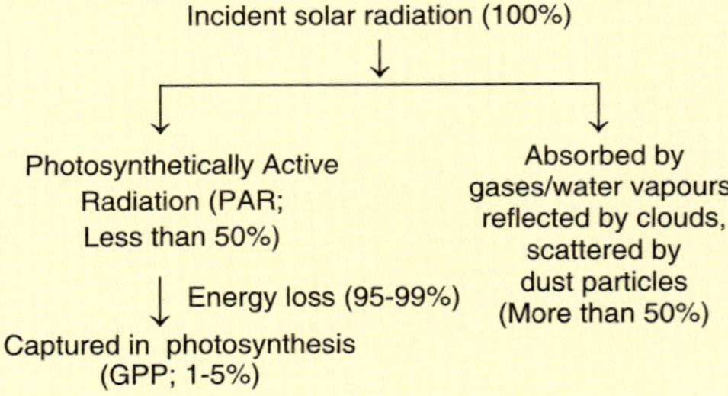

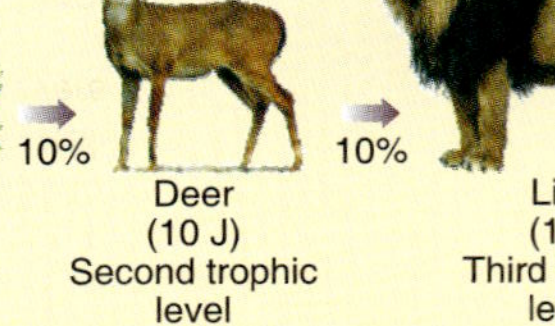

Law of 10% Energy Transfer in Ecosystem.

- The 10% law is followed in the energy transfer between trophic level.
- Only 10% is passed to the next trophic level because almost 90% of the energy is lost to the environment as heat.
- Here, the second law of thermodynamics is applied in the ecosystem.

Test 1

Syllabus: Concept of Biodiversity; Patterns of Biodiversity; Importance of Biodiversity

NCERT Page 216 to 221

For deeper insight, **Scan the QR Code**

Chapter 13

Biodiversity

- **Biodiversity**, is the occurrence of various types of life forms in different ecosystem with a whole range of variants (biotypes) and genes, adapted to different climates, environments along with their interactions and processes.
- Term '**Biodiversity**' was coined by **Walter G Rosen** (1985) and popularised by **Edward Wilson** (1992).
- Diversity is present at all levels of biological organisation ranging from the micro-molecules within the cells to biomass.
- Biodiversity is of great ecological, economic and aesthetic

Levels of Biodiversity

1 Genetic Diversity

- It is the diversity of various types of genes, chromosomes and alleles within the same species.
- Variation in genes increases with increase in size and environmental parameters of habitats.
- India has 50,000 genetically different strains of rice and 1000 varieties of mango.
- *Rauwolfia vomitoria* (Poison devil's pepper): Potency and concentration of the chemical reserpine.

2 Species Diversity

- Diversity at species level.
- E.g. Western ghats have greater amphibian species diversity than Eastern ghats.
- Species richness: Species per unit area.
- Species evenness: Number of individuals of different species.

3 Ecological Diversity

Biodiversity on wider scale includes variations in biological communities, ecosystem and interaction among these levels.

- It is of three types: alpha, beta and gamma diversity.
- **Alpha** (α) **diversity** (within community diversity) number of species in given community or habitat.
- **Beta** (β) **diversity** (between community diversity) develops due to change in a habitat or community along environmental gradients, e.g., altitude, latitude, etc.
- **Gamma** (γ) **diversity** total richness of species in all the habitats found within a region, geographical area or landscape.
- Ecosystem diversity is quite high in India.
- Ecosystem diversity is quite low in small countries like Norway.

Global Biodiversity

- According to IUCN (2004), total number of plant and animal species are slightly more than 1.5 million.
- **Robert May** places the global diversity at about **7 million**.
- Among all species, 70% of them are animals, while plants comprise of 22% of total diversity .

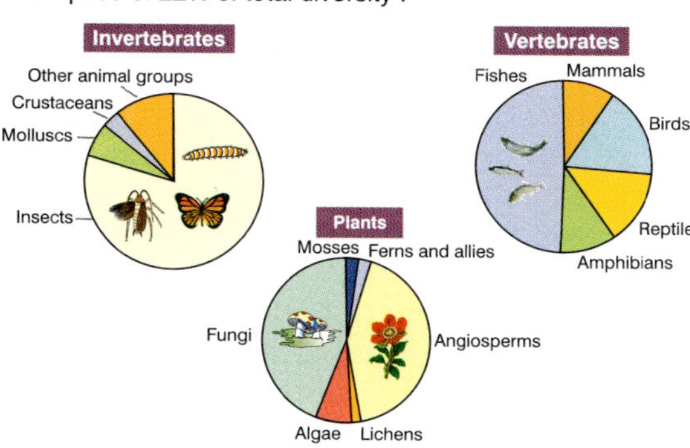

- Prokaryotes are not considered in the estimates of global species diversity.
- The conventional taxonomic methods are not suitable or sufficient for identifying prokaryotic species; many species are simply not culturable in labs.

Biodiversity in India

- India is one of the 12 mega biodiverse countries of the world.
- India has only 2.4 percent of the land area of the world.
- It has 8.1 percent of the global species biodiversity.
- There are about 45,000 species of plants and 90,000-1,00,000 species of animals.
- Many species are yet to be discovered.
- Only 22 percent of the total species have been recorded so far according to Robert May's global estimate.

Importance of Species Diversity to Ecosystem

- **Stable community**
  - Does not show too much of variations in the year to year productivity
  - Resistant to seasonal disturbances
  - Resistant to alien species.
- The maintenance of diversity is important due to the following reasons:
  - Ecological stability
  - Productivity
  - Ecosystem health
- **David Tilman**
  - More species showed less year to year variation in total biomass.
  - Increased diversity contributed to higher productivity.

Patterns of Biodiversity

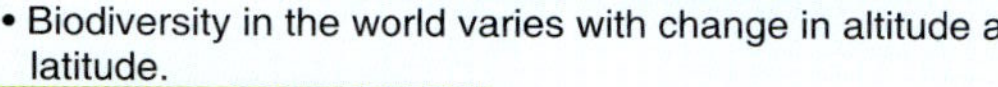

- Biodiversity in the world varies with change in altitude and latitude.

1. Latitudinal gradients

- Decrease in species diversity from equator towards poles.
- With very few exceptions, tropics (latitude range 23.5° N to 23.5° S) harbour more species than temperate or polar areas.
- Tropics region > Temperate region > Polar region.
- Causes of greater biodiversity in tropics:
  (i) Speciation
  (ii) Constant tropical environment
  (iii) More solar energy availability

Low diversity
Equator | High diversity | Equator
Low diversity

2. Species-area relationship

- Given by **Alexander von Humboldt.**
- Observed that species richness increased with increasing explored area but only upto a limit.

$\log S = \log C + Z \log A$

Where,
S=Species richness
A=Area
Z=Slope of the line
C=Y-intercept

- The value of Z ranges between 0.1 to 0.2 in a comparatively smaller region.
- Large areas, like continent shows the slope to be much steeper and Z value range between 0.6 and 1.2.
- Z value for frugivorous birds and mammals in the tropical forests is found to be 1.15.

$S = CA^Z$; log-log scale ; $\text{Log } S = \log C + Z \log A$; Species richness → ; Area →

Graph showing species-area relationship (Note that on log scale, the relationship becomes linear)

The Rivet Popper Hypothesis

- Paul Ehrlich proposed this hypothesis ; suggests the importance of species richness in the maintenance of the ecosystem.
- The rivets of an aeroplane were compared with species in an ecosystem.
- If the passengers start to pop the rivets from the wings of the aeroplane, it would not be able to fly.
- Loss of rivets on the wings (key species that drive major ecosystem functions) is more serious threat.
- If species present in an ecosystem are reduced, then the ecosystem will collapse.

Test 2

Syllabus

Loss of Biodiversity; Biodiversity conservation; Hotspots, endangered organisms, extinction; Red Data Book, Biosphere reserves, National parks and sanctuaries, Sacred Groves.

NCERT Page 221 to 225

For deeper insight, **Scan the QR Code**

Loss of Biodiversity

- The **IUCN Red list** (2004) reported extinction of 784 species (including 338 vertebrates, 359 invertebrates and 87 plants) in last 500 years.
- Recent extinctions includes dodo (Mauritius), thylacine (Australia), stellar's sea cow (Russia) etc.
- At present, percentage of threat of extinction among organisms is:
  31 percent of gymnosperms
  32 percent of amphibians
  12 percent of birds species
  23 percent of mammals

'Evil Quartet' of Biodiversity Losses:

- **Habitat loss and Fragmentation**
- Primary cause for extinction of species.
- **Over-Exploitation**
- Nature is over exploited by man for the natural resources; many species became extinct.
- **Invasion of Alien species**
- Alien species become invasive, compete with the native species and causes extinction of the indigenous species.
- **Coextinctions**
- As a host species becomes extinct, the plant and animal associated with it in an obligatory manner, also become extinct.

Mass Extinction

Extinction of species at a faster rate in short geological period of time. At present, sixth mass extinction is going on, and referred to as **Anthropogenic Extinction.**

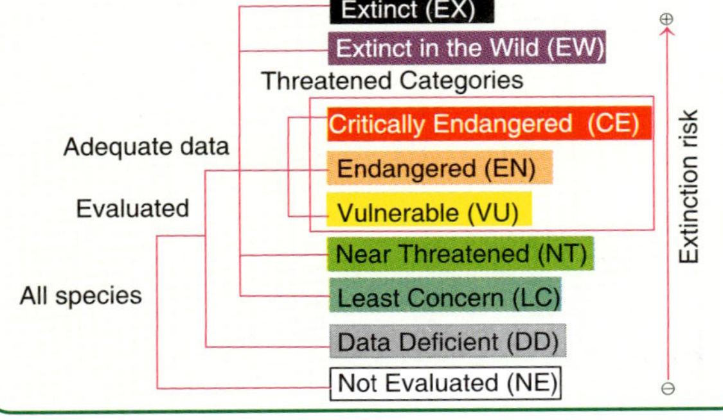

Conventions on Biodiversity

- **The Earth Summit**
- Held in Rio de Janeiro in 1992.
- Objectives- Conservation of biodiversity and Sustainable utilisation of the benefits from biodiversity.
- **The World Summit on Sustainable Development**
- Johannesburg, South Africa.
- **190 countries;** commitment to reduction in biodiversity loss at all levels by 2010.

Biodiversity Conservation

- Reasons to conserve biodiversity are grouped in three categories:

(i) **Narrowly utilitarian** argument says that conservation of biodiversity is important, as it provides countless direct benefits to humans. Some of the benefits of nature are food (cereal, pulses), firewood, construction material, medicinal and industrial products.

(ii) **Broadly utilitarian** says that biodiversity plays a major role in ecosystem services that nature provides. The Amazon forest produces 20% of the total oxygen present in the earth's atmosphere.

(iii) **Ethical** argument for conserving biodiversity is that we owe to plants and animals with whom we share this plant, therefore conserving them is our moral duty.

- Conservation strategies are broadly of two types-*In-situ* conservation and *Ex-situ* conservation

In-Situ Conservation

Biodiversity Hotspots

- High degree of endemism.
- **Number of ' Hotspots'**
- There are 34* hotspots in the globe. • Three are in india - (i) Western Ghats, (ii) Indo-Burma Region, (iii) Himalayan Region

Protected areas

- **National Parks** are larger areas of scenic and national beauty maintained for scientific, educational and recreational use.
- India has 90* National parks. The first National park was Jim Corbett (1936).
- **Wildlife Sancturies**
- Wild animal / fauna can take refuge without being hunted. Other activities are also allowed.
- India has 448* wildlife sancturies.
- **Biosphere Reserve**
- These are a special category protected areas of land and/or coastal environments, wherein people are an integral component of the system.
- There are 14* biosphere reserves in India.
- These are the representative examples of natural biomes and contain unique biological communities within.

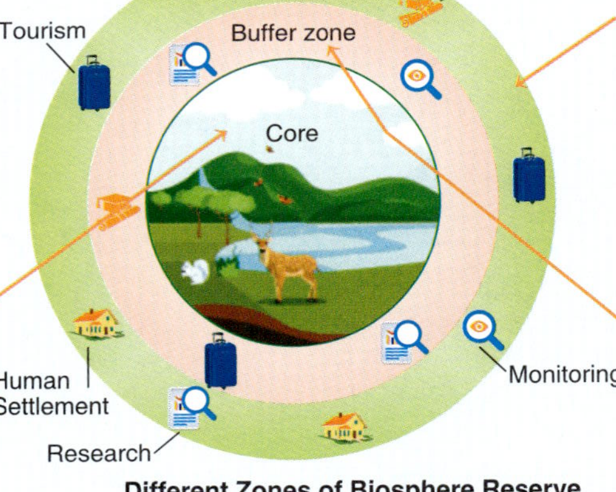

Different Zones of Biosphere Reserve

Sacred Groves in India

- Khasi and Jaintia hills in Meghalaya.
- Western Ghat regions of Karnataka and Maharashtra.
- Aravalli Hills of Rajasthan.

Ex-Situ Conservation

- Botanical gardens, zoological parks and arboretum are the conventional methods of *ex situ* conservation.
- **Cryopreservation** (-196° C in liq. N_2) is a method of conservation by storage of live cells, tissues and other biological sample at ultra low temperatures for a very long period.
- Plants are propagated using tissue culture method (micropropagation) .
- Seeds of many different genetic strains of commercially important plants are kept viable for long periods in seed banks.

* Currently, there are 36 biodiversity hotspots, 106 national parks, 573 wildlife sanctuaries and 18 biosphere reserves in India.

MEDACE

OMR SHEET

ROLL No.

1	1	1	1	1	1	1	1	1	1
2	2	2	2	2	2	2	2	2	2
3	3	3	3	3	3	3	3	3	3
4	4	4	4	4	4	4	4	4	4
5	5	5	5	5	5	5	5	5	5
6	6	6	6	6	6	6	6	6	6
7	7	7	7	7	7	7	7	7	7
8	8	8	8	8	8	8	8	8	8
9	9	9	9	9	9	9	9	9	9
0	0	0	0	0	0	0	0	0	0

TEST BOOKLET No.

1	1	1	1	1	1	1
2	2	2	2	2	2	2
3	3	3	3	3	3	3
4	4	4	4	4	4	4
5	5	5	5	5	5	5
6	6	6	6	6	6	6
7	7	7	7	7	7	7
8	8	8	8	8	8	8
9	9	9	9	9	9	9
0	0	0	0	0	0	0

TEST BOOKLET Code

Q No.	Response			
001	a	b	c	d
002	a	b	c	d
003	a	b	c	d
004	a	b	c	d
005	a	b	c	d
006	a	b	c	d
007	a	b	c	d
008	a	b	c	d
009	a	b	c	d
010	a	b	c	d
011	a	b	c	d
012	a	b	c	d
013	a	b	c	d
014	a	b	c	d
015	a	b	c	d
016	a	b	c	d
017	a	b	c	d
018	a	b	c	d
019	a	b	c	d
020	a	b	c	d
021	a	b	c	d
022	a	b	c	d
023	a	b	c	d
024	a	b	c	d
025	a	b	c	d
026	a	b	c	d
027	a	b	c	d
028	a	b	c	d
029	a	b	c	d
030	a	b	c	d
031	a	b	c	d
032	a	b	c	d
033	a	b	c	d
034	a	b	c	d
035	a	b	c	d
036	a	b	c	d
037	a	b	c	d
038	a	b	c	d
039	a	b	c	d
040	a	b	c	d
041	a	b	c	d
042	a	b	c	d
043	a	b	c	d
044	a	b	c	d
045	a	b	c	d
046	a	b	c	d
047	a	b	c	d
048	a	b	c	d
049	a	b	c	d
050	a	b	c	d

Q No.	Response			
051	a	b	c	d
052	a	b	c	d
053	a	b	c	d
054	a	b	c	d
055	a	b	c	d
056	a	b	c	d
057	a	b	c	d
058	a	b	c	d
059	a	b	c	d
060	a	b	c	d
061	a	b	c	d
062	a	b	c	d
063	a	b	c	d
064	a	b	c	d
065	a	b	c	d
066	a	b	c	d
067	a	b	c	d
068	a	b	c	d
069	a	b	c	d
070	a	b	c	d
071	a	b	c	d
072	a	b	c	d
073	a	b	c	d
074	a	b	c	d
075	a	b	c	d
076	a	b	c	d
077	a	b	c	d
078	a	b	c	d
079	a	b	c	d
080	a	b	c	d
081	a	b	c	d
082	a	b	c	d
083	a	b	c	d
084	a	b	c	d
085	a	b	c	d
086	a	b	c	d
087	a	b	c	d
088	a	b	c	d
089	a	b	c	d
090	a	b	c	d
091	a	b	c	d
092	a	b	c	d
093	a	b	c	d
094	a	b	c	d
095	a	b	c	d
096	a	b	c	d
097	a	b	c	d
098	a	b	c	d
099	a	b	c	d
100	a	b	c	d

DECLARATION BY THE CANDIDATE

I declare that particulars and signature on this OMR Answer sheet are mine and are Name as in Attendance Sheet. I fruther declare that particulars filled in and Signature as well as the circles darkened on this ORIGINALCOPY is same as in OFFICE COPY.

Signature with time (in running handwriting)

CANDIDATE's NAME (in running handwriting)

MOTHER's NAME (in running handwriting)

FATHER's NAME (in running handwriting)

CANDIDATE LEFT HAND IMPRESSION

SIGNATURE OF INVIGILATOR'S WITH TIME

1

2

MEDACE

OMR SHEET

ROLL No.

1	1	1	1	1	1	1	1	1	1
2	2	2	2	2	2	2	2	2	2
3	3	3	3	3	3	3	3	3	3
4	4	4	4	4	4	4	4	4	4
5	5	5	5	5	5	5	5	5	5
6	6	6	6	6	6	6	6	6	6
7	7	7	7	7	7	7	7	7	7
8	8	8	8	8	8	8	8	8	8
9	9	9	9	9	9	9	9	9	9
0	0	0	0	0	0	0	0	0	0

TEST BOOKLET No.

1	1	1	1	1	1	1
2	2	2	2	2	2	2
3	3	3	3	3	3	3
4	4	4	4	4	4	4
5	5	5	5	5	5	5
6	6	6	6	6	6	6
7	7	7	7	7	7	7
8	8	8	8	8	8	8
9	9	9	9	9	9	9
0	0	0	0	0	0	0

TEST BOOKLET Code

Q No.	Response	Q No.	Response
001	(a) (b) (c) (d)	051	(a) (b) (c) (d)
002	(a) (b) (c) (d)	052	(a) (b) (c) (d)
003	(a) (b) (c) (d)	053	(a) (b) (c) (d)
004	(a) (b) (c) (d)	054	(a) (b) (c) (d)
005	(a) (b) (c) (d)	055	(a) (b) (c) (d)
006	(a) (b) (c) (d)	056	(a) (b) (c) (d)
007	(a) (b) (c) (d)	057	(a) (b) (c) (d)
008	(a) (b) (c) (d)	058	(a) (b) (c) (d)
009	(a) (b) (c) (d)	059	(a) (b) (c) (d)
010	(a) (b) (c) (d)	060	(a) (b) (c) (d)
011	(a) (b) (c) (d)	061	(a) (b) (c) (d)
012	(a) (b) (c) (d)	062	(a) (b) (c) (d)
013	(a) (b) (c) (d)	063	(a) (b) (c) (d)
014	(a) (b) (c) (d)	064	(a) (b) (c) (d)
015	(a) (b) (c) (d)	065	(a) (b) (c) (d)
016	(a) (b) (c) (d)	066	(a) (b) (c) (d)
017	(a) (b) (c) (d)	067	(a) (b) (c) (d)
018	(a) (b) (c) (d)	068	(a) (b) (c) (d)
019	(a) (b) (c) (d)	069	(a) (b) (c) (d)
020	(a) (b) (c) (d)	070	(a) (b) (c) (d)
021	(a) (b) (c) (d)	071	(a) (b) (c) (d)
022	(a) (b) (c) (d)	072	(a) (b) (c) (d)
023	(a) (b) (c) (d)	073	(a) (b) (c) (d)
024	(a) (b) (c) (d)	074	(a) (b) (c) (d)
025	(a) (b) (c) (d)	075	(a) (b) (c) (d)
026	(a) (b) (c) (d)	076	(a) (b) (c) (d)
027	(a) (b) (c) (d)	077	(a) (b) (c) (d)
028	(a) (b) (c) (d)	078	(a) (b) (c) (d)
029	(a) (b) (c) (d)	079	(a) (b) (c) (d)
030	(a) (b) (c) (d)	080	(a) (b) (c) (d)
031	(a) (b) (c) (d)	081	(a) (b) (c) (d)
032	(a) (b) (c) (d)	082	(a) (b) (c) (d)
033	(a) (b) (c) (d)	083	(a) (b) (c) (d)
034	(a) (b) (c) (d)	084	(a) (b) (c) (d)
035	(a) (b) (c) (d)	085	(a) (b) (c) (d)
036	(a) (b) (c) (d)	086	(a) (b) (c) (d)
037	(a) (b) (c) (d)	087	(a) (b) (c) (d)
038	(a) (b) (c) (d)	088	(a) (b) (c) (d)
039	(a) (b) (c) (d)	089	(a) (b) (c) (d)
040	(a) (b) (c) (d)	090	(a) (b) (c) (d)
041	(a) (b) (c) (d)	091	(a) (b) (c) (d)
042	(a) (b) (c) (d)	092	(a) (b) (c) (d)
043	(a) (b) (c) (d)	093	(a) (b) (c) (d)
044	(a) (b) (c) (d)	094	(a) (b) (c) (d)
045	(a) (b) (c) (d)	095	(a) (b) (c) (d)
046	(a) (b) (c) (d)	096	(a) (b) (c) (d)
047	(a) (b) (c) (d)	097	(a) (b) (c) (d)
048	(a) (b) (c) (d)	098	(a) (b) (c) (d)
049	(a) (b) (c) (d)	099	(a) (b) (c) (d)
050	(a) (b) (c) (d)	100	(a) (b) (c) (d)

DECLARATION BY THE CANDIDATE

I declare that particulars and signature on this OMR Answer sheet are mine and are Name as in Attendance Sheet. I fruther declare that particulars filled in and Signature as well as the circles darkened on this ORIGINALCOPY is same as in OFFICE COPY.

Signature with time (in running handwriting)

CANDIDATE's NAME (in running handwriting)

MOTHER's NAME (in running handwriting)

FATHER's NAME (in running handwriting)

CANDIDATE LEFT HAND IMPRESSION

SIGNATURE OF INVIGILATOR'S WITH TIME

1

2

MEDACE

OMR SHEET

ROLL No.

1	1	1	1	1	1	1	1	1	1
2	2	2	2	2	2	2	2	2	2
3	3	3	3	3	3	3	3	3	3
4	4	4	4	4	4	4	4	4	4
5	5	5	5	5	5	5	5	5	5
6	6	6	6	6	6	6	6	6	6
7	7	7	7	7	7	7	7	7	7
8	8	8	8	8	8	8	8	8	8
9	9	9	9	9	9	9	9	9	9
0	0	0	0	0	0	0	0	0	0

TEST BOOKLET No.

1	1	1	1	1	1	1
2	2	2	2	2	2	2
3	3	3	3	3	3	3
4	4	4	4	4	4	4
5	5	5	5	5	5	5
6	6	6	6	6	6	6
7	7	7	7	7	7	7
8	8	8	8	8	8	8
9	9	9	9	9	9	9
0	0	0	0	0	0	0

TEST BOOKLET Code

Q No.	Response			
001	a	b	c	d
002	a	b	c	d
003	a	b	c	d
004	a	b	c	d
005	a	b	c	d
006	a	b	c	d
007	a	b	c	d
008	a	b	c	d
009	a	b	c	d
010	a	b	c	d
011	a	b	c	d
012	a	b	c	d
013	a	h	c	d
014	a	b	c	d
015	a	b	c	d
016	a	b	c	d
017	a	b	c	d
018	a	b	c	d
019	a	b	c	d
020	a	b	c	d
021	a	b	c	d
022	a	b	c	d
023	a	b	c	d
024	a	b	c	d
025	a	b	c	d
026	a	b	c	d
027	a	b	c	d
028	a	b	c	d
029	a	b	c	d
030	a	b	c	d
031	a	b	c	d
032	a	b	c	d
033	a	b	c	d
034	a	b	c	d
035	a	b	c	d
036	a	b	c	d
037	a	b	c	d
038	a	b	c	d
039	a	b	c	d
040	a	b	c	d
041	a	b	c	d
042	a	b	c	d
043	a	b	c	d
044	a	b	c	d
045	a	b	c	d
046	a	b	c	d
047	a	b	c	d
048	a	b	c	d
049	a	b	c	d
050	a	b	c	d

Q No.	Response			
051	a	b	c	d
052	a	b	c	d
053	a	b	c	d
054	a	b	c	d
055	a	b	c	d
056	a	b	c	d
057	a	b	c	d
058	a	b	c	d
059	a	b	c	d
060	a	b	c	d
061	a	b	c	d
062	a	b	c	d
063	a	b	c	d
064	a	b	c	d
065	a	b	c	d
066	a	b	c	d
067	a	b	c	d
068	a	b	c	d
069	a	b	c	d
070	a	b	c	d
071	a	b	c	d
072	a	b	c	d
073	a	b	c	d
074	a	b	c	d
075	a	b	c	d
076	a	b	c	d
077	a	b	c	d
078	a	b	c	d
079	a	b	c	d
080	a	b	c	d
081	a	b	c	d
082	a	b	c	d
083	a	b	c	d
084	a	b	c	d
085	a	b	c	d
086	a	b	c	d
087	a	b	c	d
088	a	b	c	d
089	a	b	c	d
090	a	b	c	d
091	a	b	c	d
092	a	b	c	d
093	a	b	c	d
094	a	b	c	d
095	a	b	c	d
096	a	b	c	d
097	a	b	c	d
098	a	b	c	d
099	a	b	c	d
100	a	b	c	d

DECLARATION BY THE CANDIDATE

I declare that particulars and signature on this OMR Answer sheet are mine and are Name as in Attendance Sheet. I fruther declare that particulars filled in and Signature as well as the circles darkened on this ORIGINALCOPY is same as in OFFICE COPY.

Signature with time (in running handwriting)

CANDIDATE's NAME (in running handwriting)

MOTHER's NAME (in running handwriting)

FATHER's NAME (in running handwriting)

CANDIDATE LEFT HAND IMPRESSION

SIGNATURE OF INVIGILATOR'S WITH TIME

1

2

OMR SHEET

ROLL No.

1	1	1	1	1	1	1	1	1	1
2	2	2	2	2	2	2	2	2	2
3	3	3	3	3	3	3	3	3	3
4	4	4	4	4	4	4	4	4	4
5	5	5	5	5	5	5	5	5	5
6	6	6	6	6	6	6	6	6	6
7	7	7	7	7	7	7	7	7	7
8	8	8	8	8	8	8	8	8	8
9	9	9	9	9	9	9	9	9	9
0	0	0	0	0	0	0	0	0	0

TEST BOOKLET No.

1	1	1	1	1	1	1
2	2	2	2	2	2	2
3	3	3	3	3	3	3
4	4	4	4	4	4	4
5	5	5	5	5	5	5
6	6	6	6	6	6	6
7	7	7	7	7	7	7
8	8	8	8	8	8	8
9	9	9	9	9	9	9
0	0	0	0	0	0	0

TEST BOOKLET Code

Q No.	Response				Q No.	Response			
001	a	b	c	d	051	a	b	c	d
002	a	b	c	d	052	a	b	c	d
003	a	b	c	d	053	a	b	c	d
004	a	b	c	d	054	a	b	c	d
005	a	b	c	d	055	a	b	c	d
006	a	b	c	d	056	a	b	c	d
007	a	b	c	d	057	a	b	c	d
008	a	b	c	d	058	a	b	c	d
009	a	b	c	d	059	a	b	c	d
010	a	b	c	d	060	a	b	c	d
011	a	b	c	d	061	a	b	c	d
012	a	b	c	d	062	a	b	c	d
013	a	b	c	d	063	a	b	c	d
014	a	b	c	d	064	a	b	c	d
015	a	b	c	d	065	a	b	c	d
016	a	b	c	d	066	a	b	c	d
017	a	b	c	d	067	a	b	c	d
018	a	b	c	d	068	a	b	c	d
019	a	b	c	d	069	a	b	c	d
020	a	b	c	d	070	a	b	c	d
021	a	b	c	d	071	a	b	c	d
022	a	b	c	d	072	a	b	c	d
023	a	b	c	d	073	a	b	c	d
024	a	b	c	d	074	a	b	c	d
025	a	b	c	d	075	a	b	c	d
026	a	b	c	d	076	a	b	c	d
027	a	b	c	d	077	a	b	c	d
028	a	b	c	d	078	a	b	c	d
029	a	b	c	d	079	a	b	c	d
030	a	b	c	d	080	a	b	c	d
031	a	b	c	d	081	a	b	c	d
032	a	b	c	d	082	a	b	c	d
033	a	b	c	d	083	a	b	c	d
034	a	b	c	d	084	a	b	c	d
035	a	b	c	d	085	a	b	c	d
036	a	b	c	d	086	a	b	c	d
037	a	b	c	d	087	a	b	c	d
038	a	b	c	d	088	a	b	c	d
039	a	b	c	d	089	a	b	c	d
040	a	b	c	d	090	a	b	c	d
041	a	b	c	d	091	a	b	c	d
042	a	b	c	d	092	a	b	c	d
043	a	b	c	d	093	a	b	c	d
044	a	b	c	d	094	a	b	c	d
045	a	b	c	d	095	a	b	c	d
046	a	b	c	d	096	a	b	c	d
047	a	b	c	d	097	a	b	c	d
048	a	b	c	d	098	a	b	c	d
049	a	b	c	d	099	a	b	c	d
050	a	b	c	d	100	a	b	c	d

DECLARATION BY THE CANDIDATE

I declare that particulars and signature on this OMR Answer sheet are mine and are Name as in Attendance Sheet. I fruther declare that particulars filled in and Signature as well as the circles darkened on this ORIGINALCOPY is same as in OFFICE COPY.

Signature with time (in running handwriting)

CANDIDATE's NAME (in running handwriting)

MOTHER's NAME (in running handwriting)

FATHER's NAME (in running handwriting)

CANDIDATE LEFT HAND IMPRESSION

SIGNATURE OF INVIGILATOR'S WITH TIME

1

2

MEDACE

OMR SHEET

ROLL No.

1	1	1	1	1	1	1	1	1	1
2	2	2	2	2	2	2	2	2	2
3	3	3	3	3	3	3	3	3	3
4	4	4	4	4	4	4	4	4	4
5	5	5	5	5	5	5	5	5	5
6	6	6	6	6	6	6	6	6	6
7	7	7	7	7	7	7	7	7	7
8	8	8	8	8	8	8	8	8	8
9	9	9	9	9	9	9	9	9	9
0	0	0	0	0	0	0	0	0	0

TEST BOOKLET No.

1	1	1	1	1	1	1
2	2	2	2	2	2	2
3	3	3	3	3	3	3
4	4	4	4	4	4	4
5	5	5	5	5	5	5
6	6	6	6	6	6	6
7	7	7	7	7	7	7
8	8	8	8	8	8	8
9	9	9	9	9	9	9
0	0	0	0	0	0	0

TEST BOOKLET Code

Q No.	Response				Q No.	Response			
001	a	b	c	d	051	a	b	c	d
002	a	b	c	d	052	a	b	c	d
003	a	b	c	d	053	a	b	c	d
004	a	b	c	d	054	a	b	c	d
005	a	b	c	d	055	a	b	c	d
006	a	b	c	d	056	a	b	c	d
007	a	b	c	d	057	a	b	c	d
008	a	b	c	d	058	a	b	c	d
009	a	b	c	d	059	a	b	c	d
010	a	b	c	d	060	a	b	c	d
011	a	b	c	d	061	a	b	c	d
012	a	b	c	d	062	a	b	c	d
013	a	b	c	d	063	a	b	c	d
014	a	b	c	d	064	a	b	c	d
015	a	b	c	d	065	a	b	c	d
016	a	b	c	d	066	a	b	c	d
017	a	b	c	d	067	a	b	c	d
018	a	b	c	d	068	a	b	c	d
019	a	b	c	d	069	a	b	c	d
020	a	b	c	d	070	a	b	c	d
021	a	b	c	d	071	a	b	c	d
022	a	b	c	d	072	a	b	c	d
023	a	b	c	d	073	a	b	c	d
024	a	b	c	d	074	a	b	c	d
025	a	b	c	d	075	a	b	c	d
026	a	b	c	d	076	a	b	c	d
027	a	b	c	d	077	a	b	c	d
028	a	b	c	d	078	a	b	c	d
029	a	b	c	d	079	a	b	c	d
030	a	b	c	d	080	a	b	c	d
031	a	b	c	d	081	a	b	c	d
032	a	b	c	d	082	a	b	c	d
033	a	b	c	d	083	a	b	c	d
034	a	b	c	d	084	a	b	c	d
035	a	b	c	d	085	a	b	c	d
036	a	b	c	d	086	a	b	c	d
037	a	b	c	d	087	a	b	c	d
038	a	b	c	d	088	a	b	c	d
039	a	b	c	d	089	a	b	c	d
040	a	b	c	d	090	a	b	c	d
041	a	b	c	d	091	a	b	c	d
042	a	b	c	d	092	a	b	c	d
043	a	b	c	d	093	a	b	c	d
044	a	b	c	d	094	a	b	c	d
045	a	b	c	d	095	a	b	c	d
046	a	b	c	d	096	a	b	c	d
047	a	b	c	d	097	a	b	c	d
048	a	b	c	d	098	a	b	c	d
049	a	b	c	d	099	a	b	c	d
050	a	b	c	d	100	a	b	c	d

DECLARATION BY THE CANDIDATE

I declare that particulars and signature on this OMR Answer sheet are mine and are Name as in Attendance Sheet. I fruther declare that particulars filled in and Signature as well as the circles darkened on this ORIGINALCOPY is same as in OFFICE COPY.

Signature with time (in running handwriting)

CANDIDATE's NAME (in running handwriting)

MOTHER's NAME (in running handwriting)

FATHER's NAME (in running handwriting)

CANDIDATE LEFT HAND IMPRESSION

SIGNATURE OF INVIGILATOR'S WITH TIME

1

2

OMR SHEET

ROLL No.

1 1 1 1 1 1 1 1 1 1
2 2 2 2 2 2 2 2 2 2
3 3 3 3 3 3 3 3 3 3
4 4 4 4 4 4 4 4 4 4
5 5 5 5 5 5 5 5 5 5
6 6 6 6 6 6 6 6 6 6
7 7 7 7 7 7 7 7 7 7
8 8 8 8 8 8 8 8 8 8
9 9 9 9 9 9 9 9 9 9
0 0 0 0 0 0 0 0 0 0

TEST BOOKLET No.

1 1 1 1 1 1 1
2 2 2 2 2 2 2
3 3 3 3 3 3 3
4 4 4 4 4 4 4
5 5 5 5 5 5 5
6 6 6 6 6 6 6
7 7 7 7 7 7 7
8 8 8 8 8 8 8
9 9 9 9 9 9 9
0 0 0 0 0 0 0

TEST BOOKLET Code

Q No.	Response	Q No.	Response
001	a b c d	051	a b c d
002	a b c d	052	a b c d
003	a b c d	053	a b c d
004	a b c d	054	a b c d
005	a b c d	055	a b c d
006	a b c d	056	a b c d
007	a b c d	057	a b c d
008	a b c d	058	a b c d
009	a b c d	059	a b c d
010	a b c d	060	a b c d
011	a b c d	061	a b c d
012	a b c d	062	a b c d
013	a b c d	063	a b c d
014	a b c d	064	a b c d
015	a b c d	065	a b c d
016	a b c d	066	a b c d
017	a b c d	067	a b c d
018	a b c d	068	a b c d
019	a b c d	069	a b c d
020	a b c d	070	a b c d
021	a b c d	071	a b c d
022	a b c d	072	a b c d
023	a b c d	073	a b c d
024	a b c d	074	a b c d
025	a b c d	075	a b c d
026	a b c d	076	a b c d
027	a b c d	077	a b c d
028	a b c d	078	a b c d
029	a b c d	079	a b c d
030	a b c d	080	a b c d
031	a b c d	081	a b c d
032	a b c d	082	a b c d
033	a b c d	083	a b c d
034	a b c d	084	a b c d
035	a b c d	085	a b c d
036	a b c d	086	a b c d
037	a b c d	087	a b c d
038	a b c d	088	a b c d
039	a b c d	089	a b c d
040	a b c d	090	a b c d
041	a b c d	091	a b c d
042	a b c d	092	a b c d
043	a b c d	093	a b c d
044	a b c d	094	a b c d
045	a b c d	095	a b c d
046	a b c d	096	a b c d
047	a b c d	097	a b c d
048	a b c d	098	a b c d
049	a b c d	099	a b c d
050	a b c d	100	a b c d

DECLARATION BY THE CANDIDATE

I declare that particulars and signature on this OMR Answer sheet are mine and are Name as in Attendance Sheet. I fruther declare that particulars filled in and Signature as well as the circles darkened on this ORIGINALCOPY is same as in OFFICE COPY.

Signature with time (in running handwriting)

CANDIDATE's NAME (in running handwriting)

MOTHER's NAME (in running handwriting)

FATHER's NAME (in running handwriting)

CANDIDATE LEFT HAND IMPRESSION

SIGNATURE OF INVIGILATOR'S WITH TIME

1

2

OMR SHEET

ROLL No.

1	1	1	1	1	1	1	1	1	1
2	2	2	2	2	2	2	2	2	2
3	3	3	3	3	3	3	3	3	3
4	4	4	4	4	4	4	4	4	4
5	5	5	5	5	5	5	5	5	5
6	6	6	6	6	6	6	6	6	6
7	7	7	7	7	7	7	7	7	7
8	8	8	8	8	8	8	8	8	8
9	9	9	9	9	9	9	9	9	9
0	0	0	0	0	0	0	0	0	0

TEST BOOKLET No.

1	1	1	1	1	1	1
2	2	2	2	2	2	2
3	3	3	3	3	3	3
4	4	4	4	4	4	4
5	5	5	5	5	5	5
6	6	6	6	6	6	6
7	7	7	7	7	7	7
8	8	8	8	8	8	8
9	9	9	9	9	9	9
0	0	0	0	0	0	0

TEST BOOKLET Code

Q No.	Response				Q No.	Response			
001	a	b	c	d	051	a	b	c	d
002	a	b	c	d	052	a	b	c	d
003	a	b	c	d	053	a	b	c	d
004	a	b	c	d	054	a	b	c	d
005	a	b	c	d	055	a	b	c	d
006	a	b	c	d	056	a	b	c	d
007	a	b	c	d	057	a	b	c	d
008	a	b	c	d	058	a	b	c	d
009	a	b	c	d	059	a	b	c	d
010	a	b	c	d	060	a	b	c	d
011	a	b	c	d	061	a	b	c	d
012	a	b	c	d	062	a	b	c	d
013	a	b	c	d	063	a	b	c	d
014	a	b	c	d	064	a	b	c	d
015	a	b	c	d	065	a	b	c	d
016	a	b	c	d	066	a	b	c	d
017	a	b	c	d	067	a	b	c	d
018	a	b	c	d	068	a	b	c	d
019	a	b	c	d	069	a	b	c	d
020	a	b	c	d	070	a	b	c	d
021	a	b	c	d	071	a	b	c	d
022	a	b	c	d	072	a	b	c	d
023	a	b	c	d	073	a	b	c	d
024	a	b	c	d	074	a	b	c	d
025	a	b	c	d	075	a	b	c	d
026	a	b	c	d	076	a	b	c	d
027	a	b	c	d	077	a	b	c	d
028	a	b	c	d	078	a	b	c	d
029	a	b	c	d	079	a	b	c	d
030	a	b	c	d	080	a	b	c	d
031	a	b	c	d	081	a	b	c	d
032	a	b	c	d	082	a	b	c	d
033	a	b	c	d	083	a	b	c	d
034	a	b	c	d	084	a	b	c	d
035	a	b	c	d	085	a	b	c	d
036	a	b	c	d	086	a	b	c	d
037	a	b	c	d	087	a	b	c	d
038	a	b	c	d	088	a	b	c	d
039	a	b	c	d	089	a	b	c	d
040	a	b	c	d	090	a	b	c	d
041	a	b	c	d	091	a	b	c	d
042	a	b	c	d	092	a	b	c	d
043	a	b	c	d	093	a	b	c	d
044	a	b	c	d	094	a	b	c	d
045	a	b	c	d	095	a	b	c	d
046	a	b	c	d	096	a	b	c	d
047	a	b	c	d	097	a	b	c	d
048	a	b	c	d	098	a	b	c	d
049	a	b	c	d	099	a	b	c	d
050	a	b	c	d	100	a	b	c	d

DECLARATION BY THE CANDIDATE

I declare that particulars and signature on this OMR Answer sheet are mine and are Name as in Attendance Sheet. I fruther declare that particulars filled in and Signature as well as the circles darkened on this ORIGINALCOPY is same as in OFFICE COPY.

Signature with time (in running handwriting)

CANDIDATE's NAME (in running handwriting)

MOTHER's NAME (in running handwriting)

FATHER's NAME (in running handwriting)

CANDIDATE LEFT HAND IMPRESSION

SIGNATURE OF INVIGILATOR'S WITH TIME

1

2

MEDACE

OMR SHEET

ROLL No.

1	1	1	1	1	1	1	1	1	1
2	2	2	2	2	2	2	2	2	2
3	3	3	3	3	3	3	3	3	3
4	4	4	4	4	4	4	4	4	4
5	5	5	5	5	5	5	5	5	5
6	6	6	6	6	6	6	6	6	6
7	7	7	7	7	7	7	7	7	7
8	8	8	8	8	8	8	8	8	8
9	9	9	9	9	9	9	9	9	9
0	0	0	0	0	0	0	0	0	0

TEST BOOKLET No.

1	1	1	1	1	1	1
2	2	2	2	2	2	2
3	3	3	3	3	3	3
4	4	4	4	4	4	4
5	5	5	5	5	5	5
6	6	6	6	6	6	6
7	7	7	7	7	7	7
8	8	8	8	8	8	8
9	9	9	9	9	9	9
0	0	0	0	0	0	0

TEST BOOKLET Code

Q No.	Response				Q No.	Response			
001	a	b	c	d	051	a	b	c	d
002	a	b	c	d	052	a	b	c	d
003	a	b	c	d	053	a	b	c	d
004	a	b	c	d	054	a	b	c	d
005	a	b	c	d	055	a	b	c	d
006	a	b	c	d	056	a	b	c	d
007	a	b	c	d	057	a	b	c	d
008	a	b	c	d	058	a	b	c	d
009	a	b	c	d	059	a	b	c	d
010	a	b	c	d	060	a	b	c	d
011	a	b	c	d	061	a	b	c	d
012	a	b	c	d	062	a	b	c	d
013	a	b	c	d	063	a	b	c	d
014	a	b	c	d	064	a	b	c	d
015	a	b	c	d	065	a	b	c	d
016	a	b	c	d	066	a	b	c	d
017	a	b	c	d	067	a	b	c	d
018	a	b	c	d	068	a	b	c	d
019	a	b	c	d	069	a	b	c	d
020	a	b	c	d	070	a	b	c	d
021	a	b	c	d	071	a	b	c	d
022	a	b	c	d	072	a	b	c	d
023	a	b	c	d	073	a	b	c	d
024	a	b	c	d	074	a	b	c	d
025	a	b	c	d	075	a	b	c	d
026	a	b	c	d	076	a	b	c	d
027	a	b	c	d	077	a	b	c	d
028	a	b	c	d	078	a	b	c	d
029	a	b	c	d	079	a	b	c	d
030	a	b	c	d	080	a	b	c	d
031	a	b	c	d	081	a	b	c	d
032	a	b	c	d	082	a	b	c	d
033	a	b	c	d	083	a	b	c	d
034	a	b	c	d	084	a	b	c	d
035	a	b	c	d	085	a	b	c	d
036	a	b	c	d	086	a	b	c	d
037	a	b	c	d	087	a	b	c	d
038	a	b	c	d	088	a	b	c	d
039	a	b	c	d	089	a	b	c	d
040	a	b	c	d	090	a	b	c	d
041	a	b	c	d	091	a	b	c	d
042	a	b	c	d	092	a	b	c	d
043	a	b	c	d	093	a	b	c	d
044	a	b	c	d	094	a	b	c	d
045	a	b	c	d	095	a	b	c	d
046	a	b	c	d	096	a	b	c	d
047	a	b	c	d	097	a	b	c	d
048	a	b	c	d	098	a	b	c	d
049	a	b	c	d	099	a	b	c	d
050	a	b	c	d	100	a	b	c	d

DECLARATION BY THE CANDIDATE

I declare that particulars and signature on this OMR Answer sheet are mine and are Name as in Attendance Sheet. I fruther declare that particulars filled in and Signature as well as the circles darkened on this ORIGINALCOPY is same as in OFFICE COPY.

Signature with time (in running handwriting)

CANDIDATE's NAME (in running handwriting)

MOTHER's NAME (in running handwriting)

FATHER's NAME (in running handwriting)

CANDIDATE LEFT HAND IMPRESSION

SIGNATURE OF INVIGILATOR'S WITH TIME

1

2

MEDACE

OMR SHEET

ROLL No.

1	1	1	1	1	1	1	1	1	1
2	2	2	2	2	2	2	2	2	2
3	3	3	3	3	3	3	3	3	3
4	4	4	4	4	4	4	4	4	4
5	5	5	5	5	5	5	5	5	5
6	6	6	6	6	6	6	6	6	6
7	7	7	7	7	7	7	7	7	7
8	8	8	8	8	8	8	8	8	8
9	9	9	9	9	9	9	9	9	9
0	0	0	0	0	0	0	0	0	0

TEST BOOKLET No.

1	1	1	1	1	1	1
2	2	2	2	2	2	2
3	3	3	3	3	3	3
4	4	4	4	4	4	4
5	5	5	5	5	5	5
6	6	6	6	6	6	6
7	7	7	7	7	7	7
8	8	8	8	8	8	8
9	9	9	9	9	9	9
0	0	0	0	0	0	0

TEST BOOKLET Code

Q No.	Response				Q No.	Response			
001	a	b	c	d	051	a	b	c	d
002	a	b	c	d	052	a	b	c	d
003	a	b	c	d	053	a	b	c	d
004	a	b	c	d	054	a	b	c	d
005	a	b	c	d	055	a	b	c	d
006	a	b	c	d	056	a	b	c	d
007	a	b	c	d	057	a	b	c	d
008	a	b	c	d	058	a	b	c	d
009	a	b	c	d	059	a	b	c	d
010	a	b	c	d	060	a	b	c	d
011	a	b	c	d	061	a	b	c	d
012	a	b	c	d	062	a	b	c	d
013	a	b	c	d	063	a	b	c	d
014	a	b	c	d	064	a	b	c	d
015	a	b	c	d	065	a	b	c	d
016	a	b	c	d	066	a	b	c	d
017	a	b	c	d	067	a	b	c	d
018	a	b	c	d	068	a	b	c	d
019	a	b	c	d	069	a	b	c	d
020	a	b	c	d	070	a	b	c	d
021	a	b	c	d	071	a	b	c	d
022	a	b	c	d	072	a	b	c	d
023	a	b	c	d	073	a	b	c	d
024	a	b	c	d	074	a	b	c	d
025	a	b	c	d	075	a	b	c	d
026	a	b	c	d	076	a	b	c	d
027	a	b	c	d	077	a	b	c	d
028	a	b	c	d	078	a	b	c	d
029	a	b	c	d	079	a	b	c	d
030	a	b	c	d	080	a	b	c	d
031	a	b	c	d	081	a	b	c	d
032	a	b	c	d	082	a	b	c	d
033	a	b	c	d	083	a	b	c	d
034	a	b	c	d	084	a	b	c	d
035	a	b	c	d	085	a	b	c	d
036	a	b	c	d	086	a	b	c	d
037	a	b	c	d	087	a	b	c	d
038	a	b	c	d	088	a	b	c	d
039	a	b	c	d	089	a	b	c	d
040	a	b	c	d	090	a	b	c	d
041	a	b	c	d	091	a	b	c	d
042	a	b	c	d	092	a	b	c	d
043	a	b	c	d	093	a	b	c	d
044	a	b	c	d	094	a	b	c	d
045	a	b	c	d	095	a	b	c	d
046	a	b	c	d	096	a	b	c	d
047	a	b	c	d	097	a	b	c	d
048	a	b	c	d	098	a	b	c	d
049	a	b	c	d	099	a	b	c	d
050	a	b	c	d	100	a	b	c	d

DECLARATION BY THE CANDIDATE

I declare that particulars and signature on this OMR Answer sheet are mine and are Name as in Attendance Sheet. I fruther declare that particulars filled in and Signature as well as the circles darkened on this ORIGINALCOPY is same as in OFFICE COPY.

Signature with time (in running handwriting)

CANDIDATE's NAME (in running handwriting)

MOTHER's NAME (in running handwriting)

FATHER's NAME (in running handwriting)

CANDIDATE LEFT HAND IMPRESSION

SIGNATURE OF INVIGILATOR'S WITH TIME

1

2

MEDACE

OMR SHEET

ROLL No.

1	1	1	1	1	1	1	1	1	1
2	2	2	2	2	2	2	2	2	2
3	3	3	3	3	3	3	3	3	3
4	4	4	4	4	4	4	4	4	4
5	5	5	5	5	5	5	5	5	5
6	6	6	6	6	6	6	6	6	6
7	7	7	7	7	7	7	7	7	7
8	8	8	8	8	8	8	8	8	8
9	9	9	9	9	9	9	9	9	9
0	0	0	0	0	0	0	0	0	0

TEST BOOKLET No.

1	1	1	1	1	1	1
2	2	2	2	2	2	2
3	3	3	3	3	3	3
4	4	4	4	4	4	4
5	5	5	5	5	5	5
6	6	6	6	6	6	6
7	7	7	7	7	7	7
8	8	8	8	8	8	8
9	9	9	9	9	9	9
0	0	0	0	0	0	0

TEST BOOKLET Code

Q No.	Response	Q No.	Response
001	a b c d	051	a b c d
002	a b c d	052	a b c d
003	a b c d	053	a b c d
004	a b c d	054	a b c d
005	a b c d	055	a b c d
006	a b c d	056	a b c d
007	a b c d	057	a b c d
008	a b c d	058	a b c d
009	a b c d	059	a b c d
010	a b c d	060	a b c d
011	a b c d	061	a b c d
012	a b c d	062	a b c d
013	a b c d	063	a b c d
014	a b c d	064	a b c d
015	a b c d	065	a b c d
016	a b c d	066	a b c d
017	a b c d	067	a b c d
018	a b c d	068	a b c d
019	a b c d	069	a b c d
020	a b c d	070	a b c d
021	a b c d	071	a b c d
022	a b c d	072	a b c d
023	a b c d	073	a b c d
024	a b c d	074	a b c d
025	a b c d	075	a b c d
026	a b c d	076	a b c d
027	a b c d	077	a b c d
028	a b c d	078	a b c d
029	a b c d	079	a b c d
030	a b c d	080	a b c d
031	a b c d	081	a b c d
032	a b c d	082	a b c d
033	a b c d	083	a b c d
034	a b c d	084	a b c d
035	a b c d	085	a b c d
036	a b c d	086	a b c d
037	a b c d	087	a b c d
038	a b c d	088	a b c d
039	a b c d	089	a b c d
040	a b c d	090	a b c d
041	a b c d	091	a b c d
042	a b c d	092	a b c d
043	a b c d	093	a b c d
044	a b c d	094	a b c d
045	a b c d	095	a b c d
046	a b c d	096	a b c d
047	a b c d	097	a b c d
048	a b c d	098	a b c d
049	a b c d	099	a b c d
050	a b c d	100	a b c d

DECLARATION BY THE CANDIDATE

I declare that particulars and signature on this OMR Answer sheet are mine and are Name as in Attendance Sheet. I fruther declare that particulars filled in and Signature as well as the circles darkened on this ORIGINALCOPY is same as in OFFICE COPY.

Signature with time (in running handwriting)

CANDIDATE's NAME (in running handwriting)

MOTHER's NAME (in running handwriting)

FATHER's NAME (in running handwriting)

CANDIDATE LEFT HAND IMPRESSION

SIGNATURE OF INVIGILATOR'S WITH TIME

1

2

OMR SHEET

ROLL No.

1	1	1	1	1	1	1	1	1	1
2	2	2	2	2	2	2	2	2	2
3	3	3	3	3	3	3	3	3	3
4	4	4	4	4	4	4	4	4	4
5	5	5	5	5	5	5	5	5	5
6	6	6	6	6	6	6	6	6	6
7	7	7	7	7	7	7	7	7	7
8	8	8	8	8	8	8	8	8	8
9	9	9	9	9	9	9	9	9	9
0	0	0	0	0	0	0	0	0	0

TEST BOOKLET No.

1	1	1	1	1	1	1
2	2	2	2	2	2	2
3	3	3	3	3	3	3
4	4	4	4	4	4	4
5	5	5	5	5	5	5
6	6	6	6	6	6	6
7	7	7	7	7	7	7
8	8	8	8	8	8	8
9	9	9	9	9	9	9
0	0	0	0	0	0	0

TEST BOOKLET Code

Q No.	Response	Q No.	Response
001	a b c d	051	a b c d
002	a b c d	052	a b c d
003	a b c d	053	a b c d
004	a b c d	054	a b c d
005	a b c d	055	a b c d
006	a b c d	056	a b c d
007	a b c d	057	a b c d
008	a b c d	058	a b c d
009	a b c d	059	a b c d
010	a b c d	060	a b c d
011	a b c d	061	a b c d
012	a b c d	062	a b c d
013	a b c d	063	a b c d
014	a b c d	064	a b c d
015	a b c d	065	a b c d
016	a b c d	066	a b c d
017	a b c d	067	a b c d
018	a b c d	068	a b c d
019	a b c d	069	a b c d
020	a b c d	070	a b c d
021	a b c d	071	a b c d
022	a b c d	072	a b c d
023	a b c d	073	a b c d
024	a b c d	074	a b c d
025	a b c d	075	a b c d
026	a b c d	076	a b c d
027	a b c d	077	a b c d
028	a b c d	078	a b c d
029	a b c d	079	a b c d
030	a b c d	080	a b c d
031	a b c d	081	a b c d
032	a b c d	082	a b c d
033	a b c d	083	a b c d
034	a b c d	084	a b c d
035	a b c d	085	a b c d
036	a b c d	086	a b c d
037	a b c d	087	a b c d
038	a b c d	088	a b c d
039	a b c d	089	a b c d
040	a b c d	090	a b c d
041	a b c d	091	a b c d
042	a b c d	092	a b c d
043	a b c d	093	a b c d
044	a b c d	094	a b c d
045	a b c d	095	a b c d
046	a b c d	096	a b c d
047	a b c d	097	a b c d
048	a b c d	098	a b c d
049	a b c d	099	a b c d
050	a b c d	100	a b c d

DECLARATION BY THE CANDIDATE

I declare that particulars and signature on this OMR Answer sheet are mine and are Name as in Attendance Sheet. I fruther declare that particulars filled in and Signature as well as the circles darkened on this ORIGINALCOPY is same as in OFFICE COPY.

Signature with time (in running handwriting)

CANDIDATE's NAME (in running handwriting)

MOTHER's NAME (in running handwriting)

FATHER's NAME (in running handwriting)

CANDIDATE LEFT HAND IMPRESSION

SIGNATURE OF INVIGILATOR'S WITH TIME

1

2

OMR SHEET

ROLL No.

1	1	1	1	1	1	1	1	1	1
2	2	2	2	2	2	2	2	2	2
3	3	3	3	3	3	3	3	3	3
4	4	4	4	4	4	4	4	4	4
5	5	5	5	5	5	5	5	5	5
6	6	6	6	6	6	6	6	6	6
7	7	7	7	7	7	7	7	7	7
8	8	8	8	8	8	8	8	8	8
9	9	9	9	9	9	9	9	9	9
0	0	0	0	0	0	0	0	0	0

TEST BOOKLET No.

1	1	1	1	1	1	1
2	2	2	2	2	2	2
3	3	3	3	3	3	3
4	4	4	4	4	4	4
5	5	5	5	5	5	5
6	6	6	6	6	6	6
7	7	7	7	7	7	7
8	8	8	8	8	8	8
9	9	9	9	9	9	9
0	0	0	0	0	0	0

TEST BOOKLET Code

Q No.	Response	Q No.	Response
001	ⓐ ⓑ ⓒ ⓓ	051	ⓐ ⓑ ⓒ ⓓ
002	ⓐ ⓑ ⓒ ⓓ	052	ⓐ ⓑ ⓒ ⓓ
003	ⓐ ⓑ ⓒ ⓓ	053	ⓐ ⓑ ⓒ ⓓ
004	ⓐ ⓑ ⓒ ⓓ	054	ⓐ ⓑ ⓒ ⓓ
005	ⓐ ⓑ ⓒ ⓓ	055	ⓐ ⓑ ⓒ ⓓ
006	ⓐ ⓑ ⓒ ⓓ	056	ⓐ ⓑ ⓒ ⓓ
007	ⓐ ⓑ ⓒ ⓓ	057	ⓐ ⓑ ⓒ ⓓ
008	ⓐ ⓑ ⓒ ⓓ	058	ⓐ ⓑ ⓒ ⓓ
009	ⓐ ⓑ ⓒ ⓓ	059	ⓐ ⓑ ⓒ ⓓ
010	ⓐ ⓑ ⓒ ⓓ	060	ⓐ ⓑ ⓒ ⓓ
011	ⓐ ⓑ ⓒ ⓓ	061	ⓐ ⓑ ⓒ ⓓ
012	ⓐ ⓑ ⓒ ⓓ	062	ⓐ ⓑ ⓒ ⓓ
013	ⓐ ⓑ ⓒ ⓓ	063	ⓐ ⓑ ⓒ ⓓ
014	ⓐ ⓑ ⓒ ⓓ	064	ⓐ ⓑ ⓒ ⓓ
015	ⓐ ⓑ ⓒ ⓓ	065	ⓐ ⓑ ⓒ ⓓ
016	ⓐ ⓑ ⓒ ⓓ	066	ⓐ ⓑ ⓒ ⓓ
017	ⓐ ⓑ ⓒ ⓓ	067	ⓐ ⓑ ⓒ ⓓ
018	ⓐ ⓑ ⓒ ⓓ	068	ⓐ ⓑ ⓒ ⓓ
019	ⓐ ⓑ ⓒ ⓓ	069	ⓐ ⓑ ⓒ ⓓ
020	ⓐ ⓑ ⓒ ⓓ	070	ⓐ ⓑ ⓒ ⓓ
021	ⓐ ⓑ ⓒ ⓓ	071	ⓐ ⓑ ⓒ ⓓ
022	ⓐ ⓑ ⓒ ⓓ	072	ⓐ ⓑ ⓒ ⓓ
023	ⓐ ⓑ ⓒ ⓓ	073	ⓐ ⓑ ⓒ ⓓ
024	ⓐ ⓑ ⓒ ⓓ	074	ⓐ ⓑ ⓒ ⓓ
025	ⓐ ⓑ ⓒ ⓓ	075	ⓐ ⓑ ⓒ ⓓ
026	ⓐ ⓑ ⓒ ⓓ	076	ⓐ ⓑ ⓒ ⓓ
027	ⓐ ⓑ ⓒ ⓓ	077	ⓐ ⓑ ⓒ ⓓ
028	ⓐ ⓑ ⓒ ⓓ	078	ⓐ ⓑ ⓒ ⓓ
029	ⓐ ⓑ ⓒ ⓓ	079	ⓐ ⓑ ⓒ ⓓ
030	ⓐ ⓑ ⓒ ⓓ	080	ⓐ ⓑ ⓒ ⓓ
031	ⓐ ⓑ ⓒ ⓓ	081	ⓐ ⓑ ⓒ ⓓ
032	ⓐ ⓑ ⓒ ⓓ	082	ⓐ ⓑ ⓒ ⓓ
033	ⓐ ⓑ ⓒ ⓓ	083	ⓐ ⓑ ⓒ ⓓ
034	ⓐ ⓑ ⓒ ⓓ	084	ⓐ ⓑ ⓒ ⓓ
035	ⓐ ⓑ ⓒ ⓓ	085	ⓐ ⓑ ⓒ ⓓ
036	ⓐ ⓑ ⓒ ⓓ	086	ⓐ ⓑ ⓒ ⓓ
037	ⓐ ⓑ ⓒ ⓓ	087	ⓐ ⓑ ⓒ ⓓ
038	ⓐ ⓑ ⓒ ⓓ	088	ⓐ ⓑ ⓒ ⓓ
039	ⓐ ⓑ ⓒ ⓓ	089	ⓐ ⓑ ⓒ ⓓ
040	ⓐ ⓑ ⓒ ⓓ	090	ⓐ ⓑ ⓒ ⓓ
041	ⓐ ⓑ ⓒ ⓓ	091	ⓐ ⓑ ⓒ ⓓ
042	ⓐ ⓑ ⓒ ⓓ	092	ⓐ ⓑ ⓒ ⓓ
043	ⓐ ⓑ ⓒ ⓓ	093	ⓐ ⓑ ⓒ ⓓ
044	ⓐ ⓑ ⓒ ⓓ	094	ⓐ ⓑ ⓒ ⓓ
045	ⓐ ⓑ ⓒ ⓓ	095	ⓐ ⓑ ⓒ ⓓ
046	ⓐ ⓑ ⓒ ⓓ	096	ⓐ ⓑ ⓒ ⓓ
047	ⓐ ⓑ ⓒ ⓓ	097	ⓐ ⓑ ⓒ ⓓ
048	ⓐ ⓑ ⓒ ⓓ	098	ⓐ ⓑ ⓒ ⓓ
049	ⓐ ⓑ ⓒ ⓓ	099	ⓐ ⓑ ⓒ ⓓ
050	ⓐ ⓑ ⓒ ⓓ	100	ⓐ ⓑ ⓒ ⓓ

DECLARATION BY THE CANDIDATE

I declare that particulars and signature on this OMR Answer sheet are mine and are Name as in Attendance Sheet. I fruther declare that particulars filled in and Signature as well as the circles darkened on this ORIGINALCOPY is same as in OFFICE COPY.

Signature with time (in running handwriting)

CANDIDATE's NAME (in running handwriting)

MOTHER's NAME (in running handwriting)

FATHER's NAME (in running handwriting)

CANDIDATE LEFT HAND IMPRESSION

SIGNATURE OF INVIGILATOR'S WITH TIME

1

2

OMR SHEET

ROLL No.

1	1	1	1	1	1	1	1	1	1
2	2	2	2	2	2	2	2	2	2
3	3	3	3	3	3	3	3	3	3
4	4	4	4	4	4	4	4	4	4
5	5	5	5	5	5	5	5	5	5
6	6	6	6	6	6	6	6	6	6
7	7	7	7	7	7	7	7	7	7
8	8	8	8	8	8	8	8	8	8
9	9	9	9	9	9	9	9	9	9
0	0	0	0	0	0	0	0	0	0

TEST BOOKLET No.

1	1	1	1	1	1	1
2	2	2	2	2	2	2
3	3	3	3	3	3	3
4	4	4	4	4	4	4
5	5	5	5	5	5	5
6	6	6	6	6	6	6
7	7	7	7	7	7	7
8	8	8	8	8	8	8
9	9	9	9	9	9	9
0	0	0	0	0	0	0

TEST BOOKLET Code

DECLARATION BY THE CANDIDATE

I declare that particulars and signature on this OMR Answer sheet are mine and are Name as in Attendance Sheet. I fruther declare that particulars filled in and Signature as well as the circles darkened on this ORIGINALCOPY is same as in OFFICE COPY.

Signature with time (in running handwriting)

CANDIDATE's NAME (in running handwriting)

Q No.	Response			
001	a	b	c	d
002	a	b	c	d
003	a	b	c	d
004	a	b	c	d
005	a	b	c	d
006	a	b	c	d
007	a	b	c	d
008	a	b	c	d
009	a	b	c	d
010	a	b	c	d
011	a	b	c	d
012	a	b	c	d
013	a	b	c	d
014	a	b	c	d
015	a	b	c	d
016	a	b	c	d
017	a	b	c	d
018	a	b	c	d
019	a	b	c	d
020	a	b	c	d
021	a	b	c	d
022	a	b	c	d
023	a	b	c	d
024	a	b	c	d
025	a	b	c	d
026	a	b	c	d
027	a	b	c	d
028	a	b	c	d
029	a	b	c	d
030	a	b	c	d
031	a	b	c	d
032	a	b	c	d
033	a	b	c	d
034	a	b	c	d
035	a	b	c	d
036	a	b	c	d
037	a	b	c	d
038	a	b	c	d
039	a	b	c	d
040	a	b	c	d
041	a	b	c	d
042	a	b	c	d
043	a	b	c	d
044	a	b	c	d
045	a	b	c	d
046	a	b	c	d
047	a	b	c	d
048	a	b	c	d
049	a	b	c	d
050	a	b	c	d

Q No.	Response			
051	a	b	c	d
052	a	b	c	d
053	a	b	c	d
054	a	b	c	d
055	a	b	c	d
056	a	b	c	d
057	a	b	c	d
058	a	b	c	d
059	a	b	c	d
060	a	b	c	d
061	a	b	c	d
062	a	b	c	d
063	a	b	c	d
064	a	b	c	d
065	a	b	c	d
066	a	b	c	d
067	a	b	c	d
068	a	b	c	d
069	a	b	c	d
070	a	b	c	d
071	a	b	c	d
072	a	b	c	d
073	a	b	c	d
074	a	b	c	d
075	a	b	c	d
076	a	b	c	d
077	a	b	c	d
078	a	b	c	d
079	a	b	c	d
080	a	b	c	d
081	a	b	c	d
082	a	b	c	d
083	a	b	c	d
084	a	b	c	d
085	a	b	c	d
086	a	b	c	d
087	a	b	c	d
088	a	b	c	d
089	a	b	c	d
090	a	b	c	d
091	a	b	c	d
092	a	b	c	d
093	a	b	c	d
094	a	b	c	d
095	a	b	c	d
096	a	b	c	d
097	a	b	c	d
098	a	b	c	d
099	a	b	c	d
100	a	b	c	d

MOTHER's NAME (in running handwriting)

FATHER's NAME (in running handwriting)

CANDIDATE LEFT HAND IMPRESSION

SIGNATURE OF INVIGILATOR'S WITH TIME

1

2

MEDACE

OMR SHEET

ROLL No.

1	1	1	1	1	1	1	1	1	1
2	2	2	2	2	2	2	2	2	2
3	3	3	3	3	3	3	3	3	3
4	4	4	4	4	4	4	4	4	4
5	5	5	5	5	5	5	5	5	5
6	6	6	6	6	6	6	6	6	6
7	7	7	7	7	7	7	7	7	7
8	8	8	8	8	8	8	8	8	8
9	9	9	9	9	9	9	9	9	9
0	0	0	0	0	0	0	0	0	0

TEST BOOKLET No.

1	1	1	1	1	1	1
2	2	2	2	2	2	2
3	3	3	3	3	3	3
4	4	4	4	4	4	4
5	5	5	5	5	5	5
6	6	6	6	6	6	6
7	7	7	7	7	7	7
8	8	8	8	8	8	8
9	9	9	9	9	9	9
0	0	0	0	0	0	0

TEST BOOKLET Code

Q No.	Response				Q No.	Response			
001	a	b	c	d	051	a	b	c	d
002	a	b	c	d	052	a	b	c	d
003	a	b	c	d	053	a	b	c	d
004	a	b	c	d	054	a	b	c	d
005	a	b	c	d	055	a	b	c	d
006	a	b	c	d	056	a	b	c	d
007	a	b	c	d	057	a	b	c	d
008	a	b	c	d	058	a	b	c	d
009	a	b	c	d	059	a	b	c	d
010	a	b	c	d	060	a	b	c	d
011	a	b	c	d	061	a	b	c	d
012	a	b	c	d	062	a	b	c	d
013	a	b	c	d	063	a	b	c	d
014	a	b	c	d	064	a	b	c	d
015	a	b	c	d	065	a	b	c	d
016	a	b	c	d	066	a	b	c	d
017	a	b	c	d	067	a	b	c	d
018	a	b	c	d	068	a	b	c	d
019	a	b	c	d	069	a	b	c	d
020	a	b	c	d	070	a	b	c	d
021	a	b	c	d	071	a	b	c	d
022	a	b	c	d	072	a	b	c	d
023	a	b	c	d	073	a	b	c	d
024	a	b	c	d	074	a	b	c	d
025	a	b	c	d	075	a	b	c	d
026	a	b	c	d	076	a	b	c	d
027	a	b	c	d	077	a	b	c	d
028	a	b	c	d	078	a	b	c	d
029	a	b	c	d	079	a	b	c	d
030	a	b	c	d	080	a	b	c	d
031	a	b	c	d	081	a	b	c	d
032	a	b	c	d	082	a	b	c	d
033	a	b	c	d	083	a	b	c	d
034	a	b	c	d	084	a	b	c	d
035	a	b	c	d	085	a	b	c	d
036	a	b	c	d	086	a	b	c	d
037	a	b	c	d	087	a	b	c	d
038	a	b	c	d	088	a	b	c	d
039	a	b	c	d	089	a	b	c	d
040	a	b	c	d	090	a	b	c	d
041	a	b	c	d	091	a	b	c	d
042	a	b	c	d	092	a	b	c	d
043	a	b	c	d	093	a	b	c	d
044	a	b	c	d	094	a	b	c	d
045	a	b	c	d	095	a	b	c	d
046	a	b	c	d	096	a	b	c	d
047	a	b	c	d	097	a	b	c	d
048	a	b	c	d	098	a	b	c	d
049	a	b	c	d	099	a	b	c	d
050	a	b	c	d	100	a	b	c	d

DECLARATION BY THE CANDIDATE

I declare that particulars and signature on this OMR Answer sheet are mine and are Name as in Attendance Sheet. I fruther declare that particulars filled in and Signature as well as the circles darkened on this ORIGINALCOPY is same as in OFFICE COPY.

Signature with time (in running handwriting)

CANDIDATE's NAME (in running handwriting)

MOTHER's NAME (in running handwriting)

FATHER's NAME (in running handwriting)

CANDIDATE LEFT HAND IMPRESSION

SIGNATURE OF INVIGILATOR'S WITH TIME

1

2

OMR SHEET

ROLL No.

1	1	1	1	1	1	1	1	1	1
2	2	2	2	2	2	2	2	2	2
3	3	3	3	3	3	3	3	3	3
4	4	4	4	4	4	4	4	4	4
5	5	5	5	5	5	5	5	5	5
6	6	6	6	6	6	6	6	6	6
7	7	7	7	7	7	7	7	7	7
8	8	8	8	8	8	8	8	8	8
9	9	9	9	9	9	9	9	9	9
0	0	0	0	0	0	0	0	0	0

TEST BOOKLET No.

1	1	1	1	1	1	1
2	2	2	2	2	2	2
3	3	3	3	3	3	3
4	4	4	4	4	4	4
5	5	5	5	5	5	5
6	6	6	6	6	6	6
7	7	7	7	7	7	7
8	8	8	8	8	8	8
9	9	9	9	9	9	9
0	0	0	0	0	0	0

TEST BOOKLET Code

Q No.	Response				Q No.	Response			
001	a	b	c	d	051	a	b	c	d
002	a	b	c	d	052	a	b	c	d
003	a	b	c	d	053	a	b	c	d
004	a	b	c	d	054	a	b	c	d
005	a	b	c	d	055	a	b	c	d
006	a	b	c	d	056	a	b	c	d
007	a	b	c	d	057	a	b	c	d
008	a	b	c	d	058	a	b	c	d
009	a	b	c	d	059	a	b	c	d
010	a	b	c	d	060	a	b	c	d
011	a	b	c	d	061	a	b	c	d
012	a	b	c	d	062	a	b	c	d
013	a	b	c	d	063	a	b	c	d
014	a	b	c	d	064	a	b	c	d
015	a	b	c	d	065	a	b	c	d
016	a	b	c	d	066	a	b	c	d
017	a	b	c	d	067	a	b	c	d
018	a	b	c	d	068	a	b	c	d
019	a	b	c	d	069	a	b	c	d
020	a	b	c	d	070	a	b	c	d
021	a	b	c	d	071	a	b	c	d
022	a	b	c	d	072	a	b	c	d
023	a	b	c	d	073	a	b	c	d
024	a	b	c	d	074	a	b	c	d
025	a	b	c	d	075	a	b	c	d
026	a	b	c	d	076	a	b	c	d
027	a	b	c	d	077	a	b	c	d
028	a	b	c	d	078	a	b	c	d
029	a	b	c	d	079	a	b	c	d
030	a	b	c	d	080	a	b	c	d
031	a	b	c	d	081	a	b	c	d
032	a	b	c	d	082	a	b	c	d
033	a	b	c	d	083	a	b	c	d
034	a	b	c	d	084	a	b	c	d
035	a	b	c	d	085	a	b	c	d
036	a	b	c	d	086	a	b	c	d
037	a	b	c	d	087	a	b	c	d
038	a	b	c	d	088	a	b	c	d
039	a	b	c	d	089	a	b	c	d
040	a	b	c	d	090	a	b	c	d
041	a	b	c	d	091	a	b	c	d
042	a	b	c	d	092	a	b	c	d
043	a	b	c	d	093	a	b	c	d
044	a	b	c	d	094	a	b	c	d
045	a	b	c	d	095	a	b	c	d
046	a	b	c	d	096	a	b	c	d
047	a	b	c	d	097	a	b	c	d
048	a	b	c	d	098	a	b	c	d
049	a	b	c	d	099	a	b	c	d
050	a	b	c	d	100	a	b	c	d

DECLARATION BY THE CANDIDATE

I declare that particulars and signature on this OMR Answer sheet are mine and are Name as in Attendance Sheet. I fruther declare that particulars filled in and Signature as well as the circles darkened on this ORIGINALCOPY is same as in OFFICE COPY.

Signature with time (in running handwriting)

CANDIDATE's NAME (in running handwriting)

MOTHER's NAME (in running handwriting)

FATHER's NAME (in running handwriting)

CANDIDATE LEFT HAND IMPRESSION

SIGNATURE OF INVIGILATOR'S WITH TIME

1

2

MEDACE

OMR SHEET

ROLL No.

1	1	1	1	1	1	1	1	1	1
2	2	2	2	2	2	2	2	2	2
3	3	3	3	3	3	3	3	3	3
4	4	4	4	4	4	4	4	4	4
5	5	5	5	5	5	5	5	5	5
6	6	6	6	6	6	6	6	6	6
7	7	7	7	7	7	7	7	7	7
8	8	8	8	8	8	8	8	8	8
9	9	9	9	9	9	9	9	9	9
0	0	0	0	0	0	0	0	0	0

TEST BOOKLET No.

1	1	1	1	1	1	1
2	2	2	2	2	2	2
3	3	3	3	3	3	3
4	4	4	4	4	4	4
5	5	5	5	5	5	5
6	6	6	6	6	6	6
7	7	7	7	7	7	7
8	8	8	8	8	8	8
9	9	9	9	9	9	9
0	0	0	0	0	0	0

TEST BOOKLET Code

Q No.	Response	Q No.	Response
001	a b c d	051	a b c d
002	a b c d	052	a b c d
003	a b c d	053	a b c d
004	a b c d	054	a b c d
005	a b c d	055	a b c d
006	a b c d	056	a b c d
007	a b c d	057	a b c d
008	a b c d	058	a b c d
009	a b c d	059	a b c d
010	a b c d	060	a b c d
011	a b c d	061	a b c d
012	a b c d	062	a b c d
013	a b c d	063	a b c d
014	a b c d	064	a b c d
015	a b c d	065	a b c d
016	a b c d	066	a b c d
017	a b c d	067	a b c d
018	a b c d	068	a b c d
019	a b c d	069	a b c d
020	a b c d	070	a b c d
021	a b c d	071	a b c d
022	a b c d	072	a b c d
023	a b c d	073	a b c d
024	a b c d	074	a b c d
025	a b c d	075	a b c d
026	a b c d	076	a b c d
027	a b c d	077	a b c d
028	a b c d	078	a b c d
029	a b c d	079	a b c d
030	a b c d	080	a b c d
031	a b c d	081	a b c d
032	a b c d	082	a b c d
033	a b c d	083	a b c d
034	a b c d	084	a b c d
035	a b c d	085	a b c d
036	a b c d	086	a b c d
037	a b c d	087	a b c d
038	a b c d	088	a b c d
039	a b c d	089	a b c d
040	a b c d	090	a b c d
041	a b c d	091	a b c d
042	a b c d	092	a b c d
043	a b c d	093	a b c d
044	a b c d	094	a b c d
045	a b c d	095	a b c d
046	a b c d	096	a b c d
047	a b c d	097	a b c d
048	a b c d	098	a b c d
049	a b c d	099	a b c d
050	a b c d	100	a b c d

DECLARATION BY THE CANDIDATE

I declare that particulars and signature on this OMR Answer sheet are mine and are Name as in Attendance Sheet. I fruther declare that particulars filled in and Signature as well as the circles darkened on this ORIGINALCOPY is same as in OFFICE COPY.

Signature with time (in running handwriting)

CANDIDATE's NAME (in running handwriting)

MOTHER's NAME (in running handwriting)

FATHER's NAME (in running handwriting)

CANDIDATE LEFT HAND IMPRESSION

SIGNATURE OF INVIGILATOR'S WITH TIME

1

2

OMR SHEET

ROLL No.

1	1	1	1	1	1	1	1	1	1
2	2	2	2	2	2	2	2	2	2
3	3	3	3	3	3	3	3	3	3
4	4	4	4	4	4	4	4	4	4
5	5	5	5	5	5	5	5	5	5
6	6	6	6	6	6	6	6	6	6
7	7	7	7	7	7	7	7	7	7
8	8	8	8	8	8	8	8	8	8
9	9	9	9	9	9	9	9	9	9
0	0	0	0	0	0	0	0	0	0

TEST BOOKLET No.

1	1	1	1	1	1	1
2	2	2	2	2	2	2
3	3	3	3	3	3	3
4	4	4	4	4	4	4
5	5	5	5	5	5	5
6	6	6	6	6	6	6
7	7	7	7	7	7	7
8	8	8	8	8	8	8
9	9	9	9	9	9	9
0	0	0	0	0	0	0

TEST BOOKLET Code

Q No.	Response				Q No.	Response			
001	a	b	c	d	051	a	b	c	d
002	a	b	c	d	052	a	b	c	d
003	a	b	c	d	053	a	b	c	d
004	a	b	c	d	054	a	b	c	d
005	a	b	c	d	055	a	b	c	d
006	a	b	c	d	056	a	b	c	d
007	a	b	c	d	057	a	b	c	d
008	a	b	c	d	058	a	b	c	d
009	a	b	c	d	059	a	b	c	d
010	a	b	c	d	060	a	b	c	d
011	a	b	c	d	061	a	b	c	d
012	a	b	c	d	062	a	b	c	d
013	a	b	c	d	063	a	b	c	d
014	a	b	c	d	064	a	b	c	d
015	a	b	c	d	065	a	b	c	d
016	a	b	c	d	066	a	b	c	d
017	a	b	c	d	067	a	b	c	d
018	a	b	c	d	068	a	b	c	d
019	a	b	c	d	069	a	b	c	d
020	a	b	c	d	070	a	b	c	d
021	a	b	c	d	071	a	b	c	d
022	a	b	c	d	072	a	b	c	d
023	a	b	c	d	073	a	b	c	d
024	a	b	c	d	074	a	b	c	d
025	a	b	c	d	075	a	b	c	d
026	a	b	c	d	076	a	b	c	d
027	a	b	c	d	077	a	b	c	d
028	a	b	c	d	078	a	b	c	d
029	a	b	c	d	079	a	b	c	d
030	a	b	c	d	080	a	b	c	d
031	a	b	c	d	081	a	b	c	d
032	a	b	c	d	082	a	b	c	d
033	a	b	c	d	083	a	b	c	d
034	a	b	c	d	084	a	b	c	d
035	a	b	c	d	085	a	b	c	d
036	a	b	c	d	086	a	b	c	d
037	a	b	c	d	087	a	b	c	d
038	a	b	c	d	088	a	b	c	d
039	a	b	c	d	089	a	b	c	d
040	a	b	c	d	090	a	b	c	d
041	a	b	c	d	091	a	b	c	d
042	a	b	c	d	092	a	b	c	d
043	a	b	c	d	093	a	b	c	d
044	a	b	c	d	094	a	b	c	d
045	a	b	c	d	095	a	b	c	d
046	a	b	c	d	096	a	b	c	d
047	a	b	c	d	097	a	b	c	d
048	a	b	c	d	098	a	b	c	d
049	a	b	c	d	099	a	b	c	d
050	a	b	c	d	100	a	b	c	d

DECLARATION BY THE CANDIDATE

I declare that particulars and signature on this OMR Answer sheet are mine and are Name as in Attendance Sheet. I fruther declare that particulars filled in and Signature as well as the circles darkened on this ORIGINALCOPY is same as in OFFICE COPY.

Signature with time (in running handwriting)

CANDIDATE's NAME (in running handwriting)

MOTHER's NAME (in running handwriting)

FATHER's NAME (in running handwriting)

CANDIDATE LEFT HAND IMPRESSION

SIGNATURE OF INVIGILATOR'S WITH TIME

1

2

MEDACE

OMR SHEET

ROLL No.

1	1	1	1	1	1	1	1	1	1
2	2	2	2	2	2	2	2	2	2
3	3	3	3	3	3	3	3	3	3
4	4	4	4	4	4	4	4	4	4
5	5	5	5	5	5	5	5	5	5
6	6	6	6	6	6	6	6	6	6
7	7	7	7	7	7	7	7	7	7
8	8	8	8	8	8	8	8	8	8
9	9	9	9	9	9	9	9	9	9
0	0	0	0	0	0	0	0	0	0

TEST BOOKLET No.

1	1	1	1	1	1	1
2	2	2	2	2	2	2
3	3	3	3	3	3	3
4	4	4	4	4	4	4
5	5	5	5	5	5	5
6	6	6	6	6	6	6
7	7	7	7	7	7	7
8	8	8	8	8	8	8
9	9	9	9	9	9	9
0	0	0	0	0	0	0

TEST BOOKLET Code

Q No.	Response				Q No.	Response			
001	a	b	c	d	051	a	b	c	d
002	a	b	c	d	052	a	b	c	d
003	a	b	c	d	053	a	b	c	d
004	a	b	c	d	054	a	b	c	d
005	a	b	c	d	055	a	b	c	d
006	a	b	c	d	056	a	b	c	d
007	a	b	c	d	057	a	b	c	d
008	a	b	c	d	058	a	b	c	d
009	a	b	c	d	059	a	b	c	d
010	a	b	c	d	060	a	b	c	d
011	a	b	c	d	061	a	b	c	d
012	a	b	c	d	062	a	b	c	d
013	a	b	c	d	063	a	b	c	d
014	a	b	c	d	064	a	b	c	d
015	a	b	c	d	065	a	b	c	d
016	a	b	c	d	066	a	b	c	d
017	a	b	c	d	067	a	b	c	d
018	a	b	c	d	068	a	b	c	d
019	a	b	c	d	069	a	b	c	d
020	a	b	c	d	070	a	b	c	d
021	a	b	c	d	071	a	b	c	d
022	a	b	c	d	072	a	b	c	d
023	a	b	c	d	073	a	b	c	d
024	a	b	c	d	074	a	b	c	d
025	a	b	c	d	075	a	b	c	d
026	a	b	c	d	076	a	b	c	d
027	a	b	c	d	077	a	b	c	d
028	a	b	c	d	078	a	b	c	d
029	a	b	c	d	079	a	b	c	d
030	a	b	c	d	080	a	b	c	d
031	a	b	c	d	081	a	b	c	d
032	a	b	c	d	082	a	b	c	d
033	a	b	c	d	083	a	b	c	d
034	a	b	c	d	084	a	b	c	d
035	a	b	c	d	085	a	b	c	d
036	a	b	c	d	086	a	b	c	d
037	a	b	c	d	087	a	b	c	d
038	a	b	c	d	088	a	b	c	d
039	a	b	c	d	089	a	b	c	d
040	a	b	c	d	090	a	b	c	d
041	a	b	c	d	091	a	b	c	d
042	a	b	c	d	092	a	b	c	d
043	a	b	c	d	093	a	b	c	d
044	a	b	c	d	094	a	b	c	d
045	a	b	c	d	095	a	b	c	d
046	a	b	c	d	096	a	b	c	d
047	a	b	c	d	097	a	b	c	d
048	a	b	c	d	098	a	b	c	d
049	a	b	c	d	099	a	b	c	d
050	a	b	c	d	100	a	b	c	d

DECLARATION BY THE CANDIDATE

I declare that particulars and signature on this OMR Answer sheet are mine and are Name as in Attendance Sheet. I fruther declare that particulars filled in and Signature as well as the circles darkened on this ORIGINALCOPY is same as in OFFICE COPY.

Signature with time (in running handwriting)

CANDIDATE's NAME (in running handwriting)

MOTHER's NAME (in running handwriting)

FATHER's NAME (in running handwriting)

CANDIDATE LEFT HAND IMPRESSION

SIGNATURE OF INVIGILATOR'S WITH TIME

1

2

MEDACE

OMR SHEET

ROLL No.

1	1	1	1	1	1	1	1	1	1
2	2	2	2	2	2	2	2	2	2
3	3	3	3	3	3	3	3	3	3
4	4	4	4	4	4	4	4	4	4
5	5	5	5	5	5	5	5	5	5
6	6	6	6	6	6	6	6	6	6
7	7	7	7	7	7	7	7	7	7
8	8	8	8	8	8	8	8	8	8
9	9	9	9	9	9	9	9	9	9
0	0	0	0	0	0	0	0	0	0

TEST BOOKLET No.

1	1	1	1	1	1	1
2	2	2	2	2	2	2
3	3	3	3	3	3	3
4	4	4	4	4	4	4
5	5	5	5	5	5	5
6	6	6	6	6	6	6
7	7	7	7	7	7	7
8	8	8	8	8	8	8
9	9	9	9	9	9	9
0	0	0	0	0	0	0

TEST BOOKLET Code

Q No.	Response				Q No.	Response			
001	a	b	c	d	051	a	b	c	d
002	a	b	c	d	052	a	b	c	d
003	a	b	c	d	053	a	b	c	d
004	a	b	c	d	054	a	b	c	d
005	a	b	c	d	055	a	b	c	d
006	a	b	c	d	056	a	b	c	d
007	a	b	c	d	057	a	b	c	d
008	a	b	c	d	058	a	b	c	d
009	a	b	c	d	059	a	b	c	d
010	a	b	c	d	060	a	b	c	d
011	a	b	c	d	061	a	b	c	d
012	a	b	c	d	062	a	b	c	d
013	a	b	c	d	063	a	b	c	d
014	a	b	c	d	064	a	b	c	d
015	a	b	c	d	065	a	b	c	d
016	a	b	c	d	066	a	b	c	d
017	a	b	c	d	067	a	b	c	d
018	a	b	c	d	068	a	b	c	d
019	a	b	c	d	069	a	b	c	d
020	a	b	c	d	070	a	b	c	d
021	a	b	c	d	071	a	b	c	d
022	a	b	c	d	072	a	b	c	d
023	a	b	c	d	073	a	b	c	d
024	a	b	c	d	074	a	b	c	d
025	a	b	c	d	075	a	b	c	d
026	a	b	c	d	076	a	b	c	d
027	a	b	c	d	077	a	b	c	d
028	a	b	c	d	078	a	b	c	d
029	a	b	c	d	079	a	b	c	d
030	a	b	c	d	080	a	b	c	d
031	a	b	c	d	081	a	b	c	d
032	a	b	c	d	082	a	b	c	d
033	a	b	c	d	083	a	b	c	d
034	a	b	c	d	084	a	b	c	d
035	a	b	c	d	085	a	b	c	d
036	a	b	c	d	086	a	b	c	d
037	a	b	c	d	087	a	b	c	d
038	a	b	c	d	088	a	b	c	d
039	a	b	c	d	089	a	b	c	d
040	a	b	c	d	090	a	b	c	d
041	a	b	c	d	091	a	b	c	d
042	a	b	c	d	092	a	b	c	d
043	a	b	c	d	093	a	b	c	d
044	a	b	c	d	094	a	b	c	d
045	a	b	c	d	095	a	b	c	d
046	a	b	c	d	096	a	b	c	d
047	a	b	c	d	097	a	b	c	d
048	a	b	c	d	098	a	b	c	d
049	a	b	c	d	099	a	b	c	d
050	a	b	c	d	100	a	b	c	d

DECLARATION BY THE CANDIDATE

I declare that particulars and signature on this OMR Answer sheet are mine and are Name as in Attendance Sheet. I fruther declare that particulars filled in and Signature as well as the circles darkened on this ORIGINALCOPY is same as in OFFICE COPY.

Signature with time (in running handwriting)

CANDIDATE's NAME (in running handwriting)

MOTHER's NAME (in running handwriting)

FATHER's NAME (in running handwriting)

CANDIDATE LEFT HAND IMPRESSION

SIGNATURE OF INVIGILATOR'S WITH TIME

1

2

MEDACE

OMR SHEET

ROLL No.

1	1	1	1	1	1	1	1	1	1
2	2	2	2	2	2	2	2	2	2
3	3	3	3	3	3	3	3	3	3
4	4	4	4	4	4	4	4	4	4
5	5	5	5	5	5	5	5	5	5
6	6	6	6	6	6	6	6	6	6
7	7	7	7	7	7	7	7	7	7
8	8	8	8	8	8	8	8	8	8
9	9	9	9	9	9	9	9	9	9
0	0	0	0	0	0	0	0	0	0

TEST BOOKLET No.

1	1	1	1	1	1	1
2	2	2	2	2	2	2
3	3	3	3	3	3	3
4	4	4	4	4	4	4
5	5	5	5	5	5	5
6	6	6	6	6	6	6
7	7	7	7	7	7	7
8	8	8	8	8	8	8
9	9	9	9	9	9	9
0	0	0	0	0	0	0

TEST BOOKLET Code

Q No.	Response				Q No.	Response			
001	a	b	c	d	051	a	b	c	d
002	a	b	c	d	052	a	b	c	d
003	a	b	c	d	053	a	b	c	d
004	a	b	c	d	054	a	b	c	d
005	a	b	c	d	055	a	b	c	d
006	a	b	c	d	056	a	b	c	d
007	a	b	c	d	057	a	b	c	d
008	a	b	c	d	058	a	b	c	d
009	a	b	c	d	059	a	b	c	d
010	a	b	c	d	060	a	b	c	d
011	a	b	c	d	061	a	b	c	d
012	a	b	c	d	062	a	b	c	d
013	a	b	c	d	063	a	b	c	d
014	a	b	c	d	064	a	b	c	d
015	a	b	c	d	065	a	b	c	d
016	a	b	c	d	066	a	b	c	d
017	a	b	c	d	067	a	b	c	d
018	a	b	c	d	068	a	b	c	d
019	a	b	c	d	069	a	b	c	d
020	a	b	c	d	070	a	b	c	d
021	a	b	c	d	071	a	b	c	d
022	a	b	c	d	072	a	b	c	d
023	a	b	c	d	073	a	b	c	d
024	a	b	c	d	074	a	b	c	d
025	a	b	c	d	075	a	b	c	d
026	a	b	c	d	076	a	b	c	d
027	a	b	c	d	077	a	b	c	d
028	a	b	c	d	078	a	b	c	d
029	a	b	c	d	079	a	b	c	d
030	a	b	c	d	080	a	b	c	d
031	a	b	c	d	081	a	b	c	d
032	a	b	c	d	082	a	b	c	d
033	a	b	c	d	083	a	b	c	d
034	a	b	c	d	084	a	b	c	d
035	a	b	c	d	085	a	b	c	d
036	a	b	c	d	086	a	b	c	d
037	a	b	c	d	087	a	b	c	d
038	a	b	c	d	088	a	b	c	d
039	a	b	c	d	089	a	b	c	d
040	a	b	c	d	090	a	b	c	d
041	a	b	c	d	091	a	b	c	d
042	a	b	c	d	092	a	b	c	d
043	a	b	c	d	093	a	b	c	d
044	a	b	c	d	094	a	b	c	d
045	a	b	c	d	095	a	b	c	d
046	a	b	c	d	096	a	b	c	d
047	a	b	c	d	097	a	b	c	d
048	a	b	c	d	098	a	b	c	d
049	a	b	c	d	099	a	b	c	d
050	a	b	c	d	100	a	b	c	d

DECLARATION BY THE CANDIDATE

I declare that particulars and signature on this OMR Answer sheet are mine and are Name as in Attendance Sheet. I fruther declare that particulars filled in and Signature as well as the circles darkened on this ORIGINALCOPY is same as in OFFICE COPY.

Signature with time (in running handwriting)

CANDIDATE's NAME (in running handwriting)

MOTHER's NAME (in running handwriting)

FATHER's NAME (in running handwriting)

CANDIDATE LEFT HAND IMPRESSION

SIGNATURE OF INVIGILATOR'S WITH TIME

1

2

WELCOME LETTER

Dear NEET Aspirant,

Welcome to MED ACE family !!!

MED ACE is India's first and only **Hybrid kit** which is scientifically developed to provide **Rapid Revision, Practice** and **Assessment**, simultaneously.

Examinations like NEET are not only meant to test our knowledge, rather our study skills are also tested through them. In simpler words, our ability to do work to deal with difficult situations, to withstand mental pressures and stress are also checked and tested.

This kit is scientifically shaped to provide a **Strong Learning Management System** to boost the **Revision, Practice** and **Assessment** related skills of NEET Aspirants.

Some achievements can take a lifetime to attain while others can be completed in the course of a day.

At Arihant, we always believe
"Exams are not Hurdles, rather these are stepping stones to success".

Do share your feedbacks and comments at
info@examwitharihant.com
Team Arihant is anxiously waiting for your feedbacks and comments.

Thanks for choosing Arihant MED ACE kit in your journey of success.

Team Arihant

FEATURE ELABORATION GUIDE

MEDACE

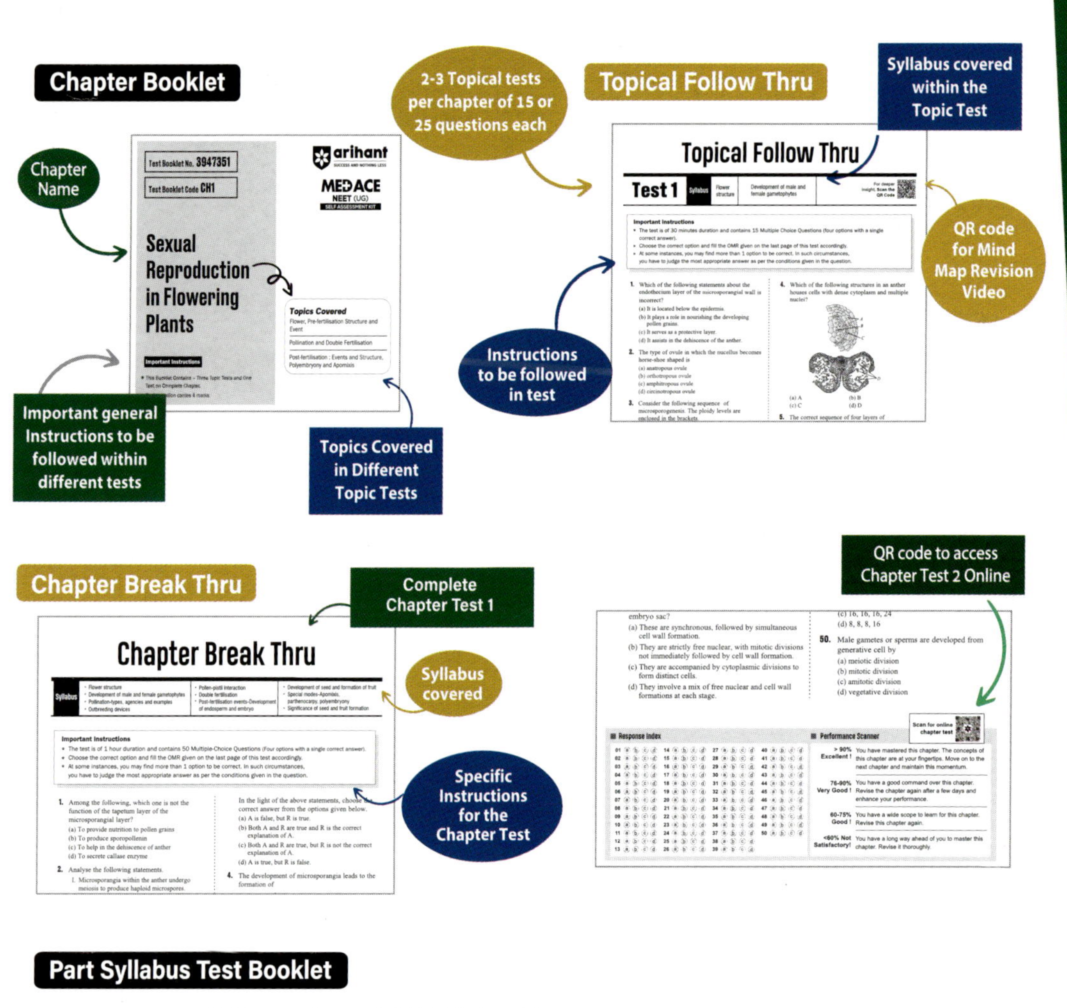

MED ACE

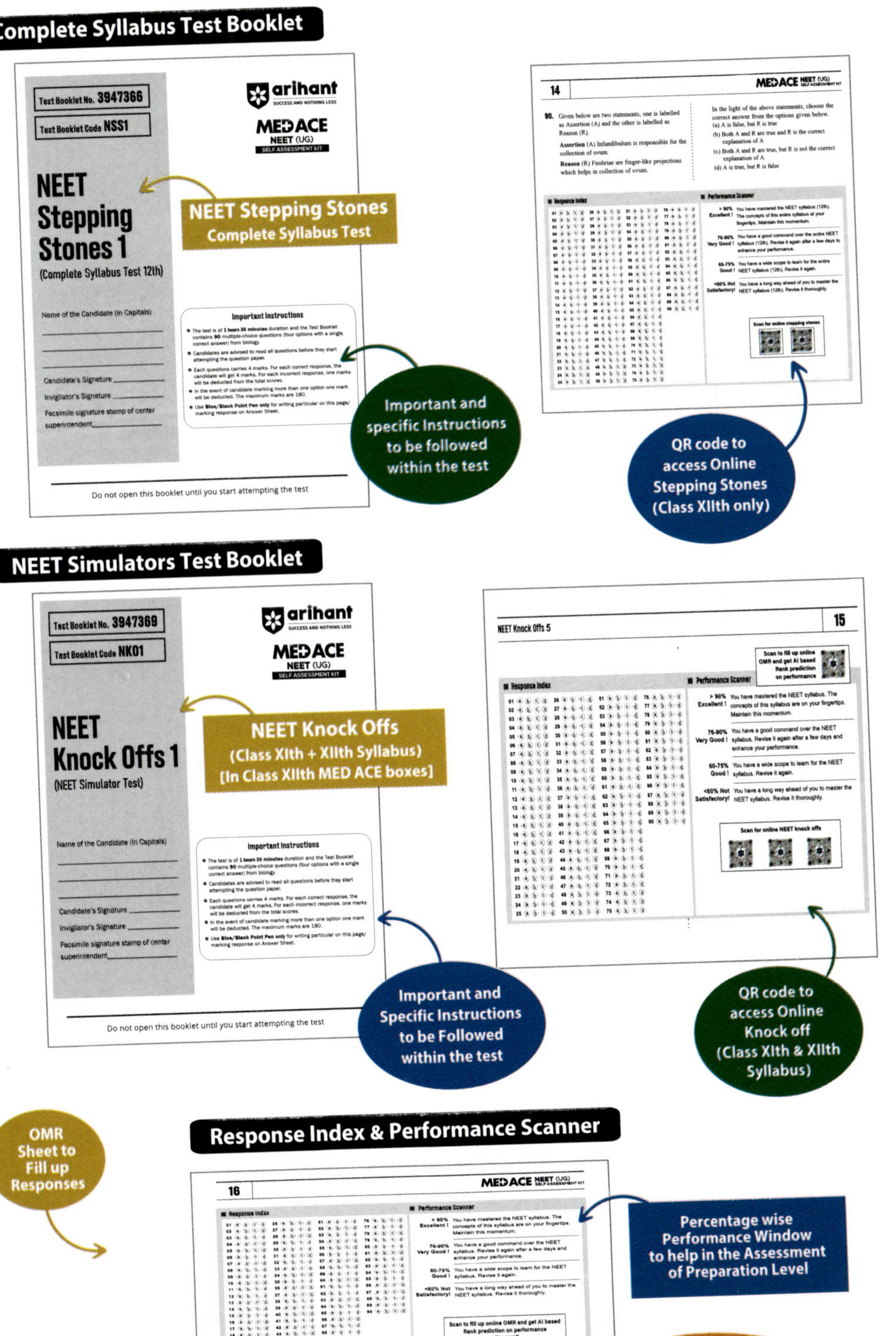

Complete Syllabus Test Booklet
NEET Stepping Stones 1
(Complete Syllabus Test 12th)
NEET Stepping Stones
Complete Syllabus Test
Important and specific Instructions to be followed within the test
Do not open this booklet until you start attempting the test
QR code to access Online Stepping Stones (Class XIIth only)
NEET Simulators Test Booklet
NEET Knock Offs 1
(NEET Simulator Test)
NEET Knock Offs
(Class XIth + XIIth Syllabus)
[In Class XIIth MED ACE boxes]
Important and Specific Instructions to be Followed within the test
QR code to access Online Knock off (Class XIth & XIIth Syllabus)
OMR Sheet to Fill up Responses
Response Index & Performance Scanner
Percentage wise Performance Window to help in the Assessment of Preparation Level
QR Code to Fill up online OMR and get AI based Rank prediction on Performance

YOUR PROBLEM OUR SOLUTIONS

We change your way of Exam prep.

Dear NEET Aspirant,

you can ask any of your queries while using our MED ACE kit by scanning the **given QR code.**

Steps to use

Step 1 Scan the QR code.

Step 2 Enter the details after selecting the language as English/Hindi with the help of below given information.

a. Book code - given at the back side of box/book below the ISBN.

9789359983615 Code: C1041 ₹-----.00

b. Booklet No.- given at the top of each booklet.

3947351

c. Fill page number and Question number in the respective field boxes.

d. Describe your Doubt/Query in your own words (either in Hindi or English).

e. Attach Image (optional).

Step 3 Click/Tap on "Submit" button. You will receive a confirmation on your whatsapp.

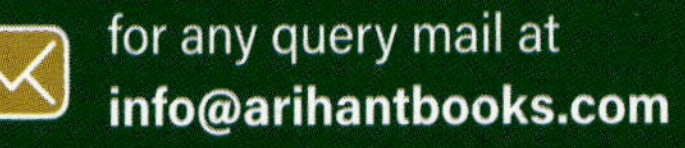

for any query mail at
info@arihantbooks.com

BIOLOGY XIIth

CONTENT LIST

S. No.	Chapters Name	Test Booklet Numbers	Test Booklet Codes
01	**Sexual Reproduction in Flowering Plants** • Test 1 • Test 2 • Test 3 • Chapter Test	3947351	CH1
02	**Human Reproduction** • Test 1 • Test 2 • Test 3 • Chapter Test	3947352	CH2
03	**Reproductive Health** • Test 1 • Test 2 • Chapter Test	3947353	CH3
04	**Principles of Inheritance and Variation** • Test 1 • Test 2 • Test 3 • Chapter Test	3947354	CH4
05	**Molecular Basis of Inheritance** • Test 1 • Test 2 • Test 3 • Chapter Test	3947355	CH5
06	**Evolution** • Test 1 • Test 2 • Test 3 • Chapter Test	3947356	CH6
07	**Human Health and Diseases** • Test 1 • Test 2 • Test 3 • Chapter Test	3947357	CH7

S. No.	Chapters Name	Test Booklet Numbers	Test Booklet Codes
08	**Microbes in Human Welfare** • Test 1 • Test 2 • Chapter Test	3947358	CH8
09	**Biotechnology : Principles and Processes** • Test 1 • Test 2 • Test 3 • Chapter Test	3947359	CH9
10	**Biotechnology and Its Applications** • Test 1 • Test 2 • Test 3 • Chapter Test	3947360	CH10
11	**Organisms and Populations** • Test 1 • Test 2 • Chapter Test	3947361	CH11
12	**Ecosystem** • Test 1 • Test 2 • Chapter Test	3947362	CH12
13	**Biodiversity and Conservation** • Test 1 • Test 2 • Chapter Test	3947363	CH13
14	**Syllabus Part Thru 1**	3947364	SPT1
15	**Syllabus Part Thru 2**	3947365	SPT2
16	**NEET Stepping Stones 1**	3947366	NSS1
17	**NEET Stepping Stones 2**	3947367	NSS2
18	**NEET Stepping Stones 3**	3947368	NSS3
19	**NEET Knock Offs 1**	3947369	NKO1
20	**NEET Knock Offs 2**	3947370	NKO2
21	**NEET Knock Offs 3**	3947371	NKO3
22	**NEET Knock Offs 4**	3947372	NKO4
23	**NEET Knock Offs 5**	3947373	NKO5
24	**NEET Chronicles 1**	3947374	NC1
25	**NEET Chronicles 2**	3947375	NC2

CONTENT LIST

S. No.	Chapters Name	Test Booklet Numbers	Test Booklet Codes
01	**Sexual Reproduction in Flowering Plants** • Test 1 • Test 2 • Test 3 • Chapter Test	3947351	CH1
02	**Human Reproduction** • Test 1 • Test 2 • Test 3 • Chapter Test	3947352	CH2
03	**Reproductive Health** • Test 1 • Test 2 • Chapter Test	3947353	CH3
04	**Principles of Inheritance and Variation** • Test 1 • Test 2 • Test 3 • Chapter Test	3947354	CH4
05	**Molecular Basis of Inheritance** • Test 1 • Test 2 • Test 3 • Chapter Test	3947355	CH5
06	**Evolution** • Test 1 • Test 2 • Test 3 • Chapter Test	3947356	CH6
07	**Human Health and Diseases** • Test 1 • Test 2 • Test 3 • Chapter Test	3947357	CH7

S. No.	Chapters Name	Test Booklet Numbers	Test Booklet Codes
08	**Microbes in Human Welfare** • Test 1 • Test 2 • Chapter Test	3947358	CH8
09	**Biotechnology : Principles and Processes** • Test 1 • Test 2 • Test 3 • Chapter Test	3947359	CH9
10	**Biotechnology and Its Applications** • Test 1 • Test 2 • Test 3 • Chapter Test	3947360	CH10
11	**Organisms and Populations** • Test 1 • Test 2 • Chapter Test	3947361	CH11
12	**Ecosystem** • Test 1 • Test 2 • Chapter Test	3947362	CH12
13	**Biodiversity and Conservation** • Test 1 • Test 2 • Chapter Test	3947363	CH13
14	**Syllabus Part Thru 1**	3947364	SPT1
15	**Syllabus Part Thru 2**	3947365	SPT2
16	**NEET Stepping Stones 1**	3947366	NSS1
17	**NEET Stepping Stones 2**	3947367	NSS2
18	**NEET Stepping Stones 3**	3947368	NSS3
19	**NEET Knock Offs 1**	3947369	NKO1
20	**NEET Knock Offs 2**	3947370	NKO2
21	**NEET Knock Offs 3**	3947371	NKO3
22	**NEET Knock Offs 4**	3947372	NKO4
23	**NEET Knock Offs 5**	3947373	NKO5
24	**NEET Chronicles 1**	3947374	NC1
25	**NEET Chronicles 2**	3947375	NC2